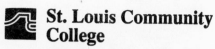

# WHO'S WHO IN
# COMEDY

# WHO'S WHO IN

# COMEDY

## COMEDIANS, COMICS AND CLOWNS
## FROM VAUDEVILLE TO TODAY'S STAND-UPS

**RONALD L. SMITH**

Facts On File
*New York • Oxford*

**Who's Who in Comedy: Comedians, Comics and Clowns from Vaudeville to Today's Stand-Ups**

Copyright © 1992 by Ronald L. Smith

Facts On File, Inc.          Facts On File Limited
460 Park Avenue South        c/o Roundhouse Publishing Ltd.
New York NY 10016            P.O. Box 140
USA                          Oxford OX2 7SF
                             United Kingdom

**Library of Congress Cataloging-in-Publication Data**
Smith, Ronald L., 1952–
Who's who in comedy : comedians, comics, and clowns from
  vaudeville to today's stand-ups / Ron L. Smith.
        p.   cm.
Includes bibliographical references and index.
        ISBN 0-8160-2338-7
    1. Comedians—Biography.   I. Title.
        PN1583.S6   1992
        792.7′028′0922—dc20
                                                    91-42881

A British CIP catalogue record for this book is available from the British Library.

Facts On File books are available at special discounts when purchased in bulk quantities for businesses, associations, institutions or sales promotions. Please call our Special Sales Department in New York at 212/683-2244 (dial 800/322-8755 except in NY, AK or HI) or in Oxford at 865/728399.

Text design by Donna Sinisgalli
Jacket design by Soloway/Mitchell and Ronald L. Smith
Composition and manufacturing by the Maple-Vail Book Manufacturing Group
Printed in the United States of America

10 9 8 7 6 5 4 3 2 1

This book is printed on acid-free paper.

# CONTENTS

# INTRODUCTION

This book has taken five years to complete. This would be the place for anecdotes mentioning all of the famous stars I've interviewed, as well as my talks with bewildered relatives of long-dead stars who couldn't believe anyone still cared enough to try and get some obscure facts straight. But every extra paragraph would only take away from what's important: the comedians.

My research was sometimes painstaking to the point of absurdity—such as the time I tracked down French- and German-language biographies of the clown Grock just to spot a familiar set of words and numerals that might be the elusive birth date I hadn't found in any English newspaper article. Or my search for Gummo Marx's son to find the one Marx Brother birth date unavailable elsewhere. A chronicle of how the book was put together might be amusing, but the comedians are more so.

In fact, there would be no introduction except that I was advised that scholars would want to know some details on who was picked for the *Who's Who* and why. I will do so—and leave for any disappointed fans the notion that had there been no introduction, your one favorite obscure missing comedian would have made it!

## WHO IS WHO

Who was picked for the *Who's Who*? Funny people, of course. But funny in the fullest sense of the word—comedians representing a full spectrum of styles from sophistication to slapstick, from family entertainers to risqué mavericks. There are famous comedians but also unique and deserving lesser-known stars who made significant contributions to comedy.

Due to space limitations, it was impossible to acknowledge movie stars who have occasionally performed memorable comedy, such as Dustin Hoffman *(Tootsie)*, Marilyn Monroe *(Some Like It Hot)*, Barbra Streisand *(The Owl and the Pussycat)*, the "team" of Spencer Tracy and Katharine Hepburn *(Adam's Rib)* and James Stewart *(Harvey)*. These performers are amply covered in other reference works and generally are not regarded by critics and fans as "comedians."

Also covered in other volumes are the various character actors and actresses, such as Edward Everett Horton and Una O'Connor, who brought comic relief and comic support to many movies. This book also does not chronicle the many "straight" actors and actresses who have appeared in hit sitcoms, a list that includes everyone from Donna Reed to Judd Hirsch. Also difficult to categorize were the stars of Broadway musical comedy, such as Gertrude Lawrence, Maurice Chevalier and Julie Andrews.

## LENGTH OF ENTRIES

Should the most important comedians get the biggest entries? In this book, that's not always the case. It sometimes takes longer to describe a visual joke than quote a gag, or to cover a colorful star with a string of controversies than someone who lived a sedate and downright dull life. Often it took longer to explain the comic style or merits of a lesser-known or faded star than one who is recognized more instantly.

Because so much material, including full biographies, is available on many major performers, it was important to compensate by giving slightly more detailed accounts to the comedians who are less covered in other reference books. I also felt that it was better to have fuller biographies of a lesser number of comedians than to try to squeeze a hundred more names in but limit everyone to useless "thumbnail" sketches.

## STYLE OF ENTRIES

This is not an encyclopedia in the purest sense of the word. It would be a grotesque disservice to chronicle comedians—most of them fun-loving, unpretentious and iconoclastic—with the standard chronology and pointless references to marital status, year of high school graduation or other factual inania. While I've inserted as many facts as possible, the text is designed to answer two basic questions: Who is this person? and What makes this person funny?

## AND NOW, A WORD FROM GROUCHO

Groucho Marx said in 1959, "My guess is that there aren't a hundred top-flight professional comedians, male and female, in the whole world."

If one figures that each generation might produce 100 great comedians to entertain them, then the approximately 450 herein representing the 20th century is a pretty accurate number.

Groucho went on to say: "They are a much rarer and far more valuable commodity than all the gold and precious stones in the world. But because we are laughed at, I don't think people really understand how essential we are to their sanity. If it weren't for the brief respite we give the world with our foolishness, the world would see mass suicide in numbers that compare favorably with the death rate of the lemmings."

He knew what's what.

Here's "who's who."

# WHO'S WHO IN
# COMEDY

## ABBOTT and COSTELLO

**Bud Abbott: William Abbott, October 2, 1895–April 24, 1974**
**Lou Costello: Louis Francis Cristillo, March 6, 1908–March 3, 1959**

Masters of fast-paced wordplay routines and aggressive lay-it-in-their-lap slapstick (to use Bud's phrase), Abbott and Costello were the most popular comedy team of the 1940s.

Abbott, a theater manager turned performer, had been around show business since his childhood. His Lutheran father was a press agent for the Barnum Circus and later an advance man for burlesque's Hurtig and Seamon shows. His Jewish mother, Rae Fisher, was a bareback rider.

Costello originally hoped for a career in sports, despite his five-foot-four-inch height and increasingly chunky build. He did some boxing, worked as a stunt man in films and finally broke into comedy by answering a job for a "Dutch comedian" in a vaudeville house. He worked with a few partners and was part of Lyons and Costello when he met Bud Abbott in 1936. Bud had been half of Abbott and Evanston.

Their teaming was not very dramatic. Lyons wasn't the best straight man in the world, and Abbott, after seeing the duo in action, simply approached Lou about forming a partnership. They worked out some routines, won encouraging notices at the Steel Pier in Atlantic City in 1937 and began touring the vaudeville circuit. They made it to Broadway with the variety revue *The Streets of Paris,* and that led them to radio.

They were a surprise hit on "The Kate Smith Show," performing burlesque routines that were unknown to most radio listeners. The bits "Who's on First," "Slowly I Turned" and "Watts Are Volts" were not written by the duo but refined by them, polished by repetition, enhanced by their chemistry and turned into gems. The team became known for many variations on word misunderstanding ("Gold ore what" and "Teller in the bank," among others), but balanced this with visual comedy: Bud's comically crude manhandling of the clumsy, exasperating Costello and the chubby fellow's well-timed pratfalls. Lou's tumbles were often as splashy and reckless as a belly flop into water, yet performed on a hard wood stage.

After being "tested" as comic relief for the 1940 film *One Night in the Tropics,* Bud and Lou starred in the hit *Buck Privates,* which was really just an assemblage of their routines, including "The Dice Game," "Go Ahead, Play the Radio," "Borrowing $50" and so on. The film helped turn slumping Universal Studios into a major film company, and the prolific team followed their hit with 34 films in 16 years.

Critics sometimes complained the team had no warmth, that their movies were just burlesque bits

The biggest box-office attraction of the 1940s, Abbott and Costello also had enormous success on radio and television with classic routines such as "Who's on First?" and "Slowly I Turned." Photo from the author's collection.

strung together. The same might be said of The Marx Brothers or Hope and Crosby, who rarely showed each other great love and affection. Actually, Bud's snarl of irritation and slaps to his wayward partner showed some kind of caring—even if it was that of an angry parent. Perhaps unintentionally, Bud was funny in his outrageously dour fault-finding and disregard of Lou's feelings. In *Rio Rita,* when Lou painfully catches himself on a cactus and can't get loose, Bud can only snarl at him for "stealing the lady's plant." Costello's character was at least two-dimensional, half the brash loudmouth and half the good-natured child. In *Keep 'Em Flying* he cries in frustration, "Oh, poison ivy!" Then, apologetically: "Now you made me say a rash word." His catch phrase: "I'm a ba-a-a-ad boy!"

Lou was so completely undisciplined in his yelling and tumbling and childlike behavior that viewers sided with Bud and reacted with laughter when he slapped the guy around. In real life Lou was forever ad-libbing and extending comic routines beyond their limits. It was Bud who had to give him the back of his hand or a dour "Talk sense, Costello" to keep him from singing opera parody or falling down longer than the audience could take. While Lou allowed Bud to dominate on stage, off stage he made most of the career decisions and was the mover and shaker in everything from contract talks to publicity stunts.

Through the 1940s, the team sometimes feuded, though never to the point of a showdown. Part of it was the natural difference of artistic opinions between the ambitious and adventurous Lou and the more quiet, conservative Bud. Lou's ego was a factor; as the team became more famous, he wanted top billing and more money for being the funny one. Another part of the problem was Lou's ill health and unhappy home life. In 1942 rheumatic fever caused him to stop working. It took nine months before he was even ready to resume the less-demanding Abbott and Costello radio show. On November 4, 1943, three hours before air time, a call came in at the studio: Lou Costello Jr., Lou's son, was dead, drowned in a swimming pool accident. November 5 would have been the child's first birthday.

Though literally sick at heart from grief and his previous illness, Lou insisted on going on. After the show, Bud Abbott appeared solo in front of the studio audience to say: "I would like to take a moment to pay tribute to my best friend and to a man who has more courage than I have ever seen displayed in a theater. . . . Just a short time before our broadcast started, Lou Costello was told that his baby . . . had died. In the face of the greatest tragedy which can come to any man, Lou Costello went on tonight so that you, the radio audience, would not be disappointed. There is nothing more that I can say except that I know you all join me in expressing our deepest sympathy to a great trouper. Good night."

Costello's marriage was shaky after the tragedy; Lou reportedly blamed his wife for not supervising the baby better. Lou's problems at home didn't help his enthusiasm for his films, which usually involved being slapped around and playing the stooge. He wanted parts that were more sympathetic and heroic. Mild-mannered Bud allowed his role to be diminished when the team made *Time of Their Lives* and *Little Giant,* films in which the boys weren't a team at all. Costello was the star, Abbott just a supporting player. During this time of crisis and bruised feelings, Lou was only barely restrained from retitling the team Costello and Abbott.

Gradually the problems were ironed out, but the team's box office appeal had suffered. Ironically, this turned out well for the team. Lou had misgivings over starring in their next film, complaining about the script. Lacking the power now to veto it, due to the last, less successful films, he and Bud reluctantly began filming. And *Abbott & Costello Meet Frankenstein* became one of their biggest hits.

Bud and Lou moved smoothly to television in the early 1950s, but the aging Abbott, troubled for decades by epilepsy, could no longer keep up physically with his younger partner. The duo split up in 1957. Lou made one film, *The 30 Foot Bride of Candy Rock*, before his death. Due to their own lack of business sense and the incompetence of their accountant, Abbott and Costello were seriously in debt in the 1950s. Fans couldn't believe that after they had raised so many millions for America during the war effort, and had contributed so much to charity, they were being hounded by the IRS into ruin. The IRS stood firm. The government showed no mercy and, in fact, never recognized the duo until the fall of 1991 when Bud and Lou were suddenly honored with a commemorative postage stamp.

Late in life, Abbott came out of retirement and briefly teamed with a virtual Costello imitator named Candy Candido, but he simply wasn't up to the demands of touring and performing. He later was able to supply his own distinctive voice for a series of Abbott and Costello television cartoons, but lived modestly in his semiretirement, weakened by a variety of illnesses.

Slowly the view of comedy theorists and critics began to change, and in the 1960s many of the films of Abbott and Costello, notably *Buck Privates, Who Done It?* and *Abbott and Costello Meet Frankenstein* were rightfully dubbed "classics." Costello was now acknowledged as a master at slapstick and an engaging personality, and Bud the ultimate straight man and amusing in his own unique and gruff way. Together they could not be matched in performing a routine with split-second timing.

Bud lived to see the first stages of this reappraisal of Abbott and Costello. Fans visiting his home were always treated warmly, and he always obliged with an autograph. When asked about his partner, Bud would stoically insist, "We never had any arguments. Lou was the greatest."

AUDIO: *Abbott and Costello on Radio* (Radiola), *Buck Privates* (Radiola), *Abbott and Costello* (Memorabilia), *Abbott and Costello Christmas Stocking* (Holiday), *Who's on First* (Nostalgia Lane), *Hey Abbott* (Murray Hill), *Abbott and Costello* (Nostalgia Lane)

BOOKS: *Bud and Lou* (Thomas, 1977), *Lou's on First* (C. Costello, 1981), *The Abbott and Costello Book* (Mulholland, 1975), *The Official Abbott and Costello Scrapbook* (Cox and Lafflin, 1990), *Abbott and Costello in Hollywood* (Furmanek and Palumbo, 1991)

BROADWAY: *Streets of Paris* (1939)

FILMS: *One Night in the Tropics* (1940), *Buck Privates* (1941), *In the Navy* (1941), *Hold That Ghost* (1941), *Keep 'Em Flying* (1941), *Ride 'Em Cowboy* (1942), *Rio Rita* (1942), *Pardon My Sarong* (1942), *Who Done It?* (1942), *It Ain't Hay* (1943), *Hit the Ice* (1943), *Lost in a Harem* (1944), *In Society* (1944), *Here Come the Coeds* (1945), *The Naughty Nineties* (1945), *Abbott and Costello in Hollywood* (1945), *Little Giant* (1946), *Time of Their Lives* (1946), *Buck Privates Come Home* (1947), *The Wistful Widow of Wagon Gap* (1947), *The Noose Hangs High* (1948), *Abbott and Costello Meet Frankenstein* (1948), *Mexican Hayride* (1948), *Africa Screams* (1949), *Abbott and Costello Meet the Killer, Boris Karloff* (1949), *Abbott and Costello in the Foreign Legion* (1950), *Abbott and Costello Meet the Invisible Man* (1951), *Comin' Round the Mountain* (1951), *Jack and the Beanstalk* (1952), *Lost in Alaska* (1952), *Abbott and Costello Meet Captain Kidd* (1952), *Abbott and Costello Go to Mars* (1953), *Abbott and Costello Meet the Keystone Kops* (1955), *Abbott and Costello Meet the Mummy* (1955), *Dance With Me, Henry* (1956)

TV: "The Abbott and Costello Show" (1952–53)

VIDEOS: *Heyyyy Abbott, Best of the Abbott & Costello Shows* Vols. 1–3, *Abbott and Costello Live, Best of Abbott and Costello Live*

## GOODMAN ACE and JANE ACE

**Goodman Ace: Goodman Aiskowitz, January 15, 1899–March 25, 1982**
**Jane Ace: Jane Epstein, October 12, 1900–November 11, 1974**

A journalism major from the Kansas City Polytechnic Institute, Goodman Ace switched from theater critic for the *Kansas City Post* to a gag writer for Jack Benny. Eventually he got his own local radio show, "Ace Goes to the Movies," which included film reviews and comedy patter with his wife, Jane.

Response to the Aces was wild, and in 1932 they switched to network radio. In 1933 they moved to New York for a 15-minute show three times a week. They made a comedy short, *Easy Aces*, in 1935 and also starred in a series of short documentaries and travelogues, offering brief introductions. In 1943 their radio show's format changed to a standard half hour. Like Burns and Allen, Goodman and Jane were a straight man–dizzy lady duo. Jane's brand of silliness was mainly malapropisms. Her classics were: "We're all cremated equal," "You could've knocked me down with a fender," "We're insufferable friends" and "Time wounds all heels."

Unlike George Burns, who never fought with Gracie, there were lifelike moments of exasperation from Goodman Ace. Jane: "I'll divorce you!" Goodman: "Promises, promises!" Mostly theirs was a friendly, mild program; their scripts, like those for Fred Allen's show, praised for intelligence and consistent quality. Goodman Ace enjoyed wry little throwaways à la Fred Allen: "He said he was 99% sure, but that 1% must have got him." This contrasted nicely with the more obvious tone of Jane's dizziness: "I didn't do it of my own violation. I was talked into it . . . and you know me, when somebody talks me into something . . . I'm completely uninhabited!"

The radio show's initial run was from 1932 to 1945. It returned for 1948 and '49, and then in December 1949 moved to television on the Dumont network. Jane retired in 1950 after the short run of the "Easy Aces" television series. The book *Ladies and Gentlemen, Easy Aces* collected their best scripts.

Goodman Ace went back behind the scenes as a comedy writer for radio and television shows starring Tallulah Bankhead (1950–52), Perry Como (1955–59) and Sid Caesar (1963–65), earning as much as $10,000 a week for his efforts—the highest salary of any comedy writer at the time.

Ace retained his acerbic qualities. Once Ace saw quiz show producer Bill Todman carrying some prizes into the studio. He dropped boxes containing toasters and percolators as he walked in. He couldn't gather them up fast enough to avoid Goodman Ace, who shouted, "Hey, Todman, you dropped your script!"

Milton Berle once said to him, "Goodie, you must have a list of hates longer than my arm." Ace answered, "I have a list longer than your arm. I also hate midgets who are shorter than your arm."

BOOKS: *The Book of Little Knowledge* (Goodman Ace), *The Fine Art of Hypochondria* (Goodman Ace), *Ladies and Gentlemen, Easy Aces* (Goodman Ace, 1970) TV: "Easy Aces" (1949–50)

# DON ADAMS

**(Donald Yarmy, April 13, 1926–   )**

Though Don Adams played a laughable spy on television's "Get Smart" winning three Emmy awards, (1967–69), the little guy was really tough. After attending De Witt Clinton High School in the Bronx, he joined the marines. He served four tough years, contracting black water fever at Guadalcanal.

Adams moved to New York to battle club and television bookers. He performed stand-up comedy at Le Reuban Bleu and The Latin Quarter, but making money consistently was a struggle. At one point he took $350 to become Mae West's opening act. There was a catch: When he auditioned his routines for her, she began cutting his best lines. After he bombed with his truncated routines, he was ready to give up. Fortified after smoking marijuana for the first time (courtesy of sympathetic band members), he tried again. He recalled: "The second show came and I was paralyzed . . . I had no idea where I was. . . . They pushed me out and I started screaming 'Good evening Ladies and Gentlemen . . .' and when I came to, I was still screaming 'Ladies and Gentlemen.' I screamed it for eight minutes!"

It wasn't a disaster: Mae West loved it! Her whole plan was to make sure the opening act wasn't funny. "I went on tour with her," Adams said. It turned out to be a miserable experience, but for another reason: "I put back the punch lines and it didn't make any difference."

Eventually Don crashed "The Arthur Godfrey Talent Scouts" show and managed to get an audition. From there he appeared on "The Perry Como Show," where he developed the catch phrase: "You really know how to hurt a guy."

With Bill Dana writing for him, Adams scored with a number of stand-up routines, including "The

Bengal Lancer" and "The Detective." The detective was a parody of all the films where a smug gumshoe gathers the suspects around to name the murderer: "You can't be the inspector. You must be the murderer. And if you're the murderer, then you're the inspector. And if you're the inspector . . . I must be on the wrong case."

Don's detective was loosely modeled on William Powell. In his early days, Adams (and then-partner Jay Lawrence) did a mimicry act. Now he modified his impression of the stagey Powell, accentuating the actor's imperturbable confidence to the point of silliness.

When Bill Dana got his own series in 1963, as bellhop José Jimenez, Adams turned up as Glick, the hotel detective. A year later he became Maxwell Smart—bearing the same steely if short-sighted vision as Glick, his voice taking on the comical edge of misplaced arrogance.

Though Adams was capable of some cute comic takes and moved well, it was his voice and his attitude that made Maxwell Smart click. There was nothing physically memorable about Max—not compared to his verbal humor and the five catch phrases he used. Fans loved them all. "Sorry about that, Chief" and "Missed me by that much!" became part of the nation's speech pattern. Max's chagrin over being duped was always blamed on some kind of "trick," as in: "the old inflatable-head-in-the-coat trick!" In moments of peril he displayed ludicrous bravado: "I'll be risking my life . . . and loving it!" But most of all, there was "Would you believe . . ." where Max's cool would slowly melt. In a typical moment of crisis, he tells a villain, "At this moment, seven coast guard cutters are converging on us." The villain isn't falling for it. "Would you believe . . . six? How about two cops in a rowboat?" The formula was repeated often. On another boat in another sea: "This yacht happens to be surrounded by the 7th Fleet!" "I find that hard to believe." "Would you believe the 6th Fleet?" "I don't think so." "How about a school of angry flounder?"

The show lasted five years. Both during and after, Adams performed stand-up, but added to his versatility by lending his distinctive voice to a cartoon series, "Inspector Gadget" (he'd previously been the voice of 1960s cartoon star "Tennessee Tuxedo"). After hosting an unusual quiz show ("Don

Adams' Screen Test") where contestants had to act out scenes from movies, Adams went on to try his luck in a number of sitcoms, most notably "Check It Out," playing the head of a supermarket. The syndicated show was recorded before a studio audience. "It's like opening night of a play every week. It's nerve-wracking but stimulating . . . I'm having fun. That's the main thing."

Periodically, in commercials and in made-for-television films, Adams returned to play Maxwell Smart—and loving it.

AUDIO: *Don Adams* (Signature, reissued on Roulette as *The Detective*), *Roving Reporter* (GNP Crescendo), *Get Smart* (UA), *Live? In Las Vegas* (UA)
BROADWAY: *Harold* (1962)
FILMS: *Murder Can Hurt You* (narration only, 1980), *The Nude Bomb* (1980), *The Return of Maxwell Smart* (1988)
TV: "The Bill Dana Show" (1963–65), "Get Smart" (1965–70), "The Partners" (1971–72), "Don Adams Screen Test" (1975), "Check It Out" (1985–87)
VIDEO: *Inspector Gadget*

## JOEY ADAMS

**(Joseph Abramowitz, January 6, 1911– )**

A Borscht Belt stand-up comic with a penchant for insults, Adams was popular in the 1950s when he hosted a few quiz programs. For the next 30 years he was better known for starring on a New York radio show, assembling joke books and producing a syndicated joke column loaded with gags such as: "Divorces are arranged so lawyers can live happily ever after." "A psychiatrist is a talent scout for a nuthouse." "The best way to prove girls are dynamite is to try to drop one."

Adams' lone album was a studio effort with his wife, Cindy (who emerged in the 1980s as a powerful gossip columnist for the *New York Post*). She speaks first: "What is it you don't like about my father?" "My wardrobe." "For your information, Daddy never wears your old suits." "Sure, only my new ones." "Neither does he complain about the size. Happens they fit him perfectly. It's just that they're a little snug on Mother, that's all." "I don't

Best known as a syndicated joke writer, Joey Adams was also a popular figure in the Borscht Belt and on quiz shows in the 1950s. Photo by the author.

Oriental artifacts and had a strong knowledge of each individual piece.

For Joey's 80th birthday party, Cindy helped gather an astonishing collection of celebrities, including Jackie Mason, Joan Rivers, Alan Alda, Beverly Sills, Kurt Vonnegut, Jerzy Kosinski, Helen Gurley Brown, Robin Leach, Donald Trump, Bess Myerson, Leona Helmsley and Imeldo Marcos, who was chosen to sing "Happy Birthday."

Over the decades Adams has made many famous stars and political figures laugh. There was always an audience for him, especially when he took over from George Jessel as a professional "roastmaster," doing Jolson imitations, telling jokes and acting the part of implacable master of ceremonies. Joey's all-purpose wisecracks thrown at Burt Reynolds during a roast: "Burt Reynolds is a big star. I know because before the dinner he came up to me and told me, 'I'm a big star. . . .' I hear Burt has finally found true romance. He's in love with himself."

AUDIO: *Cindy and I* (MGM)
BOOKS: *Cindy and I* (1957); *The Joey Adams Joke Book (1952), Encyclopedia of Humor (1968),; You Could Die Laughing (1968), Strictly for Laughs* (1982), *From Gags to Riches (1946), Joey Adams Joke Diary (1979), The Borscht Belt, Roast of the Town* (1985)
FILMS: *Ringside* (1949), *Singing in the Dark* (1956)
TV: "Back That Fact" (1953)

know, I've tried every diet there is." "Yeah, between meals." "Yeah, well, I know how I can get rid of 110 pounds immediately." "How?" "Dump you!"

Along with Bob Hope and Henny Youngman, Adams was often perceived as a rather cold, relentless joke-teller. Others knew that despite his gruff exterior, Adams had another side to his nature. In 1948 he produced *Singing in the Dark,* a sentimental film about a nightclub comedian (Joey) befriending a cantor (Moishe Oysher). He was once president of the American Guild of Variety Artists, joined with Martin Luther King Jr. for civil rights marches in Birmingham in 1963 and traveled the world for charitable causes. And while it was fashionable to consider Adams just another Borscht Belt comic and Friar's Club tummeler, a visit to Adams' home proved that he knew what really was fashionable and what really was art. He was proud of his collection of

## JACK ALBERTSON

### (June 16, 1910–November 25, 1981)

"Discovered" by television audiences in "Chico and the Man," Jack Albertson's comedy career began many decades earlier. He spent years in vaudeville and played straight man to Phil Silvers, Bert Lahr and Milton Berle. His performance of the burlesque classic "Floogle Street" with Joey Faye appears on the album *They're Still Laughing.*

Among his early movie roles was a comic vignette as the postman who rerouted the mail to Macy's "Santy Claus" in *Miracle on 34th Street.* He turned up in 1960s sitcoms, playing the tough but tolerant Lieutenant Stoner on "Ensign O'Toole." He began making a name for himself as a dramatic actor, winning a Tony and an Oscar for the Broadway and film version of *The Subject Was Roses.*

Finally, aged "just right" by life's pleasures and aggravations, Jack Albertson won his greatest fame late in life as the slightly battered, slightly bitter garage owner Ed Brown on "Chico and the Man."

It was a classic comedy concept—the grumbling curmudgeon versus the younger generation. Following the leads of Archie versus Meathead on "All in the Family" and father versus son on "Sanford and Son," the show worked with a gentler twist, as the salty old "Man" ultimately becomes father figure and friend to "Chico," his Latin assistant (Freddie Prinze).

Prinze learned a lot about teamwork from the veteran Albertson, who had appeared in recent revivals of *The Sunshine Boys* and had won an Emmy as a guest star on "The Cher Show." Prinze was sweet as Chico, but it was Albertson who gave the show its bite, making crustiness as delicious as the edge of an apple pie.

Prinze may have also identified with Jack personally. Albertson had grown up the tough way. He left school early, working in pool halls, literally sleeping on subways, taking small stage parts with encouragement from his sister Mabel (later a popular sitcom actress in mother-in-law roles). He knew what it was like to struggle out of a tough environment.

"Chico and the Man" was a great success—Albertson won an Emmy for his role in 1975, making him one of a select group to earn the Emmy, Academy Award and Tony. But the show's success was too much for young Prinze, who killed himself in January 1977. The show sputtered along without him; fans were too shocked by the loss of Freddie to find the show funny any more.

Yet fans still wanted to see more of Albertson. He was rushed into another series, "Grandpa Goes to Washington," which didn't prove the right vehicle for him. He continued to be in demand for comedy and occasional dramatic parts. Fans were hoping for another series, but instead were saddened by Albertson's death just a few years after his last show was canceled.

AUDIO: *Top Banana* (Capitol), *The Subject Was Roses* (Columbia), *Seventeen* (RCA), *They're Still Laughing* (RCA)

BROADWAY incl.: *The Subject Was Roses* (1964), *The Sunshine Boys* (1972)

FILMS incl.: *Top Banana* (1952), *Man of a Thousand Faces* (1957), *Don't Go Near the Water* (1957), *The Shaggy Dog* (1959), *Lover Come Back* (1961), *Son of Flubber* (1963), *The Patsy* (1964), *How to Murder Your Wife* (1965), *The Subject Was Roses* (1968), *Willy Wonka and the Chocolate Factory* (1971), *The Comedy Company* (1978), *Dead and Buried* (1981)

TV: "Room for One More" (1961), "Ensign O'Toole" (1962), "Chico and the Man" (1974–78), "Grandpa Goes to Washington" (1978)

## ALAN ALDA

### (Alphonso D'Abruzzo, January 28, 1936–   )

"I really like his passion. I like his appetite. He throws himself into what he does. I like his dedication to his work, his responsibility, and I like his ability to cut through his own seriousness with a self-deprecating joke."

That was Alan Alda talking about Benjamin Franklin Pierce, a character named after a famous American and a less famous president, and nicknamed "Hawkeye" after a character in *The Last of the Mohicans*. The quote could just as easily be Hawkeye talking about Alan Alda.

Since Alda shaped the character, ultimately writing and directing episodes of his television show "M*A*S*H," it's not surprising that "Hawkeye" was more than a funny man. Viewers watched him grow and evolve. They cared about him.

At first "Hawkeye" was mostly Groucho Marx—a Dr. Hackenbush. The supposedly Maine-bred Pierce spoke like a Jewish comedian, uttering an occasional "oy" and joking that the "M" in "M*A*S*H" was for "meshuggah." An early episode even had him imitating Groucho for a comedy sketch with a prostrate patient:

NURSE: Doctor, Doctor, can you give him a hand?

HAWKEYE: I'd rather give *you* one . . . did you take his pulse? I thought I told you to take his wallet! Sorry, kid, you should've booked ahead—you should've booked the rest of the body as well!

The link between Groucho and Hawkeye was not always subtle. Groucho to Margaret Dumont in *Duck Soup*: "I hear they're going to tear you down and put up an office building where you're standing." Hawkeye on the attack: "I wish somebody would tear him down and put up a human being." In *A Day at the Races* Groucho tells his dance partner: "If I hold you any closer I'll be in back of you." In a "M*A*S*H" episode a nurse dances with Hawkeye and says, "You couldn't get any closer." He answers, "Not unless I was behind you."

Audiences knew Alda was not like his iconoclast character. Magazine articles stressed his devotion to his family. He had a wife and three daughters and commuted on weekends back home to New Jersey as often as he could. He often talked about causes he cared about, including feminism, equal rights and human rights. He also grew up with strong family ties (his father was musical comedy star Robert Alda).

Alda's background in comedy went back to the days when he followed his vaudevillian father around the country. In the days of burlesque, Alda recalled "I remember going onstage as a joke in someone's act when I was three years old. I was around the theater all day long, and the strippers and the chorus dancers would sort of make me a mascot." When he was 16 he joined a summer stock company in Pennsylvania, picking up tips from stars such as Mae West and Buster Keaton. He later joined the Compass improvisational troupe in Hyannis: "The favorite thing I did was an impersonation of President Kennedy, which I did as a press conference. I worked very hard on that . . . after I stopped doing that impersonation, I thought it would be fun to do William Buckley." Later the Fordham University graduate briefly joined the New York version of the Second City improv company and appeared on "That Was the Week That Was."

Alda starred in Broadway's *The Owl and the Pussycat* and was nominated for a Tony for *The Apple Tree*. In films, Alda drifted far from his comedy and satire roots. When he got the call to do "M*A*S*H" he was filming the grim prison drama *The Glass House*.

"M*A*S*H" proved to be a pioneering, successful combination of comedy and drama. As he said, "I think the best drama has some laughter in it, and the best comedy has some places where you cry." Alda won Emmys for acting (1974, 1982), directing (1977, 1982) and writing (1977, 1982). From about $250,000 a year at the start, Alda's annual salary grew to $5 million.

In the last years of the show's run, Alda's ardent feminism began to show in episodes that ridiculed Hawkeye's womanizing. At first praised for his liberal views (he was applauded for writing and starring in the political film *The Seduction of Joe Tynan*), Alda found himself criticized as "wishy washy" for his views. Fans evidently had grown tired of reading about how disappointingly nice and uncharismatic he was in real life, compared to Hawkeye Pierce. Though his film *The Four Seasons* was a success, his subsequent efforts at starring, writing and directing, including *Sweet Liberty* and *A New Life*, received lukewarm attention, as did the two sitcoms he produced, 1974's "We'll Get By" and 1984's television version of *The Four Seasons*. The dry spell ended with his excellent notices as the egotistical director in Woody Allen's *Crimes and Misdemeanors*, though his next film project, *Betsy's Wedding*, received mixed reviews and did mildly at the box office. In 1992 he was nominated for a Tony award for his performance in Neil Simon's *Jakes Women*.

Of his image as a nice, bland guy Alda admitted, "I'm dull! All of the stuff I could tell you that would be interesting is in my movies. That's what makes the movies interesting and me dull."

BROADWAY: *Only in America* (1959), *Darwin's Theories* (1960), *Purlie Victorious* (1961), *A Whisper in God's Ear* (1962), *Fair Game for Lovers* (1964), *The Owl and the Pussycat* (1964), *The Apple Tree* (1966), *Jake's Women* (1992)

FILMS incl.: *California Suite* (1978), *Same Time Next Year* (1978), *The Four Seasons* (1981), *Sweet Liberty* (1987), *A New Life* (1988), *Crimes and Misdemeanors* (1989), *Betsy's Wedding* (1990)

TV: "That Was the Week That Was" (1964), "M*A*S*H" (1972–83)

# ALLEN and ROSSI

**Marty Allen: March 23, 1922–**
**Steve Rossi: May 25, 1932–**

Following the breakup of Martin and Lewis, a number of comics tried to take their place using the formula of Italian singer and wacky man-child. There were duplications (Mitchell and Petrillo, among others) but no really new variation until Allen and Rossi came along.

Steve Rossi was the genial straight man and singer, a mild Dean Martin type. Unlike Jerry Lewis, a wiry slapstick clown, Marty Allen was bug-eyed and huggable, his catch phrase a shyly forced "Hello dere!" He was the quiet little kid who, seemingly well behaved, suddenly came up with the darndest things. Typical sassy shock dialogue: "Do you come from a large family?" "I got 18 brothers and 12 sisters." "What does your father do?" "I don't know, but whatever it is he better cut it out!"

Allen and Rossi were frequent guests on television's "The Ed Sullivan Show," and their first album was a best-seller in 1962. That was quick work for the relatively inexperienced team. The duo met only three years earlier. Marty, a journalism major from the University of Southern California, was working as Nat King Cole's opening act. Aspiring singer Steve Rossi, who attended Loyola University on a music scholarship, had worked as a straight man in a Mae West revue. He became straight man to Marty Allen after Nat King Cole brought them together.

Together they created a mild, silly brand of comedy heavy on prepared formula interviews. Marty usually played a variety of incongruous characters (as Bill Dana was doing when he played José Jimenez the bull fighter, skindiver, karate expert, etc.). Marty was everything from a mechanical man to a Playboy bunny to "Rocky" Allen, the punch-drunk fighter:

"Tell me, how many fights have you had?" "Hundreds." "How many did you lose?" "Hundreds." "How do you explain that?" "Can't win 'em all . . ." "What's your trickiest punch?" "Left hook." "What's so tricky about that?" "I use my right hand." "Hey, Rock, I don't see any marks on your face." "I had my nose fixed." "Oh, did they straighten it?" "They put it between my eyes." "Well, why do you wear a mouthpiece?" "Cause I ain't got time to brush after every meal. . . ."

As the 1960s wore on, Marty's little-kid act became less of a novelty, and the team tried to incorporate more adult-oriented political material. It didn't suit Marty's naive, jovial style. The civil rights issue wasn't exactly enhanced with Steve interviewing Marty

as black activist James Meridith: "Hello dere." "James, now that you're safely enrolled in Mississippi University, what do you want to get out of college?" "Me!"

The team's only movie, *The Last of the Secret Agents,* was not successful. Marty Allen went out as a single, guesting on quiz shows and taking film roles. After Rossi's album *A Man in Love* failed to ignite his solo career, he teamed with aging vaudevillian Joe E. Ross and later Slappy White. As an interracial duo, Rossi and White made a few ripples, but they broke up after one album. Next came Allen and Rossi with *Bernie* Allen.

An ex-Bronx luncheonette owner, Bernie literally drove a cab into show business. One evening he picked up Rocky Graziano for a fare and kept him so entertained with jokes that Rocky helped him get into show business. In nightclubs Bernie was billed as "the World's 32nd Greatest Entertainer." He bore an exaggerated resemblance to Marty Allen, which may have prompted unwary fans to buy the lone Bernie Allen–Steve Rossi album *Sex Is* . . . In November 1972 *Variety* panned "the tastelessness of Allen's material . . . It seems incredible that references to 'colored boy' and 'fairies' could still be acceptable fodder." Bernie went on to team with his daughter Marilyn.

In 1983 the original Allen and Rossi finally reteamed, finding a warm welcome in Vegas and Atlantic City casinos. Allen's second wife Katie Blackwell joined in for songs and comedy and Rossi began to try some jokes too, along with impressions of such singers as Johnny Mathis and Luciano Pavarotti. Marty reported, "We all work throughout the act. And Steve and I do our regular routines—the drunk, the football player, the fighter. We've updated the gags. For instance, the fighter is asked if he'd fight Mike Tyson, and he says, 'Sure, I got a minute.' "

AUDIO: *Hello Dere* (ABC Paramount), *One More Time Hello Dere* (ABC Paramount), *Too Funny for Words* (Reprise), *In Person* (Mercury), *Great Society* (Mercury), *Batman and Rubin* (Mercury), *Truth About the Green Hornet* (Roulette), *Dedicated to Our Armed Forces* (Roulette)
FILM: *Last of the Secret Agents* (1966)

## DAYTON ALLEN

### (September 24, 1919–   )

Goofy pontificator Dayton Allen gained fame as one of the "men in the street" on television's old "Tonight Show" hosted by Steve Allen. His catch phrase was "Why not!" (pronounced "whoooooyyy not?")—his voice a cross between an Ed Wynn fool and a Steve Martin "excuuuuuse me" wise guy.

A typical introduction from Steve Allen leading to a stalwartly dizzy monologue: "This is the start of national headache week. Therefore we decided it is only fitting that tonight's lecturer be a world-famous surgeon. Here is Dr. Harvey L. Dayton."

Dayton: "Whoooy not? Being a very famous surgeon, I have even worked in hospitals. Sometimes I would aid in helping around! Surgery to me is more than just a way to make a good fast buck. Here's a for instance. The technical advances in operating have been really swell. Clean gloves, nice lights and a bunch of other stuff! There are certain unwritten rules in surgeon work, like—don't get cute. Before operating always wash your hands—if they're very dirty."

Dayton grew up in New York City. One of his school friends was a kid named Art Carney. Like Carney, Allen began his show biz career in radio. In 1935 WINS hired him as a disc jockey. Discovering a lucrative market in voiceovers and cartoon voices, Allen was the voice of various New York–based kiddie-show characters, appearing on "Winky Dink and You" for five years and playing "Flub-a-Dub" on "Howdy Doody." Dayton was also the voice of Deputy Dawg, Heckle and Jeckle, and many early Terrytoons cartoon characters. He continued to be popular voiceover performer through the 1980s and into the 1990s.

Of course he was still known best as the "Why not?" man. The catch phrase began as a stalling ad lib to an interview question. After it caught on, Allen used it for television commercials and saw novelty toys, a book and a record spin off the "Why not?" phenomena. In its day, fans were shouting "Why not?" as often as *Mad* magazine's famous "What me worry?" An interviewer, confused by the sense and nonsense of people parroting catch phrases, asked Dayton why. He got the answer: "Why not?"

AUDIO: *Why Not?* (Grand Award)
BOOK: *Why Not?*
TV: "The Steve Allen Show" (1958–61)

## FRED ALLEN

### (John Florence Sullivan, May 31, 1894–March 17, 1956)

The billboard in front of the vaudeville house read: "Freddy James, The World's Worst Juggler. His patter whilst Juggling is Very Humorous." Freddy had no luck with blunt objects, but between dropping things, he'd slip in a blunt wisecrack: "I know a man who is so deceitful he puts salt on his toupee to make people think he has dandruff."

Eventually "Freddy James" took the name of his manager, Edgar Allen, and Fred Allen forged his own identity as one of the first cynical, cerebral, satiric stand-up comedians.

Fred Allen's salty approach was iconoclastic. The ancestor of Ernie Kovacs and David Letterman, Allen "put on" the audience constantly. Often he'd come on pretending to be a ventriloquist, performing despite the dummy falling apart in his hands. He liked to put a sign on stage before he went on: "Mr. Allen is Quite Deaf. If You Care to Laugh and Applaud Please Do So Loudly."

Reaching Broadway in *The Passing Show* of 1922 and later *Greenwich Village Follies* of 1924, Allen was still experimenting with comic styles. In 1926 he even teamed with straight man Bert Yorke. Then, for *Disappointments of 1927*, he did a vaudeville sketch with his wife, Portland.

Allen's style was further shaped on radio, where he starred in 1932's "Linit Bath Club Revue." The biggest radio star then was Ed Wynn, who wore funny costumes, told raucous one-liners and invited a live audience in to whoop it up. "Analyzing the comedians' problem in this new business," Fred later wrote, "it seemed to me that the bizarre-garbed, joke-telling funster was ogling extinction. The monotony of his weekly recital of unrelated jokes would soon drive listeners to other diversions. . . . I thought that a complete story told each week or a series of episodes and comedy situations might be a welcome change."

Allen's style was laid-back and dry, easy to take week after week. He developed sketches, running gags and such regular features as reviewing listener mail: "Our postcard tonight comes from Mr. John W. Dunn . . . he says, 'A friend of mine has been in the hospital . . . I have bought him some fruit, a dozen bananas, but I haven't had time to get down to the hospital to eat the fruit at my friend's bedside. The bananas are turning black. What should I do?' It is perfectly permissible, Mr. Dunn, to eat the fruit at home. You can mail the banana skins to your friend in the hospital to prove you have been thinking of him."

Allen made fun of the whole "show biz" process, booking such guests as "Captain Knight," whose stupid pet trick was to accidentally let an eagle loose in the studio. "Probably looking for a taxidermist to give himself up," Allen ad-libbed.

Allen invented the "Mighty Allen Art Players" for satiric sketches, including his "One Long Pan" Chinese detective routines. He played straight man to denizens of "Allen's Alley" such as Mrs. Nussbaum, Ajax Cassidy, Senator Claghorn and Titus Moody, setting up jokes with tongue-in-cheek enthusiasm. Titus Moody speaks first: "My wife lost an ear." "Your wife lost an ear? In an accident?" "She was carryin' a basket of corn from the barn." "And?" "My wife lost an ear." "Fine." Allen's wife Portland (1906–90) appeared on his show, but like Jack Benny's wife Mary, she didn't seem in it for the fame as much as to stay close to her husband.

Allen's detached style and hostility toward pretension influenced many comics, most obviously Dick Cavett, who often lapsed into the raspy Allen cadence when uncomfortable or bored with a cliché-spewing guest. Fred's cutting wit was a rarity in radio. It may seem mild now, but in his day these lines were dangerously caustic:

"California is a great place to live if you're an orange. . . . To me, an advertising agency is 85% confusion and 15% commission. . . . An NBC vice president is a gentleman who doesn't know what his duties are and by the time he finds out, he is no longer there. . . . An associate producer is the only guy in Hollywood who will associate with a producer."

Fred's mock "feud" with Jack Benny, a running gag that lasted for a decade, was insult comedy raised to an art form. "Benny was born ignorant and has been losing ground ever since!" Fred declared. Jack conceded Fred's brains, but not his body: "With those bags under his eyes his face looks like an old pair of pants with the pockets inside out."

Allen's gaunt face suggested the many hours he spent writing his own material on what he called "the treadmill to oblivion." The few gag writers he used were literary, including the young Herman Wouk. More of a wit than a physical comic, he never made the transition to films. It was only after his death that one effort, *It's in the Bag,* came to be appreciated as a minor classic. His radio show was popular, but his dry wit made him less of a draw than a Jack Benny or Bob Hope. When quiz shows became his competition in the late 1940s, Allen bitterly watched his ratings go down. He savagely parodied quiz shows that had to "give away things" to keep audiences amused. He loved radio, though, and feared television, pessimistic about a medium where comics couldn't be witty, only Berle-esque.

When radio gave way to television, Allen was ironically rescued by a variation on quiz shows, "What's My Line?" There he could shoot out occasional one-liners. He could also command $100,000 for his autobiography, which he was feverishly trying to finish despite high blood pressure and heart problems. He suddenly collapsed and died on St. Patrick's Day, while walking his dog across the street from Carnegie Hall. Steve Allen substituted for Fred on the next broadcast of "What's My Line?" On the show, Steve mentioned that many thought Fred was his father. Steve added, "Last night when I heard the sad news, I couldn't have been more depressed if the answer had been yes."

AUDIO: *World of Fred Allen: Comedy Highlights* (Nostalgia Lane), *Down in Allen's Alley* (Radiola), *The Famous Fred Allen Show* (Memorabilia), *Texaco Star Theater* (Radiola), *The Fred Allen Show* (Radiola), *The Fred Allen Show* (Mar-Bren), *Linit Bath Club Revue* (Radio Archives), *Salad Bowl Revue* (Radio Archives), *Fred Allen Looks at Life* (Bagdad), *Tribute to Fred Allen* (Chase and Sanborn, Promotional)
BIOGRAPHIES: *Fred Allen: His Life and Wit* (R. Taylor, 1990), *Fred Allen's Radio Comedy* (Havig, 1990)

BOOKS: *Much Ado About Me* (1956), *Treadmill to Oblivion* (1991), *Fred Allen's Letters* (1965)

FILMS incl.: *Thanks a Million* (1935), *Love Thy Neighbor* (1940), *It's in the Bag* (1945), *We're Not Married* (1952), *O. Henry's Full House* (1953)

TV: "Colgate Comedy Hour" (1950), "Chesterfield Sound Off Time" (1951–52), "Judge for Yourself" (1953–54), "What's My Line" (1954–56)

## STEVE ALLEN

### (December 26, 1921–    )

He was born with a long, long name: Steven Valentine Patrick William Allen. His credits would become even longer as a talk show host/comedian/author/actor/musician. But to millions of fans, he is simply Steve Allen, that simplicity reflecting the personality of a man who never let his gift of genius lift him over the common man.

A symbol of nice guys finishing first, Allen has earned the distinction of being one of the best-liked and most respected comedians of all time. Lenny Bruce characterized him as "the most moral comic I ever met . . . a good, good man," and almost everyone agreed with that assessment. Utilizing a deceptively easy style, he appealed to the hip and to the heartland. His wit delighted the intellectuals but was not beyond the reach of everyone else. He expressed opinions openly, which gratified free thinkers, but at the same time never offended anyone. His humor could be silly or satiric or both at the same time.

Allen grew up in show business. His parents, Billy Allen and Belle Montrose, were a vaudeville team. Montrose continued alone after Allen's death following an appendicitis operation in 1923. Milton Berle called Belle "the funniest woman in vaudeville," and though his early years were tough and marked by a lot of travel and confusion, Steve decided on a show business career too.

He worked nightclubs with a partner, Wendell Noble, but had better luck as a disc jockey with his own show in Phoenix in 1948. He went to New York two years later. After Jerry Lester's "Broadway Open House" left television, Allen took over that late-night time spot with his unique "Tonight Show," a program that mixed sketches, songs, guest appearances by bright new comics and interviews into a pioneering new style, one that would influence Johnny Carson, David Letterman and many more talk show hosts and comedians.

Allen created "the Answer Man," the first man to figure out the question to any answer. Such as the answer: "Butterfield 8-3000." The question? "How many hamburgers did Butterfield eat?" Allen delighted in taking cameras out of the studio to interview people in the street. Sometimes he'd let the camera merely spy on passersby while he created his own narration to their everyday actions. He made "funny phone calls" to strangers, played "stump the band" with the studio audience and pioneered a new brand of "stunt comedy," which ranged from organizing a pie fight with the entire studio audience to covering himself in tea bags and dunking himself in a giant cup. Allen's quick wit enabled him to keep the show fresh and unpredictable as he ad-libbed with the audience. Question: "Do they get your program in Boston?" Answer: "Well, they see it but they don't get it."

Steve's theories on comedy, from brief axioms ("Tragedy + Time = Comedy") to full essays, have filled several books. After "The Tonight Show" he periodically returned to television with talk shows in different formats. He also guest-hosted other talk shows. His opening lines—filling in for Merv Griffin—show his trademark "parenthetical" technique of spontaneously transforming straight lines into whimsical comedy:

"You're probably wondering where Merv is. (I know I am.) Well, Merv was in a hot poker game last night (and he lost the show). No, Merv came down with the bug (that's something you get from watching Watergate). But the real story is that it's Merv's mother's birthday, and so he had to go to San Quentin to visit her. No, seriously, I'm filling in for Merv because he had a slight accident. I ran over him. Actually, Merv is sick, but game trouper he is (did you know Merv was once a game trouper. . . .)."

If anyone could have influenced Steve's style in verbal humor, it was probably Groucho Marx. Steve himself noted how closely some of his remarks resembled things Groucho might have said. It wasn't Groucho but Steve who explained why he refused to join a particular social organization: "I was invited to sit on the committee, and if there's anything I'd like to do to that committee it's sit on it." And when a sexy starlet said, "I have a healthy constitution," it was Grouchoesque Steve who answered, "You certainly do, and the amendments to it are pretty impressive too."

Allen's impressive credits mounted over the years as he authored sociological studies, mysteries and novels. Even a minor Steve Allen ad lib became a part of the language when, as a panelist on "What's My Line?" he asked, "Is it bigger than a breadbox?" He wrote musical revues *(Seymour Glick Is Alive and Sick)*, Broadway shows *(Sophie)* and won a place in the *Guinness Book of World Records* for writing more than 4,000 songs, including the hits "This Could Be the Start of Something Big" and "Grazy Waltz." Steve once said, "My main gift is for music." But in comedy, few names have been as important over the past 40 years as Steve Allen. It was a rare year when Allen didn't host his own television or radio show, publish a valuable comedy book or star in an important comedy project.

Despite all his honors as a comedy legend, Allen remains characteristically humble. When he received an award for his "contributions to television," he told the crowd, "Yeah, that's right. Last year alone I contributed more than $3,000."

AUDIO incl.: *Man in the Street* (Signature), *Funny Fone Calls* (Dot, re-issued by Casablanca), *More Funny Fone Calls* (Dot, re-issued by Casablanca)

BOOKS: *Funny People* (1981), *Bob Fables* (1955), *Fourteen for Tonight* (1955), *The Funny Men* (1956), *Wry on the Rocks* (1956), *The Girls on the Tenth Floor* (1958), *The Question Man* (1959), *Mark It and Strike It* (1960), *Not All of Your Laughter Not All Your Tears* (1962), *Letter to a Conservative* (1965), *The Ground Is Our Table* (1966), *Bigger Than a Breadbox* (1967), *A Flash of Swallows* (1969), *The Wake* (1972), *Princess Snip-Snip and the Puppykittens, Curses* (1973); *What to Say When It Rains* (1975), *Schmock! Schmock!* (1975), *Meeting of Minds Vols. 1–5* (1989), *Chopped-up Chinese, Ripoff—The Corruption that Plagues America* (1979), *Explaining China* (1980); *The Talk Show Murders* (1982), *Beloved Son* (1982); *More Funny People* (1982), *Murder on the Glitter Box* (1990), *How to Be Funny* (1988), *Dumbth* (1979), *Murder in Manhattan* (1990)

A television pioneer, a prolific songwriter and a famed analyst of comedy, Steve Allen has appeared in 15 television shows and has written over 4,000 songs and more than 30 books, including *Funny People* and *More Funny People*. Photo from the author's collection.

FILMS: *Down Memory Lane* (1949), *The Benny Goodman Story* (1956), *The Big Circus* (1959), *College Confidential* (1960), *Where Were You When the Lights Went Out* (1968), *The Comic* (1969), *Heart Beat* (1980), *Amazon Women on the Moon* (1987)

## WOODY ALLEN

### (Alan Stewart Konigsberg, December 1, 1935–   )

The most famous combination writer/director/comedian since Charles Chaplin, Woody Allen began his career contributing gags to Earl Wilson's newspaper column. He was still a student at Brooklyn's Midwood High School when he penned them. A typical line Wilson used: "Woody Allen says he ate at a restaurant that had OPS prices—over people's salaries."

He told biographer Eric Lax that his adopted name had "all the glamorous appeal of show business one imagines in Flatbush." His father, Martin, told another writer that "the kids on the block named him 'Woody' because he was always the one to bring

From a brilliant joke writer and stand-up comic, Woody Allen has become an accomplished screenwriter and director with classics such as *Annie Hall, Manhattan, Hannah and Her Sisters* and *Crimes and Misdemeanors.* Photo from the author's collection.

the stick out for the stickball game. He was always athletic."

Contrary to his image, Woody Allen was indeed a good baseball player with the local Police Athletic League. He recalled, "I was not a good student, no good in math, Spanish, history or anything. I didn't study . . . I lived in the movies. I'd go seven days a week and sometimes sat through two or three shows. The movies served as my education."

He was only 17 when he became a full-time comedy writer at NBC. Before long he was contributing gags to "Your Show of Shows" and earning $1,700 a week on the staff of Garry Moore's show. Woody gave up the writing life for stand-up com-

edy, influenced by Mort Sahl's comedy-in-the-form-of-therapy style. It was agony, but Allen learned—in front of a live audience—to capitalize on his timidity by turning every gulp for air and every stutter into a calculated comic device. By combining disciplined one-liners with the more conversational and confessional styles of Sahl and Shelley Berman, Allen became a unique hybrid.

From 1964 to 1968 he rose to the top of his profession. His wife jokes had a thinking man's edge. From an appearance on television's "That Was the Week That Was" in 1965: "I had a bad marriage. My wife and I thought we were in love, but it turned out to be benign." Many of his lines became instant classics. "I used to steal second base—and feel guilty and go back. . . . I was thrown out of NYU. On my metaphysics final I looked within the soul of the boy sitting next to me. . . . I don't believe in the afterlife, but I am bringing a change of underwear."

An earlier generation of "sicknik" comics had begun to call attention to their alienation. Allen was part of the next generation trying to survive despite the alienation. "Not only is God dead, but try getting a plumber on a Saturday night." Life was less meaningless to Woody if he at least had a hot-looking girlfriend and took in a Bogart movie now and then. Many of his fans had a similar hope; and when Woody began making films, some hoped to find *their* dream date standing alone on line at *Play It Again Sam.*

Allen always resented the tag of filmdom's most famous "nebbish." Though his horn-rimmed glasses, messy hair and five-foot-six, 125-pound body made him seem the spindly "loser," he sought an image closer to that of his film idol, Bob Hope. He wanted to be the dashing coward. For all his fumbling and foolery, he made sure to "get the girl." Allen's unique combination of intellectuality, wit, humor and lust did indeed make him a sex symbol for some women and a role model for some men. In the late 1960s and early '70s he was the perfect cult hero for his time, when sexual revolution and social liberation promised a new life for those in quiet desperation. Woody's character was neurotic and self-doubting, but fueled by fantasies of grandeur, ready to rob banks (*Take the Money and Run*) or overthrow a country (*Bananas, Sleeper*) in order to be the star of his own fantasies (*Play It Again Sam*).

Allen phased out stand-up in the late 1960s and with each new movie made new strides toward the mastery of his art. From visualized one-liners (*Take the Money and Run*) he experimented with political satire (*Bananas*) and moved to deeper comedy with a touch of romance (*Love and Death*, a film that still had Groucho Marx-influenced comebacks and Bob Hope–styled cowardice, but featured a character with more than a few dimensions).

He reached his peak with the Academy Award-winning *Annie Hall*. Not only were there the usual quota of hostile one-liners and sight gags, but there was humor and drama drawn from the heart. The film captured the era perfectly and it marked a major change in Allen's comic identity. In the past, including his stand-up days, he was the lustful little intellect who said of one lady, "When I see a girl that beautiful, I want to write a poem . . . cry . . . jump on her!" Now he was able to write poignantly from a woman's point of view and create a screen romance beyond the stereotyped women of his earlier films. The focus of the film was not Woody, but Annie Hall, and as such, it propelled co-star Diane Keaton to instant stardom.

Allen's next film, *Manhattan*, was a plateau just slightly below the level of *Annie Hall*. The bittersweet film was again concerned with failed relationships, but there were still moments of visual comedy, including the boating scene in which Woody discovers the romance of the Central Park lake—as well as the reeking glop that Woody pulls out of it.

The 1970s had come to an end and with it an end to Woody Allen's first era of film work. A generation grew up with Woody, sharing his preoccupation with light-hearted sex and the playboy lifestyle (*What's New Pussycat, Everything You Always Wanted to Know About Sex . . .*), fantasizing about ruling the world (*Casino Royale*) and over a decade coming to grips with earning a living (*The Front*) and finding an enduring relationship (*Annie Hall*).

If growing up was difficult for Allen, it was doubly so for his fans. Quite a few expected him to continue with light-hearted sex comedies. They went to revival houses to rerun Woody's earlier hits. Woody's serious drama *Interiors* had perplexed many fans, as did *Stardust Memories*, which presented fans as nerdy, neurotic pests and Allen as an agitated genius who (to judge from the film style) was in the same league as Fellini or Bergman.

To quite a few fans, the heroic Woody of the 1970s—sexy, lovable, forgivably shy and neurotic—was replaced by a different Woody in the 1980s—aging, cold and reclusive. Fans resented Woody's habit of appearing in public hiding underneath hats ludicrously pulled down over his eyes. On television's "Saturday Night Live," Bill Murray often chided "the Wood-man" for such behavior. As Mort Sahl pointed out, "Woody wants his privacy. He's hired a dozen publicity men to tell you that."

In the 1980s occasionally Woody Allen produced a film of genius, or at least a film with sparks of his old comic stylings. *Broadway Danny Rose* was a charming valentine to the old show biz world of agents and comics that had begun to fade away in the 1960s and '70s. The startling mock documentary *Zelig* took three years to make and featured intricate cinematography in telling the tale of a human chameleon who absorbed the personalities and even faces of others because "it's safe to be like the others. I want to be liked." Its originality and audacity had critics comparing it to the documentary style of *Citizen Kane* and the pure cinema of silent and foreign films. *Hannah and Her Sisters* was Allen's biggest box office hit of the 1980s and earned him yet another Oscar, for Best Screenplay.

Despite Allen's problems including a few box office failures, he still had great critical support, a core following of fans, and was still influencing the world of comedy. The zany style of early Woody Allen films influenced any number of anything-goes films, while *Annie Hall* spawned a variety of "sensitive" screen comedies starring everyone from Albert Brooks to Billy Crystal. Woody's best-selling books of short humor, themselves influenced by S. J. Perelman and Robert Benchley, became the style of choice for a new generation of humorists. His writing offered cheeky and wry aphorisms ("It is impossible to experience one's own death objectively and still carry a tune") as well as fey literary satire: "O'Shawn was a mystic and, like Blake, believed in unseen forces. This was confirmed for him when his brother Ben was struck by lightning while licking a postage stamp. The lightning failed to kill Ben, which O'Shawn attributed to Providence, although it took his brother seventeen years before he could get his tongue back in his mouth."

The new generation of stand-up comics had grown up listening to Woody's records, and leading "surrealist" and "neurotic" stars Steven Wright and Richard Lewis pointed out their indebtedness.

Still, despite his smoothed personal life (his relationship with Mia Farrow was a lasting success, he had a child, and he even lost his trademark floppy hat disguise in public), Allen had to remain on the defensive. After making another serious and largely unappreciated film, *September* (and then remaking it with new cast members), Allen declared: "I have to be taken seriously. . . . Certain ideas occur to me that are not comic and that's the long and the short of it. . . . I just want to feel free to create any kind of work that occurs to me." *September* was followed with another drama, *Another Woman,* which had comedy fans seriously concerned.

As the 1980s drew to a close, Allen returned to the Woody of old, appearing in a typical role: the mother-pecked fellow in the most praised segment of *New York Stories.* The short film delighted many fans who were glad to see "the old Woody" back. He even took a break from writing/directing to star in someone else's comedy, *Scenes from a Mall,* opposite Bette Midler.

As the 1990s began Allen was drawing praise for one of his best films ever, *Crimes and Misdemeanors.* The film was not only effective as drama, it had some light moments and the most quotable Woody Allen one-liner in years, his hapless admission that "the last woman I was in was the Statue of Liberty." The film was nominated for two Academy Awards (Best Director and Best Screenplay). *American Film* magazine noted, "Allen in his comedies in the 60s and early 70s was keyed into the country's radical mood; he set the tone for the hippest movie humor . . . with this film, he's moved into . . . a resonance with modern urban despair. . . . Woody Allen is facing up to his own hopelessness and he wants us to recognize it as our hopelessness too."

Allen continues to have the artistic luxury of writing, directing and (more often than not) starring in the projects of his choosing. With this creative security—and his undeniable genius for comedy and filmmaking—there is no doubt that he will continue to be at the forefront of his craft and a major influence on comedy itself.

AUDIO: *Woody Allen* (Colpix, reissued by Bell), *Woody Allen Volume 2* (Colpix), *Woody Allen Volume 3* (Capitol), *Woody Allen, the Nightclub Years* (United Artists, reedited as *Woody Allen: Stand-up Comic* and later reissued by Casablanca)

BIOGRAPHIES: *Films of Woody Allen* (Benayoun, 1987), *Woody Allen, Clown Prince of American Humor* (Adler and Feinman, 1975), *On Being Funny: Woody Allen and His Comedy* (Eric Lax, 1975), *Woody Allen* (Bendazzi, 1976), *Woody Allen, A Biography* (Guthrie, 1978), *Woody Allen* (Lebrun, 1979), *Loser Take All: The Comic Art of Woody Allen* (Yacowar, 1991), *Woody Allen, An Illustrated Biography* (Palmer, 1980), *Love, Death and the Meaning of Life* (Hirsch, 1981), *Woody Allen* (Postel, 1991), *Woody Allen: Joking Aside* (McKnight, 1992), *Woody Allen: New Yorker* (McCann, 1990), *Woody Allen: A Biography* (Lax, 1991)

BOOKS: *Getting Even* (1971), *Without Feathers* (1975), *Side Effects* (1980), *Four Films by Woody Allen* (1982), *Three Films by Woody Allen* (1987), *Hannah and Her Sisters* (1986)

BROADWAY: *Play It Again Sam*

FILMS: *What's New Pussycat* (1964), *What's Up Tiger Lily?* (1966), *Casino Royale* (1967), *Take the Money and Run* (1969), *Bananas* (1971), *Play It Again Sam* (1972), *Everything You Always Wanted to Know About Sex But Were Afraid to Ask* (1972), *Sleeper* (1973), *Love and Death* (1975), *The Front* (1976), *Annie Hall* (1977), *Interiors* (1978), *Manhattan* (1979), *Stardust Memories* (1980), *A Midsummer Night's Sex Comedy* (1982), *Zelig* (1983), *Broadway Danny Rose* (1984), *The Purple Rose of Cairo* (1985), *Hannah and Her Sisters* (1986), *Radio Days* (1987), *September* (1988), *Another Woman* (1988), *New York Stories* (1989), *Crimes and Misdemeanors* (1989), *Alice* (1990), *Scenes from a Mall* (1990), *Shadows and Fog* (1992)

PLAYS: *Don't Drink the Water, Play It Again Sam, The Floating Light Bulb*

## JEFF ALTMAN

### (August 13, 1951–   )

In a fancy restaurant, Jeff Altman suddenly whipped off his shirt. The table shielded his lower half, making him look completely naked to everyone in the crowd. "I only had my shirt off for 15 seconds," Altman recalled. But his shaken dinner partner, David Letterman, has never forgotten it.

A harmless-looking explosive, Altman looks ordinary—but acts completely insane. Like his biggest influence, Jonathan Winters, and his friend Robin Williams, Altman seems rather benign—until he steps into character, playing punch-drunk boxer Leonard Moon, the raving "Dog Man" or his tense and combative "Father." The latter is close to genius; Altman hurtles past Don Knotts in presenting a nervously excitable figure quivering with rage. As "Father" he sweatily pulls at the waistband of his pants, girding up his courage, and shouts trembling threats at his son: "I'll flip you like a cheese omelette, I'll lay you out like wholesale carpet, buddy boy!"

In the course of a performance, as on his 1990 Showtime Special *Sweet and Meaty*, Altman swings manically between his crazed characters and deliberately crazy non sequiturs. At one point he ran up to the camera lens and shouted, "Do you see a large, goat-headed zebra in my nose?"

Serious and thoughtful off stage, Altman, a graduate of Johns Hopkins University, can see the philosophical side of comedy. "I think people are about as happy as they feel they have control over the world and themselves. I think very often depression is linked to feelings of being out of control. Being a performer is a way of controlling the world and the lives of people. We go on stage and make people laugh. It's controlling someone in a good way. . . . A lot of people would say, and I might agree to some degree, frustration, unhappiness and free-floating anxiety is part of what makes people creative. I think to be a comic you're either very sensitive to the environment or slightly introspective."

He started in show business with a magic act and later added comedy. His career took off with a Jimmy Carter parody album, guest spots on television's "Mork and Mindy," "WKRP in Cincinnati" and "Archie Bunker's Place," and a regular role on the short-lived variety show "Cos." Bill Cosby's series folded quickly, but a much bigger disaster was "Pink Lady and Jeff," an Asian attempt at "Tony Orlando and Dawn." Altman literally interpreted for Mie Nemoto and Kei Masuda, the duo called Pink Lady. They sang and coyly mangled the language, while Altman, in an uncomfortable tux, tried to maintain order.

Altman returned to stand-up, made films and became a well-known face in television commercials.

The *New York Times* in August 1988 reported that he made more than $25,000 a day doing commercials and was one of the country's most sought-after pitchmen. His wife, Leslie Ackerman, appeared in the spots he did for Toll House Cookies. He appeared with his idol Jonathan Winters in a Showtime cable special in 1988. He followed it with his own cable special in 1990 *(Sweet and Meaty),* a starring role in the television comedy "Nurses" and his first solo comedy album, which of course included Father's favorite insults: "I'll flip you like a cheese omelette . . . I'll sink you like a three-foot putt, I'll hit you so hard your kids'll be born dizzy . . . I can stop you like a bad check!"

AUDIO: *I'll Flip You Like a Cheese Omelette* (Mercury)
FILMS incl.: *American Hot Wax* (1978), *Easy Money* (1983), *Doin' Time* (1985), *Soul Man* (1986)
TV: "Mary Hartman, Mary Hartman" (1975–77), "Cos" (1976), "Pink The Starland Vocal Band Show" (1977), "Pink Lady and Jeff" (1980), "Solid Gold" (1982–83), "Nurses" (1991)
VIDEO: *Rodney Dangerfield: It's Not Easy Being Me; Laughing Room Only*

## DON AMECHE (See THE BICKERSONS.)

## AMOS and ANDY (See also TIM MOORE.)

**Andy Brown: Charles Correll, February 3, 1890–September 26, 1972**
**Amos Jones: Freeman Gosden, May 5, 1899–December 10, 1982**

In the duo's prime, movie theaters would stop the film and put on the radio so that listeners wouldn't miss Amos and Andy. Now the name that once was beloved by a nation is tainted by charges of racism.

First teamed in North Carolina in 1919, Freeman Gosden and Charles Correll made their radio debut in New Orleans in 1920. On January 12, 1926 over WGN in Chicago they starred in a radio show called "Sam and Henry." Sam and Henry were a typical comedy team, one member smart and the other dumb. Also typical for the era, they adopted ethnic personalities. The "funny accents" most popular back then were Irish, Italian, Jewish, German and

Southern black. Since they knew the South well, they chose the latter.

A key to success as a team is likability. Audiences cared about Sam and Henry. The scripts evolved from gags strung together into stories that were often handled soap-opera style with multipart adventures. Victor recorded Sam and Henry in 1926 issuing "Sam 'n' Henry Rollin' the Bones" and "Sam 'n' Henry at the Dentist." When the team attempted to leave WGN for better pay at rival WMAQ, they became Amos and Andy. They moved to network radio on August 19, 1929 and stayed on the air through 1951.

Fans of the show insisted the show was good for race relations, presenting blacks as unthreatening, nonviolent and good-natured, with the same foibles as everyone else. Others were embarrassed by the duo's use of dialect (especially coming from whites impersonating blacks) and resented characters that seemed too dumb (Andy) or shifty (Kingfish).

Actually, the problem was not Amos and Andy. It was the lack of anything *besides* Amos and Andy. When raucous, ethnic television shows such as "Sanford and Son" or "The Jeffersons" appeared, there were at least sitcoms from Bill Cosby or blockbuster films such as *Roots* for counterbalance. Few blacks were on radio balancing out the comedy of Amos and Andy catch phrases such as "Ize regusted" and "ain't dat sumpin'." Oddly enough, while blackface was still accepted (*The Jolson Story* was a huge hit in 1946), Gosden and Correll had no success in blackface in their lone Amos and Andy film, *Check and Double Check*. Listeners evidently had their own ideas about what the duo looked like, and these two white guys didn't fit in with them.

Through the 1930s and '40s, Amos and Andy remained intensely popular. An estimated 40 million people tuned in to listen to the show—out of the total U.S. population of 100 million.

When radio gave way to television, Gosden and Correll hand-picked the black actors and actresses for the roles, including Spencer Williams as Andy, veteran comic Tim Moore as Kingfish and Alvin Childress as Amos. Childress was the first to be cast for the television version. He always insisted, "I didn't feel it harmed the Negro at all. . . . Actually the series had many episodes that showed the Negro with professions . . . attorneys, store owners, and

so on, which they never had in TV or movies before." The show had a short run and for years was so frowned upon by civil rights activists that it was banned from rerun syndication. The controversy extended into the 1980s when videocassettes were released to the general public, and many debated whether the shows were any better or worse than more recent sitcoms "Sanford and Son," "Good Times" and "The Jeffersons."

The big plus for the series was that it used blacks. Many who championed the show still protested the radio series because it starred whites as blacks. In the 1950s Gosden and Correll used their comical voices for "Calvin and the Colonel," a cartoon series. But in their lifetime, the two elderly men who had once been the most beloved stars of radio found themselves worse than has-beens, their life's work over 40 years bitterly attacked and derided. They seemed to give up on trying to defend themselves and lived in obscure retirement.

Amos and Andy did influence subsequent generations of sitcom writers and performers. Fans of "The Honeymooners" recognized that the debt to Amos and Andy was strong, up to the inclusion of "The Raccoon Lodge," a variation on Kingfish and Calhoun's "Mystic Knights of the Sea." "The Odd Couple," "Sanford and Son" and many others were influenced by "Amos and Andy," both in sitcom plots and the character comedy that explored the friendship and friction of two men who sometimes insulted each other or schemed against each other but—underneath it all—remained good friends.

On his 1960s variety show, Dean Martin regularly lapsed into winking dialect for throwaway lines ("I gonna go to de couch" or "Nobody 'splained it to me"). Johnny Carson used it through the 1980s. In 1989 Carson told a joke about the government spending $500 million for Stealth bombers. An official claimed the "sticker price" on the bomber was reasonable. Carson said, in a broad Kingfish accent, "The trouble is, Andy, we're the stickee!" During the laughter he walked over to a ringsider, a black woman, and said with an apologetic smile, "I know that stuff went out years ago . . ."

AUDIO: *Amos and Andy Story* (Radiola), *Amos and Andy Best Loved Shows* (Murray Hill), *Amos and Andy Classics* (Murray Hill), *Legendary Amos and Andy*

(Murray Hill), *Rare Amos and Andy* (Murray Hill), *The Christmas Show* (Radiola), *Amos and Andy* (Radiola), *Amos and Andy* (Mar-Bren), *Amos and Andy* (Radio Greats), *Amos and Andy* (Yorkshire), *Amos and Andy 1943* (Memorabilia), *Amos and Andy 1949* (Memorabilia), *Amos and Andy 1955* (Memorabilia), *Original Broadcasts* (Golden Age), *Rarest Amos and Andy* (Radiola)

BOOKS: *All About Amos and Andy and Their Creators* (Freeman and Gosden, 1929), *Holy Mackerel* (Andrews and Juilliard, 1986), *The Adventures of Amos 'n' Andy: A Social History* (Ely, 1991)

FILMS: *Check and Double Check* (1930), *Big Broadcast of 1935* (1935)

TV: "Calvin and the Colonel" (1961–62), "Amos and Andy" (all black cast), 1951–53

VIDEOS: *Amos and Andy: Anatomy of a Controversy; Amos and Andy TV Episodes* (Vols. 1–16)

## MOREY AMSTERDAM

### (December 14, 1912–  )

Dubbed "the Human Joke Machine," little Morey Amsterdam could spout one-liners on any topic shouted out from the audience.

Originally planning on a career in serious music, Morey was an accomplished cellist. He mixed music and comedy in writing a few popular novelty hits in the 1940s. He adapted an old Trinidad ditty into The Andrew Sisters' "Rum and Coca Cola" and wrote "Why Oh Why Did I Ever Leave Wyoming," "Oh, My Achin' Back" and "I Can't Get Offa My Horse." His signature tune, "Yuk a Puk," was a series of everchanging gags strung together with a nonsense chorus: "It's easy to grin when your ship comes in and life is a happy lot. But the man who's worthwhile is the man who can smile when his shorts creep up in a knot. Yuk a puk, yuk a puk, yuk a puk. . . ."

Amsterdam wrote some yucks for Will Rogers, worked on radio through the 1940s and became a panelist on the early television quiz show "Stop Me If You've Heard This One." He had his own series in 1948. The jokes and music were set at the "Golden Goose Cafe," where Morey had comic troubles with Charlie the waiter (Art Carney) and Lola the cigarette girl (Jacqueline Susann).

Amsterdam's most famous role was Buddy Sorrel on television's "Dick Van Dyke Show." The imp played a veteran comedy writer, which was a good excuse for his running stream of one-liners. He even had his own foil on the show, bald Richard Deacon as producer Mel Cooley. Amsterdam's yuk-a-puckish charm and cheerful delivery prevented his insult comedy from really causing much damage. In a typical skirmish Buddy insults Mel in front of comedy writer Sally Rogers (Rose Marie):

BUDDY: I wish you'd kept your hair and lost the rest of you.

SALLY: Watch it, Buddy, he'll turn on you.

BUDDY: What's the difference, he's the same on both sides!

Amsterdam continued his stand-up career after the series ended. He slowed down at 69 after he underwent a triple-bypass heart operation. Amsterdam told reporters after the operation, "I am a very very lucky man. God was with me and I give Him thanks." He went on to other roles, including a stint guest starring on the soap opera "The Young and the Restless" in 1990.

Married for more than 50 years, Amsterdam said the secret of a long-lasting relationship was simple. Never bicker. "It's a waste of time. Next day, you've forgotten what you argued about. One day Kay said, 'You're no fun to fight with.' And we haven't had that problem since." He added, "She is more than a wife, she's a very close friend. . . . A thousand times I've said to Kay, 'If I ever complain about you, take me out and shoot me because I've got nothing to complain about!' "

AUDIO: *Morey Amsterdam's Party Album* (three 78-rpm discs, Crown), *Yuk-a-Puk* (Signature, reissued as *The Next One Will Kill You* by Roulette), *Funny You Should Ask* (Marsh), *Uncle Morey's Mixed Up Stories* (Golden)

BOOKS: *Keep Laughing* (1959); *Morey Amsterdam's Book for Drinkers or Betty Cooker's Crock Book* (1977)

FILMS incl.: *Machine Gun Kelly* (1958), *Don't Worry We'll Think of a Title* (1966), *Horse in the Grey Flannel Suit* (1968), *Wholly Moses* (1980)

TV: "Stop Me If You've Heard This One" (1948), "The Morey Amsterdam Show" (1948–50), "Broadway Open House" (1950), "Battle of the

Ages" (1952), "Who Said That?" (1954), "Keep Talking" (1958–60), "The Dick Van Dyke Show" (1961–66), "Can You Top This" (1969–70)

VIDEO: *George Burns Wit and Wisdom*

## EDDIE "ROCHESTER" ANDERSON

### (September 18, 1905–February 28, 1977)

In the 1930s, most black comedians were stereotyped as servants of some kind. On radio, Eddie Anderson's "Rochester" served Jack Benny, but his attitude was a sarcastic "It serves you right!"

When they had exchanges, Rochester was the one who usually got the laughs. Rochester greeting Jack on his arrival: "Your dentist and your barber called." "What did they say?" "Both gave me the same message—you can pick 'em up tomorrow." Rochester also had ample opportunity to tell his own gags. Describing his new girlfriend to Jack, he said, "Mr. Benny, did you ever see a Hershey bar with all the almonds in the right places?"

That line would not be out of place on "Sanford and Son" or "Good Times"—black television shows of the 1970s. But for some people, the character of Rochester was an uncomfortable stereotype. In his autobiography Jack Benny wrote that he got more complaints from Southern whites who were upset by Rochester's sass. According to Benny, an episode in which Rochester sparred with Jack and knocked him out "brought the heaviest mail we ever received on the program. . . . I was amazed . . . to me I was just doing a comedy show. Would it have been funny if I had knocked out Rochester?" He added, "You don't hate a race when you're laughing with it. You couldn't hate Rochester . . . you loved Rochester."

Eddie Anderson came from a show business family. His mother was a circus aerialist, his father a song and dance man (half of the team of Anderson and Goines). Anderson quit high school to appear in a 1919 revue called *Struttin' Along*. For a few years he was one of the Three Black Aces and played the Apollo Theater and the Cotton Club in Harlem. In 1932 he made his film debut in *What Price Hollywood?* He had bits parts in many films, including the little role of elevator operator in *Three Men on a*

*Horse.* In 1937 he accepted a quick booking to do the voice of the Pullman porter Rochester Van Jones on a Jack Benny show. The pay was $50. But when Anderson's comical voice was heard, a new character was born, one whose fame would last well over the next 50 years. Rochester's exasperated gravelly voice contrasted with Benny's placid delivery like a saw biting into a violin.

Anderson stayed with Benny through radio, films and television, but made a few memorable appearances on his own, including the film *Cabin in the Sky* in 1943. He even recorded a few novelty tunes in the early 1940s. Though he suffered some comic indignities in films (taking several falls in *Topper Returns*), he usually was allowed to register his own indignation. Having a tough time as Topper's chauffeur, he huffs, "I'm goin' back to Mr. Benny! Nothin' like this ever happened to him!" He got a chance to do a song and dance number in *Star Spangled Rhythm*. Eyeing one lady, he sang, "You ain't only classy, you're highly Selassie!"

Working for W. C. Fields in *You Can't Cheat an Honest Man* was also different from working with Benny. They were together in a scene that called for endless retakes. Abruptly Fields refused to do another and locked himself away from the crew—with sidekick Anderson. When the director called, Fields shouted, "This time *we're* not ready," and spent an hour drinking martinis with Rochester. When the two men finally emerged, the set was dark. The crew had given up and gone home.

Rochester's son Bill grew up to play football for the Chicago Bears in the early 1950s. In 1954 his wife died at only 42. In 1958, while rehearsing a Jack Benny show, Rochester suffered a heart attack. He was never the same after that. Fans got their last good look at him when he played a cameo role as a cab driver in *It's a Mad Mad Mad Mad World*.

FILMS: *You Can't Take It with You* (1938), *Gone With the Wind* (1939), *You Can't Cheat an Honest Man* (1939), *Man About Town* (1939), *Buck Benny Rides Again* (1940), *Topper Returns* (1941), *Tales of Manhattan* (1942), *Meanest Man in the World* (1943), *Cabin in the Sky* (1943), *It's a Mad Mad Mad Mad World* (1963)

TV: "The Jack Benny Show" (1953–65)

## FATTY ARBUCKLE

### (Roscoe Conkling Arbuckle, March 24, 1887– June 29, 1933)

Yesterday Fatty Arbuckle was one of America's favorite film stars. Today most people know his name only in connection with the worst scandal in early film history.

After living in near poverty in Kansas, Arbuckle and his family moved to California when he was two. Arbuckle joined Leon Errol's vaudeville troupe while in his teens, and the 266-pounder earned a good living on stage. He concentrated on film work in 1913, the year he joined Mack Sennett. Eclipsing Ford Sterling as Sennett's top comedian, Roscoe Arbuckle became "Fatty," a nickname he disliked. If it was used once too often by a reporter, he'd quietly say, "I have a name, you know."

His name grew as big as he. When Arbuckle left Sennett, he signed a deal for $1,000 *a day* from Paramount, plus a Rolls-Royce as a signing bonus.

Fatty's films were loaded with belly laughs and inventive gags. Not merely a fat guy falling down in Sennett slapstick, Roscoe Arbuckle used his expressive face, puckish personality and graceful choreography to create a character America loved. He created grand sight gags (such as the floating bedroom in the short subject *Mable and Fatty Adrift*) and, like Keaton and Chaplin, had serious theories about the art of comedy. One, later used by The Marx Brothers, was to test key scenes before live audiences. Arbuckle reshot sequences, regardless of expense, if they didn't get the reaction he wanted. He dropped gags that were too esoteric or too risqué, wanting comedy that children and their parents could enjoy.

Arbuckle's image was good clean fun. Off camera, he was so shy he insisted his wife turn out the lights before they made love. When a starlet came into his dressing room to ask about her costume—and casually began removing it to try on her second choice— Fatty left the room immediately. He had her fired from his picture.

Years before Chaplin scored with *The Gold Rush,* Fatty had hits with feature films *The Round Up, The Life of the Party* and *Brewster's Millions.* The hardworking comedian had to film three features simul-

taneously to keep up with demand. But that demand ebbed after Monday, September 5, 1921.

The legend, as told in *Hollywood Babylon* and other books, is that Arbuckle raped actress Virginia Rappe after inviting her to a big Hollywood party. Rumor had it he ruptured her bladder with a bottle and that, mortally wounded, she was taken from the room naked and gasping, crying out the name of her attacker.

What actually happened was clearly documented in the trial transcripts and in the pioneering 1976 book by David Yallop, *The Day the Laughter Stopped.* Virginia Rappe, a minor starlet notorious for her loose lifestyle, crashed the party. She had undergone five abortions and was a few months pregnant once again. She also had venereal diseases that caused severe infections, bladder problems and a "running abscess."

After soaking up the bootleg liquor at Arbuckle's party, she got so drunk she began throwing up. Several women assisted her as she rested between 3 P.M. and 9 P.M., periodically dozing, then throwing up. They tried homemade remedies, which ranged from standing her on her head to dunking her nude in cold water. Ice, wrapped in towels, was placed on her head and stomach. She was seen by a doctor and also by the house detective, who wanted to make sure she was not going to put the hotel in a compromising position.

The next morning a doctor examined her and noted, "Patient gives history of having been intoxicated last night. She does not remember just what happened, complains of pain in abdomen, vomiting, some trouble with the urine." If Virginia didn't remember what happened, that was fine with Maude Delmont. Delmont, a crafty woman with an eye for crooked deals, was determined to make herself Virginia's friend and make them both some money.

On Wednesday, September 7, she wired her lawyer: "We have Roscoe Arbuckle in a hole here. Chance to make some money out of him." Virginia Rappe had made no statements about Arbuckle until she was coached by Maude Delmont. Theorists aren't sure if Virginia became part of the plot or was convinced by Maude that Fatty might have taken advantage of her while she was passed out. Either way, she was ready to file suit. But she died

September 9, officially of peritonitis caused by her ruptured bladder.

Maude Delmont didn't get money from Arbuckle, but she enjoyed instant stardom when she began manufacturing lies and innuendos about the incident. She was never put on the stand (since her story conflicted greatly with that of other witnesses), but before Fatty could get a fair trial the public had made up its mind. Women's rights activists literally spat on him as he walked to court. Although he was emphatically exonerated after a nightmare of botched trials and confusion, Paramount Pictures and the "watchdog" for the industry, Will Hays, still refused to allow Arbuckle to work. The public wanted a scapegoat, and Arbuckle served nicely.

Paramount stuck Fatty's newest film, *Leap Year*, in the vault. Ironically, this preserved the film far better than most other silent movies. While many of his films were lost or damaged, *Leap Year* has become one of his more accessible efforts.

Two hundred thousand dollars in debt due to court costs, Fatty went back to vaudeville where he faced, and won over, the crowds who came to see him. Using his father's first and middle names, Arbuckle became director William Goodrich. He wrote and directed portions of two Buster Keaton films, *Sherlock Jr.* and *Go West*. Arbuckle had given Keaton his first break in films and now Buster returned the favor. Others were sympathetic too. In the film *Hollywood*, Fatty's friend director James Cruze brought Arbuckle in for a poignant cameo. He played an actor who finds a sign on the casting director's door: "No Work Today."

In 1931 Fatty told his public, "Just let me work. . . . I think I can entertain and gladden the people that see me. All I want is that. If I do get back, it will be grand. If I don't, well, okay." Finally he got his wish. His first film for Vitaphone, *Hey Pop*, reused gags from his best silent films. Another, *In the Dough*, featured good old-fashioned pie fighting. He went to his New York hotel to celebrate his comeback and the signing of a new movie deal.

After dinner and some backgammon with friends, Fatty and his wife went up to their room at 2 A.M., still laughing over the evening's fun and renewed fortune. His wife recalled, "He went to bed, still laughing. I went into the bathroom, and when I came back I talked to him, and he didn't answer.

He was very peaceful. . . . Then I realized he was dead."

One of the few consolations of Arbuckle's miserable fate is that the scandal kept his name alive, long enough to be exonerated and long enough for comedy fans to take a renewed interest in his work. The average person who has no knowledge of Harry Langdon, Charlie Chase or even Harold Lloyd has heard of Fatty Arbuckle, for better or worse. The worst is over. The best is still ready to be screened.

BIOGRAPHIES: *The Day the Laughter Stopped* (Yallop, 1976), *Frame-Up* (Edmonds, 1991)
FILMS: incl.: *Passions, He Had Three* (1913), *Help Help! Hydrophobia!* (1913), *For the Love of Mabel* (1913), *Fatty's Day Off* (1913), *The Woman Haters* (1913), *Fatty's Flirtation* (1913), *A Robust Romeo* (1914), *The Knockout* (1914), *Mabel and Fatty's Wash Day* (1915), *Mabel and Fatty's Simple Life* (1915), *Mabel and Fatty's Married Life* (1915), *Fatty's Reckless Fling* (1915), *Fickle Fatty's Fall* (1915), *Mabel and Fatty Viewing the World's Fair* (1915), *He Did and He Didn't* (1916), *His Wedding Night* (1917), *The Butcher Boy* (1917), *Oh, Doctor!* (1917), *Good Night, Nurse!* (1918), *The Bell Boy* (1918), *Camping Out* (1918), *A Desert Hero* (1918), *The Cook* (1918), *The Hayseed* (1919), *A Counry Hero* (1920), *The Round-up* (1920), *The Life of the Party* (1920), *The Dollar a Year Man* (1921), *A Traveling Salesman* (1921), *Gasoline Gus* (1921), *Brewster's Millions* (1921), *Leap Year* (1921), *Freight Prepaid* (1921), *Hey, Pop* (1932), *In the Dough* (1933), *How've You Been?* (1933)
VIDEOS incl.: *Original Keystone Comedies, Mack Sennett Comedies*

# EVE ARDEN

## (Eunice Quedens, April 12, 1912–November 12, 1990)

Smoothing the edges off previous spinster comedians such as Edna May Oliver, Eve Arden won the hearts of even the worst school-hating students when she became radio and television's winsomely attractive sitcom teacher, "Our Miss Brooks."

She had a way with an indulgent wisecrack, issued from her comically pursed lips. As the single Miss Brooks, she was forever hoping to marry biology teacher, Mr. Boynton. Too bad he was so dense. As she once said, "Maybe I could dump a bowl of rice over his head and whistle the wedding march." Miss Brooks had no trouble handling her young students. A typical left-handed compliment for perennial fool-student Walter Denton: "Why, Walter, I didn't know you had it in you, and I wish you'd put it back."

Arden had the same attitude two decades later when she played the school principal in *Grease*. She told one foil: "If you can't be an athlete, be an athletic supporter."

Arden's show business career began at seven when she sang a comic dialect tune "No Kicka My Dog" at an amateur show. In her teens she joined a theatrical troupe in San Francisco. It was deceptively simple. She simply walked in and asked for a job. When she got an offer to go to New York in 1934, she left her boyfriend and secure California home behind, suffering nightmares on the cross-country train ride.

For Broadway, she felt she had to exchange her real name Eunice Quedens (which she pronounced "Kwa-denz") for something classier. She got her inspiration while sitting in her manager's office. She picked "Eve" from the character in a book she happened to be reading. And next to her book "lay a package of the products of Elizabeth Arden, a lady of such accomplishment that I recognized the name as a symbol of quality and aspiration. Voilà! Eve Arden! Also, there was no other Arden in show business, I thought. Only later did I learn, by seeing it emblazoned in lights on a burlesque house outside of Boston, that not only was there an Arden, but an Eve Arden, who appeared nightly adorned in a single white fox fur."

Arden did well in revues (in a *Ziegfeld Follies* sketch she played mother to Fanny Brice's Baby Snooks and in *Parade* she offered "My Escape from the Soviets"). She co-starred with Danny Kaye in *Let's Face It*. Her film career began slowly, though *Stage Door* won her some praise from amused co-star Katherine Hepburn. For *A Day at the Circus* Eve had to do many of her own stunts, including hanging upside down during some dialogue with Groucho Marx. As she recalled in her book, Groucho "seemed more inclined to play than work that day. Seven spoiled takes later . . . I was furious. I requested permission to descend." She stalked over to Groucho and, fixing him "with a steely eye, I said, 'Let's get it now, shall we?' And we did. And became good friends."

She had more to do in subsequent films, including Ernst Lubitsch's *That Uncertain Feeling* and *Mildred Pierce*, in which she broke the tension by remarking on the title character's nasty daughter: "Alligators have the right idea. They eat their young." She was nominated for an Academy Award. The line would later be adopted for use by everyone from The Smothers Brothers to Roseanne Arnold. In films, Arden admitted, "I was always the girlfriend of the heroine."

She became a star with "Our Miss Brooks." She didn't seem to enjoy it that much, disappointed that her most famous character was "hard-boiled, unsentimental—and not me." She won an Emmy Award for her work and had a lot of fan adulation, but sometimes it was a bit misplaced. At the maternity hospital, being shaved just prior to giving birth, the nurse suddenly dropped her shaving basin and shouted, "Oh, could I please have your autograph!"

Arden went on to try a few more sitcoms and later appeared in stock productions of *Mame* and *Hello Dolly*. She even played Vegas in the early 1960s, putting together an evening of songs and comic impressions of Bette Davis, Loretta Young, Zsa Zsa Gabor, Jackie Kennedy and Marlene Dietrich. Her last series was "The Mothers In Law," displaying her amusing disdain for her co-star, plump comic foil Kaye Ballard. Ballard recalled, "She had an air of sophistication, class and wit. She was ladylike even doing a pratfall."

She guested on television's "Maude" but worked mostly on stage, in *Critics Choice* with Rue McLanahan and Ed Nelson, *Absurd Person Singular* and in 1983 *Moose Murders*. In 1985, after her husband's death, she published her memoirs, *Three Phases of Eve*, which included a discussion of her years in therapy and the bittersweet last years of her marriage. Sounding a bit unaware of her accomplishments, she remarked she was still hoping "to contribute something worthwhile to this sad and wonderful world."

AUDIO: *Our Miss Brooks* (Radio Archives), *Our Miss Brooks* (Memorabilia), *Our Miss Brooks* (Radiola; other side of the lp is "The Great Gildersleeve")

AUTOBIOGRAPHY: *Three Phases of Eve* (1985)

BROADWAY: *Ziegfeld Follies* (1934), *Parade* (1935), *Ziegfeld Follies* (1936), *Very Warm for May* (1939), *Two for the Show* (1940), *Let's Face It* (1941)

FILMS incl.: *Stage Door* (1937), *Having a Wonderful Time* (1938), *Marx Brothers at the Circus* (1939), *Ziegfeld Girl* (1941), *That Uncertain Feeling* (1941), *Whistling in the Dark* (1941), *The Doughgirls* (1944), *Mildred Pierce* (1945), *Kid from Brooklyn* (1946), *My Reputation* (1946), *Night and Day* (1946), *The Lady Takes a Sailor* (1949), *We're Not Married* (1952), *The Lady Wants Mink* (1953), *Our Miss Brooks* (1956), *Sgt. Deadhead* (1965), *A Very Missing Person* (1971), *All My Darling Daughters* (1972), *The Strongest Man in the World* (1975), *Grease* (1978), *Under the Rainbow* (1981), *Pandemonium* (1982)

TV: "Our Miss Brooks" (1952–55), "The Eve Arden Show" (1957–58), "The Mothers in Law" (1967–68)

## ALAN ARKIN

### (Alan Wolf Arkin, March 26, 1934–    )

Alan Arkin has come a long way from playing the recorder on *When Dalliance Was in Flower,* a late 1950s album of folk songs by Ed McCurdy. The liner notes at the time called him "a television and stage actor, delivery boy, dude ranch entertainer, pot washer and baby sitter." As a member of The Tarriers, he co-wrote and sang "The Banana Boat Song," the calypso tune that had too many listeners singing along with cries of "Day-o! Daaaay-o!"

In the early 1960s Arkin joined the Second City improvisational group in Chicago. He characterized improv comedy as "a release valve . . . a way of screaming endlessly and getting paid for it." A fine writer as well as performer, he wrote many of the group's famous routines, including "Museum" with Barbara Harris.

In "Museum" he's a beatnik singing a particularly terrible tune: "Here I am in Chicago! Sittin' in an art gallery! I just flew in from New York City in a drivin' rain! And it's a bad scene in New York. But I swear to God it's a worse one in Chicago! That's

why I'm gonna split for Denver, Colorado . . . thassa end o' my song!" He meets an uptight liberal (Barbara Harris) with a crush on him. His attitude? "We only live once or twice, might as well make the most of it."

Arkin appeared in *From the Second City* in New York in 1961 and starred in several other Broadway shows, winning a Tony Award for *Enter Laughing* in 1963. Though he received fine reviews for his dramatic part in *The Heart Is a Lonely Hunter,* Arkin was more often cast in comedies, playing a variety of roles including a Puerto Rican father *(Popi),* a Russian *(The Russians Are Coming, The Russians Are Coming)* and a deadpan French detective *(Inspector Clouseau).* The actor admitted that he enjoyed the diversity and that his many characters were "a way of escaping from myself. It was a way of getting as far away from myself as I possibly could." He added, "I did that until *Catch 22.* I was afraid to unleash my own personality on an audience until *Catch 22* and I only did it then because [director Mike] Nichols really wanted me to do that." Over the years Arkin's best parts have contrasted his average looks and deadpan demeanor with death-defying slapstick situations. One of his best roles was as the dentist who gets mixed up with South American revolutionaries in *The In-Laws* co-starring Peter Falk.

He had trouble finding such a good role again. Ironically, he said his favorite part was one he signed for—and lost. It was the part of the judge in *The Bonfire of the Vanities.* As shooting began in 1989, Morgan Freeman was given the role. He explained, "Blacks were not properly shown in the film and the only sympathetic role they could use was the one I was to play. It was my favorite part in the past decade."

Fortunately for Arkin, he would have a fresh start in the 1990s. His ability to play men with an almost ludicrous sense of calm led to his role as the laidback, balding father who isn't too shocked by the offbeat *Edward Scissorhands,* and was the scientist who creates a backpack that can make a man fly in *The Rocketeer.* The superhero Rocketeer wears it and asks, "How do I look?" Arkin: "Like a hood ornament."

AUDIO: *When Dalliance Was in Flower* (Elektra), *Folk Songs Once Over Lightly* (Elektra), *From the Second*

*City* (Mercury), *The Second City Writhes Again* (Mercury), *Best of the Baby Sitters* (Vanguard)

BOOK: *Halfway Through the Door* (1979)

BROADWAY incl.: *Heloise* (1958), *From the Second City* (1961), *Man Out Loud, Girl Quiet* (1962), *Enter Laughing* (1963), *Luv* (1964), *The White House Murder Case* (1970)

FILMS incl.: *The Russians Are Coming, The Russians Are Coming* (1966), *Inspector Clouseau* (1968), *Popi* (1969), *Catch 22* (1970), *Little Murders* (1971), *Last of the Red Hot Lovers* (1972), *Freebie and the Bean* (1974), *The Seven Percent Solution* (1976), *The In-Laws* (1979), *Simon* (1979), *Chu Chu and the Philly Flash* (1981), *Improper Channels* (1981), *A Matter of Principle* (1983), *Return of Captain Invincible* (1984), *Bad Medicine* (1985), *Joshua Then and Now* (1985), *Coupe de Ville* (1990), *Edward Scissorhands* (1990), *The Rocketeer* (1991)

## DESI ARNAZ

### (Desiderio Alberto Arnaz y de Acha, March 2, 1917–December 2, 1986)

Intentionally and unintentionally, Desi Arnaz got loads of laughs for loving Lucy. Playing straight man to Lucille Ball, his stern mispronunciations were highlights of the scripts. Desi as Ricky Ricardo: "I dun't care. . . ." Lucy: "You *dunt?*" Desi: "No, I dun't!" In fact, those lines were the tag ending for their feature film *Forever Darling*. Audiences laughed at Desi's habit of ranting in Spanish whenever Lucy did something too bizarre to be believed. His pop-eyed looks of surprise and his ridiculously fake "ha, ha, ha" laugh whenever he thought he'd gained the upper hand were also familiar parts of Desi's comedy.

Before television's "I Love Lucy" Desi was known as a bandleader and singer. Bob Hope said when Desi was on his show, "Everytime he went to the mike, an enchilada fell out of his mouth. He couldn't get a laugh. Then, after ["I Love Lucy"] I met him one day and said, You're getting laughs. How do you figure it." It was while filming the musical *Too Many Girls* that Desi met Lucy. Filming began July 1, 1940. They were married on November 30.

In 1946 Arnaz had a hit tune banging a drum bare-chested and belting "Babalu!" He followed it with another hit, "Cuban Pete." When Lucy was approached to do a television sitcom, she insisted on having Desi play her husband. They both realized it was a way to anchor their strained marriage.

It was Desi's idea to film the show in front of a live audience, even if CBS forced the duo to take a pay cut to help cover expenses. Lucy and Desi didn't have to worry about money when the series became a hit. CBS later bought the rights to the first 180 episodes from Desi for $4,500,000. Unfortunately, Desi's philandering and the strains of doing the show doomed the marriage. Desi was divorced by Lucy in 1960. As Arnaz put it, "The more we fought, the less sex we had, the more seeking others, the more jealousy, the more separations, the more drinking, which led right back to more fights, less sex and more seeking others." Columnist James Bacon later recalled it this way: "When Desi would get drunk, he was wild. If he was out carousing, he wouldn't call in one whore, he'd call in 18. One night when I was with him in Palm Springs, he didn't do anything but sit on the floor naked and sing Babaloo with all these whores around. . . . Lucy put up with it quite a bit, but then it just became too embarrassing."

While Lucy went on to star in more sitcoms, Desi concentrated on business. He hosted a drama series, "Desilu Playhouse," and turned a two-part episode on Elliot Ness into the long-running "Untouchables" series. He helped guide Desilu Studios to more profits and later became the producer of the Eve Arden sitcom "The Mothers in Law." He even guest-starred a few times as a wayward bullfighter.

Desi married Edie Hirsch, and late in life he was able to look back on the years of "I Love Lucy" with unexpected good humor. He made a memorable comeback on an episode of "Saturday Night Live," describing how the show was nearly called "I Hate Lucy" and "I Love Loose Change." He began accepting occasional sitcom parts, including an episode of the series "Alice."

After his death, daughter Lucie Arnaz remarked that Desi was much funnier in real life than Lucy, but he "never got the acclaim that I think he deserved. . . . He was a naturally funny kind of guy . . . he always used to see things funny. So it's kind of depressing that he ended up a drunk."

AUTOBIOGRAPHY: *A Book* (1976)

BROADWAY: *Too Many Girls* (1939)

FILMS incl.: *Too Many Girls* (1940), *Four Jacks and a Jill* (1941), *Father Takes a Wife* (1941), *The Navy Comes Through* (1942), *Cuban Pete* (1946), *Holiday in Havana* (1949), *The Long, Long Trailer* (1954), *Forever Darling* (1956)

TV: "I Love Lucy" (1951–57), "Lucy-Desi Comedy Hour" (1957–60), "Westinghouse Desilu Playhouse" (1958–60)

## ROSEANNE ARNOLD

### (November 3, 1952–   )

At the height of Roseanne Arnold's fame, gossip columnist Liz Smith asked: "Roseanne: Slob or role model?"

Not since Carroll O'Connor's "Archie Bunker" had the American public simultaneously embraced—and been repulsed—by the star of a number-one sitcom. Archie Bunker did it via racism. Arnold did it via gluttony, arrogance and sloth.

Born in Salt Lake City, Arnold's tumultuous childhood began with facial paralysis from Bell's palsy at age three and a fall at age five that knocked her teeth through her lip and required an hour and a half of surgery. Emotionally she was paralyzed by being Jewish in a Mormon city. She called the Mormons "the Nazi Amish" and said they tormented her and beat up her brother. Her mother's compromise of having Roseanne study both religions only left the young girl confused. At 16 Arnold was hit by a car and was in a coma for days, with her legs requiring plastic surgery. Bedeviled with nightmares after that, she was ultimately placed in Utah State Hospital for eight months of psychiatric therapy. Her mother recalled, "Life was not easy for Roseanne. It wasn't easy for me either, because I'd never met anyone like her."

In May 1971 Arnold had a child at a Salvation Army home for unwed mothers. The child was given up for adoption. She married in 1974, later living with her husband Bill Pentland and her three kids in a trailer in Denver. A housewife and part-time cocktail waitress, Arnold's first attempt at comedy came when she read some material over the phone to radio talk host Alan Berg. "I actually peed my pants because I was so scared," she recalled.

In 1980 she tried stand-up comedy, toughening up to survive the bad nights of silence or jeers. She won the "Denver Laff-Off" in 1983 and moved out to the West Coast. Another fat woman, Totie Fields, had shown guts on stage. Contemporary comic Judy Tenuta had success with putdown humor, calling herself "Goddess." Columnists Peg Bracken and Erma Bombeck had both gotten laughs with caustic humor about housewives sick of their chores. Roseanne put these styles together, adding her own distinctive touches.

"I always had entertained folks that I knew with my bitching," she recalled. So she bitched in a flat nasal voice. She tossed out nasty comments taken as jokes. On housework: "I figure by the time my husband comes home at night, if those kids are still alive, I've done my job." On sex with her husband: "Like, I'm gonna turn off 'Wheel of Fortune' for that?"

The bluntness was startling, the shock produced laughter. She made it to "The Tonight Show" in August 1985, again in November and by 1987 starred in her own HBO special. The following year her sitcom became an unexpected top-10 hit. Blue-collar viewers responded strongly to Arnold's self-described attempt at becoming the female Ralph Kramden. Her humor consisted mostly of sarcastic grumbling. When a kid on the show cried, "Mom, I've got a knot in my shoelace," her answer was: "Wear loafers." But there was enough warmth coming from co-star John Goodman (playing her husband) to balance the cheap shots. The *Daily News* decided "the real star of Roseanne is John Goodman and everyone knows it." *TV Guide* agreed he was "Roseanne's beefy better half—and the best explanation for this show's runaway success." His good humor would eventually help steer Arnold toward a more realistic and less biting performance.

Arnold's difficult personality, her insecurities as a star and her lack of experience as an actress produced tensions on the set of her show. People were fired, people were hired—and Arnold soon replaced Joan Rivers as the tabloid press's favorite target. Her response was to flaunt her stardom and act even more obnoxious than she was. "I do offensive things," she said. "Like I belch at the audience

Despite the many controversies surrounding her, Rose-anne Arnold continues to be a popular star on television and in stand-up. Photo from the author's collection.

and swear and fart and stuff. That's who I am. That's my act." She thumbed her nose at critics, shouting "You're looking at one happy, fat bitch. I'm fat and I'm proud of it!"

Arnold made tabloid headlines constantly in 1988 and 1989. She mooned her bare behind at the crowd at an Oakland A's baseball game, one of her daughters required alcohol abuse treatment and reporters discovered the daughter she'd given up for adoption before Arnold could locate her. Her marriage broke up and her new husband was Bill Pentland's best friend, chunky stand-up comic Tom Arnold. Arnold then made headlines for his cocaine abuse and treatment. Tom and Roseanne tattooed each other's name on their butts and conducted interviews together, chortling over their habit of making love noisily in unlikely places. They were not perceived as a "class couple," and the public's love/hate of Arnold now extended to her pugnacious hubby, who dominated interviews with sweaty defenses of Roseanne's antics and bright-eyed cheerleading. Columnist Marilyn Beck wrote, "I've been absolutely swamped with

letters from readers who feel Roseanne should be crowned 'The Tackiest of '89.' "

The next year, 1990, proved even tackier. Arnold's variety of controversies ranged from mildly nauseating (her *Vanity Fair* photo shoot frolicking in a bathing suit and beach mud) to tastelessly foolish (an ear-splitting rendition of "The Star Spangled Banner" at a July San Diego Padres game that included her spitting and grabbing her crotch in parody of baseball player vulgarity). The latter even provoked the ire of President Bush, who called the incident "disgraceful." When the latest executive producer on Arnold's show, Jeff Harris, tried to limit Tom Arnold's influence in dictating script changes, Tom tried to strangle him. As Arnold recalled, "After he strangled him, I said 'You have a slight problem. You think this is a democracy. It's not. It's a Queendom. You're outta here." For simple star versus star controversy there was Roseanne inflamed over Arsenio Hall's fat jokes, declaring, "Arsenio Hall is America's first black nerd . . . a triangle-headed Eddie Murphy look-alike mother. . . ." They later made up.

Arnold's autobiography was roasted by book reviewers, and her first film, *She Devil*, was treated to similar hellfire. As she often did, Barr hid behind feminist philosophy when it came to accepting blame for failure. The problem, she insisted, was that men couldn't deal with a movie featuring strong female characters. "Our movie depicts strong bitchy women who don't just sit around. And no, I don't think they are too bitchy. Women can never be too bitchy!" She could think of only one solution: "I'm going to have to grow a penis."

Arnold's 1990 HBO special was another embarrassing exercise in self-indulgence, and deliberate obnoxiousness. If critics disliked her off-key rendition of "The Star-Spangled Banner" she would get even by singing several songs, even worse, on the special. Her television series, however, continued to do well in the ratings and in its accurate, often warm and sympathetic depiction of blue-collar living, displayed Arnold at her best. Arnold did have an attractive side, and could actually seem cute and almost cuddly at times.

Fans were with her as she explained how a tabloid did more than simply "invent" a front-page story declaring she was being investigated for child abuse—

they set her up by phoning in the fake charge themselves. And when the tabloids hired an insider on Arnold's TV show to rifle through Tom's briefcase and steal love letters for subsequent publication, the couple spent hundreds of thousands of dollars to sue—and win. They emerged on talk shows both looking thinner and healthier, their comedy far less strident. They could even poke fun at themselves, joking about the public perception of them. But just to keep everyone off balance, after a decade as "Roseanne Barr," Roseanne made her professional name "Arnold," a tribute to her husband who had converted to Judaism for their marriage. And when there had been no major conflict for a few months, Roseanne suddenly remembered something. She declared she had been sexually molested in early childhood. Her parents took a lie detector test and passed it, her father declaring "I never had any incestuous relationships with her and"—his voice breaking into sobs—"I don't understand."

Roseanne Arnold continues to confuse, outrage, amaze and amuse fans and foes alike, both with her private life and her stand-up and television comedy. As Carroll O'Connor demonstrated as Archie Bunker, it's possible to win laughs and affection even playing a character with some grating character flaws. Interviewed by David Letterman in November of 1990, she said, "I'm in therapy . . . all I can do is try and get better!"

AUDIO: *I Enjoy Being a Girl* (Hollywood)

AUTOBIOGRAPHY: *Roseanne: My Life as a Woman* (1990)

FILMS incl.: *She Devil* (1989), *Look Who's Talking Too* (1990)

TV: "Roseanne" (1988–   ), "Little Rosey" (1990)

VIDEOS: *The Roseanne Barr Show; Rodney Dangerfield: It's Not Easy Being Me*

## ARTHUR and DANE

**George K. Arthur: Arthur Brest, April 27, 1899– )**

**Karl Dane: October 12, 1886–April 13, 1934**

An early "Mutt and Jeff" comedy team, tall Karl Dane battled little fool George Arthur through a series of minor comedies in the late 1920s.

Though Arthur and Dane are not well known now, their gags are still getting laughs—in other comedians' films. An Arthur and Dane gag from *China Bound* saw hulking Karl Dane deflect bullets with a shovel; the bit was used with a slight variation by Groucho Marx in *The Big Store*. Another gag of the duo's, the old "fake head" trick, was used by Harpo Marx as he walked into a room backward in *Duck Soup*. Dane's gag from *China Bound* in which he flexes one fist then socks the villain with the other was used by Harpo in *Horse Feathers*.

George K. Arthur moved to America from Scotland. Dane, as the name suggests, was born in Denmark. After their films of the late 1920s, the duo split up. It proved to be a poor decision for Karl Dane. Though he had a semicomic part as a tobacco-spitting soldier in *The Big Parade* in 1925, he found few solo parts after he left George Arthur. Dane was reduced to running a hot dog stand near a film studio where many of his friends worked. One night Dane relived his old triumphs by gathering up his old press clippings and notices. He read them, laid them on a table, and put a bullet in his head.

Arthur became a producer, staging many shows at the Hollywood Playhouse in 1933. The following year he recorded songs for Brunswick. In 1935 he was arrested for stealing a necklace from an English banker in Cannes and duping an 18-year-old society girl, Mary Jopling, into bringing it through customs. He didn't let the arrest interfere with the scheduled opening of his next New York stage production, *Grand Guignol Horror Plays*. More memorable than the show was his publicity campaign. He declared that anyone suffering from fright could avail themselves of the nurse, doctor or mortician on duty!

By 1936 the restless Arthur was ready to stay out of the spotlight. He told reporters, "I don't think anyone is interested in me. I've completely cut the theater world out of my life . . . half the publicity about me is all wrong anyway, so say what you like." Arthur eventually became a film distributor, importing comedy short subjects (including Marcel Marceau's early pantomimes) and feature films. In 1962 he loaned some imports to the Museum of Modern Art for a special showing—and included one of his own—*Shove Off*. As for his career, he said "I don't miss acting. And I hope the bug never bites

entic

my child." Into his 90s, he was living in retirement in New York City.

FILMS: incl.: *Rookies* (1927), *Circus Rookies* (1928), *Detectives* (1928), *All at Sea* (1929), *Hollywood Revue* (1929)

## BEATRICE ARTHUR

### (Bernice Frankel, May 13, 1926–   )

An imposingly tall (five foot ten) and solidly built woman, Bea Arthur could get laughs with glares and disdainful frankness, her voice deep enough to be mistaken for someone named Frank. She had her best success on television as the strong-willed "Maude" and later as the disapproving ringleader of "The Golden Girls."

Arthur grew up in Cambridge, Maryland and graduated from the Franklin Institute of Sciences and Art in Philadelphia. After World War II she went to New York to study acting. She married director Gene Saks in 1950, and the two struggled for years to make it in show business. Bea played Lucy Brown in a revival of *Mack the Knife* in 1954 and won some praise in *The Shoestring Revue* of 1955, singing a tune called "Garbage." Arthur briefly co-starred on television's "The George Gobel Show" in 1959. When Saks' career took off after directing *A Thousand Clowns*, Bea went into semiretirement. After Saks became ill with hepatitis, she became the bread-winner for a few years, playing Yente the Matchmaker in *Fiddler on the Roof*.

Bea spent many years playing character comedy parts on Broadway and in films. Though she won a Tony Award for her work in *Mame* in 1966, she was not well known nationally until she became "Maude," Edith Bunker's no-nonsense cousin on "All in the Family." At first Bea didn't want the part. Norman Lear, who remembered her from the "Garbage" revue song nearly two decades earlier, sent a writer out to help her create a believable character. The writer spoke with Bea's husband. Arthur recalled, "Gene told him what he loved about me and what he hated about me. And that's how Maude was born. In some ways, I am Maude. Like her, I'm a liberal—sometimes a pretty misguided liberal, I suppose."

Beatrice Arthur has been a formidable sitcom star; first dueling Archie Bunker in episodes of "All in the Family" and then starring in "Maude" and "The Golden Girls." Photo from the author's collection.

Maude was indomitable, the first person on the show capable of dueling Archie Bunker to a draw. "You know what I like about you Archie?" she asks. "What?" "Nothing." Her confidence seemed steely. She could fix her gaze on him and utter a withering "Still fighting mental health?" In the spin-off series, Maude's catch phrase was a stinging "God'll get you for that."

As the show progressed through its first few seasons, Bea Arthur was able to turn Maude from a simple but memorable "tough lady" to a complex person with plenty of insecurities and problems. As "All in the Family" did, "Maude" tackled difficult issues, including abortion and alcoholism, mixing laughter and tears. Of the famous abortion episode in 1972, she recalled in 1976, "I never thought of a fetus being an unborn child. When the script arrived I didn't question it. All I thought was: 'Oh my God, of course.' I can't imagine anything more heart-breaking in this world than an unwanted child." Arthur won an Emmy in 1977. When "Maude" ended, so did her marriage to Gene Saks. The couple had two children.

Arthur's next series was not a success. She played a hotel owner in "Amanda's," which was loosely based on John Cleese's "Fawlty Towers." In 1981 she went back to New York to appear in Woody Allen's *The Floating Light Bulb*. Allen had great respect for her, telling her "Listen, you can change anything you want. If there's a word you don't like or a line. . . ."

In 1985 she returned to television success as one of "The Golden Girls," the tall, stern woman dominating the ensemble cast of Betty White, Rue McLanahan and Estelle Getty. Once again Bea Arthur's comedy was based on scornful sarcasm. White as Rose: "Those burglars were probably looking for drugs!" Bea as Dorothy: "We have Maalox and estrogen. How many thieves do you know who have gas and hot flashes?"

With co-stars McLanahan and White, Bea became an ardent spokeswoman against the fur industry. "I think fur coats should have a label on them saying how they became fur coats. People don't know the indignity, the horror that animals go through." While the tabloids insisted the stars feuded constantly, Bea said of her new family, "We really do get along. We don't socialize of course . . . but we are professionals who respect one another. I can't imagine working with anyone I don't get along with." She retired from the show in 1992. Her character got married. She said, "It's better than having me killed off in a car wreck!"

AUDIO: *Jewish American Princess* (Bell)
BROADWAY: *Yerma* (1947), *Dog Beneath the Skin* (1947), *No Exit* (1948), *Six Characters in Search of an Author* (1948), *The Owl and the Pussycat* (1948), *The Creditors* (1949), *Heartbreak House* (1949), *Three Penny Opera* (1954), *Shoestring Revue* (1955), *Nature's Way* (1957), *Ulysses in Nighttown* (1958), *Mame* (1966), *Fiddler on the Roof* (1966), *The Floating Light Bulb* (1981)
FILMS incl.: *Lovers and Other Strangers* (1969), *Mame* (1974), *History of the World Part I* (1981), *My First Love* (1988)
TV: "The George Gobel Show" (1959), "Maude" (1972–78), "Amanda's" (1983), "The Golden Girls" (1985–1992).

# JEAN ARTHUR

## (Gladys Georgianna Greene, October 17, 1905– June 19, 1991)

After making little impression in more than 25 silent movies, mostly westerns, Jean Arthur brought her unique sexy "squeaky voice" to talkies. Her first hit was *The Whole Town's Talking*. The mood was set in one of her opening scenes as a harried office worker. "You're late!" complains her boss. "For what?" she answers. Unlike most wisecracking dames in screwball comedies, she paid for that remark by getting fired. Audience sympathy never left Jean Arthur for the rest of the film—and the rest of her career. Unlike some other stars of screwball comedies who were overtly sexy or outrageously witty, Jean Arthur tended to play the average girl: nice, low key, minus any affectations. She was rarely the purveyor of screwball slapstick. It just *happened* to her. Such as the coat that was dropped onto her from a building as she was riding in an open-topped bus in *Easy Living*. Her reaction: "Say, what's the big idea, anyway?"

Sometimes it was hard to tell if she was being innocent or just acting innocent. In *The Ex-Mrs. Bradford* ex-husband William Powell doesn't quite know how to take Arthur's latest proposition. "I'm going to marry you again . . . for your sake so you wouldn't have to pay me alimony." In private life Jean was also a bit enigmatic. She was shy, which some co-workers mistook for being aloof.

Her charm in realistic romantic comedy made her a favorite of both Preston Sturges and Frank Capra. It was Capra who gave one of the better descriptions of the unique Arthur voice: "low, husky—at times it breaks pleasingly into the higher octaves like a thousand tinkling bells." Some scripts included a few jokes written in expressly for her vocal comedy. In *The Ex-Mrs. Bradford* there's a scene in which she tries, twice, to imitate an authoritative male on the phone, only to be betrayed by her cracking soprano.

Arthur received an Academy Award nomination for *The More the Merrier* in 1943, a fitting cap on a decade of excellent work in comedy. Over the next decade her film career waned. Her last movie was 1953's *Shane*. In 1965 she guested on television's "Gunsmoke," and the reaction was so positive she decided to come out of retirement for her own sitcom, "The Jean Arthur Show." She played Patricia Marshall, a comically talkative mom who couldn't resist sharing her son's legal cases. The show was adjourned in just three months. Fortunately, her classic comedies of the 1930s and '40s have lasted much longer.

BIOGRAPHY: *Jean Arthur* (Pierce and Swarthout, 1990)
BROADWAY: *Foreign Affairs* (1932), *The Man Who Reclaimed His Head* (1932), *The Curtain Rises* (1933), *Peter Pan* (1950)
FILMS incl.: *Biff Bang Buddy* (1924), *The College Boob* (1926), *The Poor Nut* (1927), *Half Way to Heaven* (1929), *Paramount on Parade* (1930), *The Virtuous Husband* (1931), *Get That Venus* (1933), *Most Precious Thing in Life* (1934), *The Whole Town's Talking* (1935), *If You Could Only Cook* (1935), *Public Hero Number One* (1935), *Mr. Deeds Goes to Town* (1936), *More Than a Secretary* (1936), *The Ex-Mrs. Bradford* (1936), *History Is Made at Night* (1937), *Easy Living* (1937), *You Can't Take It with You* (1938), *Only Angels Have Wings* (1939), *Mr. Smith Goes to Washington* (1939), *Too Many Husbands* (1940), *Talk of the Town* (1942), *The More the Merrier* (1943), *A Lady Takes a Chance* (1943), *The Impatient Years* (1944), *Shane* (1953)
TV: "The Jean Arthur Show" (1966)

## JOHN ASTIN

### (March 30, 1930–   )

"Tish! That's French!"

With a manic gleam in his eye, John Astin as Gomez Addams would kiss and nibble his wife's hand—right up to the shoulder. All it took to set him off were a few soft-spoken French words. Or anything that even sounded French.

The classic 1960s sitcom "The Addams Family" offered Astin his most memorable comic role as the "mysterious and ooky" head of the household. Whether ruminating about his fortunes ("Consolidated Lint" and "Amalgamated Fuzz" were his prize stocks), or putting his cigar out by snuffing it into his jacket pocket, Gomez was endearingly strange. He was a food connoisseur ("What's an aardvark without an apple in its mouth? It's like a martini

without the egg!") He liked relaxation on a bed of nails: "When I stretch out on that thing I want my pores to really open up." He had toy locomotives in his basement, which he loved to blow up: "Of course! Why else would a grown man play with trains?"

In her autobiography, ex-wife Patty Duke's description of John pointed out some similarities between Astin and Gomez Addams. Like Gomez, Astin was basically mild-mannered, often absentminded and oblivious to others when immersed in thought. If Gomez was not alarmed by son Pugsley's interest in dynamite, the real-life John only offered a mild warning when two of his sons set off a real Molotov cocktail in the backyard. If Gomez had exotic cultural interests, so did John, a vegetarian who built a Buddhist shrine in the middle of his house. Patty's description of John could have matched a Morticia description of Gomez: "extremely handsome . . . tall and slender with a great voice and eyes that can look like a Frenchman's bedroom eyes or those of a bassett hound."

Astin, a graduate of Johns Hopkins, often appeared on Broadway in the 1950s, but in the '60s he played straight man to Marty Ingels in television's "I'm Dickens He's Fenster." He auditioned for "Lurch" on "The Addams Family" but executive producer David Levy thought that, with a mustache, he'd be a better Gomez.

After "The Addams Family," Astin starred in a pilot, "Sheriff Who?" as a lovable villain who each week knocked off a different hero. Another pilot was filmed and the combination later released as a made-for-television movie, *Evil Roy Slade*. Astin remained reliably droll in guest roles (a Hugh Hefner–type publisher on an "Odd Couple" episode) and starred in the short-lived "Operation Petticoat." He starred briefly as "the Riddler" on "Batman," subbing for Frank Gorshin.

Astin and Patty Duke worked together in a television movie *Two on a Bench*. They married, had two sons and spent five years touring the country in a series of plays, including *A Shot in the Dark, The Marriage Gambol* and *My Fat Friend*.

Over the years Astin's appearance changed radically. He grew a beard, donned glasses and looked more like a balding college professor than a sitcom star. He moved behind the scenes to direct television shows. After the Duke-Astin marriage ended, John returned to sitcoms. He was back to his familiar look (clean-shaven and dark haired), playing Ed LaSalle on Mary Tyler Moore's short-lived "Mary" series. He still gets calls for "ooky" comedy parts from time to time, including a grinning ex-mental patient on "Night Court" and the crazed Professor Gangreen in *Return of the Killer Tomatoes*, a man angry over having a nonhunchbacked assistant: "It doesn't look right for a noted misanthrope of my stature!"

BROADWAY: *Major Barbara* (1956), *Threepenny Opera* (1956), *Ulysses in Nighttown* (1958), *Tall Story* (1959)

FILMS incl.: *That Touch of Mink* (1962), *The Wheeler Dealers* (1963), *The Spirit Is Willing* (1967), *Candy* (1968), *Evil Roy Slade* (1971), *Get to Know Your Rabbit* (1972), *Viva Max* (1972), *Miss Kline We Love You* (1974), *Freaky Friday* (1977), *Life in the Pink* (1977), *Return of the Killer Tomatoes* (1988), *The Saint: The Blue Delac* (1989)

TV: "I'm Dickens He's Fenster" (1962–63), "The Addams Family" (1964–66), "The Pruitts of Southampton" (1967), "Operation Petticoat" (1977–78), "Mary" (1985–86) "Eerie Indiana" (1992)

## PHIL AUSTIN (See FIRESIGN THEATRE.)

## AVON COMEDY FOUR (See SMITH and DALE.)

## DAN AYKROYD

### (July 1, 1952–   )

One of the original stars of television's "Saturday Night Live," Dan Aykroyd didn't achieve the fame of his flamboyant co-stars Chevy Chase and John Belushi. Part of the problem was that while he was sometimes manic, he was more often enigmatic, playing characters without much inner depth, from Beldar, a monosyllabic "Conehead" from outer space, to a variety of dislikable, oily television commercial pitchmen. His best imitations were of people with robotic delivery styles (Rod Serling), clipped and hesitant speech patterns (Jimmy Carter) or harsh inhumanity (Richard Nixon). Appearances he made

A fine sketch writer and performer on the original "Saturday Night Live," Dan Aykroyd has mostly given the gags to his co-stars in hit films such as *Ghostbusters*. Photo from the author's collection.

on talk shows underlined his serious and reserved nature.

Though viewers didn't respond emotionally to Aykroyd, the laughs were often as loud for him as anyone else. The Canadian comedian wrote much of his own material, like the fake commercial for "Bass-o-Matic," an electric blender. As delivered in his intense announcer's style: "Yes, fish eaters, the days of troublesome scaling, cutting and gutting are finally over, because Super Bass-o-Matic '76 is the tool that lets you use the whole bass with no fish waste and without scaling, cutting or gutting. Here's how it works . . ." Here he dumps a whole fish into the blender. Once it's been reduced to raw soup: "It's just that simple . . . ready to pour. Order now!"

Aykroyd won an Emmy in 1977 for his writing on "Saturday Night Live." He moved on to films with his close friend John Belushi, co-starring with him in *1941* and *The Blues Brothers*. A Blues Brothers album of terse rocking blues sold over a million copies, but the movie was not a big hit. Aykroyd carved out a successful career in films, but rarely did viewers come specifically to see him. Aykroyd's biggest successes were ensemble films such as *Ghostbusters* and *Driving Miss Daisy* in which he was only one helpful cog in the wheel. His characters in such films were rarely well defined and audiences were often drawn to a co-star instead (Eddie Murphy in *Trading Places*).

Aykroyd didn't do well with mainstream films *(My Stepmother Is an Alien)* and was embarrassing in *Caddyshack II,* in which he attempted a cheerfully goofy character more suited to Chevy Chase or John Belushi. Another attempt at zany, multicharacter comedy fizzled in *Loose Cannons,* with the *New York Times* reporting "Whenever he's in a situation with which he can't cope, he assumes the identities of such characters as the Lone Ranger, the Roadrunner, Goofy and Captain Kirk. It's not a brilliant idea."

While his film version of *Dragnet* was not a box office success, Aykroyd gave an impressive performance and was able to match his stiff, impersonal style to the deadpan parody of hard-nosed cop Joe Friday. Aykroyd had an affinity for the part. Years earlier he spent four years studying criminology at Carlton University. He said at the time that Joe Friday was, "next to Clouseau, the most famous cop in the world. I've studied his speech inflections, his mannerisms, his walk. During filming, I'd listen to tapes of the old shows. I even started dreaming in character. If there ever was a character I'd always wanted to play, it was this one."

Aykroyd's admiration for the all-business cop was also reflected in his early jobs. He recalled in 1991, "I learned a certain work ethic from holding a lot of part-time jobs while I was still in high school—everything from delivering mail to unloading box-cars. To this day, I still have that blue-collar mentality. I'm a company man and no matter what I'm doing, I feel like an employee who is told what to do and loves taking orders."

For a while he seemed to have his best luck at home. He and his actress wife, Donna Dixon, had their first child, Danielle, on November 18, 1989. He earned a measure of critical acclaim from his serious role in *Driving Miss Daisy*. Columnist Marilyn Beck praised him for taking "a new, refreshing direction in a career that's had more downs than ups lately." Financially, *Ghostbusters II* was the last film he really needed to make. After the original movie took in $235 million, he made sure to get a large hunk of the second one's profits. With Bill Murray the love interest for Sigourney Weaver, Aykroyd retreated further into his new role of chubby-faced fat-headed comic relief, but occasionally showed some of his old "Saturday Night Live" edge. In this kid-oriented film, he did get to call a room full of brats "ungrateful little Yuppie larvae."

Conservative estimates from "Entertainment Tonight" indicated he received $15 million for his ghost busting, enough to allow him to pick and choose future movie roles. When he didn't find anything suitable, he wrote and directed his next film himself, another zany (and critically unappreciated) effort, *Nothing But Trouble*.

FILMS incl.: *Love at First Sight* (1975), *1941* (1979), *The Blues Brothers* (1980), *Neighbors* (1981), *It Came from Hollywood* (1982), *Doctor Detroit* (1983), *Trading Places* (1983), *Twilight Zone, The Movie* (1983), *Ghostbusters* (1984), *Spies Like Us* (1985), *One More Saturday Night* (1986), *Caddyshack II* (1988), *Ghostbusters II* (1989), *Driving Miss Daisy* (1989), *Loose Cannons* (1990), *Nothing But Trouble* (1991), *My Girl* (1991), *This Is My Life* (1992)

TV: "Saturday Night Live" (1975–79)

VIDEOS: *Saturday Night Live* (various volumes); *The Best of Dan Aykroyd*

B

## JIM BACKUS

**(February 25, 1913–July 3, 1989)**

Master of the manic cackle, Jim Backus was known for his trademark laugh that could express surprise and delight (as the lovable old Mr. Magoo), cheery eccentricity (as "Gilligan's Island's" buoyant Mr. Howell) or leering bad intentions (his stand-up creation "the Dirty Old Man"). A man who could cackle in three different ways showed a lot of talent. And cackling was only a small part of it.

Backus was originally a popular comic character on a variety of radio shows. In the early days of television he played Mr. Dithers on "Blondie" (his wife, Henny, played Mrs. Dithers) and was well known for his role as Judge Bradley Stevens, the man whose sitcom confession was "I Married Joan." His ability to play believable but funny characters helped him avoid typecasting. He acted in dramas in the 1950s, taking a key role in *Man of a Thousand Faces* and playing James Dean's father in *Rebel Without a Cause*.

By then Backus had already begun lending his voice to the cartoon character Mr. Magoo, giving the nearsighted old man a trademark wheedling mumble and dry chuckle. Everyone loved the Academy Award-winning Mr. Magoo, including James Dean. Dean slipped an in-joke Magoo imitation into *Rebel Without a Cause* in a scene with Sal Mineo holding a candelabrum.

Far from an anonymous cartoon voice star, Backus was a recognizable performer with his dark, round eyebrows and short-cropped graying hair. Backus was writing autobiographies as early as 1958 *(Rocks on the Roof)*. Through the 1950s and '60s he developed a character distinctly different from Magoo, a rich Harvard type with a tongue-in-cheek accent. The character was filthy rich "Hubert Updyke" on "The Alan Young Show." A typical concern of Hubert's: "I have to get a new Cadillac . . . the ashtrays are full."

His popularity continued to grow when he turned Updyke into "Thurston Howell III" on "Gilligan's Island." Once again, as he had with the curmudgeonly Magoo, Backus' warmth and charm turned a potentially unsympathetic and irritating character into something lovable. His ridiculously rich and self-centered Thurston was the show's most original character, the only source of satire on the program. Howell: "Do you think I began a dozen international corporations by stooping to thievery?" The Professor: "Of course not." Howell: "Shows how naive you are. How else do you get to the top of the corporate ladder?"

Backus continued to play Thurston Howell in subsequent "Gilligan" television movies and Magoo in everything from a charming television musical *(Mr. Magoo's Christmas Carol)* to light-bulb commercials.

In the 1970s he cut an album, *The Dirty Old Man*, using his cackle for some leering laughs. Years earlier he had recorded a successful novelty single, "Delicious," a laughing record featuring Jim and an unnamed lady giggling, drinking champagne and shouting "Delicious" as they got progressively more and more plastered.

The laughs were fewer for Backus in the 1980s. He resented the lack of residuals for "Gilligan's Island" and was plagued with illnesses. When talk shows brought about nostalgic reunions of the "Gilligan's Island" cast, Backus was always there, though his frailness was evident. Yet he never disappointed his many fans. Prompted by the doting talk show host, he would do a bit of "Mr. Magoo" and would always manage to muster at least one trademark laugh.

AUDIO: *Mr. Magoo* (Wonderland), *The Little Prince* (Pip), *Magoo in Hi-Fi* (RCA), *The Dirty Old Man* (Dore)

BOOKS: *Rocks on the Roof* (1958), *What Are You Doing After the Orgy?* (1962), *Forgive Us Our Digressions* (1988), *Only When I Laugh; Backus Strikes Back* (1984)

FILMS incl.: *Hollywood Story* (1951), *Pat and Mike* (1952), *Androcles and the Lion* (1953), *Francis in the Navy* (1955), *Rebel Without a Cause* (1955), *Man of a Thousand Faces* (1957), *Macabre* (1958), *It's a Mad Mad Mad Mad World* (1963), *The Wheeler Dealers* (1963), *Billie* (1965), *Where Were You When the Lights Went Out* (1968), *Hello Down There* (1969), *Now You See Him, Now You Don't* (1972), *Pete's Dragon* (1977), *Rescue from Gilligan's Island* (1978), *Good Guys Wear Black* (1979), *Chomps* (1979), *Castaways on Gilligan's Island* (1979), *Harlem Globetrotters on Gilligan's Island* (1981)

TV: "Hollywood House" (1949–50), "I Married Joan" (1952–55), "The Jim Backus Show" (1960), "Talent Scouts" (1962), "Famous Adventures of Mr. Magoo" (1964–65), "Gilligan's Island" (1964–67), "Continental Showcase" (1966), "Blondie" (1968–69)

## LUCILLE BALL

### (August 6, 1911–April 26, 1989)

The most beloved, most enduring star in sitcom history, Lucille Ball was a natural talent, if not a

The most beloved comedienne in the history of television, Lucille Ball. Photo from the author's collection.

natural-born redhead. Born in Jamestown, New York, she went to New York to attend drama school, but the best student in class was somebody else—Bette Davis. Lucy dyed her hair blond, changed her name to Diane Belmont and became a model instead.

A car accident confined her to a wheelchair for two years. She then went back to modeling, becoming the poster girl for Chesterfield cigarettes and joining the decorative chorus girls backing Eddie Cantor in *Roman Scandals* and *Kid Millions*.

At Columbia Lucy took bit parts, even in a Three Stooges short (*Three Little Pigskins* in 1934). At RKO she received $50 and some recognition for *That Girl from Paris* in 1936. She had little to do in The Marx Brothers' *Room Service* and played Edgar Bergen's love interest in the mild *Look Who's Laughing Now*, doing a nurse sketch with Charlie McCarthy. She was delightful in *The Affairs of Annabel*, and even made a sequel. *Too Many Girls* in 1940 wasn't much— but the co-star was. She married Desi Arnaz that year.

It was at MGM for the bland *DuBarry Was a Lady* that she turned from blond to redhead. Her career continued to grow, but her marriage began to crumble. She filed for divorce in 1944, but gave Desi another chance. *Easy to Wed* in 1946 led to her own radio show, "My Favorite Husband," playing housewife Liz Cooper. Richard Denning played her husband. When plans were being made to bring Lucy to television, she decided her co-star had to be Desi. It was the only way of saving their marriage.

Lucy and Desi toured together in the summer of 1950, doing sketches that incorporated suggestions by Buster Keaton. Ultimately they convinced nervous CBS brass that viewers would accept a white woman and a Hispanic male as a sitcom duo. Lucy and Desi worked hard on the show, hiring the best writers, using an innovative three-camera approach filming before a live audience and rehearsing each show as a play.

The result, "I Love Lucy," was a hit, with Lucy bringing enthusiastic slapstick and funny faces to the staid sitcom format, combining all the punch of a live Milton Berle show with the kind of character comedy that had made Burns and Allen enduring stars. The show's highlights touched all bases, including: the mechanical (Lucy trying to gobble up chocolates going past her on a fast assembly line); the raucous (Lucy's battle with a female grape stomper); the situational (her embarrassing attempts to meet famous stars, like William Holden or John Wayne); and the personal (the domestic cat-and-mouse games with Desi). The ensemble cast of Lucy, Desi, Vivian Vance and William Frawley became "family" to millions of viewers, week after week.

*Time* magazine put her on the cover, applauding her "cheerful rowdiness." The key to Lucy's personality was a childlike desire to please Desi, her father-husband, and a childlike habit of getting caught by her own schemes and curiosity. Her most famous trademark was a ridiculously juvenile open-mouthed cry. The twist was that, though she behaved less like a housewife and more like a little girl playing house, Lucy was a woman—with charm, sexuality and a residue of the down-to-earth cynic that characterized her "tough, wise-girl" years in films.

Marital problems contributed to the end of "I Love Lucy." The tension on the set caused by Desi's nights of drunkenness and infidelity proved too much. Lucy tried to keep the marriage going, for their two children, for the millions who believed in the love of Lucy and Ricky Ricardo on "I Love Lucy" and for her own belief in that fantasy.

Recalling her divorce from Desi, Lucy said in 1988, "The fact that he still embarrassed me by cheating and everybody knew it, I certainly didn't relish that. . . ." Lucy felt it "was part of the Latin mentality . . . if you don't talk about it, it doesn't exist." After dozens of second chances, divorce proceedings began in March 1960.

Lucy had a hit on Broadway in *Wildcat* and in 1961 married Gary Morton. The following year Lucy bought out Desi's shares in Desilu Productions. She was an astute businesswoman, the wealthiest woman in show business; her assets were worth an estimated $50 million.

Lucy Ricardo was gone, but there would be Lucy Carmichael, Lucy Carter and Lucy Barker—roles she would play in three more sitcoms. These were tamer and sillier, but still a delight for her fans. For 20 years she was a regular sight on Monday nights. She was 75 when she starred as Lucy Barker in "Life with Lucy," playing a widow who takes over her husband's hardware store. The show reunited her with the 80-year-old Gale Gordon, who played her husband's partner. He had played the glaring banker Mr. Mooney on both "The Lucy Show" and "Here's Lucy." "Our type of comedy seems to be in favor again," she said. "After Vivian passed away I had no thought of doing this again at all. Then the cycle went around. Family shows came back . . . when Cosby hit, I thought, 'The time is here!' Then 'Golden Girls' and the movie *Cocoon* came along. . . ."

Unfortunately, at 75, the idea of Lucy still fumbling about and acting cute just didn't work. The scripts were written in the style of her old sitcoms, which seemed out of date. The show was canceled and soon after, in September 1987, Lucy admitted, "It's no fun anymore . . . I think, when people see me in the old reruns and then see me now, they're reminded of their own mortality. And they don't like that very much. It doesn't bother me, though."

Lucy looked as vibrant as ever when she appeared on the March 29, 1989 Academy Award telecast. But on April 18 she was hospitalized for a heart operation to replace her aorta. She seemed to be on the mend, but suddenly died of cardiac arrest due to a ruptured abdominal artery.

A nation mourned. Color shots of vintage 1950s or '60s Lucy adorned the covers of most every major magazine. Lucy once said, "Getting into trouble and then getting out of it will always be the essence of comedy." So it is that reruns of Lucy will always be popular. Lucy knew her place in history, and it was untarnished by her one sitcom flop. She said, "I've been seen around the world by more people than any other actress on TV."

AUDIO: *Wildcat* (RCA), *Mame* (Warner), *My Favorite Story* (20th Century Fox), *I Love Lucy* (Radiola)

BIOGRAPHY: *Lucy: The Bittersweet Life of Lucille Ball* (Morella and Epstein, 1973), *The Lucille Ball Story* (Gregory, 1974), *Loving Lucy* (Andrews and Watson, 1982), *Lucy* (Higham, 1987), *Lucy in the Afternoon* (Brochu, 1991), *Lucy and Desi* (Harris, 1991)

BROADWAY: *Wildcat* (1960)

FILMS incl.: *Roman Scandals* (1933), *Moulin Rouge* (1934), *Hold That Girl* (1934), *Kid Millions* (1934), *I Dream Too Much* (1935), *Top Hat* (1935), *Chatterbox* (1936), *That Girl from Paris* (1936), *Stage Door* (1937), *Room Service* (1938), *The Affairs of Annabel* (1938), *Annabel Takes a Tour* (1938), *That's Right, You're Wrong* (1939), *Too Many Girls* (1940), *Look Who's Laughing* (1941), *Du Barry Was a Lady* (1943), *Thousands Cheer* (1943), *Abbott and Costello Meet Hollywood* (1945), *Without Love* (1945), *Ziegfeld Follies of 1946* (1946), *Easy to Wed* (1946), *Dark Corner* (1946), *Two Smart People* (1946), *Lured* (1947), *Miss Grant Takes Richmond* (1949), *Sorrowful Jones* (1947), *Her Husband's Affairs* (1947), *Fancy Pants* (1950), *A Woman of Distinction* (1950), *The Fuller Brush Girl* (1950), *The Long, Long Trailer* (1954), *Forever Darling* (1956), *The Facts of Life* (1960), *Critic's Choice* (1963), *Yours Mine and Ours* (1968), *Mame* (1974), *The Stone Pillow* (1985)

TV: "I Love Lucy" (1951–57), "The Lucy-Desi Comedy Hour" (1957–60), "The Lucy Show" (1962–68), "Here's Lucy" (1968–74), "Life with Lucy" (1986)

VIDEO: *I Love Lucy Collectors Edition* (multivolumes)

## ROSEANNE BARR (See ROSEANNE ARNOLD.)

## BELLE BARTH

### (Annabelle Salzman, April 27, 1911–February 14, 1971)

A risqué "red hot mama," Belle Barth resembled her idol Sophie Tucker, except that for the early 1960s her one-liners were downright dirty and her parodies well below the belt: "The farmer in the dell, the farmer in the dell—I had a cherry once but now it's shot to hell!"

The most endearing thing about Belle was her parody of ladylike manners and naiveté, beginning a joke with a dainty "My next story is a little risqué. . . ." In the 1950s and early '60s she was especially good at contrasting a coquette's conversational sweetness with the sudden brawling howls of a Brooklyn bordello madam. Audiences were shocked at her sudden putdowns of ringsiders ("Shut yer hole, girlie, mine's makin' money") and bawdy observations: "I always say the most difficult thing for a woman to do is try to act naive on the first night—of her second marriage. She hollers it hurts, and he's gotta tie his feet to the bed he shouldn't fall in and drown!"

Using her husband's last name, the ex-student from Manhattan's Julia Richmond High played in vaudeville through the 1930s, doing impressions of Sophie Tucker, Al Jolson, Harry Richman and even Gypsy Rose Lee. She appeared often in the Catskills. She aged into her bawdy old broad act, with songs, stories and plenty of Yiddish curse words tossed around for the amusement of her Miami-based fans. They figured she knew what she was talking about; she was married five times.

Adult comedy was tolerated in the 1950s and early '60s as long as it was confined to small clubs, contained no religious gags and was only "whiz bang" vulgar. Barth's obscenity arrests generally came at times when she was too caught up in the laughs and too loaded with booze to tone herself down. As *Variety* noted, she was not "a crusader . . . once during a performance at Carnegie Hall, N.Y. she was warned that there was 'fuzz' in the audience. She immediately deleted the rougher stuff in her routine with disastrous audience results. A similar adverse audience reaction occurred when Basin Street East, N.Y. asked Miss Barth to clean up her act because the spot was afraid to lose its liquor license. Nobody had come to hear Miss Barth deliver straight ballads."

The red-hot comic mama played her own Belle Barth Pub in Miami and sojourned to Las Vegas often. She was working at Caesars Palace in 1970 when she became ill. She died of cancer soon after. Though she was often overly brash and coarse in her later years, she was rather appealing in her prime. Her trademark was a smile and a coy "If I embarrass you, tell your friends!"

AUDIO: *If I Embarrass You Tell Your Friends* (After Hours), *My Next Story Is a Little Risqué* (After Hours), *In Person* (Laugh Time), *Wild Wild Wild Wild World* (Record Productions), *Her New Act* (Riot), *If I Embarrassed You, Forget It* (Riot), *Hell's Belle* (Laff), *The Customer Comes First* (Laff), *I Don't Mean to Be Vulgar But If It's Profitable* (Surprise), *Book of Knowledge Memorial Album* (Laff)

## ORSON BEAN

### (Dallas Burrows, July 22, 1926–   )

Mild-mannered and cheerful, Orson Bean reflected, "The most important thing in my life has always been to be happy. I spent most of my life trying to find out how to be the happiest bastard who ever lived. . . . I don't mean that I've always been happy, but when I wasn't, I wasn't satisfied with that. It wasn't the way I wanted to present myself."

Consequently, Bean's comedy included making paper eucalyptus trees on stage while telling shaggy dog stories and singing whimsical songs. A founding member of the Laurel and Hardy club *Sons of the Desert,* Bean was inspired by gentlemanly comedy. Sadly, the Vermont-born comedian's early years were filled with tragedy. Unhappy at home, he moved out as soon as he could. When he did, his mother committed suicide. She left behind a note that said in part, "my son won't come to visit."

Bean was a rising star in the late 1950s, one of the first to record a comedy album (on Fantasy Records, later Lenny Bruce's label). He had come upon his new name by trial and error. He used to open with a joke: "Hi, I'm Dallas Burrows, Harvard '49–Yale 0." When it failed to generate enough laughs, a band member in a local club suggested it was because he didn't have a funny name. After a few tries, it was "Orson Bean" that got the laugh.

His enduring routines include the tale of an Australian who has an affair with an ostrich, an Armenian hunting for his mother and a football game between ants and elephants. In the latter, an ant runs downfield with the ball when an elephant squashes him to death. "A low murmur of disap-

proval spread through the crowd. The umpire ran out onto the field and said, 'Why'd you step on him for?' The elephant said, 'I was only trying to trip him!' "

Blacklisted during the Communist scare in the 1950s, Bean's career was nearly destroyed. Yet a smiling, impish Orson Bean returned, unscathed, years later, appearing on the quiz show "To Tell the Truth" for many years and resuming his stand-up career. Bean appeared in everything from a lighthearted "Twilight Zone" television episode to "Mary Hartman, Mary Hartman" as Reverend Brim.

A man of eclectic interests, he founded the Fifteenth Street School in 1964 in New York, wrote a book on orgone therapy, appeared in off-Broadway plays in the 1980s, and performed in summer stock (notably as Mr. Appleby in a revival of *Damn Yankees* in 1986). He remains in demand for talk show appearances as well, all due to his engaging personality and sense of fun—what might be called the power of being positively, eccentricly unique.

AUDIO: *At the Hungry i* (Fantasy), *I Ate the Baloney* (Columbia)

BOOKS: *Me and the Orgone* (1978), *Too Much Is Not Enough* (1985)

BROADWAY: *Men of Distinction* (1953), *The School for Scandal* (1953), *Almanac* (1953), *Will Success Spoil Rock Hunter* (1955), *Mister Roberts* (1956), *Say Darling* (1959), *Subways Are for Sleeping* (1961), *Never Too Late* (1962), *I Was Dancing* (1964), *Ilya Darling* (1967), *A Round with Ring* (1969), *A Christmas Carol* (1983), *40 Deuce* (1984), *The Show Off* (1985)

FILMS incl.: *Instant Karma* (1991)

TV: "I've Got a Secret" (1952), "The Blue Angel" (1954), "Keep Talking" (1959–60), "To Tell the Truth" (1964–67, 1990–91), "Mary Hartman, Mary Hartman" (1977–78)

## STYMIE BEARD (See OUR GANG.)

## JOHN BELUSHI

### (January 24, 1949–March 5, 1982)

Raised to larger-than-life status after his death by drug overdose, John Belushi's fame rests primarily with his brawling, angry, intense comedy sketches from television's "Saturday Night Live" and the one movie that captured the almost lovable craziness behind the viciousness—*Animal House.*

Born in Chicago to Albanian parents, Belushi was an aggressive child. He recalled that in sixth grade his gym teacher became so exasperated with him she kicked him right between the legs. In high school he was on the wrestling squad and became the captain of the football team. He also was in a rock band singing "Louie Louie," something that impressed a fellow student who would soon become his wife, Judy Jacklin.

After dropping out of college, Belushi became a member of Chicago's Second City improvisational troup (1971–72). He first achieved some national attention with *Lemmings* in 1972, the record album and off-Broadway revue that grimly satirized the Woodstock generation. Belushi was the ghoulish master of ceremonies of the show championing suicide: "Okay, we all know why we came here. A million of us. To off ourselves . . . if your buddy's too stoned to off himself, roll him up in a sleeping bag and drag him over to where the tractors can run him over. . . ." After writing, directing and performing on the "National Lampoon Radio Hour" and appearing in the 1975 off-Broadway *National Lampoon Show,* Belushi became one of the original "Not Ready for Prime Time Players" on "Saturday Night Live."

He specialized in aggressive comedy characters, from a psycho Samurai warrior to a swarthy Greek diner chef who would cook only cheeseburgers. His favorite impersonations were the grinding rock singer Joe Cocker and actor Marlon Brando. Belushi could even satirize his own fierce intensity. Sitting alongside Chevy Chase during "Weekend Update" news segments, he'd toss out his disgusted catch phrase "But nooooooo!" and end up literally tossing his burly body under the desk in unspeakable frustration.

Together with friend Dan Aykroyd, Belushi formed The Blues Brothers, a sinister-looking rhythm-and-blues duo that fans weren't sure whether to take seriously or not. At one point Belushi was a hot star in four mediums at once—his *Briefcase Full of Blues* album with Aykroyd went Gold, his tours with Aykroyd were a hot ticket, his film *National Lampoon's Animal House* was a hit and "Saturday Night Live" was as popular as ever.

Belushi's uncompromising, blustery and often obnoxious comedy style was a colorful and potent contrast to the slick Chevy Chase, the cool Jane Curtin and the childlike Gilda Radner. His personality off stage was challenging and aggressive, and his feuds with Chase and Curtin were often just below the boiling point.

Fans cheered Belushi as they would a disruptive "class clown." That was exactly the role he played as Bluto Blutarsky in *Animal House.* In the film he performed some gross slapstick; a highlight was his impression of a pimple (by filling his mouth with mashed potatoes and "popping" the gunk out by pinching his cheeks).

Big things were expected of Belushi, and the driven comic expected much more, convinced he could tackle not only comedy but dramatic and romantic roles. However, fans were indifferent to the romantic comedy *Continental Divide* and were put off by the offbeat *Neighbors.* Belushi's career was slipping, but some had faith in him. John Landis, director of *The Blues Brothers,* said, "If he doesn't burn himself out, his potential is unlimited." Belushi sensed he was on a dangerous course admitting "It comes along with a certain kind of lifestyle. . . . Everything becomes more heightened, takes on more urgency and the tendency to self-destruct heightens too. . . . I get nervous and I am capable of doing something to blow it on purpose."

If Belushi's comedy on "Saturday Night Live" was full tilt, joyously rude and swaggering, it hardly matched the intensity of his private life. Known for his formidable drug intake, he seemed able to take anything without serious damage. In the early morning hours of May 5, Belushi shared some cocaine with Robin Williams and Robert DeNiro and then went back to his rented bungalow. He shared it with a woman named Cathy Smith, who had endeared herself to him with her cocaine and heroin connections. Some time between 3 and 6 A.M., Cathy Smith injected the restless comedian with a "speedball" of heroin and cocaine. He finally fell asleep, and he never woke up.

For months headlines raged over his death, and it became a symbol of Hollywood's rampant drug abuse. Smith eventually pleaded guilty to manslaughter and served a short sentence. Belushi's death cast a pall over reruns of "Saturday Night Live," especially episodes such as the one that featured Dan Aykroyd admonishing the audience, "This just in from the National Drug Abuse Association. Cocaine and heroin do not mix. If you must snort, don't shoot." The Belushi story was even turned into a best-seller—*Wired*—and a film of the same title.

The "me generation" was exemplified by 1970s comics such as Chevy Chase and Steve Martin, who overstated their egotism and preened over their superiority. But the darker side of the "me generation" was demonstrated by Belushi and his comic slob-bullying, unapologetic selfishness and raging excesses. His best work, much of it still brash and hilarious, is in video stores. But some of the laughs are lessened knowing that Belushi isn't living the good life in California but residing at Abel's Hill Cemetery in Chilmark, Masssachusetts.

BIOGRAPHIES: *Wired* (Woodward, 1984), *Samurai Widow* (J. Belushi, 1990)
AUDIO: *Lemmings* (Blue Thumb/Banana), *The Blues Brothers* (Atlantic), *Briefcase Full of Blues* (Atlantic)
FILMS: *National Lampoon's Animal House* (1978), *Goin' South* (1978), *Old Boyfriends* (1979), *1941* (1979), *The Blues Brothers* (1980), *Neighbors* (1981), *Continental Divide* (1981)
TV: "Saturday Night Live" (1975–79)
VIDEOS: *Things We Did Last Summer; Saturday Night Live; Best of John Belushi*

## ROBERT BENCHLEY

### (September 15, 1889–Nobember 21, 1945)

A mild-mannered humorist who utilized embarrassed smiles and an air of gently flustered chagrin in his comic lectures and movie roles, Robert Benchley achieved fame both as a performer and a writer. He was naturally funny off stage as well as on.

Off stage: Benchley, on vacation in Venice, sent a telegram to a friend: "Streets flooded. Please advise."

On stage: Benchley played a boozing author in the film *China Seas*. Falling off a cruise ship's gangplank, he calls out, "These streets are in deplorable condition!"

Born in Worcester, Massachusetts, Benchley graduated from Harvard in 1912 and took jobs with several publishing houses and newspapers. He and Dorothy Parker shared an office at *Vanity Fair* in 1919. The door read: "Utica Prop Forge and Tool Company."

Working as a drama critic for *Life* (1921–29) and *The New Yorker* (1929–39), Benchley was noted for his tart reviews. For "Abie's Irish Rose" he simply wrote "Hebrews 13:8." In the Bible, that passage read: "Jesus Christ, the same yesterday, and today, and forever."

In 1922 he wrote sketches for the show "The 49ers." For "The Music Box Revue" of 1923 he performed a monologue, "The Treasurer's Report." He used it in vaudeville and filmed it as a short in 1927. Benchley's 1928 short *The Sex Life of the Polyp* was a light, amusing hit, and between 1935 and 1943 he wrote and starred in a series, including the Academy Award–winning *How to Sleep* in 1936. Other favorites were *A Night at the Movies* (1937), *How to Sub-Let* (1939) and *Keeping in Shape* (1942). The 1950 book *The Reel Benchley* collected comic moments from his short films.

In most of these, the pear-shaped Benchley assumed the part of a modest, slightly nervous lecturer tossing off absentminded asides while forcing a smile. "If you remember, in our last lecture we took up the subject of how to stay awake. And on looking about me, I notice that many of you did not seem to catch the idea. Today, therefore, we are taking up the subject of 'How to Sleep,' and I am hoping for a little better response. . . ."

In *The Courtship of the Newt* (1938) he referred to the newt's courting cycle, which "opens on the 10th of March and extends on through the following February—leaving about ten days for general overhauling and redecoration."

On radio and on records, he liked to deliver whimsical "Flying Broom" travelogues. A fragment from a tour of India: "We notice a native family clustered around a crude hut. There is a baby playing in the dirt. He is n-a-k-e-d. Or as they say in India, naked. The child has his mother's eyes, his mother's nose, and his mother's mouth. Which leaves his mother with a pretty blank expression. . . ."

Throughout his career he was well known for best-selling books featuring his short humor. As a character actor Benchley's charm enhanced many film comedies, whether he played friend (to Robert Paige in *Her Primitive Man*) or foe (to Fred Allen in *It's In the Bag*).

Benchley's generally gentle personality was noted by Woolcott Gibbs, who said, "Whenever he was aware of a sense of insecurity or inadequacy in anyone he met, he was their admiring ally before the world. This committed him to many bores, and some men and women used him shamelessly. He knew it, but was helpless. Perhaps it was a price he had agreed to pay for the luxury of knowing that he had failed very few people in kindness."

Even his practical jokes were inoffensive. A short time after his doctor explained that the pills he was taking could cause side effects, Benchley summoned the physician to his home. When the doctor arrived, there lay Benchley—half of his body covered with feathers.

AUDIO: *Benchley's Best* (Audio Rarities), *Best of Benchley Read by Bob Elliott* (Caedmon Records), *The World of Robert Benchley Read by Henry Morgan* (Listening Library)

BIOGRAPHIES: *Robert Benchley* (N. Benchley), *Robert Benchley* (Rosmond)

BOOKS: *Of All Things* (1921), *Love Conquers All* (1922), *Pluck and Luck* (1925), *The Early Worm* (1927), *20,000 Leagues Under the Sea or David Copperfield* (1976), *The Treasurer's Report* (1938), *No Poems or Around the World Baackwards and Sidways* (1932), *From Bed to Worse* (1934), *My Ten Years in a Quandary* (1976), *After 1903—What?* (1938), *Inside Benchley* (1976), *Benchley Beside Himself* (1976), *The Reel Benchley* (1950)

FILMS incl.: *Dancing Lady* (1933), *Social Register* (1934), *Live Love and Learn* (1937), *Broadway Melody of 1938* (1938), *Foreign Correspondent* (1940), *Nice Girl* (1941), *The Reluctant Dragon* (1941), *You'll Never Get Rich* (1941), *Bedtime Story* (1941), *The Major and the Minor* (1942), *I Married a Witch* (1942), *Flesh and Fantasy* (1943), *Her Primitive Man* (1944), *National Barn Dance* (1944), *See Here Private Hargrove* (1944), *It's in the Bag* (1945), *Weekend at the Waldorf* (1945), *Hollywood Victory Caravan* (1945), *The Stork Club* (1945), *Duffy's Tavern* (1945), *Road to Utopia* (1945), *Snafu* (1946), *Blue Skies* (1946)

## WILLIAM BENDIX

### (January 4, 1906–December 14, 1964)

Almost a caricature of a Runyonesque mug, William Bendix was a comical 200-pound hulk with a huge oval face dominated by a big broken nose. His small mouth added to the quizzical expression that made him popular in dumb-ape roles. It was his mild, hoarse voice and gentle personality that saved him from a steady diet of stereotyped roles and ultimately led to his comedy success in television's "The Life of Riley."

Born in a tenement on Third Avenue and 45th Street in New York City, Bendix left P.S. 5 in the Bronx to get a job and help support his family. His father, Oscar, was a musician but not nearly as successful as his uncle Max, who once conducted the Metropolitan Opera orchestra.

Bendix was a bat boy for the New York Giants at the Polo Grounds and also for the Yankees. One of his chores was going up into the stands to get Babe Ruth hot dogs during the game. Bendix played semipro baseball for a while. His only brush with acting as a child was when, at five, he did some extra work at Vitagraph Studios in Brooklyn. His father worked there briefly as a handyman.

At 22 Bendix married, and his father-in-law set him up as the manager of a Newark grocery store. It was only when the store folded during the depression that Bendix joined the New Jersey Federal Theater Project. His best role was Policeman Krupp in a Theater Guild production of *The Time of Your Life*. He went to Hollywood and played a bartender in *Woman of the Year* and a cab driver in *The McGuerins of Brooklyn*. His career began to gain momentum. He showed promise in both comedy (stealing a few scenes from Lou Costello as a dumb cop in *Who Done It?*) and in drama (as the poor stooge whose life falls to pieces aboard Hitchcock's *Lifeboat*).

He became Chester Riley on radio in 1944, and "The Life of Riley" lasted eight years. During that time he also made some of his best films. He co-starred with Bing Crosby in *A Connecticut Yankee in King Arthur's Court*, starred in *Kill the Umpire* and was memorable in the highly fictionalized *Babe Ruth Story*.

After a brief contractual problem was resolved, he took over for Jackie Gleason and made the television version of "Riley" a hit. His Durante-like catch phrase was "What a revoltin' development this is!" He always said comedy was tougher than drama. "You've always got to strive for laughs as a bumbler. . . . Once I was a psychopathic killer . . . you don't have to worry about making the audience like you."

Bendix succeeded Jackie Gleason in *Take Me Along* on Broadway in 1960 and made many more films in addition to television appearances. In the late 1960s he remarked, "I've had a long varied, pleasant, eventful career. I don't hate anybody and I don't have any bitter thoughts. I started out without any advantages, but I've been lucky and successful and I've had fun."

FILMS incl.: *Woman of the Year* (1942), *Brooklyn Orchid* (1942), *The Glass Key* (1942), *Who Done It?* (1942), *Taxi Mister* (1943), *Lifeboat* (1944) *The Hairy Ape* (1944), *It's in the Bag* (1945), *Don Juan Quilligan* (1945), *Sentimental Journey* (1946), *The Blue Dahlia* (1946), *The Dark Corner* (1946), *Where There's Life* (1947), *The Babe Ruth Story* (1948), *The Life of Riley* (1949), *The Big Steal* (1949), *A Connecticut Yankee in King Arthur's Court* (1949), *Kill the Umpire* (1950), *Detective Story* (1951), *Idle on Parade* (1959), *Boys' Night Out* (1962), *For Love or Money* (1963), *Young Fury* (1965)

TV: "The Life of Riley" (1953–58), "The Overland Trail" (1960)

## BILLY BENEDICT (See THE EAST SIDE KIDS.)

## JACK BENNY

### (Benjamin Kubelsky, February 14, 1894–December 26, 1974)

Jack Benny's style was epitomized by the first line he ever uttered on radio. In 1932, on Ed Sullivan's local WHN show in New York, he said, "This is Jack Benny talking. There will be a slight pause while you say 'Who cares?' "

The timing of his lines and his mild chagrin at being the butt of the jokes were keys to his enduring success. In stand-up he was one of the first "natural" comedians, coming out in a suit and tie and telling jokes in a conversational manner. On radio and television Benny was a pioneer "reaction" come-

A master of timing, from the exasperated aside to the comic stare, Jack Benny was an enormously popular radio and television comedian whose average-man foibles touched and amused millions. Photo from the author's collection.

dian—getting laughs more from the way sidekicks deflated his vanity and satirized his stinginess than from any wisecracks uttered in return. Some of his most memorable laughs came from reaction lines. His answer to "Your money or your life" was just a perfectly timed "I'm thinking it over." He topped a Fred Allen insult with chagrin: "You wouldn't have said that if my writers were here."

Born in Chicago but raised in Waukegan, Illinois, Jack studied the violin and in his late teens was an accompanist for a local vaudeville house. He was offered a job as accompanist to the young Marx Brothers, but his parents made him turn it down. Eventually they let Jack team with a safe, motherly 40-year-old pianist named Cora Salisbury. Eventually Benny became a solo performer. His stage name was Ben Benny, but entertainer Ben Bernie complained.

From "Ben Benny, Fiddle Funology" he became "Jack Benny, Aristocrat of Humor," adopting a breezy, sophisticated air. He even sang an occasional novelty tune, like the prohibition lament "After This Country Goes Dry, Goodbye Wild Women, Goodbye." He was featured in the Broadway show *The Great Temptations,* but the *Herald Tribune* called him just "a pleasant imitation of Phil Baker." In early films, like *The Big Broadcast of 1937,* he's rather slick and self-assured, and in many he's smooth and sarcastic, especially *George Washington Slept Here,* in which he wisecracks and slow-burns his way through the story of a man roughing it in a falling-down suburban home. Year after year he developed and refined the self-deprecating patter and fall-guy personality that would win him sympathetic laughs.

In 1932 Benny got his own radio show, but his peak years began in the middle and late 1930s. By that time he had assembled a cast of supporting players that included his wife, Mary Livingstone (whom he married in 1927), announcer Don Wilson, band leader Phil Harris, Eddie "Rochester" Anderson, Dennis Day and Mel Blanc. Almost all got an equal chance to toss verbal stones at the fragile glass targets of Jack's preening narcissism and woeful thrift.

Known to be one of the nicest men in show business, the one thing that truly bothered Jack was fans thinking he really was a tightwad. At one point he ordered his writers to cut down the "cheap jokes" to one per show. Only in retrospect was it remotely amusing to him when, after having failed to return a full bottle for a urine specimen, his nurse angrily remarked, "You never give anything away, do you!"

While other radio comedians burned out quickly with boisterous jokes and wild catch phrases, Benny guided his writers into well thought out scripts that often included running gags from week to week. His catch phrases were too mild to wear out their welcome—his fidgety, frustrated "Now cut that out!" or his contemplative "Hmmmm."

Benny was a pioneer in building and topping the laughs, taking one gag and sprouting several more from it—then twisting back to get a few more in before the surprise finish. A typical example from an old radio show:

BENNY: When I started in radio, I was 22.

DON: What are you talking about? I knew you then and you had gray hair.

BENNY: Don, I was born with gray hair. I was worried about the doctor bill. I'm glad I didn't pay

him. Slapping me when my back is turned. And, Don, after all these years who do you think is sitting in the audience this very moment?

DON: The doctor?

BENNY: No, his lawyer. The case comes up in court Wednesday.

Benny remained on radio through 1955. While he often joked about his limited film success, he did star in at least one authentic classic, *To Be or Not to Be* with Carole Lombard. His television shows, in various formats, lasted from 1950 to 1965. Benny was a regular visitor into American homes for over 30 years, rarely missing even one week. An exception was the Sunday after Carole Lombard's plane crash. Jack couldn't bring himself to perform the show. Another time, on Yom Kippur, Jack balked at performing. He told his writers that it wasn't because he himself was especially religious. He said, "I wouldn't like the Gentiles to think I didn't respect my religion."

In the 1960s Benny continued to perform regularly in television specials and on talk shows. On a "Dick Cavett Show" he mentioned one of his greatest sources of pride—the school in Waukegan named after him. The sports team was "the 39'ers," a reference to one of Benny's longest running gags—his vainglorious insistence on being 39. Remarkably, Benny looked fairly close to 39 or 49 even when he was in his 70s. He performed almost to the end, always a big draw at live concerts around the country.

At his death. President Ford wrote, "If laughter is the music of the soul, Jack and his violin and his good humor have made life better for all men."

AUDIO: *Greatest Original Broadcasts* (MF Records), *The Horn Blows at Midnight* (Radiola), *The Radio Fight of the Century: The Fred Allen–Jack Benny Feud* (Radiola), *The Jack Benny Story* (Radiola), *Jack Benny 1933* (Mark 56), *Jack Benny 1936* (Mark 56), *Jack Benny 1940* (Mark 56), *Jack Benny Original Radio Broadcast* (Nostalgia Lane), *The Jack Benny Show* (Radiola), *The Jack Benny Show* (Yorkshire), *The Radio Feud Continues* (Radiola), *The Jack Benny Roast* (Friar's Club)

BIOGRAPHIES: *Jack Benny* (Fein, 1976), *The Jack Benny Show* (Josefsberg, 1977), *Sundays at Seven* (Benny, 1990)

BROADWAY: *Great Temptations* (1926)

FILMS incl.: *Hollywood Revue of 1929* (1929), *Medicine Man* (1930), *Broadway Melody of 1936* (1936), *It's in the Air* (1935), *Big Broadcast of 1937* (1936), *Artists and Models* (1937), *Artists and Models Abroad* (1938), *Man About Town* (1939), *Buck Benny Rides Again* (1940), *Love Thy Neighbor* (1940), *Charley's Aunt* (1941), *To Be or Not to Be* (1942), *George Washington Slept Here* (1942), *The Meanest Man in the World* (1943), *It's in the Bag* (1945), *The Horn Blows at Midnight* (1945), *It's a Mad Mad Mad Mad World* (1963), *A Guide for the Married Man* (1967)

VIDEOS: *The Jack Benny Program; Reel Moments of Laughter*

## MICHAEL BENTINE (See THE GOONS.)

## GERTRUDE BERG

**(Gertrude Edelstein Berg, October 3, 1899–September 14, 1966)**

The ultimate "Jewish mother" in the days when the term meant warmth, affection and only slight "noodging," Gertrude Berg spent 25 years playing alter ego Molly Goldberg, the character she first developed for radio in 1929. Molly based the character on herself and the people she knew. She was born in the then–middle-class neighborhood of Harlem, New York and was well acquainted with the struggling immigrants of the Lower East Side.

Berg had written scripts for her father, Jacob, who ran a Catskill Mountains resort. After her marriage in 1918, she continued writing and attended Columbia University. She wrote for the Jewish Art Theater, and when her husband began having trouble in business, she decided to try to sell a radio script. Her first effort, "Effie and Laurie," was about two salesgirls in a department store. CBS bought it, but the series only lasted four months. Her next idea was the dialect comedy "The Rise of the Golbergs." She was so anxious that NBC understand the humor, she performed it for the radio executives herself. Then they insisted she be the star. The cast eventually featured Menasha Skulnik as Uncle David, Everett Sloan as her son Sammy and James R. Waters as her husband, Jake.

Over the years Molly Goldberg relied less and less on dialect, and the show was given over to charming character comedy. Many who appeared on the show, including Joseph Cotton and Marjorie Main, were not even Jewish. Berg's salary eventually rose from $75 a week to $7,500. The show was initially offered in five-minute installments every night, a comic soap opera. Listeners of all persuasions tuned in religiously and enjoyed Molly's catch phrase, "So who's to know?"

"The Goldbergs" left the air in 1934, but after her next series "House of Glass" failed, Gertrude found a sponsor willing to bring "The Goldbergs" back. It stayed on the air for another nine years. She once wrote, "Anything I say grows out of my own experience. . . . It is impossible to improve on reality. . . . The good radio story should never escape reality and the problems of real people. . . . It's not a strange phenomenon that certain radio serials go on for years and remain favorites. These programs reflect a definite characteristic of American life, and the stories they tell always have some relationship to actual events that occurred in one way or another in the listener's life."

A movie version and television series appeared in the 1950s, with *Time* magazine reporting it was still "sugary smooth as butter, pastry-thin [in] plot and heavily spiced with Bronxisms. What keeps this confection from cloying is author Berg's tart recognition of human frailties and her blunt but understanding sense of humor."

The 1950s were not understanding times. Philip Loeb, Molly's husband on the show, was suspected of being a Communist by McCarthy supporters. The sponsor, General Foods, canceled its ads and the show temporarily left the air. After wobbling back in 1952 on NBC, "The Goldbergs" managed to sneak over to the Dumont network for a last season in 1954. Philip Loeb committed suicide in 1955.

Gertrude Berg, who had won a Best Actress Emmy in 1950, continued on, appearing on Broadway in several plays and even taking a shot at another sitcom. She recorded an album, *How to Be a Jewish Mother,* (based on the Dan Greenberg book), just a year before her death in 1966.

AUDIO: *How to Be a Jewish Mother* (Amy)
AUTOBIOGRAPHY: *Molly and Me* (1961)

BROADWAY: *Me and Molly* (1946), *A Majority of One* (1959), *Dear Me the Sky Is Falling* (1963)
FILMS incl.: *Make a Wish* (1937), *Molly* (1951), *Main Street to Broadway* (1953)
TV: "The Goldbergs" (1949–55), "The Gertrude Berg Show" (aka "Mrs. G Goes to College") (1961–62)

# EDGAR BERGEN

## (February 16, 1903–September 30, 1978)

A ventriloquist on radio? Only Edgar Bergen could manage that. He made his dummy, Charlie McCarthy, seem real. In fact, despite occasional "I'll slice you into a venetian blind" jokes from W. C. Fields, Charlie was treated like a real boy. No dummy had such a distinctive voice, unique mannerisms (including a gasping "heh heh" laugh) and a catch phrase: "I'll clip ya so help me I'll mow ya down."

At 11, the Chicago-born Edgar began learning how to throw his voice and do magic tricks. He sketched the face for the dummy he wanted, and the head was built for him in 1920 for $35. He unveiled his ventriloquism skills in a high school talent show. After attending Northwestern University, he went into vaudeville. At his first performance, the manager of the theater was so pleased with his work that aside from the $3 for five shows, he tipped him a quarter. Bergen was delighted: "That's the only time anyone in show business ever paid me more than I contracted for."

Around 1930 Bergen (with Charlie billed separately) appeared in some Vitaphone shorts. Charlie didn't have his trademark monocle and top hat yet, but he was very much the girl-chasing little wise guy. "Let's play post office," he tells a lady in *Nut Guilty*. "That's a child's game," she says. "Not the way I play it!" Bergen insists, "It's up to us to teach this woman the difference between right and wrong." Charlie agrees: "Well, you teach her what's right and I'll hold her for further examination!"

One reason that Charlie seemed real was that he often appeared in vaudeville sketches: nurse skits, courtroom capers, etc. He didn't simply rest on Bergen's knee all the time. Charlie and Edgar adapted the sketches to film and made sure to have scenes in which Charlie was seated nowhere near Edgar,

seeming to react like any of the flesh-and-blood performers.

After guesting on Rudy Vallee's radio show, Bergen and McCarthy got their own series, which lasted for 20 years. For six of them, it was the number-one show in the country. Guest episodes with W. C. Fields, Fred Allen and Marilyn Monroe are among radio's comedy classics, still available on disc and tape. The Fields feud with McCarthy continued in the movies. Fields' dislike of kids definitely extended to the wooden one: "You'd better come out of the sun, Charles, before you get unglued." "Do you mind if I stand in the shade of your nose?" "Quiet, you termite flophouse . . . Charles, is it true your father was a gate-leg table?" "If it is, your father was under it!"

The show sometimes included appearances by Edgar's daughter, Candy (dubbed "Little Dextrose" by Bergen's wry British bandleader, Ray Noble). Bergen expanded his family to include dummies Effie Klinker and dopey Mortimer Snerd. Mortimer's goofy speaking voice influenced many (including British comic Spike Milligan's radio character Eccles), but the 4-foot-tall, 30-pound Charlie remained the biggest star. He even received a special Academy Award.

A pleasant personality, Bergen sometimes made solo film appearances, including *I Remember Mama* in 1948. He hosted a television quiz show in the 1950s, "Do You Trust Your Wife," which was revamped into Johnny Carson's "Who Do You Trust." Bergen wrote the *Encyclopedia Britannica* entry on how to throw your voice and in the 1960s appeared often on "The Red Skelton Hour," with Skelton imitating Fields in sketches with Edgar and Charlie.

In 1978, suffering from heart problems, Bergen announced his retirement. He said Charlie McCarthy would spend his eternity at the Smithsonian Institute. Of course, Charlie had something to say in all of this: "How can you retire when you haven't worked since you met me?"

On stage, Friday evening, September 29, Bergen told the crowd, "All acts have a beginning and an end . . . and I think that the time has come for me." Edgar Bergen died peacefully in his sleep some time during the night.

Bergen's daughter emerged as a comedy star with "Murphy Brown" in the late 1980s, and in 1991

Edgar Bergen and Charlie McCarthy were all over America in a way that Bergen could never have imagined. The duo was immortalized on a U.S. postage stamp.

AUDIO: *The Chase and Sanborn Show* (Mark 56), *Chase and Sanborn 102nd Anniversary* (GRC), *Edgar Bergen* (Mark 56), *Edgar Bergen and Charlie McCarthy* (Memorabilia), *The Edgar Bergen Show* (Radiola), *Charlie McCarthy Rides Again* (Radiola), *Fractured Fairy Tales* (Radiola), *Lessons in Ventriloquism* (Juro), *Bergen and McCarthy* (Murray Hill), *Fields on Radio* (Columbia), *The Great Radio Feuds* (Columbia), *Fred Allen Vintage Radio Broadcasts* (Mar-Bren), *Jest Like Old Times* (Radiola), *Great Radio Comedians* (Murray Hill)

FILMS incl.: *The Goldwyn Follies* (1938), *You Can't Cheat an Honest Man* (1939), *Charlie McCarthy Detective* (1939), *Look Who's Laughing* (1941), *Here We Go Again* (1942), *Song of the Open Road* (1944), *I Remember Mama* (1948), *One Way Wahine* (1966), *Don't Make Waves* (1967), *The Muppet Movie* (1979)

TV: "Do You Trust Your Wife?" (1956–57)

## MILTON BERLE

### (Mendel Berlinger, July 12, 1908–  )

"Good evening, ladies and gentlemen. I'm sorry I'm calling you ladies and gentlemen when you *know* what you are. . . ."

Brash, corny, anything-for-a-laugh, Milton Berle was everyone's "Uncle Miltie," the television superstar who made faces, wore garish costumes, brawled with guests in free-for-all slapstick and machine-gunned jokes until the audience was helpless with laughter. Berle's comedy wasn't always pretty—especially when he turned up in drag—but he was always boldly funny.

Berle was born in Harlem, 68 West 118th Street. His family was desperately poor. One of Milton's bitterest memories was when, at age four, there was almost nothing to eat in the house for Milton and his brothers. "It was one of the worst days of my life. Also the longest. The three of us were so weak with hunger we just lay around the flat, waiting for Mom to come home. It got later and later. Finally, long after dark, Mom came in. Crying and hollering,

Milton Berle, television's first great comic pioneer. "Uncle Miltie"'s fame goes beyond his well-known penchant for drag comedy and his legendary joke-stealing. Photo from the author's collection.

we rushed her, demanding something to eat. All she had was four bagels which she'd gotten for two cents because they were leftovers. We each got a bagel plus one third, carefully divided . . . then we all went to bed and cried, because we were so hungry and miserable. . . ."

Berle's stage-struck mother, Sarah, got him into show business. She took him to Fort Lee, New Jersey to be an extra in silent films. Berle claimed his screen debut was as the baby Marie Dressler held to her heart in *Tillie's Puncture Romance*, and that he was in *The Perils of Pauline:* "I was the kid on the top of the moving train, running with it. . . . Pearl White was holding on to me and, to this day, a lot of comics wish I'd never been saved!"

In 1920, only 12 years old, he joined the cast of *Floradora* stealing scenes by deliberately dancing off-stride from the rest, trying jokes and techniques taught to him by his mother. The following year he and Elizabeth Kennedy became Kennedy and Berle, working their way through vaudeville. When she got married, he went solo. He eventually evolved his own comedy sketch in 1927, "Memories of Milton," playing the patsy to several women who gave him hard-luck stories. A master of ceremonies at The Palace in 1931 and a rising star in *The Earl Carroll Vanities* and in *The Ziegfeld Follies*, Berle turned to radio in 1936. By the 1940s he had his own radio show, but it was on television that he would achieve his greatest fame.

In 1948 he starred on "The Texaco Star Theater," wowing audiences with all the vaudeville bits he had picked up over the years. He was on the covers of both *Time* and *Newsweek* on the same day, May 16, 1949. A perfectionist, he directed the show's director, advised the makeup man, moved the cameramen around and supervised the writers. Though it was a strain and made him a few enemies, it paid off. When Berle arrived in 1948, there were half a million television sets in use in the country. The following year, a million. By 1954, 26 million. The demand seemed to come from Milton Berle's supply of jokes and funny faces.

Branded the "thief of bad gags," Milton did indeed believe that nobody could tell a joke better than he. Berle's on-stage persona was labeled brash to the point of obnoxiousness, the epitome of "show biz phony." Off stage Berle was usually characterized as honest, direct, considerate and generous. Some glimpses of the other side of Milton Berle were seen by fans in his dramatic appearances in movies and on Broadway, notably his brilliant work on stage in *The Goodbye People*.

Though tastes have changed somewhat, Berle's vintage television clips have found an audience on video. It's hard not to be bludgeoned into giggles by Berle's relentless aggression. To a woman getting to her seat: "You can sit down, madam. We saw the dress." A double dose to a woman with a feather in her hat: "That looks like the feather that signed the Declaration of Independence. And the guy with her looks like he signed it!"

Berle knew what the critics said about him. In his own starring movie, *Leave 'Em Laughing,* he's even upbraided by his agent for being a selfish and superfluous gagster: "Jack Benny, Bob Hope, Red Skelton—what've they got? A style of their own. What've you got? You've got all their material and

no style. You're a parrot with skin on." In the film, Bert Lahr also took him to task: "They've got to like you, feel sorry for you. Do they? People forget jokes . . . what sticks with them when they leave the theater are the nice things the comic does, like spending his last dime on flowers for a girl who don't know he's alive. . . . A joke ain't everything."

Fans seemed to recognize the passion to please that was behind Berle's bombast. They knew that his desire to be in front of an audience was heartfelt and joyous. They tuned in for more every week. He was proud to say that there was no laugh track on his show: "We *made* the audience laugh." They roared over some gags over and over, like his catch phrase "Makeup!" followed by the huge dusty powder puff smashed in his face. His 1951 contract with NBC was an astounding $200,000 a year for 30 years. "And I lived, thank goodness, to 1981 when the contract was up and they paid me for 30 years."

Berle was not the top comic in the land after the 1950s, but he remained a popular talk and variety show guest and was always in demand for live performances. In the 1980s he was also called upon more often for made-for-television dramas, including *Doyle Against the House* and *Family Business*.

Berle's heart operation in 1985 slowed him down only temporarily. In 1986 he was up and around, playing a series of concerts with Henny Youngman. He said of the operation, "It has really improved my sex life. I can hardly wait to tell my wife about it. I went to an honest doctor, he would never operate on someone unless he needed the money. And the hospital was very well suspected. I mean respected. They spent $5 million on a new recovery room—and it hasn't been used yet!"

In 1987 Berle began gathering his old Berle clips for "The Second Time Around," a series of television specials and videocassettes. The reaction to Berle was typical. *People* magazine found him "as overbearing as ever—age (he's 81) clearly hasn't introduced him to humility." Audiences just ran out and picked up the tapes. In 1989 Berle put out a joke book crammed with some of the best from the millions in his computer gag file.

Young comics asking advice from Berle were told to answer three questions on stage: "Who am I? What am I doing here? Why am I here?" He added, "Comedy is a lonely art. When you make a personal appearance you're alone . . . alone on the stage. If the laughs don't come, you have egg on your face. That's lonely. There's another kind of loneliness, even now. Maybe you don't feel like being funny . . . maybe your mind is on other things. . . . You feel isolated."

While known to be serious off stage, and his autobiography was filled with regrets, in public Berle remained the complete ham, ready to step in front of the public for most any reason. It wasn't just the money ($400,000) but the chance to sneak into folks' living rooms that made him do a commercial for BVDs: "At my age, I've done just about everything in my BVDs." He added, "Waiting for me to retire is like leaving the porch light on for Jimmy Hoffa. I could never think of it. A retired person with nothing to do is a dead person."

AUDIO: *Uncle Miltie* (Radiola), *Milton Berle on Radio* (Mark 56), *Songs My Mother Loved to Sing* (Roulette)

AUTOBIOGRAPHY: *Milton Berle: An Autobiography* (1974)

BOOKS: *B.S. I Love You* (1988), *Out of My Trunk* (1945), *Milton Berle's Private Joke File* (1989)

BROADWAY: *Earl Carroll Vanities* (1932), *Saluta* (1934), *Ziegfeld Follies* (1936), *See My Lawyer* (1939), *The Goodbye People* (1968)

FILMS incl.: *New Faces of 1937* (1937), *Radio City Revels* (1938), *Tall Dark and Handsome* (1941), *Rise and Shine* (1941), *Whispering Ghosts* (1942), *Over My Dead Body* (1942), *Margin for Error* (1943), *Always Leave Them Laughing* (1949), *Let's Make Love* (1960), *The Bellboy* (1960), *It's a Mad Mad Mad Mad World* (1963), *The Oscar* (1965), *The Happening* (1967), *Who's Minding the Mint* (1967), *Where Angels Go Trouble Follows* (1968), *Hieronymus Merkin* (1969), *Seven in Darkness* (1970), *Lepke* (1975), *The Muppet Movie* (1979), *Off Your Rocker* (1980), *Broadway Danny Rose* (1984), *Pee Wee's Big Adventure* (1986), *Side by Side* (1988).

TV: "The Milton Berle Show" (1948–56), "Milton Berle in the Kraft Music Hall" (1958–59), "Jackpot Bowling" (1960–61), "The Milton Berle Show" (1966–67)

VIDEOS: *Berle the Second Time Around* (3 vols.); *Milton Berle Show: His Famous Dragnet Parody; Milton Berle Invites You to an Evening at La Cage; Best of Milton Berle* (2 vols.)

## SHELLEY BERMAN

### (Sheldon Berman, February 3, 1926–   )

His albums were titled *Inside, Outside* and *The Edge*, and they were drawn from his heart, soul and mind. Shelley Berman's monologues often resembled one-act plays, artistic and theatrical. Some of them were intense and dark, others sentimental and poignant. Trained as an actor, he was one of the first stand-up comedians whose work was intended as "art" and received on just those terms. He performed "concerts," not nightclub "gigs."

The Chicago-born performer had always strived for an acting career. An early trip to New York was a disaster. He "froze" at auditions. He wrote comedy for Steve Allen's show but ultimately returned home to work as a cab driver and later a drugstore manager. In the summers he performed with local stock companies. In 1955 he replaced Severn Darden in Chicago's Compass Players improvisational group. "At first I thought the idea was to go up and ad-lib funny. It took me at least a month, I think, to learn that you don't go up with the intention of being *funny*. You go up with the intention of playing out an action . . . the *funny* will happen."

Other members of the group included Nichols and May, the only performers of the era who, like Berman, were successfully experimenting with "serious" comedy. Berman actually hoped to join Nichols and May as a comedy trio, but they refused, exacerbating the "love-hate" rivalry between Berman and Nichols. Ironically, it was after Elaine May refused to join him in acting out an improv suggestion from the audience that he created, alone, his first important routine, "The Morning After the Night Before."

The bit was about a man suffering through a hangover and learning, in a grossly embarrassing phone call from the party host, that he made a complete fool of himself and worse: "How did I break a window? I see. Were you very fond of that cat? It's lucky the only thing I threw through the window was a cat! Oh . . . she's a very good sport, your mother. . . ."

Berman's monologue device—the phone call—would be copied by many other comedians. No one, however, could copy the kind of routines Berman did with it. His other classics included "Franz Kafka on the Telephone" (a modern nightmare of trying to get information from a phone operator), "The Hotel Room" (a stark drama of hysteria as a hotel guest discovers himself in a black room with no windows or even a door to get out again) and "The Cut Finger," (in which a man alone in a strange city telephones everyone from a vet to a gynecologist while wondering if he'll eventually bleed to death). His comedy often had life-or-death emotions, such as his call as a man trying to get help for a woman dangling from a building ledge.

Experimenting with all types of stand-up, Berman could as easily ad lib (he did a bit as a child psychiatrist fielding questions from the audience), put together a frenzied ten-minute tirade on airlines or indulge in intimate, neurotic confessionals, such as his famous complaint against buttermilk or his sudden psychosexual need to pull the case off the pillow he nuzzled the night before.

For such bleak and offbeat routines, *Time* magazine lumped him in with Lenny Bruce and Tom Lehrer as one of the "sick" comedians of the day. And, adding insult to the injury, the magazine wrote that he had a face "like a hastily sculpted meatball."

Mostly critics praised Berman as a virtuoso satirist of modern angst and anxiety—an intellectual performer. Berman's sensitivity was well known. At a time when nightclubs were raucous places and comics were supposed to machine-gun jokes, he demanded an end to such distractions as the drone of blenders mixing drinks at the bar. Berman's reputation for being "difficult" seemed to be proven in 1963 when he appeared in an NBC documentary *Comedian Backstage*. During one of his best routines, the sentimental "Father and Son," a phone rang offstage. The cameras followed him when, after the show ended, he stormed around complaining about the ringing phone. Irritated and piqued, he deliberately grabbed the phone and dumped it off the hook, showing how it *should* look when he was on stage.

For decades Berman insisted that his fall from popularity was caused by reaction to the television special. Back in the 1960s this extremely minor incident was indeed a cause célèbre. Standards for star behavior were rather strict. Another problem was that Berman had begun to run out of new

material. Bob Newhart was now doing phone bits and Woody Allen was creating neurotic one-liners. The year after *Comedian Backstage*, Berman recorded his last concert album.

Berman's enthusiasm for stand-up waned. He found other pursuits. He wrote a few novelty books, including 1966's *Cleans and Dirtys*, a dissection of language. He discovered: "A big boob is a clean. Two big boobs is a dirty. . . . Zelda is a clean. Fanny is a dirty. . . . Sailboat is a clean. Frigate is a dirty. . . . Desk is a clean. Drawers is a dirty. . . . Vertical is a clean. Horizontal is a dirty. . . . Comma is a clean. Period is a dirty. Giggle is a clean. Titter is a dirty."

Through the years Berman accelerated his acting career. He appeared in films and in stock productions of such shows as *Fiddler on the Roof, The Rothschilds* and *The Odd Couple*. Berman's luck in television was mixed. He recalled being offered the part of Lou Grant on "The Mary Tyler Moore Show." He said, "My management made a very big mistake and said there wasn't enough money." Moore, a great fan of Berman's, eventually hired him for a guest spot. He later turned up as "Mel Beach" on the series "Mary Hartman, Mary Hartman." In 1992 Berman premiered *First Is Supper*, in New York. The play for the National Jewish Theater is about life in Chicago in the late 1920s. He continues to guest in both comic and dramatic roles on television. Occasionally Berman has mounted a comeback tour with stand-up comedy or appeared on a "comedy club" television show. For short television appearances he usually offers a reworking of his "embarrassing moments" routine from years earlier—instantly accessible to all.

AUDIO: *Inside Shelley Berman* (Verve), *Outside Shelly Berman* (Verve), *The Edge of Shelley Berman* (Verve), *Personal Appearance* (Verve), *New Sides* (Verve), *Sex Life of the Primate* (Verve), *Great Moments in Comedy* (Verve), *Let Me Tell You a Funny Story* (Metro), *A Family Affair* (United Artists)

BOOKS: *Cleans and Dirtys* (1966), *A Hotel Is . . .* (1972)

BROADWAY: *Slightly Delinquent* (1954), *The Girls Against the Boys* (1959), *A Family Affair* (1962)

FILMS incl.: *The Best Man* (1964), *The Wheeler Dealers* (1964), *Divorce American Style* (1967), *Every Home*

*Should Have One* (aka *Think Dirty*) (1970), *Beware! The Blob!* (1972), *Teen Witch* (1989)
TV: "Mary Hartman, Mary Hartman" (1977–78)
VIDEO: *The Young at Heart Comedians Special*

# SANDRA BERNHARD

## (June 6, 1955–  )

"Performance art is nonsense," John Simon once wrote. "It's something that anybody without any training, any culture, or any genius can do. If it's bizarre enough, it works."

It has worked especially well for bizarre Sandra Bernhard, who carved out a career on the sheer force of her personality. Her act, which can be subtitled "The Importance of Being Sandra," is based mostly on preening recitations and self-absorbed psychodrama, the actress stage-center and self-centered. She has developed a hardcore cult who share her rages and outrages.

Born in Flint, Michigan, Bernhard spent her teen years in Scottsdale, Arizona, where she developed into a strange-looking creature, 5 foot 10 inches and 106 pounds, with a big nose and thick lips. "The kids called them 'nigger lips' all the time. I didn't look like anybody else, and that scared people. I was stared at from the time I was able to remember." She described her teen years as "isolated, alienating and very stark . . . real neurotic with deep-seated insecurities and fears."

A manicurist in Beverly Hills for five years, Bernhard turned the anger and insecurity inside out, developing a theatrical streak, performing stand-up in the late 1970s. Her career took off after she played the alarming and aggressive girl obsessed with Jerry Lewis in *The King of Comedy*. She was equally alarming and aggressive on talk shows. Her ability to fluster David Letterman consistently with her hot-and-cold sexuality made her a welcome guest time after time. He seemed amazed by her bohemian lifestyle and the probably apocryphal anecdotes she used to elicit his titters and stares. Once she described how, so dreadfully bored while making a film in Budapest, she allowed a grimy masseur to have sex with her while she pretended to sleep.

In New York it was not comedy clubs but performance art theaters that embraced and nourished Bernhard. Like her friend pop singer Madonna, Bernhard had a fondness for performing in her underwear and intriguing ringsiders with hints of steamy sexuality. She'd tell a gaping fan, "I'm very attracted to you, I feel I could really open up to you . . . and yet there's something about you that makes me want to hurt you. I'd really like to smash your face!" She told disdainful one-liners ("I saw Jerry Lewis kick one of those kids he was supposed to be helping") and offered unabashed narcissism: "I love sleeping on a full-length mirror."

Like Madonna, Bernhard played both sides of the feminist/sex object equation. She described her first album cover (posed in a bra and slip) as "a comment on women who are manipulated by the media, by men." For her one-woman performance film, she stripped down to a G-string for a dance number. Of her appearances on Letterman's show, she said, "I just observed how he treated the typical actress that came out. Most of them floundered, so I figured I'd better do something. I took the natural dynamic between us and pushed it over the top."

Bernhard insisted, "I'm not a real egotistical person . . . I'm really the antithesis of my performances in my personal life. I don't drink or do drugs and I hate overindulgence and insanity." For her overindulgence on stage the *New York Times* complained that her performances were "only slightly more polished than those one might do in private in front of a mirror, imagining oneself a star." But now she doesn't have to imagine she is a star. With her shows, her film appearances and even a book, she has become one. As she said with grand amusement, "I'm creating my own myth."

AUDIO: *I'm Your Woman* (Mercury), *Without You I'm Nothing* (Enigma)
BOOK: *Confessions of a Pretty Lady* (1988)
FILMS: *The King of Comedy* (1983), *Casual Sex* (1988), *Track 29* (1988), *Heavy Petting* (1989), *Without You I'm Nothing* (1990), *Hudson Hawk* (1991)
TV: "The Richard Pryor Show" (1977) "Roseanne" (1991)
VIDEOS: *Best of the Big Laff Off' An Evening at the Improv*

## JOE BESSER (See also THE THREE STOOGES.)

### (August 12, 1907–March 1, 1988)

A rolypoly comic with silly, sissy mannerisms, Joe Besser said he came upon his unique style in the late 1920s: "Since I always came across childlike, I decided to create a character everyone could identify with. The character I went with was an overaged Lord Fauntleroy who always thought the world was crashing down on him; his only defense became his exasperated mannerisms and catch phrases like 'Ooh, you crazy y-o-u!' and 'aw, shut uuuup!'" In moments of great pique, Joe tended to squeal and pinch, and promise worse: "Oooh, I'll haaaarm you!"

The stage-struck Besser left his Orthodox Jewish home to become an assistant to Thurston The Magician. Later he moved on to vaudeville sketches, teaming up with straight man Richy Craig Jr. and later Sam Critcherson in the 1930s. In a typical sketch he came out wearing two coats. Sam: "Hey, Joe, where are you going?" "Ooh, you're such a dumb! I'm going to paint my house . . . don't you see what it says on the paint can? It says for best results put on two coats!"

In the 1940s Joe joined Olsen and Johnson's "Sons of Fun" show on Broadway. "I waited 21 years for this break," he said at the time. Ed Sullivan wrote in his popular newspaper column, "Out of the maelstrom of sound and fury there emerged on opening night a genial comedian who ran away with the show . . . Joe Besser." Columnist Dorothy Killgallen predicted he'd be "the next comedian to hit the laughter jackpot of the nation."

Besser first developed his character "Stinky" in occasional guest spots on television's "Alan Young Show," then perfected it (wearing an oversized Lord Fauntleroy suit) on "The Abbott and Costello Show." There was no attempt at illusion—the laugh was in a fully grown adult mincing about as a devilish brat. It was Besser at his bizarre best.

When Shemp Howard died in 1955, Besser was invited to take his place as one of The Three Stooges. Joe toned down his minty brand of comedy (which didn't fit that well with Moe and Larry's style), and the boys made some mild comedies that alternated between slapstick and sitcom. In 1958 Joe chose to stay home with his wife rather than tour with the boys.

"I have been sorry ever since that I left the Stooges," Joe wrote the author. "We enjoyed working together and had a lot of fun." Besser went on to play a comic handyman on "The Joey Bishop Show," lent his distinctive voice to a variety of cartoon characters and guested in television sitcoms. He was the only member of The Three Stooges alive and well enough to be around for the momentous day in 1983 when the gang got their own star in the Hollywood Walk of Fame. He looked up, saw a few clouds in the sky and told the crowd that they must be "the boys" looking down in appreciation.

AUTOBIOGRAPHY: *Not Just a Stooge* (1984)
BROADWAY: *Sons of Fun* (1941), *If the Shoe Fits* (1946)
FILMS incl.: *Hey Rookie* (1944), *Eadie Was a Lady* (1945), *Talk About a Lady* (1946), *Feudin, Fussin and a Fightin* (1948), *Africa Screams* (1949), *The Desert Hawk* (1950), *Sins of Jezebel* (1953), *Abbott and Costello Meet the Keystone Kops* (1955), *Say One for Me* (1959), *The Rookie* (1959), *Three Stooges Fun-A-Rama Compilation* (1959), *Let's Make Love* (1960), *The Errand Boy* (1961), *With Six You Get Eggroll* (1968), *Which Way to the Front* (1970)
TV: "The Ken Murray Show" (1950–51), "The Abbott and Costello Show" (1951–52), "The Joey Bishop Show" (1962–65), "The Houndcats" (voice only, 1972–73), "Jeannie" (voice only, 1973–75), "Yogi's Space Race" (voice only, 1978–79)
VIDEO: *Best of Spike Jones Volume 2*

## THE BICKERSONS

**John: Don Ameche, Dominic Felix Amici, May 31, 1910–**
**Blanche: Frances Langford, April 4, 1914–**

John Bickerson, blustering at his wife in the kitchen: "And stop using my pants for a pot holder!"

Blanche Bickerson: "Why? That's what you use them for!"

In 1946 "The Bickersons" emerged as radio's funniest fighting couple. The very name became a slang term for any married couple in trouble, and "Bickerson"-styled comic strips and sitcoms proliferated, many based on the antics of John and Blanche. Some seemed so close to The Bickerson spirit that writer Philip Rapp had to sue. There was an out-of-court settlement with Jackie Gleason over "The Honeymooners."

Don Ameche was John Bickerson and Frances Langford was Blanche. Langford was born in Lakeland, Florida and sang while at Southern College. After some throat problems her soprano turned into a husky contralto. This became an advantage when she sang sultry numbers like "I'm in the Mood for Love" (as she did in the film *Every Night at Eight*). She went to radio on Rudy Vallee's show and followed that with a Broadway musical *Here Goes the Bride*. After singing "Night and Day" at a party for Cole Porter, she was signed to a movie contract and appeared in a half-dozen musicals. In 1941 she became a regular on "The Bob Hope Show," developing a flair for comedy. She joined him on overseas visits to entertain the soldiers during World War II.

As Blanche, the underrated Langford showed a deceptively wide range of emotions. The show was far from being a one-joke session of insults. Audiences laughed as she whined, complained and frustrated John with her whimsies and demands for attention, but they were sympathetic toward her since she was often justified. They knew that she wasn't a shrew, but a clearly attractive woman who, like her husband, was getting hopelessly ground into the machinery of marriage. A running gag on the show was her inability to savor a victory calmly. After getting her husband to agree to something, she wouldn't let it lie. "You say you'll do it? Do it *now,*" she'd cry, even though *now* was the middle of the night.

Sometimes Blanche could only wail: "It's hard to make you believe I'm right when you know I'm wrong!"

For years, Don Ameche set up jokes for the greatest comedians in radio: W. C. Fields, Spike Jones, Mae West and Edgar Bergen. Then he got a chance to create a unique comic character himself: the alternately snoring and snarling John Bickerson, hapless husband to Blanche in the long-running "Bickersons" sketches on radio and television.

Ameche grew up in Kenosha, Wisconsin, where his father ran a saloon. "It was brutal. It scared the hell out of me. I was so petrified all the while I was a child. . . . it was no fun living with someone who had a revolver in his trousers every day and a poison-tipped stiletto in the house. The lowest class people drank in his saloon." Once the saloon bar-

tender was arrested for shooting a man in the bar. Papa Amici knew what to do: He stabbed the bartender with a scissor, then went to court, pointed to the wound, claimed "self-defense" and got his man off.

While studying law at Georgetown University, Ameche began appearing in college plays. He co-starred with Texas Guinan in vaudeville and by 1929 was a full-time actor, eventually hosting "Grand Hotel" and "The First Nighter" on radio. It was while working on "The Chase and Sanborn Show" that he played straight for West, Fields, Bergen and many more. He had a chance to sing comic parodies and clown on "The Spike Jones Show," but was best loved as frustrated John Bickerson, hopelessly trying to deal with his wife Blanche:

"Blanche, what did you do with that $24?" "I spent it. I bought some perfume . . . it's called 'Perhaps.'" "'Perhaps'? For $24 they should give you 'Positively'! I can't understand why you throw my money away. . . ." "Before you married me you told me you were well off." "I was, but I didn't know it. Good night, Blanche."

One of John's trademarks was a ridiculously hilarious snore, which turned from low-pitched drones to high giggles, yelps and doglike howls.

Ameche and Langford appeared together on a 1951 television daytime talk/variety program but did not confine themselves to work as a comedy team. In films Ameche occasionally played in comedies, including the 1930s series of shorts *The Naggers* with Jack and Dorothy Norworth, but for years was best known as an affably handsome leading man, the star of two memorable film biographies (as Alexander Graham Bell and Stephen Foster). His favorite film was 1943's *Heaven Can Wait*, directed by Ernst Lubitsch. In the late 1950s Ameche conquered Broadway starring in the musical *Silk Stockings*. Nearly 30 years later he was bigger than ever, starring in 1983's *Trading Places*, and then *Cocoon*, as an old man rejuvenated by a "fountain of youth." An amusing highlight was Ameche topping the kids as an impeccable disco dancer. In recognition of his fine job and nearly 50 years of similar performances, the ever young and always gracious Ameche won an Academy Award.

One of his memorable recent roles was as the Italian immigrant in *Things Change*. A hard worker all his life, he considers having a fling in Vegas with a sudden windfall. "Is good to work, Jerry. But is also good to play. The ant and the grasshopper: once upon a time, there was an ant and a grasshopper. All summer long the ant work hard. The grasshopper, he play the violin. He dance. Winter come, the ant grew fat. The grasshopper he's cold. The grasshopper eat the ant."

Frances Langford was married to Jon Hall from 1938 to 1955. The couple divorced and she married Ralph Evinrude, president of the Evinrude motor company. She retired to enjoy travel and sports with her husband, but occasionally returned to television for a "Bickersons" sketch. In the late 1950s she and Ameche recorded a pair of albums. Her active lifestyle was temporarily curtailed due to open heart surgery in March 1978. In 1990 she was persuaded to reunite with Bob Hope for a television special honoring their early years entertaining the troops.

"The Bickersons" radio episodes, still fresh, funny and contemporary, were reissued several times. Of these enduring shows she recalled, "Our lines had to be delivered so fast we didn't have time to read idiot cards. We had to memorize and rehearse every line. The jokes were so fast there wasn't even room for laugh tracks, so we did without them. . . . It was the first of the 'at home' comedies—comedies about ordinary folks."

Few folks were quite so ordinary—but as universal—as The Bickersons.

AUDIO: *The Bickersons* (Columbia), *The Bickersons Fight Back* (Columbia), *Bickersons Re-Match* (a reissue of the first two albums, Columbia), *The Bickersons* (Radiola), *The Bickersons Three-Album Set* (Radiola)
TV: "The Don Ameche–Frances Langford Show" (1951)

## JOEY BISHOP

### (Joseph Gottlieb, February 3, 1918–   )

A glum stand-up comic with a number of sad-sack lines ("In kindergarten, I flunked sandpile"), Joey Bishop's hip twists on the down side of life made him a nightclub favorite through the 1950s and '60s. "We were very poor when I was a kid. I remember one winter, it snowed and I didn't have a sled. I used to go down hill on my cousin. And you know, she wasn't bad."

Born in the Bronx, Bishop's first break in show business was winning $3 in a 1936 amateur contest imitating radio comics Joe Penner and Jimmy Durante. He formed The Bishop Brothers comedy trio soon after, recalling "Bishop was the name of a guy we knew who owned a car." After World War II service he became a solo impressionist, doing James Cagney, Fred Allen, Al Jolson and others. He favored a low-key, subtle and often ironic approach. After doing the standard "hitching up the pants" pantomime for his Cagney impression, he said, "Five thousand a week and he can't afford a belt."

His career took off in Chicago in the late 1940s, working the Chez Paree with singer Tony Martin. Bishop cultivated his style of soft-spoken, nonthreatening humility. He claimed to be the first comedian to address the audience as "folks" in nightclubs, a ploy to create a friendly bond with the crowd. He began working club dates with Frank Sinatra and in the 1950s reached national audiences thanks to appearances on Jack Paar's television show. As Bob Newhart would later do even more successfully, Bishop parlayed his brand of put-upon moroseness from stand-up into a sitcom. Audiences were sympathetic to Bishop's wounded look and easygoing personality. His softly clipped delivery was easily identifiable, and would even be used for the character of the ant-chasing aardvark on a segment of the "Pink Panther" half-hour cartoon show.

As a member of Frank Sinatra's Rat Pack, Bishop turned up in a few films in the mid-1960s. After guest-hosting the "Tonight Show" 208 times, in 1967 he went up against Johnny Carson with a late-night talk show. Viewers found his mild, deadpan demeanor a bit soporific at that hour. Ironically, his announcer on the show—Regis Philbin—would become a master of the talk show format. Bishop returned to nightclubs with his familiar brand of conversational comedy. A typical opening line: "This is a nice family crowd—so many middle-aged men with their daughters!" Though Jackie Vernon would zero in on sad-sack comedy, and Jackie Mason added a spicier accent to the concept of soft-spoken irony, Biship's deadpan style is unique. The capable entertainer can still win over an audience when he chooses to perform.

FILMS incl.:*The Naked and the Dead* (1958), *Onionhead* (1958), *Ocean's 11* (1960), *Pepe* (1960), *Sergeants*

*Three* (1963), *Johnny Cool* (1963), *Texas Across the River* (1966), *A Guide for the Married Man* (1967), *Who's Minding the Mint?* (1967), *Betsy's Wedding* (1990)

TV: "Keep Talking" (1958–60), "The Joey Bishop Show" (1961–64), "The Joey Bishop Show" (1967–69), "Liar's Club" (1976–78)

## MEL BLANC

**(Melvin Jerome Blank, May 30, 1908–July 10, 1989)**

A master of comical voices, Mel Blanc got laughs imitating tough-talking rabbits, broken down cars and monosyllabic Mexicans. He was a key performer on "The Jack Benny Show" and was the voice of many of Warner Brothers' greatest cartoon characters. Yet for years few knew who he was. People drew a blank. Appreciation for him grew through the 1950s and '60s, and finally today the genius of Mel Blanc is being truly appreciated.

Short and balding, with prominent circles under his eyes, Blanc hardly resembled his zany creations. He flourished on radio doing everything from horses to the famous broken-down Maxwell car on "The Jack Benny Show." He could even get laughs out of straight lines. He was the railroad announcer whose running joke over the years was his stop-start pronunciation of "Cucamonga" in: "Train leaving on Track Five for Anaheim, Azusa and Cuc-amonga." He could get laughs merely uttering a syllable. As the Mexican, Cy, he told Benny precious little: "Your name is Cy?" "Sí." "You have a sister?" "Sue." "Sue?" "Sí." "What does she do?" "Sew." He used the Mexican character on many other shows. He was "Pedro" on a Judy Canova broadcast talking about his señorita: "I got her a flashy dress made out of ostrich feathers! It tickled her vanity!"

As hilariously memorable as these characters were, Mel's main contribution to comedy was in cartoons. He turned a number of radio stars into cartoon characters, doing a speeded-up Roscoe Ates (Porky Pig), a blustery Kenny Delmar (Foghorn Leghorn), a spluttering Joe Penner (Sylvester the Cat and Daffy Duck) and a ridiculously romantic Charles Boyer (Pepe Le Pew). His greatest voice was Bugs Bunny—patterned after a variety of Bronx-accented wise guys.

Each Warners character had a distinctive speech pattern and a catch phrase. Bugs Bunny's "What's up, Doc," for example, was invented by cartoon creator Tex Avery in 1940 based on a line he remembered being used at his North Dallas high school. Blanc used lisps (Sylvester with his "Thufferin' Thuccotash!" and Daffy Duck with his "You're dethpicable!"), reverse lisps (Tweety's "I tawt I taw a puddy tat") and stutters (Porky Pig with his "Th-th-that's all folks!"). His characters had a startling range from the gentle Tweety-Pie to the rip-roarin' Yosemite Sam. Outside the Warner lot (where he first turned up in the 1930s as a violinist in their music department), Blanc was also briefly the voice of Woody Woodpecker. In the 1960s he was Barney Rubble for television cartoon series "The Flintstones."

Though Blanc briefly had his own radio show in 1947 and made a few film appearances (most notably *Neptune's Daughter* in 1949), he became more recognizable to the public in the 1950s when he played Professor Le Blanc (the French violin teacher) and the stone-faced Cy on Jack Benny's television show. In the 1950s and '60s he recorded several novelty albums featuring eccentric singing, usually as his cartoon characters. His best was *Party Panic*, which offered "I'm Just Wild About Animal Crackers," "K-K-K-Katy" and "I Tawt I Taw a Putty Tat." In occasional talk show appearances he would imitate animals and some of the Warners cartoon characters he'd made famous. Blanc continued doing Warner cartoon voices for records, commercials and occasional shorts and contributed his all-star voices to the film *Who Framed Roger Rabbit?*

He lived to see the publication of his autobiography and the release of *A Tribute to Mel Blanc*, a collection of some classic Warners cartoons on videocassette. Above the dates and the notation "Man of 1000 Voices, Beloved Husband and Father," Mel Blanc's tombstone in Hollywood Memorial Park reads: "That's All Folks."

AUDIO: *Party Panic* (Capitol), *I Taut I Taw a Puddy Tat* (Capitol), *Bugs Bunny Songfest* (Golden), *Bugs Bunny and His Friends* (Capitol), *Bugs Bunny in Story Land* (Capitol), *Bugs Bunny and the Tortoise* (Capitol), *Woody Woodpecker's Family Album* (Decca)
AUTOBIOGRAPHY: *That's Not All Folks* (1988)

TV: "The Jack Benny Show" (1950–65), "Musical Chairs" (1955), "The Bugs Bunny Show" (1960–62), "The Flintstones" (1960–66)

## BOB and RAY

**Robert Elliot: March 26, 1923–**
**Raymond Goulding: March 20, 1922–March 24, 1990**

Some people laughed at everything Bob and Ray did. Others didn't get it at all. The duo's satire was on the very edge of subtlety, but since it's difficult for something subtle to have a discernible edge, it's no wonder the team had more of a cult following than great national fame.

Bob and Ray both worked at WHDH radio in Boston. In May 1946 they teamed for "Matinee with Bob and Ray." They enjoyed parody but had to be careful about being too bold or offensive. Consequently they often relied on nuance and tongue-in-cheek humor. In satirizing radio interviews, commercials and specific soap operas, often only fans tuned in directly to their wavelength got the jokes.

Their best routines mirrored the banality of the world around them. On radio the average listener wasn't always sure who was Bob and who was Ray because they were both adept at playing straight man or interview subject, and in their view, both interviewer and interviewee were equally inane. If reporter Wally Ballou was intensely stupid for doing a man-in-the-street interview with a cranberry grower—while police sirens wailed for nearby mayhem and a juicier story—so was the cranberry grower, who kept up the conversation and didn't even know his own subject. If the hapless "Komodo Dragon Expert" knew only four barely interesting facts about the subject, what of the obtuse interviewer who kept asking the same questions over and over?

In the best Bob and Ray routines, humdrum lives and homely moments of would-be glory were magnified: a man calling attention to himself for his ability to imitate vegetables; a commercial for "The House of Toast"; the dubious thrill of visiting a pair of "nonidentical Siamese twins," one parroting the other out of synch by one frustrating second. They captured the pathetic in everyday life, as in their portrayal of vegetable collector Parnell W. Garr: "I'm always reading in the paper about somebody who's grown a hubbard squash in the shape of an elephant—or something like that. So I usually hop the next plane to go dicker with the owner about buying it for my collection." It doesn't matter that his collection is almost completely rotten.

Bob and Ray were most popular on radio but branched out for recordings and funny commercials. They started their own ad agency in 1956 and had great success with a long-running series of cartoon television ads as "The Piel Brothers," selling the company's beer. They briefly had their own television show in the early 1950s, were on "The Today Show" in 1966 and 1967, and had a summer series called "Happy Days" in 1970. They turned up in the film *Cold Turkey*, taking several roles parodying newscasters and television personalities including Walter Cronkite (Walter Chronic) and Arthur Godfrey (Arthur Lordly).

Always on some New York radio station between national hookups, they went to Broadway in 1970 for an acclaimed two-man show of their best material.

While Bob and Ray didn't need to be seen to be appreciated, their looks enhanced the comedy. Columnist Gerald Nachman was impressed with "Ray's watery-eyed pink balloon head and Bob's gruff beetle-browed glower." Burly Ray made his characters seem even more obtuse, more like the ungainly mental lummoxes they were. His imposing size suggested the violence lurking under the surface of the failed ballplayers, crooked politicians and frustrated truffle hunters he played. Balding, feverish Bob was perfect for overly serious but inept reporters like Wally Ballou and Biff Burns, or such bland idiots as the winner of a "beautiful face" contest.

In the 1980s the team were broadcasting nationally for National Public Radio. The *Wall Street Journal* reported in June 1984, "For two guys who use no sex, no ethnics, no politics, no funny accents no funny clothes, no dirty words and no jokes about their wives, Bob and Ray are enjoying a remarkable renaissance." They celebrated their 40th anniversary in 1986 and released (on cassette only) *A Night of Two Stars*, which was nominated for a Grammy Award.

"We get rediscovered every generation," Bob noted mildly. He also admitted, "I don't know know why . . . we've always been strong on the East Coast and the West Coast and medium strong in between."

In 1990, after nearly two years of illness, Ray died of kidney failure at his Manhasset, Long Island home. Bob recalled at the time, "I think the main reason we worked well together was that we really appreciated each other, as opposed to some comedy teams. We had no rivalry, just great mutual respect. We always got along well." Bob went on to cameo roles in films (he was a bank guard in Bill Murray's *Quick Change*) and appeared on his son Chris' television series.

Bob and Ray left behind hundreds of homely heroes, including Mary Backstayge, Noble Wife; Doctor Merton Chesney; Mary McGoon; Augustus Winesap; Mr. Trace, Keener than Most Persons; child star Fat Baby Moxford; Mr. Science; Mug Mellish; Ramses Fletch; Illegal Left Turn Bronson; Word Carr; philosopher Wing Po; and the Slow Talkers of America.

They had a favorite way of ending their broadcasts:

"And now this is Ray Goulding, saying . . . write if you get work." "And Bob Elliott reminding you to hang by your thumbs. Good night, folks."

AUDIO: *Bob and Ray on a Platter* (RCA), *Bob and Ray Throw a Stereo Spectacular* (RCA), *Bob and Ray Present Wally Ballou* (Genesis), *Any Time You're Ready, C.B.* (B&R), *Mary Backstage, Noble Wife* (Radiola), *Paint the Town Spred* (Columbia/Glidden), *The Two and Only* (Columbia), *Vintage Bob*

Known primarily as radio performers, Bob and Ray pioneered subtle, satiric comedy based on the inanities of daily life. Photo by Darryl Pitt.

*and Ray* (Genesis), *Write If You Get Work* (Unicorn), *Bob and Ray, A Night of Two Stars* (Mind's Eye), *The Best of Bob and Ray* (Radioart)
BOOKS: *Write If You Get Work: The Best of Bob and Ray* (1975); *From Approximately Coast to Coast, It's the Bob and Ray Show* (1983); *The New! Improved! Bob & Ray Book* (1985)
BROADWAY: *The Two and Only* (1970)
FILMS: *Cold Turkey* (1971), *Author! Author!* (1982)
TV: "Bob and Ray" (1951–53), "Club Embassy" (1952), "The Name's the Same" (1955), "Happy Days" (1970)

# VICTOR BORGE

### (Borge Rosenbaum, January 3, 1909–   )

"Laughter is the shortest distance between two people," Victor Borge once said. His classic classical music comedy traveled all around the world and to hundreds of thousands of admirers.

At Carnegie Hall and similar venues, Borge had bright and sophisticated audiences roaring over his routines as a befuddled, genially absentminded concert pianist. He was perplexed over sheet music that sounded all wrong (he had placed it upside down on the stand), puzzled when his memory seemed to fail him and a classical piece segued into a silly pop standard, and peeved when the heavy lid of the keyboard suddenly slapped down. Borge offered a variety of audio, visual and audio-visual gags that would become standards. Though the premiere comedian of classical music, even nonclassical music fans could appreciate his satires on the solemnity of a classical recital.

In addition to the music, there was the words. Borge became equally well known for his wry and whimsical lectures on famous composers. They were all delivered with the eccentric stop-start delivery that was the natural result of having to learn English phonetically when he arrived in America in the 1940s. A few words on Bach: "Bach had approximately 20 to 30 children. I guess that goes for Mrs. Bach too. It takes time to raise about 25 to 30 kids. I know, I have two myself. Mine are twins, though. Both of them. Can't think of their names. They don't come when I call them anyway." Some of his

The grand comic pianist, Danish-born Victor Borge has made comedy a universal language around the world. Photo from the author's collection.

gags had nothing to do with music at all. He recalled a great man in his family: "My father invented the burglar alarm. Which unfortunately was stolen from him."

Borge was born in Copenhagen, Denmark. He studied to be a classical pianist and played with the Copenhagen Philharmonic in his teens, but the perfectionist demands of memorizing and playing concertos made him perpetually tense and nervous. He decided to play it for laughs—deliberately fumbling at the keyboard, then creating jokes to go with the musical humor. He became a top star in Denmark, even making films. It all changed during World War II when Borge had to flee the country, the target of S.S. men outraged at his anti-Hitler gags. Lines such as: "What's the difference between a Nazi and a dog? The Nazi usually lifts his arm. . . ."

In America, Borge learned English from the movies. He told jokes phonetically when he guested on radio, and rapidly moved on to films. In 1943's *Higher and Higher* with Frank Sinatra, he played a handsome but eccentric pianist with a mock-serious demeanor. "Lovely thing you're playing, Victor," says an admirer. "What is it?" Victor rises carefully from his seat and looks around. "The piano," he answers. "I often wondered what made an excellent musician like you take up the piano." "Well, you see, my teacher couldn't play any other instrument. That is why."

Borge's problems learning English led to a pair of routines that any nightclub comedian would have envied. In one clever bit he wondered what would happen if, by some kind of inflation, numerical words were raised by one number, so that "create would be cre-nine, and so fifth." Then he told a nonsensical story loaded with these new words, ending with a dramatic confrontation between Bob, Anna and the Latin lover "Don Two," (raised from Juan): "Bob grabbed from the table in front of him a piece of mari-nine-ted herring. But Anna warned, 'Don't throw it, remember you are an officer in the United States Air-fiveces.' 'Don Two,' he retorted. 'Are you two?' 'I am two, three.' Then he left and when he was one and halfway through the door, he turned. 'Anna,' he said as he wiped his fivehead, 'if I can't have you . . . I will remain double!' "

His other beloved routine was "phonetic punctuation." He reasoned that on the printed page, one could see the periods, commas and question marks. Why not in conversation? And so he told a story—with every bit of punctuation marked by outrageous sound effects.

Borge had his own television show in 1951 and a few years later made history, starring in 849 performances of *Comedy in Music*, his one-man show. It remains in the *Guinness Book of Records* as the longest run for a single performer on Broadway. For more than 30 years after, fans were still agreeing with *New York Times* critic Brooks Atkinson who had announced after the Broadway triumph that Borge was "the funniest entertainer in the world."

He continued to perform in his 80s, now taking some of the burden off himself by utilizing stooges— a man to play comically feuding piano duets with him and a soprano he could insult and make faces at while accompanying her operatic selections. He also enjoyed conducting "pops" concerts and, on occasion, performing classical music "straight" for all the fans who craved a complete prelude or etude. Even a 1988 heart operation couldn't slow down

Borge's busy schedule and love of performing. After the operation he remarked, "I'm really fine now. Except when I look in the mirror!"

Borge went on to release new audio and video versions of his concerts. While punsters always seemed dutybound to report this superstar a "Great Dane," he certainly was the pride of Denmark, knighted by his grateful homeland. Probably the only other person from Denmark general audiences are aware of is Hamlet, the melancholy Dane. Borge didn't mind being called "the unmelancholy Dane." As he said, "This gloomy Hamlet stuff is for the bards!"

AUDIO: *Caught in the Act* (Columbia), *Comedy in Music* (Columbia), *Borge's Back* (MGM, reissued as *Great Moments in Comedy*, Verve), *Brahms, Bizet and Borge* (Columbia), *A Victor Borge Program* (Columbia), *Piccolo, Saxie and Company* (Columbia), *Hans Christian Andersen* (Decca), *Victor Borge at His Best* (PRT), *My Favorite Intervals* (Pye), *To Denmark the Legend* (Private Pressing), *Victor Borge in Concert* (Gurtman & Murtha, cassette)

BOOKS incl.: *My Favorite Comedies in Music* (1981), *My Favorite Intermissions* (1991)

FILMS incl.: *Miss Muller's Jubilee* (1936), *Higher and Higher* (1943)

VIDEO: *Victor Borge on Stage with Audience Favorites*

## BOWERY BOYS (See THE EAST SIDE KIDS, LEO GORCEY and HUNTZ HALL.)

## EDDIE BRACKEN

### (February 7, 1920– )

Though a veteran actor with many credits, Eddie Bracken is best remembered for his two classic films with director Preston Sturges: *The Miracle of Morgan's Creek* and *Hail the Conquering Hero.*

After work as a child actor, including a few "Our Gang" comedies, Bracken moved on to vaudeville and finally Broadway for the 1936 play *So Proudly We Hail.* He made several film comedies, mostly playing bumbling and nervous rube types, before

Sturges cast him in *The Miracle of Morgan's Creek*, a double-edged classic of slapstick and satire.

He played the timid and stuttery Norval, a fellow who never had much luck with the opposite sex: "I knew a girl once who told me to jump in the lake and when I came back she was gone." He's so smitten with the local good-time girl, pregnant Trudy Kockenlocker (Betty Hutton), he's willing to marry her and protect her dubious honor even though he's not the father of her child. In handling the risqué comic situation, Bracken gave one of his most energetic performances, the nervous and timid hero trying to do almost anything, however dangerous or embarrassing, to win his girl.

*Hail the Conquering Hero* offered Bracken in a similar role, as Woodrow Lafayette Pershing Truesmith, dreaming of glory but rejected by his draft board. Once again the jittery, thin and unheroic-looking character must muster enough guts and anger to stand up for himself. Asked to pick his favorite films, Bracken always named *Hail the Conquering Hero* and *Miracle of Morgan's Creek*, saying "It's hard to separate the two."

Bracken's subsequent films suffered greatly in comparison to his work with Sturges and, as he aged, he had some problems finding a new identity beyond his particular brand of bumbling but pluckily all-American boy. He had better luck on Broadway some years later, taking over for Tom Ewell in both *The Seven Year Itch* and *The Tunnel of Love*. The stage would provide Bracken with steady work through the years.

He admitted that it was also easy for fans to confuse his work with that of similar performers. He recalled, "I went to see Donald O'Connor on stage and he introduced me to the audience. He said, 'I work eight hours dancing, now I'd like you to meet the man who gets the credit!'" In the 1970s he was seen around the country in productions of several comedies, including *The Odd Couple*. In 1989 he played "Captain Andy" in a PBS production of *Show Boat*.

AUDIO: *Archy and Mehitabel* (Columbia), *Peter and the Wolf* (Harmony)
BROADWAY: *So Proudly We Hail* (1936), *What a Life* (1938), *Too Many Girls* (1939), *Shinbone Alley* (1957), *Beg Borrow or Steal* (1960)
FILMS incl.: *Too Many Girls* (1940), *Life with Henry* (1941), *The Fleet's In* (1942), *Star Spangled Rhythm* (1942), *The Miracle of Morgan's Creek* (1944), *Hail the Conquering Hero* (1944), *Out of This World* (1945), *Bring on the Girls* (1945), *Duffy's Tavern* (1945), *Hold That Blonde* (1945), *Ladies' Man* (1947), *Fun on a Weekend* (1947), *The Girl from Jones Beach* (1949), *Summer Stock* (1950), *Two Tickets to Broadway* (1951), *We're Not Married* (1952), *About Face* (1952), *A Slight Case of Larceny* (1953).
TV: "I've Got a Secret" (1952), "Make the Connection" (1955), "Masquerade Party" (1957)


## DAVID BRENNER

### (February 4, 1945–   )

At the turn of the 1970s, "The Ed Sullivan Show" was a memory and the old-fashioned comedians he booked were dying out, along with their wife jokes. Most younger stand-ups, including George Carlin and Richard Pryor, were rebelling against the conventional styles.

Almost alone among the younger performers was David Brenner, strongly influenced by the Sullivan-styled comedians and waiting for his chance to perform standard family-oriented comedy like they did. As it turned out, there still was a big market for a young, clean performer. While most young stars couldn't appear on television with their dirty jokes and drug-tinged humor, there was David Brenner getting on "The Tonight Show" on January 8, 1971 after only a few years in stand-up. He would log an amazing 150 guest spots over the next 15 years and guest-host another 75 times.

Back then contemporaries considered Brenner a "sellout," but audiences appreciated this newcomer who told *real* jokes they could understand. Such as the one about his tough South Philadelphia neighborhood: "It was a tough neighborhood. The gang from Third Street would always fight the gang from Fifth Street. They'd throw things at them. And what they used to throw at them were the kids from Fourth Street."

After a career as a television producer following his years at Temple University, Brenner had given himself one year to make it in stand-up. Show business was in his blood thanks to his vaudevillian father. But, Brenner decided, if it didn't turn out to be "a way of reaching my financial goals," he'd try something else. As it turned out, there was a goldmine in Brenner's straight brand of comedy and his personality as a guy just like his audience: hard-headed, working class and down-to-earth. His most famous joke was about riding the subway to work: "I sat down on a newspaper on the subway, and a guy asked if I was reading it. I said yes, stood up, turned the page and sat down again."

In 1986 he hosted his own talk show, "Night Life." Brenner insisted he would succeed as a perfect contrast between the other rising talk show hosts of the day, Joan Rivers and David Letterman. He believed Rivers was too wild, "a bombastic woman who talks about putting a diaphragm on her head and going into the shower." Letterman was merely "an acerbic, put-down, pick-on-the-small guy" type who only appealed to "10% of America." As it turned out, Brenner was perceived as much blander than Rivers, a goofy nerd compared to a zealous yenta. And Yuppies preferred the coolness of Letterman to Brenner's blue-collar attitude. The show was canceled in June of 1987 and his standing was so badly damaged that Garry Shandling and Jay Leno eased past him as the most popular guest hosts for "The Tonight Show."

Brenner failed to bring his 1989 one-man show to Broadway after a two-week tryout but still retained his popularity as a casino and resort headliner. He wrote a few chatty, anecdotal books that his fans appreciated and even had his own "David Brenner Day" in Philadelphia. For some added diversion he opened the Amsterdam Billiard Club in New York City, complete with 30 pool tables. By the 1990s he was clearly no longer the bright young boy rushing to the head of the class, but he remains a professional and always dependable class act.

BOOKS: *Soft Pretzels with Mustard* (1983); *Revenge Is the Best Exercise* (1984); *Nobody Ever Sees You Eat Tunafish* (1987); *If God Wanted Us to Travel* (1990)
VIDEO: *I Hate to Work Out*

# FANNY BRICE

## (Fannie Borach, October 29, 1891–May 29, 1951)

Broadway's original "Funny Girl," Fanny Brice began her career at 14, singing at an amateur show at Keeney's Theater in Brooklyn. She won $10 for her rendition of "When You Know You're Not Forgotten by the Girl You Can't Forget." When she decided to go into show business full time she changed her name from Borach (rhyming with "more ache") to the more neutral Brice.

After Irving Berlin gave her the novelty tune "Sadie Salome," Brice concentrated on Jewish dialect comedy, achieving popularity in burlesque and vaudeville. Her other novelty hits included the saga of an adopted Jewish girl ("I'm an Indian!"), "Oh How I Hate that Fellow Nathan," "Goodbye Becky Cohen," "Mrs. Cohen at the Beach," "The Sheik of Avenue B" and the ironic "Second Hand Rose."

Only 18 when she began appearing in editions of *The Ziegfeld Follies,* Brice was still known for dialect and comic versions of vamps Theda Bara and Madame Pompadour. She burlesqued their sultry looks with funny faces and improbable dialogue: "I'm a bad voman, but I'm dehm good company!"

Brice combined physical comedy and dialect for "Becky Is Back in the Ballet" and had hits with routines that called for eccentric mime. Her "Dying Swan" routine was built around knock-kneed choreography and her insanely perky wide-mouthed grin. Fanny learned her dance skills from other chorus girls, paying them with sexy lingerie swiped from her mother's dresser drawer.

Fanny could play a variety of characters (including W. C. Fields' wife in a Ziegfeld sketch). Her first extended appearance similar to her famous Baby Snooks character was the little girl "Babykins" in a sketch in 1930's *Sweet and Low.* Some historians felt her characterization owed much to Rachel "Ray" Dooley who played baby roles in early Ziegfeld productions in the 1920s. (Supposedly the reason Brice accepted the part was that her dentures were bothering her and she had developed a lisp!) In 1934 she became "Baby Snooks," the most devilishly comic brat Broadway had ever seen. Some of her gags were pure vaudeville:

BABY SNOOKS: Remember I asked you, "What's the shape of the world?"

DADDY: Yes?

BABY SNOOKS: Well, teacher said "stinko" ain't the right answer!

Audiences were always warmly receptive to Fanny, which was part of her stage philosophy: "Make them comfortable. Because if they wanted to be nervous they could have stayed home and added up the bills." They also knew enough about her private life to feel sympathy for her. Fanny was married and divorced three times. The first, to a barber named Frank White, was a brief mistake she made at 18. Her second husband was con man Nicky Arnstein, who bilked $5 million from Wall Street in a scandal that sent him to jail. Her torch ballad, "My Man," underlined her hopeless devotion to him. They were divorced in 1927. She married Billy Rose the following year, but the marriage ended in 1938 after he had been unfaithful. On stage the sad ballads continued: "I've been singing about this bum for 15 years under different [song] titles. He's always the same lowlife, always doing me dirt but I keep loving him just the same. Can you imagine if I really ever met a guy like that? Why I'd—it's no use talking. That's my type."

Three films would tell Fanny Brice's story: *The Rose of Washington Square*, *Funny Girl* and *Funny Lady*. They all concentrated on the drama and not the comedy.

In 1937 she began appearing regularly on radio, starring in "Good News of 1938" and then "Maxwell House Coffee Time." She got her own "Baby Snooks Show" in 1944. Unlike Red Skelton, whose "Mean Widdle Kid" was just one of many characters, Fanny was only "Baby Snooks." Nearing 60, and having played little else but Snooks since 1937, Fanny was worried. Most radio shows were being adapted to television. Could she make the transition?

The answer never came. In 1951, at the dawn of the television era, Fanny suffered a stroke. After several days in a coma, she died. The greats of show business mourned her passing. Eddie Cantor recalled her as both tender and tough: ". . . nothing ever bothered her. She had no worries and no nerves. . . . She was always the most truthful, candid person, and she could wither you with one line. Once she told off a certain producer who had a habit of saying 'You can have my right arm.' 'Look, kid,' Fanny told him, 'I happen to know that in your desk you have a whole drawer full of right arms.' "

Fanny Brice once summed up her own private life in one epigram: "I never loved a man I liked and never liked a man I loved."

AUDIO: *Baby Snooks* (Radiola), *The Return of Baby Snooks* (Radiola), *Baby Snooks* (Mar-Bren), *Baby Snooks* (Memorabilia), *The Baby Snooks Show* (Yorkshire), *Makin' Whoopee* (Pro-Arte), *Fanny Brice and Helen Morgan* (RCA), *Original Funny Girl* (Audio Rarities)

BIOGRAPHY: *The Fabulous Fanny* (Kratkov, 1953)

BROADWAY: *Ziegfeld Follies* (1910, 1911), *The Honeymoon Express* (1913), *Nobody Home* (1915), *Ziegfeld Follies* (1916, 1917, 1920, 1921, 1923), *Why Worry* (1918), *The Music Box Revue* (1924, 1925), *Fanny* (1926), *Fioretta* (1929), *Sweet and Low* (1930), *Billy Rose's Crazy Quilt* (1931), *The Ziegfeld Follies* (1934, 1936)

FILMS: *My Man* (1928), *Night Club* (1929), *Be Yourself* (1930), *The Great Ziegfeld* (1936), *Everybody Sing* (1938), *The Ziegfeld Follies* (1945)

## ALBERT BROOKS

### (Albert Lawrence Einstein, July 22, 1947–   )

While he mystified some "Tonight Show" viewers and movie audiences, Albert Brooks became a cult favorite for his stand-up comedy in the 1970s and his films in the 1980s and '90s.

Brooks was born in Los Angeles and attended Beverly Hills High School. He later studied drama at Carnegie Tech. The son of Harry Einstein, a comedian who performed Greek dialect routines as Parkyakarkus, Brooks knew comedy well enough to satirize it. He turned up on the summer television show "Dean Martin Presents the Golddiggers" in 1969 doing a fake ventriloquist act and by 1972 was a frequent guest on "The Tonight Show." The early 1970s was a tough time for a young monologist. With few comedy clubs around, the options were to either play the casinos and follow the old-fashioned style of a Jack Carter (young David Brenner chose this path) or open for rock acts and try for the hip stance of a George Carlin.

Brooks wasn't comfortable with either option. Instead, he chose to satirize the artificiality of traditional stand-up and find ways for he and the audience to subtly think their way through the routines. On "The Tonight Show" he once came out and began to read from the phone book (his tongue-in-cheek take on the cliché of a great comedian being able to get laughs from just a list of names). Another time he performed mime (while telling the audience every move he was making). Another routine was little besides Albert fretting over "running out of material." While the audience squirmed with silent embarrassment, Brooks dropped his pants, pelted himself with a pie and broke eggs over his head. Gradually they began to laugh at his comic desperation.

Brooks performed the kind of smiling, deliberately artificial "noncomedy" that, in a more high-powered vaudeville mode, would win fame for "wild and crazy" Steve Martin.

For mild and Yuppie Albert Brooks, these experiments gained him the reputation as a clever "comedian's comedian" and little beyond a cult following. Many audience members simply didn't warm up to his parody of smugness and self-importance, figuring the joke was really on them. Probably Brooks' most accessible routine was a musical parody in which (impersonating various idiots at an audition) he attempted to find an alternative to the dull and unsingable "Star Spangled Banner." One of the entries was a cheesy cabaret singer offering a cheery "Hey! World! Look at Us!" A favorite was the blue-collar hopeful who began his anthem, "While we stand here waiting for the ball game to start. . . ."

Brooks made some short films for television's "Saturday Night Live," many involving his put-on character of an annoying egocentric, but his brand of West Coast subtlety clashed with the live and acerbic action on the rest of the show. He went on to write and direct several films that tended to divide critics and audiences. Many didn't care for Brooks' style, which was to play annoying and obtuse types, from the ridiculous director of documentaries who aggravates the family he tries to film in *Real Life* to the overbearingly obsessive man who tries to win his girl back, nearly causes her to lose her mind instead and makes a shambles of *Modern Romance*.

*Crow* magazine probably summed up *Lost in America* best: "The nastiest indictment of the Yuppie mentality so far. Albert Brooks' unpleasant and depressing story of a man and his wife dropping out of the rat race and hitting the road with a $200,000 'nest egg' and a Winnebago is a one-sour joke comedy, but so claustrophobic and unrelenting it is probably the best of that genre. Weeks later, you will find yourself laughing at lines you barely noticed the first time."

Brooks received an Academy Award nomination for his role in *Broadcast News*, a part in which some audience members were not sure if he was kidding (or satirizing) or not. A very typical line: "Wouldn't it be great if neediness and desperation were a turn-on?"

Having dealt extensively with the plight of the upper middle class and the insincere on earth, Brooks began the 1990s wondering if there was any cosmic relief in heaven. He wrote, directed and starred in *Defending Your Life*, playing yet another self-absorbed self-conscious, selfish type. Having some troubles in the afterlife of "Judgment City," he had to wonder if he was "the dunce of the universe" for the way he handled things back on earth.

Brooks received the same mixed criticism from those who were on his wavelength and those who were unamused. The only criticism that bothered him was when he was accused of whining.

"Please don't say whine," he told an interviewer. "Nobody could associate 'whine' with anything but a kid you want to throw out of the car. Whining is complaining with no redeeming features. Let's use another word. Let's use 'plead.' I plead: 'Let's change things, things are horrible here, help!' Did anyone accuse The Elephant Man of whining? He just said 'Help me!'"

AUDIO: *Comedy Minus One* (ABC), *A Star Is Bought* (Asylum)

FILMS incl.: *Taxi Driver* (1976), *Real Life (1979)*, *Private Benjamin* (1980), *Modern Romance* (1981), *Unfaithfully Yours* (1984), *Lost in America* (1985), *Broadcast News* (1987), *Defending Your Life* (1991)

TV: "Dean Martin Presents the Golddiggers" (1969), "Saturday Night Live" (1975–76)

## FOSTER BROOKS

### (May 11, 1912–   )

Billed as "The Lovable Lush," Foster Brooks offered a new variation on drunkard comedy. Unlike the staggering, rubber-legged Leon Errol or the deceptively stewed W. C. Fields, Brooks portrayed a repulsively realistic alcoholic, slurring his words, pretending to be sober and then clearing the room with a series of gaseous burps. Well dressed, with wavy white hair and a trimmed beard parted in the middle, the contrast between his dignified appearance and his delirious behavior added to the laughs.

Born in Louisville, Kentucky, a disc jockey most of his life, Brooks' comedy career began after he was a hit telling jokes and acting as master of ceremonies at a golf tournament that Perry Como attended. Como helped him along, as did Dean Martin, who booked him often on his late 1960s variety series. Brooks was perhaps the only comic around who could make the twinkly-eyed, tippling Martin seem sober by comparison. For his variety show guest spots Brooks usually appeared as a monologist, but sometimes went on as a bombed television executive or tipsy husband in sketches. Questioned about being drunk, he might cock a bleary eye at his antagonist and announce, "I must say that I have a very good reason for bein' loaded." Then after an unsteady pause: "I been drinkin' all day!"

Occasionally Brooks was able to play a literal "straight" role, usually on a drama series (notably "Murder She Wrote"), but primarily he was a nightclub and casino stand-up star. While some were offended by yet another comedian seeming to glorify alcohol abuse, Brooks' portrayal had some supporters. Bill Cosby insisted there wasn't anything glamorous about "the lovable lush." He wrote some liner notes for a Brooks album, stating: "Foster Brooks will make you see your uncle, your father, a close friend of yours, or your boss. Buy this record and play it for a drunken friend of yours and say to them 'here you are.'"

AUDIO: *The Lovable Lush* (Decca), *Foster Brooks Roasts* (Roast Records)
FILMS incl.: *Super Seal* (1977), *Cracking Up* (1983), *Odd Balls* (1984)

## MEL BROOKS

### (Melvin Kaminsky, June 28, 1926–   )

Aggressive, bombastic and outrageous: Critics used these adjectives over and over to describe Mel Brooks and his work. Each phase of his career was marked by wildman antics. Brooks himself recalled that when he was writing for television's "Your Show of Shows," he was "aggressive . . . a pit bull terrier. I was unstoppable. I would keep going until my sketch was in the show."

When he broke into the performing side of show business, it was as "The 2000 Year Old Man." Once again Mel seemed to not only go for belly laughs but for the throat. Of his first album of comic outrages he declared, "People used to listen to that record and laugh their guts out. They used to get lockjaw from laughing so much . . . hernias . . . appendicitis . . . cardiac arrest . . . killed a whole family in Iowa, nine people actually died from laughing so much."

And finally, as the writer, director and star of his own films, Brooks was known primarily for his bold brand of gag writing. The highlight of *Blazing Saddles* was flatulent cowboys producing a cacophony of wind. *The Producers* was cheered for the horrifyingly tasteless production number "Springtime for Hitler."

Critics paid less attention to the other side of Brooks. "The 2000 Year-Old Man" character was warm, lovable and at times almost eloquent. *Blazing Saddles* contained strong satire on race relations. *The Producers* tackled greed, anti-Semitism and Broadway standards of taste. *High Anxiety,* considered merely "a parody," was extraordinarily witty in laughing with Hitchcock and not at him. Though Brooks has rarely been acknowledged for his keen satiric eye, many scenes in the film marked a comic genius at work (such as the way Brooks duplicated the shower scene in *Psycho* via an effeminate man who "stabbed" at Brooks with a newspaper in the shower, and the ink running down the drain, all painstakingly shot in the Hitchcock style).

The dual side of Brooks' nature was expressed in a remark he made about "The 2000 Year Old Man." It began seriously and ended with a typical no-nonsense gag: "When I became [the old man], I

Mel Brooks, perhaps comedy's biggest extrovert. His comic talents were behind the classic album *The 2000 Year Old Man*, the hit show "Get Smart" and hilarious films such as *The Producers, Blazing Saddles* and *Young Frankenstein*. Photo from the author's collection.

could hear 5000 years of Jews pouring through me. Look at Jewish history. Unrelieved lamenting would be intolerable . . . so, for every ten Jews beating their breasts, God designated one to be crazy and amuse the breast beaters! By the time I was five I knew I was that one."

"That one" was born in Brooklyn. His father died when he was two, leaving his mother to support him and three older brothers by working in the garment district. The youngest and smallest of the family, Mel learned to joke to gain acceptance, and after World War II went to the Catskill resorts as a drummer. He became a "social director" at Grossingers, entertaining guests with everything from jokes to periodic falls into the swimming pool.

It was not as a performer but as a writer that Brooks began earning big money. He wrote for Sid Caesar's "Your Show of Shows." Brooks was so serious about his comedy that he once tried to throw a punch at the tall, powerful star. Caesar sternly announced, "This time, I will let you live. But if you feel that strongly about the joke, I'll put it in the script." Once the high-strung Caesar dangled Brooks out a Chicago hotel window. (Years later Brooks' film company produced *My Favorite Year,* which was a fictionalized rendering of those hectic times). Brooks was sometimes as manic. He literally mugged another star on the show, Howard Morris, taking his wallet for a laugh. At an Emmy awards ceremony, when a writing award went to the staff of "The Phil Silvers Show," he jumped on top of a table and began shouting "There is no God!"

Brooks was making $2,500 a week but the pace was killing him. He suffered panic attacks, insomnia and vomiting. He sought psychiatric help, but as the 1950s ended, so did his marriage to dancer Florence Baum. The couple had three children. (Brooks later married actress Anne Bancroft.)

With Carl Reiner, who co-starred in "Your Show of Shows," Brooks sometimes entertained at parties. His bits as "The 2000 Year Old Man" were so hilarious many suggested the duo hit the club circuit with them. Steve Allen helped them book time in a small studio, and after inviting a small audience of friends to make it seem more like a "party" setting, an album was recorded in two hours. It became a sensation in 1960 and remains one of the best comedy albums ever released. It was loaded with Brooks' painfully funny truths: "I have over forty-two thousand children—and not *one* comes to visit me." "Tragedy is if I cut my finger. Comedy is if you walk into an open sewer and die."

Reiner and Brooks made two more albums in the next two years. Then in 1963 Brooks made his Academy Award-winning short, *The Critic.* It was a deceptively simple piece—just a crotchety guy complaining about modern art. Yet the laughs came from two directions—from Brooks poking fun at the boorishness of the critic's loud commentary and from the potent satire of the flaws in modern art appreciation (since the critic's remarks were often justified).

The novel Brooks had been working on finally became a film, *The Producers,* which won an Academy Award for Best Original Screenplay. Many were appalled by it at the time, but it has since become recognized as one of the best comedies of the 1960s.

In 1970 he wrote and directed *The Twelve Chairs,* a film rich in warmth, gentle satire and philosophical truths as it was in visual comedy and zany gags.

Through the 1970s, the two champions of film comedy were Brooks and Woody Allen. Inevitably, the two were placed in competition. Brooks had the biggest hit, the box office smash *Blazing Saddles.* The satire of a town's stupidity and prejudice was lost amid the huge belly laughs of sight gags, blunt cursing (then still a shock novelty in comedy) and the antics of Brooks himself in his first major starring role as Governor Lepetomaine (the name of a French legend known for his flatulent stage act).

The success of the film as a Western parody led Brooks to follow up with a horror film parody, *Young Frankenstein.* Once again the response was very positive, and Brooks had another big hit with a variety of gags, puns and moments of his trademark "bad taste" (the Frankenstein monster stumbling around singing the Fred Astaire tune "Putting on the Ritz").

Brooks' next attempt at artistic cinema, perhaps in response to Woody Allen's newest efforts, was *Silent Movie,* a daring exercise that tried to do something Chaplin had abandoned after *Modern Times.* A modern silent film was a daring experiment and it often succeeded, but critical response was mixed and audiences seemed to have trouble adjusting to the idea.

Brooks' reputation as a broad parodist continued. *History of the World Part I* had plenty of zany gags (at the Last Supper, Brooks the waiter asks, "Separate checks?"). It also had satiric twists, especially in the vignette with Brooks as a greedy, powerful monarch shouting his wildly enthusiastic catch phrase "It's *good* to be the king!" *Variety*'s review was typical, complaining Brooks "hasn't strayed far beyond his three favorite butts for humor: sex, excrement and Jews."

The two sides of Mel Brooks seemed to jar against each other in the flawed *To Be or Not to Be,* another conscious attempt at work pathos and drama into his comedy. His subsequent *Spaceballs* was much more escapist and silly. It seemed that Brooks had simply decided that he should separate the comic and the serious. Under his own name, he could market crazy comedy. With his company Brooks-films he could produce more artistic work. Brooksfilms released two of the most poignant, serious and disturbing films ever made: *The Elephant Man* and *Frances.*

In 1991 Brooks was back after a long absence. He wrote, directed and starred in *Life Stinks,* a story that tried to find humor in homelessness. He insisted, "As long as you make something really genuinely gut-wrenching gut busting spitting out funny, it's gonna work. I don't care what it's about." It had a longer life in video rental than at the box office, where it joined the perennial classics in the Brooks catalog.

The best of Mel Brooks continues to earn laughs all over the world. Brooks knows the answer for that: "The biggest laughs I get are physical comedy, and it travels all around the world." He also admits that there are some who will never appreciate visual comedy or his particular brand of blunt humor. His mother was one such person. She was proud to tell her friends that her son was a star, but that was about it: "One of the heartaches of my life was that my mother was never really aware of the bizarre nature of my comedy. She thought maybe I shouldn't say such bad things or do such bad things; that maybe I was in bad taste. She never really *got* my comedy, but she got my fame."

AUDIO: *The 2000 Year Old Man* (Capitol), *2001 Year Old Man* (Capitol), *At the Cannes Film Festival* (Capitol), *2013 Year Old Man* (Warner Bros.), *The Incomplete Works of Reiner and Brooks* (Warner Bros.), *The Producers Soundtrack* (RCA), *Mel Brooks' Greatest Hits* (Asylum)

BIOGRAPHIES: *L'ultima follia di Hollywood* (Bendazzi, 1977), *Mel Brooks* (Giusti, 1980), *Mel Brooks* (Adler and Feinman, 1976), *Seesaw, A Dual Biography of Anne Bancroft and Mel Brooks* (Holtzman, 1979), *Mel Brooks and the Spoof Movie* (Smurthwaite), *Method in Madness* (Yacowar, 1981)

FILMS incl.: *Putney Swope* (1969), *The Producers* (1968), *The Twelve Chairs* (1970), *Blazing Saddles* (1974), *Young Frankenstein* (1975), *Silent Movie* (1976), *High Anxiety* (1977), *History of the World Part 1* (1981), *To Be or Not to Be* (1984), *Spaceballs* (1987), *Look Who's Talking Too* (voice only, 1990), *Life Stinks* (1991)

VIDEOS: *An Audience with Mel Brooks, Comedy Music Videos* (compilation), *The 2000 Year Old Man* (Animated Cartoon)

## BROTHER THEODORE

### (Theodore Gottlieb, November 11, 1906–    )

On a black stage illuminated by one spotlight, the foreboding Brother Theodore grimaces and says, "In this best of all possible worlds—everything is in a hell of a mess." With the audience laughing uneasily, weird shadows distorting his features, he continues, describing "the degrading aftereffects of living," his alternately glum and raging expressions horrifyingly funny. Even in his 80s, the small but muscularly stocky man commands the stage with powerful vitality. His craggy features blaze with intensity, his eyes pop from their sockets and he speaks "with a tongue of madness" in a darkly brooding German accent.

For over 30 years he's lectured on life and death, all punctuated with twists of absurdist humor and deranged philosophy. "The best thing," he insists, "is not to be born. But who is as lucky as that? To whom does it happen? Not to one among millions and millions of people."

It seemed that Theodore was born lucky. His German family was extraordinarily wealthy, and he had the best of everything, though his autocratic and disciplinarian father sometimes made life difficult for the young man who preferred to study "useless" things, such as art and philosophy, in college. Then, during the 1930s, the philosophy in Germany changed: "Suddenly . . . we were Jewish pestiferous rats that had to be exterminated." The Nazis took the family's money, mansion and finally their lives. Theodore was the only family member to survive Dachau, where he saw the tortures firsthand and Nazi guards "roaring with laughter" watching men eaten alive by vicious dogs.

Escaping to America, Theodore worked as a janitor at Stanford University and toiled for three years in a shipyard in San Francisco. He put his savings into a serious one-man concert that flopped miserably. No one came to hear his soliloquies or his

A haunting philosophical performer, Brother Theodore was the only member of his family to survive the Dachau concentration camp. Photo by the author.

version of "The Tell-Tale Heart." After seven years of struggling in poverty, his wife left him for his best friend. Theodore's only son went with her.

In the 1950s Theodore finally found his element, working small and bohemian theaters in New York. His serious Grand Guignol monologues of tortured souls and horror had become exaggerated for comic effect. His midnight shows had a strong following and the cult gradually extended to the mainstream. He made 36 appearances on "The Merv Griffin Show," and it was Griffin who dubbed the dour performance artist/comedian "Brother" Theodore, based on the priestlike black turtleneck he wore.

Over the next 30 years, while Lenny Bruce and Lord Buckley died and theater-based purveyors of dark comedy such as Nichols and May and Shelley Berman went into semiretirement, Theodore retained a cult following, performing his monologues of guilt, frustration and existentialist fear mostly in one small Greenwich Village theater. National interest in him was revived in the 1980s by his two dozen appearances on "Late Night with David Letterman." The elusive and eccentric performer retained his self-described "defeatest attitude" and routinely turned down nightclub offers around the country. He had to be persuaded by friends and admirers to accept a few of the film offers that came his way, including the brief but high-paying role in the Tom Hanks movie *The Burbs*.

In real life—very much the brilliant but gloomy personality he seems to be on stage and in talk shows—he set up a meeting with the author with this sepulchrally entoned warning: "Please call the day before to confirm this. Anything might happen to you or to me." Before undergoing a nasal operation in 1990 to correct the breathing problems he suffered ever since he had his nose broken by the Nazis at Dachau, he was characteristically gloomy. He remarked, "If I die, best wishes for the rest of your life. If I don't—I'll phone you."

Like many humorists, Theodore is often surprised when the reaction to his honest commentary is laughter. But it was Theodore's art that enabled humor to rise out of frustration, out of rage, inner chaos and hopeless tragedy. As he always says, without really trying to be funny, "Madness is a very healthy sickness. If it were not for my madness, I would have gone insane long ago."

AUDIO: *Entertainment of Sinister and Disconcerting Humor* (Proscenium), *Coral Records Presents Theodore* (Coral)

FILMS incl.: *The Invisible Kid* (1988), *The Burbs* (1989)

VIDEO: *Billy Crystal: Don't Get Me Started*

## BROWN and CARNEY

**Wally Brown: 1898–November 13, 1961**
**Alan Carney: December 22, 1911–May 2, 1973**

Abbott and Costello had several imitators; the most successful were Brown and Carney. Brown, the thin, curly-haired straight man, had been in vaudeville for years. The chubby Carney had shown some promise in films, notably *Mr. Lucky* with Cary Grant in 1943. In 1944 the duo starred in *Adventures of a Rookie,* their version of Bud and Lou's *Buck Privates*.

Within five minutes they were trying a wordplay routine, a hypothetical question about "A & B driving to Chicago." Carney is immediately befuddled: "Where'd they get the gas to drive to Chicago?" "Look, they had gas. A had a B book, B had an A book, they both had an uncle who died and left them a C book. Believe me, they had gas. . . . Now look, A & B are driving to Chicago. A leaves an hour ahead of B. . . ." "Why did A leave an hour ahead of B . . . why didn't they drive together? Say, look at all the tires they would've saved." "Look, they couldn't ride together, they didn't know one another. They'd never met. And I'm beginning to be sorry I ever met you. . . . Let's assume you are A. You leave an hour ahead of B." "I'm a what?" "What?" "I'm a what?" "You're just A." "How can I just be A, I've got to be something." "You are A *nothing!*"

The film was unimpressive and the duo showed little promise. Carney was fat and dumb but not cute about it as Costello was. Brown lacked Abbott's ferocity. They persisted for a few more films, including *Zombies on Broadway* co-starring Bela Lugosi. Since Carney wasn't much at slapstick, the visual gags mainly consisted of Carney somnolently wandering around as a bulge-eyed zombie (thanks to Lugosi's secret formula). The duo occasionally took a stab at more Abbott and Costello wordplay: "I'll have a rum punch." "I think I'll have something tripical." "You mean tropical." "No, I mean tripical. I'll have a tripical rum punch. I'm thirsty!"

After the duo split up, Wally Brown appeared as a character actor in films including 1948's *Family Honeymoon* and 1954's *The High and the Mighty* and did some sitcom work. Carney tried to start over again in vaudeville with a new partner, Little Jack Little. Then he went on to television (including the 1953 series "Take It From Me"), Broadway (*Fanny* starring Walter Slezak) and films (notably 1959's *Lil Abner*, 1963's *It's a Mad Mad Mad Mad World*, and his last, *The Love Bug Rides Again* in 1973). He was at the Hollywood Park racetrack in Van Nuys when he won the daily double—and then had a heart attack.

FILMS incl.: *Adventures of a Rookie* (1944), *Rookies in Burma* (1944), *Step Lively* (1944), *Zombies on Broadway* (1945), *Genius at Work* (1945)

## JOE E. BROWN

### (July 28, 1892–July 6, 1973)

Though Joe E. Brown is known primarily for having a large, wide mouth (his catch phrase was "You said a mouthful!") audiences weren't aware of it during the first decade of his career. He was an acrobat, and all people saw was a body bouncing around the stage and flying through the air.

Brown ran away from home at nine to join a circus. He became one of The Five Marvelous Ashtons. When they broke up in 1906 he played semi-pro baseball, nearly earning a place with the Pittsburgh Pirates. He then joined the Bell-Prevost Trio, taking the show-biz expression "break a leg" literally. After that experience he tried acting. He appeared on Broadway in 1918's *Listen Lester* and developed his comedy reputation through the 1920s. His first hit was the film *Hold Everything,* originally a Broadway show with Bert Lahr. Lahr placed an ad in *Variety* claiming Brown had stolen his mannerisms. Two decades later, Brown explained in his autobiography that he hadn't tried to steal from Lahr and that, in fact, Lahr's own mannerisms were borrowed from another comedian.

Brown was a big star during the depression, making films that emphasized the Ohio-born comic's midwestern roots and spunk. Like Harold Lloyd, he played a bumbler who had enough ego and talent to straighten out and be a hero, usually in some athletic way (winning a swimming meet or a baseball game, etc.). Now Brown's brand of All-American hero seems dated, his pluck irritating, his comic bumbling tedious, his use of rube terms such as "golly" and "gosh" too hokey to ring true. While Lloyd used sight gags and thrill visuals to offset his bland personality, Brown relied on his trademark yelps (gradually widening his mouth to yowl "Hhhhhhelllp!" or "Aaaaaaaaay!" in moments of panic). At the time audiences couldn't get enough of it, (he did four yells in a row in one scene in *The Circus Clown*), but today more than once in a film is too much.

A top-10 moneymaking star in 1932, 1935 and 1936 (his more enduring efforts were *Elmer the Great* and *Midsummer Night's Dream* as Flute), Brown wore himself down doing bond rallies during World War II. In two months in Detroit, touring in *The Show Off,* Brown made over 100 appearances. The tireless comic liked to take over the box office and sell tickets to his own show, to the surprise and delight of his fans. On October 8, 1936 in Detroit, Brown was at the box office joking with some reporters when the phone rang. He was told that his oldest son, Captain Don E. Brown, had been killed in a plane crash. A moment earlier he had been talking proudly about his sons. Now he could only rest his head on the ticket counter and cry. There was no show that night.

Brown entertained the troops overseas and wrote a book: *Your Kid and Mine.* In 1946 he recorded a baseball sketch on two 78's and subsequently toured in *Harvey* (replacing Frank Fay) and as Captain Andy in *Show Boat.* During the Korean War, Brown once again used his celebrity status to raise money. A clip of Brown making a pitch in a Fox Movietone newsreel turns up in an episode of television's "M*A*S*H." The comedian urges viewers, "Have a heart—give some blood."

Brown wrote his autobiography in 1956, but his most famous screen role was yet to come. In *Some Like it Hot* he plays the wealthy and unperturbable Mr. Farnsworth, ready to marry Jack Lemmon in drag. Lemmon tries to tell him the truth: "For three years I've lived with a saxophone player." "I forgive you." "We can never have children!" "We can adopt some." "You don't understand. I'm a man!" "Well, nobody's perfect."

Brown's health began to fail in the 1960s; his last roles were mostly cameos. In *Comedy of Terrors* he played a gravedigger who gets frightened and . . . opens his mouth for one long loud cry. He gave his wide-mouthed yelp in *It's a Mad Mad Mad Mad World,* as well. The bits brought joy to his old fans, who remembered him as a nice guy and a wholesome comedian. His success in the 1930s earned him a place in comedy history; his comic face and catch phrases are still immortal. And for his work during the country's war efforts, Brown must be ranked as one of the film industry's great patriots.

AUTOBIOGRAPHY: *Laughter Is a Wonderful Thing* (1956)
BROADWAY: *Listen Lester* (1918), *Jim Jam Jems* (1920), *Greenwich Village Follies* (1921), *Betty Lee* (1924), *Captain Jinks* (1925), *Twinkle Twinkle* (1926), *Courtin' Time* (1951), *Show Boat* (1961)

FILMS incl.: *On with the Show* (1929), *Painted Faces* (1930), *Song of the West* (1930), *Hold Everything* (1930), *Top Speed* (1930), *Going Wild* (1931), *Sit Tight* (1931), *Broad Minded* (1931), *Local Boy Makes Good* (1931), *Fireman Save My Child* (1932), *The Tenderfoot* (1932), *You Said a Mouthful* (1932), *Elmer the Great* (1932), *Son of a Sailor* (1933), *A Very Honorable Guy* (1934), *Circus Clown* (1934), *Six Day Bike Rider* (1934), *Alibi Ike* (1935), *Midsummer Night's Dream* (1935), *Sons o' Guns* (1936), *Earthworm Tractors* (1936), *Polo Joe* (1936), *Riding on Air* (1937), *Fit for a King* (1937), *Wide Open Faces* (1938), *The Gladiator* (1938), *Beware Spooks* (1939), *So You Won't Talk* (1940), *Shut My Big Mouth* (1942), *Joan of the Ozarks* (1942), *Casanova in Burlesque* (1944), *Show Boat* (1951), *Around the World in 80 Days* (1956), *Some Like it Hot* (1959), *Comedy of Terrors* (1963), *It's a Mad Mad Mad Mad World* (1963)

## LENNY BRUCE

### (Leonard Alfred Schneider, October 13, 1925– August 3, 1966)

In 1960, as Lenny Bruce's controversial stand-up career was on the upswing, Walter Winchell called him "America's #1 Vomic."

In 1966, as Lenny Bruce's controversial stand-up career was sputtering downward, Dick Gregory declared, "Lenny Bruce, 2000 years from now will be one of the names that will still be remembered. He's to show business what Einstein was to science."

Twenty years later Dick Cavett said, "He was a dazzling performer at his best, and I don't know why that isn't enough for people."

Even after so many decades, after 800 pages of biography by Albert Goldman, a film bio and play, and after dozens of posthumous audio and video releases, Lenny Bruce remains the most controversial figure in the history of comedy. Not only do some have moral quarrels with his lifestyle (as earlier generations did with Chaplin's and Arbuckle's), and not only is there mystery surrounding his death (as there is with comedienne Thelma Todd), there is still debate over the simplest premise for any stand-up performer: whether he was funny or not.

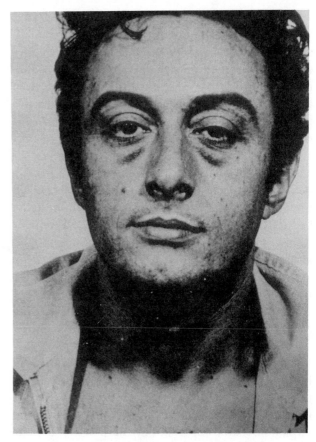

Police photo of Lenny Bruce, stand-up comedy's most controversial and influential figure. Bob Dylan sang of him: "He fought a war on a battlefield where every victory hurt." Photo from the author's collection.

Born in Wantagh, New York, his parents divorced, Lenny grew up neurotic, hungry for affection, bewildered by the rules and regulations of the adult world and the confusion of two separate worlds—his father's and his mother's. He leaned toward his mother's world. She was Sally Marr, a sometime stand-up comic and entertainer who occasionally took him to burlesque shows. She took him to "Arthur Godfrey's Talent Scouts" on April 18, 1949. Lenny tied for first place and began a grinding career doing straight schtick, impressions and master-of-ceremonies work in strip clubs. He married a red headed stripper, Harriet Jolliff, who had worked as Honey Michel and Honey Harlowe.

Bruce raised money any way he could and once was arrested (and acquitted) for impersonating a priest soliciting funds for a leper colony. Around 1953 he worked briefly as a screenwriter. He managed to star in *Dance Hall Racket*, a stilted low-budget exercise redeemed only slightly by his lively imitation of a murderous small-time hood. Honey had a bit part as a gun moll. Their daughter Kitty was born in 1955, but within a few years the family was shattered by divorce and drug abuse.

Lenny's comedy was changing, turning hipper and "sicker." He fused old-fashioned gags with a newfound irreverence: "My mother-in-law broke up my marriage. My wife came home and found us in bed together." The more critics objected, the wilder Lenny got. A favorite early (1959) routine was an airline bit on John Graham, the man who blew up a plane with 40 people and his mother aboard for the insurance money. Lenny summed it up: "For this the state sent him to the gas chamber, proving actually that the American people are losing their sense of humor."

Lenny then went on to prove his own sense of humor and his innate ability to satirize human nature as he re-created the scene—the pathetic con man Graham handing his mother the gift box and impatiently shouting "Fill out the policy!" and the naive mother who believes her son can do no wrong ("It's a music box!" "Yeah, you'll get a bang out of it"). He moves on to chronicle the pesty passengers who elicit laughter from the audience and no sympathy. After the explosion the pilot is concerned only about his job ("Are we gonna get yelled at!") while the stewardess whines that the surviving passengers are becoming "cranky."

While some of the humor was in the sick concept, much of it was in Lenny's charismatic ability to create vivid, satirically etched characters. Everybody aboard the plane came to life, every homely detail intact. He didn't spare himself either. In the bit Lenny sketched in a portrait of himself—alone, making faces at himself in the airplane bathroom. It was part of Bruce's nature to bare himself to his audience. While Mort Sahl pioneered many of the techniques Lenny adopted, Mort's attitude was more like a therapist talking to a patient, or the patient on the couch. Lenny was in the confessional, sometimes as priest, sometimes as penitent.

Bruce's most memorable routines had both aggressive and vulnerable moments. In "To Come," he shocked the 1950s audience by declaring "to is a preposition, come is a verb." But in the course of his fierce routine (accompanied by drums) he talked about impotence and love ("I can't come," " 'Cause you don't love me, that's why you can't come." "I love you. I just can't come. That's my hangup. . . .") In another routine, he challenges the audience: "Would You Sell Out Your Country?" Then he adds, "I don't have to think twice. I know me, Jim. The flag goes right down the toilet." And he describes a torture scene, a patriot who won't spill his country's secrets—until he discovers he's about to be given a hot lead enema.

Sometimes Bruce used more poignant observation than harsh satire, as in his portrait of home folks in Lima, Ohio: "They show me how the house used to look . . . how dirty the other people were who lived there . . . we cleaned for months . . . yeah, that's a very lovely closet. It's nice the way the towels are folded . . . they always have a piano nobody plays. The function of the piano is to have that brown 8x10 picture of that shlub in the army saluting. . . ."

One of the reasons Lenny Bruce was so important to comedy was the complexity of his work. Something as simple as a parody of "The Lone Ranger" had shock comedy ("Masked man's a fag! Bet you got mascara under that mask!"), satire ("I like what they do to fags in this country—they throw them in jail with a lot of men, very clever!") and vulnerability (as the hero admits "I *must* have a 'thank you, masked man . . .' ").

Audiences encouraged Lenny toward more "free-form" comedy. He wanted to do less set "bits" and one-liners and more observational material drawn, like a jazz musician, from his feelings and emotions of the moment. When some of his sexual or religious material received negative criticism, it only goaded him into more furious assaults. He took on any topic that he felt uncomfortable talking about, whether it was how to remove snot from suede or deciding if Jacqueline Kennedy was running for cover or "going for help" when the shots were fired in Dallas.

Bruce didn't have all the answers. He even questioned his own business—where an entertainer could earn $50,000 a week while a schoolteacher made next to nothing.

Anti-Bruce forces were powerful. While there wasn't much that could be done to silence him for religious or political material, when it came to "dirty words," the law was clearly on their side. "What's *wrong* with appealing to prurient interests?" Lenny wanted to know. He wondered why Las Vegas was the entertainment capital of the country when the big attraction was "tits and ass." His use of those terms was shocking at the time—ironic considering that his use popularized the term and its slang abbreviation "T&A."

He joked, "If anyone believes that God made his body, and that body is dirty, the fault lies with the manufacturer." But it was no joke to those who were offended by Lenny Bruce. Lenny was busted for obscenity several times—and in his struggle to not only free himself but change the attitudes and laws on obscenity he found himself in legal quicksand, his money and strength draining away. Lenny had his weaknesses to begin with, and among them were drugs. The narcotics busts always seemed to occur around the same time as the obscenity arrests, exacerbating Bruce's problems and his increasing paranoia.

Bruce struggled on, his stage act becoming increasingly obsessed with dissecting law and language, trying to make sense of the nonsense. *Variety* reported that he made $108,000 in 1960 and only $6,000 in 1964. He was bankrupt in 1965 and dead in 1966. In his last days he had experimented with LSD, taken sleeping pills and worried his friends with his heroin abuse. Nobody was in the house when Lenny died. He had been typing; the electric typewriter was on, and he had been in midsentence: "Conspiracy to interfere with the fourth amendment const. . . ."

He was found by his friends, in the bathroom, a needle in his arm. It seemed strange. Lenny would not have simply thrown a sash around his arm and jabbed the needle in. None of the paraphernalia he used to shoot up, including a spoon and matches, were around. When the police arrived, they arranged the body for some photographs and added a few touches—such as a box of syringes found under the sink. There remain conflicts between the police reports and eyewitness testimony. Confusion over such basic facts as whether the drug was morphine or heroin, and whether the injection was administered by Lenny (accidentally or as a suicide attempt) or by someone else, have left the death of Lenny Bruce as controversial as his life.

In 1971 the Broadway show *Lenny* sparked a Lenny Bruce revival, and in the early, radical half of the decade students clamored for the reissue of his albums and previously unavailable works. Lenny was nominated for more Grammy awards posthumously than during his lifetime. The 1974 film version of *Lenny* brought even more attention to Bruce, along with Albert Goldman's biography.

In the passing years other comedians utilized elements of Lenny's style and teachings, often with broader and more cartoonish strokes. Some young listeners complain they simply can't "get" the original. They didn't grow up going to Jewish candy stores and were too young to understand the guilt trips involved in growing up in the repressed 1950s. They never saw the films Lenny satirized and didn't understand the jazz lingo or Yiddishisms strewn through his bits. They had no ear for routines without big payoffs and were used to far "dirtier" material. They enjoyed George Carlin's more accessible bits on dirty words and Richard Pryor's version of the "I'm going to piss on you" bit.

But for many, Lenny Bruce remains not only an original; he is still funny, still provocative and one of the few comedians whose "sound" is so charismatic it can be heard over and over for the sheer pleasure of his characterizations and word-weaving.

Many songs have been written about Lenny Bruce, ranging from performers such as Grace Slick (with The Great Society) to Bob Dylan and Tim Hardin. Paul Simon collaged the news report of his death with a chorus of "Silent Night." And on another number he declared, "I learned the truth from Lenny Bruce!"

Songs are sung for those who are bigger than life and bigger than death. Legends. In his lifetime, he once said, "I'm not a comedian. I'm Lenny Bruce." Now no writer, no critic, no friend and no foe can ever write about him as just a comedian. Because he was Lenny Bruce.

AUDIO: *Interviews for Our Time* (Fantasy), *The Sick Humor of Lenny Bruce* (Fantasy), *I Am Not a Nut, Elect Me* (Fantasy), *Lenny Bruce: American* (Fantasy), *Lenny Bruce Is Out Again* (Philles), *The Best* of *Lenny Bruce* (Fantasy), *The Real Lenny Bruce* (Fantasy), *Thank You Masked Man* (Fantasy), *Lenny Bruce at the Curran Theater* (Fantasy), *Carnegie Hall* (United Artists, aka *The Midnight Concert*), *The Berkeley Concert* (Bizarre, reissued by Enigma), *Law, Language and Lenny Bruce* (Warner), *To Is a Preposition, Come Is a Verb* (Douglas, aka *What I Was Arrested For*), *The Essential Lenny Bruce: Politics* (Douglas), *Why Did Lenny Bruce Die* (Capitol)

AUTOBIOGRAPHY: *How to Talk Dirty and Influence People* (1965)

BIOGRAPHIES: *Lenny Bruce* (Kofsky, 1974), *Ladies and Gentlemen, Lenny Bruce* (Goldman, 1974), *Honey: Lenny's Shady Lady* (H. Bruce, 1976), *Lenny Bruce: The Making of a Prophet* (W. K. Thomas, 1989)

BOOKS: *Stamp Help Out, The Essential Lenny Bruce* (Cohen, 1970), *The Unpublished Lenny Bruce* (K. Bruce, 1984)

FILMS: *Dream Follies* (1953), *Dance Hall Racket* (1954)

VIDEOS: *The Lenny Bruce Performance Film, Lenny Bruce Without Tears, Tribute to Lenny*

## LORD BUCKLEY

### (Richard Buckley, April 5, 1906–November 13, 1960)

A comedian smoking marijuana on stage? Leading a group of nude people through the lobby of a busy hotel? Championing the causes of Jesus Christ and the Marquis de Sade in the same show? If the idea sounds mind-boggling in the 1990s, imagine what it was like in the 1950s. That's when Lord Buckley did it.

Lord Buckley's cool lifestyle off stage and his mind-blowing "hipsomatic" monologues on stage made him a charismatic cult figure in the 1950s. His antics were known to a select few during his own lifetime, but he became a legend after his death. One of his comedy albums was strategically placed on the cover of Bob Dylan's *Bringing It All Back Home,* while George Harrison later wrote the song "Crackerbox Palace" about Buckley. Dylan, in early 1960s stage performances, covered a Buckley monologue called "Black Cross," the story of Hezekiah Jones, a black farmer killed by racists.

Early in his career, working nightclubs in Chicago, Buckley (billed as Dick Buckley; "Lord" was for his hip gigs only) developed a straight act of comedy and Svengali-like audience participation. In one of his most popular bits he invited audience members on stage, sat them down, and as they opened and closed their mouths (to his signal of tapping them on the neck) he ad-libbed "Amos and Andy"-style dialect routines. He even did it on a 1949 "Ed Sullivan Show" using celebrity members of the audience, including New York Yankee Phil Rizzuto, Brooklyn Dodger Gene Hermanski, Hermanski's wife and actor John Derek. Tapping Rizzuto: "If it wasn't fo' me, de Yankees wouldn't be no place . . . when a team's got the greatest shortstop in the world on their side, ain't nobody be messin' with 'em that's for sure." Hermanski: "Well, tomorrow's another day, my dear boy, remember that. . . ." Hermanski's wife: "I'm hip, he's got somethin' there." Derek: "You ain't lyin', baby . . . ain't nothin' ah like better than a hip chick." The wife: "I'm hip yo' hip." Derek: "I'm hip yo' hip I'm hip!" Hermanski: "Hip hip, hooray . . ."

In the 1950s, in select nightclubs, he offered his own brand of black dialect, which he termed "hipsomatic." The California-born comic looked like English royalty and spoke with what seemed like a British accent. But after his whimsical introduction to the audience ("m'lords and m'ladies of the Royal Court . . .") he lapsed into a funky black/beatnik lingo all his own, retelling philosophical truths about Christ ("the Naz"), discussing "the Bad Rapping of the Marquis de Sade" and twisting classic poems and poetic themes for modern audiences.

The idea of an aristocratic gent doing dialect wasn't new. George A. Moore was a vaudevillian who performed black dialect while wearing top hat and tails. Buckley may have seen the man work, since Moore (who died in December 1940) began his career in Chicago and toured the circuits regularly. But what Buckley did with the idea was startling and new, both his concepts and swinging delivery. His analysis of Poe's "The Raven" was simple: "Poe didn't want the bird, he didn't need the bird, he didn't dig the bird . . . if they knocked the bird on him post paid he wouldn't have dug it . . . when you don't want the bird, when you don't need the bird, when you don't have no possible *use* for the bird [gives a razzing 'bird' noise into the microphone]—that's when ya get it!"

Many tales have been told about Buckley's onstage eccentricities (the marijuana use) and his even more colorful off-stage moments (the time he baffled his landlady by dressing up his guests and friends in ballet tights and offering her free dance lessons in lieu of the rent money). With such a reputation, Buckley often raised the suspicions of nightclub owners. They never knew what he was going to do next. The police felt the same way, especially when they couldn't follow every word of his fast-paced routines about sex and religion, or the rumors of drug use. When he died of a stroke in 1960, *Variety* reported that the affliction "was said to have been brought on by the picking up of his police permit to work in New York by the N.Y. Police Dept. on an old charge . . . he was working at the Jazz Gallery, N.Y. when the police lifted his cabaret card several weeks ago."

Buckley's hip monologues and philosophy of peace and love reached a whole new audience in the 1960s thanks to the existing recordings he made and new ones unearthed by admirers such as Frank Zappa and George Harrison, who admitted, "He was very important to me during the sixties." In "Crackerbox Palace" (the name of one of Buckley's many homes), Harrison said he was referring to Buckley when he sang the line "Know that the Lord is well and inside of you."

It was not in the psychedelic 1960s but a decade earlier that Lord Buckley ended his show with this benediction: "The flowers, the gorgeous mystic multicolored flowers are not the flowers of life. People, yes, people are the true flowers of life . . . and it has been a most precious pleasure to have temporarily strolled in your garden."

AUDIO: *Lord Buckley: Friends, Romans and Countrymen* (RCA), *The Best of Lord Buckley* (Crestview), *Euphoria* (Vaya), *In Concert* (World Pacific), *Buckley's Best* (World Pacific), *Way Out Humor* (World Pacific), *Blowing His Mind* (World Pacific, reissued by Demon Verbals), *Bad Rapping of the Marquis de . Sade* (World Pacific, reissued by Demon Verbals), *A Most Immaculately Hip Aristocrat* (Straight, reissued by Enigma)
BROADWAY: *The Passing Show of 1946*
FILMS: *We're Not Married* (1952), *Spartacus* (1960)

## BUNNY and FINCH

**John Bunny: September 21, 1863–April 26, 1915**
**Flora Finch: 1869–January 4, 1940**

The first successful "comedy team" in film history, Flora Finch joined with John Bunny for a series popularly dubbed the "Bunnyfinch" shorts. Mostly domestic comedies, the humor was in slim and excitable Flora dominating her drunk, philandering, rolypoly old hubby. The lovable rascal Bunny said (via subtitles) in *Polishing Up:* "Here's to our wives and sweethearts—may they never meet."

Finch began her career as a Shakespearean actress and was a respected stage performer in England. She went to Hollywood in 1909 and was soon working regularly with John Bunny. They turned out over 200 short comedies.

"I didn't aim to be a comedian," Bunny once said, "but nature was agin' me. How could I hope to play Romeo with a figure like mine? It was many years before I learned to yield gracefully to the fate for which nature had endowed me."

Bunny looked a bit like W. C. Fields, an older gent sporting short gray hair, a prominently round nose and a ruddy complexion suggesting one drink too many. Like Fields, Bunny had an affection for Charles Dickens, starring in a 1912 hour-long film of *A Tale of Two Cities* and in *The Pickwick Papers* the following year. Considered a major comic star with or without Finch, he earned up to $1,000 a week for his solo projects. In 1914 he even had a song written in his honor, "That Funny Bunny Rag," with a photo of him on the sheet music.

Bunny hoped to parlay his fame into a hit stage production, *Bunny in Funnyland*, but the show was a disaster. Bunny had put a lot of money into the production, and after it folded, friends claimed he was literally a broken man. He was booked to begin making more films but died before he could make a celluloid comeback.

Flora had her own series a few years after Bunny's death, but it was not as great a success. Her solo films include *The Starring of Flora Finchurch* (1915), *Prudence the Pirate* (1916), *His Better Half* (1919), *When Knighthood Was in Flower* (1923) and *Monsieur Beaucaire* (1924). She also appeared on stage (notably *We've Got to Have Money* on Broadway in 1923), but her star had permanently dimmed.

She had a cameo role as a miner's wife in Laurel and Hardy's *Way Out West*.

FILMS incl.: *Bunny's Mistake* (1913), *Bunny's Birthday Surprise* (1913), *Bunny's Scheme* (1913), *Bunny Buys a Harem* (1914), *Pigs Is Pigs* (1914), *Love, Luck and Gasoline* (1914), *Polishing Up* (1914), *Bunny in Bunnyland* (1915)

## CAROL BURNETT

### (April 16, 1933–    )

One of the greatest actresses in modern comedy, Carol Burnett performed everything from raucous slapstick and movie parodies to realistic slice-of-life characters and pathos-drenched mime.

Born in San Antonio, Texas and raised in California, she had a traumatic childhood. She said, "My mother and father were divorced when I was six years old. Both were alcoholics . . . they were constantly splitting and getting back together." Burnett was raised by her grandmother, an uninhibited, fun-loving woman who had six husbands and shared Carol's fantasy-love of movies. Though they were desperately poor, they went to films as often as they could. "We'd see about eight movies a week. We were on welfare—that's all we spent our money on." Carol worked as an usherette to earn spending money.

Her teen years were little better than her childhood years. She recalled, "I never had a boyfriend. I was athletic, but I was five foot six, gangly, a string bean, 90 pounds wringing wet, buck teeth, long, stringy brown hair. . . . If a very popular boy would say hello to me, I wouldn't trust it. I'd think somebody had put him up to it as a joke."

Carol edited the school newspaper at Hollywood High and in 1952 went to UCLA, thanks to the support from an anonymous benefactor ("To this day I don't know who sent the money"). Carol was a journalism major at first. Her mother remarked: "No matter what you look like you can always write."

Carol later majored in theater and so impressed a wealthy businessman at a party by a routine she and another student did that he gave them each $1,000 to go to New York and try to make it in show business. She and Don Saroyan went to New York in 1954. They married but were separated several years later.

Her first television appearances were in comedies. She was Buddy Hackett's girlfriend on "Stanley," but on "The Paul Winchell Show," she recalled, "I was the girlfriend of the dummy Knucklehead Smiff. I would have to sing to him." In 1957 she developed a nightclub act that included a parody of Eartha Kitt. Carol would go out in a bathrobe instead of a negligee, singing "Monotonous." Another tune got her an appearance on Jack Paar's show: "I Made a Fool of Myself over John Foster Dulles" (then secretary of state under President Eisenhower). She won good reviews for 1959's off-Broadway *Once Upon a Mattress* (which later went to Broadway) and, after subbing for ill guest Martha Raye on "The Garry Moore Show," became a regular. She won a 1962 Emmy for her work on Moore's show, then left to star on Broadway in the musical *Fade Out, Fade In*. She won another Emmy for a television special in 1963, "Carol and Company," and the following year appeared in a disastrous television variety series "The Entertainers," a badly planned and executed show that crumbled apart while its stars, Burnett and Bob Newhart, ducked for cover.

On "The Garry Moore Show" the young star had proven her abilities in clowning and slapstick in the Martha Raye/Lucille Ball mold. Some sketches hinted at her talent in sketch comedy similar to Imogene Coca. On Broadway she proved her charisma and was clearly able to carry a production with her acting, singing and comedy skills. She put all this together, adding her own distinctive personality, on her long-running comedy-variety series "The Carol Burnett Show," produced by second husband Joe Hamilton.

Burnett could play virtually any type of character in a sketch, developing several alter egos, including a serio-comic charlady, the gum-chewing secretary Mrs. Wiggins and the psychotic silent film actress Nora Desmond. Burnett's love of movies and her fascination with the stars of the 1930s and '40s led her to a series of classic movie parody sketches that relied less on the writers' jokes than on her talent for faces, gestures and voices. Unlike most sketch comedy of the era, Bob Hope's work in particular, Carol preferred visual and character humor to wisecracking. In fact, fans probably can't recall a single funny "line" on the show, compared to such visual gems as her walk down the stairs in a satire of *Gone With the Wind* in which she wore a dress made from an old curtain—complete with curtain rods. The verbal joke was merely the icing: "I saw it in the window and I just couldn't resist."

Carol's original characters were not parodies of common people; she was clearly one of them. Everyone could identify with the housewives and girlfriends she played in domestic sketches. She created more true, believable characters in one television season than most actresses do in a lifetime. Audiences loved Carol and she loved them, as evidenced by what—for almost any other comedian—would have been a nauseatingly sugary routine: opening the show by turning up the lights and talking with the audience. Carol said, "They tell you when you're right and they tell you when you're wrong. And they're never wrong."

As tastes changed a bit from the broad slapstick and breezy parody of the 1960s into the '70s, Carol concentrated more on realistic domestic sketches, ultimately arriving at the dour housewife Eunice Higgins in a series of playlets with her co-star Harvey Korman. Carol won additional Emmy awards in 1972, 1974 and 1975, continuing to delight audiences with a seemingly unlimited array of comic talent. Actually, she did have one limitation, monology: "I never really got up and by myself did jokes that much. I was terrified to get up and perform alone. I didn't like to do that. For me to get up and try to tell a joke, it's sad."

For a decade "The Carol Burnett Show" remained a habit for comedy fans, even though the variety show format had become antiquated and all the other stars of the genre had long since departed the airways. In the 1980s there were several changes for Carol Burnett. After years of shyness she had begun standing up for herself, the most public example being her successful lawsuit against *The National Inquirer* for some gossipy lies it had printed. In 1981 she underwent a "sliding horizontal osteotomy" to strengthen the look of her chin and jaw, though many had always found the self-deprecating star rather attractive.

Carol divided her time between serious movies (the television film *Friendly Fire*), comedies (*The Four Seasons*) and her autobiography, which she wrote during the two years she lived by herself in a New York hotel. A few personal problems marred the '80's for her. She and Joe Hamilton divorced. The substance abuse problems of one of her three daughters, Carrie, were highly publicized in the early 1980s but were later successfully resolved. Carol and Carrie starred in a 1988 film together, *Hostage*.

Fans admired "the new" Carol Burnett, the one who held her own opposite Elizabeth Taylor in the television movie *Between Friends* and the one who played an alcoholic in *Beatrice*, a praised production that was even broadcast in Russia. But they couldn't help but wonder when the comic Carol they knew and loved best would return. They were tantalized by a 1989 special with Julie Andrews that included some old-fashioned pie fighting. Carol enjoyed the messy comedy thoroughly: "You feel cleansed once you do something like that. Absolutely purged."

Carol had been hesitant about returning to television: "I did not want to be in a situation comedy where I would do the same person week after week. . . . I love doing different kinds of characters and playing dress-up. Putting on different makeup and wigs." Her solution was a sitcom in which she'd play a different character each week. Later she returned to her original format for a new season of comedy. She said, "I started to realize I didn't have to do [slapstick], that I was a mature woman who could still be funny without crossing my eyes all the time. It was a sense of insecurity that made me do that, and a growing security that made me stop."

Though the variety format was too antiquated to succeed and the show was canceled, Burnett has remained in demand for movies and TV specials. Fans have never stopped admiring Carol Burnett, who over the years ended her shows with a little tug on her ear and a few lines of her closing song: "I'm so glad we've had this time together. . . ."

AUDIO: *If I Could Write a Song, Julie and Carol at Carnegie Hall, Fade Out, Fade In* (ABC Paramount), *Once Upon a Mattress*
AUTOBIOGRAPHY: *One More Time* (1987)
BIOGRAPHY: *Laughing Till it Hurts* (Taraborelli, 1988)
MONOGRAPGH: *Carol Burnett and Joe Hamilton: An American Film Institute Seminar on Their Work* (1977)
FILMS incl.: *Who's Been Sleeping in My Bed* (1963), *Pete 'n Tillie* (1972), *The Front Page* (1974), *A*

*Wedding* (1978), *The Grass Is Always Greener Over the Septic Tank* (1978), *The Tenth Month* (1979), *Friendly Fire* (1979), *Chu Chu and the Philly Flash* (1981), *The Four Seasons* (1981), *Annie* (1982), *Between Friends* (1983), *Hostage* (1988), *Noises Off* (1992)

TV: "Stanley" (1956–57), "Pantomime Quiz" (1958–59), "The Garry Moore Show" (1959–62), "The Entertainers" (1964–65), "The Carol Burnett Show" (1967–79), "Mama's Family" (1983–84), "Carol and Company" (1990–1991)

VIDEO: *My Personal Best: Best of the Carol Burnett Show,* vols. 1 & 2

## BURNS and ALLEN (See also GEORGE BURNS.)

**George Burns: Nathan Birnbaum, January 20, 1896–**

**Gracie Allen: Grace Ethel Cecile Rosalie Allen, July 26, 1902–August 28, 1964**

The most beloved husband-and-wife act in comedy history, Burns and Allen thrived on a deceptively simple format: smart man serves up straight line, dizzy lady lobs it back with a twist. From their television series:

BURNS: Isn't that boiling water you're putting in the refrigerator?

ALLEN: Yes, I'm freezing it. Then whenever I want boiling water all I have to do is defrost it.

What made the team such a lasting success in vaudeville, radio, films and television was the guileless charm of Gracie Allen and the underrated skills of George Burns, who shared his chagrin with the listeners via low-key, dryly gruff asides and a mordant gaze at the audience. Like their friend Jack Benny, they were so easy to take and so true to life that they were welcomed year after year, while more frantic acts burned out.

They teamed in 1923. George, a veteran of many vaudeville acts, logically chose to be the funny one. As it turned out, audiences laughed more at Gracie than George, so they switched roles. Audiences were enchanted by Gracie—and so was George, who hoped to make her his wife, despite the fact that he'd been married before and she already had a boyfriend. For a frustrating year George tried to encourage Gracie to see him as more than just a comedy part-ner. She didn't take him seriously and kept her boyfriend. Finally George decided it was do or die. He told Gracie "Agree to marry me within ten days or we split up." As he recalled later, "I think, until that moment, she didn't believe I was serious about marrying her." After a big argument, George stormed out, shouting "You don't even know what love means!" That night Gracie called up George and said, "You can buy the wedding ring if you want to." She admitted to having cried that night: "You're the only boy who ever made me cry," she told him. "And I decided that if you could make me cry, I must really love you."

They married on January 7, 1926, becoming husband and wife (and, in the privacy of their own home, "Nattie" and "Googie"). That she was Irish Catholic and he Jewish did not matter in the slightest. Neither did the "defects" that shy Gracie was highly concerned about. Gracie never wore short-sleeved dresses due to scars she suffered as a child when she knocked a pot of boiling tea onto her left arm. She had one blue eye and one green eye and limited vision in one of them due to glass fragments that stuck in her eye after she knocked over a glass lamp in another childhood accident. The vivacious Gracie may have seemed carefree on stage, but before shows she was often nervous and had severe migraine headaches requiring rest and absolute quiet.

Burns and Allen rose steadily through vaudeville, starred in a series of short films beginning in 1929, played The Palace in 1930, and in 1932 got their own radio show. It stayed on the air for 18 years. Through the 1930s they co-starred in a number of feature films. Along the way the duo "grew up" professionally, their gags moving away from playful boyfriend and coquettish girlfriend to domestic husband-and-wife comedy. They were now clearly a married couple together for better or for Gracie's dizzy worst. As George once said, "We often think the way Gracie talks, but we pride ourselves that we never talk the way Gracie thinks."

From the film *International House:* "You know, you're very smart. To what do you attribute your smartness?" "Three things. First, my very good memory. And the other two things I forgot. . . ." "Did you ever go to school?" "Oh yes, I did." "Well, what school did you go to?" "I'm not allowed to tell." "You're not allowed to tell?" "The school pays me $25 a week not to tell."

Gracie's humor required skill and timing to deliver. A real "Dumb Dora" could not have even remembered the complicated messes Gracie had to make sound real: "There's so much good in the worst of us, and so many of the worst of us get the best of us, that the rest of us aren't even worth talking about."

Burns and Allen moved to television in 1950 and stayed on the air until Gracie retired. The show has become a rerun favorite, surprisingly modern (thanks to George's habit of talking to the viewers, something video critics now call "breaking the fourth dimension"). Gracie's retirement was such big news in 1958 that she made the cover of *Life* magazine on September 22. Her death in 1964 was front-page news and was flashed on the huge news tickers erected at the World's Fair. In the 1950s George wrote a hit book about their life together, *I Love Her That's Why*. Thirty years later he found that he and the audience still shared that love. *Gracie: A Love Story* was a number-one best-seller across the country.

AUDIO incl.: *Burns and Allen* (Nostalgia Lane), *The New Burns and Allen Show* (Radiola), *Burns and Allen* (Mark 56), *Burns and Allen Show* (Memorabilia), *Burns and Allen* (Murray Hill)

BIOGRAPHIES: *I Love Her, That's Why* (Burns, 1955), *Gracie: A Love Story* (Burns, 1989), *Say Goodnight, Gracie* (Blythe and Sackett, 1990)

FILMS incl.: *The Big Broadcast* (1932), *International House* (1933), *College Humor* (1933), *Six of a Kind* (1934), *We're Not Dressing* (1934), *Many Happy Returns* (1934), *Love in Bloom* (1935), *Here Comes Cookie* (1935), *Big Broadcast of 1936* (1936), *College Holiday* (1936), *Big Broadcast of 1937* (1937), *A Damsel in Distress* (1937), *College Swing* (1938), *Honolulu* (1939), *The Gracie Allen Murder Case* (1939), *Mr. and Mrs. North* (1941), *Two Girls and a Sailor* (1944)

## BURNS and SCHREIBER

**John Francis Burns, November 15, 1933–**
**Avery Schreiber, April 9, 1935–**

Chubby, amiable, woolly-haired Avery Schreiber and severe, straight, slick Jack Burns were a pair of opposites who attracted national attention in the late 1960s and early '70s. Their most enduring routine featured Jack as a bigoted foot-in-mouth WASP climbing into friendly Avery Schreiber's cab:

"By the way, your name on the nameplate there. You're of the Judeo-Hebraic persuasion." "You mean I'm a Jew." "Hey, I don't go in for name calling! But lemme tell ya, pound for pound Hank Greenberg was one of the greatest ballplayers who ever lived." "What about Sandy Koufax?" "Don't tell me he's one of them too. . . . Listen, this country is made up of individuals. But I'll tell you what I hate, I hate those people who make derogatory remarks about someone's ancestry . . . 'he's a dago, he's a wop, he's a hebe.' You know who says that the most? Your hunkies."

Long before "All in the Family" and Archie Bunker, the team of Burns and Schreiber presented the routine under the heading "The New Emerging Bigot." Burns was the thick-headed fool who told the parent of an albino child, "You can never be *too white*." And Schreiber was forever trying to gently lead Burns toward the truth. The trouble was that Burns wasn't paying attention. Their catch phrase was not a phrase at all, but the frustrating "Huh?" "Yeah." "Huh?" "Yeah." "Huh?" "Yeah!" cadence of Burns and Schreiber trying to communicate.

The duo met in Chicago in 1962. Schreiber, a Chicago native, was working with the Second City improvisational troupe. He had studied drama at the Goodman Theater following service in the army. Boston-born Burns, an ex disc jockey, had spent a few years as George Carlin's straight man and later as a member of The Compass Players in St. Louis. Together Burns and Schreiber evolved a number of fine routines, including the cab driver and the conventioneer, a bit with Burns as a frantic faith healer and a touching tableau with Burns as a lonely man seeking comfort from a talking machine (played by Schreiber). The team made it to Jack Paar's show in 1964, had their own "Our Place" summer variety show in 1967 and recorded an album.

The promising duo split up in the late 1960s with Schreiber finding television sitcom work as the comically evil Captain Manzini on "My Mother the Car" and Jack Burns briefly replacing Don Knotts as the irritating deputy on "The Andy Griffith Show." They reteamed in the early 1970s once again finding a ready audience for their polished sketches. They had a new summer show and put out more records. Shortly thereafter, they broke up.

Schreiber stayed in front of the camera, appearing in character comedy parts for sitcoms and movies, taking the lead in a West Coast version of *Volpone* and playing in *Dreyfuss in Rehearsal* on Broadway. Fans probably remember him best for his series of high-profile humorous Dorito corn chips commercials. Burns became head writer for ABC's "Fridays" series, wrote and produced "The Muppet Show" in England, scripted *The Muppet Movie* and produced the CBS sitcom "We've Got Each Other."

AUDIO: *Second City Writhes Again* (Mercury), *In One Head and Out the Other* (Columbia), *Pure B.S.* (Little David), *The Watergate Comedy Hour* (Hidden)

## BOB ''BAZOOKA'' BURNS

### (Robin Burns, August 2, 1893–February 8, 1956)

Championed as the heir to Will Rogers, Bob Burns was a rural comedian with blunt features and a ready, enthusiastic personality. Perhaps George "Goober" Lindsay would be the most similar modern version. The burly six-foot, two-inch 200-pounder didn't exactly fulfill his destiny, but he was quite popular during the late 1930s and early '40s. Trivia buffs might consider him most famous as the inventor of the word "bazooka."

Born in Van Buren, Arkansas, Burns was not a hillbilly, despite his accent. His father was a civil engineer, and for several years Bob studied engineering at the University of Arkansas. Music was his first love, having played mandolin, piano and trombone with The Silver Tone Cornet Band in Van Buren. It was there that he invented the "Bazooka" in 1905. While rehearsing in a plumber's shop, Burns put a few gas pipes together and blew. What came out was a blast: "I found I could make about three fuzzy bass notes. The other boys all laughed and I suppose I was just like all other boys— if you laugh at them they'll do it ag'in. I spent the rest of that night figurin' out the bazooka."

Burns practiced on his wind instrument and discovered he was windy enough to make music. "There's an expression for a guy who's windy—'he blows his bazoo too much.' So this thing was a bazoo. And then I added the "ka" because it was a musical instrument, like the balalaika and harmonica."

Burns added a whiskey funnel to the end and increased the range by sliding the length of pipe up and down like a trombone. He worked his way up from New Orleans to New York, but didn't make much money. After serving as a marine sergeant during World War I, Burns tried working for a carnival, attempted a blackface vaudeville act, then returned to music with his comical bazooka.

In 1935 Burns won a spot on Rudy Vallee's show and later guested often with Bing Crosby. Crosby gave Bob a role in his film *Rhythm on the Range*. When Will Rogers died, the Southern-accented Burns immediately seemed the fitting replacement, even though his corny comedy was not in the Rogers tradition. Burns' homely anecdotal style, from the film *Big Broadcast of 1937* includes the following: "I never could understand to save my life why you women can't be satisfied with the way you are. I've got one aunt down home, my Aunt Duddy, and she's in her late 50s and that woman never put a nickel's worth of cosmetics on her face for her life. And, right today, she's got a complexion like a peach. Yella and fuzzy."

Burns' comedy, which seems rather overbearing and windy these days (including his occasional bazooka playing), slid out of favor after some starring film roles and his own radio series in the early 1940s. According to word origin specialist Charles Earle Funk, during World War II Bob's musical instrument led to the naming of a new weapon. A General Somervell was present at the testing of the powerful gun and said, "That damn thing looks just like Bob Burns' bazooka."

FILMS incl.: *Rhythm on the Range* (1936), *Big Broadcast of 1937* (1937), *Wells Fargo* (1937), *Radio City Revels* (1938), *The Arkansas Traveler* (1938)

## GEORGE BURNS (See also BURNS and ALLEN.)

### (Nathan Birnbaum, January 20, 1896–   )

"If there was a Mt. Rushmore for comedians," Bob Hope said in 1989, "Burns would be the first one on it."

For years fans and critics considered Gracie the only star of the Burns and Allen team. But George proved them wrong, making his comeback at 79 with the film *The Sunshine Boys* and becoming the "grand old man of comedy." Photo from the author's collection.

George Burns has become a living legend, mostly by outliving the other living legends. In the 1930s, '40s and '50s the modest comedian insisted it was his partner Gracie who had all the talent. In the 1960s and '70s he was really considered just another elderly vaudevillian, less obnoxious than Cantor, more amusing than Jessel, but certainly not as beloved as Jack Benny or as revered as Groucho Marx. After these and other friends passed away, Burns became the only link to the good old days. Then he became more than that, redefining the crustiness and chagrin of his straight-man days with Gracie to become the dryly caustic, sagely witty grand old man of comedy, performing one-man shows of songs, anecdotes and jokes and continuing in his 90s to appear on talk shows.

Burns was seven when he joined the Pee Wee Quartette and not much older when he invaded vaudeville. "I think I loved being in vaudeville more than any other part of my career," he once wrote. "Vaudeville was that place where people who said they would do anything to be in show business, did. . . . Whatever type of act the booking agent was looking for happened to be the type of act I did. I sang, I danced, I worked with Captain Bett's seal, I worked with a dog, I did a song and dance act with

a dog, I worked alone, I worked with a partner. . . . As long as I could put on my makeup and go out on stage I was happy."

Billy Lorraine was one of his partners, but his ultimate partner was Gracie Allen. Burns and Allen prospered for decades. George's style was so self-deprecating and the laughs so centered on Gracie that only lately have audiences come to realize that Burns was not only perfect as a straight man, but wryly amusing in his role as the long-suffering husband. In the 1960s, after Gracie's retirement, audiences couldn't accept Burns in a sitcom on his own or with new partners Carol Channing (on tour) and Connie Stevens (the sitcom "Wendy and Me"). The nostalgia craze of the late '60s led Burns to try an album of rock songs sung in his humorous rasp, but the "old gramps is as hip as the kids" image just didn't fit. As the years wore on, Burns developed as a raconteur, but he relied mostly on the same old anecdotes about his vaudeville years, sang the same old songs (always with his trademark of cutting off the endings) and brought up the names of Cantor, Jolson and Jessel too often for younger viewers to care about.

Burns did what he could: "If I get a laugh, I'm a comedian. If I get a small laugh, I'm a humorist. If I get no laughs, I'm a singer. If my singing gets big laughs, then I'm a comedian again."

Everything changed in 1975 after he won an Academy Award for his work in the hit film *The Sunshine Boys*. He was a last-minute replacement for the original choice, the late Jack Benny. Burns was wonderful as the realistic, stoic but lovable old vaudevillian dubiously about to reteam with his hyper ex-partner (Walter Matthau). He followed it with films that further explored this facet of Burns' personality. In *Oh God*, George delivered dry-eyed philosophical lines, his unperturbable rasp and gentle demeanor suggesting so well that one must be hard-headed and realistic about life's miseries—but soft-hearted and humorous enough to appreciate its joys. He recalled, "I got nervous when I was asked to play God. We're both around the same age but we grew up in different neighborhoods."

Now, in his stand-up routines, Burns used not only the anecdotes about vaudeville and Gracie, but pearls of wit and wisdom, observations on life. In the past he had come close to being everyone's windy grandfather, about to tell that one joke once too often. Now, with a twinkle in his eye, he triumphed year after year, delighting nervous audiences when his trademark occasional stutter kicked into gear and he effortlessly sang and told jokes. As he grew older, talk show audiences became obsessed with asking George about how much he missed Gracie or what the secrets were for long life. They were able to rejoice and smile as George sailed past 80, 85, 88, 90, 95 and on, as funny, wise, and lively as ever.

Years earlier Jack Benny had said, "George Burns is so old his birth certificate is on a rock." But here was George Burns, wryly acknowledging his longevity: "Thanks for the standing ovation. I'm at the point now where I get a standing ovation just for standing." Into the 1990s, George Burns displayed something better than the crusty "indomitable spirit" that feisty old people often claim as the secret for endurance. He displayed understated humor and a disdain of sentiment. As he said in 1991, "It's great to be 95 and get out of bed and have something to do. I don't think I can make any money in bed."

AUDIO incl.: *An Evening with George Burns* (Pride, import), *George Burns Sings* (Buddah), *I Wish I Was 18 Again* (Mercury)

AUTOBIOGRAPHIES: *I Love Her That's Why* (1955); *Living It Up* (1976); *The Third Time Around; Gracie: A Love Story* (1989); *All My Best Friends* (1989)

BOOKS: *How to Live to Be 100—or More* (1984); *Dr. Burns' Prescription for Happiness* (1984); *Dear George* (1985); *Wisdom of the 90s* (1991)

FILMS incl.: *The Sunshine Boys* (1975), *Oh God* (1977), *Sergeant Pepper's Lonely Hearts Club Band* (1978), *Just You and Me Kid* (1979), *Going in Style* (1979), *Oh God Book II* (1980), *Two of a Kind* (1982), *Oh God, You Devil* (1984)

TV: "The Burns and Allen Show" (1950–58), "The George Burns Show" (1958–59), "Wendy and Me" (1964–65), "The George Burns Comedy Week" (1985)

## RED BUTTONS

### (Aaron Chwatt, February 5, 1919–  )

Red Buttons was a red-hot star in the 1950s but, like several comedians who leapt into the new media

of television, he crash-landed when he ran out of material. After achieving success as a serious actor, he returned to comedy and was once again a popular performer in nightclubs and on television.

Born on the Lower East Side, nicknamed "Irish" for his red hair, Buttons sang on street corners and in the choir of Cantor Joseph Rosenblatt. After attending Evander Childs High School in the Bronx he went to work in Ryan's, a City Island tavern. His uniform (with 48 buttons) and his flaming hair led to his nickname. In the Catskills he worked the resorts with straight man Robert Alda. Then, in 1939, he became one of the youngest comedians in burlesque. He was eager to move on to Broadway, but the show he was in couldn't open. The actors didn't bomb—the Japanese did. The premiere had been scheduled for December 8, 1941, the day after the attack on Pearl Harbor.

Red made his Broadway debut in *Vicki* the following year, followed it with more Broadway work and made some films, including *Winged Victory*. He played a comical soldier who led his fellow GIs on a tour of the barracks ("Pneumonia Gulch!") and the mess hall: "Ptomaine Tavern . . . the wheatcakes we leave are used by the navy as depth bombs!"

Buttons starred in a video biography of Joe E. Lewis and in 1951 made a startling appearance on Milton Berle's show. In a sketch, Berle ripped Red's break-away suit off. And Red's underwear as well. The kind of national exposure Red Buttons really wanted was his when he got his own television show and, on September 28, 1953, the cover of *Newsweek* magazine.

Although he was an amiable comic in gentle sketches (an early character was the likable "Kupke Kid" and his catch phrase was the cheerful "Ho Ho Ho" of his theme song, "Strange Things Are Happening"), Buttons worked at the same hectic pace as the more frenzied slapstick comics of the era. "World War II was a skirmish compared to what I went through," he recalled. He left television exhausted by the stress and strain of doing his series.

Some thought Red would never be funny again. He wasn't right away. He turned from comedy and accepted a straight role in the film *Sayonara*. From then on Buttons was able to balance comedy with occasional straight parts, receiving a Golden Globe nomination for his work in *Harlow* and giving a brilliant performance as an aging sailor battling physical exhaustion during a dance marathon in *They Shoot Horses Don't They.*

A reliable stand-up comedian over the next three decades, Buttons was especially successful in the 1970s when he appeared often on Dean Martin's televised "Roast" specials. A new generation unfamiliar with his old characters, such as "The Kupke Kid," enjoyed the old pro's mock agitation and impassioned appeals for all the famous people through history who "never got a dinner." He made a catch phrase out of it, crying with an enthusiasm deliberately bordering on self-parody, that "Richard the Third, who said to Richard the Second, 'Your number is up,' *never got a dinner!* Michelangelo's girlfriend, who said to Angelo, 'Forget about paint, let's put a mirror on the ceiling'—*never got a dinner.*"

After so many years in show business, Red finally "got a dinner" himself. Of his tumultuous career he admitted, "I've been on the Ferris wheel, believe me. I've been stuck at the bottom and stuck at the top." The dinner, a Friar's "Man of the Year" banquet, was held on May 16, 1987 at the Waldorf Astoria. Many celebrities were on hand, including Lucille Ball and Jackie Mason. Red received a letter from President Ronald Reagan. It read, in part, "I am pleased to join your many friends and colleagues in congratulating you . . . one of America's most beloved comedians. You have shared your gift for laughter and your extraordinary talents with us. On behalf of your multitude of fans, thank you for those gifts." Many others wrote letters too. Johnny Carson's was brief: "Dear Red: You finally got your dinner—now shut up!"

AUDIO: *Poems for My Daughter* (Wonderland), *Gay Purree* (Warner Brothers), *Fun House* (Harmony)
BROADWAY: *Vicki* (1942), *Winged Victory* (1943), *Barefoot Boy with Cheek* (1947), *Hold It* (1948), *A Midsummer Night's Dream* (1956)
FILMS incl.: *Winged Victory* (1944), *Sayonara* (1957), *Imitation General* (1958), *The Big Circus* (1959), *Hatari* (1962), *The Longest Day* (1962), *Stagecoach* (1966), *They Shoot Horses Don't They* (1969), *Who Killed Mary What's Her Name* (1971), *The Poseidon Adventure* (1972), *Movie Movie* (1978), *CHOMPS* (1979), *When Time Ran Out* (1980), *Leave 'Em*

*Laughing* (1981), *Reunion at Fairborough* (1985), *18 Again* (1988)
TV: "The Red Buttons Show" (1952–55), "The Double Life of Henry Phyfe" (1966)

## RUTH BUZZI

### (July 24, 1936– )

An endearing and versatile sketch performer, Ruth Buzzi developed one particular character that she made famous: the huffy, self-protective spinster Gladys Ormphby on television's "Rowan and Martin's Laugh-In."

Ruth was born in Rhode Island and raised in Wequetequock, Connecticut, where her father ran a business selling graveyard monuments. In 1954 she joined the Pasadena Playhouse and two years later starred in *Jenny Kissed Me* with Rudy Vallee in San Francisco. She went back to the East Coast in 1960, appearing one year later in the off-Broadway play *Misguided Tour.* She developed her first major character playing "Shakuntula," a clumsy, wide-eyed grinning idiot who was less than helpful as a magician's assistant. The funny girl with the Fanny Brice grin, prominent jaw and flexible body for hilariously awkward poses retained the "Shakuntula" character for instant laughs and began to develop more.

It was during a summer stock production of *Auntie Mame* that Ruth played "Agnes Gooch." The stage directions called for her to "schlump" on stage. She did, creating a shambling walk and adding a strained, choking voice. This was the beginning of Gladys Ormphby. Joan Rivers recalls working with Ruth in off-Broadway revues in the early 1960s. Ruth "stayed alive cleaning apartments. She would ride the subways with her spaghetti mop and bucket, dressed . . . [in a] hairnet, the baggy sweater, rolled stockings, fat shoes. That made everything endurable. She was not a cleaning lady. She was an actress pretending to be a cleaning lady."

Ruth made her first television appearances in 1964's "The Entertainers" as Shakuntula, with Dom Deluise as the magician. DeLuise recalled, "She was marvelous. She wore thrift-shop bloomers, cotton socks at half mast underneath her harem pants and blotches of rouge that didn't quite hit the center of her cheeks. I did all the talking, she did all the listening. She got the big laughs. At playing desperate ladies, she had no peer."

She followed "The Entertainers" with sketch work on "The Carol Burnett Show" and "The Steve Allen Comedy Hour," and was a semiregular on "That Girl" as Margie "Pete" Peterson. But it was as the desperate but self-denying Gladys Ormphby that she made her mark on "Laugh-In." Producer George Schlatter loved that character, insisting she do almost nothing but Ormphby sketches in her first year on the show. Her nemesis was Arte Johnson as the dirty old man, Tyrone. There was an odd chemistry to this odd couple—the repulsive old man relentlessly trying to date (or just annoy) the equally homely old spinster. Ruth brought some humanity and vulnerability to the stereotypical role. There was a definite hurting throb in her voice as she deflected the old man's advances. Of course, she stayed on to keep listening: lonely but not enough to give in.

In real life Ruth was already a happily married woman. She was glad to also have the chance to play other roles on "Laugh-In," even if they were broadly done caricatures of hookers, secretaries and housewives. She remained with the show through its entire run. She continued to work on variety shows, later enjoying success in the children's field with a Saturday morning series co-starring Jim Nabors and Arte Johnson. Over the years she's played older eccentrics on television and in Disney movies, proving her durability, though not always given a chance to show her versatility.

FILMS incl.: *Freaky Friday* (1977), *The Apple Dumpling Gang Rides Again* (1979), *North Avenue Irregulars* (1979), *Chu Chu and the Philly Flash* (1981), *The Being* (1984), *The Bad Guys* (1985), *Dixie Lanes* (1988)

TV: "The Entertainers" (1964), "The Steve Allen Comedy Hour" (1967), "That Girl" (1967–68), "Rowan and Martin's Laugh-In" (1968–73), "Baggy Pants and the Nitwits" (1977–78)

VIDEO: *Miss Casino Comedy Show*

## JOHN BYNER

**(John Biener, 1937– )**

Originally a slightly offbeat impressionist, John Byner was popular in nightclubs and 1960s variety shows doing both standards (Frank Sinatra, Lyndon Johnson and Ed Sullivan), less-covered actors (Robert Stack) and originals (Felix Fossadeedee, a mild-mannered fellow whose voice seemed like a cross between Donald Duck and Wally Cox). Byner's cool extended to routines as "Lennie Jackie," a satire of Vegas lounge comics doing formula gags from memory: "My luck is so bad that if I bought a suit with two pair of pants, I'd get the half that eats!"

Born in Rockville Center, New York, John's mother was an attendant in a mental hospital and his father a semiemployed mechanic who died when John was 12. After navy service, Byner worked as a truck driver. With a wife and four children to support, he tried show business, entering a "JFK Sound-alike" contest. He won. At 27 he got his first shot on television's "Ed Sullivan Show" and was on his way. Through the 1970s Byner varied his stand-up appearances with guest roles in sitcoms (he was Detective Donahue on "Soap"). He made enough money to buy, with his manager, a $300,000 island in the South Pacific. He sometimes stayed there for half a year at a time.

In 1979 Richard Dawson filmed a pilot called "Bizarre," a collection of offbeat sketches. ABC didn't want it, but Showtime Cable did, producing it in Canada with Byner as the host. In October 1980, the *New York Daily News* complained the show "points up everything that's wrong with cable television," citing sketches involving nudity. *People* magazine agreed about the "bare-breasted women . . . sophomoric sketches, lascivious language and unpardonable puns," but declared Byner "en route to becoming this decade's Ernie Kovacs." The show attracted a strong cult following over the years as Byner livened things up with his impressions of everyone from Ghandi to "Mr. Godwrench, Faith Healer to Cars." For club dates, Byner adds current standards such as Julio Iglesias, Dr. Ruth and Mister Rogers. In 1990 he began hosting "Comedy on the Road," featuring young stand-up performers at work.

When he isn't on the road, he's home with his third wife, whom he met on the set of a film he made in Europe, *Transylvania 6-5000*. He played an insane butler, while his bride, a tall blond Yugoslavian named Kesenija Prohaska, played a mummy. "It was 3 A.M. and she was in this box [coffin], and it was cold on the set and she was uncomfortable and nervous, and I talked to her and tried to relax her and pretty soon we were friends and then we fell in love. The moral is, never unwrap a mummy on a cold morning in Yugoslavia."

AUDIO: *The New First Family 1968* (Verve), *The Out of the Ordinary World According to Byner* (Dr. Pepper)

FILMS incl.: *The Great Smokey Roadblock* (1976), *The Man in the Santa Claus Suit* (1978), *Murder Can Hurt You* (1980), *The Black Cauldron* (voice, 1985), *Transylvania 6-5000* (1985), *Go Go Dancer* (1990)

TV: "The John Byner Show" (1972), "Soap" (1978–80), "Bizarre" (1980–86), "Comedy on the Road" (1990–   )

# C

## SID CAESAR

### (September 8, 1922–   )

One of the few comedians specializing in both silence and gibberish, Sid Caesar could get laughs from miming a man eating popcorn in a movie theater or playing a wacky lecturer speaking in fractured foreign languages. His routines created in the golden age of television in the 1950s went on to become classics, later reissued for films and revived by Caesar himself for Broadway 30 years later.

Caesar's first career was music. At 14 he joined a band playing saxophone. By 1942 he was playing and recording with Shep Fields. While in the coast guard he formed a band with composer Vernon Duke. In between numbers he did jokes, imitations and double-talk. When Duke went on to work on a coast guard show called "Tars and Spars," he recommended Caesar for comedy sketches. The show toured the country for a year and was made into a film, which features Caesar doing a monologue complete with sound effects. He made his comedy debut at The Copa in 1947 and was a hit in the Broadway revue *Make Mine Manhattan*.

In 1949 "American Broadway Review" was retitled "Your Show of Shows." The original live Saturday night revue, it stayed on television through 1954. As Jack Klugman recalled, "Every single week, they did it live. They did these magnificent sketches. I don't know how. And today, they tape a show and it takes forever." Caesar was the leader, his energy and creativity a key to unlocking the talents of his writers, a staff that at one time or another included Mel Brooks, Neil Simon, Larry Gelbart and Woody Allen. Sometimes no writer could save a sketch when things went haywire; it was up to Caesar's ad-libbing skill.

Once he started dressing up in a leopard loincloth and sandals only to be told the sketch order was changed. He rushed on stage wearing a suit jacket over the crazy costume. Pointing to the shoes, he said to the other businessmen: "Well, you know how sometimes you get a present and feel obligated to wear it at least once? And besides, it looked like rain this morning!"

The grind of doing the live weekly show led to alcoholism—a bottle of scotch a day. His temperment was, at times, a bit over the edge. While staying at The Palmer House in Chicago, he was urged by Mel Brooks to take a break. "Let's go out," Mel asked. Caesar took Mel out: He hauled him out the window and dangled him from 18 floors up. Brooks also recalled the time in Central Park that Caesar and his wife went horseback riding: "His wife Florence was thrown from the horse and he *punched* the horse. And it was never the same after that." The scene inspired a horse-punching moment in Mel's *Blazing Saddles*.

Caesar won two Emmy awards (1951 and 1956), but it seemed to have come at too high a price. His career slowed until the success of his Broadway show *Little Me* (1962) and his starring role in *It's a Mad Mad Mad Mad World* a year later. Even so, the decade after "Your Show of Shows" was not a happy one, and it led Caesar to ask the question that became the title of his autobiography, *Where Have I Been?*

In 1978 he vowed to change his life. He recalled saying to himself, "Sid, do you want to live or do you want to die?" He began to make a recovery, as recounted in his book. He was proud to finally say "The problems I had with alcohol are gone. That's it. That's all. You don't carry it around. There's nothing wrong with having a couple of drinks, for people who can control it. I don't do it because I can't control it." Exercise helped Sid greatly. "I got hooked on exercise in conjunction with diet. If you just exercise all you're doing is making hard fat. And if you just diet and don't exercise all you're making is lean flab."

The film *My Favorite Year,* produced by Mel Brooks, was a hail to Caesar, though the character (played by Joseph Bologna) was "King Kaiser" and the show retitled "The Comedy Cavalcade." Caesar thought Bologna wasn't bad (and affirmed that the drunk Peter O'Toole played was based on Errol Flynn, who did show up drunk for a show), but he wasn't happy with the intimation that the star was no writer. "No one ever handed me a script to do. I worked on every line with the writers every day before each show went on the air."

The fame of "Your Show of Shows" was rekindled for younger audiences by a 1973 film that compiled ten golden routines including such favorites as the mechanical Swiss clock and the brawling parody of "This Is Your Life."

In 1987 Caesar, Milton Berle and Danny Thomas starred in a television movie *Side by Side*. In the spring of 1988 they played Las Vegas and Atlantic City together in a "Legends of Comedy" show. In 1989 Caesar brought his *Sid Caesar and Company* show to Broadway, a nostalgic look back at sketches such as "The Penny Candy Gum Machine" (written 40 years earlier by Caesar himself) and material from "Your Show of Shows." The following year he reteamed with Imogene Coca for nightclub work, proving that classic comedy is classic forever. "The chemistry is the same," he said. "It's like we took a

Television's manic funnyman on "Your Show of Shows" during the "Golden Age of Comedy," Sid Caesar is a master of pantomime and dialect comedy. Photo from the author's collection.

long weekend off, like Rip Van Winkle. We just pick up where we left off."

He said, "Comedy is the truth. You can identify with the truth. Truth doesn't change . . . when we were poor, being poor, you can make fun of it because you have to make fun of it. You have to laugh at yourself. You find yourself laughing at things other people would cry at."

Caesar was cheered for bringing his great comedy from "then" back into "now." He added, ". . . do you know how precious that now is? You enjoy that now, enjoy it as much as you can, because no matter how much you want to hold on to that now, it's going to be a was, and if it's a bad now, you're going to have a bad was . . . they pile up in shoulda-coulda—I shoulda, I coulda—you must face reality. I faced reality. It's really not that hard . . . life has to be lived and enjoyed, and if you don't, you're a fool."

AUDIO: *Best of Comedy Relief*
AUTOBIOGRAPHY: *Where Have I Been?* (1982)

BROADWAY: *Make Mine Manhattan* (1948), *Little Me* (1962–63), *Sid Caesar and Company* (1989)

FILMS incl.: *Tars and Spars* (1946), *It's a Mad Mad Mad Mad World* (1963), *A Guide for the Married Man* (1967), *The Busy Body* (1967), *The Spirit Is Willing* (1967), *Ten from Your Show of Shows* (1973), *Silent Movie* (1975), *The Cheap Detective* (1978), *Grease* (1978), *The Fiendish Plot of Fu Manchu* (1980), *Over the Brooklyn Bridge* (1984), *Stoogemania* (1985), *Side by Side* (1987), *The Emperor's New Clothes* (1989)

TV: "Admiral Broadway Revue" (1949), "Your Show of Shows" (1950–54), "Caesar's Hour" (1954–57), "Sid Caesar Invites You" (1958), "The Sid Caesar Show" (1963–64)

VIDEO: *Your Show of Shows Vols. 1–8*

## GODFREY CAMBRIDGE

### (February 26, 1933–November 29, 1976)

Godfrey Cambridge was the first black stand-up comic to let loose with uninhibited racial comedy. His act was joyously, rebelliously filled with black slang and biting ironies. Back in the early 1960s, he followed Dick Gregory and Bill Cosby to national fame on television variety shows and nightclubs. He seemed to combine the styles of his two contemporaries. He was outgoing and friendly, like Cosby, but his subject matter was stinging and angry, like Gregory.

He described the time he was nearly knocked down by a car. The driver explained, "I didn't see you." Cambridge, in hilariously blustery disbelief: "Didn't see me? Big and black as I am he didn't see me?" At the time, some critics and audience members were a bit uncomfortable with Cambridge's unapologetic ethnicity. Just as Jews in the early 1960s complained to Jackie Mason that his accent was "too Jewish," some blacks were concerned with Cambridge's unapologetic flamboyance. In one routine he declared that the town of Yuma, Arizona was named by a black man. The black man, shot by a white sheriff, uttered his last dying words: "You mu . . ."

Very popular in Las Vegas, Cambridge told general jokes as a beleaguered everyman, then led audiences to understand that not every man had his added problems. A routine about swimming pools might begin with a gag about how embarrassed he felt about showing his 300-plus pounds in a swimsuit. Then he'd mention a swimming pool down South: "The black pool and the white pool are the same—except there's no water in the black pool. And the diving board is higher."

Cambridge was not from the South. In fact, his childhood was free from overt prejudice. His parents came from British Guiana and at his affluent Flushing High School in Queens he was viewed as an exotic foreign exchange student. He said it was later, at Hofstra University and struggling as an off-Broadway actor, that he experienced racial taunts and the mounting indignities that made him turn to extroverted comedy for release.

One of his classics was a black man's "Why Lord" speech to God: " 'Lord! Why did You make me so dark!' And the Lord says, 'My boy'—and he was wrong from the get-go, ya know, He says, 'the reason I made you so dark is so that when you're running through the jungle, the sun would not give you sunstroke.' He says, 'Lord! Why did you make my hair so coarse!' He said, '. . . so that when you're running through the jungle . . . your hair would not get caught in the brambles.' He said, 'Lord! Why did you make my legs so long?' '. . . so that when you're loping through the jungle, you would run very fast . . . any further questions?' 'Yeah, Lord—what the hell am I doin' in Cleveland?' "

Cambridge hit his stride shortly after Cosby, winning a Grammy nomination for his first album in 1964. He earned $33,000 a week in Las Vegas and began making films, including the cult classic *Watermelon Man*, about a white whose life changes drastically when his skin turns black. He also starred in some of the first big-budget movies intended for black audiences; including *Cotton Comes to Harlem* and *Come Back, Charleston Blue*. His ability to tread a line between humor and sorrow was evident in much of his acting work, both in guest spots on television (such as "O'Hara, U.S. Treasury") and films such as *The President's Analyst* in which he played a government agent who discovers a certain therapy in his license to kill.

Cambridge's weight helped make him boisterously unforgettable and imposing on stage, but it was a liability to his health and to his chances for getting good film roles. He was constantly dieting and gaining the weight back again. In 1976, while filming the television movie *Victory at Entebbe,* he suffered a sudden and fatal heart attack. He was playing the role of the mad Ugandan President Idi Amin. "An act of God," Amin claimed.

For many who recall Cambridge's stand-up years and enjoy his surviving films, he fulfilled some of the prophecy of his Flushing High School yearbook. Under his photo it read: "Unforgettable Godfrey Wonder Boy Cambridge, a laugh, a chat, a gay retort, perhaps sometimes a pun, a friend to all who knew him, a smile for everyone."

AUDIO: *Ready or Not* (Epic), *Them Cotton Pickin' Days Are Over* (Epic), *Toys with the World* (Epic), *Godfrey Cambridge Show Live in Las Vegas* (Epic)

BOOK: *Put-Downs and Put-Ons*

BROADWAY: *Take a Giant Step* (1956), *Androcles and the Lion* (1958), *Shakespeare in Harlem* (1959), *The Blacks* (1961), *Purlie Victorious* (1961), *The Living Premise* (1963), *How to Be a Jewish Mother* (1967)

FILMS incl.: *The Last Angry Man* (1959), *Gone Are the Days* (1963), *The Troublemaker* (1964), *The Busy Body* (1967), *The President's Analyst* (1967), *The Biggest Bundle of Them All* (1968), *Bye Bye Braverman* (1968), *The Watermelon Man* (1970), *Cotton Comes to Harlem* (1970), *The Biscuit Eater* (1972), *Come Back, Charleston Blue* (1972), *Beware the Blob* (aka *Son of the Blob*) (1972), *Friday Foster* (1975), *Scott Joplin* (1976)

## JOHN CANDY

### (October 31, 1950– )

Born in Ontario, John Candy hoped for a career as a hockey player until a knee injury hobbled that dream. He went to Centennial Community College in Toronto, majoring in journalism. While working as a salesman, he joined a local theater group and in 1971 was in "Creeps," a revue that co-starred Dan Aykroyd. Candy joined the Second City improvisational troupe in Chicago and then starred, with the Toronto branch, in the syndicated "SCTV" show. He won two Emmy awards as he took on impressions of bulky celebrities (Luciano Pavarotti, Orson Welles, Divine and Tip O'Neill) and created original characters, such as polka fan "Yosh Shmenge."

A member of the original "SCTV" show, John Candy has since become a colorful star and co-star in films such as *Uncle Buck, Splash* and *Planes, Trains and Automobiles.* Photo from the author's collection.

In early film roles, viewers saw a rather sour Candy. Rather than playing cherubic types (in the Fatty Arbuckle and Dom DeLuise mold), he tended to provide imposing contrast to the smaller, weaker comics in the cast. One of his better roles was as the gruff, slobbish half-human sidekick to little spaceman Rick Moranis in the Mel Brooks comedy *Spaceballs.* Another, playing a brash salesman opposite quiet and mortified Steve Martin in *Planes, Trains and Automobiles,* flirted with pathos.

Candy continued to play aggressive types in an age when antagonistic and "slob" comedy was very popular (Roseanne Arnold and "The Simpsons" leading the way on television). The ad campaign for 1989's *Uncle Buck* enthused: "He's crude! He's crass!" Critic Kathleen Carroll wrote in the *New York Daily News* that *Uncle Buck* was "another one-joke comedy . . . ultimately so bland and predictable."

From time to time Candy has tried to vary his diet of unpalatable screen roles, most notably in

*Only the Lonely,* a film that attempted to add a dash of romance to his screen character.

FILMS: *Silent Partner* (1978), *The Blues Brothers* (1980), *Stripes* (1981), *Going Berserk* (1983), *Strange Brew* (1983), *National Lampoon's Vacation* (1983), *Splash* (1984), *Brewster's Millions* (1985), *Volunteers* (1985), *Summer Rental* (1985), *Armed and Dangerous* (1986), *Find the Lady* (1986), *Little Shop of Horrors* (1986), *Spaceballs* (1987), *Planes, Trains and Automobiles* (1987), *The Great Outdoors* (1988), *Who's Harry Crumb?* (1989), *Uncle Buck* (1989), *Home Alone* (1990), *Nothing But Trouble* (1990), *The Rescuers Down Under* (1990), *Only the Lonely* (1991), *Once Upon a Crime* (1992)

TV: "Second City TV" (1977–79), "SCTV Network 90" (1981–83), "Camp Candy" (1989)

VIDEO: *Big City Comedy, The Last Polka, Comedy Music Videos*

## JUDY CANOVA

### (Juliette Canova, November 20, 1916–August 5, 1983)

A hillbilly comedienne born in Florida, Judy Canova sang country tunes on radio with her mother and brother Zeke as The Canova Cracker Trio. Eventually teamed with her sister Anne as The Happiness Girls, the duo went to New York dressed as stereotyped rurals.

Though Judy had secret ambitions of being a straight singer, her face and figure typed her in comedy. The Happiness Girls often appeared on Rudy Vallee's radio show. Judy slowly emerged as the most talented member of the family, going to Hollywood for the film *In Caliente* mugging and maiming the tune "The Lady in Red."

The Canovas enjoyed a 13-week guest stint on "The Edgar Bergen Show" in 1938, but Judy's solo work, which had included the 1936 *Ziegfeld Follies,* began to dominate. She starred on Broadway in 1939's *Yokel Boy* with Buddy Ebsen and then made the film *Scatterbrain* in 1940 for Republic, her first starring role. The corn was never greener than in the scene in which she washed the floor with brushes attached to roller skates—a bit that goes back to Joseph Coyne in the 1907 Broadway show *The Girl from Kay's.*

Judy became Republic's top female star. She premiered her own radio show in 1943. The "Hee Haw" of its day, it stayed on the air for a decade.

"Don't you know the Order of the Bath?" Judy: "Why sure, on Saturday night it was Pa first, and then all the kids in the order of their ages."

Trying to sell bubble bath to a woman: "I tried some of that there bubble bath soap once. I sat in the bath for three hours drinkin' that stuff and I couldn't blow a single bubble!"

Canova's character was the homely, man-hungry stereotype. On one show someone declares, "Being denied the companionship of men is sometimes a healthy thing." Judy: "Take a look at the healthiest girl in California!"

In her heyday, hayseed Canova earned $8,000 a week. Her popularity began to diminish in the 1950s after she completed a series of films for Republic Studios. In real life, the gal who could never find a man was married four times. And in real life, her wish to be taken seriously surfaced in interviews. Her description of herself: "Moody and generally unhappy. I'm a comedienne."

AUDIO: *Miss Country USA* (Craftsman), *Featuring Judy Canova* (Viking), *Country Cousins* (Crown)

BROADWAY: *Calling All Stars* (1934), *The Ziegfeld Follies* (1936), *Yokel Boy* (1939)

FILMS incl.: *Going Highbrow* (1935), *In Caliente* (1935), *Artists and Models* (1937), *Thrill of a Lifetime* (1937), *Scatterbrain* (1940), *Puddin' Head* (1941), *Sleepytime Gal* (1942), *True to the Army* (1942), *Joan of Ozark* (1942), *Chatterbox* (1943), *Sleepy Lagoon* (1943), *Louisiana Hayride* (1944), *Singing in the Corn* (1946), *Honeychile* (1951), *Oklahoma Annie* (1952), *The WAC from Walla Walla* (1952), *Untamed Heiress* (1954), *Carolina Cannonball* (1955), *Lay That Rifle Down* (1955), *Adventures of Huckleberry Finn* (1960), *Cannonball Run* (1976)

## CANTINFLAS

### (Mario Moreno Reyes, August 12, 1913–   )

In Mexico, the verb "cantinflear" means to talk gibberish—to speak in grand non sequiturs and say nothing. It may have come from "cantina," the word for a saloon and a place where people stagger out talking nonsense. A "cantinflas" is a funny character. And the greatest Latin comedian of them all was the epitome of a funny character: Cantinflas.

He was born Mario Moreno Reyes, and in his teens he worked in a variety of traveling shows. His parents were not happy with his decision to go into show business, so he took the name "Cantinflas."

As Cantinflas, the vaudevillian made the rounds, rising in popularity enough to make a film in 1941, *Neither Blood Nor Sand,* a parody of Tyrone Power's current *Blood and Sand* epic. Over the next two decades Cantinflas would make nearly 20 films for his Posa Films company, earning $100,000 a month in royalties. The man with the two tiny flecks of mustache posed on either side of his upper lip was a great star throughout Latin America and groomed for "cross-over" appeal.

*Around the World in 80 Days* and the star-studded *Pepe* failed to make Cantinflas an instant American star. He couldn't live up to Charlie Chaplin's announcement that he was "the world's greatest comedian," billing that had English-speaking audiences expecting a lot. In 1957 *Coronet* magazine reported, "To North Americans conditioned to the Bob Hope–Jack Benny brand of humor, Cantinflas may appear somewhat short of funny. . . . Cantinflas, in his classic role as the underdog, is funny mostly to other underdogs. And these form the vast majority in Mexico."

Cantinflas explained his film persona to interviewer Joe Hyams in 1960: "Cantinflas always tries to help everybody else, but what he needs most is someone to help him. But he never asks for himself. The Latin people have a difficult life, many problems. When they go to a theater to see Cantinflas he makes their problems seem small because his are so big. But he works them out and he hurts no one doing it. . . . Cantinflas wants nothing for himself. Only for you. So he doesn't get the girl. There is no sadness because you know he will get another girl. I don't want anybody to cry or be sad for Cantinflas."

AUTOBIOGRAPHY: *Cantinflas: Apologia de un humilde*
FILMS incl.: *Neither Blood Nor Sand* (1941), *Romeo and Juliet* (1944), *Ahi Esta El Detalle* (1946), *Around the World in 80 Days* (1956), *Pepe* (1959), *The Illiterate*

*One* (1960), *El Profe* (1972), *Don Quijote* (1976), *Condominium Janitor* (1976), *El Ministro Y Yo* (1978), *El Patrullero 777* (1978)

## EDDIE CANTOR

### (Isidore Itzkowitz, January 31, 1892–October 10, 1964)

Frank Fay once said, "Eddie Cantor must get very tired of having himself around." Milton Berle added: "Cantor had to fight for his laughs . . . Cantor wasn't born a funny man." George S. Kaufman wrote: "Cantor's humor is painted on like his blackface." Even the gracious Steve Allen agreed: "Eddie Cantor's humor bore no distinctive earmarks. It was simply the humor of the day." And, playing a Cantor look-alike in the film *Thank Your Lucky Stars,* Cantor himself grumbled, "You know, I can't stand that pop-eyed baboon!"

What made Cantor great? Enthusiastic salesmanship. His overpowering stage presence included, in a *New York Times* description, "prancing about, clapping his hands, rolling his eyes, [and] gay enthusiasm." His trademark was his set of huge "banjo eyes," which were accentuated in blackface when he refused to black up near his sensitive eyes, leaving huge white spaces. His style, which some now find irritating, silly and effeminate, was considered comic and charming years ago. The greatest star of Cantor's day, Al Jolson, regularly mugged effeminately and sang while making goofy, pouty-lipped faces and bulging eyes. Like Jolson, Cantor "sold" his songs, his biggest hit a line of salesmanship: "Potatoes Are Cheaper, Tomatoes Are Cheaper, Now's the Time to Fall in Love." Another hit was "Makin' Whoopee," the laughs coming again from Cantor's mincing delivery and the doubt that he ever made "whoopee" himself. Though he performed monologues on stage and on 78 rpm records, on radio he seemed more often the querulous straight man, arguing in a high-pitched voice with such stooges as The Mad Russian.

Eddie's parents both died before he was two. He was raised by his grandmother, Esther Kantrowitz. *Variety* and the *New York Times* have given his real name as Isidor Iskewitch, with Joe Franklin and Leslie Halliwell choosing Edward Israel Iskowitz.

Cantor, in *Take My Life,* says it was Isidore Itzkowitz. Back then he couldn't pronounce his grandma's simpler name and was registered in school as Isidore Kantor. He didn't stay in school much. He spent most of his time in poolrooms or on streets singing and doing comic impressions for spare change. He entered amateur contests and got into showbiz as an assistant to a juggling team, Bedini and Arthur. He joined "the" Gus Edwards troupe, doing a schoolroom sketch with cast-member George Jessel, and formed duos, first with Sammy Kessler in 1913 and then Al Lee in 1914. On his own, he finally got signed for Broadway's *Ziegfeld Follies* in 1917.

The ingratiating Cantor soon became one of Broadway's biggest stars. His first hit on his own was 1923's *Kid Boots,* which ran for three years. He made a silent film version of it with Clara Bow. *Whoopee* followed in 1928, running through 1930, netting Cantor $5,000 a week. In 1930 he made a movie short, *Insurance,* loaded with corny gags from his vaudeville days and the tune "Now That the Girls Are Wearing Long Dresses Men Can Keep Their Minds on Their Work." He had hits in the 1920s with bouncy novelties ("Yes We Have No Bananas") as well as bouncy straight tunes ("If You Knew Susie"). He received an amazing quarter of a million dollars to re-sign with Brunswick Records.

Though it was Jolson who made the first sound film, Cantor made one of the first lavish all-color musicals, *Whoopee* in 1930. It featured his hit "Makin' Whoopee" and presented him as a mild-mannered hypochondriac: "Last week I looked so terrible two undertakers left a deposit on me." Loaded with odd bits of vaudeville ("Where are you from?" "We moved"). Jewish in jokes and a dash of slapstick, it gives a good idea of what was endearing about Cantor. There were also some good moments in *Roman Scandals,* including the scene in which he goes back in time only to be seized by murderous Roman soldiers: "This is no fooling? I'm really living in Rome? If this is really Rome, you can't kill me 'cause I haven't been born yet! It wouldn't only be murder, it would be birth control!"

Cantor's cheerful optimism and impudence was a tonic during the depression, and though he lost all of his money in the stock market crash, he earned it back quickly with hit records and Broadway shows.

His better films show his enthusiasm and drive, and the comedy of a little man struggling against tough situations. He premiered on radio in 1931 and stayed on the air for 20 years. Though his image was lighthearted, Cantor himself was not. During the dark days when the notorious Father Coughlin's anti-Semitic speeches were carried on radio, Cantor spoke up against him. It cost him his radio show for a while, but Cantor held firm. Later his films were banned by several Arab countries. Cantor answered, "I have no desire to make any people laugh who have made my people cry. If our friends in the Middle East want to boycott my pictures, I just won't buy their camels."

A heart attack slowed him in 1952 and his health problems multiplied. He was given an honorary Academy Award in 1956 but within a few years was rarely able to make any public appearances at all. When his wife, Ida, died in 1962, he was too ill to attend the funeral.

He nostalgically recalled his show biz friends in the 1963 book *As I Remember It,* and died the following year, remembered fondly by a still large number of friends and fans. Talk show host Joe Franklin recalled one piece of advice he got from Cantor in 1953, which he posted on his office door: "It's Nice to Be Important, But It's More Important to Be Nice." Another person who recalled him with nostalgic appreciation was Allen Ginsberg, the poet. He remembered the way Cantor closed his show with the wistful "I love to spend this hour with you, as friend to friend, I'm sorry it's through." He said: "It was a really sad Jewish moment that was the high point of the week, I guess because he was Jewish and a national comedian, and everybody in the family identified with him."

AUDIO: *Best of Eddie Cantor* (Vik), *Date with Eddie Cantor* (Audio Fidelity), *Ida Sweet as Apple Cider* (Camden), *Ol' Banjo Eyes Is Back* (Pelican), *Sings* (Decca), *Makin' Whoopee* (Pro Arte)

AUTOBIOGRAPHIES: *My Life Is in Your Hands* (1928), *"Take My Life," As I Remember Them* (1963)

BOOKS: *Caught Short: A Saga of Wailing Wall Street* (1929); *Yoo Hoo Prosperity* (1929); *Your Next President* (1932); *Between the Acts; Who's Hooey; World's Book of Best Jokes*

BROADWAY: *Ziegfeld Follies* (1917, 1918, 1919), *Brevities* (1920), *Make It Snappy* (1922), *Kid Boots* (1923), *Whoopee* (1928)

FILMS incl.: *Kids Boots* (1926), *Special Delivery* (1927), *Glorifying the American Girl* (1929), *Whoopee* (1930), *Palmy Days* (1931), *The Kid from Spain* (1932), *Roman Scandals* (1933), *Kid Millions* (1934), *Strike Me Pink* (1936), *Ali Baba Goes to Town* (1937), *Forty Little Mothers* (1940), *Thank Your Lucky Stars* (1943), *Hollywood Canteen* (1944), *Show Business* (1944), *If You Knew Susie* (1948), *The Story of Will Rogers* (1952), *The Eddie Cantor Story* (1953)

TV: "The Colgate Comedy Hour" (1950–54), "Eddie Cantor Comedy Theater" (1954–55)

## GEORGE CARLIN

### (May 12, 1937–   )

Through five decades in comedy, George Carlin has not varied his personal style. He remains a likable monologist able to balance a clowning, zany streak with the sharp-edged wit to dissect words and emotions with cutting irony. Yet through these five decades, Carlin has changed emotionally and physically, reflecting the tumultuous shifts in culture and lifestyle from the 1950s to the 1990s.

He offered engaging nightclub patter in the 1950s and early '60s, cheerfully "hippy-dippy" humor in the late '60s, more crusading comedy in the '70s, slightly mellowed humor in the early '80s, and then more disillusioned, angry observations into the '90s. Yet through it all, his style has remained distinctly and identifiably his own.

Each step of the way Carlin produced gems of monology. There were his early, solid and silly routines from "The Indian Sergeant" ("Cut out the horseplay. You guys playin' with the horse—cut it out!") to Al Sleet, the weatherman who announced: "Tonight's forecast: dark!" These were followed by Lenny Bruce-like, banned-on-radio routines ("The Seven Words You Can't Say on TV") and gently philosophical and ironic observations ("A Place for My Stuff"). He was also known for comic querulousness, his Andy Rooney–styled questioning of words and phrases: "Undisputed heavyweight champion? Well, if it's undisputed, what's the fight-

Stand-up great George Carlin popularized the "Seven Words You Can't Say on TV." Photo from the author's collection.

ing all about? Selling like hotcakes? Is this the biggest-selling item?"

Born in New York City, Carlin grew up the "class clown." After quitting high school and nearly getting tossed out of the air force, he became a disc jockey in Louisiana. At 20 he moved on to WEZE in Boston and met comedian Jack Burns. They formed a partnership and eventually went out to California, where an impressed Lenny Bruce helped them find work. Some routines were standard (George as a punch-drunk boxer), but others dabbled in the new freedom of "sick" comedy (a television commercial for the "Lolita Kit" that lets little girls "pick up a little cash after school").

Carlin went solo in 1962 and soon became a television regular, known for rubber-faced comedy (his first album cover contained dozens of funny faces taken in a subway photo booth) and clean, inoffensive material. In the late 1960s he and another "straight" comic, Richard Pryor, began to pursue comedy in the Lenny Bruce tradition. It began in 1970 when he was fired for using a four-letter word in concert at The Frontier Hotel in Las Vegas. A short time later a few satiric comments on the Vietnam War caused a storm at the mainstream Playboy Club.

Carlin was no longer willing to work in the restrictive casinos and nightclubs of the day. He found his audience at rock concerts. The change liberated his comedy and changed his delivery a bit. Since he had to work huge theaters opening for rock stars, he had to reach the crowd by using a lot of facial and physical cartooning. He noted, "You have to raise your voice above the din to be heard, to get their attention." He also tended to "talk down" to the crowd and acted out phrases ("I sent awaaaaaay for it"). Critics sometimes insisted Carlin's controversial routines (such as "The Seven Words You Can't Say on TV") were a lot milder and cuter than Lenny Bruce. That might have been true, but audiences got the message. So did the authorities, who, in a supposedly more liberal age, tried to censor Carlin as they had Bruce.

In 1972 Carlin was arrested in Milwaukee at an outdoor concert. The police worried that some children might be hearing his comedy. The disorderly conduct charge was later thrown out. When a radio station played a Carlin routine, announcing beforehand that the routine might be objectionable to some people, the Federal Communications Commission fined it. The case went all the way to the Supreme Court, where the radio station lost. Carlin continued to perform his "countercultural" routines and in the early 1970s was supported by enthusiastic fans who bought millions of his albums (his *AM & FM* and *Class Clown* discs were certified gold in 1973 and *Occupation Foole* went gold in 1976).

Carlin was a tireless stand-up performer through the 1970s. In the mid-1980s some of the wear and tear began to show. Ironically, he and Richard Pryor had similar problems, cocaine abuse and a heart attack. While Pryor made fun of it all on stage, Carlin kept the experience private. He told the author in 1989, "I feel vaguely embarrassed and presumptuous to present my life and my story as the subject for an evening's entertainment. My imagination is aroused more by the things that are out there in the world that all of us deal with . . . language has always been a favorite subject for me. . . . I don't find my own story important."

For a time his stand-up turned more aggressive and bitter, with growling routines about the mindless violence of football and even some rare ringsider abuse ("You're wearing an earring, sir? How about a Kotex? Are you wearing one of them too?"). What seemed to be eating at him was an unfulfilled desire: "I always wanted to be a movie actor like Danny Kaye. My plan was to become a radio disc jockey first and then go into nightclubs as a comedian. My theory was, if I was a good enough comedian, they'd have to let me in the movies the way they let him in."

Carlin was able to land his first important role in a movie, a burned-out hippie in *Outrageous Fortune*. He later starred in the hit *Bill and Ted's Excellent Adventure*. Whether he made films or maintained his heavy schedule performing stand-up, he had enthusiastic audiences waiting. Rather modestly, he characterized himself simply as "just someone who is open to things that surprise and delight and make you wonder; things that are ironic or absurd. I like contemplating silliness."

Though still young, in 1990 Carlin was perceived as "The Grand Old Man of Counterculture" in a *New York Times* review. Television interviewer Bob Costas asked him, "Do you think you're as funny now as you were in the 1970s and '60s?" He answered, "I'm doing my best work. I'm the only one that can ever really be the judge because I do it for myself. The fact that the audience is there is wonderful, but I do it for me. And I'm thinking better than I ever have, my observations I think stand out in better. . . . I'm having more fun with it than I ever have. I know that."

AUDIO: *The Original George Carlin* (ERA, aka *At the Playboy Club with George Carlin and Jack Burns* and *Killer Carlin*), *Take Offs and Put Ons* (RCA), *AM and FM* (Little David), *Class Clown* (Little David), *Occupation Foole* (Little David), *Toledo Window Box* (Little David), *An Evening with Wally Lando* (Little David), *On the Road* (Little David), *Indecent Exposure* (Little David), *A Place for My Stuff* (Atlantic), *The Carlin Collection* (Little David), *Carlin on Campus* (Eardrum), *Playin' with Your Head* (Eardrum),

*What Am I Doing in New Jersey* (Eardrum), *Parental Advisory: Explicit Lyrics* (Eardrum)

BOOK: *Sometimes a Little Brain Damage Can Help* (1984)

FILMS incl.: *With Six You Get Eggroll* (1966), *Car Wash* (1976), *Americathon* (1979), *Outrageous Fortune* (1986), *Justin Case* (1988), *Bill and Ted's Excellent Adventure* (1988), *Working Trash* (1990), *The Prince of Tides* (1991), *Bill and Ted's Bogus Journey* (1991)

TV: "The Kraft Summer Music Hall" (1966), "That Girl" (1966–67), "Away We Go" (1967), "Tony Orlando and Dawn" (1976), "Apt 2C" (1986), "Shining Time Station" (1991)

VIDEOS: *Carlin Live on Campus; Carlin at Carnegie Hall; Playin' with Your Head; A Toast to Lenny Bruce; Saturday Night Live: George Carlin*

## ALAN CARNEY (See BROWN and CARNEY.)

## ART CARNEY

### (November 4, 1918–    )

"Piggy Wiggy Woo" isn't as famous as "Hey there, Ralphie boy!" but that was the beginning of Art Carney's career—singing "Piggy Wiggy Woo" with Horace Heidt's Orchestra.

Shy and quiet in his school, in Mount Vernon, New York, Carney was noticed only when he imitated the teachers and did some comedy for the other kids. That got him an audience—the principal. He was left back one year. When he finally graduated, he found a job in a jewelry store, and might have stayed there for years if not for a brother who worked for the MCA agency. He got a booking with Horace Heidt and slowly Art blossomed as a singer/comedian. He even appeared in the Heidt film *Pot o' Gold* in 1941.

Hoping to establish a career on his own, Carney tried stand-up comedy and impressions but couldn't work up an act that would withstand hecklers and boozers. He found a better atmosphere for his talents in radio. He was versatile enough for comedy and drama, and his imitation of Roosevelt on "March of Time" was a great success.

Drafted into the Army in 1944, Carney could have found an easy job entertaining the troops, but it was his nature to take the hand dealt him. It led him to Normandy where an exploding shell slammed him to the ground and smashed through his right thigh. He limped out of the hospital nine months later, one leg slightly shorter than the other.

Carney appeared on Henry Morgan's radio show in the late 1940s and moved on to become a regular on Morey Amsterdam's television show (playing a waiter). More television work followed, including some bit parts on Jackie Gleason's series "Cavalcade of Stars." The Gleason/Carney chemistry clicked, and when the two teamed up for sketches as Ralph the bus driver and Ed Norton the sewer worker, television had its equivalent of Laurel and Hardy. Carney agrees with the comparison: "Sure, it's all absolutely there. We were the Brooklyn-type version, the same sort of fumblers. I'd always loved Laurel and Hardy, I could see their shorts over and over again, and people are always telling me they have the same feeling about the Honeymooners shows. You know the plots, you sit back and even though you know exactly what's coming it doesn't matter, you still enjoy it. Even more *because* you know it."

The one prime season of "The Honeymooners" produced dozens of classic episodes and a strong cult that delighted in Carney's unique trademarks. He made his friend fume and audiences chuckle over his time-wasting habit of rolling up his sleeves, adjusting his posture and testing the flexibility of his fingers before doing something as simple as playing the piano or writing something on a piece of paper. He won laughs with a simple, goofy cry of "Hey there, Ralphie boy!" And he was a source of great wisdom: "As we say in the sewer, time and tide wait for no man."

Eventually, for Carney's artistic and emotional well-being, he had to leave his complying, second-banana role with Gleason. He played opposite Siobhan McKenna as a philandering husband in *The Rope Dancers* on Broadway. He appeared in television versions of *Harvey* (1958) and *Our Town* (1959). He was in a "Twilight Zone" Christmas episode that even those who hate Christmas sentimentality enjoy. He often starred on television drama shows including "Studio One" and "Kraft Theater." Though critics applauded Carney, he tended to see only the flaws in his performance. One of his quirks was to get a haircut after a show, whether it was needed or not. He said at the time it was "a compulsion. I feel sort of dirty from the show—and I want to start off clean again."

In 1960 he starred in nine television specials and then went to Broadway in *Take Her She's Mine*. In 1965 he starred as the original Felix Ungar opposite Walter Matthau in *The Odd Couple*. He was a real-life Felix, insisting his magazines and his spare change be stacked neatly on his desk. He also had a full medicine chest loaded with cures for real or imagined ailments. Carney's real-life ailments led him to drop out of the show, his agent citing "depression and nervousness." Carney, mild-mannered and overly considerate of others, never complained or raised a fuss when other actors had tantrums or made demands. He kept his anger inside, as well as his own worries, self-doubt and nervousness. In the evenings, he drank. And after many years, it had taken its toll.

Carney recovered in a Connecticut sanitarium. Old friend Jackie Gleason helped out, casting Art in new "Honeymooners" sketches on his show. His alcoholism under control, Carney was once more the classic "Ed Norton." Then he began to add new characters. Young viewers knew him as "The Archer" on "Batman" in 1966. In 1974 he won an Oscar for *Harry and Tonto*, a key role in which he played a crusty, humorous and realistic comedy character. It would be followed by many more serio-comic films including *Going in Style* and *The Late Show*. While he would still be "Ed Norton" to many, there were now an equal number of fans who recognized him simply as Art Carney.

In accepting his Academy Award, Carney recalled the director saying "Don't be afraid of playing an old man—you are one!" He later recalled, "It took me 37 years to star in my first picture. I got top billing over a cat. When I did *Tonto* I needed lots of makeup. Now, for all elderly parts, I hardly use any at all . . . playing elderly parts makes me happy for all seniors. Life is available to anyone, no matter what age. All you have to do is grab it. I grabbed it."

Carney has won six Emmy awards, five for his work with Jackie Gleason and one for supporting James Cagney in *Terrible Joe Moran*. In 1985 Carney and Gleason reteamed for *Izzy and Moe*, a television "buddy" movie about aging crimefighters. Gleason's

death ended rumors of a new "Honeymooners" special. Ironically, Gleason's discovery of old kinescope "Lost Honeymooners" sketches from his early variety shows led to a syndicated collection of episodes that were added to the originals in syndication.

Carney was amazed to see his fan mail increase over the years. Ed Norton was never too far from his thoughts. And he still owned the famous battered Ed Norton hat from the show. It wasn't a prop. As he once said, "It's mine. I bought it in 1935 when I was in high school."

Though it was rough at times, Art Carney's star has remained bright for over 40 years, on television, in films and on stage. "Everything in this whole business is timing," he once said. "I don't just mean timing your performance. I mean, your life's timing."

BROADWAY: *The Rope Dancers, Take Her She's Mine, The Odd Couple* (1965)

FILMS incl.: *The Yellow Rolls Royce* (1964), *A Guide for the Married Man* (1967), *Harry and Tonto* (1974), *W. W. and the Dixie Dance Kings* (1975), *Won Ton Ton The Dog That Saved Hollywood* (1976), *Lanigan's Rabbi* (1976), *The Late Show* (1977), *Scott Joplin* (1977), *House Calls* (1978), *Movie Movie* (1978), *Sunburn* (1979), *Going in Style* (1979), *Terrible Joe Moran* (1984), *The Undergrads* (1984), *Izzy and Moe* (1985), *Miracle of the Heart* (1986), *Night Friend* (1987), *Where Pigeons Go to Die* (1990)

TV: "The Morey Amsterdam Show" (1948–50), "Cavalcade of Stars" (1950–52), "Henry Morgan's Great Talent Hunt" (1951), "The Jackie Gleason Show" (1951–55), "The Honeymooners" (1955–56), "The Jackie Gleason Show" (1956–57, 1966–70), "Lanigan's Rabbi" (1977)

VIDEO: *Fairie Tale Theater: The Emperor's New Clothes; The Honeymooners Hidden Episodes 1–17; My Man Norton*

## JACK CARSON

### (John Elmer Carson, October 27, 1910–January 2, 1963)

A little bit too heavy (six foot two and 200 pounds) to be a leading man, Carson was usually cast as the good-natured lug or the insufferable wise guy. One film, *Girl Crazy,* offered both sides of his personality. He starts out as the hilarious lug (due to a sitcom misunderstanding, he's surprised to find Myrna Loy seemingly attracted to him). Then he turns into the obnoxious boor (once smitten, he won't leave her alone).

Born in Manitoba, Canada, Carson went to Carleton College in Minnesota. He toured in vaudeville, partnering with Dave Willock as Willock and Carson. After working as a singer and master of ceremonies at the Tower Theater in Kansas City in 1935, he went to Hollywood to appear in musical comedies. Early in his career critics compared him to Jack Oakie, at least in general size and build. He had a tougher edge than Oakie, which enabled him to play the heavy in comedy (he was Red Skelton's arrogant competition in *The Good Humor Man*) and in a few successful dramas (he needled James Mason cruelly in *A Star Is Born*).

Though he could play in a wide variety of films, Carson admitted in the late 1950s that he preferred comedy: "I'm best at making people laugh, at entertainment. They don't want me for the morbid oversexed stuff Hollywood is turning out nowadays."

Carson married for the fourth time in 1961. In August 1963, while playing in a New Jersey summer stock production of *Critic's Choice,* he became ill. Cancer was diagnosed and he died only a few months later.

BROADWAY: *Of Thee I Sing* (1952)

FILMS incl.: *You Only Live Once* (1937), *Stage Door* (1937), *Too Many Wives* (1937), *It Could Happen to You* (1937), *The Toast of New York* (1937), *Crashing Hollywood* (1938), *Bringing Up Baby* (1938), *Everybody's Doing It* (1938), *Go Chase Yourself* (1938), *Having a Wonderful Time* (1938), *Mr. Smith Goes to Washington* (1939), *Destry Rides Again* (1939), *Young As You Feel* (1940), *Sandy Gets Her Man* (1940), *Mr. and Mrs. Smith* (1941), *The Strawberry Blonde* (1941), *Love Crazy* (1941), *The Bride Came COD* (1941), *Blues in the Night* (1941), *The Male Animal* (1942), *Princess O'Rourke* (1943), *Thank Your Lucky Stars* (1943), *Arsenic and Old Lace* (1944), *Make Your Own Bed* (1944), *Hollywood Canteen* (1944), *Roughly Speaking* (1945), *April Showers* (1948), *Two Guys from Texas* (1948), *It's a Great Feeling* (1949), *The Good Humor Man* (1950), *The Groom Wore Spurs* (1951), *Dangerous When Wet* (1953), *Red Garters* (1954), *A Star Is Born* (1954), *Phfft* (1954), *Ain't Misbehavin'* (1955), *Rally Round the Flag Boys* (1958), *King of the Roaring 20s* (1961)

TV: "All Star Revue" (1950–52), "The U.S. Royal Showcase" (1952)

## JOHNNY CARSON

### (October 23, 1925– )

Johnny Carson's 30-year tenure as host of "The Tonight Show" has made him a legend. He has become as famous as his three main influences, the men who he chronicled in his college thesis on the art of radio comedy. Carson combines the warm, pleasant, day-to-day appeal of Jack Benny, the naughty wise-guy spirit of Bob Hope and the wit of Fred Allen into a package uniquely his own.

From his late-night time slot at 11:30, he spent three decades sending a nation to bed with a monologue of jokes, sketches and amusing interviews with the biggest and brightest stars. Through the years and many traumatic experiences for the country (assassinations and disasters) and for himself (ranging from death threats to three divorces), nothing seemed to affect the cool, self-assured and professional style Carson exhibited each night. At first critics labeled Carson the opium of the masses or America's night-light, but over the years they began to appreciate his considerable skills as a comedian, his mastery of monology, his ability in sketch and character comedy, and his light, witty touch with celebrity interviews. He soon took his place among the most liked, most durable and most trusted figures television has produced, including Lucille Ball, Walter Cronkite and Ed Sullivan.

Born in Corning, Iowa, Carson grew up in nearby Avoca and later in Norfolk, Nebraska. A shy kid, he learned magic tricks to call attention to himself and win admirers, and as "The Great Carsoni" even made some spare change with local shows. After World War II he worked on Omaha radio and television. Good-looking, respectful but possessing a naughty streak, he recalled getting in trouble even back then for stunts and jokes: "One of the first jokes I ever told: A guy went to Mars. His friend

Johnny Carson, the king of the late-night talk show. His record of 30 continuous years of television comedy may never be broken. Photo from the author's collection.

said, 'Are the people any different?' He said, 'No, the men look like men. The women, hell, there's a little difference. The breasts are on the back.' The guy says, 'That's crazy.' His friend said, 'It's wonderful for dancing!' "

After a long drive to California, using up much of his savings, Carson struggled before finding work as an announcer. He went to television with the local "Carson's Cellar," an experimental comedy show in 1951 to 1953, and began writing for Red Skelton. When Skelton knocked himself out on a prop door, Carson went on in his place, earning good reviews. Subsequent quiz and variety shows were disappointing, but "Who Do You Trust?" a daytime show with comedy interviews similar to Groucho Marx's "You Bet Your Life," won him increasing fame and attention.

Carson remained with the show, turning down a role in the new Broadway musical *Bye Bye Birdie* (it went to Dick Van Dyke). He and Van Dyke were later up for the same role in a sitcom. Dick won out and "The Dick Van Dyke Show" became a hit. But Carson would get his chance at stardom when he replaced Jack Paar as host of "The Tonight Show."

Carson offered a distinct change from Paar. He was cool, in control and self-assured. He steered the show away from controversy, favoring guests who could ad lib and entertain. He resurrected some aspects of "The Tonight Show" when it was hosted by Steve Allen. He performed in sketches and had regular segments for the alter egos he developed, such as the aging "Aunt Blabby," redneck "Floyd Turbo," failed magician "El Moldo," television pitchman "Art Fern" and the most popular, seer and psychic "Karnak the Magnificent."

While the influence of past comics and contemporaries was obvious (there was a strong dash of Jonathan Winters in "Aunt Blabby" and Gleason's voice in "Art Fern"), Carson, in turn, influenced a new generation of comedians. They admired his effortless, relaxed monolgue style. Many were in awe of his ability to walk out and perform "cold" five to eight minutes of untried material. Part of his style was to winkingly make the audience his co-conspirators in putting the routine over. If he started a joke with "It was so hot today . . ." someone would eventually shout "How hot was it?" In an aside he might point out that he was going for "the biggie," or that he was "heading for the dumper" after a few bombs in a row. The audience shared Johnny's predicament and were rooting for him. Over the years he raised the sophistication level of his audience by conditioning them to accept political jokes and offbeat gags; this kind of humor was previously available only in nightclubs via a Mort Sahl or Jonathan Winters.

Carson became so well known for his monologues and for "The Tonight Show" that he rarely ventured from it, playing Las Vegas resorts from time to time but rarely starring in a television special or film. He was offered Gene Wilder's role in *Blazing Saddles*, but turned Mel Brooks down. He explained, "I'm on every night playing myself, so it would be hard to make the transition."

For 30 years competing networks tried to shake viewers from their habit of watching "The Tonight Show" to no avail. While occasionally a talk show host won a few nights with a particular guest or some controversial publicity, none could rival Johnny Carson.

Carson's gags could be silly. During one of his bitter divorces he announced on the air that he would never marry again: "I resolve if I ever get hit in the face again with rice, it will be because I insulted a Chinese person." He could cover political subjects sharply but without offending the audience: "Did you know Richard Nixon is the only president whose formal portrait was painted by a police sketch artist?" And he was also capable of handling questions from the audience. Question: "What is the difference between Nebraska and California?" Carson: "Manure is cheaper in Nebraska and there's less of it."

Carson remained a man of paradox: friendly and smiling on television but shy and serious in person. He admitted feeling more comfortable performing in front of 20 million people than mixing with a half-dozen people at a party. Critics and fans were surprised to realize that after seeing him almost nightly for 30 years, they actually knew very little about him. Some of the intricacies of Carson's personality have been explained in biographies. Some are still elusive—which is part of the reason why, with a little cool and mystery to go with his warmth, humor and charm, Carson remains a personality viewers could watch year after year.

Carson had announced his May 1992 retirement a year in advance. As the day approached, the tributes began to pour in. Perhaps the simplest came from Elizabeth Taylor, who had never been a guest on his program. Making her belated debut on a February 1992 show, she said, "I'm not plugging anything. I have nothing to sell. I really wanted to come on the show and thank you for 30 years of brilliant entertainment."

AUDIO: *Introduction to New York and the World's Fair* (Columbia), *Magic Moments from The Tonight Show* (Casablanca)

BIOGRAPHIES incl.: *Here's Johnny* (Ephron, 1968), *Heeere's Johnny* (Lardine, 1975), *King of the Night* (Leamur, 1989), *Johnny Tonight* (Tennis, 1980), *Johnny Carson* (R. Smith, 1987)

BOOKS: *Happiness Is a Dry Martini, Misery Is a Blind Date* (1967)

BROADWAY: *Tunnel of Love* (1958)

FILM: *Looking for Love* (1963)

TV: "Earn Your Vacation" (1954), "The Johnny Carson Show" (1955–56), "Who Do You Trust?" (1957–62), "The Tonight Show *Starring Johnny Carson*" (1962–92)

## JACK CARTER

### (Jack Chakrin, June 24, 1923–   )

Flashy and glib, Jack Carter became known in the late 1950s and '60s as one of the newest of the brash "top banana" comics, the motormouths who put over one-liners with frenzied charm. Often billed as "the Jack of all tirades" he replaced Phil Silvers on Broadway in *Top Banana* and starred in his own fast-paced variety shows. Before Milton Berle, he was one of the hosts of television's "Texaco Star Theater" and along with Jackie Gleason was a regular host of "Cavalcade of Stars."

The Brooklyn-born stand-up comic was very popular through the 1960s, appearing more than 50 times on "The Ed Sullivan Show." With mimicry, jokes, a bombastic song and a brightly charged smile, the woolly-haired comic was a frequent guest on many variety programs. When viewing tastes changed and variety shows became few, Carter's national visibility lessened, but he continued to tour in nightclubs, resorts and casinos.

In addition to stand-up work, Carter took occasional film roles (he played George Jessel in *Rainbow*), directed sitcoms (including several episodes of "Here's Lucy") and often appeared in television dramas, receiving Emmy nominations for two "Dr. Kildare" episodes. More recent credits include "Magnum P.I.," "Fantasy Island," "Amazing Stories," "The New Mike Hammer" and "Murder She Wrote." He starred in stock productions of *Last of the Red Hot Lovers, A Thousand Clowns, Little Me* and *Critic's Choice*. In the late 1980s he toured as Fagin in *Oliver* and appeared in the musical *Sugar* in Los Angeles. In 1989 he and Mickey Rooney were signed for a tour as *The Sunshine Boys*.

Though audiences appreciated him and could identify him easily thanks to his comic aggressiveness (similar to that of Phil Silvers) and his Milton Berle–like tendency toward comic fretfulness, Carter admitted that his average looks and lack of a defined character prevented him from becoming a true comic superstar. "For a performer, I'm very untheatrical. Milton Berle steals gags, Joe E. Lewis drinks, Buddy Hackett talks out of the side of his mouth in that beautiful nasal voice. What have I got going for me? Somebody up there doesn't like me, and I think it's me."

AUDIO: *Broadway ala Carter* (Aamco)

FILMS incl.: *The Horizontal Lieutenant* (1962), *Viva Las Vegas* (1964), *The Extraordinary Seaman* (1969), *Rainbow* (1974), *The Sex Symbol* (1974), *Hustle* (1975), *Amazing Dobermans* (1976), *The Happy Hooker Goes to Washington* (1980), *Alligator* (1980)), *History of the World Part I* (1981), *Funny Farm* (1982), *Hambone and Hillie* (1984)

TV: "American Minstrels of 1949" (1949), "Jack Carter and Company" (1949), "Cavalcade of Stars" (1949), "The Jack Carter Show" (1950–51)

## DANA CARVEY

### (April 2, 1955–    )

An impressionist/actor, Dana Carvey has become one of the more versatile members on television's "Saturday Night Live" in the late 1980s and early '90s, perfecting both mimicry of personalities and his own characters. He seems to specialize in know-it-alls. From real people, such as the loud Robin Leach and the lecturing George Bush, to his own creations, such as Hans the loud bodybuilder and the lecturing "Church Lady," Dana has carved out a gallery of self-important people.

He admits, "That's what the real fun of playing these characters is. It's making fun of those people who really feel they have the truth and the answers for everybody. Self-righteous, arrogant, 'I'm superior to you' people drive me nuts." Carvey even did an imitation of "Saturday Night Live" co-star Dennis Miller. Another favorite is Andy Rooney, spouting; "Ya ever wonder why people's faces are made of flesh? Why can't people's faces be made of Play-Doh? That way, if someone said something that annoyed you, you could just reach out, and, well mess up their face a little."

Born in Missoula, Montana, Carvey grew up in San Carlos, California and began performing stand-

up comedy in San Francisco in 1978. He found some acting work as well, taking small parts in films (a waiter in *This Is Spinal Tap*) and the role of Mickey Rooney's grandson in *One of the Boys*. A sitcom pilot, "Whacked Out" co-starring Desi Arnaz Jr., never made it to series even with Lucille Ball urging the audience to laugh. Carvey got married in 1983 and a few years later won recognition for playing the likable probation officer in *Tough Guys* with Kirk Douglas and Burt Lancaster.

On "Saturday Night Live" Carvey has been able to use his mild personality to underline his satire. Jay Leno enthused, "He's got a real pie-in-the-face AM sense of humor and a sophisticated FM routine for people who appreciate their comedy when it's more subtle." His two most popular routines, as George Bush and The Church Lady, are both broad and quietly satiric at the same time. Through the gags, Carvey's gestures and expressions capture the characters' underlying tensions. He gives Bush a lot of restless hand movements and the catch phrase, "It wouldn't be prudent." He explains that he arrived at Bush by performing "a cross between Mister Rogers and John Wayne's cadence."

The Church Lady, with her tensely twisted half smile and feverish sense of etiquette and propriety, is based on someone Carvey and his Lutheran family met in church: "I remember when my family would be late to church, we'd be kind of embarrassed, and we'd have to say, 'Hey, we had a barbecue, lighten up!' And those church ladies would go, 'Oh, I see, we come to church when it's conveeeeenient!'"

As the moderator of a television talk show called "Church Chat," the Church Lady (rarely called by her name, Enid Strict), interviewed guests with tongue-in-cheek sarcasm and cold friendliness. To one sexy actress, she huffed, "We like ourselves, don't we? Yes, especially with our bosoms pressed together and offered for the explicit viewing of the chestal area. Who dressed you this morning, Sally? Could it be—Satan?" When Rob Lowe appeared as a guest, fresh from a scandal involving pornographic videotapes he made with an adoring fan, The Church Lady took him over her knee as the crowd laughed and applauded. "Get out of his buttocks, Satan!" she shouted.

Her catch phrase is the artificially pleasant and dryly mocking "Isn't that special?" It made Carvey the most "special" member of the new "Saturday Night Live" cast. A few years later Carvey topped himself by topping his head with a long blond wig and playing a nerd convinced of his own hipness in the show's "Wayne's World" segments. These parodies envisioning a goofy, self-indulgent cable show—run by "babe"-obsessed mall teens—yielded a subsequent book and hit 1992 movie.

FILMS incl.: *This Is Spinal Tap* (1984), *Racing with the Moon* (1984), *Tough Guys* (1985), *Moving* (1988), *Opportunity Knocks* (1990), *Wayne's World* (1992)
TV: "One of the Boys" (1981), "Blue Thunder" (1984), "Saturday Night Live" (1986– )

## DICK CAVETT

### (November 19, 1936– )

In his days as a budding stand-up performer, Dick Cavett tried to bring to nightclubs erudite if not cerebral humor, the kind of wry wit he had loved when he was a child, listening to Fred Allen's radio show. Cavett talked about the bride who arrived at her wedding pregnant: "So everyone threw puffed rice." And he mentioned eating in a Chinese-German restaurant: "The food was great but an hour later you're hungry for power."

Born in Kearney, Nebraska, he never lost his fondness for his roots: "One of the most beautiful areas of the world is the Sand Hills of Nebraska. You travel through dreamy, rolling, beautiful countryside, seeing cattle and isolated windmills, and quiet." He did not live a rural lifestyle, however, adding, "I hate to disappoint Easterners by not knowing how to milk a cow." He graduated from Yale and developed a combination of down-to-earth boyishness and urban sophistication.

After writing for "The Tonight Show" under Jack Paar, Cavett achieved some measure of attention as an up-and-coming stand-up star, one of the few (along with Woody Allen and David Steinberg) to favor soft-spoken and intellectual humor. Cavett got his own talk show on daytime television in 1968 and the next year went opposite Johnny Carson. Cavett had admired Carson years earlier. They met for the first time when Johnny was a professional magician in Nebraska and Dick an avid student.

Cavett's ratings hardly matched Carson's, but his show became a lively forum for the lost art of prickly, controversial conversation. Not since Paar's heyday did newspapers breathlessly quote the outrageous opinions and witty rejoinders bandied about by such regular guests as Norman Mailer, Groucho Marx and Mort Sahl. Cavett emerged as an amusing host who could embrace intellectuality one minute and prick the pretensions of it the next.

Cavett continued to perform monologues to open each show, still favoring Fred Allen–style wit: "My ABC show censor is affected by his job. He goes to the zoo and tries to shame monkeys by looking at them. . . . I'm not very self-conscious about my height but I was recently insulted by *Playgirl* magazine. They offered me half a centerfold."

Cavett has returned to star in periodic talk shows both for networks, syndication and cable. In the late 1980s he briefly turned to radio as host of "The Comedy Hour," spinning comedy albums and interviewing favorite comedians. Of his recurring role as talk show host he said, "It always seems like a tremendous long treadmill, like being in the waves and when one knocks you down you get up and try again." He always tried again. "Just when I come to the point where I say this has got to stop for a while, something will come up that makes me think this is just about the best job you could ever have."

AUTOBIOGRAPHIES: *Cavett* (1974), *Eye on Cavett* (1983)
BROADWAY: *Otherwise Engaged* (1977)
FILMS incl.: *Jimi Hendrix* (1984), *Nightmare on Elm Street III* (1987), *After School* (1988), *Moon Over Parador* (1988)
TV: "The Dick Cavett Show" (1968 daytime; 1969–1972 late night), "ABC Late Night" (1973–74), "The Dick Cavett Show" (1975), "The Dick Cavett Show" (PBS, 1978–81, USA cable 1986–87, NBC Cable 1989– )

## CHARLES CHAPLIN

### (April 16, 1889–December 25, 1977)

Around the world there is one symbol of comedy: Charles Chaplin. All a movie house needs to do is flash a poster of the little tramp with a cane—or just a close-up of his sadly expressive eyes and his little mustache—and people know that there's comedy waiting for them inside.

"I am known in parts of the world by people who have never heard of Jesus Christ," said Charles Spencer Chaplin. He remains the first true genius films have produced—writing, directing, acting, producing, even supplying the music for his movies.

Born in London, his career began at five when, after his mother was booed off stage during the nadir of her singing career, little Charlie came out to sing and clown in her place. The glory of that moment was soon snuffed by tragedy. His father had long since gone, and soon his mother was taken away to an asylum for the mentally ill. Some have theorized that Chaplin's tenderness toward his helpless mother translated into all the films in which the woman is an idealized heroine who usually is taken from him in a bittersweet ending.

Years in a Dickensian workhouse for orphans traumatized the boy. It was a long time before he got another chance to shine in a stage's spotlight. It happened after half brother Sydney joined Fred Karno's vaudeville troupe and took his young brother along. Chaplin soon became the star of the show, and on a visit to America, he stayed to join Mack Sennett for $150 a week.

After a shaky start and a lot of insecurity in the new country and new medium of film, Chaplin developed his character of "The Little Tramp." He wrote: "I wanted everything a contradiction: The pants baggy, the coat tight. The hat small and the shoes large. I was undecided whether to look old or young, but remembering Sennett had expected me to be a much older man, I added a small moustache, which, I reasoned, would add age without hiding my expression. . . . the moment I was dressed, the clothes and the make-up made me feel the person he was . . . a tramp, a gentleman, a poet, a dreamer, a lonely fellow, always hopeful of romance and adventure. He would have you believe he is a scientist, a musician, a duke, a polo player. However, he is not above picking up cigaret butts."

Volumes have been written on the art of Chaplin's modest short films. At the time, "art" was second to laughter as far as the public was concerned. They just loved little Charlie. And Chaplin himself insisted that "art" was second to money. He wanted financial success desperately, and got it when he left

Often called the first genius of film and comedy's grand master, Charlie Chaplin not only acted in his movies, he wrote, directed and created the musical scores. Photo from the author's collection.

Sennett for Essanay in 1915 ($1,250 a week), Mutual in 1916 (a contract for $250,000) and First National in 1918 (for $1,000,000). The studios got a bargain, for nearly each film was a classic, loaded with wildly inventive comedy and something new—pathos. Chaplin was not a human slapstick machine, he was a grand comic actor, and audiences felt his struggles as a little man in a big world, his complex emotions that could be wistful one minute, angry the next, sentimental in one scene, downright cruel in another.

Chaplin's genius could be dissected and described by relating virtually any five-minute segment of one of his films. But perhaps the essence of Chaplin can come through in one anecdote from actor David Niven. A director was fretting over how to stage a comedy scene in a serious drama. He asked Charlie for advice: How would he shoot a scene in which somebody falls on a banana peel? Do you show a close-up of the peel? Do you show the person walking first? Charlie answered, "Neither. You show the fat lady approaching, then you show the banana peel, then you show the fat lady and the banana peel together, then she steps over the banana peel and disappears down a manhole."

Chaplin had the temperament of genius, working and loving with fierce intensity. "I know he appeared stand-offish and superior," Stan Laurel recalled. "He wasn't, he wasn't at all . . . he is a very, very shy man. You could even say he is a desperately shy man." At times his love life got more headlines than his films, especially his stormy marriage to second wife 16-year-old Lolita McMurry (Lita Grey); his subsequent marriage to Paulette Goddard; and the ridiculously unjust scandal caused by a 1941 paternity case where, though medical evidence proved he was not the father, he was forced to pay child support. Chaplin the Casanova and Chaplin the outspoken political theorist (he was an alleged Communist) began to sour the public's appreciation for Chaplin the comedian. When Chaplin left the country on a vacation in 1952, he was suddenly barred from returning. Chaplin, his bride Oona O'Neill (daughter of playwright Eugene O'Neill) and their children (eventually eight—there were two more from his earlier marriage to Lita Gray) would take up permanent residence in Switzerland.

Chaplin's creative output diminished greatly during the 1940s, after his Academy Award–nominated first "real" talkie, *The Great Dictator*. Audiences in the 1940s did not understand the black humor of *Monsieur Verdoux*, the tale of a murderous bluebeard having difficulty with his latest subject (Martha Raye). It was a box-office failure. The political climate of the 1950s (when praising a blacklisted "Red" could be dangerous) was probably the main reason the bittersweet *Limelight*, Chaplin's portrait of an aging clown, was neglected when it was first released. Some had the temerity to challenge his title as the world's greatest comedian. Groucho Marx delighted in telling writers how envious Chaplin was of him: "You can talk," said Charlie, whose sound comedies were obviously short on verbal wit.

An aging Chaplin simply couldn't make a comeback with the frail situation comedy *The Countess from Hong Kong*. Once it was clear that there would be no more works of any kind from Chaplin, and

with the release (after many years) of his complete works to theaters, the old master was finally removed from the blacklist. He went back to the United States for an emotional tribute on April 10, 1972 and an honorary Academy Award. "Words seem . . . so futile, so feeble," he told the emotional crowd. In 1975 he was knighted. Today a statue of Chaplin (dressed in street clothes, not in his familiar "Tramp" outfit) stands in Trafalgar Square.

Sometimes the great Chaplin was still insecure. When he wasn't recognized often enough in a museum, the white-haired comedian told his daughter Geraldine, "I used to be famous, you know." But when Chaplin's films were reissued to theaters and brought to videocassette, the excitement proved that Chaplin's films were still masterpieces. Familiarity with Chaplin's work has tarnished him slightly— viewers who see modern comedies that have stolen his techniques or his sight gags are less impressed when viewing the originals, especially if these are the "public domain" versions that are flickery and difficult to watch. Critics who grew up studying Chaplin's films have sometimes taken him for granted, saving their praise for new discoveries or rediscoveries.

Chaplin is indeed an artist in every sense of the word and a great cultural figure. Just 20 minutes of Charlie Chaplin, vintage 1917, instantly recalls the only words that matter, the ones that were lavished on him the moment his image hit the screen. He was—and is—"the funniest man in the world."

AUTOBIOGRAPHIES: *Charlie Chaplin's Own Story; My Trip Abroad; My Wonderful Visit; My Autobiography; My Life in Pictures*

BIOGRAPHIES: *Charlie Chaplin: His Life and Art* (Bowman, 1974), *The Charlie Chaplin Fun Book* (A. Brown, 1915), *My Father Charlie Chaplin* (C. Chaplin Jr., 1960), *My Life with Chaplin* (Grey, 1966), *I Couldn't Smoke the Grass on My Father's Lawn* (M. Chaplin, 1966), *The Little Fellow* (Cotes and Nicklaus, 1966), *The Charlie Chaplin Scream Book* (Dell 1915), *Books on/by Chaplin* (Eriksson, 1980), *Charlie Chaplin's Parade* (Gold, 1930), *The Legend of Charlie Chaplin* (Haining, 1983), *Sir Charlie* (Hoyt, 1977), *Charlie Chaplin* (Huff, 1972), *The Movies and Charlie* (Jacobs, 1975), *Chaplin and the American Culture* (Maland, 1991), *Charlie Chaplin*

(McCabe, 1978), *Focus on Chaplin* (McCaffrey, 1971), *The Films of Charlie Chaplin* (McDonald, Conway and Ricci, 1965), *Chaplin* (Manvell, 1924), *The Immortal Tramp* (Minney, 1954), *The Great God Pan* (Payne, 1952), *Charlie Chaplin, Early Comedies* (Quigley, 1968), *The Chronicles of Charlie Chaplin* (Reed, 1917), *Chaplin* (J. Smith, 1984), *Chaplin, Last of the Clowns* (Tyler, 1985), *Chaplin* (Gifford, 1974), *Chaplin's Films* (Asplund, 1973), *Charlie Chaplin's One Man Show* (Kamin, 1984), *Chaplin, the Mirror of Opinion* (Robinson, 1984), *Chaplin: His Life and Art* (Robinson, 1985), *Chaplin vs. Chaplin* (Sullivan, 1965), *Chapliniana* (Geduld, 1987), *Charlie Chaplin, King of Tragedy* (Von Ulm, 1940)

FEATURE FILMS: *The Gold Rush* (1925), *The Circus* (1928), *City Lights* (1931), *Modern Times* (1936), *The Great Dictator* (1940), *Monsieur Verdoux* (1947), *Limelight* (1952), *A King in New York* (1970), *A Countess from Hong Kong* (1967)

SHORT FILMS incl.: *The Knockout* (1914), *Caught in a Cabaret* (1914), *Caught in the Rain* (1914), *A Busy Day* (1914), *Laughing Gas* (1914), *The Face on the Barroom Floor* (1914), *Dough and Dynamite* (1914), *His Prehistoric Past* (1914), *His New Job* (1915), *A Night Out* (1915), *The Champion* (1915), *In the Park* (1915), *Work* (1915), *A Night in the Show* (1915), *The Tramp* (1915), *The Floorwalker* (1916), *The Fireman* (1916), *The Vagabond* (1916), *One AM* (1916), *The Count* (1916), *The Pawnshop* (1916), *Behind the Screen* (1916), *The Rink* (1916), *Easy Street* (1917), *The Cure* (1917), *The Immigrant* (1917), *The Adventurer* (1917), *Shoulder Arms* (1918), *The Kid* (1921), *The Idle Class* (1921)

## GRAHAM CHAPMAN (See MONTY PYTHON'S FLYING CIRCUS.)

## CHARLEY CHASE

### (Charles Parrott, 1893–June 20, 1940)

A pencil-thin mustache gave him a dapper appearance, but the mild-mannered and nattily dressed Charley Chase was usually the victim of situations that tested his placidly smooth confidence and pushed him into slapstick mishaps.

Born in Baltimore, Chase was a song-and-dance man in vaudeville and performed monologues in an Irish accent. After working with Mack Sennett and directing comedies using his real name, Charles Parrott, Chase achieved his best success at Hal Roach Studios. He was similar to another Roach protégé, Harold Lloyd. Both used optimistic "average American" characters of the day (which may explain why both have had less appeal for modern viewers than the cartoonish-looking Chaplin, Laurel and Hardy, or cynical Keaton).

Chase's character was warmer than Lloyd's, his comedy often coming from embarrassing situations, his fluster accompanied by a shy little smile. He could do well in both domestic comedy as a hen-pecked married man and in situation comedy as a lighthearted, devil-may-care single. Unfortunately, he also tended to play obnoxious characters (*The Heckler*) and silly asses (the scoutmaster in *Midsummer Mush*), neither type guaranteeing much fan support.

A star in both the silent and sound eras, Chase made over 200 short films, yet no one ever considered syndicating them with the same zeal as Laurel and Hardy or the Our Gang series. Though several were and still are sparkling comedies, most are dated in style and attitude. Chase's brief appearances in feature films have done little to spark interest in him. One of his better known roles was as a silly conventioneer in Laurel and Hardy's *Sons of the Desert*.

When Chase's luck ran out with Roach, he went to Columbia where he starred in shorts and directed some of the early Three Stooges films. Some of his better efforts were *The Pip from Pittsburgh* (1931), *Fallen Arches* (1933) and *The Chases of Pimple Street* (1934). He drank heavily in the 1930s, despite warnings from his doctors. His death in 1940 was not particularly well publicized at the time.

BOOK: *The Films of Charley Chase* (Chaim)

FILMS incl.: *Ship Ahoy* (1919), *All Wet* (1924), *His Wooden Wedding* (1925), *Mighty Like a Moose* (1926), *What Women Did for Me* (1927), *The Way of All Pants* (1927), *Never the Dames Shall Meet* (1927), *The Real McCoy* (1930), *The Pip from Pittsburgh* (1931), *One of the Smiths* (1931), *What a Bozo* (1931), *The Tabasco Kid* (1932), *Midsummer Mush*

(1933), *Sons of the Desert* (1933), *The Chases of Pimple Street* (1934), *Kelly the Second* (1936), *The Wrong Miss Wright* (1937), *South of the Boudoir* (1940), *The Heckler* (1940)

VIDEO: *Hal Roach Comedy Classics Volumes 1 and 2*

## CHEVY CHASE

### (Cornelius Crane Chase, October 8, 1943–  )

Smug but cute Chevy Chase was the first big star to emerge from television's "Saturday Night Live." It was the start of the "me generation," and no one was more disarmingly bold about it than the man who began the show's "Weekend Update" mock newscasts with: "I'm Chevy Chase—and you're not!"

Boyishly handsome, teasingly coy, oozing a smart aleck's confidence and poker-faced naughty-boy bravado, Chase began developing his style in the late 1960s when he was briefly a part of Channel One, an underground comedy troupe. Their best work was gathered for *The Groove Tube* movie of 1970. Early on Chase demonstrated ways of making bratty, annoying sass pay off. He did "face ballet," twisting his face into a variety of grins and grimaces, moving his eyes and lips in time to recorded music. He offered "facial sarcasm," mimicking other performers (behind their backs, of course). He resurrected ancient comedy devices—such as the pratfall—and made them fresh with his showoff's enthusiasm.

An English major from Bard College, Chase grew up admiring Ernie Kovacs, Charlie Chaplin and Sid Caesar. He wasn't the class clown: "Real class clowns were obvious. I was very subtle, but I did get into trouble." Both a comedy writer and performer, Chase's credits included the off-Broadway show *Lemmings* in 1973, the "National Lampoon Radio Hour" and writing for The Smothers Brothers in 1974. "I was hired as head writer on "Saturday Night Live," he recalled, "but not as a performer. But Lorne [Michaels, the producer] wanted me to perform the stuff I was writing. . . . my experience mugging in front of the camera at Channel One . . . enabled me to play the camera well, particularly the newscast."

As the only performer with a regular solo spot (the "Weekend Update" comedy news), Chase quickly

Chevy Chase's good looks and wise guy personality made him a favorite among "Saturday Night Live" fans in the 1970s and film fans into the 1990s. Photo from the author's collection.

established his stardom, offering irreverent editorializing: "Gerald Ford: if he's so dumb, how come he's president?" Occasionally he made the most of deadpan subtlety. He was effective—heard but not seen—in a sketch playing a shallow "Land Shark" trying to gain access to a woman's apartment with cheesey excuses: "Candygram."

Chase was so popular he was rumored to be the top choice for host on "The Tonight Show" should Johnny Carson retire. Chase had his eye on a film career instead, and it began with some commercially successful romantic comedies (*Foul Play* and *Seems Like Old Times*).

Over the years he has aged into the role of hapless parent in a series of *National Lampoon's Vacation* films that led many to shake their heads over Chase's decline from a "cutting edge" comic into a bumbling cartoon of himself. One of the few modern comedians to insist on performing slapstick, Chase has paid the price for his pratfalls. An addiction to Percocet (prescribed after back problems) landed him in the Betty Ford Clinic in 1986. While there, he met both Mrs. Ford and his old comedy target President Gerald Ford, who for years had watched Chase do pratfalling impressions of him. Chase said Ford "acted very fatherly . . . and gave me advice, to the effect of 'Stick with it.' "

Easy slapstick became a big part of his film identity (a gag in *National Lampoon's European Vacation* has his car backing into Stonehenge, knocking the stones over like dominoes). Each new film, especially in the *Vacation* series—earned millions, but no critical praise. In 1989 he signed a contract with Warner Brothers worth over $20 million on a four-picture deal.

*People* magazine called him "terminally tiresome" and panned *National Lampoon's Christmas Vacation*, insisting laughing "depends on how much humor you find in dog drool, burping, intestinal gas, breast jokes (the mere mention of 'hooters' and 'nipples' is presumed, it would seem, to lead to guffaws), explosions, obscene gestures, obscene comments, broken windows, tantrums, car crashes, fires and threats."

Chase, now a family man himself with three kids at home, seemed well suited to his *Vacation* pictures. In the late 1980s, there was no way he could appease fans and critics demanding the anti-Establishment humor of his early days. It was out of style; conservatives were far more vocal than liberals. On a December 1989 "Tonight Show" Nancy Reagan, promoting her autobiography, was the first guest. After she left, Chase came out and told host Johnny Carson, "I actually have the book and I think that it's a good thing that she did that. Because for eight years to not be able to say anything significant . . . for that matter, Ron wasn't able to either. . . ." The boos seemed to outweigh the cheers. Carson replied, "Pretty gutsy. You wait till she's gone."

Hosting the 1988 Academy Awards show, Chase began the proceedings with "Good evening, Hollywood phonies." It got a laugh, but after one too many mild and mellow movies, he was ripe for being considered one of them. He wasn't even parodying phonies anymore. He had sincere empathy for his *Vacation* film character, Clark Griswold. He described him as "a well-intended incurable optimist

Dad, who is emotionally a child." After many light-hearted efforts, Chase spent a lot of time bringing the more complex *Memoirs of an Invisible Man* to the screen. He admitted, "to have to carry broad comedies for years after years after years—it can get boring."

In the spring of 1990 Chase was given an honorary doctorate from Bard College. He told the grads, "Avoid smoking, drugs, Bensonhurst, the Gaza Strip, bungee jumping, humorless people . . . and never call me!"

AUDIO: *National Lampoon Lemmings* (Banana), *National Lampoon Golden Turkey* (Epic), *The White Album* (Label 21)

FILMS incl.: *Groove Tube* (1974), *Tunnelvision* (1976), *Foul Play* (1978), *Caddyshack* (1980), *Oh Heavenly Dog* (1980), *Seems Like Old Times* (1980), *Modern Problems* (1981), *Under the Rainbow* (1981), *Deal of the Century* (1983), *National Lampoon's Vacation* (1983), *National Lampoon's European Vacation* (1985), *Fletch* (1985), *Spies Like Us* (1985), *Three Amigos* (1986), *Caddyshack II* (1988), *Funny Farm* (1988), *Fletch Lives* (1989), *National Lampoon's Christmas Vacation* (1989), *Memoirs of an Invisible Man* (1992)

TV: "Saturday Night Live" (1975–76)

VIDEOS: *The Best of Chevy Chase; Ernie Kovacs—Television's Original Genius; Saturday Night Live*

# CHEECH and CHONG

## Richard Marin, July 13, 1946–
## Tommy Chong, May 24, 1938–

The Bob and Ray of the scruffy drug culture, Cheech and Chong favored "recognition humor" based less on jokes than on creating familiar characters and situations that their audiences found true to life. A favorite sketch for fans was about a drug dealer trying to get a drugged-out dope to open a door: "It's Dave, let me in, man!" "Dave? Dave's not here." "No, man, I'm Dave!! Dave!!" "Dave?" "Yeah, man, it's Dave! Dave!" "Dave's not here."

Draft-dodging Richard Marin met ex-rock songwriter ("Does Your Mama Know About Me") Tommy Chong in the latter's Vancouver topless club. The hippies put on comedy sketches between the nude dance numbers, swiping old sex jokes and stealing from The Committee and other improv groups. With few comedy clubs around and nightclubs catering to conservative suit-and-tie stand-ups, Cheech and Chong opened the bill for rock acts. They were able to penetrate the hostile crowd by imitating comic casualties of the drug culture and doing "class clown" sketches, such as their parody of Catholic schoolteacher Sister Mary Elephant who loses her cool and begins to shout at her students, "SHUT UP!"

Some of their better sketches played off the character of a laid-back hippie (Chong) dealing with an excitable little Chicano. According to Chong, his partner "resisted that, he didn't want to do it, because he's a very well-educated Mexican American. I think there was a concerted effort on the part of a lot of Chicanos to leave that image behind. There's a real big difference between the Cheech character and Richard Marin. And he resisted, but I kind of talked him into it, and . . . he did it. . . . So I was really proud to have instigated Cheech to do that character."

Chong got his own laidback character from the guy who manned the lights when they worked in Vancouver: "He was like our critic . . . we'd do a bit and we'd come off stage and he'd say, 'That wasn't funny, man. That sucked. That was embarrassing, man.' And I just loved his attitude."

Critics hated Cheech and Chong's records and films. They didn't understand or know the ugly druggies and dopes the guys were satirizing, and the material seemed tedious and obnoxious. Even more irritating was the team's lack of skill in comedy basics: Their comedy "takes" were broad, their slapstick wooden and their attempts at ethnic accents outside the Latino or drug culture pathetic. To the critics' chagrin the team's early record albums went gold and their first movies were hits. Chong admitted, "There was a lot of bad acting" in the early films, "but what happened is it became the style."

The duo's popularity faltered as the hilarity of the 1960s and '70s pot-dominated drug culture turned to the tragedy of the cocaine/crack era of the '80s. They made only three albums between 1976 and 1985. Their hippie comedy became woefully dated and even gross-out adolescent humor couldn't save them (their last album had a report on a sushi bar serving "half-blind baby seal . . . just cook the back half and toast the flippers"). Of the team's breakup in 1985, Cheech said simply, "We had our own opinions on the way to proceed. Maybe the twain shall meet."

Cheech appeared solo in *Born in East L.A.* in 1987 and 1989's *Rude Awakening*, but the reviews remained negative. Of the latter, critic Roger Ebert declared Cheech's "patented 'Wow, man!' routine . . . is growing seriously old." Tommy Chong starred in 1990's *Far Out Man*, but the *Daily News* wrote that it was a "largely lame homemade melange of mostly archaic rock, sex and smoke jokes." Most film fans seemed more receptive toward Tommy's daughter, actress Rae Dawn Chong.

AUDIO: *Cheech and Chong* (Ode), *Big Bambu* (Ode), *Los Cochinos* (Ode), *Wedding Album* (Ode), *Let's Make a New Dope Deal* (Warner), *Sleeping Beauty* (Warner), *Cheech and Chong's Greatest Hit* (Warner), *Get Out of My Room* (MCA)

FILMS incl.: *Up in Smoke* (1978), *Cheech and Chong's Next Movie* (1980), *Cheech and Chong's Nice Dreams* (1981), *Things Are Tough All Over* (1982), *It Came from Hollywood* (1982), *Still Smokin'* (1983), *Yellowbeard* (1983), *Cheech and Chong's The Corsican Brothers* (1984)

VIDEO: *Get Out of My Room*

## CLARK and McCULLOUGH

### Bobby Clark, June 16, 1888–February 12, 1960
### Paul McCullough, 1883–March 25, 1936

Who was the comedian with the funny walk, seedy jacket, fast and punny delivery, waggling cigar and painted-on makeup? Who was the comedian who played in sketches and shows written by S. J. Perelman, Morrie Ryskind and George S. Kaufman? Groucho Marx, of course. And . . . Bobby Clark. Both were huge stars on Broadway—Clark stayed there. Now only a handful of short films made by Clark and his partner Paul McCullough support the accolades theater critics gave them.

The duo teamed in 1905. Both were born in Springfield, Ohio where they took classes in acrobatics together at the YMCA. In 1906 they worked as tumblers with Ringling Brothers. They were initially called The Jazzbo Brothers and later Sunshine and Roses. They didn't talk much at first, concentrating on visual gags and acrobatics. As Clark and McCullough, appearing in burlesque in 1917, they developed their trademark of fast-paced patter to go along with the slapstick. They enjoyed courtroom farce and had an early hit with a boxing routine with an elaborate "trick ring" with a trampoline in it that let Bobby literally jump over his opponent's head. Another involved sketch, now a cliché but fresh at the time, had Bobby the Lion Tamer confused between McCullough in a fake skin and a real lion. "That's great, you're sure fooling the audience," he'd shout to the real lion. "What a performance. You even smell like a lion!" Ultimately, he had to race around the stage trying to get away from the vicious beast. "That's the real lion in there with you!" he's told. His curtain line: "This is a hell of a time to tell me!"

The team headlined on Broadway through the 1920s, using their tried-and-true sketches in "The Music Box Revue" and similar variety shows. Clark had evolved a complete character by then—a freewheeling, lecherous, smiling demon sporting a cane and odd painted spectacles. It was during his strenuous slapstick days that Clark realized painted-on glasses were more expedient than real prop glasses. He kept the painted-on look through all his short films with his bulky, bearlike friend McCullough.

In the 1930s they made a series of two-reelers for RKO, many of them fast and zany. To a female co-star in Iceman's Ball wild Bobby cried, "You know, it's women like you who make men like me make women like you make men like me!" Their breezy style was evident in another classic, Odor in the Court, a farce that featured the men as lawyers: "No case too small, no fee too large." Their wacky streak showed in Kickin' the Crown Around, about a kingdom where there's prohibition—against the sale or consumption of salami!

During the 1930s Clark was clearly the star and McCullough had less and less to do. In some shows Bobby sang and clowned while McCullough sat out half the sketches. It's unclear whether McCullough was not physically well enough to perform and needed the rest or whether the lack of important work pushed him further into depression. Whichever it was, in 1936 his problems were serious enough to require treatment in a Massachusetts sanitarium.

One day in the small town of Medford, McCullough went into a barber shop for a shave. After it was over, he suddenly grabbed the razor and flayed at his neck and wrists. He died in the hospital two days later.

A shaken Clark said, "I think it was just something Paul couldn't help. Something that had been with him all the time and he didn't even know it."

A few months later Clark appeared alone in The Ziegfeld Follies of 1937. He went on to perform in many more sketch-oriented revues, singing such risqué songs as "Robert the Roue from Reading PA" and clowning as the top-billed star in Streets of Paris, a revue that featured a new team, Abbott and Costello. Clark's Broadway work continued through the 1940s, with Cole Porter writing songs especially for him in Mexican Hayride. He showed his versatility in comedy classics as well, including a well-received revival of The Rivals. He enjoyed his last stage show in 1956, playing the devil in a road company of Damn Yankees, a fitting end for a man known for impishly devilish stage comedy.

BROADWAY incl.: *The Music Box Revue* (1922), *The Music Box Revue* (1924), *The Ramblers* (1926), *Strike Up the Band* (1930), *Here Goes the Bride* (1931), *Walk a Little Faster* (1932), *Thumbs Up* (1934), *Ziegfeld Follies* (1936), *The Streets of Paris* (1939), *Star and Garter* (1942), *Mexican Hayride* (1944), *As the Girls Go* (1948)

FILMS incl.: *Two Flaming Youths* (1927), *Clark and McCullough in the Interview* (1928), *Clark and McCullough in the Honor System* (1928), *The Bath Between* (1929), *The Diplomats* (1929), *Knights Out* (1929), *All Steamed Up* (1929), *False Roomers* (1931), *A Melon Drama* (1931), *Scratch as Scratch Can* (1931), *The Iceman's Ball* (1932), *The Millionaire Cat* (1932), *Jitters the Butler* (1932), *The Millionaire Cat* (1932), *The Druggist's Dilemma* (1933), *Kickin' the Crown Around* (1933), *Bedlam of Beards* (1934), *In a Pig's Eye* (1934), *Odor in the Court* (1934), *Flying Down to Zero* (1935), *The Goldwyn Follies* (Clark alone, 1938)

## ANDREW DICE CLAY

### (Andrew Clay Silverstein, 1958)

Dubbed "The Hoodlum of Humor," Andrew Dice Clay began his career with dirty jokes and nursery rhymes swiped from old party albums. One of his most famous rhymes was: "Little Miss Muffet sat on a tuffet eating her curds and whey. Along came a spider and sat down beside her and said, 'What's in the bowl, bitch?' It didn't seem to matter that these lines, word for word, appear on a 25-year-old Sylvia Stoun lp.

What helped put over these ancient gags was his persona of the swaggering punk (complete with black leather jacket, greasy hair and a cigarette dangling from his mouth). It too was not original, most of it swiped from Henry Winkler's "Fonz" character on television's "Happy Days." His lack of originality annoyed other comics, but his appeal could not be ignored by club owners who found big crowds craving his antics.

Eventually Clay began to develop some original material, emerging as the white counterpart to Eddie Murphy. His first major national exposure was a 1988 HBO cable television special. Clay shared Murphy's reverse-racist riffs, putdowns of women and gays, and delight in colorful street slang. Clay's support was huge among lower-class whites who shared his comic frustrations and anger. One of Clay's most famous lines was not a joke but a complaint: "If you can't speak the language, get the fuck outta the country!" It drew cheers. Clay, like Murphy, ignored the criticism and pointed to his top-selling records and sellout concerts as proof of his worth. Celebrities in the audience included Cher, Bruce Willis, Sylvester Stallone and Billy Idol.

Clay's rising fame was fueled by controversy. If feminists complained about his abusive routines, he could point to the many women in the audience who were either turned on by his macho diffidence or appreciated his supposed satire of it. When MTV banned Clay from their channel after he deliberately performed some tasteless gags on an awards show, he responded, "MTV wants to tease everybody with sex. Look at how Madonna was rubbing herself and what Cher was wearing . . . and then they tell me not to say anything. It's unbelievable . . . I don't talk about drugs, sell crack or go around murdering people . . . I just make people laugh." And when Sinead O'Connor and Nora Dunn walked off "Saturday Night Live" when he was the guest host and a female keyboard player walked off when he appeared on "The Arsenio Hall Show," Clay switched gears and played the victim, sobbing to Hall, "When-

ever somebody is on top, they try to bring him down."

The Clay controversy extended to ABC's talk show "Nightline." Ted Koppel said of Clay, "He describes his sexual technique as, and I quote, 'So I say to the bitch, lose the bra or I'll cut you.' Is that funny?" Defender Lorne Michaels answered, "Obviously, the way you just said it, no . . . but the fact of it is . . . he's a character when he's on stage, he's a comedian. These things function as a safety valve." On a talk show with Diane Sawyer, Clay stressed that he was not his character: "If I was Dice to you right now, I'd be saying 'So let me ask you something honey, you live alone? You wearin' panties?' That's what Dice would do. He shocks." Sawyer answered, "Everybody asks me that all the time."

He was the target of endless attacks. From the *New York Times* in 1989: "aggressively hostile . . . downright vicious . . . the contempt expands to include anyone different—blacks, gays, the homeless, all those who might not fit into the macho, beer-drinking universe of a white lower middle class neighborhood. Indian and Pakistani citizens are described as 'urine-colored' . . . the audience is more unsettling than the star . . . raising clenched fists every time Dice gets off another offensive sally . . . he seems to ignore the fascistic reverberations." In 1990 the paper called him "a foul-mouthed, sexually obsessed, low-class bigot and misogynist." His personal life suffered (his ex-wife Kathy Swanson filed a $6 million breach of contract suit against him) and his "star" attitude enraged the pros of the business. When he gave Joan Rivers only four minutes' notice that he wasn't appearing on her daytime talk show, she shared her anger with her audience and then declared that if he was watching, "I want you to take one of those four-letter words out of your act—and add 'YOU' to it!"

The criticism got to Clay. When he couldn't bluff it out by staying in character, he went to the other extreme, insisting he was just playing a character. When he wasn't able to deflect attacks over his abuse of various ethnics in his act, he revealed what insiders had known all along, that he was ethnic himself, Andy Silverstein, a kid who attended Kingsborough Community College in Brooklyn and played drums in a bar mitzvah band. After the "Saturday Night Live" and "Arsenio Hall" debacles in the spring of 1990, Clay's hot streak turned ice cold. His debut film *The Adventures of Ford Fairlane* bombed and his follow-up concert film, the arrogantly titled *Dice Rules,* was put on hold for a year.

Clay has retained his core of fans and they have made his concerts sell-outs. He eventually cut down on the more overt ethnic slurs and gay baiting, concentrating more on dirty jokes that had guys in the audience cheering and the women (the main subjects of his comic complaints) chuckling too. *Time* magazine theorized "perhaps proving they are tough is as important to them as it is to men." In the 1990s he is still a big draw, just not such a big shot anymore. Says Clay, "People are nasty. Maybe that's why my humor has got a lot of attitude to it, 'cause nobody likes to see people do good."

AUDIO: *Dice* (Def American), *The Day the Laughter Died* (Def American), *Dice Rules* (Def American)

FILMS incl.: *Night Patrol* (1985), *Private Resort* (1985), *Pretty in Pink* (1986), *Casual Sex* (1988), *The Adventures of Ford Fairlane* (1990), *Dice Rules: The Concert Movie* (1991)

TV: "Crime Story" (1988)

VIDEOS: *Redd Foxx's Dirty Dirty Jokes; Rodney Dangerfield: Nothing Goes Right; Andrew Dice Clay Live*

## CLAYTON, JACKSON and DURANTE (See JIMMY DURANTE.)

## JOHN CLEESE (See also MONTY PYTHON'S FLYING CIRCUS.)

**(October 27, 1939–   )**

Imposingly tall, usually performing his lunacy with a severe, straight face, John Cleese dominated the Monty Python troupe and had a hand in two of their most popular sketches—as the glaring, angry owner of a dead "ex-parrot" and as the seriously dedicated "Minister of Silly Walks." He also portrayed one of the show's few continuing characters—a stern BBC newscaster whose catch phrase was a monotonous "And now for something completely different."

Cleese went on to become the most successful solo comedian of the bunch, starring in a number of hit films and the television series "Fawlty Towers," which became almost as much of a cult classic as the Python series.

Less imposing early in life, Cleese recalled, "I was an immensely weak boy and consequently was bullied a lot." Born in Weston-super-Mare, a resort in Bristol Bay, England he studied law at Downing College, Cambridge and earned a degree. At the same time he starred in comedy revues that ultimately became *The Cambridge Circus,* a show that went to Broadway in 1964. (While in New York Cleese sat in on the recording of the Doud and Robin album *Welcome to the LBJ Ranch;* fans can see him in the audience on the album cover). The best sketch featured Cleese as a prosecuting attorney: "Would I be right in imagining that your wife recently returned from the West Indies?" "Yes." "Jamaica?" "Objection!"

Cleese appeared on Broadway in *Half a Sixpence* and then went back to England to work as both writer and actor on the radio series "I'm Sorry I'll Read That Again" and on the 1967 television series "At Last The 1948 Show" with Graham Chapman and Marty Feldman. A highlight of the latter was Cleese singing "I've Got a Ferret Sticking Up My Nose . . . how it got there I can't tell, but now it's there it hurts like hell. And what is more it radically affects my sense of smell."

Cleese also worked as a writer and performer on David Frost's "Frost Report." Eventually he, Chapman and others from the Frost show teamed to form Monty Python's Flying Circus. After the show's run ended, and in the midst of various Python movies, Cleese co-wrote and co-starred in "Fawlty Towers," a series about a petty, frustrated hotel owner (Basil Fawlty). The show raised situation comedy to new heights of raging intensity. When faced with a problem caused by his own ego, pomposity, narrow morality or sneering misogyny and misanthropy, Basil Fawlty was driven into hilarious extremes of crazed fury or masochistic smiling delirium. He would either beat (usually Manuel, the servant) or be beaten (by his nattering, sharp-tongued wife). Sometimes the frustrations would literally double him over, turning the nearly six-and-a-half-foot tower of strength into a fist-clenching, impotent, hapless mute.

Cleese's therapist, Robin Skynner (who co-wrote a book on family life with Cleese), described Fawlty as "paranoid. He blames everyone else . . . how stupid and inconsiderate other people are, while preserving an image of himself as morally perfect.

People like this need to use their opponents as dustbins, somewhere they can dump all the bits of themselves they can't accept. So, they need to hate their opponents, to keep themselves sane. And he's depressed, too, though he couldn't admit it. He spends his life sending out signals to everyone else that it's their fault for making his life so miserable."

Cleese's solo film career was not initially successful. His first films were strangely tied to archaic British comedy traditions. The slow-paced *Clockwise*, for example, chronicled the frustrations that gradually undo the efficiency of a pompous headmaster. But the comically sadistic *A Fish Called Wanda* firmly established Cleese's film stardom. He parlayed it into a series of lucrative radio and television commercials that emphasize his mellower, less angry personality.

In an interview for the British magazine *Blitz*, Steve Martin was asked, "Do you think you're the funniest man in the world?" Steve answered: "No. John Cleese is."

AUDIO: *The Complete Fawlty Towers* (BBC), *Sorry, I'll Read that Again* (EMI), *A Poke in the Eye with a Sharp Stick* (Transatlantic), *The Mermaid Frolics* (Polydor)

BROADWAY: *Cambridge Circus* (1964), *Half a Sixpence* (1965)

FILMS incl.: *Interlude* (1968), *The Best House in London* (1968), *The Rise and Rise of Michael Rimmer* (1970), *The Magic Christian* (1970), *The Statue* (1971), *The Love Ban* (1972), *Time Bandits* (1981), *Whoops Apocalypse* (1981), *The Secret Policeman's Other Ball* (1982), *Privates on Parade* (1983), *Yellowbeard* (1983), *The Secret Policeman's Private Parts* (1984), *Silverado* (1985), *A Fish Called Wanda* (1988), *Erik the Viking* (1989), *An American Tale: Fievel Goes West* (1991)

VIDEOS: *Romance with a Double Bass; Fawlty Towers, Vols. 1 and 2*

## STANLEY CLEMENTS (See THE EAST SIDE KIDS.)

## DEL CLOSE

### (March 9, 1934–   )

One of the legends of the Second City improvisational troupe and the creator of several cult classic record albums, Del Close began his career doing summer stock in Wisconsin as a teenager. Born in Manhattan, Kansas, he eventually joined the Compass Players, a St. Louis improvisational group. When a New York version was formed in 1956, he was in the cast along with Severn Darden and Paul Mazursky.

After "two years of absolutely humiliating defeat" working solo, he returned to improv work and moved to Broadway in *The Nervous Set*, playing a bizarre yogi. His solo song was the teasing "How Do You Like Your Love," a list of strange experimentation: "Some lovers love on a bicycle, some hang from a chandelier. Some like it cold as an icicle. I once knew a man who called a panda 'dear.' "

Joining the Second City group, Close evolved his most famous character, Brigadier General J. C. Clevis, but fans knew Close was funny without playing any roles at all. In 1964, during the dangerous days when prosecution for obscenity was a serious concern, someone shouted to him from off stage, "Del! Del! Lenny Bruce got busted for obscenity!" Del turned in surprise and said, "No shit?"

Close eventually left the group in 1965. "Actually I was fired. I was too high too often and it was affecting my work." He went west and spent five years with Peter Bonerz, Leigh French and Howard Hesseman as members of The Committee. He rejoined Second City in the early 1970s, becoming known for both his acting and his work as a director.

Though Close's solo career never took off, his solo albums are still fondly remembered. His *How to Speak Hip* album was a classic of jazz-tinged beatnik comedy. A quick definition: "A nod—that's like a very hip nap." And some philosophy: "Flip out at least once. Then you wouldn't have that to worry about. Dig, once you get used to it, insanity can be the most natural thing in the world."

AUDIO: *The Nervous Set* (Columbia), *The Second City Writhes Again* (Mercury), *How to Speak Hip* (Mercury), *Do It Yourself Psychoanalysis Kit* (Mercury), *Pieces of Eight* (Offbeat)

## IMOGENE COCA

### (November 18, 1908–   )

One of television's most versatile comediennes, Imogene Coca could play winsome, impish ladies, comic romantic leads or a variety of housewives from the tearful and inept to the aggressive and sarcastic. She could win laughs with or without dialogue. Whether she was creating an original character with her crooked grin and bright eyes, or doing a parody of a famous film star, Imogene Coca was on target.

"In the kind of comedy I've done," she said, "you're playing a real situation, which is then exaggerated. But if you don't feel the reality of the character and the character's emotions, then it's not funny."

Coca's father was the conductor at the Chestnut Street Opera House in Philadelphia. Her mother had been a dancer. Imogene studied dance, played the piano and made her first stage appearance in a school play as "an Evil Germ." By the time she was nine, she was in vaudeville, tap dancing. When it came time for her to choose high school or show business, she quickly packed herself off to New York where she got work as a dancer in Broadway shows (*When You Smile*, 1925). She worked her way up to the "New Faces of 1934" revue. Backstage, Imogene borrowed a coat from one of the performers. It was so big for her, she started ad-libbing pantomime, creating an instant comedy sketch that was soon part of the show.

She continued to work on stage, perform her solo cabaret act and star in "Buzzy Wuzzy," a 15-minute television variety show for ABC that lasted exactly a month. In 1949 she appeared in the "Admiral Broadway Revue"—which co-starred Sid Caesar. The next season they were together for "Your Show of Shows." The 90-minute television program aired live on Saturday nights, and many sketches from it have become comedy classics. There were several men getting laughs—Caesar, Carl Reiner, Howard Morris—but only one woman. Imogene Coca had to play all the female parts. The Emmy-Award-winner was worth every bit of her $10,000-a-week salary. Some felt she was worth more—perhaps the same $25,000 Sid Caesar received.

Imogene had her own show in 1954, but format changes (from sitcom to variety show and back again) doomed it. She and Sid Caesar both had trouble living up to the legendary old show. Even their reunion on "Sid Caesar Invites You" was unfavorably compared to the superlative "Your Show of Shows."

Through it all, the public still loved Imogene Coca, whose shy good nature, spritely warmth and unassuming grace showed through even in the brassiest husband-and-wife sketch or the broadest pantomime. Her next two series didn't have long runs. There was nothing wrong with "Grindl," the sitcom in which she played a plucky maid, that good writing couldn't have fixed. The same went for the kid-oriented Stone Age comedy "It's About Time," a kind of live-action version of "The Flintstones."

Imogene continued to appear in clubs, played Granny's 100-year-old mother in *The Return of the Beverly Hillbillies*, and moved to Broadway for *On the Twentieth Century*. She played Aunt Edna opposite Chevy Chase in *National Lampoon's Vacation*, victim of a bizarre sight gag: dying and being strapped to the roof of the car. "I hated the part," she admitted, "but Chevy and all of them were so nice."

She enjoyed touring in summer stock and dinner theater, often appearing with her second husband, actor King Donovan, whom she married in 1960. Donovan died in 1987.

One of her favorite roles was in *Plaza Suite*, which had a scene about a marital breakup: "It's both funny and terribly moving. That's what I like—the things that combine great poignancy with almost farcical moments of humor."

In 1990 she reteamed with Sid Caesar for several sellout months of concert performances. "We're not a team," she reminded reporters. During a keep-in-touch phone call, they started having such a great time they decided to get back together for a show: "If he calls me or if I call him we start to laugh, because we're both terrible on the phone. We say hi, and then there's a dead silence . . . he called me and I must have laughed for five minutes. And so did he. And we never did finish the conversation. . . . We both are aware of the fact that we're very shy."

BROADWAY: *Shoot the Works* (1931), *New Faces of 1934* (1934), *New Faces of 1936* (1936), *Who's Who* (1938), *The Straw Hat* (1939), *All in Fun* (1940), *Concert Varieties* (1945), *The Girls in 509* (1958), *On the Twentieth Century* (1978)

FILMS incl.: *Under the Yum Yum Tree* (1963), *Ten from Your Show of Shows* (1973), *Rabbit Test* (1978), *The Return of the Beverly Hillbillies* (1981), *National*

*Lampoon's Vacation* (1984), *Nothing Lasts Forever* (1985)

TV: "Buzzy Wuzzy" (1948), "Admiral Broadway Revue" (1949), "Your Show of Shows" (1950–54), "The Imogene Coca Show" (1954–55), "Sid Caesar Invites You" (1958), "Grindl" (1963–64), "It's About Time" (1966–67)

## MYRON COHEN

### (July 1, 1902–March 10, 1986)

Classic dialect stories—jokes with a beginning, middle and end—were Myron Cohen's specialty, delivered with modesty and warmth. A former garment industry salesman, Cohen used to tell jokes to his customers. He told the story of a traveling salesman who came to a woman's front door to admit "I'm so sorry, when I parked my car I ran over your cat. I'm so sorry. I'd like to replace him." The woman said, "Well, don't just stand there—there's a mouse in the kitchen!"

Born in Poland and raised in New York, Cohen decided to try telling the jokes on stage. A short time later he was able to leave his job at Wullscheger and Company to work full time in the Catskills, Miami Beach and such clubs as The Copacabana, in 1952. His tales were predominantly Jewish, as was his audience, but his stories spoke of universal human nature.

"I hope you'll think this is funny," he might begin. "A little woman, way up in years: now the Good Lord sees fit to take her. The husband is at the bedside, and with what little strength she can summon up she pleadingly says to her husband, 'Tomorrow for the funeral, do me a favor. Let my mother ride with you in the first car. Please, it's my last request.' He says, 'Let her drop dead and go with you in your car!' " After the laughs, there's the topper: "He says, 'All right, I'll let her go, but it's gonna spoil my whole day!' "

A sad-looking, bald little man, Cohen's easygoing delivery and richly evocative variety of Jewish accents made his classic stories amusing time and again, even if people had heard them before. Like Jack Benny, he was a master at setting up a long, anecdotal story and wringing every laugh out of it. He filled two books with jokes in 1958 and 1959,

then recorded a pair of classic albums for RCA Victor.

Cohen worked through the 1970s and gave his last performance in 1984. He had a heart attack in September 1985 but didn't let it affect his lifestyle too much. He still had a Rob Roy at lunch and an occasional cigarette. As columnist Cindy Adams recalled, he and "his wife Miriam were married a lifetime. When she passed on three years earlier, he didn't care about sticking around."

AUDIO: *Variety Yiddish Theater Compilation* (Banner), *Myron Cohen* (Audio Fidelity), *Everybody Gotta Be Someplace* (RCA), *It's Not a Question* (RCA, both albums reissued together as *This Is My Myron Cohen*)

BOOKS: *Laughing Out Loud* (1958), *More Laughing Out Loud*

## CLAUDETTE COLBERT

### (Lily Chauchoin, September 13, 1903– )

It didn't take long for Claudette Colbert to become one of the queens of screwball comedy. She won an Academy Award for the film *It Happened One Night* opposite Clark Gable and went on to star in many more classics for such esteemed directors as Litvak (*Tovarich*), Lubitsch (*Bluebeard's Eight Wife*), Cukor (*Zaza*), Van Dyke (*It's a Wonderful World*) and Sturges (*The Palm Beach Story*).

Born in Paris, Claudette moved to America when she was nine. She worked on Broadway before going to Hollywood in 1927, getting her start in the silent film *For the Love of Mike*. Her first major success was 1931's *The Smiling Lieutenant* opposite Maurice Chevalier. She surprised viewers as Poppaea, bathing in asses' milk for *The Sign of the Cross*, and delighted them as *Cleopatra* in 1934.

Her career, which had taken an exotic turn, came back to earth for *It Happened One Night*. Viewers looking for a little of Colbert's trademark sprightly sex appeal found it in the classic scene in which she hitchhikes and stops a car cold—by raising her dress and showing plenty of leg. In *Midnight*, after losing at roulette in Monte Carlo, wearing her fancy evening gown, she tells cab driver Don Ameche, "Here's how things stand. I could have you drive me around town and then tell you I left my purse at home on the grand piano. But there's no grand piano, no home—and the purse? Twenty-five centimes with a hole in it!"

Of the screwball heroines, she was the one most likely to take an aggressive chance for love and/or money. Her man was sometimes unsure whether she was genuine or a golddigger playing him for a chump. Her wisecracks put them off balance too, and she knew it. "Men don't get smarter as they grow older," says the charming, independent coquette in *The Palm Beach Story,* they just lose their hair." This film proved to be one of her enduring hits, despite a contrived ending.

In other films, she continued to keep her men off balance. In *Bluebeard's Eighth Wife* Gary Cooper thinks he's conquered her. After several martinis, she seems to be begging "Kiss me." Cooper is smug: "What does a nice girl say?" Colbert answers, "Please . . . please . . ." Only when they kiss does he discover she'd taken a bite from an onion a moment before.

Colbert's years in screwball comedy ended in the 1940s, but she went on to do some television work and often appeared in stage comedies on Broadway. Honored in 1984 by the Film Society of Lincoln Center, she declared she was still taking acting roles: "I just tell myself I'm 60 and I have 30 years to go." That year she and Rex Harrison starred in the London revival of *Aren't We All.* They brought it to Broadway the following season. She enjoyed travel and entertaining in her apartment overlooking New York's Central Park. She was working well into her later years and was still giving interviews at age 87 (and making sure the writers got her age right). She admitted to writer James Brady in 1990, "If I have a quality, it is that I'm honest and not self-conscious about things like my ears (she wears a hearing aid) or my age. Because there they are, and why should I apologize?" Writers and fans were delighted to see that Colbert had no reason to apologize for anything—and that she was unchanged—still fascinating, exciting and thoroughly unique.

BROADWAY: *The Kiss in a Taxi* (1925), *The Barker* (1927), *Within the Law* (1928), *Tin Pan Alley* (1928), *Dynamo* (1929), *The Marriage-Go-Round* (1958), *Julia, Jake and Uncle Joe* (1961), *The Irregular Verb to Love* (1963), *The Kingfisher* (1978), *A Talent for Murder* (1981), *Aren't We All* (1985)

FILMS incl.: *For the Love of Mike* (1927), *The Smiling Lieutenant* (1931), *The Wiser Sex* (1932), *Tonight Is Ours* (1933), *I Cover the Waterfront* (1933), *Imitation of Life* (1934), *It Happened One Night* (1934), *Cleopatra* (1934), *The Bride Comes Home* (1935), *The Gilded Lily* (1935), *Private Worlds* (1935), *She Married Her Boss* (1935), *I Met Him in Paris* (1937), *Tovarich* (1937), *Bluebeard's Eighth Wife* (1938), *It's a Wonderful World* (1939), *The Palm Beach Story* (1942), *No Time for Love* (1943), *So Proudly We Hail* (1943), *Since You Went Away* (1944), *Practically Yours* (1944), *Guest Wife* (1945), *Without Reservations* (1946), *The Egg and I* (1947), *Family Honeymoon* (1949), *Bride for Sale* (1949), *Let's Make It Legal* (1951), *Texas Lady* (1955), *Parish* (1961)

## DABNEY COLEMAN

### (January 2, 1932–   )

Dabney Coleman entertains audiences with characters that are vain, mean, smug, curmudgeonly and corrupt. Unlike the broad burlesque of the past masters, Coleman makes his con artists and love-to-hate villains realistic, leaving viewers with only the barest glint in his eye to detect the merriment behind the miscreant.

Born and raised in Texas, a graduate of the Virginia Military Institute, Dabney Coleman worked as a magazine model and played faceless roles on 1960s television. He had so little of his trademark acerbic personality back then that he didn't get walk-on but "lie-on" roles. (He played a corpse—Dan Duryea's dead son—in an obscure television show.) He was killed twice in two episodes of "The Outer Limits."

As he aged, his receding, thinning hairline, mousy mustache and beady eyes led to his being cast in roles calling for a sneak and a weasel. He was Mayor Jeeter, selling "Condos for Christ" for two seasons of "Mary Hartman, Mary Hartman," and "Fast Eddie" Murtaugh on "Apple Pie." He made an impression on audiences as the stereotypical nasty boss in the film *9 to 5,* a leering bully ultimately put into bondage by three of his put-upon female office workers. The same year he starred in the film *Pray TV,* playing the stereotypical "Marvin Fleece," a greedy sleaze who turns television station KRUD into K-GOD for a money-making scheme.

Coleman's first starring sitcom was "Buffalo Bill." He played a heel, a boss who refused to see any side to an issue that might inconvenience him ("You're telling me there's no redeeming qualities in toxic waste?"). The show was short-lived but had a strong cult following. Next he played the glib, aging, hard-bitten "Slap Maxwell," an old-fashioned sports columnist. Slap may have been going down, but he intended to go out with style. His simmering reaction to golfers: "They ride in little carts like a panzer division . . . they splash the landscape in red pants, peach pants, lime green pants of polyester . . . they hack and gouge . . . at journey's end they sneer into their gin fizzes." It was another short-run show with a cult of enthusiastic followers.

In subsequent films and television roles producers attempted to refine Coleman's egocentric comic identity, trying to match the earthy bluntness or insulting bluster with touches of vulnerability and insecurity: smarm with charm. For television's "Drexel's Class" he was in a Fieldsian element: the curmudgeon with kids. Though he often portrayed dour and cagey types, Coleman admitted in 1990, "Things have been going pretty good the last six, seven, eight years. In the beginning, I don't think I gave stardom a hell of a lot of thought. I became an actor to act, not to be a star."

Coleman is popular on talk shows, insulting the hosts and usually getting back far worse than he dishes out. While promoting his film *Short Time*, he declared that his role called for some warmth and sensitivity. Johnny Carson shot back, "Sensitivity? That must have been a stretch for you."

FILMS incl.: *The Trouble with Girls* (1969), *I Love My Wife* (1970), *Bad Ronald* (1978), *North Dallas Forty* (1979), *Nothing Personal* (1980), *How to Beat the High Cost of Living* (1980), *Melvin and Howard* (1980), *9 to 5* (1980), *Pray TV* (1980), *Modern Problems* (1981), *On Golden Pond* (1981), *Tootsie* (1982), *Cloak and Dagger* (1984), *The Muppets Take Manhattan* (1984), *The Man with One Red Shoe* (1985), *Dragnet* (1987), *Hot to Trot* (1988), *Where the Heart Is* (1990), *Short Time* (1990), *Meet the Applegates* (1991)

TV: "That Girl" (1966–67), "Mary Hartman, Mary Hartman" (1976–78), "Apple Pie" (1978), "Buf-

falo Bill" (1982–84), "The Slap Maxwell Story" (1987–88), "Drexel's Class" (1991)

## JERRY COLONNA

### (Gerardo Luigi Colonna, October 17, 1904–November 21, 1986)

His face was a live caricature: a thick mustache springing out over a fiercely toothy smile and thick eyebrows flexing over bulging wide eyes. His manic expression seemed to flash "eccentric!" the moment he walked on stage. When he spoke, his clipped, ingratiating delivery got laughs for the mildest of jokes. When he sang he didn't need jokes at all. His trademark was holding notes for insanely long intervals. His histrionic version of "You're My Everything," which featured about 20 or 30 seconds of "You," an outragous trill over the "r" and a swooping slide into "my-everything" never ceased to amaze and amuse.

A musician with Ozzie Nelson, Benny Goodman and Artie Shaw, Colonna played trombone for the CBS orchestra, including classical pieces conducted by Eugene Ormandy. He was in the orchestra for Bing Crosby's 1937 radio show but was soon up front as a supporting comic for Bob Hope, Fred Allen and others. He played a quack psychiatrist in Fred Allen's *It's in the Bag* and appeared with Hope from 1938 through the 1960s not only for radio shows but for each year's overseas treks to entertain the troops.

The eye-rolling glib purveyor of nonsense regularly bewildered the normally implacable Bob Hope, as in this sequence, with Colonna calling him from a pay phone: "Hope, hello! Colonna is this!" "Colonna, why are you talking backwards?" "Put the nickel in upside down." "That wouldn't have anything to do with it, Colonna. [After hearing the sound of an animal growling] What's that, Colonna?" "I'm pulling the buffalo out by his tail." "That's impossible!" "I don't ask questions, I just have fun!"

His catch phrase on Hope's show was a breezy opening cry of "Greetings, Gate!" Another well-used phrase was his grinning bark of "Whattssa matter? You crazy or something?" Another catch phrase, written for him by Jack Douglas, was "Who's Yehoodi?" which poked fun at the name of violinist

Yehudi Menuhin. Colonna and most listeners were unaware that Menuhin's father had chosen the name to proudly combat anti-Semitism with what pointedly translates into "the Jew."

A trademark manic bit of Colonna's was to shout "Hello" in a sketch, then "Goodbye," then grin, stare and add, "Short day, wasn't it?" There was more than a touch of Groucho Marx to Colonna's brand of challengingly abrupt nonsequiturs. From 1937 to 1940 Colonna recorded a series of novelty tunes, including "Hector the Garbage Collector," "You're My Everything," "Where Is My Wandering Boy Soprano Tonight?" and "The Yogi Who Lost His Will Power."

Colonna appeared on the syndicated 1956 "Super Circus" show for children and guested on many television variety shows. He was never the same after a stroke in 1966. He was still noticeably weak when he made a guest appearance with Bob Hope on television in 1976. When Jerry died a decade later, Hope recalled, "He was a dear friend, a great entertainer whom I traveled all over the world with for 25 years. He provided millions of laughs for millions of people. He delighted the entire world with his unique style of comedy—a great loss to the entertainment industry. I'll miss him."

AUDIO: *Music for Screaming* (Decca), *Jerry Colonna Entertains at Your Party* (Bravo), *Let's All Sing with Jerry* (Liberty)

BOOKS: *Who Threw That Coconut?*; *The Loves of Tullio*

FILMS incl.: *52nd Street* (1937), *College Swing* (1938), *Naughty But Nice* (1939), *Comin' Round the Mountain* (1940), *Road to Singapore* (1940), *Ice Capades* (1941), *Star Spangled Rhythm* (1942), *Priorities on Parade* (1942), *Atlantic City* (1944), *It's in the Bag* (1945), *Road to Rio* (1947), *Kentucky Jubilee* (1951), *Meet Me in Las Vegas* (1956), *Road to Hong Kong* (1961)

TV: "The Jerry Colonna Show" (1951)

## CHESTER CONKLIN

### (Jules Cowles, January 11, 1886–October 11, 1971)

A diminutive silent comic whose broom mustache obliterated his mouth almost completely, Chester Conklin wasn't muffled early in his career. He studied elocution and won a prize in a recital.

Born in Oskaloosa, Iowa, he worked as a circus clown and appeared in vaudeville as a Dutch comedian. He was in many Charlie Chaplin films in 1914, including *Dough and Dynamite*. When Chaplin first created his "Tramp" costume, he borrowed Fatty Arbuckle's pants and Conklin's coat. So even if Conklin was never a big star, indirectly he at least made a great contribution to comic history.

The shambling little cherub with the big mustache, steel-rimmed glasses and thinning hair proved humorous contrast to bulky Mack Swain in Swain's "Ambrose" film series, and over the years there was always a supporting comic role for him as any type of bungler or boob, with an occasional eccentric cop thrown in for a change of pace. He appeared in Ed Wynn's 1927 *Rubber Heels,* four early W. C. Fields films (including *Her Majesty Love* in 1931) and reunited with Chaplin for *Modern Times* in 1936 and *The Great Dictator* in 1940. He was the white-haired, white-mustached Mayor Gurgle in *Li'l Abner* the same year.

Conklin worked less often in the 1940s and in 1954 was found working in a J. W. Robinson department store as Santa Claus. By then one of the few survivors of silent film comedy, and still recognizable with his bulky mustache, the little man was given some more cameo parts in screen comedies. Conklin's surprising career never completely stopped. It seemed as if he was ready for permanent retirement when he went to live in the Motion Picture Country House. But the 79-year-old comic left after marrying 75-year-old June Gunther. They set up house together and Conklin even returned to pictures, taking a part in *Big Hand for the Little Lady*.

FILMS incl.: *Making a Living* (1914), *Dough and Dynamite* (1914), *Ambrose's Sour Grapes* (1915), *A Clever Dummy* (1917), *The Village Chestnut* (1918), *Skirts* (1921), *The Nervous Wreck* (1926), *Tell It to Sweeney* (1927), *Two Flaming Youths* (1927), *Rubber Heels* (1927), *Fools for Luck* (1928), *Tillie's Punctured Romance* (1928), *Her Majesty Love* (1931), *Hallelujah, I'm a Bum* (1933), *Modern Times,* 1936), *Every Day's a Holiday* (1938), *The Great Dictator* (1940), *Li'l Abner* (1940), *Hail the Conquering Hero*

(1944), *The Perils of Pauline* (1947), *Big Hand for the Little Lady* (1967)

# TIM CONWAY

## (December 15, 1933–   )

A pudgy, balding, babylike bumbler on television sitcoms in the 1960s, Tim Conway first made a name for himself playing Ensign Charles Parker on "McHale's Navy." He was the chubby-cheeked dope who sputtered a few confused syllables, pouted in bewilderment and ultimately showed a dimwitted resolve to obey orders.

Initially a "reluctant" performer, Conway had originally worked behind the scenes as a television show director in Cleveland. (He was born in Willoughby, Ohio.) Off stage he was interested more in athletics than theatrics. He participated in Golden Gloves tournaments and had his nose broken half a dozen times—the last occasion was while rocking on a wooden horse and smashing face first into its mane.

After "McHale's Navy," Conway recorded a pair of comedy albums in 1967 and 1968 but still ended up playing a sitcom bumbler on "Rango," a Western parody that sported a (pre-*Blazing Saddles*) raving theme song by Frankie Laine. He hosted the one and only episode of the legendary bomb television show "Turn-On."

Conway got a chance to present a wider variety of comical blank-faced dopes when he joined the cast of "The Carol Burnett Show." Among audience favorites was the straight-faced Swedish office manager with the semiscatalogical name, "Mr. Tudball." Known to break up his co-stars with deadpan ad libs and improvised pantomime, Conway's talents were thoroughly appreciated by Burnett. She said, "The man is a comedy genius. I think Tim, had he been in silent films, would have been as big as any of them. He comes up with incredible pieces of business; he's a brilliant schtick artist, an almost lost art."

After winning three Emmy awards for the Burnett show, Conway returned to films as the title character *The Billion Dollar Hobo* and wrote and starred in *They Went That-Away*. He then teamed up with Don Knotts for a few light, typically bumbling family-oriented comedies. In 1985 he and Harvy Korman, his friend from his days on "The Carol Burnett Show," tried for a film partnership that, though not too successful, extended over the years to include television appearances and commercials. In 1989 Conway played Felix to Tom Poston's Oscar Madison in a touring company of *The Odd Couple* and the following year starred in a "Candid Camera"–style special, "Tim Conway's Funny America," playing practical jokes on unsuspecting citizens.

Conway's major successes seemed to be in the 1960s ("McHale's Navy") and the '70s ("The Carol Burnett Show"). In the late '80s, he was once again in demand for variety show appearances thanks to a new character, "Dorf." This was a ludicrously serious lecturer on sports who had the handicap of being able to wear bermuda shorts as full-length pants.

While there is something tasteless about making fun of a man whose legs are so short his knuckles could touch the ground and he is forever tipping forward or backward to balance himself, audiences find it inexplicably hilarious. Conway achieves the effect by standing in a hole, his shoes on his knees. He racked up big sales with a series of "Dorf" videocassettes in the late 1980s and early '90s. Conway wryly notes "Harvey [Korman] said my career was over and this piece of crap saved me. Which is probably true."

AUDIO: *Are We On* (Liberty), *Bull* (Liberty), *Geraldine, Don't Fight the Feeling* (10-minute sketch with Flip Wilson)

FILMS incl.: *McHale's Navy* (1964), *McHale's Navy Joins the Air Force* (1965), *The World's Greatest Athlete* (1973), *The Apple Dumpling Gang* (1975), *Gus* (1976), *The Shaggy D.A.* (1976), *The Billion Dollar Hobo* (1978), *They Went That-Away* (1978), *The Apple Dumpling Gang Rides Again* (1979), *The Prize Fighter* (1979), *Private Eyes* (1980), *The Longshot* (1985)

TV: "The Steve Allen Show" (1961), "McHale's Navy" (1962–66), "Rango" (1967), "The Tim Conway Show" (1970), "The Tim Conway Comedy Hour" (1970), "The Carol Burnett Show" (1975–79), "The Tim Conway Show" (1980–81), "Ace Crawford, Private Eye" (1983)

VIDEO: *Dorf on Golf; Dorf's Golf Bible; Dorf and the First Games of Mount Olympus; Dorf Goes Auto Racing; Faerie Tale Theater: Rip Van Winkle*

## JACKIE COOGAN

### (October 26, 1914–March 1, 1984)

He achieved fame as a comedy star when he was four. Then again when he was 50. But there were a lot of lean years in between for Jackie Coogan.

Jackie's vaudevillian parents put him into their stage act when he was barely old enough to walk. When Charlie Chaplin saw him, he knew this was the boy to star in his next film, *The Kid*. It turned out to be one of Chaplin's best early films, and Coogan's performance was one of the finest ever by a child actor. Coogan had warm memories of Chaplin as both friend and teacher, but after *The Kid*, filmmaking became more work than play. His parents cashed in on his success by booking him for film after film. They earned over $2 million from his film work in the silent film era.

Coogan continued to work in his teens, though his years of stardom were behind him. Eventually he gave up acting and attended Villanova College and the University of Southern California. In 1935 his father was killed in a car accident. In 1938 Coogan had to sue his mother and stepfather for his earnings. He got no money, only the grim satisfaction that the outrageous misuse of child labor would not happen again. Inspired by his case, the Child Actors Bill became law in May 1939. It stipulated that half a child's earnings be set up in a trust fund, not squandered by greedy guardians.

Coogan tried a comeback in vaudeville. He married his stage partner Betty Grable in 1938 and made a film that year called *This Way Miss*. After their divorce (he married three more times) and service in World War II, Coogan made some kind of living with a nightclub act. The highlight was a parody of *The Kid*, in which he dressed up in his old kid togs and Ben Blue played Chaplin.

Into the 1950s Coogan struggled to earn a living in the remaining vaudeville houses. He told Milton Berle, "When I was three years old I sat in the lap of the Queen of England. Where do I go from there!" He wasn't asking for sympathy. And he

didn't get much. The route continued down, but Coogan never quit. He fought for supporting roles in films and on television, became a sidekick to Russell Hayden in 1951's "Cowboy G-Men" children's series and turned up as a second banana to Allyn Joslyn on the sitcom "McKeever and the Colonel." With this decent credit and enough determination to shave his head for the audition, Coogan won the part of Uncle Fester in "The Addams Family."

For a new generation Coogan was not "The Kid," he was the hilariously bizarre Uncle Fester, the man who wore a long black coat with a fur collar and could make light bulbs glow in his mouth. In retrospect, his Uncle Fester was Curly Howard doing *Night of the Living Dead*. He pitched his voice high enough to squeak and flashed a perky smile behind his foreboding, white-skinned, black-eyed face. The character was so enduring that 23 years after the show was canceled a video game arrived called "Fester's Quest," featuring a miniature cartoon version of Uncle Fester battling various dungeon demons.

In the 1970s Coogan's poor health kept him from taking as many roles as he would have liked. He was on a dialysis machine late in life, but was able to get off it temporarily to fly to New York and appear as part of an "Addams Family" reunion show staged by ABC's "Good Morning, America." In the green room after the show, a staffer came by with a photo of Jackie from *The Kid*. He held it in front of the old man and said condescendingly, "Jackie—do you know who this is?" "That's me, and Mr. Chaplin," he said as he dutifully autographed the photo. If there was any anger or resentment in Jackie Coogan, it never showed.

FILMS incl.: *A Day's Pleasure* (1919), *The Kid* (1920), *Peck's Bad Boy* (1921), *My Boy* (1922), *Oliver Twist* (1922), *Circus Days* (1923), *Little Robinson Crusoe* (1924), *A Boy of Flanders* (1924), *The Rag Man* (1925), *Johnny Get Your Hair Cut* (1926), *The Bugle Call* (1927), *Tom Sawyer* (1930), *Huckleberry Finn* (1931), *Home on the Range* (1935), *This Way, Please* (1938), *College Swing* (1938), *Million Dollar Legs* (1939), *Kilroy Was Here* (1947), *The Joker Is Wild* (1957), *High School Confidential* (1958), *Sex Kittens Go to College* (1960), *Girl Happy* (1965), *A Fine Madness* (1966), *The Shakiest Gun in the West* (1968),

Cook and Moore represented British comedy at its naughty, radical best. Photo from the author's collection.

*Human Experiments* (1969), *The Phantom of Hollywood* (1974), *Sherlock Holmes in New York* (1976), *Dr. Heckyl and Mr. Hype* (1980), *The Escape Artist* (1982)

TV: "Pantomime Quiz" (1950–55), "Cowboy G-Men" (1952), "McKeever and the Colonel" (1962–63), "The Addams Family" (1964–66)

VIDEO: *Comedy, A Serious Business*

## COOK and MOORE (See also DUDLEY MOORE.)

**Peter Cook, November 17, 1937–**
**Dudley Moore, April 19, 1935–**

The original bad boys of British comedy, Cook and Moore's irreverent satire and devilish sense of fun made them big stars in the 1960s and early '70s.

Cook began producing revues while still a student at Cambridge, and wrote for London shows *Pieces of 8* and *One Over the 8*. He was involved in the radical comedy newspaper *Private Eye* and opened The Establishment Club in England, booking Lenny Bruce there in 1962. It was back in 1959 that he joined with Dudley Moore, Jonathan Miller and Alan Bennett to star in *Beyond the Fringe*, the famous series of sketches that arrived on Broadway in 1962 and again for a new production in 1964.

Cook was at the forefront of the era's radical comedy. While some lines in the show may seem mild now, they were dangerous at the time, especially one about Christ on the cross (with the thieves alongside him grousing that he's higher up and

"getting all the attention"). "Aftermyth of War" was an especially biting sketch on Neville Chamberlain's passive reaction to Hitler. At one point the emotionless Officer Cook tells a soldier, "The war's not going very well. . . . I want you to lay down your life, Perkins. We need a futile gesture at this stage. . . . Goodbye, Perkins."

Cook and Moore were successful through the 1960s on their own. Never too far from the standard comedy team in format, Cook was severe, caustic and bullying, with cuddly Dudley Moore the self-proclaimed "complaint sort of twit." Their film *Bedazzled* became a cult classic. Fans on both sides of the Atlantic eagerly bought the record albums based on their British television shows, most marked by rather good-natured sketches involving struggles between the low working class (Dudley) and the high and effete (Peter).

In 1974 their two-man show *Behind the Fringe*, premiered as *Good Evening* in the United States. The classic "bad taste" sketches included Moore playing a cheerfully naive one-legged man applying to cruel and dour casting agent Cook for the role of Tarzan, and their version of the birth of Jesus: "Was the Holy Ghost there?" "Hard to say. He's an elusive little bugger. . . ." "Three wise men arrived?" "Three bloody idiots. In they come and call themselves Maggie!"

Cook and Moore worked less often together in the 1970s and '80s. While Moore continued to make successful films, Cook had less impact in America, though in England his monologues as everything from a severe judge to the "mistry Mr. Wisty" continued to find an appreciative audience. Cook was involved in the American television show "The Two of Us" (1981–82), won an Emmy for producing *Concealed Enemies* in 1984 for American Playhouse and appeared in several films including *Find the Lady* (1986), *Without a Clue* (1988) and *Getting It Right* (1989). He even turned up in a 1989 cola commercial playing the very British proprietor of a house for sale (haunted by Madelyn Kahn).

The team occasionally worked together for benefits and made several albums under their alter egos "Derek and Clive," a pair of drunken, lower-class types engaging in shockingly scatological banter (their *Come Again* album offers a long fantasy about Joan Crawford strewn with four-letter words). Though some fans were appalled, many enjoyed the duo's deliberate rudeness. However, Cook and Moore's ability to surprise fans didn't rely on dirty words. Peter Cook as a blind man: "I'm blind, but I am able to read thanks to a wonderful new system known as broil. I'm sorry—I'll just feel that again. . . ."

AUDIO: *Beyond the Fringe* (Capitol), *Beyond the Fringe '64* (Capitol), *The World of Pete and Dud* (Decca), *Once Moore with Cook* (Decca), *Not Only Peter Cook, but Also Dudley Moore* (Decca), *Goodbye Again* (Decca), *Peter Cook and Dudley Moore Cordially Invite You to Go to Hell: Bedazzled* (20th Century Fox), *Behind the Fringe* (Atlantic Import), *Good Evening* (Island), *Derek and Clive Ad Nauseam* (Virgin), *Derek and Clive Come Again* (Virgin), *Derek and Clive Live* (Island), *Derek and Clive's Greatest $hits* (Krass), *Six Fabulous Filthy Favourites* (Krass), *The Clean Tapes* (Cube)

BOOK: *The Dagenheim Dialogues* (1971)

BROADWAY: *Beyond the Fringe* (1962, 1964), *Good Evening* (1974)

FILMS incl.: *Bedazzled* (1967), *The Bed Sitting Room* (1969), *Those Daring Young Men in Their Jaunty Jalopies* (aka *Monte Carlo or Bust*) (1969), *The Hound of the Baskervilles* (1977)

VIDEO: *Saturday Night Live: Cook and Moore*

## JOE COOK

### (Joe Lopez, 1890–May 15, 1959)

W. C. Fields praised him as the "biggest of the nut headliners," but since most of his best work was done on the stage and based less on jokes than on personality and charisma, Joe Cook's ability to make people laugh is difficult to measure. One gets no clue from his most famous routine, "Why I Will Not Imitate Four Hawaiians," which on paper seems flatter than a Don Ho record:

"I will give an imitation of four Hawaiians. This is one [whistles], this is another [tinkles mandolin], and this is the third [marks time with foot]. I could imitate four Hawaiians just as easily but I will tell you the reason why I don't do it. You see, I bought a horse for $50 and it turned out to be a running horse. I was offered $15,000 for him and I took it. I built a house with the $15,000 and when it was finished a neighbor offered me $100,000 for it. He said my house stood right where he wanted to do a well. So I took the $100,000 to accommodate him. I invested the $100,000 in peanuts and that year there was a peanut famine, so I sold the peanuts for $350,000. Now why should a man with $350,000 bother to imitate four Hawaiians?"

On stage Cook displayed such dazzling raw talent that *New York Times* reviewer Brooks Atkinson, having just seen him in *Rain or Shine*, simply gushed, "Joe Cook is the greatest man in the world." The film version, directed by Frank Capra, is the main surviving example of Cook's talent.

Cook was orphaned when he was four. His father, a painter, drowned while trying to rescue one of his students. His mother died shortly after, on Christmas Eve. The boy lived in Evansville, Indiana with his adoptive mother, Anne Cook. Young Joe put on shows in the family barn and at 12 went out with Dr. Rucker's Traveling Medicine Show. Over the years he mastered riding a unicycle, balancing on a ball; sharp shooting; playing the saxophone, banjo and trumpet; juggling; and sleight-of-hand magic tricks.

Only 15, Cook went to New York with a con man's brashness (a photograph that showed him juggling 17 balls at once—with unseen wires holding them in place) and the billing "A One-Man Vaudeville Show." Amid the tricks, Cook developed whimsical nonmonologues and throwaways that surprised and disarmed Broadway audiences. He included Rube Goldbergian props and worked with stooge Dave Chasen (later a famous restaurant owner) in many revues. In one bit Cook worked with an acrobatic team—all dummies. Cook balanced them, fell over them and ran riot with them about the stage.

In addition to touring and Broadway, Cook appeared on radio's "Colgate House Party." Parkinson's disease slowed him in 1940. A short time later he retired, enduring his disease as best he could. The master of circus tricks spent his last days almost completely paralyzed.

BOOK: *Why I Will Not Imitate Four Hawaiians* (1930)

BROADWAY: *Half Past Eight* (1918), *Hitchy-Koo* (1919), *Earl Carroll Vanities* (1923, 1924, 1925), *Rain or Shine* (1928), *Fine and Dandy* (1930), *Hold Your Horses* (1933), *Off to Buffalo* (1939), *It Happens on Ice* (1940)

FILMS incl.: *Rain or Shine* (1930), *Hold Your Horses* (1933), *Sound of Laughter* (1964)

## JACKIE COOPER (See OUR GANG.)

## PAT COOPER

### (Pasquale Caputo, July 31, 1929–   )

Originally critics felt Pat Cooper was "the Italian Sam Levenson." He specialized in warm, if somewhat excitable recollections of his childhood and family growing up in Red Hook, Brooklyn. His father was a bricklayer from Bari, Italy. Cooper dropped out of Manual Training High School and for 12 years worked as a bricklayer as well, driving a cab in the winter.

Back in the early 1960s he said, "My stuff is an exaggeration of the truth. When I was a kid and my mother spanked me, it wasn't the least bit funny. But today, I can speak of it with humor as I describe her left-hooking me from any angle."

Typical New York–accented humor from Pat Cooper: "I got a genuine Eye-talian mother. Four feet eleven! If they five feet they Turks! She has a bun ovah hee-ah, a knitting needle over hee-ah, a gold tooth over hee-ah. That'sa my momma . . . black dress, black stockings and black shoes. I say, 'Poppa, why they wear black?' He says, 'In case anybody dies, they're ready!' "

After getting a break in 1963 on television's "Jackie Gleason Show," Cooper put out a string of successful record albums. Some had catchy covers such as *Spaghetti Sauce and Other Delights,* which parodied Herb Alpert's album cover for *Whipped Cream and Other Delights.* Alpert featured a sexy nude girl in whipped cream. Here was Pat, ridiculous in his Clark Kent black glasses, sitting nude in marinara sauce.

In the 1970s and '80s, Cooper heightened his comically angry persona and became known as a don't-get-me-started! comedian who could ad lib a seemingly out-of-control tirade about any subject. He brought his combative comedy to resorts and clubs around the country. Briefly co-billed on a tour with Jackie Mason in the late '70s, he and Mason shared a similar identity as ethnic, opinionated and outrageous. While Mason would go on to Broadway fame, Cooper opened for Lola Falana, Tony Bennett, Steve Lawrence and similar mainstream performers. He's become a ubiquitous figure in the East Coast and is often known to turn his up his high-decibel complaints and cajoling for frequent guest spots on local New York radio shows.

AUDIO: *Our Hero* (United Artists), *Spaghetti Sauce and Other Delights* (United Artists), *More Saucy Stories* (United Artists), *You Don't Have to Be Italian* (United Artists), *Our Hero: The Best of Pat Cooper* (BVM, CD compilation)

FILMS: incl.: *Fighting Back* (1982)

## IRWIN COREY

### (January 29, 1912–   )

A wide-eyed but lovable wildman with a windy, whimsical streak, Irwin Corey spent nearly 50 years playing his "Professor" character, lecturing in his large frock coat and string tie, his hair mussed, his fingers jabbing the air to make a dramatic, nonsensical point.

In the early 1940s, he began working The Village Vanguard and Le Ruban Bleu. At the time he described his alter ego as just a "poor-soul absent-minded professor . . . lost in the clouds." His puckish sense of humor included a lecture on Sir Isaac Newton's discovery of the law of gravity: "There he was, walking through his apple orchard, and he saw an apple falling down from a tree, which amazed him. Because—up until that time—until the law of gravity was passed, all apples fell up!"

In the 1960s, inspired by his friend Lenny Bruce, Corey spiced up his act with political and social satire. His eyes gleaming with mischief, the seemingly absentminded professor snuck in some sharp barbs amid the babbling. "Is there life after birth?" the Professor asked on one talk show. He thrust a finger in the air and gave out with one of his trademark long cries of "Yeeeeesss!" Then added: "President Nixon is a great example of afterbirth."

Banned from television in the '70s due to both his radical comedy and his eccentric, unpredictable personality, Corey worked the less glamorous end of the nightclub circuit, made a few films and bitterly denounced "sellout" comedians (such as Woody Allen and Rodney Dangerfield) who played it safe and got television exposure. The bizarre little Professor turned up in some unexpected places in that decade. In 1974 he was sent by Viking Books to pick up Thomas Pynchon's National Book Award and say a few words. A few years later he was *Screw* magazine's pick to run for president.

Corey starred as an angel in *Stuck on You* in 1982, recorded a new album and, with cable television a rising force, staged a comeback in this new forum for his free-wheeling, often R-rated remarks. The Smothers Brothers booked him occasionally on their 1989 variety show, and national viewers once again were able to see the master monologist at work.

His trademark was one few comics would dare attempt. The Professor would come out on stage not with a joke, but with silence. After staring at the audience, alternately serious and bewildered, he'd slap his forehead as if unable to think of what he wanted to say. Then he'd seem to clear his throat and start. But change his mind. After an excruciating minute of delay, with the audience giggling and laughing, he'd sternly declare, "However . . ."

He may seem to have started in the middle or lost the beginning, but before long the audience had to agree with him: "Remember, wherever you go—there you are!"

AUDIO: *At the Ruban Bleu* (Jubilee), *Win with Irwin* (Atlantic), *World's Foremost Authority* (Viva), *I Feel More Like I Do Now* (Gateway), *Flahooley* (Capitol)

BROADWAY: *New Faces of 1943* (1943), *Heaven on Earth* (1948), *Happy as Larry* (1950), *Flahooley* (1951), *Mrs. McThing* (1952), *The Good Soldier Schweik* (1963), *Seven Scenes for Yeni* (1963)

FILMS incl.: *How to Commit Marriage* (1969), *The Comeback Trail* (1974), *Car Wash* (1976), *Thieves* (1977), *Stuck on You* (1982), *Crackers* (1984)

TV: "The Andy Williams Show" (1969–70), "Doc" (1975–76)

VIDEO: *The Hungry i Reunion Concert* (Pacific Arts)

## CHARLES CORRELL (See AMOS and ANDY.)

## BILL COSBY

### (July 12, 1937–   )

Bill Cosby's warm family comedy first won over audiences in the early 1960s. Back then his anecdotal monologues offered humor from the child's point of view as he imitated their voices and put on beguiling faces of wide-eyed innocence or smirky naughtiness. Later his tales came from the parents' viewpoint, his visage comically stern, his style leaning toward frustrated lectures.

Either way, Cosby has never veered from his aim in presenting healthy, wholesome humor that could often be healing and even educational. The way he does it, as "Cool Cos"—everybody's big brother and friend—is unique. His style of comedy, though, goes back to the descriptive antics of Mark Twain, whose stories were often read to Cosby by his mother.

Cosby reinvented his childhood when he hit his stride as a monologist in 1964 to 1965. His father, in reality, had disappeared when Cosby was a teenager. His Philadelphia home life was marred by poverty and the death of a brother at six. He turned his life around after navy service, earning an athletic scholarship to Temple University. He left to gamble on a career in comedy.

After a few low-selling albums, Cosby began gaining ground and suddenly he found himself cast—with no acting experience—in the hit television series "I Spy." Ironically, by avoiding racial humor in both his monologues and on television, he became a powerful symbol of the black man as equal. Cosby won a record six straight Grammy awards (1964–69) for his comedy albums. Over a dozen went on to become certified gold best-sellers. For three straight years he won Emmy awards for "I Spy."

Bill Cosby is one of the most successful comedy stars of all time. He won a record six consecutive Grammy awards for his comedy albums more than a decade before he was America's favorite father on "The Cosby Show." Photo by the author.

Through the decades, Cosby navigated rough waters, years when the radical black power movement and raging civil rights controversies made him seem disappointingly neutral and when more radical performers such as Richard Pryor made headlines. Yet through it all, Cosby stuck to his convictions and emerged as an enduring comedian, a legend in his own time.

Twenty years after his first splashy fame, Cosby had the greatest success of his life with "The Cosby Show," which was the number-one-rated series through most of its first six years. The time was once again ripe for the cycle of "family" entertain-

ment. Cosby, a respected scholar (he went back to school and earned his Ph.D. in 1977) as well as cool kid at heart, appealed to all ages.

In 1987 *Forbes* magazine estimated his earnings at $100 million for the year. It seemed accurate. Without much fanfare, Cosby donated $20 million to Spelman College in Atlanta. A 1988 deal for the syndication rights to "The Cosby Show" was placed at over $500 million. Not only was he number one as a moneymaking comedian, with the number-one show, his book *Fatherhood* was the number-one bestseller of 1986, selling 2.5 million hardcovers. His follow-up books did almost as well. He was also a ubiquitous pitchman for Jell-O, Coke and Kodak.

Cosby's books are filled with the same observational humor as his monologues. In "Time Flies" he addressed the problem of getting older:

"Although I just can't take the plunge into bean sprouts or alfalfa, one day I did put a few carrot sticks and celery stalks into a bag and I took a healthful walk in the park. After a while, I sat down on a bench beside an old man, who was both smoking and eating a chocolate bar, two serious violations of a longevity diet. 'Do you mind my asking how old you are?' I said. 'Ninety-two,' he replied. 'Well, if you smoke and eat that stuff, you're gonna die.' He took a hard look at my carrots and celery, and then he said, 'You're dead already.' "

Being the top star on television and an "establishment" figure left Cosby open to jibing criticism from younger stars. Eddie Murphy liked to mimic what he perceived as the Cosby professorial smugness in concert and clean public image. Cosby set the record straight: "In his act he says I chastised him for cursing, which is not true. I chastised him because I had heard from enough people as I followed him on the road that Eddie was telling audiences, whenever he got upset with them, how much money he made. I said that isn't the right thing to do."

Cosby then found himself competing with another bad boy in comedy, cartoon character Bart Simpson, the bratty star of "The Simpsons" television show. In 1990 it was front-page news when the sullen and grousing Simpson clan, the latest hot fad in the television industry, were rescheduled opposite the wholesome Cosby family. Cosby won. His strategy was simple: to work harder. He maintained the level of the show's scripts and with his advisers made sure to avoid the "preaching" some viewers detected in his coverage of sex, drugs and other family problems. Cos joked about the competition to the media and on his show allowed one of his family to sport a "Bart" Halloween mask in one episode. Of the "new wave" of "nasty" sitcoms, including "The Simpsons" and "Married with Children," Cosby remarked, "The mean-spirited and cruel think this comedy is on 'the cutting edge.' But what is entertaining about that?"

One of the most respected and best-loved comedians of all time, Bill Cosby has continued his steady course in comedy, dividing his time among television, stand-up concerts, books, a variety of unpublicized educational and philanthropical pursuits, and an occasional movie. *People* magazine declared, "To the millions who watch his show and read his books, Cosby has become the decade's antidote to sleaze and cynicism, the self-appointed ombudsman of American morality. . . . He's as smart as six lawyers, rich enough to buy Arabia and practically as famous as God." For all that, he has never varied from his hectic schedule of daily work.

"It's not a killing schedule, not at all," said Cosby. "I love this work . . . my mind is always working. I enjoy the fact that I have an outlet. . . . When people remind me that I have all the money in the world, and I'm happy, and ask me when I'm going to retire, I don't understand."

AUDIO: *Bill Cosby Is a Very Funny Fellow . . . Right* (WB), *I Started Out as a Child* (WB), *Why Is There Air?* (WB), *Wonderfulness* (WB), *Revenge* (WB), *To Russell, My Brother Whom I Slept With* (WB), *200 MPH* (WB), *It's True, It's True* (WB), *8:15 12:15* (Tetragrammaton), *Bill Cosby: Sports* (Uni/MCA), *Live at Madison Square Garden* (Uni), *When I Was a Kid* (Uni/MCA), *For Adults Only* (Uni/MCA), *Inside the Mind of Bill Cosby* (Uni/MCA), *Fat Albert* (MCA), *Bill Cosby Is Not Himself These Days, Rat Own!* (Capitol), *Disco Bill* (Capitol), *My Father Confused Me* (Capitol), *Bill's Best Friend* (Capitol), *Bill Cosby Himself* (Motown), *Bill Cosby/Hardheaded Boys* (Nicetown), *Those of You with or Without Children, You'll Understand* (Geffen), *Silver Throat Sings* (WB), *Hooray for the Salvation Army Band* (WB), *Bill Cosby Presents Badfoot Brown* (Uni), *Bill Cosby Presents Badfoot Brown and the Bunions Bradford Funeral and Marching Band* (MCA), *At Last Bill Cosby Really Sings* (Partee), *Bill Cosby Cutups* (Motown), *Best of* (WB), *Best of Volume Two* (WB), *Cosby Classics/Cosby Kids* (WB), *Bill* (MCA), *Bill Cosby Talks to Children About Drugs* (MCA), *Oh Baby* (Geffen)

BIOGRAPHY: *Cosby* (R. L. Smith, 1987)

BOOKS: *Fat Albert's Survival Kit* (1975); *Bill Cosby's Personal Guide to Tennis Power* (1975); *Fatherhood* (1987); *Time Flies* (1988); *Love and Marriage* (1989)

FILMS: *To All My Friends on Shore* (1972), *Man and Boy* (1972), *Hickey and Boggs* (1972), *Uptown Saturday Night* (1974), *Let's Do It Again* (1975), *Mother, Jugs and Speed* (1976), *Piece of the Action* (1977), *Top Secret* (1978), *California Suite* (1978), *The Devil and Max Devlin* (1979), *Bill Cosby Himself* (1983), *Leonard Part 6* (1987), *Ghost Dad* (1990)

TV: "I Spy" (1965–68), "The Bill Cosby Show" (1969–71), "The New Bill Cosby Show" (1972–73), "Cos" (1976), "The Cosby Show" (1984–1992)

VIDEOS: *Bill Cosby 49; A Toast to Lenny Bruce*

## WALLY COX

### (December 6, 1924–February 15, 1973)

Best remembered as the 1950s television character "Mr. Peepers," Wally Cox made a career of playing shy, mild-mannered, gently twerpish little men. He was almost a stereotype of the birdwatcher or bookworm, complete with glasses and a bland, secret smile. The quivery, piping voice that he used when standing up for himself (while his entire body seemed about to give way) was another trademark. Cox grew up in New York exaggerating his meekness for comic effect: "I was a perfect subject for getting beaten up. So I contrived a method whereby I could give the correct answers and make the guys laugh, without simultaneously offending the teacher. I had to dance between eggs."

Encouraged by friends, including Marlon Brando, Cox began performing. *Variety* wrote in January 1949 that though "still among the ranks of parlor entertainers, he has a comedic approach that's somewhat out of the ordinary." Perhaps inspired by Brando's streetwise personality, he developed offbeat monologues about accidentprone "Dufo": "We used to play roof tag. Everybody has to run over the roofs. Everybody has to run under the radio wire. So everybody runs under the wire but Dufo. It gets him right in the neck. What a crazy guy."

He performed Dufo monologues in the Broadway show *Dance Me a Song,* but it was as unassuming and gentle high school science teacher "Mr. Peepers" that Cox achieved fame. The show was a marked contrast to the era's more boisterous slapstick sitcoms. Its success was purely in the believable, human comedy of Cox. As one of the show's writers, Jim Fritzell, recalled; "Wally *was* Mr. Peepers. He spent all of his spare time studying insects . . . he read *Scientific American.* That was Wally. And as far as the nervousness—well, that was genuine too. See, Wally was never too sure of himself."

Cox never duplicated the success of "Mr. Peepers," but he did supply the voice for the enduring cartoon character "Underdog." His style influenced a generation of comics and his unique voice remains a delight to hear, on records and in cartoons. He later divided his time among writing books, being married (three times), various artistic hobbies and regular appearances on the quiz show "The Hollywood Squares."

BOOKS: *Mr. Peepers: Sort of a Novel* (1955), *My Life as a Small Boy* (1961), Ralph Makes Good (1965), *The Tenth Life of Osiris Oaks* (1972)

FILMS incl.: *State Fair* (1962), *The Yellow Rolls Royce* (1964), *A Guide for the Married Man* (1967), *The One and Only Genuine Original Family Band* (1968), *The Cockeyed Cowboys of Clico County* (1970), *The Boatniks* (1970), *The Barefoot Executive* (1971)

TV: "School House" (1949), "Mr. Peepers" (1952–55), "Underdog" (1964–73)

## LOU COSTELLO (See ABBOTT and COSTELLO.)

## BING CROSBY

### (Harry Lillis Crosby, May 2, 1903–October 14, 1977)

Bing Crosby's success as a singer has dwarfed his credits in humor, which are certainly equal to or better than many who have devoted an entire life-time to comedy. The Hope and Crosby comedy team of the 1940s was one of the top box office attractions. Among Crosby's biggest solo hits is the comedy classic *A Connecticut Yankee in King Arthur's Court,* due in part to his special brand of low-key charm. Into the 1960s, Crosby even had his own sitcom.

Born in Tacoma, Washington, Crosby was lead singer for Paul Whiteman in the late 1920s but was already dabbling in comedy, making some shorts for Mack Sennett in 1931. Even as his recording and radio career took off, he had roles in such light-hearted films as *We're Not Dressing* and W. C. Fields' *Mississippi.* He often satirized his own image. In *The Big Broadcast* he plays himself, but the famous singer isn't so famous to everyone. Asks Stu Erwin, "Are you a singer by profession?" In the film Crosby seemed to sense that simply singing into a microphone would not be enough of him. He says in one scene, "You sing into a little hole year after year and then you die."

Into the 1940s he and Bob Hope played friendly rivals in a series of movies in which Crosby's cool wisecracks contrasted with Hope's frantic cowardice. In *The Road to Utopia* Bing is sure that Bob is going to cause an avalance by continuing to hiccup. "Scare me," Bob cries. "I can't," deadpans Bing. "I don't have a mirror."

While some fans were surprised years later when Bing's son Gary painted a disparaging picture of his father as "the hollow man," icy and cruel, there was nothing very compassionate about Crosby in his movies with Hope. As his contemporary Bud Abbott did with Lou Costello, Crosby often tried to take advantage of partner Hope. In *The Road to Morocco* he sells Hope into slavery and is willing to swap his partner's life to marry Dorothy Lamour. In *The Road to Utopia* he doesn't care if the dog he and Hope own is blown up by a stick of dynamite.

On radio, Hope and Crosby continued their feud. In a typical broadcast Bob crows, "I'm on for Swan Soap this year." "Yeah," answers Bing, "too bad it's not something you use." "Hey, Lump Lap, you've got two chins, would you like to try for one?" "Let's face it, Nostril King, before I sang my song, this show was laying a swan egg."

In the 1960s Crosby did a bit of drag comedy in *High Time* and made *The Road to Hong Kong,* his final film with Hope. He briefly starred in a television sitcom and later coasted through guest roles on television variety shows, more often singing sentimental songs.

In the 1970s, up through his death in 1977, Crosby continued to host his own popular television Christmas special every year.

AUDIO: *Crosby and Hope on Radio* (Radiola)

BOOKS: *Bing Crosby: A Discography of Radio Program Lists & Filmography* (Morgareth, 1987), *Going My Way* (G. Crosby, 1983), *My Life with Bing* (K. Crosby, 1983), *The Films of Bing Crosby* (Bookbinder, 1977)

FILMS incl.: *The Big Broadcast* (1932), *College Humor* (1933), *We're Not Dressing* (1934), *Mississippi* (1935), *Big Broadcast of 1936* (1936), *Anything Goes* (1936), *Double or Nothing* (1937), *The Road to Singapore* (1940), *The Road to Zanzibar* (1941), *The Road to Morocco* (1942), *Holiday Inn* (1942), *Duffy's Tavern* (1945), *Bells of St. Mary's* (1945), *Blue Skies* (1946), *The Road to Utopia* (1946), *The Road to Rio* (1947), *A Connecticut Yankee in King Arthur's Court* (1949), *The Road to Bali* (1952), *White Christmas* (1954), *The Country Girl* (1954), *High Society* (1956), *High Time* (1960), *The Road to Hong Kong* (1962), *Robin and the Seven Hoods* (1964), *Stagecoach* (1966)

TV: "The Bing Crosby Show" (1964)

## NORM CROSBY

### (September 15, 1927–   )

A comic who tries to establish a "rapaport" with the "masculine men and fenneman ladies" in the audience, Norm Crosby is the most successful stand-up star in gently confused malaprop comedy. Of course, his act contains a lot of solid jokes to support the dizzy twists of tongue that sometimes leads audiences to give him what he craves: "a standing ovulation."

Born in Boston, Crosby went to the Massachusetts School of Art, but before he could finish, he enlisted as a radar operator in the coast guard. While on antisubmarine patrol in the North Atlantic, he suffered hearing losses due to a concussion from depth charges.

After working in a shoe store, Crosby landed a job as an assistant master of ceremonies at a summer resort hotel. He worked hard to perfect his "imperfect" delivery style and became a regular in top nightclubs around the country in the 1960s. He appeared often on "The Ed Sullivan Show" and other variety series. In the 1970s he hosted one of the first "comedy store" television series spotlighting young talent, "The Comedy Shop."

A series of 1978 commercials humorously trying to explain "natural light beer" made him an even more nationally recognizable figure, but Crosby spent more time in less commercial pursuits. In 1979 he became the first national chairman for the Council for Better Hearing and Speech and by 1988 was its public information ambassador. He was a tireless worker for the City of Hope Hospital and for causes ranging from muscular dystrophy to the El Paso Cancer Treatment Center.

The modest stand-up star earned a star in the Hollywood Walk of Fame, and on February 24, 1982, he saw it placed on the sidewalk between two of his favorite performers, Jack Benny and Red Skelton.

In 1989 Crosby starred in a Showtime cable sitcom called "The Boys," which was about friends at a Friar's-type club. He said, "Having me play myself makes the Excalibur Club plausible . . . the producers decided I should play me so that we could have a recognizable person in show business who could make the club credible. I can actually bring in celebrities to visit the club . . . and it's believable. We can talk about my trips to Vegas and my telethon and it's credible. But I'm really just being me. I'm not doing my act, I'm just being Norm Crosby."

He was also himself in a new series of beer ads, but this time he admonished the audience, "If you're drinking—and talking like me—you're not in control!"

AUDIO: *She Wouldn't Eat the Mushrooms* (Epic)

TV: "The Beautiful Phyllis Diller Show" (1968), "Liar's Club" (1976–78), "The Comedy Shop" (1978), "The Boys" (1989)

## BILLY CRYSTAL

### (March 14, 1947–   )

The youngest "old-timer" in show business, Billy Crystal has never forgotten his comedy roots, which were buried deep in the 1950s. While most stand-up comics his age took on countercultural topics (Robin Williams) or addressed modern life (Whoopi Goldberg), Crystal has remained 30 years behind the times, parodying 1950s actors (Fernando Lamas), movies (*The Bible* starring Yul Brynner), comedians (his "Buddy Young Jr." character) and his childhood in imitations of his home movies and his grandparents.

Clean cut, curly haired and cute, Crystal looks like "the nice grandson" of any grandma's dreams. As even Charles Bronson said to him, "I like you. You're not like the other pig comics." In a market dominated by abrasive newcomers, Crystal, along with David Brenner and Garry Shandling, had great success in replacing aging 1950s comics in resorts, casinos, fairs and other family venues. That he was clearly the best looking of the bunch, rarely covered anything controversial and had the talent to break up his show with mime and different characters helped him rise to the top. His advice to aspiring comics was simple: "Don't curse if you don't have to. Think television."

Crystal's awe for show business began in childhood when celebrities such as Billie Holiday visited the home of his father, a music producer, and his uncle, who was an executive for Decca and the founder of Commodore Records. With his father providing the costumes, Billy and his brothers used to dress up like the Nairobi Trio of the Ernie Kovacs Show. Billy's later style of comedy—precocious, gentle and sometimes coy—clearly came from trying to please a doting family audience.

His father's death from a heart attack when Billy was 15 was worse than devastating. Billy and his father had had an argument just before it happened; his last memory was of conflict. Billy later realized that the experience "forced me to become a man before I should have."

In school, Billy wasn't the class clown. "I was the class comedian. The difference was that the clown dropped his pants at halftime. The comedian was the one who talked him into it." A wiry athlete, Crystal was on his high school baseball and wrestling squads. He attended Nassau Community College and worked the college circuit as part of a three-man improvisational troupe, Three's Company. When Billy happened to entertain solo at a college party, two agents saw him and expressed interest.

A versatile "nice guy" comedian, Billy Crystal has won fans as a star of both romantic comedies and stand-up. Photo from the author's collection.

Crystal landed some acting roles (he played Mike's best friend on a 1976 episode of television's "All in the Family") and won his first fame as a comic actor playing gay Jodie Dallas on "Soap." It was one of the first times a homosexual character appeared in a continuing series role. Some fans were surprised that Billy (married since college) wasn't really gay. These were probably the same people who were surprised that in the movie *Rabbit Test* he wasn't really pregnant.

Billy's comedy variety show lasted just five weeks in 1982, but when he got the chance to join "Saturday Night Live," he made the most of it, filling the screen with a flurry of characters, many aided by latex makeup. A consummate pro, Crystal made sure each creation had a memorable catch phrase. Loudmouth Buddy Young Jr. threatened, "Don't get me started." Crystal's black jazz musician character asked, "Can you dig that? I knew that you could." The goofy street kid Willie said, "I hate when that happens!"

Most successful of them all was "Fernando," the utterly insincere and foolish interviewer who would tell anyone and everyone, "You look mahvelous!"

The character was based on actor Fernando Lamas, who once said on a talk show, "It's better to look good than to feel good." Lamas died before the "Fernando" character became popular. His widow, Esther Williams, reacted to the parody with irritation, then acceptance. This distressed Billy, who said, "I don't want to hurt anybody's feelings." He insists all his characters "have an underlying sweetness and sadness at the same time." This is Crystal's charm—his slickness tempered by sentiment, his aggression tempered by boyish enthusiasm.

Taking over host duties for Academy Awards broadcasts in the late 1980s, and early '90s, Crystal has earned praise for his easy presence and mild irreverence. On the 1990 broadcast he sang, "Gee it's great—in a segregated state—to be driving Miss Daisy back home." Comfortable in front of crowds of any size, he set a record of sorts in May 1990 when he led some 30,000 fans at Shea Stadium in a group recitation of "Take my wife—please."

Crystal's warm and schmaltzy 1991 HBO special, *A Visit to Moscow*, earned critical praise. "It's as good as anything I've ever seen on HBO, by far," said Rob Reiner. It included a travelogue in front of Lenin's tomb ("Hi. Bob Vila, for 'This Old Tomb.' Just kidding!") and his version of a Russian singer, "Nicky Nukie and the Meltdowns." In live performance, he coaxed the crowd to do "the wave," and told them, "Growing up in the United States, we were taught that you were the enemy. You were taught that we were the enemy. And we're both wrong. It's the French!"

Crystal's had some of his best recent success making films. Once a student in Martin Scorcese's film class at New York University, Crystal came to understand the media, moving from the standard (*Running Scared*, a buddy cop film with Gregory Hines) to co-writing *Memories of Me* and starring in Rob Reiner's romantic comedy *When Harry Met Sally*. *City Slickers* was another effort that played on his sympathetic character who means well, has heroic dreams and an overpowering amount of energy. In real life, Crystal admitted that he had a bit too much energy. An insomniac, he added, "If I get three hours, I'm okay."

He plans to concentrate on writing and directing more films in the future, trading in on his new leading man status. Or, as *People* magazine put it,

"Onscreen he is a modern girl's modern man—sensitive, romantic, warm, someone you can trust."

In addition to his film work, Crystal works as a fundraiser and spokesperson for Comic Relief. Almost every year, Crystal, Whoopi Goldberg and Robin Williams host a "Comic Relief" special on HBO that raises millions of dollars for the homeless.

AUDIO: *Mahevlous!* (A&M), *Best of Comedy Relief* (Rhino)
AUTOBIOGRAPHY: *Absolutely Marvelous!* (1986)
FILMS incl.: *Rabbit Test* (1978), *Running Scared* (1986), *Throw Momma from the Train* (1987), *The Princess Bride* (1987), *Memories of Me* (1988), *When Harry Met Sally* (1989), *City Slickers* (1991)
TV: "Soap" (1977–81), "The Billy Crystal Comedy Hour" (1982), "Saturday Night Live" (1984–85)
VIDEOS: *All-Star Toast to the Improv; Big City Comedy; Best of Comedy Relief; Don't Get Me Started; Faerie Tale Theater: The Three Little Pigs; A Comic's Line; Comic Relief 3; Likely Stories Volume 3; Midnight Train to Moscow*

## JANE CURTIN

### (September 6, 1947–    )

An original member of television's "Saturday Night Live," Jane Curtin had previous comedy experience while a drama student at Northeastern University and as a member of The Proposition improvisational group in Cambridge, Massachusetts. She was with them for four years before moving on to touring companies of plays such as *The Last of the Red Hot Lovers*.

Despite her background in ad-libbing and playing a number of characters, Curtin was often cast on "Saturday Night Live" as the straight woman to the more emotional and flamboyant Gilda Radner, who had been hired first. When she did get the comedy spotlight, Jane played unemotional types: an uptight, overly efficient newscaster, sneering housewives, sour hostesses and irritated sophisticates. Perhaps her most popular character was Mrs. Conehead, the cold and mechanical creature from outer space who always had a scientific explanation for American customs and products. Her definition of a taco: "a folded starch disc encasing vegetable substances and shredded flesh of hooved mammals."

Curtin's favorite comedy stars of the past tended to be cool and sarcastic. When she was invited by the Museum of Broadcasting to present an evening of sitcoms under the banner "Comedians' Choice: Acts and Influences," she chose Ann Sothern in "Private Secretary" and Eve Arden in "Our Miss Brooks."

On "Saturday Night Live" some of the laughs came from Jane's chafing against the unrefined or downright boorish. She glared with undisguised disgust at Radner's Roseanne Rosanadanna and simmered with indignity over Dan Aykroyd's insults ("Jane, you ignorant slut!") during their parodies of the "60 Minutes" debates between Shana Alexander and James Kirkpatrick. On the set, cast and crew noted the real disdain the quiet-living Curtin had for slob co-star John Belushi. Sometimes Curtin found it difficult to remain aloof from the chaotic comic behavior that went on both backstage and in front of the camera.

A notorious highlight of the show was the one episode in which Curtin suddenly responded to years of being typed as the show's classy ice queen. During a "Weekend Update" segment, she suddenly pulled her blouse open, exposed herself in a black bra and shouted "Try these on for size, Connie Chung!" One of the most level-headed members of the original cast, Curtin is married and lives quietly in Connecticut.

The only member of "Saturday Night Live" to score a success with a second television series, Curtin won two Emmy awards for "Kate and Allie." Though she played a divorced woman on the show, she didn't intend that to be her real-life fate. Part of her negotiations for the show included filming it in New York, so she could maintain her home life. Curtin was pleased to see that without giving interviews or losing her privacy to the tabloids, she was able to maintain a successful show business career.

After the series ended she appeared on Broadway in *Love Letters*. Married since 1975, she had a bit of trouble recalling the whole idea of love letters: "I'm not big on correspondence . . . I always found letter writing to be tedious. Besides, I didn't have that many boyfriends, and the ones I had used the phone." Jane went on to try another sitcom, "Working It Out," which didn't exactly work out. Interviewers got some decent copy about the plot line for the new show but nothing much on the star. She shrugged and admitted that her life at home with her husband and daughter was "boring. I like it, but it doesn't make good copy."

BROADWAY: *Love Letters* (1989)

FILMS incl.: *How to Beat the High Cost of Living* (1980), *O.C. and Stiggs* (1987), *Suspicion* (1987), *Maybe Baby* (1988)

TV: "Saturday Night Live" (1975–80), "Kate and Allie" (1984–88), "Working It Out" (1990)

VIDEOS: *Bob and Ray, Jane, Laraine and Gilda; Mr. Mike's Mondo Video; Saturday Night Live; The Best of Gilda Radner; The Best of John Belushi; The Best of Chevy Chase; The Best of Dan Aykroyd*

D

## BILL DANA

### (William Szathmary, October 5, 1924–   )

One Christmas in the late 1950s, a little Hispanic fellow appeared on "The Steve Allen Show." The audience broke up when he announced in a small nasal voice, "My name . . . José Jimenez." His occupation? Teaching sidewalk Santas to say "Jo Jo Jo." Soon José was the country's newest comedy sensation, and so was the writer who created him and played him: Bill Dana. Dana, who had written stand-up material and sketches for Don Adams (including the "Would you believe . . ." catch phrase) now had one of his own: "My name . . . José Jimenez." For years, all he had to do was open with those four words to get a huge laugh.

Though at first a lot of the humor was in José's funny accent, his enduring appeal was in his cute, confused demeanor and his personality as a sympathetic Walter Mitty who took on all kinds of jobs (astronaut, skin diver, lion tamer) only to get himself into comic trouble. Almost all of Dana's José Jimenez routines required a straight man. As "José the Rancher," there was this typical exchange: "What is the name of your ranch?" "The name of my ranch is the Bar 9, Circle Z, Rocking O, Flying W, Lazy R, Crazy 2, Parallelogram O." "Do you have many cows?" "No. Not many survived the branding."

Born in Quincy, Massachusetts and a graduate of Emerson College, Bill Szathmary borrowed his mother's first name (Dena) when he began performing as half of a comedy team with Gene Wood. He felt more comfortable behind the scenes and became a writer. He recalled, "Once I got on stage and got my first laugh everything was fine, but up to that time was sheer terror. I said to myself what am I doing this for, it's too scarey. When I met Don Adams and began writing for him, it was like being a fight manager. You rub the guy's shoulders, but he's the guy who's going out there and getting beat up. So I just loved that!" As a writer he had confidence. "If it makes me laugh I'm almost 100% positive that the audience is gonna enjoy it." He had been writing for Steve Allen's show when he came up with the José Jimenez character. Steve felt that only Bill could perform it properly, and the encouragement sparked his renewed career in front of the camera.

Though the José character did confuse his "h's" and "j's" and spoke with a sharp accent, the jokes were never ethnic. As "José the Submarine Officer" with Steve Allen as straight man: "Congratulations on your tremendous feat." "Thank you, but they're only size eight." "You stayed underwater for 84 days. How come?" "I didn't want to come up before the submarine." "Under water all that time, did you begin to hate your friends?" "Just one time. During the third riot." "In those 84 days you were submerged, did you have any mechanical trouble?" "Only with the ballast valve that lets you go up."

"How long did you have that problem?" "83 days."

The José phenomenon, which included novelty books and many records, yielded a television sitcom. For two years viewers watched the adventures of José, working as a hotel bellhop and dealing with a snide manager (Jonathan Harris) and an inept house detective (Don Adams). Though José had a menial job, Bill Dana was always careful to maintain his character's dignity. Around that time he refused to film a Pontiac commercial when it called for José to be comically arrested for speeding.

Dana's José Jimenez records were hits through the early and mid-1960s, a time when gentle comedy from Bill Cosby and The Smothers Brothers was also popular. Dana figured that from record sales and $35,000 a week in club dates, José brought him close to $20 million over the years. Still, only a portion of his nightclub act included José (with straight man Don Hinckley). The rest of the hour featured Dana's own easygoing sketches and anecdotes. Dana was a strong enough entertainer on his own to host his own two-hour variety show live from Las Vegas in 1967. It was syndicated by the United Network, which was attempting to establish itself against the "big three" networks.

The show failed and as the 1970s began, ethnic comedy fell out of favor. Sensitive Hispanic groups began objecting to José Jimenez. Dana, admitting he was "a Jungarian Hew," decided to satirize his own ethnic group with a Jewish comedy album called *Hoo Hah*. Gradually stand-up comedy took a backseat to his other interests—packaging books for his own "Light Stuff" company, composing music, forming an ad agency and continuing his lucrative career as one of the nation's best comedy writers. The episode of "All in the Family" he wrote, guest-starring Sammy Davis Jr., was a certifiable classic.

The climate for José changed in the late 1980s. Nostalgic audiences were glad to have him back and most seemed to understand the love and warmth behind the character. In deference to José's several decades in America, Dana softened the character's accent and created a more fluid speech pattern. Dana was booked for several television appearances and club dates but admitted to the author in 1988, "I am basically a writer-performer. If I only had one career to choose, it would be writer. But the gratification from performing—there's no equal, the pri-

Bill Dana has endeared himself to millions as the little guy who called himself "José Jimenez." Photo from the author's collection.

mal stroke that people give you. That nice little warm fuzzy pat on the back if you do well before them. There's no way of getting that from your word processor."

Living in Hawaii, enjoying his music and the freedom to perform as José on a limited basis, Dana continues to spend most of his time writing comedy. He believes so strongly in the power of humor that he wrote a book on the subject with Dr. Laurence Peter. His viewpoint: "Comedy is my religion. I'm a jokist. . . . I think this is my own grasp at sanity, to try and understand all of this stuff that's going on. There's gotta be some big cosmic joke. So when I see people interested in comedy . . . I look at them as acolytes. I'm so delighted to see people doing it, because that is the ultimate avenue of healing for everything. To have a sense of humor."

AUDIO: *Pat Harrington Kookie as Ever* (Signature, reissued on Roulette), *My Name José Jimenez* (Signature, reissued on Roulette), *José Jimenez the Astronaut* (Kapp, also released as *Bill Dana at the Hungry i*), *José Jimenez the Submarine Officer* (Kapp, also released as *More José Jimenez*), *José Jimenez in Orbit* (Kapp), *José Jimenez Talks to Teenagers* (Kapp), *Our Secret Weapon* (Kapp), *José Jimenez in Jollywood* (Kapp), *Bill Dana in Las Vegas* (Kapp), *Hoo Hah!* (Capitol), *Bill Dana Presents Joey Forman as the Mashuganishi Yogi* (A&M), *José Supersport* (Puente), *The Best of José Jimenez* (GNP-Crescendo), *José Can You See* (Rhino)

BOOK: *The Laughter Prescription* (1982)

TV: "The Steve Allen Show" (1959–60), "The Spike Jones Show" (1960), "The Bill Dana Show" (1963–65), "No Soap Radio" (1982), "Zorro and Son" (1983)

## RODNEY DANGERFIELD

**(Jacob Cohen, November 22, 1921–  )**

"I don't get no respect," Rodney Dangerfield complains. Good comedy springs from the truth. And this is the truth. Rodney looks like a loser. There are bags under his bulging eyes, his heavyset body weighs him down just getting to center stage and sweat pours from him as he nervously loosens the tie that seems more like a noose. He can't get a break. He said that whenever he goes into an elevator, the operator says one word: "Basement?" And when he was a kid and played hide and go seek, it was no fun at all: "They wouldn't even look for me!"

His miseries on stage were only a slightly cartooned version of his miseries off stage. He had a rough childhood. His name back in Babylon, New York was Jacob Cohen, and he grew up tormented by anti-Semitism and a longing to fit in with the crowd. His parents were separated and money was tight. The boy had to deliver groceries to the houses of the kids he went to school with. "I wanted to date certain of the girls, but I never asked them. I felt I wasn't good enough." After graduating from high school, he drove a laundry truck.

Calling himself Jack Roy, he decided to follow his father (billed as Phil Roy) into show business. "Comedy is a camouflage for depression . . . a lot of people from split homes go into show business

Rodney Dangerfield, the stand-up comic who "gets no respect," suddenly found himself a screen star with the blockbuster success *Back to School*. Photo from the author's collection.

because they want applause. . . . in my particular case, it was a question of: accept me, tell me I'm okay. Tell me I'm as good as the rest." As a comic, he never earned more than $8,000 a year. Others seemed to go on to better things. He was a loser. And he had a wife and family to support. So he quit the business and became a salesman.

Hitting 40, writing a few jokes now and then for star comedians, he had a restless urge to give show business one last chance. Not wanting to come back as the failed Jack Roy, he needed a new name. A club owner thought up Rodney Dangerfield: "I was depressed enough to keep the name." There were a few losers in stand-up, including Jackie Vernon, but Rodney became something different—a loser fighting to be a winner, grousing over every indignity, his "I don't get no respect" coming out of anger more than self-pity. His one-liners bristled with chagrin and irony: "I broke up with my psychiatrist. One day I told him I had suicidal tendencies. He told me from now on I had to pay in advance."

Through the 1960s and '70s, Rodney's gut message hit home. A guy who knew what it was like to be an outsider, Rodney in the 1970s was well known for being friendly to fans and encouraging to other comics. He was one of the few big names who gave novice joke writers a chance, always willing to look at new material and pay a decent price for a gag.

Dangerfield continued to work hard. He was invited back on "The Ed Sullivan Show" and Johnny Carson's "Tonight Show" over and over because he was constantly turning over fresh, audience-tested, well-constructed jokes. Rodney's fame continued to grow. He cut a rap record and video, had good luck with his own Dangerfield's nightclub in New York and after only a few film appearances struck gold with the smash hit *Back to School*. He was suddenly one of the nation's hottest comics. The film grossed $90 million dollars.

The loser was suddenly a winner. But, unfortunately true to his image, he told an interviewer, "It's too late to do cartwheels." Success had come too late and he could not hide his bitterness. Among his deepest regrets was that his longtime manager had died before his breakthrough film was released. Rodney's pain and pessimism coupled with the awesome success seemed to throw him temporarily off balance.

With new management came a new look, a thick lawn of dyed blond-yellow hair. The new management felt that Rodney was worth more than the $5 million he was going to get for *Caddyshack II*—and the resulting lawsuit left him without the key follow-up film he needed. The new management refused interview requests, which only confirmed the suspicions of many that Dangerfield was beginning to indulge too deeply in the joys of star power. The new management brought him to Broadway for a critically roasted one-man show. And under the new management he made a few vulgar and poorly scripted cable specials that had fans shaking their heads.

He filmed a pilot for "Where's Rodney?" about a 12-year-old who asks Rodney for advice in times of crisis. Somehow, the concept didn't sell. Meanwhile his next film project, *The Scout*, went through three directors. And for the first time, Rodney began getting bad publicity, including a costly fight over money demands for canceled performances at a Las Vegas casino. He claimed he couldn't perform after his eye was injured in the steam room at Caesars Palace in March 1988. The casino refused to pay him for the missed shows. In September 1990 he finally won the case, getting $725,000 of the $5 million he had demanded, but it had come at a high cost. During the trial the casino contended he had "severe problems with cocaine, marijuana and alcohol abuse," and the remarks were quickly picked up by the tabloid press.

Breaking five years of silence, he consented to a *New York Post* interview to complain "[The casino] had no case, so they blasted out stuff about me on alcohol and drugs to degrade me and abuse me and debilitate me. . . . my right eye is still suffering. I have to use ointment and drops daily and it's still not good. . . . I had first-degree burns on my lids and couldn't see out of my eye and they wouldn't pay me for shows I couldn't do. What compassion. I'd worked Vegas for 20 years and never missed a show."

One sign of his old self was his compassion and support for young comics, including protégé Sam Kinison, dubbed "The Beast of Burden." Meanwhile, Dangerfield continued to suffer from his own burdens. One young comic remembered, "He called me at 3 A.M. once. He said, 'Can't sleep, right? Sure. We give 'em everything on stage and we go home and have nothing.'"

In stand-up, working the crowd, Dangerfield is still in top form, still raging about life's indignities and still remembering where it all began. "I was an ugly kid . . . one year they tried to make me a poster boy for birth control. . . . My mother had morning sickness after I was born."

AUDIO: *The Loser* (Decca, reissued by Rhino), *I Don't Get No Respect* (Bell, reissued by Arista), *No Respect* (Casablanca), *Rappin' Rodney* (RCA)
BROADWAY: *Rodney Dangerfield* (1987)
FILMS incl.: *Caddyshack* (1980), *Easy Money* (1983), *Back to School* (1986), *Rover Dangerfield* (1992), *Ladybugs* (1992)

VIDEO: *It's Not Easy Being Me; Saturday Night Live: Rodney Dangerfield; Nothing Goes Right*

## JOAN DAVIS

### (Madonna Josephine Davis, June 29, 1907–May 23, 1961)

"What a girl, what a whirl, what a wife!" That was the description of Joan Davis sung by an energetic choir during the opening credits of television sitcom "I Married Joan."

Davis's show business whirl began at age six when she performed in amateur contests. In one of her first she was booed during a recitation and pelted with vegetables. Her father's advice: "Better be funny, not serious. . . . Keep moving! It spoils their aim."

She came back the following week and won the crowd over with comedy and songs. She swiftly headed out on the vaudeville circuit as "The Toy Comedienne." When she was no longer a toy, the teenager "retired" and on her parents' advice returned to school, graduating from St. Paul's High School.

Joan returned to show business after some unrewarding jobs as a store clerk. She developed a new act that included slapstick bits borrowed from old Chaplin films and a juggling act with trick dishes. She teamed up with Si Wills in 1931, and for four years "Wills and Davis" worked the dwindling vaudeville circuit. One thing they accomplished was to get married.

In 1935 the team moved west. Joan wanted to break in with Mack Sennett, who was still making comedy shorts. When she failed to get an audition, she sought out Sennett at a Hollywood party and began doing comedy bits. Fortunately, Sennett was amused. He put her juggling dish routine in his next short, *Way Up Thar*. Her career was on its way, but it had its ups and downs. After disappointments at RKO she and her husband returned to the stage, but Wills and Davis bombed at The Palace. Returning west, moving to 20th Century Fox, she had bit parts in 11 films in 1937, starting with *The Holy Terror*.

She developed a reputation for rough-and-tumble comedy, occasionally singing and offering some eccentric dance steps. In *The Great Hospital Mystery*

she juggles a bedpan. In *Hold That Co-Ed* she took tumbles in a comic scene playing football. At first she was typed as garish comic relief, almost a second string Martha Raye imitator. She had an early trademark bit, a literal knock out. When overwhelmed by comic problems, she didn't make funny faces or noises, she just socked herself in the jaw.

She moved to Universal Studios where she had a meaty co-starring role in *Hold That Ghost* with Abbott and Costello. In the film she plays a pleasant-looking woman whose profession just happens to be screaming on radio horror shows. She plays "straight" to Lou Costello in a routine involving a candle he swore was moving, but in the film's musical highlight, she matches him in a hilarious dance routine.

Around the same time Davis was getting laughs performing song parodies on Rudy Vallee's radio show. She became a regular, appearing in sketches as Rudy's most ardent fan (much to his comic chagrin). When he left for military service, Joan took over the show. In 1943 she teamed with Jack Haley for a radio sitcom. Her energetic personality and vocal dexterity (she had a range from a throaty whisper to a wailing scream) soon placed her in the top 10. In 1945 she was able to command $1 million a year and a move from NBC to CBS for "Joanie's Tea Room." By 1949 she was starring in "Leave It to Joan" and ready to leave radio for television.

All of her sitcom roles had revolved around the basic "man-hungry" premise, with Joan flirting, mugging, singing and shouting to get the attention of a likely male. Sometimes she did it with Martha Raye comic brassiness, other times with a dash of high-decibel Gracie Allen naiveté and enthusiasm. But for her 1952 sitcom debut she was no longer the old sex-starved Joan Davis. She was married (to Jim Backus, as Judge Bradley Stevens) and was now more of a Lucille Ball type, getting into all kinds of mischief that taxed her hubby's patience, love and affection. In a bit of interesting casting, Joan's daughter, Beverly Wills, played her sister.

Davis had been far more successful on radio than Lucy, but Lucy had made the switch from radio to television a year earlier and was now comedy's queen. Davis was ready to meet the challenge, calling on her years of experience in making funny faces and taking wild pratfalls. Her sitcom was loaded with slapstick, everything from hanging off ladders to tumbling inside a clothes dryer. She drew many fans for her own unique personality, but she couldn't sustain such a frantic pace in physical comedy and the scripts lacked the charm and freshness of "I Love Lucy." After a respectable run of four years, the show folded.

Joan had been a top star for many years, keeping at it, as she said, with "a mixture of gall, guts, and gumption." Several times she tried for a comeback, but none of her subsequent sitcom ideas sold. She might have won her way back eventually, but to the shock of her fans, the rough-and-tumble slapstick star died suddenly of a heart attack in 1961. Her daughter, Beverly Wills, died in a fire in 1963.

FILMS incl.: *Millions in the Air* (1935), *Love and Hisses* (1937), *Hold That Co-Ed* (1938), *Two Latins from Manhattan* (1941), *Hold That Ghost* (1941), *Yokel Boy* (1942), *Show Business* (1944), *She Gets Her Man* (1945), *She Wrote the Book* (1946), *If You Knew Susie* (1948), *Make Mine Laughs* (1949), *The Traveling Saleswoman* (1950), *Love That Brute* (1950), *The Groom Wore Spurs* (1951), *Harem Girl* (1952)
TV: "I Married Joan" (1952–55)

## DORIS DAY

### (Doris von Kappelhoff, April 3, 1924–    )

The female "Movie Box Office Champ" for 1959 was Doris Day. Her light comedies also made her the top film star in 1960, and again from 1962 through 1965. But while audiences of all ages chuckled at her sitcom antics in romantic comedies, critics were less than complimentary.

Not only underrated but routinely insulted, Day was forever being chided as the "oldest American virgin" for the chaste 1960s romantic comedies that seemed to get most of the laughs from the battle between a suave bachelor and the old-fashioned nice girl. Even "serious" film critics lapsed into exasperated vulgarity describing her appeal. Critic David Thomson in *The Biographical Dictionary of Film:* "She hoped to suggest that the world was OK, that wholesome blonde girls with cheerful voices and big tits were destined to meet nice guys who would woo them chastely and tunefully."

Ironically, Day's films so effectively captured the silliness and frustration of the era's repressive dating rituals that they were almost satires. Viewers in the 1970s and early '80s began to hunt up her old films as "camp," hooting over every cliché. They chortled at the previous era's concept of beauty (round face, pug nose, short hair). They even got cruel laughs out of unfortunate double entendres regarding Rock Hudson. In *Pillow Talk,* he teases Day about her prospective date with him in disguise: "Well, must I spell it out . . . well, there are some men who just are very devoted to their mothers, you know, the type that likes to collect cooking recipes and bits of gossip."

Day's initial fame was not in comedy. Born in Cincinnati, Ohio, she was a dancer until a car accident limited her mobility. She sang at Barney Rapp's Little Club in Cincinnati and was soon making records. She moved to films in 1948 with *Romance on the High Seas,* replacing Betty Hutton. She tended to make musicals, though at times she had undemanding dramatic parts that allowed her to sing at least one song no matter how terrible and/or incongruous ("Que Sera Sera" from *The Man Who Knew Too Much*). The musical comedy *The Pajama Game* in 1957 gave some hint of her talents as a comedy actress and light, humorous, romantic films followed, with Day opposite Gene Kelly (*The Tunnel of Love*) and Clark Gable (*Teacher's Pet*). Her own favorite film is *Calamity Jane,* which displayed her spunky, Betty Hutton–influenced side. "That's the real me," she says.

She next joined Rock Hudson for what was practically a "comedy series." Though they weren't exactly a team, Hudson and Day were certainly the most successful film couple since William Powell and Myrna Loy, and fans eagerly awaited each new movie. Hudson was handsome, charming and did have a likable light touch, but like most of Day's costars in the 1960s, he usually didn't get the laughs. Audiences were sympathetic and rooted for him, but most of the attention was centered on "will she or won't she" Doris.

In the 1960s she moved to television. After playing a sitcom mom during her show's first three seasons, she tried to update her image. The kids were dropped and the show concentrated on her life as a career woman. It wasn't a bad idea, but it worked better for Mary Tyler Moore a few years later. Moore had a wholesome streak but seemed to avoid leaving quite the saccharine aftertaste of the blond, sunny Day.

Towards the end of the decade Day was no longer interested in sitcom problems. She devoted herself to real-life issues. She said, "I love the movies and I'm grateful for my career, but the movies are gone. There's no future or past, there's only what's going on now." She formed The Doris Day Animal League and in the 1980s had a syndicated talk show that featured celebrities and their pets. She was a firm supporter of animal rights. "When are women going to stop with that ego baloney of fur coats?" she asked.

She said in 1990 that convicted murderers, not animals, should be used to test AIDS drugs. "I can't bear anything innocent being used. I think they should experiment on murderers. . . . Why not? They owe society something. Don't stand aghast at that. They're sitting there having three meals a day, and we're paying for it. What the hell are they going to do for society to pay us back?"

BIOGRAPHY: *Her Own Story* (1975); *The Sentimental Journey* (Hotchner, 1976), *The Films of Doris Day* (Young, 1977)

FILMS incl.: *Tea for Two* (1950), *Lullaby of Broadway* (1951), *On Moonlight Bay* (1951), *April in Paris* (1952), *By the Light of the Silvery Moon* (1953), *Young at Heart* (1955), *The Pajama Game* (1957), *The Tunnel of Love* (1958), *Teacher's Pet* (1958), *Pillow Talk (1959)*, *Please Don't Eat the Daisies* (1960), *Lover Come Back* (1962), *That Touch of Mink* (1962), *The Thrill of It All* (1963), *Move Over Darling* (1963), *Send Me No Flowers* (1964), *Do Not Disturb* (1965), *The Glass Bottom Boat* (1966), *Caprice* (1967), *With Six You Get Eggroll* (1968), *Where Were You When the Lights Went Out* (1968)

TV: "The Doris Day Show" (1968–73)

## THE DEAD END KIDS (See THE EAST SIDE KIDS.)

## DOM DELUISE

### (August 1, 1933–    )

Chubby and cuddly with a ready smile and a zany gleam in his eyes, Dom DeLuise usually plays com-

ically ingratiating types. He was a harmless sidekick for Burt Reynolds and Mel Brooks in films and a barber on his own television series. Whatever the role, he seems ready to bend over backward to be useful, even if the inevitable result is a pratfall.

Dom's first part was in a school play when he was seven. He remembered, "I was cast as a penny. The part called for me to roll under a bed as soon as the curtain went up and stay there until I was found in the very last scene. It was my hardest role to date. I detested having to be quiet and out of the action for so long."

DeLuise's first successful character was "Dominick the Great" on Garry Moore's old television show. He was the fretting, faltering, deliberately bad magician moving his bulk around the stage with mock daintiness and self-confidence, his smile going wan at the edges each time a trick failed. He used the character on "The Entertainers," performing with Ruth Buzzi as his assistant.

The self-deprecating, genuflecting DeLuise style made him popular in a variety of feature films. He was a charming scene stealer, easily recognizable thanks to his dumpling physique and the faint meringue whisp of hair adorning the top of his balding head. Dom's cheery, nonthreatening presence suggested humility as well as humor. That vulnerability audiences saw and appreciated in Dom DeLuise was something he appreciated in others. "I had my picture done by Al Hirschfeld," he recalled. "When I sat with him I said, 'What does it feel like to be the greatest cartoonist in the world?' He said, 'Dom, every time I sit down in front of that blank paper, I think I've lost it.' And I think that's the most wonderful thing. I mean, here he is with the greatest skill and he still has some self-doubt."

DeLuise's had a starring role in the semidramatic *Fatso*, directed by Anne Bancroft. It failed to launch him as a solo star but solidified his reputation as a fine actor. He continued to perform varied roles in films over the years and he briefly starred in his own syndicated television show, playing a sympathetic barber listening to guest-star comic customers. Occasionally he's been allowed to depart from his excellent if stereotypical happy, fat and fawning roles to play everything from a hilariously tempermental director (*The World's Greatest Lover*) to a greed-crazed manic (*The Twelve Chairs*). He surprised audiences with an effete Peter Lorre parody (*The Cheap Detective*) and shocked them with a drag performance in *Haunted Honeymoon*. Perhaps it was that experience that inspired him to grow the beard he's worn from the mid-1980s on.

BOOK: *Charlie the Caterpiller*

FILMS incl.: *Fail Safe* (1964), *The Glass Bottom Boat* (1966), *The Busy Body* (1967), *What's So Bad About Feeling Good* (1968), *The Twelve Chairs* (1970), *Norwood* (1971), *Every Little Crook and Nanny* (1972), *Blazing Saddles* (1974), *The Adventures of Sherlock Holmes' Smarter Brother* (1975), *Silent Movie* (1976), *The World's Greatest Lover* (1977), *Sextette* (1978), *The End* (1978), *The Cheap Detective* (1978), *Fatso* (1980), *Cannonball Run* (1981), *History of the World Part I* (1981), *The Best Little Whorehouse in Texas* (1982), *Johnny Dangerously* (1985), *Haunted Honeymoon* (1986), *Going Bananas* (1987), *Loose Cannons* (1990), *An American Tale: Fievel Goes West* (1991)

TV: "The Entertainers" (1964–65), "The Dean Martin Summer Show" (1966), "The Dom DeLuise Show" (1968), "The Glen Campbell Goodtime Hour" (1971–72), "The Dean Martin Show" (1972–73), "Lotsa Luck" (1973–74), "The Dom DeLuise Show" (1988), "Candid Camera" (1991)

## WILLIAM DEMAREST

### (February 28, 1882–December 28, 1983)

A longtime vaudevillian, William Demarest began his career at 13 playing the cello on New York City street corners. He starred with Olsen and Johnson in *Monkey Business* in 1925, and appeared in vaudeville and Broadway revues that showcased his talents as a musician, acrobat and comedian.

As a film comic in the 1930s and '40s, Demarest usually played the slow-burning, hard-boiled type. He was a great favorite of Preston Sturges and had key scenes in several of his comedies. In *The Miracle of Morgan's Creek* he played the cantankerous, long-suffering Officer Kockenlocker, who has trouble with his daughters. He declared in the film that some girls are "so homely they hang around the house like Spanish moss." In *Hail the Conquering Hero* he offered some typically feisty advice to 4-F

soldier Eddie Bracken: "They say opportunity's only got one hair on its head and you got to grab it while it's going by!"

Demarest knew all about opportunity. Between comedy parts he worked as a talent scout. One of his better discoveries was actress Jane Wyman. The film industry respected Demarest. He received an Academy Award nomination for his serio-comic role in *The Jolson Story*, using slow burns of chagrin as Al Jolson's sidekick and mentor.

Demarest received an Emmy nomination for his portrayal of Uncle Charley on television's classic sitcom "My Three Sons." He was the lovable curmudgeon to the end. The show was canceled in 1972, but Demarest was far from forgotten. He earned a star in the Hollywood Walk of Fame in 1979.

FILMS incl.: *The Gay Old Bird* (1927), *Simple Sis* (1927), *The Bush Leaguer* (1927), *The Jazz Singer* (1927), *The Butter and Egg Man* (1928), *Many Happy Returns* (1934), *Fog Over Frisco* (1934), *Circus Clown* (1934), *Mind Your Own Business* (1936), *Charlie Chan at the Opera* (1936), *Oh, Doctor* (1937), *Blonde Trouble* (1937), *One Wild Night* (1938), *The Gracie Allen Murder Case* (1939), *Mr. Smith Goes to Washington* (1939), *Laugh It Off* (1939), *The Great McGinty* (1940), *The Lady Eve* (1941), *The Devil and Miss Jones* (1941), *Sullivan's Travels* (1941), *The Palm Beach Story* (1942), *All Through the Night* (1942), *My Favorite Spy* (1942), *Hail the Conquering Hero* (1944), *The Miracle of Morgan's Creek* (1944), *Along Came Jones* (1945), *The Jolson Story* (1946), *Perils of Pauline* (1947), *Jolson Sings Again* (1949), *He's a Cockeyed Wonder* (1950), *Never a Dull Moment* (1950), *The Lady Wants Mink* (1953), *Here Come the Girls* (1953), *Jupiter's Darling* (1955), *Pepe* (1960), *Son of Flubber* (1963), *That Darn Cat* (1965), *Won Ton Ton, The Dog Who Saved Hollywood* (1976)

TV: "Love and Marriage" (1959–60), "My Three Sons" (1965–72)

## BOB DENVER

### (January 9, 1935–   )

Television's most cheerful goof, Bob Denver, like filmdom's Huntz Hall, made a career out of childlike charm and galling stupidity. As Maynard G. Krebs ("The Many Loves of Dobie Gillis") he was incredibly dumb. Given a quarter, he shouts "Joy for joy! That's almost fifteen cents!" As Gilligan, hapless fool of "Gilligan's Island," it was hard to tell if he was stupid or just fond of stupid jokes. Either way, the results were the same. While out fishing, the Skipper shouts to him, "I got a bite!" Gilligan: "Where?"

These were the jokes, and they rarely got better. Bob Denver not only made this kind of thing amusing, but he made the characters last a lifetime. Born in New Rochelle and raised in Los Angeles, Bob had little interest in acting. He was planning to major in law at Loyola University when he took his first role as a seaman in a class production of *The Caine Mutiny*.

His first important television role was as beatnik Maynard G. Krebs, the goofy, goateed counterpoint to straightman Dobie Gillis. His pleasantly blameless behavior and catch phrase, "You rang?" made him the hit of the show. From there, he won the title role on "Gilligan's Island." Once again, the humor was not in the gags but the character comedy—the relationship between the parental "Skipper" and Gilligan, who behaved like a little boy. His catch phrase was "You can't make me, you can't make me," followed by a quick fade and a shot of Gilligan forced to do the chore, still calling out one last "You can't make me!"

The show was a big hit among kids. They thoroughly loved and identified with Gilligan, someone dumbly cheerful when left to do what he wanted (usually nothing) and fretfully petulant when given responsibility. Critics, old enough to have their own petulant or deliberately silly children, were not amused. Denver did admit, "Little kids seem to love 'Gilligan's Island.' It doesn't take a mature intellect to laugh at a monkey running off with Gilligan's dinner or a guy getting hit on the head by a coconut."

After "Gilligan's Island," Denver had shorter runs in a pair of sitcoms, "The Good Guys" and "Dusty's Trail." Playing on his appeal among younger audiences, he moved on to Saturday morning kiddie fare with "Far Out Space Nuts." Like most comedians who rely on the comedy of innocence, aging was an enemy. Childlike behavior seems more like an aberration in people over 40. Even more of a problem

was his ever-increasing identification as Gilligan thanks to its phenomenal longevity in reruns. It was not surprising that Denver was seen less often except for reunion "Gilligan's Island" television movies.

Denver, never big on Hollywood anyway, seemed content to hold on to his privacy and enjoy his homes in Hawaii and Las Vegas. He married four times and had four children.

Meanwhile, fans still dream about life on "Gilligan's Island," and critics still wonder why. As Johnny Carson said in a 1988 monologue: "There was a report on the effects of television on teenagers. According to the study, by the age of 17 the average teenager has seen Bob Denver fall out of that hammock 758 times."

FILMS incl.: *A Private's Affair* (1959), *Take Her She's Mine* (1963), *For Those Who Think Young* (1964), *Who's Minding the Mint* (1967), *Did You Hear the One About the Traveling Saleslady* (1968), *Rescue from Gilligan's Island* (1978), *Castaways of Gilligan's Island* (1979), *The Harlem Globetrotters on Gilligan's Island* (1981), *The Invisible Woman* (1983), *High School USA* (1983), *Bring Me the Head of Dobie Gillis* (1987)

TV: "The Many Loves of Dobie Gillis" (1959–63), "Gilligan's Island" (1965–67), "The Good Guys" (1968–70), "Dusty's Trail" (1973)

## JOE DERITA (See THE THREE STOOGES.)

## DANNY DE VITO

### (November 17, 1944)

In his first major film he was short and crazy: Five-foot-tall Danny De Vito played one of the asylum inmates in *One Flew Over the Cuckoo's Nest*. Since the film used some real sanitarium residents, some viewers weren't sure if De Vito, as the perpetually smiling Martini, was acting or really out of his mind.

Born in Neptune, New Jersey, De Vito's career began on stage. He played Martini in the original off-Broadway production of *Cuckoo's Nest* and appeared in many more shows, including *Line of Least Existence*, with eventual "Taxi" co-star Judd Hirsch.

When De Vito moved to television, as one of the ensemble cast of "Taxi," viewers loved the comic grossness of his role as sleazy Louie DePalma, who insults the "loser" cab drivers at New York City's Sunshine Cab Company and behaves even worse toward his dates. In one episode he tried to take advantage of a girl for a one-nighter: "There she was—dejected, desperate and stoned. Everything I could hope for in a woman."

In another episode, after peeking at Elaine (Marilu Henner) in the ladies' room, he tries to apologize. "I was treatin' you like a sexual object," he admits. Then he adds, "Thank God I watched that Donahue show about broads." He couldn't even be pleasant with his own mother. After banishing her to a nursing home, he decides he wants her to come back and live with him. "Ma, when you're not there it's so quiet, I can hear the toilet running. I'm sorry for gettin' mushy." She asks, "If I come home, will you be nice to me?" His answer: "For a while."

His mother on the show was played by his real-life mother, Julia De Vito. Another performer on the show was Rhea Perlman, who appeared occasionally as Louis De Palma's girlfriend, Zena. After living together for 11 years, Danny and Rhea were married during a lunch break from "Taxi." For the occasion he did an impression of Our Gang's Alfalfa and sang "I'm in the Mood for Love." Danny won an Emmy for Best Supporting Actor in 1981, and the show had such a strong cult following that when ABC canceled it, NBC picked it up for another year.

Following "Taxi" and bit parts in films (he had one line in *The World's Greatest Lover*), De Vito emerged as a solid box office comedy star. He seemed to work best playing off a straight man. He was coupled with Joe Piscopo in *Wise Guys*, Richard Dreyfuss in *Tin Men*, Billy Crystal in *Throw Momma from the Train* and, for pure comic contrast, hulking Arnold Schwarzenegger in the box office smash *Twins*. *Twins* secured his fame—and (based on his percentage of the box office take) earned him an estimated $28 million. Somewhat typecast, he announced, "Maybe 10 or 12 more vulgar movies and then I'll do the straight ones. I've been saying for years that I want to tailor my career after Jimmy Stewarts'—be the guy who rescues the town from the flood and walks off into the sunset with Jane Wyman. But it ain't worked like that."

De Vito has always been interested in directing. He helmed some episodes of "Taxi" as well as some episodes of the 1985 sitcom "Mary." After directing a made-for-TV movie *The Ratings Game*, he directed (as well as co-starred in) *Throw Momma from the Train*. It was a hit and enabled him to again co-star and direct, this time the equally successful nasty slapstick *War of the Roses*. De Vito was so serious about his new position as a true director that for the laser disc version of the film, he included a track of narration to help explain his directorial point of view. Not all of his comments were of a deeply artistic or serious nature. Reviewing one scene, he announced, "Boy, am I fat in this picture!"

*War of the Roses* marked De Vito as both a highly marketable director and performer and has led to more lucrative offers. In addition to more films in which he's been the formidable co-star rather than supporting player (the Penguin in *Batman Returns*), he's had a chance to star in his own film comedies (he played "Larry the Liquidator" in the Wall Street comedy *Other People's Money*).

BROADWAY: *Shoot Anything with Hair That Moves* (1969), *License* (1969), *The Jar* (1969)

FILMS incl.: *Scalawag* (1973), *One Flew Over the Cuckoo's Nest* (1975), *The Van* (1976), *Car Wash* (1976), *The World's Greatest Lover* (1977), *Goin' South* (1978), *Going Ape* (1981), *Terms of Endearment* (1983), *Romancing the Stone* (1984), *Ruthless People* (1986), *Wise Guys* (1986), *Tin Men* (1987), *Throw Momma from the Train* (1987), *Twins* (1988), *War of the Roses* (1989), *Other People's Money* (1991), *Batman Returns* (1992)

TV: "Taxi" (1978–83)

# PHYLLIS DILLER

## (Phyllis Driver, July 17, 1917–   )

Often called "the First Lady of Stand-Up," Phyllis Diller arrived after pioneers Jean Carroll and Moms Mabley, but surpassed them and became the first female superstar of monology. Through the 1960s, she had hit records, played all the top clubs, made films and starred in her own television series. Thirty years later she can still command packed houses. Asked for the secret to her success, she said, "I never tried to be a phony, never tried to be a star.

The first lady of stand-up comedy: Phyllis Diller became a hit in the 1960s and remains a big star into the 1990s. Photo by the author.

A lot of performers try to be someone else. I never did. I don't know if that's the answer to my longevity in a very competitive business but it's the only answer I can think of."

A student at Bluffton College, the girl from Lima, Ohio had talent as a writer (she had written comedy for the school newspaper) and also as a singer and pianist. After marrying Sherwood Diller (oddly, there was an actress already named Phyllis Diller who starred in a 1934 film called *Maniac*), her aspirations for a musical career ended and she became a full-time housewife, raising five kids.

Feeling unfulfilled and needing some extra cash to help support the family, Diller began writing for the local *San Leandro News Observer*. She began writing comic articles and decided to put them into monologue form. She made her debut at the legendary Purple Onion nightclub at the age of 37.

Initially she created the character of a campy chanteuse, singing sophisticated songs ("I'd Rather Cha-Cha Than Eat"), lampooning such "chi chi" topics as Yma Sumac records and *Vogue* magazine, and offering arch one-liners: "I'm dedicated to culture. I honestly believe there's absolutely nothing wrong with going to bed with a good book—or a friend who's read one." She managed to get on Groucho Marx's "You Bet Your Life" as a budding comic/contestant, but her career wasn't taking off.

Bob Hope saw her perform in 1959. He saw promise in her, even though she bombed. "I bombed marvelously. I never flagged. . . . he saw courage. . . . He says, 'You are great.' From then on I had what's called high self-esteem." She developed the confidence to try more personal, conversational material based on her housewife lifestyle: "I was making a pudding and I knew something was wrong. I couldn't get the spoon out. Well, the Food and Drug Administration people showed up. They wanted to stir it and the whole room went around! And then they wanted to take it to their lab to test it. They had to. One of their guys was now stuck in it!"

She created a series of jokes about husband "Old Fang Face," shortened to "Fang." The "Fang" character became an audience favorite, long after she divorced Sherwood Diller in the mid-1960s. The only subject that took more abuse than Fang was herself: "My Playtex Living Bra died—of starvation. I've turned many a head in my day, and a few stomachs. I never made 'Who's Who' but I'm featured in 'What's That?' "

Like her idol, Bob Hope, she developed a one-liner style that gave the customers more jokes for their money. She livened up the gags with eccentric costuming. In the 1960s she favored the outlandishly harried housewife look: garish clothes, a blond fright wig, gloves and a cigarette holder. In subsequent decades she dropped the cigarette holder, disgusted by smoking. She began wearing outfits that were simply on the lunatic fringe of fashion. Most of all, there was her trademark, a loonlike, cackling laugh. She said it developed "probably out of desperation and nervousness" as she waited for the audience to get the gag.

Diller co-starred in several films with Bob Hope, but it was at the nadir of his movie career and did nothing to promote hers. A sitcom series about a newly poor eccentric on Long Island missed as well, but in stand-up she remained a hot attraction. A frustrated singer since her college days, she finally got the chance to record a "straight" album of pop and rock tunes and in the 1970s replaced Carol Channing in *Hello Dolly* on Broadway. She was proud to sing a few songs that had previously been removed because Channing "didn't have the register." From time to time Diller appeared at the piano for serious concerts with symphony orchestras.

Known for her generosity, Diller performed often for charity, always shared her comic theories with young comedians and was always willing to talk about "the secrets" of her success. She pointed to Claude Bristol's book *The Magic of Believing* as a strong influence on her life and recommended it to those in need of direction. "I'm for mental attitude being up and positive," she said. "When something goes wrong, it isn't going to stay that way."

In the 1980s she was almost as well known for her plastic surgery as her comedy. She underwent a nose job, teeth straightening, cheek implants, tucks, even breast lifts. The latter surgery surprised most fans. She laughed and admitted, "I convinced everyone I was flat. I was 38D. I had nursed the world." Back in the early 1960s she had even shot a nude test photo session for *Playboy*. One of Diller's more pioneering beauty procedures was having her eyelids tattooed black so she wouldn't have to bother applying eyeliner. She was one of the first stars to acknowledge the "changes" and to offer advice and encouragement for anyone thinking about similar procedures.

Always active, always performing, Diller enjoys her travel schedule. Single since the 1960s, eligible and attractive without her "fright" stage makeup on, she always seems to be in the company of a handsome escort. When she is alone, it is definitely by choice. Gracious to fans despite the constant interruptions for autographs and questions that made

them "the bane of my existence," she favored wearing disguises to the cruelty of simply walking away. She's sometimes gone out in public wearing a nun's habit. She may have gotten the idea after playing Sister Mary Regina in a stock production of *Nunsense* in 1988.

Diller received honorary doctorates from National Christian University and Kent State, both institutions that praised her enviable life achievements. A realist, she always believed she had to get the most out of her one go-round: "My mother taught and ran a church. She spoon-fed me fundamental religion. . . . I didn't buy it. . . . And I'm fearless. I don't mind dying. I'm going to die and I'm not going anywhere. I'm going to be truly dead!"

As a comic (the "tough-and-punchy" term she prefers to "comedienne"), few could be so lively. She comes out with energy, good nature and her ecstatic laugh, blitzing the audience with sight, sound and one-liner fury: "I went to this plastic surgeon. He took a look at me and just wanted to add a tail! He said my face looked like a bouquet of elbows! My foot doctor sent me to a blacksmith! Lloyd's of London refused to insure my face. They told me— what the hell more could happen to it?"

BOOKS: *Housekeeping Hints* (1966), *Marriage Manual* (1967), *The Complete Mother* (1968), *The Joys of Aging and How to Avoid Them* (1981)
FILMS incl.: *Splendor in the Grass* (1961), *Boy, Did I Get a Wrong Number* (1966), *The Fat Spy* (1966), *Eight on the Lam* (1967), *The Private Navy of Sgt. O'Farrell* (1968), *Did You Hear the One About the Traveling Saleslady?* (1968), *The Adding Machine* (1969), *The Sunshine Boys* (1975), *Boneyard* (1991)
TV: "The Pruitts of Southampton" (1966–67), "The Beautiful Phyllis Diller Show" (1968), "The Gong Show" (1976–80)
VIDEOS: *The Minsky Follies; How to Have a Moneymaking Garage Sale; Laughing Room Only*

## JACK DOUGLAS

### (Douglas Crickard, 1908–January 31, 1989)

An ex-vaudevillian who once teamed with Cliff Arquette in the late 1930s, Jack Douglas divided his time between careers as a stand-up comic, talk show raconteur, television producer and best-selling humorist. He began his show business career with master of ceremonies work on radio (WEAF in 1937) and drumming (for Al Vann's orchestra). Very much a precursor to Pat McCormick and Jonathan Winters, Douglas pioneered offbeat humor. After joining Bob Hope in 1939, Hope dubbed him "the Mad Dog" of his writing staff. Douglas could not be restrained. Once, during half-time at a football game, Douglas suddenly grabbed the microphone away from Bob and shouted to the crowd, "This is a stickup! Nobody move!"

His first book, 1949's *No Navel to Guide Him*, offered weird chapters such as "How to Train an Aardvark." It was reissued a decade later as *My Brother Was an Only Child* and became a hit. By that time Douglas had won an Emmy for his writing on "The George Gobel Show" and was now working for Jack Paar. Paar recalled, "My biggest and wildest jokes were usually his. One was the line about the starlet who decided to commit suicide glamorously—by jumping into twenty gallons of lanolin. She softened to death."

Douglas first appeared on Paar's show to plug the book. His spontaneous gags and curmudgeonly comedy made him a welcome guest over and over. The book sold 100,000 copies and helped revitalize Douglas' stand-up career. He suffered a heart attack in 1959 after finishing an engagement at New York's Hotel Duane but was back soon after, appearing at The Bon Soir in the early 1960s and even appearing in stock productions such as *Teahouse of the August Moon* in 1961.

Douglas continued to appear as a talk show raconteur, revered as one of the funniest writers in America. This was an amazing feat considering that he wasn't writing the tired, dry and quaint volumes of humor that were usually praised by book reviewers, but borderline sick material with vaudevillian timing. One volume opened with: "This book is bound in old Moroccan leather—so if your old Moroccan grandfather is missing. . . ."

Douglas gags were caustic: "Anyone can be a yogi. All you need are a dirty sheet and two broken legs." In stand-up he had surreal visions: "I'm on the Emergency Redi-Whip Team. . . . It's not what you think. These jet planes, they're still having trouble with the landing gear. So we get out to the airport and spread the stuff on the runway nice and smooth. We were at La Guardia last night and the plane landed at Idlewild."

Through the years he wrote books, produced adventure shows ("I Search for Adventure" and "Bold Journey") and mellowed a bit in his talk show appearances, now discussing his suburban life with his wife Reiko and his pet wolves. In private life, Douglas was still authentic in his idiosyncracies. His driveway seemed like something out of a Warner Brothers cartoon, with periodic signs saying "Stop," "No Trespassing," "Get Out of Here" and "This MEANS YOU!" He dumped crates and lumber in his swimming pool so that if a stray squirrel or rabbit fell in, the creature would have a "fighting chance."

Douglas was hired by George Bush to write jokes for him during the 1988 presidential campaign. It was a strange twist to a long, iconoclastic career that ended barely a year later when Jack died of pneumonia.

AUDIO: *Jack Douglas and the Original Cast* (Columbia)
BOOKS: incl.: *My Brother Was an Only Child; Never Trust a Naked Bus Driver; A Funny Thing Happened to Me on My Way to the Grave; The Adventures of Huckleberry Hashimoto; The Neighbors Are Scaring My Wolf; Shut Up and Eat Your Snowshoes; What Do You Hear from Walden Pond; The Jewish-Japanese Sex and Cook Book and How to Raise Wolves; Benedict Arnold Slept Here; Going Nuts in Brazil*

## RUTH DRAPER

**(December 2, 1884–December 30, 1956)**

For the average person, "Ruth Draper" is a vaguely familiar name, usually summoned up in reference to Lily Tomlin or Whoopi Goldberg. Part of the reason for Draper's obscurity is that hers was performance art at a time when there was no such thing. For decades a small but vocal group of theater devotees and acting students attended Draper's solo shows, praising her ability to create monologues and act them out in a variety of characters. Unlike Tomlin, Draper was not presenting humor that happened to be artistic, she was offering art that sometimes happened to be humorous. Even now Draper's albums are never placed in the "comedy" section of a store or library but in the "spoken arts" section.

Schooled by a governess, raised by a socially prominent family that hosted many influential figures of the day, Draper was ever the precocious child, called upon for recitations. She devised her own monologues based on characters she knew. Draper recalled, "What I had as a child I've never lost—the child's ability to pretend to be what he imagines he is. But it is the audience who must supply the imagination."

After performing at private gatherings—for such public figures as Paderewski, Henry James and King George V—Draper began her career. She was markedly different from another pioneering female monologist, Beatrice Herford, who performed in London (1895) and in America into the 1930s. Herford favored chatty, slice-of-life humor pieces: Beatrice playing a woman tending a sick friend, or visiting the doctor or becoming a hairdresser: "Soap in your eyes? Take this towel. There was a little girl in here the other day and she kept rubbing her eyes. I told her to take them out and keep them in her lap."

Draper's approach was far more theatrical. She began her American career by presenting a sketch, "The Actress," at New York's Comedy Theater. While vaudeville demanded fast jokes and instant laughs, the world of theater was more indulgent. She performed on a bare stage, with only a shawl or a hat to help her weave her illusions. Joyce Grenfell recalled, "Ruth's 'dramas' (her word for them) had plots. Her work was composed at a period when there was plenty of time to introduce characters, establish them, allow them to develop, and finally reveal them as full-length portraits. What she wrote and performed with total mastery were little plays of great intensity. . . . She recorded well, but I felt that all her warmth was fully revealed only in her stage performances; then she was vulnerable, passionate, gentle, tender, loving and wholly approachable."

Draper's subtle comic performances were reviewed less often in *Variety* than *The Literary Digest*. They wrote that she was "very funny but at the same time . . . hardly exaggerated, or exaggerated only so much as keen, friendly observation will exaggerate any human act."

Draper toured the world, her sketches becoming polished gemstones over the years. She was performing at New York's Playhouse Theater in a four-week run at the time of her death. She had opened to good reviews on Christmas Day. A few nights later, on her way home from the theater, she asked to be driven around Rockefeller Plaza so she could see the famous Christmas tree. She died in her sleep that night.

AUDIO: *The Art of Ruth Draper* (Spoken Arts)
BIOGRAPHY: *The Art of Ruth Draper* (Zabel, 1960), *The Letters of Ruth Draper* (Warren, 1979)

## MARIE DRESSLER

### (Leila Marie Koreber, November 9, 1869–July 28, 1934)

Marie Dressler was one of the first of the homely, humongous heroines in film comedies, still best remembered as the overpowering Tillie in the first silent comedy feature, *Tillie's Punctured Romance*.

Born in Ontario, Dressler's first experience with slapstick was at age five, playing Cupid in a church play. She posed on a pedestal, fell off and fell in love with the sound of the laughter. Her parents didn't mind if she wanted to go into show business as long as she didn't use the family name. She adopted the name of a long-dead aunt, "Marie Dressler."

She made her stage debut in *Under Two Flags* in 1886. Blossoming to a full 200 pounds, she impressed Maurice Barrymore, who insisted, "The first chance you get, do comedy. You can't miss!" Dressler recalled that the idea made sense: "I was too homely for a prima donna and too big for a soubrette." She honed her skills performing in comic operas. At the turn of the century, when minstrel acts were popular and blacks were ridiculed with impunity, she wore dark makeup and sang "All Coons Look Alike to Me" and other songs.

A few years later Dressler was making fun of herself with such comic songs as "A Great Big Girl Like Me." She was one of Broadway's top laugh-getters, known for taking bruising pratfalls night after night in such fancifully named shows as *Higgledy Piggledy* and *Twiddle-Twaddle*. The latter featured a vegetable fight that usually ended with the audience flinging stray bits of food all around the house. In 1910 she created the part of the housebound Tillie Blobbs in a play called *Tillie's Nightmare*. In this Cinderella tale of a long-suffering houseworker and her idle sister she sang "Heaven Will Protect the Working Girl."

In 1913 she moved on to vaudeville for "Marie Dressler's All-Star Gambols" and became one of the highest paid stars on stage, earning $2,500 a week. She regularly met presidents and royalty. When Mack Sennett considered filming a full-length comedy, he didn't have a star big enough to interest backers. So he brought in the Broadway superstar for $35,000. It was an amazing price for Sennett, who fought with his star comics over a few hundred a week.

*Tillie's Punctured Romance* was a big hit, with up-and-coming star Charlie Chaplin as her suitor and Mabel Normand as the other woman who couldn't believe Charlie would be interested in "one of Ringling's elephants." Sadly, interest in Marie waned after the mild sequels *Tillie Wakes Up* and *Tillie's Tomato Surprise*. Her stage career stalled too, in part due to her active role in the 1919 Actors Equity Strike, which angered producers.

They refused her work and insisted she was too old for raucous "Tillie" parts and that the public was too "sophisticated" for her brand of hokum. In 1925 she retired, declaring "I've had my name in electric lights for 28 years. . . . I am glad to be through with the terrible nerve strain of theatrical work." She tried to sell real estate, but it didn't work out.

Fortunately, a few people hadn't forgotten Marie Dressler, and when she really needed a break, she got a bit part in 1927's *The Joy Girl*. She rebounded with *The Callahans and the Murphys*. It was written by Frances Marion (a woman named after her ancestor, the Revolutionary War's "Swamp Fox") who was returning the favor after Dressler had nursed her through an illness and had also given her an interview that helped boost her early writing career.

The film vaulted Dressler back to prominence, though Irish groups protested the brawling stereotypes in the film and a scene in which Dressler and her comic partner Polly Moran engaged in a wet and wild beer brawl. Moran and Dressler eventually formed a comedy team and made four subsequent films together: *Caught Short, Reducing, Politics* and *Prosperity*.

Marion went on to write several of Dressler's best screen vehicles, including *Dinner at Eight* and *Min*

*and Bill*, co-starring Wallace Beery, who also teamed with Dressler for several films. Dressler won an Academy Award for her role in the latter. A controversial biography of Greta Garbo in 1990 insisted there was a romance between the Swedish superstar and the motherly-looking matron. They appeared together in *Anna Christie*. Briefly married, Dressler would leave her estate to her sister, Bonita.

Once a has-been, Dressler was once again a superstar. Titanic in silent films, as an energetic harridan; she emerged now as a battered but unbowed old broad. She stood her ground with great comic dignity. She recalled, "I may have stood on my head and knocked my co-stars around as if they were ninepins, still I always did it with refinement."

Dressler earned the cover of *Time* magazine in 1933. Her fans included President Roosevelt, who signed a scroll commemorating her 64th birthday. In the weak film *Hollywood Revue* she saved the day by singing "I'm the Queen." She mugged her way through the lyrics: "I'm the Queen! Once as Lady Godiva I was seen! The poor horse died, of course. Not of shame or deep remorse—'twas my weight that killed the horse. Still, I'm the Queen!"

Though ill with cancer for two years, the queen of comedy continued to make films. In the classic *Dinner at Eight* she played a retired actress ("I'll have my double chins in privacy!"). She utilized many comic tricks, including a priceless double take when Jean Harlow announces "I was reading a book the other day." She also had the best line in the film. The heavyset homely lady is discussing modern times with sleek Harlow. Jean remarks, "Do you know, machinery is going to take the place of every profession?" Dressler: "My dear, that is something you need never worry about."

AUTOBIOGRAPHIES: *The Life Story of an Ugly Duckling* (1924), *My Own Story* (1934)
BROADWAY: *Princess Nicotine* (1893), *Madeleine* (1895), *The Lady Slavey* (1896), *Hotel Topsy Turvy* (1898), *The Man in the Moon* (1899), *Miss Print* (1900), *The King's Carnival* (1901), *The Hall of Fame* (1902), *King Highball* (1902), *Higgledy Piggledy* (1904), *Twiddle Twaddle* (1906), *The Boy and the Girl* (1909), *Tillie's Nightmare* (1910), *Roly Poly* (1912), *Marie Dressler's All-Star Gambols* (1913), *The Passing Show*

*of 1921* (1921), *Cinderella on Broadway* (1921), *The Dancing Girl* (1923)

FILMS incl.: *Tillie's Punctured Romance* (1914), *The Callahans and the Murphys* (1927), *Bringing Up Father* (1928), *The Patsy* (1928), *Hollywood Revue of 1929* (1929), *Let Us Be Gay* (1930), *Min and Bill* (1930), *Reducing* (1931), *Emma* (1932), *Prosperity* (1932), *Christopher Bean* (1933), *Tugboat Annie* (1933), *Dinner at Eight* (1933)

## DUFFY and SWEENEY

**Jimmy Duffy, 1888–March 15, 1939**
**Fred Sweeney, 1896–December 10, 1954**

When hard-drinking Jimmy Duffy met hard-drinking Fred Sweeney, the results were intoxicating. Duffy and Sweeney were known for wild and violent comedy antics, the kind of knockabout brawling that one might expect from brains pickled in alcohol. In their most popular bit, Duffy would doze off during Sweeney's monologue. Rudely awakened by Sweeney, Duffy would slap his friend in the face. In classic stooge fashion, Duffy would quickly apologize to avoid any further mayhem. And Sweeney, in the spirit of friendship, would accept the apology; then smack Duffy just to even the score. Sweeney, now ready to continue the act, couldn't imagine that Duffy would hold a grudge. Until he got socked again.

Audiences were amused by all that violence. They loved how the men used courtly politeness and called each other "Mister"—before landing the punches. Vaudeville scholars claim Gallagher and Shean began using the "Mister" trademark after seeing how effective it was for Duffy and Sweeney.

Sometimes, when the team's violence was especially gratuitous, their slapstick was met by dull silence. On one such occasion, Duffy went out to the footlights and announced to the audience that he and Sweeney were going to "go through the aisles with a baseball bat and beat the bejesus out of you." This got the dangerous duo banned from E. F. Albee's vaudeville houses.

One of the classic stories in vaudeville is the one about their reinstatement. Duffy went to Albee's office with a little boy in tow. Pleading poverty, he pointed to the child and asked, "Are you going to let him starve?" Albee was touched. And, fortunately for Duffy, the theater owner never learned that the kid was not his son. Another time Albee discovered Duffy was drunk. "I'm sorry to see you like this," Albee said sternly. "Are you sure you're sorry?" asked the wobbling Duffy. "Yes, I'm very sorry!" snapped Albee. "Well," said Duffy, "if you're very sorry, then I'll forgive you."

The duo broke up after the 1920s. Duffy, who had earlier teamed with his parents (Duffy, Sawtelle and Duffy) and Mercedes Lorenz, did some writing for Earl Carroll's *Vanities* but fell on hard times. Duffy's alcoholism worsened until he was found dead on the corner of 47th Street and 8th Avenue in New York. Sweeney appeared in bit film parts. Bob Hope and Bing Crosby were especially fond of the old vaudevillian and used him in several pictures. Sweeney died of tuberculosis in 1954.

## MARGARET DUMONT

**(October 20, 1889–March 6, 1965)**

One of the classic concepts in comedy is the upsetting of dignity. But it's not that simple. If it was, then Margaret Dumont would be an unknown. As the prime target for much of The Marx Brothers' comedy (she was also the victim of W. C. Fields and Abbott and Costello and appeared with Laurel and Hardy and Jack Benny, among others), Margaret Dumont was powerfully, aristocratically and foolishly dignified. The great dowager and grand duchess of comedy, Margaret Dumont's haughty and invincible demeanor invited comic disaster.

Born in Brooklyn, originally billed as Daisy Dumont, the actress had her first major success playing Trixie Fluff in *The Summer Widowers* on Broadway in 1910. She married successful businessman John Moller and lived in fashionable homes in Palm Beach and Paris. She retired from the stage, resuming her career only after her husband's death.

After appearing at the Casino de Paris in Paris and in many Broadway roles, some featuring her opera-trained voice (she sang "I Want to Be Loved Like a Leading Lady" in the show *The Girl Behind the Counter*), she was discovered by George Kaufman in a show called *The Four Flushers* and cast in the original Broadway production of *Cocoanuts*.

She appeared in many subsequent Marx Brothers films and later was cast as a foil for others. Groucho, who was always called Julie (short for Julius) by Dumont, said, "She never understood any of the jokes. She said, 'What are they laughing at, Julie?'" It's true that she often didn't understand specific lines, such as Groucho's crack "I'm fighting for your honor—which is more than you ever did." But she did understand her role, which was, in her words, that of "the ultra-ultra social climber, the fluttery, helpless creature who always had people running in circles . . . so shallow and so absurd." She recalled that when she first worked with The Marx Brothers in *Cocoanuts,* "I thought the society leader funny, but whenever I tried to clown Groucho would say, 'I like you dignified.'" In a 1942 interview she explained her philosophy in comically playing it straight: "I'm not a stooge. I'm a straight lady—the best straight woman in Hollywood. There's an art to playing straight. You must build up your man, but never top him, never steal the laughs from him." Of Groucho, who was prone to pulling chairs out from under her during stage productions and surprising her with frogs on the dinner table, "He roughed me up a good deal, but he never hurt me. He was an artist."

Typical of the verbal abuse heaped on Dumont is this battle with Groucho Marx from *Duck Soup:* "As chairwoman of the reception committee, I welcome you with open arms." "Is that so? How late do you stay open?" "I feel you are the most able statesman in all Freedonia." "Well, that covers a lot of ground. Say, you cover a lot of ground yourself. You better beat it, I hear they're going to tear you down and put up an office building where you're standing . . . not that I care, but where is your husband?" "Why, he's dead." "I'll bet he's just using that as an excuse." "I was with him till the very end." "No wonder he passed away." "I held him in my arms and kissed him." "Oh I see. Then it was murder!"

Physical abuse was fun too. In an outrageous scene in *Animal Crackers,* Harpo bashes her repeatedly in the stomach with Chico gleefully jeering she "can't take it there." And in *Duck Soup* all the brothers attack her. When she loudly bleats an anthem to her country, "Freedonia," they start pelting her with fruit. Off stage, The Marx Brothers showed her even less respect. Groucho recalled that while touring in tryous for *A Night at the Opera,* the brothers got the better of her during a train trip. "We took off all her clothes. She screamed so loud you couldn't hear the train whistle."

Dumont, who did affect a certain haughty star grandeur off stage, played the dowager throughout her film career and brought it to television as Mrs. Rhinelander on "My Friend Irma." Just a week before her death, she appeared opposite Groucho in a comedy sketch on television's "Hollywood Palace." She once said, "My association with The Marx Brothers was fun while it lasted. I wouldn't take a million dollars for the experience, but I wouldn't give a cent to do it again. Making pictures with them is truly living dangerously."

BROADWAY: *The Summer Widowers* (1910), *Go Easy Mabel* (1922), *The Rise of Rosie O'Reilly* (1923), *Cocoanuts* (1925), *Animal Crackers* (1928), *Shoot the Works* (1931), *Tell Her the Truth* (1932)

FILMS incl.: *The Cocoanuts* (1929), *Animal Crackers* (1930), *The Girl Habit* (1931), *Duck Soup* (1933), *A Night at the Opera* (1935), *Anything Goes* (1936), *The Life of the Party* (1937), *Youth on Parole* (1937), *Wise Girl* (1937), *A Day at the Races* (1937), *At the Circus* (1939), *The Big Store* (1941), *Never Give a Sucker an Even Break* (1941), *The Dancing Masters* (1943), *Up in Arms* (1944), *The Bathing Beauty* (1944), *The Horn Blows at Midnight* (1945), *Stop, You're Killing Me* (1952), *Auntie Mame* (1958), *Zotz* (1962), *What a Way to Go* (1964)

TV: "My Friend Irma" (1952–53)

## THE DUNCAN SISTERS

**Rosetta Duncan, November 23, 1900–December 4, 1959**
**Vivian Duncan, June 17, 1902–September 19, 1986**

One of the more unusual vaudeville sister teams, The Duncans were famous for an interracial blackface act. Vivian played the dainty white Eva, shocked by Rosetta as her tough-talking black playmate Topsy: "I is mean an' ornery. I hate everybody in the world and I only wish there were more people in the world so I could hate 'em too!"

In childhood the sisters played local church functions and then kicked around vaudeville for years, first in *Kiddies Revue* and later the 1917 revue *Doing Our Bit*. It was in 1923 that they reworked *Uncle Tom's Cabin*, added their own gags and songs, and called it *Topsy and Eva*. The show went to Broadway in 1924 and was later staged throughout Europe. They had hits with a few songs from their show, such as "Remembering" and "I Never Had a Mammy."

*Topsy and Eva* was enough of a stage hit to warrant a film version in 1927. D. W. Grifith called Rosetta "the female Charlie Chaplin," but the silent film didn't exactly do justice to the girls' singing and dialect clowning. They returned to the stage. They seemed set for life, having made over a million dollars in the 1920s. Vivian remembered how it disappeared in 1929 thanks to "goldmines with no gold, worthless stock, the fickleness of Wall Street and signatures on too many dotted lines."

The aging Duncan Sisters went back to vaudeville, utilizing some of their famous old "Topsy and Eva" and sometimes performing some novelty numbers in little-girl gowns. Their comic songs included "I Gotta Code in By Dose," "The Cuspidor My Father Left to Me," "The Prune Song," and "Tell Me Pretty Maiden." The latter was filmed in their only talkie, *It's a Great Life*.

The sister act was touring Illinois when Rosetta was killed in a car accident. She had swerved to avoid an oncoming car and crashed into a guard rail. Vivian Duncan briefly teamed up with comic Alice Tyrrell to sing some of the old Duncan Sisters songs. She died suffering from Alzheimer's disease in 1986.

BROADWAY: *Tip Top* (1920), *Topsy and Eva* (1924)
FILMS: *Topsy and Eva* (1927), *It's a Great Life* (1929)

## IRENE DUNNE

### (December 20, 1904–September 4, 1990)

A popular star of screwball comedy, Kentucky-born Irene Dunne began her career as a singer, training at the Indianapolis Fine Arts Academy and Chicago Musical College. Passed over by the Metropolitan Opera, she took roles in Broadway and touring musicals.

She expanded her range in films. For only her second movie, *Cimmaron*, she received an Academy Award nomination. Dunne's classic beauty and genteel reserve served her well as the heroine in a series of tear-jerker dramas. After returning to musicals via the films *Roberta* and *Show Boat*, she starred in *Theodora Goes Wild*, the first of her successful sophisticated comedies. She received another Academy Award nomination playing the "notorious" author of a racy novel.

The following year she starred in what genre fans consider one of the best screwball comedies ever made, *The Awful Truth*, co-starring Cary Grant. She was again nominated for an Academy Award in this story of a divorcing couple and their various breakups, new romances and court battles. The film included the archly dry humor that was typical of her style. In a nightclub scene, she observes a dancer perform a saucy number that ends with a gust of wind lifting her skirt. She remarks, "I guess it was easier for her to change her name than for her whole family to change theirs."

*My Favorite Wife*, another Grant and Dunne teaming, is on similar ground: a husband plans to remarry after his wife is lost at sea. Then she turns up alive. In that one she demonstrated coy aloofness and tart disdain. Rather than telling "the other woman" that she is Grant's wife, she puts on a hokey Southern accent and pretends to be merely "a friend" of his. She'd rather teach the guy a lesson than reunite with him and her long-suffering children.

All of her poised archness and pretty poison posing didn't go unnoticed by critics. Some resented her coolness and her ability to keep the hero off balance with her beauty and her games. Most screwball film heroines were more manic (Lombard) or vulnerably warm (Arthur). In evident exasperation, critic James Agee wrote, "I am not among those who take to Irene Dunne—as a rule she makes my skin crawl."

Others believed her to be an underrated and inspiring comedienne. Lucille Ball, a starlet at the time, watched Dunne work and was impressed with her careful experimentation in finding just the right expression, just the right way to deliver a line. For one sequence, Ball recalled, "I watched her do . . .

32 takes and 25 must have been different. She really worked on how to do that scene."

The aging actress gradually shifted back into soap operas and dramas, an exception being *Life with Father*. Despite her image in light romantic comedy, Dunne led a quiet life, married for 37 years to a dentist, Dr. Francis Griffin, who died in 1965. As columnist Earl Wilson once noted of the dignified Dunne, "She was too much of a lady to be good copy." After she stopped making films, Dunne devoted herself to charity work and in 1957 became a delegate to the United Nations. Though closely allied with Republican causes, she surprised many by declaring that "the extreme right is just as dangerous as the extreme left." As in her sometimes enigmatic movie roles, she was never as predictable as people thought.

BROADWAY incl.: *Lollipop* (1924), *City Chap* (1925), *Sweetheart Time* (1926), *Yours Truly* (1927), *Luckee Girl* (1928), *She's My Baby* (1928)

FILMS incl.: *Leathernecking* (1930), *Cimarron* (1931), *Back Street* (1932), *Symphony of Six Million* (1932), *No Other Woman* (1933), *Age of Innocence* (1934), *Magnificent Obsession* (1935), *Sweet Adeline* (1935), *Roberta* (1935), *Show Boat* (1936), *Theodora Goes Wild* (1936), *The Awful Truth* (1937), *Joy of Living* (1938), *Love Affair* (1939), *My Favorite Wife* (1940), *Anna and the King of Siam* (1946), *Life with Father* (1947), *I Remember Mama* (1948), *The Mudlark* (1950), *It Grows on Trees* (1952)

## JIMMY DURANTE

### (February 10, 1893–January 28, 1980)

A comedy original, the flamboyant "Schnozzola" was the ultimate comical song-and-dance man. Clutching his fedora and doing a stiff-legged strut across the stage, he'd smile and sing his novelty classics "Inka Dinka Do" and "Can Broadway Do Without Me?" He had plenty of songs, and as for jokes, his catch phrase said it all: "I gotta million of 'em!"

Born on the Lower East Side of New York, his father a barber, Durante quit school at the age of eight to work in a variety of menial jobs. He began his career as a piano player in 1910, working every-

Despite his comic frustrations and stupefactions, Jimmy Durante was almost always a cheerful and smiling entertainer. Photo from the author's collection.

thing from gangster-ridden gambling dens in Harlem to secret gay cabarets on the Bowery. It would take another 10 years before "Big Nose" the piano player got up the nerve to tell jokes between the songs. A few years later he had his own speakeasy, Club Durant, and two partners, Lou Clayton and Eddie Jackson. After the club closed in 1925, they performed at other tough venues visited by the likes of Legs Diamond and Mad Dog Coll, later playing The Palace and starring on Broadway in *Show Girl* in 1929 and *The New Yorkers* in 1930. That year they made their film debut in *Roadhouse Nights*. Their biggest hit was a song called "Wood," in which they raucously piled the stage with items made of wood, singing its praises while nearly buried in timber.

Durante was always the star, so it was no surprise that he eventually went solo. It was an amicable split, with Clayton, Jackson and Durante occasionally reteaming for variety show dates, and Clayton becoming Jimmy's manager. Durante's star continued to rise and he had a hit song in the show *Strike Me Pink,* strutting about singing, "I'm Jimmy da Well Dressed Man." The film *Jumbo* from 1935 (a Durante line in the show called it "da greatest show dis side of oblivion") featured the tune "Laugh," with typically mangled lines: "Laugh . . . when things are catastrophic. Ya gotta laugh . . . an' take it philostrophic."

Durante became the epitome of a star "personality." He was a unique character who brought life to almost any song or gag. One of the favorites of impressionists in the 1950s and '60s, Durante had a uniquely gruff voice and Brooklynese accent. He played the comic tough guy loaded with misplaced aggression and huffing outrage ("Everybody wants ta get inna the act!"). He contrasted it with heart-of-gold good nature, ending an outburst with coy embarrassment, twinkling eyes, a little half smile and a teeth-chattering laugh ("aaaah-cheh-cheh-cheh!"). That bit was so popular he opened his film *What, No Beer?* with a full face closeup and that trademark laugh.

As the lovable streetcorner stooge, Durante was usually the loser. "I'm walkin' down the street and I bumps into a guy. So I apologizes. But he ain't satisfied! He demands an autopsy. I sees an openin'—I'm flat on my back!" As just an average guy (albeit with a grossly long and large nose), he also got a lot of mileage out of mangled malaprops and low-I.Q. confusion. In the musical *Red Hot and Blue* he had this dialogue trying to comfort Ethel Merman: "Don't cry. Don't be lugubrious!" "What does lugubrious mean?" "Go ahead and cry."

Durante made the most of comical frustration and aggravation. It led to his wide-eyed catch phrase, "I'm mortified!" In his stupefied state of mind he'd sing another popular novelty song he made uniquely his own: "Didja ever have da feelin' dat ya wanted ta go an' still had da feelin' dat ya wanted ta stay?"

Durante's unique style influenced many, from Jackie Gleason to Rose Marie. Before him, most comedians using anger for laughs did it purely from slow-burn takes and tantrum rage. Edgar Kennedy, James Finlayson, Eric Campbell and the rest were not portraying happy men. But Durante, blustery

and aggravated though he was, would simultaneously laugh at himself and his antagonists. His fury was funny because even he could see the ridiculousness of it all. His charismatic personality was captivating; people wished they could imitate him and learn his secret for happiness.

The ebullient Durante, who had his nose insured with Lloyds of London for a million dollars, was the subject of a hit book in 1951, *Schnozzola.* He won an Emmy in 1952, but his fame continued well into the 1960s. While some old-time stars were strictly a nostalgia act on such shows as *Hollywood Palace,* Durante's brawling, interrupting comedy style was as lively as ever. Though he had a hit with a contemplative version of "September Song," Durante was basically the last of the red-hot Grandpas, always the smiling, frisky clown.

The ancient but ageless star would leave the stage with a heartfelt shout, "Goodnight, Mrs. Calabash, wherever you are!" Jimmy never explained what it meant. A producer of Durante's radio show, Phil Cohan, told inquiring reporters that it began as a running gag, and that the writers planned to explain to listeners that Mrs. Calabash was a slow racehorse that still hadn't crossed the finish line yet. Somehow, Cohan said, the writers forgot to explain it and Durante just kept using it.

After his death, friends and co-workers saw no reason to deny the truth. "Mrs. Calabash" was Jimmy's affectionate nickname for his first wife. It came from a Mrs. Calabash who owned the boardinghouse where the couple lived after their honeymoon. It was only after his wife's death in 1943 that he began to say if he'd said who it was, it would've seemed maudlin. And once he remarried, it would have been a great insult to his second wife.

AUDIO: *Jimmy Durante on Radio* (Radiola), *At the Copa* (Roulette), *At the Piano* (Decca), *Club Durante* (Decca), *Favorites* (Decca), *The Very Best of Jimmy Durante* (MGM), *In Person* (MGM), *One of Those Songs* (Warner Bros.)

BIOGRAPHIES: *Schnozzola* (Fowler, 1951), *Goodnight, Mrs. Calabash* (Cahn, 1963), *I Remember Jimmy* (Adler, 1980)

BROADWAY: *Show Girl* (1929), *The New Yorkers* (1930), *Strike Me Pink* (1933), *Jumbo* (1935), *Policy* (1936),

*Red Hot and Blue* (1937), *Stars in Your Eyes* (1939), *Keep Off the Grass* (1940)

FILMS incl.: *The Passionate Plumber* (1932), *Speak Easily* (1932), *The Wet Parade* (1933), *What No Beer?* (1933), *Palooka* (1933), *Hollywood Party* (1934), *Carnival* (1935), *Little Miss Broadway* (1938), *You're in the Army Now* (1941), *The Man Who Came to Dinner* (1941), *Two Girls and a Sailor* (1944), *It Happened in Brooklyn* (1947), *The Great Rupert* (1950), *Milkman* (1950), *Pepe* (1960), *Jumbo* (1962), *It's a Mad Mad Mad Mad World* (1963)

TV: "All Star Revue" (1950–53), "Colgate Comedy Hour" (1953–54), "The Jimmy Durante Show" (1954–56), "Jimmy Durante Presents the Lennon Sisters" (1969–70)

# E

## EAST SIDE KIDS (See also LEO GORCEY and HUNTZ HALL.)

Street gangs usually aren't too funny, but for three decades a New York bunch led by Leo Gorcey got lots of laughs, whether they were called The Dead End Kids, The East Side Kids (their first series that emphasized comedy) or the all-comedy Bowery Boys.

The boys (Leo Gorcey, Huntz Hall, Billy Halop, Gabriel Dell, Bobby Jordan, Bernard Punsley and Sidney Lumet) were first assembled for the Broadway show *Dead End.* All but Lumet were invited to go to Hollywood for the film version. (Lumet, of course, later became a film director.) The serio-comic teenagers turned up in a variety of Warner Brothers crime films, including Humphrey Bogart's *Crime School* and James Cagney's *Angels with Dirty Faces.* They were called The Dead End Kids at first, with a few forming a splinter group called The Little Tough Guys.

In 1940 the key players reunited as The East Side Kids for Monogram Studios, and it was then that they began getting laughs, the comedy centering around tough-guy and malaprop language mangler Leo Gorcey and his goofy stooge Huntz Hall. The low-budget, hour-long gang comedies had almost jokeless scripts, relying mostly on strong character humor and the enduring theme of a gang of comic lowlifes tweaking authority while displaying laughable bravado (until, at the end, they managed to triumph in a brawling free-for-all). Aside from Gorcey and Hall, the key "gang" members were:

**Bobby Jordan** (April 1, 1923–September 10, 1965) was the youngest and most innocent-looking one, thin but mousy. He was the one to suffer in early melodramatic plots involving cruelty at the hands of reform school directors or cops.

**Bernard Punsly** (July 11, 1922–   ) was a short, nondescript member who would join in the fights after Gorcey called out "Routine 5!" or some other code. He became a doctor in Torrance, California.

**Bennie Bartlett** (August 16, 1927–   ), another lesser member, was a "filler" to make the gang look large; he played "Butch."

**Ernest "Sammy" Morrison** (December 20, 1912–1989) was the obligatory black member of the gang. He actually had the best comedy training. He was dubbed "Sunshine Sammy" back in 1919 when he was reportedly the first black actor to sign a movie contract, co-starring in Hal Roach comedies, notably with Harold Lloyd. When theaters balked at comedies starring the precocious black child himself, Roach created the "Our Gang" comedies for him. When he outgrew the gang in 1924 he toured in a stage act, created a jazz band and in the 1940s joined The East Side Kids as "Scruno." For one of the few times in his life, Morrison had to suffer through racial gags. In a haunted house: "Man, it sure is dark in here . . . I can't even see myself!"

Huntz Hall and Leo Gorcey never grew up. They were mischief-making "teens" well into their 40s. Photo from the author's collection.

He had a successful career away from show business in the 1950s and '60s.

**David Gorcey** (February 6, 1921– ), Leo's younger brother, had little to do besides join in when there was a brawl. In the 1950s he suddenly changed his screen billing to "David Condon," using his mother's maiden name for a few years. On his own he starred in the obscure western *Prairie Moon,* then became the head of a halfway house for alcoholics and drug addicts as the Reverend David Gorcey.

**Billy Halop** (February 11, 1920–November 9, 1976) was the original leader of the gang in the early "Dead End" films. First a child star on radio ("Bobby Benson of the B-Bar-B" and "Skippy") he was edged out of the gang by the more comical tough guy Gorcey. After World War II he found little work; he suffered from a drinking problem, a nervous breakdown and heart troubles aggravated by heavy smoking. He made a comeback as Munson, owner of Archie Bunker's cab company on "All in the Family," and wrote an autobiography, *There's No Dead End.*

**Gabriel Dell** (Gabriel del Vecchio, October 4, 1919–July 3, 1988) usually played himself, "Gaby," the one member of the gang smart enough to have a steady job and steady girlfriend. Off screen he could be just as troublesome as his pals. One day he set off the Warner Brothers studio sprinkler system with a match, causing $25,000 worth of damage. He left the gang in 1950 to appear in the Broadway musical *Tickets Please.* He starred in more Broadway and off-Broadway productions (including the lead in *The Sign in Sidney Brustein's Window* in 1964) and replaced Alan Arkin during the latter half of the run of *Luv*. A regular on Steve Allen's show (1956–61) as a sketch performer and impressionist, he often guested on sitcoms in the 1970s and '80s and appeared in two short-lived sitcoms of his own, "The Corner Bar" and "A Year at the Top." He co-wrote and starred in the private eye parody *The Manchu Eagle Murder Caper*. In 1979 he played in a stock production of *Luv* co-starring Huntz Hall. He continued to perform, but the debilitating effects of leukemia curtailed his career in the mid-1980s.

**Stanley Clements** (July 16, 1926–October 16, 1981) played Duke, the new gang leader after Gorcey retired in 1956. Generally he was just a grim, head-shaking straightman for Hall. The series ended with Clements in 1958. He appeared in a few subsequent films, including *That Darn Cat,* as well as episodes of "Kojak" and "Cannon" television shows.

**William Benedict** (April 16, 1917–  ) played "Whitey," empty-headed and blank-faced. As the dopiest member of the group besides Huntz Hall, he sometimes played Hall's foil in comic scenes. He went on to play Toby, the informant on "The Blue Knight" television series, and had bit parts in films including *The Sting* (1973) and *Farewell My Lovely* (1975). "People ask me what it was like working with the Bowery Boys," Benedict remarked in 1991. "It was like being on a three-day drunk riding the rollercoaster."

AUDIO: *The East Side Kids* (Murray Hill)

BIOGRAPHY: *The Bowery Boys* (Hayes and Walker, 1984)

FILMS incl.: (as The Dead End Kids) *Dead End* (1937), *Crime School* (1938), *Angels with Dirty Faces* (1938), *Little Tough Guy* (1938), *Angels Wash Their Faces* (1939), *They Made Me a Criminal* (1939), *You're Not So Tough* (1940); (as The East Side Kids) *Boys of the City* (1940), *Pride of the Bowery* (1940), *Bowery Blitzkrieg* (1941), *Spooks Run Wild* (1941), *Let's Get Tough* (1942), *Ghosts on the Loose* (1943, aka *East Side Kids Meet Bela Lugosi*); (as The Bowery Boys) *Bowery Bombshell* (1946), *Hard Boiled Mahoney* (1947), *Ghost Chasers* (1951), *Bowery Battalion* (1951), *Loose in London* (1953), *Bowery Boys Meet the Monsters* (1954), *Hold That Hypnotist* (1957), *Up in Smoke* (1957)

## JAMES EDMONDSON (See PROFESSOR BACKWARDS.)

## BOB EINSTEIN

### (November 20, 1940–  )

Bob Einstein didn't sound like a comedy star and he didn't look like one. In fact, he was mainly a comedy writer when The Smothers Brothers brought him before the camera to play "Officer Judy" in a few sketches. "Officer Judy" was little more than a grim, deadpan authority figure, tall and humorless with a hoarse, worn-out voice. He'd stoically warn the radical brothers to behave themselves, and they'd react with satirical levels of fear and respect for his power.

Initially an ad copywriter for radio and television commercials, it was Tommy Smothers who first gave Einstein a break in comedy writing. The Emmy Award–winning writer's deadpan style was in contrast to the comedy of his father Harry (who worked under the name of Parkyakarkus) and his brother, the more animated and boyish Albert Brooks. He remained known as a writer until he wrote himself the role of "Super Dave Osborn."

He premiered the character on the cable series "Bizarre" and eventually got his own cable series on Showtime. It's had an astonishingly long run for what is essentially a one-joke concept.

Like "Officer Judy," this character is also solid but humorlessly stolid. He is the hard-headed stuntman who needs that hard head, since every one of his stunts ends in well-deserved disaster. A cult developed around the dense, deadpan Dave, and fans delighted in seeing his death-defying stunts bring him as near to death as possible. Unlike slapstick performers of old who would bounce back unscathed, Dave would often remain frozen in pain, able to mumble only a few deadpan words of chagrin to his supporters. Typical of his sadomasochistic stunts was the time he jumped off a building, convinced, as always, that he would emerge unmarked. When he landed, embedded in the dirt, he could only moan, "I have a minute to live." When the ambulance came and ran him over, the audience couldn't stop laughing. The punch line: "Could you take me right to the graveyard?"

BOOK: *This Is My First Magic Book, I'm a Little Nervous* (1970)

TV: "The Smothers Brothers Comedy Hour" (1967–69), "Pat Paulsen's Half a Comedy Hour" (1970), "The Sonny and Cher Hour" (1973–74), "The Smothers Brothers Show" (1975), "Joey and Dad" (1975), "Van Dyke and Company" (1976), "Bizarre" (1985–87), "Super Dave" (1987–   )

## LEON ERROL

### (July 3, 1881–October 12, 1951)

One of the better known "drunk acts" of the 1940s, Leon Errol appeared in countless feature films as a realistically befuddled boozer: his legs rubbery, his brain pickled, but his face registering dour discomfort more often than a cheerful high. Additionally, he starred in a series of nearly 100 film shorts (1938–1951), usually playing a henpecked husband opposite Dorothy Granger. The plots centered on Errol's attempts to flee the house, get bombed and spend his money on showgirls. The films eventually settled into static domestic comedy, though in his first series (1934–37) he was more experimental, including lively visual comedy and crisp vaudeville dialogue. The early *Should Wives Work?* received an Academy Award nomination.

The Australian-born comedian moved to the U.S. by way of San Francisco. His first major comedy sketch, which was featured prominently in 1906's "The Baltimore Beauties" burlesque show, featured Tom Kennedy as a ventriloquist and Errol as his live dummy. Later Errol and his wife formed their own eccentric dance team and got a break appearing in *The Ziegfeld Follies of 1911* and the next four editions of the show.

Errol had a few continuing roles in films. He played Knobby Walksh, Joe Palooka's manager, in a series of movies for Monogram. He also played the twin roles of Uncle Matt and Lord Basil Epping in the "Mexican Spitfire" comedy series with Lupe Velez. He co-starred in *Never Give a Sucker an Even Break* with fellow ex-Ziegfeld star W. C. Fields. In *The Noose Hangs High* with Abbott and Costello he played a genial, befuddled eccentric. He was often at his best when only mildly stewed—which allowed for a more lovable character and some sly throwaway gags. In *Higher and Higher* he plays a rich father. Asked "Did you have more than one daughter?" he pauses for a moment to carefully consider the question. Then he blithely mutters, "Well, that of course I wouldn't know. My wife took care of those matters. . . ."

BROADWAY incl.: *Ziegfeld Follies* (1911–15), *The Century Girl* (1916), *Hitchy-Koo* (1917–18), *Sally* (1920), *Louie the 14th* (1925), *Yours Truly* (1927), *Fioretta* (1929).

FILMS incl.: *Only Saps Work* (1930), *Finn and Hattie* (1931), *Alice in Wonderland* (1933), *We're Not Dressing* (1934), *The Captain Hates the Sea* (1934), *Girl from Mexico* (1939), *Mexican Spitfire* (1939), *Mexican Spitfire Out West* (1940), *Never Give a Sucker an Even Break* (1941), *Where Did You Get That Girl?* (1941), *Mexican Spitfire's Baby* (1941), *Mexican Spitfire's Blessed Event* (1943), *Higher and Higher* (1943), *Invisible Man's Revenge* (1944), *Babes on Swing Street* (1944), *What a Blonde* (1945), *Joe Palooka* (1946), *Joe Palooka in the Knockout* (1947), *Joe Palooka in the Big Fight* (1949), *Joe Palooka in the Counterpunch* (1949), *The Noose Hangs High* (1948), *Footlight Varieties* (1951)

# F

## PETER FALK

**(September 16, 1927– )**

John Garfield crossed with Groucho Marx, Peter Falk achieved his greatest fame playing a variety of stoop-shouldered detectives, his seedy grit matched with offbeat wit. In *The Cheap Detective*, he delivered this throwaway at the start of a phone conversation: "Hello? Georgia? I just had you on my mind."

Born in Ossining, New York, where his father owned the Falk Department Store, Falk received his degree in public administration from Syracuse University. Ironically, many of his acting roles cast him as a street-tough, semi-educated wise guy. He received Academy Award nominations for his thug role in *Murder, Inc.*, and as a guy tough enough to chew through a glass in the gangster comedy *Pocketful of Miracles*. He was the schemer/dreamer trying to mastermind *The Brink's Job*, the shyster manager of female wrestlers in *All the Marbles* and a mob boss in *Cookie*. One of his best roles was as an eccentric, reckless agent in the classic *The In-Laws*. His insistent, gruff but irresistible con job on co-star Alan Arkin led them deep into comic disaster. An underrated comic actor, Falk got laughs without histrionics. He turned one word of advice in avoiding flying bullets ("Serpentine!") into a catch phrase viewers laughed at on their way out of the theater. Falk and Arkin reteamed for *Big Trouble* in 1986.

Falk perfected his unmistakable style of wily humor and grating-yet-ingratiating humility on "Columbo," television's long-running serio-comic detective series. He was so successful in the part he could command $2 million for four 90-minute episodes. The part was originally offered to Bing Crosby. Wearing a seedy raincoat (his own, bought in 1967), often needing a shave, speaking in a self-deprecative rasp and always displaying ample foibles (including the catch phrases, "Just one more thing" and "Am I bothering you?"), Falk's rumpled Columbo was a friendly, funny character viewers never seemed to tire of. His look was enhanced by a slightly askew stare that was always aped by impressionists. This was the result of a tumor at age three that caused him to lose his right eye. The tragedy, after about 40 years of time, now lent itself to his humor.

Falk would play variations on Columbo in both *The Cheap Detective* and the parody *Murder by Death*. He demonstrated more diversity in later films. In *Cookie* he played a more elegant gangster, "based on John Gotti . . . that hood in New York. He's the guy who runs New York, the head mob guy." For *Tune in Tomorrow* he was cast as an eccentric writer given to semipithy statements: "Art is two cannibals on a desert island. Eat or be eaten!"

On television, Falk was still "Columbo," as eccentric as ever. Some were surprised that the character would be brought back in the 1990s, but not Falk: "What's there not to like about the man?" he asks.

"Columbo is this ass-backward Sherlock Holmes . . . childlike and shrewd at the same time. He says things only a child would say, because he isn't self-conscious, like wondering why soap in a rich man's house is shaped like a lemon. . . . What a character. . . ." Of his famous catch phrase he admits, "The challenge came in doing the line in different ways so it didn't become a forced gag in every show." In one 1990 movie, he literally sniffs around the murder scene, rising up from the corpse under the table to spy, with delight, a platter of cheese. The corpse will go to the morgue—and the cheese to Colombo's house: "Make sure the boys put that aside!" he says. He also made sure to take care of his old Columbo raincoat: "It's threadbare. I have to put a saucer of milk out for it every night. I don't wear it every day because it'll fall apart, but I wear it once or twice every show." Though he played Columbo on and off for decades, Falk never seemed to tire of the role. "That guy tickles me," he said. "He'll always tickle me. It's fun doing him."

BROADWAY: *The Iceman Cometh* (1956), *Saint Joan* (1956), *The Lady's Not for Burning* (1957), *The Passion of Josef D* (1964), *Prisoner of Second Avenue* (1968)

FILMS incl.: *Murder, Inc.* (1960), *Pocketful of Miracles* (1961), *It's a Mad Mad Mad Mad World* (1963), *Robin and the Seven Hoods* (1964), *The Great Race* (1965), *Luv* (1969), *Columbo: Murder by the Book* (1971), *Mikey and Nicky* (1976), *Murder by Death* (1976), *The Brinks Job* (1978), *The Cheap Detective* (1978), *The In-Laws* (1979), *All the Marbles* (1981), *Big Trouble* (1986), *Happy New Year* (1987), *The Princess Bride* (1987), *Wings of Desire* (1988), *Vibes* (1988), *Cookie* (1988), *In the Spirit* (1990), *Tune in Tomorrow* (1990)

TV: "Trials of O'Brien" (1964), "Columbo: NBC Mystery Theater" (1971–78), "Columbo: ABC Mystery Movie" (1989–    )

# JAMIE FARR

## (Jameel Farah, July 1, 1934–    )

The most famous "drag act" since Milton Berle, Jamie Farr's swarthy complexion, sad-sack face, huge nose and hairy body made him instantly laughable as "M*A*S*H" 's Corporal Klinger, a man trying to get out of the Korean War by wearing dresses. Ironically, he was the only cast member who served in Korea during the war.

No matter what Klinger did—from hang-gliding in a nightie and fuzzy pink slippers to posing as the Statue of Liberty for General MacArthur—he never got arrested.

As an actor, Jamie Farr spent 20 years where he "couldn't get arrested," toiling in obscurity as a banana-nosed extra, playing well-meaning delivery boys ("The Dick Van Dyke Show"), sailors ("The Red Skelton Show") and others. He had bit parts in films: Thaddaeus in *The Greatest Story Ever Told* (he met his wife Joy Richards during filming) and Santini in *The Blackboard Jungle*.

"M*A*S*H" didn't seem like an instant ticket to fame. For the first year or two, Farr was not a regular on the television show. The character evolved. At first Klinger was a nasty, psychopathic individual who used gay slang (calling other men "Mary"). Farr helped reshape the character into a hapless, ordinary guy driven to comic extremes to get out of the army. Klinger metamorphized into a cheery Sergeant Bilko type, sans dresses. Farr gave Klinger some of his own autobiography (both were born Lebanese in Toledo). But while Klinger's family was nefarious, Farr's father was a butcher who put in 14 hour days to keep the family together. And while Klinger seemed to have had a streetwise lifestyle back in Toledo, Jamie was a good student—class president in high school, manager of the basketball team and a leading player on the tennis team.

Farr has become a ubiquitous quiz show panelist, an occasional guest on sitcoms and for a while performed stand-up as well. He remains best known for his "M*A*S*H" role. As Father Mulcahy said in one episode, "Klinger, the Lord moves in mysterious ways—but you take the cake."

FILMS incl.: *Blackboard Jungle* (1955), *Happy Hour* (1985)

TV: "Dear Phoebe" (1954–55), "Chicago Teddy Bears" (1971), "M*A*S*H" (1973–83), "The Gong Show" (1976–80), "After M*A*S*H" (1983–84)

# FRANK FAY

## (Francis Fay, November 17, 1897–September 25, 1961)

Frank Fay was the prototype for the smooth, brash, good-looking wise-guy comedian. His sarcasm, swagger and smart-aleck patter conquered audiences. They loved him. But most people who actually knew him hated him.

Born in San Francisco, Fay was a child actor in Chicago (*Babes in Toyland* in 1903). He made his way to Broadway for 1906's *Redemption of David Corson*. After teaming with Johnny Dyer, Fay went out as a single in 1917, becoming one of the first stand-ups to perform without relying on comic makeup, dialect or costumes. Fay is also generally credited with being the first comedy master of ceremonies. It was probably his own ego that led him to tell jokes between the acts.

He was most famous for routines sarcastically dismembering popular songs. Many comics copied the idea. Pointing out the idiocy in the lyrics for "Tea for Two," he'd sing a line, then stop and rip it to shreds:

"*Just tea for two, and two for tea—ain't that rich? Here's a guy, he's probably got enough tea for two, so he's gonna have two for tea. If a third person walks in they stab him . . .* Nobody near us, to see us or hear us. *Who wants to listen to two people drinkin' tea? . . .*"

Fay sometimes used stooges in his act, notably Patsy Kelly. She'd come out to be insulted. "Where have you been?" "At the beauty parlor." "I see. And they didn't wait on you?" Fay's style strongly influenced Ted Healy and Milton Berle, who adopted his brash try-and-stop-me attitude and his storytelling technique that relied on parenthetical wisecracking.

His habit of smoothly squelching interruptions and irritations around him with a self-assured putdown was picked up and perfected by Bing Crosby. Jack Benny adopted Fay's habit of registering chagrin with a withering glare. *Variety*'s description of Fay's innovations sounds like Jack Benny: "He made it on style . . . his timing and delivery were rated masterly."

As a human being, Fay wasn't rated at all. Fred Allen noted, "If Fay's ego had been acid he would have consumed himself." Fay was an insult comic on stage and off. His cheery greeting to Bert Lahr: "What's the low comedian doing today?" The best at bullying comedy, he once challenged an unprepared Groucho Marx to come out of the audience, get up on stage and "have some fun." When Groucho refused, Fay shot him an icy stare. "You do need your brothers, don't you." When Milton Berle did offer a duel of wits, Fay is credited with coming up with the classic "I never fight with an unarmed man."

An unwary Bert Wheeler once came up on stage, only to be destroyed by a fast and unavoidable stream of Frank Fay insults. Before leaving the stage, Wheeler asked one question: "Now would you like to see me get a laugh like you've never gotten in your whole life?" Fay nodded. Wheeler punched him in the face. Fay once irritated an entire courtroom. Asked to testify on one occasion, he was asked his profession. He answered, "I'm the greatest comedian in the world!" After all, he explained, he was under oath.

Often under the influence of alcohol, Fay was often in drunken brawls. Since he fought just as badly drunk as sober, wags insisted the only person he could beat up was his third wife—Barbara Stanwyck. She was a starlet when they wed in August 1928. They went to Hollywood so he could star in films, but while his bombed (a humiliation for the man who played a record 100 shows at The Palace in 1926), Stanwyck's were smash hits. The dutiful wife tried to help her husband. She invested $125,000 in the 1933 Broadway show *Tattle Tales* and even appeared in it with him to help insure its success. It flopped. Fay's ego had gotten the better of him. As Jack Benny later recalled, Fay "rarely changed his act or polished it. He never bothered to remove jokes or lines that were dated. His attitude toward the audience was 'You people are lucky to see the great Frank Fay no matter what I do.'" At the time, columnist Louella Parsons added fuel to the fire: "Frank Fay is being selfish and thinking only of himself . . . Barbara is making all the sacrifices."

Back home in Hollywood, Mr. and Mrs. Fay adopted a baby to save the marriage. Instead, wife-beater Frank had a new target. One day in a drunken tantrum he threw the child into the swimming pool.

One night at a big Hollywood nightclub Fay punched Barbara in the face and knocked her down. She wrote him a letter: "I love you just as much as it is possible for a woman to love a man. . . . I cannot imagine life without you. . . . You are always right about everything. . . . Please, Frank, love me—whatever you do."

All Fay did in response was get drunk and beat her up some more. Finally, in 1935 she divorced him. Jack Oakie bought the home she and Fay had shared. The only thing he wanted to know about the property was whether to call it "Santa Barbara" or "Santa Fay."

Fay's career continued to nose dive. He wasn't kidding when he wrote his autobiography *How to Be Poor* in 1935. After sporadic nightclub work, Fay's luck changed briefly in 1944. His show *Harvey* was a surprise hit. But cast members filed complaints with Actor's Equity over his abusive personality and anti-Semitic remarks. Jimmy Stewart made the movie *Harvey,* and Fay made few ripples afterward. His star had been dim for years when it finally went out in 1961.

AUDIO: *Be Frank with Fay* (Bally)

AUTOBIOGRAPHY: *How to Be Poor*

BROADWAY: *Jim Jam Jems* (1920), *Fables* (1922), *Pinwheel Revel* (1922), *Artists and Models* (1923), *Harry Delmar's Revels* (1927), *The Conflict* (1929), *Tattle Tales* (1933), *Frank Fay's Vaudeville* (1939), *Laugh Time* (1943), *Harvey* (1944)

FILMS incl.: *The Show of Shows* (1929), *The Matrimonial Bed* (1930), *Under a Texas Moon* (1930), *God's Gift to Women* (1931), *Bright Lights* (1931), *Star over Broadway* (1935), *Nothing Sacred* (1937), *Spotlight Scandals* (1943), *The Love Nest* (1951)

# JOEY FAYE

## (Joseph Palladino, July 12, 1909–    )

One of the classic stars of burlesque, short and chubby Joey Faye appeared in variations of all the grand old chestnuts of the stage, from "Who's on First" to "Crazy House." He worked in vaudeville and in burlesque through the 1930s and kept it alive over may decades with a variety of new stage productions and revivals.

Born in New York City, the son of a barber, Joey was always telling jokes and even had his own column in the DeWitt Clinton High School newspaper, *Palladino's Panics.* After entering amateur shows with partner Bobby Falich (they called themselves The Faye Brothers), Joey worked the Catskills and vaudeville, breaking into burlesque with a Minsky show. He began to collect scripts and jokes, amassing a huge collection of vaudeville and burlesque sketches that would serve him well over the years. Producers looked to him when they wanted to stage or adapt classic routines, and often some burlesque lines from Joey turned up in "legitimate" stage works. A gag from *The Man Who Came to Dinner* came right out of one of Faye's old burlesque bits. A teetotaler upbrades a drinker, insisting "Whiskey will ruin you! Look at me, I'm 51 and people take me for 30, because I have never taken a drink of whiskey in my life." Joey answers, "I had an uncle who drank whiskey every day of his life and lived to be 83. When he died, we buried him, and then three weeks later we opened the grave again, and he *still* looked better than you do!"

Faye toured in productions of *Room Service* and *The Man Who Came to Dinner* and went to Broadway for many hits in the 1940s, culminating in his own television show in 1950. He remained active in television and films, and in 1963 he and Mickey Deems starred in 200 15-minute episodes of the syndicated "Mack and Myer for Hire." Starting with "Anatomy of Burlesque," the show he wrote, directed and starred in in 1957, Faye toured regularly in a variety of similar shows that brought back the flavor of old-fashioned sketch comedy. He produced *That Wonderful World of Burlesque* in 1975, and when the burlesque comedy *Grind* played on Broadway, Joey was naturally a prominent cast member. Appropriately enough for a guy surrounded by strippers for so long, Faye became a familiar face on television in the 1980s as the apple in Fruit of the Loom underwear ads. A comic known to colleagues as "the fastest sneeze in the West," he performed comic sneezes in Marcal Tissue commercials as well as sitcoms and variety show sketches.

Through the 1980s Faye guest-starred on television (including a Benny Hill special) and continued to tour the country with revivals of classic comedy sketches, several starring his second wife, Judy

Faye. When not on the road, he and his wife enjoyed their home on Staten Island, New York. Visitors ringing their door didn't hear a bell or buzzer; instead there was a raucous rendition of "Roll Out the Barrel."

BROADWAY: *Sing Out the News* (1938), *Laughter over Broadway* (1939), *Strip for Action* (1942), *The Milky Way* (1943), *Boy Meets Girl* (1943), *Allah Be Praised!* (1944), *The Duchess Misbehaves* (1946), *Tidbits of 1946* (1946), *High Button Shoes* (1947), *Top Banana* (1951), *The Tender Trap* (1954), *Little Me* (1962), *Guys and Dolls* (1965), *Man of La Mancha* (1969), *Lyle* (1970), *Grind* (1985)

TV: "Broadway Spotlight" (1949), "54th Street Revue" (1950), "Joey Faye's Frolics" (1950)

## MARTY FELDMAN

### (July 8, 1933–December 2, 1982)

A human Punch puppet, British wildman Marty Feldman had ragged reddish-brown hair, a hooked nose, curved jutting ears, a fiendish grin and bulging eyes (due to a thyroid condition). One of those eyes sailed off slightly to one side, which added to his frighteningly funny appearance. His own view: "I'd say I look like Dada on legs."

At 15 Feldman played trumpet in a dance band. After touring France in *Saucy Girls of 1952* and appearing in an act called "Morris, Marty and Mitch," he switched to writing, contributing to BBC radio and television shows "Educating Archie," "Round the Horne" and "The Frost Report." Following the 1966 David Frost series, he joined other Frost writers John Cleese and Graham Chapman on 1967's "At Last the 1948 Show." Like Cleese, Feldman began to perform some of the material he wrote, and soon he had his own show, "Marty."

In the late 1960s the eccentric comedian's sketches were showcased on Dean Martin's summer replacement "Golddiggers" series. Marty and his wife, Lauretta, moved to America to promote the subsequent "Marty Feldman Comedy Machine," a show ahead of its time for American television. It featured gleefully destructive, old-fashioned comedy—such as the three-minute music sketch in which deranged percussionist Feldman disrupts his entire orchestra, wildly clanging his cymbals as he chases an elusive fly all over the stage.

Feldman's strange humor included such songs as "The Great Bell," with its chorus: "Rum tiddle tiddle tum tiddle tiddle, scum on the water. Lint in your navel and sand in your tea." The throwaway line at the end guaranteed that Americans would not hear it in 1970: "Get your hand off my knee, Vicar, I'm trying to play the piano!"

In his sketches, the one-man Monty Python played a variety of old men, thugs and demented loonies. One sketch had him crying out: "You want to know how it will be? I'll tell ye! The heavens will open up, blood will come raining down. Ha ha ha! And there will be plagues of frogs and locusts. Hee hah! And the Earth will crack, and the seas boil over! Ha ha! And nameless abominations will come forth . . . there'll be storms, there'll be sleet, and fire will engulf the whole Earth!" The camera pulls back. Feldman composes himself. He's a weatherman: "The rest of the night will be fine."

Feldman's widest fame came in two Mel Brooks films, as the grotesque Igor in *Young Frankenstein* and as Joe Eggs, the aviator-helmeted pal of Mel Funn in *Silent Movie*. It seemed Americans liked him best as a modern Ben Turpin, a human sight gag. But there was more to Marty than that. Of working with Brooks he admitted, "It's very exciting, but you wouldn't want to do it every day. His is a two-dimensional, comic-strip world, the world of The Three Stooges, The Ritz Brothers . . . the world I relate to is the world of Buster Keaton and Laurel and Hardy."

He wanted to experiment. "There's never a guarantee comedy will work till the moment you do it. There's no way I can personally guarantee to make them laugh. I could make them sad if I talked about the human condition . . . but humor—it's like a trapeze without the safety net."

Unfortunately, on his own this proved too true. His spoof, *The Last Remake of Beau Geste*, came as the rage for Brooksian film parody was over. Feldman directed and co-wrote *In God We Trust*, with Richard Pryor as God, but the response was not encouraging. Later Feldman joined some of his old Python friends for *Yellowbeard*, a film with too many comics and not enough script.

On the last day of filming *Yellowbeard* in Mexico City, he said on the set, "I'm glad it's over. Now I can get some well-deserved rest." Once back at his hotel, he suffered a heart attack. He managed to gasp a few messages to his loved ones before he died. The film was dedicated to Marty; but the enduring tribute to him is in his earlier films, as well as the radio scripts, television sketches and record albums he left behind.

AUDIO: *I Feel a Song Going Off* (British Decca), *Marty* (Pye)

FILMS incl.: *Every Home Should Have One* (1969), aka *"Think Dirty", The Bed Sitting Room* (1969), *Young Frankenstein* (1973), *Silent Movie* (1976), *Adventures of Sherlock Holmes' Smarter Brother* (1976), *The Last Remake of Beau Geste* (1977), *In God We Trust* (1979), *Yellowbeard* (1982)

TV: "Dean Martin Presents the Golddiggers" (1970), "The Marty Feldman Comedy Machine" (1972)

## FERNANDEL

### (Fernand Joseph Constandin, May 8, 1903– February 26, 1971)

France's most famous comedian through the 1930s, '40s and '50s, Fernandel made over 100 films. Only a few were imported to America. He starred as the priest Don Camillo in a few 1950s comedies, played the village idiot in *Le Rosier de Mme. Husson* (translated as *Mrs. Husson's Rosebush,* but released in America as *The Virgin Man*) and had five roles in *The Sheep Has Five Legs.*

Acting was originally just a hobby for bank employee Fernand Constandin. He began using the stage name "Fernandel" in 1931. His wife, Henriette, used to call him "le Fernand d'Elle" ("my Fernand"). *Le Rosier de Mme. Husson* was his first hit, a farce about a small town unable to find a woman who has kept her virtue long enough to win the year's chastity prize. The honor goes instead to the fool Fernandel. Not so foolish after all; after winning the prize he spends the money on women!

The actor's career remained 99% comedy. His only drama was the unsuccessful film *Murder.* Fans knew what they wanted; they wanted to see the amusingly long face, twinkling little eyes and toothy grin of Fernandel in farces. His fame grew over the years, and eventually American filmmakers began to take notice.

In 1949 Fernandel posed for *The Frenchman,* a comic photo book by Philippe Halsman. This was a perfect introduction to him for Americans. Funny faces were a universal language, and the book was merely a set of silly portraits. There was one question about the French per page ("Would a Frenchman let a Kinsey researcher interview him?" "Do you know that 4 and a half million pairs of falsies were sold last year?") and on the following page, a close-up of Fernandel's response: the appropriate grin, groan, gasp or grimace. After his "Don Camillo" series in the early 1950s, Michael Todd used him in *Around the World in 80 Days* and Bob Hope co-starred with him in the bland *Paris Honeymoon;* but neither film established Fernandel as a box office attraction stateside.

Fernandel occasionally performed on stage in America; his last appearance in this country was a concert of comedy and music at Carnegie Hall in 1968. He remained a beloved comic legend in France, where he was awarded the Legion of Honor.

AUDIO: *Sonopresse, Felice Aussie*

BIOGRAPHIES (in French): *Fernandel* (Plume, 1976), *Fernandel* (Jelot-Blanc, 1981)

FILMS incl.: *Fric Frac* (1939), *La Fille du Puisatier* (1940), *The Red Inn* (1951), *Forbidden Fruit* (1952), *The Little World of Don Camillo* (1952), *The Return of Don Camillo* (1953), *The Sheep Has Five Legs* (1954), *Paris Holiday* (1957), *Fernandel The Dress Maker* (1957), *The Cow and I* (1959), *La Cuisine au Beurre* (1963), *L'Homme à la Buick* (1967)

## STEPIN FETCHIT

### (Lincoln Theodore Monroe Perry, May 30, 1896–November 19, 1985)

It seemed like good luck: Lincoln Perry named himself after a Baltimore racehorse, Stepin Fetchit. But over the years, the name would symbolize the demeaning roles blacks sometimes played in 1930s and '40s movies. His good comedy work was denigrated by those convinced that he got his laughs the easy, lazy way—with a shuffling step and fetch.

The Jamaican comedian (some sources list 1902 as his birth date) began his career in 1914 in minstrel shows. He worked with a partner for a while, the duo known together as "Step and Fetchit." One of his early solo film successes was 1929's *Hearts in Dixie,* featuring an all-black cast. Its main attraction was Fetchit as "Gummy," the man who moved on amazingly bendable "gum legs."

Fetchit co-starred in several Will Rogers films, including *Judge Priest* and *Steamboat Round the Bend.* Fetchit claimed in 1971, "I was the first Negro militant. When people saw me and Will Rogers together like brothers, that said something to them." He made more films, toured the black vaudeville circuit, and entertained GIs in army bases during World War II.

Into the late 1950s and '60s, Stepin Fetchit was shunned. Being a comic known for laziness and slow talking was one thing—being a black comic known for those traits was another. Few cared about his claims of having broken through color barriers or demanding (and getting) comparable pay for his work. "All the things that Bill Cosby and Sidney Poitier have done wouldn't be possible if I hadn't broken that law," he said. "I set up thrones for them to come and sit on."

Today black authors Alain Locke and Sterling A. Brown applaud Fetchit's *Hearts in Dixie* performance for showing "the emotional vibrancy of the race." Author Gerald Weales of the University of Pennsylvania wrote: "Fetchit was unique. He still is. Watching him now, I am amazed at his skill as a performer, the effects he can get from the smallest gesture, the most incomprehensible mutter. . . ." Fetchit did know how to wring chuckles from a glance, a grumble or a downtrodden lope. He also had some decent gags. In *Judge Priest,* Will Rogers asks him, "Why aren't you wearing shoes?" Says Fetchit: "I'll save 'em in case my feet wear out." Still, there's no denying that Fetchit shuffled along a fine line between comedy and offense.

The old film comedian was granted a few film appearances late in life by a few forgiving admirers, but it really was too late. So was his claim of being the first black actor to become a millionaire; he had filed for bankruptcy in 1947 and had many lean years thereafter. Late in life and then after his death, Fetchit's place in film comedy remains firm—despite the "lucky" name that remains a source of controversy.

BROADWAY: *Three After Three* (1939), *Walk with Music* (1940)

FILMS incl.: *In Old Kentucky* (1927), *Show Boat* (1929), *The Ghost Talks* (1929), *The Big Fight* (1930), *The Prodigal* (1931), *Stand Up and Cheer* (1933), *Charlie Chan in Egypt* (1935), *Dimples* (1936), *On the Avenue* (1937), *Elephants Never Forget* (1939), *Zenobia* (1939), *Miracle in Harlem* (1948), *The Sun Shines Bright* (1953), *Amazing Grace* (1974), *Won Ton Ton The Dog Who Saved Hollywood* (1976)

## TOTIE FIELDS

### (Sophie Feldman, May 7, 1930–August 2, 1978)

In the 1960s Totie Fields told as many self-deprecating fat jokes as Phyllis Diller did ugly jokes. The difference was in the attitude. Diller accepted her fate and literally laughed at herself. Loud and raucous, Totie belted out the gags with comically exaggerated angst. "It's hard to be sexy when your feet are swollen right over the shoes! You think it's easy pushing fat Jewish feet into thin Italian shoes?"

Unlike Diller, who consciously peppered her monologues with one-liners, Fields tended toward a more conversational approach. She appeared often on television variety shows of the day and played Vegas, but her style worked best in Catskill resorts. There she was a superstar. With her catch-phrase cry "Am I right? Am I right?" her observational gags and complaints had the ladies nodding in mirthful agreement. The men laughed too, recognizing the same kind of brawling "yenta" they met every day back home in the Bronx. The crowd loved her ringsider tummeling and fat jokes. She was everyone's extroverted next-door neighbor, their funny best friend, someone they could believe went to the beauty parlor on the corner and not only shopped at King Kullen but collected coupon books.

Born in Hartford, Connecticut, Sophie Feldman sang on the radio at age four. The child couldn't pronounce her own name. "Sophie" came out "Totie," and it stuck to her. So did food. She weighed nearly 200 pounds, a hefty load for a woman barely five feet tall. Inspired by another hefty Sophie from

Connecticut, Sophie Tucker, Fields pursued a show business dream. She played anywhere, even strip clubs. At one Boston joint she met a struggling comic named George Johnson. They married and kept on struggling. Totie thrived in the Catskills, and by 1963 the pudgy but tough comic made it to New York's Copa and—in more than 20 appearances—"The Ed Sullivan Show."

She made over $200,000 a year in her prime in 1970 and headlined the Riviera Hotel at $35,000 a week. Her brand of humor remained blunt. On the game show "The Hollywood Squares," she was asked: "Do snails ever caress?" Her answer, delivered in her grumbling New York accent: "I never saw a horny snail!"

In 1976 Totie's health began to fail. She had diabetes and developed phlebitis. After her leg was amputated, no-nonsense Totie announced, "I don't want anyone feeling sorry for me." She strapped on an artificial leg and made a comeback. She won the title "Entertainer of the Year" in 1978. It would take a lot to bring down tough Totie. A lot happened to her: including an eye operation, a mastectomy and the loss of 70 pounds due to so many ailments and so much hospitalization. She died of a heart attack during her comeback year, 1978.

Totie's brand of Catskill comedy wasn't pretty. In her time, her housewife humor and brawling fat jokes rarely amused newspaper critics. Yet Totie was an ancestor to the proudly unapologetic style of Roseanne Arnold and was one of the few female comics of her day to utilize the bold sizzle-and-sputter style of such male comics as Alan King and Buddy Hackett.

AUDIO: *Totie Fields Live* (Mainstream)
BOOK: *I Think I'll Start on Monday* (1972)

## W. C. FIELDS

**(William Claude Dukenfield, January 29, 1880–December 25, 1946)**

He was "The Great Man," a legend in his own time, one of the very few stars whose art and life intertwined. There wasn't much to separate myth from legend.

The three faces of W. C. Fields: cantankerous old gent, conniver extraordinaire and, in Groucho Marx's words, "a great drunk." Photo from the author's collection.

Fields was the same on screen and off. His letters had all the grand bluster of his scripts, whether writing to his beloved son ("Thank you son for your letter of the 11th ultimo") or his less-adored wife: "Why don't you try work as an antidote for your million and one ills? Keep your troubles to yourself. When I am out on a limb I use my brain instead of yelling for help . . . you have been a lazy, ignorant, bad-tempered, arguing trouble-making female all your life. . . ."

His remarks off stage could have been uttered on stage. He disconcerted Mae West by calling her "my little brood mare" and remarking during shooting "Ah yes, she's a fine figure eight of a woman . . . exceptionally well preserved too." He embarrassed his mistress, Carlotta Monti, by raging at a bird flying overhead during a lawn party: "I know what you're up to, you white-feathered fiend! Go release your bowels on some lesser personage."

The legend of Fields has extended to biographies loaded with anecdotes real and apocryphal. Sources err in reporting even the simplest details, such as his birth date in Philadelphia (grandson Ronald Fields confirms the one given above). Of his early years, most agree that he disliked his bullying father and adored his mother, Kate, who sported not only the Fieldsian nose but the cadence as well. Ronald Fields described Kate's brand of cynical humor. She would sit on her porch and greet neighbors as they passed by: "Kate would roll back and forth on her rocker, darning socks or knitting . . . a friend would walk in front of the house. 'Oh, good evening, Mrs. Frobisher. How's Mr. Frobisher?' 'He's a little under the weather.' 'Oh! That's a shame. That's a shame.' Then mumbling to her family: 'Last night he was under the table. Two quarts of rye, no doubt.'

Though he possessed one of the most unique voices in comedy and was one of the most quotable wits, Fields' initial fame came as a juggler. His first job was in an Atlantic City theater in 1896. Stories of him running away from home to escape his father may well be apocryphal. From the turn of the century on, Fields toured the world billed as "W. C. Fields, Eccentric Juggler." His wife, Hattie, was along to introduce the act and, according to a reviewer for the *New York Telegraph* in 1901, flaunt her "black satin panties." He added comedy to his prowess and developed routines playing croquet and golf. He performed in *The Ziegfeld Follies* and in 1915 made a short film, *Pool Sharks,* which included a variation of the pool routine as well as some slapstick sadism. In one scene Fields pries a man's eye wide apart, the better to stick a finger into it. Another silent effort, *His Lordship's Dilemma,* included his golf routine.

Fields' silent film trademark was a clip-on mustache that darkened half of his upper lip. The films didn't make him a star but his stage work did, as he evolved his grandiose delivery and infinite comic nuances before a live audience. His *Ziegfeld Follies* sketches are far from lost; he adapted many for a series of 1933 shorts (*The Fatal Glass of Beer, The Pharmacist,* etc.) and often stuck them into his feature films. His 1925 *Ziegfeld Follies* sketch "The Back Porch" turned up in *It's a Gift.* Like the saucy revues of Broadway, Fields' films sometimes strayed into the risqué. For years a scene in *The Dentist* was censored; a female patient writhing and wrapping her legs around him as he attempts to deal with her stubborn cavity. Fields also filmed his Broadway

stage triumph *Poppy* twice, first as a silent (*Sally of the Sawdust*) and later a sound version.

Fields was a master stylist, his films (like his drinking) steadily paced to create a world of amusement and bemusement. The comic "high" in Fields' films was like a comic "high" in real life. Stoned or drunk, a person might well find hilarity in repeating the word "kumquat" or laboriously repeating the spelling of a name such as LaFong ("capitol L, small a, capitol F, small o, small n, small g"). Fields' art was in making this funny to a sober audience. While any drunk might fumble putting on his top hat or getting the hat mixed up with his cane, Fields made that an art too. In *The Back Dick* and *Man on the Flying Trapeze* he created a surreal world in which dizzy car chases (featuring outrageously bad rear projection) couldn't destroy his inner calm and even burglars breaking into his house turned into a bizarre comic interlude of singing and drinking. Fields erased the line between uninhibited behavior and sobriety—able to kick Baby LeRoy in the behind (*The Old Fashioned Way*) or ignore such minor problems as a quill pen stuck point-first in his head (*The Bank Dick*).

Fans loved sharing Fields' world of highs, a world where he can dally with Mae West, fall off a cliff with impunity or face the insanity of a cruel world with his own perspective: "What a gorgeous day. What effulgent sunshine. It was a day of this sort the McGillicuddy brothers murdered their mother with an ax."

When *The Christian Science Monitor* complained in 1942 about the "atmosphere of befuddled alcoholism" in one of his "distasteful" comedies, he sent them a response: "Wouldn't it be terrible if I quoted some reliable statistics which prove that more people are driven insane through religious hysteria than by drinking alcohol?"

Fields' day was not complete without the consumption of two quarts of gin. His work seems brewed rather than written, as in his radio sketch about eating camphor balls: "Every time I sneeze dozens of moths fly out. Closely followed by a bevy of silverfish, flying in V formation. Fly, fly on the wing! I sleep with my mouth closed, they crawl in through the nostrils. . . . I usually drink a couple of glasses of Flit before retiring." Actually Fields was an alcoholic who never got visibly drunk or so besotted he couldn't work. In fact, his work relied on nuance and timing, from his juggling to his flourishes with his fingers or his cane. "Show me a comic who isn't a perfectionist and I'll show you a starving man. You have to sweat and toil and practice indefinitely. A comic should suffer as much over a single line as a man with a hernia would in picking up a heavy barbell."

Fields was one of the screen's most complex comedians, twisting together meanness, tenderness, grandness and pettiness. His great moments of humor could come from subtle tedium (a sticky piece of paper adhering to his hands) or wild slapstick (the thrill car chase of *Never Give a Sucker an Even Break*). He was a cowardly family man in some films, an independent con man in others. Both sides were blurred. As a con man he was often incompetent and forever being chased by the authorities. As a beleagured family man, his pains and miseries were usually resolved during an uplifting moment of heroism at the end.

Perhaps the only comic device he never used was pathos. His tender advice to his daughter in one climactic scene was "Never give a sucker an even break." The master of pathos was Charles Chaplin, W. C. Fields' nemesis. Fields resented Chaplin for his fluid grace, calling him "that goddam ballet dancer." He knew that part of Chaplin's appeal was in portraying a downtrodden tramp and in his tenderness toward women, but Fields never altered his own comic vision just to win mass acceptance. He prided himself on his own brilliant array of comedy routines and his ability to do one thing Chaplin couldn't—talk. And lace his conversation with his patented one-liners:

"I'll be sober tomorrow, but you'll be crazy the rest of your life." "A thing worth having is worth cheating for." "A man who overindulges lives in a dream . . . he thinks the whole world revolves around him. And it usually does." "There may be some things better than sex and some things may be worse. But there is nothing exactly like it." "If at first you don't succeed, try, try again. Then quit. No use being a damn fool about it." "Women are like elephants to me. I like to look at them, but I wouldn't want to own one." "I'd rather have two girls at 21 each than one girl at 42." "Everything I do is either illegal, immoral or fattening."

It doesn't even matter that scholars credit the "women are like elephants" line to old-time newspaper columnist Frank Hubbard; the "two girls at 21" to Douglas Jerrold, a British writer who died in 1847; or the last line to critic Alexander Woolcott. Fields was the magnificent rogue; when someone asked to use the "illegal, immoral or fattening" line in a film, Fields agreed and sold his rights to the line for $200. When it was discovered Woolcott used it first, Fields refused to give back the money. "I sold you *my* rights," he explained.

Fields was a big film star in the 1930s and '40s, but became even bigger in the '60s when his antiestablishment humor won over college students who attended screenings of his lost gems and bought record albums featuring his monologues, film clips and bizarre radio appearances solo and feuding with Edgar Bergen's Charlie McCarthy.

Bartlett's book of quotations gives Fields sole credit for the catch phrase "Tain't a fit night out for man nor beast," uttered in *The Fatal Glass of Beer*. But almost everything he uttered, even "I hate you," came out funny. And while many viewers have a make-me-laugh attitude when viewing Chaplin or Keaton, and a few have trouble enjoying any black-and-white sound film from the 1930s, there are still many devotees ready to take a mental drink or two and sit back to enjoy Fields at work.

Fans enjoy not only what they see on the screen but the Fieldsian spirit behind it all. Director Gregory LaCava once asked, "Why don't you ever give a sucker, or anyone else for that matter, an even break?" Said Fields, "Most people have a feeling they are going to be reincarnated and come back to this life. Not me. I know I'm going through here only once."

AUDIO: *The Temperance Lecture/The Day I Drank a Glass of Water* (Jay Records, re-issued as *Original and Authentic Recordings* by Blue Thumb, as *Best of Friends* by Sutton and as *Fields and West* by Proscenium and by Harmony), *Original Voicetracks* (Decca), *The Magnificent Rogue* (Radiola), *W. C. Fields Original Radio Broadcasts* (Mark 56), *Poppy* (Columbia, and Mark 56), *Further Adventures of Larson E. Whipsnade* (Columbia), *The Great Radio Feuds* (Columbia), *W. C. Fields on Radio* (Columbia), *The Best of W. C. Fields* (Columbia),

*The Uncensored W. C. Fields* (Murray Hill, reissues of Columbia and Mark 56 material), *The Best of W. C. Fields* (Nostalgia Lane)

BIOGRAPHIES: *W. C. Fields, His Follies and Fortunes* (Taylor, 1949), *W. C. Fields and Me* (Monti, 1971), *The Films of W. C. Fields* (Deschner, 1966), *The Art of W. C. Fields* (Everson, 1968), *W. C. Fields, A Life on Film* (R. J. Fields, 1984), *Drat* (Anobile, 1969), *A Flask of Fields* (Anobile, 1972)

BOOKS: *W. C. Fields for President* (1971); *W. C. Fields by Himself* (a posthumous collection of letters and sketches, 1973)

BROADWAY: *Ziegfeld Follies* (1915–18, 1920–21), *George White's Scandals* (1922), *Poppy* (1923), *The Comic Supplement* (1925), *Ziegfeld Follies* (1925), *Lambs Gambol* (1925), *Earl Caroll's Vanities* (1928), *Ballyhoo* (1930)

FILMS incl.: *Pool Sharks* (1915), *His Lordship's Dilemma* (1915), *Janice Meredith* (1924), *Sally of the Sawdust* (1925), *It's the Old Army Game* (1926), *Two Flaming Youths* (1927), *The Potters* (1927), *Running Wild* (1927), *Her Majesty Love* (1931), *Million Dollar Legs* (1932), *If I Had a Million* (1932), *International House* (1933), *Tillie and Gus* (1933), *Alice in Wonderland* (1933), *Six of a Kind* (1934), *You're Telling Me* (1934), *The Old Fashioned Way* (1934), *Mrs. Wiggs of the Cabbage Patch* (1934), *It's a Gift* (1934), *David Copperfield* (1935), *The Man on the Flying Trapeze* (1935), *Poppy* (1936), *Big Broadcast of 1938* (1938), *You Can't Cheat an Honest Man* (1939), *My Little Chickadee* (1940), *The Bank Dick* (1940), *Never Give a Sucker an Even Break* (1941), *Follow the Boys* (1944), *Song of the Open Road* (1944), *Sensations of 1945* (1944)

VIDEO: *W. C. Fields: Straight Up; Best of W. C. Fields; W. C. Fields' Comedy Bag*

## FLORA FINCH (See BUNNY and FINCH.)

## LARRY FINE (See THE THREE STOOGES.)

## JAMES FINLAYSON

### (August 27, 1877–October 9, 1953)

The bald, squinting, sour-pussed nemesis of Laurel and Hardy, James Finlayson specialized in displays of comic fury and chagrin. He regularly steamed himself into what he referred to as the "double take and fade away." In his double take of rising rage, he'd screw one eye closed to get a better look, cock an eyebrow high and grimace, ready to strike. Then would come the fade-away. Usually frustrated just at the moment of action (either by a passing policeman or his own realization of ultimate futility), his steaming anger simmered away into a few withering head shakes and a disgusted sigh.

After appearing on stage in Scotland following his graduation from Falkirk College, Finlayson toured America in 1912's *Bunty Pulls the Strings* and later tried films. His balding dome, big ears, dark eyes and black mustache made him a natural for villains and slapstick husbands. Finlayson bounced from studio to studio, from Universal to Sennett, finally arriving at Hal Roach's lot in 1923. "Fin" became friendly with Stan Laurel during Stan's solo days. The two co-starred in the memorable *Smithy*, with Stan the clutzy carpenter and James the excitable foreman. When Stan temporarily retired to try gag writing, he worked on several of Finlayson's films. One of Finlayson's few starring shorts was *Yes, Yes, Nanette* as a bridegroom foiled by his wife's ex-lover (Oliver Hardy).

Finlayson's solo career never took off but as a regular in Laurel and Hardy movies, he was instantly recognizable. In some early appearances he performed quite a bit of energetic slapstick. One of his best films with the boys was *Big Business*. The little Scotsman, enraged over their repeated attempts at selling him a Christmas tree in midsummer, escalates a vicious battle of "reciprocal destruction." While they deface his house, he wrecks their car, huffing and sneering with stubborn determination.

He had no trouble matching the duo during the sound era. He was a standout in *Way Out West* as a crooked saloonkeeper and played an exasperated teacher in *Pardon Us*.

While Finlayson also worked regularly with Hal Roach's other successful star, Charley Chase, and guested with Olsen and Johnson in *All Over Town* (1937) and Clark and McCullough *False Roomers* (1931), he is best remembered as the irascible foil for Laurel and Hardy.

FILMS incl.: *Married Life* (1920), *Smithy* (1924), *Near Dublin* (1924), *Yes Yes Nanette* (1925), *Welcome Home* (1925), *The Second Hundred Years* (1927), *Ladies Night in a Turkish Bath* (1928), *Lady Be Good* (1928), *Men o' War* (1929), *Hoosegow* (1929), *Chickens Come Home* (1930), *Big Business* (1930), *The Dawn Patrol* (1931), *Pardon Us* (1931), *Our Wife* (1931), *Pack Up Your Troubles* (1932), *Fra Diavolo* (1933), *Bonnie Scotland* (1935), *The Bohemian Girl* (1936), *Way Out West* (1937), *Blockheads* (1938), *Flying Deuces* (1939), *Chump at Oxford* (1940), *Saps at Sea* (1940), *To Be or Not to Be* (1942), *Perils of Pauline* (1947), *Royal Wedding* (1951)

## FIRESIGN THEATRE

Phil Austin, Peter Bergman, Philip Proctor and David Ossman began calling themselves "Firesign Theatre" when they started broadcasting over KPFK in 1966. Their style was similar to that of Bob and Ray: They parodied radio drama and radio commercials and favored numbly absurdist characters. The biggest difference was that they took the psychedelic approach, utilizing densely layered scripts loaded with asides and throwaway jokes, drug humor and complex sound effects that made for mind-blowing headphone listening.

One of their most accessible creations was "Nick Danger," a not-so-clever detective who spouted exaggerated Raymond Chandler lines. From their second album: "It all began innocently enough on Tuesday. I was sitting in my office that drizzly afternoon listening to the monotonous staccato of rain on my desktop and reading my name on the glass of my office door: Regnad Kesin." Danger was, as he said on the *Three Faces of Al* album, "just a doomed dick with his dipstick on empty."

All four members of the group had training in writing and theater. Peter Bergman and Phil Proctor were both from Yale. Proctor won a Theater World Award in 1962 and had appeared on Broadway. Bergman wrote, directed and starred in *Flowers*, a film made in Berlin in 1965. The foursome's first album arrived in 1968.

Very popular among college students, the Firesign albums were the closest thing to radio fantasy for a new generation. Some students felt these records were best heard while high on pot or LSD. The Firesigns loaded their albums with drug references. A typical line from a western parody on their first album: "Hi Ho Electric Brew, away . . . give that nice horsey some sugar cubes . . . let me have some more of that Third Redeye." Much of this kind of humor would fall completely flat for "straight" listeners; many were at a loss to understand the incoherent wordplay and sophomoric gags: "See that bear lappin' up that good old country water? Sure makes a big hairy guy like me thirsty. That's when I wrap my lips around a tall sweaty edible bottle of Good Old Country Bear Whiz Beer. As my Daddy said, 'Son, it's in the water. That's why it's yellow.' "

"Nobody can explain exactly what we do," Ossman once said. "We keep people confused, we layer our record with intangibles, existential dualities, mystery, a new dimension . . . it's like trying to be in two different places at one time. It's like making movies in your mind." Ossman left the group in 1982, after seeing their best work reach a peak in the 1970s.

The cult for Firesign Theatre began to wane when hippies turned to Yuppies and drugs of "discovery" and "inner light" were replaced by crack. "We were jesters of the hallucinogenic era, making fun of ourselves from within," Proctor admitted in 1984. That year the trio tried a comeback, transferring their style to Ernie Kovac–style videos. Their "Eat or Be Eaten" television special premiered on Cinemax in 1985. In the late 1980s some of their better albums were rereleased on CD, including the twin favorites of most fans, *How Can You Be in Two Places at Once When You're Not Anywhere At All* and *"Don't Crush That Dwarf Hand Me the Pliers.*

AUDIO: *Waiting for the Electrician* (Columbia), *How Can You Be in Two Places at Once When You're Not Anywhere At All* (Columbia), *Don't Crush That Dwarf Hand Me the Pliers* (Columbia), *I Think We're All Bozos on This Bus* (Columbia), *Dear Friends* (Columbia), *Not Insane* (Columbia), *The Giant Rat of Sumatra* (Columbia), *Everything You Know Is Wrong* (Columbia), *In the Next World You're on Your Own* (Columbia), *Forward into the Past* (Columbia), *Just Folks* (Butterfly), *Fighting Clowns* (Rhino), *Shakespeare's Lost Comedie* (Rhino), *Carter/Reagan* (Rhino), *The Missing Shoe* (Rhino), *Lawyer's Hospital* (Rhino),

*Three Faces of Al* (Rhino), *Eat or Be Eaten* (Mercury)

BOOKS: *The Apocalypse Papers; Firesign Theater's Big Mystery Joke Book* (1974); *Firesign Theater's Big Book of Plays* (1972)

FILMS: *Zachariah* (1970), *The Martian Space Party* (1972), *Everything You Know Is Wrong* (1975)

VIDEOS: *The Case of the Missing Yolks; Hot Shorts; Nick Danger*

## REDD FOXX

### (John Sanford, December 9, 1922–October 11, 1991)

He had been kicking around for years, ever since he began his career as a street musician in St. Louis. Redd Foxx recalled, "I used to play on the corner for tips. I had a group called The Four Hep Cats. Then I sang with a group called the Five Bon-Bons. We picked the name because Bon-Bons were little chocolates."

Foxx, still John Sanford then, drifted to Newark in 1939 and spent a decade trying to break into show business. Along the way he took low-paying jobs—and sometimes took to petty crime just to eat. He spent five days in jail on Riker's Island for stealing a bottle of milk and 90 days for sneaking out of a New York restaurant without paying the bill.

Still trying to make it as a singer, Foxx cut some records in 1946, including "Let's Wiggle a Little Woogie," a smooth jazz vocal with no trace of the throaty gravel that would make him famous as a comic curmudgeon. Into the 1950s he found steadier work in comedy, teaming up with Slappy White for a while, then going solo. The years of hard living had toughened him for stand-up. The gruff-voiced comic grabbed the audience with risqué stories, quickies and streetwise putdowns: "One out of every four people is a freak. So pick out three of your friends. If they all right, it's you!"

He was Redd Foxx now. Light-skinned, he had been nicknamed "Red" years earlier. He spelled his name with a "double d, double cross so it wouldn't be a color or an animal."

Dootsie Williams' small Dooto record label released over two dozen Foxx albums in the mid and late 1950s, "adults only" discs that rarely found their way into white record stores. Gradually Redd developed a crossover following, peppering his monologues with salty racial remarks: "It's not true that all Negroes carry knives—my uncle carried an ice pick for 45 years."

In 1958 Hugh Downs gave Foxx a break, booking him on television's "Today Show." He turned up on a few sitcoms, including "Mr. Ed," "The Lucy Show" and "The Addams Family" in the late 1960s as well as "The Flip Wilson Show." Meanwhile, in stand-up he continued to issue disc after disc, tallying over 50 party records. He had his own Los Angeles nightclub. After appearing as a junk dealer in the film *Cotton Comes to Harlem*, Redd was chosen for 1971's television hit "Sanford and Son."

The show seemed to be a black answer to "All in the Family." "All in the Family," based on the British sitcom "Till Death Do Us Part," was about an irascible bigot. "Sanford and Son" was based on "Steptoe and Son," about an irascible old junk dealer with unchanging attitudes. At first there was a lot of social and racial humor. Foxx delivered reverse-racist zingers: "White woman? Don't mess around with them, boy." "Pop, this woman was about 90 years old." "Ain't nothin' uglier on earth than a 90-year-old white woman."

Eventually the show became more of a character comedy, with Foxx as a lovable curmudgeon. Redd's old stand-up pals, including Slappy White and LaWanda Page, were added, making for a lively cast. The first sitcom since "Amos and Andy" to present, with good humor, realistic, earthy black characters, it was soon the target of criticism. Some blacks complained the series focused on "low-class" slum blacks and that Foxx's rascally, cantankerous junkman character was a poor role model.

An editorial by Don Carle Gillette in *Variety* in January 1976 complained that Foxx's show "is no more complimentary to the blacks than the burnt-cork 'Amos 'n' Andy.' . . . Contending that blacks will accept caricatures of blacks from their own race, but not from whites, seems a rather flimsy explanation."

Actually the funniest running gag on the show had nothing to do with race: It was Foxx feigning a heart attack whenever backed into a corner by the sitcom plotting. "I'm comin', Elizabeth," he'd shout toward heaven and his departed wife, "it won't be long now!"

To Foxx, every line on the show had to ring true. It had to reflect real characters, even if they were exaggerated for comic effect. He questioned the show's writers, who at first were mostly white, and insisted on changing his own lines and jokes. At a big conference, an executive asked what the star's qualifications were for judging scripts. Foxx answered, "I've been black longer than anybody here."

Despite the murky undercurrent of stereotyping, "Sanford and Son" became a hit for both black and white viewers and made Redd Foxx a giant star. This produced a giant ego—a natural response given his bitterness at having to wait 30 years for his break. Foxx made headlines regularly—for marriages, divorces and demands for respect. He fought for a nicer dressing room and a golf cart to ride to and from the set. He complained bitterly when he didn't get his own television special, or when he was passed over for an Emmy: "You work for a lifetime in a business that you love, and I love it like a woman, so it hurts when it treats you this way."

The unhappy star left "Sanford and Son" for the glory of his own variety series, "The Redd Foxx Show." It was a crushing failure. So was his debut as a movie star, *Norman Is That You?* Foxx tried to make a sitcom comeback with "Sanford," minus the son. It flopped. Considered not only a difficult personality but a three-time loser (after two television bombs and a movie failure), Foxx returned to risqué comedy in nightclubs. Troubles followed. Foxx dropped $300,000 to settle his 1981 divorce from his third wife and in 1983 went bankrupt. "Material things don't mean so much," the aging star said. "You don't have that long left to enjoy them. I'd just like some peace of mind." Even his 80-year-old father couldn't live out his life in peace. He died of a gunshot wound to the chest—he shot himself, evidently by accident—in the hallway of his apartment.

After a few years, the one-time star was chastened. The man whose manager angrily refused interviews (unless Foxx was paid for them) now sought out interview opportunities. In 1986 he turned up on an ESPN boxing show, pleading for another chance to revive "Sanford and Son." In a dissipated, hoarse voice he said, "Other shows have come back. I don't understand why they can't bring back 'Sanford and Son.' I'd love to come back and do Sanford." He was even willing to work again with co-star Demond Wilson. He hadn't seen Wilson much since the young performer quit show business to become a preacher: "We don't keep in touch no more 'cause he knows I don't wanna hear it."

Trying to duplicate Jackie Mason's success, Foxx came to Broadway in 1987 with guests Slappy White and LaWanda Page. Many first-nighters walked out before it was over. The *New York Times* called Foxx "pathetically unprepared," his act "rooted in angry self-disgust and physical loathing . . . unintelligble" and "mercifully brief." In 1989 the Internal Revenue Service raided his home in Las Vegas and seized his property, ready to auction it off if he failed to pay a huge tax debt. He claimed he was "white-listed," not blacklisted—"nobody black hurt me. . . . There have got to be some whites in town that owe taxes. Why don't they go to their houses and tear it up and throw stuff all around the floor?" *People* magazine reported that after Foxx went public with his problems, he raised only $293 from friends and fans. Most were wondering what he'd done with the $500,000 he made from his last film, *Harlem Nights*. In July 1990 the IRS started its auction, selling eight of his cars for about $50,000. It kept going, claiming Foxx owed nearly $3 million in taxes and penalties.

In the summer of 1991 Foxx married for the fourth time and in the fall he attempted a comeback with a new sitcom, "Royal Family." The show was a "family comedy," which meant he had to tone down his grouchy persona and invent a suitable-for-prime-time epithet, the quickly grumbled, "mother-father!"

Asked if he had any advice for young people about to embark on a show business career, he said, "Go to school and finish college and your life will be much better. You won't have to go through the stuff I've been through." At age 68, he maintained a hectic schedule admitting, "When you work 10 to 12 hours every day it's rough . . . it's rough for me now at my age." While on the set, rehearsing a script, Foxx suffered a heart attack and died in the hospital just a few hours later.

AUDIO incl.: *Laff of the Party 1–4* (Dooto), *Laff of the Party 7–8* (Dooto), *Burlesque Humor* (Dooto), *The Sidesplitter* (Dooto), *The New Race Track* (Dooto), *Redd Foxx Fun* (Dooto), *Sly Sex* (Dooto), *Have One on Me* (Dooto), *Laffarama* (Dooto), *The Wild Party* (Dooto), *This Is Foxx* (Dooto), *He's Funny That Way* (Dooto), *At Jazzville* (Dooto), *Hearty Party* (Dooto), *New Fugg* (Dooto), *Laff Along* (Dooto), *Crack Up* (Dooto), *Naughties* (Dooto), *Laff Your Head Off* (MF), *Laff Your Ass Off* (MF), *Redd Foxx At Home* (MF), *A Whole Lot of Soul* (MF), *At His Best* (MF), *Doin' His Own Thing* (MF), *Say Like It Is* (MF), *Is Sex Here to Stay* (MF), *Where It Is* (MF), *Huffin' and a Puffin'* (MF), *I'm Curious Black* (MF), *3 or 4 Times a Day* (MF), *Mr. Hot Pants* (MF), *Hot Flashes* (MF), *Restricted* (MF), *Superstar* (MF), *In a Nutshell* (King), *Matinee Idol* (King), *Pass the Apple, Eve* (King), *Bare Facts* (King), *On the Loose* (Loma), *Both Sides* (Loma), *Live at Las Vegas* (Loma), *Up Against the Wall* (Warner), *Sanford and Son* (RCA), *Wash Your Ass* (Atlantic), *I Ain't Lied Yet* (Laff), *Redd Foxx Uncensored* (Laff), *Everything's Big* (Laff), *Laughin' at the Blues* (Savoy Jazz), *Foxx Live in '85* (Reddy Freddy)

BIOGRAPHY: *Redd Foxx B.S.: Before Sanford* (Price, 1979)

BOOK: *Redd Foxx Encyclopedia of Black Humor* (1977)

BROADWAY: *Redd Foxx* (1987)

FILMS incl.: *Cotton Comes to Harlem* (1970), *Norman Is That You?* (1976), *Ghost of a Chance* (1987), *Harlem Nights* (1989)

TV: "Sanford and Son" (1972–77), "Redd Foxx" (1977–78), "Sanford" (1980–81), "The Redd Foxx Show" (1986), "Royal Family" (1991)

VIDEOS: *In a Plain Brown Wrapper*; *Dirty Dirty Jokes*

## IRENE FRANKLIN

### (June 13, 1876–June 16, 1941)

"The Most Popular Woman Vaudeville Artist," Irene Franklin not only sang comic songs but dressed up for each part. She was convincing as a little girl, singing "I'm Nobody's Baby Now," or as an old spinster, singing "If I Don't Lock My Family Up, It's the Old Maid's Home for Me." She displayed all her funniest faces for a novelty piece called "Expres-

sion" and showed her beguiling, saucy tendencies with the risqué song about prohibition and sex, "What Have You Got on Your Hip? You Don't Seem to Bulge Where a Gentleman Ought To."

The red-headed Franklin began her career as a child actress, and before she was out of her teens she had toured the world as a vaudeville star. A capable actress, she appeared on Broadway in 1907's *The Orchid* co-starring Eddie Foy. Probably her closest contemporary was Vesta Victoria. They both enjoyed singing wry satires. But Vesta was not about to dress up in a child's dress and frilly knickers to sing "Somebody Ought to Put the Old Man Wise." Unlike later comediennes who played brawling, bawling brats (Rae Dooley and Fanny Brice), Irene sang in a low, insinuating voice, a cross between Mae West and one of the Little Rascals.

Her best-known song, "Red Head," which she co-wrote with her husband, tells the story of a mean-tempered kid who hates it when she's called "Gingerbread Head" or "Bricktop." She retaliates by kicking people in the shins. That's only the start of her mischief. In the song's next stanza, she reports the family's "brand-new house caught fire. Pa said I set it off, but he's a liar." In a spoken segment, her father breaks in, sternly warning "Don't you want to go to heaven when you die?" Irene sneers, "No, Father, I'd rather go with you."

Franklin recorded many tunes, including three 1911 numbers, "I've Got the Mumps," "I Want to be a Janitor's Child" and "The Talkative Waitress." *Variety* called her "the red-headed meteor of the two-a-day . . . satirical, and subtle, witty and beautiful . . . an unmatchable personality."

Irene's accompanist/husband Burt Green died from Bright's disease in 1922. It was a devastating loss, but Irene came back to play The Palace in 1925, 1926, 1929 and 1930. Unfortunately, as the years rolled by, few songs matched the old hits she and Green had written together. There were fewer places for the aging vaudevillian to play as well. Franklin made a few films (she played Jean Harlow's mother in *Saratoga*), but the list is a study in cinematic obscurity.

Irene, who'd raised her own two kids plus two from Green's earlier marriage, eventually remarried. She and husband Jerry Jarnegin had company one evening in 1934. The guests waited for Jarnegin to come down for dinner. He shot himself instead.

In her 60s, Irene no longer lived in Hollywood, but at the Actors Fund Home in New Jersey. One day she began to write down a few lines, which she sent to a local newspaper columnist named Louis Sobol: "Irene Franklin speaking. Perhaps you remember her. She wrote and sang 'Red Head.' She was born on June 13, Friday, and her name is spelled with 13 letters. Now another Friday, June 13, is near. Do you think anyone remembers or cares?"

Three days later, she was dead.

BROADWAY: *The Orchid* (1907), *Hands Up* (1915), *The Passing Show of 1917* (1917), *Greenwich Village Follies* (1921), *Sweet Adeline* (1929)

FILMS incl.: *Lazy River* (1934), *Change of Heart* (1934), *The President Vanishes* (1934), *Timothy's Quest* (1936), *Song and Dance Man* (1936), *Midnight Madonna* (1937), *Married Before Breakfast* (1937), *Saratoga* (1937), *Fixer Dugan* (1939)

## WILLIAM FRAWLEY

### (February 26, 1887–March 3, 1966)

He was gruff, old and dumpy. In a word, his personality was "nertz." But "Fred Mertz" was hilarious, thanks to the intentional and unintentional humor of veteran character actor William Frawley.

The co-star of "I Love Lucy" began his career as a singer. The kid from Burlington, Iowa sang in his church choir and at Elks Club functions. His mother didn't want him to go into show business, insisting on more dignified professions. So Frawley worked for a fight promoter. Later he was a boilermaker. He secretly returned to show biz with piano player Franz Rath. They worked vaudeville under the title A Man, A Piano and a Nut.

Frawley was the nut. He got nuttier in 1914 when he married his first wife, Edna Louise Broedt, and formed Frawley and Louise. *Variety's* Abel Green called it one of the "great comedy acts" of the day—until the duo divorced. In 1927 Frawley began singing and dancing in Broadway shows. A film contract followed and he lent his scowly, streetwise comic presence to a variety of hard-boiled roles. Balding,

sour-ball Frawley was cast as the fall guy—such as the detective too dumb to get the goods on Bud and Lou in *Abbott and Costello Meet the Invisible Man*.

"I played in 96 pictures," he once said. "Maybe one or two good ones." The two he referred to were *Miracle on 34th Street* and Chaplin's *Monsieur Verdoux*. In the former he was the squinty, savvy politico who advises a judge that he won't get reappointed if he rules "there ain't no Santy Claus." In the latter he had a small role as Jean La Salle. As a character man, most of Frawley's roles were small, and he spent much of his time "at liberty." When Frawley heard that Lucille Ball was casting her new sitcom, he went after the part the old-fashioned way: He called up and badgered Lucy for it. Lucy hardly even knew the old actor, but the more she thought about it, the more she figured he'd make a good Fred Mertz. (Mertz was the real name of a neighbor of "I Love Lucy" scriptwriter Madelyn Pugh.) Desi Arnaz and CBS weren't so sure. Frawley had a reputation for being a grumbler and a drinker. He got the part but was told that if he was ever late or ever drunk, he was through.

The contract didn't say anything about being abusive. The grumpy old wise guy disliked co-star Vivian Vance the moment he met her and needled her constantly. After the show ended he told a reporter, "She's one of the finest gals to come out of Kansas, but I often wish she'd go back there." Despite their personal problems, Frawley and Vance were a funny combination, as was Frawley versus everyone else. It was hard to tell if it was technique or just luck. Audiences laughed when he stood around with nothing to do and were in stitches whenever he tried to put some enthusiasm into his lines. He seemed slow and out of touch, quite a comic contrast to the other cast members. Perhaps his halfhearted attitude was not acting. He once admitted that rehearsing and performing on the show was "like eating stew every night—stale and not a bit funny."

Frawley went on to play "Bub," a grumbling old softy on television's "My Three Sons," but left the show to undergo prostate surgery and wasn't well enough to return. Two years later he suffered a heart attack and collapsed in the lobby of the nearby Hollywood Knickerbocker Hotel. To the surprise of many, the tough old man of comedy never regained consciousness. Of course, had Death come for landlord Fred Mertz years earlier, he probably would've opened the door, stared at the specter and grunted, "Ethel—it's for you."

AUDIO: *Bill Frawley Sings the Old Ones* (Dot)

BROADWAY incl.: *Merry Merry* (1925), *Bye Bye Bonnie* (1927), *She's My Baby* (1928), *Here's Howe!* (1928), *Carry On* (1929), *Sons o' Guns* (1929), *She Lived Next to the Firehouse* (1931), *Tell Her the Truth* (1932), *Twentieth Century* (1932), *Ghost Writer* (1933)

FILMS incl.: *Moonlight and Pretzels* (1933), *Shoot the Works* (1934), *The Lemon Drop Kid* (1934), *Hold 'em Yale* (1935), *Alibi Ike* (1935), *Car 99* (1935), *Three Cheers for Love* (1936), *Double or Nothing* (1937), *Blossoms on Broadway* (1937), *Something to Sing About* (1937), *Professor Beware* (1938), *St. Louis Blues* (1939), *Adventures of Huckleberry Finn* (1939), *One Night in the Tropics* (1940), *Blondie in Society* (1940), *Cracked Nuts* (1941), *Six Lessons from Madame La Zonga* (1941), *Whistling in Brooklyn* (1943), *Going My Way* (1944), *Ziegfeld Follies* (1946), *Miracle on 34th Street* (1947), *Monsieur Verdoux* (1947), *The Babe Ruth Story* (1948), *Joe Palooka in Winner Take All* (1948), *Kill the Umpire* (1950), *The Lemon Drop Kid* (1951), *Rhubarb* (1951), *Abbott and Costello Meet the Invisible Man* (1951), *Safe at Home* (1962)

TV: "I Love Lucy" (1951–57), "The Lucy-Desi Comedy Hour" (1957–60), "My Three Sons" (1960–64)

## STAN FREBERG

### (August 7, 1926–   )

One of the legends of 1950s satire, Stan Freberg's parodies seem genial now, but they were considered iconoclastic and outrageous when they first appeared. These included 45-rpm records such as "John and Marsha" (two lovers whispering and ultimately shouting each other's name in the ultimate movie passion scene) and "St. George and the Dragonet" (a million-selling send-up of television's "Dragnet").

Freberg's work, like *Mad* magazine, would shape a generation's tastes in humor. It was satire almost hidden by a goofy veneer. He pointed up the foolishness of censors by rerecording "Old Man River" and changing offensive terms ("old" to "elderly,"

"sweat and strain" to "perspire and strain"). He prodded Christmas conscience in "Green Christmas" by having Bob Cratchit complain, "Can't you just wish someone a Merry Christmas?" only to be told by an ad man: "What's the percentage in that?" Often Freberg skipped jokes in favor of weird comic visions, such as a quiz show offering as a prize "a life-size full-color inflatable latex rubber Liberace."

It was typical of Freberg's comedy sketch style to have a scene of Christopher Columbus' crew threatening Chris with rumbles of mutiny: "Rumble rumble rumble! Mutiny mutiny mutiny!"

Today much of Freberg's work seems dated because his original, visionary techniques have been used by many since. His "Tuned Sheep," who shake their heads and play "Lullaby of Birdland," seems like Monty Python, his weird commercials could be Firesign Theatre, as in the one about an astronaut promoting "Puffed Grass . . . if I didn't start off every day with a stomach full of puffed grass, I couldn't break through the sound barrier. One hundred million cows can't be wrong."

Freberg grew up in Pasadena, his father a pastor. The boy was a dreamer who listened to radio shows all night and loved the satire of Fred Allen. Neighborhood kids, more interested in sports, picked on him. One day a bunch jumped him and tied him to a tree. One grabbed a knife and slashed him across the knee. "When I look at the scar on my knee today, it reminds me that I have been a nonconformist for a long time now and that basically nothing has changed. The guys in the dark suits still wonder why I won't play ball."

He learned how to use his brains to get what he wanted. When he was in the army, he was given an ill-fitting uniform. The timid soldier told his supply sergeant, "If General Patton walks up to me, I want to look nice for him. Otherwise it'd be a reflection on you." The sergeant blinked, thought it over and gave Private Freberg a new uniform.

Freberg got a job at Warner Brothers doing cartoon voices and later, in 1949, produced "Time for Beany" a children's television show with hip humor adults could appreciate. In the 1950s he began making hit comedy records. "I just rolled a blank yellow paper into the typewriter and tried to channel the anger into satire and humor . . . outrage in its natural state is not too salable. The hard part comes in covering the social message with the candy coating of humor."

Today the candy coating seems a bit thick, a problem Freberg attributes to the bland censorship he called a "tapioca curtain" between him and his audience. Freberg shifted into advertising in the 1960s; he was one of the first to produce entertaining, offbeat commercials. His anticommercial style would soon be copied, but at the time he was the only one doing them. One standout was for Chun King Chinese food, in which an announcer declared, "Nine out of ten doctors prefer Chun King," and a photo showed nine Chinese doctors and one Caucasian.

Through the years Freberg remained primarily at the helm of his "Freberg Ltd. But Not Very" ad agency. Interest in Freberg, sparked by his autobiography, helped get his long out of print *Stan Freberg's U.S.A.* rereleased on CD in 1989. Capitol even dug into the vault and restored portions of the satire censored 30 years earlier. He produced a new special for radio in 1991.

AUDIO: *Best of the Stan Freberg Shows #1* (Capitol, reissued as *Face the Funnies*), *Best of the Stan Freberg Shows #2* (Capitol, reissued as *Madison Avenue Werewolf*), *A Child's Garden of Freberg* (Capitol, reissued as *The Best of Freberg*), *Stan Freberg with the Original Cast* (Capitol), *Pay Radio* (Capitol), *The United States of America* (Capitol), plus promotional albums issued for Bekins Van Lines, Chun King, the Radio Advertising Bureau, Madow Gold Dairy, the Oregon State Centennial and for Freberg Ltd.

AUTOBIOGRAPHY: *It Only Hurts When I Laugh* (1988)

## PAUL FREES

**(June 22, 1920–November 1, 1986)**

Impressionist Paul Frees could do them all: Lorre, Bogart, Jolson and hundreds more. But when he switched from the stage to cartoon voice work, he became a legend. He gave voices to gruff Russians (Boris Badenov), goofy Germans (Ludwig von Drake), lovable Liverpudlians (John and George on "The Beatles" cartoon series) and All-Americans (the Pillsbury Doughboy in television commercials).

Some comic cartoon voices were based on his earlier impressions. The voices he used on "The Bullwinkle Show" for Inspector Fenwick and Captain Peachfuzz were based on film stars Eric Blore and Ed Wynn. His voice for Toucan Sam in Froot Loops commercials was Ronald Colman.

Frees began his career in vaudeville at 13. Later, under the name Buddy Green, he started playing stand-up dates. In the 1940s he became one of radio's busiest performers, appearing in countless roles and acting as narrator for both "Escape" and "Suspense." The voice he used as an announcer was comparable to Orson Welles for commanding instant attention. As a "hobby," he appeared in films, though usually minor roles. Fans recall him best as Dr. Maurice Vorrhees in *The Thing*. On television he was heard but not seen as John Beresford Tipton, the man who gave away a fortune every week as "The Millionaire." He sang as everyone from Al Jolson to Chico Marx to Dick Powell on the soundtrack of *The Abominable Dr. Phibes*.

The versatile performer wrote and directed a film (*The Beatniks* in 1960), drew the charcoal sketch of Brother Dave Gardner for the cover of Dave's *Hippocracy* album and was responsible for some of Spike Jones' greatest hits, guesting as Peter Lorre for a demented rendition of "My Old Flame" and starring as Bela Lugosi, Boris Karloff and Alfred Hitchcock on the concept lp *Spike Jones in Stereo*. He recorded his own novelty album, *Poster People*, singing pop tunes as famous stars (Bogart doing "Raindrops Keep Fallin' on My Head" and Peter Lorre fracturing "Hey Jude"). The album was one of the few times in recent years that he came out from behind his low profile.

Many in the business remember him as a kind man. He was well known for his generosity to fans and to his co-workers. Jackie Vernon recalled being nervous and unsure of himself when he did a cartoon voice for the first time ("Frosty the Snowman"). It was Paul Frees who gave him the help and confidence he needed. However, Frees never sought publicity and enjoyed his privacy. He remained something of a mystery man; few knew even the basics about him—that he was married and had a son and daughter as well as two brothers and a sister.

AUDIO: *Spike Jones in Stereo* (Warner), *Best of Spike Jones* (RCA Victor), *Music from the Soundtrack of Dr. Phibes* (A.I.R.), *The Poster People* (MGM)

FILMS incl.: *Riot in Cell Block 11* (1954), *The Thing* (1960)

TV: "The Millionaire" (1955–60), "The Bullwinkle Show" (1961–62)

## FRICK AND FRACK

**Frick: Werner Groebli, April 21, 1915–**
**Frack: Hans Mauch, May 4, 1919–June 5, 1979**

Today the term "Frick and Frack" is applied to any dubious duo. Howard Cosell, in an episode of "The Odd Couple" television series, took one look at Felix and Oscar and pronounced them "Frick and Frack."

For some, the very words "Frick and Frack" have a funny, risqué overtone. Both words are close to various slang terms. In France, a "fric-frac" is a burglary. However, in Switzerland "Frick" is a town, and that's where Werner Groebli said he was born.

An ice-skating comedy team, Groebli and Hans Mauch billed themselves as Frick and Frack as part of Shipstad and Johnson's *Ice Follies* in 1939. They remained a team until 1953 when Mauch contracted a bone disease. They were considered the top entertainers in ice show comedy; other notable performers with less evocative names included Biddy and Baddy (Gigi Percelly and Steven Pedley), Hans Leiter and tramp comic Freddie Trenkler.

After the duo split up Groebli continued to perform as "Mr. Frick." He still got laughs from a classic routine in which he pretended to be caught by an invisible rope. As he slipped and slided forward, objecting strenuously to being pulled by some irresistible object, audiences laughed in wonder and surprise.

FILMS incl.: *Silver Skater* (1942), *Lady Let's Dance* (1943)

## JOE FRISCO

**(Louis Wilson Joseph, 1890–February 16, 1958)**

Originally a comic soft-shoe dancer, Joe Frisco invented "The Frisco Dance." The man from Milan,

Illinois rarely spoke on stage. He stuttered. But when he discovered that his stutter got laughs, it encouraged him to display more and more of his natural wit. On psychoanalysis: "I refuse to pay anyone $50 an hour just to squeal on my mother." On California air: "This is the only town where you wake up in the morning and listen to the birds coughing."

After performing with several partners (he was in the duo of "Coffee and Doughnuts" and the trio of Frisco, McDermott and Cox), he performed a solo act of jokes and dancing. He won applause for a new novelty dance, "The Jewish Charleston," in 1926. Frisco played The Palace in 1927, 1929 and 1930 and in 1930 made a few obscure shorts: *Happy Hottentots*, *Border Patrol* and *The Song Plugger*.

Though a capable comic on stage, Frisco's place in posterity seems to be as a colorful character off stage. He was spontaneously funny among his comedian friends, who have told endless anecdotes about him. He was a "comedian's comedian," according to Joey Adams, who recalled "he was a character who just happened to make his living in show business." Joe lived a simple life. He made money and spent it. Said Adams, "Most of his life he had no wife, never a big home with servants and cars. . . . For Joe life was a single room and a scratch sheet."

Anecdotes about Frisco's gambling—and losing—are legendary. Once Frisco boasted of a great day at the races: "I got a r-ride home." Another time he had to pawn a painting of *The Last Supper*. Asked what it was worth, Joe said, "Well, at least t-ten dollars a p-p-plate." Perhaps the most typical story concerns the time Frisco and his agent argued over what to charge for a particular engagement. The agent was going to ask the theater owner for $2,000. Frisco demanded $3,000. The agent asked Joe to come down and straighten it out in person. Said Joe: "What? And get locked out of my r-room?"

BROADWAY incl.: *Ziegfeld Follies* (1918), *Earl Carroll Vanities* (1928).

FILMS incl.: *The Gorilla* (1930), *Mr. Broadway* (1933), *That's My Man* (1947), *Riding High* (1950), *The Sweet Smell of Success* (1957)

# DAVID FROST

## (April 7, 1939– )

A popular "angry young man" of 1960s comedy in Britain, David Frost was only 23 when he helmed "That Was the Week That Was," a cheeky satirical television program that had politicians running for cover. The parson's son from a rural town in England had only recently graduated from Cambridge University.

Written by the top talent of the day, including Ned Sherrin, Peter Cook, John Braine and Peter Shaffer, the show was loaded with prickly observations, such as this one on world leaders: "Wilson's sincere. Jack Kennedy's sincere. So's Khrushchev. Give him his due, he's sincere." "True, true. Thank God there aren't any Machiavellis in world politics today." "You knew where you were with Machiavelli."

When the show came to America, Frost lined up this country's top comedy stars, including Woody Allen, Tom Lehrer and Buck Henry. Frost delivered his usual sarcastic one-liners: "A spokesman for the Republicans said today with the candidacy of Barry Goldwater, the Republican Party is on the way back. And who knows, someday it may even go forwards."

America was not quite ready for biting satire. Frost went back to England for "The Frost Report," once again surrounding himself with the best young wits he could find. Five of them went on to form Monty Python (only American Terry Gilliam was not involved). Once again Frost delivered tart monologues of wit and whimsy:

"Mr Harold Wilson said today the drain on Britain's gold reserves has finally stopped. They've all gone. Mr. Wilson added, 'We would all have had our backs to the wall—but we're so far behind with the building program that the wall isn't ready.' Parliament is opened by Her Majesty the Queen, who would be well advised to take one quick look and shut it again. . . . Abroad things are done so differently. We've just heard there's going to be a general election in Greece. And we all know which generals are going to be elected. Someone broke into the Kremlin and stole next year's election results. . . . And a group of British M.P.'s returning from Africa report that of the African leaders they met, one of them was Haile Selassie, eight were fairly Selassie and five weren't Selassie at all."

In 1969 Frost returned to America for a talk show that balanced outrageous guests like Mort Sahl, John Lennon and Phil Ochs with the kind of movie stars that led him to use his British exclamations "mahvelous" and "supah." He asked iconoclastic questions and wittily sparred with some guests, but merely burbled "What is your definition of love?" to others. His catch phrase was a cheery "Hello, good evening and welcome!"

Frost won two Emmy awards and produced a series of humorous books, but after the series ended he tended to take on more serious pursuits. One of his greatest triumphs was a series of four 90-minute talk specials in 1977 with Richard Nixon. Frost's private life settled down too. At one time considered quite a dashing, eligible bachelor, linked romantically with Diahann Carroll, Frost married Peter Sellers' widow, Lynne Frederick, in 1981.

Frost remained popular in England as both a film producer and television talk show host. In 1985, after hosting the lighthearted syndicated series "The Guinness Book of Records" he got a chance to resurrect "That Was the Week That Was." "Irreverent political and social satire hasn't been done in prime time for 20 years," he said. He gave it his best shots: "What is a liberal? A liberal finds it in his heart to forgive Jane Fonda for being in Hanoi but not for being in *Barbarella*. . . . Statistics in today's Pravda show that 88% of Russian homes have a video camera. But of those, only 5% know about it." Political satire was not of strong interest to viewers at the time, and neither was Frost's subsequent show, "Inside Edition," a syndicated "magazine" of news stories. In 1990 Frost returned to the straight talk show format with "Talking with David Frost," a successful PBS series of specials in which he spent an hour with important figures of the day, including General Norman Schwarzkopf and British Prime Minister John Major.

AUDIO: *That Was the Week That Was* (Odeon), *That Was the Week That Was* (Radiola), *David Frost Talks to Bobby Kennedy* (Douglas), *David Frost on Nursing*

(University Hospitals of Cleveland), *The Frost Report* (Janus), *David Frost in Las Vegas* (UA)

BIOGRAPHY: *Will You Welcome Now . . . David Frost* (Frischauer, 1971)

BOOKS incl.: *The World's Worst Decisions* (1983), *David Frost's Book of Millionares* (1984).

TV: "That Was the Week That Was" (1964–65), "The David Frost Show" (1969–72), "The David Frost Revue" (1971–73), "Headliners with David Frost" (1978), "That Was the Week That Was" (1985), "Inside Edition" (1988)

# DAVID FRYE

## (David Shapiro, 1934–    )

The most ferocious political impressionist of all time, David Frye didn't just mimic the voices of presidents—he twisted his face into grotesque caricatures of them. In fact, his career could be charted strictly on the attractiveness of American leaders. In the early 1960s, Frye was a struggling mimic while handsome John F. Kennedy was in the White House. In the mid-'60s, he gained fame using a chillingly benign smile and harsh Southern accent for Lyndon Johnson. He reached his peak as a jowly, shifty-eyed, lamprey-mouthed Richard Nixon. Then he faded away in the eras of mild-mannered Jimmy Carter, former leading man Ronald Reagan and George Bush.

The Brooklyn-born comedian, short and shy as a child, developed his talent for mimicry early. He had a somewhat strange reaction to the people who impressed him: "Later on I would begin to believe I was that person. I would make his facial expressions, imitate his voice. I would get vibrations from just a brief meeting with a person, maybe passing on a stairway, and hours later I would still be feeling them."

Probably the best example of the intense, serious young performer's ability to get into a subject's psyche is his Richard Nixon impression. His facial caricature was less the real Nixon and more the imagined monster Frye thought was lurking inside. His catch phrase as President Nixon went deep into what he thought to be going on in Nixon's mind—

"I *am* the president!" This was not a phrase Nixon used; it was Frye's. But once Frye put it into Nixon's mouth, people believed it had to be a Nixon original.

Frye attended James Madison High School in Brooklyn and the University of Miami, spending the late 1950s struggling with his comedy act. "I bombed miserably and went to work for my father at the Anchor Office Cleaning Company in Brooklyn, working there during the day while playing pass-the-hat spots in the Village at night." He managed to get a few television variety spots in the early 1960s, but he pinpointed a booking on "The Merv Griffin Show" in October 1966 as the turning point. He unveiled his perfected Lyndon Johnson that night and afterward found himself with a new agent and consistent nightclub bookings.

The hatred the American public was feeling toward Johnson was mirrored in the ferocious newcomer's mimicry. Johnson's fall became Frye's rise. As Johnson he drawled, "Mah fellow Americans. Ah come here tonight because ah no longer have any place to go. Ah have gone down the lonely road. Ah have stumbled and lost mah way. And all of you have followed me." Nixon was next, and the country was even more polarized. Frye fried Nixon with the first hit political album since Vaughn Meader's Kennedy era *The First Family*. It was *I Am the President*, playing off the catch phrase sweeping the country. Frye didn't let up until Nixon was destroyed. In his fourth album, the Watergate satire *Richard Nixon: A Fantasy*, he not only envisioned Nixon guilty (due to an incriminating jowl print at the scene of the crime) but delighted in the thought of the president being led kicking and screaming to death row: "I accept responsibility, but not the blame. . . . I love America, and you always hurt the one you love!"

Frye was a scorching, driven satirist, but underneath he was the same insecure little guy he was in Brooklyn. On talk shows, he seemed uncomfortable answering questions as himself. He admitted, "Being yourself . . . you feel naked, like you're going out there without your clothes on." But he also had increasing trouble becoming his characters. He would pause on a talk show panel, dig into his pocket, take a look at photos of his targets, then proceed.

All of Frye's top impressions were of strong, antagonistic people: a viciously giddy George C.

Scott as Patton; a lizard-tongued William F. Buckley Jr.; a nasally snide Howard Cosell; and a wheedling and obnoxious Truman Capote. After the death of Nelson Rockefeller (reportedly in the unlikely company of an attractive young woman), Frye imagined the ghost of the gratingly gravel-voiced politician saying: "A guy of 70 doing 69 with a 25-year-old? It could've been worse. I could've died at 25 doing 69 with a 70-year-old!"

Still uncompromising, Frye continues to tour in nightclubs and remains one of the most acidic mimics in show business.

AUDIO: *The New First Family* (Verve), *I Am the President* (Elektra), *Radio Free Nixon, WNIX* (Elektra), *Richard Nixon Superstar* (Buddah), *Richard Nixon, A Fantasy* (Buddah), *The Great Debate* (David Frye Productions)

TV: "The Leslie Uggams Show" (1969)

# G

## GALLAGHER

### (Leo Gallagher, July 24, 1947–   )

The Liberace of comedy, Gallagher relies on a teasingly fey personality and expensive props to get laughs. Audiences roar and applaud each expensive gag costume. They love it when he wheels out his latest zany invention like a boat with a Cadillac roof on it (which cost the comic $15,000 to build).

The most popular "prop comic" in contemporary comedy, Gallagher admits, "I'm a showman, a circus." He wants to top himself every time he comes out on stage, whether it's wearing giant high heel shoes or a rubbery fake "muscle" body suit.

Originally the round-faced comic with the little mustache and old fashioned hippie hairstyle was a fairly standard comic who used observational humor and quick jokes: "Blind man in a drugstore comes in, starts knocking things off the shelf with his cane. The owner says, 'Can I help you?' He says, 'No thanks, just looking.' " Gradually he shifted to prop comedy, thanks to his big "hit," a routine in which he parodied television commercials for a slicer/dicer called "Veg-a-Matic" with the watermelon-bashing "Sledge-o-Matic." For his concerts, the first rows were often decked out in rain gear to guard against being splattered by the elfish troublemaker.

As he began to get a name for himself, Gallagher decided it would be just that—one name. He refused to divulge his full name to interviewers and rarely even talked to the press. Since he was never a major television or movie star, more popular on cable and on the concert circuit, he wasn't pressed for many interviews anyway. He was born in Tampa, Florida, attended Plant High School and was a Southern regional roller skate champ. He claimed to have attended the University of Southern Florida and studied chemistry at the University of Southern California, graduating in 1969. He felt being a chemistry major had some influence on him: "You've got to be analytical about life. If yogurt goes bad, how can you tell?"

In the same way concert pianists resented Liberace, other comics blanch at the mention of Gallagher. Part of it is his smugly fey delivery. Part of it is the belief that prop comedy is "'the lowest form of stand-up." The other part is Gallagher's unabashed pursuit of large venue audiences and the biggest paydays possible (he would be the last comedian asked to appear free at a charity benefit). He would sometimes brag to a fellow comedian he'd meet on a plane flight that he'd just signed a new contract or commercial tie-in for concerts that was worth hundreds of thousands. His success could not be denied. With a half-dozen videos in release, more than most comedians, he also claimed to have performed more solo concerts to more sold-out crowds than any performer in history—including Elvis Presley.

AUDIO: *Gallagher* (United Artists)

VIDEOS incl.: *Stuck in the '60s; Melon Crazy; Book Keeper; Over Your Head; Maddest; Comedy Tonight*

## GALLAGHER and SHEAN

**Edward Gallagher, 1873–May 28, 1929**
**Al Shean: Al Schonberg, May 12, 1868–August 12, 1949**

Gallagher and Shean had a famous novelty tune that included one of the most famous catch phrases of the day: "Positively, Mr. Gallagher" "Absolutely, Mr. Shean." Unfortunately, that tune lasted about three minutes. And the team of Gallagher and Shean, compared to other great comedy teams, hardly lasted much longer.

Actually, the men had longer associations with others. Gallagher was straight man to comic Joe Barret for 15 years. During that time Shean was in The Manhattan Comedy Four with Sam Curtis, Arthur Williams and Ed Mack, and had spent the last four years teamed with Charles L. Warren. It was in 1910 that Gallagher and Shean teamed up, coming to Broadway for the 1912 musical *The Rose Maid*. Two years later the team split up.

The split lasted longer than the partnership. Together for four years, they were apart for six. They would've stayed apart if not for Al Shean's sister, Minnie Schonberg Marx—the mother of The Marx Brothers. While Minnie was known as the show biz mom who pushed her boys to stardom, she also pushed Gallagher and Shean back together in 1920, interceding for her brother, who claimed that Gallagher refused to even talk to him.

The rejuvenated Gallagher and Shean scored with a new act, "Gallagher and Shean in Egypt." It was so successful that Shean would forever wear the fez he used in that skit, which certainly was incongruous with his use of German dialect. (Shean's pronunciation of "Mr. Gallagher" was more like "Meesta Gelligah"). The duo's luck continued with their novelty tune, "Mr. Gallagher and Mr. Shean." The song, supposedly given to them by Bryan Foy (a son of Eddie Foy), was structured so that any type of nonsense dialogue could be inserted between the choruses. Typical patter from one of the original stanzas: "Oh Mr. Gallagher, Mr. Gallagher, what do you call that game they play upon the links? Where

you drive a ball to where you can't find it at all, then a caddy walks around and thinks and thinks?" "Mr. Shean, Mr. Shean, you don't even know a hazard from a green! It has become a popular game and you don't even know it's name" "Is it polo, Mr. Gallagher?" "No, lawn tennis, Mr. Shean!"

*The Ziegfeld Follies of 1922* featured the team and the song, and they starred in two more Broadway shows. Once again they were together four years. Once again they split. This time it was forever.

Gallagher met with hard times. His fourth marriage ended around the same time as his partnership. He drank heavily and retired to a sanitarium in 1927, he died two years later.

Al Shean had found work during the last split (appearing in Broadway shows, including *The Princess Pat* in 1915 and *Flo-Flo* in 1917). After the final breakup he found solo work again, not even needing the support of his now-famous nephews, The Marx Brothers. Shean's credits include the Broadway show *Father Malachy's Miracle* (1937) and a variety of films: *Music in the Air* (1934), *Traveling Saleslady* (1935), *It Could Happen to You* (1937), *Too Hot to Handle* (1938), *Broadway Serenade* (1939), *Atlantic City* (1944) and *People Are Funny* (1946). For *Atlantic City*, he performed a "Gallagher and Shean" routine with actor Jack Kenny. Sometimes for stage appearances, Shean would sing the "Gallagher and Shean" song alone—switching from straw hat to fez for each verse.

BROADWAY: *Ziegfeld Follies* (1922), *Greenwich Village Follies* (1924), *In Dutch* (1924)

## BROTHER DAVE GARDNER

**(June 11, 1926–September 22, 1983)**

A Will Rogers for the 1960s, Brother Dave Gardner drawled topical ironies. On the space race: "The only reason the Russians are apparently ahead of us in scientific development is 'cause they want to get out of their country a whole lot worse than us." Gardner's philosophies differed slightly from Will's "I never met a man I didn't like." His point of view: "Love your enemies—and drive 'em nuts."

Born in Tennessee and a student at that state's Union University in Jackson, Gardner originally favored anecdotes (such as "The Motorcycle Story"), which were more in keeping with Southern tradition. It was after he started injecting topical comedy into his act in the late 1950s that he crossed over to appearances on Jack Paar's "Tonight Show" and began making records for RCA Victor. Though he had some of Will Roger's folksiness, ex-drummer Gardner added '50s hipster slang and developed a catch phrase for expressing his amusement: "Ain't that weird?"

Colorful and uncompromising, Brother Dave got into some troubles, including a bust for pills in the early 1960s (he got out of that one by producing a doctor's prescription) and a long fight with the Internal Revenue Service in the '70s (in philosophical protest, he refused to pay taxes). Gardner's national popularity dwindled in the late '60s and '70s, though his regional appeal remained strong.

The 1980s began with tragedy—the death of Millie Gardner, his wife and manager. But the new interest in stand-up and the rise of "concert" movies with Richard Pryor and others brought offers for Gardner's services. He was a minor legend, the only Southern comedian with a reputation for biting commentary. Producer Earl Owensby filmed *Brother Dave in Concert* and planned to follow it with *Chain Gang,* starring Gardner. One day on the set in South Carolina, pausing to sign autographs, Brother Dave suddenly collapsed. He was dead at age 57.

AUDIO: *Ain't That Weird* (RCA), *All Seriousness Aside* (RCA), *Best of Dave Gardner* (RCA), *Did You Ever* (RCA), *It's Bigger Than Both of Us* (RCA), *Kick They Own Self* (RCA), *Rejoice, Dear Hearts* (RCA), *Brother Dave Gardner in Person* (Delta), *Motorcycle Story* (Delta), *Out Front* (Tonka), *It's All in How You Look at It* (Capitol), *It Don't Make No Difference* (Capitol), *Hipocracy* (Tower), *Brother Dave Gardner's New Comedy Album* (4 Star)

FILM: *Brother Dave in Concert*

## TERI GARR

### (Terry Ann Garr, December 11, 1945–   )

An actress best known for her comedy and her somewhat air-headed comical appearances on talk shows, Teri Garr was given the honor of "Teri Garr Week" on television's "Late Night with David Letterman" in 1986, guesting five nights in a row.

Garr was born in Hollywood. Her mother, a dancer and ex-Rockette, became a film wardrobe mistress. Her father, Edward, was an actor who had also worked in vaudeville. "My father was an alcoholic and was sick the whole time I was growing up," she said. "After he died, it was a struggle financially for my mother." At 13 Teri joined a ballet company in San Francisco, danced on the 1960s rock show "Shindig" and doubled for Ann-Margret in *The Swinger* in 1966. She majored in both dance and speech at Carl State College. Acting won out, and after many television appearances ("Star Trek," "McCloud," etc.) she became a regular as Cher's friend Olivia on "The Sonny and Cher Show."

After some roles in serious films (*Law and Order* with Darren McGavin and *The Conversation* with Gene Hackman), Teri found herself cast most often in comedy, directed by Mel Brooks in *Young Frankenstein* and Carl Reiner in *Oh God,* where she carved her own identity in the "flaky but sexy" territory of Madeline Kahn and Diane Keaton. She played a dizzy cocktail waitress in *After Hours* and established herself with her Academy Award–nominated supporting role in *Tootsie.* She ad-libbed one of her character's most famous lines: "Who said anything about love? I read *The Second Sex!* I read *The Cinderella Complex!* I'm responsible for my own orgasm!"

As she progressed in film comedy, she was able to create a more modern variant on the "fluttery, ditsy" blonde, one with strong will and romantic appeal. Her versatility impressed a *TV Guide* writer who chronicled her many traits: "She sighs incessantly; her eyes squint; her brows furrow; she's always wiping her bangs away. She stutters as she talks, excited and exasperated . . . she's in constant motion, and whether she's laughing, crying or just trying to talk, it's in a lilting—but just slightly edgy—voice."

Garr's light touch and her combination of sexiness and harmless humor has not only won her television and movie roles. It got her an interesting celebrity endorsement in 1990. She posed for magazine ads in little more than a cotton shirt, a wry expression and a pair of pink briefs. The caption: "What Makes Teri Garr Feel Good? Fruit of the Loom panties."

In 1991 she starred in *Good and Evil,* an offbeat "Soap"-influenced comedy series that some labeled "black" and others "tasteless" in which she played the evil daughter of a woman running a cosmetics business. She said, "I'm playing evil because I've been good too long in my life, and too many people have taken advantage of me."

Whether evil or good, Garr remains sexy without taking herself too seriously. And that's the key reason why she leans toward comedy roles over dramatic parts: "If you want to be taken seriously you have to dress seriously and look like you have thought about it. I try, but I'm not serious. People ask me 'What was your favorite role?' and I say 'Oh, *Gone With the Wind.*' You know. I'm just not serious!"

FILMS incl.: *Head* (1968), *Young Frankenstein* (1974), *Won Ton Ton* (1976), *Oh God* (1977), *Tootsie* (1982), *The Sting II* (1983), *Mr. Mom* (1983), *Close Encounters of the Third Kind* (1977), *After Hours* (1988), *Full Moon in Blue Water* (1988), *Out Cold* (1989), *Let It Ride* (1989), *Short Time* (1990), *Waiting for the Light* (1990)

TV: "Good and Evil" (1991)

## JACKIE GAYLE

### (Jack Potovsky, March 1, 1928–   )

One of the first and now one of the last "old-fashioned" Vegas comics, Gayle moved to the desert in the 1960s and became known as a reliable pro with enough fast-paced schtick to keep the audience in line. A quickie: "My car broke down and a kid asked me if I wanted a lift. I said sure, and he threw me some pills!"

Gayle's style is conversational, sometimes rising into the comic angst of Pat Cooper or Alan King as he gripes about his troubles. From his '60s days: "God bless ya. You're carrying matching Polish luggage, two A&P shopping bags. . . . Tom Jones, at him they throw room keys. Me, they throw corrective stockings. . . . Once I worked a town so small the Howard Johnson surprise flavor of the week was vanilla." Into the 1990s he is still aggravated. His dieting troubles are a real pain: "Jews never learned to say 'no thanks' to anything. You get a guy from a small town, he'll sit down: 'May I give you a piece of apple pie, Tom?' 'No thank you, watching my weight.' A Jewish guy will right away dig in and as

he's eating it will say, 'Oh well, I'll start the diet tomorrow.' We've heard all that for years. Let me tell you, if corned beef were forbidden we'd be snorting it. Jew junkies on corned beef!"

Gayle was a regular at the Playboy Clubs in the 1960s and '70s and appeared often on "The Dean Martin Roasts" series and the television talk show circuit. His late brother Marty Gale was also a comedian, known for many Jewish comedy albums. In the 1980s the stocky comedian won many acting roles. Barry Levinson, who wrote and directed the film *Tin Men*, praised Jackie as "one of the real machine-gun stand-ups. Onstage he just explodes." The film's success gave Gayle's career a great boost, which included a cable television show co-starring Norm Crosby as well as more films and stand-up dates. He starred in a special, "The Wicked Witch," with Rue McLanahan and played a businessman in a 1990 two-part episode of "L.A. Law."

Though in his early days he hung around with Sally Marr and her son Lenny Bruce (he was part of Sally's act, Sally Marr and the Escorts), he admitted that he couldn't be another Lenny even though it was a big desire. "It takes a lot to reveal yourself, to undress yourself in front of an audience, and talk about the truth. . . . I wish I had the courage." Actually he has his own brand of courage, facing a racuous, demanding Vegas audience that expects belly laughs with every line.

FILMS incl.: *The Seven Minutes* (1971), *The Tempest* (1982), *Broadway Danny Rose* (1984), *Tin Men* (1987), *Plain Clothes* (1988), *Bert Rigby, You're a Fool* (1989)

TV: "The Boys" (1989)

VIDEO: *A Toast to Lenny Bruce, The Young at Heart Comedians Special*

## BILLY GILBERT

### (William Gilbert Baron, September 12, 1894–September 23, 1971)

It seemed that for most of his career, Billy Gilbert either chased Laurel and Hardy or sneezed.

His trademark was sneezing—and the upsetting of dignity that it caused him. An imposing figure with lordly girth, a thick mustache and bulging eyes, audiences tittered with the first little nasal disturbance. An incongruous, timid little smile of embarrassment would play across his face. Then there was usually another. And another. Each one louder, each bending the huge man forward like a mountain in the midst of an avalance. He was funny even without being seen: He was the voice of "Sneezy" in Disney's *Snow White and the Seven Dwarfs.*

All sneezing aside, Gilbert was a grand comic heavy, playing excitable types opposite the teams of Todd and Pitts and Laurel and Hardy. In the former's *Bargain of the Century* (1933), he played a German-accented eccentric whose watch is destroyed during a magic trick gone wrong. His reaction? Outrageous rage, of course, grabbing a hammer and breaking every clock in the apartment until the police haul him away.

In Laurel and Hardy's *The Music Box* he played the blustery and arrogant "Professor Theodore von Schwarzenhoffen, MD, AD, DDS, FLD, FFF and F!" After feuding with the boys as they attempt to deliver a piano, he losses control during the typically berserk ending. And in the feature *Blockheads* he played the Teddy Rooseveltish big game hunter who discovers Oliver Hardy in a compromising situation with his wife. Wild-eyed and ranting, he grabs his gun and once again offers the team a wild, farcical finale.

Occasionally Gilbert tried to join a comedy team of his own, but he seemed funnier as a guest villain. He teamed with Ben Blue as The Taxi Boys and later joined Shemp Howard and Maxie Rosenbloom for three feature films. The comedy veteran was in demand throughout his career. One of the few performers to come close to the legend of being "born in a trunk," Gilbert was born in a dressing room in a Kentucky theater. His parents were both opera singers. Though he worked in burlesque and vaudeville, Billy made his mark in films, by his count appearing in over 300 shorts and features, usually playing small parts as an ingratiating waiter or a bombastic professor.

On December 9, 1942, while Gilbert and his wife, Ella, were entertaining the troups in a USO show in the Caribbean, Billy's foster son committed suicide. The boy was only 13. Beside the rifle was a note: "Grandmother wouldn't believe me." Gilbert's career faded in the '40s, as did the careers of his

chief comic tormentors, Laurel and Hardy. He did have a small role in Chaplin's *The Great Dictator* and later found work on Broadway (he took over Walter Slezak's role in *Fanny* in 1956) and even Las Vegas, where he took part in comedy revues. A stroke in 1963 literally silenced him for a year but as soon as he could, he was back making movies—*Five Weeks in a Balloon.* Though financially comfortable (he owned a few apartment buildings), Gilbert was a trouper to the end and always appreciated a hearty comic role. He appeared on Johnny Carson's "Sun City Scandals" television special the year before he died.

BROADWAY: *The Chocolate Soldier* (1947), *The Buttrio Square* (1952), *Fanny* (1956)
FILMS incl.: *Noisy Neighbors* (1929), *The Music Box* (1932), *Million Dollar Legs* (1932), *Flying Down to Rio* (1933), *One Hundred Men and a Girl* (1937), *Snow White and the Seven Dwarfs* (1937), *Blockheads* (1938), *Happy Landing* (1938), *Destry Rides Again* (1939), *The Great Dictator* (1940), *His Girl Friday* (1940), *Arabian Nights* (1942), *Crazy House* (1945), *Anchors Aweigh* (1945), *The Kissing Bandit* (1949), *Five Weeks in a Balloon* (1962)

## JACK GILFORD

### (Jacob Gellman, July 25, 1907–June 4, 1990)

Gentle and likable, the enigmatically smiling, curly-haired, button-eyed Jack Gilford was especially sympathetic when paired opposite a bigger, more aggressive comic character such as Zero Mostel, whom he worked with in many stage productions and films.

Born on the Lower East Side of Manhattan, Gilford grew up in Brooklyn after his parents divorced. His mother earned some money as a bootlegger. In 1939 he tried stand-up comedy at Cafe Society, a club that featured another young stand-up comic, Zero Mostel. Gilford's offbeat routines included everything from a monologue about a golf ball to an impression of a subway rider lulled to sleep by the moving train. He sang "California Here I Come" in Yiddish and offered a puffy-cheeked imitation of soup boiling.

In the late 1940s Gilford's acting career stalled after he, Mostel and many others were blacklisted.

His son recalled, "My father was not really political. He was just genetically predisposed to social dissent." It was on stage that he achieved popular fame, first off-Broadway and then in *A Funny Thing Happened on the Way to the Forum,* for which he received a Tony Award. He toured in productions of *The Sunshine Boys* in 1974 and *The Seven Year Itch* in 1976, among many others. His most successful film role, aside from the screen version of *A Funny Thing Happened on the Way to the Forum,* was his dramatic Academy Award–winning work in *Save the Tiger.*

On television in the 1960s and '70s, Gilford was well known for a series of Cracker Jack candy ads as well as sitcom roles playing on his character of the "nice nebbish" or the bewildered eccentric. On a memorable episode of "Get Smart," the writers paid tribute to his unique charm, giving him the role of "Simon the Likable," an agent whose weapon is niceness—the pleasant twinkle in his eye is more impossible to resist than a hypnotist's glare. He was in an episode of "The Golden Girls" shortly before his death. He still enjoyed the laughter and applause even after so many decades. He told an interviewer, "It's really hard for me to describe the exhilaration of being accepted and wanted. And if you ever find something better than being wanted, call me."

BOOK: *170 Years of Show Business* (Gilford, Gilford and Mostel, 1978)
BROADWAY: *Meet the People* (1940), *The New Meet the People* (1943), *The Live Wire* (1950), *The World of Sholom Aleichem* (1953), *Once Over Lightly* (1955), *Once Upon a Mattress* (1959), *A Funny Thing Happened on the Way to the Forum* (1962), *Cabaret* (1966), *The Sunshine Boys* (1972), *No No Nanette* (1972), *Sly Fox* (1977), *Supporting Cast* (1981), *World of Sholom Aleichem* (1982), *Palace Theater Benefit* (1983)
FILMS incl.: *Hey Rookie* (1944), *Main Street to Broadway* (1953), *A Funny Thing Happened on the Way to the Forum* (1966), *Enter Laughing* (1967), *The Happening* (1967), *Catch 22* (1971), *They Might Be Giants* (1971), *Who's Minding the Mint* (1967), *Save the Tiger* (1973), *Harry and Walter Go to New York* (1976), *Wholly Moses* (1980), *Cheaper to Keep Her* (1980), *Caveman* (1981), *Cocoon* (1985)

TV: "The Arrow Show" (1948–49), "The David Frost Revue" (1971–73), "Paul Sand in Friends and Lovers" (1974–75), "Apple Pie" (1978), "The Duck Factory" (1984)

## JACKIE GLEASON

### (Herbert John Gleason, February 26, 1916–June 24, 1987)

He was called "The Great One," homage to both his flamboyant girth and his talent. Jackie Gleason was one of the most talented comedians to work in the golden age of television. Only Lucille Ball's "I Love Lucy" has proven as classic as his "Honeymooners" series.

Gleason, like his famous alter ego Ralph Kramden, was born in a poor section of Brooklyn. (Kramden's address, 328 Chauncey Street, was Gleason's). Jackie had a brother Clarence, but he was sickly and died at 14. Jackie (named Herbert after his father) was almost as frail and undernourished. Things got worse after his father left home when Jackie was nine. His mother worked long hours as a subway token clerk. She clung to religion for support and in frightening visions would prophesize the end of the world. Every violent thunderstorm threw her into a fit of prayer, clutching her frightened son to her side. Meanwhile, her prayers for enough food to eat went unanswered.

Gleason remembered, "One morning I peeked into her room, and I saw her wrapping my Boy Scout Leggings around her legs. The snow was deep and she was going to have to walk through it to get to her job. I grew up in that minute, pal. I knew what she was going through for me." The kid left high school and earned money hustling pool. After winning a talent contest, Gleason pursued show business, the best way of making big bucks fast.

At 19, Gleason was now the breadwinner, his mother too sick to work. She developed anemia, skin diseases and a growth on her neck. She refused to see a doctor, praying for relief instead. Fifty years old and looking older, she moaned constantly with the pain. One night, as Gleason stood his vigil beside her, he heard her sigh. Then all was quiet. He had

As Ralph Kramden, Joe the bartender and Reginald Van Gleason III, Jackie Gleason was surely "the great one." Photo from the author's collection.

watched his mother die in the midst of squalor and poverty.

Jackie did anything he could for money, even working as a stuntman, nearly killing himself in high-speed auto exhibitions at a local carnival. When he managed to get jobs as a comic, he did everything for a laugh. As "Jumping Jack Gleason" he took pratfalls and did cartwheels. He conquered audiences in low-class nightclubs by turning his hostility into wisecracks, laying it in their laps with broad, cartoonish gestures. One of his most famous early lines was delivered at ringsider Sonja Henie. When the ice skating queen was introduced, he tossed an ice cube at her and sneered, "Do something!"

The rising nightclub comic was known to drink anyone under the table and brawl with the best of them. He insulted one ringsider and challenged him to a fight. Outside in a nearby alley, for one of the

few times in his career, Jackie was knocked down— and out. He didn't know the ringsider was heavyweight contender Two Ton Tony Galento.

Gleason's earthy style and brassy charisma made him a hero to the average clubgoer. He was one of them—just another working stiff. He tried to broaden his career to Broadway and films but was humbled by failures. The only thing that broadened was his waist. He made up for his starved childhood by ballooning to 285 pounds. He thrived in nightclubs and tried radio as well. Occasionally he veered from character comedy and broad jokes to something more offbeat, such as his early monologue about falling in love with a slot machine: "I looked at her and she turned green. . . . All the colors of the rainbow dashed through her neon veins." Sadly, "She only loved me for my money." And as she got older, "I'd push number three and she'd play number four . . . her neons were sagging. She was getting careless about changing her records." She ended up with slugs in her "in McGillicuddy's Saloon . . . an old slot."

Gleason got a break on television in 1949 as Chester Riley, but audiences believed only William Bendix in the role. He had better luck on "Cavalcade of Stars," moving from stand-up to sketch comedy, using all the ad libs and gut-funny schtick he'd polished over the years.

Television was Gleason's media; he signed a three-year pact with Buick for a staggering $11 million. He filled the stage with such characters as the pathetically hopeful "Poor Soul" and boisterous "Joe the Bartender." As comically suave and nasal-voiced "Reginald Van Gleason III" (evidently a parody of the fruitily cadenced grandiose actor John Gilbert), Gleason influenced many, including Johnny Carson (the "Art Fern" character). Ultimately, there was the good-natured, blustery bus driver Ralph Kramden in a series of domestic sketches with Pert Kelton.

Ralph Kramden was so popular he became one of televisions first "spin-offs," getting his own "Honeymooners" show. Though only 39 episodes were filmed, and most viewers have seen each rerun often enough to memorize the dialogue, the show remains a syndication favorite. Books, a fan club and a set of videocassettes attest to the enduring popularity of Ralph Kramden, the little boy in a grown man's body who naively dreams of instant money, throws blustery tantrums when thwarted, plays "king of the castle"—and ultimately ends each episode humbled and contrite. He may have shouted "Bang Zoom! To the moon!" at wife Alice (now played by Audrey Meadows) but in the end, he had to admit with a huge grin "Baby—you're the greatest."

Audiences thought he was the greatest—probably because he was one of the few performers who tried hard to be "pals" with them. He was forever declaring "what a dan-dan-dandy bunch" they were or uttering a winsome "You're a good group!" And while Gleason did have his ancestors (Ralph Kramden and Ed Norton were certainly updates of Laurel and Hardy, and Jackie's elbow-flexing "away we go" has been compared to similar mannerisms by Jack Oakie), audiences considered him a complete original. Critics felt the same way and were eager for him to prove it somewhere else besides television, which was still considered an inferior medium.

Gleason complied. He finally conquered Broadway, receiving a Tony Award for 1959's *Take Me Along*. And nearly 20 years after leaving Hollywood in defeat, he returned to receive an Academy Award nomination for 1961's *The Hustler*. Still, it was on "Honeymooners" reruns and subsequent television variety shows that he was best loved and so completely his flamboyant self. He didn't need the stress of the stage or screen when he could enjoy the good life of his own television schedule comfortably produced near his home in Florida. His delight in his own good fortune was expressed by a joyous and yet humble "How sweet it is!"

Gleason fought hard to enjoy the good life. In a biography of Gleason, Jim Bishop wrote that Jackie was "one of the world's most tormented and fearful men. There are half a dozen Jackie Gleasons and they are not at peace. Gleason the businessman does not admire Gleason the playboy, Gleason the Catholic hates Gleason the connoisseur of blondes. Gleason the actor has little respect for Gleason the drinker. Gleason the brooding reader has no affection for Gleason the clown."

Through the 1970s Gleason worked less and enjoyed himself more, playing golf, riding along Jackie Gleason Drive in Miami Beach and trying to make up for all the years of misery and hectic work. Deeply tanned and a bit thinner, Gleason made a few easy comedies, including the *Smokey and the Bandit* series, and rarely showed the desire to become the king of comedy again.

Heading into the 1980s, perhaps renewed in spirit and restlessly seeking to cap his career with glory, Gleason made a film comeback. He appeared opposite Art Carney in *Izzy and Moe*, co-starred with Sir Laurence Olivier in the drama *Mr. Halpern and Mr. Johnson* and won critical praise starring opposite Tom Hanks in *Nothing in Common*. He hadn't tried too hard in films since 1962's *Gigot*, his one attempt at the comedy and pathos of Chaplin. Fans were delirious when he released *The Lost Honeymooners Episodes*, tapes from his old live show that had been gathering dust. The response was so gratifying he even contemplated a series of new "Honeymooners" productions.

The Great One's death came as something of a shock, even to fans aware of his excesses in alcohol and tobacco. Fortunately, the great wealth of Gleason material—the original "Honeymooners" reruns and now the dozens of *Lost Episodes*, made it a bit easier to say goodbye—or, using his catch phrase, "And away we go."

AUDIO: *Jackie Gleason on Radio* (Radiola), *And Away We Go* (Capitol), *It's Honeymooners Time* (Murray Hill)

BIOGRAPHIES: *The Golden Ham* (Bishop, 1956), *How Sweet It Is* (Bacon, 1986), *The Great One* (W. Henry, 1991), *Jackie Gleason: An Intimate Portrait* (Weatherby, 1992)

BROADWAY: *Keep Off the Grass* (1940), *Follow the Girls* (1944), *Along Fifth Avenue* (1949), *Take Me Along* (1959)

FILM incl.: *Orchestra Wives* (1942), *Springtime in the Rockies* (1942), *All Through the Night* (1942), *The Desert Hawk* (1950), *The Hustler* (1961), *Gigot* (1962), *Requiem for a Heavyweight* (1962), *Papa's Delicate Condition* (1963), *Soldier in the Rain* (1963), *Skidoo* (1968), *How to Commit Marriage* (1969), *Don't Drink the Water* (1969), *Smokey and the Bandit* (1977), *Smokey and the Bandit II* (1980), *The Toy* (1982), *The Sting II* (1983), *Smokey and the Bandit 3* (1983), *Izzy and Moe* (1985), *Mr. Halpern and Mr. Johnson* (1985), *Nothing in Common* (1986)

TV: "Life of Riley" (1949–50), "Cavalcade of Stars" (1950–52), "The Jackie Gleason Show" (1952–

55), "The Honeymooners" (1955–56), "The Jackie Gleason Show" (1956–59), "You're in the Picture" (1961), "The Jackie Gleason Show" (1962–70)

VIDEO: *The Lost Honeymooners Episodes* (MPI)

# GEORGE GOBEL

## (May 20, 1919–February 24, 1991)

One of the biggest stars in 1950s television was a little crew-cutted, birdlike Mid-westerner with a bewildered look and a mild if slightly risqué catch phrase: "Well, I'll be a dirty bird!" It was "Lonesome George Gobel," an unassuming throwback to the Harry Langdon school of wistful, wife-dominated husbands. The offbeat performer who hoped his comedy "would prevent you from becoming too sullen" was a change of pace from the brash Milton Berle types that dominated television's golden decade of comedy.

Born in Chicago, he began his career as "Little Georgie Gobel," a singer on the National Barn Dance radio series in the 1930s. He cut singles such as 1933's "Berry Picking Time" and "A Cowboy's Best Friend Is His Horse" (with guest vocalist Gene Autry). During World War II he was a B-26 pilot instructor in the Army Air Corps and began wearing his hair in his trademark crewcut.

In the late 1940s, appearing in USO shows and nightclubs, he began to inject humor into his song introductions. These throwaways and shy, straight-faced gag lines brought laughs from his surprised audience. He developed his comic persona as the almost unintentionally funny guy who happened to wander up on stage to tell a few anecdotes about his life. He guested on "The Garry Moore Show" and eventually got his own television series.

Gobel looked funny. A short fellow with squinting eyes, a pudgy sad face and a severe blond crewcut, he looked as if he just managed to duck from under a swinging scythe. The joke was that he would probably stand there in bewilderment and not get out of the way of the next shot. On television, George's character was just that oblivious. "George," his wife says in a sketch, "you've got to go to work! You've got to win the bread!" George: "Honey, I've been going down to that bakery all week and my

number hasn't come up once. I'm beginning to think Schultz is running a crooked game down there." This kind of dialogue would often lead to his other catch phrase, a blameless "You can't hardly get them no more."

Gobel won an Emmy Award in 1954 and remained very popular on television through the decade hosting and guesting on variety shows. In the mild 1950s his little anecdotes were always loaded with straight-faced asides ("My wife and I were sitting around and talking, the way you do when the TV set's busted. . . .") and dim one-liners: "If it wasn't for electricity, we'd all be watching television by candlelight." His perturbed remarks about his wife, "Spooky Old Alice," were only slightly accurate; her name was indeed Alice. He and Alice Humecki were married in 1942 and had three children.

Alice kept careful check on George, especially since he was known, according to columnist James Bacon, as one of Hollywood's "legendary drinkers." As Gobel said, "I've never been drunk, but I've often been overserved." Bacon recalled the time Gobel, having consumed eight martinis, was entertaining his fellow golfers in the locker room after a game. President Richard Nixon was there; he'd played a few rounds that day. In the midst of the festivities, George's wife called up, demanding that he come home. "I can't leave the president of the United States," George said. His wife didn't buy the lame excuse so George put Nixon on the phone. Alice wasn't impressed. She demanded to talk to George again and admonished, "You're drinking with Rich Little!"

Gobel's career took an upswing when he became a regular on the comedy quiz show "The Hollywood Squares," his cockeyed humor amusing a new generation. Question: "According to the *L.A. Times*, where in this country will you find the greatest number of turkeys?" George: "The U.S. House of Representatives." Gobel made a sitcom comeback playing Mayor Otis Harper on "Harper Valley PTA." After that, health problems plagued him. Confined to a wheelchair, he underwent surgery for a blocked artery in his left leg. Complications arose and after a bout with pneumonia, he suffered a heart attack. "George can't talk," Alice told reporters. "It's not easy to see my husband in this condition. We figured by having the surgery he would be in better shape, but so far he's worse off than before." His family rallied around him, but the weakened comedian died exactly one month after the heart attack.

AUDIO: *Lonesome George Gobel* (Decca), *Let It Ride Original Cast Recording* (RCA)

BROADWAY: *Let It Ride* (1961)

FILMS incl.: *The Birds and the Bees* (1956), *I Married a Woman* (1957), *Benny and Barney* (1977), *Rabbit Test* (1978), *Never Late Than Better* (1979), *The Invisible Woman* (1983)

TV: "The George Gobel Show" (1954–60), "The Eddie Fisher Show" (1957–59), "Harper Valley PTA" (1981–82)

VIDEO: *The Young at Heart Comedians Special*

## WHOOPI GOLDBERG

**(Caryn Johnson, November 13, 1949– )**

When the name "Whoopi Goldberg" was suddenly flashed on a Broadway marquee in October 1984, most people had the same reaction as Robin Williams. The name sounded, he said, "like the Hasidic inventor of artificial flatulence in a bag." Who was this Jewish boy with the comical first name, how come he was getting his own show when nobody'd ever heard of him, and was he funny?

Soon enough critics supplied the answer: Whoopi was a black female performance artist with a talent for imitating everyone from Valley girls to down-and-out bums. Her stark monologues recalled Lily Tomlin, but with a streetwise edge, a lot of four-letter words and uncompromising pathos. One monologue was about a dumb "surfer chick" who made audiences laugh as she recounted her sexual experiences and naiveté; then she drew shocked silence as she described how she used a coat hanger to abort her pregnancy: "I'm not gonna be able to have kids . . . You can't drag babies around. . . . besides, I'm turning 14 next week. I've got my whole life ahead of me."

Goldberg tried to retain the aura of mystery surrounding her, but after her Broadway show, record album and cable special were all hits, reporters found out her real name. Caryn Johnson grew up in a Manhattan project: 288 Tenth Avenue in the

Stand-up comedy with both heart and soul characterizes Whoopi Goldberg, who finally got her film career on track, winning an Oscar for *Ghost*. Photo from the author's collection.

Chelsea district near West 26th Street. She attended Washington Irving High School and began performing at the Hudson Guild Community Center. She left for the West Coast to join repertory theaters while taking odd jobs as a bricklayer and mortuary beautician: "When you work in a beauty parlor, you can't talk back and you can't talk mean. But with dead people you can tell 'em how you really feel: 'I'm glad you're dead. I think you're a bitch.' You can grab their head and go, 'Hey come on. Sit up here. Let's try the Joan Crawford look on you. Nah, that doesn't work. Let's try Lucille Ball.' " As for her stage name, that remained a mystery. "My mother suggested it. I've asked her why, but she's even more private than I am. All she will say is 'Because it's ours.' "

Goldberg worked in San Diego and then Berkeley in 1981. She loved avant-garde theater, "a haven, a sanctuary for expressing thoughts that could get you arrested or taken to Bellevue." She was discovered by Mike Nichols after her one-woman *Spook*

*Show* on the Coast and brought to Broadway. She seemed like an "overnight" sensation and the Broadway elite embraced her. Well-heeled liberal audiences were eager to pay an expensive Broadway ticket price to see her. The characters Goldberg threw at these out-of-touch, guilty people shamed them and demanded their attention. *Vanity Fair* magazine ran an article on her and asked about her inspirations. She mentioned Moms Mabley and Lenny Bruce. "Moms and Lenny are saying 'Do it. It's going to piss a lot of people off.' "

Paul Simon visited her during her Broadway run and offered three words of advice: "Please—enjoy this." Despite her veneer of anger and angst, she admitted to heeding the words and making sure to have fun at big Hollywood parties and let loose. Another star, Joan Rivers, was concerned about her scruffy wardrobe and begged her to try wearing a dress once in a while. Goldberg answered, "If somebody's really interested they'll look beyond the first layers. . . . If they're lucky enough to last till I get out of my clothes, they'll get a big surprise." Joan asked, "Is your underwear sexy?" Whoopi nodded. "Yes! And tasty too."

Whoopi went from Broadway to the prestigious film *The Color Purple.* Unfortunately, her next films were box office disappointments. When she continued to be cast in film after film, Sam Kinison cracked, "an entire country is afraid to hurt one woman's feelings!" In stand-up Goldberg never duplicated the success of her one-woman show. In 1988 *Esquire* magazine called her "sanctimonious" and urged her to "Get a haircut. Get serious." Goldberg sent them a reply: "Gotta haircut. Got your magazine and [used it as toilet tissue]. Love, the Sanctimonious Whoop." In 1990 *Spy* magazine referred to her simply as a "humorless comedienne." One reason was probably the edginess in her humor; unlike Robin Williams or Billy Crystal, her frequent "Comic Relief" television show co-stars, Goldberg rarely seemed to make the audience laugh from pure joy and silliness. There was always the edge of playing a character hostile and at odds with the audience, or the edge of satire with a bitter message to teach.

Reviewing *Homer and Eddie,* yet another box office bomb, the *New York Post*'s critic wrote, "At least Goldberg didn't have to do anything to her hair to

play a vagrant," and questioned "her acting talents, such as they are assumed to be." *People,* commenting on a 1990 HBO special, added "those wondering just what it is that Whoopi Goldberg does to warrant her celebrity will be further mystified."

A regular on "Comic Relief" broadcasts, capable of showing both the same sentimentality as Billy Crystal and the frantic sensitivity of Robin Williams, Goldberg seemed to frustrate fans and critics who saw so much talent wasted. She trod familiar ground as the obstreperous, independent owner of television's "Bagdad Cafe," feuding but ultimately befriending co-star Jean Stapleton. "Am I disturbing you?" asks Jean. "Too late," growls Goldberg. "I'm already disturbed." Evidently disturbed by weekly sitcom work, Goldberg had enough very quickly and the show disappeared mysteriously from the CBS schedule. It was another dead end. Goldberg shrugged off her string of failures. "If people are disappointed in my films, that's a shame, because I've had a great time. . . . I'm pleased I'm still around. . . . I live at the beach, I drive a Sterling. I'm a happy woman. . . . My philosophy has always been to do pretty much damn well what I want. And if I can be funny I'd like to explore that and if I can be serious I'd like to explore that and I suppose it's good to do both."

At this, the nadir in her career, the *New York Times* declared, "If she were a savings and loan, the government would have taken her over by now. She's had nothing but failures since *The Color Purple.*" But once again Goldberg managed to get a movie role. *Ghost,* required an actress with enough talent to make up for the rest of the cast. Suddenly Whoopi had a box office hit. As she put it, "I didn't know my career was so far down the toilet until I read the reviews for *Ghost!*" Her comeback was complete when she won an Academy Award for Best Supporting Actress. It was the first time a black actress won that prize in over 50 years. (Hattie McDaniel had been so honored for *Gone With the Wind.*)

Whoopi closed her acceptance speech, the warmest and most articulate of the night, by declaring to the star-studded audience, "I come from New York. As a little kid I lived in the projects and you're the people I watched. You're the people who made me wanna be an actor. I'm so proud to be here, I'm so proud to be an actor, and I'm gonna keep on acting and thank you so much!"

AUDIO: *Whoopi Goldberg* (Geffen), *Fontaine . . . Why Am I Straight?* (MCA)

BROADWAY: *Whoopi Goldberg* (1984)

FILMS incl.: *The Color Purple* (1985), *Jumping Jack Flash* (1986), *Burglar* (1987), *Fatal Beauty* (1987), *The Telephone* (1988), *Clara's Heart* (1988), *Homer and Eddie* (1990), *Ghost* (1990), *The Long Walk Home* (1990), *Soapdish* (1991), *The Player* (1992), *Sarafina* (1992), *Sister Act* (1992)

TV: "Bagdad Cafe" (1990), "Star Trek: The Next Generation" (1990)

VIDEOS: *Comic Relief; Comic Relief III; Dr. Duck; Whoopi Goldberg in Concert*

## BOB GOLDTHWAIT

### (May 26, 1962–   )

Quivering and twitching like a little boy in need of a bathroom, then grimacing and screaming like a punk in need of a rubber room, Bob "Bobcat" Goldthwait became one of the more controversial stand-up comics in the late 1980s.

Many were shocked to the point of laughter at the sheer freakishness of his manic-depressive act. He was alternately frightened and ready to swoon, and so furious he seemed about to throw a tantrum. Then there was the sizable group that was simply repulsed. The *New York Times*, for example, called his character "a caricature of an overgrown, emotionally damaged child . . . not unlike watching a mental patient with strong political opinions going through primal scream therapy." They likened him to "a fulminating id." Buddy Hackett watched his act and announced, "I'm 65 years old and I'd like to punch that kid in the face."

A punk rock bassist from Syracuse, New York, Bob's between-song muttering and audience-baiting led to stand-up comedy. At first he leaned toward pathos, crying as he read outrageous "Dear John" letters to the crowd. "I was vulnerable," he recalled, "and people in the audience would start picking on me. So then I got kind of mean because I didn't want them to get the better of me up there. . . . The reason I scream in my act is 'cause I'm fright-

ened and I'm angry, and that's how you convey that emotion." Then he experimented with "performance art" comedy, elaborate put-ons that antagonized as many people as they amused.

In his completely unorthodox way, he mirrors many influences. There is a dash of W. C. Fields and Henny Youngman in one popular quickie of his: "My father's turning over in his grave. He wasn't quite dead when we buried him." He often tries for Lenny Bruce–style outrage: "How many of you made the mistake of wishing your Jewish friends 'Merry Christmas' then realizing, 'Oh sorry, I forgot, you're the ones who killed him!' " He once professed surprise that people were so upset with his on-stage screaming, since Jackie Gleason seemed to make a career out of bellowing his jokes. Some of Bob's seem to have that Gleason bombast: "You say frog legs taste just like chicken? Then *why don't you just order some goddam chicken?*"

Most of his humor centers on irony and sarcasm, observations that contain a core of fright in the shell of hardness. "I can legally kill anybody I want, and I don't think there's a court in the land that wouldn't say I was insane at the time of the crime. . . . that's all it takes to get out of jail now: I was a little insane, but I'm feeling much better. Let me start writing my book." He insisted that his most obvious difference from contemporary Sam Kinison was his focus on societal problems and a disdain for misogyny and homophobic insults. "I envision the KKK putting on a Kinison album and chortling, 'This boy's funnnny! He's really saying something now: Screw them queers.' That brand of humor isn't healing; it's boring and ignorant." He did share Sam's bluntness. When an interviewer from television's "Entertainment Tonight" asked, "How does it feel to be obnoxious?" Goldthwait answered, "How does it feel to be a stupid Yuppie dickhead?" Before the cameras blinked off he added, " 'Entertainment Tonight' is for people too stupid to read *People* magazine!"

Goldthwait's fame outside stand-up is largely based on appearances in *Police Academy* films, but he was disgusted with the quality of the humor. He called them his "Police Lobotomy" pictures. Small vulnerable, quivery and just plain strange, Goldthwait found that the character he created in stand-up had potential in films. Unfortunately, it was rare that the finished product did the character justice. Critics pointed out his fine supporting role in *Burglar* as a stuttery loser who couldn't handle his sexual frustration. In *Scrooged* he was able to play a blustery nebbish, sympathetic and sweaty until unleashed with funny fury.

AUDIO: *Meat Bob* (Chrysalis)
FILMS: *Police Academy 2* (1985), *Police Academy 3* (1986), *Burglar* (1987), *Hot to Trot* (1987), *Scrooged* (1988), *Shakes the Clown* (1992)
VIDEOS: *Share the Warmth; Is He Really Like That?; Comic Relief III*

## THE GOONS (See also SPIKE MILLIGAN and PETER SELLERS.)

Often called radio's answer to The Marx Brothers, the four "Goons" were Spike Milligan, Peter Sellers, Harry Secombe and Michael Bentine. More than comic anarchists in the Marx tradition or "madmen" perpetrating frantic nonsense, The Goons created a different world, a cartoonish fantasyland that even had its own slang. Phrases such as "Sapristi Nuckos!," "Needle noddle noo," "ying tong iddle i po" and "ya gotta go owww" were liberally sprinkled into the scripts.

More than 150 scripted episodes were aired, including such titles as "The Dreaded Piano Clubber" (1953), "Affair of the Lone Banana" (1954), "Fireball of Milton Street" (1955), "The Red Bladder" (1956), "Insurance, the White Man's Burden" (1957), "Nude Welshman" (1958), "Atomic Dustbin" (1959) and "Last of the Smoking Seagoons" (1960). The gags in dialogue were vaudevillian, including this exchange from "Affair of the Lone Banana" between lead character Seagoon (Harry Secombe) and Peter Sellers as Gravely Headstone:

"Headstone, you are a footman." "Two foot six to be exact." "How lovely to be tall. Headstone, you say Fred Nurke disappeared whilst having a bottle of tea with his mother, Lady Marks?" "True. You might say he disappeared from under her very nose." "What was he doing there?" "It was raining, I believe." "Where is her ladyship at the moment?" "Me lady hasn't got a ship at the moment." "I don't wish to know that!"

The action was fast and chaotic, each episode filled with bizarre sound effects, running gags and a delirious battle between the idiot forces of naivité and good (Seagoon and his compatriots Boy Scout and pimply lad Bluebottle and buffoon Eccles) and shyster archfiends (oily Grytpype-Thynne and dubious henchman Moriarty). Fans of The Goons were loud and loyal. Outsiders were often bewildered, since "The Goon Show" often seems like eccentric gibberish until one begins to know all the continuing characters, in jokes and catch phrases.

The Goons began broadcasting in May 1951. Michael Bentine left The Goons for a solo career in November 1952 after appearing in their film *Down Among the Z Men.* He later starred in the television show "It's a Square World" from 1959 to 1965. Like The Marx Brothers, the three surviving Goons each had a definite identity. Spike Milligan wrote and co-wrote all the scripts and played key Goon idiots Eccles and Moriarty. Peter Sellers was Grytpype-Thynne, Eccles and most everyone else, his acting talents keeping the show persuasively on the fringe of reality and away from mere nonsense farce. Harry Secombe starred as the hero, Neddy Seagoon. Together they continued through 1960. They occasionally got together for a radio performance (notably "The Last Goon Show of All" in 1972), and the team of Sellers and Milligan recorded a few albums and made films together. Over the years, the four thrived on their own. Secombe, a popular singer in England, played Mr. Bumble in the musical *Oliver,* wrote a few books and maintained his musical career, which included several "straight" record albums.

The Goons' radio broadcasts have been available on albums for decades and a market for their scripts has thrived as well. "Their humor was the only proof that the world was insane," John Lennon wrote in reviewing the *Goon Show Scripts* for the *New York Times* in 1972. "When I play them . . . I find myself explaining 'that in those days there was no Monty Python's Flying Circus, no Laugh-In . . . The Goon Show was long before and more revolutionary than 'look back in anger.' Hipper than the Hippest and Madder than *Mad,* a conspiracy against reality. . . . I love all three of them dearly."

The cult for The Goons included Lord Snowdon, the Monty Pythons troupe and Elton John, who paid $31,000 at an auction for original "Goon Show" script. The cult has remained strong, even as neophytes, drawn by the jumble of sound effects, crazed voices, corny gags and insidiously meaningful nonsense, struggle at first to get past the "initiation rite" of confusion—to ultimately accept the special confusion that is Goon madness.

AUDIO: *Best of the Goon Shows* (Parlophone), *Best of the Goon Shows #2* (Parlophone), *Dark Side of the Goon* (EMI), *First Men on the Goon* (Parlophone), *Goon Again* (Parlophone), *Goon But Not Forgotten* (Parlophone), *Goon Show Classics 1 and 2* (Pye), *Goon Show Classics 3–11* (BBC), *Goon Show Greats* (Parlophone), *Last Goon Show of All* (BBC), *Michael Parkinson Meets the Goons* (BBC), *Very Best of the Goons* (EMI), *World of the Goons* (Decca)

BOOKS: *The Story of the Goons* (Draper, Austin and Edgington, 1977), *The Book of the Goons* (Milligan, 1974), *Goon Show Scripts I and II* (Milligan, 1972)

FILMS: *Down Among the Z Men* (1952)

## LEO GORCEY (See also THE EAST SIDE KIDS.)

### (June 13, 1917–June 2, 1969)

Comical little tough guy Leo Gorcey was born in the Washington Heights section of New York, his mother Irish, his father Jewish actor Bernard Gorcey. Bernard played Papa Cohen in Broadway's *Abie's Irish Rose* and was in many films, including *The Great Dictator*. He later played Louie the sweet shop owner in his son's "Bowery Boys" comedies.

When Bernard read a casting call for young toughs to appear in a new Broadway play, *Dead End,* he suggested that Leo try out. The boy, who had been working for a plumber, not only got a part but found himself the gang leader, "Spit." After the film version, Leo and the gang began making comedies and he progressed from tough wise guy to funny wise guy. Malaprops were his specialty, delivered in his inimitable New York accent. He got chuckles from muttering things like: "I reirrigate," "by the simple process of illumination," "just a filament of your imagination" or "This is no time for sediment." In *Mr. Hex,* he declares "Money is the roost of all evil." He's sure he could earn money and be "the greatest financial lizard the Bowery has ever seen."

He was the none-too-bright leader who thought he was smart: "I said out! O-W-T!"

Gorcey, like Moe Howard of The Three Stooges, could deliver insulting, unfunny lines but make them come out comical. It was his attitude, the way he deflated the pompous with a disdainful look and a combative, Brooklynese grunt. In *Loose in London,* Gorcey was introduced to a fussy French artist. The artist: "Merci." Gorcey: "You look like you need mercy."

The script, usually weak on wit, didn't need gags as long as Gorcey, in character, could put some spit and backspin on his insults. Usually the nominal hero in the films, a jockey or boxer trying to clear his name, or a punk-turned-amateur detective to help a pal, Gorcey was "Ethelbert McGinnis" (alias Muggs) in films from 1941 to 1945 and "Terence Aloysius Mahoney" (alias Slip) from 1946 to 1956 in the Monogram/Allied Artists era. He was often a solo guest star in films, usually typecast as a tough guy, a mean drunk or a cocky jockey (he was all three in *So This is New York*).

Gorcey had a tough reputation in real life. He was married seven times and had two kids. He later wore a belt buckle engraved with the names of his wives and the amount of money they received in the divorce settlements. There was a mild scandal involving his second wife; after their separation she came to his house and he fired three shots at her, all missing. Charges against him were later dropped. His first bride, Kay, had divorced him, claiming he was cruel and abusive. Then she married Groucho Marx. She later divorced him too.

At 38, Leo decided he was getting too old to play a teen tough guy. When his father got into a car accident on August 31, 1955, and died September 11, Leo called it quits. Virtually retired from films, he lived on a ranch where he raised cattle and pigs. He played a cab driver in *It's a Mad Mad Mad Mad World* in 1963 and self-published his autobiography in 1967.

AUTOBIOGRAPHY: *Dead End Yells, Wedding Bells, Cockle Shells, and Dizzy Spells* (1967)

FILMS: incl.: *Dead End* (1937), *Crime School* (1938), *Angels with Dirty Faces* (1938), *Hell's Kitchen* (1939), *Angels Wash Their Faces* (1939), *Pride of the Bowery* (1940), *Spooks Run Wild* (1941), *Mr. Wise Guy*

(1942), *Midnight Manhunt* (1945), *Bowery Bombshell* (1946), *Spook Busters* (1946), *Hard Boiled Mahoney* (1947), *Jinx Money* (1948), *So This Is New York* (1948), *Lucky Losers* (1950), *Crazy over Horses* (1951), *Loose in London* (1952), *Bowery to Bagdad* (1955), *Crashing Las Vegas* (1956), *It's a Mad Mad Mad Mad World* (1963), *Second Fiddle to a Steel Guitar* (1965), *The Phynx* (1969)

## FRANK GORSHIN

### (April 5, 1935– )

In the early 1960s, Frank Gorshin was the nation's top impressionist. Aside from the standard subjects (James Cagney and Ed Sullivan), Gorshin offered pioneering impressions of hollowly laughing Burt Lancaster and teeth-clenched, glaring Kirk Douglas. Another standout was his Richard Widmark—nothing but sucked in cheeks and a gross, tongue-filled snorting laugh. Gorshin wasn't content with vocal mimicry; he duplicated postures and gestures and twisted his face to turn even such handsome stars as Richard Burton into hysterical caricatures.

Gorshin was an actor first, not a comic. He had appeared in a number of movies, including *Studs Lonigan* and the cult comedy *Where the Boys Are* before achieving fame on television variety shows. Afterward he still hoped to find fame beyond stand-up mimicry. He was disappointed in the short-run of *Jimmy*, the Broadway musical that starred him as New York mayor Jimmy Walker. He had better luck as the spindly, obsessively giggling "Riddler" on episodes of television's "Batman." Nobody looked or sounded like this dangerous loon, but fame in a campy adventure series still wasn't that satisfying to Gorshin. He dropped the role and in the 1970s resisted "cast reunion" appearances on talk shows.

He tried to concentrate on musicals, appearing more often on the dinner theater circuit than in clubs. He starred in *On the 20th Century* on tour with Imogene Coca, and *Ah, Wilderness!* When he starred in 1985's *Promises, Promises* at an Atlantic City casino theater, he reiterated to local columnist Martin Burden how he felt about the mimicry:

"I don't want to be just known as that guy who did Kirk Douglas and Burt Lancaster. Listen, in the eyes of some people it may be terrific that I can do these people the way I do them, but personally, inside, it's beginning to bother me. I don't mean to demean my impressions, or sound ungrateful for my ability to do them. But I've reached the time in my life where I want to do different things." While acknowledging that his national exposure as The Riddler transformed him from an opening act to a headliner, he said, "I wish people could forget it. That was such a long time ago. . . ."

Gorshin's main television exposure still comes from mimicry—the old standbys and a few new ones, such as Jack Nicholson. On a television show saluting James Cagney's lifetime achievements, Gorshin performed his famous imitation, this time a unique routine capturing, step by face-twisting step, how Cagney developed his tough grimace and his "you dirty rat!" catch phrase.

When Cagney reached the dais, the aging actor acknowledged his foremost imitator: "Oh, Frankie. Just in passing—I never said, 'mmm, you dirty rat!' What I actually did say was 'Judy Judy Judy!' " The audience gave Cagney—and Gorshin—a spontaneous burst of applause.

AUDIO: *The New First Family 1968* (Verve)
FILMS: incl.: *The True Story of Jesse James* (1957), *Where the Boys Are* (1960), *Warlock* (1959), *Studs Lonigan* (1960), *Ring of Fire* (1961), *The Great Imposter* (1961), *The George Raft Story* (1961), *Sail a Crooked Ship* (1962), *Batman* (1965), *Hot Resort* (1985)
TV: "Batman" (1966–67), "ABC Comedy Hour: The Kopycats" (1972)

## FREEMAN GOSDEN (See AMOS and ANDY.)

## GILBERT GOTTFRIED

### (February 28, 1955– )

A stand-up performer since 1970 when he was just 15, Gilbert Gottfried stayed on the lunatic fringe of stand-up until 1980, when he briefly joined the cast of television's "Saturday Night Live." He said his main claim to fame on that show was being the only person on the staff who didn't take drugs with John Belushi. He was a regular on 1983's "Thicke of the Night," appeared on his friend Richard Belzer's

Cinemax special in 1984 and slowly began to wear down resistance to his hilarious but abrasive style of squinty grimaces, screamy declarations and kvetchy, often tasteless rambles.

In 1986 he became the pitchman (or more accurately, "yellman") for an O'Henry candy bar television campaign, still in his self-described "loud, irritating" character. He experimented with print humor in the late 1980s *National Lampoon,* unfortunately during the worst period of the magazine's editorship and quality. He ended the decade hosting late-night exploitation films on USA cable, interrupting the films for sketches or just a few minutes of ranting guaranteed to wake up any dozing viewer. He began the 1990s with more films (dueling with a brat in *Problem Child* and trading insults with Dice Clay in *The Adventures of Ford Fairlane*).

Quiet and shy off stage, Gottfried is the exact opposite on stage, a cross between old-style Catskill comics and high-powered new wavers like Bob Goldthwait or Judy Tenuta.

A love-him-or-hate-him stand-up, it isn't surprising that it took nearly 15 years for national audiences to get used to his shock comedy: "I went up to Jackie Kennedy at a party and figured I'd try to break the ice by getting a little conversation going. So I said, 'Do you remember where you were and what you were doing when you heard that Kennedy was shot?'" Looking for comics hip and "on the edge," the Emmy awards producers in 1991 booked him as a presenter. He took the opportunity to deviate from the script and defend Pee Wee Herman: "I sleep a lot better since Pee Wee Herman's been arrested! Masturbation a crime? I should be on death row! Masturbation's against the law? I should've been sent to the electric chair years ago!" The Emmy producers expressed outrage and alarm.

This kind of reaction doesn't bother Gottfried. If greeted by dismay or silence, he has a comeback: "Okay, now you make *me* laugh."

FILMS: incl.: *Bad Medicine* (1985), *Beverly Hills Cop II* (1987), *Problem Child* (1990), *The Adventures of Ford Fairlane* (1990), *Look Who's Talking, Too* (1990)
TV: "Saturday Night Live" (1980–81), "Thicke of the Night" (1983)

## THEODORE GOTTLIEB (See BROTHER THEODORE.)

## RONNY GRAHAM

### (August 26, 1919–    )

One of the unsung legends in comedy, Graham was a bright star in 1950s and '60s New York revues. At a time when Julius Monk's shows and Leonard Sillman's "New Faces" revues were the equivalent of "Saturday Night Live," he was both writing and starring in key sketches. One of his most famous routines was his hip "How to Smoke a Reefer" monologue, adopting the hoarse, wise-guy character of jazz singer Harry "The Hipster" Gibson: "Now let's say this is a reefer. Let's say this is—'cause this *is!* This is not a civilian cigarette. This is standard-gauge M-1: Progressive Pall Malls. Left-wing Luckies."

Discovered by Imogene Coca, the Philadelphia-born comic scored in *New Faces of 1952* with a monologue "Oedipus Goes South." He wrote for television's "Colgate Comedy Hour," appeared on a dozen Ed Sullivan shows and received glowing reviews acting and directing Broadway's *The Tender Trap.* In cabaret comedy he was a regular at Upstairs at the Downstairs, appearing in Julius Monk's *Take Five* revue in 1957 and his own subsequent *Graham Crackers* show. He directed *Grin and Bare It,* which had the distinction of being Broadway's first all-nude play when it opened in 1970.

Over the years Graham retained a solid reputation among comedians. Bill Cosby, Bob Crane, James Komack and others sought him out for acting or writing assignments on their shows. He turned up as a consultant on "M*A*S*H" and appeared in one episode as a boozy soldier who is siphoned for a blood transfusion. Along with his contemporary Dick Shawn, Graham either didn't have the luck or the desire to reach the level of superstar. National television audiences probably knew him best as "Mr. Dirt" in a series of gasoline commercials.

In films, Graham was well respected by Mel Books, Gene Wilder and others. He worked on the screenplay of Brooks' *To Be or Not to Be* and had a part in the film. He played a director giving screen tests in Wilder's *The World's Greatest Lover.* On his own, he wrote the screenplay for *Finder's Keepers.* In 1990 he was scheduled to be in *Annie 2,* but the show folded out of town. Instead, he played James Joyce in a play premiering in New Haven, *Is He Still Dead?*

AUDIO: *Take Five* (Offbeat), *How to Be Terribly Funny* (Riverside), *New Faces of 1952* (RCA)
BROADWAY: *New Faces of 1952* (1952), *The Tender Trap* (1954), *Something More* (1964)
FILMS incl.: *New Faces* (1954), *Dirty Little Billy* (1972), *The World's Greatest Lover* (1977), *History of the World Part I* (1981), *To Be or Not to Be* (1983)
TV: "New Bill Cosby Show" (1972–73), "The Hudson Brothers Show" (1974), "The Bob Crane Show" (1975), "Chico and the Man" (1975–76)

## CARY GRANT

### (Archibald Leach, January 18, 1904–November 29, 1986)

One of the true film greats, a comic actor of great style and charm, Cary Grant was versatile in comedy. Well known for handling a subtle or sophisticated line, he was also capable of utilizing Curly Howard yowls (teetering on a rope bridge in *Gunga Din*), pop-eyed jitters *(Arsenic and Old Lace),* beautifully timed pratfalls *(Bringing Up Baby)* and even drag *(I Was a Male War Bride).*

Grant played primarily comedy roles during the first decade of his career. Off stage his personality was typical of a comedian. His friends found him to be a serious perfectionist who had to be flawless even in his hobbies, horseback riding and swimming. A lively eccentric, he wore ladies' underpants (plain, no lace), insisting they were more comfortable and easier to wash and dry. The hero of romantic comedy would marry five times, admitting "It took me a long time to mature." Like so many comedians, he seemed to wish he received as much happiness as he gave. A unique personality adulated all his life, he once admitted with some chagrin, "Everybody wants to be Cary Grant. I want to be Cary Grant."

Grant's childhood was, like Chaplin's, miserable. His father, a half-Jewish pants presser, taught him music hall songs but needed alcohol to replenish his own flagging spirits. At nine, his mother disappeared into an asylum for the mentally ill. Left alone

most of the time, the boy got into trouble, including the time the curious 14-year-old snuck into the girl's bathroom. Expelled from school, he went to work in the British music halls as an acrobat. When the troupe went to New York in 1920, he stayed—walking around on stilts with advertising on his back in Coney Island—until he won parts in plays.

He claimed his unusual, clipped British accent was initially a put-on, an attempt by the uneducated young man to affect a more upper-class style. Always modest, he insisted he was just "a kind of combination of Jack Buchanan—he was the reigning musical comedy star of those days—and Noel Coward. In other words, I pretended to be somebody I wanted to be until finally, I became that person. Or he became me."

He co-starred with Fred Allen in the show *Polly* and played opposite Jeanette MacDonald in *Boom-Boom.* Although Grant never said "Judy, Judy, Judy," in his very first film, a short called *Singapore Sue* shot in New York in 1931, he played a sailor who shouts out enthusiastically in a bar, "Hello, Judy!" As his first lines on film, he may have referred to them in passing often enough for comics to pick up on it. He himself credited Larry Storch as the Mimic who first used the "catchphrase."

He was billed as Archie Leach back then. When he finally arrived in Hollywood, he changed his name to Cary Grant. Some claim his studio chose "Cary" to link him with "Gary" Cooper. Actually "Cary" came from "Cary Lockwood," the part he played on stage in *Nikki* opposite Fay Wray. Years later he enjoyed a few in jokes about his name. In *Arsenic and Old Lace* a headstone read "Archie Leach." And in *His Girl Friday,* an outraged Grant said, "The last person who said that to me was Archie Leach, just a week before he cut his throat."

One of Cary's earliest roles was in *She Done Him Wrong* with Mae West. It was to him that she asked the classic question, "Why don't you come up sometime and see me?" Another early success was *Topper,* playing the delightfully rakish ghost George Kirby. He was the comic relief in the beloved adventure film *Gunga Din,* and from there starred in a half-dozen romantic comedies with the top leading ladies of the day.

The only comedy role he regretted was in *Arsenic and Old Lace.* Grant had a few good lines ("Insanity runs in my family. It practically gallops!"), but was annoyed to find others censored. At the end of the play, the character, learning he's not related to lunatics, shouts, "Thank God I'm a bastard!" In the film he was limited to: "Thank God I'm the son of a sea cook!" He was also dismayed at having to play the part as pure farce: "I overplayed it terribly." His theory was that playing comedy depended on "doing it as naturally as you can under the most unnatural circumstances. And film comedy is the most difficult of all. At least on the stage you know right away whether you are getting laughs or not. But making a movie, you have no way of knowing. So you try to time the thing for space and length and only hope that, when it plays in a movie house months later, you've done the timing right. It's difficult, and it takes experience." He was fond of A. E. Matthews' quote: "Dying's tough but it's not as tough as comedy."

Grant generally downplayed his abilities. For *Bringing Up Baby* he said he merely thought of how Harold Lloyd would've played the part. But Lloyd couldn't have gotten the laughs Cary did when, with nothing else to wear, he stomps toward May Robson in nothing but a woman's robe. "Why are you wearing a robe?" she huffs. He shouts, "Because I just went gay all of a sudden!"

It was only after a decade of comedy that Grant landed a meaty dramatic role, receiving an Academy Award nomination for *Penny Serenade* in 1941. He did star in several key romantic and dramatic films, notably *Notorious, Suspicion* and the Odets drama, *None But the Lonely Heart* that earned him his second (and last) Academy Award nomination. But he also continued to thrive in many delightful light comedies. Many of his supposedly noncomedy roles were rich in character comedy. He was amusing in *North by Northwest* ("Roger O. Thornhill. What does the O stand for?" "Nothing.") and had several visual comedy scenes in *Charade*, including funny faces and showering with his clothes on.

After Grant retired from films he received a 1970 Academy Award for his "unique mastery of the art of film acting." In his 70s he remained remarkably youthful and vibrant, and seemed to enjoy a more settled private life. He was devoted to his only child, a daughter (from his fourth marriage), and had found contentment with his fifth wife, a woman half

his age. However, watching films like *On Golden Pond* with a frail Henry Fonda, he began thinking more and more about death. "When I was young," he said in 1977, "I thought they'd have the thing licked by the time I got to this age. I think the thing you think about when you're my age is how you're going to do it and whether you'll behave well."

In his 80s, the shy Grant suddenly decided to meet his public and return to a form of show business. He went on the lecture circuit, offering film clips and an informal question-and-answer session afterward. One cross-country trek of speaking engagements was quite strenuous. He was in Davenport, Iowa preparing for the night's performance (with St. Louis scheduled the following day) when he told his wife, "I'm sorry—I can't go on." Suffering from chills and dizziness, he was taken to a hospital in a wheelchair. As ill as he was, he talked not of his health but of how badly he felt for the audience that would be disappointed that night. Grant lapsed into a coma and died a few hours later.

It was front-page news around the world. President Ronald Reagan wrote: "Nancy and I are very saddened by the death of our very dear and longtime friend Cary Grant. He was one of the brightest stars in Hollywood and his elegance, wit and charm will endure forever on film and in our hearts. We will always cherish the memory of his warmth, his loyalty and his friendship and we will miss him deeply."

Tributes poured in, and television specials showed film clips of classic Cary Grant in action. Once Grant was asked who did the best Cary Grant impersonation. He answered, "I do."

BIOGRAPHIES incl.: *Films of Cary Grant* (Deschner, 1973), *Haunted Idol* (Wansell, 1983), *Conversations with Cary Grant* (Nelson, 1991)

BROADWAY incl.: *Golden Dawn* (1926), *Boom Boom* (1929), *Nikki* (1930)

FILMS incl.: *This Is the Night* (1932), *Sinners in the Sun* (1932), *Merrily We Go to Hell* (1932), *Devil and the Deep* (1932), *Blonde Venus* (1932), *She Done Him Wrong* (1933), *I'm No Angel* (1933), *Alice in Wonderland* (1933), *Suzy* (1936), *Topper* (1937), *The Awful Truth* (1937), *Toast of New York* (1937), *Bringing Up Baby* (1938), *Holiday* (1938), *In Name Only* (1939), *Gunga Din* (1939), *His Girl Friday*

*(1940)*, *My Favorite Wife* (1940), *The Philadelphia Story* (1940), *Penny Serenade* (1941), *Talk of the Town* (1942), *Once Upon a Honeymoon* (1942), *The Bachelor and the Bobby Soxer* (1947), *Mr. Blandings Builds His Dream House* (1948), *I Was a Male War Bride* (1949), *Monkey Business* (1952), *Kiss Them for Me* (1957), *Operation Petticoat* (1959), *That Touch of Mink* (1962), *Charade* (1963), *Father Goose* (1964), *Walk Don't Run* (1966)

## THE GREAT GILDERSLEEVE (Harold Peary)

### (Harrold José Pereira de Faria, 1908–March 30, 1985)

Noted for his gooey, gurgling laugh, which quivered into a seesawing "eeeeeeh-uhhhhh" when perplexed, Harold Peary played Throckmorton P. Gildersleeve in films and on radio, a windy, self-important fellow who was forever trying to be the big man in his small town. He was so good-natured and harmless that audiences had to laugh and sympathize with him.

A veteran of touring shows in the 1920s when he sang baritone in musicals, Peary was "The Spanish Serenader" on local San Francisco radio in 1929. He moved to Chicago in 1935 and, two years later, on "The Fibber McGee and Molly Program," became Gildersleeve. He got his own show in 1941, often considered the first "spinoff" in radio sitcom history.

The cast included niece Marjorie and nephew Leroy (Marylee Robb and Walter Tetley), housekeeper Birdie (Lillian Randolph), Peavey the Druggist (Richard Legrand), Floyd the Barber (Arthur Q. Brain), Judge Hooker (Earle Rosse) and love interests Adeline Fairchild (Una Merkel) and Leila Ransom (Shirley Mitchell). The sitcom was so popular that Peary was invited to meet first lady Eleanor Roosevelt. She said, "Oh, yes. I believe you're the man the president listened to when I was on the air."

The "Gildersleeve" film series began in 1942. Peary was fairly comic visually, with his pudgy body, wan smile and expression of uneasy consternation, but the scripts were bland and curiously lacking in the fast insult patter that characterized Gildersleeve's bickering with other important town citizens. Each film did make sure to utilize his nervous giggle over and over. In fact, the films opened with a full head shot as he smiled and gave an "eeeeehh ahhhh" gurgle and leering laugh to the audience.

Peary become completely identified with "The Great Gildersleeve" character, but the rights to the name belonged to the radio show's sponsor, Kraft Foods. Their refusal to allow him to use the character name for other pursuits was part of the 1950 contract dispute that led him to leave the show; he was replaced by actor Willard Waterman. Many others would imitate the famous Gildersleeve character. Young television fans were probably unaware that "Captain Huffenpuff" on "Beany and Cecil" was really just an imitation of "The Great Gildersleeve."

Peary appeared often on 1950s television sitcoms, playing Herb Woodley on "Blondie" and Mayor La Trivia on "Fibber McGee and Molly." He continued to make sitcom appearances over the years, turning up on "That Girl" and "The Brady Bunch." To his fans, he was still "Gildy," and they delighted in asking him to repeat one of his radio catch phrases: "You're a haaaaard man" (uttered to anyone who was thwarting him) and "Don't ever DO that," borrowed from Joe Penner. He'd sometimes give them a trademark chuckle, in thanks for their laughter and applause for so many memorable years.

AUDIO: *The Great Gildersleeve* (Golden Age), *The Great Gildersleeve* (Mark 56), *The Great Gildersleeve* (Radiola)

FILMS incl.: *Look Who's Laughing* (1941), *Here We Go Again* (1942), *Seven Days' Leave* (1942), *The Great Gildersleeve* (1942), *Gildersleeve on Broadway* (1943), *Gildersleeve's Bad Day* (1943), *Gildersleeve's Ghost* (1944), *Clambake* (1967)

TV: "Willy" (1955), "Blondie" (1957), "Fibber McGee and Molly" (1959–60)

## SHECKY GREENE

### (Sheldon Greenfield, April 8, 1925– )

The ultimate "Vegas comedian," Shecky Greene went to the resort town back in the 1950s. Born in Chicago, he had worked in resorts near Milwaukee and had gotten a break playing Miami Beach as Martha Raye's opening act. He wasn't particularly well known

The best of the tuxedo-clad Vegas comics, brash and boisterous Shecky Greene once drove his car into a fountain in front of Caesars Palace. Photo from the author's collection.

when he arrived in Vegas, but he and the town seemed to grow wild together. The more free-wheeling and splashy Vegas became, the more frenzied was Green's ad-libbing and clowning with ringsiders.

Ralph Pearl, a major Las Vegas reporter in Greene's heyday, recalled, "Though small in stature (five foot seven) Shecky is almost that wide. He could easily have passed for a large fire hydrant. And, when aroused, he could have ripped a phone book into small pieces with his bare hands with ease. Or a Ralph Pearl into just as many pieces."

Shecky's explosions of comic violence were legend, such as the time he drove his car into the fountain in front of the Ceasars Palace casino. "No spray wax, please," he said. His admitted "drinking, carousing, gambling, turning over crap tables and busting up entire casinos" was tolerated, even encouraged in the anything-goes Vegas atmosphere. He was soon earning hundreds of thousands of dollars each year, joining the elite company of Don

Rickles and Buddy Hackett as must-see attractions for tourists.

Like a cactus in the desert, the formidable Greene needed a special location in which to thrive. His prickly barbs and blitz of ad libs, old gags, impressions, song parodies, dialect and old-fashioned face-making didn't come across on albums. He couldn't "tummel" in seven tight minutes before a television variety show audience and "work the crowd" up to a fever pitch of hilarity. The magic of Green was best appreciated in the live, party atmosphere of the casinos and similar nightclubs around the country. His career slowed only after throat surgery, cancer surgery and a 1990 hip transplant that sidelined him for a year.

Though many comedy critics frowned on the tuxedo-wearing Vegas stand-ups and their whiz-bang gags punctuated by drum "rim shots," Green was clearly the best of the lot, a riot for the blue-collar types, middle Americans and the "velvet painting and Capodamonte" crowd that came to see him. A stand-up whose roots were in the lay-it-in-their-laps style of Abbott and Costello (Greene often pointed out his physical resemblance to Lou Costello), Greene's style wasn't subtle or cerebral; he simply wanted to kill the audience with laughter and was strong enough and manic enough to be able to use the bludgeon approach. No one watching him work could deny his overpowering charisma. Jerry Lewis called him "the epitome of comic genius," and many had to agree. If critics never considered him a classy diamond, he was at least a brightly polished zircon, shining in a casino setting.

AUDIO: *A Funny Thing Happened to Me on My Way to the Moon* (Majestic), *Day at the Races* (Laff), *Shecky Green in the Lounge* (LP WH 0001)

FILMS incl.: *Tony Rome* (1967), *The Love Machine* (1971), *History of the World Part I* (1981), *Splash* (1984)

# DICK GREGORY

## (October 12, 1932–   )

Stand-up comedy wasn't perceived as a gutsy, heroic, "relevant" art form until three men began challenging audiences with hard-hitting satire. Mort Sahl handled the political revolution, Lenny Bruce challenged sexual and religious conventions, and Dick Gregory was the voice of the rising civil rights movement.

Born in St. Louis, Dick seemed destined for a sports career. He broke track records, and by the time he reached Southern Illinois University he was judged to be one of the country's best running the half mile and mile. In the army he hosted shows and performed comedy, and when he got out he rented nightclubs to produce his own shows in Chicago. Liberal audiences seeking the truth from Bruce and Sahl seemed to encourage stronger comedy. When Gregory subbed for Irwin Corey at the Chicago Playboy Club, he gave it to them.

"I understand there are a good many Southerners in the room tonight," he said. "I know the South very well. I spent 20 years there one night." Gregory told broad jokes about race, laughing at the myth of Santa Claus: "You know damn good and well ain't no white man comin' in our neighborhood after midnight." But he also told dangerously strong one-liners, such as the definition of "a Southern moderate. That's a cat who'll lynch you from a low tree." His anger and his ironic sense of humor showed in his classic tale of visiting a Southern diner: "I sit down, a blonde waitress walked over to me. I said, 'I'd like two cheeseburgers.' She said, 'We don't serve colored people down here.' I said, 'I don't eat colored people nowhere!' "

Some characterized Gregory as "the black Mort Sahl" for his political gags. Of the Johnson versus Goldwater presidential race, he said, "You got two girls and one is a full-time prostitute and the other is a weekend prostitute. If you choose the lesser of two evils and marry the weekend prostitute, you're only fooling yourself if you don't think you're marrying a whore."

Dick Gregory was pleased to see "the message" get across but restless over how much of it was sinking in. He also began to question the value of jokes in producing real change. "We didn't laugh Hitler out of existence," he said. "There will be a cure found for cancer, only it won't be good humor." Through the 1960s he shifted his energies toward writing books, marching and giving speeches.

He ran for president in 1968. His comedy performances turned into lectures, and he quit stand-up in the early 1970s.

He remains active in the civil rights movement and still makes headlines being arrested for on-site pickets and protests. He makes most of his money through lectures and his business venture, "The Bahamian Diet." Following his many protest fasts against everything from world hunger to the death penalty, the vegetarian Gregory became an expert on nutrition (and how to go from 170 pounds to 98 without killing himself).

In 1987 he was involved in the famous case of Walter Hudson, the 1,200 pounder who got stuck in his own doorway at home. Chiding Hudson for being "a waterbed with a head," Gregory helped the man slim down to 600. Sadly, the two men fought during the subsequent publicity and Hudson gained back the weight, dying on Christmas Eve, 1991.

While some wonder why Dick would sell diet products instead of more typically flying to Ethiopia to call attention to the starving there, he defends his position: "When you see businessmen in airports with the bloated bellies and bald heads—that's malnutrition, too." He still blends comedy with his lectures and his diet tips. As he says, "There are two things that burn up the poison in the body—forgiveness and laughter."

AUDIO: *Dick Gregory Talks Turkey* (Vee Jay), *Two Sides* (Vee Jay), *Running for President* (Vee Jay), *East and West* (Colpix), *We All Have Problems* (Colpix), *In Living Black and White* (Colpix), *My Brother's Keeper* (Gateway), *Light Side, Dark Side* (Poppy), *At the Village Gate* (Poppy), *On . . .* (Poppy), *Frankenstein* (Poppy), *Kent State* (Poppy), *Caught in the Act* (Poppy), *The Best of Dick Gregory* (Tomato)

BOOKS incl.: *Nigger* (1990), *From the Back of the Bus* (1962), *Write Me In* (1968), *No More Lies* (1971), *Dick Gregory's Natural Diet for Folks Who Eat* (1974)

## ANDY GRIFFITH

### (June 1, 1926–   )

"What it was, was football." That's the name of the routine that punted Andy Griffith to fame back in

1954. Capitol Records decided to record the stand-up comic's five-minute hillbilly view of football: "Both bunches full of them men wanted this funny little punkin' to play with . . . and I know, friends, that they couldn't a-eat it, 'cause they kicked it the whole evening and it never bust."

From stand-up and singing, Griffith moved to television for "No Time for Sergeants" broadcast on "The U.S. Steel Hour." He starred in the subsequent Broadway and film versions, becoming well known for his comic "hick" character, affable, grinning and humorously naive. When he landed the role of Sheriff Andy Taylor (first in a "test" episode of "Make Room for Daddy" and later on his own show, produced by Danny Thomas), he downplayed the rube clichés.

Griffith's dignity and even his shyness and solemnity became a part of Sheriff Andy's character. He may have been the "good old boy" from North Carolina (as in real life), joking with Otis the Drunk and Floyd the Barber, but he kept law and order with unchallenged strength and keen wisdom.

At the time many successful sitcoms were being shot live in front of an audience. Griffith's show was filmed like a movie. Without having to rely on one-liners and slapstick to keep the audience roaring, the writers concentrated on character. The show's laughs were very much "with" and not "at" Griffith. And the audience was always "with" him when he had to deal with the more eccentric and foolish of the supporting players.

"The Andy Griffith Show" was a number-one hit all through its run. It was Griffith who decided to call it quits. Like Dick Van Dyke, he figured he had done all he could do with the show and was ready to take on new challenges. Also like Van Dyke, Griffith stubbed his toe quickly. After a few indifferent films, the native North Carolinian saw his movie career sink slowly in the west. He returned to television but couldn't recapture the magic. In the 1970s interest in rural programs had ebbed; "Green Acres" and "The Beverly Hillbillies" were canceled. Sitcoms such as "All in the Family" were going strong.

The 1970s were a lost decade for Andy not only professionally but physically. He fought a seven-year battle with Guillain-Barre syndrome, which limited his ability to perform. Having drawn raves for his performance back in 1957's drama *A Face in the Crowd*, the aging comedian found serious roles on television in "Centennial" and "Roots: The Next Generation." When he returned to series television he played "Matlock," a serious lawyer, not a country sheriff. He showed some traces of the knowing humor and wisdom that fans loved from the old days, enough of a balance of personable humor and adventure to push the show into the top 20 and keep the network begging him each year to sign a new contract. Even old co-star Don Knotts made some appearances on the show. Andy was grateful and proud of his success and admitted that Matlock was a great role, but he added, "Andy Taylor was a wonderful character; the best experience of my professional life."

AUDIO: *Andy and Cleopatra* (Capitol), *Best of Andy Griffith* (Capitol), *Just for Laughs* (Capitol), *This Here Andy Griffith* (Capitol), *The Andy Griffith Show* (Capitol), *Shouts the Blues* (Capitol)

BROADWAY: *No Time for Sergeants* (1955), *Destry Rides Again* (1959)

FILMS: incl.: *A Face in the Crowd* (1957), *No Time for Sergeants* (1958), *Onionhead* (1958), *The Second Time Around* (1961), *Angel in My Pocket* (1969), *Hearts of the West* (1975), *Return to Mayberry* (1986)

TV: "The Andy Griffith Show" (1960–68), "The Headmaster" (1970–71), "The New Andy Griffith Show" (1971), "Salvage 1" (1979), "Matlock" (1986–   )

VIDEO: *The Andy Griffith Show*

## RAYMOND GRIFFITH

### (1890–November 25, 1957)

*Life* magazine proclaimed in 1926, "Raymond Griffith leads all comedians" for "ingenuity, imaginativeness, and originality. [He] deserves enthusiastic encouragement." The following year talkies arrived and spelled the discouraging end to his comedy career. A short time later a film library fire destroyed some of his best work. Over decades of neglect, many more of his silent comedies quietly disintegrated into dust.

Griffith's career began on the stage, but he soon moved to Hollywood to work with Mack Sennett.

His short from that era, *The Surf Girl*, is one of the few remaining examples. Griffith enjoyed writing more than performing and scripted many quick comedies. He liked to devise "smart" stunt comedy, favoring the carefully timed slapstick that Buster Keaton was then utilizing. In 1923 Griffith was lured back in front of the cameras, and he showed a few Keaton-esque touches. In *Hands Up*, he plays a Southerner supporting Robert E. Lee. He's so busy shaking Lee's hand, he ignores the building being bombed all around them. As the dust settles, he's still shaking the general's hand.

Unlike most major clowns of the golden silent era, Griffith wore no outlandish costumes and was no underdog. Well dressed, handsome and dapper, sporting a mustache and sideburns, he looked more like an extra in a Douglas Fairbanks *Zorro* film than a comedian. He had a hero's devil-may-care indifference. In *Hands Up* he amuses himself in front of a firing squad by tossing dishes up in the air and letting the men take target practice. If his career had flourished in the sound era, he probably would have been cast in William Powell or George Sanders roles as an elegant, clever fellow with humorous detachment and an eye for semishady dealings.

A throat condition reportedly kept Griffith's voice at a whisper, dooming his career in sound films. He had a memorable scene in *All Quiet on the Western Front* as a Frenchman stabbed and left for dead, but there weren't too many parts that required his silent skills. During the talkie era he mainly worked as an associate producer for Darryl F. Zanuck.

The comedian's reputation now rests almost completely on a few shorts and two key surviving films, *Hands Up* and *Paths to Paradise*. Screening these comedies, critic Walter Kerr felt that Griffith had much to offer modern audiences: "the essence of his comedy lay in his perfectly honest, undemanding, unregretted, eternally grinning iconoclasm."

FILMS incl.: *The Eternal Three* (1923), *Changing Husbands* (1924), *Open All Night* (1924), *Lily of the Dust* (1924), *Forty Winks* (1925), *The Night Club* (1925), *Paths to Paradise* (1925), *Miss Bluebeard* (1925), *Hands Up* (1926), *Wet Paint* (1926), *Wedding Bells* (1927), *Time to Love* (1927), *Trent's Last Case* (1929), *All Quiet on the Western Front* (1930), *The Great Profile* (1940)

# GROCK

## (Charles Adrien Wettach, January 10, 1880–July 14, 1959)

Ironically, though Grock is a legend in stage comedy, many know him only through an anecdote—one of the saddest ever told about comedy and the human condition.

The Swiss clown played London's Palladium in 1911 and was a featured player in variety shows around the world for decades. The happy-faced performer's outfit was usually a giant plaid jacket that came down to his ankles and a baggy pair of plaid pants that hung over his flat shoes. In his most famous routine he tried to play a violin, only to be foiled time and again. These foibles probably would not sound funny written out. Even in his heyday, critics could only say "You had to be there." As *Variety* reported of his whimsies, gestures and gags, "he does acrobatics, plays the piano, concertina, talks, sings, dances, and—oh it's no use trying to describe him . . . Grock pleases because he is Grock."

Grock viewed himself with wry deprecation: "Grock, the greatest clown in all the world, is not Grock at all. . . . he smokes 40 cigarettes a day, drinks his glass of beer, wears patent underclothes and wants nothing so much as a little peace and quiet."

Though he occasionally played the United States, Grock was a bigger hit in Europe where there was a stronger tradition for music hall, circus and mime—audiences that were accustomed to comedians from France, Italy, Germany and Spain performing visual comedy rather than attempting to learn each language. The clown king toured during the decade after World War II with his own circus. After that he was semiretired, appearing occasionally on stage and on television, spending most of his time in his Riviera mansion.

The famous story about Grock and comedy has been told often. By most accounts, Grock's show was playing a small town when a man came to a doctor's office in miserable shape. "I'm so depressed," he told the doctor, "I don't think I can go on. Life has no meaning for me. I look at everything and see only sadness." He related a litany of woes. Finally the doctor said, "What you need to do is lighten your heart. Learn to laugh. There is a brilliant clown performing this week. See him and you're sure to forget your troubles and smile. Go see Grock." The man listened and shook his head. "Doctor," he said, "I am Grock."

Whether the story is apocryphal or Grock's view improved is unknown. When he wrote his autobiography in 1931, he declared, "I am a lucky man, a very lucky man. My health is good. I am at peace within myself."

AUTOBIOGRAPHY: *Life's a Lark*
BIOGRAPHIES: *Grock* (in German, Von Ernst Konstantin, 1956), *Grock* (in French, Blaque 1948)
FILM: *Au Revoir Mr. Grock* (1950)

## ROBERT GUILLAUME

### (Robert Williams, November 30, 1927–    )

For over a decade, one word described Robert Guillaume: Benson. He played the part on two series, "Soap" and his successful spinoff, "Benson."

Television audiences know him exclusively from his role as Benson Dubois, but Guillaume had a long and respectable career on the stage. Born in St. Louis, he attended St. Louis University and Washington University. Using a more distinctive French version of his last name, he appeared in productions of classics such as *Othello* and *Golden Boy*, as well as the musicals *Finian's Rainbow, Carousel, Porgy and Bess, Purlie* and the all-black revival of *Guys and Dolls*, which earned him a Tony nomination in 1976.

In Hollywood, Guillaume appeared on many sitcoms, including "All in the Family," "The Jeffersons" and "Sanford and Son." Then came "Soap" and the continuing role of Benson, cook and servant to the Tate family. Many critics and viewers panned the show for its strong emphasis on sex, but most praised Guillaume's character as the most respectable and, given his insolent wisecracks, the funniest. He won an Emmy Award for "Soap" in 1979. When Guillaume got his own show, his character Benson jumped from an assistant to a governor to the lieutenant governor—quite a promotion.

After the long run of "Benson," Guillaume once again began turning away from his comedy image. "It's all well and good to do comedy, and I like comedy. But I'm not unmindful of the fact that comedy images are something black people have always been able to get across. Seldom, if at all, has there been any interest in a black character who is serious." He resumed his career on stage, and in 1990 he replaced Michael Crawford in the Los Angeles production of the musical *The Phantom of the Opera*. It was a time of triumph and sadness. During the run his son died of AIDS at the age of 32. "It was a terrible, terrible time," he said. "I was devastated, needless to say."

He was asked to stay with *The Phantom of the Opera* for another year, but he needed time to straighten out his home life. The following year he began a new sitcom, "Pacific Station." Once more he was his simmering, deadpan self. In a typical moment, a health food nut chides him for eating doughnuts and coffee, adding, "I would not like to see what your colon looks like!" His response: "Damn. Now I'm not gonna get a chance to show you a picture I took of it in front of the fall backdrop at Sears."

BROADWAY incl.: *Fly Blackbird* (1962), *Porgy and Bess* (1964), *The Life and Times of J. Walter Smintheus* (1970), *Guys and Dolls* (1976)
FILMS incl.: *The Kid from Left Field* (1979), *Seems Like Old Times* (1980), *Prince Jack* (1984)
TV: "Soap" (1977–79), "Benson" (1979–86), "The Robert Guillaume Show" (1989), "Pacific Station" (1991)

## SIR ALEC GUINNESS

### (Alex Guinness de Cuffe, April 2, 1914–    )

Known for his quick-change abilities (he played eight parts in *Kind Hearts and Coronets*), renowned British actor Alec Guinness had three identities as a child. He was known as Alec de Cuffe, then Alec Stiven (his stepfather's name) and finally, using his real father's name, Alec Guinness.

Though in later years he took on more dramatic roles, audiences first discovered him in comedy. In the 1950s he starred in a string of some of the most acclaimed comedies England produced, most filmed at Ealing Studios. His name at the box office assured fans of a hilarious time. *Kind Hearts and Coronets* in 1949 made him famous. In 1951's *Lavender Hill Mob* he played the leader of a larcenous mob trying to mastermind a robbery. Trivia buffs enjoy the added bonus of Audrey Hepburn in an early one-line role. That same year *The Man in the White Suit* was released, a pungent satire about a man inventing a superfiber and treated not as a hero but as a villain about to wipe out the clothing industry. And finally in 1955 the fourth of his classic Ealing comedies appeared, *The Ladykillers,* which cast Guinness as a gangleader delighting in his own wicked scheme to concoct the perfect crime.

Guinness had always shown flair in his days as an acting student, especially in mime class. He remembered, "I longed to do absurd and clownish things. My mime of an old man being blown off the end of a pier while clinging to an open umbrella (not visible), or a youth catching a large fish which he kept alive in a cardboard box because he loved it so, were barely tolerated . . . in my daydreaming . . . Buster Keaton and Stan Laurel were my heroes."

In his early comedies, Guinness would do anything for a laugh, just like his idols. In *The Man in the White Suit,* he had to climb down the side of a house. He was fitted with a belt secured with piano wire. Guinness was dubious, but he went to work: "The wire snapped when I was about four feet from the ground and I landed flat on my back. . . . No one apologised. They rarely do in films, as very few people care to take responsibility." There was a similar unfunny moment during the making of the satiric gem *The Ladykillers.* He recalled: "I had to stand on the edge of a sixty-foot-high wall. . . . 'Is this secure?' I called down. . . . 'Perfectly!' they called from below. Whereupon [the rail] snapped and I had the good fortune to fall backwards to safety, not forward to oblivion below."

An Academy Award winner for 1957's *The Bridge on the River Kwai,* Guinness, like American counterpart Jack Lemmon, was never typed by critics or fans as strictly a funny man. Over the years, he played in few comedies and even fewer classic ones. His best comic performance in his later years was in the all-star *Murder by Death,* playing a wry cameo as a blind butler. Into the 1980s, now "Sir" Alec Guinness, he was beloved as a "legitimate" actor of the stage and screen by most critics and loved by young children who knew him only for his adventure role

in *Star Wars.* But among fans of film comedy the Guinness they liked best was the one who made all those classics during England's golden age of film comedy in the 1950s.

AUTOBIOGRAPHY: *Blessings in Disguise*
BIOGRAPHIES: *Alec Guinness* (Tynan), *Alec Guinness, A Celebration* (Taylor, 1984)
FILMS incl.: *Kind Hearts and Coronets* (1949), *The Lavender Hill Mob* (1951), *The Man in the White Suit* (1951), *Father Brown* (1954), *The Ladykillers* (1955), *The Bridge on the River Kwai* (1957), *The Horse's Mouth* (1958), *Our Man in Havana* (1959), *Situation Hopeless but Not Serious* (1964), *Hotel Paradiso* (1966), *Scrooge* (1970), *Murder by Death* (1976), *Star Wars* (1977), *Lovesick* (1983), *Return of the Jedi* (1983), *A Handful of Dust* (1988)

## FRED GWYNNE

### (July 10, 1926– )

Not many monsters graduated from Harvard to star in sitcoms, write children's books and exhibit paintings. A *Munster* did it: Fred Gwynne.

Gwynne initially combined art and comedy drawing for the *Harvard Lampoon.* After he graduated in 1951, he pursued an acting career while working full time writing ad copy for the J. Walter Thompson agency. After years of stage roles he got a key role and good notices for *Irma La Douce.* With so many television shows filming in New York, he dabbled in sitcoms as well. For "The Phil Silvers Show," he was cast against type—a gaunt, pale, thin fellow who happened to be a champion food eater. Then he joined co-stars from Silvers' show, Joe E. Ross and Al Lewis, in a new sitcom, "Car 54 Where Are You."

With the glummest comic visage since Fred Allen, grim Gwynne played Officer Francis Muldoon, forever trying to control the bumbling enthusiasm of his partner, Officer Gunther Toody. Then the six-foot, five-inch actor starred in "The Munsters," with Al Lewis once again in the cast. As many actors found before him, putting on Frankenstein makeup was a horrible chore. But, with a hearty laugh, nervously fluttering fingers, a silly wide smile and bright eyes behind the jutting monster brows, Gwynne created a fresh comic character in the lovable half man, half monster, semimasculine Herman Munster. It wasn't just his comic face or gestures that won laughs; he even had a funny voice, uniquely flat and nasal, timid and whining, an unimposing contrast to his imposingly strong body.

After "The Munsters" fad faded, Gwynne recalled "waiting a year to see what would happen." Nothing much did, besides a few little sitcom parts. Gwynne didn't mind. "I was a New York actor. I wasn't Alfred Lunt, but damn it, I was worthy of something worthwhile. . . . I made a rock-solid choice. I went back and started over." He appeared in summer theater and off-Broadway productions of classic plays, winning back his reputation as a fine actor. In 1982 he appeared on Broadway in *Whodunnit* and played King Claudius in the American Shakespeare Theater production at Stratford, Connecticut. After a while Gwynne was able to look back at his two shows—now rerun classics—with tolerant amusement. In addition to stage and film roles (rarely in comedies) he pursued his hobbies—writing children's books and painting.

BOOKS incl.: *Best in Show* (1958), *What's Nude* (1960), *God's First World* (1970), *The King Who Rained*, *The Story of Ick* (1971), *Chocolate Moose* (1976), *The Sixteen-Hand Horse* (1980)

BROADWAY: *Mrs. McThing* (1952), *Frogs of Spring* (1953), *Irma La Douce* (1960), *Here's Love* (1963), *Whodunnit* (1982)

FILMS incl.: *Munster Go Home* (1966), *Simon* (1980), *The Munsters' Revenge* (1981), *So Fine* (1981), *The Cotton Club* (1984), *Water* (1985), *Murder by the Book* (1987), *Fatal Attraction* (1988), *Pet Sematary* (1989), *My Cousin Vinny* (1992), *Shadows and Fog* (1992)

TV: "Car 54, Where Are You?" (1961–63), "The Munsters" (1964–66)

# H

## BUDDY HACKETT

### (Leonard Hacker, August 31, 1924–   )

The imp of Vegas raunch comedy, Buddy Hackett peppered his routines with unabashed, cheerful vulgarity. He'd tell graphic sex anecdotes to shock the crowd into laughter—and get more by coaxing a blushing lady at ringside into using four-letter words too. Buddy's teddy-bear body, goofy grin and babyishly nasal Brooklyn voice seemed to take the harsh edge away from the jokes. From another comic, the gags would seem like bullets crashing through a plate-glass window. From Buddy, they were just spitballs bouncing off the schoolhouse door.

At a 1989 appearance at the family-oriented Westbury Music Fair, ads for Hackett's show bore warning stickers: "Adult comedy at its best." The comedy veteran had indeed changed from the 1950s and '60s when he did silly clean routines about Chinese waiters, dating and dieting.

Before he became comedy's bad boy, Buddy did some boxing in his teens using the name "Butch Hacker." The kid from Brooklyn's New Utrecht High School became a comedian in the Catskills, where he had earlier been a busboy and waiter. He moved to Broadway for a show called *Lunatics and Lovers* and followed this with a 1956 television sitcom called "Stanley," playing a newsstand owner who gets into zany problems with his boss (Paul Lynde)

and girlfriend (Carol Burnett). In nightclubs, the five-foot-six, 200-pound pudge was known for his Chinese waiter schtick, playing a stereotyped but feisty Asian attacking his customers: "Spale lib or the egg roll? No spale lib *and* egg roll, spale lib *or* egg roll . . . no, no split 'em up, I split *you* up, you round-eyed iriot! What's a 'fly lice'? Fly lice is *fly lice!* Wattsamatta, can't you speak Engrish?"

With his button eyes twinkling, his words shyly dripping out the side of his mouth, Hackett was, in Brooks Atkinson's words, "large, soft, messy." He was a natural to play babe-in-the-woods movie roles. Universal Studios hoped Buddy and Hugh O'Brien would be the new Abbott and Costello, starring them in *Fireman Save My Child*. Critics poured water on it, but Buddy went on to star in *Everything's Ducky* in 1961 and *It's a Mad Mad Mad Mad World* in 1964, still playing the fretting little boy, popping his eyes and gasping at the havoc he caused. He even sang playing the lead in Broadway's *I Had a Ball*, a show about Garside the Great, a small-time Coney Island sideshow man.

During the1960s, Hackett's little boy became blue. He said it began when he told risqué jokes to a nightclub boss, who insisted he tell them on stage. If the bosses didn't mind risking walkouts, neither did he. "Once you're fillin' the room, you do what you want," he said. At a banquet in Minneapolis, sharing the dais with then Vice President Hubert Humphrey, Hackett did a completely uncensored

"The bad boy of comedy," stand-up comedy great Buddy Hackett rose to the challenge of playing the legendary Lou Costello in the television film *Bud and Lou.* Photo from the author's collection.

show and was asked to leave. In the summer of 1970 Buddy strode onto the stage of the Kings Castle Hotel in Lake Tahoe naked, except for a jangling pendant hanging low from around his neck, swaying side to side, thigh to thigh.

For the next two decades, Buddy played Vegas and played naughty boy to Johnny Carson on television's "Tonight Show," mischievously stretching the bounds of censorship by using "correct" names for anatomical parts—and then going overboard with a deliberate (bleeped) obscenity. In 1980 Hackett tried a syndicated version of the old Groucho Marx "You Bet Your Life" show, but couldn't find the blend of cuteness and outrageousness viewers could take on a daily basis. He chose semiretirement in 1990, appearing a few times a year at Las Vegas casinos.

An underrated actor, Hackett worked only sporadically in films and episodes of television shows ("Murder She Wrote"). He won some good notices

for his role in *God's Little Acre,* and years later was highly effective in the challenging role of Lou Costello in the television film *Bud and Lou.* He was able to show sympathetically both Lou's quixotic temper and his cuddly qualities, traits Buddy shared in real life.

Mostly Hackett was content performing stand-up loaded with joy-buzzer obscenity and harmless shocks. Though in his 60s, no one thought of him as a dirty older man—just Buddy, the bad boy.

AUDIO: *How You Do?* (Coral), *The Original Chinese Waiter* (Dot, reissued by Pickwick)
BROADWAY: *Lunatics and Lovers* (1954), *Viva Madison Avenue* (1960), *I Had a Ball* (1964)
FILMS incl.: *Walking My Baby Back Home* (1953), *Fireman Save My Child* (1954), *God's Little Acre* (1958), *All Hands on Deck* (1961), *Everything's Ducky* (1961), *The Music Man* (1962), *It's a Mad Mad Mad Mad World* (1963), *Muscle Beach Party* (1964), *The Golden Head* (1965), *The Love Bug* (1969), *Scrooged* (1989)
TV: "Stanley" (1956–57), "The Jackie Gleason Show" (1958–59), "The Jack Paar Show" (1958–62), "You Bet Your Life" (1980)
VIDEOS: *Buddy Hackett in Concert* (F.H.E.), *Buddy Hackett II: On Stage* (Media)

## ARSENIO HALL

### (February 12, 1959–    )

When Arsenio Hall took over for Joan Rivers on her late-night television talk show, he was an unknown, some jiving pal of Eddie Murphy's. Critics complained that he was an amateur who belonged on public access cable. He jawed with pals in the audience and fawned over the few stars who bothered showing up. Critics were annoyed at his childish, look-at-me, I-got-my-own-show grin and his sassy I-got-my-own-show-so-I-must-be-cool finger-pointing and strutty body language. Few thought he'd catch on.

"But what was interesting," recalled his producer Jeff Yarborough, "was the phenomonal audience share, 60 or 70 percent, that he was pulling among black viewers." When Hall left Fox and returned with a new talk show, he broadened this base by featuring young movie personalities and rock stars as guests. Hall was a hit among blacks and young whites, a demographic similar to the successful rock music channel MTV. The audience cheered him like a rock star, whooping it up over each joke and bellowing "woof woof woof" (borrowed from the lynch mob–like audience cry on the boorish Morton Downey talk show that aired in the hour just before Hall's series).

In some urban cities Hall's show was moved to 11:30 to challenge Johnny Carson. Said Hall, "I'm not going after Johnny's crowd. I'm going after Johnny's crowd's kids."

As a kid in Cleveland, Arsenio dreamed of being a talk show host like Johnny Carson. The lonely child yearned for an audience. "I was an only child who spent most of my time lying in bed crying." He unintentionally followed Carson's childhood: learning magic tricks and performing them to gain money and attention. Arsenio's Baptist preacher father and mother, Annie Hall, divorced when he was six. His mother had to work two jobs to support the family, and any money he made as a magician came in handy. "I was raised by women, by my godmother, my grandmother and my mother," he says. "I don't trust men. I may have two male friends, men I've cried with, like Eddie Murphy, someone who don't want nothin' from you."

Arsenio's mother insisted he get an education. He did, graduating from Kent State. In 1979, after working as a cosmetics salesman, Hall tried stand-up comedy. At first he was so scared that he literally ran out of the Comedy Cottage in Rosemont, Illinois when he was called to the stage. "Comics are not ready to fail," he recalled, "because it hurts so much. You're alone and they're not saying, 'We don't like your material.' They say, 'We don't like *you.*' And it hurts. The whole thing is approval." He got a break when singer Nancy Wilson caught his act and saw his potential. He had few jokes but lots of personality.

Hall arrived in Los Angeles in 1980 and slowly built up his credits, turning up on HBO's 1983 *Going for Laughs* special, co-hosting Alan Thicke's talk show and becoming a regular on "Solid Gold '87." He made a few films and was particularly amusing in *Coming to America,* but he knew that stand-up and talk show hosting was what he wanted. Critics still complained that he had more personality than jokes

when he began hosting his own show. They simply couldn't appreciate his flashy style and the show's loose, goofing-around "party" atmosphere.

The show is actually similar to David Letterman's loose, goofing-around atmosphere where the stand-up monologue was less jokes and more attitude. A typical opening: "Hello! Boy oh boy! I'm the sheriff around here and [pointing to the band] this is my posse! Give it up!" The difference is that Hall doesn't appeal to Dave's hip Yuppies but to "Yabbies" (Young-and-Buying teens) and black urban "Buppies." Both hosts cater to their own interests in music, starlets and small-time comics, and both hosts mystify viewers who don't understand the attitude, nonjokes and in jokes.

As Arsenio said, "I'm a warmer brown-bread version of David Letterman. Call me the pumpernickel of late night." It got him plenty of bread—and by April 1989 over 2 million viewers under 30. If the show is style without substance, it mirrors current trends. *People* magazine wrote: "Sure he strokes his guests with powder-puff questions, but isn't that the point? Everybody's relaxed." In November 1990 the skyrocketing Hall got a star on Hollywood's "Walk of Fame," at one time an honor that came only after decades of work. "Fame comes and goes," he said, "but this will always be there." Of course, along with fame came tabloid headlines and rumors. Comic Ellen Cleghorne quipped on stage that "Arsenio Hall" was a Swahili term for "Am I gay or am I not—only Eddie Murphy knows for sure."

When Johnny Carson chose to retire, many speculated that Hall would emerge as the "King of the Night." *New York Times* television critic John J. O'Connor wrote that of all the hosts and comedians, Hall "earned special consideration" to be considered a front-runner, especially "playing the genial host with a smile a yard wide . . . ingratiating yes, but always managing to slip in telling points." O'Connor did admit, "Mr. Hall's on-camera persona can be endearing or grating, depending on your mood or his. . . . the woof-woof antics used to rev up the audience . . . could use a rest. The milking of audience hysteria might be toned down . . . and the opening monologues are embarrassingly uneven."

If people think a talk show means success for Arsenio, they are right—and wrong. "You know what success is?" Hall asked. "Success is when you look at your mom and tell her, 'Mom, whatever you want to do.' I've done that, and my accomplishments are exceeding my dreams. I am the happiest man in show business."

FILMS incl.: *Amazon Women on the Moon* (1987), *Coming to America* (1988), *Harlem Nights* (1989)

TV: "The Half Hour Comedy Hour" (1983), "Thicke of the Night" (1984), "Solid Gold" (1986), "Late Night" (1987), "The Arsenio Hall Show" (1989–)

## HUNTZ HALL (See also THE EAST SIDE KIDS.)

**(Henry Richard Hall, August 15, 1919–   )**

Huntz Hall insisted in *Loose in London,* "I'm couth!" But he was kidding. The comedy star of The East Side Kids, he had bulging eyes, fluttering hands and a talent for spouting inanities. He seemed to take delight in annoying "straight man" Leo Gorcey and everyone else with his deliberately dopey attitude. Before there was Jerry Lewis, there was teen nuisance "Horace Debussy Jones" played with unapologetic glee by Huntz Hall.

Hall grew up on New York's East Side, 30th Street and 1st Avenue, one of 16 children. He got the nickname "Huntz" from one of his brothers, who thought he looked like a typical German from the Yorkville section. Hall and his friends had novel interests, such as visits to nearby Bellevue Hospital. "We'd go over and scream at the crazy people. They'd throw things at us and we'd collect 'em."

A singer, Hall was a member of the Madison Square Quintette until his voice broke. He broke into radio acting on such shows as "Bobby Benson's Adventures" (which also featured Billy Halop) and "The Life of Jimmy Braddock." He auditioned for Broadway's *Dead End* and lost. He got a second chance when one chosen kid had trouble doing a realistic imitation of a machine gun. Huntz came back, opened his mouth and blasted away. (He would later add a sound "catch phrase" to his arsenal, air plopping out the side of his mouth from one fluttering cheek.) The play about tenement life and a street gang was a huge success. Hall and "the gang" went to Hollywood to film it.

In the subsequent movies, Hall's sullen attitude and long face typed him as the comic patsy. From his first role as "Dippy," he became "Glimpy Williams" then "Glimpy Freedhoff" then "Glimpy McClosky." Whatever Glimpy he was, he was still the same, a kid with a punchlike face that was all long nose and prominent chin, livened by a goofy stare and smirky grin. When The East Side Kids became The Bowery Boys, "Glimpy" was renamed "Horace Debussy Jones."

As the main comic of the bunch, Huntz did surprisingly little. He was no pratfall expert, rarely had a truly funny line to say and never performed any trademark slapstick or wordplay "routine" with straight-man Leo Gorcey. The films were shot too cheaply and quickly for that. Hall got laughs on personality, making the most of tried-and-true comic devices (the fluttery hands of a Hugh Herbert and the madcap aggression of Harry Ritz). He said that the only major comic who actually worked with him on developing comic technique was Shemp Howard. Somehow it all came together to form a likable character with a shade of complexity: an "innocent" dupe who could be streetwise, a girl chaser who didn't seem to know what to do with a girl, a goof with enough ego to think he was smart. He appealed strongly to kids due to his habit of irritating the parental Leo Gorcey.

GORCEY: One day the men in the white coats will come and drop a net over you!

HALL: Who needs a haircut?

Huntz, married three times, was one of the gang's mischief makers off screen. He recalls giving a "hot hat" to actor Ronald Reagan. It was a variant on the hot foot. "One day he was sitting, reading a newspaper. We rolled a piece of paper into a cone . . . gently put it on his head and lit it."

Hall was in less demand after the Bowery Boys series ended. He performed on stage often (Oscar Madison in a stock version of *The Odd Couple* and Willie in *The Sunshine Boys*) but was seen only sporadically in films and on television. Fans were happy to see him guesting in 1982's *Channel Zero,* a cable special with Chevy Chase and Martin Mull. For them, he would remain forever young as Horace

Debussy Jones, a teenager he played even as a 35-year-old. Asked how he could play such a role for so long, and at that age, he shrugged and said, "It's how you feel. If you're young at heart, you can do it."

BROADWAY: *Dead End* (1935)
FILMS incl.: *Dead End* (1937), *Crime School* (1938), *Angels with Dirty Faces* (1938), *Give Us Wings* (1940), *Spooks Run Wild* (1941), *Bowery Bombshell* (1946), *Bowery Buckaroos* (1947), *Jinx Money* (1948), *Angels in Disguise* (1949), *Lucky Losers* (1950), *Ghost Chasers* (1951), *No Holds Barred* (1952), *Loose in London* (1953), *Paris Playboys* (1954), *High Society* (1955), *Dig That Uranium* (1956), *The Gentle Giant* (1967), *The Love Bug Rides Again* (1973), *The Manchu Murder Caper Mystery* (1975), *Valentino* (1977), *The Escape Artist* (1982), *Cyclone* (1987)
TV: "The Chicago Teddy Bears" (1971)

# TOM HANKS

## (July 9, 1956–   )

In 1988 Tom Hanks wasn't sure what all the fuss was about. He didn't act like a star, or look like one: "I've got kind of a bizarre body, a big ass and fat thighs. I've got a goofy-looking nose, ears that hang down, eyes that look like I'm part Chinese and are a funny color. I've got really small hands and feet, long limbs, narrow shoulders, and a gut I've got to keep watching. My hair makes me look like a Talmudic scholar. . . . I don't think I'm ugly, but I do sometimes look in the mirror and say, 'What is with these lips?' "

His look: average. But that's exactly what made him a big comedy star in the last half of the 1980s. He was a sympathetic, believable comic hero in move comedies; neither an arrogant Yuppie nor a hopelessly stereotypical nerd.

Born in Concord, California, Hanks had a hectic childhood. His parents (his father a cook, his mother a waitress) split up when he was five and he had to follow his father from job to job, city to city. His mother remarried three more times, his father twice more.

A student at California State University, he went out to act at the Great Lakes Shakespeare Festival in Cleveland, where he won a "Best Actor" award in his second season. He played Proteus in *The Two Gentlemen of Verona* in 1978. Since his girlfriend Samantha Lewes was pregnant, he married her. They went to New York where he appeared in roles including Hortensio in *The Taming of the Shrew*. City living wasn't glamorous on 45th Street: "We lived next door to a transient hotel, and the crack fiends who lived next door to us would leave their radio playing all night long."

After appearing in the made-for-television film *Mazes and Monsters*, Hanks moved back to California. A pilot he made for "Bosom Buddies" was a surprise—it actually sold. As Hanks put it, "I had no idea what I was getting into; if somebody had told me, I would probably have choked. Really." A drag comedy, it was about two guys living in a women's residence hotel. The *Los Angeles Times*: "If there was ever a turkey, this is it." *Time* magazine said Hanks in drag looked "more like a female moose in distress." Only the *Village Voice* thought it was a "classic."

The scripts had little wit, relying on Hanks' attitude-based comebacks. When Hanks is turned on by a lady, only to be told "She thinks you're a girl," he says, "I'll settle." Hanks settled for $9,000 per episode, and 32 episodes of "Bosom Buddies." When it folded, he turned up on "Family Ties" and "Happy Days," where he met Ron Howard, who thought of him when he began filming *Splash*—after Michael Keaton, Bill Murray and John Travolta turned the lead down.

In the film about an average guy who discovers a mermaid, Hanks developed a lot of his movie personality traits. At first he was playing it a bit too smugly "brat-packish," as if it was all a put-on. Director Ron Howard told him, "You're not what the movie is about [the mermaid is], but you're the catalyst for everything that goes on here." Hanks modified the grating impudence with vulnerability and honesty. By being an ensemble player, he actually stood out even more, allowing his natural, relaxed personality to show through.

The film took in over $60 million at the box office and Hanks took off, mostly in roles that matched his self-confidence against all odds: spies in *The Man with One Red Shoe,* a crumbling house in *The Money Pit* and half the world in the Peace Corps comedy *Volunteers.* When he co-starred with Jackie Gleason in *Nothing in Common,* the old star said, "He's got it . . . not only can he deliver a line, he's got great moves. He moves like a funny guy."

Hanks tried to keep his perspective amid the money and the acclaim, but the jump to stardom came with a price. Tom's divorce became final after filming *Every Time We Say Goodbye.* In 1985 he married *Volunteers* co-star Rita Wilson.

Hanks' fame hit a new high with *Big.* The film was basically just an acting exercise: Instead of pretending you're bacon frying, throw yourself on the floor and act like a kid. But Hanks made the film sparkle. The film offered plenty of chances for Hanks to mug outrageously and prove himself another Jerry Lewis or Steve Martin, but he and director Penny Marshall knew *Big* itself was bigger. He kept things believable. It was a film starring Tom Hanks, not a Tom Hanks vehicle.

*People* magazine enthused, "If he'd been the boy next door, the girl next door might never have left home. Men like him, too, because he looks like a hang-out kind of guy . . . to kids, he's the dream big brother."

Hanks continued to play comedy roles that marked him as forever young (the boy and his dog story of *Turner and Hooch*) or an adult with too much goofy kid in him (the perplexed neighbor to a ghoulish family in *Burbs*). In the right film, he showed flashes of greatness. In *Punchline,* his serio-comic skills as a driven stand-up comic had audiences giggling and weeping. Jay Leno told Tom, "You did a great job. You captured the essence of it very very well." By now a firmly established star, he was given the plum lead role in *The Bonfire of the Vanities,* but the film was an unsteady mixture of satire, soap opera–level trash and glitz. Many thought Hanks was miscast, but he was quick to see the vulnerable and pathetic little-boy side to the "master of the universe" Yuppie he was playing.

A very hot star following *Big,* the chilly reception for *Bonfire* (following the disappointing critical response to *Joe Versus the Volcano*) did little for his career. Younger stars were now getting the parts

in teen comedies, leaving Hanks to consider the next movie.

Hanks may find a niche similar to Chevy Chase in playing middle-age men in comedies, or he might lean more toward serious films. Some critics hope he can age into a modern version of the comic actors he himself admires, such as Jack Lemmon and Cary Grant. He admitted, "I would hope to come off as a guy that's hip . . . Cary Grant. He was the embodiment of hip." But hip with a down-to-earth touch. Of his average appearance, he said, "That makes me something of a blank canvas for whatever the texture of the movie. I'm lucky. I've been labeled this Everyman. So I guess I'm appropriate for everything."

FILMS incl.: *He Knows You're Alone* (1980), *Mazes and Monsters* (1981), *Splash* (1984), *Bachelor Party* (1984), *The Man with One Red Shoe* (1985), *Volunteers* (1985), *The Money Pit* (1986), *Nothing in Common* (1986), *Every Time We Say Goodbye* (1986), *Dragnet* (1987), *Punchline* (1987), *Big* (1988), *The Burbs* (1988), *Turner and Hooch* (1989), *Joe Versus the Volcano* (1990), *The Bonfire of the Vanities* (1990), *A League of their Own* (1992)

TV: "Bosom Buddies" (1980–82)

## OLIVER HARDY (See LAUREL and HARDY.)

## VALERIE HARPER

### (August 22, 1940–   )

For three straight years Valerie Harper won supporting Emmy awards for playing Rhoda Morgenstern on television's "Mary Tyler Moore Show." A few years later she won her own "Best Actress" Emmy as star of the spin-off series "Rhoda." It was good acting: Many fans assumed that, like her lovable character, Valerie was a Jewish girl from the Bronx. Actually, she was born in upstate Suffern, New York and attended parochial school. When her parents divorced, she and her father moved to New Jersey.

Valerie attended church schools, studied ballet and eventually worked as a dancer at Radio City

Music Hall and in Broadway chorus lines for the musicals *Take Me Along* and *Subways Are for Sleeping.* She recalled that her comedy back then was unintentional, such as the time she danced in *Wildcat* and tumbled into the footlights: "I burned my arm—but the other dancers couldn't stop laughing!"

Her roommate, Arlene Golonka, was a member of the New York version of Second City and in 1963 invited Valerie to see the improvisational troupe perform. In 1964 she married one of the actors, Richard Schaal. They worked in improv together. In 1966 she appeared in some sketches on the comedy album *When You're in Love the Whole World Is Jewish,* and the husband and wife duo appeared on local television in 1968 with improv sketches on "Skitch Henderson's New York."

After more theater work in California, Harper got the call for "The Mary Tyler Moore Show." Used to performing energetically on stage, Valerie sparkled in front of the live studio audience. As good-hearted but down-to-earth Rhoda, she supplied a little sour reality to Mary's sweetness. Many applauded Moore for presenting a realistic view of single life for women in the 1970s, but a lot of the jokes came from Rhoda. She was the one who fretted before a date, "I've gotta lose ten pounds by 8:30!"

Rhoda was the one who complained, "When we used to play Mommy and Daddy when I was a kid, I always played Mommy's unmarried sister." Valerie's ad libs often ended up in the show, such as her complaint at lunch one day: "I don't know why I'm putting this in my mouth—I should just apply it directly to my hips."

Rhoda Morgenstern was so strong a character she was given her own show in 1974. For the opener she explained to viewers, "I was born in The Bronx, New York, in December of 1941. I've always felt responsible for World War II. The first thing that I remember liking that liked me back was food. I had a bad puberty. It lasted seventeen years. . . . I decided to move out of the house when I was 24. . . . Eventually I ran to Minneapolis where it's cold and I figured I'd keep better. Now I'm back in Manhattan. New York: This is your last chance!"

After "Rhoda" left the air in 1978, Harper tried to change her image and for much of the next decade took roles in everything from horror movies *(Don't Go to Sleep)* to rape drama *(An Invasion of Privacy).* She returned to sitcoms as "Valerie." She loved the new character. "She likes to laugh and have a good time. She's not a quiet, elegant character. She's terminally middle class, like me. . . . Valerie is more like me than Rhoda was. With Rhoda, I really did do a character. I worked on a thick Bronx sound and attitude." Viewers didn't get much of a chance to get to know Valerie; after a contractual dispute with NBC, Harper was fired and the show renamed "The Hogan Family." She won her case against NBC and in an ironic twist, she returned in a new sitcom, "City," scheduled opposite her old show. She played Liz Gianni, city manager to deputy manager Ken Resnick (Stephen Lee). It was a more subdued, realistic role than she had in years. Critic David Bianculli in the *New York Post* reported, "In the series, she's more Mary than Rhoda. And it works."

BROADWAY: *Story Theater* (1970)
FILMS incl.: *Freebie and the Bean* (1974), *Chapter Two* (1979), *The Last Married Couple in America* (1980), *Blame It on Rio* (1984), *Stolen: One Husband* (1990)
TV: "The Mary Tyler Moore Show" (1970–74), "Rhoda" (1974–78), "Valerie" (1986–87), "City" (1990)

## PAT HARRINGTON JR.

### (August 13, 1929–   )

A naturally amusing guy who enjoys put-ons and dialect comedy, Pat Harrington Jr.'s show biz career began as a joke. After graduating from Fordham University in 1952, he became a salesman at NBC. He enjoyed Italian dialect comedy and in 1956 happened to do some dialect gags for Jonathan Winters. Winters, at NBC to guest-host "The Jack Paar Show," invited Harrington to appear on the show.

Soon Harrington was a regular with Paar himself. Pat named his character "Guido Panzini" and, after pretending expertise in various guises, he had a hit with one particular routine, "The Italian Golf Pro." Paar, his straight man, asked him about the most difficult course he ever played: "Tanganyika Contary Club in Africa. It goes'a uppa side of Mount Kilimanjaro. Hardest hole issa third. Green there issa other side of pygmy village. If you short with a two iron, means pow! Blowgun dart inna chest!"

Harrington went on to become a regular on Steve Allen's "Tonight Show," where Guido Panzini met another regular, José Jimenez (Bill Dana). Bill and Pat cut a record together with Pat—more famous at the time (1959)—getting top billing and Dana writing some of the material and playing straight man. Pat's best bit was about surviving the *Andrea Doria* crash:

"When did you first realize you were on a collision course?" "The captain asked a question and somebody answered in Swedish." "What was the very first thing out of the captain's mouth when he knew what had happened?" "The very first thing out of his mouth? His lunch . . . I was in the bridge. I don't want to boast, but I made it to the lifeboat in 9.6 . . . the captain did it in 9.4."

For a few years, "Guido Panzini" was a hit. Few seemed to know Guido was actually someone named "Pat Harrington Jr." If the name was familiar at all, it was because of Pat Harrington Sr., a vaudeville star who sang Irish tunes, song parodies and incorporated sharp insult patter into his act. When Guido faded away, Pat Harrington Jr. remained. He played Pat Hannigan on "The Danny Thomas Show" and was busy with stand-up, sitcoms and even cartoon voice work (he was the voice of "The Inspector" in a series of cartoons based on the detective from "The Pink Panther" shorts). With his artificial handsomeness (too bright a smile, too-piercingly-bright eyes), he was often typed in guest sitcom roles and films as the ultimate in plastic young executives (notably, *The President's Analyst*).

Harrington appeared in the 1969 sitcom "Mr. Deeds Goes to Town," and ultimately attained new fame and an Emmy as Dwayne Schneider on "One Day at a Time." He played the part of the macho building superintendent given to philosophy: "Remember and don't ever forget—it is better not to have been in love than to never have loved at all."

AUDIO: *Pat Harrington as Guido Panzini* (Signature, reissued on Roulette), *Some Like It Hip* (United Artists

FILMS incl.: *The President's Analyst* (1967), *The Affair* (1973)

TV: "The Steve Allen Show" (1958–61), "The Danny Thomas Show" (1959–60), "Pantomime Quiz" (1962), "Mr Deeds Goes to Town" (1969–70), "One Day at a Time" (1975–84)


## PHIL HARRIS

### (June 24, 1904–    )

Easygoing band leader Phil Harris enjoyed a career that meandered between music and comedy and intertwined with a series of novelty song hits.

Phil's little film *So This Is Harris* won an academy Award in 1933, the first in the newly created "Best Short Subject" category. Through the 1930s jukeboxes were loaded with Harris' good-natured Dixie novelty tunes, especially "That's What I Like About the South," a cheerful nonsense number about the good life: "There you can make no mistakey. Where those nerves are never shakey. You ought to taste that layer cakey! And that's what I like about the South!"

When Harris joined Jack Benny's program he did more than lead the band. He developed a comedy character known for boozing, ridiculous displays of hip ego and a hearty delight in teasing his "boss," Jack. "Hiya, Jackson!" was Phil's annoying greeting. He'd clue in the folks at home too: "The program's been dull, but now Harris is here—so come on, all you folks, prepare to cheer!"

In 1941 Harris married Alice Faye, and in 1948 they had their own bouncing baby radio show, with Gale Gordon part of the sitcom cast. The show remained on the air to 1954. Through that period Harris still had occasional novelty hits, including "The Thing," a bouncy, semirisqué tune about a "thing" Phil discovers on the beach one day. The lyrics stop and a rap on the drums obliterates the description: "I wandered all around the town until I chanced to meet—a hobo who was looking for a handout on the street. He said he'd take most any old thing, he was a desperate man. But when I showed him the (rap rap rap) he turned around and ran!"

During the 1960s Harris eased his workload. One of his more famous turndowns was *The Music Man*, which went to Robert Preston. The Dixie novelty singer called it "too corny." His biggest success in recent years was as the voice of the bear in *The Jungle Book* cartoon feature. He recalled in 1987, "It was one of the great experiences I think in my show business life." It gave a new generation a chance to enjoy Phil's special brand of good humor, aged to perfection.

AUDIO: *At the Cocoanut Grove* (Sunbeam), *On the Record* (RCA), *Southern Comfort* (Mega), *The South Shall Rise Again* (RCA), *You're Blasé* (RCA), *Woodman Spare That Tree* (MFP)

FILMS incl.: *Melody Cruise* (1933), *Man About Town* (1939), *Buck Benny Rides Again* (1940), *Here Comes the Groom* (1951), *The Glenn Miller Story* (1954), *The High and the Mighty* (1954), *Anything Goes* (1956), *The Wheeler Dealers* (1963), *The Jungle Book* (1967), *Rock A Doodle* (1992)

## GOLDIE HAWN

### (November 21, 1945–   )

Ever since her years as the dizzy blonde on "Rowan and Martin's Laugh-In," Goldie Hawn has retained her cute, sweet, happy image. She admitted, "I wake up happy. I guess all of us like to be around people who make us happy. And that's part of my thing."

Goldie began as a go-go dancer at East Coast nightclubs and in Las Vegas. She went to Hollywood to be one of the dancers in an Andy Griffith television special. Her first important acting role was as a stereotypical giggling blonde named Sandy on the sitcom "Good Morning World." A typical line: "I have to go home and get my toast out of the clothes dryer." That was funny enough to take her to "Laugh-In."

When the nervous 22-year-old giggled and missed her lines, producer George Schlatter kept the cameras running. He had discovered somebody who could supply natural, infectious laughter. She recited jokes with all the enthusiasm and glee of a grade schooler. She almost looked the part, with

The giggling cutie from television's "Laugh In," Goldie Hawn has had her best film successes in light comedies such as *Private Benjamin* and *Foul Play*. Photo from the author's collection.

columnists comparing her to the cartoon character Tweety-Bird, thanks to her short blond hair and large eyes. Kurt Russell, who would become the man in her life, recalled that in those days she was "funny and sort of adorable and likable, but I didn't think of her as sexually attractive."

Her giggling is real. She recalled, "I've been a giggler, a laugher, since I was three years old." Her Jewish mother was "a giving woman. I'm not an entertainer because I need attention I didn't get as a baby. I got plenty." She took dancing lessons as a child, and in her teens performed her first major stage role, as Juliet in a *Romeo and Juliet* production. She appeared in musical comedies, sometimes creating spontaneous if embarrassing moments of laughter: "I was in the chorus of *Kiss Me Kate*. We were in Springfield, Massachusetts, and one of the actors was playing a strong man . . . but the strong man couldn't find his loincloth at the last minute, so he showed up in a girl's leotard. I laughed so hard I peed down my leg. . . . Everyone could see it."

Everybody could see that Goldie was one of the big stars of "Laugh-In," her effervescent personality perfectly complementing the fast-paced show of one-liners, quick sketches and songs. What people didn't realize was that Goldie had talents beyond those of a charming, chuckling joke reciter. Though she had little real dramatic training, after Goldie left "Laugh-In" she won an Academy Award for her first major film, *Cactus Flower.*

She starred in a variety of films and experimented with variations on simple comic dizziness, playing roles that called for more of an eccentric free spirit or a sexy leading lady. While there was rebellion in the 1960s, it was also the time of giggly drugs, paisley clothes and silly "Laugh-In" comedy. To an extent Goldie in that era mirrored the naiveté of the hippie lifestyle. In the '70s she matured, ending the decade with the box office hit *Foul Play* and a foray into adult comedy via Neil Simon's *Seems Like Old Times.*

For the 1980s Hawn had a huge hit as *Private Benjamin,* adding new twists to the vulnerable character of a young, silly little thing who learns to grow up and take responsibility. She followed this success with similar films in the formula, including *Protocol,* in which a silly waitress ends up a force in politics, or *Wildcats,* in which she leads a football team to success. The films reflected the women's movement at the time and her own successful struggle to become a film producer and take a firm hand in guiding her own career.

Hawn has tried to break away from her trademark dithery character, but it has not been easy. In *Overboard,* she tried to play a bitchy rich lady, but was more successful in the latter half of the film in which she was reduced to helpless vulnerability. It got mixed reviews, as did her attempt at a serious drama, *Deceived.* The varying climate of feminism and "politically correct" comedy has made it hard for anyone to predict the reception to a new Hawn film. *Bird on the Wire,* for example, was roundly attacked for its portrayal of a modern woman. Gol-

die played a lawyer who can't handle big decisions, such as which brand of bottled water to drink and whether or not she needs a manicure.

The *New York Post* railed at "Giggly Goldie. Dithery Goldie . . . Goldie who strikes a blow against feminism every time she opens her mysteriously swollen mouth and whines." Even so, film execs are still charmed by Goldie, and they also have faith in her business acumen. Walt Disney's new "Hollywood Studios" division has her signed to a seven-picture deal worth tens of millions of dollars.

BIOGRAPHIES: *Solid Goldie* (Berman, 1981), *Goldie* (Haining, 1985)

FILMS incl.: *The One and Only Genuine Original Family Band* (1968), *Cactus Flower* (1969), *There's a Girl in My Soup* (1970), *Butterflies Are Free* (1972), *Dollars* (1972), *Sugarland Express* (1973), *Shampoo* (1975), *The Duchess and the Dirtwater Fox* (1976), *Foul Play* (1978), *Seems Like Old Times* (1980), *Private Benjamin* (1980), *Protocol* (1984), *Swing Shift* (1984), *Wild Cats* (1986), *Overboard* (1988), *Bird on a Wire* (1990), *Deceived* (1990), *Alone Together* (1991), *Criss Cross* (1992), *Housesitter* (1992), *Death Becomes Her* (1992)

TV: "Good Morning World" (1967–68), "Rowan and Martin's Laugh-In" (1968–70)

## TED HEALY (See also THE THREE STOOGES.)

### (Charles Earnest Nash, October 1, 1986–December 21, 1937)

In his day, Ted Healy was considered a grand comedian and far funnier than the comics who "stooged" for him in vaudeville and in some of his feature film appearances. Now Ted Healy is virtually forgotten, and when film fans screen his movies, it's to watch his "Three Stooges," not him.

After starting his career as an impressionist doing Al Jolson and Ed Wynn, Healy became a stand-up performer, his trademark a battered hat (à la Ted Lewis). Somewhat of a snappy wise guy (his style directly influenced Milton Berle), the handsome top banana seemed to handle audiences easily with his sharp patter and songs. At 26 he married Betty Brown and the two became a comedy and dance team. Healy evolved more comedy sketches requiring heavy-duty stooges. He reportedly went through several second bananas before settling on childhood friends Moe and Shemp Howard. In 1925 Larry Fine joined and Healy had three stooges.

The act was corn and violence. In a typical sketch, the boys met Ted at center stage. "Who are you gentlemen?" Ted asks. "We're from the South." "So," Healy says, "you're from the South. Did you ever hear of Abraham Lincoln?" Moe shakes Ted's hand, saying "Glad to meet ya!" Pow—Healy smacks him in the face.

Healy was bossy and not great to work with. Moe left the act in 1927, as did Larry (only Healy and Shemp appeared in Broadway's *A Night in Spain*). Eventually the gang reunited and played Broadway in 1929's *A Night in Venice*. In 1930 they played The Palace and made a film, *Soup to Nuts. Variety* said Healy was "unfunny," and the reviewer even questioned why he was making $6,000 a week in vaudeville.

His Stooges wondered too, since he was taking most of the money. For their big film break, Healy got $1,250 a week—the boys $100 apiece. They broke up and formed their own act with Moe Howard as the boss. Healy hired three new stooges. There was a brief reconciliation (Healy and the original stooges starred in a few shorts for MGM), but when Ted's nasty disposition and drunken brawling became too much, they left him permanently. Healy's brand of comedy off screen included tossing phone books out hotel windows to frighten pedestrians. Around the same time, he and his wife were divorced. He had been cheating on her for years.

Healy was in Jean Harlow's *Bombshell* in 1933 and Gary Cooper's *Operator 13* in 1934, but the balding tough-guy comic was not successful. Constantly broke thanks to his drinking and racetrack betting, he ended up the victim of violence perpetrated by two (some reports say three) men he met in a nightclub. Healy was drinking—celebrating the birth of his son—when he got into an altercation with the strangers. Whether he challenged them to go outside or they waited for him to come out, the result was the same: The men beat Healy into the sidewalk and kicked him unconscious. Joe Frisco helped get Ted to a hospital, where he died. He left behind a bewildered wife, an infant son and no money at all.

A last tribute was paid him in the film *Always Leave 'em Laughing*. Bert Lahr, playing an aging comic, remarks that all the great clowns have died off. He names "Bill Fields, Ted Healy, Willie Howard."

Ironically, the man who seemed to slap around his co-workers and friends had a strong feeling for his audience. Between takes on a film set, he told a fellow actor, "Never treat your audience as customers—treat them as partners." The actor never forgot it, and quoted Healy's advice often. The actor—James Stewart.

BROADWAY: *Earl Carroll's Vanities* (1925), *A Night in Spain* (1927), *A Night in Venice* (1929), *The Gang's All Here* (1931), *Crazy Quilt* (1931)

FILMS incl.: *Soup to Nuts* (1930), *Meet the Baron* (1933), *Hollywood on Parade* (1933), *Dancing Lady* (1933), *The Band Plays On* (1934), *It's in the Air* (1935), *Mad Love* (1935), *San Francisco* (1936), *Sing Baby Sing* (1936), *Love Is a Headache* (1937), *Hollywood Hotel* (1937)

## SHERMAN HEMSLEY

### (February 1, 1938– )

Not many men could battle Archie Bunker successfully. It took excitable little George Jefferson to do it. As Bunker's cantankerous black next-door neighbor, Sherman Hemsley made obstreperous nastiness fun. His snide insults and sizzling anger sounded real, a bracing contrast to the broad buffoonery of bigoted Archie.

Viewers responded to Hemsley and the rest of the Jeffersons and it wasn't long before they were spun off into their own television show. The twist was that they were "movin' on up," with George now a successful businessman who could spurn Bunker's low-class Queens neighborhood to live on Manhattan's ritzy upper East Side. But Jefferson's success didn't make him any happier. He was still the resentful, steaming, scowling little man who considered a pat on the back a slap in the face and every greeting a secret insult.

George's abrasiveness was often as racist as Archie Bunker's. When George's son Lionel marries a girl who's father is white, George gets in the digs. "Want a drink?" he asks the man. "How about a white mule . . . a honky donkey!" The white characters on the show were often portrayed as idiots (Paul Benedict as Harry Bentley is the most obvious example). Mostly, the show's laughs came from George's antagonistic attitudes toward everyone and the misery of achieving money without peace of mind. Even his black maid, Florence, took insults. "Is there something you don't like about my cooking?" she asks. "Yeah," says George. "Eating it!"

Born in Philadelphia, Hemsley took dance lessons and acting classes. However, he didn't quit his day job, working in the post office. Five years later he had his mail forwarded to New York, where he joined the Negro Ensemble Company. In 1968 he was off-Broadway in *The People vs. Ranchman,* then on Broadway for two years in the musical *Purlie.* Then he moved out to California to star in a production of *Don't Bother Me I Can't Cope.* "All in the Family" had been running for three years when Norman Lear decided to cast the part of George Jefferson. He recalled Hemsley's work on *Purlie* and was delighted to find him alive and well and in California, ready to join the show. After a decade of playing George, Hemsley took some time off to develop an Atlantic City stand-up act of jokes, singing and dancing. He came back to television with another success, as Deacon Ernest Frye on "Amen."

Hemsley is still perceived as curmudgeonly George Jefferson. In real life, he is soft-spoken and there is no hint of the broad street-tough ethnic accent he often uses in his comedy. When interviewers questioned his quiet, almost aloof personality, he simply pointed out, "I never hung out with a lot of people. . . . When I first came to California, I never went to parties because I just felt uncomfortable standing around and holding a drink. Not that I was snotty or anything: I stayed alone because I knew that if I socialized there'd come a time when I'd want to be alone and wouldn't be able to be, and I needed my mind clear to think and create. I'm one-track that way. My work is my party."

He admitted there was some irony in his becoming known for feisty comic roles complete with his trademark strutting walk (a "tough walk" he remem-

bered from guys in his old Philadelphia neighborhood). Of George Jefferson and his other roles, he admitted he played "characters with a lot of energy. He insults people but deep down inside he's a lovable character. Love is the key. As long as you love or you show some kind of love the people can relate to you. You can do all the mean things but you got to come around to love and that's the connection in all of us."

BROADWAY: *The People vs. Ranchman* (1968), *But Never Jam Today* (1969), *Old Judge Mose Is Dead* (1969), *The Moon on a Rainbow Shawl* (1969), *Purlie* (1970)
FILMS incl.: *Love at First Bite* (1976), *Stewardess School* (1986), *Ghost Fever* (1987)
TV: "All in the Family" (1973–75), "The Jeffersons" (1975–85), "Amen" (1986–    )

# BUCK HENRY

## (Henry Zuckerman, Sagittarius, 1930–    )

Known as a great comic screenwriter (*Candy, The Graduate, The Owl and the Pussycat, The Troublemaker, Catch 22, First Family* and *Protocol*), for co-creating television's "Get Smart" and creating the short-lived sitcom hero "Captain Nice," Buck Henry has also enjoyed a lucrative career as a comic character actor and television personality.

His acting career began in childhood when he was part of a road production of *Life with Father.* He returned to acting following his graduation from Dartmouth in 1951. Some sources report that he attended Columbia University. Since Henry enjoys giving conflicting information to biographers (very much in keeping with his put-on style of comedy), it's not surprising that some even list his name as "Buck Henry Zuckerman," though "Buck" was a childhood nickname. He will not even reveal his birthdate, saying, "I like to keep them guessing. That way I don't get any weird cards or letters on my birthday." He's asked that only his zodiac sign be used in this book.

Buck Henry's first national exposure came with a practical joke. After appearing in a touring company of *No Time for Sergeants,* he invaded television talk shows as G. Clifford Prout, a member of SINA ("The Society for Indecency to Naked Animals").

Many believed that the stern, serious fellow in the black-rimmed spectacles was deadly serious about forcing pets to wear pants. It was the real beginning of a comedy acting career marked by roles requiring a baleful stare of disapproval, from a desk clerk in *The Graduate,* suspiciously eyeing Dustin Hoffman, to another clerk trying to make sense of John Belushi's Samurai warrior on "Saturday Night Live."

Following his SINA put-on, Henry joined The Premise improvisational troupe in 1959. He followed it with writing assignments on shows hosted by Steve Allen and Garry Moore, and was a key member of television's "That Was the Week That Was" as both performer and writer in the early 1960s. In 1964 he co-wrote and co-starred in *The Troublemaker,* with various members of off-Broadway's improv group The Premise. He went on to co-conceive "Get Smart." He said, "Mel Brooks and I wrote the pilot and created it, then I worked as story editor for two seasons. I really loved the first year, then I got tired, and it got tired, I felt."

He wrote the screenplay for *The Graduate,* amused that the biggest laugh line came from one ironic word. It was the career advice a businessman gave to the young graduate: "plastics." Henry recalled in 1991, "That's probably the most famous line I ever wrote—"plastics." A lot of people get a lot of articulation out of their quotes, but I lived off one word for a long time."

Henry continued to divide his time between screenwriting and acting. He also created a few more television shows, notably the short-lived cult favorite "Captain Nice." He cast William Daniels in the lead, an actor who had also worked in *The Graduate* and shared Henry's deadpan and intense performing style. While Henry went on to play many character roles through the 1960s, he admitted, "Nobody quite knows who I am, because every generation attaches me to something different. Real old people remember me from "That Was The Week That Was." Then there's a whole generation who think I did "Get Smart" and nothing else. And there are *The Graduate* people. And then there's a group that think I hosted "Saturday Night Live" so many times I must have worked for it, and don't know what else I ever did."

Ironically, most of Henry's best work on "Saturday Night Live" is not shown in rerun. He contributed some of the show's most notoriously "offensive" moments. On several shows he played "Uncle Roy," a lecher who lived for baby-sitting and catching glimpses (up the dresses) of his young charges (Gilda Radner and Laraine Newman). He drew fire for a sketch that found humor in silly scatological names ("Lord and Lady Douchebag") and drew the most negative mail for one of his favorite sketches, "Stunt Baby." Henry did point out that there were some fans of his work. He got mail "from people who wanted tips on how to throw their own baby out the window." He went on to do a sequel, "Stunt Puppy." His least favorite moment on the show was one of his sketches with John Belushi as the Samurai. In these sketches, Henry, in the guise of a school official or some other authority figure, would try talking logic to the excitable Samurai. Once Belushi accidentally got carried away and slashed Buck on the forehead with his sword. "He whacked me out. Blood on stage. A memorable evening."

Henry's comedy was usually subtle, enough to get past the censors the first time, if not in rerun. Once he played Charles Lindbergh. In one scene he was reading a men's magazine instead of a map. The announcer remarked that he was "jerked off—course."

Henry continues to write screenplays and take roles in films that called for a "Buck Henry" type—usually a prim or cold citizen content to be a sharp, square cog in the big wheel of society. In 1989's *Rude Awakening* he played a businessman proud of his co-op. "You mean," he is asked, "some poor people lost their low-cost housing just because you called your congressman?" Henry answers, "Yes. The system works!"

OFF-BROADWAY incl.: *The Fortress of Glass* (1952)
FILMS incl.: *The Troublemaker* (1964), *Catch 22* (1970), *The Owl and the Pussycat* (1970), *Taking Off* (1971), *Is There Sex After Death* (1971), *Heaven Can Wait* (1978), *Gloria* (1980), *Eating Raoul* (1982), *The Man Who Fell to Earth* (1987), *Aria* (1988), *Rude Awakening* (1989), *Tune in Tomorrow* (1990), *Defending Your Life* (1991), *The Player* (1992), *The Linguini Incident* (1992)
VIDEO: *Saturday Night Live*

## PEE-WEE HERMAN (Paul Reubens)

### (Paul Rubenfeld, August 27, 1952–    )

He wore a tight-fitting gray suit with his white socks showing and a red bow tie tight around his throat, looking like the typical overdressed nerd at a children's birthday party. His greasy black hair was slicked back to accentuate his round head. Imitating the Harry Langdon breed of silent film comedians, his face was floury white and his lips reddened. He moved and spoke like a *Night of the Living Dead* version of Pinky Lee. His mugging and blinking suggested a woman doing Eddie Cantor in drag.

This unlikely creature, Pee-Wee Herman, was thoroughly repugnant to many. But he became a strong cult star in the early 1980s and, after nearly finding crossover success in films, returned to his cult-star niche and popularity with a children's Saturday morning show. Buried under the makeup, and rarely giving interviews out of character, was Paul Reubens. And Paul Reubens was just another layer of protection for the man actually born Paul Rubenfeld.

Penetrating the two layers protecting Pee-Wee Herman wasn't easy for journalists, but eventually the basic facts came out. Rubenfeld was born in Peekskill, New York. The family moved to Sarasota, Florida, where his parents, Milton and Judy Rubenfeld, owned a lamp store. In sixth grade the precocious Paul starred in a production of *A Thousand Clowns*, and by the time he was in high school he played the male lead in *David and Lisa*.

After a year at Boston University, he transferred to the California Institute of the Arts. He appeared on stage with Charlotte McGinis as the Hilarious Betty and Eddie, doing puppet shows and sound effects. They went on television's "Gong Show" and won. Paul later joined The Groundlings improvisational troupe in the late 1970s and, along with another Groundling, Cassandra Peterson (later known as "Elvira, Mistress of the Dark"), had a few bit roles in Cheech and Chong films. Paul also did some cartoon voice work, playing Freaky Frankenstone in "The Flintstones." For 1982's *Pandemonium* he played the angry, geekish assistant to Canadian Mountie Tommy Smothers.

Pee-Wee debuted on national television in his own HBO special, playing the childish master of ceremonies presiding over his own variety program, featuring himself as everything from monologist to magician. The show was loaded with satirical humor from the viewpoint of a childlike adult (or a perversely adult-acting child). In a highlight scene, Pee-Wee delighted in showing off his skills as a hypnotist. He made a female stooge from the audience strip down to (gasp!) her slip. In another scene, he put mirrors on his shoes so he could look up a girl's dress; but he refused to peek if she *wasn't* wearing panties.

Pee-Wee Herman was clearly some kind of mutant from the 1950s. Pee-Wee's satire of the awkward age was the height of cool in the eyes of the '80s critics writing for alternative newspapers. Gradually others began to catch on. They began to tune in to Pee-Wee, who was soon amazing and alarming talk show hosts and basking in all his goofy, bratty, silly, spacey glory.

On talk shows there was no Paul Reubens; interviewers could talk only to Pee-Wee, the frustratingly rude and idiotic dweeb who would interrupt and shout "okay, okay, okay" and, like any seven-year-old, talk about only what was amusing him at the moment. Many were confused. Was this a brilliant satirist of childhood and the 1950s, or just another jerk act for Yuppies who'll laugh at anything if it's stupid or weird?

Some of the answers came in 1985, when the unlikely performer made the giant leap to stardom via his first starring film *Pee-Wee's Big Adventure*. Critics responded seriously, noting the film's mock Fellini-Hulot soundtrack, the comical walk that always indicated a master mime at work and the rich symbolism of a man-child living in his own world. Like some of the silent film clowns, Pee-Wee had successfully taken an awkward, pathetic little character and created his own vivid, magical world in which he was the hero. At his best, he was funny and imaginative, at his worst the hyper pest was really only as annoying as Fanny Brice's "Baby Snooks."

The experiment cost $6 million to make and grossed over $45 million. Pee-Wee mania was at its peak. He got his own Saturday morning children's show, which, of course, was being watched by almost as many perversely hip adults as kids. The show was loaded with humor children could appreciate, and

Pee-Wee's "big adventure" into television and film comedy started and nearly ended in controversy. Photo from the author's collection.

they loved his neat stage set full of junk and toys. The laughable geek pulled the same kind of "made ya look, haw haw" stunts one might find in any progressive classroom.

Some parents protested the idea of children watching effeminate Pee-Wee and resented the way he'd grimace like a lunatic and shout, "I'll show you mine if you'll show me yours!" Even without the gender confusion, parents could live without having the loud and annoying kiddie show host tell kids "When anyone says the secret word . . . SCREAM!" In a way, Herman had almost the same negative response as 1950s kiddie host Pinky Lee, the lisping little fellow who also often worked at fever pitch.

Pee-Wee told *Rolling Stone* magazine how he felt about the criticism: "I get upset, it hurts me, but then I think, 'I don't like everybody.' What I do is extreme, to a degree, and I can certainly see if people don't like it. I don't completely understand why people get so worked up about it. . . . I'm just

trying to illustrate that it's okay to be different—not that it's good, not that it's bad, but that it's all right."

The rage for and against Pee-Wee began to die down. Children went on to the next fad. His second movie, *Big Top Pee-Wee,* had nothing new except setting some kind of record—the longest movie kiss (90 seconds between Pee-Wee and Valeria Golino). His show sputtered until Pee-Wee Decided not to do another season in 1991.

In July of 1991, as the last reruns began to air, Herman was arrested in an X-rated movie house in Sarasota, Florida. Lt. Bill Stookey of the sheriff's office said that Pee-Wee was observed "manipulating his genitalia in the theater in plain view." This was front-page news, but instead of the expected "moral outrage" over a kiddie show host caught in a "sex crime," fans and newspaper editorials raged that Herman's career was being ruined for a victimless crime.

David Letterman was the first to comment. He told his audience: "I have this to say in defense of Pee-Wee Herman. At least he wasn't *talking* during the movie." Jay Leno offered a similar gag, adding "It was a case of reverse sexism! Pee-Wee was arrested for doing off stage what Madonna gets paid to do on stage!" Bill Cosby was dead serious: "I'm a concerned citizen. When I see injustice, prejudice or anything dishonest or unfair, I get upset. I feel the need to speak out . . . the media's blowing the thing out of proportion."

For his minor crime Herman accepted a fine and agreed to community service work. He made his first video appearance after the incident as an MTV video awards presenter, declaring "Heard any good jokes lately?" Director Tim Burton (who had been the director of *Pee-Wee's Big Adventure*) offered him a cameo in *Batman Returns*. While it's difficult to tell whether or not Reubens will continue the Pee-Wee Herman character, clearly there are many who are still devoted. And just as many who still aren't sure what Pee-Wee's fun is all about, who he is or what he is. Paul Reubens would never give a clue. "I have a song I sing when people heckle me, 'I Know You Are, But What Am I?' "

FILMS incl.: *Cheech and Chong's Next Movie* (1980), *Pandemonium* (1982), *Pee-Wee's Big Adventure*

(1985), *Big Top Pee-Wee* (1988), *Batman Returns* (1992)

TV: "Pee-Wee's Playhouse" (1986–91)

VIDEOS incl.: *Pee-Wee's Playhouse, Pee-Wee's Christmas Special*

## BENNY HILL

### (Alfred Hawthorn Hill, January 21, 1925–April 20, 1992)

The legendary director Hal Roach, who gave the world Harold Lloyd, Laurel and Hardy, and "Our Gang," once was asked if any contemporary comedian ranked with the classic stars of the past. "I guess there's only one," he said. "Benny Hill. But I wish he'd clean up his act."

It wasn't that Benny Hill was such an original comedian. His gift was in adapting the visual comedy of silent films and vaudeville for a modern audience. Each television generation had its own link to past traditions. Previously, grinning Red Skelton clowned in a variety of characters, getting belly laughs with old-fashioned sketches and a sense of humor that was often corny and naughty. Later, "Laugh-In" brought back blackout sketches, speeded-up videos and one-liners. And for the 1980s, Benny Hill recycled old jokes back into freshness, rejuvenated the world of novelty songs and poems, and put together mini-silent films complete with gently speeded up videos and eccentric music. From the burlesque world, he added pretty girls forever "accidentally" stripped to their underwear for leering laughs. Benny was not shy about borrowing directly; he once used a Skeltonesque clown, wall graffiti similar to material from "Laugh-In," and lines such as "Don't Waste Water—Dilute It."

In America, Skelton and "Laugh-In" were considered "low comedy" at the time. Critics had their reservations about "low" Benny, too. But viewers discovered Hill with fadlike ferocity, delighting in his nonstop parade of jokes, scantily clad women and saucy sketches. His self-written scripts, though borrowing from many sources, were carefully assembled and polished into a unique mosaic, and the action was mixed and paced to perfection and presided over by a round, cheerful fellow with twinkling eyes, a wide smile and honest charm. Even critics began to laugh in spite of themselves.

Born in Southampton, England, Benny Hill learned early on how to entertain people. At six, he would circulate among the bathers and sun-worshippers at the beach, catch their attention and amuse them with a song. He learned the art of charm and salesmanship in his job driving a milk truck. He always entertained his customers with a joke or two. He played in amateur productions, and at 17 quit his job for show business. He was a drummer with Ivy Lillywhite and Her Boys and stooged for a comedian named Hal Bryan. After performing in army shows during World War II, he once again worked as a straight man, this time to British comic Reg Varney. He admired all the comedians he'd seen in British burlesque. He recalled, "I'd watch each comic and think, you lucky devil up there, because everybody loved him, laughed at him, and with him there were always the saucy girls, the glamour, the French maids with black stockings, knickers and feather dusters, who would stick their bottoms up." Finally he went out on his own. He made it to British television with "The Service Show" in 1952 and two years later was voted "Outstanding TV Personality of the Year."

Hill starred in *Paris by Night* (1955) and *Fine Fettle* (1959), but found the stage much too confining. Television gave him the chance to experiment with special effects and play a variety of characters all at once. He became popular with his own show and, despite an occasional film appearance, was content to remain with the format, letting various countries around the world edit old shows to fit their schedules. In America, stations either ran episodes as "specials" or chopped them into half hours for syndication.

Every show seemed to have a guarantee of slapstick visual comedy and risqué jokes at the cheerful whiz-bang level: "I've been sitting listening to you so long my little bottom's gone to sleep," says Benny's wife in a sketch. "I know," he answers, "I heard it snoring." While most stand-ups and even sitcom scriptwriters avoided puns as too common and "low" a form of humor, Hill would always toss them in, the more ridiculous the better. Playing a stereotypical Chinese man, he tells an interviewer how happy he is with his wife—"breast with two nipples." "Oh," says the interviewer after a moment's pause, "blessed with two nippers!"

Hill enjoyed silly wordplay that no other show dared to try. Misreading cue cards was always good for a giggle as Benny announced a singer with "a musical bum. Oh . . . music album!" Every possible British slang term for bottoms and backsides seemed to find its way into his scripts. An entire generation had grown up without hearing vintage one-liners. Hill obliged. In a blackout scene, he calls his wife from the bar and tells her: "I said I'd be home after seven. I've only had six."

Hill was also one of the few to make full use of the makeup artist's skills. In each show he had reason to use a remarkable array of wigs, false teeth and different skin tones to supplement his reasonably good array of voices and ethnic accents. The show had no guest stars and few regulars (the notables were a wizened, ancient little patsy named Jack Wright, a glinting-eyed suave straight man Henry Magee, and a long-suffering, bulky bald chap named Bob Todd). The most prominent cast members were Hill's Angels (dancers who had a few provocative production numbers in each show) and the anonymous pretty girls who had drinks poured down their blouses and broomsticks accidentally prodded into their behinds. This comic treatment of women, not seen much since the days of Laurel and Hardy and The Three Stooges, alarmed some feminists.

Hill defended himself: "There is nothing nasty or sexist about my comedy. And the fact that I chase the girls doesn't make me a dirty old man. The whole idea is based on the premise that I fail in my pursuit. Terrible things happen to me, apart from the disappointment of being rebuffed and not getting anywhere with my advances. . . . I don't downgrade women. Quite the opposite. They downgrade me. On my shows it is always the men who suffer, never the girls. The girls score off us every time. We're always the losers."

In the 1980s Hill was a winner, his shows syndicated around the world along with videos and CDs of his songs. Despite his sudden success in America, he refused to capitalize by coming stateside for concerts or an American-made show. He continued to produce fresh episodes of "The Benny Hill Show" until the show's demise in 1989, and lived a modest rather reclusive life in the same home he'd had for decades.

AUDIO: *The World of Benny Hill* (Decca), *Benny Hill Songs* (Capitol)
BIOGRAPHY: *The Benny Hill Story* (J. Smith, 1989), *Saucy Boy* (L. Hill, 1990)
FILMS incl.: *Who Done It?* (1956), *Light Up the Sky* (1959), *Those Magnificent Men in Their Flying Machines* (1965), *Chitty Chitty Bang Bang* (1968), *The Italian Job* (1969), *The Best of Benny Hill* (1976)
TV: "The Benny Hill Show" (syndicated and specials)
VIDEOS: *The Benny Hill Show Vols. 1–5; Benny Hill's Video Spotlight; Benny Hill's Drive-in Video; Video Sideshow; One Night Video Stand*

## JUDY HOLLIDAY

### (Judith Tuvim, June 21, 1922–June 7, 1965)

Playing dumb in *Born Yesterday* brought Judy Holliday fame. But her 172 IQ and years of acting training indicated she could have played a wider variety of parts. Would she have become a great star, or remained a blond, strident variation of Gracie Allen? The question remains, asked by fans who remember the promise she showed in a half-dozen films.

Raised in Queens, New York, Judy wrote a school play, edited the school newspaper and won many literary awards. She went to Manhattan's Julia Richman High School. She broke into show business as a phone operator for Orson Welles' Mercury Theatre, but got most of her show business training in the Catskills. There, in 1938, she joined Adolph Green in a series of plays. Along with Betty Comden, Alvin Hammer and John Frank, they became The Revuers, playing the Village Vanguard and after five years of polish, going west to make films. It was in California that Judy used the translation of her Hebrew name, Tuvim and (adding an extra "l") became "Holliday."

The Revuers made *Greenwich Village* for 20th Century Fox, but when it was released in 1944, their numbers had been cut out. The troupe split up and Judy tried for a solo film career. It didn't work out, but by the time she went back to New York, Comden and Green were a success and they helped her get started again. She played a stereotypically dimwitted hooker in the comedy *Kiss Them for Me.* *Variety* applauded her "decisive triumph as this moronic but devastating nitwit. She's going places."

Nobody expected she'd be "going place" so soon. But she was so memorable in that role that, with a lucky break, she was able to go right to the top. Jean Arthur was to star in the hot new play *Born Yesterday,* but during rehearsals she complained about the coarse language in the play and asked for rewrites. Then she developed a throat problem in New Haven. An understudy went on temporarily while producer Max Gordon tried to hunt up a new star. Gordon was told about Judy and her success in *Kiss Them for Me.* He recalled, "I had missed her performance, but everything I heard and read was praise. . . . The minute she walked in, I knew she was it. I listened to her talk—even without giving her a script to read—and was certain that she would make an ideal replacement."

On short notice, Judy took over in Philadelphia, and when she arrived on Broadway, the *Daily News* headlined: "Judy Holliday Perfect as Dumb Broad in Very Funny Play." The *New York Times* reported of her role as Billie Dawn, "In one line she managed to forge the image of an intellectually vacuous young woman with a peasant shrewdness and a hard honesty: 'Do me a favor will ya, Harry?' She told her boorish lover. . . . 'Drop dead.' "

Columbia wanted a big star for the film version, but Judy had many supporters. *Born Yesterday* author Garson Kanin and Katherine Hepburn helped get her into *Adam's Rib,* which served as a kind of screen test. The results were positive, and she not only got the part in *Born Yesterday* but received an Academy Award for the role. Critics and fans loved their dumb and daffy comedy queen. But Judy didn't like being typed as dumb and daffy. Of *Kiss Them for Me, Adam's Rib* and *Born Yesterday,* Judy remarked: "I started off as a moron . . . worked my way up to imbecile . . . and have carved my current niche as a noble nitwit. Now I want a part where I can use my own hair, my own voice, and maybe even be literate."

Today many agree that there's the same 1950s shrillness about Judy Holliday's dimwit roles as Jerry Lewis's jerk portrayals: a character too black and white and crude all over to be warmly appealing. In 1956 she got a chance to star in a musical, *Bells Are Ringing,* and won a Tony Award. This was an encouraging start to more balanced roles. She made the film, but it was her last.

During tryouts of her next play, *Laurette* (about actress Laurette Taylor), Judy began feeling ill. The show closed and she underwent surgery. She came back to star in *Hot Spot,* as much to pay her bills as to try to resume her career, but had a relapse. At the time, there was more respect for a star's privacy, especially when it concerned serious illness. Fans had no idea she'd undergone a mastectomy and were unaware of her struggle with cancer. It was a shock when the ebullient actress who had made bells ring just a few years ago was pronounced dead at 43.

AUDIO incl.: *Legacy of Laughter* (AEI)
BIOGRAPHY: *Judy Holliday* (Holtzman, 1982)
BROADWAY: *Kiss Them for Me* (1945), *Born Yesterday* (1946), *Dream Girl* (1951), *Bells Are Ringing* (1956), *Hot Spot* (1963)
FILMS: *Something for the Boys* (1944), *Greenwich Village* (1944), *Winged Victory* (1944), *Adam's Rib* (1949), *Born Yesterday* (1950), *The Marrying Kind* (1952), *It Should Happen to You* (1953), *Phfft* (1954), *The Solid Gold Cadillac* (1956), *Full of Life* (1956), *Bells Are Ringing* (1960)

## HOMER and JETHRO

**Homer: Henry D. Haynes, July 27, 1920–August 7, 1971**

**Jethro: Kenneth Burns, March 10, 1920–February 4, 1989**

The men who billed themselves as "The Thinking Man's Hillbillies" were one of the few country comics with cross-over appeal. In 1959 they won a Grammy Award for their parody of "The Battle of New Orleans" called "The Battle of Kookamonga." Homer and Jethro's brand of corn was mainstream, closer to Red Skelton's than to that of more traditional country comedians. Musically, they resisted the clichés of country music (either raucous twanging or weepy violins) and favored pleasing two-part harmonies.

Many country love songs were sad drown-your-tears-in-wine laments. "Laugh about her and drink corn liquor" seemed to be Homer and Jethro's satirical viewpoint. The girls in their songs were always beasts. In their best parodies sweethearts were just sweathogs. For example, "Let Me Go, Lover" becomes "Let Me Go, Blubber."

Homer and Jethro—known back then as Henry Haynes and Ken Burns—began their career as fairly straight musicians. They joined with some other musicians as The String Dusters on WNOX in Knoxville in the 1930s. Offstage Henry and Ken liked parodying country tunes. Encouraged by friends they began performing them, becoming a duo in 1936. After World War II they began making records, including "Pal Yatchy" for Spike Jones—a parody of "Pagliacci" ("When we listen to Pal-yatchy, we get itchy and scratchy, this sure is top corn, so let's go and get some popcorn!"). Through the 1950s they were featured often on the "National Barn Dance" radio show.

Homer (on guitar) was the slim, lightly "tetched" one, and toothy Jethro (on mandolin) his bulky, head-shaking straight man. Though the team became popular after "The Battle of Kookamonga" in 1959 and made several successful albums at the time, they were most successful in the early 1960s thanks to the fad for rural comedy inspired by the hit television series "The Beverly Hillbillies." Homer and Jethro's brand of easygoing corn was really popping. They issued eight albums of musical comedy in two years (1966–67).

Aside from their songs, the boys could be counted on for silly jokes. "Jethro, gimme an E flat," Homer asks. "You know I can't play an E flat." "Well, gimme an E and I'll flatten it out myself!" They developed a catch phrase out of a series of cornflake commercials they made: "Oooh, that's corny!" At the start of the 1970s "The Beverly Hillbillies," "Green Acres" and similar shows faded out, but Homer and Jethro were still making records. Their brand of comedy had defied trends for over 30 years. In 1971 Homer suffered a heart attack just before a scheduled concert in Indiana. He died in the hospital a few hours later.

Jethro recorded some albums for Flying Fish Records (mostly straight tunes), and appeared on television's "Hee Haw" and radio's "Prairie Home Companion." When he died in 1989, his son told reporters, "He had a good time, he made a lot of people happy. That's what he was all about."

AUDIO incl.: *Barefoot Ballads* (RCA), *The Worst of Homer and Jethro* (RCA), *Life Can Be Miserable* (RCA), *At the Country Club* (RCA), *Songs My Mother Never Sang* (RCA), *At the Convention* (RCA), *Fractured Folks Songs* (RCA), *Tenderly* (RCA), *Zany Songs of the '30s* (RCA), *Playing Straight* (RCA), *Go West* (RCA), *Old Crusty Minstrels* (RCA), *Cool Crazy Christmas* (RCA), *Something Stupid* (RCA), *Wanted for Murder* (RCA), *Ooh, That's Corny* (RCA), *Cornfucius Say* (RCA), *Nashville Cats* (RCA), *Any News?* (RCA), *Homer and Jethro's Next Album* (RCA)

FILMS incl.: *Second Fiddle to a Steel Guitar* (1965)

## DARLA HOOD (See OUR GANG.)

## BOB HOPE

### (Leslie Townes Hope, May 29, 1903–   )

Bob Hope used the theme song "Thanks for the Memory" for over 50 years. Ironically, he sang that song with elegance and cool, never with real warmth or nostalgia. Unlike most of his contemporaries, including Jack Benny on radio, Red Skelton on film and Lucille Ball on television, Hope was never a "friend" to the audience. In stand-up he liked to "stare them down" and his character in sketches was always snappy and brash. It's not surprising, then, that for much of his career, audiences liked him but didn't love him, and until late in life neither fans or critics thought to return a "thanks for the memory" to Bob Hope.

America's legendary comic was born in England. He recalled, "It was my mother who discovered my nose. 'Call back the doctor,' she cried. 'He's taken the baby and left the stork.'" At four he and his family moved to Cleveland. Teased by kids as "hopeless" Les Hope, he learned to fight back literally. For a while he fought as a boxer, using the name Packy East. He worked as a song and dance man and later a master of ceremonies. He evolved into a stand-up comic and developed a technique that would separate him from most of the rest: "I learned to

Bob Hope, the enduring star of Broadway, stand-up, films and television whose patriotism and spirit has made him an American icon. Photo from the author's collection.

his own radio show. His film debut, *The Big Broadcast of 1938,* featured his theme song, "Thanks for the Memory." His film career took off after *The Cat and the Canary* in 1939. Through the 1940s Hope was one of America's biggest film stars. Film critics later theorized that he symbolized the average American male during the war years. Like the soldiers marching off to war, he evoked confidence and saw himself as slick, streetwise and just a little smarter than his opponent. But, like those men, he also had a little streak of insecurity.

In his best films, all of this was exaggerated. Hope was drafted into situations he resolved to handle, whether investigating a haunted house, tracking down a criminal or swashbuckling for his lady love. The only problem for him were lapses of comic cowardice and foolish fumbling. (In *The Princess and the Pirate* the film opens with him cheerfully announcing "I play a coward!") In the end, he always found the guts to win, usually with a combination of brain power and luck. Rarely, if ever, did his movie character dip into tenderness or pathos, either for his leading lady or for himself.

In his films he usually had a snappy comeback. In *Ghost Breakers* he's told about zombies, who walk "around blindly with dead eyes, following orders, not knowing what they do." Hope pauses and remarks, "You mean like Democrats?" His cowardice was also handled via wisecracks. He says in *The Paleface,* "Brave men run in my family."

Audiences in the 1940s appreciated snappy comedy. The lovable character humor of Laurel and Hardy was not appreciated as much as the faster, more impersonal byplay between Abbott and Costello. Of the solo comics, Hope was clearly the leader in '40s film popularity. Many of Hope's films are comedy classics, including *My Favorite Brunette* and *Monsieur Beaucaire.*

Hope was also successful teaming with Bing Crosby. Just as impersonal as Abbott and Costello, the two men found laughs in trying to undercut each other with women and cheat each other out of money. The Hope and Crosby "Road" pictures were big box office hits. Using "in" jokes and stepping out of character, the team succeeded in distracting the villains by performing a children's hand-slapping game, "patty-cake." They usually managed to make an escape, unless the villains happened to have seen the bit in a previous film.

have enough courage to wait. I'd stand there waiting for them to get it for a long time . . . my idea was to let them know who was running things. I used to defy the audience. I didn't have much talent but I had plenty of guts." Fred Allen told him, "You reek of guts." Jack Benny once said, "Bob walks like a headwaiter who is leading a guy to a good table." All through his stand-up career Hope kept the icy glare and, to the surprise of some critics and fellow comedians, he seemed to train the audience to at least force a chuckle. Sometimes he cued them by marking time with his trademark throwaway "But I wanna tell ya . . ." More often he ended the punchline with a grim stare.

Hope was a hit on Broadway in 1933's *Roberta,* followed it with *The Ziegfeld Follies,* and in 1938 had

Hope had conquered Broadway, radio and films, and put it all together when he moved to television for his own show. He opened with his usual topical monologue: "It's great to be back in New York City. I've got a nice room here. I'm staying in City Hall. Nobody else does. But I wanna tell ya. . . ." He continued with sketches that were always breezy. In one fragment he romances a guest star actress in a park: "Some park." "Some park." "Some grass." "Some grass." "Some dew." "I don't!"

Hope's influence could be seen in many comedians, from the smooth but stinging stand-up star Johnny Carson to the cheerful, handsome but distant film star Chevy Chase. Woody Allen admitted that he borrowed several characteristics of his film persona from Hope, exaggerating aspects of Hope's heroism and cowardice and embellishing on Hope's nervous "now wait a minute, let's talk this over" one-liners.

In the 1960s and '70s Hope was often criticized for his formula-written television comedy specials and monologues. The 1940s cool wise guy had completely iced over into a cold professional. He was a little too old to be a comic hero in films and his sitcom-style efforts in the 1960s failed, mostly because audiences didn't want to pay in theaters for the kind of material Hope was generating on his television specials. On television he still commanded good ratings, but his conservative stance against the Vietnam War protests and his old-fashioned comedy style made him highly unpopular with a young generation that appreciated comics who put their guts in their work (Lenny Bruce) or at least their warm humanity (Bill Cosby).

Comedians who were cheered by young fans weren't shy about pointing out Hope's flaws. Chevy Chase said in the 1970s, "Look, Bob Hope is still about as funny as he ever was. I just never thought Bob Hope was that funny in the first place." And in the '80s, David Letterman intercepted the feed of a Bob Hope interview on a local television news show and cracked to the audience, "Was that Bob 'I'm a Hundred Years Old' Hope?"

It didn't seem to matter; the general public appreciated Hope's reliable shows, knowing every second or third gag would be good and the others pleasant, and that there would be plenty of guest stars (each carefully chosen to bring in a specific segment of the audience). He continued to tour, his familiarly phrased gags still getting laughs. In October 1989, on stage in a concert with George Burns, he told the crowd, "I'm staying in a good hotel. It's a family hotel. Every guy I met in the lobby was with his niece." Despite his falling out with critics and his self-parody in later years, Hope's ratings remained high. Late in the 1980s, befitting his longevity and with the Vietnam issue a faded memory, Hope was finally accorded tributes, both for his films (now in revival houses thanks to Woody Allen's emphatic praise) and for his public service.

He was, in essence, the definition of the "American" comic. He had risen from nowhere to become a huge success; not because he was the best singer, dancer or joke-teller, or the most handsome man, but because he had all-American drive and desire. He had conquered the stage, radio, film and television, and he did it by relying not on lovability and charm but on strength and on giving the public their money's worth. He didn't give fans a lot of tender emotion from the heart, but he did work tirelessly in every war to travel the globe bringing his show to American soldiers. He was a giant when it came to loyalty, honor and philanthropy.

In 1990 Hope made a staggering million-dollar donation to the Center for Motion Picture study. That same year he was given an honorary Doctor of Humane Letters degree from the University of San Diego. Also the same year, Hope surprised some of his liberal antagonists by supporting gun control, stating "I think the violence today is a concern of every citizen, and I am for gun control. . . . I'm not going to stop until Congress does something about this. We have to be able to walk our streets and stroll in our parks. Mandatory gun registration is a step in the right direction."

Back on July 4, 1982, Hope performed a stand-up concert in St. Louis in front of 2 million people. Another comic would've been awed. Hope said, "The best I ever did before was 500,000. I must be getting better in my old age." He was ready for more, and just as he had done before and after, he went directly to the next project and the next audience. "I'll never retire," Hope once said. "Hell, if I retired I'd have to have an applause machine to wake me up in the morning."

BIOGRAPHIES incl.: *The Amazing Careers of Bob Hope* (Morella, 1978), *Bob Hope* (Faith, 1982)

BOOKS incl.: *I Owe Russia $1200* (1966), *So This Is Peace* (1946), *They've Got Me Covered* (1946), *Five Women I Love* (1966), *Confessions of a Hooker* (1986), *Don't Shoot It's Only Me* (1990)

BROADWAY: *The Ramblers* (1926), *Sidewalks of New York* (1927), *Ups-a-Daisy* (1928), *Smiles* (1930), *Ballyhoo of 1932* (1932), *Roberta* (1933), *Say When* (1934), *Ziegfeld Follies* (1936), *Red Hot and Blue* (1936)

FILMS: *The Big Broadcast of 1938* (1938), *Thanks for the Memory* (1938), *Never Say Die* (1939), *The Cat and the Canary* (1939), *The Road to Singapore* (1940), *The Ghost Breakers* (1940), *The Road to Zanzibar* (1941), *Caught in the Draft* (1941), *Nothing but the Truth* (1941), *Louisiana Purchase* (1941), *My Favorite Blonde* (1942), *The Road to Morocco* (1942), *They Got Me Covered* (1942), *The Road to Utopia* (1945), *Monsieur Beaucaire* (1946), *My Favorite Brunette* (1947), *The Paleface* (1948), *The Great Lover* (1949), *Fancy Pants* (1950), *Lemon Drop Kid* (1951), *My Favorite Spy* (1952), *The Road to Bali* (1952), *Son of Paleface* (1952), *Casanova's Big Night* (1954), *Seven Little Foys* (1954), *That Certain Feeling* (1956), *Beau James* (1957), *Paris Holiday* (1958), *Alias Jesse James* (1959), *The Facts of Life* (1960), *The Road to Hong Kong* (1962), *Critic's Choice* (1963), *Call Me Bwana* (1963), *I'll Take Sweden* (1965), *Boy Did I Get a Wrong Number* (1966), *The Oscar* (1966), *Eight on the Lam* (1967), *Private Navy of Sgt. O'Farrell* (1968), *How to Commit Marriage* (1969), *Cancel My Reservation* (1972), *A Masterpiece of Murder* (1986)

TV: "Chesterfield Sound Off Time" (1951–52), "Colgate Comedy Hour" (1952–53), "Bob Hope Presents" (1963–67)

## CURLY HOWARD (See THE THREE STOOGES.)

## MOE HOWARD (See THE THREE STOOGES.)

## SHEMP HOWARD (See also THE THREE STOOGES.)

**(Samuel Horwitz, March 17, 1895–November 23, 1955)**

The brother of Curly and Moe Howard, and the only one to enjoy a separate successful career outside of The Three Stooges, Shemp continues to enjoy a cult appeal far beyond his status as a member of that group and as a reliable, comically gruff solo performer.

In April 1989 Johnny Carson noted: "An author has written several snotty biographies claiming famous movie stars were Nazis. Now he's claiming one of The Three Stooges was a Nazi. The book is called *Mein Shemp.*"

A few months earlier David Letterman reported the Campbell's company had "Curly Noodle Soup," but added, "I'm waiting for the Shemp Broth."

For some reason, his name was exceptionally funny, and so was his face, which was essentially just plain homely: His eyes were small and squinty, like raisins in thickened oatmeal; his nose was lumpy like an old potato; and greasy hair skittered down either side of his head from the part in the middle. His ears were the size of Zweiback crackers and his voice drifted between gruff wise guy and whining stooge. Sometimes it was hard to say if Shemp was funny because he looked funny or because he was trying to be.

"Trying" was part of Shemp's comic character. In Stooge shorts he was hilarious *trying* to box a bad guy (skipping back and fourth and shaking his fists while uttering ridiculous threats), *trying* to figure out the owner of a coat by the initials stitched inside ("T.H. Who could that be? Teddy Hoosevelt?"), or *trying* to stop a baby from crying by standing on his head. In *The Brideless Groom* he *tries* to get married but, in one gruesomely funny scene, gets stuck in a phone booth and, when he presses his mug against the window, frightens his prospective bride away.

In his feature film appearances without the boys, Shemp was deliberately very trying. In *Hellzapoppin,* he had a running joke of trying to sell Olsen and Johnson various dopey items: "Wanna buy a stove? It's hot! Wanna by an anchor? Right off the boat!"

The Brooklyn boy was dubbed "Shemp" by his mother, who pronounced Sam with a slushy "sh." Shemp and his brother Moe formed a comedy team around 1917, and in 1922 the duo joined friend Ted Healy. The Three Stooges evolved when Larry Fine joined in 1925, but after many disagreements with Healy, Shemp left the group to play Knobby

Walsh in a Joe Palooka film. He was virtually the whole show, bossing other stooges around and doing a lot of comic whining and growling as Joe's manager. The Three Stooges recruited the youngest Howard brother, Curly, to take Shemp's place.

Between 1933 and 1937 Shemp exceeded the output of The Three Stooges, starring in 33 shorts, mostly for Vitaphone. A typical entry, *I Scream,* from 1934, contains gags the Stooges hadn't even thought of yet—such as the use of a stiff hand to "block" an eye poke, or a finger up the nose to pull someone along. In the 1940s Shemp stooged for other comics. He was a grousing cook in a scene with Lou Costello (*Buck Privates,* one of five Abbott and Costello films he made) and a Mickey Finn–mixing bartender in cahoots with W. C. Fields *(The Bank Dick).* In 1944 Shemp formed a quasi–Three Stooges group with Billy Gilbert and Maxie Rosenbloom and starred in three features, *Three of a Kind, Crazy Knights* and *Trouble Chasers.*

It was only in 1947, after making several solo shorts at Columbia, that Shemp rejoined The Three Stooges. He did it sadly, replacing brother Curly, who had suffered a stroke. Though it was difficult, Shemp managed to fit back into the group using his own unique arsenal of noises (an "ib-ib-ib" intake of air) and odd faces (he had a lip twitch he called "the fish mouth"). Some Stooge fans loved Shemp even more than Curly, and in 1990 Columbia began releasing a series of "All Shemp" shorts on videocassette. Shemp stayed with the trio until 1955 when, after watching a prize fight, he had a heart attack in a taxi on the way home. Years later Moe was philosophical. "If I had my choice, that's how I'd want to go. Curly had stroke, and he lingered. But Shemp . . . if you have to go, it's better to go quickly."

BROADWAY: *A Night in Spain* (1927), *A Night in Venice* (1929)

FILMS incl.: solo shorts: *In the Dough* (1933), *Close Relations* (1933), *Here Comes Flossie* (1933), *Henry the Ache* (1934), *Corn on the Cop* (1934), *Knife of the Party* (1934), *A Peach of a Pair* (1934), *While the Cat's Away* (1936), *The Choke's on You* (1936), *Boobs in the Woods* (1940), *Pick a Peck of Plumbers* (1944); Stooge shorts: *Hold That Lion* (1947), *Brideless Groom* (1947), *Sing a Song of Six Pants*

(1947), *Heavenly Days* (1948), *Who Done It* (1949), *Don't Throw That Knife* (1951), *The Pest Man Wins* (1951), *Gents in a Jam* (1952), *Rip Sew and Stitch* (1953), *Creeps* (1956); solo feature films: *The Bank Dick* (1940), *Buck Privates* (1941), *In the Navy* (1941), *San Antonio Rose* (1941), *Hold That Ghost* (1941), *Hellzapoppin* (1941), *The Invisible Woman* (1941), *Private Buckaroo* (1942), *Crazy House* (1943), *Three of a Kind* (1944), *Crazy Knights* (1944), *Trouble Chasers* (1945), *Africa Screams* (1949)

## WILLIE HOWARD

### (William Levkowitz, April 13, 1886–January 13, 1949)

Early in his career, Willie Howard had the comic look of a Punch puppet: wild hair, a long nose, sad eyes and big ears. His humor wasn't Punch-violent, though. He preferred dialect comedy and funny faces, as in his classic bit "Rigoletto," in which he would ogle a buxom female stooge as she sang opera. The bit was in the film *Millions in the Air.*

For decades his straight man was his brother, Eugene. The Howard boys were born in Germany but grew up in Harlem, New York. Their father was a cantor and they did their first singing in a synagogue. Willie joined Sammy Liebert and Thomas Dunne as The Messenger Boys Trio, adding comedy to the songs by imitating comic stars of the day such as Barney Bernard. Eugene replaced Liebert, Dunne eventually left and the brothers toured vaudeville from 1906 to 1910 with a comic act called The Messenger Boy and the Thespian. They came to Broadway in *The Passing Show of 1912,* featuring a sketch about Willie the confused immigrant and Eugene the customs man:

"Where did you come from?" "I just got off the boat." "Do you have anything to declare?" "I'm all right, I declare." "Where are your papers?" "I haven't got the papers, but I've got the makings." "Say, you're pretty fresh. . . . Have you got any relatives here?" "Yes, I've got a twin brother two years older than I am." "Is he naturalized?" "Well, one of them is a glass eye."

With this kind of material, funny faces had to help. As Willie recalled, "When you cannot get over with a line, you must trick with an absurd facial expression or a burlesque movement . . . or by a surprise pitch of the voice."

The brothers performed in many classic sketches over the years, from "The Ambulance Chaser" (Eugene convinces Willie to fake an accident for the insurance money) to "The African Explorer," performed in 1931's *Scandals* revue. Willie used Groucho-like puns basted in a thick Jewish accent. "I bagged a lion in Africa." "You bagged a lion?" "I bagged him and bagged him but he vouldn't go avay!" Another sketch, "Phoneyfibs," was adapted later by many comics. Willie dallies with his girlfriend while his wife is on the phone. The wife thinks Willie is baby-sitting a much younger girl and urges him to care for her properly: "Undress her and put her to bed," she says. Willie with a leer: "That's a damn good idea!" His best-known routine was "Pay the Two Dollars," written by Billy K. Wells. Inept lawyer Eugene insists on fighting a two-dollar fine Willie drew for spitting on the subway. After taking the case to court, he gets Willie into deeper and deeper trouble, while Willie keeps wailing, "Pay the two dollars!" Eventually Willie gets the death sentence! The sketch was reworked on radio by Jack Benny and in the film *Ziefgeld Follies* by Victor Moore and Edward Arnold.

In *Ballyhoo of 1932* Willie delivered one of his best monologues, playing a revolutionary preaching from a soapbox: "Fellow workers, the time has arrived. Our cup of bitterness, it is filled to the brim! We must throw off the yoke of oppression . . . revolt! Revolt! Comes the revolution, ve'll eat strawberries and cream!" A heckler yells he doesn't like strawberries and cream. Willie: "You'll eat strawberries and cream and like it!" Later he unveiled a new character, Professor Pierre Ginsberg, with a mustache and goatee. The humor was mostly in Willie's hilarious French/Jewish accent. When Eugene retired in 1940 (he died August 1, 1965), Al Kelly became his straight man for the bit. A typical question for the Professor: "I have an uncle who is 78 years old. He's married to a woman who is 18. They have a child just one year old. He'd like to know from you if you think he can do it again." Professor: "He wants to know from me? Do you think he did it the first time?"

A stage legend, it's hard to find Howard's work in films and on records. The scope of his talent might best be judged by the honorary pallbearers at his funeral: Milton Berle, Jack Pearl, Harry Hershfield, Ed Sullivan, Fred Allen and Bobby Clark. Nat Kahn of *Variety* wrote: "To millions of theatergoers, Howard symbolized the little fellow who was confounded by the world's complexities. And he was, by nature, always a picture of abject humility. He never fully realized the great scope of his talent."

BROADWAY: *The Whirl of the World* (1914), *The Show of Wonders* (1916), *The Passing Show of 1921* (1921), *The Passing Show of 1922* (1922), *Sky High* (1925), *George White's Scandals* (1926), *George White's Scandals* (1927), *George White's Scandals* (1928), *Girl Crazy* (1930), *George White's Scandals* (1931), *Ballyhoo of 1932* (1932), *Music Hall Varieties* (1933), *Ziegfeld Follies* (1934), *The Show Is On* (1937), *George White's Scandals* (1939), *Crazy with the Heat* (1941), *Priorities of 1942* (1942), *My Dear Public* (1943), *Star and Garter* (1944), *Sally* (1948)

FILMS incl.: *A Theatrical Manager's Office* (1927), *Between the Acts of the Opera* (1927), *Music Maker* (1929), *Millions in the Air* (1935), *Rose of the Rancho* (1936), *Broadway Melody of 1938* (1937)

## ERIC IDLE (See also MONTY PYTHON'S FLYING CIRCUS.)

**(March 29, 1943–    )**

Eric Idle was the member of Monty Python's Flying Circus most prone to playing cheerful salesmen, windy complainers and wide-eyed chatty fools. In one of his best sketches he played an irritating fellow who finds vicarious thrills in asking lewd questions of a stranger: "Your wife—does she go? Ay? Ay? Know what I mean? Know what I mean? Nudge nudge!" Eventually he self-destructs: "Well, I mean, you're a man of the world. . . . You've slept with a lady. . . . What's it like?"

Idle was one of the busiest members of the Python troupe, although the dominant star was John Cleese. As Idle pointed out, "Because of his size you cast him as an authority figure. But someone like Mike [Palin] and I would play the bulk of the character roles."

Idle worked on solo projects during his life with Python, most of them satirizing life in the British town of "Rutland." A Beatles parody, *The Rutles,* spawned a record album and a television special (Idle played Dirk McQuickley, the "Paul" role), a *Rutland Weekend Song Book,* and a book satirizing life in Rutland, the *Rutland Dirty Weekend Book.* In it Idle offered a hodge-podge of photo parodies, plays and advertisements. The highlight was "The Vatican Sex Manual," a series of nude sex position studies, all of them making sex impossible. One shows Idle touch-ing his partner's bare backside with his finger and noting "The finger should be held fully erect and nothing else."

Idle closed out the eighties starring as Ko-Ko in a production of *The Mikado* in London and briefly appeared in his own television series, "Nearly Departed" (aka "Ghost Story"). Idle played Grant Polard, a ghost unhappy with the people now living in his house. It was closer to *Topper* than *Beetlejuice,* which Eric found "loud and noisy . . . I went with Robin Williams and I kept on trying to make him leave . . . but we stuck it out loyally. He said, 'No, you have to watch this, this is American humor.' " His own favorite American sitcoms were "Sgt. Bilko" and "The Dick Van Dyke Show," but his series didn't last long enough to evolve in any direction.

The 1990 film *Nuns on the Run* offered up Idle as a bank robber who, with his partner, disguises himself as a nun ("Sister Euphemia of the Five Wounds," or just "Five Wounds" for short) and hides out in a convent. "When it comes to drag," he said, "I haven't kicked the habit." The most notable thing about the movie was the reaction of critics Gene Siskel and Roger Ebert. They panned the film so badly that 20th Century Fox banned them from ever previewing another of their films. Public opinion later changed Fox's mind. The serious controversy didn't bother Idle, who was not about to get serious about anything regarding films. "I've done some serious roles—straight parts—but they're not as challenging as comedy. There are so many straight actors and so few people who can make you laugh. I'll always be one of the few."

AUDIO: *Rutland Weekend Songbook* (Passport), *The Rutles (Warner), The Mikado* (MCA)

BOOKS: *Rutland Dirty Weekend Book* (1976), *Hello Sailor* (1974)

FILMS: *The Secret Policeman's Other Ball* (1982), *Yellowbeard* (1983), *National Lampoon's European Vacation* (1985), *The Adventures of Baron Munchausen* (1989), *Nuns on the Run* (1990), *Too Much Sun* (1991)

TV: "Ghost Story" (1988)

VIDEO: *Saturday Night Live*

## GEORGE JESSEL

### (April 3, 1898–May 23, 1981)

Nearly ten years after Jessel's death, Robin Williams was still imitating him and old-time comedians were still telling anecdotes about him. Though his few hit records are schmaltz, his starring films obscure, and his fame in stand-up rests mostly on his creaking "Phone Call to Mama" routine and a few tapes highlighting his talents as an after-dinner "toast-master," George Jessel is regarded as a star.

Born in the Bronx, he was a show business veteran by the time he was ten, helping to support his family after his father's death. His mother worked as a ticket seller at the Imperial Theater and helped him form the Imperial Trio with Walter Winchell and Jack Wiener. They used the stage names Leonard, Lawrence and McKinley.

Jessel joined Eddie Cantor in a Gus Edwards' kid sketch but at 16 outgrew the role. *Variety* reported "Jessel is growing up, and with the passing of his cuteness, it is hoped he will perforce make it up with ability." After teaming with Lou Edwards in an act called "Two Patches from a Crazy Quilt," he went solo and had a hit with his "Hello Mama" routine: "Hello, Mama, this is George. Isn't it nice to have your own phone? What? Nobody calls you? Even before you had the phone, nobody called you either? Say, Mama, how did you like that bird I sent you for your birthday? You cooked it? But

Momma, that was a South American parrot! He spoke five languages. He should have said something?"

As a comedian and singer, Jessel hit his stride in his 20s, producing his own "George Jessel's Troubles" in 1919. He co-wrote the lyrics for a hit tune "Oh How I Laugh When I Think I Cried About You" and in 1923 performed "Hello Mama" in *The Passing Show of 1923*. He recorded a single. "The Toastmaster," in 1921, along with another routine, "Professor Lafermacher."

Jessel was the toast of Broadway in 1925's *The Jazz Singer*. He claimed Al Jolson horned in on his movie deal, offering to work cheaper. The film made Jolson a star and Jessel's career skidded by comparison. Jessel had an autographed photo from George M. Cohan inscribed to "the greatest talent I ever met, greater than Jolson." Over the years few beside Cohan would agree. Jessel made films for Jewish audiences (including *Ginsberg the Great*), starred in the Jolsonesque *Lucky Boy* singing his weepy hit "My Mother's Eyes," and remained a star in vaudeville.

Most of his press coverage concerned his romances, not his comedy. His marriage to Norma Talmadge included a scandal going in (she was already married) and going out (after the divorce a drunken Jessel broke into her house with a gun and fired shots at her current lover). One of the classic Jessel anecdotes concerns the time he knocked on

Norma's door seeking a reconciliation. When she refused, he shouted, "Can I at least use the pool?"

Jessel shifted behind the scenes, producing 24 films, including the riveting drama *Nightmare Alley*. Into the 1950s and '60s, Jessel appeared on the banquet circuit and at Friar's roasts, offering old-styled bon mots. To Jayne Mansfield on the dais: "As I look at you, Miss Mansfield, I can have only one thing on my mind—General Nasser should have them for tonsils!"

In 1968 he starred in "Here Comes the Stars," a syndicated variety show. The turbulent decade saw a distinct decline in his popularity in part due to his old-fashioned humor but also his strident support of the Vietnam War and right-wing causes. On a 1971 "Today Show" he repeatedly called the liberal *New York Times* "Pravda." Interviewer Edwin Newman tossed him off the show. In hindsight, Jessel probably deserved better, but his irritating, yammery vocal style and has-been status made him less appealing and more expendable than the equally conservative Bob Hope. Jessel's endless anecdotes extolling bygone pals became increasingly more tiresome. Said Walter Winchell, "That son of a bitch started to reminisce when he was eight years old."

Ironically, the liberals who abused him for his Vietnam stance probably had no idea he was on their side in matters of civil rights. Jessel, the "Toastmaster General" to six presidents, disliked Dwight Eisenhower and complained to Milton Berle, "Eisenhower doesn't understand a joke unless it has 'darky' in it!" Once he escorted Lena Horne into a nightclub where blacks were not permitted. "Do you have a reservation?" the doorman demanded. "Yes," Jessel insisted. "Who made it?" asked the doorman. "Abraham Lincoln, you son of a bitch!"

To his admirers, Jessel's conservatism was balanced by his colorful personality. In his youth, he was associated with such stars as Pola Negri, Helen Morgan and Lupe Velez. In old age he spent all his money on gifts for showgirls who acted like prostitutes and prostitutes who looked like showgirls. Jack Benny said, "One year alone Georgie Jessel personally supported 1,250,000 Jews in Israel and 325 chorus girls in the United States."

In his later years, struggling to support himself and rarely getting bookings, he said, "If I had it to do over again, I'd get a better education, study law,

and run for public office. Entertaining people is a great, great art . . . but many times it is very transient, insecure and lonely. At my age I find myself confronted with loneliness . . . and futility." But he still wanted to put these words on his tombstone: "I tell you from the shades of darkness that it is all worthwhile."

AUDIO: *Jessel at His Best* (Audio Fidelity), *Bedtime Stories for Adults* (Riot), *Mr. Toastmaster General* (Palette), *Mr. Toastmaster* (Private Stock), *Show Biz* (RCA), *This Is My Show Business* (Show Biz), *50th Anniversary* (Cabot), *Albert Brooks' Comedy Minus One* (ABC)

AUTOBIOGRAPHIES: *So Help Me* (1943), *This Way Miss* (1955), *The World I Lived In* (1975)

BOOKS: *Elegy in Manhattan* (1961), *Halo Over Hollywood* (1963), *The Toastmaster's Guide to Public Speaking* (1969), *You Too Can Make a Speech* (1956), *Hello Mamma!*

BROADWAY incl.: *Shubert Gaieties of 1919* (1919), *George Jessel's Troubles of 1919* (1919), *The Passing Show of 1923* (1923), *The Jazz Singer* (1925), *The War Song* (1928), *Even in Egypt* (1930), *Joseph* (1930), *Sweet and Low* (1930), *Lost Paradise* (1934), *Casino Varieties* (1934), *High Kickers* (1941), *Show Time* (1942), *Red, White and Blue* (1950)

FILMS incl.: *Private Izzy Murphy* (1926), *Ginsberg the Great* (1927), *George Washington Cohen* (1928), *Lucky Boy* (1929), *Love Live and Laugh* (1929), *Stage Door Canteen* (1943), *Four Jills in a Jeep* (1944), *I Don't Care Girl* (1953), *Can Heironymus Merkin Find True Love* (1969), *The Phynx* (1970), *Diary of a Young Comic* (1979)

TV: "The George Jessel Show" (1953–54), "Here Come the Stars" (1968)

## ARTE JOHNSON

### (Arthur Eric Johnson, January 20, 1934–  )

As a helmeted German spy, he'd peek around, grin knowingly and murmur "Verrrrrry interrrresting." As an ancient lecher, he'd toddle up to a park bench and growl rude come-ons to an old maid until she bashed him.

Neither role was sympathetic, and on paper not too funny, but both characters were big hits for Arte

Johnson on television's "Rowan and Martin's Laugh-In." Though he had been on four sitcoms earlier, viewers hadn't noticed. Now they did, tuning in each week to watch Arte, the show's most versatile performer, the master of dialect and kooky disguises.

Johnson graduated from the University of Illinois School of Journalism and in 1952 worked for a New York publishing house. He became an actor the deceptively simple way: He went to an open audition and got the part of an elderly Frenchman in Broadway's *Gentlemen Prefer Blondes*. He never missed the scholarly life: "One of my college professors said that if all those graduating from universities remembered one sentence from each course they took, they'd be well educated. It's quite a remark, and I never forgot it."

Johnson worked in summer resorts, joined the cast of *No Time for Sergeants* on Broadway (by this time Andy Griffith had left the show) and began getting television sitcom parts. The five-foot four-inch comic often played shleppy little characters such as Bascomb Bleacher Jr. (on "Sally"), Stanley Schreiber (the delivery boy on "It's Always Jan") and Seaman Shatz (a sailor on "Hennessey").

The "Laugh-In" success was about time for Johnson, who had literally been eating himself up waiting for a break, having nursed an ulcer since he was in his teens. As he said at the height of his fame in 1969, "Today I'm doing most of the same characters I did 15, 20 years ago, I'm no more or less funny, or more or less talented than I was then." Johnson's German soldier with the "verrrry interesting" catch phrase was originally a character named "Wolfgang Busch." The dirty old man that he had called "Julius Andrew" six years earlier was rechristened Tyrone Horneigh. This was the slow-moving, black-coated oldie who asked lascivious questions of old maid Ruth Buzzi in a deep, hollow, lewd voice: "Wanna come with me and play mumbly peg? Wanna come with me and play hide and seek? Wanna stay right here with me and play dead?"

Although Johnson was the big promising star of "Laugh-In" he found limited success afterward. He did voiceovers for Saturday morning cartoons, including "Baggy Pants and the Nitwits" co-starring Ruth Buzzi. In films his most memorable role was the Renfieldesque little looney in the vampire parody *Love at First Bite*. As he rhapsodized in one

scene, recalling victims gone to serve his master, "Oh, how we danced on the night that they bled!" One of his better roles was a straight dramatic part as the manager of Abbott And Costello in the made-for-television *Bud and Lou*.

In 1987 Arte turned up as the master of ceremonies in a West Coast production of *Cabaret*. He pointed out that the show about decadence in Nazi Germany had something to say to America today: "The most sensitive and cultured society can turn, become a nest of sickness . . . such things are certainly happening today, all around the world. . . . it's time to look around."

AUDIO: *You're on the Air* (GNP), *Rowan and Martin's Laugh-In* (Epic), *Laugh-In 69* (Warner)
BROADWAY: *Gentlemen Prefer Blondes* (1953), *Shoestring Revue* (1955), *No Time for Sergeants* (1956)
FILMS incl.: *Miracle in the Rain* (1956), *The Subterraneans* (1960), *The President's Analyst* (1967), *Love at First Bite* (1979)
TV: "It's Always Jan" (1955–56), "Sally" (1958), "Hennesey"(1959–62), "Don't Call Me Charlie" (1962–63), "Rowan and Martin's Laugh-In" (1968–71), "Ben Vereen Comin' At Ya" (1975)

## CHIC JOHNSON (See OLSEN and JOHNSON.)

## SPIKE JONES

### (Lindley Armstrong Jones, December 14, 1911– May 1, 1965)

As the creator of the greatest aural slapstick in comedy history, the name Spike Jones conjures up the sounds of brutal brass, brackish bells, bellicose burps and the billious "birdaphone." The eyes go misty—or just sore—envisioning Spike himself leading the band, wearing painfully loud plaid suits and laconically chewing gum, his Cagneyesque face registering little emotion. Like an impassive assassin, he often had a gun handy and ready to use. He conducted his band with it and occasionally shot it off in time to the music.

Through the 1940s, Jones murdered classical music, opera and clattering Tin Pan Alley hits. His first hit was an original, 1942's "Der Fuehrer's Face," a boldly raucous literal raspberry in the face of Germany's lunatic dictator. The tune had been written for a still unreleased Donald Duck cartoon—an appropriate beginning for Spike Jones, music's wildest audio cartoonist. As with almost all his hits, Spike conducted the band but didn't sing. The eccentric vocals in this case were by Carl Grayson. Other veteran vocalists over the years were Del Porter, Paul Frees, Doodles Weaver and George Rock.

Jones was only 12 when he became a drummer in a group called The Jazzbo Four. While still attending high school, the 16-year-old wise guy from Long Beach, California had his own apartment and played professionally in bands. He eventually formed a hot Dixieland jazz band in 1934, "Spike Jones and His Five Tacks." A few years later he became a recording studio session man, playing drums for vocalists such as Lena Horne and Hoagy Carmichael. As a "hobby," Spike and his band would have fun demolishing hit songs with eccentric arrangements and bizarre instruments.

After "Der Fuehrer's Face" became a hit (and the Donald Duck cartoon, rush-released under that title, won an Academy Award), Spike went on to destroy "Cocktails for Two" in 1944, "The Nutcracker Suite" in 1945, "Laura" in 1946 and "My Old Flame" in 1947. The great hits of Spike's golden '40s were collected in two albums, RCA's *Thank You Music Lovers* (reissued as *The Best of Spike Jones*) and *Spike Jones Murders the Classics*.

Spike and his band toured, appeared in films (usually musical comedies that allowed for one or two set pieces to be inserted into the proceedings) and had their own radio show in 1949. Spike hosted his own television series in the '50s and issued a classic album of horror comedy, *Spike Jones in Stereo*. Unfortunately, as the decade wore on, his brand of humor went temporarily "out of style." He remarked, "We were too corny for straight people, too straight for corny people." Not particularly adept as a stand-up or sketch comedian, Spike had to rely on his formula of trashing hit tunes, which was difficult to do at the time. Spike fumed that the new rock and roll hits already sounded trashed.

Jones tried to make a comeback with a "straight" band, but the big band era was dead too. Spike, a heavy smoker who was known to put away five packs of cigarettes a day, died of emphysema in 1965. Only a few years later his albums were reissued and the novelty records he made—so cleverly and concisely orchestrated down to each perfectly timed burp and perfectly pitched goat bray—were finally recognized as works of comic genius. He was, forever on, considered the definitive master of musical mayhem.

AUDIO: *Spike Jones Presents a Christmas Spectacular* (Verve, reissued by Goldberg & O'Reilly), *Dinner Music for People Who Aren't Very Hungry* (Verve, reissued by Goldberg & O'Reilly), *Spike Jones in Stereo* (Warner), *Omnibust* (Liberty), *60 Years of Music America Hates Best* (Liberty), *Thank You Music Lovers* (RCA Victor, reissued as *The Best of Spike Jones*), *Spike Jones Murders the Classics* (RCA Victor), *Best of Spike Jones Volume 2* (RCA Victor), *The Very Best of Spike Jones* (United Artists), *Spike Jones on Radio* (MF), *The Spike Jones Show* (Radiola), *Vintage Radio Broadcasts* (Mar-Bren), *And the Great Big Saw Came Nearer* (Golden Spike), *The King of Corn* (Glendale, reissued by Sandy Hook), *Spike Jones and His City Slickers* (Jass), *I Went to Your Wedding* (RCA Victor, Import), *Featuring Spike Jones* (Tiara)

BIOGRAPHY: *Spike Jones and His City Slickers* (Young, 1984)

FILMS incl.: *Thank Your Lucky Stars* (1943), *Meet the People* (1944), *Bring on the Girls* (1945), *Breakfast in Hollywood* (1946), *Variety Girl* (1947), *Ladies Man* (1947), *Fireman Save My Child* (1955)

TV: "The Spike Jones Show" (1954, 1957), "Club Oasis" (1958), "The Spike Jones Show" (1960–61)

## WILL JORDAN

### (Wilbur Rauch, July 27, 1929–   )

"The mimic doesn't just exaggerate the character or just find the highlights," Will Jordan insisted. "He invents. . . . Did Ed Sullivan ever say 'R-r-really big shew?' You're wrong. He never said it. I invented it for him. . . . I also invented the famous knuckle cracks, eyes upward roll and crazy body spins."

Invention: That's what Will Jordan brought to his art. It made him the top impressionist in the 1950s and early '60s. His most famous impression was Ed Sullivan. He went one-on-one with Sullivan, on Sullivan's show, devastating him with the accuracy of his impression while the audience roared with laughter.

Jordan was born in Queens, New York and attended Flushing High School. In 1948 he began to get prestige bookings at such clubs as Le Ruban Bleu and The Village Vanguard, but "each step was down. And with the layoffs, weeks at a time, I was very discouraged." He was buoyed by winning an Arthur Godfrey Talent Scouts competition and ecstatic when, in March 1953, his Sullivan bit was a hit. Will toured in a revue called *The Best of the Town* (a play on Sullivan's "Toast of the Town" show) and recorded a "Roast of the Town" 78-rpm single. Steve Allen called him the "Greatest Comedy Impressionist in Show Biz." Jordan was then called to Broadway to supply the voice of Ed Sullivan for *Bye Bye Birdie*.

Will created facial caricature to go with the voices, twisting into an arch-eyebrowed Bing Crosby, a cheek-bulging Alfred Hitchcock or a leering Groucho Marx. He blazed a trail for visually oriented impressionists David Frye and Frank Gorshin, and would later give pointers to a kid from Canada, Rich Little.

At first Jordan found work as an actor and was a partner with Mel Brooks and several others in a little theater project. Gradually he moved on to solo work. Restlessly creative, Will grew tired of the simple mimic gimmick. He added offbeat concepts, such as Martin and Lewis doing their impressions of Karloff and Lugosi. Then he began to shift toward pure stand-up. Variety reported in 1958: "Jordan . . . is now up with character-and-situation takeoffs . . . dandy sound-effecting à la Jonathan Winters. . . . he's trigger quick . . . an attractive personality."

A "sick" comic before there was even a term for it, Jordan invented concepts that awed and inspired Lenny Bruce and Mel Brooks—such as his bit about Hitler changing his image and appearing in a musical. "Ill Will," as he was known, created a sketch about a war hero who flies into enemy territory. He did it for a simple reason—he was blind. Another movie bit was his classic "Frankenstein" parody,

ablaze with ad libs and throwaways. Dr. Frankenstein in the cemetery with his hunchback assistant: "Fritz, are you digging?" "Oh yeah man, I'm picking up on all this jazz." "No, no, Fritz, don't try to put the shovel through your sleeve . . . take off your coat . . . take out your left arm. Now take out your right arm. Now take out your . . . other arm? Hold your arms, up Fritz. You know something, Fritz? You're built like a fork."

Into the 1960s the sensitive Jordan was disheartened when other comics went on Sullivan's show and imitated Sullivan (or rather, Jordan imitating Sullivan). He couldn't come up with new routines after seeing his concepts borrowed by others. Even though Jordan's "Hitler" bit wasn't quite the same as Lenny Bruce's or Brooks' *The Producers*, Jordan felt used.

Jordan was still sharp in 1964: "Maybe we should be grateful for subways—at least they've taken crime off the street." Will could still be devastatingly funny, but in the 1970s he began to steer away from the competitive club scene. He's discovered a lucrative market in corporate functions. If a big, well-paying company needs some comedy to liven up the annual banquet or convention, Will fills the bill. He even evolved a routine designed for such affairs, dressing up as Patton to "address the troops" on sales techniques.

Will does commercials, cartoon voices and, for the 1960s nostalgia revival, Ed Sullivan (in the film *The Buddy Holly Story* and a Billy Joel rock video). When the mood suits him, he does a nightclub gig or television appearance. As a kind of tribute, Woody Allen used Will in *Broadway Danny Rose*. Years earlier Woody hosted the "Tonight Show" and had Will on as a guest. "Having you on was my pleasure," Woody said, adding that Jordan was "a genius at mimicry." He is perhaps the only mimic who, for both his ability in impressions and his creativity in writing material, can be called "genius."

AUDIO: *Ill Will* (Jubilee), *Tapped Wires* (Roulette), *All About Cleopatra* (Topical), *The New First Family* (Verve)

FILMS incl.: *The Buddy Holly Story* (1978), *I Wanna Hold Your Hand* (1978), *Broadway Danny Rose* (1984)

TV: "The ABC Comedy Hour/The Kopycats" (1970)

# K

## ISH KABIBBLE

### (Merwyn Bogue, January 19, 1908–  )

The name Ish Kabibble meant laughs on Kay Kyser's radio show. In Yiddish "Ish Kabibble" means "I should worry?" Back in 1913 Eddie Morton sang the novelty hit "Ish Ga Bibble" and, five years later, Harry Hershfeld recorded "Abe Kabibble Does His Bit," the first in a series of "Abe Kabibble" comedy 78s.

It would be quite a while before "Ish Kabibble" arrived, but when he did, he had the biggest hits of all. He sang the 1937 nonsense classic "Three Little Fishies," selling 5 million copies, and added another foolish favorite, "Mairzy Doats." He looked as silly as he sounded, sporting little-boy bangs. In real life he was pretty smart. Aside from his novelty vocals for Kyser's band, Ish Kabibble was their trumpet player, publicist and bookkeeper, also responsible for setting up hotel reservations.

Born in Pennsylvania, he graduated from West Virginia University in 1930 majoring in economics. He didn't need to major in English to read this kind of poetry on Kyser's show: "I sneezed a sneeze into the air. It fell to earth I know not where. But you shoulda seen the looks on those in whose vicinity I snoze."

By the '60s the ex-novelty singer had become a successful real estate salesman, using "Ish Kabibble" on his business card. His autobiography was published by Louisiana State University. He hadn't changed a bit. In the book he wrote: "In I come, down I sot. I wrote a book and up I got."

AUTOBIOGRAPHY: *Ish Kabibble: The Autobiography of Merwyn Bogue* (1989)
FILMS: *That's Right, You're Wrong* (1939), *Playmates* (1941), *Carolina Blues* (1944)
TV: "Kay Kyser's Kollege of Musical Knowledge" (1949–50)

## MADELINE KAHN

### (September 29, 1942–  )

An extravagant comic actress often used in Mel Brooks films for her exaggerated good looks and tongue-in-cheek romanticism, Madeline Kahn had a setback at the very start of her career. After her parents divorced, the Boston-born girl went to New York with her mother and at six made her singing debut on "Horn and Hardart's Children's Hour." She recalls: "I cried on the air and they dragged me off the second time I was on."

A decade later Kahn's career goals were more within reach. She eventually won a drama and music scholarship to Hofstra University, performing a Ruth Draper monologue at her audition. She graduated in 1964. A fine singer, Kahn played Musetta in a Washington Opera Society production of *La Bohème* and was Cunegonde in *Candide* with the New York Philharmonic.

She joined the *Upstairs at the Downstairs* musical comedy revue in 1966–67, appeared in *New Faces of 1968* and co-starred in the Danny Kaye musical *Two by Two.* She blossomed on Broadway, receiving two Tony award nominations, for *In the Boom Boom Room* and *On the Twentieth Century.*

She went on to an even more acclaimed film career. An early comic performance was in *The Dove,* a short film satirizing Ingmar Bergman movies, complete with hilarious mock-Swedish dialogue. She was a favorite of Peter Bogdonavich, who cast her in her first major film, *What's Up Doc,* and then *Paper Moon,* for which she received an Academy Award nomination.

Mel Brooks was a big fan, casting her in four of his films. For his *Blazing Saddles,* she again received an Academy Award nomination. One of the film's highlights was her Marlene Dietrich parody song, "I'm Tired," sung as a saloon hostess: "I've been with thousands of men, again and again, they sing the same tune. They start with Byron and Shelley then jump on your belly and bust your balloon! Tired! Tired of playing the game! Ain't it a friggin' shame? I'm so—let's face it, everything below the waist is kaput!"

Whether in campy comedies or more subtle satires, Kahn knows how to keep a straight face. She was excellent in slightly tilted satires, such as the detective yarns *Clue* or *The Cheap Detective.* In the latter, the air of mystery extends to everything. Peter Falk: "What time is it now?" Kahn: "I'd rather not tell you that till I know I can trust you." Kahn achieved the same blend of tasteful mania as Mel Brooks' girlfriend in *High Anxiety.*

Kahn was not able to parlay her film success into sitcoms. Her television series "Oh Madeline" was short-lived, as was "Mr. President," which featured her as George C. Scott's sister-in-law.

Over the years Kahn has taken her comedy seriously, making sure that there is always some intriguing subtlety to her comic roles. Discussing film directors who want to position the camera for a leering laugh, she said, "When they want to focus on my breasts and I say no, they think I have a hangup."

AUDIO: *Mel Brooks' Greatest Hits/High Anxiety* (Elektra), *New Faces of 1968* (Warner)
BROADWAY: *New Faces of 1968* (1968), *Promenade* (1969), *Two by Two* (1970), *In the Boom Boom Room* (1973), *On the Twentieth Century* (1978)
FILMS incl.: *What's Up Doc?* (1972), *Paper Moon* (1974), *Blazing Saddles* (1974), *Young Frankenstein* (1974), *At Long Last Love* (1975), *The Adventures of Sherlock Holmes' Smarter Brother* (1975), *Won Ton Ton, the Dog Who Saved Hollywood* (1976), *High Anxiety* (1977), *The Cheap Detective* (1978), *Simon* (1979), *The First Family* (1980), *Wholly Moses* (1980), *Happy Birthday Gemini* (1980), *History of the World Part I* (1981), *Yellowbeard* (1983), *Slapstick of Another Kind* (1984), *City Heat* (1984), *Clue* (1985), *Betsy's Wedding* (1990)
TV: "Comedy Tonight" (1970), "Oh Madeline" (1983–84), "Mr. President" (1986)
VIDEO: *Saturday Night Live: Madeline Kahn*

## GABE KAPLAN

### (March 21, 1946–   )

A low-key, curly-haired Brooklyn stand-up comic who had a lot of observational comedy routines about "the old neighborhood," Gabe Kaplan went from journeyman monologist to star thanks to a bit he called "Holes and Mellow Rolls."

It was a richly evocative routine about goofy high school kids and their penchant for "ranking contests." Dumb stuff: "I heard your mother is like the Pennsylvania Railroad—she's been laid all over the country." "Up your hole with a Mellow Roll—and twice as far with a Hershey Bar." A gem of its kind, similar in style to a rollicking Bill Cosby reminiscence (R-rated, though, which Cos never was), the routine led to a comedy album and, when seen in California by the right people, the sitcom "Welcome Back Kotter."

Kaplan found himself acting for the first time, teaching a gang of "Sweathogs," a stereotypical group of teens of varied ethnicity, including John Travolta as Vinnie Barbarino. He found himself with a hit show. It was an unlikely success story, considering Kaplan had always wanted to be a baseball player (he was "all hit and no field") and had ended up a bellboy at a New Jersey hotel.

The shy bellboy watched the comics who were booked at the hotel and was inspired. "It just hit me that to be a comic you didn't have to be an extrovert, you only had to have a funny bone basically and the presence to perform." Kaplan gave it a try. His mother went along with it, but only after she wrote a note to Woody Allen asking if the idea was plausible. (Woody wrote back assuring her it was worth a year's experimentation.)

Before the year was over, Kaplan was making progress. Comedy clubs were only beginning in the late 1960s, but there were enough for him to find an identity. His first major bit was an impression of Ed Sullivan drunk out of his mind introducing his show ("where's Topo Gigio, the little faggot mouse"). Then the quiet, almost deadpan comic began coming out of his shell for more personal comedy about growing up, doing bits about gym class, masturbation and "Mellow Rolls."

Self-described as "inhibited and shy," Kaplan was an unlikely star. A loner who "Kotter" show producer James Komack found socially inarticulate and strange, Kaplan's personality caused a few rifts on the set. His tides of enthusiasm ebbed into distant calm, leaving many confused, including his wife on the show, Marcia Strassman. Labeled "difficult" at worst, bland at best by interviewers seeking a colorful star to write about, Kaplan was an enigma. After a few seasons John Travolta emerged as a huge film star and departed. This, plus a lack of freshness in new episodes, contributed to the show's decline.

Kaplan's personality was not suited to the movies, and for a time he lived completely on the show biz fringe, spending most of his time playing (and winning) in Las Vegas poker tournaments. In 1983 he began touring in a one-man show about Groucho Marx, showing touches of brilliance in portraying the comedy legend in his prime and as a wistful but spirited old man.

Preferring the world of poker playing and golf tournaments, Kaplan kept a low profile in stand-up, in 1990 surfacing with "Sports Nuts," a call-in show

featuring interviews with athletes on Los Angeles radio station KLAC. In 1991 he demonstrated his deft skill at poker finishing 11th out of 250 players at the World Series of Poker.

AUDIO: *Holes and Mellow Rolls* (ABC Dunhill)
BIOGRAPHY: *Gabe Kaplan: A Spirit of Laughter* (Jacobs, 1978)
FILMS incl.: *Fast Break* (1979), *Nobody's Perfekt* (1981), *Tulips* (1981)
TV: "Welcome Back Kotter" (1975–79), "Lewis and Clark" (1981–82)
VIDEO: *Catch a Rising Star's 10th Anniversary Concert*

## MICKEY KATZ

### (Meyer Myron Katz, June 15, 1909–April 30 1985)

The most popular Yiddish comedy parodist, Mickey Katz is known for his albums of the 1950s and 60s of "kosherized" popular tunes. The humor was basic: "That's Amore" became "Oy That's Morris," "Ghost Riders" became "Borscht Riders" and "Witch Doctor" became "Knish Doctor." "How Much Is that Doggie in the Window" turned out "How much is that pickle in the window, the one that's on top of the pail?"

While some Gentiles bought his music for the unusual Klezmer rhythms, Katz's albums were best sellers mostly among Jews. While Allan Sherman had some crossover appeal, Katz's lack of lyrical subtlety and his use of Yiddish limited his audience. Even among Jews there was some controversy, since Katz's wheedling nasal vocals were almost offensively stereotypical.

Born in Cleveland, Katz was fortunate to attend Central Junior High School, where musical instruments were given free to underprivileged kids. After winning amateur contests with his old (1898) clarinet, he became a pro and joined several bands, including one led by Phil Spitalny. Also a monologist, Katz performed on WTAM radio in Cleveland and published a comedy book in 1929. These included Yiddish retellings of fairy tales ("Little Red Rosenberg") and famous stories ("Romeo and Juliyente"). There were even nursery rhymes, all written in dialect: "Mery had a leetle lemb, who followed her ontze de treck. A big strit car came along, smesh, cresh! Now Mery wears de lemb on de beck."

In 1934 he and his band, Mickey Katz and His Kittens, began touring. Betty Hutton once sang and danced in the group. After appearing with her for USO shows during World War II, Katz joined Spike Jones' band for two years, recording some vocals and adding some gurgling sound effects to the novelty tunes. In 1948, not thrilled by Spike's paychecks or the constant touring, he again formed his own band, began making albums and assembled touring variety shows, such as *Borscht Capades*. Though his stardom was eclipsed by Allan Sherman in the 1960s, Katz gave it one last go with "Hello Solly" in 1967, singing songs and telling classic jokes. By that time his son, Joel Grey, was established in show business, starring on Broadway in *Cabaret*. Katz never begrudged Allan Sherman the fame but always felt that he had paved the way for him by convincing major record companies that ethnic musical humor could sell.

In recent years there's been some nostalgic interest in Katz's work, but much of it seems to center around his straight music, most evident on the album *Music for Weddings, Bar Mitzvahs and Brisses*. Klezmer musicians, including Don Byron, formerly with the Klezmer Conservatory Band, had recorded his compositions. Joel Grey made some guest appearances when Byron took his Katz music on the road. Talking about an old Katz recording, Byron raved about the "beautiful voice-leading, four-part harmonies, melodies that go down to 16th notes, four-part fugues, really fancy writing." For most Katz fans, the joy was simply his bouncy melodies, ridiculous lyrics and silly comic vocals.

AUDIO: *Borscht* (RCA), *Mickey Katz* (Capitol), *The Borscht Jester* (Capitol), *Katz at the UN* (Capitol), *Katz Puts on the Dog* (Capitol), *Katz Pajamas* (Capitol), *Mish Mosh* (Capitol), *Most Mishige* (Capitol), *Sing Along with Mickele* (Capitol), *Weddings, Bar Mitzvahs and Brisses* (Capitol), *The Hits of Mickey Katz* (Capitol), *Hello Solly* (Capitol)
BOOK: *Nonzense on Who's Whoo End Wat's Wat* (1929)
BROADWAY: *Borscht Capades* (1951), *Hello Solly* (1967)

## ANDY KAUFMAN
### (January 17, 1949–May 16, 1984)

As a performance artist, Andy Kaufman was provocative and outrageous. But since the term "performance artist" was virtually unknown in the late 1970s, he was billed as a comic, which confused audiences who often found his anticomic theatrical routines obnoxious and annoying.

In his time, Kaufman was praised by critics in the same way critics raved over Andy Warhol's soup can paintings, nonevents and day-long movies. They admired his challenging and original vision—especially since they weren't paying to see it. Typical Kaufman stunts, such as reading from *The Great Gatsby* or sitting and watching his laundry go around in a portable dryer on stage, were hilarious as anecdotes—but not to sit through.

Along with a few other hip comics, such as Steve Martin and Albert Brooks, Andy Kaufman was unsatisfied by the awkward artificiality of stand-up comedy. The whole idea of coming out and telling jokes to strangers was becoming a corny cliché. Kaufman chose to go after the audience—the passive, complacent people who were accepting such entertainment. Kaufman shook them up by goading female ringsiders to come up and wrestle him, by deliberately telling bad jokes (as "The Foreign Man"), and by parodying such deadly old comic devices as funny-faced lip-synching to records.

Some hip audiences shared the joke, singing along as he did every chorus of "100 Bottles of Beer on the Wall." Other times, they threw ashtrays and screamed out curses. Often the audience didn't know what to do; they chuckled uneasily, sensing something profound in his experimentation, not about to complain that they didn't know what was going on.

In 1975 Kaufman began appearing on television's "Saturday Night Live," but after a dozen outings, a put-on poll asking viewers their opinion of him backfired. They resoundingly voted him off the show. In February 1981 Kaufman disgraced himself on the similar show, "Fridays." His idea was to stage a mock wrestling fight that would shock the audience. At first some questioned if it was real or just a joke. But either way, the consensus was that it was pretty stupid. His sister Carol recalled in *Rolling Stone* magazine, "I don't think 'Fridays' was entertainment to the average person. . . . with Andy, it all goes back to the self, the I. What am I going to get pleasure out of, not how am I going to pleasure the audience. . . . they want him to tell jokes. But no. That would be selfless."

Kaufman grew up a lonely kid involved in fantasy. He read wrestling magazines and collected Elvis Presley memorabilia. At one point he was sent to a psychologist. He was such a passive kid he'd get beaten up by a school bully and not even attempt to fight back. On stage he turned passive-aggressive. Often he'd stretch out in front of the audience and pretend to go to sleep, the crowd trying to jeer him awake.

"I just want to play with their heads," Andy remarked. He got away with it because he was so shockingly strange audiences were usually not sure what to do. Besides, no matter how obnoxious he was acting, there was a streak of vulnerability to him and a cute, bewildered look on that baby-fat young face. His most successful character, "The Foreign Man," had the wide-eyed help-me look of José Jimenez. He parlayed it into national popularity as "Latka Gravas," the foreign cab man on television's "Taxi."

Even on a fairly safe sitcom, Kaufman brought controversy. Many "Taxi" viewers felt his odd character, and episodes based on his comically weird European customs, ruined the realism of the show. Calling "Taxi" just "a vehicle" for money and exposure, Kaufman seemed content to mouth old burlesque catch phrases (such as a fast "tank you very much!") and serve up silly double entendres (in his language, the sex act was called "nik nik"). Later he began to demand scripts more in keeping with his experimental nature, such as the one in which Latka undergoes a personality crisis and turns into an irritating creep named Vic Ferrari.

Meanwhile, in stand-up, Kaufman invented Tony Clifton, an egotistical Vegas lounge singer. As Kaufman's "opening act," Clifton would keep singing until the stage was littered with debris. Kaufman insisted Clifton was real, not a character, and insisted on letting the opening act stay on for hours. It was just the latest example of Kaufman lacking the discipline to get off a worn-out put-on.

Still, the Kaufman cult included other comics. "It was great to watch the *audience* watching him," Robin Williams recalled. Comics admired Andy for his completely opposite stance—a comic who'd do anything *not* to get a laugh. While most comics wanted applause and "love," Andy seemed to enjoy being hated. David Letterman booked him, saying, "I think it's important to have guests who annoy the public." Kaufman wanted to guest on Letterman's show in December 1983 so he could perpetrate a good gag. Letterman would be scripted to ask "What did you get for Christmas, Andy?" And Andy would answer, "Cancer."

Once again, the line between Kaufman's life and his art was blurred. He didn't do the show. He did die of cancer a few months later at only 35. When the shocking news first hit, many were skeptical. They assumed it was just Andy going too far for a gag.

FILMS: *In God We Trust* (1980), *Heartbeeps* (1981)
TV: "Van Dyke and Company" (1976), "Taxi" (1978–83)
VIDEOS: *My Breakfast with Blassie; Comedy Tonight; Andy Kaufman Special; Saturday Night Live: George Carlin; Catch a Rising Star's 10th Anniversary; Sound Stage*

## DANNY KAYE

### (David Daniel Kaminsky, January 18, 1913–March 3, 1987)

One of the most charismatic comedians of the 1940s, Danny Kaye did it all and did it with charm. He was an engaging novelty singer, a believable comic actor and performed slapstick and face-making with enough puckish whimsy to amuse even sophisticates. Unlike his contemporaries, Bob Hope and Red Skelton, Kaye was not afraid to show his underlying sensitivity and intelligence, two traits that made him a favorite of critics who rarely praised comedians.

His characteristic personality in movies was "depressive-manic." As a professor, a milkman or a lazy dreamer, he was meek, pleasant and vulnerably somber over his ineptness or failures. Then, in crisis, he'd become bright, bold and vibrant, saving the

A lovable clown, Danny Kaye was known for his funny patter songs and his roles as a heroic daydreamer. Remember: "The pellet with the poison is in the vessel with the pestle." Photo from the author's collection.

day with slick comic grace and heroism. Unfortunately, many of his films have dated badly, especially the musical comedies.

Kaye's best-loved comic devices were his whimsical facial expressions (he could go instantly from tragic tears to gleeful hysteria), and his dazzling, tongue-twisting novelty songs such as "The Lobby Number" in his film *Up in Arms*. In that one he announces the credits in a matter of seconds: "Screenplay by Gluck from a stageplay by Motts from a story by Blip from a chapter by Ronk from a sentence by Dokes from a comma by Stokes from an idea by Grokes—based on a Joe Miller's Jokes!" He would make many albums of fey nonsense songs that managed to delight children as well as their more demanding parents. Often he'd insert deliberate gibberish into his songs. Critics unfamiliar with what was really a funny variation on scat-singing dubbed the result "git gat gittle." Many of the nov-

elty numbers were written by his wife, Sylvia Fine, whom he married in 1940.

Born in Brooklyn (the family name has been spelled Kominsky and Kuminsky, but the Singer and Freedland biographies confirm Kaminsky), Kaye dropped out of school in his teens and got his start in the Catskills, where he joked, sang, danced and eventually became one of The Three Terpsichoreans. In the winters he worked with straight man Nick Long. Kaye made some movie shorts in 1937 and 1938, including *Dime a Dance* and *Cupid Takes a Holiday*, but his career didn't take off until 1939 when he appeared in Broadway's *Straw Hat Revue*. His lighthearted, manic approach was pure delight. As Shelley Berman recalled, Kaye arrived "just before World War II when we were just desperate and nothing made sense."

*Lady in the Dark* was another smash hit for him, his mix of whimsy and sophistication earning lavish praise. Some were surprised that Kaye's sophistication didn't come from traditional schooling. "I don't regret never having gone to college," he once said. "Some of the biggest schlemiels in the world are college graduates. When I was 20 I was playing in the Orient—I was getting my education around the world."

At first the Broadway star had trouble making the transition to film. Movie boss Sam Goldwyn told him "Do something about your nose," complaining that Kaye looked "too Jewish." Over and over Goldwyn complained, but Kaye refused to be brainwashed. So Goldwyn settled for a hair wash and dye job. Kaye was turned into a blond. His hair remained unnaturally light through much of his film career before returning to its natural reddish brown.

Kaye's stardom continued on stage and in films through the 1940s. In 1948 he played The Palladium in England, with Winston Churchill, Laurence Olivier and the Royal Family in the audience. The English always loved his blend of silliness and sophistication, and with his songs, anecdotes and patter, he became one of the last of "The Entertainers," a dying breed of singing, dancing, joking stars exemplified by Eddie Cantor and Sophie Tucker. The following year his first biography appeared, *The Life Story of Danny Kaye*.

In 1953 Kaye starred at The Palace in a long-running one-man show and received a special Academy Award in 1954. Kaye thrived on television in the 1960s, starring in a variety show that fused the styles used by other popular hosts of the day. There were mild songs (the staple of Andy Williams) and comic sketches (the style of Red Skelton). Kaye won an Emmy for his television series and after its run was content to tour with live concerts and guest on television specials.

Kaye returned to Broadway as Noah in the musical *Two by Two*. When he injured his hip during the show's run, he kept right on going. This Noah would board his ark on crutches or even roll up the gangplank in a wheelchair if he had to.

In the 1970s and '80s he devoted most of his energies to performance and charity work on behalf of the United Nations and UNICEF. His work with children and his fondness for them made him a beloved figure all over the globe. He could have flown around the world himself, since he had a pilot's license. He delighted in taking friends up in his own small plane, dazzling them with a few plane tricks and loops. Of his UNICEF work, he commented, "I think maybe I get along so well with kids because I'm not afraid to be a child."

Once a skeptic approached Kaye and asked, "In your work for sick children, don't you think you are only interfering? Isn't this God's way of taking care of the world's overpopulation?" Kaye pondered it a moment and said, "That's a very sound theory. Why don't you apply it the next time your son is sick?"

Kaye was occasionally coaxed back to television (he played Captain Hook in a new version of *Peter Pan*) and took a straight acting role in *Skokie*, a 1981 film about a Holocaust survivor. He won a Peabody Award in 1983 and appeared around the country as a guest conductor with symphony orchestras until health problems intervened. He underwent quadruple bypass heart surgery in 1983 and a hip replacement in 1984.

In 1986 Kaye was awarded the Legion of Honor by French President François Mitterrand. Though sometimes frail due to his ailments, Kaye continued. The redhead displayed sparks of his greatness and all of his warmth when he made a rare guest appearance as a dentist on an episode of television's "Cosby Show."

Kaye's name was suddenly thrust into the spotlight in 1992 with the publication of Donald Spoto's book on Laurence Olivier, which confirmed the long-rumored ten-year affair between the two stars in the 1940s and early '50s. Rather than paint a tawdry picture, the author only noted that Kaye's appeal sexually was rather similar to his appeal as an entertainer: "Kaye was not simply amusing, but vibrantly intelligent; not merely encouraging and admiring of Olivier, but also quick-witted, original and capable of discussing the fine points of art, literature and music history. . . . Kaye also had an understanding with his wife," which allowed him such affairs without guilt.

Danny's humor was always evident, whether dressing up with Olivier as bride and groom for a private party, or playing a practical joke on Sir Laurence. At a New York airport, Olivier was detained by a gruff customs man who insisted the actor be strip-searched for contraband. Afterward the customs man pulled off his elaborately constructed latex mask and wig. Standing in front of the startled Olivier was the ever-puckish Danny Kaye.

AUDIO incl.: *Mommy Gimmie a Drink of Water* (Capitol), *Grimm's Fairy Tales* (Golden), *Entertaining* (Columbia), *Gilbert and Sullivan* (Decca), *Best of Danny Kaye* (Decca)

BIOGRAPHIES: *The Life Story of Danny Kaye* (Richards 1949), *The Danny Kaye Story* (Singer, 1957), *The Secret Life of Danny Kaye* (Freedland, 1985)

BROADWAY: *The Straw Hat Revue* (1939), *Lady in the Dark* (1941), *Let's Face It* (1941), *Danny Kaye* (1949), *Danny Kaye's International Show* (1953), *Danny Kaye* (1955), *Two by Two* (1971)

FILMS incl.: *Up in Arms* (1944), *Wonder Man* (1945), *Kid from Brooklyn* (1946), *The Secret Life of Walter Mitty* (1947), *A Song Is Born* (1948), *It's a Great Feeling* (1949), *On the Riviera* (1951), *Inspector General* (1949), *Hans Christian Andersen* (1952), *Knock on Wood* (1954), *White Christmas* (1954), *The Court Jester* (1956), *Merry Andrew* (1958), *Me and the Colonel* (1958), *The Five Pennies* (1959), *On the Double* (1961), *The Man from the Diner's Club* (1963), *The Madwoman of Chaillot* (1969), *Peter Pan* (1975), *Skokie* (1981)

TV: "The Danny Kaye Show" (1963–67)

Not even a cat on his head could make Buster Keaton—"the Great Stone Face"—blink. Keaton stands as the closest rival to Chaplin for the title "Best Silent Film Comedian." Photo from the author's collection.

## BUSTER KEATON

### (Joseph Francis Keaton, October 4, 1895–February 1, 1966)

"The Great Stone Face," Buster Keaton wore an almost constant mask of glum and grim determination. This was not very unusual, many silent film comedians relied so much on slapstick gags that they masked their faces with thick, eccentric mustaches that concealed all trace of a smile.

What was different about Keaton was his attitude. His character hoped for the best but expected the worst. He wasn't quite so stoical or cynical that he was not motivated toward success. He was just re-

alistic about it. In the film *The Navigator,* Buster christens a ship—and then shows no emotion as it sinks. In Keaton's world life is like that.

Keaton was slammed around early in life and seemed to accept it. Harry Houdini gave him his nickname, calling the boy a "rough little Buster" when he took falls and abuse in a violent slapstick comedy act put together by his acrobat parents. He was "The Human Mop" in semisadistic sketches about a pesky child and his parents. Ad copy for The Three Keatons read, "Maybe you think you were handled roughly when you were a kid. Watch the way they handle Buster!"

Keaton was punched and thrown around the stage by an often-drunk father who made it look real. Buster developed a deadpan style early. A sure-fire gag: Buster gets belted, shows no emotion, then cries "Ouch!" a good five seconds later.

Keaton learned never to laugh along with the audience. "If something tickled me, and I started to grin, the old man would hiss 'Face! Face!'—that meant 'freeze the puss'! The longer I held it, why, if we got a laugh, the blank pan or the puzzled puss would double it. He kept after me, never let up, and in a few years it was automatic."

The Keatons played vaudeville and were at The Palace in 1917. At this point, the young comic was ready to go solo. Fatty Arbuckle was in New York making a movie and Buster joined him in *The Butcher Boy.* In some early films he did show emotion (he actually laughs in *Fatty at Coney Island*), but not in his own solo films.

Keaton's ability as a gag man and movie director enhanced his value. He put his theories into practice in shorts such as *Cops,* which featured not only intricate and acrobatic slapstick but breathtaking visuals (an entire raging army of police chasing one spindly fellow down the street). Keaton graduated to features, earning acclaim for *The General* and for *Steamboat Bill Jr.,* the film that included both the famous scene of Buster in the midst of a cyclone and one quintessential visual gag both bombastic and subtle. In it Keaton walks away from a building and the wall suddenly teeters over. Buster is certain to be crushed. As the wall comes down one open window perfectly frames him and he's spared. Unlike another thrill comic, Harold Lloyd, Keaton doesn't react with wide eyes and sweat. He reacts to the detached wall falling on him—with detachment. Keaton did take pride in his work, and he did have clear-cut theories on constructing gags and keeping the audience guessing, but he was modest about it. In highlights in Lloyd's work (dangling from a building, for example) or Chaplin's work (balletlike moves in triumphing over a huge bully), the attention is on the artist as an individual: Isn't Lloyd daring? Isn't Chaplin clever? But when, usually in long shot, Keaton was running from giant boulders, battling a windstorm, eluding cops or simply gazing into the face of disaster, the viewer identified the character more as "man" than as a comedian named Buster.

Lloyd was beloved as the All-American boy, and Chaplin, with his pathos, touched viewers hearts. They were amply rewarded and lived in palacelike homes. Keaton did not fare quite as well. He was respected and admired by critics and fans but not really loved. After all, viewers were seeing him more as a symbol than the boy next door or the poor tramp on the street. Keaton continued to work and signed with MGM, but could not secure total control over his films. These new movies were disappointing and he spiraled downward, hampered by drinking and marriage woes. He and actress Natalie Talmadge broke up in 1933. That year he made his last starring film, *What, No Beer* about his efforts to become a success ("I'd give ten dollars right now to be a millionaire!"). There were a few brief, magic moments of clever visual inventions, but the film was actually dominated by co-star Jimmy Durante. A second marriage failed in 1935 while Keaton filed for bankruptcy.

Part of Keaton's problem was the talkie era. As a stoic, he worked better in silence. In silent films the viewer didn't know if the character was intelligent or stupid, he was simply a figure crossed by fate. But once he spoke, his personality had to match his lines. In *Parlor, Bedroom and Bath*, for example, he played a shy, virginal fool who is afraid of women. This was at odds with his sturdy, midwestern rasp of a voice, his athletic build and the stony face that belied emotions of desperation and confusion. The film was an adequate "French farce," but Keaton was wrong for the role. And the corny spoken gags did a disservice to Keaton, whose sight gags were

sophisticated and intricate. Sitting down to dinner, he sees something wrong: "That lobster's only got one claw." Waiter: "Sometimes they lose one in a fight, you know." "Well, why don't you bring me the winner?"

In the 1940s Keaton was primarily behind the scenes as a gag man, notably for Red Skelton in *A Southern Yankee*. The '50s were also tough. Keaton appeared in *Limelight* with Charles Chaplin, but two years later turned up working in a circus, Cirque Medrano in Paris. In 1957 he got $50,000 for *The Buster Keaton Story*, a film staring Donald O'Connor, and there was some renewed interest in him, including appearances on television's "Candid Camera," "The Twilight Zone" and commercials. In 1959 he received a special Academy Award "for his unique talents which brought immortal comedies to the screen."

The early 1960s saw Keaton return from alcohol problems and find a secure homelife in his third and final marriage His film character—realistic, hard-edged, devoid of pathos—struck a chord with modern movie audiences. After years of neglect, he was suddenly judged as the prince of comedy to King Chaplin. Keaton wasn't accorded the status of living legend, but at least he was working. In 1962 he reissued *The General* to good reviews, though he was so shy he couldn't go into the theater to hear the crowds roar with laughter. He was the subject of the experimental short *Film* in 1965 by Samuel Beckett. Most of his best appearances in old age were in virtually silent comedy roles. His last film *War Italian Style*, circulated after his death.

In the decades since, many of Keaton's films have been reissued and several books have been written about The Great Stone Face. He was the unemotional man who actually produced a wide range of emotions in his audience: escapism, existentialism, optism, pessimism and something more powerful than any "ism"—laughter.

AUTOBIOGRAPHY: *My Wonderful World of Slapstick* (1982)

BIOGRAPHIES: *Keaton* (Blesh, 1966), *Buster Keaton* (Robinson, 1969), *The Look of Buster Keaton* (Bernayoen, 1983), *Buster Keaton* (Moews, 1977)

FILMS incl.: *The Butcher Boy* (1917), *The Bellboy* (1918), *Out West* (1918), *One Week* (1920), *The Paleface* (1921), *Cops* (1922), *The Frozen North* (1922), *Balloonatic* (1923), *The Three Ages* (1923), *Sherlock Jr.* (1924), *The Navigator* (1924), *Go West* (1925), *Battling Butler* (1925), *The Seven Chances* (1926), *The General* (1927), *College* (1927), *Steamboat Bill Jr.* (1928), *Cameraman* (1928), *Spite Marriage* (1929), *Dough Boys* (1930), *Parlor, Bedroom and Bath* (1931), *Sidewalks of New York* (1931), *Passionate Plumber* (1932), *What, No Beer* (1933), *Le Roi des Champs-Elysees* (1934), *An Old Spanish Custom* (1935), *Hollywood Cavalcade* (1939), *The Villain Still Pursued Her* (1940), *Li'l Abner* (1940), *Bathing Beauty* (1944), *That's the Spirit* (1945), *That Night with You* (1945), *In the Good Old Summertime* (1949), *You're My Everything* (1949), *Sunset Boulevard* (1950), *Limelight* (1952), *Around the World in 80 Days* (1956), *It's a Mad Mad Mad Mad World* (1963), *Beach Blanket Bingo (1965), A Funny Thing Happened on the Way to the Forum* (1966), *War Italian Style* (1967)

VIDEOS: *Buster Keaton: A Hard Act to Follow; The Best of Candid Camera; Legends of Comedy; Comedy: Serious Business; A Few Moments with Buster Keaton and Laurel and Hardy*

## DIANE KEATON

**(Diane Hall, January 5, 1946–   )**

Born in Los Angeles, California, Diane Keaton starred in many dramatic films and published books of photography, but over the years the public still remembers her best as the sweet, awkward, sloppily dressed *Annie Hall*, the star of Woody Allen's greatest comedy.

Keaton won an Academy Award as Annie, the almost perfect match for Woody's modern neurotic man. Annie was vulnerable, shy, wistful, gently confused and preoccupied, and so naive and open she could actually use an expression like "oh, la-de-dah." The character seemed close to the real actress, considering Keaton's nervous talk show appearances. Her influence extended into the pop culture of the day. Her clothing actually became a fashion trend.

But some, such as John Simon, complained of her one-note comedy style: "Her work, if that is the word for it, always consists chiefly of a dithering, blithering, neurotic coming apart at the seams—an acting style that is really a nervous breakdown in slow-motion."

Keaton seemed to know she couldn't duplicate *Annie Hall* and really didn't try, opting for dramatic roles instead and indulging herself with books of photography, such as *Reservations* in 1980 and *Still Life* in 1983. After some critical success in the box office failure *Reds,* she had three bombs in a row: *Shoot the Moon* earned $4 million in rentals but cost $12 million to make, *Mrs. Soffel* brought in $2 million on a budget of $14 million and *The Little Drummer Girl* took in just $4 million on a budget of $15 million.

With her career in the doldrums, she returned to comedy with the hit *Baby Boom,* which tried to fuse her unsympathetic *Sleeper* character (now an all-business Yuppie) with a few dashes of Annie Hall confusion (the standard trying-to-diaper-the-baby routine). Keaton even resurrected a bit of the old Annie Hall "um, yeah, ahhh, mmmm" preoccupation and frazzle. The hit film seemed to arrive at the right time, but critics did find it obvious, written to a formula and too much of a cliché.

A subsequent film, *The Lemon Sisters,* tried the patience of most critics. *The New York Times* declared, "Among many candidates for the worst scene are . . . just about any of Ms. Keaton's reaction shots. . . . Just imagine Diane Keaton at her most hysterical, as an asthmatic cat lover who returns from a stay in a hospital to find that her two best friends have thrown her a cat-free welcome home party. 'Those cats need me!' she yells. 'Those cats love me!' You can make up your own lemon jokes."

BIOGRAPHY: *Diane Keaton* (Jonathan Moor, 1991), *The Diane Keaton Scrapbook* (Munshower)
BOOKS: *Reservations; Still Life* (1985)
BROADWAY: *Hair* (1968); *Play It Again, Sam* (1969)
FILMS incl.: *Lovers and Other Strangers* (1970), *Play It Again, Sam* (1972), *The Godfather* (1972), *Sleeper* (1973), *The Godfather Part II* (1974), *Love and Death* (1975), *I Will, I Will, for Now* (1976), *Harry and Walter Go to New York* (1976), *Annie Hall*

(1977), *Manhattan* (1979), *Reds* (1981), *Shoot the Moon* (1982), *Mrs. Soffel* (1984), *The Little Drummer Girl* (1984), *Crimes of the Heart* (1986), *Heaven* (1987), *Radio Days* (1987), *Baby Boom* (1987), *The Good Mother* (1988), *The Lemon Sisters* (1990), *The Godfather Part III* (1990)

## GARRISON KEILLOR

### (Gary Keillor, August 7, 1942– )

Shambling and homely, sporting a mop of unruly hair and a pair of thick glasses, Garrison Keillor found an audience of like-minded shut-ins on National Public Radio. Billed as the tallest comedian on radio, he began broadcasting fey reports about his mythical "Lake Wobegone." Each broadcast, a tongue-in-cheek, slightly warped send-up of small-town life, drew appreciative nods and knowing smiles from his fans.

Young radio listeners who had never heard of Fibber McGee and Molly's home in "Wistful Vista" were tickled by the name "Lake Wobegon" alone. Those unfamiliar with Bob and Ray found satisfaction in Garrison's similar style of fake commercials, such as the one for "Powdermilk Biscuits . . . [that give] shy people the get up and go to do what needs to be done." And those who found David Letterman too obvious appreciated Keillor's deliberately understated lameness. He meditated on Lake Wobegon "where all the women are strong, all the men are good-looking, and all the children are above average." It was the place for Ralph's Pretty Good Grocery: "If you can't find it at Ralph's you can probably get along without it."

Keillor was born in Minnesota. His mother was a strict member of the Plymouth Brethren, fundamentalists who disapproved of "dancing, drinking, card playing . . . and too-friendly association with nonbelievers." He listened to dowdy radio shows of inspirational lectures and "home folks" philosophies and the music of the Grand Ole Opry—influences that turned up, twisted, on his radio show. After receiving his B.A. from the University of Minnesota, he hosted a show for Minnesota Public Radio in 1968. He also wrote for *The New Yorker*, and, after a 1974 piece on the Grand Old Opry, decided to mix commentary and an affectation for bluegrass

music into "A Prairie Home Companion." As with most comedy that really wasn't funny, it could not have survived without a grant from the National Endowment for the Arts.

Though he lacks the "crossover" appeal for late-night talk shows or comedy club appearances, Keillor has had enough devoted fans to market over 200 "Lake Wobegon"–related products, developing a business similar to ones selling mail order cheese and fruitcake. Keillor's show lasted on radio from 1974 to 1987. When it left the air, humorist P. J. O'Rourke wrote an elegy in *Rolling Stone* magazine: "It was America's last available source of humor for wet-blanket academic types who drink sherry, wear suede elbow patches on their sport coats and poke you in the chest with their pipe stems. They will now have to go back to memorizing the captions from *New Yorker* cartoons."

After a brief, well-publicized "retirement" to Copenhagen with his wife Ulla and his four kids, Keillor returned to the airwaves in 1989 with "Garrison Keillor's American Radio Company of the Air." The vogue for his humor was past its peak. "People aren't responding," said a programming director at Philadelphia affiliate WHYY-FM.

Keillor is still peddling his particular brand of lopsided Americana, chipping away at listeners' brain cells with images that could sometimes be amusingly pathetic: "It's like what we used to do in Minnesota on real hot days—go down to the river and lay in the shallow part. If you were really still, the minnows would come by and bite the dead skin off you. Your body was attacked by tiny, tiny fish. It felt so good, it was like a message. You'd come out chewed and refreshed."

AUDIO: *Prairie Home Companion Anniversary Album* (PHC), *The Family Radio* (PHC), *News from Lake Wobegon* (PHC), *Tourists* (PHC), *Lake Wobegon Loyalty Days* (Virgin), *News from Lake Wobegon* (PHC, set of 4 CDs), *More News from Lake Wobegon* (PHC, set of 4 CDs)

BIOGRAPHY: *The Man from Lake Wobegon* (1988)

BOOKS: *Happy to Be Here* (1986), *Lake Wobegon Days* (1985), *Stories from Lake Wobegon* (1990), *Leaving Home: A Collection of Lake Wobegon Stories* (1989), *We Are Still Married* (1990)

## AL KELLY

### (Abraham Kalish, December 18, 1896–September 7, 1966)

Ironically, the master of comic double-talk got his stage name from double-talk. The kids in Abe Kalish's New York neighborhood called him "Kally," which ended up "Kelly." But as the proud, Jewish comic insisted, "I never legally changed it."

Al Kelly's change from straight comic to double-talk specialist happened in the Catskills: "During one of my routines I got mixed up and words came out scrambled. It sounded funny and I got so many laughs that I started a new language—double-talk."

Though double-talk was a comic device before Kelly, he refined it. "I differ from the rest of the double-talk boys. They just use the jumbled stuff straight, so you know it's phony. I mix it up with legitimate and familiar-sounding phrases of the topic at hand."

The double-talker worked with Lew Parker in the Catskills in the early 1930s, then with Willie Howard. Later he was a partner for Joey Adams. When that relationship soured Kelly concentrated on solo work, from brief guest spots in sketches to banquet appearances putting on people with five minutes of authoritative-sounding nonsense.

In his 1966 autobiography he explained: "You hear it fine, but you can't understand it. This makes people laugh. I don't know why. It would certainly seem that once you have heard a man talk as though his teeth were in backwards, that would be the end of it and if you heard him again it would call for a yawn, but the oftener you hear it, the funnier it is, which is the part that has baffled me. Yet, though I don't understand it, I have to respect it, because making people laugh is as important as anything I can think of."

In October 1964 Kelly celebrated his 50th anniversary in show business. He started as a singer and dancer appearing for $3 at New York City's Webster Hall. For the occasion, the *New York Times* headlined, "Al Kelly Flons 50 Fural Years." That the *Times* would put double-talk into the "paper of record" was a lasting tribute to Al Kelly's charm and skill.

Kelly was known within the comedy industry as one of the most charitable performers. He was always willing to give a free show for a worthy cause.

His last appearance was at a Friar's Club event honoring Joe E. Lewis. As Joey Adams recalled, he "was the hit of the night. As the laughter soared he sat down. There was a standing ovation. He stood up to take another bow. Seconds later he collapsed. . . . he was gone."

Joe E. Lewis later declared, "If you have to go, that's the way to do it. Leave with the cheers ringing in your ears."

AUDIO: *Funny, You Don't Look It* (RCA Victor)
AUTOBIOGRAPHY: *Al Kelly's Double Life* (Kelly and Rose) 1966
BROADWAY: *Crazy with the Heat* (1941), *Priorities of 1942* (1942), *Star and Garter* (1942), *My Dear Public* (1943), *Hilarities* (1948)
FILM: *Singing in the Dark* (1956)
TV: "Back that Fact" (1953), "The Ernie Kovacs Show" (1956)

## LEW KELLY

### (August 24, 1879–June 10, 1944)

Drug comedy didn't begin in the 1960s. As early as 1908, Lew Kelly was earning riotous applause and laughs as "Professor Dope," the dreamy, pasty-faced addict who lived in another world. The Professor might begin a monologue with a solemn declaration: "I was just run over by an auto." After a pause he explained, "I wasn't hurt, because I was under a bridge." Not quite sure how he got on stage, but definitely "on" something, Professor Dope confided, "I'm the fellow who thinks he's me but he's not."

Kelly toured the burlesque circuit with "The Behman Show" and later "Follies of the Day," developing a catch phrase, "Everything's all right but decidedly wrong." Decidedly odd were his ramblings: "I was working on the roof of the Washington Monument when the balloon ran over a tack, but I bought the picture for ten cents because it was a corner lot and no one else would eat it." A review for the *Chicago Record* in 1913 was mystified but amused by Kelly's "serious nonsense" and his report on "how to kill a gimpf by pushing an empty lake over on top of him and hurting his feelings."

Kelly later toured the country in minisketches he wrote himself, his cast including a black face actor

(Edward C. Jordan) and a female impersonator (Tom Martelle). "I was bound and gagged by pirates," he told one stooge in a sketch. "Oh, just like in a show, wasn't it?" Kelly: "No, they used new gags."

Born in St. Louis, Kelly teamed with Charles A. Mason around 1906 but became the solo "Professor Dope" shortly after. The *Kansas City Post* reported in 1908, "he has a series of dreams from the excessive use of dope which keeps the audience guessing . . . brings down the house." Kelly recalled the origin of the character: "In Portland one day I saw a dope fiend on the street, a cheerful sort of chap, who, of course, was a tragedy, but who made you laugh by seeing things harmlessly that weren't there. . . . that was the beginning of Professor Dope." He acknowledged that there were other "dope" comics before him, such as Toledo's Junior McCree, but his style was deadpan and different. "I figured a long time before I decided to try the slow-walking, erratic sort of dope fiend that I am portraying out there. Usually patrons of burlesque shows want the quick, slam-bang type of a comedian but ever since I have undertaken to portray the dope fiend, I mean the real hop smoker, I have made a success of it."

He told the *Cleveland Plains Dealer* in 1915 his technique was to outguess the audience: "If they think you'll roar, that's your cue to hold silence. If they think you'll say nothing, have something to say and have it good. When I first started the game of life I realized that to get ahead you have to do something a little differently, better, than anyone else." Kelly even toured differently. He traveled via corpse. He did it "by haunting undertaking establishments and getting a commission to ride with a corpse being taken back for burial. That was a law in those days. A corpse, to be expressed, had to be accompanied by two live men who were responsible for its safe transit."

Kelly's marriage in 1912 evidently inspired his 1914 sketch "Dope's Legacy," in which Professor Dope marries a "wicked girl with shapely legs" for inheritance money but is sidetracked trying to buy keyholes to fit a set of keys he found. In 1917's "The Thirteen Chairs," he played a detective assembling a group of suspects for the final solution. *The Newark Star Eagle* headlined his opening night with: "Watson, the needle! Lew Kelly's at Miner's!" Kelly toured London in 1919 and 1925, and remained popular on stage for many years. He made a few film appearances in the 1930s (notably the Three Stooges short *Spook Louder*) and had bit parts in three W. C. Fields movies, most prominently as Adolph Berg in *Man on a Flying Trapeze.*

FILMS incl.: *Barnum Was Right* (1929), *Laughter in Hell* (1933), *Strange People* (1933), *The Old Fashioned Way* (1934), *Six of a Kind* (1934), *The Nitwits* (1935), *Man on a Flying Trapeze* (1936), *Man from Music Mountain* (1938), *Tough Kid* (1939), *Taxi, Mister* (1942), *Lady of Burlesque* (1943)

## EDGAR KENNEDY

### (April 26, 1890–November 9, 1948)

They all aggravated him: Laurel and Hardy, Wheeler and Wolsey, Olsen and Johnson, and The Marx Brothers. All he could do about it was his famous "slow burn." His eyes squinted shut, his lips tensed with rage, and one hand slowly grinded across his forehead and bald dome in anguished chagrin.

A former vaudevillian and Keystone Kop, Kennedy arrived at Hal Roach's studio to play annoyed cops and sour relatives in Laurel and Hardy and Our Gang comedies. He worked for other studios as well, singing an opera aria as comic relief in *Night Waitress,* playing a judge in *Crazy House* with Olsen and Johnson, and turning up as "Old Naked Skull," another judge, in W. C. Fields' *Tillie and Gus.* He was a warden in *Hold 'em Jail* with Wheeler and Woosey, and the detective who needed prim and salty Edna May Oliver to solve his case for him in *The Penguin Pool Murder.* One of his most memorable battles was with Harpo Marx in *Duck Soup.* At first he seemed to be winning, but eventually his lemonade stand and hat were demolished by the mute during furious, perfectly timed slapstick. Ready to wash his hands of the whole thing, he went home to take a bath. But the moment he settled in, Harpo came rising from the suds.

Kennedy starred in *The Average Man* comedy series of domestic shorts from 1931 to 1948 with Florence Lake as his wife and Dot Farley as his mother-in-law. The shorts were popular at the time but relied heavily on Kennedy's "slow burn." The sitcom aggravations the poor average man endured were often beyond annoying—things that would have led anyone else to homicide. At least, after so many years, he had a starring role. His older brother, actor Tom Kennedy, never managed more than buffoon roles as a lovable thug or thick-witted cop. (Tom may be remembered best as a confused ship's officer chasing The Marx Brothers around the deck in *Monkey Business.*)

Edgar had a wife and two children. Though suffering from throat cancer, he kept making films. He was going to be honored with a testimonial dinner, but died two days before it was scheduled to occur. Brother Tom died in October 1965.

FILMS incl.: *Tillie's Punctured Romance* (1914), *The Knockout* (1914), *The Great Vacuum Robbery* (1915), *Skirts* (1923), *Going Crooked* (1926), *A Pair of Tights* (1928), *They Had to See Paris* (1929), *Penguin Pool Murder* (1932), *Son of the Border* (1933), *Duck Soup* (1933), *Tillie and Gus* (1933), *All of Me* (1934), *Twentieth Century* (1934), *Murder on the Blackboard* (1934), *Kid Millions* (1934), *Silver Streak* (1934), *Woman Wanted* (1935), *The Bride Comes Home* (1935), *Mad Holiday* (1936), *A Star Is Born* (1937), *Super Sleuth* (1937), *It's a Wonderful World* (1939), *Charlie McCarthy, Detective (1939), Laugh It Off* (1939), *Li'l Abner* (1940), *Margie* (1940), *Blondie in Society* (1941), *Snuffy Smith, Yard Bird* (1942), *The Falcon Strikes Back* (1943), *Air Raid Wardens* (1943), *Crazy House* (1943), *It Happened Tomorrow (1944), Mad Wednesday* (1947), *Variety Time* (1948), *My Dream Is Yours* (1949)

VIDEO: *Edgar Kennedy Slow Burn Festival; Edgar Kennedy: The Slow Burn Re-Ignites*

## THE KEYSTONE KOPS (See also FATTY ARBUCKLE, EDGAR KENNEDY and FORD STERLING.)

According to creator Mack Sennett, the police lineup for his cops were: Charles Avery, Bobby Dunn, George Jesky, Edgar Kennedy, Hank Mann, Mack Riley and Slim Summerville. Their leader, Chief Teheezel, was Ford Sterling. But as critic Walter Kerr noted, "They were flailing tailcoats and inverted spittoon helmets lurching past the camera so swiftly and so interchangeably that it can be something of a game trying to guess which members of the stock company are Kops each time around."

Several men turned up in a Kops uniform, including Fatty Arbuckle, Bobby Vernon, Eddie Sutherland, Bill Campbell, Bill Williams, Glen Cavender, Eddie LeVeque and an actor named John F. Kennedy. The formula rarely varied; it was thrill comedy, with viewers loving the way the symbols of authority bumbled and fell out of their own patrol cars as they raced along. Other studios copied the format, creating their own cop films.

Eddie LeVeque recalled, "The fast chases were trick photography. The film would be speeded up mechanically. For the collisions we used what was called a moving panorama. It was a painting with trees and telephone poles and city buildings and trolley cars. . . . Then, of course, we'd fall out of the cars and do flops, and it all looked real on the screen. . . . I took many a fall that was unnecessary, but everyone was trying to outdo everyone else. There was always that spirit of good-natured competition." Another favorite stunt was the Kop being dragged down the street—the car moving slowly, a platform with rollers underneath his back. The breakneck speed of Keystone Kops comedies was enhanced by broken film frames—deliberately cut frames were respliced so the action would seem faster and jerkier. Sennett knew all the tricks, including running film backward; two cars would pull away from each other, but run backward it seemed as if they were colliding.

*The Bangville Police* released in April 1913 is generally considered one the first "Kops" films, though various dizzy policemen had appeared together in earlier Sennett comedies. Probably the best Kops film was 1914's *In the Clutches of a Gang.* The vogue for the Keystone Kops ended fairly quickly, since all their movies were the same, but they became such a symbol of slapstick comedy that they were often resurrected for comedy shorts, such as the thrill-and-pie fight melee *Keystone Hotel* (1933), and features, such as 1955s *Abbott and Costello Meet the Keystone Kops.*

## ALAN KING

### (Irwin Alan Kniberg, December 26, 1926–   )

It's simple, said Alan King. "Everything I talk about touches a chord in the audience, that's why they laugh. . . . what happens to me makes people laugh. It's a funny world we live in. If we didn't laugh about it we'd cry."

What always happens to King is aggravation, the kind that makes the average family man go through the day with a headache and an ulcer, snarling and sneering over: the family, the plumber, the carpenter, the decorator, the house, the doctor, the lawyer, bad phone service and lost airline luggage.

Barely concealing his irritation, his eyes glaring, his mouth half flattened in silent rage but twisting at the corners in disgust, King's rage is never out of control like Don Rickles'. Instead he simmers, slow-burns and in controlled bursts of enunciated fury gathers steam and "lets 'em have it."

Always aggressive, King grew up in tough neighborhoods on the Lower East Side of Manhattan and in Brooklyn. He had seven brothers and a sister. There were many mouths to feed and not enough money. "I don't honestly think that an absence of money is funny. We went on relief when I was three years old and for nine years my father couldn't get a job in his trade." King began working after he left Boys High School in Brooklyn: "I wasn't a dropout . . . I was a throwout. I majored in truancy and class-cutting."

He was a drummer and a boxer before becoming a comic in the Catskills. He was fired from one of his first jobs, at the Hotel Gradus, when he opened with: "When you work for Gradus, you work for gratis!"

King became a regular on the club circuit, reaching his first peak opening for Judy Garland at The Palace on Broadway in 1956. Though a contemporary of Lenny Bruce and a man whose comedy was firmly based in aggression, King chose a different path, working classier clubs, talking about suburbia, reaching a middle-class audience. Hip comedy critics didn't see much heroism in King's "Ed Sullivan Show" appearances of the 1960s as he took on gardeners and stewardesses; but he was reacting to what was around him—and what was on the minds of the average guy who didn't read the newspaper as thoroughly as Mort Sahl and who considered the phone company more of a threat than Russia.

Wearing a vested suit, smoking a cigar, he was the guy who had worked hard for the good life, only to find that it wasn't so good. Take suburban schooling: "We live directly across the street from a public school, and my boys can't attend! We don't live in the zone! It's right across the street! I can

Alan King's stand-up act is a visceral explosion of complaints and one-liners. Photo from the author's collection.

spit on the school from my front door, which I've done on several occasions. They tell me the zone line runs through my house. According to the school board, if my kids slept in the garage, they could go to that school. My kids sleep in the garage? In my house I sleep in the garage!"

King had a few best-selling humor books in the 1960s and began branching out as an actor decades later. Though he appeared in movies as early as 1955's *Hit the Deck*, he had his first major co-starring role in *Just Tell Me What You Want* opposite Ali MacGraw. King was amusing as the sadistic head of a quit-smoking company in *Cat's Eye*, won fine notices when he played Nathan Detroit in a 1980 revival of *Guys and Dolls*, and was effective in a serio-comic role opposite Billy Crystal in *Memories of Me*. Active behind the scenes as well, King produced television shows, films and Broadway shows including *A Lion in Winter*. In 1990 he began an interview show at the Comedy Central Cable Network.

Not just a guy to complain about problems and not doing anything about it, King founded the Alan

King Diagnostic Medical Center in Jerusalem, and, closer to home, raised money for the Nassau (New York) Center for Emotionally Disturbed Children.

AUDIO: *Alan King in Suburbia* (Seeco), *The Best of Alan King* (Bronjo)

BOOKS: *Anyone Who Owns His Own Home Deserves It; Help, I'm a Prisoner in a Chinese Bakery*

BROADWAY: *Judy Garland's New Variety Show* (1956), *Judy Garland* (1959), *Guys and Dolls* (1965), *The Impossible Years* (1965), *Applause* (1970), *Guys and Dolls* (1980)

FILMS incl.: *Hit the Deck* (1955), *The Girl He Left Behind* (1956), *The Helen Morgan Story* (1957), *Operation Snafu* (1965), *Bye Bye Braverman* (1968), *Just Tell Me What You Want* (1979), *Author! Author!* (1982), *Lovesick* (1983), *Cat's Eye* (1985), *Memories of Me* (1988), *Enemies, A Love Story* (1989), *The Bonfire of the Vanities* (1990)

VIDEO: *Alan King Stops the Presses*

## ALEXANDER KING

### (November 13, 1900–November 16, 1965)

Where could a thief, morphine addict and failing author go to fine fame and fortune? "The Jack Paar Show." When crusty old Alexander King turned up on Paar's show one night, he delighted a nation with his iconoclastic observations and caustic humor. Paar recalled that "rambling along in a stream-of-consciousness style, he was by turns witty, irreverent, poetic, outrageous, and vitriolic." The raconteur was soon a regular, his books suddenly best-sellers. He even began making lucrative concert appearances, reading from his works and offering anecdotes about his life and times.

Typical of his colorful, curmudgeonly style (all that's missing is his argumentative Austrian accent) is this fragment from his visit to a kidney specialist: "I wanted to reach a purely human level of sympathy and understanding with him. I wanted him to like me. . . . I'm like an ancient iguana full of splenetic wrinkles. I wanted this character to respond to my personal charm. I covered him with the slime of my amiability until he looked web-footed. I got no response. . . . this squat, ovoid, red-faced man permanently submerged in his uri-

nous misgivings . . . had finally turned into a kidney."

King began his career as a painter "chiefly concerned with the most sinister nudity my fellow man exposes—his face." Later he became an art thief (the Metropolitan Museum lost 50 prints to him). Jailed twice, married four times, author of eight obscure plays, his health had deteriorated after nine years of morphine addiction. For a while he could eat nothing but rice. The aging humorist did not have much time left when he won his fame. The day after appearing on "The Today Show" to publicize his new book, *Rich Man, Poor Man, Freud and Fruit,* he died.

AUDIO: *Alexander King Reads from Mine Enemy Grows Older* (Urania), *Love and Hisses* (United Artists)

BOOKS: *Mine Enemy Grows Older; May This House Be Safe from Tigers; Is There a Life After Birth; I Should Have Kissed Her More; The Great Ker-Plunk; Rich Man, Poor Man, Freud and Fruit*

## SAM KINISON

### (December 8, 1953–April 10, 1992)

The most controversial comic in the last half of the 1980s, Peoria-born Sam Kinison was compared to Lenny Bruce for his deliberate bad taste and Richard Pryor for his dangerous raging on stage and off. For some he was a symbolic primal screamer exploding with inner pain and frustration. For others he was just a trashy lowbrow appealing to woman haters and an audience of hard rock punks.

Utilizing the bombastic, shouting style of a Pentecostal preacher (his first profession), Sam shocked audiences with earthy routines on religion. He wondered why Christ would ever want to return to earth, enacting Christ on the cross ("Somebody get a ladder and a pair of pliers!") and Christ's bitter realization afterward that he was "the only savior who can use his own hand as a whistle!" Another routine that shook people up was Sam's response to famine and starvation. His response to the Ethiopians: "Hey, we just drove 700 miles with your food and it occurred to us that there wouldn't be world hunger—if you people would *live* where the *food* is! You live in a . . . *desert!* Nothing grows here? Dammit, you see this? This is *sand*. . . . We have deserts in America, but we *don't live in 'em!*" His most famous early line, following a raging description of his failed marriages and expensive divorces, was "I don't condone wife-beating. I *understand it.*"

The difference in audience reaction depended on whether they viewed him as "The Beast of Burden" (the nickname he preferred over "Screamin' Sam") or simply "The Beast."

As "The Beast of Burden," Sam was just a frenzied, out-of-control version of loser Rodney Dangerfield. Rodney was Sam's first supporter, giving him several key career breaks, including a 1985 appearance on a *Young Comedians* HBO cable special. Sam was the cynic who couldn't imagine Christ forgiving the sins committed against him. He was the average guy whose guilt and discomfort over starvation led to shouting out an exasperated, ridiculous solution.

As "The Beast," many alarmed critics and audience members simply believed Sam was a shock comic, a man whose religious comedy had no soul, a man who made cruel fun of starving people, a man who not only hated women but advocated murder. As *L.A. Weekly* noted, "What . . . would the public reaction be if the line read, 'I don't condone *Jew*-beating—I understand it.' "

The fine line of what's funny and why was stomped on repeatedly by the short, heavyset Kinison, who had spent five tough years developing his cathartic style, demanding ringsider attention with his screams. When he was banned from The Comedy Workshop in Houston, Kinison staged a mock crucifixion and hanged himself on a cross from across the street. He seemed the perfect candidate to become the next comic martyr in the Lenny Bruce tradition.

At first, the liberal press, rock critics, comedy buffs and Bruce fans were all behind Sam. His career took off. A controversial, censored appearance on television's "Saturday Night Live" added to his notoriety in 1986. His first album sold over 200,000 copies. It was easy for Sam to blast back at his critics, and he often did it with convincing good humor. He wasn't a sadistic satanist telling jokes against Christ. His father was a preacher and Sam had been one as well. And how could he be a misogynist? He loved women. There were only two he didn't like, and they happened to be his ex-wives.

Sam Kinison's deafening shouts of rage appealed to a new wave of comedy fans in the 1980s. Photo from the author's collection.

Besides, wasn't he urging guys to take better care of their ladies so they wouldn't share his fate? He frankly and hilariously explained on stage how to please woman orally by "licking the alphabet . . . they *love* the letter T!"

As fans demanded more outrageous routines and his stardom led him into a fast lane of concerts, interviews and big deals, Kinison's woes increased. Problems on the set of his first movie led to its cancellation; Kinison lost $350,000 in salary. He lost his manager. Worse, he lost his brother, who shot himself mortally during a family reunion.

Kinison tried to live by the comic sword he was swinging. On stage just three days after the funeral, he looked up to heaven and raged, "Liberace! You dead fag! Stay away from my brother!" Like Richard Pryor (a strong influence since Sam first heard the *Bicentennial Nigger* album), Kinison was perceived as self-destructive, dangerous and a druggie. Kinison admitted only to the latter and claimed he gave up cocaine after a bad drug reaction that felt like a heart attack. A damaging article in *Rolling Stone* magazine criticized Kinison's lifestyle and insisted he was heading for self-destruction.

Complaints from gays, feminists and conservatives grew, and his career stalled as record executives, film executives, agents and publicists began to step back. Sam's audience became mostly youthful heavy metal fans, ones who just wanted to hear gross-out comedy, woman and gay bashing, and a lot of cursing. Influenced by the heavy metal musicians he was hanging out with, Sam explored rock singing and made a few semisatiric rock videos featuring heavy metal guest stars and the usual painted-up bimbos.

Gone was the challenging, iconoclastic satire. To the cheers of his foolish, party-animal followers, he raged against the inconvenience of wearing condoms and championed drunk driving: "Child killer? Attempted manslaughter? We don't want to drink and drive, but there's no other way to get home!" He thought up a routine on homosexual necrophilia not for any message but "just to see if I could think up the worst thing and make it funny." Reacting to his own fame and controversy, he spent a lot of stage time snickering over his image and made an ironic catch phrase of critics' demands for "family entertainment."

Sam had been urged to go over the edge for his comic truths. Now he analyzed the AIDS epidemic, declaring it was caused by "a few bored fags" who "had to go in the jungle, grab some monkey," have sex, "and bring us back the black plague of the 80s. Thanks guys!" Gay groups picketed his concerts, scuffling with the sellout crowds that weren't very sympathetic. When Sam hosted "The 2nd Annual International Rock Awards" on television in 1990, guest Elton John suddenly announced, "I'm doing this show under protest. I'd like to congratulate Sam Kinison on being the first pig ever to introduce a rock and roll show."

Kinison insisted, "I'm not a pig. I'm a charitable man. I have a lot of sympathy for anyone who has AIDS. . . . I don't do AIDS jokes in my act anymore. . . . I was pretty insensitive, but back then I was honestly unaware. AIDS is a horrible disease and the people who catch it deserve compassion." Then he complained, "It's acceptable to ridicule the pope or the president, but God forbid you do a joke about gays. The gay community is the last sacred cow in this society."

Kinison's popularity declined sharply in 1990. His screaming was no longer a novelty, and he had said every outrageous thing he could think of. A new bad boy, Andrew Dice Clay, was then getting the headlines. Kinison's year of misery bottomed in

June when his girlfriend was allegedly raped by his bodyguard, a 300-pound man whom Kinison had hired without a background check. Kinison had slept through the entire incident, including the four rifle shots his girlfriend fired (all missing the rapist).

The irony of the incident was not lost on the media. *People* magazine declared, "For years, primal-scream comedian Sam Kinison has built his act on the elements of psychic terror and sexual violence." So, they intimated, he and his girlfriend deserved this.

Most performers want to be liked. According to his third wife, Malika, Sam was trying to tone down gags that were leading to audience hostility and actually move toward "family entertainment" and broader appeal. Married less than a week, they were on their way to a scheduled concert in Laughlin, Nevada when their car was struck by a pickup truck that had veered across the dividing line on U.S. Highway 95 near Needles, California. Sam was driving, without a seatbelt, and was killed. He had told a columnist shortly before his death, "I can see me doing standup at Jackie Mason's age . . . if I can just stay in the business and become a name that every generation is familiar with . . . I'd like to be cast as a normal guy."

At his death, Kinison's star had been eclipsed, but he left a blazing trail. He influenced many performers and sparked the return of uncompromising comedy in the late 1980s the same way Lenny Bruce ignited it in the late 1950s and Richard Pryor in the late 1960s. His best work remains powerful, challenging and valuable.

AUDIO: *Louder Than Hell* (Warner Bros.), *Have You Seen Me Lately* (Warner Bros.), *Leader of the Banned* (Warner Bros.)
FILMS: *Back to School* (1986)
VIDEOS: *Breaking the Rules: Sam Kinison Live; Rodney Dangerfield: It's Not Easy Being Me*

## ROBERT KLEIN

### (February 8, 1942– )

Usually appearing glum and annoyed, Robert Klein began his career as an Alan King for the college crowd. In the 1960s, while King was raging about doctors and airlines, Klein was chagrined, recalling the indignities of teachers and parents—the misery of being "a child of the '50s." He bitterly recalled not being able to go to the men's room alone at five and enduring the stares of women as his mother marched him into the ladies' room. Twenty years later he was still seething: "If I had the moxie to say 'Relax, lady, I'm only five, I'm essentially impotent, I have no desire for you. . . . It's humiliating enough to be in here!' "

His first and best album, *Child of the 50's*, was loaded with bits of trauma, from air-raid drills and meeting a drunken baseball idol, to watching "Our Gang" and reading confusing stories about historical figures: "Garfield was assassinated. Shot by a disappointed office seeker, right? Don't they always say that same sentence? It's crazy. Every time you read his name: James Abram Garfield, 'Shot by a disappointed office seeker. . . .' You look in the *Encyclopedia Britannica* under Garfield, James Abram. It says, 'See Office seeker, disappointed.' "

Klein had gone from the Bronx's De Witt Clinton High School to the Yale Drama School. While struggling as an actor (he appeared on Broadway in *The Apple Tree* in the late 1960s), he taught school. Briefly a member of the Second City improvisational troupe (1965–66), Klein found his best success in stand-up, but these were strange times for a newcomer. The old school of comics were still in power, typified by Alan King appearing on "The Ed Sullivan Show." The few "counterculture" young comics, such as George Carlin, worked mostly in front of college crowds or opening for rock acts. Klein did not fit into either category. He was too straight-looking for the Carlin crowd, too brash and hip for the older audiences.

This was reflected in his comedy style. His one-liners had the caustic bitterness of Alan King, and the attacks were against safe targets: "Hawaiian Punch is 10% fruit juice. What's the other 90%? You'd be better off with paint thinner!" His more cartoonish humor, the kind of thing George Carlin's crowd might like, included his hysterical sound portrait of a car trying to start on a cold morning. The key hit the ignition with the motor whispering "please-don't-try-to-start-me" and when it turned, the motor let out a high-pitched "Leave me a-loooooone!"

While making his perilous way through the generation gap, Klein always looked to widen his appeal with acting roles. His dramatic training was appreciated. Not only did he get occasional sitcom guest spots, he appeared in several films and starred opposite Lucie Arnaz in the hit Broadway musical *They're Playing Our Song*. Always a frustrated singer, Klein insisted on performing some comic versions of 1950s doo-wop and '60s crooning in his shows.

He hosted a talk show on USA cable in the mid-1980s and performed in a one-man show as the "Child of the 50's, Man of the 80's." Klein was now the voice of the disillusioned hippies who cut their hair short and joined the establishment, as well as the middle class who already were mired in the lives of their parents, and the middle-aged looking for someone to sympathize with them. In 1991 he began hosting a variety show on the Arts and Entertainment cable channel.

Typical of his current style is this monologue on air travel: "On an airplane, order Kosher food. Jew and Gentile alike. It throws them into chaos and they deserve that. There's Kosher—the meat must be killed in a certain ritualistic way. And then there's Glatt Kosher, which is ultra conservative. The animal must be killed in a certain way and the person who kills the animal must be killed in a certain way. You have to put up with a little self-conscious banter: 'Will the Jew who ordered the Kosher meal please make himself known to flight attendant Vicki? Will the Jew . . . may I see your genitalia, sir? We have the Jew here.' "

AUDIO; *New Faces of 1968* (Warner Bros.), *I Were a High School Graduate* (Epic), *Howard Who?* (Caedmon), *Child of the 50's* (Brut), *Mind over Matter* (Brut), *New Teeth* (Epic), *They're Playing Our Song* (Casablanca), *Let's Not Make Love* (Rhino)

BROADWAY: *Passionella* (1966), *The Lady or the Tiger* (1966), *The Apple Tree* (1967), *New Faces of 1968* (1968), *Night* (1968), *Morning* (1968), *Noon* (1968), *They're Playing Our Song* (1979)

FILMS: *The Landlord* (1970), *The Owl and the Pussycat* (1971), *Pursuit of Happiness* (1971), *The Rivals* (1972), *Hooper* (1978), *Nobody's Perfekt* (1981), *This Wife for Hire* (1985), *Tales from the Darkside, The Movie* (1990)

TV: "Comedy Tonight" (1970), "TV's Bloopers and Practical Jokes" (1984), "Robert Klein Time" (1987)

VIDEO: *Saturday Night Live: Robert Klein; Child of the 50's, Man of the 80's; Pajama Tops*

## JACK KLUGMAN

### (April 27, 1922–    )

One of the most versatile actors in the golden age of television, Jack Klugman appeared mostly in dramas ("The Twilight Zone"), winning an Emmy for an episode of "The Defenders." But when he got his first series, he played a downtrodden curmudgeonly husband in "Harris Against the World."

The world was too big a target. In the 1970s, in his next series, it was Oscar Madison against Felix Ungar in Neil Simon's "Odd Couple." Klugman, who took over for Walter Matthau in the original Broadway production, was perfect as the sloppy sports writer, his already sorrowful, put-upon face aged into a soft pouchiness that accentuated his character's mild grouchiness. A master of comical frustration and misery, Klugman was versatile whether growling or sulking as he dealt with the aggravations supplied by picky, petty and pesty roommate Felix Ungar (Tony Randall).

Beyond the occasional salty comebacks or food-on-shirt slapstick, Klugman offered hilariously real character comedy, getting laughs from his grim expressions of foreboding and chagrin at the start of his troubles and the ultimate rages and moans at the results. For years after Klugman would remain best known as Oscar Madison.

Years earlier the Philadelphia-born actor was sharing a room in New York with another struggling hopeful, Charles Bronson. He worked in the post office while trying to get stage work. He appeared in *Stevedore* with Rod Steiger, but got most of his breaks on television, on "Playhouse 90" and "U.S. Steel Hour" along with the kiddie series "Captain Video" and a soap opera "The Greatest Gift." Ultimately, it was on television in the 1970s that he went from reliable character actor to major comedy star. Klugman won "Odd Couple" Emmy awards in 1971 and 1973. The man who painted broad comic strokes on "The Odd Couple" appreciated bold comedy such as "Don Rickles, Jack E. Leonard, Buddy Hackett. I laugh at Mel Brooks a lot. . . . if you want to know what makes me laugh—he does."

He married Brett Somers in 1966. They had two kids. When Oscar Madison's ex-wife turned up on episodes of "The Odd Couple," Brett played the part. Later, she became an ex-wife in real life.

After "The Odd Couple" Klugman starred in "Quincy," a crime series about a crusading coroner. Some mild humor was incidental to the part. Off stage, Klugman was crusading too. Brandon Tartikoff of NBC said, "The guy is screaming and working all hours and walking off the set—for what? Not more money, like everybody else. All he wants is a quality show."

Klugman later tried another sitcom, "You Again," but it lacked the chemistry of his earlier shows. Klugman and Randall discussed a new "Odd Couple" movie for NBC but plans were dashed in 1989 when Klugman's health problems began to flare up. In 1990 Klugman underwent cancer surgery, and one of his vocal cords had to be removed. His voice was reduced to a rasp, but the plucky actor went on television to declare that this was minor compared to the other possibilities: "Had I waited three weeks more to go to the doctor I would be dead now."

In 1991 he and Tony Randall filmed some snack food commercials together. Randall made the pitch and Klugman utilized his exquisite range of facial expressions to get the laughs. In summer 1991 fans were delighted when Klugman co-starred with Tony Randall in a one-night-only revival of *The Odd Couple* on Broadway. *Newsday* reported that "although his voice is changed considerably and he was straining at some points, he was still filthy, sloppy, hilarious Oscar Madison. And he brought the house down—or up on its feet, actually."

AUDIO: *The Odd Couple Sings* (London)

BROADWAY: *Stevedore* (1949), *Golden Boy* (1952), *Coriolanus* (1954), *A Very Special Baby* (1956), *Gypsy* (1959), *The Sudden and Accidental Re-education of Horse Johnson* (1968)

FILMS incl.: *Twelve Angry Men* (1957), *Days of Wine and Roses* (1952), *I Could Go on Singing* (1962), *Act One* (1963), *Goodbye, Columbus* (1969), *Two-Minute Warning* (1976)

TV: "The Greatest Gift" (1954), "Harris Against the World" (1964–65), "The Odd Couple" (1970–75), "Quincy" (1976–83), "You Again" (1986–87)

VIDEO: *Buy This Tape, You Hockey Puck*

## TED KNIGHT

### (Tadeus Konopka, December 7, 1923–August 26, 1986)

A hit on television's "Mary Tyler Moore Show," Ted Knight made his character, a ridiculously incompetent and egocentric television newscaster, not only laughable but likable. Ted Baxter would swagger into a room with the confident catch phrase: "Hi, guys!" But viewers could see the insecurity—the need to be one of the guys. With his wide grin and his nervous attention to his looks and silver-blond hair, he got laughs for trying to retain his dignity, charm and bravado—when they weren't there in the first place.

The ultimate in cosmetically appealing but vacant television anchormen, Ted Baxter relied completely on his scripts. "You know what makes this country great? You don't have to be witty or clever, as long as you can hire someone who is." Audiences enjoyed seeing the swaggering clown put down in almost every show, as long as he always bounced back, as boneheaded as before.

Born in Connecticut, Knight studied drama at the Randall School of Dramatic Arts in Hartford, and split his time between local theater productions and work as a disc jockey. He went out to the West Coast but film work was limited. He had a brief scene as a cop tending to Norman Bates in the last moments of Hitchcock's *Psycho*. He appeared in episodes of television's "Wild Wild West" and "The Outer Limits" and did voice work for the 1967 cartoon series "Journey to the Center of the Earth."

"The Mary Tyler Moore Show" established Knight as a television comedy star. He won two Emmy awards for his role and was soon offering variations of it. In films he tended to play more arrogant types (just waiting to be whittled down to size comically), while on television he was allowed to be more sympathetic. His first solo series, "The Ted Knight Show," about the owner of an escort service loaded with sexy ladies, lasted two months. His next offering, "Too Close for Comfort," playing dad to two grown daughters, ran three years on ABC and two additional years in syndication. The comfortable, familiar-formatted series was retitled "The Ted Knight Show" and syndicated independently. Cancer surgery slowed him down. He bravely returned to his show but died a short time later.

BROADWAY: *Some of My Best Friends* (1977)
FILMS incl.: *Psycho* (1960), *Caddyshack* (1980)

TV: "The Mary Tyler Moore Show" (1970–77), "The Ted Knight Show" (1978), "Too Close for Comfort" (1980–85), "The Ted Knight Show" (1986)

## DON KNOTTS

### (July 21, 1924–    )

Well known for playing mild-mannered, nervous little men in stand-up, television and films, Don Knotts seemed to be typed the moment he found work as an actor. After graduating from West Virginia University and serving in the army, Knotts got a role on the television series "Search for Tomorrow." It lasted three years, but he had little dialogue, playing a shy man rendered speechless by everyone except his sister. Actually, Knotts knew a lot about giving speeches and the use of his voice. Bullied as a child, the plucky kid learned ventriloquism to give himself some stature and amaze his friends.

As a stand-up comic, Don created a nervous character tied up in knots. He performed six-minute monologues as a stuttering, trembling banquet speaker, a tongue-tied announcer excitedly stumbling over his words during an exciting game and a frantic political analyst trying to make sense of election returns. The character was based on a banquet speaker he remembered from West Virginia. Knotts brought his jittery personality to "The Steve Allen Show" in "Man on the Street" segments. One of his most memorable appearances was as a twitchy expert in bomb defusal. The little man was simply known as "K.B." Naturally when pressed to explain his initials, the quiet fellow blurted, "Ka BOOM!"

From a character who simmered and crackled and then boiled over, Knotts evolved his television sitcom alter ego, Barney Fife. He got his job on "The Andy Griffith Show" after co-starring with Andy in *No Time for Sergeants* in 1955. He was eventually signed to a five-year contract playing the small-town deputy Barney Fife—bug-eyed, fish-mouthed and a tad spindly. Put in an unlikely position of responsibility, pumped up with misplaced self-confidence, Barney strained to keep his nervousness in check. Since his woes were self-inflicted and his high-strung hysteria caused by his own high opinion of his abilities, audiences laughed and sympathized with the little man who tried to be big.

Typical of his comic fretting was a scene in which he girded up to battle a formidable enemy, little kids:

"I don't like it, I don't like it one bit! I tell you, this is just the beginning. Going around breaking streetlamps . . . next thing you know they'll be on motorcycles and wearing them leather jackets. . . . They'll take over the whole town! A reign of terror . . . today's eight-year-olds are tomorrow's teenagers. . . . Nip it in the bud! . . . You've got to nip it in the bud . . . nip it! You go read any book you want on the subject of child discipline and you'll find every one of them is in favor of bud nipping."

As an Emmy-winning comedy star, and realizing that Andy Griffith was thinking of quitting the show while it was still on top, Knotts chose to star in feature films rather than renew his television contract. He starred in the pleasant comedy *The Ghost and Mr. Chicken* and others geared for children and families. He went back to Griffith's show for five guest appearances over the next few years. In one poignant episode, Barney (now with the Raleigh police department) went back to Mayberry to learn that his one steady girl, Thelma Lou, had married someone else. He said: "What's gone is gone. Can't go back . . . that's the way life is. . . ."

Knotts continued to make mild features, teaming up with Tim Conway for a few Disney movies. He returned to television, replacing Norman Fell on "Three's Company," and appeared on Yakov Smirnoff's short-lived "What a Country" sitcom. He brought his expertise to every comedy show he did. His five Emmy awards attest to his memorable, consistently reliable work. In the late 1980s he was reunited with Andy Griffith on episodes of "Matlock."

BROADWAY: *No Time for Sergeants* (1955)
FILMS incl.: *No Time for Sergeants* (1958), *Wake Me When It's Over* (1960), *The Last Time I Saw Archie* (1961), *It's a Mad Mad Mad Mad World* (1963), *Move over Darling* (1963), *The Incredible Mr. Limpet* (1964), *The Ghost and Mr. Chicken* (1966), *The Reluctant Astronaut* (1967), *The Shakiest Gun in the West* (1968), *The Love God* (1969), *How to Frame a Figg* (1971), *The Apple Dumpling Gang* (1975), *No Deposit, No Return* (1976), *Herbie Goes to Monte*

*Carlo* (1977), *Hot Head and Cold Feet* (1978), *The Prize Fighter* (1979)
TV: "The Andy Griffith Show" (1960–68), "Three's Company" (1979–84), "What a Country" (1987)
VIDEOS: *The Andy Griffith Show Collector's Series: Best of Barney; Bungling Barney Strikes Again*

## HARVEY KORMAN

### (February 15, 1927–   )

One of the most versatile men in sketch comedy, both a fine straight man and comic personality, Harvey Korman won four Emmy awards for his work on television's "The Carol Burnett Show." He could play almost anyone, from a mock Otto Preminger in Burnett's parody of *Sunset Boulevard* to Clark Gable in a sendup of *Gone With the Wind*. Korman scored well opposite Burnett in more believable parts, including a variety of ineffectual, cranky or confused husbands.

Korman was so good at playing "average" men on Burnett's show that he was rarely recognized on the street. This didn't amuse Harvey, who had spent a lifetime toiling for show business fame. He grew up in Chicago, his parents divorcing when he was four. "My childhood stunk. It was very unhappy. We were poor and there's the no-father bit." Some of the other kids in the neighborhood were jeeringly anti-Semitic and punctuated their insults with their fists. In talking to interviewers, Korman rarely dwelled on his early miseries, remarking that, in general, most comedians were all "very bright, very angry, very disturbed, very neurotic people. . . . Most of the people I've worked with who do comedy are serious, introverted, almost tragic . . . that's probably one of the reasons they go into comedy. Maybe they felt unattractive when they were little. Or maybe they were insecure . . . they became clowns as a defense against the world."

After navy service in World War II he tried to enter a journalism school but they'd filled their "Jewish quota." He went to acting school instead. After, he looked for work. "I think if I had any education I would have become a teacher or something but I didn't know how to do anything else. . . . I wasn't a leading man type or a juvenile type.

I was physically wrong for everything. I had a very bad time."

In 1960 he got a break, appearing in "Mr. & Mrs." in Chicago, written by Sherwood ("Gilligan's Island") Schwartz, then head writer for "The Red Skelton Show." Skelton's director, Seymour Berns, caught the show and suggested Harvey come to Hollywood. Harvey's career began to bloom. The six-foot-one actor was the perfect height to play comic authority figures to tall comics Skelton and Danny Kaye. Harvey became a regular on Kaye's show and then "The Carol Burnett Show." The show was so popular that 13 years after its run, he was asked to team with co-star Tim Conway for a series of comic television ads for a cold medicine. Audience identification was still strong.

For films such as *Blazing Saddles* and *The First Family,* Korman relied on his most popular sitcom character type—the small-time conniver with prissy seriousness and ninny mannerisms. His imposing height and serious demeanor were in contrast to his fey, neurotic inner personality. In *The First Family* he got laughs on that incongruousness, not on jokes. In one scene he knocks on a bathroom door to ask the occupant sternly, "Are you making la la or chee chee?" As an actor, Korman's best role was his sympathetic portrayal of Bud Abbot in the television movie *Bud and Lou.*

Over the years Korman has been firmly typed as a petty, exasperated, fretting fool. For 1989's "The Nutt House," a television show that lasted only five episodes, he played a hotel manager trying to maintain his dignity and pretense while presiding over a shambles. Touring his hotel with the new owner: "Here's the room where over 400 men and women consummated their relationships." "The bridal suite?" "No, the broom closet. . . . And here we have our famous presidential suite where seven presidents have spent the night. Two together. . . . All I can tell you is they were both Republicans."

BROADWAY: *Captain Brassbound's Conversion* (1950)
FILMS incl.: *Gypsy* (1962), *Lord Love a Duck* (1966), *Don't Just Stand There* (1968), *The April Fools* (1969), *Blazing Saddles* (1974), *High Anxiety* (1977), *Americathon* (1979), *History of the World Part I* (1981), *The Invisible Woman* (1983), *Curse of the Pink Pan-*

*ther* (1983), *Trail of the Pink Panther* (1987), *Munchies* (1987)
TV: "The Danny Kaye Show" (1963–67), "The Carol Burnett Show" (1967–77), "The Tim Conway Show" (1980–81), "Mama's Family" (1983–84)," "Leo and Liz in Beverly Hills" (1986), "The Nutt House" (1989)
VIDEO: *Evening at the Improv*

## ERNIE KOVACS

### (January 23, 1919–January 13, 1962)

One of the most startlingly original satirists of television's golden age, Ernie Kovacs got laughs the offbeat way. One of the more unexplainably hilarious features of his shows was the appearance of "The Nairobi Trio," which was nothing more than three people in gorilla masks moving jerkily like clock figures to a simple tin-whistle tune. Then one would periodically hit another over the head with drumsticks. Kovacs' pioneered trick video comedy to create his own strange comic world where he could smoke a cigar underwater, ponder a house where water pours on an angle from the sink and encounter the surreal even by opening a book. Opening his copy of *Camille,* he heard coughing. His live show was anarchistic; he was one of the first to turn the camera around and joke with the studio audience and crew, laughing at the pretense of slick production. In an age of manners and propriety, he'd open a show by announcing "Thank you for inviting me into your home. But couldn't you have cleaned it up a little?"

Born in Trenton, New Jersey, Kovacs had a wicked sense of humor even as a child. "I pretended I was frying the cat in the oven," he recalled. When his parents rushed to open the oven door, inside was a cardboard version of the cat with a sign on it that read "Phew, that was a close one." He once handed out gum to his pals—which was really a laxative.

After an affluent childhood (his parents even bought him a pony), Kovacs attended drama school in the late 1930s but was sidetracked by pneumonia and pleurisy, spending over a year and a half in a hospital. Unfit for military service, Kovacs found work as a disc jockey. Once, as a stunt, he stayed awake on the air for a full week. Kovacs had a wide-

One of the great innovators in the art of wacky video comedy, television pioneer Ernie Kovacs tried anything for a laugh, from "exploding" books to seemingly smoking a cigar underwater. Photo from the author's collection.

awake personal life thanks, in part, to his eccentric mother, who always urged girlfriends to go all the way with him. "Ernie has to have sex!" she insisted.

Through the 1940s, he appeared on a variety of radio programs, wrote a regular comic newspaper column and developed a dry style similar to that of Bob and Ray. In a parody of "Believe It or Not," he reported on the amazing case of "the wife of Paul H. Fletcher." She died in 1846 and "her husband Paul passed away from grief 74 years later!"

After a local show in Philadelphia, he moved to national television. Aside from his trademark sight gags, Kovacs gave audiences their first taste of dadaist humor, singing "Mona Lisa" in Polish and offering odd news items instead of traditional one-liners: "Mrs. Arnold Frumkin of Liver Bile, Arkansas raised a cat, a rat, a rattlesnake and a raccoon as pets in an apartment only ten feet square. Oddly enough, the animals got along very well, and shared Mrs. Frumkin equally." He indulged in bristling

"sick" comedy from time to time, including the sketch "Whom Dunnit," where panelists on a game show try to figure out who shot the contestant. "I'm sorry, panel," says Ernie, "but your time is up. The contestant is dead." The O. Henry of comedy, he specialized in quick vignettes with a twist ending: a man describes a cake as being extremely light. He lets go of it and it floats away.

His comic fantasy show, replacing "Kukla, Fran and Ollie" during the summer of 1951, was called "Ernie in Kovacsland." Television networks knew he was an original but didn't know how to use him, altering his formats, offering him a 15-minute show one year, a half hour the next, scheduling him at night, during the day and night again. Today some viewers don't see what the fuss is all about. His bits, wild at the time, seem tame and predictable, such as the famous blackout sketch in which Kovacs pats the hood of his used car and it falls through the floor.

He influenced a generation of comedians who employed his trick special effects and adopted his style of nonjoke bizarre musing. Many copied his technique of making blackout video gags from cartoon concepts. A typical Kovacs sight gag, such as a man opening a copy of *War and Peace* and observing cannon fire coming out, could easily have been a spot cartoon in a magazine. Part of Kovacs' genius was in allowing his imagination not only to run wild but run wild *outside* the rigid formats of the day. Like Harold Lloyd, Kovacs was obsessed with the mechanics of his gags. Figuring out how to do them was half the fun. He created the illusion of smoking a cigar underwater by sitting in a filled tank and, after removing his cigar from his lips, spitting out a mouthful of milk. It formed realistic "smoke clouds."

Kovacs learned to add humanity to these scientific gags, developing characters such as lispy poet Percy Dovetonsils (his parody of Alexander Woolcott and a generation of radio poets) and the pathetic Eugene, who lived in a world of amplified sound effects (his shoes squished whenever he walked). Eugene was one of the few characters at all similar to one of Kovacs' comedy idols, Jacques Tati. Always a daring innovator, Kovacs produced a half-hour silent television special in 1957 in his Eugene character and aired it directly after a raucous special starring Jerry Lewis. Over the years as

Kovacs experimented with different styles of comedy, he moved from CBS to NBC to Dumont.

These bewildering turns were nothing compared to the confusion in Kovacs' personal life. After he and his first wife divorced, she kidnapped his two daughters. He somehow maintained his funny television comedy during his tense, heartbreaking three-year hunt for them, but he nearly went broke doing it. The story was the subject of an acclaimed 1984 television movie, *Ernie Kovacs: Between the Laughter*, scripted by April Smith.

After Kovacs found his daughters, the Internal Revenue Service found Ernie. They claimed he owed half a million dollars in taxes. His compulsive gambling and extravagant lifestyle were partly to blame. Television audiences began to see even more of the bushy-browed cigar-smoking comic as he feverishly guested on variety shows, starred on quiz shows, wrote books and made films. He was paid $100,000 for his role in *Sail a Crooked Ship*, but that hardly made a dent in his debts. An underrated actor, Kovacs made a vivid impression on Alec Guinness, who worked with him on *Our Man in Havana*. He recalled Kovacs was "outrageously extrovert, wild, rash, gypsylike, and, in a Goonish way, just about the funniest man I have ever met." Guinness recalled the time he wandered past Kovacs' hotel room and saw the door open. "He was sitting at a desk typing furiously, a vast cigar jammed in his face. . . . I noticed there were about half a dozen lovely girls, all totally naked, sprawled about the room reading magazines." When Guinness offered to close the door and give him privacy, Ernie said, "What would people say? They'd think the worst. With the door open they can see for themselves it's all perfectly innocent."

January 13, 1962 was a Saturday, but there was no rest for Ernie. He had recently filmed a television pilot with Buster Keaton called "Medicine Man." He had a new film project. And he'd spent the late afternoon editing a new television special to be shown on the 23rd, his birthday. There was no rest this evening. He had to dress up and be scintillating at a party at Billy Wilder's house. Ernie wasn't big on such things, but he knew it was a good place to make connections for film work, and comics such as Lucille Ball, Milton Berle and his friend Jack Lemmon would be there.

He got to the party as soon as he could, trying to relax a bit after his long day. His second wife, comedienne Edie Adams, had arrived earlier. Kovacs was worn out by 1:30 A.M. Since Edie had come to the party in her station wagon, and there were two cars to drive home anyway, Kovacs told her to stay and enjoy the rest of the party. He left his car and took the station wagon.

It had started to rain. He hadn't gone far when the car skidded; he hit the brakes and the car spun around sideways into a telephone poll. The comedian's chest and ribs were crushed, bones stabbing into his heart, liver and lungs. He was found slumped halfway out the door of the car. Jack Lemmon came out to identify the body. Blood tests put his alcohol level at .11 percent, barely over the .10 now considered intoxicated.

Restlessly creative, a man who was forever exploring and mastering new media, from radio and television to books and films, Kovacs' motto was a parody of "Nothing in Excess." It appeared on his tombstone: "Nothing in Moderation."

AUDIO: *Ernie Kovacs* (Columbia)

BIOGRAPHIES: *Nothing in Moderation, aka The Kovacsphile* (Walley, 1987), *Kovacsland* (Ricco, 1991)

BOOKS: *Zoomar* (1957), *How to Talk at Gin* (1961)

FILMS: *Operation Mad Ball* (1957), *Bell, Book and Candle* (1958), *It Happened to Jane* (1959), *Our Man in Havana* (1960), *Pepe* (1960), *Wake Me When It's Over* (1960), *Strangers When We Meet* (1960), *North to Alaska* (1960), *Five Golden Hours* (1961), *Sail a Crooked Ship* (1961)

TV incl.: "Time for Ernie" (1951), "Ernie in Kovacsland" (1951), "Kovacs on the Korner" (1952), "The Ernie Kovacs Show" (CBS 1952–53, Dumont 1954–55), "Take a Guess" (1953), "Time Will Tell" (1954), "One Minute Please" (1954–55), "The Ernie Kovacs Show" (NBC 1955–56), "Tonight" (1956–57), "Take a Good Look" (1959–61), "Silents Please" (1961)

VIDEOS: *Kovacs!; Television's Original Genius*

# L

## BERT LAHR

**(Irving Lahrheim, August 13, 1895–December 4, 1967)**

"A comedian," Bert Lahr said, "he's got to be able to make you laugh even when he don't say a word. And if he can't make you cry as well as laugh, he's no real comedian."

A real comedian, Bert Lahr was a Broadway comedy superstar, a master of bombastic burlesque. A great actor as well, critics paid their respects to him late in his career when he starred as Estragon in Beckett's *Waiting for Godot*.

Lahr was born and raised in Manhattan, in the German section of town, 81st Street and York Avenue. He went to P.S. 77 and Monroe High School. At 15 he was already a veteran of vaudeville shows, including *Nine Crazy Kids*. In 1915 writer Billy K. Wells brought him to burlesque. He sang comic songs in 1917's *Best Show in Town* and honed his tough comic exterior. His catch phrase was a jaundiced "Some fun, ay kid?" A few years later he and his wife hit the big time with their sketch "Lahr and Mercedes—What's the Idea?"

Lahr played a cop trying to arrest an exotic Spanish dancer: "Stop, stoooop! What's the idea? What's the idea of massaging the atmosphere?" The dancer is indignant: "Are you speaking to me?" Lahr stares at her chest. "Yeah to you—and to you too. . . . It's a public nonsense to shimmy or vibrate any part of the human astronomy." "I believe you're intoxicated." "Well, if I ain't, I'm out seven bucks."

The slapstick and jokes, some bold and risqué, were only part of the appeal. The audience bought Bert Lahr, the putty-faced character who talked tough but was obviously soft-headed and soft-hearted, never quite in control. The cop-and-dancer sketch appeared in Broadway's *Harry Delmar's Revels*. The following year Lahr made the move to comic actor in *Hold Everything* in which he played Gink Shiner, punchy boxing champ.

Lahr suffered a temporary setback when Joe E. Brown was tapped for the film version. A serious man and a worrier, Lahr fired off a letter which was printed in *Variety:* "I am greatly surprised and amazed to find that Joe E. Brown so boldly lifted my original business, mannerisms, methods and phrases which I have been identified with for years. . . . This is hurting my reputation, livelihood, and future in talking pictures."

Lahr had to wait a few years for a really good film role, but when he found it, he made it a classic: the Cowardly Lion in *The Wizard of Oz*. He stole the show with his gruff clowning and amusingly timed nuance. He was tough and tender as the bewildered lion who has the tools to be king of the forest, but is held back by fear. His "Courage" solo, a number consisting of abrupt shifts between bombast and subtle bits of nonsense, was made vivid not so much by the silly lines but the way he delivered them.

Each line was different. First, New York–accented toughness: "What makes the Hottentot so hot?" Then ridiculously misplaced heroism: "Who put the ape in apricot?" Then self-assurance: "What makes the elephant charge his tusk?" Finally, with blundery tenderness: "What makes the muskrat guard his musk?" From mock elegance (he wants to be "king, *just* king!") to big-hearted self-effacement ("Ain't it the truth!"), Lahr poured 20 years of comedy experience into those few golden moments of song.

Throughout the film Lahr kept things lively. He even ad-libbed a few lines, including the scene in which snow begins to fall in the Oz poppy field: "Unusual weather we're havin', ain't it?"

Back on Broadway, Lahr resumed his tried-and-true style in *DuBarry Was a Lady*. In one scene he announces his occupation: "You asked for it: I was a ladies' maid in a gents' room!"

Lahr's tremendous energy worked best on stage, especially when he'd rely on funny faces and sounds to get laughs between the lines. In moments of pain, confusion or aggravation he'd be reduced to a wide-eyed, wide-mouthed, guttural cry of "ng-ong, ng-ong, ng-ong!" That trademark catch phrase, or "catch noise," was imitated by fans and impressionists. Lahr's unique comic cadence influenced many and was borrowed for the cowardly "Snagglepuss" on Saturday morning cartoons.

Stage success remained his, but as *Variety* later noted, "while he got great reviews almost always and enjoyed high repute in show business he never rated as a ticket-selling name." Known to be insecure and often glumly depressed off stage, Lahr was clearly frustrated by his situation. He despaired of his reputation as a comic gargoyle and was pained whenever well-meaning fans shouted to him or joked with him on the streets or in restaurants. He expected misery and got it: He did his best work in a play called *The Beauty Part,* which opened during a newspaper strike and closed with no reviews leading patrons to the theater.

Lahr did win over critics with *Waiting for Godot* and in 1964 received a Tony Award for *Foxy*. While generations of television reviewers still enjoyed the screenings of *The Wizard of Oz*, he added to his fame with a famous series of Lays potato chip commercials, portraying (in various makeups and guises), men and women who became frantic after discovering they couldn't eat "just one."

The tireless burlesque comic was still on the go, pushing himself during the filming *The Night They Raided Minsky's*. Suffering from cancer, he didn't make it through the picture. In his biography *Notes on a Cowardly Lion*, son John Lahr recounted Bert's last moments: "I heard him singing in bed. The nurse thought he was calling for help, but bending over him, she saw he was doing an old routine. The words were inaudible, but the rhythm was musical comedy. His last word, whispered two days before a quiet death, was 'hurt.' " But in his prime "Bert Lahr remained unique. His voice never lost its range, his statement never lost its hard truth. He told us about the limitations of the body, about the isolation and humble beauty of the soul. He made a most gorgeous fuss. He made us laugh, until, at times, we cried."

AUDIO: *Bert Lahr* (Mark 56), *Waiting for Godot* (Caedmon), *Two on the Aisle* (Decca), *The Wizard of Oz* (MGM)

BIOGRAPHY: *Notes on a Cowardly Lion* (J. Lahr, 1984)

BROADWAY: *Harry Delmar's Revels* (1927), *Hold Everything* (1928), *Flying High* (1930), *Hot-Cha!* (1932), *George White's Varieties* (1932), *Life Begins at 8:40* (1934), *George White's Scandals* (1935), *The Show Is On* (1936), *Du Barry Was a Lady* (1939), *Seven Lively Arts* (1944), *Burlesque* (1946), *Make Mine Manhattan* (1949), *Two on the Aisle* (1951), *Waiting for Godot* (1956), *Hotel Paradiso* (1957), *The Girls Against the Boys* (1959), *A Midsummer Night's Dream* (1961), *The Beauty Part* (1962), *Foxy* (1964)

FILMS incl:. *Mr. Broadway* (1933), *Merry Go Round of 1938* (1937), *Love and Hisses* (1937), *Just Around the Corner* (1938), *Josette* (1938), *Zaza* (1939), *The Wizard of Oz* (1939), *Ship Ahoy* (1942), *Meet the People* (1944), *Always Leave Them Laughing* (1949), *Mr. Universe* (1951), *Rose Marie* (1954), *The Second Greatest Sex* (1956), *The Night They Raided Minsky's* (1968)

# STEVE LANDESBERG

## (November 3, 1945–    )

A mild-mannered comic, tongue-in-cheek if not deadpan, Steve Landesberg is often subtle, offbeat and hip, which made him an unusual guest on late 1960s television variety shows. Some audiences didn't know what to make of his anti-show biz impressions (including his straight-faced Jolson) or his dry one-liners, but most could enjoy his most accessible character, a stereotypical German psychiatrist.

Born in the Bronx, Landesberg's father owned a grocery store near Yankee Stadium. In the late 1960s he began to work Manhattan comedy clubs. He surprised fellow performers such as David Brenner by experimenting, refusing to do the same routine twice. After years of guest stand-up work, including his first "Tonight Show" in 1971, Landesberg used his German psychiatrist routines as a regular on television's "Dean Martin Presents Bobby Darin" and played a similar character on "Paul Sands in Friends and Lovers."

As a personality, he presents an amiable, slightly eccentric countenance with his tall but stooping posture, short-cropped curly hair, flat smile and small eyes hidden behind his glasses. On talk shows he seems like Randy Newman doing Jonathan Winters, as he sleepily slips in and out of dialect characters, toying around to a semipayoff. On Pat Sajak's brief talk show in 1989, Landesberg mentioned his 1986 marriage to a Southern girl and the strangeness of country music lyrics. He started singing laconically. "I was in prison. Mah girl left me. Ah killed mah pig. . . ." His quick take on a British boxing manager coaching his fighter: "You know you're losing the fight? You know, he's killing you, really. But you're so much better looking. Why don't you spit out your mouthpiece and cast aspersions on his family members?"

Landesberg's ingratiating, quirky personality turned out to be a natural for television commercials, and his hollow, earnest voice is often heard on radio commercials as well. Not always easy to place for film work, he found the most suitable vehicle for his talent when he played Arthur Dietrich on television's "Barney Miller." He was the intellectual detective given to quiet put-ons and unassuming logic. In one episode, Dietrich is preoccupied with research on a slightly old case: "It's been kickin' around awhile—1973." Captain Miller is wide-eyed. "That was seven years ago! Nixon was president!" Says Dietrich evenly, "No, he's got an airtight alibi for this one."

Some of his lines could have been from his stand-up act. Another Dietrich gem: "Honesty is the best policy, but insanity is a better defense."

FILMS incl.: *Blade* (1973), *Leader of the Band* (1987), *Final Notice* (1990)
TV: "Dean Martin Presents Bobby Darin" (1972), "Paul Sands in Friends and Lovers" (1974–75), "Barney Miller" (1976–82)

## HARRY LANGDON

### (June 15, 1884–December 22, 1944)

Harry Langdon has often been called one of the four greats of silent films, but linking Chaplin, Keaton, Lloyd and Langdon seems a bit like Mount Rushmore with Washington, Lincoln, Jefferson and Franklin Pierce. One has tremendous sympathy for Langdon; he was a unique and endearing character and he made a few fine films, but his years in the spotlight were unfortunately brief.

Harry was born in Council Bluffs, Iowa. His parents worked for the Salvation Army. As a teen, Harry helped the family by working in a theater selling tickets. He saw enough shows to realize what he wanted to do with his life. At 13 he joined Dr. Belcher's Kickapoo Indian Medicine Show and eventually worked as a circus clown, acrobat and ventriloquist. Around 1903 he created "Johnny's New Car," a comedy act for himself and his first wife, Rose. He played an inept fumbler who can't get his car fixed and must withstand the complaints of his bossy wife. He actually wheeled a large prop car onto the stage and did so for the 20 years he toured the country with the routine.

Mack Sennett sensed that there might be a place for Harry in films and made a few amusing shorts with him, but his character emerged only when he left Sennett and started working with Frank Capra at First National. Capra called the perfected Langdon character "The Elf." Most thought "Baby Man" more appropriate. He had a round baby face and walked with a childlike hop, his bulky pants leading more than one critic to wonder if he was out of diapers. The innocent look was augmented by powdery makeup, mascara and a lipsticked pout for his frail lips. Langdon's main prop was a dented hat, clearly suggesting that something hard and heavy once landed on him and his brain never recovered.

Audiences felt sympathy for this humble babe in the woods. Women wanted to mother him. Men felt

Harry Langdon, known for his innocent, oddly childlike characterizations, dabbled in pathos as a silent film star. Photo from the author's collection.

superior to him. Children considered him their equal. With Frank Capra as one of his writers, Langdon became a brief box office sensation with *Tramp Tramp Tramp* opposite Joan Crawford and *Soldier Man.* In another highly regarded film, *Strong Man,* he played his comedy opposite a blind girl, predating Chaplin's *City Lights.* He basically played the same character in each film, the one who, in *Saturday Afternoon,* was described as "just a crumb from the sponge cake of life."

Critics expected more excellent work, and Harry tried to churn out three feature films a year. The pace was hectic by any standard. Viewers seemed to think they were seeing too much of Harry. Most film historians agree that what really doomed Langdon was "the Chaplin syndrome," his belief that only he fully understood his character, and that great comedy needed more pathos to win fans' sympathy. Confident in his own comic theories, he split with Frank Capra.

Langdon declared of his film character, "I must be wretched, and consequently ludicrous. When I do a part in a film, I must really suffer. In my

pictures I allow myself to be a victim of Fate. But a sort of Divine providence always carries me through." He even directed his films, another mistake. A typical effort, heavy on humiliation and pathos, was *The Chaser,* in which a judge, thinking he's a "chaser" (a womanizer), forces him to wear his wife's dress as punishment.

In real life Harry had major wife troubles. He was divorced, married, and divorced again. As his film career tumbled he said, "I have learned that women just must quarrel. Women are like that. I don't feel like making an audience laugh after I have had a quarrel with a woman. In order to be a good comedian I must escape the tragedy of marriage."

Hoping to change his luck, he signed to make sound films with Hal Roach in 1929. He also married for the third time. His new bride was already married when they started seeing each other, which led the woman's husband to sue him for alienation of affections and collect $15,000. The marriage failed in 1931 and Harry went bankrupt.

Fortunately for Harry, his luck began to change. He made some shorts for Educational in 1932 and moved on to Columbia where he made shorts for Three Stooges director Jules White. Harry's work was basically filler, but at least he was working. As a supporting comic he turned up in many feature films, and his next marriage, to Mabel Sheldon, proved stable and provided Harry with a son. Occasionally Harry had the promise of a major comeback. When Olsen and Johnson left the stage production of *Hellzapoppin,* Harry was going to join Jay C. Flippen in the show. Instead he lost the part to a comic named Happy Felton. He hooked up with Hal Roach again in the late 1930s as a gag writer for Laurel and Hardy, and in 1940 he starred opposite Oliver Hardy in *Zenobia.* Was this going to be the start of a real "Langdon and Hardy" team, or was it Roach's way of scaring Laurel into signing a new contract? Whatever the truth was, the film was mild and forgettable and Harry's comeback stalled again. He was only getting older, which made it very difficult for a comic relying on baby-faced looks of innocence.

Harry continued to make a decent living as a comic actor at the low-budget studios of Monogram and Republic. At Republic he made *Swingin' on a*

*Rainbow.* After a day's filming he went home with a headache. Two weeks later he was dead of a cerebral hemorrhage.

Harry left behind several classic comedies. His personality continues to amuse and fascinate fans, and his influence can certainly be felt in a variety of comedians ranging from George Gobel to Pee-Wee Herman. Probably the best assessment of Harry Langdon came from critic James Agee. His oft-quoted remark was that "Langdon had one queerly toned, unique little reed. But out of it he could get incredible melodies."

BIOGRAPHY: *Harry Langdon* (Schelly, 1982)

FILMS incl.: *Picking Peaches* (1924), *Smile Please* (1924), *Feet of Mud* (1924), *The Sea Squawk* (1925), *Boobs in the Woods* (1925), *Saturday Afternoon* (1926), *Soldier Man* (1926), *Tramp Tramp Tramp* (1926), *The Strong Man* (1926), *Long Pants* (1927), *Three's a Crowd* (1927), *His First Flame* (1927), *The Chaser* (1928), *Heart Trouble* (1928), *Hotter than Hot* (1929), *See America Thirst* (1930), *Hallelujah I'm a Bum* (1933), *My Weakness* (1933), *There Goes My Heart* (1938), *Zenobia* (1939), *Misbehaving Husbands* (1940), *Double Trouble* (1941), *All-American Co-Ed* (1941), *House of Errors* (1942), *Block Busters* (1944), *Hot Rhythm* (1944), *Swingin' on a Rainbow* (1945)

## FRANCES LANGFORD (See THE BICKERSONS.)

## LOUISE LASSER

### (April 11, 1939–   )

For a few years in the early 1970s, Louise Lasser seemed to be the neurotic and vulnerable "female Woody Allen." She had the right training for it, having gone out with Woody for five years since meeting him when she was 20 and marrying him for another four.

Just as Woody was miserable and fearful when he began in stand-up comedy, Louise recalled: "The stage terrified me. Oh, I played Dorothy in *The Wizard of Oz* in summer stock. Toto the dog bit me on stage and I got bad reviews."

Louise grew up on East 73rd Street in Manhattan. Her father was a tax expert. Her parents even-

tually divorced, and some time later her mother committed suicide. The girl from Brandeis University studied improvisation with Elaine May, substituted for Barbra Streisand during a week of *I Can Get It for You Wholesale* and in 1964 made her Broadway debut in *Henry Sweet Henry.* Her romantic life with Woody Allen led them to finally buy a $1.98 ring at a novelty shop and go through a ceremony only to be asked, "Do you take Woody Herman to be your husband?" "No," she answered.

It was only after the marriage ended that Louise turned up in Woody's films. She explained, "Woody and I never made movies when we were married because we were afraid it would ruin our marriage. . . . You don't stop caring about someone. What you like about someone at one time you always like." She offered a glimpse into their home life: "You remember what he said about my cooking? That he realized I wasn't much of a chef when he found a bone in the chocolate pudding? It's true. I am very inept in the kitchen."

Woody's films and a television commercial for Nyquil that featured her sadly weary countenance ultimately led her to Norman Lear's "Mary Hartman, Mary Hartman," a soap opera satire that developed a huge cult. It was the saga of dowdy Fernwood, Ohio and a plain woman bewildered by everything from commercials to the average townsfolk, who included murderers and flashers. "When I first read the script, I said 'I don't get it.' But they kept after me . . . so I read it again. I still didn't get it. . . . my idea of a great show is 'The Mary Tyler Moore Show.'" *People* magazine praised her "spaced-out performance," and the show's "kitchen-sink theater of the absurd . . . lasting relief from the flatulence of American television."

Fans responded to Louise as Mary Hartman, complete with her trademark bangs and braids. "All of us are basically very pure, very childlike beneath the facade," she said. "Mary was a child-woman." The adulation became too much. Louise felt suffocated by fans and fame, stopped eating and grew more and more uncomfortable with her Hollywood lifestyle. She had been in therapy for 15 years and seemed to need it more than ever. In May 1976, her nerves fraying, she made a scene in a boutique when they wouldn't honor her credit card. She was buying a $150 antique dollhouse, a gift for her wardrobe mistress. "I had a 102 temperature and a blood infection. I didn't yell, but I said very quietly like a child, I'm not leaving without my dollhouse." The store owner called the police, the police ran a check and discovered outstanding traffic violations—and, when they opened her purse, cocaine.

"The arrest was terrible for me. It was so much like Kafka. I was guilty of possession of $6 worth." Louise claimed it had been pressed on her by a fan. The incident was major news. Johnny Carson announced in a Karnak routine on "The Tonight Show": "The answer is '7-Up, Pepsi and Coke.' The question: 'Name two soft drinks and a problem for Mary Hartman.'"

Scheduled to appear on television's "Saturday Night Live" not long after, Lasser panicked and at first refused to go on just before air time. She did go on but was clearly disoriented and nervous. In a show so bad that it was never included for rerun syndication, Lasser went through her deathly paces, ending with a meandering monologue, muttering "They made me rich, famous and a known criminal."

The outcome of the cocaine arrest was a judge's order to undergo psychiatric treatment, which she already was doing; but the real cure was to get out of town. After a television movie she wrote and acted in (*Just Me and You*) missed in the ratings, she moved back to New York and took acting and art classes. After living alone and steering clear of fans and reporters as best she could, she gradually made a comeback. In 1978 she appeared in *The Goodbye People* with Sam Levene in summer stock, and the following year starred in a Marty Feldman movie. Woody Allen gave her a part in *Stardust Memories*, and she turned up on television in 1981's "Making a Living." She continued to take occasional roles on stage and in films, including a pair of screen appearances in 1989: *Sing* and *Rude Awakening*.

BROADWAY: *Henry Sweet Henry* (1964), *Marie and Bruce* (1980)

FILMS incl.: *What's New, Pussycat* (1965), *What's Up Tiger Lily* (1966), *Take the Money and Run* (1969), *Bananas* (1971), *Such Good Friends* (1971), *Everything You Always Wanted to Know About Sex But Were Afraid to Ask* (1972), *Slither* (1973), *Just Me and You* (1978), *In God We Trust* (1979), *Stardust*

*Memories* (1980), *Blood Rage* (1983), *Crime Wave* (1985), *Rude Awakening* (1989), *Sing* (1989), *Frankenhooker* (1990)

TV: "Mary Hartman, Mary Hartman" (1976–77), "Making a Living" (1981–82)

VIDEO: *Mary Hartman, Mary Hartman* (Vols. 1–2)

# HARRY LAUDER

## (August 4, 1870–February 26, 1950)

The most famous Scottish comedian, Sir Harry Lauder's reputation has outlived his work. Vaudeville authority Anthony Slide put it this way: "Viewing him on film, one is aware only of a small, grouchy-looking Scotsman putting a lot of energy but little personality into his songs, and telling jokes that must have been corny when he first used them." Today Lauder is probably best known as the singer of "Roaming in the Gloaming," which he performed with great enthusiasm and his grand Scottish burr.

Born in Portobello, Scotland, Lauder began singing in a coal mine. When his fellow workers urged him to sing before the bright lights of the stage, he began appearing in music hall revues. He was a hit with his mix of songs and comedy, and even then some people weren't sure just why he was so enjoyable. *Variety* reported in 1907, "It is impossible to catch and analyze the peculiarly elusive charm of this great artist." His "elusive" appeal meant big money. In 1908 he was earning $3,000 a week in America. Whenever he traveled over from Europe, it was to a hero's welcome. In 1911, when his ship was late to arrive due to fog, his New York audience stayed from 8:15 till 12:45 A.M. when he finally reached the theater.

Like Jack Benny several years later, Lauder cultivated a stingy image. He'd deliberately stiff a bellhop or waiter on a tip and create a loud scene—after having given the person a big tip in private beforehand. He once claimed his greatest delight was money, and "knowing that white, black, brown and yellow men have been willing to pay it out just to hear me, to see me and cheer me."

Knighted in 1919, Lauder was an institution through the '20s. A 1928 *Variety* review: "He was the rollicking comic, the comedian extraordinary. . . . The Pagliacci in the flesh. He made them laugh; he wrung them dry after he had doused them with laughter. Then he drenched them again—with tears. . . . He had a thousand people weeping." In 1929 he was paid $15,000 to sing three songs on the radio.

The Scotsman remained a durable performer up until his retirement in 1949. He died a year later. Far from forgotten, nearly 20 years after his passing Lauder was the subject of a new biography released in England, *The Great Scot*. People still recall his songs, his wit and some of his philosophy: "Happiness is one of the few things in the world that doubles every time you share it with someone else."

AUDIO incl.: *The Immortal Harry Lauder*
AUTOBIOGRAPHIES: *Roamin' in the Gloamin'; Between You and Me*
BIOGRAPHY: *The Great Scot* (G. Irving)
FILMS incl.: *Auld Lang Syne* (1933), *Song of the Road* (1936)

## LAUREL and HARDY

**Stan Laurel: Arthur Stanley Jefferson, June 16, 1895–February 23, 1965**
**Oliver Hardy: Norwell Hardy, January 18, 1892–August 7, 1957**

Laurel and Hardy were the only masters of silent comedy to be as effective in the sound era. They had it all: They looked funny, talked funny and moved funny. They made audiences laugh at outrageous extremes of slapstick: the ultimate pie fight *(Battle of the Century)*; an exploding gas stove completely caving in an apartment *(Helpmates)*; a man's neck stretched five feet and snapping back *(Way Out West)*. They could also get just as loud laughter from the subtlest character comedy—an embarrassed twiddle of a tie, a blameless grin, a doleful stare. One might "like" the other comedy greats of the day—Charlie Chaplin, W. C. Fields, the Marx Brothers, Buster Keaton. One might even admire them or worship them. But Laurel and Hardy were *loved*.

Stan Laurel was born in Ulverston, England and schooled at Tynemouth College. He was Charles Chaplin's understudy when they were both with the Fred Karno vaudeville troup in 1910. He formed his own Stan Jefferson Trio and after that toured with his wife, Mae. Disturbed at the 13 unlucky

letters in his name, he let his wife pick a new stage name. She was inspired by a drawing of a Roman general with a crown of laurels. Moving to films only a few years after Chaplin, Laurel had his own 1917 series as "Hickory Hiram" and later produced a number of hilarious spoofs of popular films including *Mud and Sand* (1922), *The Soilers* (1923) and *Dr. Pickle and Mr. Pride* (1925). He could play everything from a grinning and brash salesman (1923's *Kill or Cure*) to a slapstick-prone dimwit (1925's *Smithy*). Stan was one of many delightful if "minor" solo comedians of the day and was comfortable directing and writing gags for others. In fact, he was working primarily behind the scenes when he teamed with Oliver Hardy.

Oliver Hardy, born in Harlem, Georgia, had a fine tenor voice and amused audiences in minstrel shows and vaudeville. Around 1910 he opened a movie house. Later the six-foot-two, 250-pounder discovered he was a perfect heavy for films. After some local Florida films he moved out to California. He acquired the nickname "Babe" from an Italian barber who pinched his baby face. Hardy was "teamed" with several diminutive comics, most notably Bobby Ray in 1915's *Paperhanger's Helper,* and in 1916 he was part of *Plump and Runt* with Billy Ruge as "Runt." He played the outrageously made-up villain in Chaplin imitator Billy West's comedies (such as 1916's *The Hero*) and later worked with Larry Semon, a Laurelesque comic with a pasty baby face. Hardy played the tin woodsman in Larry's *The Wizard of Oz.*

On July 24, 1926, some real-life slapstick led to the birth of a comedy team. Out hiking, Ollie's wife tore ligaments in her leg running away from a rattlesnake. Ollie, helping around the house, decided to cook dinner for her. In the process, he scalded himself with hot grease so severely that he couldn't play the butler in a short called *Get 'Em Young.* Writer/director Stan Laurel was asked to make a "mini-comeback" in the part. Stan enjoyed it, especially after getting a raise in salary. After replacing Hardy, he suddenly found himself working with him in several more shorts.

Laurel and Hardy purists debate exactly what the first "official" Laurel and Hardy film the boys made. Some say technically it was back in 1918 when Stan made *Lucky Dog* and had a brief scene with an extra,

The fiddle and the bow: Equally hilarious in silents and talkies, Stan and Ollie became the most beloved comedy team in history. Photo from the author's collection.

Oliver Hardy. Hal Roach's publicists trumpeted "Laurel and Hardy Team Up in a Film" when *Duck Soup* (not The Marx Brothers' film) was released in 1926. *Why Girls Love Sailors* in 1927 unveiled Ollie's "tie twiddle" and stare into the camera, but biographer William K. Everson pinpoints *Do Detectives Think?* as "the first film to present Laurel and Hardy as the team we now know so well . . . workmates . . . in their traditional bowler hats."

Late in 1927 the boys offered up their first masterpiece, the epic pie fight to end all pie fights, *Battle of the Century. Two Tars* in 1928 was another gem, one of their first classics of "reciprocative violence." With polite pauses and careful thought, the boys and their antagonists take turns bashing each other and each other's cars as they wait out a frustrating traffic tieup. *Big Business* in 1929 was similar, with James Finlayson destroying their car while they attacked his house—all because of a misunderstanding over their dubious efforts at selling him a Christmas tree in the middle of summer. They also starred in a variety of "thrill" comedies, from the thrill of tottering atop an unfinished building *(Liberty)* to the thrill of accidentally stripping the skirt from Jean Harlow *(Double Whoopee)*.

With the sound era, the boys developed more and more character comedy—officious, exasperated Ollie now having to explain things to wayward, sleepily dizzy Stan. They had their share of silly gags. Ollie: "We haven't eaten for three days." Stan: "Yes. Yesterday, today and tomorrow." Audiences laughed even more at the unexplainable bits of nonsense that passed for dialogue. Stan begins: "How long did you say it would take us to get up there?" "Oh, just a jiffy." "How far is a jiffy?" "Oh, about three shakes of a dead lamb's tail." "Hmmm. I didn't think it was so far."

The team's unique mixture of subtlety and slapstick reached perfection in the Academy Award–winning short *The Music Box*. A masterpiece of simplicity, it had the slimmest plot imaginable: the boys trying to haul a piano up endless flights of stairs and into an apartment. Yet they got big laughs from the very tediousness of the process and the number of obstacles they come across in attempting to reach their goal.

Laurel and Hardy went on to star in some of the classic feature films of all time. *Way Out West* is easily their best, a blend of fast-paced gags, nonsensical wordplay and songs. Fans who grew up watching the boys on television tend to favor the often inexplicably hilarious *Babes in Toyland*. Purists usually point to *Sons of the Desert* as the epitome of timing, pace, and character as well as *Blockheads*, a delightful session of Laurel and Hardy euphoria. Throughout the last film the team exists in a world just a few beats slower and on a slightly more tilted angle than everyone else. The tipoff comes from Stan: "Remember how dumb I used to be? I'm *better* now."

One criticism of the team was their slow pace. Sometimes it was just a little too slow and mannerly. Stan Laurel, who was the "brains" of the duo off screen and deeply involved in the writing, directing and editing of the finished product, admitted that in some cases this was caused by allowing time for audience laughter in a big theater. In the 1940s the aging duo's slower pace contrasted with the slicker style of Abbott and Costello. Drifting to new movie studios that hadn't the time or the budget to craft good comedy, the team's last efforts were mild and disappointing, especially compared to Abbott and Costello, who peppered their films with the classic burlesque routines they'd perfected over ten years.

The situation was particularly disturbing to Stan, the perfectionist who watched over each day's work and constantly sought ways to improve the scripts. (Like Chaplin, his genius extended to restless womanizing and several messy divorces.) Ollie was more placid, content to leave the worries to Stan and go off to play golf. The duo did not socialize much, which may have helped them remain cordial friends all their lives.

There was always the hope that Laurel and Hardy would find some way of returning to greatness. They toured America and Europe with a stage act and endured the misery of a few more cheaply done and disappointing films. They appeared on an episode of television's "This Is Your Life" and hoped that their life as a comedy team might be extended via a series of television specials. Just as a deal was being worked out, Stan had a mild stroke. He also had high blood pressure and diabetes. He recovered, but then Ollie, now weighing well over 300 pounds, suffered a massive stroke from which he never fully recovered.

In 1961 Stan Laurel received an honorary Academy Award. Admirers from Laurel and Hardy biographers to new comedy greats Jerry Lewis and Dick Van Dyke visited the retired, serene and cheerful star. Stan was offered work, including a cameo in *It's a Mad Mad Mad Mad World*, but he turned it all down, insisting that fans would be disappointed in seeing an elderly gent instead of the young, blank-faced fellow with the blinking vacant blue eyes, weedy tufted hair and "fig bar" smile. Laurel told James Bacon, "I'm all washed up. If I was well enough to make a movie I'd be out chasing girls. You know my hobby. I married them all."

Stan kept an eye on the current comedy trends and had his own opinions. "In comedy the most important person is the person you're playing to—the person you're trying to make laugh. Too many young comedians these days forget that. A lot of them are up there performing in order to make themselves feel better, when it should be the other way around. And why don't some of them even try to use a little visual humor? They stand there and talk, talk, talk—and after a while I get the feeling that the only person they're really talking to is themselves. That's sad. That means they haven't learned the very first thing a comedian must learn—it is your audience that counts, not you."

For audiences, Laurel and Hardy films count, watched the first time for all of Stan's lovable antics, watched a second time for all the subtleties of Ollie and then watched over and over for their wonderful teamwork together; for Laurel and Hardy were the greatest comedy duo of all time.

AUDIO: *Naturally High* (Douglas), *Laurel and Hardy on Radio* (Radiola), *Best of Laurel and Hardy* (Murray Hill), *Way Out West* (Mark 56), *Trouble Again* (Mark 56), *Another Fine Mess* (Mark 56), *Original Soundtracks* (Mark 56), *Babes in Toyland* (Mark 56), *No U Turn* (Mark 56)

BIOGRAPHIES: *Mr. Laurel and Mr. Hardy* (McCabe, 1985), *Stan Laurel's World of Comedy* (McCabe, 1974), *Babe* (McCabe, 1989), *The Films of Laurel and Hardy* (Everson, 1983), *Laurel and Hardy Scrapbook* (Scagnetti, 1976), *Laurel and Hardy: Every Film They Ever Made* (McCabe, 1975), *Laurel and Hardy* (Barr, 1968), *Another Fine Mess* (Anobile, 1975), *Stan* (Guilles, 1980), *The Boys* (Nollen, 1989), *Laurel and Hardy* (Skretvedt, 1987)

FILMS incl.: shorts: *Lucky Dog* (1917), *Duck Soup* (1926), *Flying Elephants* (1927), *Do Detectives Think?* (1927), *The Second Hundred Years* (1927), *Putting Pants on Philip* (1927), *The Battle of the Century* (1927), *Leave 'em Laughing* (1928), *From Soup to Nuts* (1928), *Two Tars* (1928), *Liberty* (1929), *Wrong Again* (1929), *Big Business* (1929), *Double Whoopee* (1929), *Unaccustomed as We Are* (1929), *Berth Marks* (1929), *Men O' War* (1929), *A Perfect Day* (1929), *Blotto* (1930), *Below Zero* (1930), *Another Fine Mess* (1930), *Be Big* (1930), *Come Clean* (1931), *Helpmates* (1931), *Any Old Port* (1932), *The Music Box* (1932), *County Hospital* (1932), *Towed in a Hole* (1933), *Twice Two* (1933), *Me and My Pal* (1933), *Them Thar Hills* (1934), *Tit for Tat* (1934); features: *The Devil's Brother*, aka *Fra Diavolo* (1933), *Sons of the Desert* (1933), *Babes in Toyland* (1934), *Bonnie Scotland* (1935), *Our Relations* (1936), *Way Out West* (1936), *Swiss Miss* (1938), *Blockheads* (1938), *Flying Deuces* (1939), *A Chump at Oxford* (1940), *Saps at Sea* (1940), *Great Guns* (1941), *A Haunting We Will Go* (1942), *Jitterbugs* (1943), *The Bull Fighters* (1945), *Atoll K* (1951)

VIDEOS: *Hal Roach Comedy Classics*, (Vol. 3, 4); *Laurel and Hardy Comedy Classics* (Vols. 1–9)

# LINDA LAVIN

## (October 15, 1937– )

After a long, creditable career that included stage work and films, Linda Lavin emerged as a favorite television star with her portrayal of Alice, the New Jersey widow waitressing at Mel's Diner in Phoenix, Arizona. The pioneering sympathetic sitcom about a working woman's real-life tribulations impressed not only audiences but the star herself. She recalled, " 'Alice' opened up a world I had no idea about, the world of women working in low-paying and non-skilled jobs, who have to fight for benefits, for a quality of life often not within their reach."

Lavin's comic characters over the years had been no less real, but played for more laughs. She won a Tony nomination for *The Last of the Red Hot Lovers* on Broadway in 1969. The *New York Times* wrote, "Linda Lavin, eyebrows flaunting like telegraphed messages, mouth twitching and pouting, voice dry as thunder and with a cough like electric static, is beautiful as Elaine, the sex cat feeling kittenish and looking for a safe tin roof."

Born in Portland, Maine, Linda seemed to have inherited a lot of talent from her mother, who once sang with Paul Whiteman's orchestra and performed on local radio. Linda sang, played piano and acted in plays at Deering High School in Portland. She enrolled as a theater arts major at William and Mary College, and in a portent of her comic style in years to come played both drama (Juliet in *Romeo and Juliet*) and lighter fare (Dolly in *The Matchmaker*). She tried soloing as a jazz vocalist in Boston clubs and was in productions at the Edgartown Summer Theater in Cape Cod in 1959 before moving to New York and living at 229 West 16th Street, sharing a room with another struggling actress, Olympia Dukakis.

Lavin appeared off-Broadway in *Oh Kay!* in 1960 and sang in her first Broadway outing, Shelley Berman's musical *A Family Affair* in 1962. Lavin also appeared with the Second City improvisational troupe and worked as a single when she could get bookings. Joan Rivers recalled Lavin at The Duplex: "singing . . . very sexy in a lace body stocking." More Broadway and off-Broadway shows followed, including 1965's *The Mad Show*. She played a secretary in *It's a Bird, It's a Plane, It's Superman* and in the fall of

1966 toured in *On a Clear Day You Can See Forever*. She also appeared on the comedy lp *The Bunch*, spoofing the 1966 film *The Group*. She married her co-star in *Cop-Out*, Ron Leibman, in September 1969. She continued in stage productions through the late 1960s and replaced Valerie Harper in 1971's *Story Theater*.

Growing restless with her progress on stage, she moved out to Hollywood in 1975 for a Mike Nichols film. After it was shelved, Lavin landed television sitcom parts instead, notably the role of fiesty little Detective Wentworth on "Barney Miller." From there Lavin made a pilot that didn't sell ("Jerry") and then landed a show that lasted for nine years—"Alice."

As Alice Hyatt, Lavin had a chance to have some dramatic moments (the show was based on the Ellen Burstyn film drama), but comedy predominated. Though there was some slapstick and corn, there were also some good lines. Groucho Marx's son Arthur was one of the writers. Much of the dialogue sounded as if it could have been overheard at a real diner.

"My husband's been dead six months," Alice says in the first episode. "Don didn't believe in insurance . . . it didn't come in a six-pack." Some byplay with her son, who wants her to quit the diner to become a singer: "If you didn't have me, I bet you'd say 'Yes' just like that." "That's why I have you—because I said 'Yes' just like that."

Lavin's marriage to Ron Leibman ended during the run of "Alice," in 1981. A second marriage ended in 1990 amid painful public accounts of her ex-husband's infidelities and demand for alimony. Her career continues to flourish, in both films and on Broadway, where she won a Tony Award as Kate Jerome in Neil Simon's *Broadway Bound*. Linda Lavin still favors comedy with guts and drama to it. "What makes me laugh is desperation, self-pity, things that are funny because they're awful. That's the kind of comedy I like, covering pain with acid humor, with self-deprecation. . . . Humor is a survival button."

AUDIO: *A Family Affair* (MGM), *The Bunch* (RCA)
BROADWAY: *Oh Kay* (1960), *A Family Affair* (1962), *The Riot Act* (1963), *The Mad Show* (1965), *Wet Paint* (1965), *It's a Bird, It's a Plane, It's Superman* (1966), *Something Different* (1967), *Little Murders* (1968), *Cop-Out* (1969), *Story Theater* (1971), *Last*

of the Red Hot Lovers* (1971), *Broadway Bound* (1986), *Gypsy* (revival, 1990)
FILMS: *Like Mom, Like Me* (1978), *The $5.20 an Hour Dream* (1979), *A Matter of Life and Death* (1981), *Another Woman's Child* (1983), *See You in the Morning* (1989)
TV: "Barney Miller" (1975), "Alice" (1976–85), "Room for Two" (1992)

## EDDIE LAWRENCE

### (Lawrence Eisler, March 2, 1921–    )

One of the most enduring characters in recorded comedy is "The Old Philosopher," the alter ego of Eddie Lawrence. The Philosopher treats every ridiculous misery in life the same way. He lists the grievances with mockingly serious sympathy (as a squeamy violin plays softly in the background) then gives way to raging optimism (complete with blaring march music):

"Hey there, friend, you say your radiators didn't work all winter and now that it's summer they started up again and you can't turn them off? You say your wife sent your lightweight suits to the cleaners and that means you'll have to wear your itchy tweeds this morning when they say it'll hit 106? And . . . you opened a big cut on your cheek tryin' to even out your sideburns . . . is that what's troublin' you, friend? *Lift your head up high!* And take a walk in the sun with that dignity and stick-to-it-iveness that you'll show the world! You'll show 'em where to get off! You'll never give up, never give up, never give up— that *ship!*"

Over the years Lawrence would issue dozens of "Old Philosopher" routines, all in the same format of hapless maladies and stirring melodies. The only major change was the name of the Philosopher's friend. Quite often the greeting was "What's the matter, Bunkie?" It became a catch phrase for Eddie and the many imitators who delighted in copying the Philosopher's attitude.

Lawrence said that the Philosopher was "ad-libbed at a party. I did a character called 'Sentimental Max' when I was in the army—'how are you feeling, boy, feeling good, well that's good, sonny. The moon is shining . . .' terrible jibberish, and people laughed at the voice." Then came the philosophy: "I met this actor on Broadway once, and he told me so many terrible things—his voice was cut out of a cartoon short and stuff like that—and we both started to laugh. All these terrible things—and he bit his tongue too—a little thing like that could send you to a nut house." As the Old Philosopher, Lawrence went on to nightclubs, television and pioneering record albums.

Eddie hadn't really planned a show business career. Born in Brooklyn, a graduate of Brooklyn College, his first love was painting. He presented several art shows (he always signed his artwork using his real name) and studied with the greats of the day, including Fernand Leger. During World War II he earned a Bronze Star, then laughs when the sketches he wrote were performed by top stars visiting the troops. Eddie joined in and after the war teamed with his friend John Marley, to become "Lawrence and Marley," legendary radio personalities. He recalled, "We did a lot of stuff similar to Monty Python. It was on NBC, we did 15-minute shows. Then we were supposed to do a big show for Dream Shampoo and we didn't like the director. . . . they were so angry with us they made sure somebody else got the spot. It was a big chance but we were always bucking the establishment with the attitude and comedy. . . . we did take-offs, crazy, wild stuff. Jack Kroll, the critic in *Newsweek* wrote a review of Bob and Ray and mentioned us—'Where are those two geniuses Lawrence and Marley . . .'"

Marley went on to become a fine dramatic actor. Eddie found a lucrative career in voiceovers (he narrated many *Blondie* movies), radio (his own "Eddie Lawrence Show") and ultimately a series of hit comedy records. Along with his contemporary, Stan Freberg, Eddie blazed a new trail in audio comedy, using sound effects, music and voices to create a surreal new world.

Sometimes there were no jokes in these three-minute sound cartoons, just character comedy. In "The Good Old Days," for example, a growling man complains about life while his mild-mannered companion utters perturbed little cries of "Will you shut up?" The laughs are purely in the contrast between the two men (both voices by Eddie Lawrence). Sometimes Eddie layered enough sounds, music and voices together to create a mad minidrama such as "Eddie at the Opera," an aural Marx Brothers film filled with nonsequiturs, interruptions, sketch material and singing, a complete re-creation of a beserk opera broadcast on radio.

While Lawrence's best work was on radio and records, the compact comic with the Mel Brooks–like body and optimistic smile often played comedy character parts on stage, most notably in *Bells Are Ringing*. He also wrote plays, from the 1952 drama *The Beautiful Mariposa* to the ill-fated Broadway musical *Kelly* in 1965. Though he performed in nightclubs starting with The Village Vanguard in 1954, he later preferred to stay in New York with his wife and family. He was a legend in comedy for his pioneering work in the 1950s, but over the years simply has had too many other interests to remain focused on the Old Philosopher. This character clearly could have provided him with a lifetime of stand-up work, as "The Professor" character did for Irwin Corey. Now and then he does a stand-up show and often uses the Philosopher voice for radio commercials, but he is just as content with other pursuits.

Eddie's attitude was always a healthy one, driven by only one axiom: "Do what you feel like doing." He felt like doing over 40 "Tonight Show" appearances and seven classic comedy albums as the Philosopher and other characters, but the other characters inside Eddie include writer, playwright and the original "Lawrence Eisler," who continues to paint in his own New York studio and give critically acclaimed exhibitions.

AUDIO: *The Garden of Eddie Lawrence* (Signature), *The Old Philosopher* (Coral), *Side-Splitting Personality* (Coral), *Seven Characters in Search of Eddie Lawrence* (Coral), *Kingdom of Eddie Lawrence* (Coral), *Is That What's Bothering You, Bunkie?* (Epic), *Bells Are Ringing* (Columbia)

BROADWAY: *Threepenny Opera* (1955), *Bells Are Ringing* (1956), *Sherry!* (1967)

FILMS incl.: *Act of Love* (1953), *The Night They Raided Minsky's* (1968), *Somebody Killed Her Husband* (1978)

## CLORIS LEACHMAN

### (April 30, 1930–   )

"In Hollywood they wanted to change my name. So I opened a phone book and just picked one out. It was Leavitt. So I left it."

Initially Cloris Leachman carved out a career as a respected actress, earning an Academy Award for *The Last Picture Show.* But her name still seemed to spell comedy. As Steve Allen put it on television's "Laugh-In" in 1972: "Cloris Leachman is the basic ingredient in most standard washday detergents." Eventually she began to specialize in comedy and played a wide variety of grotesques in Mel Brooks movies. On television she was a more human monster, the snide and egotistic Phyllis on "The Mary Tyler Moore Show" and its spin-off, "Phyllis."

Born in Des Moines, Iowa, Cloris studied piano and attended Northwestern University on a scholarship. After becoming a Miss America finalist, she moved to New York to study at the Actors Studio in 1948. She appeared often on Broadway and made her film debut with *Kiss Me Deadly* in 1955. Television audiences got their first long look at her when she replaced Jan Clayton in "Lassie." The next year she herself was replaced by June Lockhart. She continued to guest on television shows, though it would be many years before she became a regular: after she joined the cast of "The Mary Tyler Moore Show" as Phyllis Lindstrom, Mary's airy neighbor and landlord. She won two Emmy awards for the role.

"Phyllis," the spin-off, tried to take some of the edge off Cloris' character of a woman-you-laugh-to-hate. The show's short run was marred by tragedy. Cast member Barbara Colby was murdered after the very first episode. Before the completion of the second season, elderly cast member Judith Lowry died. The show was canceled in its third season. Leachman would have limited success in subsequent sitcoms. Her reunion with *High Anxiety* co-star Harvey Korman in the hotel comedy "The Nutt House" lasted only five weeks.

In Mel Brooks films, Cloris Leachman was a comic woman of a thousand faces, most of them hilariously awful. She was Frau Blucher in *Young Frankenstein,* the sadomasochistic, bullet-breasted Nurse Diesel in *High Anxiety* and Madame DeFarge in *History of the World Part I.* Strange old ladies seemed to become a Leachman trademark. She played Ernie Kovacs' eccentric mother in April Smith's made-for-television movie *Ernie Kovacs: Between the Laughter,* and in the late 1980s began touring in a play about Grandma Moses, which necessitated hours of arduous makeup.

When Leachman tours in the Grandma Moses role, she's never alone. "I like hotels, but I always travel with a hot-water bottle. It's a little, warm, friendly, fat object that you cuddle up to and put anywhere you want. It just fits in all the places you need a body if one isn't there—well, almost."

FILMS incl.: *Kiss Me Deadly* (1954), *The Chapman Report* (1962), *Butch Cassidy and the Sundance Kid* (1969), *Lovers and Other Strangers* (1970), *The Steagle* (1971), *The Last Picture Show* (1971), *Young Frankenstein* (1974), *Charley and the Angel* (1974), *High Anxiety* (1977), *The Muppet Movie* (1978), *The North Avenue Irregulars* (1978), *Herbie Goes Bananas* (1980), *History of the World Part 1* (1981), *The Acorn People* (1981), *Advice to the Lovelorn* (1981), *Miss All-American Beauty* (1982), *S.O.B.* (1981), *Ernie Kovacs: Between the Laughter* (1984), *Breakfast with Les and Bess* (1985), *Deadly Intentions* (1985)

TV: "Lassie" (1957–58), "The Mary Tyler Moore Show" (1970–75), "Phyllis" (1975–77), "The Facts of Life" (1986–87), "The Nutt House" (1989)

## PINKY LEE

### (Pincus Leff, 1916–   )

A cute, spritely little burlesque comic, Pinky Lee became one of the most popular comedians for kids in the 1950s. He was an energetic children's show host known for his innocent, lisping delivery, checked suit and undersize checked hat.

Born in St. Paul, Minnesota, his given name of Pincus was quickly shortened into "Pinky." Lee entered vaudeville performing in a "School Days" sketch produced by Gus Edwards. He wore a rich-kid outfit, looking a bit like Charlie McCarthy, dressed up in top hat, tux and monocle. During the waning days of vaudeville, he and another man wore sailor suits and joining with a girl for the appropriately named team of Port, Lee and Dotty.

Lee married Bebe Dancis in 1932 and had two children. He developed his trademark attire by accident. Originally he wore a straight suit and a silly little hat. Before one show, he couldn't find the hat and had to borrow a small checkered cap from a child in the audience. It got big laughs. Later he added a mismatched checked suit.

After a decade more of burlesque and vaudeville, he starred in a show at Earl Carroll's Theater in Hollywood. After some lean years in the late 1940s, he went to London to perform at The Palladium. He returned to the United States to star in the television show "Those Two," co-starring Martha Stewart. She was later replaced by Vivian Blaine.

For all his durability and success, it was as a kiddie show host that Pinky Lee achieved his greatest fame. After "Those Two" ended, producer Larry White's son kept pestering him to bring back Pinky. White did, and millions of children grew up loving the silly antics of the oddly dressed, lisping comic. Lee claimed his character of the "pathetic little guy" was a throwback to such silent greats as Stan laurel and Larry Semon, but critics were never impressed. Parents complained that Lee was not only overexciting the kids with his breakneck pace but inciting them to adopt his peculiar mannerisms.

Pinky was working too hard to let the criticism really bother him. He produced six live shows a week, each one filled with fast-paced sketches and some momentary moments of wistful miming. It all came to a screeching halt on September 20, 1955. "I collapsed. They all thought I'd had a heart attack. Instead, I was being poisoned from a postnasal drip. My doctor asked if I could afford to quit. I had no choice." For the sake of his sinuses he moved to Tucson, Arizona to recuperate. Once he did, he was ready for a comeback. He hosted television's "Gumby Show" in 1957. He played in Las Vegas in 1958 and won good notices, even if some nights the slapstick was beyond Lee's control. Once a pony used in one burlesque scene dropped a load of manure on stage and then trampled on it, splashing the first few rows of dinner theater diners. This distracted Pinky, who was getting dressed for the finale. When he arrived on stage, and a female stooge ripped away his breakaway suit, everyone realized that he had forgotten to put on his gag checked undershorts.

Pinky returned to the kiddie comedy field with a local "Pinky Lee Show" for KABC in Los Angeles in 1964 and 1966. He hoped to stage *Little World, Hello* based on the life of comedian Jimmy Savo, but it said good-bye before it ever opened. Lee toured in burlesque revivals when the mood suited him, including Roy Radin's shows of the early 1980s. He was persuaded to come out of retirement for a

tour in *Sugar Babies* in 1989. He had a heart attack in 1989, but declared he was getting better thanks to his own brand of physical therapy: "I have a little dance floor and a cassette player and I dance every day." By that time there was a new star on the kiddie scene with an act that was suspiciously similar to prime Pinky Lee: Pee-Wee Herman. Lee brushed off the comparison. "I never knock success. He's successful at what he does and more power to him. But he's not my cup of tea."

In his heyday, critics tended to be rough on the funny-named "low" comic, but as burlesque and vaudeville shows enjoyed a revival in the 1970s and acts such as The Three Stooges began earning praise, Lee felt he was vindicated. "My kind of humor was broad and slapstick. That's what this country wants and needs right now. The last thing we need is more filthy humor."

FILMS incl.: *Lady of Burlesque* (1943), *Earl Carroll's Vanities* (1945), *Blonde Ransom* (1945), *That's My Gal* (1947), *South Caliente* (1951)
TV: "The Pinky Lee Show" (1950), "Those Two" (1951–53), "The Pinky Lee Show" (1954–57)

## TOM LEHRER

### (April 9, 1928–   )

A Harvard professor, Tom Lehrer had no idea his few years on sabbatical performing "sick" musical comedy would make him a cult legend for over 40 years. He began his career with a self-made record album intended more to amuse friends than influence people. He was merely writing deliberately cruel parodies of the day's more sappy and sentimental songs, going genre by genre from college drinking songs ("Bright College Days") to his version of a "Kiss of Fire" torch ballad, "The Masochism Tango."

That the tunes were ever heard beyond Harvard was, he recalled in 1991, "the coincidence of technology. It was cheap to make records. I'd been singing these songs around and I assumed they had no commercial value so I just custom-recorded. I looked up in the Yellow Pages and I did it . . . the total recording cost was fifteen dollars, and that was for piano, studio, tape, editing, everything. I wasn't trying to break into the market, it was just something to have around as a souvenir."

Lehrer pressed 400 copies for $700, and when the demand for this 1953 album, *Songs by Tom Lehrer,* started taking off, so did his sudden career as a performer. After returning from the army in 1957, he played concerts and a few nightclubs and earned the tag of "sick" comedian for his deliberately tasteless tunes about poisoning pigeons in the park, hometown perverts and burn-charred bodies in a nuclear holocaust. The self-described "calm and gentle and totally domesticated" professor didn't care for the "sick" identification. His aim in comedy had been to mock folk, pop and dance music and perhaps duplicate some of the funny Danny Kaye patter songs and Gilbert and Sullivan tunes that had influenced him.

He noted that during his live shows "the audience would laugh and I would act surprised that they were laughing. They were the ones who were sick because they were laughing at this. I was just doing it. Rather than my being ghoulish in the song, I would sing 'Poisoning Pigeons in the Park' really sweetly, as if it were a nice bucolic spring song, and if they laughed at the gruesome part, then that was their fault. Their problem." He performed in "this sort of deadpan, it's-up-to-you-to-get-the-joke style. That was really self-protection. There's nothing so embarrassing as a comedian who tells a joke and pauses, and there's silence."

Lehrer worked mainly to his peers, "the liberal consensus who agreed that Adlai Stevenson was a good guy and lynching was bad." Of course, even among the liberals who embraced him as they did Mort Sahl and Lenny Bruce, some were disturbed by his (now-mild) brand of shock comedy. Some were upset by "The Vatican Rag" and its religious satire: "Get down upon your knees, fiddle with your rosaries, bow your head with great respect and—genuflect! genuflect! genuflect!" Others shook their heads over his boy scout tune "Be Prepared" ("Don't solicit for your sister, that's not nice—unless you get a good percentage of her price"). And others were surprised when he came out in favor of pornography in "Smut," a tune filled with comically desperate rhyming: "Give me smut and nothing but. A dirty novel I can't shut. If it's uncut. And unsubt-le."

Always shy and reserved, Lehrer refused to put his photo on any album jacket, considering such photos "an invasion of privacy." He had to be begged to make television appearances and did so only rarely. He was happy to return to the world of academia after putting out a few albums in 1960 and made only a brief comeback in 1965 when he recorded his first album for Reprise based on material he'd given to the television series "That Was the Week That Was." His last paid concert tour was in 1967 in Sweden, Denmark and East Germany, his last public performance of any kind was at a McGovern rally in 1972.

Born in New York where he attended P.S. 6, P.S. 166 and then Horace Mann High School, Lehrer graduated from the Loomis prep school in Connecticut and went on to Harvard, where he earned his degree. He taught at Harvard and then at MIT for nine years during the 1960s. In 1971 he went bicoastal, maintaining a home in Cambridge while teaching math and music at the University of California. Over the years he watched his students come and go, while his albums remained in print. His 1953 *Songs of Tom Lehrer* album is clearly the most successful comedy disc of all time in terms of longevity, available for purchase ever since it first came out. In 1990 CD versions of his albums were issued.

Lehrer's students sometimes asked him to autograph an album, but what amused him was to discover that most were more excited over his other musical credit—having contributed nearly a dozen songs to the "Sesame Street" television show: "They're more impressed that I wrote for that show. It's like *'You* wrote 'Silent E'? It's as if I wrote 'Jingle Bells.' "

To the disappointment of his fans, Lehrer professes no interest in composing new comedy songs. One reason is the lack of clearly defined musical styles to parody effectively; the 1950s love ballads and folk tunes that had inspired his wrath are long gone. More important, he told the author, "There's no clear target, even within that 'liberal consensus.' It's hard to take a position. The audience would be split. I couldn't write 'Smut' today—there's a dichotomy within the liberal consensus of feminism vs. pornography. I'm for feminism and I'm for pornography. What can I do? To be funny you have to be shocking a little, and it's hard to be shocking now. People don't have a common body of knowledge anymore—cultural literacy—whatever you want to call it." He pointed out that the new brand of shock comedian "talks about flatulence, menstruation, genitalia. Things everybody can relate to without having to have ever read a book. And that just isn't interesting enough.

"You can't be funny if you're angry," he added. "That was one of the problems that let Lenny Bruce down, and then Mort Sahl when he got on the Warren Report. When you start getting angry then it's not funny any more. You've got to be detached and view it with a real sense of perspective to find it funny. That's the problem."

Many of the problems of Lehrer's era are still with us, which is one reason why his albums are still in print and still powerful. In 1965 Lehrer sang a song called "Pollution." One line: "Fish gotta swim and birds gotta fly—but they won't last long if they try." Tom Lehrer's songs are still considered fresh and funny, especially for those who think the world no longer is.

AUDIO: *Songs by Tom Lehrer* (Lehrer, reissued by Reprise), *More of Tom Lehrer* (Lehrer), *An Evening Wasted with Tom Lehrer* (Lehrer, reissued by Reprise), *Tom Lehrer Revisited* (Lehrer, remastered using different performance cuts by British Decca, reissued in CD form only by Reprise), *That Was the Year That Was* (Reprise)

SONG BOOKS incl.: *Too Many Songs by Tom Lehrer*

# HARVEY LEMBECK

## (April 15, 1923–January 5, 1982)

He knew comedy so well he could teach it. In fact, it's hard to tell for sure how many young comics remember Harvey Lembeck more fondly as their acting class mentor or as the tough but good-natured little co-star of 1950s sitcoms and films.

Born in Brooklyn, originally part of a dance act called The Dancing Carrolls, Lembeck's studies at the University of Alabama were interrupted by service in World War II. He enlisted in the army, transferred to the marines and ended up in the navy spending two years on a submarine. He joked about being in the service all his life, since he seemed to specialize in war comedies throughout his subsequent acting career.

After graduating from New York University in 1947, he arrived on Broadway as Insignia in *Mister Roberts* and later played Shapiro in *Stalag 17*. In the latter he played the good-natured little Brooklynite trying to keep his tough pal "Animal" (Robert Strauss) in check, sometimes with force, sometimes with a shaming, astonished remark such as: "How dumb can you get, Animal?" He and Strauss reteamed for another service comedy, *The Last Time I Saw Archie.* He was also in the service in such films as *You're in the Army Now* and *Willie and Joe Back at the Front.*

On television, Lembeck got a break when Buddy Hackett turned down the role of fretting little Corporal Rocco Barbella on "You'll Never Get Rich" (also known as "Sgt. Bilko"). It became Lembeck's duty to try to placate the scheming Bilko (Phil Silvers). (Rocco Barbella was the real name of boxing great Rocky Graziano.)

With his television show being filmed in New York, Lembeck had no reason to move from his home in Queens, where he had a wife and two kids, Michael and Helaine. Around the same time Lembeck was also working on the Broadway stage, occasionally finding other roles to play besides soldiers. He did comedy sketches with Nancy Walker in *Phoenix '55*, played Ali Hakim in 1958's *Oklahoma* and sang "Brush Up your Shakespeare" alongside Jack Klugman in the television version of *Kiss Me Kate* starring Alfred Drake.

One of Lembeck's favorite movie characters was "Erich Von Zipper," his role in a series of "Beach Party" movies. He made a lovable villain, a little guy with a ridiculous sense of imperiousness and an air of class punctured by his Brooklyn accent. A busy stage actor, he played Sancho Panza in a touring company of *Man of La Mancha* and performed the role at the White House for Lyndon Johnson.

For 15 years Lembeck ran a comedy workshop, coaching young stars, including Robin Williams and John Ritter. In 1981 he made a few appearances on television's "Mork and Mindy" and also appeared on a Lily Tomlin special, but mainly he devoted his attention to his teaching and to producing television specials featuring new talent. He was shooting an episode of "C.H.I.P.S" at the time of his death.

BROADWAY: *Mister Roberts* (1948), *Stalag 17* (1951), *Wedding Breakfast* (1954), *Phoenix 55* (1955), *South Pacific* (1957), *Oklahoma* (1958)

FILMS incl.: *You're in the Navy Now* (1951), *Willie and Joe Back at the Front* (1953), *Stalag 17* (1954), *Sail a Crooked Ship* (1962), *Beach Party* (1963), *Bikini Beach* (1964), *The Unsinkable Molly Brown* (1964), *Beach Blanket Bingo* (1965), *Ghost in the Invisible Bikini* (1966), *The Spirit Is Willing* (1967)

TV: "Sgt. Bilko" ("The Phil Silvers Show") (1955–59), "The Hathaways" (1961–62), "Ensign O'Toole" (1963–64)

## JACK LEMMON

### (John Uhler Lemmon III, February 8, 1925–   )

The deceptive "Mr. Average" of modern film comedy, Jack Lemmon was the pleasantly good-looking, nice guy star of sitcom movies from *Good Neighbor Sam* to *The Odd Couple* to *The Out of Towners*. He usually had a mildly upwardly mobile job, traces of modern neurosis and the good old American virtue of feisty determination in crisis. If he got involved in mischief *(Mister Roberts)*, schemes *(The Fortune Cookie)* or screwball insanity (his drag role in *Some Like It Hot*), his sense of righteous rage and moral indignation usually won out. Lemmon made it look so easy that it took a long time before he was given full credit as one of the best actors in comedy over the past several decades—as well as one of America's best dramatic actors.

Some of the neurosis in Lemmon's portrayals might have been with him from birth: "I was born at the Newton-Wellesley Hospital in Newton, Mass. in the elevator. I was born two months premature, with a testicle that refused to drop and acute jaundice—and the nurse quipped, 'My, look at the yellow Lemmon.' At least, that's what my mother told me."

Lemmon remembers suffering through a sickly childhood, being alone a lot. His father was a boss with the Doughnut Corporation of America, his mother a beguiling storyteller. It was no secret that his parents stayed together for the sake of the child. They eventually separated when he was at Andover. By this time Lemmon had become active in sports, breaking a school record in the two-mile run. He

enjoyed playing the piano, which remained an important outlet for his creative energies throughout his career. At harvard he was busy writing songs for Hasty Pudding Club revues.

After navy service he went to New York with $300 from his father. When it ran out, he worked in a restaurant. "I did anything to keep myself alive while I was keeping my dreams alive. I can't say it was tough. Nothing is tough when you're in your late teens and early 20's. . . . You're absorbed with achieving the goal that you want to achieve. . . . There were times when I didn't have any money and I'd sleep in free places like buildings that were condemned and had X's on the windows."

He worked as a piano man in bars, acting in early television dramas and on radio. He married Cynthia Stone in 1950. They worked together when Jack hosted "Ad Libbers," a comedy improvisation television show, and "Heaven for Betsy," where they played newlyweds.

In 1953 he played the naive, bewildered playwright Leo Davis in a revival of *Room Service* on Broadway. Columbia Pictures was impressed and signed him. Studio head Harry Cohn wanted him to change his name to Lennon, afraid critics would call his picture a lemon. Jack told Cohn that moviegoers might confuse Lennon with the Communist leader Lenin. Amid the confusion, Jack stuck to his real name, claiming that if he could endure school days being called "John U. Lemmon" he could deal with anything. His debut film was *It Should Happen to You* with Judy Holliday. They starred together in *Phfft!* as well, but it would be his role as Ensign Pulver in *Mister Roberts* that established him as a bright new star. He won an Academy Award for the part and seemed typed for a while as a slightly manic and excitable fellow, brash but sometimes frustrated into a mild comic stutter.

He and Cynthia Stone divorced in 1956, and he married Felicia Farr in 1962. Through the late 1950s and early 1960s, Lemmon progressed from bratty mischief (a warlock in *Bell Book and Candle*) to brilliant screwball comedy *(Some Like It Hot)* to serio-comic and dramatic roles *(The Apartment* and *Days of Wine and Roses)*. He racked up Academy Award nominations for all those films before settling into comfortable domestic sitcom films (many of them dated, such as *Good Neighbor Sam*). The best from that era include the classic *The Odd Couple* and others featuring friend and frequent co-star Walter Matthau.

The 1970s proved a fertile decade for Lemmon's versatility in comedy and drama. He never called attention· to it, but he was always careful about his movie roles, often making moral choices as to what he wanted to play, even if he had to work for scale to get a particular film done. He won another Academy Award for 1973's serious *Save the Tiger*, earned an Emmy nomination for his tour-de-force as *The Entertainer* in a 1976 made-for-television movie and won praise for his return to Broadway in *The Tribute* in 1978. Pure comedy wasn't neglected. He and Matthau starred in *The Front Page,* and he delivered the perfect touch of humanity and believability to another comedy of brittle neurosis and near breakdown, *Prisoner of Second Avenue.*

Lemmon repeated the formula of mixed comedies and dramas into the 1980s, always presenting something not only fresh but important. These included the powerful movie about a nuclear meltdown, *The China Syndrome,* the serio-comic morality study *Mass Appeal* and the comedy *That's Life!* with his wife Felicia Farr, which mirrored his own anxieties over turning 60. He would later enjoy the pleasures and pains of acting far older than that in *Dad.* He even found time for the Broadway revival of *Long Day's Journey into Night.*

In comedy, Lemmon always admired Chaplin and contemporary Walter Matthau. In drama, his favorites are Spencer Tracy, Laurence Olivier and Robert Donat. One of the few performers to have won Academy awards for both comedy and drama, he continues to hunt for new movie and stage roles, proud to say "I have never lost a total passion for my work." He once said, "Comedy is more difficult than drama on every level. It's more difficult to act, to write, to direct. . . . Comedy has to be . . . totally successful. A drama can hold your interest, have some highlights and you don't necessarily go out and say it missed. But if something is supposed to be funny, and we *know* it's supposed to be funny, and it doesn't end up funny, you're dead."

He was once asked how he felt about being called "the best comic actor in America" and a great serious actor as well. Lemmon reflected, "I like both. Who wouldn't? The thing I really like best was said about me by an old schoolmate of mine named Fred Jordan. Fred said I always had the grace to make a fool out of myself. I really love that."

AUDIO: *Twist of Lemmon* (Epic), *Some Like It Hot* (Epic), *Jack Lemmon Narrates E. B. White* (Riverside), *Peter and the Wolf* (Laserlight)
BIOGRAPHY: *Lemmon* (Widener, 1975)
BROADWAY: *Room Service* (1953), *Face of a Hero* (1960), *Idiot's Delight* (1970), *Tribute* (1978), *Long Day's Journey into Night* (1988)
FILMS incl.: *It Should Happen to You* (1954), *Phfft!* (1954), *My Sister Eileen* (1955), *Mister Roberts* (1955), *You Can't Run Away from It* (1956), *Operation Mad Ball* (1957), *Bell Book and Candle* (1959), *It Happened to Jane* (1959), *Some Like It Hot* (1959), *The Apartment* (1960), *The Wackiest Ship in the Army* (1960), *Pepe* (1960), *The Notorious Landlady* (1962), *Days of Wine and Roses* (1962), *Irma La Douce* (1963), *Under the Yum Yum Tree* (1963), *Good Neighbor Sam* (1964), *The Great Race* (1965), *The Fortune Cookie* (1966), *The Odd Couple* (1968), *The Out of Towners* (1969), *The War Between Men and Women* (1972), *Save the Tiger* (1973), *The Front Page* (1974), *Prisoner of Second Avenue* (1975), *The Entertainer* (1975), *The China Syndrome* (1979), *Buddy Buddy* (1981), *Mass Appeal* (1985), *That's Life* (1986), *Dad* (1989), *For Richer or Poorer* (1992)
TV: "That Wonderful Guy" (1949–50), "Toni Twin Time" (1950), "Ad Libbers" (1951), "Heaven for Betsy" (1952), "Alcoa Theatre" (1957–58)

# JAY LENO

## (James Douglas Muir Leno, April 28, 1950–   )

At first, television critics couldn't get past Jay Leno's unusual face. He had "the chin of Dudley Do-right and the facial contortions of Herman Munster," said one. "Looks like a cross between a young Elvis Presley and an upright Gerry Cooney," another reported. One called him "anvil faced." Another "pelican headed." His voice was also out of the norm for the average comic, a sometimes lispy nasal whine that rose in pitch when aggravated, but just as easily shifted low for impatient grousing. Once the comic's face and voice were described, his comedy style was next. "A barroom bouncer version of Andy Rooney," said one. "The common sense comedian," said another. "I got a write-up once where the guy said I was a thinking blue-collar comedian," Leno recalled, "which I sort of like."

After years of television talk show exposure, including regular guest-hosting for "The Tonight Show," Leno emerged as the most likable of the show's regulars, youthful and acerbic enough to please the crucial young audience the show was losing, yet genial and working class enough to keep the older audience tuning in. And so the comic with the unlikely visage became such a familiar face to American viewers that he was chosen to replace retiring host Johnny Carson.

Born in New Rochelle, New York and raised in Andover, Massachusetts, the part Scots/Irish, part Italian youngster recalled that he always got laughs, even at the age of "about three and a half. I remember a group of people. I remember the living room. I remember the tiny TV, and I remember saying 'How come girls have camel humps?' I remember my aunt—'Oh, oh.' The whole family was there—'Oh, oh' and they go running around the room. And my father and the men were laughing. And my mother . . . she's trying to act as if nothing happened." Soon Jay was the class clown in school. When the students were discussing the adventures of Robin Hood, Jay had something to add. "They killed people by boiling them in oil," he declared. "But they couldn't boil Tuck. He was a friar!"

Leno's first job was not in comedy but working for a Ford dealership. After he was fired for dropping a hubcap, Jay wrote a letter to Henry Ford II complaining about his unfair treatment. He got his job back. Later he worked as a chauffeur and got an assignment to do the driving for Jack Lemmon. Leno confessed his show biz ambitions to Jack, who encouraged him and added affably, "Maybe you'll move to Beverly Hills and we'll be neighbors." That prophecy would later come true.

By the time he graduated from Emerson College, Leno was working Boston strip clubs, performing comedy between the acts for $20 a night. "When I was a teenager, all I had to do to get on stage in clubs in Boston was bribe the bartender $50. I told him if you like my act I get the $50 back. Later I went around auditioning all over the place in Manhattan with my friend Freddie Prinze." He had trouble getting to television. One agent confided, "Your face will frighten little children." Circa 1974, sporting fashionably long hair, Leno tried out routines such as Elvis Presley doing "To Be or Not to Be." In 1975 he met David Letterman in California and the two formed a close friendship. Over the years Leno sharpened his stand-up style and relied more on commentary than zany antics. He wrote for Jimmie Walker and in 1977 made his first appearance on "The Tonight Show."

Over the next ten years Jay was known as comedy's "road warrior," relentlessly touring the country, learning to tell the same joke and get the same amount of laughter from a young urban audience or an older Vegas crowd. He had his share of troubles along the way. Opening for Muddy Waters, he was hit in the head with a ketchup bottle. The club owner remarked, "You're a professional. You should have seen it coming." Another time a ringsider shouted, "I hate you!" Reasonably, Jay answered, "How can you hate me? You don't even know me." He leaned down and asked, "Where are you from?" The man laid Jay out with one punch. Despite such moments, Jay discovered, "Everybody's got a sense of humor—a comedian's job is to find it. . . . You don't have to change your act, just your angles. Let's say you're doing a phone company joke. In Vegas you might start out saying 'I've had some trouble with the telephone company lately.' In a college you might start by saying 'Damn Nazi fascists at the phone company.' . . ."

Mort Sahl was clearly Jay's main influence as he became more and more known for "clever" comedy with topical bite. He said, "I always liked Mort Sahl better than Lenny Bruce. . . . I liked Lenny okay, but my feeling was that a lot of the time he was preaching to the converted. . . . Mort would come on a middle-class show like Ed Sullivan, and TV was as white bread as it could be in the '50s, and he would go after somebody like Joe McCarthy. He did it with such a sharp wit that even people who didn't

Topical stand-up comic Jay Leno was given the honor of following three legends, Steve Allen, Jack Paar and Johnny Carson, as the host of late-night television's most prestigious series, "The Tonight Show." Photo from the author's collection.

want to hear it said, 'Yeah, Sahl's right.' I like people who work within certain confines and can be clever within those confines." Unlike Sahl, Leno was not branded an intellectual political satirist. This was fine with him, since he thought of himself as "just an average person, and if I have any special intelligence, it's in the area of comedy. I tend to like popular things and I get confused by the same foreign films that most people get confused by." At the time the most successful stand-up performer at performing topical wit for the masses was Johnny Carson. And soon Leno would be one of Carson's favorite guest hosts of "The Tonight Show," then the only guest host and ultimately the host.

Along the way Leno picked up a few tricks in getting his point across without offending. Rather than use four-letter words, he adopted a funnier strategy. "Instead of calling someone a [four-letter name], it's funnier to call them a sodomite or penophile. It makes people laugh." Leno also learned to emulate Johnny Carson's habit of smiling and seeming to chuckle lightheartedly after squelching an audience heckler or delivering a particularly potent line. It helped the audience understand he was "just kidding." He was also not above the old Carson habit of the lightly blue one-liner: "They're operating on hemorrhoids using lasers . . . you talk about seeing the light at the end of the tunnel!"

One of the differences between Leno's approach and Carson's is Jay's love of chiding sarcasm, dressing up a cartoonish joke with mock irritation: "A woman in New York—this was in the paper today—was arrested for going topless on the beach. . . . You know, we have dead animals, we have medical waste, oil on the beach—the people who do that, they don't get arrested, right? Yet a woman walks around topless, she gets arrested. Now what would you rather have on a beach, a dead oily animal or a topless woman? Yeah! Boy! One happy note—you don't hear about beached whales anymore. I guess with all these oil slicks they just slide back into the water."

Once he was promoted to host duty, Leno quickly established a favorite new comedy feature on the show, his collection of absurd newspaper headlines, most loaded with unintentional irony: "First Annual Animal Abuse Council Benefit Pig Roast."

In 1986 Jay headlined 300 shows around the country at $15,000 minimum per show. That year he received a two-year contract to work the Sands Casino in Vegas and starred in a Showtime cable special. He had gotten a lot of television exposure thanks to both "The Tonight Show" and his many appearances on "Late Night with David Letterman." Within a year he was named the permanent host on "The Tonight Show," subbing for Carson a dozen weeks during the year and appearing every Tuesday night. Typically the down-to-earth comic made fun of his success: "Permanent guest host? That's a triple oxymoron—three words in a row that contradict the one before." In 1991 he was named the host, only the fourth since "The Tonight Show" premiered in 1954. His estimated salary: $3 million per year. He put it all into perspective quickly. "Well, when I called my mother, she said, 'Oh, I love Johnny. Why can't Johnny stay and maybe they can find something else you can do? Isn't there another time spot for you?' I said, 'Ma, whatever you do, don't talk to the press.' "

Like Carson, Leno displays coolness under pressure and a love for his work: "You get into the lights and then it's like a Zen thing. It's the most quiet, relaxed place in the world when you're on stage, because you're just there. Like you're in this cradle and you just rock back and forth. The laughs kind of hold you up and keep you going."

BOOKS: *Headlines; More Headlines; Still More Headlines*
FILMS incl.: *Silver Bears* (1978), *American Hot Wax* (1978), *Collision Course* (1987)
TV: "The Marilyn McCoo and Billy Davis Jr. Show" (1977), "The Tonight Show" (1992–  )
VIDEOS: *Dr. Duck; Jay Leno's Vanishing America*

## JACK E. LEONARD

### (Leonard Lebitsky, April 24, 1911–May 11, 1973)

The 300-pound, egg-bald comedian seemed pretty friendly: "You look like a nice bunch of people. And I'm a nice bunch of people, so maybe we'll have a good time." But when the audience didn't smile at his often lame gags, he got nasty: "When you cross the George Washington to go home, I hope the bridge falls!"

Then, the crowd laughed. For the next 20 years Jack E. Leonard perfected the first successful stand-up act based on insults, the bombing comedian hurling bombs back at the audience. That the stumbling comic's mumbled jokes and muttered insults were mostly harmless and ridiculous made the show even funnier.

As "Fat Jack" acknowledged, "An insult is only funny if it's really ridiculous, and if it's aimed at some really big shot." His insults to ringsiders were usually halfhearted and tossed out in self-defense: "The next time you go on a Halloween tour I hope your broom breaks!" The shots at celebrities were also blunt and silly. To Perry Como: "You have a very fine voice. Too bad it's in Bing Crosby's throat!"

With a hand splayed defensively across his vulnerable belly, his posture more like a poised and polite salesman, Leonard muttered his gags like a

pitcher slinging the ball underhand. The windup was hard to hear and tentative ("Well, I'd just like to say . . .") and when it finally came in, it was laughably obvious: ". . . that if there's ever a price on your head, take it."

Born in Chicago, Leonard was slim and athletic in his prime, a varsity swimmer at Northwest University. A good dancer, he performed in a variety of revues and toured with the USO during World War II. It was after the war that he developed into a stand-up star and through the 1950s and early '60s a frequent guest on television variety shows. Jack had a ready wit and was a formidable ad-libber at Friar's Roasts and other gatherings of fellow comics. He was rarely without a comeback. Once when he was about to perform on Ed Sullivan's variety show, Sullivan told him the show was running long and asked Jack to cut his routine down. "What can you do in three minutes?" Sullivan asked. Jack said, "Boil two eggs." Sullivan let him do his full routine.

Leonard was an authentic comedy character with his bulky build and bald dome and his trademark mumbling delivery. His personality was as important as his jokes. A favorite of impressionists, Fat Jack even was turned into a cartoon character, the "illegal eagle" on "The Beany and Cecil Show."

Married for 22 years, Jack remarried after his first wife died in 1967, and adopted three children. The aging Jack continued to perform, though he faded in the late '60s, replaced by the more visceral and direct Don Rickles. On his first night at The Rainbow Grill in New York City he became ill. A month later he underwent open heart surgery. Two weeks after that he was dead. Friends and fellow comics eulogized him as a great comic and a fast man with a quip—a man who in private life was quite different from his abrasive stage personality. Of course, Jack would never have admitted to having a soft spot. Rather than a "just-kidding" closing speech, he enjoyed telling the audience: "Ladies and gentlemen, if I've said anything to offend anybody here tonight, I'd like to repeat everything I've said!"

AUDIO: *How to Lose Weight* (RCA), *Rock and Roll for Kids over 16* (Vik), *Scream on Someone You Love Today* (Verve)

FILMS incl.: *Three Sailors and a Girl* (1953), *The Disorderly Orderly* (1964), *The World of Abbott and Costello* (1965), *The Fat Spy* (1965)
VIDEO: *The Arthur Godfrey Show*

## JERRY LESTER

### (February 16, 1910–   )

Jerry Lester's main claim to fame is for something he did do but didn't do. He's generally credited as the "first host" of television's "Tonight Show." But the name of the late-night series was called "Broadway Open House" at the time.

Lester, an energetic "top banana"–style comedian, got the job when "Creesh" Hornsby contracted polio and died shortly before he was scheduled to begin the show. Lester jumped in, bringing along a busty stooge named Dagmar and decades of experience in comedy.

Lester was born in Chicago and attended Northwestern University. As unlikely as it seems, Jerry studied ballet with Marcel Berger and voice with Alexander Nakutin. It was only after he tore a ligament dancing that he turned to comedy. In 1940 he was a summer replacement for Bob Hope's show and in 1941 became a regular guest on radio's "Kraft Music Hall." His own radio show followed, along with Broadway musicals and nightclub work at The Chez Paris and Copacabana. He became the master of ceremonies at The Latin Quarter, which was run by newscaster Barbara Walters' father, Lou Walters. Jerry's brother, Buddy Lester, was also a comic.

Jerry was earning big bucks and, as he recalled, living in "an apartment at 40 Central Park South, the ritziest spot in town, ten rooms on the 12th floor . . . [NBC's president] Sylvester Weaver, who was called 'Pat,' had decided he wanted to build up the night hours, which were empty of sponsors, so he thought up getting some act or acts. He hired ['Creesh' Hornsby]. The guy died a week before the first announced show was to go on the air. There was panic. One day my wife Alice began badgering me to buy her a mink coat. I asked 'How much is it?' She said, 'Forty-five hundred.' At that moment Pat Weaver called on the phone . . . he wanted me, he said the fellow that was to go on had died. I said, 'Why didn't you tell him not to?' Pat asked how

much would I charge to go on for a week. I turned to Alice and said, 'How much is that coat?' 'Forty-five hundred.' I said, 'Pat, I'll go on for three nights only, at $1,500 a night.' "

On May 29, 1950 he premiered on NBC's "Broadway Open House," with Morey Amsterdam hosting the remaining two nights. Like many other burlesque/vaudeville-style programs, it relied on skits, old gags, songs and a sexpot dumbelle to absorb the top-banana comic's double entendres. The show was a hit, further annoying critics who complained about the number of "low" comics, such as Ed Wynn, Abbott and Costello, and Milton Berle already on the tube. Within a year Lester and Dagmar were feuding, the old gags seemed even older and the novelty was gone. Lester quit the show.

He went on to other programs, but critical response was the same. In 1952 the *New York Times* caught his new series, "Saturday Night Dance Parade," and huffed, "Mr. Lester apparently fancies himself as the life of the party who can put together a couple of old jokes and play the Palace. On Saturday he dug out of the files the one about the dumb musician who thought Paganini stood for 'Page Nine.' What's more, he made a production of it. Come on, Congress, get on with that TV investigation! Between lulls Mr. Lester grimaces, gestures, smirks, screams, runs around, falls down, gets up, stands, sings, frowns, leers and sticks his tongue out. . . . He desperately needs material and, more desperately, stern discipline and direction."

Lester had his boosters, including columnist Earl Wilson, who praised Jerry's you-hadda-be-there brand of humor. Wilson once described Jerry's famous routine as a man with a broken leg playing golf: "Carefully gripping his imaginary golf club—making sure he had the right hold on the thin air—he drew back, started his swing, kept swinging—and then rolled over on the floor in a heap. . . . This silly piece of business got one of the biggest laughs I'd ever heard a comedian get. But the next piece of nonsense got even a bigger roar." This was Lester's juggling routine, bouncing five rubber balls on the floor and over his head. "We were all surprised he was that good. . . . Now he held out still another ball which he was going to add to the bunch he kept bouncing. All of us wondered whether he would be able to handle this extra ball too. Jerry finally bounced the extra ball on the floor while we looked on in suspense. . . . It hit the floor with a thick, dull thud—and flattened out until it looked like a cookie. It was a handful of putty that Jerry had shaped to look like a ball. They were howling with laughter when Jerry, with feigned anger, said, 'All right! Who threw that matzo ball in here?' "

Many 1950s comics with Lester's style had the same problem he had, changing tastes. Lester moved on to successful business careers in real estate and insurance, occasionally turning up on the straw hat trail (including a 1965 revival of *A Funny Thing Happened on the Way to the Forum*). In May 1986 Lester joined Steve Allen, Jack Paar and Johnny Carson to form a kind of Mount Rushmore of late-night television, appearing together for the first time on an NBC 60th anniversary special.

BROADWAY: *Earl Carroll's Vanities* (1940), *All in Fun* (1940), *Beat the Band* (1942), *Jackpot* (1944), *South Pacific* (1969)

TV: "Cavalcade of Stars" (1950), "Broadway Open House" (1950–51), "Chesterfield Sound-Off Time" (1951), "Saturday Night Dance Parade" (1952), "Pantomime Quiz" (1953–55)

## DAVID LETTERMAN

### (April 12, 1947–   )

Steve Martin turned the clichés of stand-up comedy around in the 1970s. David Letterman did the same thing for comedy talk shows in the '80s, literally turning things around when he had his cameras broadcast one show upside down. Viewers kept watching, quite in keeping with Letterman's comfortable brand of anarchy.

The cult hero of late-night television, Letterman, like his idol Johnny Carson, has made something unique from synthesizing the styles of other comedians. Steve Allen let his cameras roam the streets while he offered ad-lib commentary. Letterman made that a regular feature, peeking into local shops and office buildings with mock querulousness and snickers. Allen also loved stunt comedy, once turning himself into a human tea bag and being lowered in a huge cup of water. Letterman dunked his Alka-Seltzer tablet-festooned body in water. Groucho Marx

Top 10 lists, stupid pet tricks and the "thrill cam": David Letterman's "Late Night" antics have made him a hero to a generation of comedy fans and like-minded wise guys. Photo from the author's collection.

favored a detached, insulting style with people on "You Bet Your Life," and Letterman quickly became known for needling guests and putting them off balance, sometimes to the point where they vowed never to return (something he'd allude to the next night with flabbergasted surprise). Most of all (and especially evident in the early shows), Letterman copied Carson's attitude, the combination of cool urbanite and goofy, middle American. Letterman could be commanding and daunting, looking all of his six-foot, two-inch height, or he could seem four foot three with his Alfred E. Newman gap-toothed grin and the unruly mop of wavery, wavy hair that he liked to tug at and pretend was a toupee.

Carson was perceived as a lovable scamp and Letterman shared that attitude, whether in conducting comically impatient phone interviews with his own mother or throwing watermelons from a roof just to see them smash. Letterman dressed like a rebellious youth forced to wear something proper: blazer, slacks . . . and a pair of sneakers. Like a typical teen, his sense of jeering cynicism could only be broken by "neat stuff," such as playing with a "thrill-cam" video camera soaring above the audience or the appearance of a budding actress in a slinky dress. This would usually illicit a squint, a high-pitched giggle or perhaps a moan of "Oh, man!"

Two decades younger than Carson, Letterman lacks Carson's reverence for show business and has won over fans with his mock curmudgeonly intolerance for sentiment. While Carson endeared himself to audiences via cute segments holding precocious wild animals, Letterman's regular feature is "stupid pet tricks."

After a few years Letterman's anti-show biz hostility turned into a more detached amusement. He evolved a style comfortable enough to withstand nightly duty but prickly enough to keep viewers expecting the unexpected. They could always expect to see him, though. When he celebrated his 8th anniversary show on February 1, 1990, it marked his 1,255th show—not one of them helmed by a guest host. Along the way, his viewership rose from an average 2.5 million to 3.4 million.

Born and raised in Indianapolis, Letterman attended schools with names that seem like pungent parodies of middle-America normality: Broad Ripple High School and Ball State University. In high school he and a pal would throw eggs at the houses of the class's prettiest and most inaccessible girls. In college he grew a beard (but no mustache) and was thrown off the classical radio station for his tongue-in-cheek wisecracks: "That was Claire de Lune. You know the de Lune sisters. There was Claire and there was Mabel."

Letterman formed "The Dirty Laundry Company," an improvisational group that included Joyce DeWitt as a member. He debuted on local television hosting late-night movies and doing the weather. "You can only announce the weather, the highs and lows, so many times before you go insane," he said. "In my case, it took two weeks. I started clowning . . . I made up my own measurement for hail and said hailstones the size of canned hams were falling. . . . People said, 'Who is this punk and why is he making fun of the relative humidity?' "

Letterman moved on to stand-up comedy, performing in Los Angeles in 1975, where he also wrote for other comics and joined the staff for television's "Paul Lynde Comedy Hour." He remained just another young journeyman in a suit doing "The Starland Vocal Band Show" in 1977, "Rock Concert," "The Gong Show" and game shows such as "The $20,000 Pyramid." He recalled with a grim, self-effacing smile that the contestants "all lost with me." He was in the cast of Mary Tyler Moore's ill-fated "Mary" show. Finally, on November 26, 1978, he made his "Tonight Show" debut.

NBC eventually gave him a morning show, which was canceled in October 1980 (it won a posthumous Emmy). His next move would be as different as night and day. "Late Night with David Letterman" premiered on February 1, 1982. The *New York Times* wrote: "He is more of an acquired taste." The *New York Post:* "A hip generation's Carson show." The *Village Voice:* "He can push a suggestive joke without offending the sensibilities of the more conservative sleepy-pies."

Letterman acknowledged his influences, saying "I'd rather be Johnny Carson." He admitted, "I was a real fan of the Steve Allen Westinghouse show and I would be happy if I could capture a part of that feeling." Just as Steve Allen's show had a clubhouse feel, with viewers tuning in every night just to be a silent sidekick to Steve, Letterman viewers watch no matter who the guest is. They enjoy Dave's attitude, which suggests that show biz is just a sham, but that it is still better than anybody else's day job. Speaking pointedly to his generation, Letterman's speech is filled with ironically used ejaculations from 1950s television, a mocking use of "Oh my," "Oh gee," "What's the deal?" "Say, kids," and the like, all designed to underline the reality behind childhood promises and adulthood.

With occasional interruptions to ask "How much time do we have?" or to meander out into the hallway to chat with a security guard, Letterman keeps his show offbeat, a mix of planned and unplanned amusements. Jay Leno once pointed out one of the many contradictions in Letterman: "Dave is one of the few performers who can say something real vicious and have it come across as a cute aside." Or vice versa.

Letterman admits, "We may have alienated as many people as we may have won over, because there are people who hate me and hate the show." Even Dave's biggest fans cannot be sure if, when he reads one of their letters on the air or waves back when they shout to him on the street, he likes them or is making fun of them. That uncomfortable quality, a part of the show, a part of him, goes back to his own relationship with mentor Johnny Carson. Letterman recalled, "I've never been able to feel comfortable with the man. He's been very gracious to me, very nice . . . I could spend every minute of my life from now on with Johnny Carson and I don't think I'd get over that sense of awe."

Letterman has often tried to reduce any sense of awe the audience might have of him as a "star." He comes out to meet the audience before a taping. He often makes fun of his own "goofy" looks. When he makes headlines for his own foibles (endless traffic citations for speeding) or those of others (the deranged woman who was jailed after breaking into his New Canaan, Connecticut house six times, convinced she was his wife), Letterman always has a joke or two, on the show, realizing his fans would be wondering "What's the deal?"

Letterman's show became the in program to do and often featured cameos from Tony Randall, Jerry Vale, Jane Pauley, Tom Brokaw, Teri Garr, Arnold Schwarzenegger and others willing to make fun of their own fame via ignoble walk-ons.

The most consistent ritual of the show is the recitation of "The Top 10 List," an example of comedy shorthand. Rather than tell jokes the old-fashioned way, Letterman sets up a premise and lets the hip audience join him in checking off the possible variations. He might announce that the night's topic is: "Top 10 Least Popular Candy Bars." Then he reads them, from "Good and Linty," or "Mexican Monkey Brittle" to "Roger Ebert's Mystery Log." Reading with detachment, Letterman may mutter a sarcastic "I couldn't be more proud" if an easy joke gets a laugh.

The shorthand of The Top 10 List extends to the opening monologue. Letterman dispenses with the Carson staple of a long, sharp monologue in favor of a minute or two of observations and seemingly deliberate nonjokes. "I used to think my routines were pretty smart, pretty witty, pretty clever observations," he said, "but the material is secondary. Your personality and attitude are primary. If people buy and accept you as a personality and

understand your comedic viewpoint, then you can say to them, 'Here is my attitude and that attitude applies to everything and if you share this attitude then you're going to find everything I'm talking about fairly amusing.'

"I don't have that undeniable performing instinct in my veins like some guys. Robin Williams or Richard Pryor, they would get on stage six, seven times a night. . . . I get up there and have to do 20 minutes, I'm gone in 15. . . . And I don't like the comedian image—the feeling that I'm the court jester who comes out after the banquet to make people laugh. I've had debates with my comedian friends about that. They say, 'What are you talking about? You can make huge sums of money as a comic.' And I say, 'You give me Shecky Greene or David Brinkley: Which of the two is going to get more respect?' "

Respect is something Letterman seems ambivalent about. Half the time he is laughing at his own "nickel-and-dime show" and making fun of stardom, but just as often he shows unconcealed displeasure with cost-cutting memos from NBC's owner, General Electric, or the failure to be consulted when reruns of his show were sold to a cable network. Through it all, David Letterman displays the one quality that keeps the most successful talk show hosts in business year after year—the ability to keep an audience entertained every night, but wanting to know: "What's he *really* like?"

BOOK: *The Late Night with David Letterman Book of Top Ten Lists* (1985)
TV: "The Starland Vocal Band Show" (1977), "Mary" (1978), "The David Letterman Show" (1981), "Late Night with David Letterman" (1982–   )


# SAM LEVENSON

## (December 28, 1911–August 27, 1980)

An ex-schoolteacher from Brooklyn, Sam Levenson was a favorite in the 1950s and '60s for his nostalgic good humor. Most of his epigrams were middle-class truisms that left his audience nodding in agreement. On women's lib: "You've got to look like a lady, act like a man and work like a dog." On television: "The greatest spectacle of the year was my TV repairman's bill." On children: "Between the ages of 12 and 17 a parent can age 30 years."

After graduating from Brooklyn College, Levenson became a Spanish teacher at Samuel Tilden High School in Brooklyn. He turned professional comic after his after-dinner speeches and lectures had his audience laughing and encouraging him. In 1946 he stopped teaching and started performing, appearing on Ed Sullivan's "Talk of the Town" television program three years later. From there he hosted his own shows and guested on game shows.

Recognition comedy—the humor of pinpointing human attitude and emotion via anecdotes and amusing description—was not very popular in the 1950s, when audiences were accustomed to Milton Berle's slapstick. Levenson was one of the first to find success with anecdotal material, stories of neighborhood life recounted with warmth and an eye for detail. He had people nodding their heads in amusement and agreement. On his show he described everyday problems with the same irony Andy Rooney would use decades later, but without the trace of malice: "These days we all marvel at that wondrous invention the deep freeze. Do you know that there are children sitting tonight in wealthy homes, starving to death as they huddle around the kitchen table, waiting for hours and hours for lamb chops to defrost?"

As a genial stand-up performer, Levenson found the Catskills and Miami Beach lucrative territory. He also gave comic lectures to a variety of schools and social groups. Over the years he and similar low-key performers such as George Gobel and Myron Cohen had some trouble competing with younger, high-powered performers. The middle-class audience of "The Ed Sullivan Show," and the middle-age and elderly Jewish audiences who loved him no longer were a force in nightclubs during the 1970s. Levenson reached them through a series of best-selling books, including his last volume, *You Don't Have to Be in Who's Who to Know What's What*.

Levenson, complaining of chest pain, was checked into the hospital on August 17, 1980. He died three hours later, leaving a wife and two children. In good spirits up until that day, it was a rather gentle end for one of comedy's gentlest men.

AUDIO: *But Seriously Folks* (Signature)
BOOKS: *Meet the Folks* (1948), *In One Era and Out the Other* (1973), *You Don't Have to Be in Who's Who to Know What's What* (1979), *Sex and the Single Child* (1969), *Everything But Money* (1971)
TV: "The Sam Levenson Show" (1951–57), "This Is Show Business" (1951–54), "Two for the Money" (1955–57), "Masquerade Party" (1958–60), "Celebrity Talent Scouts" (1960)

## AL LEWIS

### (Albert Meister, April 30, 1923–   )

He looks like a human Punch puppet—a beaky nose, squinty button eyes, strong chin and a flat concave mouth that seems almost toothless when he gives out with one of his demented grins. As "Grandpa Munster," Al Lewis was bizarrely amusing, a vampire who happened to talk with a New York accent. For a bloodless creature, he also displayed an amazing amount of comically exaggerated pep and enthusiasm.

Though he remains best known for "The Munsters," Lewis has been a fine comic character actor for years. Born in New York City (some sources report in 1910), a graduate of the Oswego State Teacher's College, Al originally worked in a circus as a barker, clown or anything else that was needed. It was a tough job: "See, in the circus you can't bull . . . you go up on the high wire, you got to cut the butter. Otherwise you are dead. Splash, man." After World War II he lived in Italy for five years but returned to New York and show business.

For his role in Broadway's *Night Circus*, The *New York Mirror* declared, "Al Lewis stands out as a wolfish and amiable tavern keeper." From there he played Moe Shtarker in *Do Re Mi* and then became a regular as irritable, manic Leo Schnauzer on *Car 54 Where Are You*. At the time he described Leo as "always ready to explode. It's a major catastrophe if supper isn't ready on time. He reacts! He erupts!"

The character reflected Al's own aggressive nature. A self-promoter, he said in 1990, "Every day you do nothing about your potential, that's a wasted day. My secret for success is to deal with only those things that you have control over. You'd be amazed at the amount of time you have." While fans continue to watch old reruns of "The Munsters" and quote lines to Lewis, he doesn't bother watching the show. "There's more interesting things in life to do. I'm not a part of a mutual admiration society, you know what I mean? I know what I did, I know what I did good. I know next time I'll do better."

The years after "The Munsters" were tough. His marriage, which produced three sons, ended in divorce after 24 years. Universal Studios, owning the rights to the character, prevented him from doing personal appearances as "Grandpa Munster." But feisty Al Lewis simply began calling himself "Grampa" and went on to make horror comedy videos, star in quickie horror flicks, host WTBS's "Super Scary Saturday" film fests, guest on local New York talk radio shows and open his own "Grandpa's" Italian restaurant in New York City in 1987, located five blocks away from Munster co-star Fred Gwynne's house.

He remains, in makeup or not, quite a character. About the only thing that peeves him is not playing Grandpa Munster in the syndicated revival of the series: "They said I was too old to play the part. If I remember correctly, Grandpa was 316 years old!"

BROADWAY: *Panic* (1935), *The Iceman Cometh* (1956), *The Night Circus* (1958), *One More River* (1960), *Do Re Mi* (1960)

FILMS: incl.: *Munster Go Home* (1966), *The Night Strangler* (1972), *The Munsters' Revenge* (1981), *Fright Night* (1985), *Married to the Mob* (1988)

TV: "Car 54 Where Are You" (1961–63), "The Munsters" (1964–66)

VIDEOS: *Comic Cabby, Grampa's Silly Scaries, Grampa's Monster Movies*

## JERRY LEWIS (See also MARTIN and LEWIS.)

### (Joseph Levitch, March 16, 1926– )

Jerry Lewis' clowning style earned him the love of million of devoted fans. Unfortunately, there is also a large number who simply can't stand his brand of broad zany antics. Of the latter group, Lewis remarked, "People hate me because I am a multifaceted, talented, wealthy, internationally famous genius."

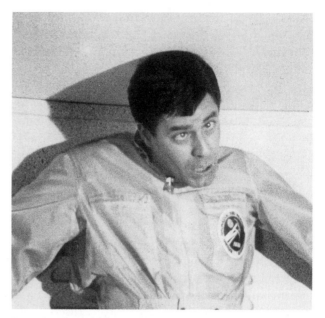

Jerry Lewis and his zany hit films in the 1950s and 1960s still appeal to the young at heart, and have influenced modern comedians Joe Piscopo, Martin Short and Pee-Wee Herman. Photo from the author's collection.

Born in New Jersey, Jerry was five when his vaudevillian parents let him on stage to sing "Brother Can You Spare a Dime." He loved the attention and applause but didn't get more of it. His parents left him with relatives while they toured. He remembered always being alone. A sickly kid who had bronchitis, mastoiditis and spinal problems, he didn't eat much and was ridiculed by his classmates for his thin, gawky frame and goofy looks. He was left back in fifth grade. The teachers were often as nasty as the kids. At Irving High School one of them reprimanded him, adding "All Jews are stupid." In a rage, Lewis overturned the man's desk.

Jerry left school for show business, developing an act that was mostly mugging and miming to records. He married his wife Patti in 1944 (they divorced in the 1980s) and had five children. He teamed with Dean Martin from 1946 to 1956 and then began making solo films, signing a $10 million deal with Paramount. He continued to have box office hits relying more and more on his same bag of stumbling, fumbling slapstick tricks, outrageous rubber-faced mugging and frenzy registered by his loud, high-pitched nasal voice. His audiences seemed to get younger and younger, to the degree where critics believed he was more of a kiddie entertainer than anything else. To kids, he was one of them: someone adults never took seriously and treated condescendingly. He was childlike, his mood swinging from reticent pouting and whining to deliberate manic obnoxiousness. Jerry mirrored the awkward, repressed '50s and early '60s. It is no coincidence that the pomaded, frustrated kid and his frantic antics faded in popularity in the mid 1960s after the arrival of long hair and new social freedom.

Lewis reached his peak between 1960 and 1963, with 1963's *The Nutty Professor* generally considered his best effort. Its plot line helped to establish some reasons behind the bursts of uncontrollably manic energy. That year Lewis went to television with a live two-hour show of production numbers, talk and improvisational comedy. The charge against Lewis, one often leveled at similarly raucous funny men, was no self-control. *Time* magazine called the result "the scriptless life of a semi-educated egocentric boor." One week during the show's very short run, Lewis quipped to a priest in the audience, "Father, would you like to give me the last rites?"

Lewis continued to make films and television appearances, but these were mostly of interest only to his most devoted fans. During the anything-goes 1970s, the comic of the '50s repression and childish rebellion made very few movies. Sometimes accused of injecting too much pathos in his later films, Lewis did have a maudlin side. He said, "Laughter is healing. Do you know how I feel about making people laugh? I have a sort of godly and spiritual feeling about it." One of his most notorious efforts was never released, *The Day the Clown Cried,* filmed in 1974. It was about a clown who had to lure children to their deaths in concentration camps.

Steve Martin's *Jerk* character success in the 1980s buoyed Jerry into something of a comeback. The time seemed right for zany comedy again. Fortunately, he did not seem to have aged a day since the 1950s, still sporting greasy black hair and a smooth complexion. He was billed as "the original Jerk" for the release of *Hardly Working* in 1981. Two years later Lewis received his best notices in years for his work in *The King of Comedy.*

Over the years critics and writers seemed to come down harder on Jerry Lewis than almost any other comedian. The reason was not just his brand of tongue-out-the-mouth goofy comedy, but his foot-in-mouth off-screen comments, some brashly egocentric, obnoxious and vulgar. Typical was a 1986 tirade against a female reviewer. Claiming that he really didn't care about any critic "particularly if it's a female," he added that her writing was probably tainted by hormone problems: "God willing, I hope for her sake it's not the case, but when they get a period it's really difficult for them to function as normal human beings."

Lewis did have reason for his outbursts against critics. Whether a true genius or not, he had an artist's temperament and resented the condescending putdowns of his "low comedy." He pointed out that not everyone could get a laugh with a funny face or a pratfall and that there was some artistic method to his brand of farcical madness. While Americans rarely gave him any kind of honor, in France he was awarded the Legion of Honor.

While he was taken for granted most of the time, Lewis had a strong influence on many comedians, from the more toned-down Bob Denver to the more hyped-up Pee-Wee Herman, to Joe Piscopo and Martin Short, who created characters spiritually based on Jerry's energetic, anything-for-a-laugh personality. Steve Allen said in the 1950s, "I believe Jerry Lewis is the funniest visual comedian since Charlie Chaplin." Forty years later, many would at least admit that visually a Jerry Lewis film is, for funnier or for worse, unforgettable.

To the many children he helped through his muscular dystrophy telethons and charity work, Lewis is unforgettable. While cynics always insisted Lewis's involvement was due to contrition over a comic personality that seemed to mimic the facial contortions of the afflicted, he proved his sincerity in year after tireless year of service to the cause. The first telethon in 1966 raised a million dollars. In 1990, the annual amount was over $40 million. On Jerry's 65th birthday, reporters asked him for his birthday wish. He didn't wish for a hit film or an Academy Award. He said he wanted to see a cure for muscular dystrophy at long last: "I would wish God to give me just as much time as it's gonna take to get the job done."

AUDIO: *Jerry Lewis Sings for Children* (Vocalion), *Just Sings* (Decca), *Big Songs for Little People* (Decca), *Jerry Lewis: Collector's Series* (Capital CD)
AUTOBIOGRAPHY: *Jerry Lewis: In Person* (1982)

FILMS incl.: *Delicate Delinquent* (1957), *The Sad Sack* (1957), *The Geisha Boy* (1958), *Don't Give Up the Ship* (1959), *Visit to a Small Planet* (1960), *The Bellboy* (1960), *Cinderfella* (1960), *Errand Boy* (1961), *It's Only Money* (1962), *The Nutty Professor* (1963), *Who's Minding the Store?* (1964), *The Patsy* (1964), *The Disorderly Orderly* (1964), *Family Jewels* (1965), *Boeing Boeing* (1965), *Three on a Couch* (1966), *The Big Mouth* (1967), *Don't Raise the Bridge, Lower the River* (1968), *Hook Line and Sinker* (1969), *Which Way to the Front?* (1970), *Hardly Working* (1981), *Cracking up* (1983), *Slapstick of Another Kind* (1983), *The King of Comedy* (1983), *Fight for Life* (1987), *Cookie* (1989)

TV: "The Colgate Comedy Hour" (1950–55), "The Jerry Lewis Show" (1963), "The Jerry Lewis Show" (1967–69)

VIDEO: *Jerry Lewis Live*


## JOE E. LEWIS

### (Joe Klewan, January 12, 1902–June 18, 1971)

In the 1940s Frank Sinatra was the ultimate saloon singer, a stylist who influenced almost every pop and jazz singer of the following generation. In that decade Joe E. Lewis was the ultimate nightclub comic, and his breezy booze-and-broads style influenced all of the Jackies and Joes who followed him into swanky night spots and Las Vegas casinos.

Ironically, it was Frank Sinatra who played Joe E. Lewis in *The Joker Is Wild*. The film centered on his years in Chicago and the time when he was victimized by some of the most spectacularly repulsive violence ever heaped on a show business personality.

Lewis was making $650 a week at the gangster-run Green Mill in Chicago. When he signed with a rival club at $1,000 a week, a contract was put out on him. The three men who did the job were convinced they'd beaten him to death; he had been pistol-whipped and punched until bits of his skull were embedded in his brain. His throat was slashed from ear to ear and the knife carved into his tongue and vocal cords.

Somehow Lewis managed to crawl out into the hallway of his hotel room and get help. Somehow he was sewn back together and, after months and months of therapy, was able to rasp out a few words. Finally he began performing again.

He was a tough guy, ever since he was a kid growing up in New York. While attending DeWitt Clinton High School in the Bronx he was already working after hours as a burlesque comic. He left school permanently and joined the marines. When he got out he gravitated to Chicago, perfected his music and comedy act, and nearly lost his life.

Lewis' return to the top was excruciatingly long and painful. In his first few years his scars were still very visible, his voice more of a croak. Later he would insist, "I'm a lucky bum. If I hadn't been cut up I would have been just another comic. The knife sharpened my brain, made me slow down too, improved my delivery."

Finally, in 1933, he had a hit with the novelty tune "Sam You Made the Pants Too Long." At the time, it was smoothly risqué: "I get the damndest breeze through my BVDs. My fly is where my tie belongs. . . . Sam you made the pants too long." By 1940 he was headlining The Copa in New York City, offering sophisticated patter, singing adult ditties, creating an easy atmosphere of good times and good fun.

He drank with the patrons, waving his glass and saluting them with his catch phrase "It is now post time!" His specialty was the dry-as-a-martini declaration: "Show me a man with both feet on the ground and I'll show you a man who can't put his pants on. . . . I've been rich and I've been poor. Believe me, rich is better. . . . I don't like to drink. It's just something I do while I'm getting drunk. . . . There are a lot more important things than money. Trouble is, they all cost money."

Dapper, confident, suave and tough, Lewis was in his element in nightclubs and enjoyed more than his share of booze and broads after hours. He used a middle initial to avoid confusion with fighter Joe Louis, but often insisted he merely borrowed his "E" from an actress who wasn't using it—Lizabeth Scott.

Lewis' brief film appearances give little indication of his appeal. In *Private Buckaroo* he is disappointingly mild and silly, offering up only one decent line. Eyeing one dubious gent: "That's the first time I saw a pair of shoes with three heels!" Lewis didn't do especially well on television variety shows either and generally shunned them. His laidback style was best in nightclubs. His one recording, late in life, gives some idea of what he was like. Unfortunately, by the time he made that disc he was no longer at the top of his game, and some of his acolytes, including smooth singer/booze comic Dean Martin, had updated his style and even made it acceptable to television audiences.

While Dean Martin was succeeding on television with his own variety show, Joe E. Lewis was succumbing to health problems. He suffered a stroke in 1966. He made a comeback and in 1970 appeared at a Friar's Club Roast, announcing "As I approach the final curtain—I leave my broads to Richard Burton." Then he collapsed. He died not long after.

Today the raconteur style of Lewis has been replaced in Las Vegas by the more manic Buddy Hacketts and Shecky Greenes. Lewis' many happy boozer gags repel audiences aware of the havoc alcohol abuse plays in daily life. The word "broad" is as dated as spats. But in his day Joe E. Lewis was the master of stand-up, even if he seemed hardly able to stand up. One time he did declare he would give up drinking: "I can see the handwriting on the floor."

At his funeral, the gathered comedians and show business personalities recalled his classic gags and his wild personality. There were few tears. They seemed to think he had fulfilled his ambition: "You only live once. But if you do it right, once is enough."

AUDIO: *It Is Now Post Time*
BIOGRAPHY: *The Joker Is Wild* (1955)
FILM: *Private Buckaroo* (1942)


# RICHARD LEWIS

## (June 29, 1947–   )

A comic basket case, Richard Lewis seems to be stooped over by his problems, pawing at his forehead, whining and groaning over a catalogue of problems related to a depressed childhood and a miserable social life.

Influenced by Woody Allen and Lenny Bruce, Lewis evolved into an unusual combination of the two. From Woody Allen he took the comedy of neurosis, the sharpness of one-liners and the kind of vulnerability women found fascinating. From Lenny Bruce he took the style of restlessly prowling the stage talking in a confessional stream-of-consciousness style. Possessing the greasy-haired angular good looks and charisma of Lenny, Lewis found himself marketable as a leading man in films and sitcoms.

Lewis admitted to the author that Woody "wrote the strongest one-liners . . . and what made it so great was it worked for his attitude and his look. . . . But Lenny, if there's anything smiliar, we're both manic, we have a lot of energy, a lot of angst coming out. . . . I was blown away by his double Berkeley album . . . he was so ahead of the field and always will be. Sadly, once I got into comedy I couldn't enjoy it, I don't like to listen to other comics, I'm so frighteningly ethical."

Born in Brooklyn, Richard graduated from Ohio State with a degree in marketing. His comedy career began in 1971 when he first began performing in local clubs. "I prepared for six weeks," he said. "Actually my father passed away and it somehow—it was like a catalyst. I was struggling, doing some copy writing, working in the Museum of Modern Art library and a sporting goods store . . . then my father passed away, and I guess it was like a void that had to be filled. I had been goofing around, writing lines for comics, and I just decided to go on stage. . . ."

Lewis' rise to popularity took time. He appeared for a few weeks on television's "Sonny and Cher Comedy Hour" in 1977 but "In one sketch, I played a rutabaga in a chef's salad dance number. My own mother literally didn't recognize me." A made-for-television film, *Diary of a Young Comic,* won some good notices but little else.

A regular on David Letterman's show since 1982, Lewis starred in a 1985 Showtime cable special *I'm in Pain,* which featured guest interview spots by Robin Williams and others. This was a turning point for him. In 1988 he starred in a new HBO special, *I'm Exhausted.* He matched a persuasive personality with sharp one-liners: "I would generally insist, before making love with a date, that we boil ourselves." "I'm a hypochondriac. My blood type is very negative." "My grandparents had a bumper sticker: 'I'd rather be weeping.'" At a time when black comics such as Eddie Murphy and Arsenio Hall were the rage, along with completely nonethnic performers such as Steve Martin, Robin Williams and Garry Shandling, Lewis was conspicuously Jewish, a link to the old tradition in comedy that included Allen and Bruce.

When he co-starred with Jamie Curtis in the sitcom "Anything But Love," a female writer for *US* magazine called him "the coolest neurotic since Woody Allen . . . [he] has charmed his way into America's heart . . . we love him because his love life makes our own more bearable . . ." The show sputtered in and out of ABC's lineup and was eventually shelved permanently. Lewis has returned to stand-up and poor Richard's ailment act continues to dwell on miserable relationships: "I want to marry the woman of someone else's dreams. . . . My ex-girlfriends are listed in 'Who's Who in Torment.' "

FILMS incl.: *Diary of a Young Comic* (1979), *The Wrong Guys* (1988), *Once Upon a Crime* (1992)
TV: "Anything But Love" (1989–90)
VIDEO: *I'm in Pain; Comic Relief II; I'm Exhausted*

## BEATRICE LILLIE

### (Constance Sylvia Munston, May 19, 1894– January 20, 1989)

One of the originators of campy comedy, dubbed "Queen Bea" in her day, Beatrice Lillie was the toast of Broadway with gay ballads and fanciful sketches, many of them tweaking the nose of society types and the aristocracy. She was married to an aristocrat (Baron Robert Peel), but "Lady Peel" referred to herself as "every other inch a lady." Critic Kenneth Tynan noted that the title "sits on her like a halo on an anarchist."

Born in Toronto, originally part of The Lillie Trio with her mother and sister, she achieved fame in London in the comedy revues of Andre Charlot, who had turned her down as a straight singer. She sang novelties such as "The Next Horse I Ride On, I'm Going to Be Tied On" and often performed in male drag with short-cropped hair, which nearly typed her as a male impersonator. Gradually she evolved her outrageous stage style, which included slinging a six-foot string of pearls around her neck and propping a huge, long-stemmed chrysanthemum between her breasts.

Charles Chaplin called her "my female counterpart," more for her spirit than anything else, since her act was basically trashing anything "refined" and turning it into the wryly "grotesque." She said, "I think it's important to be able to laugh at yourself before you can laugh at anybody else, and to detect and deflate pomposity or bad manners, anywhere up or down the social scale."

In private life, she did just that. At the hairdresser's with some chorus girl friends, she was surprised to hear a rich woman loudly remark, "Oh, if I'd known there would be *chorus girls* here today, I never would have come." Lillie found out it was wealthy Mrs. Armour, whose husband owned the famous canned meat company. On her way out, Bea told the manager "You may tell the butcher's wife that Lady Peel has finished."

On another occasion, she endured a rich woman burbling about her jewelry: "I clean my diamonds with ammonia, my rubies with Bordeaux . . . and you, Miss Lillie?" "Oh, I don't bother cleaning mine. When they gets dirty, I simply throw them away."

She could work the other side of the scale too. She was in a cab that stalled due to a St. Patrick's Day parade. "Goddam Irish, bunch of stupid Micks," the cab driver said. Lillie gave him a generous dollar tip at the ride's end, saying "Something for you, driver. Buy yourself a sense of humor."

Bea Lillie's humor endured through personal tragedies well known to her fans. Her husband died at 35 after an appendicitis operation, leaving her in debt. During World War II her son, who had volunteered for hazardous duty, was killed when his ship was under Japanese attack. When news came that he was missing in action, she posted a backstage note to her fellow actors: "I know how you all feel. Don't lets talk about it. Bless you. Now, let's get on with our work."

Lillie continued on, becoming a popular Broadway star. Eddie Cantor noted that funny ladies "like Martha Raye, Joan Davis and Lucille Ball have always been rough and ready. They go in for slapstick and we are happy about them. But for a comedienne with subtlety, whose broadest gesture may be the pointing of a finger or the lifting of an eyebrow, there is only one—Beatrice Lillie. This girl can go through an entire evening's performance without taking a deep breath while her audience is choking with laughter."

Bea could be rather impish on stage. In *The Show Is On*, she played opposite Bert Lahr. In one scene Lahr was supposed to stride up to a box office on stage, ask for a ticket and get into some comedy business with ticket-seller Lillie. "Well," he recalled, "one night when I stepped up, she slammed the window in my face and shouted, 'So sorry. Box office closed for the night.'"

Lillie's style of comedy could be quite eccentric. A quick recitation: "I was standing at the corner of the street, as quiet as quiet could be. When a great big ugly man came up—and tied his horse to me." Often her songs were coy and arch. Singing of her friend Maud: "I said, darling, look at you. And the sordid things you do. . . . Your soul's a bed where worms queue up to breed. You don't know what life's for, Maud. You're rotten to the core, Maud. And Maud agreed."

Audiences loved her bravado and battiness. Through the 1950s she starred in her own one-woman show and more Broadway musicals. Called "the funniest woman of our civilization" by Noel Coward, Lillie unfortunately outlived civilization as she knew it, and her fey enunciations and piquant rhymes went out of style. Her send-ups of mannerly "la dee da" Brits and society types had less of an audience in the 1960s, and songs such as "There Are Fairies at the Bottom of My Garden" had very limited appeal.

Lillie did not find many good roles in the '60s or '70s. *Thoroughly Modern Millie* was a dismal film farewell, allowing her very few moments to shine. She played a conniving white slaver who constantly mutters "Oh, Pook!" in moments of crisis.

Bea Lillie spent her last days in extremely poor health and without the queenly sums of money she had enjoyed in her heyday. For years she lived in obscurity, strokes robbing her of all vitality, her fans not sure if she was dead, alive, or in some horrible state in between. They chose to remember her the way she was in her prime, recalling her the way the *New York Times* once did: "When the audience roars for more and won't let the show go on, she flutters through a devastating mockery of curtsies and fond gestures of farewell."

AUTOBIOGRAPHY: *Every Other Inch a Lady* (1972)
BIOGRAPHY: *Beatrice Lillie, The Funniest Woman in the World* (Laffey, 1972)
BROADWAY incl.: *Andre Charlot's Revue* (1924), *Charlot's Revue* (1925), *Charlot's Revue of 1926* (1926),

*Oh Please* (1926), *She's My Baby* (1928), *This Year of Grace* (1928), *Charlot's Masquerade* (1930), *The Third Little Show* (1931), *Too True to Be Good* (1932), *Walk a Little Faster* (1932), *Please* (1933), *At Home Abroad* (1935), *The Show Is On* (1936), *Happy Returns* (1938), *Set to Music* (1939), *Big Top* (1942), *Seven Lively Arts* (1944), *Better Late* (1946), *Inside USA* (1948), *An Evening with Beatrice Lillie* (1952), *Ziegfeld Follies* (1957), *Auntie Mame* (1958), *High Spirits* (1964)
FILMS incl.: *Exit Smiling* (1926), *The Show of Shows* (1929), *Are You There?* (1930), *Dr. Rhythm* (1938), *On Approval* (1943), *Around the World in Eighty Days* (1956), *Thoroughly Modern Millie* (1967)

## MAX LINDER

### (Gabriel Maximilien Leuvielle, December 6, 1883–October 31, 1925)

The first major star of movie comedy, Max Linder began making films in 1906, turning out dozens of quickies in France. Though forgotten now, in the course of his pioneering work he evolved comedy bits and stylings that influenced Chaplin, The Marx Brothers and others. The famous broken mirror sequence in *Duck Soup*, in which Harpo Marx pretends to be the reflection of Groucho, was first filmed by Linder in *Seven Years' Bad Luck* in 1921. Chaplin once sent a photo of himself to Linder and signed it "To the one and only Max—the Professor—from his disciple, Charles Chaplin."

Some have failed to see any connection between Linder and Chaplin, since Linder evolved a smiling, well-dressed ladies' man character while Charlie was "the tramp." Chaplin was impressed by Linder's comic walk and bearing as well as his eye for invention. Linder was one of the first film comics to announce his presence with a funny walk. He moved like a puppet on strings, his backside jutting out, his back swaying into an ingratiating bow.

Critic Walter Kerr noted a typical example of Linder's originality and Chaplin's homage. In *Max and the Statue*, Linder passes out drunk in a museum. He's covered by a sheet and later "unveiled" as a new piece of statuary by immediately chagrined museum officials. In *City Lights*, Chaplin's little tramp falls asleep and is similarly "unveiled."

In the same film, Linder, hiding in a suit of armor, is about to be cut open by thieves convinced there's treasure inside. He "comes to life" and frightens them away. A similar gag was used in a Three Stooges short, *Gem of a Jam,* in which Curly, disguised as a plaster-covered mannequin, is about to have his head cut off by thieves looking for a hiding place for a gem.

Some of Linder's gags sound as if they could be from Chaplin films. In one film he pretended to be a pedicurist, lathering up his patron's foot like a barber. In another he buys a guard dog to make sure his wife isn't cheating—and ends up living with the dog. Ironically, when Chaplin left Essanay to sign with Mutual, Essanay imported Linder to take his place for a series of critically well-received shorts. At the time Linder was in poor health. He had retired from films in 1911 and had been severely injured by chemical warfare attacks during World War I. After three films released in 1917, illness forced him to retire again. But again, after a period of recuperation, he returned with *Seven Year's Bad Luck,* featuring the mirror sequence. He was the first to film this classic bit of comedy, though variations on it had been performed on stage as early as 1848 by Charles Manetti and Rhum at the Cirque Olympique, and by The Hanlon-Lees troupe in 1860 at Niblo's Gardens in New York.

In August 1923 Linder eloped with 17-year-old Madeleine Peters. Theorists believed Linder's health failed him again when, in November 1925, he and his young bride entered into a different kind of pact. They took poison and slit their wrists. They left behind an infant daughter, Maud. It was Maud who, years later, gathered her father's best work and restored some measure of his fame with the 1963 compilation film, *Laugh with Max Linder.*

BIOGRAPHY: *Max Linder* (Ford)

FILMS incl.: *An Unexpected Meeting* (1906), *A Rustic Idyll* (1907), *Mad Comes Across* (1917), *Max Wants a Divorce* (1917), *Max in a Taxi* (1917), *Le Petit Cafe* (1919), *Le Feu Sacre* (1920), *Be My Wife* (1921), *Seven Years Bad Luck* (1921), *The Three Must Get Their's* (1922), *Au Secours! i.e, (Help!)* (1923), *En Compagnie de Max Linder (aka Laugh with Max Linder)* (1963), *L'homme au Chapeau de Soie* (1983)

# RICH LITTLE

## (November 26, 1939–   )

The most successful impressionist in show business history, Rich Little has rarely been topped since his big break in America, a 1964 appearance on Judy Garland's television show. Occasionally another impressionist makes a splash (David Frye created a visually and viscerally more pungent Richard Nixon, and Dana Carvey did a popular George Bush), but "the man of a thousand voices" does them all, in nightclubs, television specials and commercials.

Born in Ottawa, Canada, Little won local talent shows and, with advice from top mimics of the day such as Will Jordan, he devised his own specialty act featuring 103 impressions in under four minutes. While most mimics, including Jordan and Frank Gorshin, delivered sometimes unflattering caricatures with sharp wit, the star-struck Little felt "you can be funny without being cruel . . . the voices I do best are the people I admire most."

He tends to stay away from political satire, unless he can perform it without malice. He thrived when he could do "nice guy" presidents such as Jimmy Carter, Gerald Ford and Ronald Reagan.

Fans get the same vicarious thrill Rich Little does as they watch an average guy turn himself into a star. Rich recalled the time, as a star-struck neophyte in the business, he called up George Burns to do an impression of him. Judy Garland made the call to George and then put Rich on the line. Rich, imitating Burns, rasped, "H-h-hello, George, I-I just came in to do the Garland show, and I do an impression of you." Burns said, "Gee, that's great. I'd like to hear it some time." And hung up.

It was a typical Burns joke, of course. Usually the stars Rich imitates are flattered, offering suggestions on how to be even more realistic. Through the 1960s and '70s, Little was incredibly accurate, not only duplicating a W. C. Fields or George Burns with stunning virtuosity but "solving" previously untried stars such as Johnny Carson.

He may have been too accurate with his Carson. After 1985 he was not invited back to Carson's show. Carson insisted it was only because he too could do a very good Ronald Reagan. As with most mimics who become stars, Little developed his own ego and sense of self. In the 1980s he no longer wanted to be someone else so badly. Consequently, his mimicry was not quite as sharp as it had been and he peppered his show with straight songs. Even so, his act, which now even included dramatic segments (a "tribute to Bogart" with Rich doing scenes from *The Caine Mutiny* and others), continues to roll on week after week in Vegas.

His ability to judge just the right way to approach a new celebrity voice has rarely erred. If it does, his fans are sure to tell him, even if the fans are President George Bush, his wife and children. Rich recalled that Bush's children "came to me and said, 'Rich, it stinks'—their precise words. I went to the President and his wife and asked for help. They spent a lot of time with me!" One reason politicians probably enjoy him is that however he makes them sound, he never makes them look foolish. He is completely apolitical. Little admitted, "I'm neither a Democrat nor a Republican—I eat like an elephant and think like a jackass. But I'm a Canadian, so I can't vote anyway."

AUDIO: *My Fellow Canadians* (Capital), *Scrooge and the Stars* (Capital), *Rich Little's Broadway* (Kerr), *Politics and Popcorn* (Mercury), *The New First Family 1968* (Verve), *W. C. Fields for President* (Caedmon), *Spiro T. Agnew Is a Riot* (Cadet), *Earl Doud's Celebrity Workout* (Capital), *The First Family Rides Again* (Boardwalk), *Ronald Reagan Slept Here* (Dr. Dream)

TV: "Love on a Rooftop" (1966–67), "The John Davidson Show" (1969), "The ABC Comedy Hour" (1972), "The Julie Andrews Hour" (1972–73), "The Rich Little Show" (1976), "You Asked for It" (1981–83)

VIDEO: *Rich Little's Hollywood Trivia Game*

## THE LITTLE RASCALS (See OUR GANG.)

## CHRISTOPHER LLOYD

**(October 22, 1938–   )**

There is an art to being a comic villain and a dangerous but humorous psychopath. After many years polishing his skills, actor Christopher Lloyd emerged as one of the few who could earn giggles and shivers at the same time, portraying characters on the edge of sanity or violence, wavering with comic tension.

Born in Stamford, Connecticut, Lloyd worked for the Lincoln Center Repertory Company, was part of the American Shakespeare Festival and appeared on Broadway as early as 1969 in *Red White and Maddox*. He played the lead as the semidemented, heroic iconoclast in a stock production of *A Thousand Clowns*, played Bill the night clerk in the West Coast premiere of *Hot L. Baltimore* and won over New York reviewers back in 1977 with his appearance in Brecht and Weill's *Happy End* at the Brooklyn Chelsea Theater Center. His intensity and dedication was evident even then: He performed the role on crutches after knee surgery.

Film audiences first saw Lloyd as a scary mental patient in the comedy/drama *One Flew over the Cuckoo's Nest*, which featured Danny De Vito as another inmate. De Vito and Lloyd later were reunited for the television show "Taxi," where fans applauded Lloyd's performance as Reverend Jim Ignatowski, a bizarre burnout who had somehow managed to make it through the LSD-tinged '60s. Of course, he was a still a little strange. One of his favorite foods was Spaghetti-O's mixed with herring. Other dishes seemed to defy description: "There are worms on that pizza!" "It's the fisherman's special."

Lloyd won two Emmy awards for his role in "Taxi" and returned to films where he played villains (*Star Trek III*), goofy Nazi types (*To Be or Not to Be*) and other suspicious characters (*Clue*). He admitted in 1984, "I've done a lot of dumb stuff. I'll do a film if a director is really interested in me and if I see something in the role I can get off doing. . . . I don't plan much, I try to select from whatever comes at me, whatever it may be."

Lloyd scored as the cold and calculated meanie ready to murder cartoon characters in *Who Framed Roger Rabbit* and played the open-mouthed, popeyed Uncle Fester in the film version of *The Addams Family*. He probably remains best loved for his recurring role as the magical "Doc Brown," the wideeyed scientist-wizard who, with many an absentminded look of wonder and astonishment, managed to conquer time travel in various installments of *Back to the Future*. Of that role Lloyd notes, "He reminds me more of a combination of Toscanini and Einstein . . . a wild impresario genius."

FILMS incl.: *One Flew over the Cuckoo's Nest* (1975), *Goin' South* (1978), *Schizoid* (1980), *Mr. Mom* (1983), *To Be or Not to Be* (1983), *Star Trek III* (1984), *The Adventures of Buckaroo Banzai* (1984), *Back to the Future* (1985), *Clue* (1985), *Miracles* (1986), *Walk Like a Man* (1987), *Who Framed Roger Rabbit* (1988), *Eight Men Out* (1988), *The Dream Team* (1989), *Back to the Future II* (1989), *Back to the Future III* (1990), *The Addams Family* (1991)

TV: "Taxi" (1979–1983)

## HAROLD LLOYD

### (April 20, 1893–March 8, 1971)

The all-American boy of silent screen comedy, audiences loved plucky Harold Lloyd. Unfortunately, much of his work is as dated as a Horatio Alger novel. In the 1960s when silent films began to attract newfound attention, audiences identified with cynical stoic Buster Keaton and the ragged underdog Charlie Chaplin. In the 80s some documentaries appeared on Lloyd, but the focus of attention was largely on his few thrill comedies, not the far more numerous films that had the Alger plots of boy meets girl or young man makes good.

As the title of one Lloyd biography asserted, the general public continued to know him mostly as "The Man on the Clock," dangling from the facade of a tall building in the famous, often-excerpted clip from his classic silent comedy *Safety Last*. Of course, there are even critics of this one scene who insist that it's more of a "thrill" than a real "laugh."

Stan Laurel recalled, "He hardly ever made me laugh but I admire his inventiveness. A smart comedian. The best of the straight comedians." Laurel's director, Hal Roach, agreed. The key was the word "straight." Roach pointed out that unlike Chaplin, Keaton and the others, Lloyd was really an actor doing comedy—not a comedian.

Born in Nebraska, Lloyd attended San Diego High School and made a few films in San Diego around 1913. It was with Hal Roach that Lloyd developed a comedy character, "Willie Work," which was later developed into "Lonesome Luke," a tramp imitation of Charles Chaplin. Lloyd was Chaplin inside out. Instead of a tight jacket, Lloyd used a bulky one. Instead of a thick mustache, Lloyd used two toothlike dots. Lloyd's version of heroines Mabel Normand and Edna Purviance were his wife Mildred Davis and Bebe Daniels.

Like most who imitated Chaplin's mannerisms, Lloyd was often very funny, his best just about matching Chaplin's lesser efforts. "Funnier things happen in life to an ordinary boy than to Lonesome Luke," Lloyd ultimately realized, and within a few years he found a new identity, an average clean-cut young man whose only prop was the glasses that lent him some vulnerability. "I remember hunting through a tray containing probably 30 pair before coming on the right one. I wore them for a year and a half, guarding them with my life." Lloyd eventually had 20 pairs made exactly like them. This new character was, in Lloyd's words, "quiet, normal, boyish, clean, sympathetic, not impossible to romance."

This comic Clark Kent type emerged in the feature *Grandma's Boy* in 1922. Lloyd admitted that to look at this character, "you wouldn't think this is a funny young man." Audiences didn't laugh at the mere sight of him, as they did with so many silent comics, but they identified with him back then. "I think my character represented the white-collar middle-class that felt frustrated but was always fighting to overcome its shortcomings." That was enough for audiences to like him, but the question was how to make audiences laugh at him. Hal Roach remembered Lloyd actually asking "What do I do to be funny?" The answer was get a lot of writers and gag men and work on clever sight gags and situations for his confident if slightly bumbling hero. The earnest Lloyd was so scientific about his laughs he held previews with live audiences and had the times and places of the laughs charted on a graph.

Lloyd was most memorable in thrill comedies. Sennett and Keaton had certainly done many of these, but here was an "average man" doing it, without stoicism or outlandish gesticulation. It appealed to the Walter Mitty fantasies in everyone, and the shocks seemed real: the daring young man lost amid the girders of a building under construction in *Look Out Below*, fooling around on a building

Silent screen star Harold Lloyd was admired for his inventive and thrilling stunt comedy in films. Photo from the author's collection.

ledge in *High and Dizzy* and climbing a building and hanging from the huge clock in *Safety Last*. One of his more down-to-earth classics of clever thrill comedy was *The Freshman*, in which he does his best to win a football game singlehanded. The gags were so timelessly clever the entire sequence was used over again in *Mad Wednesday* decades later.

Though he did use doubles from time to time, Lloyd himself performed many comic stunts. Many were dangerous even though, contrary to reports at the time, scaffolds and other safety measures were used to keep him from killing himself as he scampered around tall buildings.

Ironically, his worst mishap occurred not during filming but during a photo session. Between takes

of *Haunted Spooks* in 1919, Harold went to the studio for some portraits and gag photos. Spotting a prop bomb on a table, he spontaneously decided to light it and hold it up. It suddenly exploded. A dazed Harold Lloyd stared down at his right hand. His thumb had been blown off; his index finger was hanging by a blackened shred. At the hospital a full inventory of his injuries was taken, and for a time no one was sure if he'd ever perform again.

Lloyd recovered and made an art out of positioning himself so that his hand was hidden from view. By wearing a cleverly constructed glove on his hand and making sure all shots involving the hand were made from a distance, it was almost impossible to tell that he had been injured. In interviews about the accident, he never went into details, and many fans never knew that there had been such major damage.

A rising star at the time, Lloyd reached his full potential in the following years. Through the 1920s, when Chaplin and Keaton were slowing down, Lloyd was cranking out feature films. In his day, he was one of the biggest stars in film comedy, and he invested his money well. In 1927 he spent $2 million to complete his 44-room dream house, the spectacular "Greenacres" estate that included 12 gardens, 12 fountains, a 120-foot-high waterfall, a tennis court, lake and nine-hole golf course. He was semi-retired through the '30s and '40s, raising two daughters and a son. In 1952 he received an honorary Academy Award. Enormously wealthy and a bit reclusive, Lloyd had little interest in returning to films, though in 1962 he put some of his best material together for the compilation *Harold Lloyd's World of Comedy.*

He said at the time that his films had no great statements behind them, unlike those critics read into those of Chaplin and Keaton. Watching a Lloyd film, he remarked, "You came away refreshed and you didn't have to do any heavy thinking."

His best work is still refreshing. Though viewers certainly don't leave the theater with profound thoughts, they still think that he was deservedly one of the greats of his time and still able to amuse any time.

AUDIO: *Voices from Hollywood's Past* (Delos)
AUTOBIOGRAPHY: *An American Comedy* (1971)
BIOGRAPHY: *Harold Lloyd's World of Comedy* (Cahn, 1964), *Harold Lloyd* (Reilly, 1977), *Harold Lloyd, the Man on the Clock* (Dardis, 1983)
FILMS incl.: *Willie* (1914), *Willie's Haircut* (1914), *Lonesome Luke* (1915), *Luke Lugs Luggage* (1916), *Luke Locates the Loot* (1916), *Luke and the Mermaids* (1917), *Lonesome Luke's Wild Women* (1917), *Pinched* (1917), *Bumping into Broadway* (1919), *Captain Kidd's Kidds* (1919), *From Hand to Mouth* (1919), *His Royal Slyness* (1919), *Haunted Spooks* (1919), *High and Dizzy* (1921), *Now or Never* (1921), *A Sailor-Made Man* (1921), *Grandma's Boy* (1922), *Dr. Jack* (1922), *Safety Last* (1923), *Why Worry* (1923), *Girl Shy* (1924), *Hot Water* (1924), *The Freshman* (1925), *For Heaven's Sake* (1926), *Kid Brother* (1927), *Speedy*

(1928), *Welcome Danger* (1929), *Feet First* (1930), *Movie Crazy* (1932), *The Cats Paw* (1934), *The Milky Way* (1936), *Professor Beware* (1938), *Mad Wednesday (The Sins of Harold Diddlebock)* (1947), *Harold Lloyd's World of Comedy* (1962), *Harold Lloyd's Funny Side of Life* (1964)
VIDEOS: *Harold Lloyd's Comedy Classics 1916–1919, His Royal Slyness/Spooks*

## CAROLE LOMBARD

### (Jane Alice Peters, October 6, 1908–January 16, 1942)

A queen of screwball comedy and sophisticated farce, Carole Lombard had a winning combination of beauty, charm and talent. She was in the prime of her career and married to Clark Gable at the time of her tragic death.

Born in Fort Wayne, Indiana, Carole and her family moved to Los Angeles when she was seven. A tomboy, she learned boxing from her brothers and played baseball. She went to drama school with her mother's consent and began her film career as a tomboy in *A Perfect Crime* in 1921. She seemed to show the same qualities as Mabel Normand: the ability to get laughs without sacrificing her beauty and grace. In 1924 the 16-year-old quit school to work at Fox Studios.

Then came a crash. In October 1925 she was in a car accident. The windshield shattered, cutting her left cheek and leaving a half-inch scar under her left eye. Stitches were required, and it seemed as if her career was ruined; but after treatment the scars were not noticeable.

She starred in several Mack Sennett comedies in 1927 and 1928 and by 1930 was once again a lucrative property, signing a seven-year contract. The "e" became part of her name after an ad department mistake. She sang "You Appeal to Me" in *Safety in Numbers* (1930) and in 1931 made *Man of the World* with William Powell. They were married that year but divorced in 1933.

It was in 1934 that Carole scored her first big hit with *Twentieth Century.* John Barrymore was ready to cut his throat over her in that one. She told him, "If you did, greasepaint would run out of it." With ex-husband Powell, she starred in her first classic comedy, *My Man Godfrey*, in 1936. The film took some satiric and slapstick liberties with her haughty beauty (in one scene she's dunked in a shower), but her radiance was unspoiled by the picture's end. She received an Academy Award nomination and followed it with an even bigger hit, *Nothing Sacred*, which highlighted both Lombard's eccentric, feisty and independent temperament and her seductive need to be loved and wanted. The film's classic climax was her brawling bedroom fistfight with Frederic March. That year she also made *True Confession*. Accused of murder, she asks Fred MacMurray to enter a plea: "Justifiable homicide in defense of chastity."

Off screen, Lombard was an authentic screwball character. William Haines, a gay actor turned interior decorator, recalled what it was like to work on Lombard's new mansion. During one session when the two were discussing plans, Lombard realized she was late for another engagement. ". . . She wanted to continue our conversation while she changed. I was startled when she stripped completely, staring at me all the while, going on about Hepplewhite and Sheraton. She never wore a bra; oftentimes she didn't wear panties either, and this was one of those times. She saw my surprised look, and I remember her saying the cutest thing: 'I wouldn't do this, Billy, if I thought it could arouse you.' "

Lombard was uninhibited in public. She attended a formal party where the men were in black and the women in white—all except Norma Shearer, who had arrived in an attention-getting red gown. As she walked in, Carole said loudly, "Who the fuck does Norma think she is? The house madam?"

Director Sidney Salkow recalled all the facets of the Lombard personality behind the scenes: "Ruthless in her self-criticism, she welcomed my honest suggestions. . . . This dynamic golden girl enchanted me with her vibrant personality, wildly energetic drive, fantastic sense of humor, excellent mind and forthright talent. I fell in love with her and realized why everyone else in the crew had succumbed to her charms. She was easily the most diverting and unpredictable member of the troupe, ready to concoct a dozen gags a day to enliven the tediousness of the schedule. Even when her services were not required, she haunted the set, saucily offering advice to the other actors . . . even displacing

the motion picture camera operator and making skillful pan shots."

Shooting *From Hell to Heaven* in cold weather, she had to strip to a skimpy costume. She thought about it for a moment and then told the crew, "I'm not shooting till I see every one of you down to your jockey shorts!" They complied.

Director Mitchell Leisen: "We used to call her the profane angel, because she looked like an angel but she swore like a sailor. . . . She was the only woman I ever knew who could tell a dirty joke without losing her femininity." Her comments for the record were almost as frank. In 1937: "Man thinks he's dealing with an inferior brain when it comes to woman—and that makes him a sucker."

At the height of her career, Lombard was earning about a half a million dollars a year. In 1936 the Lombard legend spread into the gossip columns when she began her torrid affair with Clark Gable, who was still married at the time. David Niven recalled that Gable's wife held Clark up for a $500,000 settlement before allowing him the freedom to marry Carole in 1939. Whenever they argued, Lombard would shout, "Well, what did you expect for a lousy half million for Christ's sake. Perfection?" It wasn't a perfect marriage, but it was a colorful one, later the subject of books and movies.

Carole continued to make fine films. Even Alfred Hitchcock was entranced by her and starred her in one of his rare comedies, *Mr. and Mrs. Smith*. In 1942 Hollywood was buzzing over what was going to be her biggest hit yet, her co-starring role opposite Jack Benny in *To Be or Not to Be*.

A week after completing the film, while most stars would have been resting up, she was out selling war bonds. She did one drive in Indianapolis and then went on to New York. There she and her mother boarded an 18-passenger plane for the return to Los Angeles. "We must not take that plane," her mother said within earshot of reporters. The woman was superstitious about the numerology of taking "Flight 3" on the DC-3, and found more ominous numbers that seemed to add up to disaster. Carole had been thinking of taking a train but wanted to get home to Gable as quickly as possible. She flipped a coin to decide whether they would board the plane. She won.

The plane took off across the country. It landed in St. Louis and then touched down in Las Vegas to refuel. Back in California, Clark Gable calculated that it would be just a matter of hours before Carole arrived home. He had arranged a practical joke for her return, placing a life-size nude mannequin in her bed.

Thirty miles outside of Las Vegas there was an explosion. Minutes later the plane was reported missing. Clark Gable joined the search party as they tried to find the plane in the snowy, mountainous terrain 8,000 feet up from sea level. The plane had struck the face of Olcott Mountain, the wreck traced to the captain's errors in following the course. In the wreckage that took the lives of 19 passengers and three crew members, the charred body of Carole Lombard was recognizable only from her earrings.

*To Be or Not to Be* was indeed the greatest hit of Carole's career. Some could have envisioned her holding up an Academy Award later that year at a posh banquet. Instead, her honor was a posthumous medal from President Roosevelt. "She loved her country," he said. "She is and always will be a star, one we shall never forget nor cease to be grateful to."

BIOGRAPHY: *Gable and Lombard* (Harris, 1974), *Screwball* (Swindell, 1975), *Carole Lombard, a Bio-Bibliography* (Matzen, 1988), *Carole Lombard* (Maltin, 1976), *Gable and Lombard, Powell and Harlow* (Morella and Epstein, 1976), *The Films of Carole Lombard* (Ott, 1979)

FILMS incl.: *A Perfect Crime* (1921), *Dick Turpin* (1925), *Marriage in Transit* (1925), *The Perfect Crime* (1928), *Show Folks* (1928), *High Voltage* (1929), *Dynamite* (1929), *Big News* (1929), *Fast and Loose* (1930), *Man of the World* (1931), *It Pays to Advertise* (1931), *Up Pops the Devil* (1931), *Sinners in the Sun* (1932), *No Man of Her Own* (1932), *Virtue* (1932), *No More Orchids* (1932), *Brief Moment* (1933), *White Woman* (1933), *Bolero* (1934), *We're Not Dressing* (1934), *Twentieth Century* (1934), *Now and Forever* (1934), *Lady by Choice* (1934), *The Gay Bride* (1934), *Rumba* (1934), *Hands Across the Table* (1935), *My Man Godfrey* (1936), *The Princess Comes Across* (1936), *True Confession* (1937), *Nothing Sacred* (1937), *Fools for Scandal* (1938), *Made for Each Other* (1939), *In Name Only* (1939), *They Knew What They Wanted* (1940), *Vigil in the Night* (1940), *Mr. and Mrs. Smith* (1941), *To Be or Not to Be* (1942)

## MYRNA LOY

### (Myrna Williams, August 2, 1905–   )

Poise, charm and tastefulness don't often translate into laughs, but these words could all be applied to Myrna Loy, the stylish comic actress who *did* get laughs in "screwball" comedies of the 1930s.

Born in Montana (one of her childhood neighbors was Gary Cooper), red-headed Myrna Williams moved with her family to California where she studied at the Westlake School for Girls in Los Angeles and Venice High School. She took piano and dance lessons and eventually taught dance at the Ritter School of Expression in Culver City. She found work in films and in 1925 when her "avant-garde" friends suggested she change her name, they made a game out of it, toying with "Myrna Lisa" before ending up with "Myrna Loy."

Loy made many silent films, from a bit part in *The Jazz Singer* to a variety of Oriental roles playing on her unusual new name. "It took a long, long time to find my real niche," she said. Typical of some of her strange early work was *The Mask of Fu Manchu*, in which she played Boris Karaloff's dragonlady daughter. The nasty woman was as sadistic as Fu Manchu, supervising the whipping of unfortunate white men, shouting "Faster! Faster!"

In the 1930s she began landing breezy roles in comedies, many starring William Powell. Director George Cukor recalled, "There had been romantic couples before, but Loy and Powell were something new and original. They actually made marital comedy palatable. I remember Bill Powell when he started out as a melodramatic actor. Then, by some alchemy, he suddenly became comic. But Myrna gave the wit to the whole thing. They hit that wonderful note because he always did a wee bit too much and she underdid it, creating a grace, a charm, a chemistry."

According to the book *F.D.R., My Boss*, Myrna was President Roosevelt's favorite actress. Dillinger supposedly was a fan too, his shootout with the law occurring as he left a showing of *Manhattan Melo-*

*drama.* Cary Grant was fascinated with her on the set and admired her as an actress as well. "All the leading men agreed," he said. "Myrna was the wife everybody wanted." Of course, fantasy and reality didn't mix. Myrna suffered through four less-than-perfect marriages over the years.

While fans were enthralled by Myrna's role as Nora Charles in *The Thin Man,* and she developed an identity as "the perfect wife," the actress felt that "Nora was hardly the perfect wife in the sense of being the chaste, virginal creature that seemed to be so much admired. I wasn't like that on or off the screen. . . . I prefer Gore Vidal's description of my image, 'The eternal good-sex, woman-wife,' which removes the puritanical connotation of perfect. What man would want a perfect wife, anyway? The Charleses had enormous tolerance for each other's imperfections."

Powell and Loy were not a team off screen. "In this world today, nobody seems to understand how you can just be terribly close and love somebody a whole lot and not sleep with him. If Bill and I had been lovers, then we would have had fights. And if we'd been married, it would have been even worse."

A "liberated lady" before her time, Loy demanded that the studio pay her the same salary Powell was getting. On screen she was often just as liberated. In *Third Finger, Left Hand* she shocks her office workers by telling them she married a man during a whirlwind romance in Rio. One office Romeo is crushed: "How could you marry a man that none of us had ever seen, that you didn't know anything about? . . ." "I don't understand it myself sometimes. But there I was alone in Rio, in April . . . it was raining . . . I adore rain." "If it was so romantic why did you leave him?" "It stopped raining."

Saucy lines of dialogue, spoken with just the right amount of dry flippancy, characterized her films. In *Love Crazy,* William Powell describes an old flame: "She's married now. She's got a husband." Myrna: "Whose husband she got?" Loy also had the under-rated ability to deliver a bad old joke gracefully, as in *The Thin Man* when she asks a clue-snooping detective, "What's that man doing in my drawers?" Later, in a dinner scene she actually said, "Waiter, will you serve the nuts—I mean, will you serve the guests the nuts."

Loy was successful in other films beside comedy, notably *The Best Years of Our Lives* in 1946. She continued to make films from time to time but found other interests that were more important. She was active in politics, UNESCO and the NCDH. She joined Norman Lears' "People for the American Way" to defend against the Moral Majority. For her years of public service, Senator Howard Metzenbaum praised Myrna Loy as "a woman who has the courage to stand up for her convictions."

Loy wrote her autobiography in 1987, and once again she did not disappoint her fans. She chronicled her story with the same taste, intelligence and wit that characterized her film career and many years working for important political causes. In 1990 "The Myrna Loy Center," a 200-seat theater, was opened in Helena, Montana, not far from her childhood home in nearby Radersburg. In 1991 she made a rare and brief television appearance from her New York City apartment to acknowledge one final gesture of respect and devotion—an honorary Academy Award. Presenter Anjelica Huston told the worldwide audience that night, "She personified grace and gaiety, warmth and wit, and above all, independence of spirit."

AUTOBIOGRAPHY: *Being and Becoming* (1987)
FILMS incl.: *Pretty Ladies* (1925), *The Cave Man* (1926), *Don Juan* (1926), *So This Is Paris* (1926), *The Jazz Singer* (1927), *Ham and Eggs at the Front* (1927), *If I Were Single* (1927), *Simple Sis* (1927), *Pay as You Enter* (1928), *State Street Sadie* (1928), *Hardboiled Rose* (1929), *The Desert Song* (1929), *The Squall* (1929), *The Show of Shows* (1929), *Cock o' the Walk* (1930), *Naughty Flirt* (1931), *A Connecticut Yankee* (1931), *The Wet Parade* (1932), *Love Me Tonight* (1932), *When Ladies Meet* (1933), *The Penthouse* (1933), *Prizefighter and the Lady* (1933), *Manhattan Melodrama* (1934), *The Thin Man* (1934), *After the Thin Man* (1936), *Wife and Secretary* (1936), *The Great Ziegfeld* (1936), *Libelled Lady* (1936), *Too Hot to Handle* (1938), *Another Thin Man* (1939), *Love Crazy* (1941), *Shadow of the Thin Man* (1941), *The Thin Man Goes Home* (1944), *The Best Years of Our Lives* (1946), *The Senator Was Indiscreet* (1947), *The Song of the Thin Man* (1947), *Mr. Blandings Builds His Dream House* (1948), *Cheaper by the Dozen* (1950), *Belles on Their Toes* (1952), *From the*

*Terrace* (1960), *Midnight Lace* (1960), *The April Fools* (1969), *Airport 1975* (1974), *The End* (1978), *Just Tell Me What You Want* (1979)

## LUM and ABNER

**Lum Edwards: Chester Lauck, February 9, 1902–February 21, 1980**
**Abner Peabody: Norris Goff, May 30, 1906–June 7, 1978**

Inspired by Amos and Andy, the team of Chester Lauck and Norris Goff decided to produce their own comedy show. A local Arkansas radio station was willing to put them on the air, as long as they could come up with a pair of interesting characters.

They premiered as Lum and Abner on April 26, 1931 and stayed on the air for 23 years. Like Amos and Andy, they did a short program five nights a week, which helped create plot lines. The show took place in the mythical town of Pine Ridge, Arkansas (which became a real town when Waters, Arkansas changed its name to capitalize on the publicity). It was at the Jot-Em-Down Store run by Lum (the more intelligent one) and Abner that a variety of friends and neighbors dropped by, including Snake Ogan and dopey handyman Cedric Wehunt (played by Lauck), along with Doc Miller and cheap Squire Skimp (played by Goff).

The dialogue was realistic because in real life, Lauck and Goff were just plain folks from Arkansas. Before becoming national radio stars Lauck worked in an auto finance company and was once a bank clerk. Goff ran a grocery store with his father.

The duo appeared in a few films, making themselves up with suitably rustic touches, including a white beard for one and a brushy mustache for the other. In 1954 Goff underwent a cancer operation. He recovered but decided to retire and enjoy life. Lauck went on to work for the Continental Oil Company.

The legacy of Lum and Abner was a brand of rural comedy that would lead the way for similarly pleasant sitcoms such as television's "Andy Griffith Show." One might imagine Lum and Abner sitting on a front porch in Mayberry feuding over their checker game: "You can't move that man there, yer

cheatin!" "I am not, I'm playin' just like you do." "Oh, so you admit it, do ya!"

FILMS incl.: *Dreaming Out Loud* (1940), *Bashful Bachelors* (1942), *Two Weeks to Live* (1943)

## PAUL LYNDE

**(June 13, 1926–January 10, 1982)**

A "sick comic" in stand-up comedy, later an eccentric character actor in films, Paul Lynde was best known as the "center square" in the long-running comedy quiz show "The Hollywood Squares." On the show he displayed his two trademark styles—the desultory putdown delivered with a huffy snort of nauseated dissatisfaction and the sinister wisecrack, blurted from behind feverish eyes and a fierce, toothy smile.

In his desultory mode. Question: "True or false: There are more cattle than people in Montana." Answer: "It's hard to tell."

And the sinister wisecrack. Question: "True or false: A horse can remember something that happened to him years ago." Answer: "Yes, and that's why Roy Rogers has an unlisted telephone number."

Unfortunately, Lynde's personal life was not quite as carefree as his jokes would lead one to believe. He recalled that his father favored his brothers, who were more athletic and smarter. Overfed and overprotected, he was a chubby duckling who compensated "by being a silly goose" in school. He appeared in plays at Northwestern University but his days there were marred by tragedy: His parents died and his favorite brother was killed during World War II. After graduating in 1948 he worked as a salesman in New York, struggling to diet from 260 to 180 pounds. Once he did, he managed to get into some revues, including *New Faces of 1952*. He developed a campy comic cadence that was a bit like Gwen Verdon's. But off stage he was still prone to fits of moroseness and giddy flights of fancy. Other actors could see he was still very troubled, but few could take the time to counsel him. June Carroll once put it simply: "Paul, if you can't be a gentleman, at least be a lady."

Lynde developed "sick comedy" routines and appeared in nightclubs. One of his classics was a black comedy monologue about a hunter's hellish tour: "We'd only been tramping on the trail four or five hours when my wife began to complain of her feet. The only shoes she had with her were those high-heeled sling pumps. Heh heh, she just couldn't take it! So we had to leave her there out on the trail. On the way back I found this piece of her dress and to this day I don't know what happened to her. Heh heh."

At the turn of the 1960s, sick comedy was very popular, and Lynde recorded an album, *Recently Released.* The sick comic was actually in therapy himself, trying to cope with his ennui, depression and disgust for the nightclub environment.

The theater became his outlet, and (battling stage fright every step of the way) he scored a hit as the tense father in *Bye Bye Birdie.* He duplicated his role on film and played many more roles requiring a comically fey or painfully neurotic salesman, best friend or official. He was a mortician in *Send Me No Flowers* and in *The Glass Bottom Boat* he turned up in drag. He moved to sitcoms as the peculiar but magical Uncle Arthur on television's "Bewitched."

Still, there was little magic in his private life. In July 1965 he and a young actor named Jim Davidson had been out to a few bars. When they went back to Lynde's San Fransisco hotel room, Davidson shouted, "Watch me do a trick." He went to the window. A moment later, he was hanging from the ledge. Then he fell to his death.

Lynde was making well over a quarter of a million dollars on "The Hollywood Squares" but felt boxed in. He used his distinctive voice to play the rat in the animated film *Charlotte's Web,* and played the theatrical "straw hat circuit" in the summer, but was disappointed when his starring sitcoms failed; this was mostly the fault of mild scripts and unlikely casting.

Friends could tell he was still miserable. Though not unattractive, he couldn't look at himself in the mirror, claiming he resembled "an iguana." Lynde took pills and cocaine, and when he drank, he was often mean. When he couldn't get a table in a restaurant, even after loudly announcing his identity, he put out his cigarette on the maître d's hand. Phyllis Diller remembered his plight: "Nothing will kill you quicker than unhappiness. He really was the classic comedian who was a very sad person. Paul was tormented by the thought that he was a failure."

In death, Lynde was at least afforded some of the romance and mystery of the screen stars he had fantasized about and admired. He was found nude, with butyl nitrate on his bed side table. Death had come from a heart attack, most likely not from drug use but from his dieting and from a reported "hardening of the arteries."

AUDIO: *New Faces of 1952* (RCA), *Bye Bye Birdie* (Columbia), *Recently Released* (Columbia)

BROADWAY: *New Faces of 1952* (1952), *Bye Bye Birdie* (1960)

FILMS: *New Faces* (1954), *Son of Flubber* (1963), *Bye Bye Birdie* (1963), *Under the Yum Yum Tree* (1963), *For Those Who Think Young* (1964), *Send Me No Flowers* (1964), *Beach Blanket Bingo* (1965), *The Glass Bottom Boat* (1966), *How Sweet It Is* (1968), *Charlotte's Web* (1973), *The Villain* (1978), *Rabbit Test* (1978)

TV: "The Red Buttons Show" (1955), "Stanley" (1956–57), "The Kraft Music Hall" (1961–62), "Bewitched" (1965–72), "The Pruitts of Southampton" (1967), "The Jonathan Winters Show" (1968–69), "Hollywood Squares" (1968–82), "Dean Martin Presents the Golddiggers" (1968–69), "The Paul Lynde Show" (1972–73), "Temperatures Rising" (1973–74), "Donny and Marie" (1976–79)

# M

## MOMS MABLEY

### (Loretta Mary Aiken, March 19, 1894–May 23, 1975)

One of the most amusing and beloved "characters" in comedy, earthy Moms Mabley would go out on stage in a garish, bulky dress and start lecturing the audience as if they were her children. She was comically stern and raucously emphatic, laying down her philosophies of life and love: "Love is just like a game of checkers, children. You sure got to know which man to move! 'Cause if you move the wrong man, and he jump ya, tear your Mason and Dixon line up!"

Her favorite subject was changing times. She talked about her own problems with it: "Anybody who acts normal nowadays they're probably just not well! I'm tellin' you, I just don't understand. If I go too fast, I'll run into something, if I go too slow somethin'll run into me." Though she looked comically battered, rasping out her routines through a seemingly toothless mouth, her words were hip, her delivery feisty. A running gag was her hunt for swinging young men: "The only thing an old man can do for me is to get on a bicycle and bring me a message from a young man!" She insisted, "A woman is a woman until the day she dies. But a man's a man only as long as he can!"

Few watching her antics on stage could have believed the misery in her own life. Born in Bravard,

North Carolina, "Moms" became a mother twice while in her teens—against her will. She was raped both times, and in both cases she gave the baby up for adoption. Her fireman father was killed in the line of duty and her mother was run over by a truck after coming home from Christmas church services. At 14, the girl was earning a living in show business with no home to return to.

She got her stage name from her first real love, Jack Mabley. In later years, that name and her burlesque-style delivery led some unknowing fans to wonder if "Moms" was really a female impersonator. Clarice Taylor, who created a one-woman show called *Moms* in 1987 and had a successful off-Broadway run with it, reported that in her later years Mabley was a lesbian.

Mabley worked the black vaudeville circuit, arriving at The Cotton Club in 1923. She appeared in several Broadway revues and in 1939 was one of the first female comics to co-star at The Apollo Theater in Harlem. She evolved the "Moms" character early on, based on her grandmother. By the time white audiences discovered her, thanks to a Harry Belafonte television special *A Time for Laughter* in 1967, she looked like a grandmother and she was at her raucous peak, revitalizing even the oldest jokes with her unique delivery. She recorded many comedy albums, even though she really had to be seen to be believed (and her garbled delivery style was not always easy to understand on disc).

Some of Mom's philosophy was simple to understand: "My slogan is, by all means do what you want to do. But know what you're doin'." Moms was riding high in 1974 when she finally got the chance to star in her own film, *Amazing Grace*. Unfortunately, the strain of making the film, and her own advancing age, conspired against her. Her health weakened and she suffered a heart attack, causing a severe drop in weight. She died not long after the film was released, but to the end, she was always the remarkable Moms, joking as she imparted her words of wisdom, lovingly but firmly, without apology: "Ain't a person in the world I don't love," she said. "Nobody ever gave me nothing, and I ain't never asked, either."

AUDIO: *Funniest Woman in the World* (Chess), *At the UN* (Chess), *At the Playboy Club* (Chess), *Funny Sides* (Chess), *Best of Moms Mabley* (Chess), *Young Men Sí, Old Men No* (Chess), *Breaks It Up* (Chess), *Man in My Life* (Chess), *I've Got Someting to Tell You* (Chess), *Moms Wows* (Chess), *Moms the Word* (Mercury), *Live at Sing Sing* (Mercury), *Out on a Limb* (Mercury), *Now Hear This* (Mercury), *Her Young Thing* (Mercury), *At the White House* (Mercury), *Abraham Martin and John* (Mercury)

BROADWAY: *Swinging the Dream* (1932), *Blackbirds* (1939)

FILMS incl.: *The Emperor Jones* (1933), *Boarding House Blues*, *Killer Diller* (1947), *Amazing Grace* (1974)

## HOWIE MANDEL

### (November 29, 1957– )

A "class clown" and life-of-the-party comic, Howie Mandel rarely wins critical praise for his stand-up comedy. Like a bad boy run amok in a classroom, his humor includes swiping an audience member's chair, doing ear-splitting rooster crows and shouting out less-than-original one-liners: "I love feeding the pigeons—breast feeding them!" Critics were dismayed by his prop comedy, especially his popular routine in which he squeezed a surgeon's rubber glove over his face and then blasted it off his head by exhaling hard.

Devoted fans respond to his unpredictable, infectiously cheerful personality and the kind of antics that worked in the past for foolish bad boys of previous generations such as Jerry Lewis. His audience banter is pure smart-aleck brat: "What do you do for a living?" "Nothing." "How do you know when you're finished!" Flopping to the floor he shouts "I'm not your typical stand-up comedian!"

Born in Toronto, Mandel had a successful carpet business when he vacationed in Los Angeles and happened to visit a local comedy club. He performed on a dare and was suddenly invited to audition for a quiz show called "Make Me Laugh." The show led to a permanent show biz career. "My act is mostly improvisation," he said. "I don't really analyze my comedy, and I don't think it can be analyzed. My comedy is just me. There's no reason, there's nothing written down, I have no notes. They ask me, 'When did you first decide to put a rubber glove on your head?' I never decided. It just happened; it's just my personality. . . . I've always done it to be the center of attention, I've always acted this way. . . .

"They use this word zany. I don't think I'm crazy, or zany, I just think I'm Howie. . . . I have friends that I grew up with that were crazy and zany all through school and then become 30 years old and they're married and own a home and wear a tie every day. . . . Then there are people like me—I'm never gonna change. I do the things I did when I was five years old."

Appealing to five-year-olds, Mandel unveiled his own Saturday morning cartoon show based on one of his favorite characters, a squeaky child named Bobby. One of Mandel's first bad puns on stage was in the Bobby character. It seemed that Bobby would cry every time he sat on his potty. Asked why, he piped a line from an old Lesley Gore hit, "It's my potty and I'll cry if I want to!"

Critics were more appreciative of Mandel as an actor, especially as Dr. Wayne Fiscus on the television show "St. Elsewhere." He seemed destined for success as a film comedian, but after several box office duds and an indifferent television sitcom, he returned to venues such as Radio City Music Hall and Carnegie Hall and starred in stand-up television specials. A likable fellow in person, a charismatic performer, his juvenile comedy still drew cheers from young fans and jeers from critics, including an "F for filth" from Kay Gardella reviewing his

1989 Showtime special: "Mandel admits he has the attention span of a gnat and gets bored easily. So, unfortunately, does this critic . . . bored and outraged." The following year he starred in a syndicated television series about a fellow running a funeral home. The *Chicago Tribune* declared, "Mandel, obviously relishing his many opportunities to act the slimy fool, is up to the task. He is downright grotesque."

Mandel told the author he would only be bored and outraged if he were forced to pack his Hawaiian shirts and props and take a day job. "They say stand-up's really hard. For me it's not a hard thing. I think it would be much harder for me to go work from nine to five and sit in an office. It's much easier for me to dress the way I dress, look the way I look and do what I do. That's easier for me than doing what they say the normal person does. And they sat that I'm crazy!"

AUDIO: *Fits Like a Glove* (Warner Bros.)

FILMS incl.: *Gas* (1981), *A Fine Mess* (1986), *Walk Like a Man* (1987), *Little Monsters* (1989)

TV: "St. Elsewhere" (1982–86), "Bobby's World" (1990), "Good Grief" (1990)

VIDEO: *Paramount Comedy Theater Vols. 1–3; Howie from Maui; The First Howie Mandel Special; Howie Mandel's North American Watusi Tour*

## CHARLIE MANNA

### (October 6, 1925–November 9, 1971)

A cross between Bob Newhart and Jonathan Winters, Charlie Manna liked to perform set routines and play all the parts. Like Newhart, he took the "imagine if . . ." approach. Imagine Julius Caesar trying to reason with Brutus. Imagine an astronaut refusing to go up into space without his crayon set. Imagine how the various parts of the body talk to each other. But, closer to Winters, he generally acted out the sketches instead of making them monologues or phone calls.

He lacked the crazy cartooning of Winters and didn't have the immediately identifiable personality of the nervously low-key Newhart; he seemed like any other Jan, Corbett or Shecky when he appeared in his suit and tie on television's "Ed Sullivan Show"

in the early 1960s. But for about a decade, the pleasant-looking, likable Manna was one of the durable and reliable pros in stand-up.

Manna attended James Monroe High School in New York City, studied opera and voice at The Music School and after World War II worked with several musical groups as a singer. After Manna entertained at a party, guest Carl Reiner urged him to polish his natural comic talents and try stand-up. He helped Manna get some Catskill resort work in 1954, and by 1957 Manna was in the *Shoestring Revue* and a few years later recording comedy albums for Decca.

The first album featured one of his best routines, "Inside You." Manna plays different parts of the body, each with a different voice. The nose is nasal, the lower lip sounds like Maurice Chevalier, and the central nervous system is tense, especially when a pretty girl walks by: "Now hear this! All glands secrete! Connect me with the stomach. Any butterflies down there? Connect me with the unconscious please. Well . . . keep ringing!" Finally the whole body swings into action, including the boss: "This is the brain! B-R-A-N-E."

Over the years Manna experimented with political comedy and in 1968 thought he had a good hook with comedy about a loser character. He published a novelty book with "Tonight Show" writer Bill Majeski, *A Loser is . . .* It was filled with quickies: "A Loser is. . . . a female impersonator who doesn't know it . . . a window washer who steps back to admire his work . . . a stowaway on a kamikaze plane . . . a piano player in a marching band . . . a bra salesman who doesn't know his ABC's. . . ." Unfortunately, Manna didn't look the part—not as much as Jackie Vernon or Rodney Dangerfield did.

He always had distinctive talent in performing stand-up comedy, monologues, character sketches and even minimusicals in which he sang novelty songs. The only thing that he didn't have was a distinctive face that told people, after the laughter, that they had been enjoying and applauding Charlie Manna.

AUDIO: *Manna Overboard* (Decca), *Manna Live* (Decca), *The Rise and Fall of the Great Society* (Verve)

BROADWAY: *Shoestring Revue* (1957)

## MARCEL MARCEAU

### (Marcel Mangel, March 22, 1923–   )

The modern master of mime, for nearly 50 years Marcel Marceau toured the world with his gentle clown-tramp character Bip. Often compared to Chaplin in spirit, but clearly influenced by the traditions of mime, ballet and dance in the theatrical world, Marceau performed mostly in one-man shows, though national audiences enjoyed him on occasional television specials and a few films.

Born Marcel Mangel in Strasbourg, France, he grew up during World War II. His father was killed at Auschwitz. He and his brother joined the Resistance and worked to bring Jews to safety in other countries. He changed his name to elude the Gestapo.

After the war, Marceau studied mime in drama school and attended various acting companies before creating a "mimodrama" called *Death Before Dawn*. In 1949 he formed his own mime company. Audiences enjoyed his serio-comic works but especially his straight comedies, and giggled over Bip's efforts to walk against the wind or get out of a clear plastic box. Street mimes on every corner have since appropriated and misused Marceau's works to the point of cliché, but at the time he unveiled a whole new world of poetic comedy. Stan Laurel was an early supporter, as was Red Skelton. In the early 1960s, Skelton invited Marceau to appear with him for a few specials, giving much of America their first look at the French master. Though a rare visitor to America, he received honorary degrees from Princeton and Oregon universities.

Though he usually wore costumes more in keeping with the ballet than a Chaplin comedy, audiences had no trouble following the graceful gestures of Marceau's Bip and laughed heartily at his expressions of toothy glee or frowning outrage. The silent master even spoke to American audiences in television commercials, teaching them how to pronounce "Moet." In a hilarious comic twist, he had the only spoken line in Mel Brooks' *Silent Movie*.

Married three times, Marceau raised two sons (from his first marriage to Huguette Mallet) and two daughters (from his third marriage, in 1975, to Anne Sicco). Awarded the French Legion of Honor, he lived in France supervising the Marcel Marceau School of Mime in Paris. In 1990 he paid a visit to England for a month-long engagement at Sadler's Wells Theater. It was there that he announced a problem with partial deafness. "My ears are blocked," he said. "Fortunately I don't have to speak on stage but I do find it embarrassing." He found slight amusement that his predicament "lets me hear what I want to hear."

Marceau disliked questions about his personal life, declaring "It is beautiful to be a mystery man when you are an artist." On the subject of mime, he was never mum. "I am a silent witness of my time," he said. "There is an inside force which pushes me to re-create the dreams of man, to put this into gestures—and then I become a philosopher without wanting to be one. I become a moralist without wanting to be one. And I remain a clown wanting to be a clown. . . . I prefer silence because it leaves the door open to the whole imagination."

AUDIO: *Marcel Marceau Speaks* (Caedmon)
BIOGRAPHY: *Marcel Marceau Master of Mime* (Martin, 1978)
BROADWAY incl.: *A Soldier's Tale* (1955), *An Evening of Pantomime* (1955), *Marcel Marceau* (1956), *The Overcoat* (1960), *Marcel Marceau* (1963), *Marcel Marceau* (1970)
FILMS incl.: *Barbarella* (1968), *Shanks* (1974), *Silent Movie* (1976)

## MARCELINE

### (Marceline Orbes, 1873–November 5, 1927)

The tales of defeated, broken-hearted "Pagliacci" clowns may have been widespread in literature, but it was the tragic reality of Marceline. Born in Saragossa, Spain, he was an internationally famous clown. Not confined to the circus, Marceline played the finest venues, including five years at England's Hippodrome. He was one of the premiere attractions at the opening of the New York Hippodrome in 1905, starring in the first-act show *A Yankee Circus on Mars*. Dressed in a tux but wearing traditional clown makeup, he delighted critics. One wrote of his stage act, "part of his appeal lay in a bewildered expression, as though life puzzled him. He picked something up only to drop it. He sought to help others, but always got in the way. Children, and adults too, howled and rocked in their seats with laughter as Marceline grew entangled in the rugs . . . meanwhile dropping trays of dishes." His gestures were all so "futilely busy."

Just ten years later, the same Marceline played the Hippodrome in 1915 to far less praise. His comic routines were evidently now deemed old-fashioned. Under such conditions, it was hard for him even to perform his old standards with enthusiasm. Unable to recapture his old form, Marceline lent his name to a restaurant. When it failed, he invested his money in a second restaurant. It too failed. He and his wife separated and his remaining savings withered away.

The proud Spaniard couldn't find a way to create new material or to revive an act that was now viewed with scorn and indifference. The years passed slowly for him, but quickly enough to make his name only a dim memory for audiences. Nearly broke, he checked into the Hotel Mansfield at 226 West 50th Street in New York City. The manager recalled that in many months, "Nobody ever telephoned him; he never received mail, he never smiled or complained. We knew nothing of his business."

On November 3, 1927 he pawned his diamond ring for $15. Two days later, between midnight and 4 A.M., Marceline knelt at his bed, staring at the photographs of himself he had placed there, like cards. His first trembling pistol shot went into the wall. The second did not miss.

Marceline was found "kneeling as though in prayer" the following morning. The shots had been heard and had been ignored. Six dollars was all he had left besides the pictures of a once-loved clown.

There were no crowds at his funeral. His wife was there, telling the few reporters on hand that she had "expected something like this." She had not bought the huge wreath of roses that lay over his coffin. They were sent by someone else, someone who knew the greatness of the clown Marceline. The funeral director looked through a shuffle of papers for the card accompanying the roses. "It was sent," he said, looking up, "by Charles Chaplin."

BROADWAY: *A Yankee Circus on Mars* (1905), *Good Times* (1920), *Better Times* (1922)

## PIGMEAT MARKHAM

### (Dewey Markham, April 16, 1904–December 13, 1981)

A burly black burlesque comedian, raucous Pigmeat Markham starred in dozens of classic sketches including "Here Come De Judge." He played the world's funkiest judge: "The judge is *high* as a Georgia *pine*! *Everybody's* goin' to jail today! And to show you I don't mean *nobody* no good this morning, I'm givin' *myself* six months! And if I'm gonna do six months, Mr. District Attorney, you can imagine what *you're* gonna do!"

Born in Durham, North Carolina, Markham began his show biz career as a tap dancer before breaking into the "T.O.B.A." circuit of black vaudeville. He was in the *Sugar Cane Review* in 1925 and through the late '20s and the '30s played in many more variety shows perfecting his tried-and-true sketches. In 1935 he journeyed to the Apollo Theater in New York, sometimes appearing on the bill every week for an entire year. His nickname came from a character in an old vaudeville routine: "Sweet Papa Pigmeat, with the River Jordan at my hips, and all the women is just run up to be baptized!"

Pigmeat played "Alamo the Cook" on the brief run of the Andrews Sisters' radio show and made films that circulated mostly to black movie houses. In the 1940s, a time when "Amos and Andy" was popular on radio and snappy burlesque sketches were being adapted to film by Abbott and Costello, audiences enjoyed hearty belly laughs at Pigmeat's "low" comedy and didn't worry about any possible "stereotype" behavior in his renditions of "Open the Door, Richard" and the rest of his classics. Into the television era, Pigmeat guest-starred on "The Ed Sullivan Show" bringing his lively humor to a new generation. He issued many record albums, though they could only hint at the kind of broad gestures and costumes that were making the audiences crack up even on the straight lines.

Markham's national fame took hold after Sammy Davis Jr. popularized the old "Here come de judge" catch phrase on "Rowan and Martin's Laugh-In." Davis brought Pigmeat to Vegas with him for a $5,000-a-week taste of big-time success. A novelty tune version of "Here Come De Judge" became a top-10 hit for Shorty Long and was then covered by Pigmeat for a top-20 success. He went on to issue more albums that revelled in the funky black dialect, though now more and more people in the audience were feeling some embarrassment about his brand of broad ethnic comedy.

George Kirby wrote the notes for Markham's *Here Come the Judge* album and praised the old veteran: "This comic was one of the few greats who walked in the back door so that we young comics of today could walk in the front, and thank God he has a chance to walk in the front with us. . . . Pigmeat Markham is the greatest."

New generations enjoyed Markham's classic routines, including his variation on "Who's on First," with Pigmeat explaining the game to an old deaf man: "Ball one!" "Huh?" "The man said I got one ball!" "Ohh, the man said you got one ball. Too bad." "Ball two!" What's that?" "The man said I got two balls!" "Oh . . . ain't nothin' news about that." "Whee! I knocked up a fly!" "Say what?" "I knocked up a fly!" "Oh, you knocked up a fly. Uh-uh. It can't be done!"

Markham appeared on television variety shows but was most popular in live concert dates for predominantly black audiences. "Here Come De Judge" had brought him fame; now he could enjoy some of the fortune, collecting star billing and star payments when he toured. Living in semiretirement at home in New York until his death, he was even called upon to lecture on comedy and the golden era of vaudeville.

AUDIO: *The Trial* (Chess), *Anything Goes* (Chess), *World's Greatest Clown* (Chess), *Tune Me In* (Chess), *This'll Kill Ya* (Chess), *Save Your Soul, Baby* (Chess), *Open the Door, Richard* (Chess), *Mr. Vaudeville* (Chess), *Mr. Funny Man* (Chess), *If You Can't Be Good Be Careful* (Chess), *Here Come the Judge* (Chess), *Pigmeat's Bag* (Chess), *Hustlers* (Chess), *Crap Shootin'* (Jewel), *Would the Real Pigmeat Markham Please Sit Down* (Jewel)

FILMS incl.: *Mr. Smith Goes Ghost* (1940), *Am I Guilty* (1940), *One Big Mistake* (1940), *Fight That Ghost* (1946), *House Rent Party* (1946), *Shut My Big Mouth* (1946), *Pigmeat's Laugh Hepcats* (1947)

## PENNY MARSHALL

### (Carole Penny Marshall, October 15, 1942–  )

A television sitcom favorite as the winsomely plain Myrna Turner on "The Odd Couple" and then half of the odd couple "Laverne and Shirley," Penny Marshall turned away from the camera in the 1990s and won praise as a director. She said she was much more comfortable off camera and never enjoyed watching her own performances, insisting "I'm all nose and teeth."

Born in the Bronx, the original family named Marscharelli, Penny studied dance and at 12 was a member of a 16-girl precision tap dance troupe that appeared on television's "Amateur Hour" and "Jackie Gleason Show." After dropping out of the University of New Mexico, Penny married and had a child. Domestic bliss was short-lived. After her divorce, she turned once more to show business, teaching dance and working with the Albuquerque Light Opera.

In California, Penny joined an improvisational group called The Committee. Rob Reiner was also a member. They married in 1971. When Rob was cast as Mike Stivic on "All in the Family" Penny nearly joined him as his wife Gloria. "Unfortunately," she recalled, "I was the only one who looked like Jean Stapleton's daughter." What the casting people wanted was an actress who looked like Carroll O'Connor's daughter.

Penny appeared in various sitcoms but got her biggest break when her brother, producer Garry Marshall, cast her as the shy, plucky but insecure Myrna Turner, secretary to Oscar Madison on "The Odd Couple." She was one of the show's great supporting characters, developing a trademark goofy laugh and winning over viewers with her self-deprecating vulnerability. In one episode Felix (Tony Randall) is trying to find a quiet place for his friend Oscar (Jack Klugman) to work. He cries, "We need to isolate Oscar. He needs to be someplace where it's quiet and restful and nothing's going on!" Says Myrna: "He could come to my house any Saturday night."

The exposure on the show was important and helped her break out of her shell, but the shell was delicate. Though she won laughs from the live studio audience, she was more inclined to remember the snickers she got from other cast and crew members who liked to tease her and point out that she got the job by nepotism. Penny had recurring small roles on a few other shows of the day but couldn't shake her low-esteem. Recalling those early days, she said, "I always thought I wasn't any good."

Penny wasn't just good—she was great as Laverne De Fazio on "Laverne and Shirley," a spin-off from "Happy Days" that became one of the big hit sitcoms of the late 1970s. Unfortunately, the rigors of the show led to her divorce from Rob Reiner in 1979 and well-publicized fights with her co-star Cindy Williams.

"We didn't really know each other that well," Penny explained in a 1982 *TV Guide* interview, "and then it was like we were pushed together . . . she was being a baby and a pain. And to make her happy, somehow I had to understand. And I didn't." Cindy felt Penny was getting preferential treatment; after all, Penny's brother Garry was the executive producer, her father Tony was the producer and her sister Ronny was casting coordinator. Cindy made demands for more lines and more showcase episodes. After Cindy successfully had the show's head writers fired, Penny was steamed. For two years the duo spoke only on camera. The feud cooled down during Penny's "massive anxiety attacks" over her breakup with Rob Reiner. She was glad to find Cindy supportive and helpful.

Penny had begun to direct during her days on "Laverne and Shirley." She also directed the pilot episode of "Working Stiffs" with Jim Belushi. She developed a reputation as a skilled pro, quite the opposite of her old "Myrna Turner" image. After the original director was fired, Penny directed Whoopi Goldberg's film *Jumpin' Jack Flash.* Her next film was Tom Hanks' *Big,* which became the year's biggest hit. Interviewers expecting to find Penny Marshall happy and excited noticed she was still characteristically self-deprecating. She had not changed all that much from the shy secretary on "The Odd Couple." She still hated her voice so much that she had her housekeeper speak on her phone machine.

Penny scored another triumph directing Robert DeNiro and Robin Williams in *Awakenings.* She acknowledged that she wanted to direct more films, but certainly not become a Woody Allen type and both star and direct: "I have no interest in acting *and* directing a film. Having to look at myself for six months in postproduction is *not* my idea of a good time."

FILMS incl.: *The Couple Takes a Wife* (1972), *Let's Switch* (1975), *1941* (1979), *Love Thy Neighbor* (1984), *Movers and Shakers* (1985), *The Hard Way* (1991)
TV: "The Odd Couple" (1971–75), "The Bob Newhart Show" (1972–73), "Friends and Lovers" (1974–75), "Happy Days" (1975), "Laverne and Shirley" (1976–83)

## PETER MARSHALL (See NOONAN and MARSHALL.)

## MARTIN and LEWIS (See also JERRY LEWIS.)

**Dean Martin: Dino Crocetti, June 7, 1917–
Jerry Lewis: Joseph Levitch, March 16, 1925–**

For exactly ten years Martin and Lewis were America's hottest comedy team, first in nightclubs and later in films where they replaced the aging Abbott and Costello as box office champs. Dean Martin was the handsome big brother supervising the manic-panic antics of his childish partner, Jerry. "I get paid for doing what children are punished for," Jerry admitted. In nightclubs, he was like a bad boy unleashed, dunking cigars into drinks, bringing out gag fake teeth and making faces, yelling and squealing at the orchestra or the waiters, throwing food around, mugging and miming, while Dean tried to sing his straight tunes.

As with Abbott and Costello, in their day Martin and Lewis were loved by the public and disliked by the critics. Unlike Abbott and Costello, today critics still dislike most of their films, and it's only younger viewers who seem able to identify with Jerry Lewis' hysterical reaction to the world around him.

Lewis had been getting less than a hysterical reaction to his nightclub routines before teaming with Dean Martin. Martin, born in Steubenville, Ohio, was a tenth-grade dropout who ended up working in a steel mill. When he got up in front of a crowd in public, it was in a boxing ring as a welterweight. He fought his way to a 24-6 record while supplementing his income working for local gamblers dealing bootleg liquor. Friends admired his voice and his imitation of Bing Crosby's crooning and urged him to try it full time.

Martin did, and in 1945 he and Lewis crossed paths at a club called The Glass Hat. Jerry as the master of ceremonies managed to get some laughs playing off Dean. The good-natured singer didn't mind Lewis breaking into his act for some comedy relief, but resisted forming a partnership. Later at Club 500 in Atlantic City, Jerry was again floundering as a solo and asked Dean to come by so they could do some of the bits they had polished at the other venue. The reaction was too great to be ignored. "Martin and Lewis" teamed at last.

Their rise was meteoric. After just two years they signed a five-year movie deal with Paramount. The mania for Martin and Lewis grew into a show business phenomenon. From nightclubs they moved on to concerts. In 1951 they played the Paramount Theater, and the demand was so great they performed six shows a day. Crowds gathered in front of their hotel clamoring for more. They leaned out the window from time to time to mime gags for their roaring fans. It was the kind of scene that would be familiar to reporters covering an Elvis Presley tour or the arrival of The Beatles in America, but at the time—and for mere *comedians*—the reaction was amazing. The boys earned over $150,000 in two weeks.

Other comics, who had sweated over jokes and carefully choreographed their slapstick, bitterly resented the duo. Jack E. Leonard declared, "This is a nothing act What Martin and Lewis do isn't basically funny, but nobody else had the gall to do it." Of course, a "nonact" could not succeed year after year. The team hired good writers, including John Grant (formerly with Abbott and Costello) and newcomer Norman Lear. Their films were box office hits over and over.

But over and over the strain of touring, the strain of being together constantly and the disparity between "star" Jerry and mere "straight man" Dean began to show. Lewis, the kid, was more dependent on Dean than the older man could stand, and when Lewis talked to him about love and friendship, Dean snapped, "You can talk about love all you want—to me you're nothing but a dollar sign." The breezy early films gave way to efforts that seemed to mirror the duo's friction. In *The Stooge,* Dean played a singer who bombs without his comic partner and then apologizes to the audience: "I'm only half an act . . . I bored you and imposed upon you."

Breakup rumors circulated constantly and, on July 24, 1956, came true. Martin and Lewis announced they had played their last date together. The bitter breakup, exacerbated by the press pestering one or the other about a reconciliation, produced a feud that lasted for decades.

Darren McGavin took Dean Martin's role in *The Delicate Delinquent* and afterward Lewis enjoyed solo success. One hit, *The Nutty Professor,* contained some barbs aimed at Dean via a singer character named Buddy Love. After a shaky start, Martin developed into a modern Phil Harris, singing novelty songs, creating an amusing boozer persona and ultimately hosting his own successful variety show on television. He had several hit songs, and his good looks won him brief fame in action-adventure films. Unlike many other comedy teams, the disappointment fans felt when the team broke up was not absolute. Alone Jerry was as funny, Dean as charming, and in their prolific solo careers they gave fans double the entertainment they could have provided had they stayed together.

On a Jerry Lewis telethon held over the Labor Day weekend in 1976, Frank Sinatra turned up as a guest. He told Lewis, "I have a friend backstage who wants to say hello." Dean Martin did indeed say hello, but according to Lewis, that was about it. Subsequent letters to Dean and a gift twenty-dollar gold piece were unacknowledged. Finally, in 1989, an aging Dean Martin agreed to end the feud. He and Lewis united on stage once again, with the naive Jerry shouting "Why we broke up I'll never know!" "Me either," Dean answered mildly. "I love ya." In 1992 Lewis participated in a three-part special on the team, "Martin & Lewis: Their Golden Age of Comedy" for cable televison's Disney Channel.

AUDIO: *Martin and Lewis on Radio* (Radiola), *Martin and Lewis* (Memorabilia)

BIOGRAPHY: *Everybody Loves Somebody Sometime* (Marx, 1974)

FILMS incl: *My Friend Irma* (1949), *My Friend Irma Goes West* (1950), *At War with the Army* (1950), *That's My Boy* (1951), *Sailor Beware* (1951), *Jump-*

*ing Jacks* (1952), *The Road to Bali* (1952), *The Stooge* (1952), *Scared Stiff* (1953), *The Caddy* (1953), *Money from Home* (1953), *Living It Up* (1954), *Three Ring Circus* (1954), *You're Never Too Young* (1955), *Artists and Models* (1955), *Pardners* (1956), *Hollywood or Bust* (1956)

## DICK MARTIN (See ROWAN and MARTIN.)

## STEVE MARTIN

### (August 14, 1945–  )

Steve Martin's initial fame began with the same hysteria as fads for Silly Putty or yo-yos. The human equivalent, "wild and crazy" Steve became a stand-up comedy phenomenon in the late 1970s. Just as people couldn't explain why they enjoyed playing with Silly Putty or a yo-yo, Martin's wildly enthusiastic supporters couldn't explain why they loved watching him grin idiotically with a corny fake arrow through his head or make balloon animals, or deliberately utter a line so goofy and devoid of wit that it was hilarious. Martin was wise enough to sense when this fad appeal was waning and moved on to films and enduring fame in the 1980s and '90s as one of America's leading comedians, performing equally well in spoofs, romantic comedies and even dramas.

Born in Waco, Texas, Steve played the banjo, juggled and sometimes did Red Skelton pratfalls to amuse his classmates. He remembered the effect of a good fall: "Crash! It was like intentionally embarrassing yourself. . . . My comedy has never been about someone else slipping on a banana skin and laughing at them. Making *yourself* look stupid seems much more human."

Growing up in Orange County, California, Martin eventually got jobs playing the banjo and doing magic tricks at Disneyland and Knotts Berry Farm. At 21 he found a lucrative career as a staff writer on comedy/variety shows, knocking out gags for Sonny and Cher, Pat Paulsen, The Smothers Brothers and Glen Campbell. He quit Campbell's show to pursue his own career performing stand-up. At the time stand-up was not particularly popular, and young performers were having trouble getting ahead.

Steve Martin was once stand-up comedy's "wild and crazy guy." Now he ranks as one of Hollywood's funniest leading men, the star of such modern classics as *Roxanne* and *All of Me*. Photo from the author's collection.

Old-fashioned nightclubs were outdated and with no comedy clubs around, comedians sometimes risked their lives taking the only venues available, opening for pop and rock singers. Crafty veteran George Carlin learned to soothe them, talk down to them, make a lot of funny faces, catch their attention with jokes about dirty words and bodily functions. Martin Mull exaggerated and satirized the whole "o-kayyy, we're really havin' fun" attitude of show biz phonies. Martin made fun of the artificiality of suit-and-tie stand-up and utilized elements of both Carlin and Mull's style, in addition to his own.

He emerged with something exciting and new, the jerky "wild and crazy guy" with his put-ons, sly gags, corny schtick and so stupid-it's-hip personality. If anyone didn't get it, he had a mock-arrogant and hilariously haughty cry of "Well, excuuuuuuse me!" After several guest spots on television's "Saturday Night Live," Martin zoomed to stardom and fad success, selling a million and a half copies of his first album, 1977's *Let's Get Small*. Another album also went platinum. A year later, April 3, 1978, Steve

Martin was on the cover of *Newsweek* magazine. The fever continued to mount. A "nonbook" of whimsies and silliness, *Cruel Shoes*, sold over 200,000 copies in hardcover.

There was a price for all the fame and attention and intensive touring. "You get physically tired, emotionally tired, and start wondering what you're doing. . . . I started doing things like collapsing onstage. It was a signal. . . . It was just exhaustion. I was a wreck." Martin decided to quit stand-up while he was ahead. Summing up this phase of his career, Martin would later say, "I always felt there was a deeper meaning to what I was doing than just being wild and crazy, something more philosophical. I had a view that there was something funny about trying to be funny. . . . Now . . . I see it for what it was. It was just fun, and it was stupid and that's why it was successful." He earned up to "half a million a week. By then I thought, I've worked hard to get this act together, I've got to run it into the ground. I had to exploit it or I would have been an idiot. But I only did it for three years, and then I stopped."

For years interviewers tried to get an idea from Martin on how he put together his act. In an interview with writer Paul Morley in *Blitz* magazine, Martin analyzed his style: "With jokes the audience wait for the punch line and then decide whether to laugh or not. With me, I would deny the punch line, and just keep going, so that the tension would just build and build so much that they would have to start laughing. They would find their own place to laugh, rather than laughing at the place where you told them to laugh. And if they found their own place to laugh it would be ten times funnier than if you told them where they should laugh. It's like when you're a kid and you're laughing so hard at something and you don't know why and you just cannot stop—that's what I was going for. You couldn't leave my show going, 'and then he told the joke . . .' They could only say 'You had to be there.'"

Actually Martin did toss in a quotable joke now and then: "If I'm in a restaurant and I'm eating, and someone says 'Mind if I smoke' I say 'No, no, mind if I fart?'" Sometimes he gave a tongue-in-cheek observation or two: "I believe it's derogatory to refer to a woman's breasts as boobs, jugs, Winnebagos or Golden Bozos. And you should only refer to them as hooters. And I believe you should place a woman on a pedestal, high enough so you can look up her dress." But more often he blurred the line with prop comedy, put-ons and put-offs: "Got me a $300 pair of socks. I got a fur sink. Oh, let's see. Electric dog polisher. Gasoline-powered turtleneck sweater. And of course I bought some dumb stuff too. . . ."

What delirious fans didn't know about Steve Martin at the time was that beneath the flashy exterior there was a shy, very serious man, a philosophy major and art collector who realized how important it was to distance himself from the mad success. And as a comedy writer and keen student of humor, he knew he had done all he could with his "jerk" character. After one movie as *The Jerk*, Martin turned out experimental films that turned radically from one side of satire (*Pennies from Heaven*) to another (*The Man with Two Brains*) and yet another (*The Lonely Guy*).

There were some critics who pronounced *Pennies from Heaven* and *Dead Men Don't Wear Plaid* noble failures; and there were cults for them. Martin's film career didn't really kick off until he discovered the right balance of wild and crazy gyrations and more human, character-oriented humor. *All of Me* was a major breakthrough, and his box-office bankability increased with the hit *Roxanne*.

He married *All of Me* co-star Victoria Tennant. He rarely discusses his private life, saying only "We have got to keep our world private. Otherwise you feel like you get up to go to the bathroom and it becomes a possible anecdote for an interview." The most intimate topic he has discussed was their cuisine. "I'm a vegetarian but I eat fish, so I'm not a true vegetarian. And the same is true of her."

Martin achieved consistent success in the late 1980s with a string of successful films and always had enough fans to see him through a casting mistake (*My Blue Heaven*) or another of those noble experiments (*Three Amigos.*) Even his worst film experience was better than his off-Broadway debut in *Waiting for Godot*. As Vladimir he didn't earn the critical praise heaped on stage-trained co-stars Robin Williams, F. Murray Abraham and Bill Irwin. Calling the reviews "negative to the extreme" and "out of all proportion" he said, "I had plenty of adversity as a stand-up comic—I played dives for 15 years—I thought I had every kind of experience on stage, but this was sheer torture."

Martin returned to the crazed California coast and *L.A. Story,* another comfortable comedy. Like *Roxanne,* it was written by Martin. It began with his voiceover: "I was deeply unhappy, but I didn't know it because I was so happy all the time." Critics were happy to see Steve Martin once again grappling with serious problems in his own "wild and crazy" way. Of that line he said, "I guess it captures a mood of quiet desperation. It's very easy to go along in life working, talking, getting married, and never pausing to say 'What should I really be doing?' " He added, "Yearning to me is the most pathetic emotion. That people want something and can't get it. . . . Some people know exactly what they want to do with their lives. Some people have no clue."

While some people continued to have no clue as to his "wild and crazy" comedy style, many more caught on, and many would accost the very reserved, very private star for an autograph. Martin finally found a solution to the problem. He would hand a fan a card reading: "This certifies that you have had a personal encounter with me and that you found me warm, polite, intelligent and funny."

AUDIO: *Let's Get Small* (Warner Bros.), *A Wild and Crazy Guy* (Warner Bros.), *Comedy Is Not Pretty* (Warner Bros.), *Steve Martin Brothers* (Warner Bros.)

BIOGRAPHIES: *Steve Martin* (Lenburg, 1980), *Steve Martin* (Daly, 1980)

BOOK: *Cruel Shoes* (1979)

FILMS incl.: *The Kids Are Alright* (1979), *The Jerk* (1979), *Pennies from Heaven* (1981), *Dead Men Don't Wear Plaid* (1982), *The Man with Two Brains* (1983), *The Lonely Guy* (1984), *All of Me* (1984), *Movers and Shakers* (1985), *Three Amigos* (1986), *Little Shop of Horrors* (1986), *Planes, Trains and Automobiles* (1987), *Roxanne* (1987), *Dirty Rotten Scoundrels* (1988), *Parenthood* (1989), *My Blue Heaven* (1990), *L.A. Story* (1991), *Father of the Bride* (1991), *Housesitter* (1992)

TV: "Andy Williams Presents Ray Stevens" (1970), "The Ken Berry Show" (1972), "The Sonny and Cher Comedy Hour" (1972–73), "The Smothers Brothers Show" (1975), "The Johnny Cash Show" (1976)

VIDEOS: *Steve Martin Live* (incl. "The Absent-Minded Waiter"); *Saturday Night Live: Steve Martin; Funnier Side of Eastern Canada*

## THE MARX BROTHERS (See also GROUCHO MARX.)

**Chico: Leonard Marx, March 22, 1887–October 11, 1961**
**Harpo: Adolph (Arthur) Marx, November 23, 1888–September 28, 1964**
**Groucho: Julius Henry Marx, October 2, 1890–August 19, 1977**
**Gummo: Milton Marx, October 21, 1892–April 21, 1977**
**Zeppo: Herbert Marx, February 25, 1901–November 29, 1979**

Originally there were six Marx Brothers; Manfred didn't survive much beyond childbirth. The rest left school and their Yorkville tenement at 179 East 93rd Street in New York for show business careers. Groucho was the first, joining The Leroy Trio in 1905. Later he, brother Gummo and a singer named Mabel O'Donnell formed a trio. A quartet dubbed The Four Nightingales was formed with Groucho, Gummo, Harpo and Lou Levy. Eventually Chico replaced Levy and with stage mother Minnie Marx and their aunt Hannah, the brothers worked up a music and comedy act called The Six Mascots. Minnie's brother (Al Shean of Gallager and Shean) was doing well in vaudeville and she figured show business was the perfect career for her talented sons.

By 1914 the brothers had begun to carve out identities for themselves in a sketch called "Fun in Hi Skule." In an age of ethnic comedy, there was the German-accented teacher (Julius), the Italian kid (Leonard), an Irish boy (Adolph), and a Jewish kid (Milton). Backstage the brothers sometimes talked comedy with a stand-up comic named Art Fisher. A popular comic strip of the day called "Sherlocko, The Monk" by Gus Mager featured a monkey-faced detective and his assistant Watso. Most characters in the strip had funny names too, such as "Yanko the Dentist." Fisher began thinking up similar names for the Marx boys.

As Groucho recalled, "I was the moody one, so he called me Groucho. The harp player Adolph—

Satire and slapstick, heady madness and low-comedy mayhem: The four Marx Brothers did it all. A fifth brother, Gummo, left after the team's vaudeville days. Photo from the author's collection.

who, after Hitler's rise to power changed his name to Arthur—would be known as Harpo. The fellow who wore the gumshoes [Milton] would be known as Gummo. And the one constantly chasing the pretty chicks would be called Chicko. We didn't think much of the idea at first, but it caught on. The 'k' in Leonard's new name was accidentally dropped by a typesetter, and it became Chico." Harpo once clarified Gummo's nickname, reporting that the fellow "had a gumshoe way of prowling around backstage and sneaking up on people."

Young Herbert replaced Milton (who was a success in the garment industry) and was nicknamed "Zeppo." Harpo supplied the reason: "Herbie, since he was always chinning himself and practicing acrobatics, we named 'Zippo.' 'Mr. Zippo' was the star of a famous trained chimpanzee act. Our Zippo,

understandably, felt that we were being very unflattering, and he insisted on spelling his stage name 'Zeppo.'"

Critics began to notice the boys, but one reviewer for the *Champaign-Urbana* in Illinois singled out Harpo: "He takes off on an Irish immigrant most amusingly in pantomime. Unfortunately, the effect is spoiled when he speaks." After that, Harpo decided to keep his mouth shut. The team worked on more sketches, including "Home Again," which traveled to London in 1922.

Ultimately they arrived on Broadway with *I'll Say She Is* in 1924. Now another newspaper critic singled out Harpo. Alexander Woollcott in *The New York World* headlined his review "Harpo Marx and Some Brothers" and wrote, "Surely there should be dancing in the streets when a great clown comic comes to town, and this man is a great clown." Groucho came in second: "A crafty comedian with a rather fresher and more whimsical assortment of quips than is the lot of most refugees from vaudeville."

Thanks in part of Woollcott's impressive review, the brothers had scored a Broadway hit. They followed it with *The Cocoanuts* and *Animal Crackers.* Their style of comic anarchy was now as set as their personalities. Chico, with his crooked smile and shifty ways, destroyed dignity and pomposity by chicanery. Harpo, prankish, childlike and untamed, simply loved to have fun, even it if meant causing trouble. Groucho met his foes head-on with a steady stream of insults. The resulting anarchy sometimes left everyone in shambles—even The Marx Brothers—but in most of their classics they thoroughly triumphed over the establishment, something that would earn them more fame in the turbulent 1960s than they enjoyed when they first arrived in the '30s.

In the '30s, when films such as *Duck Soup* and *Horse Feathers* were considered more as comic romps than political or social satire, The Marx Bothers were beloved for their bracing combination of intelligent, sophisticated humor and brawling slapstick. Most anyone could find something to laugh at. Harpo contributed a great portion of the light-hearted visual comedy. Chico handled the tried-and-true ethnic humor and malaprops that had been a vaudeville staple for 30 years. Most critics came to embrace the emerged leader of the group, Groucho, who was adept at the most intellectual satire (his moody monologues in *Animal Crackers* were in parody of Eugene O'Neill). Groucho's scripts were fueled by the witty songs of Harry Ruby and Bert Kalmar and jokes written by the most respected humorists of the day, George S. Kaufman and S. J. Perelman.

Some intellectuals even felt the three Marxes were the ego (Groucho), the subconscious (Chico) and the id (Harpo). Everyone else simply liked to laugh at nonsensical antics perpetrated by cartoonish people in funny outfits. All three could claim deep psychological motivations, but all three were also grand clowns: Harpo with his demented faces and magical sight gags; Groucho with his zany singing, dancing and punchy one-liners; Chico with his amusing piano playing, outrageous Italian accent and bad puns.

The brothers had four hit films in a row until *Duck Soup,* ironically now considered one of their best, but at the time poorly received. Woody Allen once said that The Marx Brothers "for better or worse made the same picture over and over." Perhaps at this point viewers were taking them for granted. Zeppo left the act to become a Hollywood agent. Chico and Groucho tried a radio series, "Flywheel, Shyster and Flywheel."

In 1935, with the always-short-of-cash Chico leading the way, the brothers invaded Irving Thalberg's office at MGM and sat naked, toasting potatoes in his fireplace. When Thalberg arrived, he realized he had to sign these maniacs up—at least to get them out of his office. As it turned out, Thalberg was the producer the boys needed. He allowed them the luxury of trying out the film scripts in front of a live audience and added romantic subplots to attract a broader audience. The results, *A Night at the Opera* and *A Day at the Races,* were considered among their very best.

After Thalberg's death, MGM's indifference and willingness to follow a formula led the brothers downward, with each subsequent film disappointing critics and fans with increasingly milder slapstick and soggier wisecracks. Tired, both physically and mentally, of doing the same zany slapstick, both Groucho and Harpo had been threatening retirement, each time brought back by free-spending Chico and his consistent need of ready cash. After *A Night in Casablanca* the brothers vowed not to make any more films.

Harpo and Chico put together a nightclub act, and Groucho ultimately made a superstar comeback with the radio and television quiz show "You Bet Your Life." He put in only a cameo appearance in *Love Happy,* the last Marx Brothers film. The brothers did appear in *The Story of Mankind* in 1957, but not together. They teamed up later on television for an episode of "GE Theater" entitled "The Great Jewel Robbery," but as in *Love Happy,* Groucho's appearance was a token cameo.

The greatest trio in comedy, The Marx Brothers had just about everything in their arsenal, from witty lines to garrulous slapstick, from moments of satirical cruelty from Groucho to small vignettes of pathos from Harpo. They were funny both on stage and on screen, their highlights coming both from sight (the mirror scene in *Duck Soup*) sound (the why-a-duck byplay from *The Cocoanuts*) and mind (ripping up contracts in *A Night at the Opera*). They were considered irreverent and shocking in their time, and the shock-wave influence of The Marx Brothers is still being felt with each new generation of comedians. Best of all, even after running and re-running Marx Brothers films until almost every movement and word is familiar, the brothers can still raise a smile.

Off stage, the brothers were pretty much what they seemed to be. Groucho was Groucho. Chico was lighthearted and irresponsible, a card-player and womanizer, the black sheep of the family—but so charismatic and lovable all was usually forgiven. Harpo was remembered fondly as a gentle, sweet man, and no one ever had a bad word to say about him. But—he was a Marx Brother—and couldn't resist zany stunts and puckish jokes, from diving naked from Somerset Maugham's house into the swimming pool, to shaving his head to shock a golfing partner. As he told his large family of adopted kids, "If you have an impulse to do something you're not sure is right, go ahead and do it. Take a chance. Chances are, if you don't you'll regret it—unless you break the rules about mealtime or bedtime, in which case you'll sure as hell regret it. If it's a question of whether to do what's fun or what is supposed to be good for you, and nobody is hurt by whichever you do, always do what's fun. If things get too much for you and you feel the whole world's against you, go stand on your head. If you can think of anything crazier to do, do it. Don't worry about what other people think. The only person in the world important enough to conform to is yourself."

AUDIO: *The Cocoanuts* (Sandy Hook), *Night at the Opera* (Re-Sound), *Marx Movie Madness* (Radiola), *Original Voicetracks from Their Greatest Movies* (Decca), *Three Hours, Fifty Nine Minutes, Fifty One Seconds with the Marx Brothers* (Murray Hill, reissued by AAT Records as *The Best of the Marx Brothers*)

BIOGRAPHIES incl.: *The Marx Brothers* (Chrichton, 1950), *Growing Up with Chico* (M. Marx, 1986), *Harpo Speaks* (H. Marx, 1985), *The Marx Brothers Scrapbook* (Marx and Anobile, 1973), *Groucho, Harpo, Chico and Sometimes Zeppo* (Adamson, 1973), *The Marx Brothers, Their World of Comedy* (Eyles, 1966), *The Marx Brothers at the Movies* (Zimmerman and Goldblatt, 1968)

BROADWAY: *I'll Say She Is* (1924), *The Cocoanuts* (1925), *Animal Crackers* (1928), *Shoot the Works!* (1931)

FILMS: *The Cocoanuts* (1929), *Animal Crackers* (1930), *Monkey Business* (1931), *Horse Feathers* (1932), *Duck Soup* (1933), *A Night at the Opera* (1935), *A Day at the Races* (1937), *Room Service* (1938), *At the Circus* (1939), *Go West* (1940), *The Big Store* (1941), *A Night in Casablanca* (1946), *Love Happy* (1949)

FILM BOOKS: *A Night in Casablanca; Monkey Business and Duck Soup Scripts; Why a Duck* (Anobile); *Hooray for Captain Spaulding* (Anobile)

VIDEO: *The Marx Brothers in a Nutshell*

## GROUCHO MARX (See also THE MARX BROTHERS.)

### (Julius Henry Marx, October 2, 1890–August 19, 1977)

"He was an original, a true original," Woody Allen said. "Groucho Marx has always been for me the consummate artist. He looks funny, he sounds funny, he sings funny, he dances funny, he walks funny, the contents of what he says is funny, he operates within a framework that's funny. He has appeal to people who cannot read or write and is considered superbly funny by the most brilliant men in the world."

Only Charles Chaplin has been the subject of more books and more study than Groucho, but as Groucho was always quick to point out, Chaplin was a fan of his. The friendly rivalry began early in vaudeville when The Marx Brothers and Chaplin sometimes played the same bill or dallied in a whorehouse afterward. It continued when Groucho and Chaplin sometimes played tennis together. In his 70s Groucho declared, "I'm as good a comedian as Chaplin. Better, because I can talk and he can't. Sound ruined him. He made a couple of talking pictures and they were clinkers."

Of all The Marx Brothers, Groucho was most interested in pursuing a show business career. He was part of The Le May Trio in which he and another boy in drag backed up the adult singer, also in drag. Stranded in Denver when the two ran away together, Groucho struggled to make his way home. He teamed up with another obscure vaudevillian, Lily Seville, until she took his money and stranded him. Groucho realized he could trust only his own family, and with them he achieved his first fame and fortune. He was the star of their first (uncompleted) film *Humorisk* and clearly the leader in all the rest of the Marx Brothers films. George Bernard Shaw proclaimed "Groucho Marx is the world's greatest living actor."

As a solo star Groucho guested often on radio and put together a set of 78s (later released in album form) of comedy songs. One was his signature tune, "Hooray for Captain Spaulding" (from *Animal Crackers*), which unfortunately did not include some of the racier lines that appeared only in the original stage production. In that one the chorus shouts, "If he hears anything obscene, he'll naturally repel it." Groucho: "I hate a dirty joke, I do—unless it's told by someone who knows how to tell it." Chorus: "He is the only white man who covered every acre." Groucho, pointing to the nearest woman: "I think I'll try to make 'er." Chorus: "Hooray, hooray hooray!"

In the late 1940s, pessimistic about aging, unhappy about being stuck in a few poorly received solo films, Groucho viewed himself as in danger of being washed up. It was then that he consented to star in a radio game show called "You Bet Your Life." It turned out to be the perfect vehicle for him to display his skills as a master ad-libber, and became a television favorite a few years later. The show had a vague script in which Groucho was supplied with facts about the contestants, but he never met them beforehand. Instead, he and head writer Bernie Smith would plot some jokes ahead of time that might be appropriate. A female contestant: "My father is a meat distributor here." Groucho: "Your father is a meat distributor? Well, if you're any indication, he certainly knows his business." Groucho: "What's your name?" Contestant: "Shirley." Groucho: "Well, Shirley to bed, and Shirley to rise."

With this "safety net" of prepared material to fall back on, Groucho was at ease to create his own ad libs and let his mellowed but still grouchy personality shine through. Announcer: "Some special guests are ready to meet you now. As a matter of fact, when I heard about them, I asked them to do something we don't ordinarily do on the show—" Groucho: "What's that? Be amusing?" Groucho: "How long have you been married?" Contestant: "Three wonderful years." Groucho: "Never mind the won-derful years, how many miserable years have you had?"

At a time when comedians were rarely honored, Groucho appeared on the cover of *Time* magazine on December 31, 1951. His salary was over $750,000 a year. The show lasted ten years. Almost every episode of "You Bet Your Life" had a memorable Groucho gag or two. Of course, his most quoted lines were from his 1930s Marx Brothers films. He was master of the straight insult ("You've got the brain of a four-year-old boy and I bet he was glad to get rid of it") and could blast everything from a figure in power to a woman with a powerful figure: "Married! I can see you right now in the kitchen, bending over a hot stove, but I can't see the stove."

The real-life Groucho was no different. When he stood before the altar with his first wife, he had mischief on his mind. Rabbi: "We are gathered here to join this couple in holy matrimony." Groucho: "It may be holy to you, but we have other ideas!" Groucho tweaked all authority, once filling out a customs inspection form like this: Name: Julius H. Marx. Address: 21 Lincoln Road, Great Neck, L.I. Born: Yes. Hair: Not much. Occupation: Smuggler. List items purchased out of the United States: Wouldn't you like to know?

This led to a long and rigorous search of his trunk by customs officials. But that didn't dampen his spirits. After it was over he said loudly to his wife, "What did you do with the opium? Do you still have it on you?"

Groucho rarely had the occasion to tangle with politicians as he did in *Duck Soup,* but he made the most of his opportunities. At a film festival in Mexico City, a diplomat announced to Groucho and a group of stars, "On Thursday you will meet with the president of Mexico." Groucho cracked, "What assurance can you give us that on Thursday he will still be president?"

Groucho himself recalled one of his most famous remarks: "Years ago I decided to join a beach club on Long Island, and we drove out to a place called the Sands Point Bath and Sun Club. I filled out the application and the head cheese of the place came over and told me we couldn't join because I was Jewish. So I said, 'My son's only half Jewish. Would it be all right if he went in the water up to his knees?'"

Peter De Vries wrote a 1977 novel, *Madder Music,* about a man who believes himself to be Groucho. De Vries didn't find it odd, psychologically speaking, for someone to be so afflicted: "The most famous comic of our time is a walking, or I should say prowling, testimonial for Sigmund Freud. What does Freud find the two basic human drives most released in humor? Sex and aggression. And what is Groucho's chief stock-in-trade? Lechery and insult . . . hostility and desire. He wants to hit every man he knows and possess every woman he sees."

Naturally enough, the same traits that fostered the "Groucho" legend created a certain animosity. Groucho's son Arthur chronicled some of his father's foibles in *Son of Groucho.* Maxine Marx, Chico's daughter, offered this appraisal in her own book: "Daddy used to say that Groucho would insult a king to make a beggar laugh. He would insult the beggar too, if my experience was any judge." In the 1970s, the unexpurgated honesty of Groucho's interviews in *The Marx Brothers Scrapbook,* whether it was in attacking President Nixon or the talents of Zeppo, proved to be an embarrassment for some friends and family members. By that time Groucho was a legend in his own time, the hero comedian of the counterculture, and his books, and television and concert appearances were met with whole-hearted appreciation from his fans.

While he was certainly appreciated in the 1930s, and again in the 1950s, it was in his latter years that he flourished—interviewed often by magazines, the subject of endless books, even undertaking a one-man show that toured the country. One of his proudest achievements was the publication of *The Groucho Letters,* and the fact that the originals are now in the Library of Congress. Groucho's correspondence with both the greats of literature as well as his friends and fans contained some of the best examples of his wit and wisdom.

The negative aspects of Groucho were largely ignored—the three divorces (from Ruth Johnson, Catherine Gorcey and Eden Hartford) and the sometimes strained relationships between him and his three children, Arthur, Miriam and Melinda. What was celebrated was the brash and bracing character of "Groucho," the one who sang "Whatever it is—I'm against it!" The one who announced, "I do not wish to belong to any club that will accept me as a member." The one who could even find something insulting to say after being complimented. A priest once approached him, saying "I want to shake your hand and thank you for all the pleasure you've brought into the world." Said Groucho, extending his hand, "And I want to thank you for all the pleasure you've taken out of it."

After his famous 1972 one-man show tour, health problems began to slow Groucho down, but he still had a twinkle in his eye at his 85th birthday party when his brothers Gummo and Zeppo, along with such stars as Jack Lemmon, Bob Hope and Carl Reiner, paid him tribute. Said guest Peter Sellers, "Just to sit there and realize you are in the same room with Groucho Marx is a delightful experience."

Sadly, Groucho's decline was accompanied by lurid headlines describing abuses by his longtime companion, Erin Fleming. The same woman who had helped keep Groucho active and motivated was now reportedly bossing the helpless old man around. Groucho's son Arthur successfully squared off against Erin over the conservatorship of his estate and the decisions to be made regarding the ailing comedian. Groucho himself was not aware of the bitter battle, or the death of his brother Gummo on April 21. A few months later, and the fragile body of one Julius H. Marx was no more.

Groucho Marx, however, is immortal.

Of course, an iconoclast like Groucho probably would laugh at the very idea of immortality. After a lengthy interview session with *Playboy* magazine, he was asked, "One last question—what would you do if you had your life to live all over again?

Groucho answered, "Try more positions."

AUDIO: *An Evening with Groucho* (A&M), *An Evening with Groucho* (A&M Picture Disk), *Groucho!* (Mark 56), *Groucho Marx* (Memorabilia), *Groucho Marx* (Nostalgia Lane), *You Bet Your Life* (Golden Age), *Hooray for Captain Spaulding* (Decca), *Groucho Marx on Radio* (Radiola), *The Mikado* (Columbia Special Products)

AUTOBIOGRAPHY: *Groucho and Me* (1989); *Memoirs of a Mangy Lover* (1963); *The Grouchophile* (1976)

BIOGRAPHY: *Life with Groucho* (A. Marx), *Son of Groucho* (A. Marx, 1972), *Hello, I Must Be Going* (Chandler, 1978), *Groucho* (Arce, 1979), *The Secret Word Is*

*Groucho* (Arce, 1977), *Love Letters* (M. Merx Allen, 1992)

BOOKS: *Beds (1930), Many Happy Returns (1942), The Groucho Letters (1967)*

BROADWAY: *The Man Who Came to Dinner* (1941)

FILMS incl.: *Copacabana* (1947), *Mr. Music* (1950), *Double Dynamite* (1951), *A Girl in Every Port* (1952), *Will Success Spoil Rock Hunter* (1957), *Skidoo* (1968)

TV: "You Bet Your Life" (1950–61), "Tell It to Groucho" (1962)

## JACKIE MASON

### (Yakov Moshe Maza, June 9, 1930–   )

In December 1986 Jackie Mason became one of the hottest comedians in America, the first to score a success on Broadway in a one-man show since Victor Borge 20 years earlier. It was a surprise to everyone, including Jackie Mason. Jackie's controversial career had seen many highs and lows, and he had recently been at his lowest.

Ironically a "midwesterner," Jackie Mason was born in Sheboygan, Wisconsin. His father, Rabbi Eli Maza, emigrated there from Minsk. Eventually the rabbi was given a congregation in New York. There Jackie followed his father's wishes and studied to become a rabbi. Jackie majored in English at City College and graduated in 1953. While continuing his rabbinical studies, he took jobs in the Catskills as a social director. He was also the lifeguard. He told the manager, "I can't swim." The manager said, "Don't tell the guests."

Jackie began doing stand-up comedy, telling his father it was only so he could earn enough money to continue his studies. During a 1958 radio appearance in New York, host Barry Gray fumbled over the pronunciation of "Maza." Jackie instantly realized he needed a new name and joked with the host, insisting that "Jacob Maza" was really "Jackie Mason."

Jackie was ordained a rabbi in 1958, but by then he was more experienced as a stand-up comic. He gave humorous sermons for congregations in Weldon, North Carolina and Latrobe, Pennsylvania, but after getting laughs staring at a pretty woman in the front row while expounding on "the ways of the flesh," he decided to return to show business. "On my father's terms," Jackie recalled, "I was a worthless person who was living a worthless terrible life. . . . It filled me with guilt."

In nightclubs, Jackie's humor on the subject of morality was very much in the style of such new-wave comics as Lenny Bruce. Jackie in 1960: "There's a double standard about sex. Our father or mother becomes our father or mother. Beautiful . . . but how the child was created and arrived is something that is cloaked in secrecy. They're ashamed of it. They thought it was pretty clever when they did it." And on politics, he wasn't too far behind Mort Sahl: "Ask in any country, 'Where's the American Embassy?' They'll tell you 'Oh, it's just a stone's throw away.'" But Jackie didn't seem cool like Lenny, or hip like Mort, and critics weren't listening. They couldn't even hear the uniqueness of Jackie's musical staccato delivery, a cadence every bit as fascinating as the jazzy, stream-of-conscious riffs of Lenny and Mort.

Jewish audiences who came to his shows thinking he was a part of the Catskill "schtick" tradition blanched over the satiric jokes and were utterly repelled by some of his straight gags that came too close to clichés they wished would go away. "Money is not important," Jackie would tell them, "Love is important. Fortunately, I love money!"

Gentile audiences laughed at Jackie's accent and his funny voice, but they didn't get his sharper gags either. Some were offended by his "troublemaker" persona as much as Jews were, especially when he seemed unpatriotic: "President Kennedy rides around in a $12,000 car. How does he know I want to buy him such a fancy car? Special car made to order with an open top so he could stand up. If he wants to stand up he don't need a car, let him take a bus!"

On October 18, 1964 Jackie was a guest on Ed Sullivan's show, at the time the most important and influential variety series on the air. Things went well for a while. Then, off camera, the stern host held up two fingers indicating Mason had only two minutes left and should begin closing his set. Annoyed that the studio audience was distracted and no longer responding, Jackie told them, "Look at this, I'm telling jokes and he's showing me fingers. Nobody came to watch fingers . . . I'm here with jokes because nobody cares about a person standing, moving around fingers."

An ex-rabbi with strong opinions and plenty of comic chutzpah, Jackie Mason has emerged with a staggeringly successful one-man Broadway show. Photo from the author's collection.

Jackie mimicked Ed's fancy fingers. Sullivan was outraged. Already angry with Mason for ad-libbing—something comics didn't do back then—Sullivan thought that Mason had made an obscene gesture. When Jackie got off stage Sullivan began cursing at him, ending the tirade with an ad lib of his own: "You'll never work again in this business!"

The Sullivan-Mason feud made headlines and did much to permanently attach a "troublemaker" label to the young comic. After Mason filed a lawsuit and tapes of the show proved his innocence, Jackie returned to Sullivan's show on September 11, 1966. Even so, Mason's reputation remained damaged.

Jackie joked about Frank Sinatra, believing Frank had a "sickness" about having to conquer women. He joked that Sinatra couldn't continue on that way, then added self-deprecatingly, "But how long can I go on *this* way?" Mason's gags were benign, mostly playing on his own jealousy of Sinatra's good fortune.

One night Jackie was playing at a popular hotel that happened to have a special guest in residence:

Sinatra. Sinatra came in to see the show and heckle. Since Sinatra had recently married Mia Farrow and was on his honeymoon, Jackie logically asked Frank, "What's the matter, you're not busy upstairs?"

On November 6, 1966 three bullets crashed into Jackie's hotel room, hitting the bed on which he had been sitting. On February 13, 1967 a thug warned Jackie to stop the Sinatra jokes. Then he beat him up, breaking his nose.

Jackie remained an uncompromising, challenging comedian. He tried to bring a play to Broadway in 1969, *A Teaspoon Every Four Hours*. It was about a Jewish fellow who gets involved with a Gentile girlfriend. Black, in fact. The subject matter was controversial and critics tore the show apart, some tartly questioning how a common stand-up comic could be allowed in the theater. That same year Mason was censored on "The Smothers Brothers Comedy Hour" and sued CBS for $20 million.

Through the 1970s Mason worked and struggled to work, unable to find a niche, now having the tag of old-timer and has-been as well as "too Jewish" or "too controversial." In 1981 he raised $450,000 to film *The Stoolie*, a film that actually won him good reviews. Though cheaply done, the portrayal of a sleazy small-time loser was handled with some moments of humor and touching pathos. The film had limited distribution and never found an audience. Mason's next effort, *A Stroke of Genius*, co-starring Karen Black, collapsed during filming, and in 1983 Jackie went bankrupt.

Jackie didn't need the plays and movies. What he needed was an empty stage and himself. Having seen Dick Shawn win some success doing a one-man show in concert, Jackie decided to forget about nightclubs and assemble his act as a "one-man show." The result, *The World According to Me,* was a hit in Los Angeles. When it went to Broadway in December 1986, Richard Sheperd of the *New York Times* gave it a rave review. Mason was now a huge Broadway star.

Jackie hadn't changed. Others had. Jackie was still being honest, ironic and uncompromising: "I never seen four black people walking in the street and saying 'Watch out, there's a Jew over there.' Let's be honest, did you ever see anybody who was afraid to walk into a Jewish neighborhood because he might get killed by an accountant?" Jackie's asking price for a show went from $5,000 to $50,000 a night. He made records, videos and films. A comically honest commercial for Honda ("Why you need this—I don't know") won a Clio Award.

Then the controversies started all over again. In the spring of 1988 a Miami stripper and singing telegram performer put together a show called *Jackie Oh!* featuring her two-year-old daughter whom she claimed was fathered by Jackie. This didn't deter ABC from starring him in "Chicken Soup," a television sitcom about a Jewish man and his Catholic girlfriend (Lynn Redgrave). It received good notices and began with high ratings. Meanwhile, Jackie got involved with the year's mayoral race in New York, supporting white candidate Rudolph Giuliani over eventual winner David Dinkins, a man whom he thought looked "like a black model without a job."

This was a rather mild quip, considering Dorothy Parker's remark that supposedly toppled Thomas E. Dewey: "He looks like the little man on the wedding cake." And only recently Jesse Jackson had merely raised eyebrows when he called the city a "Hymietown" with too many Jews. But in the midst of a bitter mayoral race in which racial violence was a key issue, Mason's remark drew screaming headlines and the situation grew worse. Jackie, who had refused to perform in South Africa and had marched in Selma, Alabama, was called a racist for having used the term "schvartze" for black, though that is the literal word for black in Yiddish. Bob Herbert, a black columnist in the *Daily News,* called Jackie "powdery faced." Editorials for and against Jackie raged in the newspapers. Woody Allen, a Dinkins' supporter, took a moment to set the record straight: "I think that he's in no way racially prejudiced . . . the press was extremely astringent with him."

In November, "Chicken Soup" was canned by ABC. It had started out in second place and by that time was 23rd out of some 80 programs on the air, a respectable position. ABC insisted the show was doing poorly and was not a good "lead-in" for the following show, "thirtysomething." Another show flirting with top 20 status would have been moved to a new time slot.

Mason didn't complain. Instead, he toured the country with his one-man show. When he played Washington, D.C. Art Buchwald was offended: "I hate him for being so good." He was a hit in England

as well, where in 1990 Oxford University established a Jackie Mason Visiting Fellowship for the study of Hebrew. He went back to Broadway with yet another hit show *Brand New* and remains in top form.

To Jackie's point of view, a Broadway show is at least easier than nightclub work. "It's one-fifth as hard to get a laugh in a theater as it is in a club. In a theater you have an audience waiting to hear what you say; in a club you have one waiting for you to finish. A nightclub is a place for a couple to get together and there's a whole ritual going on about how he's going to start this affair with her. He's not paying $300 just to watch a Jew talk for nothing. The reason he's spending all this money is that he's trying to attack this girl. The better I am the worse he's doing because if I'm really funny he can't get out of there."

AUDIO: *I Want to Leave You with the Words of a Great Comedian* (Verve), *I'm the Greatest Comedian in the World Only Nobody Knows It Yet* (Verve), *Great Moments in Comedy* (Verve), *The World According to Me* (Warner Bros.)
BOOKS: *Jackie Mason's America* (1983), *The World According to Me* (1991), *Jackie Oy!* (1988), *How to Talk Jewish* (1990)
BROADWAY: *A Teaspoon Every Four Hours* (1969), *The World According to Me* (1986), *Brand New* (1990)
VIDEO: *Jackie Mason on Broadway*

## WALTER MATTHAU

### (Walter Matuschanskayasky, October 1, 1920– )

A grand comic curmudgeon in dozens of top film comedies, Walter Matthau creates endless expressions of indignation and chagrin from the sags, wrinkles and pouches of rubbery putty that form his unique face. More versatile than a mere sad-sack comic, Matthau can also register comic surprise, puckish rascality and complete shock. Each time he amazed critics with his latest tour-de-farce, he surpassed it with the next, turning in memorable performances for over three decades.

Matthau's father was a Catholic priest, forced to flee Russia due to religious persecution. On the way to the United States, he married Matthau's mother, a Lithuanian Jew. Walter was born in New York

City. His parents split when Walter was three; his mother worked in a sweatshop to support Walter and his brother.

Matthau appeared in school productions and, by the time he was in his teens, local Yiddish musicals. His name was a bit long for theatrical use, and it was soon shortened. Only once, for a cameo role in 1974's *Earthquake,* was he billed under his real name— Matuschanskayasky.

After graduating from Seward Park High School in 1939, where he excelled in sports, he worked as a boxing coach for the Police Athletic League. After air force service during World War II, earning six battle stars, Staff Sergeant Matthau enrolled in acting school on the GI bill. Not handsome enough to be a leading man or old enough for juicy character roles, he found his way slowly and painfully, but emerged on Broadway in the early 1950s and earned some good notices for *Will Success Spoil Rock Hunter?* in 1955.

Matthau displayed sitcom cunning in getting the best out of that stage role. After fighting with author George Axelrod over script changes, he wrote a letter to him under the name of "A. Schneider," prominent psychiatrist. The nonexistent doctor's analysis of the show and Matthau's character impressed Axelrod. "I think you're right," he told Matthau. "Look at this letter I've received from a psychiatrist."

Matthau went on to play Nathan Detroit in that year's City Center production of *Guys and Dolls* and received raves for his role as the sarcastic Maxwell Archer in the comedy *Once More, With Feeling.* He won a Tony Award for *A Shot in the Dark* in 1962 and went to Hollywood where his film career built slowly, with roles as a grim scientist *(Fail Safe),* an offbeat but stoic heavy *(Charade),* an amusingly streetwise private detective *(Mirage)* and a grumpy ship's doctor *(Ensign Pulver).*

Broadway provided Matthau with another hit when he co-starred with Art Carney in *The Odd Couple.* His role of sloppy sportswriter Oscar Madison was the first to make full use of Matthau's slow-burn temperment, baleful wisecracking and grouchy, slouchy physical mannerisms. It was not only a personal triumph, but a financial one, since he had invested a sizable amount in the production. Matthau got laughs from bombast ("Don't point that finger at me unless you intend to use it!") and from

unexpected whimsy and subtlety. During a tirade over being divorced, broke and sloppy, he answers the phone; and instead of a growl, he imitates a secretary nonchalantly answering for a law firm: "Hello, Divorced, Broke and Sloppy. . . ."

Matthau won a Tony for the role and won over movie audiences for the film version opposite Jack Lemmon. Lemmon found his co-star rather idiosyncratic, revealing that Matthau "never wanted to play Oscar, he wanted to play Felix. It's absolutely true. He wanted to go far against what was so right for him—he wanted to stretch. Walter kept telling the director, 'Switch the roles, before it's too late.' In the meantime, he was giving the performance of a lifetime in the other role." The teaming of Matthau and Lemmon led to a string of hits. He won an Academy Award for *The Fortune Cookie* co-starring Lemmon, but that role came with a high price; he suffered a heart attack during the last stages of filming. Matthau and Lemmon teamed in subsequent films including *The Front Page* and *Buddy Buddy,* and Lemmon directed Matthau in *Kotch.* Matthau's name also remained closely identified with Neil Simon as he starred in such Simon hits as *Plaza Suite, California Suite, The Sunshine Boys, I Ought to Be in Pictures* and *The Odd Couple.* While Matthau was sometimes criticized for occasional overacting in these meaty roles, off stage he was often over-humble. Of his great role as Oscar Madison, he remarked that Jack Klugman "fit the part and was better in it than I was . . . Klugman understudied me on Broadway."

Matthau grew more and more comic as he aged. His jowls fleshed out, his nose became more of a pudgy Fieldsian knob and there was a squint to his eyes. Lines accentuated his craggy features and seemed to suggest that his viewpoint in life was less do-or-die than do-it-dourly, meeting every problem with barely concealed irritation, foreboding and regret. For two roles as cantankerous older men, he was nominated for two more Academy awards— *Kotch* and *The Sunshine Boys.* In the latter he once again varied his attack, earning huge laughs not only from his grumpy antics but from his cheerfully demented delight in hollering one single word: "Enter!"

In real life, Matthau often fit his image exactly. He did feel that "there are two misconceptions about me: One that I'm an extrovert, and two that horse racing is my real passion in life." His own worst critic, he once said, "I've done 50-odd pictures and 45 have made money. But I've been semisatisfied with maybe a half dozen." In his long career, Matthau really had only one unfulfilled ambition: "To play Macbeth—nude."

BROADWAY incl.: *Twilight Walk* (1951), *Fancy Meeting You Again* (1942), *In Any Language* (1952), *Green-Eyed People* (1952), *The Ladies of the Corridor* (1953), *The Burning Glass* (1954), *Guys and Dolls* (1955), *Will Success Spoil Rock Hunter* (1955), *Once More, With Feeling* (1958), *A Shot in the Dark* (1961), *The Odd Couple* (1965)

FILMS incl.: *The Kentuckian* (1955), *Bigger Than Life* (1956), *A Face in the Crowd* (1957), *Slaughter on Tenth Avenue* (1957), *King Creole* (1958), *Who's Got the Action* (1962), *Fail Safe* (1964), *Charade* (1964), *Ensign Pulver* (1964), *Goodbye Charlie* (1964), *Mirage* (1965), *The Fortune Cookie* (1966), *A Guide for the Married Man* (1967), *The Odd Couple* (1968), *A Guide for the Married Woman* (1968), *Candy* (1968), *Secret Life of an American Wife* (1968), *Cactus Flower* (1969), *Hello Dolly* (1969), *A New Leaf* (1971), *Plaza Suite* (1971), *Kotch* (1971), *Pete 'n' Tillie* (1972), *The Front Page* (1974), *The Sunshine Boys* (1975), *The Bad News Bears* (1976), *House Calls* (1978), *California Suite* (1978), *Casey's Shadow* (1978), *Little Miss Marker* (1980), *Hopscotch* (1980), *First Monday in October* (1981), *Buddy Buddy* (1981), *I Ought to Be in Pictures* (1982), *Movers and Shakers* (1985), *The Little Devil* (1989), *The Incident* (1990), *Against Her Will* (1991)

TV: "Tallahasee 7000" (1960)

## ELAINE MAY (See NICHOLS and MAY.)

## PAT McCORMICK

### (Arley D. McCormick, July 17, 1934–   )

Pat McCormick had a great influence on American comedy, though few people are aware of it. As a writer for Jonathan Winters, Merv Griffin, Don Rickles and "The Tonight Show" under Johnny Carson, McCormick came up with bizarre material that challenged the barriers of 1950s and '60s comedy.

While "sick" comedy had been around in the '50s, and everyone from Jack Douglas to Lenny Bruce experimented with "hip" comedy, little of this material was heard by middle America. They began to hear it when Johnny Carson started to liven up his standard monologues with some of the McCormick "weirdness."

Samples of Pat's comic style in the '70s can be heard on his own album, *Pat McCormick Tells It Like It Is*. It was similar to the humor on "The Tonight Show" at the time. McCormick did a bit on "Wrinkle City," a senior citizen's home where they stage Olympic events such as "the hop, skip and trip" competition and the "false teeth toss." That kind of thing became fodder for Carson's old "Aunt Blabby." And while Carson's "Karnak" answered unusual questions, McCormick invented for himself a parody of Tonto: "Why are you cleaning your rifle, Tonto?" "Dusty Springfield!" "I understand you had a date yesterday with both Doris and Evelyn. How did you arrange that?" "Doris Day. Evelyn Knight." And if Carson sometimes brought out odd products to lampoon, Pat invented his own such as "a trained mouse to work as an operator for Cuban elevator shoes."

Not quite as masterful at voices as Jonathan Winters, McCormick was a somewhat odd and awkward sight (the mild-looking, curly-haired blond stood six foot six). He never became a major stand-up performer and for a time seemed consigned to the thankless role of Ed McMahon–like stooge for Don Rickles on Don's television show. But over the years, McCormick developed into a comedy character actor, using his imposing height and silly demeanor to play a variety of fierce but essentially harmless types. In *Smokey and the Bandit 3* he was paired with tiny Paul Williams for some visual comedy, and found himself in similar circumstances surrounded by little people in *Under the Rainbow*.

In 1990 McCormick turned up as a lawyer in Sam Kinison's rock video, "Under My Thumb." Among the ad libs he threw at the bewigged judge: "By the way, your honor, I think there's a sparrow loose in your hair!" After the song ended he declared, "Never eat in a restaurant where you see a cockroach bench-pressing a burrito!"

McCormick, a comedy legend off screen as much as on, enjoys letting his imagination loose for the fun of it. Writer Phil Berger reported a typical incident involving the always-on McCormick: "To celebrate the baptism of his baby boy, McCormick had chums of his over for a sit-down dinner. After drinks, he disappeared a moment, returning with a silver platter that he set down on the table, revealing the wee McCormick surrounded by carrot and onion trimmings. Taking hold of the infant's member, he asked 'Who wants the pope's nose?' "

AUDIO: *Pat McCormick Tells It Like It Is* (Atco)

FILMS incl.: *Buffalo Bill and the Indians* (1967), *Smokey and the Bandit* (1977), *A Wedding* (1978), *Hot Stuff* (1979), *Scavenger Hunt* (1979), *Smokey and the Bandit II* (1980), *History of the World Part I* (1981), *Under the Rainbow* (1981), *Pandemonium* (1982), *Smokey and the Bandit 3* (1983), *Doin' Time* (1984), *Beverly Hills Vamp* (1988), *Rented Lips* (1988)

TV: "The Don Rickles Show" (1968–69), "The New Bill Cosby Show" (1972–73), "Gun Shy" (1983)

## PAUL McCULLOUGH (See CLARK and McCULLOUGH.)

## SPANKY McFARLAND (See also OUR GANG.)

**(George McFarland, October 2, 1928–　　)**

Chubby, cute and wise beyond his years, Spanky McFarland was the major star of the "Our Gang" comedies during the sound era. Among his qualities were some Oliver Hardy mannerisms of innocent chagrin. Since Laurel and Hardy also worked for Hal Roach Studios, this was not surprising. But as Spanky recalled, "It was just a characteristic that [the director] developed in me. . . . I wasn't trying to emulate anybody . . . but I was aware of them; I knew who they were. . . . Laurel and Hardy liked the kids and they would come over and watch us work for a while."

Born in Dallas, Spanky appeared in print ads when he was just a baby. A few years later the chubby tot was signed to replace aging Fat Joe Cobb in the "Our Gang" comedies. His five-year contract netted him $100 a week. In Dallas the boy was known as "Sonny." Just why director Robert McGowan renamed him "Spanky" is a mystery. "I don't have any story to go with that. McGowan liked it

and Roach approved it. I made the [screen] test and got lucky and stayed for 13 years."

After he outgrew "Our Gang," McFarland had his fill of show business and actually asked his parents if he could move back home. After the air force, he recalled working "in a cluster of nondescript jobs," including a hamburger cook and a truck driver. He became a kiddie show host for "Our Gang" shorts on a Tulsa television station. Married, with two children, McFarland later became a successful salesman, moving to New Jersey in 1966 to work for Philco-Ford, then returning to Ft. Worth and completing his career with Magic Chef.

Today Spanky often goes out on lucrative college tours, lecturing and showing film clips. The ex-salesman insisted that for him, "Our Gang" was really business, a job he did as a child. He did not find it either a traumatic or an exciting experience. "You know, it wasn't like I thought I was doing something unusual, because it was normal for me to get up and go on the set and shoot a picture and go to school three hours a day and go home."

McFarland turns down most film offers, though he did appear in a brief role as the governor of Texas in *The Aurora Encounter*. Of his days in "Our Gang" he said, "I wouldn't take a million dollars for the experience, and I wouldn't take a penny to do it again."

FILMS incl.: *Day of Reckoning* (1933), *Kentucky Kernels* (1935), *O'Shaughnessy's Boy* (1935), *The Trail of the Lonesome Pine* (1936), *General Spanky* (1936), *Johnny Doughboy* (1943), *The Woman in the Window* (1944), *The Aurora Encounter* (1984)

## FIBBER McGEE and MOLLY

**Fibber McGee: Jim Jordan, November 16, 1896– April 1, 1988**
**Molly: Marian Driscoll, April 15, 1898–April 7, 1961**

The radio sitcom "Fibber McGee and Molly" got its biggest laughs from a sound effect—the opening of Fibber's messy closet—and the cacophony of junk tumbling out of it. But the amusing human nature episodes based on Fibber's small-town lifestyle and his dream-schemes of glory made for plenty of smiles and chuckles, enough to keep the beloved show on the air for decades.

Both Jim Jordan and Marian Driscoll were from Peoria, Illinois. Though he had tried for a career as a singer, Jim was a mailman when he married Marian, a piano teacher, in 1918. He became an insurance salesman and together they sang in church. After some local bookings they got a break in 1925 as The O'Henry Twins, doing local radio commercials. In 1927 they appeared on "The Smith Family" on WENR in Chicago and in 1931 starred in "The Smackouts," in which Jim owned a grocery store that was always smack out of everything. In 1935 they began "Fibber McGee and Molly," with writer Don Quinn giving them the same hometown sensibilities Paul Rhymer did for "Vic and Sade." One difference was the colorful expressions Fibber liked to use for laughs. Rather than telling fat Dr. Gamble to take a seat, in one episode he said, "Kick your case of corn cures into a corner and compose your corpulent corpus on a convenient camp chair." McGee's love of such novelty dialogue and bad puns usually earned him Molly's catch phrase complaint, "Tain't funny, McGee."

Basically Fibber was just an average guy, a likable dreamer and occasional truth-stretcher with fallible self-importance and always failing big ideas. The concept of the poor working guy hatching crackpot plots for glory would become the basis for not only "Fibber McGee" but "The Honeymooners" and many other sitcoms. Fibber's wife, like many others, greeted his schemes with tolerance but a doleful lack of personal involvement. As Molly, Marian Jordan often got in some one-liners, a rarity for sitcom wives. She favored her own brand of comic language: "Abigail just rang up another no-sale on her social register." She also created several characters for the show, including a precocious brat with a slow, teasing catch phrase, "I betcha." In the early 1940s, The Jordans were tops at domestic comedy, earning $3,500 a week.

The show and the few movies made about Fibber McGee and Molly remain pleasing and likable, though they rely quite a bit on insult comedy. Here's a scene between McGee and his chubby, windy friend Throckmorton Gildersleeve. McGee speaks first:

"That offer you had from a friend is a fake." "Why must it be a fake?" "Because you haven't got

a friend!" "Why, you anemic little anthropological aberration." "Who's an anthropologic abbreviation? . . . He can't call me that and get away with it! I'll sock his face so far down into his oxfords he'll be known as puss in boots." "Why, you bumptuous little barfly, I could smack you down with a wet noodle!" "Think he could? Neither do I!"

The show was one of the first to launch "spin-offs." "The Great Gildersleeve" soon had his own show, as well as the maid, "Beulah." As radio faded in the early 1950s, the aging Jordans faded too. Their show was whittled down to 15 minutes, then disappeared. Molly suffered a heart attack in 1953, and after some radio work for the program "Monitor," the Jordans retired in 1957. A television version of "Fibber McGee and Molly" starred Bob Sweeney and Cathy Lewis. After Molly's death, Jordan married Gretchen Steward in 1962. In his 90s, Jordan died after he collapsed in his home.

On tape and on record, Fibber McGee and Molly are still alive and well at home at "79 Wistful Vista."

AUDIO: *Fibber McGee and Molly* (Murray Hill), *Fibber McGee and Molly* (Nostalgia Lane)

FILMS: *This Way Please* (1938), *Here We Go Again* (1942), *Look Who's Laughing* (1941), *Heavenly Days* (1944)

## VAUGHN MEADER

### (Abbott Vaughn Meader, March 20, 1936–   )

"A living reminder of a tragedy" is how Vaughn Meader described himself in 1979. He was doing then what he did for over a decade before and after—trying for a comeback in comedy, touring with his country music and hoping for some acting assignments.

Abbott Vaughn Meader did not have an easy life from the start. His father died when he was 18 months old. The bright spots in his struggling school years were talent shows that won him applause for his imitations of country singers. After attending Brooklyn High in his native Boston, he was stationed in Germany for army service. It was there that he joined a GI band and married his German-born wife.

Back home, Meader tried to find a niche in show business. He got into stand-up, and with his pleasant looks and natural Boston accent put together a routine impersonating President Kennedy. Others did Kennedy, but Meader looked the part; he got a break, a chance to star on a comedy album called *The First Family*. There was no reason to expect more than modest success. The jokes were very mild. The biggest gag was President Kennedy's complaint that his kids were playing with his bath toy ("The rubber swan . . . is mine!").

*The First Family* became a "fad" success. People didn't dislike Kennedy—they didn't want to hear harsh satire of him; they seemed to buy it as a way to get close to the Kennedy magic. They wanted to have fun with Kennedy and his clan and "join" the first family. Kennedy himself was noted for his humor, and this was the first time in recent memory that there were children in the White House. As if leafing through the Kennedy family album and chuckling along with John, Jackie and the kids, listeners enjoyed amusing "audio snapshots" of the lively family at play: the relatives playing touch football; Jackie conducting a White House tour; the little kids acting cute; the president joking optimistically about the day's problems.

Recorded on October 22, 1962, by November 19 the *New York Times* reported over 200,000 copies sold and that factories were working overtime to make more. By Christmas it was a million-seller, astonishing for any record at the time, much less a comedy disc. On March 18, 1963 Meader and company put out volume 2. But already there were disturbing warning signs that told Meader his luck was beginning to run out.

A nightclub tour doing "First Family" routines radio-style in front of a live audience with a full cast failed miserably. Meader tried to get solo bookings and was finding himself typed as just a Kennedy mimic. Searching for a way out, he signed with Verve Records and put together an album of sketches on everything from the high cost of funerals to a satire of the Ku Klux Klan. He wanted to prove that he could be funny without using any Kennedy jokes. Recording was finished in early November 1963.

One day in late November, church bells suddenly began tolling in the afternoon and schoolchildren were dismissed early and told to go home. All the television channels were broadcasting the same numbing news: the youngest president ever elected, John F. Kennedy, had been gunned down in Dallas. That night Lenny Bruce took the stage. He paused and shook his head: "Poor Vaughn Meader!"

Bruce got laughs. Vaughn Meader didn't. Meader became an "unperson." The hot-selling comic had taped material for the December 4 "Grammy Awards" show. It was cut. Shelley Berman was called to take his place, but Berman refused, declaring that Meader was a fine stand-up with plenty of apolitical material. The Grammy committee booked Diahann Carroll instead. Meader's December 16 week as a guest on television's "To Tell the Truth" was canceled. "The Joey Bishop Show" canceled him. Nightclubs canceled him. And the album that he had hoped would brighten his future was ignored. The sight of a man who looked like Kennedy was too painful for a nation that had not experienced an assassination for many generations.

On January 4, 1964 The Blue Angel, the club that had given him his start years earlier, booked him for some shows. They supported him, but the audience didn't. Meader kept trying. Staging "The Populace" revue at Cafe Au Go Go in October 1964, he changed his hairstyle and even worked on a neutral New York accent. Critics praised him, but nobody was buying. The second album on his Verve contract went unnoticed, even though the humor was far sharper than *The First Family*. In one sketch he played a speaker nominating a candidate at a political convention: "A man who is in the tradition of Abraham Lincoln—he too is tall and ugly. I would like to nominate a man who is honest and courageous. I'd like to, but this party doesn't have one of them kind of people. My candidate does not know the meaning of the word compromise, does not know the meaning of the word appeasement, does not know the meaning of the word cowardice—and has done quite well despite his lousy vocabulary."

Meader faded into obscurity. Now and then someone wondered "whatever became of Vaughn Meader" and hunted him out. In the 1960s, his money gone, he drifted to the Bronx, then a commune in Los Angeles and a cabin in Maine. He was leading a drug-filled hippie lifestyle in the '70s when an old friend, comedy album producer Earle Doud, starred him as Jesus Christ on *The Second Coming*, an lp that tried to score a topical hit after the success of *Jesus Christ, Superstar*. It was not very funny and Meader, unable to do more than any other sitcom actor could with dull jokes, did not win further jobs from it. Occasionally his name and notoriety were exploited, as in 1974 when he turned up in the film *Linda Lovelace for President*, but mostly he found work outside the world of show business.

Periodically Meader was interviewed and he recited a list of his current projects, ranging from a serious play about John F. Kennedy to albums of country tunes. His last comedy appearance was a cameo on *The First Family Rides Again*, a Rich Little album about Ronald Reagan. Ironically *The First Family* has remained a very influential disc; its memorable fad success spawning presidential parody albums every four years. The best Meader could do was find some way of getting before the public every few years—to at least answer the perennial question: "Whatever became of Vaughn Meader?"

AUDIO: *The First Family* (Cadence, reissued by GNP), *The First Family Volume 2* (Cadence), *Have Some Nuts* (Verve), *If the Shoe Fits* (Verve), *Take That!* (Laurie), *The Second Coming* (Kama Sutra), *The First Family Rides Again* (Boardwalk)

## AUDREY MEADOWS

### (Audrey Cotter, February 8, 1924–   )

A singer in light comedies and an attractive if eccentric co-star on Bob and Ray's television show, nobody pictured the cheerful and charming Audrey Meadows as the frumpy, feisty Alice Kramden of "The Honeymooners." Jackie Gleason didn't even want to test her for the role. "Are you kidding?" he told her. "You're too good looking!"

Audrey washed off her makeup, donned a dowdy housedress and had photos taken of herself slaving in a messy kitchen. When Gleason saw the pictures, he knew he had found his Alice Kramden. On the screen, she added the other Alice trademarks: the stooping, round-shouldered posture, flat and nasal voice and the look of a perpetually put-upon woman with her patience running on empty.

Alice Kramden was sarcastic and sullen at times, but she was also forgiving, endearing and loving. She was not a nasty nag, slapstick woman-child or happy housewife—all predominant stereotypes in domestic 1950s sitcoms. Alice Kramden was unique; and so was Audrey Meadows.

Audrey grew up in Wuchang, China. A Communist uprising in 1927 forced her family to leave. They traveled the world before settling back in the US in 1929. She arrived knowing more Chinese than English. She recalled that she was a shy outsider, "too small for my age, and always underweight." A childhood accident—falling through a skylight—left her with a leg so scarred and damaged she had to wear white stockings. Her response to teasing from other kids was to show no emotion. She learned to control her reactions and keep to herself.

Following the lead of older sister Jayne, Audrey got into show business. Audrey Cotter became Audrey Meadows, which helped avoid any confusion with actress Audrey Totter. Trained in opera, she had a recital at Carnegie Hall at 16, sang in nightclubs and for the USO, and managed to get a role in the touring company of *High Button Shoes*. From there she replaced Rose Marie in the Broadway run of *Top Banana*.

On television she was known for her appearances on Bob and Ray's early show "Club Embassy." In one offbeat sketch she sang opera while standing on her head. Though they were both popular in show business by this time, Audrey and her sister Jayne rarely worked together. A few recordings ("Hot Potato Mambo" and "Dear Ralph") are about all that remain of the Meadows Sisters as a duo. They were too busy working with male partners. Jayne teamed with husband Steve Allen and Audrey became Alice Kramden to Jackie Gleason's Ralph.

Just as Ralph exasperated Alice, Gleason sometimes exasperated Audrey. Gleason was notorious for favoring ad libs over rehearsing. One time Audrey put on her toughest nasal voice and scolded him before filming began: "I'm going out there with you—but I'm not going to say anything. If you don't need rehearsing, then you're good enough to do without my lines too!" She relented only slightly during the episode, making up a few lines and throwing Gleason off balance several times. Afterward, like his character Ralph Kramden, Jackie was contrite. The following evening he threw a party for his gutsy co-star.

"The Honeymooners" went along smoothly after that, with most shows built around long-suffering Alice playing both wife and mother to big shot/little boy Ralph. Most shows offered at least one verbal skirmish between "the king of the castle" and his wife. Ralph: "Before I let you go to work, I'd rather see you starve. We'll just have to live on our savings." Alice: "That'll carry us through the night, but what will we do in the morning?"

Audrey appeared in several films, worked with Sid Caesar on *It's a Living* and co-starred on the sitcoms "Too Close for Comfort" and "Uncle Buck." Still, fans remember her best for her Emmy-winning performances as Ralph's wife, Alice. The role of Alice Kramden was not glamorous. To some actresses, it seemed like a thankless job not worth taking. Audrey took it—and "Honeymooners" fans have been thanking her for it ever since.

BROADWAY: *Top Banana* (1952)
FILMS incl.: *That Touch of Mink* (1962), *Take Her, She's Mine* (1963), *Rosie!* (1968)
TV: "Bob and Ray" (1951–52), "Club Embassy" (1953), "The Jackie Gleason Show" (1952–55), "What's in a Word?" (1954), "What's Going On?" (1954), "The Name's the Same" (1955), "The Honeymooners" (1955–56), "The Jackie Gleason Show" (1956–57), "Keep Talking" (1958–59), "Masquerade Party" (1958–60), "Too Close for Comfort" (1982–83), "Uncle Buck" (1990)

## JAYNE MEADOWS

**(Jane Cotter, September 27, 1923–   )**

Able to parody glamorous stars—while retaining her own star glamour—Jayne Meadows began her career as a beauty in 1940s films before establishing herself in comedy, often as a guest on husband Steve Allen's talk and variety shows.

Born in Wuchang, China, her father an Episcopalian minister and missionary, Jayne and sister Audrey spoke Chinese more often than English until the family finally returned to the United States when she was seven. Her father changed parishes a few times in New England before settling in Sharon, Connecticut, where Jayne attended St. Margaret's School. Billed as Jayne Cotter, she enchanted Broadway audiences in a pair of comedies *Another Love Story* and *Kiss Them for Me* before moving to Hollywood. Producer Hal Wallis raved she "has the power of a young Bette Davis." Unfortunately the actress, married back then to a screenwriter named Milton Krims, recalled being "very shy and frightened and turned down many fine roles in those days. . . . I was very neurotic. Today I am totally free of fear and cannot believe that that girl was me."

Jayne flourished on television beginning with her long stint as a panelist on "I've Got a Secret" in 1952, the year she met Steve Allen. By then therapy had made Jayne the assured one, especially by comparison. "When I was first dating Steve, he'd walk into a room so nervous, so insecure, that he'd talk to no one but me. On the stage, he's the master, the one in control . . . a comedian, in my opinion, is someone denying emotions. It's 'Don't get close to me because I might get too vulnerable.' " They dated for two years before marrying on July 31, 1954.

Jayne continued to appear on stage, including a farce called *The Gazebo* in 1958. With Steve's praise as "the best straight woman in the business," she worked more and more with him on television sketches and in his "Meeting of Minds" television specials, playing everyone from Cleopatra to Marie Antoinette. She also played royalty in Steve's musical version of *Alice in Wonderland*. Though she can comfortably and humorously play royalty, Jayne is never her airy, preening image. On many important, down-to-earth topics, she's been ahead of her time. She said back in 1971, "I don't see how you can wear a fur coat without feeling, literally, like a murderer. . . . I feel very sad for women who continue to purchase real fur coats. They are lacking a woman's most important requisites, heart and sensitivity."

BROADWAY: *Spring Again* (1941), *Another Love Story* (1943), *Many Happy Returns* (1945), *Kiss Them for Me* (1945), *The Gazebo* (1958)

FILMS incl.: *Kiss Them for Me* (1945), *Undercurrent* (1946), *Lady in the Lake* (1946), *Dark Delusion* (1947), *Song of the Thin Man* (1947), *The Luck of the Irish* (1948), *Enchantment* (1948), *The Fat Man* (1951), *David and Bathsheba* (1951), *It Happened to Jane* (1959), *College Confidential* (1960), *Now You See It Now You Don't* (1968), *Alice in Wonderland* (1985)

## ANNE MEARA (See STILLER and MEARA.)

## BETTE MIDLER

### (December 1, 1945–    )

From flamboyant chanteuse in an obscure gay club to heroine starring in hit Disney comedies, Bette Midler had a long and bumpy ride. Born in Hawaii, Midler's family was originally from Paterson, New Jersey. Her father was a house painter. Her mother named her after Bette Davis, unaware that the actress didn't favor a silent 'e' for her first name.

The chubby Jewish girl was quite different from the rest of the girls in the poor Hawaii neighborhood. To get attention she was the class clown. Midler dropped out of the University of Hawaii, where she had studied drama, and ended up working in a pineapple factory. She flirted with a singing career, got a bit part in 1965's *Hawaii* and moved to Hollywood when filming resumed there. "People who are damaged, they go into this business. People who are healthy don't go into show business. It's the nut jobs that go into show business, the ones who need that applause and need to be told they're okay."

Bette moved to New York where she sold gloves at Stern's, go-go danced in New Jersey and became an understudy in *Fiddler on the Roof*, later taking over the role of Tzeitel for three years. In 1971 at The Continental Baths, a combination health club/nightclub for gays at the Ansonia Hotel on New York's West Side, Bette cavorted before towel-clad men singing campy nostalgia numbers and show tunes, mixing the music with self-parody jokes about her enormous breasts. As peculiar-looking as Barbara Streisand, as charismatic as Judy Garland and utilizing an energetic and arch delivery that suggested Margaret Hamilton imitating Tallulah Bankhead, she was quickly adopted as a new favorite among the gays and the trendy. Calling herself "the last of the truly tacky women," she created her own myth, labeling herself "The Divine Miss M."

Midler managed to cross over to the general public with some hit records (earning a Grammy in 1973) and a Broadway show that won a special Tony in 1974 (Divine Madness). She was firmly in front of the big nostalgia boom with "The Boogie Woogie Bugle Boy of Company B," her version of a big band hit from Abbott and Costello's *Buck Privates*. She reached a peak with her brand of trash and vaudeville when she played The Paladium in London in 1978. In response to a sign "We Love Your Tits," she flashed on stage.

Despite her antic image, that year she shocked critics into taking her seriously by earning an Oscar nomination for her gut-wrenching portrayal of a tragic Janis Joplin–style singer in *The Rose*. Some of the insecurity and fragility she showed as that character still remained in real life. She bore the scars of family trauma. Her sister, Susan, was hit by a car in 1968, her brother Daniel needed special care due to mental retardation, and her mother died of cancer in the 1970s. Her father was not supportive: "Daddy was a yeller, the original curmudgeon—negative and undermining . . . I was constantly fighting for some self-esteem and even after I became famous, he'd say, 'Yeah, well, it will be gone tomorrow.'"

Midler resumed her campy ways with more film and stage appearances promoting her cheeky brand of "Divine Madness," but when trends changed she didn't. The film *Jinxed* was exactly that, and she went through a nervous breakdown and several years of inactivity. She married Martin Von Haselberg in 1984 and in 1986 they had a daughter, Sophie. She released a comedy album that year loaded with catty swipes at celebrities and the somewhat self-depreciating big-breast jokes: "Got myself a little mail scale, the kind they weight postage and cocaine on. Unhooked my bra, flopped one of those suckers down . . . I won't tell ya how much they weigh, but it costs $87.50 to send 'em to Brazil . . . third class!" It seemed that the talented Midler was going to languish as a cult attraction.

*Down and Out in Beverly Hills* was a surprise hit for her, a comeback film that made her a viable box office name once gain. Her breezy brand of outrageousness won over fans in subsequent hits *Ruthless People* and *Outrageous Fortune,* and after reestablishing her stardom in comedy, she once again dabbled with pathos in the film *Beaches.* She even won another Grammy for the theme song from that film, "Wind Beneath My Wings," and resumed her straight pop music career with a new album in 1990.

Now that she has won movie stardom, she seems less inclined to return to her stage act of camp and stand-up comedy. "Now everybody is vulgar. How dare Madonna *wear* a corset in public. I'm totally offended. I did worse. I did better—and worse. I was brilliant. . . ."

AUDIO incl.: *Bette Midler* (Atlantic), *Songs for the New Depression* (Atlantic), *Mud Will be Flung Tonight* (Warner Bros.)

BIOGRAPHY: *The Divine Bette Midler* (Spada, 1984)

BOOKS: *A View from a Broad* (1980), *The Saga of Baby Divine* (1983)

BROADWAY incl.: *Fiddler on the Roof* (1966–69), *Salvation* (1970), *Bette! Divine Madness* (1973), *Clams on the Half Shell* (1975)

FILMS incl.: *The Rose* (1978), *Divine Madness* (1980), *Jinxed* (1982), *Down and Out in Beverly Hills* (1986), *Ruthless People* (1986), *Outrageous Fortune* (1987), *Big Business* (1988), *Beaches* (1988), *Stella* (1990), *Scenes from a Mall* (1990), *For the Boys* (1991)

VIDEOS: *Mondo Beyondo; Art or Bust; The Bette Midler Show*

## MILLER and LYLES

**Flournoy E. Miller, April 14, 1887–June 16, 1971**
**Aubrey Lyles, 1884–July 28, 1932**

"Miller and Lyles are funny," said the *New York Times* review of *Running Wild* in 1923, "deeply funny, and possessed of a fine unction." The reviewer was also happy that the black duo avoided stereotypical comedy: "There is, to be sure, the traditional superstition scene, but there is not so much as a line about shooting craps."

Over at the *New York Post,* the reaction was completely different: "The comedy is almost too stale to be very amusing." The reviewer missed the comfortable stereotypical comedy, unable to accept the idea of a "strikingly sophisticated" show. "The least negroid of any of the mulatto comedies," it featured "an octoroon singing a Tin Pan Alley 'Mammy' song as an italian prima donna would sing it." This was "almost too much."

Miller was born in Tennessee and first met Lyles when they were both students at Fisk University in Nashville. With the more experienced Miller doing most of the writing, the duo developed comedy routines that, after years in vaudeville, led them to England for the "Charlot Revue" in 1915 and to Broadway in the '20s. They hoped to get their own radio show. They complained that they were turned down by WGN in Chicago when the station discovered they weren't minstrels but were really black. At the time, it was common for black performers to wear blackface makeup as did whites when portraying people of color. According to Miller's recollections, it was after his team was rejected that WGN brought in "Amos and Andy." He said the team stole two Miller and Lyles catch phrases: "I'se regusted" and "It all depends on the sitch-ation yo' is in."

While there's no firm evidence to determine who first used those catch phrases, there's no question that the team of Miller and Lyles did originate a classic comedy routine that has since been adapted and readapted by many vaudeville and burlesque performers. In "The Interruption Routine," the comedy comes from the comic anticipating what his partner is about to say.

"What's wrong with your car is—" "It ain't that. But you think maybe—" "Oh, I know it couldn't be that. What you need is—" "I just got one of them last week—" "No, I mean the one that costs about—" "Is you crazy? I can't afford that much!"

Despite their problems with others who either borrowed comic concepts or stole jokes outright, and despite the confusions over ethnic comedy that led some critics to praise them for their mainstream humor and others to complain that they weren't "black" enough, the team continued to appear on

Broadway and other prestigious venues. Their problems may have contributed to Aubrey Lyles' gastric ulcers, among his other health problems. After the team appeared in *Sugar Hill* in 1931, Lyles checked into Dr. Wiley Wilson's Sanitarium on 200 West 138th Street, where he died of tuberculosis.

Flournoy Miller continued to perform in the 1940s, teaming with Mantan Moreland for several films, including *Harlem on the Prairie* (1938), *Lady Luck* (1940), *Mantan Runs for Mayor* (1946) and *She's Too Mean to Me* (1948). Moreland inherited the famous "Interruption Routine" and used it with subsequent partners, including Nipsey Russell and Livingood Pratt.

BROADWAY: *Shuffle Along* (1921), *Running Wild* (1923), *George White's Scandals* (1925), *The Great Temptations* (1926), *Rang Tang* (1927), *Great Day!* (1929), *Sugar Hill* (1931)

# DENNIS MILLER

## (November 3, 1953–   )

Utilizing a sneering nasal voice and piercing pebble eyes, Dennis Miller's brand of mocking hipness won him some success in stand-up and greater fame for his "Weekend Update" news segments on television's "Saturday Night Live." He replaced Chevy Chase's '70s coyness with what he called "low-key, nonthreatening cynicism," a sulking and prickly brand of hostility.

At his best, Miller's grousing and sarcasm melts pretension like acid through butter. On born-again Christians: "I'm a little indignant when they tell me I'm going to hell if I haven't been born again. Pardon me for getting it right the first time." On drunk drivers: "There are two groups of people in the world now. Those that get pathetically drunk in public—and the rest of us poor bastards who are expected to drive these pinheads home." On female gymnasts: "The women's uneven parallel bar event. I think I'm gonna be a little skeptical the next time a woman tells me I'm being too rough in bed. I'm watchin' these girls bang their cervix off a frozen theater rope at 80 miles per hour. You don't see men in that event, okay . . ."

Born in Pittsburgh, Miller graduated from Point Park College with a journalism degree. He hosted "Punchline," a magazine show for teens in Pittsburgh, and performed comic essays on "PM Magazine." After stand-up work in Pittsburgh in the late 1970s, he went to New York in 1980, moved out to Los Angeles in 1983 and then won a spot on "Saturday Night Live" for the 1985–86 season: "What can I say? 'Weekend Update' was a job I'd always wanted . . . and now I do it. I don't want to sound saccharine, because I hate people who do that, but then, how many people get to have the exact job they always wanted? I used to watch Chevy do it years ago and I thought, 'Wow, I'd be good at that. My strengths are an ability to be pretty unflappable, to deliver reams of material at a fairly fast rate and to be able to think myself out of a box canyon quickly and not look ruffled doing it.'"

Miller wasn't ruffled by critics who sometimes found a shallowness to his political humor and his brand of iconoclasm for its own sake. In October 1989, for example, President Bush signed a pro-environment bill protecting the spotted owls in a national forest. Miller found something negative: "After a year in office it's nice to see George is confronting the hard issues head on, huh?"

Like any iconoclast, Miller seems to resent being liked and enjoys his reputation for being as difficult on screen as off. His catch phrase to end his "Weekend Update" segments was one of studied disconcern and lofty disdain. Whether audiences laughed or hissed, he didn't care. In the end, he could simply take the money and take a walk. Exit line: "I am outta here!" He was "outta" the show at the end of the 1991 season, opting for stand-up work, television concert specials and a syndicated talk show.

AUDIO: *The Off-White Album* (Warner Bros.)
TV: "Saturday Night Live" (1985–91), "The Dennis Miller Show" (1992–   )
VIDEO: *Dennis Miller Live*

# SPIKE MILLIGAN (See also THE GOONS.)

## (Terence Alan Milligan, April 16, 1918–   )

Red Skelton once said, "A clown is a warrior who fights gloom." For Spike Milligan's fans, no one could be more of a heroic warrior, sometimes shining with mad bravado, sometimes showing the pathos of the walking wounded. His poetry flirted between whimsically silly and painfully sensitive. His stand-up was always serio-comically tinged with the personality of a desperate-to-please vaudevillian, the kind who calls out "folks . . . we can still be friends, folks!" as he offers up funny faces, snatches of song and anything and everything to keep them happy. His film appearances, from *Postman Knocks* to *Bed-Sitting Room* to *The Great McGonagall*, have moments of high hilarity, but in many scenes the mask of comedy cracks to show Spike's quiet introspection, sadness, doubt and—worst of all—anguish—the kind of existential anguish that led to his nervous breakdowns.

Born in India (the family went back to England when he was seven), Spike played trumpet in a big band in the 1930s. During World War II army service (the subject of a multivolume series of memoirs), Milligan emerged with a music and comedy act. A typical low point was an evening in front of a rowdy crowd that ended with Spike saying "You hate me, don't you?" The crowd roared *"Yes!"* Spike stomped his trumpet flat, leaving the stage to suffer severe depression.

Milligan created his own world when he scripted and costarred on radio's legendary "Goon Show." In 1987 he recalled the experience "broke up my marriage and put me in mental hospitals five times." What he put on the airwaves was comic genius, battles in which ridiculous good battled even more ridiculous evil in a land of real and imagined conflicts. The show, sometimes called an audio version of The Marx Brothers, became a strong influence on a generation of comedians such as the Monty Python troupe, and Milligan in particular became a cult hero as he went on to star in British plays and musicals, appear on British television and perform solo comedy on stage. He began his prolific career as an author, writing books of poetry and prose, some hastily dashed off and slipshod, others crackling with brilliance. From his Goon show in the 1950s through his 1960s books and the novel *Puckoon* and including his television work in the '70s and '80s, Milligan emerged as the modern giant of British comedy, truly beloved and deservedly legendary.

Throughout his career Milligan has always taken chances, no matter how painful. He once admitted, "I've always had to fight through the Benny Hills in the wilderness. They are like the main bunch of the army, they know the obvious and what they think the audience wants—bums, knickers, tits, funny double-entendre jokes, things like that. But in the long term, to live on a diet of that becomes boring, so what I try to do is to do what the patrols do, I try to go out into enemy territory where nothing has happened before, and of course, you get shot at like mad out there, but I would rather be up there, trying to make or to do something different than what is here already."

A good portion of Milligan's later work included literate nonsense poems and stories for kids. He once said, "Adults don't understand me. I always loved escaping into the kids' world." General audiences in America rarely saw him on television except for a wonderfully madcap appearance on "The Muppet Show" in which the white-haired star threw himself about with all the merry abandon of one of the sponge muppets, using his mobile face to act out a news and weather report.

On stage Milligan—tall, wild-eyed, usually sporting a homeless man's thin white beard—is very much the ragged old vaudevillian, mixing declarative odes with monologues. A typical little poem: "There are holes in the sky where the rain gets in—but they're ever so small. That's why rain is thin!" One of his ecology-minded recitations: "They chop down 100-foot trees to make chairs. I bought one. I am six foot one inch. When I sit in the chair, I'm four foot two. Did they really chop down a 100-foot tree to make me look shorter?"

His eccentric tales, usually acted out with a great variety of accents and manic enthusiasm, include one about a great man: "My uncle was a great man. He told me so himself. He said 'I am a great man!' And who was I to argue. . . . He walked with a pronounced limp. L-I-M-P, pronounced 'limp.' . . . He was plagued with a completely bald head. When he folded his arms he looked like the pirate flag. He met a Hindu holy man who said, 'For ten rupees, I can cure the gentleman's head of the dreaded baldness.' The treatment involved the great man sitting naked in a darkened room, with a mixture of cow dung and treacle spread on his head. It didn't work. My uncle hit the holy man. And then he ripped off his loincloth. Alas, the poor Hindu died of overexposure. My uncle took to wearing a northern wig. One day a hawk swooped down and removed it. In a hairless frenzy, Uncle swore, threw rocks, his boots, his dentures and part of his truss. Alas, the hawk flew beyond his reach. Carrying a ladder, and wearing a handkerchief over his clawed head, he searched every bird's nest for 50 miles around. To no avail. Years later, a Burmese naturalist reported a strange find. A hawk's nest made from a northern wig. Even stranger—it wasn't my uncle's."

AUDIO incl.: *Milligan Preserved* (Parlophone), *The Bridge on the River Wye* (Parlophone), *How to Win an Election* (Philips), *Best of Milligan's Wake* (Pye), *Muses with Milligan* (Decca), *World of the Beachcomber* (Pye), *A Record Load of Rubbish* (BBC), *He's Innocent of Watergate* (Decca), *Treasure Island* (Starline), *Badjelly the Witch* (Polydor), *Live at Cambridge University with Jeremy Taylor* (Spark), *Songs from Q 8 with Ed Welch* (UA), *Adolf Hitler My Part in His Downfall* (Columbia), *Puckoon* (EMI), *Unspun Socks from Chicken's Laundry* (Ridedrop)

AUTOBIOGRAPHIES incl.: *Adolf Hitler, My Part in His Downfall* (1971), *Rommel? Gunner Who?* (1974), *Monty: His Part in My Victory* (1976), *Mussolini, His Part in My Downfall* (1978), *Where Have All the Bullets Gone?* (1985), *The Spike Milligan Letters* (1977), *The Spike Milligan Letters Vol. 2* (1984)

BIOGRAPHY: *Spike Milligan* (Scudamore, 1985)

BOOKS incl.: *A Dustbin of Milligan* (1961), *The Little Pot Boiler* (1963), *A Book of Bits* (1965), *The Bedside Milligan* (1965), *Milligan's Ark* (1971), *Goon Show Scripts* (1972), *Book of the Goons* (1971), *The Great McGonagall* (1975), *The Milligan Book of Records* (1975), *Goblins* (1978), *The Q Annual, 101 Best and Only Limericks* (1982), *There's a Lot of It About* (1983), *Goon Show Cartoons* (1982), *The Melting Pot* (1983), *Puckoon* (1976), *The Bedsitting Room* (1970), *Small Dreams of a Scorpion* (1972)

FILMS incl.: *Let's Go Crazy* (1951), *London Entertains* (1951), *Down Among the Z Men* (1952), *Super Secret Service* (1953), *The Case of the Mukkinese Battlehorn* (1956), *Watch Your Stern* (1960), *Suspect* (1960), *Invasion Quartet* (1961), *Postman's Knock* (1962), *The Bed Sitting Room* (1969), *The Magic Christian*

(1970), *Rentadick* (1972), *Alice's Adventures in Wonderland* (1972), *Adolf Hitler, My Part in His Downfall* (1973), *The Three Musketeers* (1974), *The Great McGonagall* (1974), *Man About the House* (1974), *Monty Python and the Holy Grail* (1974), *The Last Remake of Beau Geste* (1977), *The Hound of the Baskervilles* (1978), *The Life of Brian* (1979)

TV incl.: "The Frankie Howerd Show" (1953), "A Show Called Fred" (1956), "Milligan at Large" (1963), "Milligan's Wake" (1963), "Muses with Milligan" (1965), "The World of the Beachcomber" (1969), "Q5" (1969), "Q6" (1976), "Marty Feldman's Comedy Machine" (1972), "Q7" (1977), "Q8" (1978), "Q9" (1980), "There's a Lot of It About" (1982)

## MONTGOMERY and STONE

### David Craig Montgomery, March 20, 1870–April 20, 1917
### Fred A. Stone, August 19, 1873–March 6, 1959

One of the first popular comedy duos at the turn of the century, Montgomery and Stone sometimes worked in blackface, but had their best success when they left off the burnt cork. They won raves for playing The Tin Man and The Scarecrow in their own *Wizard of Oz* production (1902) and later stared in *The Red Mill* (1903) and George Ade's *The Old Town* (1910). President Taft made a point of catching them in that show when it toured in 1912.

David Montgomery, from St. Joseph, Missouri, worked for the Burlington Railroad before becoming a blackface dialect comic and singer. Long-legged, lanky Fred Stone, born in Denver, Colorado, had worked as a circus clown, high-wire star and trick rider. The duo teamed in Galveston, Texas in February 1895.

Their stage productions always featured specialty show-stoppers. Stone performed his lariat dance and high-wire scenes and was noted for his physical comedy. Montgomery tended to draw praise mostly for his dialect monologues, notably as a Japanese ambassador in *The Old Town*. The team toured the country frequently and occasionally made records, including "Moriah" and "Travel Travel Little Star" in 1911.

Most reviewers felt Fred Stone was the funnier of the duo. Typical was the March 2, 1908 notice in the *St. Louis Star* for *The Red Mill:* "Stone . . . simply convulses the audience . . . he doesn't seem to have such a thing as a backbone, and his contortions, together with his dancing and funny voice, form a combination that spell one word. That is *scream.* . . . Montgomery is also excellent, but he serves more as a foil for Stone's fun." Sometimes Stone drew praise for dong nothing. In *The Wizard of Oz,* he amazed audiences by staying motionless on a fence pole for half an hour until he "came to life" for his first comedy scenes.

Montgomery wrote some of their material and noted in 1907, "The best scenes are accidental. I was sitting in my dressing room . . . when I noticed a cockroach crawling along the wainscoting. All at once it occurred to me that it would be a good idea to put that cockroach in the Englishman's soup when it came time to serve him in the first act of *The Red Mill.* A few weeks later I got the idea that it would be a good scheme to crush the cockroach under my foot after removing him from the soup, and now that faithful insect is a nightly martyr to the cause of merriment."

Stone had his own off-stage merriment. In April of that year, he paid an $8 fine for throwing "half a bushel of potatoes, a few beets, some spinach, and a head of cabbage" at some small boys who were in front of his house at 352 West 46th Street, honking the horn of his parked car. Stone evidently did not direct his slapstick anger at Montgomery. "Dave and I have been together 23 years," Stone said, "we have shared the same dressing room. We have been together morning, noon and night for all the playing months of the years and in all that time we haven't had as many quarrels as the average man and wife have in a week." One reason for their harmony was their habit of taking separate vacations.

Dave Montgomery died in Chicago following an unsuccessful operation. According to an Associated Press story filed on April 21, Stone was at his bedside. "Fred," the story quoted the dying man as saying, "you've sacrificed enough for me in recent years. I know that you've been the whole show for a long time—that people went to see you and I've simply been paid as part owner of the old trade-

mark." Stone wouldn't allow these self-effacing words to pass for his partner's final obituary. He told reporters after it was over, "I've seen the gamest little fellow I know fight to a finish for life's biggest stake—life."

Stone went on to a very successful solo career that included films (*The Goat* and *Under the Top* in 1918) and more stage appearances (*Jack o' Lantern* in 1917 and *Tip Top* in 1920).

BROADWAY incl.: *The Wizard of Oz* (1903), *The Old Town* (1912), *Lady of the Slipper* (1912), *Chin Chin* (1916)

## MONTY PYTHON'S FLYING CIRCUS (See also JOHN CLEESE, ERIC IDLE and MICHAEL PALIN.)

**Graham Chapman, January 8, 1941–October 4, 1989**
**John Cleese, October 27, 1939–**
**Terry Gilliam, November 22, 1940–**
**Eric Idle, March 29, 1943–**
**Terry Jones, February 1, 1942–**
**Michael Palin, May 5, 1943–**

A dead parrot, a transvestite lumberjack, the Minister of Silly Walks, a soccer team composed entirely of wooden-legged Long John Silvers and a joke so funny it kills everyone who hears it; these, and many more bizarre and inspired creations, were all part of "Monty Python's Flying Circus," a silly, sinister, sly, sadistic and satiric sideshow in the form of a British television series. The name of the show became the collective name for its stars, usually referred to simply as "Monty Python" or "The Pythons."

Graham Chapman recalled, "Both we as a group and our concept had been loosely referred to as a 'circus' jokingly and otherwise . . . we felt 'python' appropriate because it's a snake which constricts, crushes and then consumes it's prey; 'flying' had a First World War sound to it; and 'Monty' would be the name for a terrifically bad theatrical agent." It all made slightly more sense than the original name for the show, "Owl Stretching Time."

Aside from American cartoonist Terry Gilliam, the troupe consisted of five British comedy writers

John Cleese presents an "ex-parrot" to store owner Michael Palin. Bizarre farce and biting satire have made Monty Python's Flying Circus a cult legend. Photo from the author's collection.

who had all worked together on David Frost's "The Frost Report" in 1965. They formed The Pythons after Cleese and Chapman finished a series called "At Last the 1948 Show" (where the Python catch phrase, "And now for something completely different," originated). The others had been working together on a children's show called "Do Not Adjust Your Set."

While Monty Python would prove to be unique and original, their influences were clear: the film world of The Marx Brothers; the radio world of The Goon Show; and the television anarchy and satire of Spike Milligan's "Q5." But there was method to the madness. Well-schooled comedy writers, the group knew how to construct traditional sketches and novelty tunes. As The Marx Brothers had done with such set pieces as "the stateroom scene" in *A Night at the Opera*, the trial scene in *Duck Soup* or "why a duck?" in *The Cocoanuts*, The Pythons took vaudeville concepts and twisted them for the 1970s:

two men screaming at each other at "The Argument Clinic"; a restaurant sketch with a suicidal waiter; an inane waitress barking out a menu loaded with Spam. As Milligan and The Goons had done, The Pythons created their own world of continuing characters (they could all play an amazing number of convincing different roles, including drag). The anarchy was loosely glued together with continuing fake BBC announcements and Terry Gilliam's imaginative cartoon collages. He was the only Python member whose best work was behind the scenes; he had far less air time than the others.

The show premiered in Britain at 11 P.M. on October 15, 1969. Before long it achieved cult status, and a few years later the series premiered on educational television stations in America. Fans watched over and over, able to recite verbatim such classics as John Cleese's complaint as the perturbed owner of a dead parrot. To the pet shop clerk: "It's expired. This is a late parrot! It's a stiff! Bereft of life it rests in peace! If you hadn't nailed it to the perch it would be pushing up daisies! This is an ex-parrot!" Fans made catch phrases out of most any fondly remembered line, from "Nobody expects the Spanish Inquisition!" to the bellow of "Dimsdale!" The troupe put out dozens of inventive episodes of the show, but eventually, as John Cleese recalled, "I felt we were just repeating ourselves." Six of the last episodes were done without him. Then it was time to look for a new challenge: full-length feature films.

They delighted fans right from the start with *Monty Python and The Holy Grail*. There was irresistible silliness (Michael Palin as the squeaky "Knight Who Says 'Ni'"). There were improbable lines that became cult catch phrases ("What? The curtains?"). And there were ghoulish moments of black humor (a feisty knight who ridiculously insists on battling even after his arms and legs are slashed off). There was satire ("retreat" for King Arthur is a cry of "Run away! run away!"). Subsequent movies offered more hilarity for fans and more "blasphemy" for the unamused. The religious satire *The Life of Brian* dismayed some Christians, but John Cleese pointed out, "The purpose of the film was to make fun of the way *some* people follow religious leaders." Added the cheeky Eric Idle, "There wasn't any 'Carry on Crucifying' so we broke new ground." The team broke new ground even on record. Their album *Monty Python's Matching Tie and Handkerchief* was "trick tracked." One side had two sets of grooves. Listeners putting the needle down could never be sure what they'd be hearing.

By this time, the various creative forces that made up Python were eager to shed that identity for more individual projects. With solo films and various book projects, there was a four-year gap between *The Life of Brian* and their next (and last) original feature film, the dark satire *The Meaning of Life*. Some sketches were as wild as ever (John Cleese as an instructor in a sex education class), but the highlight was another musical number, this one about Catholicism's contribution to the population explosion entitled "Every Sperm Is Sacred."

The Pythons separated after their hunt for *The Meaning of Life*. It had been a tough film to make. As Terry Gilliam noted, "Everybody had been going his own way. It was more difficult to get everybody to agree on things." The various members once more were caught up in other projects. As with The Beatles, incessant talk of reunions persisted, until one of the group died—Graham Chapman, who had been fighting cancer throughout 1989. That was also the year of their 20th anniversary. It marked two decades of exciting television, records and films—and the group's farewell. Twenty years was an enviably long run for any comedy group. They were now history, following The Marx Brothers and The Goons in having reinvented comedy technique and created a world that satirized the madness all around with uniquely mad humor.

AUDIO: *Monty Python's Flying Circus* (Pye), *Another Monty Python Record* (Charisma), *Monty Python's Previous Record* (Charisma), *The Worst of Monty Python* (reissue of the two Charisma albums by Kama Sutra), *Monty Python Matching Tie and Handkerchief* (Arista), *Monty Python Live at the Theatre Royal* (Charisma Import), *Monty Python and the Holy Grail* (Arista), *Monty Python Live at City Center* (Arista), *The Monty Python Contractual Obligation Album* (Arista), *Monty Python's Instant Record Collection* (Arista), *The Life of Brian* (Warner Bros.), *The Meaning of Life* (MCA), *The Final Rip-off* (Virgin)

BIOGRAPHIES: *From Fringe to Flying Circus* (Wilmut, 1985), *Monty Python's Complete and Utter Theory of the Grotesque* (Thompson, 1982), *Monty Python: The Case Against* (Hewison, 1981), *The Life of Python* (Perry, 1983), *The First 200 Years of Monty Python* (Johnson, 1989)

BOOKS: *Monty Python's Big Red Book* (1991), *The Brand New Monty Python Book* (also in softcover as *The Brand New Monty Python Paperbook*) (1973), *Monty Python and the Holy Grail* (1977), *Monty Python's Life of Brian Scrapbook* (1991), *Monty Python's The Meaning of Life* (1983), *Monty Python: Just the Words* (1989)

FILMS: *And Now for Something Completely Different* (1971), *Monty Python and the Holy Grail* (1975), *The Life of Brian* (1979), *Monty Python Live at the Hollywood Bowl* (1982), *The Meaning of Life* (1983)

VIDEO: *Monty Python's Flying Circus Vols. 1–17*

## DUDLEY MOORE (See also COOK and MOORE)

### (April 19, 1935–   )

Nicknamed "Cuddly Dudley" in the late 1970s, little Dudley Moore enjoyed a short period of unlikely superstardom in romantic comedies. Few fans of his big hits, *10* and *Arthur*, had any idea that he'd already been around for many years and that the comedy he had been most associated with was far more bold and biting.

Moore's early years were neither cute nor funny. He was a serious piano student who played in the local church. He was short and had a clubfoot, which caused him more emotional pain than physical discomfort. He recalled, "If I had been able to hit somebody in the nose, I wouldn't have been a comic." The little fellow fought back with jokes and developed a personality that relied on an almost desperate ebullience.

After attending Magdalen College, Oxford University on a music scholarship, he earned his B.A. in 1957. Subsequently, he performed in British jazz bands and created music and then comedy for satirical productions such as the fondly remembered *Beyond the Fringe*, which featured Peter Cook, Alan Bennett and Jonathan Miller. After two Broadway shows as a foursome, Cook and Moore became a team, and together they made a series of successful movies and records. Moore's first major solo film was *30 Is a Dangerous Age, Cynthia* about a pianist who intends to marry and write a musical before he turns what he considers the milestone age of 30. As it turned out, solo stardom was another decade away. Moore wrote the music for films (including *Staircase* in 1969) and starred in the 1969 British stage version of Woody Allen's *Play It Again Sam*. He reteamed with Peter Cook for more movies and a 1971 stage show gag-named *Behind the Fridge* which arrived on Broadway as *Good Evening* in 1972.

Dudley was the cuter half of the team, and on his own he had more appeal for American audiences than his partner. He developed a becoming vulnerability to go with his coy smiles and got his big American movie break playing an inept fetishist in *Foul Play*. In the film his ludicrously garish bachelor pad is loaded with automated gadgets and a wayward inflatable doll. His moments of slapdash slapstick were in the style of Blake Edwards, who cast him in *10* as second choice to George Segal. Once more playing a sympathetic role as a plucky if desperate fellow on the make for Bo Derek, the second-rate comedy was a surprise hit, due in part to the fad for "this year's model," Derek. The film popularized corn-row hairstyles, Ravel's "Bolero" for sex, the term "ten" for geeks to apply to beautiful women and, last but not least, Dudley Moore.

"Cuddly Dudley" went on to another big hit with *Arthur*, cementing his image as a lovable fellow despite all kinds of weaknesses. It was another surprise hit. Moore was nominated for an Academy Award, and magazines around the nation wrote of him as a new sex symbol, much in the same way that unlikely Woody Allen had been written up years earlier. The idea was no publicity concoction. After all, Moore had been married to Suzy Kendall (1966–68) and Tuesday Weld (1975–80) and was now shocking the press by dating another "this year's model," statuesque Susan Anton. Moore was big news in the tabloids and on interview shows.

Moore's charm and ebullience, so obviously an elaborate put-on (as it had been since childhood), couldn't stand up to such overexposure in the press and in films. Audiences had enjoyed his brand of cheeky insincerity and deliberate lightheartedness but now seemed ready for something else. It didn't help that Moore ran into some bad luck with poor choices in both dramatic films and comedies. Moore had fewer films in the late 1980s but at least had diversion at home, thanks to his third marriage, to another statuesque beauty, Brogan Lane.

The five-foot-three, 140-pounder is no longer a box office superstar or hot sex symbol, but he remains a very capable comic actor who can make even ordinary movies worth watching. The mellowed Moore returned to his first love, music, in 1991. He and conductor Sir George Solti co-starred in a cable television series for Showtime called "Orchestra!" designed to teach audiences all the nuances of music in an amusing fashion. As far as Moore could see, the most the average person knew about classical music was that "Bolero" made good background music for sex. It did in his film *10*, when Sir George Solti's version suddenly became a big hit. "When my sales of 'Bolero' shot up, I didn't know why—and then I saw *10* and I understood." When Moore and Solti first met, Solti thanked him for those added sales. After doing "Orchestra!" the precociously versatile performer considered his options: "Acting, music—brain surgery!"

BOOK: *Dudley Moore's Musical Bumps* (1986)
FILMS incl.: *The Wrong Box* (1966), *Thirty Is a Dangerous Age, Cynthia* (1967), *Bedazzled* (1968), *The Bed-Sitting Room* (1969), *Foul Play* (1978), *10* (1979), *Wholly Moses* (1980), *Arthur* (1981), *Lovesick* (1983), *Romantic Comedy* (1983), *Best Defense* (1984), *Micki and Maude* (1984), *Unfaithfully Yours* (1984), *Like Father Like Son* (1987), *Arthur 2: On the Rocks* (1988), *Crazy People* (1990), *Blame It on the Bellboy* (1922)

## GARRY MOORE

**(Thomas Garrison Morfit, January 31, 1915–   )**

Though now known more for the talented stars he brought to his show than for his work on the show itself, crew-cutted Garry Moore was a popular comedian in the 1950s and '60s, able to perform well in sketches as well as sing specialty numbers.

Born in Baltimore, he originally wanted to become a writer, and co-wrote a play with F. Scott Fitzgerald (one that unfortunately was never published). He was a writer for a local Baltimore radio station when a comedian failed to show up for a scheduled show. Moore substituted and before long was a full-time performer and announcer.

Moore's personable one-to-one radio style kept viewers tuned in. He even went to them when he decided to change his name. He sponsored a contest to choose a new show business name, and a Pittsburgh woman won $100 for coming up with Garry Moore. After starring in a morning radio show, "Everything Goes" in 1942, the mild, amusing Moore was paired with excitable Jimmy Durante for a successful radio series (1943–47). "That's mah boy!" was Durante's catch phrase as he watched the likable young star. Moving up to his own show, Moore went to television in 1951 with a very successful afternoon program and began hosting the quiz show "I've Got a Secret."

When he began to host and perform on his own television variety shows, he assembled a supporting cast that included the affable announcer Durward Kirby and promising newcomer Carol Burnett. Moore retired in the 1970s and rarely gave interviews. He was still fondly remembered for his literate, dry style exemplified by this routine he did on going to sleep:

"How many of you had trouble getting to sleep last night? I did. . . . Oh, I dozed off for maybe eight or nine hours . . . but after that, I just lay there. . . . There are . . . psychological methods of inducing sleep. You can bring on drowsiness simply by listening to a monotonous, repetitious noise . . . just pick up the phone and call your mother-in-law. . . . A doctor from the University of Chicago has some advice. . . . He says: 'Note carefully the exact position you were lying in this morning when you woke up. Then tonight, when you're ready to go to sleep, get in that same position.' That's going to be pretty tough for our guitarist, Carl Kress. This morning when he woke up, he found himself curled up at the bottom of the stairs with a paper hat on his head."

AUDIO: *Jimmy Durante and Garry Moore* (Radio Memorabilia)
BIOGRAPHY: *The Garry Moore Show* (Sanford)
TV: "The Garry Moore Show" (1950–51, 1958–64, 1966–67), "I've Got a Secret" (1952–64)

## MARY TYLER MOORE

### (December 29, 1936–   )

A modern sitcom housewife in the 1960s, then the role model for independent single women the '70s, Mary Tyler Moore starred in two of the best television shows of all time. She did it with a deceptively small arsenal of comic devices. Like Bob Newhart, she was a "reaction" comedian. Fans trying to recall a specifically funny thing she did would have to point to her squeaky "Oh, Rob!" in reaction to problems on "The Dick Van Dyke Show" and the equally comic/pathetic "Oh, Mr. Grant!" on her own sitcom. She relied not on flashy wit, comebacks, pratfalls, or funny faces, but on gently exaggerated reactions to real-life problems. At a time of booming laughtracks, she felt it was okay just to raise a smile. Probably her most memorable sitcom moment was on the "Mary Tyler Moore Show" when, reacting to the peculiar solemnity of a clown's funeral, she can't stop herself from laughing. Unlike most other comedians who might overplay the laughing, Moore presented a sympathetically accurate picture of the kind of nervous giggles that might befall someone in real life.

Though Moore had some influences, and utilized a bit of the Dick Van Dyke stutter and at times Carol Burnett's weakly dazed smile, she created a bond with audiences by playing herself, which allowed viewers to share her comic vulnerability. As Laura Petrie on "The Dick Van Dyke Show," viewers could understand the timidity and reservations of a housewife trying to do more than take care of the house and the kid. And as Mary Richards on her first solo sitcom, Moore once again was perfectly cast as a woman trying to control her insecurities and her life as a single career woman. In both cases, viewers knew that she was in a similar situation, first as a real-life housewife and later as a true career woman guiding her own production company.

Born in Brooklyn, Mary was raised strictly in several Catholic schools. Her idol was Leslie Caron: "Caron had all those teeth, and I was so self-conscious about my big mouth. But there she was, adored for her big mouth, plus she was a brilliant dancer." After a somewhat embarrassing stint as "Happy Hotpoint," the dancing sprite who frolicked atop kitchen appliances in commercials on television's "Ozzie and Harriet Show," Mary worked as a dancer on variety programs. In 1957 she was hired for "Richard Diamond," a David Janssen detective series. But all viewers saw of the detective's assistant were her legs. The camera stayed on them whenever Mary spoke, "I spoke in a very low sexy voice," she recalls. "I don't do that anymore."

She left the show, spending time at home with her one-year-old son, Richard, taking guest spots when she could get them. She auditioned often, but it was frustrating. She nearly got the role of Danny Thomas' daughter on a sitcom, but Thomas insisted "Nobody could believe that a daughter like mine would have a nose like yours!" In 1961, when casting calls had failed to produce a suitable wife for Dick Van Dyke on a new sitcom, producer Danny Thomas was stymied. An aide said to Danny, "Can you think of more?" Thomas thought his assistant meant "Moore." So, he called Mary Tyler Moore.

Thrust into the spotlight, surrounded by such comedy pros as Dick Van Dyke, Morey Amsterdam, Rose Marie and Carl Reiner, Moore soon was holding her own, as in a stand-out moment of visual comedy in an episode in which she accidentally takes strong tranquilizers and goofs her way through a dinner party. Many episodes seemed designed to play off her charming brand of suburban angst. Plots included: Laura Petrie fretting when a painter uses his imagination and creates a nude portrait of her; Laura getting her toe caught in the bathtub faucet; Laura learning judo and bruising her husband's ego—and back—by flipping him to the floor.

After Van Dyke decided to quit the show and make films, Moore tried films as well. Both she and Van Dyke suffered through some failures that had them running back to television at the turn of the 1970s. She became Mary Richards, a slightly insecure but plucky career woman dealing with a modern "singles" lifestyle. In real life, Moore's first marriage had broken up and she was now married to studio executive Grant Tinker. In one memorable early show she handled a touchy subject for single women: how to explain being sexually active without sounding "easy." "I've been around," she says with self-assurance. Then, with a little embarrassment: "Well, not *around*. But nearby."

She had earned two Emmy awards for the Van Dyke show. She doubled that on her own. In fact,

"The Mary Tyler Moore Show" ended up earning 27 Emmy awards. An unprecedented three shows were spun from it—sitcoms "Rhoda" and "Phyllis," along with the acclaimed dramatic series "Lou Grant."

Unfortunately, Moore herself could not spin another success from the sitcom world. "I'm not an actress who can create a character," Moore once said. "I play me." If that was indeed the case, then her problems with series television in the late '70s and '80s came from the inability to find a sitcom character and situation that mirrored her private life, or mirrored it in a way that viewers could respond to. Her 1978 variety show was canned after three weeks, and another version blending music, songs and a sitcom plot about her hectic lifestyle was dropped after three months. Fans still loved her; she was comic royalty, a cross between Carol Burnett and Jacqueline Onassis, someone warm and lively but also dauntingly attractive and distant.

As the '80s began, Moore could not possibly find sitcom success playing herself. Her private life was riddled with trauma and tragedy. In 1980 her only son killed himself playing Russian roulette. Evidently troubled over his girlfriend, he called out "She loves me," "She loves me not" with every pull of the trigger. Also in 1980, doctors informed Mary that she had diabetes. One year later, her divorce from Grant Tinker became final.

It was not surprising given these circumstances that success in her professional career came from dramatic roles. She won an Academy Award nomination for *Ordinary People* and a special Tony for the Broadway production *Who's Life Is It, Anyway?* She starred in dramatic films about a dying child (*Six Weeks*), heart disease (*Heartsounds*) and breast cancer (*First You Cry*).

In 1983, Mary found marital happiness again, marrying a young cardiologist named Robert Levine. Moore hoped to once again find success with a sitcom, but she admitted, "Always with me is the ghost of Mary past." Her two hit sitcoms were still running and rerunning five days a week in syndication. Every time she tried a new one, critics and fans compared it to her previous work. A new problem was the faster pace of television in the 1980s. In the '60s "The Dick Van Dyke Show" was given a full year to find an audience and polish its characters, and was allowed a second season even after finishing almost last in the ratings. Now shows were discarded before the writers and stars could become comfortable with the characters and see what worked and what didn't.

Moore was also entering a difficult time in terms of age. She was no longer the young housewife or the young career woman, but not ready to become a "Golden Girl" either. She found better options in the film world, making television movies that experimented with everything from black comedy to a new look at the life of Mary Todd Lincoln.

Moore remains active in charity work for the Juvenile Diabetes Foundation. She insists she would not do another series "Unless the rules of the game change and somehow I am allowed to decide, with the network what the time period would be I wouldn't do it again—it's a complete waste of time."

BIOGRAPHIES: *Mary Tyler Moore* (Steffoff, 1986), *Love Is All Around* (Alley and Brown, 1989)

BROADWAY: *Breakfast at Tiffany's* (1966), *Who's Life Is It, Anyway?* (1980), *Sweet Sue* (1987)

FILMS incl.: *X-15* (1962), *Thoroughly Modern Millie* (1967), *Don't Just Stand There* (1968), *What's So Bad About Feeling Good?* (1968), *Change of Habit* (1969), *Ordinary People* (1980), *Six Weeks* (1982), *Finnegan Begin Again* (1985), *Just Between Friends* (1986), *Gore Vidal's Lincoln* (1988), *The Last Best Year* (1990), *The Merry Widow* (1991)

TV: "Richard Diamond, Private Detective" (1959), "The Dick Van Dyke Show" (1961–66), "The Mary Tyler Moore Show" (1970–77), "Mary" (1978), "The Mary Tyler Moore Hour" (1979), "Mary" (1985–86), "Annie McGuire" (1988)

## TIM MOORE (See also AMOS and ANDY.)

### (Harry R. Moore, December 9, 1887–December 13, 1958)

The real star of television's "Amos and Andy" didn't play Amos or Andy. Tim Moore played the rascal George "Kingfish" Stevens, one of the sitcom world's most hilarious connivers. It was "Kingfish" who took over the show with his schemes and chicanery. A loveable con man, he had a toothy smile of possible sincerity. When things went wrong, he put on a frowning pout of possible contrition. Though he could get chuckles when he used either facial expression, he ultimately was known for his catch phrase, a rumbling "Holy mackerel, Andy." For decades after, admiring comedians such as Johnny Carson sometimes used it for a quick laugh.

Moore was born in Rock Island, Illinois, a place "Amos and Andy" co-creator Charles Correll called home for a while. One of 13 children, Moore left school at 11 having, as he recalled, "excelled in nothing but recess." He joined a vaudeville act called Cora Miskel and Her Gold Dust Twins (as one of the twins) and later worked for Dr. Mick's Pruritia Medicine Show. In his teens he was a racehorse jockey but when he outgrew it, he tried boxing. He billed himself as Young Klondike. Back home in Rock Island, now 17, he met and married his first wife, Benzonia David.

Moore left the ring for full-time comedy. He was in a vaudeville revue *Rarin' to Go* and went on to Broadway shows in the 1940s. He also worked The Apollo and in one of his novelty acts played a Scotsman, complete with kilt. After touring as a duo with Vivian Harris and opening for jazz bands fronted by Charlie Barnett and Jimmy Lunceford, Moore retired in 1946 and went back home to 719 Fifth Avenue in Rock Island. Traced there by Charles Correll and oldtime black vaudeville star Fluornoy Miller, Moore was persuaded to move to television as "Kingfish."

To fans, Moore remained closely linked with his old sitcom, and when his name got into the papers, the name "Kingfish" always seemed to accompany him, as in June 1956 when the headline read: "The Kingfish Re-Marries." Moore's first wife had died some six months earlier; the new bride, Vivian J. Cravens, was 30 years younger than he. There was a somewhat comic period of adjustment for the couple. In January 1957 Mrs. Moore had him arrested, charging that he fired a shot during an argument over roast beef. Moore had come home only to discover that her son, daughter and son-in-law had polished off the last of the leftovers. "Where's the rest of that roast beef!" he was quoted as yelling. "I'm tired of this family mooching off me!"

Moore, fined $100, didn't deny the charge. In an interview with writer Joe Hyams he admitted that he was annoyed at his wife's relatives emptying both refrigerators in the house and was especially bothered by his big stepson: "My stepson had two years of college—he majored in loafing." In his version of the fracas, he assembled the relatives together to complain about the roast beef mooching: "Then Big Stoop started to get up so I pulled out 'Betsy' and threw one across his bow. He sat down right quick!"

All was relatively quite after that. Moore died a year later. His wife died in 1988. Though his death was not major news at the time, it reached Fats Waller's lyricist Andy Razaf, who wrote a short poem eulogizing him. The first stanza read: "He was a maker of laughter, a master of his art/ Who blessed the earth with joy and mirth/ Even with tears in his heart."

BROADWAY: *Lucky Sambo* (1925), *Blackbirds* (1928), *Blackberries* (1932), *Lew Leslie's Blackbirds of 1939* (1939), *Harlem Cavalcade* (1942)

TV: "Amos and Andy" (1951–53)

## MORAN and MACK

**Moran: George Searchy, October 3, 1881–August 1, 1949**
**Moran: John Swor: 1883–July 15, 1965**
**Mack: Charles Sellers, 1887–January 11, 1935**

One of the most successful blackface duos of their day, Kansas-born Moran and Mack were The Two Black Crows, making hit records of corny gags told in slow Negro dialect.

Charles Mack's original partner was John Swor, and the team was called Swor and Mack. After Swor left, George Moran came in and the team was officially Moran and Mack. They went to Broadway in 1917's *Over the Top* and were a hit in a number of shows. They still had their problems from time to time. In Syracuse, New York Mack was arrested for failing to pay his wife's alimony. The amount was too much for partner Moran, so Mack dashed off a telegram to W. C. Fields, who was working in *The Ziegfeld Follies* in New York. "Please send me $500," Mack wrote, "I'm in jail up here." Fields sent a telegram back: "If it's a good jail, I'll join you."

Via hit records in 1927, Mack and Moran's routines became famous all over the country. The comedy was mostly in characterization; the gags were quite feeble on paper. A typical vignette has Mack talking about his luck as a farmer: "We bought 1000 pigs at 75 cents apiece and fattened them up all summer." "What did you sell them for in the fall?" "Seventy-five cents apiece." "You sold them for the same price you bought 'em for? You can't make any money that way." "We found that out."

The duo's discs included 1927's "The Early Bird Catches the Worm" and "No Matter How Hungry a Horse Is, He Cannot Eat a Bit" and in 1928 "Two Black Crows in Jail" and "Two Black Crows in Hades." The team came to the movies in 1929 with *Why Bring That Up?* The title was also their catch phrase, uttered amid the slow-moving, slow-witted dialogue. The phrase was so popular in 1936 Dr. J. F. Montague used it when he wrote a book called *Why Bring That Up?* The doctor's book was about seasickness.

The team was making lots of money, but it all seemed to end up in Charlie Mack's pocket. As legal "owner" of the "Moran and Mack" name, and claiming to be the main writer, he dealt himself a higher salary. George Moran left in protest and was replaced by Mack's old partner, John Swor. Swor, who had recently been in a blackface act called Swor and Conroy (with Frank Conroy) was persuaded to perform under the "George Moran" name, and the new version of Moran and Mack made the film *Anybody's War* in 1930.

It turned out to be everybody's war. Mack and Swor began bickering, John Barton replaced Swor and eventually the original Moran returned. By then Amos and Andy were the top blackface combo and Moran and Mack became ancient history. Mack Sennett had plans for reviving the team, but on the way to New York Sennett, Moran and Mack were in a car accident; Charlie Mack was killed.

George Moran found limited work as a solo. W. C. Fields helped him out, hiring him to play the stoic Indian named Clarence in *My Little Chickadee* and bank robber Loudmouth McNasty in *The Bank Dick*.

While Amos and Andy remained popular for decades thanks to their warm personalities and realistic scripts, there was never much nostalgic interest in Moran and Mack, two reasonably good dialecticians reciting some fair, and some fairly terrible, gags.

MORAN: Do you believe in spirits, lazy boy?

MACK: I sure does. I went to de spiritualist's last night. He's de feller made my boss Mr. Horowitz change his name. . . . He conjured up a spirit for Mr. Horowitz, and right after that, Mr. Horowitz went by de name of plain Mr. Horror! You see, de ghost, he scared him out of his witz!

If Moran and Mack are forgotten, it is perhaps just as well. Charlie Mack seemed to think so. His choice for an epitaph: "Why bring that up?"

AUDIO: *Moran and Mack/Smith and Dale* (Timestu)

BROADWAY: *Over the Top* (1917), *The Ziegfeld Follies* (1920), *The Passing Show* (1921), *Greenwich Village Follies* (1924), *Greenwich Village Follies* (1926), *No Foolin'* (1926), *Earl Carroll's Vanities* (1926, 1927)

FILMS: *Two Flaming Youths* (1927), *Why Bring That Up?* (1929), *Anybody's War* (1931), *Hypnotized* (1932)

## POLLY MORAN

### (Pauline Therese Moran, June 28, 1883–January 25, 1952)

A silent film clown who favored raucous comedy, Polly Moran's "low" style was perfectly suited to her times. She was very popular in Mack Sennett comedies circa 1915 and made a comeback teamed with Marie Dressler in the early 1930s.

Born in Chicago, she quit school to join a touring company and starred in light opera and musical comedy. While playing vaudeville on the Orpheum circuit and in Europe, she developed her own "nut" solo act as an eccentric singer and comedienne. She joined Mack Sennett in 1915. There was nothing subtle about her rather plain features and toothy grin, or her man-chasing manners. And there was nothing subtle about the result, which usually was a blow to her dignity and a pratfall to the floor. The buxom comic would do anything for a laugh. She once blackened her eyes with makeup, insisting she hurt herself jumping rope without a bra.

Martha Raye and many others would take on Moran-style roles, but in her day Polly got big laughs as everything from messy housewives to garrulous "Sheriff Nell," comic terror of the old West. After slow years in the late 1920s she made a comeback with *The Callahans and the Murphys*, co-starring Marie Dressler. The two played a pair of battling, hard-

drinking Irish women, which drew protests from various Irish groups. They especially resented the classic scene in which the two ladies splashed beer down each other's shirts. Polly and Marie continued to make knock-'em-out comedies in the late '20s and early '30s with Moran—the antagonistic troublemaker of the two—usually the one to take the flop in the mud or the pie in the face.

After Dressler's death, Moran's comic parts became smaller and smaller. She drifted back to two-reelers in 1936. On July 15, 1936 newspapers headlined the story that she had her second husband, Martin Malone, arrested. He had tried to kill her, screaming in a drunken tirade that someone had called him "Mr. Polly Moran." She said that he fired a gun at her but it jammed. She wanted a divorce. A month later she changed her story: "He never threatened me with a gun. I thought it would be a good lesson to the boy if I told officers to take him away and lock him up. I thought it would teach him not to be playing with guns." The truth evidently lay somewhere in between. He was fined $100 by a judge and set free.

Polly had invested well from her silent film years. She had a nine-room mansion with two servants and a chauffeur. Still, she longed to make more films. Republic Studios hoped to duplicate the Dressler/Moran successes by teaming Polly with grouchy Englishwoman Alison Skipworth, but there was not much interest in their two films, *Two Wise Maids* and *Ladies in Distress*. She remained in semiretirement until 1949 when she began a mild "comeback" with a role in *Adam's Rib*.

FILMS incl.: *Ambrose's Little Hatchet* (1915), *Madcap Ambrose* (1916), *She Loved Him Plenty* (1918), *Skirts* (1921), *Bringing Up Father* (1928), *Hollywood Revue* (1929), *Caught Short* (1929), *Reducing* (1930), *Politics* (1931), *Prosperity* (1932), *The Passionate Plumber* (1932), *Alice in Wonderland* (1933), *Two Wise Maids* (1937), *Adam's Rib* (1949), *The Yellow Cab Man* (1950)

## RICK MORANIS

### (April 18, 1953–   )

A plucky species of nerd, five-foot-two Rick Moranis seems lost behind his glasses, his wide mouth opening and closing like a speechless puppet. He's won audience sympathy in a variety of supporting roles. He was the tiniest member in *Ghostbusters,* played an intergalatic and infinitesimal menace as "Dark Helmet" in Mel Brooks' *Spaceballs,* played the doofus who accidentally raises a man-eating plant in *Little Shop of Horrors* and starred as the perplexed father who had to cry *Honey, I shrunk the kids!*

Moranis originally worked as a disc jockey in his native Canada. "At 25," he said, "I started performing comedy on stage . . . I came down to L.A. from Toronto in 1977 and played The Comedy Store and The Improv. I did very well. But I didn't have my immigration card . . . so I went home."

Back home he wrote and appeared on Canadian television shows and ultimately joined "SCTV," displaying his versatility in many different parody roles. He and cast member Dave Thomas won some fame on their own as The McKenzie Brothers, the Cheech and Chong of beer humor. Their comedy was mostly in monosyllabic rankings of each other ("You're a knob!" "Hose head!" "Take off!") and the recognition comedy of two goofs acting like geeks (or vice versa). Thomas admitted the comedy "was operating on such a moronic, low level it really became insulting to the intelligence to keep it up." The one-joke concept ended after a few albums and a movie, *Strange Brew.*

For all the characters Moranis played in improv, it turned out that he was the best playing a simple goof character. In the film *Spaceballs,* he got laughs from a simple running gag—the plucky little villain's helmet clanking down on him every time he was ready to fight. "I'd put my visor down and [director Mel Brooks] would see my body quivering from laughter. The clock was ticking, the delay was costing money, and Mel would say 'Get it out of your system.' I asked him why he was so accommodating about our laughing, and he'd say [Carl] Reiner was a laugher too. . . . I would guess that working on 'Your Show of Shows' was exactly like 'SCTV.' I was laughing a lot on the set."

While he had little to do in the original *Ghostbusters,* Moranis had key scenes in the sequel and became a hot prospect for solo stardom with *Little Shop of Horrors* and *Honey, I Shrunk the Kids.* Almost everyone liked the latter, except "SPELL," the Society of the Preservation of English and Literature," which gave the film their 1989 Dunce Cap Award. They

pointed out that the film should have been called *Honey, I Shrank the Kids.*

Moranis got his own Saturday morning children's show and co-starred with Steve Martin in the disappointing *My Blue Heaven.* Bad reviews didn't seem to bother Moranis. What does annoy him is when critics insist he's just a one-note comic doing a nerd act. He urges them to take a closer look at his film roles: "All of the characters, if you get analytical, are very different."

AUDIO: *The Great White North* (Mercury), *Strange Brew* (Mercury), *You, Me, the Music and Me* (Canadian Import)

FILMS: *Strange Brew* (1983), *Ghostbusters* (1984), *Streets of Fire* (1984), *The Wild Life* (1984), *The Breakfast Club* (1985), *Little Shop of Horrors* (1986), *Club Paradise* (1986), *Spaceballs* (1987), *Ghostbusters II* (1989), *Parenthood* (1989), *Honey, I Shrunk the Kids* (1989), *My Blue Heaven* (1990), *Honey, I Blew Up the Kid* (1992)

TV: "Second City TV" (1980–81), "SCTV Network 90" (1981–82), "Rick Moranis" (1990)

## HARRY MORGAN

**(Harry Bratsburg, April 10, 1915–   )**

A sitcom favorite since his early role as Pete Porter on both television's "December Bride" and "Pete and Gladys," Harry Morgan had rarely played comedy as a radio performer. His uniquely flat-but-vibrant nasal voice seemed to type him for villainous roles, such as the spooky announcer for radio's "Mystery in the Air" program.

Morgan got into show business after taking public speaking courses during pre-law studies at the University of Chicago. During the depression, he supplemented a job selling office equipment with acting roles. After local work in Washington, D.C. he was invited to go to the Westchester Playhouse for summer stock in Mt. Kisco, New York. He played Duke Mantee in *The Petrified Forest* (Bogart's role in the film) and was picked for Broadway after co-starring with Frances Farmer in *At Mrs. Beam's.* He played "Pepper White" in *Golden Boy,* still billed as Harry Bratsburg. Times were tough and parts were not always easy to get. Morgan once accepted a part in a play promoting food stamps, written by New York

Mayor Fiorello LaGuardia; all he got out of it was dinner with the mayor and eight dollars.

He journeyed to California hoping for film work. Henry Fonda helped him land movie roles, including a part in the classic western *The Ox-Bow Incident.* Initially billed in films as "Henry Morgan," he had to change that name to avoid confusion with the radio comedian. As Harry Morgan he played villains, criminals and often very serious and steely army types. He was an army major to Ronald Reagan's captain in the Korean War drama *Prisoner of War* in 1954. That year he lent his dour nasal twang to the role of perpetual complainer Pete Porter on "December Bride." He was always grousing about his (unseen) wife Gladys: "When they wanted a siren for air raid alerts they asked Gladys if she'd stand on the City Hall roof and scream." Harry recalled in 1960, "Pete was popular, especially with men. I spoke to all men with latent hostility to wives and mothers-in-law. Guys used to stop in the street and congratulate me."

Morgan was thoroughly typed as the agitated man with the horrible wife. Once, when his real-life wife Eileen was suffering from a very red sunburn and had covered her face with suntan goop, Harry heard a passing couple murmur, "My God! He's not kidding, is he?"

Ultimately audiences wanted to see just how terrible Pete's wife really was. But when he and the attractive actress Cara Williams starred in the spin-off show "Pete and Gladys," the comedy was considerably toned down. Morgan's Pete became a more genial comic character. His next role was also amusingly light. He co-starred as Bill Gannon, partner to Joe Friday on "Dragnet." Though the show was basically dramatic, and Jack Webb insisted that Harry adopt the businesslike "Dragnet monotone," fans remember Morgan as comic relief, forever spouting inanities—recipes, cooking advice, reports on his wife's doings—to the slow burn of Sergeant Friday.

Morgan went on to achieve probably his greatest fame as Colonel Potter on "M*A*S*H." He won an Emmy for his role as the no-nonsense but folksy leader of the medics. As with his role on "Dragnet," he managed to find the elusive line between a comical personality and an authoritative one. Typical of this trait was a scene in which, observing that his jeep has been flattened by a tank, he puts it out of its misery by grimly firing a single bullet into it. Fans enjoyed the colorful expressions the oldtimer often used. Having to discipline a wayward soldier, he announced, "I'm gonna duck walk his carcass from now to Saint Swithin's Day!"

He said in 1989, "Of all the television series I did . . . the first one was my favorite . . . but I think probably Colonel Potter is closer to the real me, because I had a free rein to do whatever I wanted to do with that character."

Morgan enjoys the same western lifestyle as Colonel Potter, the same love of horses. Married over 40 years, father of four children, he raises quarter horses on a California ranch. One of the few actors to be spun off twice into starring sitcoms, he not only went from "December Bride" to "Pete and Gladys," but also from "M*A*S*H" to "After M*A*S*H." Then, Morgan starred in his tenth series, playing the cheerful rascal father to Hal Linden on "Blacke's Magic." He livened up the adventure series with his spirit, charisma and twinkling eyes. Viewers discovered once again something "M*A*S*H" co-star Loretta Swit noticed years earlier with great delight: "He's a leprechaun, a menehune, an imp—all those wonderful puckish figures that bring magic into your life."

BROADWAY: *Golden Boy* (1937), *The Virginian* (1937), *The Gentle People* (1939), *Thunder Rock* (1939), *Night Music* (1940), *Heavenly Express* (1940), *Cream in the Well* (1941), *The Night Before Christmas* (1941), *Hello Out There* (1941)

FILMS incl.: *The Loves of Edgar Allan Poe* (1942), *The Ox-Bow Incident* (1943), *A Bell for Adano* (1945), *It Shouldn't Happen to a Dog* (1946), *The Big Clock* (1948), *My Six Convicts* (1952), *High Noon* (1952), *What Price Glory* (1952), *Stop You're Killing Me* (1952), *The Glenn Miller Story* (1954), *The Bottom of the Bottle* (1956), *Teahouse of the August Moon* (1956), *It Started with a Kiss* (1959), *Inherit the Wind* (1960), *John Goldfarb, Please Come Home* (1964), *What Did You Do in the War Daddy?* (1966), *The Flim Flam Man* (1967), *Support Your Local Sheriff* (1969), *Viva Max* (1969), *Support Your Local Gunfighter* (1971), *The Barefoot Executive* (1971), *Sidekicks* (1974), *The Apple Dumpling Gang* (1975), *The Shootist* (1976), *Dragnet* (1987), *The Apple*

*Dumpling Gang Rides Again* (1979), *The Incident* (1990), *Against Her Will* (1991)

TV: "December Bride" (1954–58), "Pete and Gladys" (1960–61), "The Richard Boone Show" (1964), "Kentucky Jones" (1964–65), "Dragnet" (1967–70), "The D.A." (1971–72), "Heck Ramsey" (1972–74), "M*A*S*H" (1975–83), "After M*A*S*H" (1983–84), "Blacke's Magic" (1986)


## HENRY MORGAN

### (Henry Lerner Van Ost, March 31, 1915–   )

James Thurber said of him: "He wishes everybody were dead, but not in heaven with the angels." In other words, few radio personalities were as saltily downright caustic as the curley-haired, bullet-nosed Henry Morgan. He opened his shows with a curt "Good evening, anybody." His targets for satire: anybody.

Morgan was born in New York City, where he began his radio career as an announcer on WMCA in 1933. He drifted to WCAU in Philadelphia and got his first show over WEBC in Duluth called "Strictly Masculine." His comedy career really started when he finally returned home. "I began as a monologist on WOR in 1938 and was a sort of cult personage among a double handful of the literate. This lasted until some time in '43 when I joined the air corps, as it was known then, and did my best to save my country—or, at any rate, that part of it which consisted of greater metropolitan downtown Santa Ana, California. . . . I was in a radio unit and did programs designed, according to the dimwit colonel in charge, to keep up the morale of the American people. I was made a corporal. He was the husband of Rosalind Russell and known to his flock as 'The Lizard of Roz.'"

In 1945 he went to NBC with his own "Here's Morgan" program, a show notorious for Morgan's tampering with the commercials. "One sponsor was Adler's Elevator Shoes. Their slogan was 'Now you can be taller than she is.' One 'revised' commercial went 'These elevator shoes will make you almost two inches taller than she is. You, of course, will still be a klutz.'" The sponsor asked Morgan to be more positive, and so he was. He assured listeners, "You

*can* be two inches taller—if you're able to stand up in them." The client sold loafers in "seven awful colors. I recited the colors and then said that I wouldn't be caught dead in any of them. The client complained so the next night I apologized. I said, 'Last night I said I wouldn't be caught dead in those loafers. Old man Adler complained, so I'm sorry I said it. The truth is I would be caught dead in them."

The "Here's Morgan" show was a dim ancestor to "Late Night with David Letterman" and other similar programs. The host played strange music, lampooned his sponsors and dryly urged listeners to turn the dial and find something better. When his show was doing well enough for the network to insist on a full orchestra, a large cast and other improvements, Morgan was characteristically grouchy. He said on the air: "This program was written under the influence of, I am sorry to say, money." One of the show's highlights was "The Question Man," in which he'd give answers to viewer mail: "From Mr. J. D. of Jackson Heights. I am making a study of multiple birth statistics. Can you tell me how often triplets are born?" "Once."

Morgan also had a penchant for sneering lectures, tart monologues and punography. His routine on "The Invention of Time" reported on two brothers: "First they tried to measure time by burning candles. Frank started at one end, Dick at the other, and they invented the process of burning the candle at both ends. One day Frank and Dick accidentally sat on their candles. This was known as burning their ends at both candles. . . . They cut notches in a candle. When the flame reached the first notch, it was lunchtime. When it reached the second notch, dinnertime. And at the third notch, it was night and bedtime. They called this process 'Burnas Notches.'"

Morgan's film career never progressed beyond the neglected *So This Is New York,* produced by Stanley Kramer, which excellently captured his simmering brand of long-suffering sarcasm. As a midwesterner stuck in New York, he indulged in dry, low-key wisecracks, discovering that in the street "New Yorkers walk on tiptoe. Yours." He even had some dry sight gags, handling the constant tip demands from cap drivers and bellboys by eventually wearing a change-maker on his belt.

Like David Letterman in the 1980s, Morgan in early decades was branded an anarchist and a wise guy. The Life Savers company was upset when Morgan called the hole in their candy "unethical," and Schick Razors somehow didn't find the humor in Morgan's version of their slogan: "Push, pull, click click—ouch ouch."

Television viewers got a look at Morgan when, in 1953, he became an acerbic panelist on "I've Got a Secret." He was with the show for 15 years, in part thanks to producer Mark Goodson and host Garry Moore, who protested when CBS demanded he be removed due to both his wisecracks and the era's "Red Scare" blacklisting. He occasionally dabbled in theater (he played in *The Man Who Came to Dinner* in summer stock) and at one time wrote a satiric column for *Penthouse* magazine. Morgan always maintained some kind of local radio show in New York. He was on WOR radio for many years and moved to WNEW in 1983. In 1985 the station released him. The problem was a lack of sponsors. They couldn't find one daring enough to put up with Henry Morgan.

AUDIO: *The Henry Morgan Show* (Memorabilia), *The Best of Henry Morgan* (Command), *The Best of Morgan* (Judson, reissued as *Here's Morgan*) (Riverside), *The Saint and the Sinner* (Offbeat)
BOOK: *Dogs* (1976)
FILMS: *So This Is New York* (1939), *So This Is Hollywood* (1947)
TV: "On the Corner" (1948), "Henry Morgan's Great Talent Hunt" (1951), "Draw to Win" (1952), "I've Got a Secret" (1952–67), "That Was the Week That Was" (1964), "My World and Welcome to It" (1969–70), "I've Got a Secret" (1976)

## HOWARD MORRIS

### (September 4, 1919–    )

A little comic wild man, Howard Morris delighted television audiences as a regular on the legendary "Your Show of Shows." He may well be remembered best for one quintessential vignette from that series. In a parody of "This Is Your Life," Sid Caesar plays the surprised guest and little Howard one of his old friends. Overcome with emotion, the teary, bawling Morris embraces Caesar and won't let go, clamped to the tall man's leg like a shivering poodle.

Roles calling for strange little characters were Morris' specialty. After playing various emotionally strained roles with Sid Caesar, he played the berserk and dangerous little Ernest T. Bass on "The Andy Griffith Show" and later a histrionic professor opposite Mel Brooks in the film *High Anxiety*.

After attending De Witt Clinton High School in the Bronx and New York University, Morris joined the Washington Players and spent two years doing Shakespeare for a summer theater in Cooperstown. During the war, Sergeant Morris appeared in plays with the U.S. Army Special Services, from *What a Life* as Henry Aldrich, to *Hamlet* as Laertes. Major Maurice Evans led the company. After the war Evans brought *Hamlet* to Broadway, Howard was on his way. After several more Broadway shows, he moved to television for "The Admiral Broadway Revue." The producers were looking for a little fellow, and the five-foot-six-inch Morris was perfect. He recalled, "They needed a little guy called Weasel who was light enough to be picked up by the lapels." That show, starring Sid Caesar, led to "Your Show of Shows" and to years of Howard Morris' literal ups and downs as a little comic foil. He left Caesar in 1957. "I was an actor before all of those wonderful years with Sid put the 'comic' label on me," he said at the time. He wanted to appear in dramas, but knew he was "up against stiff resistance" due to his image. "Frankly I don't know if I can get away with it."

He appeared in a television production of *Twelfth Night* with Maurice Evans in 1957 but tended to drift back into lighter fare. He played the leprechaun Og in 1960's *Finian's Rainbow* at New York's City Center. After starring in Cameron Mitchell's syndicated "Beachcomber" series, he played the looney Ernest T. Bass, the scruffy, hillbilly wildman whose antics were in sharp contrast to laidback Andy Griffith. With guidance from Sid Caesar and Carl Reiner, Morris became a sitcom director, supervising episodes of "The Dick Van Dyke Show," "Hogan's Heroes" and "Get Smart," as well as 1960s comedic films *Don't Drink the Water, Who's Minding the Mint?* and *With Six You Get Eggroll*.

He soon found a lucrative career directing television commercials for McDonalds, Liquid Plumber and Kodak. "Funny is funny," he said, insisting that doing a perfect 30-second spot was often more gratifying than appearing in an imperfect movie: "It's a medium that demands perfection." Morris hasn't acted often in films or on television in the past 20 years. When he does it is memorable. Morris played Professor Lillolman, an eccentric but ultimately brilliant specialist in psychosomatic illness who counseled (or, rather, yelled at) Mel Brooks in *High Anxiety*. He was also featured in both comedy scenes and moments of pathos in *Life Stinks*.

Of the fondly remembered "Your Show of Shows," Morgan said, "I'm terribly proud to have been a part of it, of course, but to be nostalgically revered is a little frightening. We're still alive but people talk about us the way they talk about Laurel and Hardy and others who are gone. It's scary . . . I think we filled the needs of people for that time, but times have changed."

BROADWAY incl.: *Hamlet* (1945), *Gentlemen Prefer Blondes* (1949), *Finian's Rainbow* (1960)
FILMS incl.: *Boys' Night Out* (1962), *Who's Minding the Mint?* (1967), *With Six You Get Eggroll* (1968), *Don't Drink the Water* (1969), *Ten from Your Show of Shows* (1973), *High Anxiety* (1977), *Goin' Coconuts* (1978), *Munsters' Revenge* (1981), *History of the World Part I* (1981), *Portrait of a Showgirl* (1982), *End of the Line* (1988), *Transylvania Twist* (1988), *Life Stinks* (1991)
TV: "Your Show of Shows" (1951–54), "Caesar's Hour" (1954–57), "The Beachcomber" (1962)
VIDEOS: *The Andy Griffith Show Collector's Series: The Best of Ernest T. Bass, Volumes 1 and 2*

## ZERO MOSTEL

**(Samuel Joel Mostel, February 28, 1915–September 17, 1977)**

A bombastic, comic actor who bludgeoned audiences with broad, farcical gestures and grimaces, hefty, zero-shaped Zero Mostel usually tempered his overpowering style with just the right flourishes of delicacy and understatement. Like the flower-loving Ferdinand the Bull, Mostel's 90% brute force and lilting 10% of whimsy proved a combination audiences responded to with laughter and love.

The public was deprived of a major talent when Zero Mostel was blacklisted. The energetic comedian gave one of his best performances in the stage and screen versions of *A Funny Thing Happened on the Way to the Forum*. Photo from the author's collection.

Born in Brooklyn, one of eight children, Mostel grew up in Moodus, Connecticut where his rabbi father supervised a kosher slaughterhouse. Ten years later the family returned to New York City, where Mostel graduated from Seward Park High School in 1931. He majored in English at City College and graduated in 1935. After briefly attending New York University trying for his master's degree, he taught art and lectured on painting. In 1942 he tried his stand-up comedy and impressions at The Cafe Society Downtown. The club's press agent, Ivan Black, helped find a catchy first name. Mostel often told interviewers that he got his nickname in school due to low grades. Some writers assumed he chose it from his zero-shaped body and printed the theory as fact. The mundane truth is that Ivan Black tossed out comic names currently in use, like Groucho, Chico and Harpo. It led to "Zero." As Black said, "After all, here's a guy who's starting from nothing."

Zero created some original characters for his stand-up routines, such as Senator Polltax T. Pellagra, a politician with isolationist policies and outrageous attitudes: "As to the most grievous problem facing America today—the so-called Japanese attack on

Hawaii—I'd like to ask, what the hell was Hawaii doing in the Pacific Ocean, anyway?" As Mostel's fame grew, some conservative columnists attacked him for his humor. Conservatives also objected to his outspoken support of the National Negro Congress and the Refugee Appeal of the Joint Anti-Fascist Refugee Committee. Mostel appeared on Broadway in *Keep 'Em Laughing* and played heavies in some Hollywood films, but the McCarthy era blacklist caught up with him and crushed his career.

For a while Mostel gave art exhibitions. His mother came to one and remarked, "When you were a little boy, you drew like a man. Now you're a man, you draw like a little boy." Married in 1944, Mostel had two sons in the '50s. His son Josh (born December 21, 1957) would begin making film comedies in the late 1980s.

Mostel could find acting work only off-Broadway. As it turned out, he won great critical acclaim in small and experimental plays he might never have considered doing otherwise. Burgess Meredith cast him in *Ulysses in Nighttown* in 1958, and Mostel followed this with *Rhinoceros* in 1961.

While low comics such as Red Skelton, Charlie Callas and Jerry Lewis made silly faces and got clobbered by critics, Mostel's image as an intellectual, painter and avant-garde actor probably helped him win favorable reviews even when indulging in broad clowning. In a world in which comedians were traditionally jeered for making funny faces, Mostel was often the subject of magazine photo essays. The glory of his grimaces were even featured in an entire book published by *The New York Times* in 1963. When he sang novelty songs in his walruslike bawling voice, they were the whimsies of a composer such as Harry Ruby, not an Allan Sherman or Tom Lehrer, both routinely panned by serious reviewers of the day. Mostel often gave lectures on humor, declaring it an art form "against hypocrisy, against pretense, against falsehood and humbug and bunk and fraud . . . against all evils masquerading as true and good and worthy of respect."

Mostel went from his Tony Award–winning *Rhinoceros* to big Broadway musicals, braying the anthem "Comedy Tonight" in *A Funny Thing Happened on the Way to the Forum,* and then perfecting his blend of hearty slapstick and heartfelt sincerity in the serio-comic musical *Fiddler on the Roof.* He won Tony awards for both shows and was truly a larger-than-life giant of the New York stage, not only celebrated, but beloved. He was instantly identifiable thanks to his charisma, his voice, his zero-shape, and the peculiar hairstyle that allowed a few sparse wet strands of hair combed up from the back to cover his balding dome.

Mostel then conquered the film world, albeit briefly, as the charismatic, flamboyant Max Bialystock in Mel Brooks' *The Producers.* The overpowering combination of Mel Brooks' words and Mostel's bombastic performance was cheered by a huge cult that continues to find rich laughter in almost every minute of the film, particularly such lines as "When you got it, flaunt it! flaunt it!" and "He who hesitates is poor!"

Mostel's greatest triumphs were sadly behind him after that; it was another case of a unique personality unable to find suitable stage and film roles. There were some interesting performances and heroic failures along the way, but the road ended in Philadelphia, where Mostel was readying a show called *The Merchant* for Broadway. He had been dieting excessively and gone from 300 to 215 pounds. After complaining of dizziness, he checked into a local hospital. Doctors could not find anything radically wrong with him. He left the hospital but was readmitted a few days later with the same symptoms. "I feel dizzy—you better call a nurse," he told a visitor. But it was too late. Mostel died of an aortic aneurysm.

Ironically, fans had their last look at Mostel in *The Front,* co-starring Woody Allen, a film in which his character did not meet with a happy ending. But until the sad finale, the film had served as a reminder of Mostel's greatness, his ability to blaze with fiery comic bravado one minute and then glow softly the next, with poignant expressions of unforgettable pathos.

AUDIO: *Peter and the Wolf* (Lyrichord), *Zero Mostel Sings Harry Ruby* (Vanguard)

BIOGRAPHY: *Zero Mostel* (Brown, 1989)

BOOKS: *Zero Mostel Reads a Book* (Frank, 1963); *Zero Mostel's Book of Villians* (1976); *One Hundred Sev-*

*enty Years of Show Business* (Gilford and Mostel, (1978)

BROADWAY AND OFF-BROADWAY: *Keep 'em Laughing* (1942), *Top Notchers* (1942), *Concert Varieties* (1945), *Beggar's Holiday* (1946), *Flight into Egypt* (1952), *A Stone for Danny Fisher* (1954), *Once Over Lightly* (1955), *The Good Woman of Setzuan* (1956), *Good as Gold* (1957), *Ulysses in Nighttown* (1958), *Rhinoceros* (1961), *A Funny Thing Happened on the Way to the Forum* (1962), *Fiddler on the Roof* (1964), *The Latent Heterosexual* (1968)

FILMS incl.: *Du Barry Was a Lady* (1943), *Panic in the Streets* (1950), *Mr. Belvedere Rings the Bell* (1951), *Sirocco* (1951), *The Model and the Marriage Broker* (1951), *A Funny Thing Happened on the Way to the Forum* (1966), *Great Catherine* (1968), *The Producers* (1968), *The Great Bank Robbery* (1969), *The Angel Levine* (1969), *The Hot Rock* (1972), *Rhinoceros* (1973), *Foreplay* (1975), *The Front* (1976)

## MARTIN MULL

### (August 18, 1943–   )

In 1989 *Playboy* magazine asked Dave Barry, "Are you the funniest WASP in America?" The Pulitzer Prize–winning columnist and author answered, "No. That would be Martin Mull."

Mull is at least the quirkiest. A subtle cross between Randy Newman and Steve Martin, he spent much of the early and mid-1970s singing bent ballads to a cult audience, a mix of redneck country, jive and swing, all out of fashion at the time. The lyrics guaranteed his obscurity. Some were deliberately strange: "Ventriloquist love! It ain't such a groove. Whenever I kiss you your lips never move." A few were guaranteed to offend: "So let's get Jesus Christ a football, let him even up the score, let him run it through the crossbars and be on the cross no more. . . ."

Making matters worse (but, of course, funnier) was Martin's smug attitude. Part of it was ego and confidence, but another part was a defense mechanism against an ambivalent or hostile crowd. Long before Steve Martin or Chevy Chase, Mull was spicing up his act with such sarcastic asides as this: "Well. We sure have had fun, haven't we? I swear,

it's just been fun, fun, fun, fun, fun! We're all fun people. You know what I mean? It's fun . . . and I'm having a fun time . . . it's really fun, and it has been fun. Funny at times, just fun at others. . . ."

The fun began in Ohio, where Martin was born. The family moved to New Canaan, Connecticut, and Martin seemed a typical All-American boy, a member of the football team and a capable track star. His attentions shifted slowly over the years. Rather than attend a college on an athletic scholarship, he opted for the Rhode Island School of Design. He received his M.A. and had some avant-garde art exhibits, but had better luck with a pick-up band called Soup and songwriting. In 1970 "Marty Mull" wrote an answer to "A Boy Named Sue"—"A Girl Named Johnny Cash"—for Jane Morgan. It was about a girl who was given a strange name by her drunken father: "I was working in a diner, in a hairnet servin' hash. And on my little apron was embroidered 'Johnny Cash.' I coulda had my pick of men if I was named Lucille. But when they saw my uniform they laughed and ate their meal. So I'd just drink my coffee black in back behind the trash, and curse that lousy drunkard who had named me Johnny Cash. . . ."

That year Mull's first marriage began to unravel. His wife recalled later, "We had no money. Martin had to take public transportation to the gigs carrying his guitar and not get paid, and play to an empty house." She admitted it was his "very large ego that sustained him for a long time." In 1975 he toured with Steve Martin (they wrote a song, "Westward Ho!" together, which appeared on Mull's *Sex and Violins* disc) and his cult kept growing. He turned down the band leader's job on television's "Saturday Night Live," but accepted acting assignments in the quirky "Mary Hartman, Mary Hartman" comedy soap opera, which turned out to be his big break. He played villain Garth Gimble, eventually impaled on his own aluminum Christmas tree. On the spin-off show "Fernwood 2-Night" he played Barth Gimble, a talk show host of deep shallowness: "A lot of times when a star does rise to the top, the first thing they do is buy their parents a beautiful big ranch home in Arizona. But I couldn't really do that, because I said, hey, where's the man's dignity in a case like that, living in a house that he didn't pay for. So I did something else. I got my father a job."

Mull phased out his singing after putting out several low-selling discs. He developed his satirical point of view on WASPs into *A History of White People in America,* a series of video specials in 1985 that later became books as well. Martin, who had loved to parody all-American mediocrity in his songs, found that his "seriously wimpy hair" and bland, blond looks made him the perfect star for his own tongue-in-cheek white-bread parodies. His squints, smirks and officious style recalled the style shy, sly Robert Benchley used in his lectures.

Mull has put his charming/sleazy unctuous and oily act to work as a compelling, comic pitchman in an endless string of television and radio commercials. He's played hapless dads, con men and comical creeps in films, and after briefly starring in his own CBS sitcom as a psychiatrist, joined Roseanne Barr Arnold's sitcom playing her coffee shop boss.

Whether guesting on a talk show, appearing in a film or a television sketch, Mull's persona is the same. To borrow the title of one of his records: "I'm Everyone I've Ever Loved." Or as he'd tell the crowd after a show, "Thank you all for coming, or however you reacted."

AUDIO: *In the Soop with Martin Mull* (Vanguard), *Martin Mull* (Capricorn), *Martin Mull and His Fabulous Furniture* (Capricorn), *Normal* (Capricorn), *Days of Wine and Neurosis* (Capricorn), *No Hits Four Errors* (Capricorn), *I'm Everyone I've Ever Loved* (ABC), *Sex and Violins* (ABC), *Perfect/Near Perfect* (Elektra)

BOOKS: *White People in America* (1985), *A Paler Shade of White* (1986)

FILMS incl.: *FM* (1978), *Serial* (1980), *My Bodyguard* (1980), *Take This Job and Shove It* (1981), *Mr. Mom* (1983), *Private School* (1983), *Clue* (1985), *Flicks* (1985), *Lots of Luck* (1985), *The Boss' Wife* (1986), *Home Is Where the Hart Is* (1987), *O. C. & Stiggs* (1987), *Rented Lips* (1988), *Think Big* (1989), *Ski Patrol* (1990), *Far Out Man* (1990), *Love in Venus* (1991), The Player (1992)

TV: "Mary Hartman, Mary Hartman" (1976–77), "Fernwood 2-Night" (1977–78), "Domestic Life" (1984), "His and Hers" (1990), "Roseanne" (1991)

VIDEOS: *History of White People in America Vols. 1 and 2; Portrait of a White Marriage; Seals and Crofts and Martin Mull Live; All Star Toast to the Improv, Big City Comedy; Martin Mull Live*

## RICHARD MULLIGAN

### (November 13, 1932–   )

A tall, horse-faced comic actor who seemed to look physically and act emotionally as if he'd gotten his head stuck between elevator doors, Richard Mulligan hit his stride playing sympathetic wrecks in Blake Edwards movies.

Born in the Bronx, Mulligan belonged to a gang. But, since his father was a cop, it wasn't a street gang. As he recalls, "There was one qualification—you had to be funny." Mulligan hoped for a career as a playwright. At a Miami audition for one of his plays, a local theater director liked the reading better than the writing and cast him in *Beyond the Horizon* by Eugene O'Neill. Eventually Mulligan went to Broadway in *All the Way Home,* and had several more stage productions before moving out to California.

Goofily handsome in the Dick Van Dyke tradition, Mulligan co-starred with Mariette Hartley in the short-lived 1960s television western spoof "The Hero" and later enjoyed a cult following (and an Emmy Award) for his role as Burt Campbell on "Soap." He was a bit quirky not only on camera but off. Billy Crystal remarked at the time, "He makes odd noises in his throat that makes it sound like there's a seal loose on the set."

Mulligan went on to play a variety of out-of-control characters, from a mental patient *(Teachers)* to a suicidal film maker in *S.O.B.* He returned to television for another sitcom success, playing the head of the family on "Empty Nest."

Mulligan admits his personality is far from sitcom dad or film zany: "I'm a very low key, very soft fellow, very quiet about everything."

BROADWAY incl.: *Nobody Loves an Albatross* (1963), *Mating Dance* (1965)

FILMS incl.: *One Potato Two Potato* (1964), *The Group* (1966), *Little Big Man* (1970), *The Hideaways* (1973), *The Big Bus* (1976), *Scavenger Hunt* (1979), *S.O.B.* (1980), *Trail of the Pink Panther* (1982), *Teachers*

(1984), *Doin' Time* (1984), *Micki and Maude* (1984), *The Heavenly Kid* (1985), *A Fine Mess* (1985), *Meatballs Part II* (1987), *Guess Who's Coming for Christmas?* (1990)

TV: "The Hero" (1966–67), "Diana" (1973–74), "Soap" (1977–81), "Reggie" (1983), "Empty Nest" (1989–  )

## EDDIE MURPHY

**(April 3, 1961–  )**

Twenty million, thirty million—*Forbes* magazine wasn't counting the assets for some fat cat businessman. The magazine was counting up the take for a cool cat comedian: Eddie Murphy. He and Bill Cosby ended the 1980s earning more each year than almost any other entertainers. "Ol' Cos," like a veteran baseball pitcher, had spent decades achieving superstardom. Murphy, like a rookie "phenom," seemed to come out of nowhere to conquer the comedy world while barely out of his teens.

Eddie was born in Brooklyn. His parents divorced when he was three. For a time after his father's death he and his brother Charles were placed in foster care. His mother remarried when Eddie was nine, and the family settled in Roosevelt, Long Island. Eddie went to Roosevelt Junior-Senior High School and performed at the Roosevelt Youth Center talent shows in 1976. Admittedly growing up in an environment far removed from the racism and taunts that Richard Pryor knew as a child, Eddie's idol was Elvis Presley, whom he thought "had more presence and charisma than anybody who ever existed." When he got into comedy, the young kid played Richard Pryor albums, which were loaded with all of that cool cursing.

On stage Murphy was Pryor without the hatred and bitterness. Murphy talked about sex like Richard did, cursed like Richard did, and made faces like Richard did. And when the cycle for angry young men ebbed and audiences wanted a smiling new face, Murphy took over for Richard. He rose quickly, performing at New York's Comic Strip for affluent East Siders who found his street jive an amusing novelty.

Shortly after, he was a regular on television's "Saturday Night Live" and the hit of the show. He

Eddie Murphy was one of the hottest film stars of the 1980s, a comic superstar who followed the trail blazed by Richard Pryor. Photo from the author's collection.

began creating sketch characters, fusing Little Richard and Richard Simmons for "Little Richard Simmons," mimicking Stevie Wonder and Bill Cosby, and parodying Buckwheat of "Our Gang" and Gumby. Eddie didn't ignore racial problems, but he presented them with surprisingly good humor in the ironic "Mr. Robinson's Neighborhood" sketches and in his parodies of militant blacks such as "Raheem Abdul Muhammad."

Murphy not only became a hot television star, he became a superstar on the concert circuit. With his open leather jackets, gold chains and entourage, Murphy sold out concerts in the largest venues around the country. The star carried himself not as a mere comic but a cross between a rock idol and the heavyweight champ of the world. Eddie left "Saturday Night Live" to become a box office champ in films.

Though his film *48 Hrs.* was loaded with clichés and violence, it became a huge hit, as did *Trading Places.* Eddie signed a $15 million deal with Paramount and scored his biggest hit in the one film that captured all of his charisma, swagger and good humor, *Beverly Hills Cop.*

The hysteria for Eddie Murphy intensified and the young star did his best to remain level-headed. Still, the press, unable to gain access to the new superstar, wrote with a certain hostility about his seeming arrogance, $3.5 million home in New Jersey, hostile bodyguards and nubile girls all desperate to please the flaunting star/sex symbol. As with most comedians who earned fame through questionable material, the more it was questioned, the worst it became. At first Murphy cheerfully joked about Bill Cosby calling him up and telling him to clean up his four-letter act. Now his stand-up show was intentionally dubbed "Raw" and the goofy putdowns of women, gays and Asians became more hostile.

Murphy was not very concerned with white Middle America's desire for him to continue with his "Saturday Night Live" characters or his lighthearted action films with white co-stars. He began making films geared more for black audiences and featuring black co-stars. He turned from comedy records to recording such R&B songs as "Put Your Mouth on Me" and "Love Moans," which were beyond the tastes of his white liberal supporters. Instead of being cheerfully *Delirious*, the title of his new concert film was *Raw*, and it was cautiously panned by white critics. Female critics were more hostile. So were some audience members: A man was killed in a drive-in shootout in California on opening night, and according to *Variety* "unruly" crowds proved disruptive at several other venues. *Premiere* magazine calculated that *Raw* averaged a profanity every 10 seconds, compared to 53 seconds for *Blazing Saddles* and one every three minutes 20 seconds for *Rocky.*

Murphy's first black-oriented film, *Coming to America*, was viewed as benign, sophomoric (the requisite phallic jokes) and middling. Then *Harlem Nights* was a critical bomb. "There's not an original idea in the movie," said critic Roger Ebert, "and the modern four-letter dialogue is distracting in a period picture." Partner Gene Siskel found it "shockingly embarrassing, with gross amounts of racist dialogue directed at both whites and blacks, a sexist portrayal of women." *Rolling Stone* magazine called the "rude, crude and misogynistic" film one of the worst movies of the year. Janet Maslin in the *New York Times*

huffed Eddie "can continue to write his own ticket, since audiences will so eagerly pay to see him no matter what he happens to do."

As Murphy partied in chic nightclubs headlines followed, calling attention to alleged skirmishes with women, fans and photographers. An ex-manager sued him demanding money. Gay groups protested his concerts. The kid who once couldn't do anything wrong was now the big star who couldn't do anything right. Eddie asked for a little understanding. In 1988 he said, "All I want to say is that I'm just as screwed up as everybody else, no better, no worse, and I'm just as capable of sinning or of doing good as anybody else. I've done some real mean things and I've done some kind things, too . . . I'm an abstainer of drugs and alcohol, and although I have lavished money, cars and a house, I'm still a manic depressive. I still go up and down. Everybody does . . . sometimes I'll wake up and want to cry, and not really have any reason."

More scandals hit Murphy. He was accused of being selfish, taking $8 million dollars for starring in *Coming to America*, while his three co-stars, Arsenio Hall, James Earl Jones and John Amos, shared $1 million. Then he was accused of being a plagiarist. Columnist Art Buchwald successfully sued Paramount, claiming the film was based on material he had submitted earlier. Murphy himself was cleared, but the studio lost the case and had to pay up. He was even accused of turning his back on his own people when he announced that *Harlem Nights* would not be shot on location in Harlem.

To restore his star luster, Murphy found himself in a sequel, *Another 48 Hrs.*, which was greeted with mild approval and the hope for better work in the future. The fad for Murphy had risen and slumped at the start and end of the 1980s, but into the 1990s Murphy remains a big box office name in films and a powerful attraction whenever he chooses to tour in stand-up comedy.

FILMS incl.: *48 Hours* (1982), *Trading Places* (1983), *Eddie Murphy: Delirious* (1983), *Best Defense* (1984), *Beverly Hills Cop* (1984), *The Golden Child* (1986), *Eddie Murphy: Raw* (1987), *Beverly Hills Cop II* (1987), *Coming to America* (1988), *Harlem Nights* (1989), *Another 48 Hrs.* (1990), *Boomerang (1992)*
TV: "Saturday Night Live" (1981–84)
VIDEO: *The Best of Eddie Murphy: Saturday Night Live*

## BILL MURRAY

### (September 21, 1950– )

Cold and dangerous with his glaring stare and rough complexion, Bill Murray replaced Chevy Chase's sassy arrogance with a much more sinister and sarcastic show of comic bravado. Though he was a harsh contrast to the recently departed Chase when he arrived on televison's "Saturday Night Live" in January 1977, eventually audiences began to catch on to his style. His best sketches included parodies of gratingly self-confident lounge singers and smug reporters. His memorable version of a movie columnist included a moment when he glared directly into the camera for a one-to-one chiding of Woody (dubbed "The Wood Man") Allen for being reclusive. Murray wasn't afraid of portraying sleazy, mocking characters. He predated Dennis Miller's nasty-smug "I am outta here" with his joshing dismissal "Now get outta here!"

Born in Wilmette, Illinois, one of nine children, Bill attended parochial school and enrolled as a pre-med student at Regis College in Denver. Not exactly a model student, he was once arrested at O'Hare Airport in Chicago for possession of marijuana, but received probation.

·Bill's older brother Brian Doyle-Murray was a member of "The Second City Troupe" in Chicago. Eventually Bill gave up college to join him. Together they began working on "The National Lampoon Radio Hour" in 1974 and the subsequent touring *National Lampoon Show* through 1975. Bill moved to "Saturday Night Live" that year—"Saturday Night Live with Howard Cosell." The variety show folded quickly, and it took nearly two years before he got his chance on "Saturday Night Live."

The show was in a transitional phase that saw the gradual defection of not only Chase, but John Belushi and Dan Aykroyd as well. For a while, the macho Murray was called upon to become the backbone of the show. He took over both on screen and off. A master of both the icy glare and the strident tantrum, he tried to keep the writing on target and dominated many of the sketches. He even swept away co-star Gilda Radner into a brief love affair.

In films Murray tempered his abrasiveness, showing some of the laidback, laconic tolerance of a Jack Nicholson. (Ironically, he played the Nicholson role in the remake of *Little Shop of Horrors*.) His summer camp comedy *Meatballs* was a commercial hit. Other youth-oriented comedies cemented his stardom, though he was prouder of the critical acclaim for his role in *Tootsie*. For a while he had dramatic aspirations, which led to the disastrous *Razor's Edge*. Despite the flop, Murray was a box-office name, enough to propel interest in such fizzled experiments as *Scrooged*, the bank robbery yarn *Quick Change* and his role as Richard Dreyfuss' infuriating psychiatric patient in *What About Bob?* Critic Pauline Kael wrote of his screen persona, "He looks capable of anything, yet he isn't threatening; he'd just do something crazy."

On talk shows he revels in his image as the mordant put-on artist, unpredictable enough to tear someone down with his sharp tongue or perhaps his bony fist. Even if he is obviously "just kidding," his demeanor is unsettling; and always good for uneasy chuckles.

The man whose demeanor was so foreboding on early episodes of "Saturday Night Live" retains a strong following amoung younger viewers, thanks to his blockbuster series of *Ghostbuster* comedies. Married with two sons, the comic ghostfighter said, "I believe in ghosts, but most of them are waiters. They take your order and vanish."

FILMS incl.: *Next Stop, Greenwich Village* (1976), *Meatballs* (1979), *The Jerk* (1979), *Mr. Mike's Mondo Video* (1979), *Caddyshack* (1980), *Coming Attactions* (1980), *Where the Buffalo Roam* (1980), *Stripes* (1981), *Loose Shoes* (1981), *Tootsie* (1982), *Ghostbusters* (1984), *Nothing Lasts Forever* (1984), *The Razor's Edge* (1984), *Little Shop of Horrors* (1986), *Ghostbusters II* (1989), *Quick Change* (1989)
TV: *Saturday Night Live* (1977–80)
VIDEO: *Bill Murray Live from the Second City*

## JAN MURRAY

### (Murray Janofsky, October 4, 1917– )

A slick and good-looking stand-up comedian who played clubs such as The Copa in the 1960s and went on to casinos and vacation resorts in subsequent decades, Jan Murray is not only admired by audiences for his consummate professionalism on stage, but by other comedians as well. Steve Allen noted that "perhaps the most interesting thing about

Jan's work is that, as richly funny as he is on stage, he is even more so in a room. At the typical Hollywood comedians' party, with perhaps a dozen funny men in the room, as often as not it will be Jan [getting the laughs] . . . He is by no means merely a jokesmith but rather a commentator analyzing the events of his experience, actual or alleged."

Born in the Bronx, Jan quit De Witt Clinton High School to help out his family. A turning point was a job in a doll factory, poking out the bubbles in the doll's heads as they went by him on the assemble line: "The first day I went to work at 8 A.M., and after poking out the bubbles in about two thousand doll's heads, I figured it must be time for lunch. I looked up at the clock and it was 9 A.M. I decided then and there I would never work in a factory for my livelihood."

Doing routines he memorized from watching vaudeville shows, Jan was a hit at local Bronx social clubs and moved on to Catskill resorts. Debunking the myth that comedians only feud with each other and steal jokes, he reported that his early career was helped by many big stars: "For instance, back in 1940 I was a kid playing a little nightclub in Miami Beach. Al Jolson walked in one night and saw the act. For the next two weeks he invited me to his home, came to the club and guided and advised me. He pointed out all my mistakes and taught me not to resort to off-color material." He also remembered the advice from Bert Wheeler: " 'Jan,' he said, 'you're a talented and a wonderful young comedian. You'll make it big some day if you have the perseverance and remember two important things. Never fight too hard for billing and for money. When you deserve it, they'll bill you as a star and pay you like one.' "

By 24 he was a regular at the "class" clubs of the day, The Copa in New York, the Chez Paree in Chicago and many others. He married his wife Toni, a "Copa Girl," in 1949 and raised four children.

In 1950 Murray hosted television's "Songs for Sale," and became one of the first comedians enlisted to turn quiz show hosting into ad-libbed entertainment. He hosted many shows and even produced a few. Meanwhile, he continued club work and guest spots on "The Ed Sullivan Show," "Hollywood Palace" and late-night talk shows.

Utilizing his rough good looks and the forceful charisma that allowed him to take control of an audience, Murray guested on action television shows ("The Man from UNCLE") and played the hero in the film *Who Killed Teddy Bear?* a grim detective thriller about a perverted murderer. Through the years he added more television acting (episodes of "Ellery Queen," "Night Stalker," "Fantasy Island," "The Fall Guy," "Hunter," "It's a Living") and dinner theater (*A Thousand Clowns, The Odd Couple, Guys and Dolls*) to his lucrative Las Vegas and Atlantic City stand-up. Occasionally he opened for headliners, if they were of the Frank Sinatra/superstar caliber.

In the 1980s he contrasted the new styles of comedy with the old: "In my day putdown humor was mostly about ourselves—I'd do jokes about how thin I was, how dumb I was. Now it's directed at ethnic groups, other groups, politicians. My comedy has always been gentler. . . . The biggest change I've noticed is language. There seems to be no restrictions on it now . . . I may say a naughty word occasionally, but when I do I apologize to the audience."

Murray's humor remains general and gentle. Though perceived as one of the old-fashioned stand-ups who told one too many "wife" jokes, his usually have a wry twist: "Sorry I'm late. That stupid wife of mine! She didn't shovel the snow from the driveway this morning. Forgot to put on the snow tires. And halfway to New York I realized she hadn't dressed me."

AUDIO: *Jan Murray's Funny Fables and Fairy Tales*

BROADWAY: *Music in My Heart* (1947), *Guys and Dolls* (1966)

FILMS: *Who Killed Teddy Bear?* (1965), *Thunder Alley* (1965), *The Busy Body* (1966), *Tarzan and the Great River* (1967), *Fear City* (1985)

TV: "Songs for Sale" (1950–51), "Go Lucky" (1951), "Sing it Again" (1951), "Blind Date" (1953), "Dollar a Second" (1953–57), "Jan Murray Time" (1955), "Treasure Hunt" (1956–59), "Chain Letter" (1966)

# N

## JIM NABORS

### (June 12, 1932–   )

"Gahhhhh-leeee!" For years, Jim Nabors' goofy, wide-eyed Gomer Pyle was one of the hit country boys of television. First on "The Andy Griffith Show" and then on his spin-off "Gomer Pyle, U.S.M.C.," Nabors played a simpleminded but good soul ("Fool me once, shame on you, fool me twice, shame on me!").

Born in Sylacauga, Alabama, Nabors looked and sounded the part of Gomer, who surfaced during the third year of Griffith's show as a gas station mechanic. "Andy saw me in a nightclub," Nabors recalled in 1990, "and I had never acted before. And George [Lindsay] and I were friends, and he got mad at me because he had read for the Gomer Pyle part." At first the producers thought Nabors' mannerisms were too outrageous, but Griffith insisted, "There are a lot of ol' boys back home like that."

Gomer was spun-off into his own show playing a marine whose Pollyanna optimism, childlike honesty and do-gooder tendencies made him the bane of pushy, scheming Sergeant Carter (Frank Sutton). His catch phrases, which he ad-libbed during various scenes, included his elongated "Golly," an astonished cry of "Shazam!" and "Sur-prise! Sur-prise! Sur-prise!", which usually meant that it was some-one else's turn to be amazed by a well-meaning act gone wrong.

Nabors developed a second career that was so completely different from Gomer it was unintentionally hilarious. Like Frank Fontaine, who had success as both a goofy-eyed comic and a gooey-voiced baritone, Nabors issued over two dozen albums singing often overly ripe versions of such pop hits as "Bridge Over Troubled Water."

Nabors and Ruth Buzzi starred in "Lost Saucer," a 1975 children's show Saturday mornings. In 1986 he guested in the made-for-television film "Return to Mayberry" and continues to tour with an act mixing songs and some moments of Gomer Pyle. More often he chooses to stay home in Hawaii where the bachelor raises macadamia nuts and flowers.

FILMS incl.: *The Best Little Whorehouse in Texas* (1982), *Stroker Ace* (1983), *Cannonball Run II* (1984)
TV: "The Andy Griffith Show" (1963–64), "Gomer Pyle, U.S.M.C." (1964–69), "The Jim Nabors Hour" (1969–71)

## BOB NEWHART

### (George Robert Newhart, September 5, 1929–   )

Bearing the worried, haunted look of a dog that doesn't know why he's been kicked, Bob Newhart became one of the best "reaction" comedians in sitcoms, leaving his cast members to be stupid, obnoxious and pushy while the meek inherited the laughs.

His style was somewhat similar when he first became a star performing monologues, most of them one-way phone calls. "I'm not really saying anything funny," he insisted. "What you're laughing at is what's unheard, which is what the other person is saying . . . on paper it's not funny." While some felt he owed a debt to Shelley Berman, Newhart cited other influences: "I learned timing from Jack Benny. He was so brave: He'd take all the time it took. I was also influenced by the almost Pinter-like quality of Bob and Ray. They would have these people that were boringly dull, just going on and on."

Newhart's routines were often stoic studies in chagrin and disbelief: phone calls to Abner Doubleday insisting nobody would ever want to play baseball; a study of a man trying to defuse a bomb (despite phone instructions describing a lethal wire as grayish blue, the other bluish gray); and the classic look at a driving instructor reacting to his pupil: "Now that was a wonderful turn . . . one little thing. Uh, this is a one-way street. Well, now, now, it was partially my fault. You were in the left-hand lane, and you were signaling left, and I more or less assumed you were going to turn left. . . . Oh, now we hit someone, Mrs. Webb. Remember you were going to watch the rearview mirror? The red light blinded you? The flashing red light blinded you? The flashing red light—on the car you hit blinded you? Yes, Officer, she was just telling me about it."

Newhart was born in Chicago and graduated from Loyola University in 1952. He had a degree in accounting but noted, trying to salvage some pride, that he was never a C.P.A. He got into comedy working with a partner, Ed Gallagher: "We did a kind of poor man's Bob and Ray." They syndicated a five-minute comedy spot, which was bought by only three radio stations in 1958, located in Northampton, Massachusetts; Jacksonville, Florida; and Idaho Falls. On his own a short time later, Newhart's radio comedy attracted the attention of Warner Brothers. The "comedy boom" was on, spurred by Shelley Berman, and labels were hunting for new talent to put on disc.

Newhart, unsure and edgy, made his nightclub debut and his first album at the same time, but fortunately his brand of low-key nervousness suited his character: the mild-mannered average man dealing glumly with the frustrations of modern life. While 1960s "sickies" such as Lenny Bruce and Jonathan Winters seemed to live outside the norm, Newhart was perceived as Mr. Normal. But his satire was often biting, as in a routine about a would-be suicide coaxed off a building ledge ("This your first time?") and a bitter look at an employee's retirement party. Newhart's stuttery timidity and self-effacing calm blunted the edge to his work, an edge more obvious in a strong, angry contemporary like Shelley Berman.

Newhart had to explain "a pet peeve runs through my humor—the impersonal corporate bigness in modern life, and the individual getting lost." Later he said of his stand-up days, "Humor was the only way I could retain my sanity. I saw these indifferences around me and the only thing I could do was make fun of them. And once you'd made fun of them, you could go on to the next inconsistency . . . it really is for your own sanity that you become a comedian."

His albums went gold, he won several Grammy awards in 1960 (Best New Artist, Best Comedy Album, Best Artist of the Year) and was rushed to television. His variety show won an Emmy but failed to catch on. Another, with Carol Burnett ("The Entertainers"), was a shambles.

Newhart's film career was never particularly strong. He tended to be typed as odious yes-men and company snitches. He was creepy Willard Gnatpole, the company man out to nab lovable crook Peter Ustinov in Hot Millions. In Cold Turkey he was conniving weasel, Merwin Wren, out to make a killing with a tobacco company publicity scheme ("Bottom line—this may be the greatest thing since creation"). His major starring part was, unfortunately, in the tasteless and boring First Family.

In 1972, well after his initial fame died down and years after his last record album, his new sitcom was scheduled after the hit "The Mary Tyler Moore Show." The show had a comfortable success in that time slot for years. It was about a Chicago psychologist (Bob Hartley) grimly saddled with dopey friends, bent clients and a cloying wife. As with "The Mary Tyler Moore Show," Newhart's series left the air while still drawing respectable ratings. In 1982 Newhart returned as Dick Loudon, former ad man and do-it-yourself book author and now owner of the Stratford Inn in Vermont, saddled with a new group of homely fools, notably the brothers Larry, Darryl and Darryl. Newhart knew audience identification with his everyman character was still strong: "I think there's an identification with the character. I think that women watch and say, 'My God, that's exactly what Norm would have done.' And then the men watch, and think, 'Oh, God, I would have done it just that way.'"

The show continued on for many years, ironically having its best showing for its last episode—the first time in seven years that it hit number one. Newhart announced he'd probably try another sitcom after a brief vacation. He added, "I've basically been doing the same thing for 25 years and getting away with it!"

AUDIO: *The Button-Down Mind* (WB), *The Button-Down Mind Strikes Back* (WB), *De-Luxe Edition* (first two albums as a double set, WB), *Behind the Button-Down Mind* (WB), *The Button-Down Mind on TV* (WB), *Bob Newhart Faces Bob Newhart* (WB), *The Windmills Are Weakening* (WB), *This Is It!* (WB), *Best of Bob Newhart* (WB), *Best of Bob Newhart* (Murray Hill), *Very Funny Bob Newhart* (Harmony)
BIOGRAPHY: *Bob Newhart* (Paige, 1977)
FILMS incl.: *Hell Is for Heroes* (1962), *Hot Millions* (1968), *On a Clear Day You Can See Forever* (1970), *Catch 22* (1970), *Cold Turkey* (1970), *Thursday's Game* (1971), *Little Miss Marker* (1980), *First Family* (1980), *The Entertainers* (1991)
TV: "The Bob Newhart Show" (1961–62), "The Entertainers" (1964), "The Bob Newhart Show" (1972–78), "Newhart" (1982–90), "Bob" (1992–)

# NICHOLS and MAY

**Mike Nichols: Michael Igor Peschkowsky, November 6, 1931–**
**Elaine May: Elaine Berlin, April 21, 1932–**

Masters of cerebral comedy and stark, angst-ridden improvisation, Mike Nichols and Elaine May united as members of the Compass Players, an improvisational group favored by intellectuals, free thinkers and the students at the nearby University of Chi-

cago. Nichols, a student at the university himself, recalled seeing an "evil, hostile girl" glaring at him while he was performing. Late one night he recognized her at a railroad station and decided to be creatively aggressive. "May I sit down?" he asked in a clipped German accent. The woman answered, in her own European spy dialect, "If you weesh." Nichols had met his match. Together they went back to Elaine May's place for cream cheese–covered hamburgers.

Nichols' father, Nicholaiyevitch Peschkowsky, fled to Berlin where Michael was born. Then he fled with his family to America just before World War II. Mike, bald due to a childhood illness, attended the University of Chicago, then went to New York to study acting with Lee Strasberg. He next returned to Chicago, meeting Elaine May. Elaine's father was Yiddish actor Jack Berlin. She learned show business firsthand when he took her along with him on jobs across the country. Later she was tutored by Maria Ouspenskaya.

Two brittle wits oozing harsh sarcasm, Nichols and May performed rigid sketches that were stark as bone, but dripping blood. These included the pathetic confrontation between "Mother and Son," in which the son is guiltily reduced to a sniffling baby (probably the first painful "Jewish mother" routine); "The Funeral Parlor," in which a crisply efficient "grief lady" relentlessly flays at a weeping mourner; and "The Telephone," in which a man tries desperately to get his lost dime back from an inhuman, mechanical-voiced phone operator.

The duo took themselves so seriously that once, in the midst of an intense sketch, Mike smacked Elaine and she clawed him, drawing blood. The psychodramas were often based too closely on the duo's personalities. Elaine was openly hostile, admitting "I feel in opposition to almost everything." Mild-mannered Mike liked to keep performing the same safe routines. Eventually, the strain was too much. After 300 performances on Broadway, Nichols and May broke up. Many thought Mike and Elaine also divorced; they were never husband and wife. Elaine was twice married, while Mike made headlines when he married news anchor Diane Sawyer.

The appeal of Nichols and May remained strong; the age of anxiety they felt in the 1950s and early 1960s grew stronger in the passing decades. Many

An influential, intellectual comedy team in the 1950s, Nichols and May each became respected stage and screen directors in their own right. Photo from the author's collection.

could identify with the neurotic couple in one sketch who equate pleasure only in terms of lessened pain: "I have my problems in relating . . . a relationship is so difficult." "For the last two hours I've really had my anxiety allayed."

Despite requests from nostalgic fans, the duo rarely unite except for occasional charity events. Nichols disliked performing. He told author Jeffrey Sweet, "Something I felt with Elaine always when we were in front of an audience was almost arrogance. A feeling that 'I can handle you guys.' I got to where I was completely comfortable with an audience. That has since left me to such an extent that I can't do anything in front of an audience anymore."

Elaine May directed *A New Leaf* (1971), *The Heartbreak Kid* (1972) and more recently *Ishtar* (1987). In 1990 she made a comeback co-starring with Marlo Thomas in *In the Spirit*, written by her daughter Jeannie Berlin, who also appeared in the movie. The following year she wrote a new play, *Mr. Gogol and Mr. Preen*. Mike Nichols divides his time between Broadway (Tony awards for directing *Barefoot in the Park* in 1964, *The Odd Couple* in 1965, *Plaza Suite* in 1968, *The Prisoner of Second Avenue* in 1972 and *The Real Thing* in 1984) and directing films (an Oscar for *The Graduate* in 1967). Nichols' interest in young comedians led him to direct Gilda Radner's *Gilda Live!* on Broadway and lead Whoopi Goldberg from obscurity to her own Broadway hit.

AUDIO: *An Evening with Nichols and May* (Mercury), *Improvisations to Music* (Mercury), *Nichols and May Examine Doctors* (Mercury), *Best of Nichols and May* (Mercury), *Retrospect* (Mercury)
BROADWAY: *An Evening with Nichols and May* (1960)

## LESLIE NIELSEN

### (February 11, 1922–  )

After becoming a comedy star in the hits *Airplane* and *Police Squad,* Leslie Nielsen admitted, "I think I was always a closet comedian." As for his ability to appear in both the drama *(Nuts)* and comedy *(Naked Gun)* at the same time, he said, "That's my profession—that's what I'm supposed to know how to do."

Nielsen was born in Saskatchewan, Canada, and grew up 100 miles south of the Arctic Circle in Fort Norman. His father was a Royal Canadian Mounted Policeman. Nielsen remembered that at the fort it was "60 below zero for four months straight." Nielsen trained at Lorne Greene's Academy of Radio Arts in Toronto and New York's Neighborhood Playhouse. After working as a disc jockey, the handsome leading man starred in a few light comedies *(Tammy and the Bachelor)* but was usually cast as a stalwart hero *(Forbidden Planet)*. Having served as an aerial gunner in the Royal Canadian Air Force, Nielsen was suited to playing heroic General Francis Marion, "The Swamp Fox," in a series of television shows for Walt Disney; Lieutenant Price Adams, leader of "The New Breed" police squad; and Police Chief Sam Danforth on "The Protectors." He guested on dozens of drama and adventure shows, almost never in comedy roles.

Nielsen didn't make a name in comedy until he starred in *Airplane!,* a movie stocked with dramatic actors such as Peter Graves and Lloyd Bridges. The film was loaded with sight gags, silly jokes and dumb wordplay, but the seriousness of the stern, adult cast made the childish comedy all the funnier.

Nielsen always had charm and a streak of vulnerable humor to him. As "The Swamp Fox," he'd perform some bit of derring-do, such as jumping from a second-floor balcony, and land with a weary shudder. In *Forbidden Planet* he had several moments of chagrin, especially when his brain capacity was questioned by co-star Walter Pidgeon. In several dramatic roles, Nielsen seemed to have the ability to take himself less than seriously. This aspect of his personality was exploited in *Airplane!* and subsequent comedies. In that film he deadpanned a catch phrase that might have drawn groans from most anyone else:

NIELSEN: Can you fly this plane and land it?

ROBERT HAYS: Surely you can't be serious!

NIELSEN: I am serious. And don't call me Shirley.

He was picked to star as Lieutenant Frank Drebin in the *Police Squad!* television series and was clearly no longer merely a dramatic actor doing comedy straight. Whether drooling madly and spit-talking through a dental device, or uttering a subtle "well" in moments of barely concealed confusion, Nielsen now displayed all the tricks of a seasoned laughgetter. His discipline as an actor allowed him to let the audience find the joke. He didn't give away the gag by overemphasizing the final line. "I'd just come from the stockyards. We'd gotten reports that hundreds of cows had been senselessly slaughtered in the area, but I couldn't find any evidence. I stopped off for a hamburger and checked in with headquarters." He was nominated for an Emmy for "Outstanding Lead in a Comedy Series."

Along with Peter Falk's quizzical Columbo and Peter Sellers' Clouseau, Nielsen's Lieutenant Drebin became one of the funniest lawmen in recent comedy—and, with the top-10 box office receipts of *The Naked Gun* and its sequel proving it—one of the most successful.

BROADWAY: *Seagulls over Sorrento* (1952)

FILMS incl.: *Forbidden Planet* (1956), *The Opposite Sex* (1956), *Tammy and the Bachelor* (1957), *Harlow* (1965), *Beau Geste* (1966), *The Reluctant Astronaut* (1967), *Dayton's Devils* (1968), *How to Commit Marriage* (1969), *The Poseidon Adventure* (1972), *Airplane* (1980), *Prom Night* (1980), *The Creature Wasn't Nice (aka Spaceship)* (1981), *Wrong Is Right* (1982), *Creepshow* (1982), *Nuts* (1987), *The Naked Gun* (1988), *Repossessed* (1990), *The Naked Gun 2½: The Smell of Fear* (1991), *Change of Heart* (1991), *All I Want for Christmas* (1991)

TV: "Wonderful World of Walt Disney" (1958), "The New Breed" (1961–62), "Peyton Place" (1965), "The Protectors" (1969–70), "Bracken's World" (1970), "The Explorers" (1972–73), "Police Squad!" (1982), "Shaping Up" (1984)

## MABEL NORMAND

### (Mabel Normand, November 10, 1894–February 23, 1930)

The queen of silent film comedy, versatile and vivacious Mabel Normand sparkled in romantic comedy, drawing room farce and slapstick. The phrase "comedy is not pretty" didn't exist at the dawn of silent comedy when Mabel was its brightest female star. She was called "the female Chaplin," not because she used his mannerisms, but because she was almost as popular as he, directed a handful of her own films and in later years yearned to move from pure slapstick to more personal and emotional comedy.

Various sources differ on her birthplace (Boston, Quebec or Providence, Rhode Island) and birth date (1892, 1894 and 1897 have been given), but there's no confusion about her climb to film stardom. After working for Butterick as a pattern maker, she became a model for leading artists of the day (Charles Dana and James Montgomery Flagg). From there she started making films in New York, including *The Squaw's Love* for D. W. Griffith in 1911. At Biograph she met aspiring director Mack Sennett and together they began making Keystone comedies—and love. The love affair between Mack and Mabel was later the subject of a 1974 Broadway musical.

Though barely five feet tall and 100 pounds, Mabel was a hardy slapstick star. She could take it and dish it out too. She's credited with throwing the first pie in silent comedy—a shot at Fatty Arbuckle in *A Voice from the Deep*, released in the summer of 1913. (Published reports, including Sennett's, claiming the initial target was Ben Turpin have since been disproved.)

Chaplin's star began to rise at Keystone a year later. He and Mabel co-starred and co-directed some films together, but he balked when she was assigned to direct him in his early efforts. Though he had little directing experience himself, Chaplin recalled, "charming as Mabel was, I doubted her competence as a director; so . . . there came the inevitable blow-up." Chaplin left Sennett for Essanay Studios and complete control. Sennett didn't mind too much. It would've been worse losing Mabel. "Mabel Normand could do everything Chaplin could do," Mack Sennett said. "To me, she was the greatest comedian that ever lived."

Normand rarely played man-hungry uglies or garishly made-up fools. She was a heroine in comedy, as Harold Lloyd was a hero, displaying charm and vulnerability even in moments of thrill comedy danger. She had her own "Mabel Normand Feature Film Company" at Sennett and scored a huge hit with the full-length *Mickey*. After she learned of Sennett's affair with Mae Busch, Mabel left Sennett and signed with Goldwyn for $1,000 a week. Unfortunately, her own erratic lifestyle led to her decline and she went back to Sennett a few years later. Then her decline turned into a landslide.

On February 1, 1922 director William Desmond Taylor was killed. Taylor was involved in the drug world and other nefarious enterprises, but most thought his death had something to do with his love life. He was having affairs with Mabel, actress Mary Miles Minter and Minter's mother. Tipped off to his sudden death by Taylor's next-door neighbor (comedienne Edna Purviance), Mabel, along with studio executives, rushed to his home to destroy love letters and other scandalous evidence. It was no use. They couldn't find all the love notes, "souvenir" lingerie and other items Taylor had hidden. And there were witnesses claiming that Mabel was the last to see him alive (shots were heard ten minutes after she left). Though Mabel was not convicted, the scandal of her relationship with Taylor and the rumors of her cocaine use caused many to demand that she retire from films. The case was never solved (Sidney D. Kirkpatrick's book *A Cast of Killers,* based on King Vidor's notes, theorized a solution).

Sennett supported Mabel and she made more films, but her career sputtered until, on January 1, 1924, it was dealt another blow. While visiting millionaire Courtland S. Dines, along with Edna Purviance, there was a gunshot. Dines was wounded and Mabel's chauffeur was arrested. The man, Joe Kelly, was actually a wanted convict named Horace Greer. The peculiar event did nothing to enhance Mabel's reputation.

Comedy's first female star, a hit in some 21 features between 1917 and 1923, was now reduced to a few roles in short subjects at Hal Roach's studio. On September 17, 1926 she married Lew Cody at 4 A.M. after a party. He was dying and she had tuberculosis, requiring blood transfusions at a sanitarium. She died a few years later. One of Hollywood's most energetic stars had completely worn out.

BIOGRAPHY: *Mabel* (Fussell, 1982)
FILMS incl.: *The Fatal Chocolate* (1912), *Mabel's Stratagem* (1912), *A Red Hot Romance* (1913), *Mabel's Blunder* (1914), *Mabel at the Wheel* (1914), *My Valet* (1915), *Wished on Mabel* (1915), *Mabel, Fatty and the Law* (1915), *Mabel and Fatty Adrift* (1915), *Mickey* (1917), *Sis Hopkins* (1918), *Peck's Bad Girl* (1918), *Back at the Woods* (1918), *Sis Hopkins* (1919), *The Pest* (1919), *The Slim Princess* (1920), *Molly O* (1921), *Suzanna* (1922), *The Extra Girl* (1923), *One Hour Married* (1926), *Raggedy Rose* (1926), *Should Men Walk Home?* (1927)
VIDEO: *Keystone Comedies I–III* (Republic)

## DON NOVELLO (See FATHER GUIDO SARDUCCI.)

## LOUIS NYE

### (May 1, 1919–   )

Often cast as a slightly nervous businessman or timorously effete official, comic character actor Louis Nye remains strongly identified with one particular creation, Gordon Hathaway, the minty Madison Avenue ad man who was a frequent "man in the street" guest on Steve Allen's "Tonight Show." His catch phrase was a simpering "Hi Ho, Steverino!"

A typical visit from Gordon standing in Allen's Alley: "I'm just old Gordon Hathaway, and I'm from Manhattan. And I'm Mr. Universe! Hi Ho, Steverino." "Are you ready for tonight's question about summer romances?" "Summer romances? (singing) La la laa, la la laa, I looove you. Well, all right. Let's have it, oh *romantic* idol of millions." "Gordon, how do you feel about summer romances?" "Oh! Oooh, I'm all for them! In fact Mother and Dad got married as a result of summer romance." "They did?" "Of *course* they did, fella. Sure! It was at a resort hotel, a *beautiful* romance between a hotel guest and a bell hop. Oooh!" "Gordon, didn't your mother's family mind your mother marrying a bellhop?" "Slow down, Slim! Mother was the bellhop!"

Though a potentially offensive stereotype character, Nye's Gordon Hathaway never received many angry letters of protest. Steve Allen noted at the time, "I think it is Louis' air of carefree, airy innocence and basic niceness that explains this." Of Gordon, Nye said, "I never did like that character. He had no depth. He was just another mustache, another beard, as we say in the business, that kept people from being aware that there really was an actor named Louis Nye." The character was based on an army officer he knew "who felt you had to be nice and happy, amusing all the time. We despised him. He'd say 'Hi guys, 30-mile hike tomorrow— hope you'll all be there, ha ha!' "

Born in Hartford, Connecticut (some sources report 1922), Nye worked in radio on serials such as "Crime Doctor," and appeared in some Broadway shows before finding local television work in New York, including Jack Paar's morning show. Married, with a son, he developed a stand-up comedy act in the late 1950s after scoring well on Steve Allen's show. He favored dialect comedy (captured on his second album, *Nye in Your Eye*). Still, for years he played variations on Hathaway, joyfully simpering and trembling with divine delight. He played Sonny Drysdale, banker Drysdale's preciously foppy and too-too rich son on "The Beverly Hillbillies" and has been a frequent silly, affected but effective sitcom performer on many shows since.

AUDIO: *Man on the Street* (Signature), *Heigh Ho Madison Avenue* (Riverside), *Here's Nye in Your Eye* (United Artists)

BROADWAY: *Inside U.S.A.* (1948), *Touch and Go* (1949), *Flahooley* (1951), *Charley's Aunt* (1970)

FILMS incl.: *Facts of Life* (1960), *Zotz* (1962), *The Wheeler Dealers* (1963), *Who's Been Sleeping in My Bed* (1963), *Good Neighbor Sam* (1964), *Guide for the Married Man* (1967), *Won Ton Ton, The Dog Who Saved Hollywood* (1976), *Harper Valley PTA* (1978), *Full Moon High* (1982)

TV: "The Steve Allen Show" (1956–61), "The Ann Sothern Show" (1960–61), "The Beverly Hillbillies" (1962), "The Steve Allen Comedy Hour" (1967), "Happy Days" (1970), "Needles and Pins" (1973), "The $1.98 Beauty Show" (1978–80)

# O

## JACK OAKIE

**(Lewis Delaney Offield, November 12, 1903–January 23, 1978)**

Once the model of the plucky, cheerful, round-faced college boy—with just the right amount of smug sass—Jack Oakie's comic reputation has suffered with changing times. Few viewers can relate to *College Humor* (1933), *College Rhythm* (1934) or *The Collegiate* (1936), now-obscure films once deemed fresh and funny depictions of the age's latest trends. Jack even had his own "Jack Oakie's College" radio show.

Oakie's fame among average viewers rests with two films: W. C. Fields' *Million Dollar Legs* and Chaplin's *The Great Dictator.* While Oakie was little more than a pleasant, typically optimistic lunk in the former, he was excellent in the latter, playing Benzino Napaloni, the Dictator of Bacteria, a hilarious parody of Mussolini. He was nominated for an Academy Award for the role. Oakie's reputation among comedy scholars runs deeper. A well-known scene stealer, Oakie filled his performances with double takes and eye-catching looks of consternation or surprise. His comic gestures and movements influenced Jackie Gleason and several other comedians.

Born in Missouri, raised an Okie from Muskogee, Oklahoma, Jack adopted the nickname for show business. Previously he'd been a New York stockbroker dabbling in amateur theatricals. After some Broadway work as a chorus boy, dancing in *Little Nelly Kelly*, Oakie performed in vaudeville with Lulu McConnell.

Oakie arrived in Hollywood for *The Fleet's In* with Clara Bow (1928). As Oakie aged, the wisecracking side of his amiably pesky college boy personality won out. Opposite Lucille Ball in *The Affairs of Annabel*, he plays a press agent whose cockeyed schemes somehow work out right. "You must've been born on a lucky day," he's told. "Yeah," he cracks, "it was mother's day!"

Jack was lucky in June 1948. Booked on a flight that happened to include his ex-wife Venita Varden, Oakie canceled his reservation when the studio needed him for last minute retakes. The plane crashed and Varden was one of the fatalities. In the 1950s and '60s, Oakie's wise investments allowed him to act only when he wanted to. And he didn't particularly want to. He told writer James Bacon, "I bought A.T.&T when it was called American Smoke Signals." The estate he bought for $30,000 was worth a fortune. He wouldn't even part with nine acres of it for a million: "If I sold off those nine acres, it would mean that I'd have to put trunks on when I go in the swimming pool!"

Oakie's last public appearance was a rare guest spot on a Johnny Carson television special in 1975.

BOOK: *Jack Oakie's Double Takes* (1980)

BROADWAY incl.: *Little Nelly Kelly* (1922), *Innocent Eyes* (1924)

FILMS incl.: *The Fleet's In* (1928), *The Dummy* (1929), *Sweetie Pie* (1929), *Hit the Deck* (1930), *Paramount on Parade* (1930), *The Sap from Syracuse* (1930), *Make Me a Star* (1932), *Million Dollar Legs* (1932), *If I Had a Million* (1932), *Once in a Lifetime* (1932), *Sailor Be Good* (1933), *College Humor* (1933), *Alice in Wonderland* (1933), *Shoot the Works* (1934), *Big Broadcast of 1936* (1935), *King of Burlesque* (1935), *Collegiate* (1936), *That Girl from Paris* (1936), *Super Sleuth* (1937), *The Toast of New York* (1937), *The Affairs of Annabel* (1938), *The Great Dictator* (1940), *Rise and Shine* (1941), *It Happened Tomorrow* (1944), *The Merry Monahans* (1944), *That's the Spirit* (1944), *Bowery to Broadway* (1944), *When My Baby Smiles at Me* (1948), *Around the World in 80 Days* (1959), *The Rat Race* (1960), *Lover Come Back* (1962)

## CARROLL O'CONNOR

### (August 2, 1924–   )

"All in the Family" was the talk of the television world shortly after its premiere in 1971. Based on the British "Till Death Do Us Part," the show shocked American audiences who'd never seen a crackling, issue-oriented sitcom. The most controversial aspect of the show was O'Connor as Archie Bunker—the "lovable bigot" who railed against the changes in his conservative lifestyle. Sometimes his quips were couched in cute malaprops ("Capital punishment is a known detergent for crime"). Mostly they were driven home with hammer-headed zeal: "What about my rights? I know I got a lot going against me. I'm white, I'm Protestant, and I'm hard working—but can't you find one lousy amendment that protects me?"

Arriving during the heated years of antiwar feeling, Richard Nixon, women's lib, the sexual revolution, hippies vs. straights, growing ethnic unrest and fractured family life, "All in the Family" hit every topic hard. People debating these issues suddenly began debating the methods of comedy used by O'Connor and company. Most agreed on one

thing: Archie was true to life, something new in the world of sitcoms.

O'Connor noted, "Most of the fathers you've seen in television comedies are emasculated comic-strip characters that nobody has ever really touched or talked to. They're larger or smaller than life; if they're flawed, they're sweetly flawed. [Archie's] flaws—racism and bigotry—involve him in the real world, not the make-believe. This is a monumental character in American literature, not just a stick figure on television."

Though not known for comedy at the time, O'Connor studied the greats and it helped him create a unique character: "I got a lot of help from Jackie Gleason, Wallace Beery, Jimmy Cagney—I just shamelessly imitated those guys. I knew it wouldn't come out like them, it would come out of me as me."

Born in New York, O'Connor graduated from the National University of Ireland and then earned a master's at the University of Montana. After three years at the Dublin Gate Theatre Company and performances of Shakespeare at the Edinburgh Festival, he appeared on stage in London and Paris before arriving back in New York in 1954. Work was sporadic. For the next three years, he was a substitute English teacher in city public schools. Eventually he established himself as an actor, displaying versatility in stage and film work that rarely provided "star" exposure. O'Connor also wrote scripts and plays, including a three-act comedy *Ladies of Hanover Tower*. His big break was "All in the Family."

As he and the show grew in popularity, O'Connor battled for more money and more control, and there was always the annual question of whether he'd sign for another season. Ironically, he was the last to leave the show, turning it into "Archie Bunker's Place" and netting a record-shattering $250,000 salary per episode. O'Connor won four Emmy awards for "All in the Family" and diversified with a Las Vegas act of songs and comedy. He recorded an album of tunes that included "It's All Over Now," with his lyrics to the music played during the closing credits of "All in the Family."

Most assumed O'Connor would be typed for life as Archie Bunker, even though he took pains to drop the Bunker Queens accent and speak on erudite subjects during talk show appearances. Proving his great talent as an actor, O'Connor swapped the Queens dialect for a Southern twang and had a new hit television series, a belated adaptation of the film *In the Heat of the Night*. He was briefly sidelined by heart surgery but soon returned to the show. "I was feeling fine after the operation and four weeks later they told me they'd done six bypasses. I thought: They did six? I could have croaked! I got a telegram from Burt Lancaster saying 'Did you have to do me one better?'"

In 1991 O'Connor and the rest of the "All in the Family" cast reunited for a television special looking back on their historic show.

AUDIO: *All in the Family* (Atlantic), *All in the Family 2nd Album* (Atlantic), *Archie and Edith Side by Side* (RCA Victor), *For Old P.H.A.R.T.S.* (Audio Fidelity), *Remembering You* (A&M)

BROADWAY: *Ulyssses in Nighttown* (1958), *The Big Knife* (1959), *Heartbreak House* (1963)

FILMS incl.: *Cleopatra* (1963), *What Did You Do in the War Daddy?* (1965), *Not with My Wife You Don't* (1966), *Waterhole Three* (1967), *Marlowe* (1969), *Kelly's Heroes* (1970), *Doctor's Wives* (1971), *Law and Disorder* (1974), *Brass* (1985)

TV: "All in the Family" (1971–79), "Archie Bunker's Place" (1979–83), "In the Heat of the Night" (1988–   )


# OLSEN and JOHNSON

**John Sigvard Olsen, November 6, 1892–January 26, 1963**
**Harold Ogden Johnson, March 5, 1891–February 28, 1962**

"Chic" Johnson and "Ole" Olsen never got much respect, not even from their film company. In *Crazy House*, they walk into the studio full of bravado. Chic pushes the secretary's intercom and tells the boss inside, "Universal's number-one comedy team is here." The boss smiles: "Oh, Abbott and Costello, send them right in!"

The two comedy teams had surface similarity. Both enjoyed corny, burlesque-style gags and were a typical "fat and skinny" combination. The difference, and a big one, was that Bud and Lou had distinct personalities. Tall straight man Olsen was pleasant and competant. Chubby Chic was like any other burlesque comic except for one faint trademark, an annoying giggly laugh.

Olsen, a pianist, was born in Indiana. Violinist Johnson was from Chicago. They met as part of a group called The College Four. They teamed up as a musical duo, adding prop comedy to their repertoire. Gags were everything. Chic would fire a gun into the air and a chicken would plop onto the stage. Olsen: "It's a good thing cows don't fly!" A moment later down came a cow.

Olsen and Johnson assembled more props, more stooges, and created a traveling revue. They tried novelty records (1923's "Oh Gee, Oh Gosh, Oh Golly, I'm in Love") and films (*Oh Sailor Behave*, featuring Chic's "Laughing Song"), but their success remained mainly in the midwestern corn belt. When their *Anything Goes* revue reached Buckeye, Arizona, it coincided with the annual "Helzapoppin'" local carnival. Ole and Chic asked for the rights to use the name (with an extra "l" thrown in during the bargaining) and headed back East, bringing *Hellzapoppin* to Broadway in 1938.

Critics weren't pleased with Olsen and Johnson's low comedy but audiences loved *Hellzapoppin*, the "Laugh-In" of its day. It was a kind of "interactive" evening of madness that careened off the stage right into the laps of the crowd. Actors were planted in various seats to spark uproars in the audience. In a way, Olsen and Johnson were even more chaotic than Broadway's mad Marx Brothers.

Their influence was substantial. *Mad* magazine's love of running gags and crowded cartoon panels full of teeming action and wacky signposts could be traced to *Hellzapoppin*, in which a woman periodically ran through the theater yelling for her husband, a plant was regularly wheeled across the stage (growing larger each time) and gag announcements filled the air. Olsen and Johnson didn't need dynamic personalities when they had all these comic fireworks at their disposal.

*Hellzapoppin* closed after becoming the longest-running musical in Broadway history up to that time. The film version was toned down, but still resembled a visual *Mad* magazine loaded with throwaway sight gags (a sled with "Rosebud" on it) and disruptive signs: "Attention—if Stinky Miller is in the audience—Go Home."

The formula remained for Olsen and Johnson's next show, *Sons o' Fun,* and their next film, *Crazy House,* which was loaded with fast-paced corn ("Want to buy an oven? It's hot!"). There was a good dose of comic anarchy, especially at the finale. Chic shoots the hero and heroine, announcing "This is one picture that isn't going to have a happy ending!" The team's irreverence continued in *Ghost Catchers,* where they did a routine parodying the moving-candle bit in Abbott and Costello's *Hold that Ghost.* They predated Ernie Kovacs with another gag: Chic shoots a picture of a sailboat on his hotel room wall and it sinks. A moment later in comes a sailor, carrying a fish, and saying "I was on that ship!" Ole shoots him, shouting "The captain always goes down with his ship!"

Olsen and Johnson couldn't maintain a film career on gags alone and lacked the strong characters necessary for audience identification. The team faded back to touring shows after their splashy film successes. They were still a big draw around the country. They were briefly on television in 1949 with "Fireball Fun for All," but were better seen and disbelieved live, dazzling the crowd with elaborate props and silly throwaways.

After 1959's *Hellza-Splashin'* aqua-comedy revue, the duo split up. Chic Johnson died in Las Vegas in 1962. Olsen died the following year in Albuquerque, New Mexico, but a short time later his body was flown to Las Vegas and buried alongside that of his partner. Even though quite a few fans never knew which guy was which, the names Olsen and Johnson still mean laughs. And many still remember what they said after every show: "May you live as long as you want. May you laugh as long as you live."

BROADWAY: *Hellzapoppin* (1938), *Sons o' Fun* (1941), *Laffing Room Only* (1944), *Funzapoppin* (1949), *Pardon Our French* (1950), *Hellza-Splashin'* (1959)

FILMS: *Oh Sailor Behave* (1930), *Fifty Million Frenchmen* (1931), *Gold Dust Gertie* (1931), *Country Gentlemen* (1937), *All over Town* (1937), *Hellzapoppin* (1941), *Crazy House* (1943), *Ghost Catchers* (1944), *See My Lawyer* (1945)

TV: "Fireball Fun for All" (1949)

## OUR GANG (See also SPANKY MCFARLAND, ALFALFA SWITZER and BUCKWHEAT THOMAS.)

Reaction to Our Gang has always been mixed. Some people love watching these cute little kids and find the comedy naively charming. Others think they look like robot midgets and find the stagy acting sickening and almost perverse. Whatever the personal reaction, there's no denying the enduring success of Our Gang (later dubbed The Little Rascals when their shorts moved to television).

The series began in 1922, spurred by the success of a black child named Frederic "Sunshine Sammy" Morrison (1913–1989) who had been in many Hal Roach shorts the years before. The early members, in addition to Morrison, were: Mickey Daniels, Jackie Condon, "Fat" Joe Cobb, Peggy Cartwright, Jackie Davis, Farina (Allan Hoskins), and Mary Kornman.

Members of the gang were replaced as they aged. Notable substitutions were Norman "Chubby" Chaney for Joe Cobb, Matthew "Stymie" Beard for Farina and Jean Darling for Mary Kornman. Other new members included Jackie Cooper, Robert Blake (known back then as Mickey Gubitosi) and Dickie Moore. Their adult antagonists included veterans of the Hal Roach studio, Billy Gilbert in various guises and Edgar Kennedy as a sour-faced cop. June Marlowe (who died March 10, 1984) played the lovely schoolteacher Miss Crabtree whom the kids had a crush on. There was also Petey, the dog with the circle around his eye.

The performers most fans remember were active in the 1930s: chubby Spanky McFarland, Scotty Beckett, Darla Hood, Billy "Buckwheat" Thomas and Alfalfa Switzer. The "golden age" for the ageless rascals was between 1934 and 1942 when these kids were part of the gang. Some of the shorts, such as *Beginner's Luck,* a look at a hapless kiddie talent show, or *Teacher's Beau,* in which the kids worry about the arrival of a new teacher, are hard to resist. The series ended completely in 1944.

The Our Gang comedy style was similar to that of the other stars of the Hal Roach Studios, Laurel

Three little comic giants from Our Gang: Spanky McFarland, Darla Hood and Alfalfas Switzer. Photo from the author's collection.

and Hardy, who were known for both leisurely routines and fast slapstick. The kids could be painfully stilted in reciting their lines, plodding around with awkward deliberation. But they could also whip things into a frenzy of slapstick for a finale. Probably the most unique thing about the gang, as a team, was that it was interracial.

"There was no prejudice at Hal Roach's Studio," Sammy Morrison recalled. Though some episodes were tainted with stereotypical dialogue or actions, generally the black child in the group was an equal to his white playmates. When King World bought the syndication rights to the series in 1964 for $300,000, the films were edited to remove moments that seemed offensive and Our Gang became a consistent rerun favorite.

The series also had at least one female member at all times. The most famous of them was Darla Hood (November 4, 1931–June 13, 1979) who made 132 shorts with the group. The gang, as Darla recalled, was for boys only. She wasn't teased or abused—she was usually ignored. They played ball while she played with dolls. She found Alfalfa a spoiled brat, but the gang member she liked least was Petey the dog, "the ugliest black-and-white short-haired dog I ever saw in my life . . . it would have been more fun to work with a cute dog like Daisy in the 'Blondie' series." She outgrew the series in

1945 but remained in show business as a singer. She dubbed the songs for Linda Darnell in *Letter to Three Wives* and for other actresses as well. In the 1960s, semiretired as a wife and mother of two, she made $25,000 singing the mermaid's jingle on "Chicken of the Sea" commercials.

Most of the kids in the series made the transition to non-show biz adulthood quite well, such as Albert "Bob" Guardia, an early member who worked for the Reno Police Department for 22 years. Jackie Cooper went on to star and direct sitcoms. A few died young. Chubby Chaney (1918–36) was so obese it affected his health. He died during glandular surgery, weighing 300 pounds. "Wheezer" Hutchins died during World War II and "Froggy" McLaughlin died in a motorcycle crash. Scotty Beckett, arrested for drunken driving (1954) and drugs (1957), attempted suicide in 1962 and killed himself in 1968. Stymie Beard (January 1, 1925–January 8, 1981) made a few films after leaving the group, including *Stormy Weather* at age 18, but encountered stormy weather after that. He turned to drugs and stole to support his habit. He said he was "too scared to get a gun and hold anybody up." In and out of jail for possession of heroin and petty theft, he joined Synanon in 1966. He found a new job, got married and occasionally took acting assignments on shows such as "Sanford and Son" and "All in the Family." "Sunshine Sammy" Morrison, who died in 1989, joined the "East Side Kids" in his teens and, after working for an aerospace company in California, appeared in episodes of "The Jeffersons" and "Good Times." Eugene "Pineapple" Jackson (who replaced "Sunshine Sammy") joined the Harlem Tuff Kids in the late 1930s and played Uncle Lou on the sitcom "Julia."

BIOGRAPHY: *Our Gang* (Maltin, 1977)

FILMS (shorts) incl.: *Free Eats* (1932), *Spanky* (1932), *Birthday Blues* (1932), *Mike Fright* (1934), *Teacher's Beau* (1935), *Our Gang Follies of 1936* (1935), *Beginner's Luck* (1935), *Teacher's Beau* (1935), *Bored of Education* (1936), *Spooky Hooky* (1936), *Male and Female* (1937), *Our Gang Follies of 1938* (1937), *Hide and Shriek* (1938), *Practical Jokers* (1938), *Alfalfa's Double* (1940), *Robot Wrecks* (1941), *Come Back Miss Pipps* (1941), *Mighty Lak a Goat* (1942)

VIDEOS: incl.: *Little Rascals on Parade; Little Rascals Volumes 1–14*

## JACK PAAR

**(May 1, 1918–   )**

Intriguing and exasperating, mesmerizing and boring, wisecracking one minute and weeping the next, Jack Paar was a minor comic who became a major star during his controversial tenure as host of "The Tonight Show."

Born in Canton, Ohio, Paar recovered from a bedridden year with tuberculosis to become a light-heavyweight wrestling champ in high school. He also wrote for the school newspaper (until he was fired). A radio announcer at 16, he earned most of his experience at WGAR in Cleveland. His four-year stay there ended during Christmas. His boss gave no bonuses that year, claiming he was investing the money in a new railroad invention. Paar was out the door after snapping "I hope it's not the wheel—they already have that."

Jack's early comedy act was built on snide remarks: "A funny thing happened to me on the way to the theater. A sweet old lady walked up to me on the street and asked, 'Will I get an electric shock if I put my foot on that streetcar track?' 'No,' I replied, 'not unless you throw your other foot up over the trolley wire.' " During World War II he entertained the troops with such lectures as "How to Cheat at War" and "How to Avoid Venereal Disease Where There Isn't Any." He joked, "The captain is censoring the mail again this week, so let's cut down on those big words. . . . We're taking the rearview mirrors off the jeeps and putting them on your hats so you can see the lieutenants during combat."

A glowing article on Paar appeared in *Esquire* and netted him a film contract with RKO, sight unseen. When he was seen, the studio sighed. One of his few films was *Love Nest* with Marilyn Monroe. He found her "not as attractive as many and not as likable as most," which seemed to be Hollywood's reaction to Paar. He returned to radio, getting his break as Jack Benny's 1947 summer replacement. He moved to daytime television (1953–56) and had a brief prime-time series.

Taking over for Steve Allen on "The Tonight Show," Paar concentrated on conversation. Stuttery, earnest and intimate, his chatty style was well suited to cozy home viewing. He brought on guests who had rarely been on television in an informal setting: Bobby Kennedy, John F. Kennedy, Fidel Castro and Richard Nixon. He encouraged frisky exchanges among his celebrity guests. In the 1940s people could only read about the witty banter at such places as The Algonquin Hotel, where Dorothy Parker, Robert Benchley and Alexander Woolcott exchanged barbs. Now, before millions, Alexander King, Oscar Levant and Paar exchanged gossip and deadly ad libs.

Unlike the gentlemanly Steve Allen, Paar was not above inviting guests to leave (Mickey Rooney) or making ribald jokes at a guest's expense. When dumpy Elsa Maxwell's bra strap drooped past her dress sleeve, Paar cried out, "Your holster's beginning to show, dear . . . you'll start an avalanche!" While in the 1990s a line like that is more acceptable, back then it was controversial and outrageous.

Quotes from the previous Paar show were on everyone's lips the next morning and the erratic host with the barbed wisecracks and weepy streak of emotion became the talk of the town. His sincerity ("I kid you not" was a catch phrase) was surpassed only by his ego. He showed home movies, feuded with Ed Sullivan and others, and provided the kind of bracing, humorous, unpredictable talk show action that would never be seen again on television, though disciple Dick Cavett often came close.

On February 11, 1960, showing the wear and tear of his job, Paar walked off in midshow, saying "there must be a beter way of making a living than this," leaving his host duties to startled sidekick, announcer Hugh Downs. What had ticked Jack off was the censorship of a mildly risqué story about a Swiss schoolmaster who misunderstood a British visitor's request for information on the "W.C." He thought she meant "wayside chapel," not knowing "W.C." is a British euphemism for the bathroom, or "water closet." Paar quoted the supposed letter: "The W.C. is situated nine miles from the house. . . . It is capable of holding 229 people and is open on Sunday and Thursday only. . . . I would suggest that you come early, although there is plenty of standing room as a rule. . . . A good number of people bring their lunch and make a day of it. . . . It may interest you to know that my daughter was married in the W.C., and it was there that she met her husband. I can remember the rush there was for seats. There were ten people to a seat usually occupied by one. . . ."

Paar returned to the show, but not for long. After a less strenuous prime time talk/variety show, he chose seclusion, travel and semiretirement. A return to the talk show wars in 1973 failed. Paar was out of touch with the times (the guests were older, his home movies staler, his anecdotes longer). After his latest book of anecdotal memoirs had disappointing sales, he appeared as a guest on Merv Griffin's show complaining "I guess the next event in my life will be my death."

Fortunately, his forecasting was premature. Paar participated in NBC's 30th anniversary show, had a high-rated special featuring clips from his old show and was invited back on the talk show circuit, where he proved his ability as an irresistable comic conversationalist with dozens of amusing anecdotes to offer. As the father of the authentic "talk" television show, he was treated with the utmost respect, guesting on Johnny Carson's show in 1987 and Pat Sajak's program in 1989.

AUDIO: *The Best of What's His Name* (Ramrod), *Jack Paar Tonight* (NBC)

BOOKS: *I Kid You Not* (1960); *My Saber is Bent* (1961); *Three on a Toothbrush; P.S., Jack Paar* (1983)

FILMS incl.: *Easy Living* (1949), *Love Nest* (1951)

TV: "Up to Paar" (1952), "Bank on the Stars" (1953), "The Jack Paar Program" (1954), "The Jack Paar Show" (1957–62), "The Jack Paar Program" (1962–65), "ABC Late Night" (1973)

## MICHAEL PALIN (See also MONTY PYTHON'S FLYING CIRCUS.)

### (May 5, 1943–   )

The most boyishly naughty member of Monty Python's Flying Circus, Michael Palin exhibited a sly grin and a cheerfully insane sense of fantasy. His most popular characters included a manic version of Cardinal Richelieu, a happy transvestite lumberjack and Ximinez, the frisky torturer who appeared whenever anyone used the catch phrase "I didn't expect the Spanish Inquisition."

Like many a Python character, Ximeniz was an adult whose childishness was ridiculously obvious. He took delight in listing all his tortures, or trying to: "Nobody expects the Spanish Inquisition! Our chief weapon is surprise . . . surprise and fear. Fear and surprise. Our *two* weapons are fear and surprise—and ruthless efficiency. Our *three* weapons are fear and surprise and ruthless efficiency and an almost fanatical devotion to the pope. Our *four* . . . no . . . I'll come in again. . . ."

Palin recalls, "I always used to overplay everything, go absolutely over the top. Then, after some criticism from the other Pythons—we knew each other well enough to be rude to each other—I drew in my horns a little." For John Cleese he often played amusingly understated straight parts, such as the pet shop owner trying to avoid giving a refund to his customer, even though the man was sold a dead parrot. Oddly enough, in his solo career, Palin at first moved away from the sparkling, puckish parts that made him so popular with Python and chose more subdued roles, underplaying his part as the dull boy Eric Olthwaite in the 1977 to '79 "Ripping Yarns" television series and starring as a clergyman in the film *The Missionary*.

Palin attended Brasenose College, Oxford, and at the Oxford University Dramatic Society met up with future Python member Terry Jones. They performed together in 1964's Oxford Revue and after graduation wrote for "The Ken Dodd Show," "The Two Ronnies" and "The Frost Report." Along with Eric Idle, they wrote and co-starred in "Do Not Adjust Your Set." Palin and Jones also starred in a six-part series, "The Complete and Utter History of Britain."

Aside from their subsequent Monty Python work, Palin and Jones wrote a 1973 BBC special about a man falling into a vat of chocolate, and in 1975 Palin co-starred in a television version of "Three Men in a Boat." Then came "Ripping Yarns." One memorable episode took a look at life in a rather rough boy's school; the students are allowed to be nailed to the walls, and it's an "amazing bit of luck" to be allowed out of school for a while after being shot in the stomach.

While Palin's films (including *Jabberwocky, Brazil* and *The Missionary*) failed to find an audience beyond cultists, he had hits with *Time Bandits*, in which he played two roles, and *A Fish Called Wanda* with John Cleese. Though he got laughs from stuttering, and his makeup included facial scratches and bandages, the basic mature Palin style was evident. He played a "dogsbody," bullied and abused, forced to endure everything from near suffocation via french fries up his nose to the painful overacting by co-star Kevin Kline, until he finally gets his revenge. In 1990 the mellowed comedian starred in a mild seven-part documentary on the travails of travel, "Around the World in 80 Days." It appeared on cable television in America.

AUDIO: *Funny Game, Football* (Charisma), *A Poke in the Eye with a Sharp Stick* (Transatlantic), *The Secret Policeman's Ball* (Island)
BOOKS: *Bert Fegg's Nasty Book of Knowledge, Ripping Yarns* (1991), *More Ripping Yarns, Time Bandits, The Missionary, Small Harry and the Toothache Pills, The Limerick Book, Cyril and the House of Commons, Cyril and the Dinner Party, The Mirrorstone, Around the World in 80 Days* (1990)
FILMS incl.: *Jabberwocky* (1977), *Time Bandits* (1981), *The Missionary* (1982), *A Private Function* (1984), *Brazil* (1985), *A Fish Called Wanda* (1988)
VIDEO: *Saturday Night Live: Michael Palin*

## FRANKLIN PANGBORN

### (Janauary 23, 1893–July 20, 1958)

As a specialist in prissy and fussy comic characters, Franklin Pangborn seemed to spend most of his career in a snit. With his lips pursed tightly and his eyes glaring balefully, he was the foil for everyone from W. C. Fields and Jack Benny in movies to Jack Paar on television.

His most memorable role was Snoopington the bank examiner in Fields' *The Bank Dick*. His straight-laced devotion to duty made him the perfect patsy for the wicked Fields, who did everything from break his pince-nez glasses to nauseate him with a dose of heavily tainted liquor. Pangborn's ridiculous resilience and insistence on coming back for more made the laughs bigger every time. Whether playing an irritated landlord *(George Washington Slept Here)* or the chairman of the reception committee *(Hail the Conquering Hero)*, Pangborn was always the disapproving model of propriety, ready to maintain dignity at all cost.

Pangborn's career began on stage. He co-starred with Nazimova in *The Marionettes* and with Pauline Frederick in *Joseph and His Brethren*. In the 1930s and '40s he settled down in Hollywood, living quietly among the discreet gay clique that included William Haines and Jimmy Shields, making his trademark appearances in film comedies.

Though his prime work in films was in the '40s, Pangborn was still around in the '50s. He was Jack Paar's first announcer on "The Tonight Show." Paar loved "that gay little guy . . . I thought it would be a riot to have someone like him be the announcer. It was funny but only for shock. It didn't last more than two weeks because dear Franklin could not ad lib in character. He was an actor who could only read lines. We had no script, so back he went to Hollywood. And then Hugh Downs took over."

Pangborn's comic pangs, caused by his perpetual petulance, endure because he endured. His stubborn dignity made him the perfect target for comic antagonists; but they, and the audience, would not have had much fun if he ever gave in.

FILMS incl.: *Getting Gertie's Garter* (1927), *The Sap* (1929), *Lady of the Pavements* (1929), *Cheer Up and Smile* (1930), *International House* (1933), *Design for Living* (1933), *Imitation of Life* (1934), *She Couldn't Take It* (1935), *$1,000 a Minute* (1935), *Mr. Deeds Goes to Town* (1936), *The Luckiest Girl in the World* (1936), *My Man Godfrey* (1936), *Step Lively Jeeves* (1937), *Stage Door* (1937), *Topper Takes a Trip* (1939), *The Bank Dick* (1940), *Where Did You Get That Girl* (1941), *Never Give a Sucker an Even Break* (1941), *Sullivan's Travels* (1941), *George Washington Slept Here* (1942), *The Palm Beach Story* (1942), *Crazy House* (1943), *His Butler's Sister* (1943), *Hail the Conquering Hero* (1944), *The Horn Blows at Midnight* (1945), *Down Memory Lane* (1949), *Mad Wednesday* (1947), *The Story of Mankind* (1957), *Oh Men Oh Women!* (1957)

# PARKYAKARKUS

## (Harry Einstein, 1904–November 24, 1958)

Among the plentiful ethnic comedians on radio was the comical Greek "Parkyakarkus." He was Harry Einstein, who had earlier in his career performed under the name Harry Parke. Most of Parkyakarkus's best work was on radio's "Eddie Cantor Show." He turned up in Eddie's film *Strike Me Pink* as well. In one of the film's highlights Parkyakarkus shows his strength by tearing a phone book in half. "Wait a minute!" shouts Cantor. "You're tearing one page at a time!" Parkyakarkus: "I ain't in a hurry."

In 1958 "Parky" appeared on the dais at a Friar's Roast for Lucille Ball and Desi Arnaz. As himself (sans accent) he got bigger laughs than most of the famous speakers. Though some of the in jokes might

not seem hysterical now, they led to huge laughs and table-banging that night. With the audience laughter in parentheses he welcomes. . .

My very dear and very close friends Miss Louise Balls (laughter) and Danny Arnaz (laughter). Danny (loud laughs from Desi), we are particularly delighted to welcome you into our club, because we know what a prominent club man you are (laughter). I have the great satisfaction of belonging to several exclusive clubs with him. Such as The Diners Club (laughter), the Book of the Month Club (laughter) and the Automobile Club of Southern California (laughter). I tried to get into the Los Angeles Country Club—but they don't take actors (laughter, thunderous applause). But you must not think that the Friar's Club is an easy club to get into. Quite to the contrary, it is most difficult. Before a prospective candidate is even issued an application, he must first satisfy us, beyond any question of a doubt, that he is either a resident (laughter) or a nonresident of the State of California (laughter, table banging, applause). He then must be proposed by and then vouched for by at least two men who are listed in the phone book (laughter). . . . After the candidate is deemed to be worthy, he is then allowed to write out a check in the amount of the initiation fee. But he is still not yet a Friar. There is a further waiting period (laughter). We wait for the ink to dry on the check (laughter). But in spite of all this kidding we have managed to put together a pretty good club made up of the very cream of show business people . . . outstanding doctors, many famous lawyers, several fine judges and quite a few defendants (laughter, applause). . . . If one should be interested in nature, we have a splendid bird-watching group. No matter what time you come into our club, you'll always see two or three of our members standing around looking for pigeons (laughter, applause). So Desi, we sincerely hope that you'll be using the facilities of our club very often. And Lucy, while ladies' nights at the Friars are traditionally Thursdays and Saturdays, we love you so you can come any time. Thank you very much."

"Parky" received lavish applause. Art Linkletter, the master of ceremonies, stood up and said,

"I've seen Harry at a dozen of these Friar's benefits and affairs. Every time he finishes, I always ask myself why isn't he on the air in prime time." The crowd applauded again. They were still applauding when Parkyakarkus slumped against Milton Berle and then leaned forward. Berle shouted to Art Linkletter, "Is there a doctor in the house?

The audience laughed—until a few doctors rushed to the dais. The stricken comedian's wife rushed from the audience and put a nitroglycerine pill in his mouth. An ambulance took him to the hospital, but it was too late. Back at the Friar's Club, Lucille Ball was too overcome to speak. Desi Arnaz told the crowd, "This was an evening that comes to you once in a lifetime. It means so much, then all at once it doesn't mean a damn thing."

Two of Parkyakarkus' four sons became comedians—Albert Einstein (as Albert Brooks) and Bob Einstein (better known as his character "Super Dave Osborne"). Neither were at the Friar's event, but a recording of the show is a cherished possession. Brooks said in 1991, "The interesting thing to me was that he finished. He could have died in the middle. He could have done it on the way over there. But he didn't. He finished. And he was as good as he'd ever been in his life."

AUDIO: *Parkyakarkus* (REM)

FILMS incl.: *Strike Me Pink* (1936), *The Life of the Party* (1937), *Night Spot* (1938), *Glamour Boy* (1940), *The Yanks Are Coming* (1942), *Sweethearts of the USA* (1944), *Earl Carroll's Vanities* (1945), *Out of This World* (1945)

## PAT PAULSEN

### (July 6, 1927–    )

In the early 1960s, gaunt and solemn Pat Paulsen carved out a modest career as an offbeat humorist and songwriter. His one-liners were strange ("I took biology two years in a row just to eat the specimens"). His nonroutines were weird, such as his demonstration of "finger shadows." He'd shove his hand in front of a light and project "fist with arm attached."

After dropping out of San Francisco City College, Paulsen had struggled as an actor in small theater productions until he began to perform solo in stand-up comedy. He met The Smothers Brothers while performing in Pasadena and sold them a novelty song, "(I Fell in a Vat of) Chocolate."

It was on television's "The Smothers Brothers Comedy Hour" that viewers got to know Paulsen through his no-nonsense reading of guest "editorials." On gun control: "Without guns, how are we gonna shoot anybody? We need guns. You never can tell when you're walking down the street and you'll spot a moose. Suppose a man comes home early and finds another man with his wife? What's he supposed to do? Poison him? . . . . Guns are not the real problem. The real problem is bullets. . . ." Once he declared, "We can win the war on poverty—by shooting 400 beggars a week."

His catch phrase, in rebuttal to those who disagreed with him, was a hilariously unsmiling cry of "Picky, picky, picky!" He won an Emmy for his work on "The Smothers Brothers Comedy Hour" in 1968 and went on to greater glory as the brothers' candidate for the presidency. Born in South Bend, Washington, he joined the marines at 17 and served in Guam and in China.

Paulsen's stand-up comedy speeches were so successful, he actually got some votes in the 1968 presidential election. A comedy special he made destroyed the opposition on television that night—a paid political broadcast from Hubert Humphrey. Later Pat recalled, "Humphrey looked me in the eye and said I cost him the election, that all those write-in votes probably would have gone to him." In 1970 Pat starred in his own brief comedy series and in 1972 the semiserious star got 1% of the vote in the Republicans' New Hampshire primary.

Paulsen's comedy career took many turns over the years. He owned a summer theater in Michigan and from 1975 on starred there in *Harvey, Beyond Therapy, God's Favorite* and many other shows. In films, Paulsen's sad-sack face might have made him a popular "loser" type in films, but his cynical, sarcastic attitude clearly rejected sympathy. His curmudgeonly visage made him an interesting choice as the veteran cop opposite Murray Langston in the film *Night Patrol*, a parody in the *Police Academy* mold.

In the 1970s he formed the Picky-Q-Picky ranch in Cloverdale, California and by 1980, as "The Pat Paulsen Vineyards," produced respected wines. Unfortunately, the '80s were an unhappy time for the hangdog comedian. The Internal Revenue Service decided to disavow a tax shelter and socked him for $270,000; he was soon in debt for over a million dollars. According to *Entertainment Tonight,* his third ex-wife "bilked hundreds of thousands of dollars" from him and was ordered to make restitution and pay him $233,337. He said, "I loved her and I trusted her . . . I shouldn't have trusted her."

Paulsen confided to Tom Smothers, "If I could just get the money and the women straightened out, the rest of my life would be easy." Smothers answered, "The rest of you life? After money and women what else is there?"

Paulsen has fought the debts with a hectic schedule of nightclub appearances and acting roles in local stage productions. And every four years he can always be counted on to wage a high-profile comic presidential campaign. His offbeat comedy and put-ons continue to confuse people who aren't sure if he is liberal or conservative, kidding or serious. He replies, "It's been my theme in life to confuse people. They deserve it. It's my whole reason for living."

AUDIO: *Pat Paulsen for President* (Mercury), *Live at the Ice House* (Mercury), *The Hexorcist* (ABC)

FILMS incl.: *Where Were You When the Lights Went Out?* (1968), *Harper Valley PTA* (1978), *Blood Suckers from Outer Space* (1984), *Night Patrol* (1985), *They Still Call Me Bruce* (1987)

TV: "The Smothers Brothers Comedy Hour" (1967–69), "The Summer Smothers Brothers Show" (1968), "Pat Paulsen's Half a Comedy Hour" (1970), "The Smothers Summer Show" (1970), "Joey and Dad" (1975), "The Smothers Brothers Show" (1975), "The Smothers Brothers Show" (1988–89)

VIDEO: *Pat Paulsen on Wine*

## JACK PEARL

### (October 29, 1895–December 25, 1982)

One of the most amusing German dialect comics of his generation, Jack Pearl was "Baron Munchausen," or simply "The Baron," teller of tall tales. His ridiculous lies would have even outraged the original Baron von Munchausen. When the whoppers got progressively more outlandish, his straight man would protest. And Jack would fire back his catch phrase: "Vas you dere, Sharlie?"

Pearl grew up on the Lower East Side of New York City. As a child he co-starred in one of the many vaudeville versions of Gus Edwards' "School Days" sketch. Walter Winchell and George Jessel were also in the cast, which drew laughs from various ethnic characters in the classroom. When another boy, Danny Murphy, left, Jack inherited his role, which required a German accent. It was in 1930, after a brief teaming with Ben Bard and a series of stage shows, that Pearl worked his accent into "The Baron," with Cliff Hall as his straight man.

For a while audiences couldn't get enough of his eccentric humor and ridiculously exaggerated German accent. "I went to correspondence school," he'd say, trilling the "r" and pronouncing "school" as "shkool." "They threw me out from there . . . I played hooky." "You played hooky from a correspondence school? How is that possible?" "I sent them an empty envelope!"

One of the hottest comics of the early 1930s, Pearl starred on Broadway, had his own radio show and was groomed for film stardom in *Meet the Baron.* Jimmy Durante was his flustered sidekick in that one, with The Three Stooges in supporting roles. Unfortunately, the film showed his character to be amusing but one-dimensional.

As the '30s wore on, Pearl wore out his welcome, his outrageous accent out of date and in questionable taste considering the rise of Nazi Germany. Ironically, he'd been afraid to disappoint the crowd by not exclaiming "Vas you dere, Sharlie?" at some point during every sketch.

Pearl was hoping to turn his luck around with *Yokel Boy* on Broadway. Phil Silvers was a co-star. Silvers claimed in his autobiography that preview audiences were "bored with Dutch dialect at $4 a seat" and that Pearl was ruining the show. During one performance, Silvers started marching around the stage. "Vat iss dat?" the distracted Pearl had to ask. "The parade passing you by," snapped Silvers. It was true; Silvers replaced Pearl as the star of *Yokel Boy.*

Silvers later regretted his cruelty, but the cruel truth was that Pearl had fewer and fewer opportunities for work in the 1950s and '60s. It was a sad fate for the comedian; as The Baron, Pearl was a lovable character, forever getting comically exasperated when people questioned his fanciful stories and corny jokes. For some old-fashioned laughs and nostalgia, Jackie Gleason used him on his old variety show; but otherwise the television horizon was barren for The Baron. The golden age of radio turned out to have been his golden age as well.

AUDIO: *They're Still Laughing* (Capital), *Golden Age of Comedy* (Evolution)

BROADWAY incl.: *The Dancing Girl* (1923), *A Night in Paris* (1926), *Artists and Models* (1927), *Pleasure Bound* (1929), *International Revue* (1930), *Ziegfeld Follies* (1931), *Pardon My English* (1933), *One Flight Down* (1937), *All for All* (1943)

FILMS incl.: *Meet the Baron* (1933), *Hollywood Party* (1934)

## MINNIE PEARL

### (Sarah Ophelia Colley, October 25, 1912–   )

A dowdy wardrobe, a straw hat with the price tag dangling from it and a hearty cry of "How-deeee!" were the trademarks of country's classic comedienne, Minnie Pearl. Much of her humor contrasted her sunny, naive personality and her plain looks. "It may not show," she'd tell the audience, beaming brightly, "but love has kicked me in the face!"

Born in Centerville, Tennessee, Minnie attended Ward-Belmont College in Nashville and studied drama. She became an acting teacher and in 1934 joined a touring group, appearing in dozens of plays. In 1938 she performed some monologues at the Pilots Club, in Aiken, South Carolina, unveiling a new character, a comical, man-starved spinster type. She seemed ready to hit the big time, but after her father's death, Minnie had to return home to care for her mother.

She earned money by giving singing lessons but, at 28, lost the momentum in pursuing her career. Her big break came when she revived her comic spinster character for an appearance at a local bank-

er's convention. Many influential people were in the audience, and later she was invited to appear on WSM radio and "The Grand Ole Opry."

Minnie went on to become the top woman in country comedy, opening her shows with a sincere and cheery "How-deeee! I'm just so proud to be here!" She did get laughs from playing a stereotypical spinster, but Minnie (who married World War II flying ace Henry Cannon in 1947) told all kinds of comfy, corny jokes. Like Red Skelton, her character was strong enough, and lovable enough, to insure a fresh welcome long after some jokes had gone just a little bit stale. She admitted in 1991, "People say 'I know your punchlines.' Maybe it's because they do know them they feel safe. They know I won't throw 'em a curve."

Fans feared the worst after she underwent breast cancer surgery and a mastectomy in 1985, and a second mastectomy only six months later. She staged a comeback and the grateful ex-patient worked for the Nashville Centennial Medical Center. A new facility was named for her: the Sarah Cannon Cancer Center. Comparing herself and her alter ego, she said in 1990, "I feel really good now. You know, Sarah Cannon may have aged a bit, but Minnie Pearl's eternally young."

Invited to appear on the 1988 cable broadcast of *Comic Relief III* Minnie told the same kinds of jokes that had folks laughing on "The Grand Old Opry" television show and the long-running "Hee-Haw" series. She talked about her uncle: "He ain't a failure, he just started at the bottom—and he likes it there!" Then she mentioned her brother: "He is the kind of a feller, if you see him pushin' a wheelbarrow, he'll have it upside down. You say, 'Turn it over.' He'll say, 'Uh, uh! They'll put something in it!' " And then she talked about the current state of her lovelife: "I'm in love! I'm in love with Pee-Wee Herman! He called me a breath of spring! Well-he didn't use them words. He said I looked like 'the end of a hard winter!' "

AUDIO: *Lookin' fer a Feller* (Nashville), *Howdy!* (Sunset, reissued by Everest and by Pickwick as *Laugh Along*), *Howdee!* (Starday), *America's Beloved* (Starday), *Country Music Story* (Starday), *Cousin Minnie Pearl* (Starday)

AUTOBIOGRAPHY: *Minnie Pearl: An Autobiography*

FILMS incl.: *Forty Acre Feud* (1965), *Second Fiddle to a Steel Guitar* (1965), *That Tennessee Beat* (1966)

TV: "Grand Ole Opry" (1955–56), "Hee Haw" (1969–75)

## HAROLD PEARY (See THE GREAT GILDERSLEEVE.)

## PENN and TELLER

**Penn Jillette, March 5, 1955–
Ray Teller, February 14, 1948–**

Master magicians of hip, shock comedy, Penn and Teller get laughs with their self-described "cruel tricks" played on the audience and on each other. Their national fame began with a series of appearances on David Letterman's late-night television show. Instead of a rabbit coming out of a top hat, the unorthodox magicians unleashed thousands of cockroaches. And instead of flawlessly performing the old cut-the-woman-in-half trick, the tall, grinningly sadistic Penn seemingly cut right into his little partner Teller, spilling quarts of stage blood and animal organs onto the floor. On the same show Teller stuck out his tongue, which was neatly snipped in half with a scissors as blood poured down the side of his face.

In the 1960s and '70s, magicians on television variety shows were always corny. The ones who deliberately joked up their act with mistakes were often cornier. Penn and Teller turned it all around by appealing to a cooler crowd, the audience that shuddered and laughed at each new put-on and wondered "Who *are* these guys?"

Teller, the short, silent partner, was born in Philadelphia. "I was a loner kid who started to hide myself away and do weird things." He developed a magic act that was a lot more interesting to him than his day job for six years, teaching Latin at Lawrence High School near Trenton, New Jersey. He stopped speaking on stage early on. "If you shut up and are very intense people feel foolish heckling you."

Penn, born in Greenfield, Massachusetts, attended Greenfield High School and then toiled as dishwasher in a Howard Johnson's restaurant. He turned to street juggling and magic. When he and

Teller teamed, they decided to modernize the standard stunts. Said Penn, "Magicians are guys with bad haircuts, treating some women badly, treating animals badly, relying entirely on props. . . . I thought magic and juggling were cool at the age of 12 and uncool at 15. Women think it's a dorky thing to be, and pulling out a deck of cards on a date would be a major handicap. . . . If a women realizes she's out with a magician, the date's over. Give Bruce Springsteen a deck of cards, and give me a guitar, and see which of us scores quicker."

As the act developed, the six-foot-six, burly but goofy-looking Penn became the slick spokesman for the group and the slight, mild-mannered Teller went mute. Their first major success was an off-Broadway show in April 1985. It won them an Obie Award and brought them to Broadway in December 1987. Keeping the audience off balance—sometimes laughing, sometimes gasping—Penn and Teller often satirized the entire magic genre. Along with levitation and fire eating, there was comic sadism—Teller flailing upside down in a straitjacket while Penn read "Casey at the Bat." Their parody of a famous Houdini trick had Teller submerged in a tank of water, drowning while his oblivious partner did card tricks. Another bit featured Penn's knife juggling. "I like a front row with guts," he'd leer. The cheerfully arrogant magician would sometimes preface a bit with: "This isn't a very good piece but I bothered to learn it and you're certainly going to watch it."

The duo starred in their own 1987 Showtime TV special, *Penn and Teller's Invisible Thread* and an Emmy-winning PBS offering, "Penn and Teller Go Public." They reached for film stardom with *Penn and Teller Get Killed,* but it turned out to be a confusing, darkly offbeat mix of suspense and subtle in jokes.

They went on to create do-it-yourself videos and books so fans could perpetrate dirty tricks on their friends. On their video, they had a segment where a man reads the news—until his image is literally wiped right off the screen via special effects. All the home magician had to do was put on the VCR, pretend it was a real newscast and then casually spray the screen with a glass cleaner and start wiping at the appropriate time.

Teller likes the idea of people fooling their friends, but figures fooling all of the people all of the time was even better: "A very important thing for people to see and learn is that Penn and I, who are not particularly intelligent, can take an audience of well-educated people and twist them around our fingers. We so thoroughly distort what appears to be reality that they should leave the theater thinking, 'if these two bozos can do it, imagine what somebody like Reagan can do.'"

BOOK: *Cruel Tricks for Dear Friends* (1989)
BROADWAY: *Penn and Teller* (1987), *The Refrigerator Tour* (1991)
FILMS incl.: *My Chauffeur* (1986), *Penn and Teller Get Killed* (1989)
VIDEO: *Cruel Tricks for Dear Friends*

## JOE PENNER

**(Josef Pinter, November 11, 1904–January, 10, 1941)**

He had some of the most popular catch phrases in radio. He had one of radio's funniest voices. He was a big star. But today, very few remember Joe Penner.

One reason is his humor was mostly in his delivery. Unlike a Fred Allen, he hasn't survived as a quotable wit. And that delivery, as funny as it was, became tiresome quickly. Penner's unique voice was goofy and nasal, the words slushing out with a juicy lisp. Several mimics adapted it for cartoon characters. There's a bit of Penner in Warner Brothers, "Sylvester the Cat" and much more in Hanna-Barbera's "Secret Squirrel." The silly voice helped him put over ridiculous jokes. A typical radio scene had him about to enter a hotel. He reads a sign: "The Fractured Arms Hotel—stop here, we'll give you a break!" Then he gets into an argument with the desk clerk. Clerk: "I'll give you a beautiful suite of rooms." Penner: "Well, I can't take it. . . . Doctor's orders! I have to stay away from suites!"

Born in Budapest, Penner was nine when he arrived in America. His father worked in an automobile factory in Detroit. Penner worked in burlesque and vaudeville, scoring a hit in 1926's *Greenwich Village Follies* on the road. He turned up on radio on Rudy Vallee's show with his nonsense and

catch phrases, and was soon hosting "The Bakers' Broadcast" in 1933.

Some of Penner's catch phrases were authentically funny, such as his perturbed whine "Don't ever dooooo that!" and his elongated insult "You natttt-thhhhty man!" He also had a "hee-yuk, yuk" laugh and the non sequitur question, "Wanna buy a duck?" He used it in this typical example of aggressive nonsense: "Do you wanna buy a duck?" "What?" "Do you wanna buy a duck?" "No, I don't want any ducks. . . ." "Well, do you wanna buy a duck's egg?" "I don't eat duck eggs." "These ain't for eating—they're for throwing!"

By 1936, after several top-10 years, Penner's ratings began slipping badly. There was no chance for him in films. Lucille Ball played the dumpy little comic's wife in *Go Chase Yourself*. As she said in the movie: "Oh, he's just nondescript. That's the best way to describe him." Worse than that, his character was an unsympathetic, obtuse dope. Physically he lacked the charm of a Lou Costello or even a Frank McHugh. In *The Day the Bookies Wept*, he played a neuter who'd rather supervise his pet pigeons than kiss his bride-to-be Betty Grable! The plot wasn't bad (his bum horse races superbly only when drunk), but viewers had to agree with him when he muttered, "Sometimes I think people are dumber than human beings."

The man who once earned over $13,000 for one week's work in vaudeville struggled to keep his radio show going through format changes, sponsor changes and even a "Penners of Park Avenue" sitcom format. He was still fairly young, but seemed to be wearing down with strain and worry. He hoped to change his luck with the Broadway-bound *Yokel Boy*. One night he and his wife went out with Martha Raye and the show's general manager, Robert Crawford. After dinner, they stayed out till 3 A.M. The next morning Mrs. Penner let Joe sleep and went out. At 4:40 P.M. Crawford called and Mrs. Penner back from her walk, went to wake Joe. Crawford heard her scream over the phone. Joe Penner never woke up. He had died of a heart attack some time during the night.

FILMS incl.: *College Rhythm* (1933), *New Faces of 1937* (1937), *Go Chase Yourself* (1938), *Mr. Doodle Kicks Off* (1938), *The Day the Bookies Wept* (1939), *Mil-*

lionaire *Playboy* (1940), *Glamour Boy* (1940), *The Boys from Syracuse* (1940)

# EMO PHILIPS

## (Philip Soltanec, February 7, 1956–   )

One of the strangest stand-up comedians to emerge in the 1980s, Emo Philips created his own unique character that some, groping in vain for comparison, likened to a combination of the awkward child-man Pee-Wee Herman and the spacey wit Steven Wright. Like Pee-Wee, Emo took innocence to an alarming Village Idiot extreme. Like Wright, clever one-liners were a trademark: "I'm not a fatalist, but even if I were what could I do about it?"

Wearing pajama tops and baggy pants—or perhaps one of his thrift shop items such as a fancy gold smoking jacket and mismatched slacks—beanpole-thin Emo slowly lopes onto the stage like a shy child, blinking his wide eyes, sleepily running his hand over his forehead and his unique skewed Dutch boy hairstyle. Using a breathy, somewhat high and hollow voice, his cadence uneven and slow, he talks about his misfortunes: "I was in a bar a few nights ago, moving from stool to stool, trying to get lucky . . . but . . . there wasn't gum under any of them . . . and I heard giggling behind me . . . I turn around. These two guys, for the last half hour or so, have been throwing darts into my head. . . . It's a good thing I heard them. . . . I said . . . 'Look, you bums.' I was angry now. I said, 'As soon as this game is over, hit the road.' As I left the bar . . . one thing stuck in my mind. That is, that there's lots of weirdos in this world."

The sublimely weird comedian was born in Chicago but grew up in Downer's Grove, Illinois with sisters, Kiki and Susan. His father was a postal worker who died in 1978. Emo left the University of Illinois in 1976 and began performing. He went through several name changes (he felt "Soltanec" sounded too satanic) before arriving at Phil Kidney and then Emo Philips. "The way I started out, I had three minutes and went to a small place and I tried it out. One thing out of that three minutes got a laugh, so I kept that one thing and the next day I wrote three more minutes. Maybe two things got a laugh. And I kept this process going until after two

years I had half an hour of good material. Then I fell down a staircase and hit my head and forgot everything and had to start over."

At first, audiences simply responded to the strangeness, laughing at the forlorn child-man's hapless tales. But along the way Emo began to assert his sly wit and an undercurrent of anger. A report on being stopped for a traffic ticket turns into bizarre but pointed satire. "I said, 'Officer, I'm taking my mom to the hospital. She OD'd on reducing pills.' He said, 'I don't see any woman with you.' I said, 'I'm too late. . . .' He said, 'You're under arrest. You have the right to remain silent. Do you wish to retain that right?' I thought, 'Ooooh! A paradox. . . .' " Told to walk a straight line, he innocently remarks, "Well, Officer Pythagoras, the closest you could ever come to achieving a straight line would be by making an electroencephalogram of your own brain wave."

Like his friend Judy Tentua, Emo usually is in character for his interviews, deflecting questions with the same innocence and slyness used on stage. Asked by the author to analyze his absurdist humor and his combination of tragedy and comedy, he sighed, rubbed his eyes and said, "There's always a fine line between comedy and tragedy. Especially when I do a show. And boredom is always an undercurrent. I never thought of myself as unique really. I just try to talk about life and help others. I want people to see my show and walk out afterwards saying to themselves, 'Well, we got that over with.' "

AUDIO: *E=MO2* (Epic), *Live from the Hasty Pudding Theater* (Epic)
FILMS incl.: *UHF* (1989)
VIDEO: *Emo Philips Live at Hasty Pudding*

# BRONSON PINCHOT

## (May 20, 1959–   )

One of the few to steal a scene from Eddie Murphy, Bronson Pinchot's career took off after he played Serge, a particularly effete art dealer in *Beverly Hills Cop.* He owed his success partially to a makeup woman on the set of an earlier, more obscure film, *The Last Resort.* Pinchot was entranced by her Israeli accent and described how she "set out to become the most elegant, fashionable, sexiest, mysterious Mata Hari who ever lived. She had developed a speech that was so elegant and syrupy. . . . I did a deliberately imperfect re-creation of it."

Despite the exotic sound of this and Pinchot's subsequent characters, he was not born in Europe but in New York. He was raised in California. His parents were divorced in 1965 and the psychological pain was matched by physical misery. His mother had to go on welfare between typing jobs. "I never sat down in a restaurant until I was seventeen. We were just lucky not to be in a ditch."

After graduating first in his high school class and attending Yale, Pinchot appeared in off-Broadway roles and had his first good luck finding a part in the film *Risky Business.* That led to other small roles, then *Beverly Hills Cop* and instant acclaim. Since the Serge character was obviously homosexual and foreign, Pinchot was up for similar roles on television. After playing a gay character on the sitcom "Sara," he became the comical immigrant Balki Bartokomous on the hit show "Perfect Strangers."

Based on the traditional foreigner of Bill Dana's "José Jimenez" and Andy Kaufman's "Latka," the humor was often in misunderstanding American language and customs. The goat herder from the mythical Mediterranean country of Mypos could turn a phrase and twist it too. "It ain't over," he once declared, "till the fat lady eats!"

The name Balki is a Pinchot in joke. As a nine-year-old, his sister called a "balcony" a "balki," much to the annoyance of other members of the family. He admitted that the character "looks at the world like a four-year-old . . . mentally he has not been touched by that veil of self-consciousness that happens when you're four and a half or five years old." What made Balki more rounded and interesting beyond the humor of the naive foreigner was his childlike honesty and directness and a thoughtful, caring interest in his friends. The traits belonged to Pinchot, who offstage displayed serious interests and collected exotic antiques and literary letters.

Aside from verbal humor, Pinchot, along with co-star Mark Linn-Baker, showed skill in visual humor, displaying comic flexibility in an episode about learning how to skate and fine timing in a show that featured them as reluctant orderlies trying to change a bed with a fat patient lying unconscious in it.

Pinchot's first major starring film role came in *Second Sight,* when he played a channeler trying to help solve a case. The biggest laugh occurred during filming. Accidentally walking on broken glass, Pinchot began cursing, forgetting that the scene he was shooting was being filmed in the Cathedral of the Holy Cross in Boston. The embarrassment ended when the archbishop tossed him and the crew out. "I don't blame the guy," Pinchot said later. "Thank God he didn't see the scene where I psychically determine that the cardinal has hemorrhoids. That was a blessing." The film was not a success and *Zoya's Apartment,* a 1990 stage production in New York, also failed to impress critics. But Pinchot's popularity on television did not waver, nor did the impression of many that he still shows a great deal of talent and potential for films and television in the future.

BROADWAY: *Poor Little Lambs* (1982), *Zoya's Apartment* (1990)

FILMS incl.: *Risky Business* (1983), *The Flamingo Kid* (1984), *After Hours* (1985), *The Last Resort* (1985), *Beverly Hills Cop* (1985), *Second Sight* (1989), *Blame It on the Bellboy* (1992)

TV: "Sara" (1985), "Perfect Strangers" (1986–  )

## MINERVA PIOUS

### (March 5, 1903–March 17, 1979)

"Ahh, Mrs. Nussbaum." "You were expectin' maybe Emperor Shapiro-hito?" One of the funniest dialect comics on radio, Minerva Pious played Mrs. Pansy Nussbaum in a series of memorable "Allen's Alley" sketches with Fred Allen: "Ah, Mrs. Nussbaum, that's a pretty gown you have on." "It is mine cocktail dress." "I didn't know you went to cocktail parties." "We are only living once . . . life is a deep breath. You are exhaling, it is gone. . . ." "How true. I didn't know you were given to tippling." "Tippling? I am reading everything Tippling is writing . . . Gunga's Din. . . ." "No, no, tippling is drinking." "I am drinking only . . . a Catskill Manhattan." "What is a Catskill Manhattan?" "A glass beet soup with inside floating a small boiled potato."

Born in Odessa, Russia, Pious grew up in Bridgeport, Connecticut: "My father didn't believe in college for women . . . but I taught myself typing and took a job as a secretary. . . . I sort of edged in [to show business] by way of radio. I suppose my father thought it was more refined because people didn't see your face or figure, only your voice. . . . A friend of mine wrote several comedy scripts with a part for me. . . . He got a 15-minute program on WRNY in 1933. Fred Allen heard us and liked us."

It was writer Harry Tugend who helped her get onto Fred Allen's "Town Hall" handling dialect parts. She stayed with him through 1949. He used her for all types of roles besides Pansy Nussbaum. She recalled in the 1970s, "Women's lib would have approved of Allen . . . though he was shy in the presence of women, he had great admiration for women who succeeded against heavy odds in what he himself referred to as a man's world." She appeared on other radio shows as well, using many other dialects. She guested on "Easy Aces," "The Kate Smith Show" and played Gypsy Rose Rabinowitz on Sammy Kaye's radio series.

She married Bernie Hanighen in the 1940s. In 1948 she became a foster mother to a 12-year-old Italian war orphan, Giuseppe di Lillo. Part of her care for him included paying for a new artificial leg that helped him to walk.

Pious played Mrs. Nussbaum in Fred Allen's film *It's in the Bag,* which remains her most notable movie role. She turned up on Broadway from time to time and appeared in *The World of Sholom Aleichem* in England in 1955. In later life she worked in soap operas ("The Edge of Night") and television commercials. The plump five-foot-tall lady had a sense of humor about her looks. A publicist handed her a questionnaire to fill out (not intended for publication). She wrote: Dress size: "12." Shoe size: "6M." Bust: "32." Waist: "29." Hips: "Wow!"

The expert at Jewish dialect and malaprop comedy surprised fans who met her in person, because she spoke flawless English. "Accents are as distinc-

tive as the color of your hair," she once said. Her ability to do them, in all different gradations, was part of her art. Television audiences got a last glimpse of her in 1972 when she appeared with the rest of the "Allen's Alley" cast in a PBS special, "The Great Radio Comedians."

AUDIO incl.: *Down in Allen's Alley* (Radiola), *Funny You Don't Look It* (RCA), *That Funny Smoking Album* (Dorsyl)
BROADWAY: *Love in Our Time* (1941), *Dear Me, The Sky Is Falling* (1963), *The Last Analysis* (1964)
FILMS incl.: *It's in the Bag* (1945), *The Ambassador's Daughter* (1956), *Joe Macbeth* (1956), *Love in the Afternoon* (1957)

## JOE PISCOPO

### (June 17, 1951– )

"I'm like a lotta guys from Jersey," said Joe Piscopo, "I just want to cruise through life, enjoy it, don't hurt anybody, have a lot of fun." Especially effective at rock venues and open air concerts where he can assemble his own backup band, he relied on his blue-collar one-of-the-guys stand-up comedy, celebrity impressions and parodies of rock singers and drummers. "Social consciousness jokes are . . . boring," he insists. "Audiences today want a little irreverence and just to be entertained."

Piscopo achieved national fame on television's "Saturday Night Live" for his ability to mimic Frank Sinatra, Jerry Lewis and David Letterman, complete with lifelike makeup. The humor was in the accuracy of his mannerisms and the duplication of catch phrases. Since he had great admiration for all three men, the jokes were always mild. "Piscopo, you fracture me," said an indulgent Sinatra, who heard him do rock songs in the Sinatra style. Said Piscopo, "When I do Sinatra, it's very special to me. My father's such a big Sinatra fan."

Born in Passaic, his father a lawyer, Piscopo's grades in high school were not spectacular. While attending Jones College in Florida, Piscopo worked as disc jockey on the local radio station, branched out into dinner theater and later stand-up. He appeared in a television pilot, "A Dog's Life," in which all the actors wore dog costumes. In 1979 NBC signed him to a development deal and he arrived on "Saturday Night Live."

The show was at its low ebb in popularity, rescued to some degree by Piscopo's impressions and Eddie Murphy's sass. They became friends and later recorded a hilarious "Honeymooners" rap single with Eddie as Ed Norton and Joe as Ralph Kramden. After Murphy left the show, Piscopo felt he was the program's big star. He agonized when the writers handed in material he felt would embarrass him, but objected to the alternative: appearing in fewer sketches. His contract ultimately was not renewed.

The springboard of "Saturday Night Live" led to a series of beer commercials that helped keep Joe's face in the public eye: "The spots are more entertainment than selling a product," he said when criticized. "It's a classy campaign." The commercials, which featured Piscopo in garish, stereotypical makeup as a hugely fat black rap singer and an Oriental martial arts devotee, were appreciated by fans of those genres and diehards who missed the broad style of comedy personified by Piscopo's idol, Jerry Lewis.

Piscopo's early film efforts didn't ignite interest. An avid weight-lifter, a new, muscularly "pumped-up" Piscopo starred in *Dead Heat,* a buddy/cop/horror/comedy, which missed at all genres and failed to boost him into the handsome comic hero territory of Michael Keaton and Steve Guttenberg.

He remains active with live shows and commercials, but critics still downgrade Piscopo's "average Joe" personality and his tendency to broadly overplay his comedy to audiences whose first choice is probably watching monster truck competitions. To his credit, Piscopo keeps his shows free of gratuitous drug references and profanity. Calling himself "a comedic actor who does characterizations," he continues to amuse audiences with the definitive Sinatra and Letterman impersonations. He continues to maintain his muscular build and appeared on the cover of *Muscle and Fitness* magazine promoting good health and good habits: "I abhor all drugs. I have never done steroids or cocaine; I don't even smoke dope. . . . I wouldn't know a steroid from a hemorrhoid."

AUDIO: *I Love Rock and Roll* (Columbia), *New Jersey* (Columbia)

BOOK: *The Piscopo Tapes* (1984)

FILMS incl.: *Johnny Dangerously* (1984), *Wise Guys* (1986), *Dead Heat* (1988)

TV: "Saturday Night Live" (1984)

VIDEOS: *The Joe Piscopo Video; Live; New Jersey; Catch a Rising Star's 10th Anniversary*

## SNUB POLLARD

### (Harold Fraser, November 9, 1886–January 19, 1962)

A little fellow with a Kaiser Wilhelm mustache turned upside down, Snub Pollard was a familiar face in silent comedies but is now known primarily for one brilliant short film, *It's a Gift.*

Born in Australia, Pollard was touring with an Australian repertory group when he broke into films with Hal Roach. Like another Roach comedian, Stan Laurel, Pollard had tearfully watery eyes and could produce a sympathy-invoking gaze of meek woe. Around 1919 Pollard began to star in his own quickly done movies. *Start Something* was a success that year, but nothing would rival *It's a Gift,* which he made in 1923.

In this gimmick comedy loaded with inventive sight gags, Snub played an inventor leading a carefree, carefully controlled lifestyle thanks to his labor-saving creations. His appliances, hooked up with elaborate strings and pulleys, cooked and served him breakfast. His small, bullet-shaped car required no gasoline: he merely held up a huge magnet and followed behind the metal bumper of the car in front of him. The film was a highlight of the silent film compilation *The Golden Age of Comedy.*

Pollard never left show business. He turned up in Jerry Lewis comedies, appeared in small television roles (including "Gunsmoke") and had a cameo in the film *A Pocketful of Miracles.* He was the comedian who threw a chocolate cream pie at Jimmy Cagney in *Man of a Thousand Faces.* Just before his death he appeared at a reunion event featuring several of the surviving Keystone Kops.

FILMS incl.: *His Royal Slyness* (1919), *The Dippy Dentist* (1920), *Insulting the Sultan* (1920), *Hook, Line and*

*Sinker* (1922), *The Stone Age* (1922), *The Courtship of Miles Sandwich* (1923), *It's a Gift* (1923), *Sold at Auction* (1923), *The Big Idea* (1923), *Are Husbands Human?* (1925), *The Yokel!* (1927), *Cockeyed Cavaliers* (1934), *The Perils of Pauline* (1947), *Man of a Thousand Faces* (1957), *Who Was That Lady* (1960), *A Pocketful of Miracles* (1961)

## TOM POSTON

### (October 17, 1921–   )

Tom Poston first amused the nation in the "Man on the Street" segment of the old Steve Allen "Tonight Show" as a man who couldn't remember his name. The sleepy-looking sad sack with the large, moist eyes and doleful expression was completely befuddled. For decades to come, he would continue playing woozy emptyheads and dummies in a variety of television comedies, including "Mork and Mindy" and "Newhart."

Born in Columbus, Ohio, a chemistry major at Bethany College, Poston was in an amateur tumbling group called The Flying Zebleys. After air force service in World War II, he studied acting on the GI Bill and opened a stock company with his brother in Rehobeth Beach, Maryland.

He went to Broadway in 1946, using his acrobatic skills to play a cadet who tumbles down the stairs in *Cyrano de Bergerac*. Poston replaced Orson Bean during the run of *Will Success Spoil Rock Hunter* in 1955 and later replaced Peter Ustinov in *Romanoff and Juliet*. He worked on television shows in New York as well, including "Tom Corbett Space Cadet" and a soap opera called "Hawkins Falls."

It was on Steve Allen's show that he made his first major impression on America. The Allen stock company of comics provided Tom with as many laughs as the audience. He contrasted it with "Saturday Night Live": "They are incredibly talented. But have you noticed, no one on that show ever breaks up. Do you suppose they don't really think of it as funny?"

Poston had a starring film role in the offbeat but misfire horror/comedy *Zotz!*, and remained a comedy co-star on television, sitcoms and as a panelist on "To Tell the Truth" for years. Rarely given enough dramatic work to suit him, in the early 1980s

Poston enjoyed returning to the Buck's County Playhouse in Pennsylvania where he played Lenny in *Of Mice and Men*, Tevye in *Fiddler on the Roof* and the lead in *Cyrano de Bergerac*.

Most fans couldn't imagine him as anything but a comic blank. Rarely did he play more colorful comic characters. One was the dizzy grump Franklin Delano Bickley on "Mork and Mindy." In the film *Cold Turkey* he was a sorrowful drunk: "I tipple. I drink—I mean, I drink all the time. You better stand up or I'll fall on you."

In 1989 he played grumpy Oscar Madison to Tim Conway's Felix Unger in a touring company of *The Odd Couple*. Still, he had his best success with such characters as the vacuous George Utley on "Newhart." Poston doesn't seem to mind playing obnoxious characters, dopes and drips. Of his role as Utley, he joked, "I'm going to ask the producers if I can play him even dumber!" The glassy-eyed comic relished playing a comic sidekick: "Which would you rather be, the star of a flop, or supporting Bob Newhart in a hit?"

BROADWAY incl.: *Cyrano de Bergerac* (1947), *Stockade* (1954), *Best of Burlesque* (1957), *Drink to Me Only* (1958), *Come Play with Me* (1959), *Golden Fleecing* (1959), *The Conquering Hero* (1961), *Come Blow Your Horn* (1962), *Mary, Mary* (1963), *But Seriously* (1969)

FILMS incl.: *City That Never Sleeps* (1953), *Zotz!* (1962), *Soldier in the Rain* (1963), *The Old Dark House* (1963), *Cold Turkey* (1970), *The Happy Hooker* (1975), *Rabbit Test* (1978), *Up the Academy* (1980), *Carbon Copy* (1981)

TV: "The Steve Allen Show" (1956–59), "To Tell the Truth" (1958–67), "The Steve Allen Show" (1961), "On the Rocks" (1975–76), "Newhart" (1982–90)

## WILLIAM POWELL

### (July 29, 1892–March 5, 1984)

A silent film tough guy and villain, William Powell became one of the great stars of screwball comedy. Some thought him the epitome of sophistication; he wasn't, and that was the secret to his grand appeal.

Powell always retained his rough edge. Even his looks, which on the surface seemed rather handsome, were tempered by a tendency toward frowns, glares and gritted teeth.

His character was the worldly wise guy, someone who learned his manners from "hanging out" with rich people. His attitude was tolerantly wry, with an undercurrent of disapproval and mild annoyance. Many of his best roles traded in on this dual identity. In *The Thin Man* he was the charming but hard-drinking Nick Charles, who fought for justice but was known and respected by hoods. In *My Man Godfrey* he played a rich man who chucked it all to live with bums, rising again to teach a rich family a lesson as their surprisingly urbane butler. As he told a group of partiers, "I was curious to see how a bunch of empty-headed nitwits conducted themselves. My curiosity is satisfied. I assure you, it will be a pleasure to go back to a society of really important people." In *I Love You Again,* he played the dual role of a wise-guy con man who, after amnesia, becomes a dull and stuffy model citizen. After another clunk on the head he sees the world through the comic perspective of a renegade outsider now a beloved insider.

Born in Pittsburgh, Powell went to drama school in New York. Edward G. Robinson was a classmate. He appeared on Broadway as early as 1912 and was first married in 1915. His first film was *Sherlock Holmes* with John Barrymore in the title role. He was a villain opposite Clara Bow in *My Lady's Lips* and didn't really have a meaty hero role until he became Philo Vance in the early sound film *The Canary Murder Case.*

He starred with Carole Lombard in the comedy *Man of the World* in 1931, the year they were married. They divorced in 1933. Soon after Powell found his ideal match on screen, Myrna Loy. Their first effort, *Manhattan Melodrama*, became famous, but only because John Dillinger was shot coming out of a theater screening it. Powell received an Oscar nomination for *The Thin Man*, his second film with Myrna Loy.

Powell's great romance was with Jean Harlow, whose death was a severe blow to him. They were together in *Libeled Lady*, along with Myrna Loy. The same year he teamed with ex-wife Carole Lombard for *My Man Godfrey.* Powell's variations on *The Thin Man* series included *Star of Midnight*, a mystery/romance opposite Ginger Rogers, and *The Ex Mrs. Bradford,* with Jean Arthur as his ex-wife. He earned another Academy Award nomination for *The Great Ziegfeld.* Powell added quite a bit to his roles, but was always modest about it: "I take that scene to bed with me and read it and read it. I figure out every bit of business that might go well with that scene. That's all subject to the director's approval, of course. But I can't hop right on a set and ad lib bits of business."

Powell, who married for a third time in 1940, aged gracefully from the Loy leading man to a family man. He received another Academy Award nomination for *Life with Father.* In *Mr. Peabody and the Mermaid* he acknowledged a milestone: "Fifty—the old age of youth, the youth of old age." After his memorable role as the salty ship's doctor in *Mr. Roberts,* Powell retired and enjoyed his later years. He said simply, "When the offers come, I ask myself, why would I do it? For the glory? The ham in me has been pretty well burned out with the years. For the money? I'd just be put into a higher tax bracket. So I just say no."

BIOGRAPHIES: *Gentleman: The William Powell Story* (Francisco, 1985), *The Complete Films of William Powell* (Quirk, 1986)

BROADWAY incl.: *Going Up* (1917), *Mary Stuart* (1956)

FILMS incl.: *Sherlock Holmes* (1922), *My Lady's Lips* (1925), *The Great Gatsby* (1926), *Beau Geste* (1926), *She's a Sheik* (1927), *Feel My Pulse* (1928), *The Four Feathers* (1929), *The Canary Murder Case* (1929), *The Greene Murder Case* (1929), *Man of the World* (1931), *Ladies Man* (1931), *The Kennel Murder Case* (1933), *Manhattan Melodrama* (1933), *The Thin Man* (1934), *After the Thin Man* (1936), *The Great Ziegfeld* (1936), *The Ex-Mrs. Bradford* (1936), *My Man Godfrey* (1936), *Libeled Lady* (1936), *The Emperor's Candlesticks* (1937), *The Baroness and the Butler* (1938), *Another Thin Man* (1939), *I Love You Again* (1940), *Love Crazy* (1941), *Shadow of the Thin Man* (1941), *The Thin Man Goes Home* (1944), *The Heavenly Body* (1944), *Ziegfeld Follies* (1946), *Life with Father* (1947), *Song of the Thin Man* (1947), *The Senator Was Indiscreet* (1947), *Mr. Peabody and the Mermaid* (1948), *Take One False Step* (1949), *Dancing in the Dark* (1949), *The Girl Who Had*

*Everything* (1953), *How to Marry a Millionaire* (1953), *Mister Roberts* (1955)

## FREDDIE PRINZE

### (Frederick Pruetzel, June 22, 1954–January 29, 1977)

A puppy-cute, charismatic young stand-up performer, Freddie Prinze was plucked, seemingly overnight, from New York's comedy clubs to television. His meteoric rise to superstardom via the television sitcom "Chico and the Man" ended with a crash that made front-page news around the nation.

A self-proclaimed "Hungarican" (Hungarian father, Puerto Rican mother), Freddie tried to work out some of his confusion over identity through acting. He attended New York's High School of the Performing Arts and at 17 starred in productions of *Bye Bye Birdie* and *West Side Story*. Even then he was experimenting with Valium and cocaine. His family had experienced tragedy early; his five-year-old sister Alice drowned in a swimming pool.

Freddie's need to be loved and to be famous led to his nickname "The Prince" and his adopted stage name, which became "Prinze" ("to be unique"). His stand-up comedy was, like that of Bill Dana's José Jimenez, geared to be lovable. The gags about his Puerto Rican lifestyle were delivered with a sugary smile and large moist eyes: "You oughta hear my mother talk about her wedding: 'It was so beautiful, you should have been there.' I said to her, 'Ma, I was!'" His catch phrases were a softly coy: "Is not my job," and a colleague Jimmie Walker's "Dyn-o-Mite," a grinning "Lookin' good!"

Under pressure in the 1970s to give minorities more visibility, talent scouts eagerly booked Jimmie Walker and Prinze, who guested on Jack Paar's comeback talk show and then Johnny Carson's "Tonight Show" on December 6, 1973. Producer James Komack saw him and signed him for "Chico and the Man." He was a bright new star, but it was the same old story: too much too soon.

Prinze's own problems with his confused ethnic background were exacerbated by the show's controversies. Mexicans protested the show, angry at a Puerto Rican playing a Mexican, upset that "Chico"

meant "boy" in Spanish. They even attacked the un-Mexican theme music of José Feliciano. Worse than this was the problem of the superstardom that took Prinze beyond his wildest expectations. He needed more drugs to keep up with it, not less. Even the best parts of stardom eventually proved destructive. Jimmie Walker recalls: "He had too many women. I don't know how he found the time to sleep with all of them." He romanced Lenny Bruce's daughter, Kitty. She loved him but later said, "Comedians aren't men or women, they're melancholy children."

Freddie married the twice-divorced Katherine Cochran in October 1975, having met her just eight months earlier. Their son was born in March 1976. His exhausting work schedule and his inner pain continued, despite psychiatric counseling. He had taken so much cocaine it had affected his nose. He gobbled handfuls of Quaaludes. His marriage fell apart. And then everything else followed.

On one of his many bad nights his therapist came by at 1:30 A.M. for a talk. Later his business manager turned up at 3:00 A.M. to further counsel Freddie through this. Freddie showed his manager the suicide note he'd written: "I must end it. There's no hope left. I'll be at peace. No one had anything to do with this. My decision totally. Freddie Prinze." His manager called up his therapist, who said, "He's just crying out for attention and help, but I'm not concerned about his doing harm to himself." After all, Freddie had talked of suicide before and had even play-acted shooting himself in front of friends.

Freddie called Katherine to say good-bye. Just a month earlier she had filed for divorce. In another month he was to be in court to answer a charge of driving while under the influence of drugs. He made more calls. Then he grabbed a gun. His manager begged him to put it down and insisted that suicide was not the way out. He even told Freddie that his wife and baby wouldn't get any insurance money if he went out that way. Freddie seemed to listen. Suddenly he put the gun to his head and fired.

For the next 37 hours, Freddie Prinze lingered in a coma. Then he died.

His friend David Brenner said, "He was so drugged out on ludes and wine he didn't know what he was doing." Co-star Jack Albertson eulogized him: "None of us truly realized the extent of his anxieties, perhaps because of his mercurial ability to abandon despondency and soar to self-mocking hilarity. He lived for laughter. I can pay him no more sincere tribute than to admit that he had grown from a new kid in a rehearsal hall into a professional colleague on stage faster, more gracefully, than any actor that I have encountered in nearly half a century of the theater."

While some stars left behind a legacy of work, Prinze had hardly tapped his full potential. His pain, his confusion, and his gruesome death have overwhelmed what survives—a few seasons of amiable humor on a sitcom, one mild disc of stand-up and the memory of a nice-looking kid with a few jokes and a shy smile.

BIOGRAPHY: *The Freddie Prinze Story* (Pruetzel, 1978)
FILM: *The Million Dollar Rip-Off* (1976)
FILM BIOGRAPHY: *Can You Hear the Laughter?* (1979)
TV: "Chico and the Man" (1974–77)

## PROFESSOR BACKWARDS

### (James Edmondson, 1911–January 29, 1976)

Several vaudevillians wrote or recited backward, including Harry Kahane and a novelty star billed as "Sessukikima," but none was as successful as "Professor Backwards," Jimmy Edmondson. The laughs were simple but sure-fire: how funny it sounded when the professor took an audience member's name, instantly wrote it backward, then spoke the garbled name out loud.

Raised in Jacksonville, Florida, his father a Baptist minister, Edmondson worked in the printing department of the *Jacksonville Journal*, learning to set type backward. This got him into *Ripley's Believe It or Not* and, having added some showmanship, "Major Bowes Amateur Hour" on radio around 1934. He said on the show, "About two years ago I had a nightmare. I saw everything backwards, I saw people walking backwards, talking backwards, singing backwards . . . and the next morning when I woke up I just started talking backwards."

Audiences laughed when he recited names backward and even sang "Show Me the Way to Go Home" backward. Edmondson freshened up the act with jokes. "I kill myself with my own material," he said back in the 1930s, "and it's so easy to write too. I had an argument with the telephone operator the other day. I said to her, 'What do ya think I am, a dope?' She said, 'Just a minute, please, I will give you the information.' See what I mean?"

Life wasn't so funny when, in August 1939, he got into a fight with a vaudevillian named Vincent Fitzgerald. According to a witness, Edmondson grabbed a sickle from a hardware store display and slammed it into Fitzgerald's side. But according to Edmondson's wife (also a witness), Fitzgerald started the fight, insulted after Edmondson kidded him about his "Punch and Judy" act. She insisted Fitzgerald "fell on the blade." Edmondson got out of the scrape after having been charged with first-degree manslaughter.

Jack Paar recalled working with him, though in his book *P.S. Jack Paar* he calls him "Jimmy Edwards." Wrote Paar, "He was a good performer, but he lived on Cracker Jack and wouldn't even rent his own room, choosing instead to move in with me and sleep on a chair rather than spend his money for a night's lodging." Paar recalled how the Professor avoided paying for long-distance calls to find out what his touring schedule would be. He'd call his agent, ask for himself and ask where Professor Backwards could be reached the following week. He got the city, the hotel and the room number. That last number was actually the price for the gig.

The Professor divided his act between backward novelties and straight gags: "I had a brand-new Mercury. I loaned it to my brother last week. I said, 'Treat it like your own.' He sold it." There was always a segment of audience participation, in which he'd mention funny words backward ("Motel backward is let 'em!") and get laughs from his pungent backward pronunciations. Any word the audience shouted out he instantly reversed. "Polyethelene" he pronounced, "Eenie litty, ya lop!" He could get laughs simply reading a dictionary—as long as it was done backward.

The Professor appeared on variety shows in the 1960s but worked most often in the South, living in College Park, a suburb of Atlanta. The next time his name was heard on national television it was in announcements of his murder.

With the cooperation of the *Atlanta Constitution,* whose reporters were closest to the case, this is the full story of the crime:

Three times married, three times divorced, his house burglarized several times, Edmondson had moved to 4185 Herschel Road in College Park after his old home burned down. Around midnight on January 28, Edmondson had his 24-year-old housekeeper Michelle Sipp arrested for drunkenness after an argument. She was released and returned to Edmondson's house.

Some time in the early-morning hours of January 29, 1976 three men were let into the Edmondson home. Two of the men took Edmondson captive, forcing him to write a check they could cash in the morning. The third man, Michael Gantt, had sex with the housekeeper in another room.

Edmondson was taken out in the morning so that he could okay the check he had written for the men. They had demanded $5,000 but Edmondson had somehow persuaded them to accept a check for $300. It isn't clear whether the thugs had decided to bring Edmondson to the bank and get him to withdraw more money, or whether Edmondson had come up with the idea in order to get himself out of the house and into a public place where he might get help.

They drove off in his 1973 Cadillac. Down the road the plan suddenly changed. Gantt shot him three times in the head. His body was dumped facedown in the muddy gravel of Watts Road. It was found around 1 P.M.—a half hour before the housekeeper finally called the police. She claimed she had been warned by the men not to call sooner; she was arrested.

The housekeeper claimed innocence and declared her tryst that night with Gantt was actually rape. By the time of the trial, she had become the star witness for the prosecution.

Despite various defenses (Gantt claimed he heard voices after a 1969 car accident), the trio were each sentenced to 20 years for armed robbery and mandatory life in prison for the murder.

It was the lot of Professor Backwards, and his style of entertainment, to get more laughs than sympathy at his bloody demise. On "Saturday Night Live," the news of his death was treated as a one-

liner for their "Weekend Update" segment from Chevy Chase: "Professor Backwards was slain in Atlanta yesterday by three masked gunmen. According to reports, neighbors ignored the professor's cries of 'pleh, pleh.' "

AUDIO: *Laugh with Professor Backwards* (Jumbo)

## PROFESSOR DOPE (See LEW KELLY.)

## RICHARD PRYOR

### (December 1, 1940–   )

The most controversial stand-up comedian of the late 1970s, Richard Pryor fused together several styles of comedy. From the old Pigmeat Markham "open the door, Richard" school, he enlarged upon black dialect. From Lenny Bruce he learned how to deal with racial or sexual tensions without flinching from painful truths. And in the tradition of clowning contemporaries such as Bill Cosby and George Carlin, he put it all together with manic faces and voices that made a one-man concert seem more like a three-ring circus.

It wasn't just the language that made Pryor infamous, though he was far more graphic than the latest trail blazer, George Carlin. Pryor was the first comedian since Lenny Bruce to wrestle with dangerous racial humor; most of it seemed to amuse black audiences and secondarily any whites who might dare to be hipped to his point of view. Fellow comedians, critics and liberals flocked to hear "the truth," while other whites called his act offensively "reverse racist" at worst, merely rambling and obscene at best. The more controversy there was, the bigger Pryor's star became, with many acclaiming him a genius, while others, quoting one of his comedy album titles, felt *That Nigger's Crazy.*

Pryor was born in Peoria, Illinois. Interviewers asking about his childhood years generally got evasive answers, hazy recollections or a few angry or pathetic recollections that might have been fact or fiction. Lenny Bruce was often the same way, even in his autobiography. One undisputed fact was that his parents separated and he was raised by his grandmother. After tough years on the streets. Pryor left high school and joined the army. Afterward, he became a master of ceremonies, comic and, following Bill Cosby's lead, a mildly swinging performer welcomed on television variety shows of the day. At the turn of the 1970s he grew tired of the safe and phony routines he was doing, dropped out and emerged with a tougher, hipper identity.

In 1972 he earned an Academy Award nomination for his acting in *Lady Sings the Blues*. He won a 1973 Emmy as a writer ("The Lily Tomlin Special") and worked on Mel Brooks' movie about a black sheriff out west, *Blazing Saddles*. In 1974, 1975 and 1976 he won Grammy awards for his hot, controversial comedy and was nominated the next four years in a row. He won twice more in 1980 and 1981.

Among his many accomplishments, Pryor reintroduced stark drama to stand-up (his "Mudbone" monologues and other routines that did not go for the laugh every 20 seconds) and fractured ground rules on censorship (unlike Lenny Bruce or George Carlin, no one seemed ready to risk a riot by arresting Richard). The first stand-up comic to achieve box office success with a "performance" film, Pryor proved to the show business industry that people would be willing to watch one man on screen for 90 minutes. A flood of stand-up films, videos and cable television specials followed, for Pryor and for those who came after.

Pryor's more orthodox movie comedies of the day were hits too. His mousy presence—the quivering voice, the popping eyes, the disbelieving and fearful expression—were not that far removed from black stereotypes in older films. The difference was that in addition to mirroring real fear and vulnerability, Pryor's film characters were hip and heroic. *Silver Streak,* his first film where he teamed with Gene Wilder, gave him his biggest hit, a "crossover" success among fans of all types.

Under pressure to constantly top himself, his own anger, suspicions and confusion led to open and potent iconoclasm and outrageousness. Aside from whatever he said on stage, off stage he made headlines by insulting talk show hosts, ridiculing other performers and inciting the occasional murder: "If you're black and still here in America," he said on "The Tonight Show" in 1979, "get a gun and go to

Richard Pryor, America's most controversial stand-up comedian of the 1970s. Dick Gregory said the three geniuses of comedy were Mark Twain, Lenny Bruce and Richard Pryor. Photo from the author's collection.

South Africa and kill some white people." His behavior set new standards for celebrity frankness. Ten years before angry boxer Larry Holmes said almost the same thing, Pryor shocked the crowd at a 1977 Human Rights Foundation benefit by saying "Kiss my happy, rich black ass." At that same event, he sneered at homosexuals for mincing about "on Hollywood Boulevard while Watts was burning down."

Pryor's personal life was even more of a shambles. His latest wife had to run for cover when he opened fire at his own car in the midst of an irrational shooting spree. Pryor's drug use led to a heart attack. And, on June 9, 1980, he tried to kill himself. Trying to get the truth out of Pryor was difficult at the time. At first he insisted he had accidentally set fire to himself while pouring a drink. Later, the accepted theory was that he had been freebasing cocaine when the mixture exploded. Finally, in 1986, he told Barbara Walters that he'd lied: "My lawyer had made a statement—he didn't know the truth . . . he was trying to cover my ass. So I was trying to cover his ass. . . . I wanted to say it was no accident, I got crazy one night and wanted to kill myself. . . . I remember pouring rum all over myself . . . I was ashamed of myself . . . I could only end up in a room smoking a base pipe."

Pryor made a miraculous recovery from almost certain death, and to his surprise, the outlaw comic received overwhelming support from his peers and his fans. His life-and-death struggle was front-page news around the country.

The struggle back to stardom remained. Pryor had a lot of trouble getting his comic act together. Perhaps the anger that had fueled so much of his work had been eroded by the outpouring of affection after the accident. Perhaps, as he said, going "straight" without alcohol or drugs had dried up some of his wild imagination. There was also the inhibiting factor of the long layoff and the slight concern that fans might notice a few scars or see a new vulnerability in this once-burned and now shy performer.

Pryor did make a successful comeback and even created a routine about his burn experience and recovery, but by now there was another hot new comedian around: Eddie Murphy. In the less tense early 1980s, Murphy's happy sense of outrage and fresh, Pryor-influenced inventions eclipsed the now-familiar routines of his idol. Several mediocre comedies weakened Pryor's box office appeal. Asked how he felt about Murphy's success, Pryor remarked: "Pissed off . . . I don't like it at all. . . . My wife helped me. . . . she said, 'You was number 1 for a long time.'"

His reunion film with Gene Wilder, See No Evil, Hear No Evil, and Harlem Nights with Eddie Murphy were roasted by critics. Fans hoped that if he wasn't enjoying great movie success, at least his personal life was straightening out. Unfortunately, peculiar health problems began to surface. He looked emaciated on a "Tonight Show" appearance in 1986, as he alarmed host Johnny Carson by intimating that he had some kind of fatal disease, such as AIDS: "I

thought Richard, it's finally caught up with you. I thought I had one of them and I was going to die . . . my right eye is blind. You could hit me on this side and I wouldn't see it coming." Gossip writer Liz Smith quoted an ex-wife as saying he had used needles during his period of drug abuse. Pryor himself had once talked about homosexual experimentation but said it had happened many years ago. In March 1990 he suffered a second heart attack, this time while golfing in Australia.

On April 1 of that year Pryor, whose previous brides varied between white and black, remarried his fifth wife, Flynn, a Jehovah's Witness. She said he had proposed after returning from Australia: "He told me he wanted to spend his last days around people who love him." In May 1991 Pryor's spokesman, Guy McElwaine, confirmed that for the past five years Pryor was suffering from multiple sclerosis, but that it was in remission. In June he underwent triple heart bypass surgery. A month later critics noticed his weakened physical condition as he struggled through the summer 1991 release *Another You,* his fourth teaming with Gene Wilder.

AUDIO: *Craps* (Laff), *Pryor Goes Foxx Hunting* (Laff), *Down 'n' Dirty* (Laff), *Are You Serious* (Laff), *Who Me? I'm Not Him* (Laff), *Who Biz* (Laff), *Black Ben* (Laff), *Wizard of Comedy* (Laff), *Outrageous* (Laff), *Insane* (Laff), *Holy Smoke* (Laff), *Rev. Du Rite* (Laff), *Very Best* (Laff), *Blackjack* (Laff), *Supernigger* (Laff), *Live* (Laff), *L.A. Jail* (Tiger Lily), *Live* (Phoenix), *Richard Pryor* (Dove/Reprise), *That Nigger's Crazy* (Partee/Reprise), *Is It Something I Said?* (Reprise), *Bicentennial Nigger* (Warner Bros.), *Richard Pryor's Greatest Hits* (Warner Bros.), *Wanted: Live in Concert* (Warner Bros.), *Live on the Sunset Strip* (Warner Bros.), *Here and Now* (Warner Bros.)

FILMS incl.: *The Busy Body* (1968), *Wild in the Streets* (1968), *Dynamite Chicken* (1971), *Lady Sings the Blues* (1972), *Wattstax* (1973), *Uptown Saturday Night* (1974), *Some Call It Loving* (1974), *The Bingo Long Travelling All Stars and Motor Kings* (1976), *Car Wash* (1976), *Silver Streak* (1977), *Greased Lightning* (1977), *Which Way Is Up* (1977), *California Suite* (1978), *The Wiz* (1978), *Blue Collar* (1979), *Richard Pryor Here and Now* (1978), *Richard Pryor Live in Concert* (1979), *In God We Trust* (1980), *Wholly Moses* (1980), *Stir Crazy* (1980), *Bustin' Loose*

(1981), *Some Kind of Hero* (1982), *The Toy* (1982), *Richard Pryor Live on the Sunset Strip* (1982), *Superman III* (1983), *Richard Pryor: Live and Smokin'* (1985), *Brewster's Millions* (1985), *Jo Jo Dancer, Your Life Is Calling* (1986), *Critical Condition* (1987), *Moving* (1988), *See No Evil, Hear No Evil* (1989), *Harlem Nights* (1990), *Another You* (1991)

TV: "The Richard Pryor Show" (1977), "Pryor's Place" (1984)

## EDNA PURVIANCE

### (October 21, 1894–January 13, 1958)

Chaplin's leading lady in most of his classic short films, Edna Purviance was rarely called on to make audiences laugh, but always offered personality, warmth and just the right, light touch of romantic charm to her roles.

She was born in Lovelock, Nevada, where few thought her odd name (rhymes with "appliance") would ever be on anyone's lips. She was recommended to Chaplin on sight alone after working as a secretary and part-time stage actress in San Francisco.

It was opposite Edna, in 1915, that Chaplin produced his first true masterpiece of comedy and pathos, *The Tramp*. That the little fellow would be smitten with Edna, the farmer's daughter, was not surprising. While many silent film heroines seem overly sweet or stilted, Edna Purviance remains a model of natural, guileless grace. His heartbreak over her remains as poignant now as it did then.

In real life, Edna and Charlie enjoyed a grand romance. He was "Boodie" and she was "Modie" in their private world. A letter to her from Chaplin in March 1915: "My heart throbbed this morning when I received your sweet letter. It could be nobody else in the world that could have given me so much joy. Your language, your sweet thoughts and the style of your love note only tends to make me crazy over you. I can picture your darling self sitting down and looking up wondering what to say, that little pert mouth and those bewitching eyes so thoughtful. If I only had the power to express my sentiments. . . ."

The often sentimental comedies Chaplin and Edna made won over audiences and critics who declared him the master of film comedy. Back in 1914 Mack Sennett wanted his actors to go out and "Be funny!" Edna inspired something else. She would smile to him on the set before a take and say, "Go on, be cute!"

To his lifelong regret, Chaplin's mistress—work—took time away from Edna. They drifted apart and after she briefly found another lover, their relationship was never the same. Chaplin found a new leading lady for *The Gold Rush* in 1925, while in 1926 Edna's career stalled with *Sea Gulls*, a film produced by Chaplin and directed by Josef Von Sternberg. Edna may have been fine in it, but the film itself was deemed so bad, Chaplin ordered all copies destroyed.

Edna grew a bit too matronly for heroine roles. In 1946 Chaplin considered casting her as Madame Grosnay in *Monsieur Verdoux*. Sadly, he discovered "the part required European sophistication, which Edna never had." She appeared as an extra in the ballet audience of *Limelight* in 1952. The wistful superstar kept Edna on his payroll as long as she lived. She never married. She kept scrapbooks of his achievements and occasionally wrote him letters. They were signed "your truest and best admirer" and, just a few years before her death, "love always, Edna."

FILMS incl.: *The Tramp* (1915), *The Bank* (1915), *The Vagabond* (1916), *The Pawnshop* (1916), *Behind the Screen* (1916), *Easy Street* (1917), *The Immigrant* (1917), *Shoulder Arms* (1918), *The Kid* (1921), *A Woman of Paris* (1923), *Limelight* (1952)

## MAE QUESTEL

### (Mae Kwestel, September 13, 1912–   )

Betty Boop, Olive Oyl, Little Audrey, Winky Dink and Casper the Friendly Ghost: Mae Questel did them all. No woman has had greater success with comic voices in cartoons. But, as Mae points out to her fans, "I like being me and not just a voice." She enjoyed stepping out from behind the anonymous microphone and was typed playing an eccentric, tough, strident-voiced Jewish mother, proud and feisty. She played Mrs. Portnoy in novelty book and record parodies of *Portnoy's Complaint* in the 1960s and ended the '80s playing Woody Allen's mother in *New York Stories*.

Born in the Bronx, a graduate of Morris High School, Mae lived a placid life at 1165 Anderson Avenue. This changed after she had won a talent contest imitating the "Boop-Boop-a-Doop" girl, singer Helen Kane. Mae appeared often in vaudeville, and in 1930 Frank Loesser wrote a novelty tune for her, "I'm the Kind of Girl You Can Bet Is Chased." She appeared at The Palace as part of an unusual trio; her co-stars were a piano player named Fred Coots and baseball star Waite Hoyt. Her act included impressions of Fanny Brice, Maurice Chevalier and Marlene Dietrich, but it was her Helen Kane mimicry that proved the most lucrative.

In 1931 she parlayed the Kane imitation into the voice for the Betty Boop cartoons. Two years later,

parodying ZaSu Pitts, she gave voice to Popeye's sweetheart, Olive Oyl. She recorded "Sweet Betty, Don't Take My Boop-Oop-a-Doop" away in 1933, and more novelties, including "Animal Crackers in My Soup" (1935) and "At the Codfish Ball" (1936). Many of the Betty Boop cartoons featured Mae's vocals, including the tune "Keep a Little Song Handy" in "Betty Boop's Crazy Inventions" and "We'll Have a Bushell of Fun" in "Grampy's Indoor Outing." In addition to hundreds of cartoons, Mae co-starred on radio shows from "Perry Mason" to "The Henry Morgan Show" and, replacing Shirley Booth, "Duffy's Tavern." She guested regularly on television too, from "The Goldbergs" to "The Bob Newhart Show." On Broadway she played Gertrude Berg's friend in *A Majority of One* and Nancy Dussault's cute, advice-giving mom in *Bajour*. She even made records, not only for her cartoon character alter egos, but albums like *Faustus and Everyman*.

Television audiences probably knew the flesh-and-blood Mae best as the gabby, pesky, mistress of chuzpah, "Aunt Bluebelle" in a series of paper towel commercials. Never one for retiring, and hardly a retiring personality, the comedienne used her vocal talents in *Who Framed Roger Rabbit* and won fine notices for her work as Sadie Millstein in *New York Stories*. She first met Woody Allen when she recorded "Chameleon Days" for his film *Zelig*. The ageless Questel ("rhymes with compel," she said), mother of two sons, lives in New York with her second husband, always ready for a good role accentuating her humorously spirited personality. She said in 1990, "I feel like an old bag but I don't act like one!"

AUDIO: *Mrs. Portnoy's Retort* (Musicor), *Faustus and Everyman* (Caedmon), *Betty Boop Soundtracks* (Mark 56)

BOOK: *Mrs. Portnoy's Retort*

BROADWAY: *Doctor Social* (1948), *A Majority of One* (1959), *Enter Laughing* (1963), *Bajour* (1964)

FILMS incl.: *Wayward* (1932), *A Majority of One* (1961), *It's Only Money* (1962), *Funny Girl* (1968), *Move* (1970), *Hot Resorts* (1984), *Who Framed Roger Rabbit* (1988), *New York Stories* (1988)

TV: *Stop Me If You've Heard This One* (1949)

# R

## GILDA RADNER

### (June 28, 1946–May 20, 1989)

A childlike sense of fun made Gilda Radner seem like a sister, a daughter or a friend. In some ways a type of Lucille Ball for the 1970s, her fans found her more than a comedienne. They loved her.

Born in Detroit, she was named after Rita Hayworth in the movie *Gilda.* Her father died when she was 14, but he was affluent enough to will her a substantial amount of money, which helped her continue her education at the University of Michigan, where she majored in drama. She moved to Canada with her boyfriend and got her first important role in a Toronto production of *Godspell. National Lampoon Show* followed in 1974, and the next year she was the first person signed for "Saturday Night Live"—without an audition.

Free to invent characters and comic fantasy, she described it as "a time when all of life was there only for me to find out what was funny about it." The sweetly impish five-foot-six performer won an Emmy for her work on the show in 1978 and developed an array of original personalities. One was Emily Litella, the little old lady with a dozen malaprops who confused "endangered species" with "endangered feces" and "Soviet Jewry" with "Soviet jewelry." Litella was given guest editorials on such matters as statehood for Puerto Rico: "What's this I hear about making Puerto Rico a steak? The next thing they'll be wanting is a salad, and then a baked potato!" After being corrected, she always ended up with a cheery chirp: "Nevermind."

In the hands of another performer, Emily would've been unforgivably annoying. The same is true of Roseanne Roseannadanna, the gum-chewing editorialist who loved to gross out other cast members by discussing personal hygiene problems and then closing with her triumphant catch phrase, "It's always something!" There was also Gilda's tragic-comic nerd girl Lisa Loopner and six-year-old Judy Miller. Gilda also had a talent for mimicry, appearing in sketches as Lucille Ball and creating "Baba Wawa," a parody of newscaster Barbara Walters that was so good-natured even Walters had to laugh.

Gilda was one of the best-liked performers on the show, rarely displaying an ego. She turned down film offers (Olive Oyl in the Robin Williams film *Popeye*) and a $50,000-a-week prime-time series that would have taken time away from the show. Co-star Jane Curtin recalled, "Performing was the most important part of Gilda's life at that time. She was not involved in any relationships that were giving her what she needed, and performing was. She had an aggressiveness born out of energy that needed someplace to go."

Gilda was a whirlwind of activity, culminating in the one-woman stage show *Gilda Live* on Broadway and another stage production, *Lunch Hour* by Jean Kerr. After a brief romance with co-star Bill Murray, she was briefly married to a member of the show's band, G. E. Smith. When the original cast members of "Saturday Night Live" began to drift from the show, Radner finally left for her long-awaited film career. Unfortunately, her film *The First Family* was a bomb and her role as a 28-year-old man-crazed, carrot-sucking virgin an embarrassment.

*Hanky Panky* co-starred Gene Wilder, who became her second husband in 1984. The film characters of the Radner and Wilder team, two vulnerable adult children, required solid scripts and careful direction to work. They were finding their way through thrill comedy, romantic comedy and farce when, during the making of *Haunted Honeymoon*, she complained of what at first seemed to be flu symptoms. She developed cramps and pains in her legs but for ten months doctors insisted there was nothing wrong, blaming her ailments on her high-strung nerves.

Finally, ovarian cancer was the diagnosis; a malignant tumor was found in October 1986. After chemotherapy she seemed to get better, and in December 1987 she graced the cover of *Life* magazine, hopeful of recovery. She began working on a book about her struggle, a heartbreaking account that, given her sweet and childlike nature, made her seem even more like the helpless girl in the clutches of a bad dream: "I would wake up sweating and out of breath, running from a nightmare that didn't end when I woke up. I would cry in deep moans, wailing like a wounded animal—getting louder and louder to try to drown out what had happened, what I looked like, what could be."

The cancer returned and she was weakened again. She still retained her sense of humor. Husband Gene Wilder recalled that at home she would pretend to be fussy Roseanne Roseannadanna shouting at the cancer cells inside her body. "Hey! What are you tryin' to do in here? Make me sick?" One of her last appearances was an Emmy-nominated episode of "It's Garry Shandling's Show." At the time Gene Wilder described how fans were reacting to Gilda's fight: "When I walk down the street—in any city—people come up and just take my arm—'How's she doing'—they don't have to say Gilda. They stop and say, 'Tell her I'm praying for her.' "

Gilda's book was called *It's Always Something*, not because of her Roseanne character, but because of the inspiration for the line. "My father really used to always say 'It's always something.' I thought, I wonder if I could make that popular." In the book she tried to include some light moments. She wrote, "Cancer is probably the most unfunny thing in the world. But I'm a comedienne, and even cancer wasn't going to stop me from seeing the humor in what I was going through."

The laughter stopped one Saturday morning in May 1989. By that night, almost everyone had heard the news of her death. The host of "Saturday Night Live" that night was Steve Martin. He promised the audience a full show of laughs—and then showed a clip of a past show—a comic dance number featuring Gilda and himself. When it ended, to thunderous applause, his eyes were wet and mournful, his lips about to quiver.

Reporters looked to members of "Saturday Night Live" for comment. Lorne Michaels, producer of the show, said "I think she had everything in her life. I think she . . . got to do the work she loved. I think she was with the man she loved. And I think she had a full life."

AUDIO: *It's Always Something* (Simon and Schuster Audio), *Live from New York* (Warner Bros.)
AUTOBIOGRAPHY: *It's Always Something* (1989)
BOOK: *Roseanne Roseannadanna's Hey Get Back to Work Book* (1983)
BROADWAY: *Gilda Live* (1979), *Lunch Hour* (1980)
FILMS incl.: *The Last Detail* (1973), *Gilda Live* (1980), *The First Family* (1980), *Hanky Panky* (1982), *It Came from Hollywood* (1982), *The Woman in Red* (1984), *Movers and Shakers* (1985), *Haunted Honeymoon* (1985)
TV: "Saturday Night Live" (1975–80)
VIDEOS: *The Best of Gilda Radner; Gilda Live*

# TONY RANDALL

## (Leonard Rosenberg, February 26, 1920–   )

Tony Randall is noted for playing self-pitying sad sacks and vibrantly eccentric fussbudgets. His quirky career has encompassed almost every form of show business, remarkable considering his own appraisal of himself: "I think a great many people would find me extremely difficult to work with. I'm terribly demanding. I expect everyone to be good. If they're lackadaisical, disinterested or not *good,* I'm simply murder on them."

Born in Tulsa, Oklahoma, his father an art dealer, Tony majored in speech and drama in Northwestern University. He was on Broadway as early as 1941 in *A Circle of Chalk* and married Florence Mitchell the following year. After four years in the Signal Corps, Lieutenant Randall appeared in summer stock and on radio, and landed his first important national exposure in a television show he didn't want to do: "Mr. Peepers." It was, he later realized, "the turning point in my career."

After playing Mr. Peepers' friend Harvey Weskit, Randall went on to more Broadway shows and musicals. Though hardly known for it, Randall's singing remained a source of pride for him. In the late 1950s and early '60s he recorded three albums, two featuring eccentric songs of the '20s, the other mixing bizarre comedy and novelty, including "Nature Boy" sung in an Indian accent.

In films, Randall developed his identity as a humorously sulky or mildly pesky friend of the leading man, particularly in Rock Hudson–Doris Day movies. He perfected woeful expressions of wounded pride and nauseous dejection, which would have led to fatal typecasting without the flip side, his overbearing pluck. "I don't know how fast he moves," he simmers, sizing up a love rival in *Pillow Talk,* "but it takes an early bird to get the best of a worm like me!"

As Felix Ungar on television's "Odd Couple," Randall perfectly balanced the giddy, childlike, obsessive personality of the manic Felix with the moping, whining depressive side of Ungar. Never afraid to look embarrassingly foolish, always adding the necessary touch of believability, Randall made Felix Ungar into one of the greatest sitcom characters of all time; matched perfectly by his equally brilliant co-star Jack Klugman, whom he'd met years earlier performing in an episode of "Captain Video."

Most viewers can recall their favorite Ungarism. It could be verbal; the prissy fellow self-delightedly declaring "You should never assume—because when you assume, you make an ASS of U and ME." It could also be physical; his arm caught in the air as his back goes into a spasm. It could even be a stare;

his look of chagrin into the camera as Oscar reaches over and wipes his wet hands on his shirt.

With the show in reruns, sometimes three times a day in certain cities, Randall never quite got over playing Felix but never seemed to mind. He said he enjoyed being recognized on the street, "except when stupid people call me Oscar!"

Randall won an Emmy for his role in 1975. He subsequently played Judge Franklin on his short-lived "Tony Randall Show," which lacked a co-star to chafe against his exaggerated sensibilities. Then he played the gay Sidney Shorr on "Love, Sidney," which suffered when the network balked at confirming the character to be homosexual. A fairly average sitcom without the challenging premise, it quickly disappeared.

Through the 1980s, Randall divided his time between old fascinations (hosting "Live from the Met" opera telecasts) and newfound eccentricities. He became a regular on "The Tonight Show," developing a Howard Cosellian habit of confounding Johnny Carson with little-known dictionary terminology. He appeared on the show over 100 times in the 1980s and is now a regular on "Late Night with David Letterman."

Witty, always capable of shifting from pomposity to pensiveness, Randall remains an amusing talk show raconteur and put together a book of show business anecdotes in 1989 called *Which Reminds Me.* The following year he began what was to be his crowning achievement in theater, raising enough money to create a national American repertory company, the National Actors Theater. He donated a million dollars to the cause and raised as much through charity events and a 1991 one-night only revival of *The Odd Couple* on Broadway.

He once confided that despite his achievements, he felt a certain sense of disappointment: "I never did what I set out to do—I wanted to be a classical actor." He vowed to do something about that by establishing a serious theater company in the tradition of the national theaters in England and other countries. Always on the lookout for an unusual stage role, he took over the part of Rene Gallimard in Broadway's *M. Butterfly.* Gallimard was the French diplomat who was romantically involved with a Chinese opera star, whom he didn't realize (even after 20 years) was male, not female. Randall said,

"It was the best I've ever been in my whole life. . . . The most flattering thing is that when it was announced I was going into the show, people asked which of the two roles I was going to play."

AUDIO: *Acts, Sings, Caricatures* (Imperial), *Vo Do De Oh Doe* (Mercury), *Warm and Wavery* (Mercury), *The Odd Couple Sings* (London), *Oh Captain!* (Columbia)

BOOK: *Which Reminds Me* (1989)

BROADWAY: *Inherit the Wind* (1955), *Oh Captain!* (1958), *Hello Charlie* (1959), *Utbu* (1966), *M. Butterfly* (1989)

FILMS incl.: *Oh Men! Oh Women!* (1957), *Will Success Spoil Rock Hunter* (1957), *The Mating Game* (1959), *Pillow Talk* (1959), *The Adventures of Huckleberry Finn* (1960), *Let's Make Love* (1960), *Lover Come Back* (1961), *Boys' Night Out* (1962), *Island of Love* (1963), *The Brass Bottle* (1964), *The Seven Faces of Dr. Lao* (1964), *Send Me No Flowers* (1964), *Fluffy* (1965), *The Alphabet Murders* (1966), *Hello Down There* (1968), *Everything You Always Wanted to Know About Sex But Were Afraid to Ask* (1972), *Foolin' Around* (1979), *Scavenger Hunt* (1979), *Sidney Shorr: A Girl's Best Friend* (1981), *The King of Comedy* (1983)

TV: "One Man's Family" (1950–52), "Mr. Peepers" (1952–55), "The Odd Couple" (1970–74), "The Tony Randall Show" (1976–78), "Love, Sidney" (1981–83)

VIDEO: *Rand McNally Video Trip: New York*

# MARTHA RAYE

## (Margaret Theresa Yvonne Reed, August 27, 1916–   )

Wide-mouthed, good-natured and bursting with energy, Martha Raye's style in the 1940s and '50s seems a bit dated now and her boisterousness is a bit hard to take, but at the time she was one of America's top comediennes, who mirrored the era's spunky optimism.

Born in Butte, Montana, Martha performed with her parents (the team of Reed and Hooper) between 1919 and 1929: "I thought I was having a wonderful life. I never realized I was being culturally deprived, that I was having a lousy upbringing. We were too busy making a living to worry about stuff like that. So I guess I grew up insecure, with no home ties. And maybe that's why I'll always be insecure and worried about finding happiness. But I do remember those as happy years, even when we didn't have enough to eat."

Ebullient and rather pretty, at 15 she became a solo vocalist with the Paul Ash Orchestra, inspired by the loud style of the day as exemplified by Ethel Merman. But, unlike another raucous singer, Betty Hutton, Martha began to specialize in novelty tunes and comedy rather than musicals. The name Martha Raye was borrowed from a Manhattan phone book. Between singing engagements Martha worked at the Cedars of Lebanon Hospital in Los Angeles as a nurse's aide.

Raye appeared in several Broadway revues, including *Earl Carroll's Sketchbook* and *Calling All Stars*, appeared on radio with Al Jolson, Eddie Cantor and Bob Hope and was in Al Jolson's musical *Hold on to Your Hats*. She starred in nightclubs and, on the basis of her work at The Trocadero, was given her film debut by director Norman Taurog in *Rhythm on the Range*. She signed a five-year deal with Paramount.

In early films she tended to sing brash novelty tunes, including "Vote for Mr. Rhythm" in *Big Broadcast of 1937*. Paramount tried to change her image, going for musical comedy glamour in 1938s *Give Me a Sailor,* but dropped her in 1940 when the experiment failed. Raye rebounded playing man-hungry types, sometimes with amusing peskiness, other times with a broad lack of restraint. She had a hilarious double role as a waitress girlfriend for Lou Costello—and a sister who couldn't stand him—in *Keep 'em Flying*. Unlike other film boy-chasers, Raye's comical bad luck had less to do with her looks than her aggressive "unfeminine" personality. Most audiences found her rather attractive, and so did Costello in the film; one kiss from her turned the slice of bread he was holding into toast.

Raye was Mischa Auer's love interest in *Hellzapoppin* and for a while played a few straight musicals that her studio vainly hoped would change her image into a more romantic comedy star. During World War II she, Kay Francis, Mitzi Mayfair and Carole Landis toured overseas for the USO. Their story became the basis for the film *Four Jills and a Jeep.*

Martha Raye was a great talent. The problem was in finding the right parts that offered some vulnerable contrast to her brassy talent at slapstick, drunk routines and rubber-mouthed mugging and miming. Charles Chaplin saw some interesting qualities in Martha, and chose her as the charming, aggravating target of a suave murderer in *Monsieur Verdoux.* Unfortunately, while critics praised the film, it was too offbeat to be a hit at the time.

Raye's career was resuscitated by Milton Berle and 1950s television, where slapstick and raucous comedy had staged a comeback. Following guest spots with Berle, Martha had her own television show, which became a top-10 success. When the vogue for slapstick television waned late in the '50s, Raye turned up on Steve Allen's show, appeared in summer stock and staged yet another comeback in 1962's *Jumbo* as Jimmy Durante's fiancée. A few years later, in 1967, she made another comeback taking over Carol Channing's role on Broadway in *Hello Dolly.*

If Raye's career was bumpy, it was matched by an equally chaotic personal life. She was married six times, mismatched with Bud Westmore, David Rose, Neil Lang, Nick Condos, Edward Begley and Robert O'Shea. The last marriage resulted in a major scandal in August 1956. She was accused of alienating the affections of Mrs. O'Shea when she fell in love with her husband. Officer Robert O'Shea had been guarding Martha against kidnap threats after a suspicious explosion in her kitchen. She settled with Mrs. O'Shea out of court for $20,000, divorced her fifth husband and married O'Shea. It lasted two months.

Raye's fans always loved her. She seemed to have warmth and affection for everyone, wearing not only a St. Christopher medal but a St. Genesius medal and a Star of David. In the early 1970s she was on Saturday morning television in the kiddie show "The Bugaloos" as Benita the Witch. In 1976, with an assist from Rock Hudson, Martha took over for Nancy Walker on "McMillan and Wife." In the 1980s she joined the hit television series "Alice," playing Vic Tayback's mother. Tolerant of being known for having a comically big mouth, she be-

came the spokeswoman for a denture company, revealing her bright, wide smile. Of course, with her luck she ended up taking on David Letterman in a futile lawsuit after he lampooned the ads.

Raye was unexpectedly the subject of tabloid headlines in 1991. Though she was often so weak she required a wheelchair, the 74-year-old star married a man who was 44. Reporters questioned his sincerity and her ability to make decisions. She had suffered a stroke the year before. Later that year her husband made headlines demanding millions from Bette Midler, claiming her film *For the Boys* was based on Raye's life.

Over the years, one thing about Martha Raye remained constant: her sense of duty to her country and its soldiers. In World War II, Korea and Vietnam, she not only entertained the troops, she received two Purple Hearts from putting her life in danger to tend to wounded soldiers personally. She used her nurse's training to help in triage, cleaning the wounds as the soldiers were brought in off the line for medical treatment. She was in Vietnam twice in 1965, twice in 1966 and yet again in 1967. In 1968 she received the Jean Hersholt Humanitarian Award.

The soldiers never forgot. In 1990 and 1991 several Vietnam veterans groups rallied behind her and began petitioning for her to receive the Congressional Medal of Freedom. Their hearts went out to the woman who did more than just clown or sing "Mr. Paganini," "Big Foot Pete" and her other novelty hits. While her own battles for her career and her own happiness would have been enough for most anyone, Martha Raye believed there was never enough time to work for something even more important to her—others.

AUDIO: *Here's Martha Raye* (Epic), *Together Again for the First Time* (with Carol Burnett) (Tetragrammaton), *The Voice* (Discovery), *Girls of the 30s* (Pelican), *Here Come the Girls* (Epic)

BROADWAY incl.: *Hold on to Your Hats!* (1940), *Hello Dolly!* (1967)

FILMS incl.: *Rhythm on the Range* (1936), *The Big Broadcast of 1937* (1937), *Waikiki Wedding* (1937), *Mountain Music* (1937), *Double or Nothing* (1937), *Artists and Models* (1937), *The Big Broadcast of 1938*

(1938), *Tropic Holiday (1938) Never Say Die* (1939), *The Boys from Syracuse* (1940), *Keep 'Em Flying* (1941), *Hellzapoppin* (1941), *Four Jills in a Jeep* (1944), *Monsieur Verdoux* (1947), *Jumbo* (1962), *Pufnstuf* (1970), *Concorde* (1979)

TV: "All Star Revue" (1951–53), "The Martha Raye Show" (1955–56), "The Bugaloos" (1970–71), "McMillan and Wife" (1976–77), "Alice" (1982–84)

## CARL REINER

### (March 20, 1922–   )

One of the giants of modern comedy, Carl Reiner has written, directed and acted in classic films and television shows since 1948. In the '90s he's finally begun to get the recognition he deserves for his 40 years of brilliance. In 1991 he received a "Lifetime Achievement" honor during the nationally televised "Fifth Annual American Comedy Awards." The reason the honor arrived late was obvious, even in his moment in the spotlight, the modest star talked mostly of his past co-workers and family.

But after playing straight man to Mel Brooks and Sid Caesar, writing and directing "The Dick Van Dyke Show" and working on classic comedies with Steve Martin, the spotlight deservedly remained on Carl Reiner that night, and the audience gave him a monumental ovation.

Reiner grew up in New York and attended Evander Childs High School. He was in the Signal Corps during World War II. His special services unit, which included Sergeant Howard Morris and Major Maurice Evans, appeared in GI revues in the Pacific. Returning to the States, Reiner turned a straight role into accidental comedy. Playing the king in a production of *Hamlet* in Opelika, Alabama, he forgot his lines and started double-talking. Typically for the low-key and amiable Reiner, the whole thing was funny only to him—the audience had no idea he was deviating from the lofty text.

In 1943 Reiner married his wife, Estelle and raised three kids. In the late '40s, following a road tour in *Call Me Mister*, Reiner moved to television in a variety of revues and, ultimately, "Your Show of Shows." Reiner seemed to work in the shadows of Sid Caesar on that show, usually playing straight man. At the start of the '60s he lobbed straight lines to Mel Brooks, who bashed them to comic pieces as "The 2000 Year Old Man." The fun began after Reiner saw an interview segment on "We the People Speak" and joked about it in the staff room of "Your Show of Shows." He turned to Brooks and said, "Here's a man who was actually at the scene of the crucifixion, isn't that right, sir?" Brooks muttered, "Oh boy . . ." and they were off. The duo of Reiner and Brooks had several hit records, but once again, the fans were attracted to Brooks, the bombastic star, while only those in the business knew how important Reiner's contributions were.

Reiner wrote the autobiographical novel *Enter Laughing*, which became a Broadway show and eventually was made into a film. Further drawing on his golden decade as a comedy writer, he created a television pilot for a sitcom. First called "Head of the Family," it originally starred Reiner as comedy writer Robert Petrie and Barbara Britton as his wife. It became a legendary hit—once the roles were taken by Dick Van Dyke and Mary Tyler Moore. Reiner wrote many of the show's finest episodes and took the role of Van Dyke's boss, the irascible television star Alan Brady. Reiner began racking up more Emmy awards and nominations than even the Academy could count. Of his various Emmys, which number about a dozen, he remarked that they're "all sitting at home, quietly oxidizing."

Still the perfect ensemble player, even as the boss, Reiner allowed most of the laughs to come from Van Dyke's reactions rather than his own bluster. For those who would like some idea of how Reiner would have played a family man in a sitcom, the best evidence is probably *The Russians Are Coming, The Russians Are Coming* the film he made around the same time as Van Dyke's show. Also at the same time, he hosted a television quiz show, "The Celebrity Game." Down to earth about "fame" and creating "an image," for some broadcasts he wore his toupee and some times he didn't bother.

Through the '70s and '80s Reiner established himself as an important comedy director. Having had previous hits with the cult classics *The Comic* and *Where's Poppa?* he directed Steve Martin in *The Jerk, The Man with Two Brains* and *Dead Men Don't*

*Wear Plaid*. The latter also featured Reiner as a Nazi (of the berserk Otto Preminger type). Reiner's best effort of that era was *All of Me*, the first film that fully integrated Steve Martin's wild-and-crazy physical comedy with a logical story line and a pleasing character.

Always a gentle and self-effacing personality, Reiner attended a press screening of *All of Me* and, sans entourage, asked several people in the lobby, "Was it funny? Did you like it?" To a chorus of congratulations he asked again, "You really liked it?" When a *New York Times* interviewer asked him about comedy directing, he answered, "When you cast good people in a good script, you don't have a lot to do."

Reiner was also behind one of George Burns' greatest hits, *Oh God* and a string of lighthearted efforts, including *Bert Rigby You're a Fool, Sibling Rivalry, The One and Only, Summer Rental* and *Summer School*. While some films won praise and some didn't, Reiner approaches them with all the same enthusiasm: "At my age you don't just take anything that comes along, because you're going to have to spend a year with it. It's got to be funny."

In addition to his films, Reiner remains an eccentric raconteur on talk shows. In his first appearance on Dennis Miller's talk show in 1992, Reiner declared, "You know how dogs and hyenas urinate in the corner of the yard? I'm going to urinate in as many places as necessary to know that I'm welcome here. I want to stake my territory!"

Quite often fans would ask Reiner if he would consider an update of "The Dick Van Dyke Show," reassembling the classic cast. Reiner admitted he had thoughts about it, but said such a reunion special would hardly be what the average fan expected: "We thought it would be a black comedy where everybody had a terminal disease, but, in situation comedy style, they keep it from each other; everybody's a martyr and at the end we all expire. We started writing dialogue for it and we got hysterical. Of course everybody was telling us that we were sick."

When told that he probably had many years ahead of him, since comedians are always laughing, he answered, "Comedians are stressful people. They're upset with what's wrong with the world.

Orchestra conductors live longest, because they do aerobics when they're working."

AUDIO: *The 2000 Year Old Man* (Capitol), *2000 and One Years* (Capitol), *At the Cannes Film Festival* (Capitol), *2013 Year Old Man* (Warner Bros.), *The Incomplete Works of Reiner and Brooks* (Warner Bros.)

BROADWAY: *Inside USA* (1948), *Alive and Kicking* (1950)

FILMS incl.: *Happy Anniversary* (1959), *The Gazebo* (1959), *Gidget Goes Hawaiian* (1961), *It's a Mad Mad Mad Mad World* (1963), *The Act of Love* (1965), *The Russians Are Coming! The Russians Are Coming* (1966), *A Guide for the Married Man* (1967), *The Comic* (1969), *Generation* (1969), *Ten from Your Show of Shows* (1973), *Oh God* (1977), *The End* (1978), *Skokie* (1981), *Dead Men Don't Wear Plaid* (1982)

TV: "The Fashion Story" (1948–49), "The 54th St. Revue" (1949), "Eddie Condon's Floor Show" (1950), "Your Show of Shows" (1950–54), "Caesar's Hour" (1954–57), "Sid Caesar Invites You" (1958), "Keep Talking" (1958–59), "The Dick Van Dyke Show" (1961–66), "The Celebrity Game" (1964–65), "Good Heavens" (1976), "Sunday Best" (1990)

## ROB REINER

### (March 6, 1945–   )

For years known either as Rob, son of Carl Reiner, or "Meathead," son of Archie Bunker, Rob Reiner has emerged as one of the most credible and bankable directors in film comedy. When his romantic comedy *When Harry Met Sally* became a box office hit, *Rolling Stone* magazine confirmed, "Reiner's fifth feature, following *This Is Spinal Tap, The Sure Thing, Stand by Me* and *The Princess Bride* (not a loser in the bunch) is a ravishing, romantic lark brimming over with style, intelligence and flashing wit."

Style, intelligence and flashing wit were not things Reiner showed during his somewhat hapless years as one of the stars of *All in the Family*, the sensational television sitcom that ignited controversies and scored number-one ratings through most of the 1970s. He played Mike Stivic, aka "Meathead," who often fed straight lines to Archie Bunker. Championing

R-rated films, Mike insisted, "The fact that they go to bed—they make love—it's part of life!" Archie: "So's throwing up, but I ain't paying three bucks to see it!"

Reiner generated some laughs from Mike's goofy smile of embarrassment or his hapless rages, but like his father, Carl Reiner, Rob's clever ensemble work was overshadowed by the stronger players in the cast. He might set up a line with a hilarious outburst ("You know, Arch, you eat my heart out! Little by little, day by day, you *eat my heart out!*"). But it was the star, O'Connor who effortlessly got the laugh: "I don't care."

Reiner attended the University of California for two years forming an improvisational company called The Session (with Richard Dreyfuss) and, at 21, joined the staff of television's "Smothers Brothers Comedy Hour" as a writer (partnered with Steve Martin). He appeared as a delivery boy in a 1967 episode of "Batman" with Cesar Romero and Burgess Meredith, turned up on "That Girl" and "Gomer Pyle" episodes, and worked with the improvisational group The Committee (where he met his wife Penny Marshall). He and Penny appeared together as lovers in an episode of "The Odd Couple." It was Norman Lear who selected Rob for "All in the Family." As Reiner recalled, Lear "was the first person to ever recognize that I had any talent at all, who thought I was funny, even."

Reiner won Emmy awards in 1974 and 1978 for "All in the Family," but in the '80s turned his attentions to directing.

As a director, he used many experiences from real life to color his stories. *Stand by Me* was praised for its handling of kids' problems. As Reiner admitted, it came from his own childhood, which, though rewarding, had its share of pain. "I felt very isolated and misunderstood." *When Harry Met Sally* came out of Reiner's own experiences following the end of "All in the Family" and his divorce from Penny Marshall in 1979. "I was not ready to be involved with anybody, and I was back in the dating world, and had needs like anybody else. And I found myself always caught in these awkward relationships with women where you'd have sex and then it would be uncomfortable. I wanted the contact with a woman, but I wasn't ready to totally commit to a full-time relationship. And I wondered could I just be friends

with a woman, because I wanted that contact and it seemed like sex always came in somehow and messed things up, whether from having it—nor not having it." He met his current wife, Michele Singer, on the set of the movie.

Reiner won over critics when he later directed serious films, but like his father, he still favors comedy over tragedy. Having grown up surrounded by comedians, and currently having many as his friends, he added, "Comedians are the brightest people in the world. They observe life in a way nobody else does. I don't know a comedian who hasn't experienced a tremendous amount of pain, and they are, to me, the most insightful people there are."

Of fans who continue to greet him with a happy cry of "Meathead," he shrugs and says, "That thing's always followed me around. No matter what happens to me—if I win the Nobel Prize, it would say Meathead Wins Nobel. That monicker will be around forever."

AUDIO: *All in the Family* (Atlantic), *All in the Family 2* (Atlantic), *Peter and the Wolf* (UA)

FILMS incl.: *Enter Laughing* (1967), *Where's Poppa* (1970), *Halls of Anger* (1970), *Thursday's Game* (1974), *Fire Sale* (1977), *Million Dollar Infield* (1982), *This Is Spinal Tap* (1984), *Postcards from the Edge* (1990)

TV: "All in the Family" (1971–78), "Free Country" (1978)

# DON RICKLES

## (May 8, 1926–  )

A caricature of the average man out of control, raging Don Rickles won laughs with his feverish, sweaty delivery and his pained personality. It was funny watching his anger and irritation take him over the edge. The laughs came from the shock of his uninhibited fury, whether he was being ludicrous ("You hockey puck!") or ludicrously accurate (telling a woman in an ostentatious fur coat, "You look like an old beaver in heat"). Whether on a talk show or a nightclub stage, the audience never knew who or what the next target would be.

Often, especially in the 1960s, Rickles' targets were members of ethnic and sexual minority groups and the remarks were notoriously blunt. He got snickers with an aside to a male ringsider. "That was a good one, wasn't it, queer?" Many in the audience shared Rickles' evident dislike for particular targets; but he could not have become the king of insult comedy if the ultimate joke wasn't on himself.

Rickles's career in comedy began after he grew tired of working as a salesman for Metropolitan Life Insurance. *The New Yorker* recalled that he was "shy and terrified," but tried show business anyway, encouraged by his mother. His father died when Don was still growing up. Rickles tried everything, from a New York drama school (Jason Robards Jr. was a classmate) to the hard knocks of comedy clubs. Billed as Don "Glasshead" Rickles, the balding comic's best routine was a Peter Lorre imitation. He recalled of his early years in comedy, "I did impersonations—badly. . . . I got my start in strip joints—in dumps. What happened was that I could never tell a joke. To this day, I still can't tell a joke. In these clubs, I found myself trying to tell jokes and do impressions and that wasn't making it for me, so I just started talking to the audience." He also yelled at the audience, his ad libs funnier than his act, his feisty personality coming out from behind the stale prepared gags.

Jack E. Leonard had achieved success with insult comedy, but Rickles' style was different. Leonard was more benign, nonthreatening in his dumpling build and his mumbling delivery. He offered a lot of prepared gags. In the 1960s, Rickles was more energetic, more unpredictable, working over the audience with ad libs that relied more on raw shock observation than joke humor.

When Rickles was in a lather, he didn't soft-soap anyone, even Frank Sinatra. In fact, Rickles made his reputation at a nightclub when he spotted Sinatra and shouted, "Your voice is gone, it's all over for you, you're making a fool of yourself!" Instead of taking offense, Sinatra laughed at the nervy young comic. As Rickles later admitted, "Attitude is important—it's all attitude. Some people can say 'you're an idiot' and it doesn't come out funny."

Sinatra was an early friend of Rickles, as was Dean Martin, who booked Don for celebrity roast television appearances that were a big boost to his career. Rickles' battles with Johnny Carson on "The Tonight Show" probably showed him off best to national audiences. Celebrities especially enjoyed being singled out at Don's shows, perhaps purging their own feelings of guilt over being stars. The way Don insulted them, they could be embarrassed but unhurt, like being hit with a pie. The first time Bob Newhart came to see Rickles, Don shouted, "Bob Newhart is a stammering idiot and his wife is a former hooker from Bayonne!"

A capable actor, Rickles was able to win occasional film and television roles. He was a heavy in *The Rat Race* and played an aggravated small-time crook in prison on "The Dick Van Dyke Show." He often demonstrated a bizarre sense of humor off stage. During the filming of *Run Silent Run Deep,* he and co-star Jack Warden stripped naked in Clark Gable's dressing room and began embracing when the star walked in.

Through the 1960s, Rickles' on-stage shock comedy regularly drew complaints from critics deeply troubled by the minority insults. Rickles insisted these gags only showed up bigotry as ridiculous, but even fellow Las Vegas bad boy Buddy Hackett was moved to remark, "He's the furthest thing from the truth." Over the years Rickles mellowed slightly and stayed more with remarks keyed less to race than to physical features. To a fat person: "What do you eat for dinner? Furniture?" He might also kibbitz with ringsiders on a variety of safe subjects, including marriage: "Marriage is a beautiful thing. It's better than laying in a dam watching a beaver eat your jacket or something. . . . My wife is laughs, she puts a cigarette in her navel and makes it puff!"

He seemed to do best attacking celebrities. At celebrity roasts he devastated other stars with remarks that were often painfully funny and honest. He deflated the inflated, shouting at Orson Welles, "Who makes your tents?" He voiced the same irritation with child actor Ricky Schroeder that others felt: "You were great in *The Champ,* sniveling and whining." He put the knock to an easy target such as Ernest Borgnine: "Look at you—anybody else hurt in the accident?" He even sharpened his knife for a stab at comedy's greatest institution: "Bob Hope's so popular, when he was in Vietnam they were shooting at him from both sides."

Notorious as a high-paid Las Vegas attraction and a sparring partner on talk shows, Rickles became so well known he rarely got the acting roles he craved, ones that would add some variety to his career. The occasional parts he got, such as his role as a manic ventriloquist on a 1990 episode of "Tales from the Crypt," were keyed to his overboard personality. His sitcoms and television variety shows never lasted, lacking the special chemistry that he relied on. Reviewing his variety show, Jack Gould in The *New York Times* complained that "for a quick-witted performer, he was ill at ease in the confinement of a prestructured format . . . in his many appearances with Johnny Carson . . . Mr. Rickles has been a frequent winner with his extemporaneous deflation of the famous and his often-refreshing departures from humbug. But the key to that success has been the presence of someone with whom he could exchange quips."

Into the '90s Rickles remains popular in nightclubs and on "The Tonight Show," where years earlier Johnny Carson had dubbed him "Mr. Warmth." He remains the king of insult comedy.

One thing is evident. His audience knows it's all an act. Few have ever sought him out after a show to confront him. "There was only one time I really got hurt by a fan," Don admitted. "In 1979. I brought a guy on stage and had some fun with him—and he bit me! But he didn't mean it. I kissed him, for a joke—and he kissed back—a little too strong!"

AUDIO: *Hello Dummy* (Warner Bros.), *Don Rickles Speaks* (Warner Bros.), *Magic Moments from the Tonight Show* (Casablanca), *Heeeere's Johnny: Don Rickles Friars Roast* (Bootleg)

FILMS incl.: *Run Silent Run Deep* (1958), *The Rabbit Trap* (1959), *The Rat Race* (1960), *Enter Laughing* (1967), *The Money Jungle* (1968), *Where Its At* (1969), *Kelly's Heroes* (1970)

TV: "The Don Rickles Show" (1968–69), "The Don Rickles Show" (1972), "C.P.O. Sharkey" (1976–78), "Foul-Ups, Bleeps and Blunders (1984–85)

VIDEO: *Buy This Tape You Hockey Puck*

## BILLIE RITCHIE

### (September 14, 1878–July 6, 1921)

Known as a Chaplin imitator and the only movie comedian to have been severely bitten by ostriches,

Billie Ritchie is a somewhat bizarre footnote to silent comedy in general and Chaplin in particular.

Born in Glasgow, Scotland, Ritchie was a clown in the Pinder and Ords Circus in Scotland in 1893. His climb to fame began when he joined the Fred Karno troupe around 1903. He played the drunk in Karno's popular sketch "A Night in an English Music Hall" and traveled to America with it, billed as "The Different Drunk" in 1908 and "The Original Drunk" five years later. He worked with partner Rich McAllister in the classic sketch, playing the drunk heckler sitting in the audience and ultimately falling onto the stage to start a comic fight.

When Charles Chaplin, also an ex-member of the Karno players, became a movie star, Ritchie moved to California and found work at L-KO studios in 1914. L-KO executive Henry Lehrman was an old enemy of Chaplin's and delighted in copying The Little Tramp character, using Karno-trained Billie Ritchie. Ritchie played the role to the hilt, duplicating the Chaplin makeup and costume. He never called himself an imitator; he even went so far as to suggest Chaplin had copied him. He had a build like Chaplin's, saying "I stand about 5 feet 7 1/2 inches, my hair is black, and I weigh about 140 pounds." Of his film style he added, "The average audience of grown-ups prefer refined comedy, but the slapstick variety is the type that appeals to the young ones. . . . You can safely figure that half the audiences at picture houses are the juvenile element, and consequently it is safe to play to their preferences in comedy. That is why so many broad farces and knock-about acts are used. They are sure to get a laugh. . . . in the matter of makeup, I have adopted a certain style and stuck with it. . . . the makeup I use for the L-KO comedies is strictly original with me . . . I have played for a great many years in this particular makeup."

Some reviewers of the day seemed to regard him as Chaplin's equal. The *Fort Wayne Journal* reviewed *Bill's Blighted Career*, declaring the star "the world champion screen comedian who can provoke more laughter with a mere uplift of his eyelid than the average comedian could in a half hour of strenuous effort." However, Billie couldn't sustain interest after wise viewers began seeing through his imitations.

He continued making films until he fell victim to his own slapstick. He was violently attacked by a group of irascible ostriches while shooting one of his comedies. He showed some pluck in attempting a comeback, but each new slapstick film only aggravated his various injuries and worsened his health. He died a few years after the ostriches got to him.

FILMS incl.: *A Meeting for Cheating* (1915), *Bill's Blighted Career* (1915), *Almost a Scandal* (1915)

## THE RITZ BROTHERS

**Al: Abraham Joachim, August 27, 1901–December 22, 1965**
**Jimmy: Samuel Joachim, October 5, 1904–November 17, 1985**
**Harry: Herschel Joachim, May 22, 1907–March 29, 1986**

They were three zanies—but not Three Stooges and not three Marx Brothers. While the look-alike boys had some fine moments in films, audiences accustomed to the more pronounced eccentricity and personality of the other teams have paid them little attention over the years. To modern viewers, Al, Jimmy and Harry look like a trio of Huntz Halls, or three Danny Kayes on drugs.

The Ritz clan grew up in Brooklyn, with Al starting out as a dancer in vaudeville and his brothers joining him later. Originally billed as The Collegians when they played Coney Island in 1925, they claimed to have gotten the name Ritz off a laundry truck when their agent insisted on a name change. Expert eccentric dancers, they clowned in 1926's *George White's Scandals* and 1932's *Earl Carroll's Vanities*. A few years later they made a short, *Hotel Anchovy,* an entertaining, nonsensical romp in which they played aggressive bellboys bewildering both guests and other employees.

Darryl Zanuck enjoyed the film, but instead of signing them to make their own movies, he sandwiched their novelty numbers and routines into a series of otherwise tame and forgettable Alice Faye musicals. They had similar guest spots in *The Goldwyn Follies,* playing animal trainers ("When you think of animals—think of us!") and doing a set piece, "Serenade to a Fish." In *One in a Million* starring Sonja Henie, they do their impressions of Boris Karloff, Peter Lorre and Charles Laughton—on skates.

The boys made a few uneven feature films in the late 1930s, with *The Three Musketeers* considered the best. They had some trouble finding good scripts with Zanuck at 20th Century Fox and after the disastrous *Gorilla* and *Pack Up Your Troubles,* they packed up for Universal, co-starring with The Andrews Sisters in their first film, *Argentine Nights.* With Abbott and Costello doing so well at Universal at the same time, the brothers were neglected and, within a few years and a few films, back in vaudeville.

The team played Las Vegas in the 1940s, retired periodically in the '50s, but were still performing together up until 1965. That year Al Ritz had a heart attack while on tour in New Orleans. Harry and Jimmy continued without him.

Though their reputation languished in the '50s and '60s, stars influenced by The Ritz Brothers often spoke out in their defense. Many, from Sid Caesar to Huntz Hall, have acknowledged a debt to Harry Ritz. Sid Caesar: "Harry brought a whole new dimension to comedy. When he told a joke, he told it with his whole body." Harry, the last surviving Ritz Brother, was given a cameo role in Mel Brooks' *Silent Movie.* In an episode of television's "M\*A\*S\*H," the officers raise their glasses high and decide on a toast. Hawkeye (Alan Alda) said, "Let's drink to something important! To the Ritz Brothers!"

BROADWAY: *George White's Scandals* (1926), *Earl Carroll's Vanities* (1932), *Casino Varieties* (1934)
FILMS incl.: *Hotel Anchovy* (1934), *Sing Baby Sing* (1936), *One in a Million* (1937), *On the Avenue* (1937), *You Can't Have Everything* (1937), *Life Begins at College* (1937), *The Goldwyn Follies* (1938), *Kentucky Moonshine* (1938), *Straight Place and Show* (1938), *The Three Musketeers* (1939), *The Gorilla* (1939), *Pack Up Your Troubles* (1939), *Argentine Nights* (1940), *Behind the Eight Ball* (1942), *Hi Ya Chum* (1943), *Never a Dull Moment* (1943), *Blazing Stewardesses* (1975), *Won Ton Ton, the Dog That Saved Hollywood* (1976), *Real Life* (1979)

## JOAN RIVERS

**(Joan Molinsky, June 8, 1933–   )**

One of the most successful women in stand-up comedy, Joan Rivers had a career marked by years of

The Ritz Brothers: Al, Jimmy and Harry. Somehow their appeal hasn't lasted as has that of other trios, such as The Marx Brothers and The Three Stooges. Photo from the author's collection.

struggle, insecurity, self-doubt and pain. The struggles continued and intensified as she moved on to films, Broadway and television talk shows. Tragedy and controversy surrounded her, but did not stop her. Her bond with her audience remains deep and strong. Neil Simon wrote, "The deeper the personal pain the richer the vein of humor . . . she not only wears her heart on her sleeve, she passes it out to the audience for personal inspection."

Raised in the affluent suburb of Larchmont, New York, her father a doctor, Joan felt inadequate and insecure, a pudgy frog compared to neighborhood princesses. After high school she landed a bit role in the film *Mr. Universe,* but finished out her schooling at Barnard College, graduating with a B.A. in 1954. An early marriage ended in divorce after six months.

Searching for a niche in show business, Rivers worked behind the scenes for television's "Candid Camera," played strip clubs as comedienne Pepper January, and joined a comedy team for some USO tours as Jim, Jake and Joan. She was briefly with the Second City improvisational group in 1960. In 1964, using the name of the agent who had suggested she change her name, Joan Rivers emerged with a local Greenwich Village cabaret act similar to Woody Allen's. She tried to appeal to intelligent audiences with flights of fancy, including gags about her blond wig (which came alive and became her pet until it was run over by a car) and the nasty

houseplant in the kitchen that would drink her soup. She told self-deprecating jokes about being single and a loser: "I was the ugliest child ever born in Larchmont, New York! Oh, Please! The doctor looked at me and slapped my mother. . . . My parents hated me. They said why can't you be like the girl next door? We lived next door to a cemetery." If the framework was Woody's, it was the soul of Lenny Bruce that brought out the best in her comedy. She said, "I learned from Lenny that you could tell the truth on stage."

Johnny Carson gave her national exposure on "The Tonight Show" in February 1966. She was now married to a producer, Edgar Rosenberg. She became a solid name in stand-up and wrote a syndicated column for the *Chicago Tribune* between 1973 and 1976 and a best-selling book, *Having a Baby Can Be a Scream,* in 1974. Still, she was struggling to reach the top of her profession, and her efforts to branch out were fraught with tension. She wrote the television movie *The Girl Most Likely To* but recalled that she threw up after watching the finished product: "How's that for liking yourself?" The show was the highest-rated made-for-television film ever made up to that time, but she suffered to create it. When she made her first theatrical film, *Rabbit Test,* she suffered even more, working furiously during production and in endless stressful promotion. The reason was not only her hyper personality; she and her husband Edgar invested their savings and mortgaged their home to make it.

In stand-up, Rivers' self-deprecating comedy began to change. For one thing, she underwent several beautifying surgical procedures. Also, now that she was a star, she confided to her audience about the stars she was meeting. Her gossipy little swipes at celebrities drew huge laughs. The anger that Joan had long turned inward was now set on the pompous and the pretentious. A dieter who suffered to keep her weight off, Joan naturally tossed jokes at Elizabeth Taylor, a beautiful woman who was letting herself go: "She has more chins than a Chinese phone book." With her catch phrase (now a government-registered trademark) "Can we talk?" Joan told her truths—wild, exaggerated, sometimes strident—but truths nevertheless.

Audiences roared and wanted more. The more outrageous she was, the more successful she became. In 1983 Joan was named permanent guest host on

"The Tonight Show" for Johnny Carson's nine weeks of vacation time. Her monologues became wilder, the audience cheering the most daring and at times tasteless remarks. Joan, one of stand-up's nicest, most sensitive, most caring stars, got caught up in all of this, logically believing that at worst, she was simply giving people a good laugh. At best, she was a crusader. After all, wasn't it *after* the insults that Liz Taylor went on a diet that brought her front-page magazine coverage?

In 1983 the workaholic performer had a Grammy-nominated record and her own line of greeting cards, and in 1984 a book of sex jokes based on a slut character she invented: *The Life and Hard Times of Heidi Abromowitz* sold over half a million copies. Her autobiography *Enter Talking* also was a best seller. Her voice was now perpetually hoarse from her nonstop concert schedule.

Clearly a comedy superstar, Rivers was shocked to learn that in the event of Johnny Carson's retirement, she was not even on the "top 10" list of

Getting better looking every day: Joan Rivers, stand-up comedienne turned talk show host. Photo from the author's collection.

replacements. She joined the Fox network, receiving a contract for three years and $10 million. When she phoned Johnny Carson to tell him, he hung up on her. He'd already heard the news and was fuming over her "betrayal" of him. The Carson-Rivers feud was front-page news. It simmered over the next month by Rivers' prescheduled promotions for her autobiography and then was set ablaze when her new show went on the air in October 1986. The show premiered successfully and had good ratings in key cities, but the network didn't have as many affiliates as NBC and Carson. Joan's ratings couldn't match his, and the panic at Fox and the network's subsequent interference with Joan and her husband Edgar Rosenberg (the show's producer), led to misery and stress. In May 1987 Fox fired Rivers, sending her star status hurtling downward. Three months later, physically ill and emotionally devastated, Rosenberg killed himself in a Philadelphia hotel room.

No one could possibly put into words what Joan Rivers went through. But a writer named Ben Stein in *GQ* magazine gave it a shot. Using an assumed name, he described Rivers as joking about Edgar's death and intimating she was about to divorce him anyway. Weak with grief and trembling with shame and rage, Joan Rivers tearfully read a prepared statement vowing to fight back and file charges. Eventually the magazine settled out of court, issuing a statement regretting "any inadvertent imputation of negative or inappropriate conduct."

By all accounts not only alone but "terrified," Rivers was not only without a husband but without the man who managed her career for the past two decades. She gave up her California home and moved to New York, busying herself with the chores of setting up her new living quarters. She tried to anchor herself with the best therapy possible: return to work. She became the "center square" on the quiz show "The Hollywood Squares." On June 21, 1988 she joined the cast of *Broadway Bound.* This was her first major appearance as an actress, and she was taking up the challenge at a fragile time in her life. She met the challenge, winning impressive reviews from the tough New York critics.

In stand-up Joan returned to a mix of self-deprecation and saucy wisecracks: "Girls on the beach in string bikinis—it looks like they're flossing their behinds." "There are no lesbians in prison. They're all in pro-tennis." "A robber broke into my house and said, 'One bark and you're dead.'" "John F. Kennedy Jr.? Dumb! He failed the [bar] exam twice and one of the questions was name a dead president."

Her daytime show mixes jokes, girl talk and emotional interviews with stars and people with dramatic or tragic stories to tell. In 1989 she earned a star in the Hollywood Walk of Fame, and in June 1990 an Emmy award. In a moving acceptance speech she declared, "I didn't think I was going to win. I'm not being cute—I have no speech prepared. . . . Two years ago I couldn't get a job in this business. I could not get a job. My income dropped to one-sixteenth of what it was before I was fired. And people said I wouldn't work again. And my husband had a breakdown, and it's so sad that he's not here, because it was my husband Edgar Rosenberg who always said, 'You can turn things around.' And except for one terrible moment in a hotel room in Philadelphia when he forgot that. . . ." Through the tears she continued, "This is really for him. Because he was with me from the beginning. And I'm so sorry he's not here today."

The audience wept with Joan Rivers as they had so often laughed with her. They laughed with her when she started out as "the female Woody Allen." And they applauded her even more when she emerged as a unique comic star with her own identifiable style.

Joan Rivers once said, "My whole career has been just hard, hurting little steps." But those little steps were always forward.

AUDIO: *Mr. Phyllis and Other Funny Stories* (Warner Bros.), *The Next to Last Joan Rivers Album* (Buddah, reissued by Arista), *What Becomes a Semi-Legend Most?* (Geffen), *Zingers from the Hollywood Squares* (Event)
BOOKS: *Having a Baby Can Be a Scream* (1978), *The Life and Hard Times of Heidi Abromowitz* (1984), *Enter Talking* (1986), *Still Talking* (1991)
BROADWAY: *Fun City* (1971), *Broadway Bound* (1988)
FILMS incl.: *The Swimmer* (1968), *The Girl Most Likely To* (1973), *Rabbit Test* (1978), *The Muppets Take Manhattan* (1984), *How to Murder a Millionaire* (1990)

TV: "The Late Show" (1986–87), "The Joan Rivers Show" (1989–  )
VIDEO: *Joan Rivers Salutes Heidi Abromowitz*

## WILL ROGERS

### (November 4, 1879–August 15, 1935)

The first comedian ever to be honored by a U.S. postage stamp, and the only one twice honored, Will Rogers remains the most respected and admired humorist of 20th century America. History books that refuse to mention stars of radio and films always find a place for Will. Most people are aware of his famous folksy line: "I never met a man I didn't like." Unfortunately, fewer and fewer can recall anything else about him.

Since most of the surviving radio broadcasts are poorly preserved and filled with dated references, he is ironically more famous as a historical figure than as a comedian. More people have probably seen James Whitmore's smooth one-man show of Will Rogers monologues, *Will Rogers U.S.A.*, Robert Hays in a made-for-television biography, or Keith Carradine's 1991 Broadway show, *The Will Rogers Follies* than ever saw Will himself. It's a strange fate for a man who was not only a Broadway star and popular in silent films, but the movie world's box office champ in the early 1930s.

Born in Oolagah, Indian territory in Oklahoma (Claremore is considered his hometown), Rogers' ancestry included Indian blood "and just enough white to make my honesty questionable." After completing about four grades at the Kemper Military School in Missouri, Rogers became a cowboy and later starred in rodeos as The Roping Fool. He transferred his rope tricks to the vaudeville stage. As he began his act one night, he shyly ad-libbed, "Swingin' a rope's all right—if your neck ain't in it." It got a big laugh and he began to slowly inject more of his natural wit into his act.

Rogers moved to Broadway and starred in a succession of *Ziegfeld Follies* productions, performing in sketches and perfecting his monologue style, which was a nervous, gum-chewing drawl, the gags slipping out between awkward pauses, stop-start mumbles and parenthetical asides. Today listeners sometimes have trouble picking the jokes out of the

He never met a man he didn't like. And there were very few who didn't like the homespun wit of Will Rogers. Photo from the author's collection.

rambling, but it was a style that worked well for Rogers, allowing him to inject a lot of sly and daring humor into his work. Though now considered "folksy" and "beloved," in his day many acknowledged the outdoorsman could be a bit savage.

Fellow *Follies* star W. C. Fields affirmed that "Will's humor was of a peculiar sort. In 1918 when 29 people were killed in a New York, New Haven & Hartford [train] wreck, Will commented: 'I see the NY, NH&H have started their spring drive.' When three people jumped off the Brooklyn Bridge Will remarked: 'They're condemning the bridge on account of too many people using it as a springboard.' "

From an early 78 rpm record: "Now folks, all I know is what little news I read every day in the paper. I see where another wife out on Long Island in New York shot her husband. Season opened a month earlier this year. Prohibition caused all this. There's just as many husbands shot at in the old days, but women were missin'. Prohibition has improved their marksmanship 90%. Never a day passes in New York without some innocent bystander being shot. You just stand around this town long enough and be innocent and somebody's gonna shoot ya."

Will later developed his talent for political barbs but admitted, "Personally, I don't like the jokes that get the biggest laughs. . . . I like the ones where, if you are with a friend, and hear it, it makes you think. And you nudge your friend and say, 'He's right about that.' "

In addition to radio work, Rogers had a newspaper column that was syndicated all over the country. His political one-liners earned him the most notoriety: "I never lack for material for my humor column when Congress is in session." "With Congress, every time they make a joke it's a law, and every time they make a law it's a joke." "I don't belong to any organized political party. I'm a Democrat."

For his time, he was extraordinarily irreverent. Mrs. Woodrow Wilson was rumored to be the power behind the president. With president and Mrs. Wilson in the audience, Rogers cracked, "Our president's going to Europe again. I don't believe he wants to go, but the old gal's got her clothes made and I guess he'll just have to tag along." Introduced to Calvin Coolidge, he smiled and said, "Excuse me—I didn't quite get the name." Of course, the very likability of Rogers and his commonsense fairness made him a favorite of politicians even as he kidded them. Like Bob Hope years later, some of his gags were so generalized and breezy, few could be offended: "The nation is prosperous on the whole, but how much prosperity is there in a hole?" With lines like that, James Thurber complained Rogers was "about as daring as an early Shirley Temple movie."

At his best, Rogers remains sharp and timeless. A few words on college: "Does college pay? Of course. If you're a halfback or a basketball player they pay you very well, I understand. College athletes are always saying to me, 'When should I turn pro?' And I say, 'Not until you've earned all you can in college.' "

When James Whitmore quoted lines like that in his "Will Rogers U.S.A." show, many began to realize that the sugar-coated image of the great comedian was concealing some acidic wit. Perhaps Rogers' most famous quote was misleading. In fact, it may have been misquoted. According to Bennett Cerf in his 1948 book *Shake Well Before Using*, Rogers did not exactly say he *never* met a man he didn't like. Cerf quoted Rogers as writing: "When I die, my epitaph, or whatever you call those signs on gravestones, is going to read, 'I joked about every prominent man of my time, but I hardly ever met a man I didn't like.' I am proud of that. I can hardly wait to die so it can be carved."

Rogers was one of the best-liked comedians of his time. His newspaper columns and vaudeville fame led to silent films that often sparkled with acrobatic slapstick, especially in comic westerns that took advantage of his riding and roping. In the sound era he was the undisputed box office champ for 1933, 1934 and 1935. (Clark Gable followed in 1936.) Will wasn't around to compete that year. A restless world traveler who often ran missions of mercy to communities stricken by floods, hurricanes and other disasters, Rogers died in an airplane crash in Alaska.

A nation went into mourning. Newsreel footage confirms for today's audiences the steady stream of mourners filing past his coffin. The parade of soldiers on horseback and the cannon salutes into the empty air were all a tribute to the only comedian who held the stature of a president in the eyes of his country: Will Rogers.

AUDIO: *Will Rogers Says* (Columbia), *Will Rogers* (Golden Age), *Will Rogers* (Distinguished), *I Never Met a Man I Didn't Like* (American Heritage), *Original Radio Broadcasts* (Mark 56), *Timely Topics* (Pelican), *Will Rogers* (Murray Hill), *The Wit and Wisdom of Will Rogers* (Caedmon)

AUTOBIOGRAPHY: *The Autobiography of Will Rogers* (Day, Rogers)

BIOGRAPHIES: *Will Rogers: His Life and Times* (Ketchum), *Our Will Rogers* (Lait), *Will Rogers Scrapbook* (Sterling), *Best of Will Rogers* (Sterling), *Will Rogers* (O'Brien), *Will Rogers* (Rollins), *Boys' Life of Will Rogers* (Keith), *My Cousin Will Rogers* (Trent), *Will Rogers: His Wife's Story* (B. Rogers), *Folks Say*

*of Will Rogers* (Payne), *Will Rogers in Hollywood* (Sterling), *Will Rogers* (Alworth)

BOOKS incl.: *The Illiterate Digest* (1974)

BROADWAY: *The Wall Street Girl* (1912), *Midnight Frolic* (1915), *Ziegfeld Follies* (1916, 1917, 1918, 1922, 1924), *Lambs Gambol* (1925), *Will Rogers* (1926), *Three Cheers* (1928), *Ah, Wilderness!* (1934)

FILMS incl.: *Laughing Bill Hyde* (1918), *Jes Call Me Jim* (1920), *Honest Hutch* (1920), *Guile of Woman* (1921), *The Headless Horseman* (1922), *Tiptoes* (1927), *A Texas Steer* (1927), *They Had to See Paris* (1929), *So This Is London* (1930), *A Connecticut Yankee* (1931), *Young as You Feel* (1931), *Business and Pleasure* (1932), *State Fair* (1933), *Doctor Bull* (1933), *Handy Andy* (1934), *David Harum* (1934), *Judge Priest* (1934), *Life Begins at Forty* (1935), *Steamboat Round the Bend* (1935), *Doubting Thomas* (1935), *In Old Kentucky* (1935)

## ANDY ROONEY

### (January 14, 1919–   )

A curmudgeon whose comic essays delight millions, Andy Rooney has become one of the highest paid humorists of all time, earning an estimated $800,000 a year for just "A Few Minutes with Andy Rooney" at the end of each "60 Minutes" television broadcast.

Born in Albany, New York, Rooney attended Colgate University and after World War II service collaborated with Bud Hutton on three books, *Air Gunner* (1944), *The Story of the Stars and Stripes* (1946) and *Their Conqueror's Peace* (1947). A writer for Arthur Godfrey's radio show (1949–55), Rooney freelanced gags for Victor Borge, Sam Levenson, and Herb Shriner, and was with "The Garry Moore Show" through 1964. He wrote and produced news specials through the 1960s, including "Of Black History" narrated by Bill Cosby. His first on-camera appearance was reading a war essay on 1971's "The Great American Dream Machine." His rather painful, grinding voice led to voiceover work—for an aspirin company.

After narrating specials, including *Mr. Rooney Goes to Washington* and *Mr. Rooney Goes to Work*, he landed his first essay spot on "60 Minutes" in 1978. He became a regular in 1979. Heartland America was amused by his old-fashioned iconoclasm; his whining and grousing about newfangled customs and language harkened back to the old days of cracker-barrel wit. Critics felt he belabored the obvious, as he did in one of his most famous pieces in which he and his cameras went on a hunt to find the mythical "Mrs. Smith" of the company manufacturing "Mrs. Smith's Frozen Pies." After he interviewed spokesmen and snooped around the factory, he proved his point—that the homey-sounding matron *did not* really sit around baking those thousands of pies.

Rooney, an Emmy winner back in 1969 as a writer, won two more in 1981 and 1982 for his comedy. His catch phrase ("Ever notice . . .") became a favorite with impressionists from Joe Piscopo to Johnny Carson, who also delighted in mimicking Rooney's whining voice and reliance on a distinct comic formula: "I hate baseball . . . to be honest with you, I'll tell you it may be because I was never very good at the game. I always threw a baseball like a girl. Is that okay to say now? Or does that suggest girls don't throw baseballs very well? . . . But I have other reasons for not liking baseball too. For one thing, the players all spit too much. Every time I try to watch . . . someone's spitting at me. . . . Baseball has been called 'The National Pastime.' It's just the kind of game anyone deserves who has nothing better to do than try to pass his time . . . what does 'pastime' mean anyway? And why doesn't it have two 't's?"

Rooney's books, which collected his argumentative essays, became best-sellers. But again, not with critics. *People* magazine reviewed his *Not That You Asked* collection by asking "Does it ever bother you when a book drones on and on with one pointless anecdote after another and your head is filled with the well-known voice of the author—which is to say the sound of brakes sorely in need of relining?"

After a decade of attacking pie companies and baseball games with impunity, the middle-of-the-road iconoclast got into trouble after declaring that the idea of two men having sex together seemed "repugnant." Gays demanded his removal from "60 Minutes." A gay newspaper, *The Advocate*, asked him for an interview. He granted it and was shocked when they quoted him as being not only homophobic but racist. He supposedly said, "I've believed all along that most people are born with equal intelli-

gence, but blacks have watered down their genes because the less intelligent ones are the ones that have the most children. . . . they drop out of school early, do drugs and get pregnant."

No tape recorder verified the remarks, but the story had its desired effect. Rooney's anti-gay comments hadn't been deemed strong enough to get him kicked off the air, but the antiblack remark stirred up a storm. CBS immediately suspended Rooney. But to the surprise of many, both Rooney's fans and foes were outraged by CBS's knee-jerk reaction. A 50-cent-a-call hotline 900 number on NBC's "Inside Edition" showed 129,000 calls supporting Rooney, only 8,000 against. Celebrities (including the revered CBS newsman Walter Cronkite) spoke out for Rooney, and as the front-page controversy raged, newspapers editorialized in his favor. The *New York Post* declared, "What evidence is there that Andy Rooney actually made the remarks attributed to him. . . . there's no question *The Advocate* had a motive for trying to destroy Rooney's career. . . . Why would CBS choose to believe an inexperienced reporter for a magazine manifestly determined to 'get' Rooney in the absence of a tape of the controversial interview, and in the face of Rooney's denials?" Other interview subjects came forward declaring that this particular *Advocate* writer "twisted" their words in misquotes.

Faced with overwhelming disapproval and a sharp dip in the ratings for "60 Minutes," CBS returned Rooney to the program, his 90-day suspension lasting only 22 days.

AUDIO: *Not That You Asked* (Random House Sound Editions)
BOOKS incl.: *A Few Minutes with Andy Rooney* (1987), *A Few Minutes More with Andy Rooney* (1981), *Not That You Asked* (1990), *Word for Word* (1987), *Pieces of My Mind* (1985)
TV: "60 Minutes" (1978–   )

## MICKEY ROONEY

**(Joe Yule Jr., September 23, 1920–   )**

A brash, self-confident, aggressive little dynamo, entertainer Mickey Rooney began his career as a child actor, and, in the course of a tumultuous career, has attained and reattained stardom in every decade since.

After precocious work in vaudeville, the bratty but cute kid star made silent films and over 50 shorts between 1927 and 1933 as "Mickey McGuire," based on a popular comic strip of the day. He even changed his name to the character's.

After the series ended, Mickey seemed washed up as a child star. He changed his name (his mother was inspired by performer Pat Rooney) and tried to make a comeback on the stage. He returned to stardom after winning the plum role of "Puck" in an all-star version of *A Midsummer Night's Dream*. Despite horsing around during rehearsals—and suffering a broken leg that forced the cameras to shoot the semimobile star from behind trees—Rooney completed filming and won rave reviews.

In 1937 Rooney became Andy Hardy, the film world's ultimate teenager. Ann Rutherford, a co-star in his "Andy Hardy" films, recalled, "It was Mickey who replaced Clark Gable as America's top box office draw. I don't know what made him so magnetic. It was a chemistry, certainly, and a marvelous sense of abandonment. He was the embodiment of every darling, hateful, mischievous boy in America—the perennial Huck Finn and Tom Sawyer rolled into one." Rooney also starred in 1938's *Boys Town*. He won a special Oscar that year for his ability to convey "the spirit and personification of youth, and as a juvenile player setting a high standard of ability and achievement."

Off screen he began setting new records for ability and achievement in dating and/or marrying beautiful stars. Though a mere five foot two and not handsome, Rooney became a notorious ladies' man and rebelled against studio rules about keeping such matters private. The All-American sitcom boy even dared to be seen gambling at the race track. He didn't break rules as much as he rolled over them, a charismatic fast talker with unlimited energy. He married Ava Gardner in 1942, then a stunning but virginal starlet of 19. Both were too young for marriage, and before long the extroverted Mickey and the shy Ava began to drift apart.

Rooney married again and again, and in his raunchy 1991 biography declared that among his affairs was one with Lana Turner that led to pregnancy

and an abortion. Turner responded with an icy statement declaring that they had never even dated at all. Rooney insisted he was telling the truth and added that he also had an affair, at age 19, with Norma Shearer.

Rooney's career was as stormy as his marital situation. In the late 1940s Rooney grew out of the Andy Hardy sitcoms, as he'd grown out of his "Mickey McGuire" role. Once again he was considered a has-been.

Once more he stormed back, this time trying television (a 1954 series "Hey Mulligan") and films that made good use of his brash comic style. He also won some good notices for dramatic work. Even more dramatic were the newspaper headlines involving Rooney's fifth wife, Barbara, whom he married before his divorce from wife number four was final. In 1958 Barbara's nude body was hauled out of the swimming pool by a female friend. It was reportedly just one of her several sleeping pill/suicide attempts. She ultimately had an affair with Mickey's chauffeur. She and Rooney separated in 1965, but when she considered taking him back, the jealous chauffeur shot and killed her and then took his own life.

On December 1, 1959, a drunk and belligerent Rooney had a notorious run-in with talk show host Jack Paar. In those days, any question about a relationship was considered rather tasteless and suggestive. "What kind of woman was Ava Gardner?" Paar asked. Rooney shot back, "More of a woman than you'll ever know." It got worse. Finally Paar asked, "Are you enjoying my show tonight?" "Not necessarily," said Mickey. Paar replied, "Then would you care to leave?"

The audience applauded as Rooney walked off. Behind his back Paar declared, "It's a shame, he *was* a great talent." The truth, a little more complicated, was that whatever was driving his erratic personality, his talent was still there, just untapped in a spate of mediocre films and sitcom appearances. Even *It's a Mad Mad Mad Mad World* failed to provide Rooney with anything more than some obvious little-man-throws-a-big-fit humor. Rooney kept going and the near misses continued. He played a Ben Turpin-esque sidekick for Dick Van Dyke in *The Comic*, but the film was not well received.

The little man's biggest comeback was in the Broadway musical *Sugar Babies*. The show, a lavish look at the days of vaudeville and burlesque, was a vehicle as bouncy and as rollicking as Rooney himself. He would star in various touring companies of *Sugar Babies* over the years. Not only was he able to remain in the play year after year, he was finally able to stay married. Since the mid-1970s he had settled down with his eighth wife. The complete list: Ava Gardner, Betty Rase, Martha Vickers, Elaine Mehnkenm, Barbara Thomason, Margie Dane, Carolyn Hockett and Janice Chamberlain.

Rooney began making films again, and in 1983 was once again awarded an honorary Academy Award. In 1990 Rooney and Donald O'Connor decided to unite for a summer tour in *The Sunshine Boys*. That year he premiered a syndicated television show based on his film *The Black Stallion*. The show was a success and fans saw the hyper comic on talk shows once again as well, offering up frantic anecdotes and corny gags at bewildering speed. He said, "In many ways I haven't changed a bit. I am still the same self-absorbed guy. . . . I like to do what I want, when I want, where I want, without much thought for the wants of others. The people around me fare best when they do not challenge me."

The man whose career began with kid comedies and the teen Andy Hardy series has returned to family entertainment. He said that there was a need for more shows like his. "In my lifetime, I have seen many changes. Times change, people change, trends change. Boy, do trends change. . . . Nowadays a quick flip through the channels is not such an easy task when there are kids present. Today's family situation comedies all too often rely on an adorable six-year-old to deliver a well-rehearsed double-entendre while the adult cast giggles along. . . . Gone are the days I so fondly remember when my family and I would sit in front of the television and watch programs that entertained as well as educated. We laughed at the antics of Sid Caesar . . . and wondered about the marvels of the underwater depths as shown to us by Jacques Cousteau. Television, however, isn't what it used to be." He felt few television shows were offering "feel good" entertainment. But he did think of an interesting alternative: "Maybe someone should find a barn and the children could put on a show. I've done it. It's not impossible."

AUDIO: *Sings George M. Cohan* (RCA Victor), *Sugar Babies* (Broadway Entertainment)

AUTOBIOGRAPHIES: *I.E., an Autobiography* (1965), *Life Is Too Short* (1991)

BROADWAY: *A Midsummer Night's Dream* (1934), *Sugar Babies* (1979)

FILMS incl.: *Orchids and Ermine* (1932), *The Life of Jimmy Dolan* (1933), *Broadway to Hollywood* (1933), *Manhattan Melodrama* (1934), *A Midsummer Night's Dream* (1935), *Ah, Wilderness* (1935), *Little Lord Fauntleroy* (1936), *Captains Courageous* (1937), *Love is a Headache* (1938), *Judge Hardy's Children* (1938), *You're Only Young Once* (1938), *Love Finds Andy Hardy* (1938), *The Adventures of Huckleberry Finn* (1939), *Andy Hardy Gets Spring Fever* (1939), *Judge Hardy and Son* (1939), *Young Tom Edison* (1940), *Strike Up the Band* (1940), *Life Begins for Andy Hardy* (1941), *Andy Hardy's Private Secretary* (1941), *Andy Hardy's Double Life* (1942), *A Yank at Eton* (1942), *Thousands Cheer* (1943), *Andy Hardy's Blonde Trouble* (1944), *Love Laughs at Andy Hardy* (1946), *Killer McCoy* (1947), *Summer Holiday* (1947), *Words and Music* (1948), *All Ashore* (1953), *Operation Madball* (1957), *Andy Hardy Comes Home* (1958), *Platinum High School* (1959), *Requiem for a Heavyweight* (1962), *It's a Mad Mad Mad Mad World* (1963), *How to Stuff a Wild Bikini* (1965), *Skidoo* (1968), *The Comic* (1969), *Pulp* (1972), *Pete's Dragon* (1977), *Find the Lady* (1979), *The Black Stallion* (1979), *Leave 'em Laughing* (1981), *Bill* (1981), *Bill: On His Own* (1983), *The Care Bears Movie* (1985), *My Heroes Have Always Been Cowboys* (1991)

TV: "The Mickey Rooney Show: Hey Mulligan" (1954–55), "Mickey" (1964–65), "NBC Follies" (1973), "Mickey Rooney's Small World" (1975), "One of the Boys" (1982), "The Adventures of the Black Stallion" (1990)

# ROSE MARIE

## (Rose Marie Mazetta, August 15, 1923–   )

"I play me in almost everything I do," Rose Marie admits. "I play a part to the best of my ability to get a joke out, to sell it and to do it best." As the veteran comedy writer Sally Rogers, Rose Marie earned three Emmy nominations on television's "The Dick Van Dyke Show." She played a realistic version of an aging manhunter, her wisecracks helping preserve her dignity as she dated a wide assortment of doubtful contenders.

Occasionally an episode allowed her to do a bit of song and dance, which she handled with the enthusiasm of a female Jimmy Durante. Younger viewers had no idea that it was in just this mode—hip, aggressive and jazzy—that she first achieved her fame. She was called "Baby Rose Marie" back then.

Discovered by a talent scout while singing on a beach in Atlantic City, she was brought to radio in 1927 to sing "What Can I Say, Dear, After I Say I'm Sorry." She had her own NBC radio show in 1930 and remained on the air, co-starring on a 1936 variety show on WHN in New York with Al Shayne. Her father, a Broadway and vaudeville star who worked under the name Frank Curley, helped her learn her songs.

Unlike sugary child stars of the day, Rose Marie sang fast-paced blues songs using startlingly adult phrasing and mannerisms. The rollicking little girl in the Dutch boy bangs can be seen doing her stuff in the W. C. Fields' comedy *International House*. She was so good some people insisting she had to be a midget in disguise.

Rose Marie "retired" in her teens, but staged a comeback in the late 1940s. She guest starred on Morey Amsterdam's early television show, appeared on stage in *Top Banana* with Phil Silvers in 1951 and played New York nightclubs. In the clubs she mixed one-liners about the town ("Where else can you wake up and hear the birds coughing?") with novelty tunes such as "I Wish I Could Sing Like Durante" and "Be a Beggar, Be a Thief—Be Anything But Please Don't Be Mine." She toured the country with the act, made some films, but won major newfound fame as the slightly cynical and amusingly pushy Sally Rogers on "The Dick Van Dyke Show." Many episodes revolved around her attempt to get a husband. Tragically, her own husband, Bobby Guy, died in 1964 of a blood infection. They'd been married 19 years and had a daughter, Georgiana.

"We were a little too close," said Rose Marie. "When I lost Bobby, I lost half my life."

Somewhat typed as the aggravated spinster with a rueful glare and frowning mouth, she continued to guest on sitcoms and became a regular on "The Hollywood Squares" quiz show with grim answers to dumb questions: "True or false, according to *The Magazine of the Midlands*, the average wild hippo is really quite gentle." "In that case—I'm available." In the 1980s, Rose Marie returned to her old forte: singing. She joined the *4 Girls 4* touring show with co-stars Margaret Whiting, Rosemary Clooney and Helen O'Connell. In December 1990 she played the fairy godmother in a West Coast revival of Rodgers and Hammerstein's *Cinderella*, co-starring Steve Allen and Jayne Meadows as the king and queen. Sitcom fans were delighted to have her back in guest spots on "Murphy Brown" in 1991.

AUDIO: *Funny You Should Ask* (Marsh)
BROADWAY: *Top Banana* (1951)
FILMS incl.: *International House* (1933), *The Big Broadcast* (1935), *Dead Heat on a Merry Go Round* (1966), *Cheaper to Keep Her* (1980), *Lunch Wagon* (1980)
TV: "My Sister Eileen" (1960–61), "The Dick Van Dyke Show" (1961–66), "The Doris Day Show" (1969–71)

## JOE E. ROSS

### (Joseph Roszawikz, March 15, 1914–August 13, 1982)

Pouchy and gargoyle-faced with a big nose and bright little eyes, Joe E. Ross had an almost Neanderthal look. He sounded tough too, with his raspy gravel voice. But the comedy came from his short, stocky build, pussycat disposition and enthusiastic ineptness, which included pained expressions of chagrin and his gasping "Oooh! Oooh" catch phrase. He even recorded a song titled "Oooh! Oooh!"

"I was born in New York," Ross said, "on the Lower East Side. Most comedians say they were born on top of a candy store. Now, I can't say that. My folks *owned* the candy store." He told his friends his Polish real name was pronounced "rose-a-weeks" but since nobody asked him to write it, the spelling above is an approximation.

After leaving school at 16, Ross became a singing waiter in a Manhattan speakeasy. "I used to sing heartbreaking songs to the hoodlums. They'd cry in their beer. With a voice like mine I guess I was lucky they didn't shoot me." He appeared in burlesque comedy shows and tried stand-up comedy doing jokes along with impressions (Wallace Beery) and nonimpressions (James Cagney's brother).

Phil Silvers' writer Nat Hiken discovered him performing in Miami, and the aging comedian was cast as the well-worn but naively wide-eyed Mess Sergeant Ritzik on television's "Sgt. Bilko." From there he became Gunther Toody, the cop whose good intentions always went awry on "Car 54, Where Are You?" He played Gronk, a caveman in the sitcom "It's About Time" and briefly teamed with Steve Rossi for nightclub work, but his fame remained with the reruns of "Car 54." He traded on it heavily in later years, promoting his risqué solo stand-up comedy act.

A hapless fall guy in comedy, Ross amused his fellow comedians with an equally lame personal life. Milton Berle: "Joe E. Ross measured his life in hookers. At his death, street corners in Hollywood were draped in black." Berle mentioned the time Ross invited a woman to stay in his apartment though he didn't even know her name. "I think she's Doreen because that's the name on some of her medicine bottles," he told Berle one day. A few days later she took everything of value in the apartment and left. All the police had to work with were a few nude Polaroids Ross had taken of her. Joe E. asked one of the cops, "Can I keep the ones with me in them?"

Ross's basic Runyonesque sweetness and likeability despite his obtuseness kept him performing right up to the end, though he now played small and obscure clubs. He suffered a heart attack while performing for a group of people in a clubhouse located in his apartment building.

AUDIO: *Should Lesbians Be Allowed to Play Professional Football?* (Laff), *Toody Tales* (Golden), *Memorial Album to Joe E. Ross: The Big Itch Volume II* (Mr. Manicotti)

FILMS incl.: *The Bellboy* (1960), *All Hands on Deck* (1961), *Tony Rome* (1967), *Love Bug* (1968), *Judy's Little No-No* (1969), *The Boatniks* (1970), *How to Seduce a Woman* (1974), *Slumber Party '57* (1977)

TV: "The Phil Silvers Show" (1955–59), "Car 54, Where Are You?" (1961–63), "It's About Time" (1966–67)

## ROWAN and MARTIN

**Dan Rowan, July 2, 1922–September 22, 1987**
**Dick Martin, January 30, 1923–**

The stars of one of the wildest, craziest and most influential television shows of the late 1960s were a pair of conservatively dressed nightclub comedians in their 40s. For years Rowan and Martin had appealed to well-heeled patrons of swanky nightclubs, not a bunch of kids and hippies.

Dan Rowan, born in Beggs, Oklahoma, had been a writer at Paramount Studios in the 1940s before joining the air force during World War II. Dick Martin, born in Battle Creek, Michigan, was classified 4F during the war and, before teaming with Rowan in 1952, had written comedy for radio shows. Together they wrote for another team, Noonan and Marshall, before deciding to perform their material themselves.

With the exception of *Once Upon a Horse,* a 1958 film that Universal hoped might spark them as the new Abbott and Costello or Martin and Lewis, the duo toiled for years in relative obscurity. They performed on national television from time to time with tame sketches such as their "spy" routine, in which Rowan would pass on instructions and Martin parroted them, getting them all wrong. In other sketches the somewhat dour, tolerantly amused Rowan would stand, cigarette in hand, and endure the goofy clowning of Martin, which included nudges, winks and jokes that he himself liked to snicker at. "In every family there's one person you can't stand," Dick Martin once said. "That's me, with Dan as my brother-in-law."

The team put out their first album in 1960 but didn't ignite much of a fire. Dick was a semiregular on "The Lucy Show" between 1962 and 1964, after which the team became regulars on Dean Martin's show and replaced him during the summer of 1966. Then came "Laugh-In," their legendary show of fast-paced one-liners, sketches and songs. They favored light, silly stuff. In one sketch Martin remarks, "Caesar killed Brutus." Dan: "Caesar didn't kill Brutus." "Oh, I'm glad he pulled through." "No, no, you're historically incorrect. Brutus killed Caesar." "I heard it the other way around." "You heard that Caesar killed Brutus?" "That's funny, so did I!"

The duo developed their own catch phrases, including Dick's breezy "You bet your bippy!" and "Look that up in your Funk and Wagnall's!" The show often ended with a Burns and Allen salute/parody: "Say good night, Dick." "Good night, Dick."

"Laugh-In" mirrored the newfound frisky interest in recreational sex and drugs, and only occasionally took a broad and essentially harmless swipe at politics or the Vietnam War. Unlike "The Smothers Brothers Comedy Hour," the show was so mild President Richard Nixon appeared for a cameo, shouting another "Laugh-In" catch phrase, "Sock it to *me?*" As Dan Rowan remarked, "There is nothing left to revere in this country, so it's pretty hard to be irreverent."

As it turned out, their conservative presence lent the only stability to a program dominated by madcaps such as Ruth Buzzi, Arte Johnson and Goldie Hawn. After the show ended, the team gradually drifted apart. In 1978 Dick Martin began working on Bob Newhart's sitcoms as a writer, director and producer. Rowan and Martin's last major appearance together was in 1981's "The First Annual Ultra Quiz."

Rowan subsequently retired, devoting himself to travel and to correspondence with writers such as John D. MacDonald, who knew him to be a serious, concerned and thoughtful man. Not long before his death from lymphatic cancer, Rowan's book *A Friendship,* was released. Dick Martin had been in touch with Dan during the last months. He told reporters, "It was sad, but he was philosophical. He said, "I've had a good run. I've had a ball.""

AUDIO: *Rowan and Martin at Work* (Trey, Atco), *The Humor of Rowan and Martin* (Epic), *Rowan and Martin's Laugh In* (Epic)

FILMS incl.: *Once Upon a Horse* (1957), *The Maltese Bippy* (1969)

TV: "Rowan and Martin's Laugh-In" (1968–73)

## PAUL REUBENS (See PEE-WEE HERMAN.)

## RITA RUDNER

### (September 17, 1955– )

Feminine and funny, Rita Rudner has brought something new to stand-up comedy: poise, charm and grace. Her attractive appearance is in comic contrast to her jokes, many influenced by Woody Allen and Steven Wright. Using a deceptively straightforward, sweet-voiced delivery, she fries minds with odd concepts ("chopsticks with Velcro on the bottom") and a catalog of strange things that happened to her: "One of my first office jobs was cleaning the windows on the envelopes."

Blinking her large, luminous eyes, she sometimes chooses jokes that seem to fit within the "ditsy" stereotype, but usually they evidence more wit than ditz: "They caution pregnant women not to drink alcohol. It may harm the baby. I think that's ironic. If it wasn't for alcohol most women wouldn't be that way."

Quiet but firm on stage, Rudner was a change from the Totie Fields/Joan Rivers school of raucous aggression or tough Elayne Boosler feminism. Rita recalled that it took time to get over that barrier. "In 1984 I played Atlantic City. I might as well have been from Mars. I'd get on stage, and they were used to seeing very loud women, who were either screaming, or fat. I could hear a collective 'What is this?' So I bought a real sparkly dress, so at least if they didn't understand the jokes they'd understand the dress."

Despite her reputation as "educated Rita," purveyor of intelligent, well-constructed jokes, she said she did not do well at school. She was a professional dancer. "I graduated when I was 15, but I stayed out of school a lot because I was in shows, and my dad wrote in that I was sick. Because I was a dancer it was painful for me to have to sit all day. And college? No, I didn't even want to hear about it."

The Miami-born dancer was in the touring company of *Zorba* plus Broadway shows *Mack and Mabel, The Magic Show, Follies* and *Promises Promises.*

After playing Lillie St. Regis in Broadway's *Annie,* Rudner began performing comedy at New York clubs. She figured it was better to write and perform her own material than wait for a playwright, a theater and audition calls. She told the author, "Everything was funny . . . in between the jokes I was telling! People were laughing at me, and none of it had to do with the jokes I'd written. But right away I liked it. Then I tried to figure out what was funny . . . why would anyone laugh once I stop talking?" She learned, "You could have the most brilliant jokes but if the audience doesn't like you, it doesn't work." She worked hard. "I work at comedy, but I've always been very disciplined. Having been a ballerina, that's the most diciplined life you can lead, so this is nothing!"

Her ballerina abilities helped her stand her ground on stage, holding her head up, radiating a kind of fluorescent brilliance both bright and cool. The coolness was actually shyness, which audiences seemed to understand. They could sense the vulnerability behind her wide-eyed stare of amazement.

Rudner won over audiences on "Late Night with David Letterman," "The Tonight Show," HBO's "Ladies of the Night" and television's "Funny People" series, ultimately getting her own Ace Award–nominated HBO specials. In 1990 she starred in a six-part British comedy series on the BBC. Though married in 1989, many of her best jokes remain on familiar subjects such as dating, which young comedy clubgoers can relate to: "You know how I end relationships? If I never want to see a man again, I just say, 'I love you . . . I want to marry you . . . I want to have *your* children.' Sometimes they leave skid marks."

Steve Martin once noted, "Comedy is not pretty." But that was before Rita Rudner. Rudner fascinates critics who point out either her beauty or her comic talent. But the biggest compliment, she says, is when they realize the two terms are not mutually exclusive: "How about . . . attractive *and* funny?"

FILMS incl.: *Gleaming the Cube* (1988)
TV: "Funny People" (1988)

## MARK RUSSELL

### (Mark Ruslander, August 23, 1932–   )

With sledgehammer pounding at the piano and an obvious, lay-it-in-their-laps delivery, Mark Russell's political comedy is not subtle. In the early 1960s, coming a few years after Mort Sahl's rise to prominence, Russell began making albums and touring. Based at the Shoreham-Americana in Washington, he remained best known locally, where politicians, patrons and columnists stopped by for drinks and parodies of the latest news. While Sahl was often intellectual and over the heads of the audience, it was easy to understand Russell's cracks.

Decades later the Russell formula of song parody remained the same: Take a public-domain tune and slip in the gags. "My Bonnie" as sung by Ronald Reagan: "My ship of state's practically grounded, for want of a policy plan. I deny all the charges—unfounded—since the state of my ship hit the fan. . . . bring back, bring back, oh bring back my Teflon to me, to me. . . ."

Russell was always musically inclined. The ex-marine began his nightclub career as a pianist influenced by Charlie Drew and later Tom Lehrer. "At first, I did some Lehrer things, and then they went off so well that I started writing my own."

Russell's national fame began to spread in the late 1970s when he began doing PBS television specials. Each special featured Russell standing up at his piano and knocking out his tunes with the kind of garrulously cynical "yowzah" showmanship of Gig Young in *They Shoot Horses Don't They.*

He calls himself "a political cartoonist for the blind," and he is right. Audience members have to be obtuse indeed not to get Russell's broad gags. From 1986: "The Supreme Court ruled that homosexuality is a crime! Give me your tired, your poor, your straight! Now, we don't know how our founding fore-persons felt about this subject. Did Patrick Henry once say, 'I know not the course others may take but as for me, give me liberty or give me Fred?' We don't know! I don't think we ever had a president who was gay. A couple of 'em bordered on the *jovial.* But the criminality in question, defined by the court, is sodomy. Taken from the ancient city of Sodom. You can still commit

Gommorah—as long as it's practiced between two consenting Philistines."

Russell continues presenting PBS specials. Like a lion tamer firing his gun constantly and flailing his whip, Mark Russell continues to overact and overreact to the point of overkill, but his fans feel it is justified. After all, desperate times call for desperate measures.

AUDIO: *Up the Potomac Without a Canoe* (Columbia), *The Face on the Senate Floor* (Weet), *The Wired World of Watergate* (Deep Six), *Assault with a Deadly Peanut* (Deep Six)

TV: "Starland Vocal Band Show" (1977), "Real People" (1979–84)

## NIPSEY RUSSELL

### (October 13, 1925–    )

For nearly 50 years Nipsey Russell has charmed audiences with his genial stand-up, toothy smile and penchant for comical rhymes.

Born in Atlanta, Georgia, Nipsey attended Washington High School and the College Conservatory of Music, now affiliated with the University of Cincinnati. A student of classical literature as well as foreign languages, Russell matched his distinguished credits in college with meritorious service during World War II.

After the war, Captain Russell spent 1946 to 1948 working in Montreal and in 1949 joined "The Show Goes On," a television series starring Robert Q. Lewis. Through the 1950s fashionable East Side residents of New York journeyed to Harlem's "Baby Grand" club to see Nipsey's stand-up act. Billed as "Harlem's Son of Fun," Nipsey wore a white straw hat and tended to tell a lot of lighthearted adult gags. He issued several albums of what now would be considered PG-rated material. His risqué patter included a rhyme about a tattooed lady: "She decided she would like to add my picture. But she couldn't find a vacant place, you see. So she tattooed my poor face—in a most undignified place—and every time she sits down she sits on me. . . . Now you wonder why I'm feeling so lowdown, and why my attitude is absolutely wrong. I'd like to romance

and kick her right square in the pants. But if I did I'd kick myself right in the jaw."

Nipsey did just enough political material to maintain his own integrity, such as the one about the integration problems in Little Rock: "I told the kids, go to school with your heads held high—and with machine guns and dynamite!" Some of the lines go back to his early days at The Apollo, when he told the crowd, "He who turns the other cheek will get hit with the other fist." He recalled, "I used to say, 'We've always had integration in the South—we just want it now in the daytime. . . .' I did those jokes at the Apollo in '43, '44, '45."

After appearing at a 1959 Carnegie Hall benefit for Martin Luther King Jr., Jack Paar booked Nipsey for "The Tonight Show." This major television exposure led to more club dates and more record albums. Russell's one-liners tended to be sunny, à la Will Rogers: "New York is a funny town. You can drown in whiskey and starve to death. Everybody says have a drink, nobody says have something to eat." But at the start of the 1960s, it was Dick Gregory, with a far sterner delivery and stronger political commentary who captured white liberal audiences.

For Nipsey, it was an indignity to be considered an "also ran" in Gregory's shadow. In the *New York Post* in 1964, three years after Gregory's rise, Russell was still burning: "I have letters from people who told me after Gregory made it that they actually felt guilty about not hiring me first . . . let me be arrogant and egotistical for a moment. If I *had* been first, some of these others couldn't have made it. They would have been compared to me."

Russell did have a few "firsts" in the '60s: the first black comic to host a quiz show ("Missing Links"); and one of the first to have a co-starring role in a sitcom (he played an officer on 1961's "Car 54, Where Are You?").

In the radical late '60s and early '70s, when Dick Gregory gave up comedy for the lecture circuit and Richard Pryor was blowing audiences away with reverse-racism, Russell's kindly comic rhymes seemed out of touch. He got little respect from critics. Even his name bothered some, since it seemed to go back to burlesque black names: "Mantan" Moreland, "Slappy" White or "Pigmeat" Markham. He insisted

Nipsey was his real name and that was that: "My mother just liked the way it sounded."

In 1978 he and Phil Foster appeared in a stage version of *The Odd Couple*, and over the years Russell starred in several touring comedies, including *A Funny Thing Happened on the Way to the Forum* in Atlantic City in 1990. Russell is still a favorite in casinos, always including his trademark little poems along with the jokes. He said, "I think people like the rhymes because as the four-liner starts you're paying attention and trying to figure out what comes next. Then the last line has the humor in it. It's worked for 25 years, so I keep doing it."

AUDIO: *Confucius Told Me* (Borderline/Humorsonic), *Things They Never Taught Me in School: Laff Lectures* (Borderline/Humorsonic), *Birds and the Bees* (Borderline/Humorsonic), *Guzzling and Giggling Party* (Borderline/Humorsonic), *The Lion's Tale* (Borderline/Humorsonic), *Sing Along* (Borderline/Humorsonic), *Ya Gotta Be Fast* (Borderline/Humorsonic), *Best of Nipsey* (Borderline/Humorsonic), *Star of the Jack Paar Show* (Surprise)

FILMS incl.: *The Wiz* (1978), *Wildcats* (1986)

TV: "Car 54, Where Are You?" (1961–62), "Missing Links" (1963), "ABC's Nightlife" (1965), "Barefoot in the Park" (1970–71), "The Dean Martin Show" (1971–73), "Dean Martin's Comedy World" (1974), "Masquerade Party" (1974–75)

## ROSALIND RUSSELL

### (June 4, 1907–November 28, 1976)

"I played the same role over and over," Rosalind Russell once said, "the overtailored, padded shouldered, pompadoured, funny-hatted, sleek and tough career woman with the flip lines and the flinty heart that somehow melts in the clutches of the man I needed all the time—in the last reel, of course."

Born in Waterbury, Connecticut, Russell received her B.A. from Barnard College, attended drama school and made the long climb from summer stock to Broadway to films. She had not done much comedy until George Cukor cast her into *The Women* giving her a memorable catfight scene opposite Paulette Goddard. Russell went on to develop the sleek-

and-tough comic character that was her trademark and starred in the classic comedy *His Girl Friday*, paired with Cary Grant.

Like many comic actresses of the day, Russell wanted to experiment with drama. But after *Sister Kenny* (1946), *Mourning Becomes Electra* (1947) and the Joan Crawfordish *The Velvet Touch* (1948), she and the critics had enough. She declared, "I've no desire to return to tragedy—ever." She left films for stage comedies and critics enthusiastically responded to her 1950 tour in *Bell, Book and Candle*. Her biggest hits followed: *Wonderful Town* and *Auntie Mame*.

Brooks Atkinson in the *New York Times* led the praise. He wrote of her performance in *Wonderful Town*: "Rosalind Russell cannot run for President until 1956, but it would be wise to start preparing for her campaign at once. For she can dance and sing better than any President we have had. She is also better looking and has a more infectious sense of humor." *Newsweek* added: "Rosalind Russell is a grand comedienne. . . . whether she is curling a hopefully sneering lip at the presumptuous, singing (not at all badly) a comic ditty, or just throwing herself all over the stage with an unself-conscious abandon." Russell's follow-up hit, *Auntie Mame*, was brought to the screen, rekindling her movie career, which thrived with another key role, the Jewish mother in *Gypsy*.

Russell's private life was hardly boisterous or madcap. In 1941 she married Fred Brisson and the couple stayed together for the next 35 years. She underwent a mastectomy in 1961 and recovered well, but arthritis gradually slowed her career. Her last film was the television movie *The Crooked Hearts* in 1972. Russell's fight with cancer led to chemotherapy in 1975. She suffered further health problems, but characteristically dismissed most of them with wry wit. She sent this poem to those concerned about her: "There is nothing whatever the matter with me. I'm just as healthy as I can be. Well, I do have arthritis in both my knees. And when I talk, I talk with a wheeze. My pulse is weak and my blood is thin. But I'm really well—for the shape I'm in."

Russell required hip replacement surgery in 1976, which only added to her growing problems. The indomitable star finished her autobiography but died that year of cancer. Lucille Ball said, "Roz showed so much courage here that God must have needed her fighting spirit somewhere else."

That fighting spirit lives on in her many stylish comedies. That spirit was best exemplified by the (uncensored) stage version of *Auntie Mame*. Audiences could not forget Roz Russell's famous line in that one: "Live, live, live! Life is a banquet and most of you poor sons-of-bitches are starving to death!"

AUDIO incl.: *Wonderful Town* (Decca), *Gypsy* (Warner Bros.)

AUTOBIOGRAPHY: *Life Is a Banquet* (1979)

BIOGRAPHY: *Rosalind Russell* (Yanni)

BROADWAY incl.: *Company's Coming* (1931), *Wonderful Town* (1953), *Auntie Mame* (1956)

FILMS incl.: *Evelyn Prentice* (1934), *Forsaking All Others* (1934), *Reckless* (1935), *Rendezvous* (1935), *It Had to Happen* (1936), *Craig's Wife* (1937), *Manproof* (1937), *Four's a Crowd* (1938), *The Women* (1939), *Fast and Loose* (1939), *His Girl Friday* (1940), *Hired Wife* (1940), *No Time for Comedy* (1940), *The Feminine Touch* (1941), *They Met in Bombay* (1941), *Take a Letter, Darling* (1942), *My Sister Eileen* (1942), *What a Woman* (1943), *Roughly Speaking* (1945), *She Wouldn't Say Yes* (1945), *Tell It to the Judge* (1949), *Picnic* (1956), *Auntie Mame* (1957), *Five Finger Exercise* (1962), *Gypsy* (1962), *The Trouble with Angels* (1966), *Oh Dad Poor Dad* (1967), *Where Angels Go, Trouble Follows* (1968), *Rosie!* (1968), *The Unexpected Mrs. Pollifax* (1970), *The Crooked Hearts* (1972)

## MARGARET RUTHERFORD

### (May 11, 1882–May 22, 1972)

Her father was a murderer. Her mother died when she was three. Her adopted son scandalized the world by changing his sex and marrying a black man. Like her most famous screen character, the eccentric old Miss Marple, Margaret Rutherford led a life of well-mannered civility, which was interrupted by some strange and bewildering events.

Margaret's father committed patricide, "his throat, beard, hands, night dress, legs and feet dripping with blood," according to a newspaper account of the murder scene. Declared insane, he was committed to an asylum. Eventually released, he shortened his real name (William Rutherford Benn) and moved to India.

Margaret, subject to bouts of depression and worry brought on by the knowledge of insanity in her family, recalled, "I was often lonely and never quite totally happy, but I knew that I had to cling on and have faith." She worked as a teacher for years while trying to land jobs in amateur theatrical productions, and was over 40 before she scored a major success as an actress, getting laughs in 1935's *Short Story*. She played Bijou Furze in *Spring Meeting* in London in 1938 and had hits with *The Importance of Being Earnest* and *Blithe Spirit* in 1941.

She married Stringer Davis in 1945 (the "Mr. Stringer" of her later Miss Marple films) and over the years scored major successes in comic parts, both on stage and screen. She aged into a plump old lady with a bulldog jaw, melty jowls and craggy wrinkles around her eyes. She was delightful even when playing harsh roles, such as glaring, huffy "Chairman of the Positive Thought Rally" in 1953's film *Runaway Bus*. "Don't call me madam, miss!" she warns an employee at the airport. "Do I look like a madame?"

Her most famous role was as Miss Marple, the amateur sleuth who found herself engaging in improbably hilarious antics, especially considering her age and girth. The films' highlights were always incongruous moments, such as engaging in the latest dances or emoting on "Dangerous Dan McGrew" (in an attempt to audition for a murderous acting company).

Strangely, her most famous role was not one that initially appealed to her. "I never wanted to play Miss Marple," she wrote in her autobiography, "I never found murder amusing. I don't like anything that tends to lower or debase or degrade." Agatha Christie wasn't pleased either. She wanted a more "fragile"-looking woman, something closer to the detective in her stories and novels. Yet the end result was a series of four highly amusing mystery-comedies. Miss Marple became Rutherford's most famous role, beyond the Duchess of Grand Fenwick in *The Mouse on the Moon*, Madame Arcati in *Blithe Spirit* or her Academy Award-winning performance in *The V.I.P.s.*

In her later years she found herself not on the movie review page but in the gossip section. Her adopted son, a hermaphrodite raised as a male, had undergone corrective surgery to become female. "Gordon" Langley Hall was now "Dawn." Sex change operations were few at the time, and this one was given major coverage in England's tabloids. Margaret and her husband issued a simple statement: "Gordon has been a fine man so we see no reason why he would not be a fine woman." Interracial marriages were also a shock for the time; and when Dawn married a black man, John Simmons from South Carolina, there was another uproar. Dawn told the full story in her biography of Rutherford, *Margaret Rutherford: A Blithe Spirit.*

Fortunately, the 1960s ended placidly for Rutherford, whom Charlie Chaplin called "my favorite actress." She completed her autobiography in 1972 and died that year. Robert Morley visited her in her last days at the hospital. "She had an unhappy last few weeks," he admitted, "but a very happy and fulfilled life before that."

AUTOBIOGRAPHY: *An Autobiography* (1992)

BIOGRAPHIES: *Margaret Rutherford: A Blithe Spirit* (Simmons, 1983), *Margaret Rutherford* (Keown, 1956)

BROADWAY: *Short Story* (1935), *Blithe Spirit* (1941), *The Importance of Being Earnest* (1947), *Ring Around the Moon* (1950), *The Way of the World* (1953), *Time Remembered* (1955), *Farewell, Farewell Eugene* (1960), *Dazzling Prospect* (1961)

FILMS incl.: *The Demi Paradise* (1943), *English Without Tears* (1944), *Blithe Spirit* (1945), *Miranda* (1947), *Meet Me at Dawn* (1948), *While the Sun Shines* (1950), *The Happiest Days of Your Life* (1950), *Her Favorite Husband* (1951), *The Importance of Being Earnest* (1952), *Castle in the Air* (1953), *Runaway Bus* (1953), *Miss Robin Hood* (1953), *Curtain Up* (1953), *Mad About Men* (1954), *Trouble in Store* (1956), *An Alligator Named Daisy* (1957), *The Smallest Show on Earth* (1957), *I'm All Right Jack* (1960), *On the Double* (1961), *Murder She Said* (1962), *Mouse on the Moon* (1963), *Murder at the Gallop* (1963), *The V.I.P.s* (1963), *Murder Ahoy* (1964), *Murder Most Foul* (1965), *A Countess from Hong Kong* (1967), *Arabella* (1968)

S

## MORT SAHL

### (May 11, 1927–   )

Mort Sahl broke the mold of the nightclub comedian in a suit and tie, telling wife jokes, exuding show biz polish. As everyone from Lenny Bruce to Woody Allen to Jay Leno have admitted, it was Mort who influenced them; dressing casually in slacks and a sweater; talking about things that actually mattered; and getting his points across with a unique delivery that was nervous, staccato-sharp, hip and intimate, the opposite of the swaggering top-banana comic.

Born in Montreal, Sahl and his family soon moved to Los Angeles. There the boy won an American Legion Americanism Award while a member of the ROTC. His father had been a court reporter and later an administrator with the FBI. Mort, attending Belmont High School, hoped to go on to West Point but was drafted and ended up in an Alaskan air force base. He got into trouble for editing the newspaper *Poop from the Group* and was given 83 days of KP in a row. Still, he remained solidly establishment-oriented, and after his air force years majored in city management and traffic engineering at the University of Southern California, graduating in 1950.

After a few aimless years of writing and nearly starving, Sahl's girlfriend suggested he try stand-up in San Francisco at the hip Hungry i. She told him, "The audiences are all intellects, which means if they understand you, great, and if they don't, they

will never admit it. . . ." They didn't admit it. As Sahl recalled, the audience "threw pennies at me—and peanuts onto the stage. They were really savage." But the club owner didn't have the heart to fire him, and so Sahl persisted and eventually the audience began to understand what he was doing.

They had been confused by Mort's mordant observational style. Instead of fast jokes, he offered satirical descriptions. He told the crowd about conservatives dressing in charcoal gray suits "because modern science was looking for a color more somber than black." He said these men usually wore a tie with "a large stick pin that seemed to go through the body." While previous generations of comics set up their jokes with mechanical precision and blasted the punchline, Mort left it to the audience to be smart enough to find the humor. It took them a moment to get a quick satiric jab, such as his mention of "a magazine of obscure poetry—called 'Whither.' "

The name "Hungry i" meant "hungry intellectual," and instead of fat jokes, skinny jokes or homely jokes, Mort gave the crowd some intellectual lines: "I took a course at Cal called Statistical Analysis. And there was a guy in the course who used to make up all his computations and he never used Sigma. He used his own initials. 'Cause he was the standard deviation."

One of his most popular bits at the time, predating Woody Allen's *Take the Money and Run*, was

Mort Sahl, one of the most innovative men in comedy. His iconoclastic, stream-of-consciousness style influenced many comedians, including Lenny Bruce and Woody Allen. Photo from the author's collection.

about a bank robber who comes up against an intellectual teller. The robber hands him a note that says, "Act normal." The teller writes back, "Define your terms."

Sahl's delivery, one that fascinated Lenny Bruce, Woody Allen and so many more, was made up of free association, nervous digression, jazzlike improvisations, one-word references, parenthetical stream-of-consciousness commentary and a mosaic of adlibs and suddenly remembered set routines. Sometimes he seemed like a hip patient on a psychiatrist's couch, other times the cool shrink himself. His trademark was the rolled-up newspaper he carried on stage (a convenient place to hide new gags and reminders of topics to cover). A nervous giggle and a dry, sarcastic laugh sometimes helped key the audience into "getting" a particular line.

Sahl's stop-and-start cadence kept audiences off balance and intrigued: "I wanted to say a few words— I have a lot of hostility tonight to bring out here— I wanted to say something on the president's press conference and this being a primitive form of the-

ater—my attempts to entertain you and take your minds off the fact that there was an explosion in the shaft and we're trapped. Boy. Clichés . . . right? Exciting . . . Captain Beech arrived in the *Triton*. He had been underwater for 83 days. And he came up and that took our minds off the U-2. And President Eisenhower gave Captain Beech a medal for being one of the few officers whose whereabouts he knows. And then nobody knew what to say. It's like 'One of Our Aircraft Is Missing.' And one of our presidents, in the opinion of many."

In the late 1950s and early '60s, it was unheard of to attack the president that way. Sahl was labeled "Will Rogers with fangs." Rogers used to say, "I never met a man I didn't like." Mort challenged, "Is there any group I haven't offended?"

Fortunately for Sahl, the time was right for his type of comedy, and the liberal press, nightclub reviewers and patrons at the hip clubs he played were all on his side. He dared to come up with such lines as "I'm not so much interested in politics as I am in overthrowing the government." His jokes against Senator McCarthy, President Eisenhower and Vice-President Nixon were quoted in magazines all over the country, including a cover story in *Time* magazine—a rare honor for a comedian back then. Sahl became one of the first comedians to have best-selling record albums. At a time when topical humor was unavailable on late-night television, people bought Mort's albums as they would a weekly news magazine, and he seemed to come out with them almost as often.

Whatever Sahl said stirred controversy: "Maybe the Russians will steal our secrets—then they'll be two years behind." "I'm for capital punishment. You've got to execute people. How else are they going to learn?" "I went to my dressing room between shows and an attorney for the NAACP was waiting for me. He wanted to know why I don't have any Negroes in my act."

Writers searching for a word to describe him came up with "iconoclast," and Mort was exactly that. He said at every election that it didn't matter who was elected—"I will attack him." John F. Kennedy was elected—and Mort attacked. On his album *The New Frontier* he told of fans surprised at his Kennedy jokes. "We thought [Kennedy's election] was what you wanted." His salty response: "You didn't have to do it for *me!*"

Ed Sullivan refused to let Mort tell Kennedy gags on his show. Sahl's bookings declined. Vaughn Meader's lighthearted *First Family* parody album sold millions of copies; Sahl's *The New Frontier* a fraction of that. Ironically, after Kennedy's death, when Sahl was one of the first and most vocal proponents of a conspiracy theory, his audiences still turned away. Sahl couldn't accept this. He had himself risked his life by attacking Senator McCarthy and President Eisenhower. Now he was once again risking his own safety by challenging the Warren Commission—and nobody would even listen.

Told repeatedly by nightclub and television bookers to stop talking about a conspiracy, Sahl tried to see their point of view. He said, "According to Gallup 88% of the American people don't believe in the Warren Report. I certainly wouldn't want it on my conscience that I disturbed the faith of the remaining 12%." Although Sahl's income sank from $400,000 a year to $19,000, he refused to stop talking about the Warren Report, which led some to declare that he'd lost his sense of humor along with Lenny Bruce, whose club routines now centered mostly on his own legal battles. Lenny died on the battlefield. For years, Mort was agonizingly missing in action.

With the escalation of the Vietnam War and the sinking popularity of Lyndon Johnson, Sahl's brand of fierce satire was suddenly back in fashion in the late 1960s. Acolytes such as The Smothers Brothers booked Mort for their television shows, and he put out one of his best albums, *Anyway Onward*. With Richard Nixon in the White House, Sahl's comeback was complete, though there were now many comedians daring to perform political satire, and the competition included not only The Smothers Brothers but the broad parodies of Nixon mimic David Frye.

Sahl never forgot the backstabbing he endured during the Kennedy years nor the bleakness of the period following Kennedy's death. He published a memoir/autobiography *Heartland* that many critics found extremely bitter. Admirers like Dick Cavett, Merv Griffin and Steve Allen booked Sahl for television appearances in the 1960s and '70s, and he

was still fiercely uncompromising, often getting into heated battles with other guests on the shows as well as audience members.

Through the '60s Sahl had occasionally taken on acting roles, both in films and on television shows including "Thriller" and "Emergency." By the '80s he talked about "failing upward," earning a good salary for writing film screenplays for top stars, though not a single script made it to the screen. He continued to tour and even tried a one-man Broadway show in 1988, but ran up against a unique new problem: His enduring influence had ultimately led Johnny Carson, Jay Leno and others to tackle topical humor without pulling the punches. And it was all free on television, no cover, no minimum. A strong cult of older fans and respectful new ones still attended Sahl's shows, but his was no longer the only quotable voice of political wit.

Sahl seemed to lean a bit more to the conservative right in the 1980s and '90s. Though he clearly is offering an older, more conservative satirical viewpoint, Sahl is still very much the iconoclast who spares nobody. A typical line circa 1990: "If anybody comes up to you and says 'My kid is a conservative—why is that?' you say, 'Remember in the '60s when we told you if you kept using drugs your kids would be mutants?' "

In concert, Sahl is as sharp as ever. He called President Bush "a living heart donor," while doubting Jesse Jackson as the moral successor to Martin Luther King: "I think his slogan is . . . 'I Have a Scheme' " Sahl's one-liners still have punch: "What is a moderate Iranian? One who's run out of ammunition." And looking back on our forefathers he announced, "Two hundred years ago we had Jefferson, Washington, Ben Franklin and Tom Paine, and there were four million people. Today we have 220 million, and look at our leaders. . . . Darwin was wrong."

AUDIO: *Mort Sahl at Sunset* (Fantasy), *The Future Lies Ahead* (Verve), *Mort Sahl 1960* (Verve), *A Way of Life* (Verve), *At the Hungry i* (Verve), *The Next President* (Verve), *Great Moments in Comedy* (Verve), *The New Frontier* (Reprise), *On Relationships* (Reprise), *Anyway Onward* (Mercury), *Sing a Song of Watergate, Apocryphal of Lie* (GNP Crescendo)

BROADWAY: *The Next President* (1958), *Mort Sahl on Broadway* (1988)

FILMS incl.: *In Love and War* (1958), *All the Young Men* (1960), *Johnny Cool* (1963), *Doctor You've Got to Be Kidding* (1967), *Don't Make Waves* (1967), *Nothing Lasts Forever* (1984)

VIDEOS: *Hungry i Reunion Concert; Laughing Room Only*

## SOUPY SALES

### (Milton Supman, January 8, 1926–    )

He's had hit records, hit television and radio shows, was on Broadway and made generations laugh at classic corn and goofy gags. He makes it look easy, thanks to a smiling, easygoing style, but it takes a unique personality to make it work. Soupy Sales can be silly without being juvenile and corny without insulting an audience's intelligence. Like the right kind of pie for throwing, Soupy has a soft exterior and a sturdy core; he keeps things loose and messy on stage—but is always in complete control of his comedy.

Sales earned his nickname as a child in West Virginia; the other kids quickly turned his last name, Supman, into "Soup." At six he got laughs in a school play: "The first time I ever heard laughter and applause—wow, it really felt good." He received his B.A. in journalism, "but when I found out how much newspapermen made, I said no, no! I can't do that!" After writing radio ad copy and sketches for disc jockeys, he became a radio performer and learned stand-up comedy in burlesque and strip clubs: "I didn't work dirty, or do things 'low' comics did. A 'low' comic would do dirty jokes and look down the girl's blouse. But the 'high' comics did 'Who's on First' or 'Crazy House.' That's what I went for." Inspired by Abbott and Costello and the *Hellzapoppin* comedy of Olsen and Johnson, Soupy's kiddie comedy shows of the late 1940s and '50s adopted the same formula.

"*Hellzapoppin* was about trying to get through a show with all that crazy stuff going on. That's what I did on my show. I was always playing straight to [puppets] White Fang, Black Tooth, the guy at the door. I was just a guy trying to get through the day with all the stuff happening around me." Of course, he didn't look like such an ordinary guy, with his floppy ties, top hats and penchant for telling corny gags. He'd tell the kids, "Keep your chin up—it'll keep the milk from dropping on your clothes." He'd say, "You show me a sculptor who works in the basement—and I'll show you a low-down chiseler!" For gags like that, he'd get a well-deserved pie in the face.

After local shows in Cincinnati, Cleveland and Detroit, he moved out to Los Angeles in 1960. There his rejuvenation of slapstick comedy made him a cult star. Big stars dropped by for pie-in-the-face comedy. Frank Sinatra was one of the first. Soupy recalled, "I never would have suggested it. To expect somebody to want to be hit in the face with a pie would be nuts 'cause it's a mess. I was the one that got hit." (Soupy prefers shaving cream to real pies: "They're easier to clean.") But after Sinatra, everyone wanted to be pie-eyed. And Soupy had a hit television show, Soupy dolls, toys, even a comic dance craze with his hit song "The Mouse." He became a souper-star. Everyone loved Soupy. And with good reason.

On stage and in person, Soupy exudes openness and friendliness, with his twinkling eyes, enthusiastic personality and that easygoing West Virginia accent. "I've always said it doesn't cost any more to be nice. I like people. I always did. I think if people take the time to ask for an autograph, or a picture, then what's wrong with that?"

When he moved to New York, Soupy's success continued, despite a few backfired gags. While most jokes attributed to Soupy are apocryphal, it's true that for a gag on a New Year's show (January 1, 1965) he did tell kids to "tiptoe into the bedroom" and send in those "green pieces of paper" from their parents' wallets. "But I never did it to get any money, it was just a joke. The punch line was 'If you send me those pieces of paper, you know what I'm gonna send you? A postcard from Puerto Rico!'" Soupy was suspended for a week, until protests from his fans brought him back.

Soupy had a regular feature, an interrupting man at the door. One day he heard the knock and went to the door—only to find a topless dancer going through some gentle gyrations. Viewers at home didn't see the gag perpetrated by show staffers; the woman was off camera. But the incident was filmed by another camera, uncensored, and the gag has since become a staple of various "blooper" video tapes.

Soupy went on to try Broadway, syndicated television shows in 1965 and 1978, and appear on quiz shows. Into the 1980s he hosted a popular comedy show on NBC radio in New York. Fans who grew up with Soupy still love him, and he's found a lucrative career in stand-up, appearing in nightclubs all around the country, "still Soupy after all these years."

As with Laurel and Hardy, The Three Stooges and other geniuses of slapstick, Soupy finally earned some respect. In 1990 he received an honorary degree, Doctor of Arts, from his alma mater, Marshall University.

AUDIO: *The Soupy Sales Show* (Reprise), *Up in the Air* (Reprise), *Spy with a Pie* (ABC Paramount), *Do the Mouse* (ABC Paramount), *Bag of Soup* (Motown), *Still Soupy After All These Years* (MCA)

BROADWAY: *Ice Capades* (1966), *Come Live with Me* (1967)

FILMS incl.: *The Two Little Bears* (1961), *Critic's Choice* (1963), *Birds Do It* (1966)

TV: "The Soupy Sales Show" (1955), "The Soupy Sales Show" (1962), "The Soupy Sales Show" (1965–67), "What's My Line" (1968–75), "The Soupy Sales Show" (1978–79), "Sha Na Na" (1978–81)

VIDEO: *The Best of the Soupy Sales Show* (Vols 1–3)

# FATHER GUIDO SARDUCCI

## (Don Novello, January 1, 1943–   )

While many found Don Novello's "Father Guido Sarducci" character a boring, one-joke creation, there were enough supporters to create a vocal cult that kept the good father busy with nightclub and television work for two decades. Few modern comedians persisted with only one character so successfully.

Novello, born in Ashtabula, Ohio, was originally an ad man for five years. He experimented with writing a rock opera about a two-headed baby (*Spe-cial Eddie*) and then went out to California to write comedy for a local UHF television station in San Francisco. He created his comic stand-up identity in 1973, becoming Father Guido Sarducci, contrasting his clerical garb and floppy black hat with hip, pink-tinted sunglasses. His stereotyped Italian dialect comedy was tempered with caustic one-liners and his grim chain smoking. The whole thing "just sort of came together. The hat is something like that worn by some priests in the Vatican. . . . The coat I bought in a St. Vincent de Paul thrift shop for $7.50 and I'm still wearing it."

As the gossip columnist for *l'Osservatore Romano* and the weekly *Vatican Inquirer*, the Sarducci act featured comic lectures toying with religious satire but loaded with a lot of harmless silliness. His report on the hazards of sock changing: "A professor from Argentina did this-a research. He found that body heat has to do with longevity and then found-a that if you could keep-a the body heat near the body you will live longer. What happens is alot of heat-a leaks out between one's toes and if you don't change your socks, the heat stays in the feet area and you could live longer . . . put a new sock on over the old sock so no heat escapes when you change-a your socks."

Over the years Sarducci appeared often on late-night talk shows, was briefly a regular on "Saturday Night Live" and in the late 1980s starred in cable television specials, including Showtime's "Father Guido Sarducci Goes to College" and Cinemax's "The Pope's Tour." The only time anyone seemed to seriously object to the Sarducci religious satire was when, in 1981, the Father went to the Vatican to take some publicity pictures. He was arrested for impersonating a priest.

Aside from some work on the old "Smothers Brothers Comedy Hour," where he did some straight monologues, Don Novello rarely performed as anything but Father Guido Sarducci. An exception was his role as the publicist for the Corleones in *The Godfather Part III*. The lack of variety and constant work as Sarducci unfortunately locked a fine comic mind into one direction. Proof of Novello's versatility is his 1977 book, *The Lazlo Letters*. He wrote put-on letters to Richard Nixon and various other politicians pretending to be an archconservative and offering insane, often fascistic advice—and getting back warm letters of congratulations. Even his most inane letters were answered. He wrote the U.S. Treasury to find out how much $500,000 in pennies would weigh (an official wrote back "about 340,000 pounds"). When he asked Queen Elizabeth what her last name was ("We just call you Queen Elizabeth over here. Queen Elizabeth who?") he got a response from her lady-in-waiting: "The Queen has no surname, but belongs to the House of Windsor." Sometimes his questions were hard to answer. To Ray Kroc of McDonald's: "I see where you're up to 10 billion hamburgers sold. How many more do you have to go?"

Despite the cult response to his Lazlo Toth character, Novello continues on as Father Guido Sarducci, though not all of his teachings supply aid and comfort to his flock. According to the Father heaven isn't so heavenly: "There's no breakfast served after eleven."

AUDIO: *Live at St. Douglas Convent* (Warner Bros), *Breakfast in Heaven* (Warner Bros.)
BOOKS: *The Lazlo Letters* (1977), *The Blade* (1984)
BROADWAY: *Gilda Radner Live* (1979)
FILMS: *Tucker* (1988), *Godfather Part III* (1990)
TV: "The Smothers Brothers Show" (1975), "Saturday Night Live" (1978–80)
VIDEOS: *Saturday Night Live: Buck Henry; Saturday Night Live: Eric Idle; Saturday Night Live: Michael Palin; Father Guido Sarducci Goes to College*

## JIMMY SAVO

### (1896–September 6, 1960)

Though forgotten today, stage star Jimmy Savo was dynamic enough in his time to be immortalized in a poem by e. e. cumings. In part:

Is poet is
(childlost
so; ul
) foundclown a
—line a
bird

An amusing, sometimes eloquent pantomime comic, little Jimmy Savo began his career as "The Boy Wonder Juggler" of vaudeville. His father had run a shoe repair shop at 97th Street and Third Avenue in New York. The Bronx-born performer became a comic when he subbed in a vaudeville sketch. He ad-libbed some bits of business. "My first entrance was coming down a flight of steps. The other comedian used to walk down the steps, but I hopped down with both feet together. I got my first laugh." The biggest laugh of the night came while holding a prop muff. He had no idea until later why the crowd was laughing. "It was the way I held the muff. It seemed the particular way I held it was the trademark of certain ladies of that period."

After World War I Savo played the prestigious Palace Theatre in New York and Broadway in the 1920s. He became known for novelty pantomimes, including his acted-out version of popular songs like "River Stay 'Way From My Door." He was also a pretty fair monologist with some quotable gags: "I don't mind a man going around telling lies about me, but he'll hear from me if he dares to tell the truth."

After winning over the critics with *The Boys from Syracuse*, Savo eventually got his own one-man mime show on Broadway, *Mum's the Word*. It was the highlight of his career, but a quick highlight. It lasted only a week. In 1946 a tumor required that his right leg be amputated. Despite this handicap to his miming, he continued to perform for many years, wrote the novel *Little World Hello* in 1947 and briefly had his own television show in 1949. A half-completed autobiography was published posthumously.

AUTOBIOGRAPHY: *I Bow to the Stone* (1963)
BOOK: *Little World Hello* (1947)
BROADWAY: *Listen, Lester* (1918), *Vogues of 1924* (1924), *Murray Anderson's Almanac* (1929), *Earl Carroll's Vanities* (1930), *Lambs Gambol* (1932), *Parade* (1935), *The Would-be Gentleman* (1936), *The Boys from Syracuse* (1938), *Mum's the Word* (1940), *Wine, Women and Song* (1942), *What's Up* (1943)
FILMS incl.: *Once in a Blue Moon* (1934), *Merry-Go-Round of 1938* (1937)
TV: "Through the Crystal Ball" (1949)

## SAVOY and BRENNAN

**Bert Savoy, Everett McKenzie, 1888–June 26, 1923**
**Jay Brennan, 1882–January 14, 1961**

Campy comedy was the specialty of effeminate female impersonator Bert Savoy. Most female impersonators in vaudeville at the time, such as Julian Eltinge, astonished audiences with their accuracy; but Savoy's aim was to make them laugh with broad parody. Some old-timers believed that Bert's coy catch phrase "You *must* come over!" was adapted, along with his exaggerated mannerisms, by Mae West.

An ex-chorus boy from Boston, Savoy became a solo female impersonator working in tough, female starved outposts in Montana and Alaska. He returned East and teamed with several partners, ultimately Jay Brennan in 1913. At the time there were some other female impersonators, including The Russell Brothers, who appeared as "Our Irish Servant Girls." But when Savoy teamed with Jay Brennan they evolved a more unique "boy-and-girl" act, one that allowed Savoy to accentuate campy coquettishness by playing off a "straight" man.

They polished their routines to a high gloss and played The Palace three years later. Savoy was married, but it was a marriage of convenience that ended in 1922 when the woman took all of the money out of their bank account and carted off as much of their belongings as she could fit in a truck.

On stage Savoy offered gags about female ways and wiles that were sometimes just barely fit to print. He told an interviewer, "It's the women that lead me on to say the awful things I say on the stage. Out in front they lead me on with their knowing laughter, and from home they write or telephone me little feminine things which they have heard and which they think will betray womankind in our act. . . . You know the type of woman that knows everything and knows nothing; that wants to make you believe how bad she is and never gives herself the chance to be bad—laughs herself out of it. I'm that way myself."

On stage the slim, fashionably flat-chested, elegantly dressed Savoy frolicked with the too-handsome, nattily dressed Brennan, while audience members snickered. "The house detective said a man jumped out of a tenth-story window at three o'clock this morning," announced Brennan. "The man must have been listening at our keyhole!" gasped Savoy.

The act came to an end one summer afternoon at Long Beach, New York. Bert and vaudevillian Jack Vincent, along with another male couple, were strolling toward the beach when a severe storm blew up. Before they could make it to shelter, Savoy and Vincent were struck by lightning. They died at Long Island College Hospital. One paper reported that Savoy was in the water at the time and drowned. As Harpo Marx recalled, "The next day a New York columnist had written an obituary for him in the form of a love letter. Also on the following day, so the legend goes, all the pansies at Coney Island were wearing lightning rods."

Brennan teamed with another impersonator, Stanley Rogers and successfully played The Palace in 1924. They remained together until 1929. Brennan later became a scriptwriter in Hollywood (*Expensive Husbands,* 1937). The lifelong bachelor died in 1961.

BROADWAY: *Greenwich Village Follies* (1920), *Greenwich Village Follies* (1922)

## AVERY SCHREIBER (See BURNS and SCHREIBER.)

## HARRY SECOMBE (see THE GOONS.)

## GEORGE SEGAL

**(February 13, 1934–  )**

A good-looking, glib performer especially effective in romantic comedies and films satirizing the mystery or adventure genre, George Segal developed his comic style from watching Cary Grant. Like Grant, Segal's slant was not to take things too seriously—to create a character that was carefree, charming on his own terms. "Cary Grant began it in movies and there hasn't been anything new since. While Grant is talking to someone in the film, he's also talking to you, the audience. The idea is that you circle around your character and get in a glancing blow now and then. You've got to do it with consummate ease, the way Joe DiMaggio used to get to the center field fence in Yankee Stadium to make a catch."

Segal learned to manipulate audiences by performing magic shows for his school friends and neighbors in Great Neck, Long Island. "I started out earning $5 a show and by the time I chucked it all my going rate was $15. It helped put spending money in my pockets." He attended Haverford College and transferred to Columbia University, graduating in 1955.

After some success as a banjo player and singer in a variety of bands, including his own group (Bruno Lynch and His Imperial Jazz Band), Segal found acting work. He started at the bottom, as a janitor at off-Broadway's Circle in the Square. He moved from understudy to a featured player in an off-Broadway production of *The Iceman Cometh*. Drafted, Segal gave Uncle Sam a few years of service before returning to New York and to the improvisational company The Premise. After several more Broadway shows Segal began making films.

After his Academy Award-nominated performance in *Who's Afraid of Virginia Woolf* and his portrayal of a charismatic con man in *King Rat,* his career drifted more and more toward comedy. He said, "I've done a lot of dramas in my life, but I prefer comedies. In comedy, you're always learning. There's only one way to do it—the way that gets a laugh. For someone who lacks discipline in his life as I do, it's nice to get the discipline of making comedy."

In the late 1960s and '70s, Segal was one of the most likable of leading men, using his boyish charms and semismooth guile on a variety of top female co-stars. He was the boyish, flustered son to Ruth Gordon in *Where's Poppa?* and the neurotic author who learned some lessons in life from Barbra Streisand in *The Owl and the Pussycat*. He matured into a likable schemer in two more hits, *The Duchess and the Dirtwater Fox* opposite Goldie Hawn and *Fun with Dick and Jane* co-starring Jane Fonda. Typically in all four films, the women were in charge, usually flustering hero Segal.

In the early 1970s Segal starred in late-night variety show specials for NBC. Occasionally he appeared in a drama or took time off for a special project. In 1978 he performed in a Chanukah play at Yeshiva University. Why did he take time off from his busy schedule? "I am a Jew," he answered. "The day I was born I was 5000 years old."

In the '80s he moved on to play slightly more mature roles (a father in *Carbon Copy*), but retained his boyish streak. He's also retained his banjo and continued to enjoy himself performing tunes in nightclubs and on late-night talk shows.

AUDIO: *The Yama Yama Man* (Phillips), *Leave It to Jane* (Strand), *The Premise* (Vanguard)
BROADWAY: *Don Juan* (1956), *Our Town* (1959), *Leave It to Jane* (1959), *Gideon* (1961), *Rattle of a Simple Man* (1963), *The Knack* (1964), *Requiem for a Heavyweight* (1985)
FILMS incl.: *King Rat* (1965), *Who's Afraid of Virginia Woolf* (1965), *Bye Bye Braverman* (1968), *No Way to Treat a Lady* (1968), *Loving* (1970), *The Owl and the Pussycat* (1970), *Where's Poppa?* (1970), *The Hot Rock* (1972), *A Touch of Class* (1973), *Blume in Love* (1973), *California Split* (1974), *The Black Bird* (1975), *The Duchess and the Dirtwater Fox* (1976), *Fun with Dick and Jane* (1977), *Who is Killing the Great Chefs of Europe?* (1978), *Lost and Found* (1979), *The Last Married Couple in America* (1980), *Carbon Copy* (1981), *Zany Adventures of Robin Hood* (1984), *Stick* (1985), *Killing 'em Softly* (1985), *Many Happy Returns* (1986), *All's Fair* (1989), *For the Boys* (1991)
TV: "Take Five" (1987)

## JERRY SEINFELD

### (April 29, 1954–   )

Through the late 1980s Jerry Seinfeld quietly became one of the most dependable of the new suit-and-tie young comics, a group that included David Brenner, Jay Leno and Garry Shandling. Thin, pleasant, slightly wall-eyed, the clean-cut Seinfeld favored family-oriented observational comedy. On Halloween: "You're seven years old and you're *working* for candy!" On retirement: "My parents moved to Florida last year. They didn't want to, but they're 60, and that's the law."

"It's not that I'm a prude," said Jerry. "I'm a purist. I want to find true quality humor, that's the quest, not to just get laughs. . . . I just think my material should be funny on its own and not rely on the gratuitous laughs profanity gets."

Born in Brooklyn, raised in Massapequa, Long Island ("an Indian name which means 'by the mall' "), Jerry recalled he wasn't the class clown. Everybody was: "Everybody in school was always fooling around. After we graduated, they went off and got jobs. I kept fooling around." He graduated from Queens College and in the late '70s began performing in comedy clubs. While many contemporaries went "full-tilt bozo" in free-form comedy, or challenged the censors with X-rated material, Seinfeld, growing up watching smooth family-oriented comics such as Alan King and Jan Murray, realized the satisfaction, and big money, in playing resorts, casinos and the top nightclubs. One of his best-known bits revolved around losing socks in the laundry; items considered hilarious by fans and notorious by his scornful colleagues.

By 1981 he was appearing on television's "Tonight Show" and later opening for Kenny Rogers, Andy Williams and Dionne Warwick. In 1987 he had his first HBO solo special. More talk show appearances followed as well as a heavy touring schedule. In 1990 he hosted a comedy special on NBC and was rewarded with a critically praised sitcom as himself: a somewhat conservative-looking single guy, middle class but hip and humorous, trying to get along with dates, friends and family. As John J. O'Connor in the *New York Times* put it, "Mr. Seinfeld is definitely a nerd, a pleasant, good-looking young fellow who gives the impression that he might have a decent career as a stockbroker except for a compulsion to tell jokes."

He remains "family entertainment," offering up little moments of everyday truth: "You go to the store and buy Grape Nuts. No grapes, no nuts. What's the story?" He continued asking his audience vital questions: "Has any turtle ever outlived a shaker of turtle food?" It is all inoffensive, but Seinfeld would not be surprised to find someone objecting. After all, he says, *Nothing* in life is fun for the whole family."

TV: "The Seinfeld Chronicles" (1990), "Seinfeld" (1990–  )

VIDEOS: *Evening at the Improv, Rodney Dangerfield: It's Not Easy Being Me*

## PETER SELLERS (See also THE GOONS.)
### (September 8, 1925–July 24, 1980)

"I have the feeling that the film character enters my body as if I were a kind of medium," Peter Sellers once said. "It's a little frightening." Worse than that, without a film character to play, Sellers felt he had no identity at all. "I have no personality of my own whatsoever," he declared.

One of the greatest actors in film comedy, Sellers was believable in dozens of different accents and disguises. While critics were dazzled by it all, biographers had a tougher time; they had to try to penetrate "the mask behind the mask," discovering a complex man whose extremes ranged from insufferable ego to painful insecurity and sensitivity.

His mother was Jewish, his father Protestant. He had little religious instruction and years later complained, "Why didn't they commit me as a child, why have they left me to grope like this? I don't know whether I'm a Jew or a Gentile. I'm nothing." His parents were both struggling vaudevillians. He made his stage debut when only a few weeks old and grew up surrounded by dancers, singers and comedians. "I had quite a unique childhood," he recalled. "I'm sure it's stood me in good stead. I mean it encouraged the resilience, the durability; it forged the humor, I suppose, because without a sense of humor in those days we would have all gone under a dozen times a week."

While his father continued to tour, his mother settled down to run an antique shop. Peter attended a nearby Catholic school, St. Aloysius College and served with the RAF in India during World War II. Originally a drummer, Sellers got into radio after phoning BBC producer Roy Speer, impersonating popular radio comedian Kenneth Horne. His voice disguised, Horne-Sellers told Speer all about the great new talent, Peter Sellers. "How do I get in touch with Sellers?" asked Speer. "You are in touch," came the reply. "I'm Sellers . . . it was the only way I could get through." "What do you do?" "I obviously do impressions."

Sellers displayed great abilities as a mimic, but when he joined friends Spike Milligan and Harry Secombe for 1951's "Goon Show," he achieved fame by creating characters uniquely his own. The legendary radio show specialized in zany comedy and

Peter Sellers was most popular as the bumbling Inspector Clouseau in the *Pink Panther* films. But his brilliance for characterization is even more evidenced by his work with The Goons and by his multiple roles in films such as *Dr. Strangelove* and *The Mouse That Roared.* Photo from the author's collection.

a bewildering cast of insane characters. The show was "antiestablishment," and Sellers was clearly one of the cheeky rising stars of a bold, free new comic style. It extended to real life. Sitting behind the Queen of England at the premiere of *West Side Story*, he called out, "Lady, would you mind taking your crown off?"

Sellers played dozens of parts on the radio show, and when he began to make films, proved that he could do it all visually as well. American audiences discovered Sellers in British imports such as *The Mouse that Roared*, and were amazed at the number of characters he could portray effortlessly. He played three parts in that one and three in his Oscar-nominated *Dr. Strangelove.*

He also played one character that year—Inspector Clouseau in *The Pink Panther*. Sellers made the film comedy a classic farce simply by adopting a unique French accent and approaching the zaniness around him with deadpan seriousness. Audiences snickered even at the straight lines, when the idiot detective would declare, "I suspect everyone and I suspect no one." Clouseau's single-minded dedication, as portrayed by Sellers, yielded laughs from throwaway lines. "Telephone call for you, Inspector Clouseau." "Ah yes. That will be for me."

Peter Ustinov had been the first choice for Clouseau, but now the part belonged to Sellers. A sequel was quickly put together, *A Shot in the Dark*, and Sellers was now acknowledged as one of the brightest stars in comedy. Then, during the filming of his next comedy, *Kiss Me Stupid*, he suffered a massive heart attack that nearly killed him. Ray Walston replaced him in the film, and for a while it seemed he would never work again.

When he did, he would suffer through nine flops in a row and watch his asking price sink from a million dollars a picture to one-third of that. Today some of those films are now acknowledged as cult classics. Fans marvel at the genius of Sellers in the lightweight running gag *The Party*, enjoy him in Neil Simon's giddy *After the Fox*, and savor the neglected gem *Hoffman*, which was the first film Sellers made that was in any way close to the real man.

The problems and the disappointments tore at Sellers, who battled mightily with the twin demons of self-doubt and self-assurance. He had the temperament of genius, often warring with those around him and seeking refuge in the extremes of extravagance and yoga meditation. He knew he had a bad reputation, but believed "it's a reputation mostly put about by those mediocre people who will always resent and try to cut down a man's talent. It's like Spike Milligan says, and God knows he's right, the world is full up with mediocrity and you find it everywhere, and when you brush with it you brush up venom."

Despite their many differences, Sellers and director Blake Edwards had one thing in common in 1975: the need for a hit. They reteamed for *The Return of the Pink Panther*. It was in fact a big hit and it led to more Panther films. Even though each one was loaded with more and more painfully predictable gags and slow, uneven direction, Sellers' Clouseau (whose accent became more and more outrageous each time out) was still irresistible.

The gods of comedy smiled on Sellers. At least he thought so. He was convinced that the spirit of Dan Leno, England's legendary stage star from the turn of the century, was guiding his career from "the other side." Leno died years before Sellers was even born but, as Sellers told his biographer Peter

Evans, "He follows me around everywhere. For years I felt his help, especially with my timing, before I knew who it was. He has been great for me. . . . he has given me some wonderful advice . . . sometimes I ask for help, sometimes it just happens."

Sellers' career was resuscitated by Clouseau, and he went on to star in several amusing films, including *Murder by Death*. Still, he knew there was something missing: the one film, the one character that he was truly destined to play. It wasn't Clouseau. It was Chance, the vacuous lead character of the Jerzy Kosinski novel *Being There*. After years of pursuit, he finally got the rights to the novel, and with a slight bow to Stan Laurel (the voice and mannerisms based loosely on the classic comedian), Sellers turned in the performance of his life. Friends and co-workers sensed that Sellers, not in the best of health, was fading even as he completed his masterpiece.

As had been the case with many Sellers films, from *The Party* through *Murder by Death* and the Panther series, critics expected so much of Sellers they gave his new effort mixed reviews. It was only in hindsight that they declared *Being There* a gem and Sellers deserving of an Academy Award. It was an honor Sellers desperately wanted but did not get.

Sellers' sudden death, from a heart attack, was front-page news all over the world. Tributes poured in from actors, directors and writers. In a few years Sellers' face would appear on a British postage stamp. Everyone praised his genius in comedy. Of Sellers, the man, there was little to say. Who was Peter Sellers? It seemed that nobody really knew.

AUDIO: *The Best of Sellers* (Angel), *Peter Sellers and Sophia Loren* (Angel), *Songs for Swingin' Sellers* (EMI), *The Songs of Sellers* (MFP), *Sellers Market* (United Artists), *An Evening with Peter Sellers* (BBC), *He's Innocent of Watergate* (Decca), *How to Win an Election* (Philips), *Bridge on the River Wye* (Odeon), *Fool Britannia* (Ember)

BIOGRAPHIES: *Peter Sellers, The Mask Behind the Mask* (Evans, 1980), *Peter Sellers: The Authorized Biography* (Walker, 1981), *P.S. I Love You* (M. Sellers, 1983)

FILMS incl.: *Penny Points to Paradise* (1951), *Down Among the Z Men* (1952), *Orders Are Orders* (1954), *The Lady Killers* (1955), *The Smallest Show on Earth* (1957), *The Naked Truth* (1958), *Tom Thumb* (1958),

*Carlton-Browne of the F.O.* (1958), *Up the Creek* (1958), *The Mouse That Roared* (1959), *I'm All Right, Jack* (1959), *The Battle of the Sexes* (1960), *Two-Way Stretch* (1960), *The Millionairess* (1961), *Mr. Topaze* (1961), *Only Two Can Play* (1962), *Lolita* (1962), *Waltz of the Toreadors* (1962), *Heavens Above* (1963), *The Wrong Arm of the Law* (1963), *The Pink Panther* (1963), *Dr. Strangelove* (1963), *The World of Henry Orient* (1964), *A Shot in the Dark* (1964), *What's New Pussycat?* (1965), *After the Fox* (1966), *The Wrong Box* (1966), *Casino Royale* (1966), *The Bobo* (1967), *Woman Times Seven* (1967), *The Party* (1968), *I Love You Alice B. Toklas* (1968), *The Magic Christian* (1969), *Hoffman* (1970), *There's a Girl in My Soup* (1970), *Where Does It Hurt?* (1972), *Alice's Adventures in Wonderland* (1972), *The Blockhouse* (1973), *The Optimist* (1973), *Soft Beds and Hard Battles* (1973), *The Great McGonagall* (1974), *Return of the Pink Panther* (1975), *Murder by Death* (1976), *The Pink Panther Strikes Again* (1977), *The Revenge of the Pink Panther* (1978), *The Prisoner of Zenda* (1979), *Being There* (1979), *The Fiendish Plot of Dr. Fu Manchu* (1980)

# LARRY SEMON

## (July 16, 1889–October 8, 1928)

One of the strangest-looking silent film comedians, Larry Semon had the wide eyes and ghostly white face of Harry Langdon and the jutting ears, long face, tufted hair and puckish little mouth of Stan Laurel. The big nose was Langdon and Laurel's combined.

Born in Mississippi, raised in Savannah, Georgia, Semon became a cartoonist for the *New York Sun* and wrote film scripts for Vitagraph comedies. In 1917 he began making his own shorts as both star and writer. He developed his stock company (Oliver Hardy and Fatty Alexander were his villains and foils, Dorothy Dwan his leading lady), and produced quality films through the late teens and early '20s.

Like Laurel, he was a perfectionist and a worrier, working carefully to set up his gags. Like Chaplin, he would throw away yards and yards of film footage if it wasn't performed to his liking. Like Lloyd and Keaton, he injected fast-paced thrill comedy and chase scenes into his work: buildings collapsed; people toppled into the mud; and windows were made for swan dives. Unlike Lloyd and Keaton, Larry didn't mind skipping work for days while his double handled most of the action in long shots.

For a time Semon was almost as popular as Laurel, Chaplin, Lloyd and Keaton, earning $1,250 a week. In the end, though, his problems were the same as Harry Langdon; he relied too much on his bizarre appearance. His mask of a face, his childishness and tiptoe fey walk became wearying, and he became more out of synch with what viewers wanted to see. In 1924, having left Vitagraph in disputes over money and budgeting, Semon lost momentum and his tried-and-true gags seemed simply redundant. In 1925 he played the Scarecrow in his ambitious version of *The Wizard of Oz*.

Semon invested heavily into one last effort that was never completed. The best he could do was a few short films instead. He suffered a nervous breakdown during the summer of 1928 and died of pneumonia a few months later, a half million dollars in debt.

FILMS incl.: *Rough Toughs and Roof Tops* (1917), *Spooks and Spasms* (1917), *The Simple Life* (1918), *Babes and Boobs* (1918), *Spies and Spills* (1918), *The Simple Life* (1919), *The Stage Hand* (1920), *The Fall Guy* (1921), *No Wedding Bells* (1923), *The Perfect Clown* (1925), *The Wizard of Oz* (1925), *Stop Look and Listen* (1926), *Spuds* (1927), *A Simple Sap* (1928)

## GARRY SHANDLING

### (November 29, 1949–   )

At first Garry Shandling was just another mild-mannered nerdish stand-up comic telling safe jokes on television's "Tonight Show." His self-deprecating material wasn't much different from anyone else's, much of it concentrated on his dating woes: "I just broke up with my girlfriend because she moved in with another guy. I said, 'That's where I draw the line,' and I dumped her, sort of."

In 1991 the nasal, frozen-faced comic hosted "The Grammy Awards." Discussing the issue of excessive sex in rock videos, he declared, "Who's to say what's obscene? Frankly, what most people find obscene—I would pay for."

He looked as if he got what he deserved, with his blow-dried puff-mat of hair, small eyes and a thick grillwork of teeth sandwiched between rubbery lips. Joining David Brenner as a reliable, clean and harmless comic suitable for family consumption, Shandling guested often on "The Tonight Show" beginning in 1981. In 1983 he began guest-host duties. His first assignment was subbing for Albert Brooks, the scheduled guest host. It was typical of Shandling's comic personality to be the guest host for a guest host.

Other comics of his generation were not impressed. Bob Goldthwait: "A lot of guys do material about how they can't get a date. If that's Garry Shandling's problem he could buy sex. I've got bigger worries."

Growing up, the Shandling family had big worries. Garry was born in Chicago but the family moved to Tuscon for the health of his brother Barry. The boy died there at 13 of cystic fibrosis. Garry was ten at the time. Garry developed an interest in comedy, especially in the albums by Reiner and Brooks, but majored in marketing at the University of Arizona. After he wrote some jokes for George Carlin, he decided to move to Los Angeles in 1973 and write jokes full time. He wrote episodes of "Sanford and Son," "Three's Company" and "Welcome Back Kotter."

Shandling had more trouble with cars than girls in 1977. He got into a minor traffic accident. While examining the damages with the other driver, a third car suddenly plowed forward, crushing him between the two cars, causing nearly fatal internal injuries. Fortunately Shandling had a strong constitution and, despite his meek appearance, was committed to exercise and a healthy lifestyle, including a vegetarian diet. Once back on his feet, Shandling was motivated to get his career into high gear. Following his breakthrough on "The Tonight Show," he hosted his own *Alone in Las Vegas* Showtime special in 1984 and followed it with his *25th Anniversary Special*. In 1986 he and Jay Leno were named permanent guest hosts on "The Tonight Show" but he resigned to star in his own television series.

Back in 1968, Woody Allen got laughs, female admirers and male commiserators for playing a fantasy-filled, unappealing but surprisingly wiry and plucky neurotic. Twenty years later Shandling was the hip loser too, filling his sitcom show with in jokes and moments of fantasy, most of it keyed to his clever reworking of the old "Burns and Allen Show" device of talking directly to the viewer and sharing the joke with them. For an episode in which he planned a surprise party, he coached the studio audience on how to yell "Surprise" and then said "Okay, now you at home . . . ."

Shandling had experimented with the idea much earlier. On the "Dr. Duck" comedy video of the early 1980s, a sequence featured Shandling describing a date with beauty contest winner Miss Maryland—and then acting it out. He's suddenly there with Miss Maryland, complete with her sash, whispering to the viewer, "Do you believe this? I'm underdressed. . . . Do you believe this? She's sitting on the roof of the car waving to people."

The laidback California hipness on the show included a throwaway theme song: "This is the theme to Garry's show, The theme to Garry's show. Garry called me up and asked if I would write his theme song. . . . How do you like the theme to Garry's show?"

Shandling's show became a cult hit but that was all. From Showtime cable it moved to the Fox network, where it sank to the bottom at the ratings, one listing placing in 80th out of 81 shows. In 1990 he decided to call it quits. He said, "Frankly, I'd really like to do something in which I'm not playing Garry Shandling."

TV: "It's Garry Shandling's Show" (1986–90)
VIDEOS: *Dr. Duck; Garry Shandling Alone in Vegas; Comic Relief III; The 25th Anniversary Special*

## DICK SHAWN

### (Richard Schulefand, December 1, 1923–April 17, 1987)

A charismatic entertainer, Dick Shawn was (along with Jonathan Winters) picked to be one of the big stars in comedy when he hit his stride in the 1950s. It was all a matter of finding a way to harness his talent for zany characters and weird hip free-form. For average viewers, he succeeded only twice in the next 30 years: as a distraught hippie in *It's a Mad*

Dick Shawn: His style of comedy was so bizarre that when he literally died on stage one night, audience members thought it was a joke. Photo from the author's collection.

*Mad Mad Mad World* and as the horrifyingly zany Hitler in *The Producers*.

Born in Lackawanna, near Buffalo, New York, Shawn recalled that "as a youngster, I was one of the shyest kids you ever saw. I was a real loner. I never felt comfortable with people. Baseball was my only interest. I was never without my black baseball cap, and I used to wear it with the peak way down over my eyes. I think that's why I remember so little of my childhood. I never *saw* anything."

He attended Fosdick Masten High School and the University of Buffalo. It was there that he first amused an audience. The six-foot-one athlete was in a frustrating basketball game and got some big laughs when, through accident and then irritation, he committed three fouls in 20 seconds. A good college baseball player as well, he missed signing with the Chicago White Sox when he was drafted in 1944. He performed in army shows in the Philippines and starred in *Objective U.S.A.* with Don Knotts.

He finished his schooling at the University of Miami and won a talent contest that got him to television's "Arthur Godfrey Show." After working at Catskill resorts and Camp Tamiment in the Poconos, he tried nightclubs and endured nights that were "real grim. No smiles, no applause, no nothing."

He got his big break opening for Betty Hutton at The Palace in 1953. As Jonathan Winters would do initially, Shawn created minisketches to house his outlandish characters. One routine about Southerners crying for "Massa Richard" to come back from the North with guns demonstrated his overpowering charisma and his trademark ability to literally wail with a concept. The *New York Times:* "Dick Shawn's cyclonic burlesque of ageless Southern loyalty is a funny escapade." The gag had a running nonjoke; an old man waiting for his son, going wild with excitement, then muttering, "Nope. It ain't him." Another routine that established him as one of the bright new neurotic comics was a study of the word "schizophrenia" that ended up with screams of "schizo-phreenee!" over and over.

Shawn opened for Marlene Dietrich at the Hotel Sahara in 1955 and went to Broadway for a series of successful performances in musicals. One of the few to really utilize Shawn's manic brand of frantic cool was Mel Brooks, who cast him in *The Producers.* Shawn played the corny hepcat who accidentally adlibs his way to glory by turning a serious play about Hitler into a hilarious musical farce.

Unfortunately for Shawn, there weren't many roles as wild and crazy. His fans seemed disappointed when the talented and rather good-looking star appeared in more "normal" roles, as he did replacing Zero Mostel in *A Funny Thing Happened on the Way to the Forum,* touring with Jack Carter in *The Odd Couple* and replacing Ron Liebman in *Room Service* on Broadway.

Shawn periodically performed a one-man show that mixed hip nonsense songs, sketches and even pantomime. With his white hair and penchant for put-ons, he seemed to new fans like an older, stranger Steve Martin. He preferred theaters to nightclubs: "In the theater you can do concepts, in nightclubs they want jokes." In 1983 he put together a 40-week tour of the United States with a show called *The (Second) Greatest Entertainer in the World.* Shawn didn't work from a script. "I figure if it's any good I'll remember it. The brain is so small, it can hold just so much information and I never crowd it with things that don't make an improvement, because I don't want anything to fall out. . . .

"People tend to intellectualize about comedy. Even psychiatrists have written heavy stuff on the subject and all they're reporting is what they see. Not the how of it. Poets, painters, comics, nobody knows the source of their talent, hidden perhaps in their first childhood observations of life. I just do what I feel. In the case of the comic actor, the statement may become blurred, for he himself in performance *is* the statement. Take in a comic's act attentively enough and alert audiences will be able to tell what kind of childhood he had."

Shawn once said, "I think of my relationship with an audience as a love affair. It lasts only a little while but I always look forward to a happy ending. For both of us." He was performing at the University of California at San Diego one night, telling a gag about nuclear war. He was his manic self as he began to imagine the holocaust. "Nobody would survive," he explained, "*except* the audience in the little sheltered theater!" Then he shouted, "And I would be your leader!"

He fell forward, flat on his face. He lay there while the audience laughed. Shawn's son Adam was in the audience and he knew this was no act.

In writing about Dick Shawn's death, *New York Post* columnist Cindy Adams recounted what the comedian said about trying to find the right audiences for his brand of comedy: "I can't work places like Vegas or the Catskills where people are belching. Maybe I belong in colleges. At least if I die, I die in front of intelligent people who know what I'm talking about."

AUDIO: *The Producers* (RCA), *Sings with His Little People* (20th Century Fox), *Mel Brooks' Greatest Hits* (Elecktra)

BROADWAY: *The Egg* (1962), *Peterpat* (1965), *Fade Out Fade In* (1965), *I'm Solomon* (1968), *Room Service* (1970)

FILMS incl.: *The Opposite Sex* (1956), *Wake Me When It's Over* (1960), *It's a Mad Mad Mad Mad World* (1963), *A Very Special Favor* (1965), *What Did You Do in the War Daddy?* (1966), *Penelope* (1966), *The Producers* (1968), *The Happy Ending* (1969), *Evil*

*Roy Slade* (1971), *Looking Up* (1977), *Love at First Bite* (1979), *Young Warriors* (1983), *Angel* (1984), *The Secret Diary of Sigmund Freud* (1984), *Beer* (1985), *The Check Is in the Mail* (1986), *Maid to Order* (1987), *Rented Lips* (1988)

TV: "Mary" (1978), "Hail to the Chief" (1985)

VIDEOS: *The Tommy Chong Roast; Live at Harrah's; Best Chest in the West*

## AL SHEAN (See GALLAGHER and SHEAN.)

## JEAN SHEPHERD

### (July 26, 1923–  )

With a quiet, confidential, almost conspiratorial delivery, Jean Shepherd developed a cult following on radio for his anecdotes about growing up, his army days, family and the little moments of heroism and lameness that make up daily life. With the same one-to-one impact as a *Catcher in the Rye* and the observational style of the later David Letterman, Shepherd described his father (who always insisted the government had a pill that turned water into gasoline), the American Dream (the failure of "Brunner's Triangular Doughnuts") and his beloved Chicago White Sox ("a White Sox fan measures victory in terms of defeat. Like if the White Sox lose 6–5 that's a good day").

A psychology major at Indiana State, Shepherd went into radio in 1949 and to New York in 1955. He remained on radio, locally and/or nationally, through 1978. His radio work was often ahead of its time, including his classic bit on Cracker Jack and its slogan, "The more you eat the more you want." A child's innocence is corrupted by a little sticky piece of Americana: "I got my mouth full of this sticky stuff, and at first it tasted sweet and made me kind of sick, kind of funny and sick." Then the poor kid realizes, "The more you eat the more you want," and starts spending all his money on the stuff. The homely tale ends with addiction: "They are not kidding, man. I'm on this stuff for four years. When you first start, you think you're just doing it to get the magic fit-all-finger ring. But it's just a come on, like all the rest of life. The more you eat the more you want."

During his radio years Shepherd dabbled in stand-up and made several comedy albums. He had a series of PBS television specials in the 1970s and '80s. Moving on to screenplays he wrote *A Christmas Story*, filmed in 1983 and starring Darren McGavin and Melinda Dillon. He said he didn't miss his radio fame. "I never look back. I have not a grain of nostalgia. I left radio not because I didn't like it anymore, but because I got offers to do films. It was time to move on. It was a lot of hard work, yet it sounded so effortless to people. . . . after a while, I thought, hey, I'm just giving this stuff away."

He's made audio tapes of his classic stories including "Ollie Hopnoodle's Haven of Bliss." Other uniquely named projects included: "The Phantom of the Open Hearth," "The Great American Fourth of July and Other Disasters" and "The Star-Crossed Romance of Josephine Cosnowski." Shepherd's books of short stories have won praise. The *New York Times Book Review* declared, "It is Shepherd's gift and his burden to be addicted to America. He's a piece of flypaper upon which the dust and flotsam of this peculiar civilization have been gathering for years."

At his best, Jean Shepherd is everyone's reassuring big brother—someone who doesn't have the answers but does have some questions. Like this declaration: "Ever look at the people around you and say, 'How the hell did I ever wind up with these idiots?' "

AUDIO: *Jean Shepherd and Other Foibles* (Elektra), *Will Failure Spoil Jean Shepherd* (Electra), *Live at the Limelight* (Quote), *The Declassified Jean Shepherd* (Mercury), *Shepherd's Pie* (Four Audio tapes)

BOOKS: *In God We Trust All Others Pay Cash* (1991), *Wanda Hickey's Night of Golden Memories and Other Disasters* (1976), *The Ferrari in the Bedroom* (1987), *A Fistful of Fig Newtons* (1987)

BROADWAY: *New Faces of 1964*

## ALLAN SHERMAN

### (Allan Copelon, November 30, 1924–November 21, 1973)

He was only 48 when he died, his body weakened by desperate dieting and chronic emphysema. He was subsequently forgotten, his novelty albums and books out of print. A few years later nostalgic listeners took out the old records and rediscovered the skill and wit behind Allan Sherman's deceptively simple comic songs, most reflecting the plain middle-class Jewish world that discovered him in the early 1960s.

In 1962 Sherman had a hit with his summer camp tune "Hello Muddah, Hello Faddah." His own childhood lacked that simple combination. His parents divorced when he was six and he was left with the decision to choose between them. He elected to live with his mother. He didn't see his father again for a decade. His mother, who had been previously married and divorced at 16, was a "swinger" who paraded endless "uncles" through the house. Even the house didn't stay put. The Shermans moved so often Allan attended 20 different schools. He grew into a fat, hook-nosed and mortally sensitive young man.

Sherman attended the University of Illinois in 1941 and, after he was discharged from the army due to asthma, went back to school where he staged shows including a musical parody of Adolf Hitler. He got married, wrote material for comedians, but flopped as a stand-up himself. To make the humiliation of his performing debut complete, his mother was ringside—drunk.

His big break came when he sold a concept for a quiz show. It became "I've Got a Secret." Unfortunately, he gave away lucrative residual rights that would have made him a fortune. The saving grace was that he latched on as the show's producer. He also produced "Masquerade Party" and wrote comic parodies for Perry Como's show. Many variety shows got a lift from Allan Sherman's ability to punch up weak scripts at the last minute. Sherman went on to produce Steve Allen's syndicated talk show, but a combination of backstage in-fighting and his own lack of ability in the format led to his firing. Suddenly the production and writing work dried up completely and he was in serious financial trouble.

A natural comic, Sherman couldn't help being funny at parties. Sherman made a one-shot novelty single in 1951 parodying Frank Loesser's "A Bushel and a Peck" with "A Satchel and a Seck." It got nowhere, but Sherman kept writing Jewish novelty tunes. These reflected his own conflicts and pride: "There was a time when I couldn't find roots be-cause I was ashamed to look where they were. When you are running around Madison Avenue . . . you carefully avoid mentioning your grandfather the ladies' coat presser. . . . When you're at a cocktail party in the Waldorf Towers and they pass you the goose-liver pâté, you very carefully neglect to point out that Lindy's chopped chicken liver tastes a lot better to you. You cover up the old roots because something in your own upbringing has convinced you that they are weeds."

His Jewish roots clashed against his California surroundings, so he turned "76 Trombones in the Big Parade" into "76 Sol Cohens at the Country Club" and "How Are Things in Glocca Morra" to "How Are Things with Uncle Morris." He created an entire new version of *My Fair Lady* complete with deeply ethnic references (including the Jewish word for horseradish, "chrein," as in "the chrein in Spain tastes good with two cents plain"). Lerner and Lowe refused permission for him to perform the parody and Capitol Records insisted "we don't think there's a market for this type of thing."

Still, whenever Allan performed at parties, stars such as Harpo Marx and Jack Benny roared with laughter and urged him to record his tunes. Finally Warner Brothers gave him a $1,500 advance, told him to use public-domain folk songs—and after a few frantic weeks of work and an hour recording the disc on August 6, 1962, Sherman had a surprise hit.

Unlike some Jewish comedians, Sherman didn't really make fun of his roots. Just because a knight was "Sir Greenbaum" didn't make him less heroic. A list of Jewish names substituted for Irish ones ("Shake Hands with Your Uncle Max My Boy") didn't mean they were homely by comparison. And a garment worker became heroic as he went "trampling through the warehouse where the drapes of Roth are stored." Sherman was proud (and funny) as he compared old Jewish business partners to "Streets of Laredo" gunfighters, or loudly extolled "seltzer" over plain water. His voice, homely yet soaring heroically, made the songs even funnier.

Many of his tunes were simply silly ("You're Getting to be a Rabbit with Me," "Eight Foot Two, Solid Blue" and "I'm Called Little Butterball"), and eventually the formula became predictable. But for several years Sherman had a string of hit albums. And

Allan Sherman's novelty tunes made comedy greats such as Harpo Marx and Jack Benny roar with laughter. Photo from the author's collection.

he couldn't handle it. The very insecure and jittery fat man recalled, "I was drinking two bottles of Scotch every day. I couldn't sleep. Or eat. . . . I got those terrible depressions. And muscle spasms. I was in a whirling madness. Nothing in life had prepared me for the insane success."

By the time he was ready to accept the applause, it was all over. The Allan Sherman fad faded, his marriage crumbled, his Broadway play *The Fig Leaves Are Falling* flopped and few bought his exhaustively researched satirical book on American sexuality, *The Rape of the A\*P\*E (American Puritan Ethic)*. Those wondering "whatever happened to Allan Sherman" found the answer in his obituary.

Now the proud and the silly songs of Sherman are considered classics. Sherman's comic spirit lives on stubbornly, just like the assimilating Jews of his *My Fair Lady* parody: "We have often walked West End Avenue. And you'll find us on a parkway known as Moshulu. Living gaily there. Like Israeli there. Oh it's grand on the streets where we live. We've got Scarsdale men. We've got Great Neck men. And just lately we've been sneaking into Darien. Strange new noses there. Friends of Moses there. Near the goys on the streets where they live . . . ."

AUDIO: *My Son the Folksinger* (Warner Bros.), *My Son the Celebrity* (Warner Bros.), *My Son the Nut* (Warner Bros.), *Allan in Wonderland* (Warner Bros.), *For Swingin' Livers Only* (Warner Bros.), *My Name Is Allan* (Warner Bros.), *Live* (Warner Bros.), *Togetherness* (Warner Bros.), *Peter and the Commissar* (RCA), *More Folk Songs by Allan Sherman and His Friends* (Jubilee), *Best of Allan Sherman* (Rhino), *Gift of Laughter* (Rhino), *My Son the Greatest* (Rhino)
AUTOBIOGRAPHY: *A Gift of Laughter* (1965)
BOOK: *The Rape of the A\*P\*E* (1991)

## MARTIN SHORT

### (March 26, 1951–   )

A short, boyish comic actor who can somtimes get away with a semiromantic role in addition to zany character parts, Martin Short was born in Hamilton, Ontario, 40 miles west of Toronto, Canada. His father was vice president of the Steel Company of Canada, and his mother was the concertmaster of the Hamilton Symphony. He had four brothers (one of whom died in a 1962 car accident) and a sister. His mother died in 1968, his father two years later.

A pre-med student at McMaster University, Martin ultimately earned his B.A. in social work and spent a year working with mentally retarded patients before taking a shot at show business. In 1972 he won a part in a Canadian production of *Godspell* with Gilda Radner. He dated her but ended up marrying her understudy, Nancy Dolman. He joined the Second City improvisational troupe in 1977.

After some sitcom work, Short returned to Canada for television's "SCTV," and from that improv show he went to "Saturday Night Live." The main difference between the two, for Short, was that "Saturday Night Live" was live, not taped. His year with the show was "the most insanely hectic" of his career.

On both shows Short excelled in sketches requiring new, original characters. Fans clamored for more of lawyer Nathan Thurm, show business superstar Jackie Rogers Jr. and tuft-headed Ed Grimley. Short became an amusing raconteur on talk shows with impressions of Bette Davis, Katharine Hepburn, Jerry Lewis and fellow Canadian, David Steinberg.

Short's forays into films, playing a comic hero, did not make much of an impression on critics or fans, who never forgot his earlier work. He performed in cable specials using his characters, on talk shows and even starred in a Saturday morning series, à la Pee-Wee Herman, based on his Ed Grimley character. The kids still loved his "I must say" catch phrase as in "I'm having a very decent time, but I believe I'm going mental, I must say!" Grimley didn't want to remain confined to Saturday morning. His ambition was to get on a television quiz show: "What if I freeze—freeze bad—on the simplest of names? But what if I did know the answer! I would be a winner, and they would have to take me home in an ambulance because I would be collapsing from my own joy, I must say! Oh, let it turn out that way! I would just go mental!"

FILMS incl.: *Sunset Limousine* (1983), *Three Amigos* (1986), *Really Weird Tales* (1986), *Inner Space* (1987), *Cross My Heart* (1987), *Three Fugitives* (1989), *The Big Picture* (1989), *Pure Luck* (1991), *Father of the Bride* (1991)

TV: "The Associates" (1979–80), "I'm a Big Girl Now" (1980–81), "SCTV" (1982–84), "Saturday Night Live" (1984–85)

## PHIL SILVERS

### (Philip Silversmith, May 11, 1912–November 1, 1985)

Usually playing a twinkle-eyed con man with a gladda-see-ya grin, balding Phil Silvers was one of the great, hyper top-banana comics of the 1950s and '60s, pushy, peppy and perpetually in motion. Since his schemes always failed and his bravado usually wilted under attack, audiences didn't mind Silver's slickness and con man's egotism. He was brash but lovable.

"I can make any villain lovable and sympathetic," Phil once said. "Maybe it's because when I was a boy I wanted to grow up to be a man who could fix horse races or something." Born in the Brownsville section of Brooklyn, he hung around with tough kids and thugs on Pennsylvania Avenue. His father was a tinsmith who tried hard to raise Phil along with five brothers and two sisters. Silvers was kicked out of grade school and sent to reform school PS 61, a badge of honor to his friends. He quit school at 12 and the following year joined the Gus Edwards

"School Days" vaudeville show. He was a singer back then but also a complete wise guy. Milton Berle remembers: "My mother admired his sweet soprano voice. He was the only show business kid my mother allowed me to associate with. . . . the first time we went out together, Silvers rewarded my mother's trust and benevolence by taking me to a whorehouse in Newark."

Ex-child star Jackie Cooper reports the time that Phil got a hooker for him, Mickey Rooney and Sidney Miller. The woman wanted $20 for each man. Con-man Silvers insisted that since she was getting four customers without having to go to four different parts of town, she was saving cabs. He talked her down to $5 each, a group rate.

After five miserable years as a stooge for the team of Joe Morris and Flo Campbell, Silvers worked the Catskills and became a star comic with Minsky's burlesque circa 1934. The balding comic wore black glasses, a necessity but also a great prop for what he thought was "sort of a blank face." In 1939 he got a shot on Broadway in *Yokel Boy* and went to Hollywood, making nearly two dozen films in sidekick roles. "I always seemed to play the same part. I was always Blinky, the hero's friend, who in the last reel told Betty Grable that the guy really loved her." "Blinky" was funnier off camera. Phil once dated a fashionable beauty who objected to his glasses. She wanted him to have a classier, sleeker look. She insisted he not wear the glasses for their next date. He showed up in his tuxedo, holding a white cane and a seeing-eye dog.

Silvers was using his "gladda see ya!" catch phrase as early as *Cover Girl* in 1944 (to Eve Arden, who didn't seem impressed or glad). Over the years he polished and perfected his pushy steamroller style and his fast-talking, hilariously insincere delivery. He had Broadway hits with *High Button Shoes* and then *Top Banana,* a hit show loosely based on the personality of Milton Berle. Silvers noted that the term "top banana" went back to an old vaudeville patter routine: "I have three bananas here, and I'll give you one." "You have only two bananas." "I have three—one banana. Two bananas. One and two is three." "You eat the third."

Phil moved to television as Sergeant Bilko, the con man of Fort Baxter, headquartered in Roseville,

Kansas. The show would be the prototype for dozens of service comedies and sitcoms, where a lovable troublemaker tries to get ahead by simultaneously flattering and flim-flamming the boss and pulling all kinds of you'll-never-get-rich schemes. The bilking Ernie Bilko (the name half inspired by a minor league ballplayer of that name) was the first of the great antiestablishment hucksters, but at the time he was mostly involved in minor, harmless diversions, such as trying to con his colonel into giving him money for a poker game. Bilko wasn't completely serious when he'd snap his fingers and shout, "Where would Al Capone be today if he wasn't willing to take chances!"

Silvers won two Emmy awards in his first year, as Best Comedian and Best Actor in a Continuing Series. He was earning $5,000 a week doing the show, then went back to Broadway for *Do Re Mi*. Phil's luck, and the times, changed after that. A sitcom in which he was factory foreman Harry Grafton failed. In hindsight he realized that viewers were against a wise guy whose grafting could hurt fellow workers; he wasn't "bucking the system" as an underdog. He appeared in the film *It's a Mad Mad Mad Mad World* but his role wasn't really geared to his zippy personality.

Silvers made a stage comeback in the early 1970s, earning a Tony Award for a revival of *A Funny Thing Happened on the Way to the Forum*. The show seemed tailored to his brand of abusive but ridiculous harangue: "You'll never learn, you'll be a eunuch all your life!"

Twice married and divorced (his first wife was 1942 Miss America Jo Carroll Dennison, the second Evelyn Patrick), Silvers continued to be bedeviled by tension and nerves, having trouble controlling his anxieties during the nightly grind of his new musical. An insomniac with a history of panic attacks, hypochondria and endless worry, the aging star reached his nadir on Monday, July 31, 1972. Phil wrote about it in his autobiography. "Awoke early, tired and restless. Called several friends for lunch. Everybody was out. Suddenly the room began to revolve like a carnival funhouse. I threw myself on the bed. I was soaking wet, as if I'd just showered. I tried to stand up—and couldn't. This was worse than my old whammies . . . it was a stroke. A minor one, they assured me, but major

enough to close *Forum*. . . . If I had been onstage, or alone in the street, it could have been my final curtain. Why me? Why now after I was back on top of my career?"

Silvers, a legendary compulsive gambler (and usually the loser), was now on the way down as far as Hollywood was concerned. Though he recovered from the stroke, producers hesitated to cast him, worried about his health, afraid he couldn't carry off bowl-'em-over-with-blather con-man roles. He appeared in some sitcom episodes, but fans looking for Silvers in *The Cheap Detective* couldn't afford to blink. He played a cab driver who, even given the current cab rates for "time not in motion," couldn't have earned more than fifty cents for his few seconds on the screen. Silvers tried to keep busy even if it meant working in low-budget comedies with inferior scripts. Work was what he wanted, and Silvers got his wish. For a few more years he was able to step before the cameras and make audiences laugh.

AUDIO: *Do Re Mi* (RCA), *High Button Shoes* (RCA), *Top Banana* (Capitol)

AUTOBIOGRAPHY: *This Laugh Is on Me* (1937)

BROADWAY: *Yokel Boy* (1939), *High Button Shoes* (1947), *Top Banana* (1951), *Do Re Mi* (1960), *A Funny Thing Happened on the Way to the Forum* (1972)

FILMS incl.: *Hit Parade of 1941* (1940), *Tom Dick and Harry* (1941), *You're in the Army Now* (1941), *Lady Be Good* (1941), *All Through the Night* (1942), *My Gal Sal* (1942), *Just Off Broadway* (1942), *The Lady Takes a Chance* (1943), *Cover Girl* (1944), *Four Jills in a Jeep* (1944), *Don Juan Quilligan* (1945), *A Thousand and One Nights* (1945), *Top Banana* (1954), *It's a Mad Mad Mad Mad World* (1963), *A Funny Thing Happened on the Way to the Forum* (1966), *Follow That Camel* (1967), *Buona Sera, Mrs. Campbell* (1969), *The Boatniks* (1970), *The Chicken Chronicles* (1977), *The Happy Hooker Goes to Washington* (1977), *The Cheap Detective* (1978), *Racquet* (1979), *Goldie and the Boxer* (1979), *There Goes the Bride* (1979), *Wholly Moses* (1980), *The Happy Hooker Goes to Hollywood* (1980)

TV: "The Arrow Show" (1948–49), "The Phil Silvers Show" (a.k.a. "Sgt. Bilko") (1955–59), "The New Phil Silvers Show" (1963–64), "The Beverly Hillbillies" (1969–71)

# RED SKELTON

### (Richard Red Skelton, July 18, 1913–   )

He bills himself as merely "one of America's clowns." But America loves the one and only Red Skelton. He was on prime-time television for 21 straight years. The only performers to match or beat this record were not comedians; they were James Arness (21 years on "Gunsmoke") and Ed Sullivan (24 years as a variety show host).

One of the most underrated stars in comedy, throughout his television years Red filled the stage with memorable characters (including "Clem Kadiddlehopper," "The Mean Widdle Kid" and "Freddie the Freeloader") and was virtually the only modern comedian to do silent pantomime for the masses. It was a minor miracle that 1950s and '60s audiences stayed tuned to their set to watch Red portray a flower growing in the sun, bending in the wind and rain, and spindling downward in death. But critics were dismayed by Skelton's passion for corny gags, his middle-American sentimentality, his habit of giggling at his own jokes and the slapstick "low" comedy that reflected his main influences. They had been sparing in their praise when he made films in the 1940s (including classic comedies *The Fuller Brush Man, A Southern Yankee* and *The Yellow Cab Man*) and remained impassive until the late '70s when, missing what they had taken for granted, they joined his fans in giving him standing ovations at his stand-up concerts.

Skelton grew up in Vincinnes, Indiana. According to biographer Arthur Marx, the middle name Red was actually put on his birth certificate. Skelton's father, a circus clown, died before Red was born. In his childhood Red sold newspapers and went to vaudeville shows whenever he could. One day a kindly gent bought all of his papers so he could see the evening's show. The man was the star of the program: Ed Wynn. Red was captivated by Wynn's clowning style. Wynn created an atmosphere of euphoria, his own giggles encouraging the audience to smile and laugh. Everyone seemed to enjoy Wynn's zany costumes and pun-filled jokes.

Red worked carnivals, burlesque and, during the depression, "walkathons" and dance marathons. He learned to pull out all the stops and go for basic belly laughs. He started with basics: crossed eyes,

Red Skelton modestly calls himself "one of America's clowns." Photo from the author's collection.

goofy voices, Joe Miller jokes and pratfalls. He polished these to the point of art, and then added more surefire gags, more characters and spectacular tumbles that over the years would eventually break practically every bone in his body. In 1936 he developed his first big routine, the slapstick demonstration of "Donut Dunking." Later his wife, Edna, adapted a routine from an old Harry Tugend script written for a Fred Allen show, and he had an even bigger hit with the result, "Guzzler's Gin." Red played a radio announcer demonstrating, with each drink and ever-increasing drunkenness, what a "nice, smooooooth" drink Guzzler's was.

He became a big star on radio with his "Scrapbook of Satire," premiering in October of 1941. He had a cheerfully homely catch phrase, "I dood it!" Red's first screen success was *Whistling in the Dark,* which utilized the formula of hit Bob Hope films of the day—the nice, jittery young man beset by criminals. A series of "Whistling" films followed in which he played a defective radio detective named "The Fox."

Red's manager was his first wife, whom he called "Mummy," and on whom he'd been dependent for many years. In 1942 they divorced, with Skelton enthusiastically looking for glamorous replacements. Edna remained on as his manager and friend, which perturbed his second wife, Georgia ("Little Red").

In many of the 1940s films, Red played a soft-hearted, soft-headed type, inept and self-deprecating. In *Merton of the Movies* someone remarks, "He still thinks the world is a wonderful place and everybody's sweet and kind and decent like him." The films were often uneven blends of riotous slapstick, corn, stolid acting and aw-shucks pathos. Part of the problem was his studio, MGM, run by the notoriously humorless Louis B. Mayer. Red was often stuck in bland musicals and low-budget comedies that weren't tailored to his strengths. It was while on loan to Columbia that he made his first classic film, *The Fuller Brush Man*. MGM got the hint and hired Buster Keaton to create gags for their next Skelton vehicle, *A Southern Yankee*. Later they aped *The Fuller Brush Man* with the similarly styled *The Yellow Cab Man*. He went on to television in the 1950s, winning his greatest fame and thriving week after week, wringing laughter out of often slender monologue jokes, keeping the sketches fresh by utilizing one of a dozen different comic characters.

Groucho Marx said back in the '50s, "I think the logical successor to Chaplin is Skelton . . . the most unacclaimed clown in show business. I've seen most of the great, legendary clowns of the circus but I must confess I've rarely seen one who could amuse me for more than a minute." Groucho pointed out that with "one prop, a soft battered hat," he could convert himself into a dozen characters. "No grotesque makeup, no funny clothes, just Red. There is no one around who can take a comic fall as completely and as magnificently as he can. He also sings, dances, delivers a deceptively simple comic monologue and plays a dramatic scene about as effectively as any of the dramatic actors, Method or otherwise . . . we need all the pure comedians like Red we can get."

Considered one of the most naturally gifted stars in comedy, reporters soon discovered Skelton was authentically zany in real life. His anything-for-a-laugh style was the same off camera and on. During a visit to the White House, Red lunged for Franklin Roosevelt's glass and with dead seriousness said, "Careful what you drink, Mr. President, I got rolled in a place like this once!" At a Hollywood party,

David Niven sat next to Red at the dinner table and pointed out that there was a caterpillar in Red's salad. "Mmm, nice!" Red said. He popped it into his mouth and ate it.

Skelton's quirks were well known to friends and fans, from his inability to eat anything but raw tomatoes before a show to his phobia about full bathtubs (he had to sit in the empty tub first and then turn on the water). He reportedly wrote hundreds of short stories, but refused to let anyone see them. Like Chaplin, he enjoyed composing and conducting music, and while he never had a hit, he recorded a few albums and wrote his own introductory theme song for his stand-up concerts. One of his most intriguing habits was the quasi-Oriental ritual in which he would say a prayer for an enemy and, from that day forward, consider the person deceased.

Skelton rarely gave interviews; when he did, he kept it lighthearted, and joking. "I know I'm nuts, but as long as I make 'em laugh they're not gonna lock me up!" What fans knew of his private life only confirmed their picture of him as the ultimate heartbroken clown. They knew of his fatherless childhood and in 1958 they shared his grief when his only son, Richard, died of leukemia.

In the 1960s, Red's marriage to Georgia, became more and more shaky. In 1966 she attempted suicide. At the time the incident was described as "an accidental shooting." Her alcoholism worsened and eventually she and Red divorced, and he remarried in 1973. In 1976, on the 18th anniversary of her son Richard's death, Georgia committed suicide.

Red's television show and his concert act always included elements of pathos and seriousness. In the 1960s he had a hit single with his heartfelt recording of "The Pledge of Allegiance," stopping to explain the meaning behind each word. Through the decades audiences always expected a performance of his classic "Old Man at the Parade" pantomime, a stirring, literal salute to America.

When Red left television in the '70s, it was not because of ratings. It was demographics. CBS wanted to change their image, scuttling all their "rural" sitcoms such as "Green Acres" and "Beverly Hillbillies" and canceling shows that didn't appeal to upscale advertisers. Red's audience was not really 30-something urban types but middle Americans, kids and old folks. After two decades of this weekly attention, the love and laughs and affection, an abrupt corporate decision had taken it all away.

Red spent most of the next decades touring the country and appearing live at resorts, casinos and county fairs. Once in a while Skelton ventured into the big cities. The comedian once taken for granted and dismissed by critics seeing him free on television each week was finally treated with respect. His shows at Carnegie Hall were reviewed with the reverence due one of the living legends in comedy. Yes, the corny gags were still there, the habit of laughing at his own jokes and the sentimental moments of heart-tugging mime. But few other comedians could create such an atmosphere of goodwill and happiness; few could take the simple prop of a soft hat and twist it magically into a dozen shapes or create wonderful mime out of thin air. He exuded warmth, decency, humanity and fun, and by evening's end received a standing ovation.

The overwhelming critical praise for his Carnegie Hall shows led him back to television with a series of special concerts on HBO, later released on home video. A Chaplin for the masses, Red remains the video Pagliacci who painted clowns (always red-headed ones), spoke his philosophy at Ed Wynn's funeral ("A clown is a warrior who fights gloom") and always ends his shows with a humble benediction that usually goes something like this:

"I sincerely hope I haven't said or done anything to offend anyone. If I have, I didn't mean it. . . . It is a lot of fun to try and make people laugh. Regardless of what your heartache might be, while laughing, for a few seconds you have forgotten your troubles. Perhaps in a moment of sorrow, you'll remember something I've said or done, and it will bring a smile again. . . . Good night, and may God Bless."

AUDIO: *Red Skelton's Rogue's Gallery* (Radiola), *Red Skelton on Radio* (Mark 56)
AUTOBIOGRAPHY: *I Dood It* (1943)
BIOGRAPHY: *Red Skelton* (Arthur Marx, 1979)
FILMS incl.: *Having a Wonderful Time* (1938), *Whistling in the Dark* (1941), *Lady Be Good* (1941), *Maisie Gets Her Man* (1942), *Panama Hattie* (1942), *Whistling in Dixie* (1942), *I Dood It* (1943), *Whistling in Brooklyn* (1943), *DuBarry Was a Lady* (1943),

*The Bathing Beauty* (1944), *Ziegfeld Follies* (1946), *The Show Off* (1946), *Merton of the Movies* (1947), *The Fuller Brush Man* (1948), *A Southern Yankee* (1948), *Neptune's Daughter* (1949), *Watch the Birdie* (1950), *Three Little Words* (1950), *The Yellow Cab Man* (1950), *Excuse My Dust* (1951), *Lovely to Look At* (1952), *The Clown* (1953), *The Great Diamond Robbery* (1953), *Half a Hero* (1953), *Susan Slept Here* (1954), *Public Pigeon No. 1* (1957), *Those Magnificent Men in Their Flying Machines* (1965)
TV: "The Red Skelton Show" (1951–71)
VIDEO: *Red Skelton's Christmas Dinner; Red Skelton's Funny Faces; Red Skelton: King of Laughter*

## MENASHA SKULNIK

### (May 15, 1892–June 4, 1970)

One of the greatest stars of Yiddish theater, Menasha Skulnik was also popular on radio (Uncle David on "The Goldbergs" for 19 years) and made many television and Broadway appearances as well.

Born in Warsaw, Menasha ran away to join a circus when he was ten. In Philadelphia in 1913, he joined a Yiddish stock company and began getting comic parts. It happened by accident. In one play he was supposed to stand up to his girlfriend's father; but the man was so tall and he was so short (five feet four) that audiences laughed. Audiences laughed at his name too, but he said, "Menasha is my right name. Long before I ever heard of Menasha, Wisconsin, I was Menasha Skulnik. My name comes out of the Bible. The Old Testament hero Joseph not only had a coat of many colors but a son named Menasha."

Skulnik sounded funny, looked funny and acted funny. He knew exactly what he was in comedy: "I play a schlemiel, a dope. Sometimes they call me the Yiddish Charlie Chaplin and I don't like this. Chaplin's dope is a little bit of a wise guy. He's got a little larceny in him. I am a pure schlemiel, with no string attached."

Called the "East Side's Chaplin" by the *New York Evening Journal* in 1935, Skulnik earned $2,000 a week in Yiddish theater by the 1940s. Stars such as Fred Allen and Ray Bolger would watch his miming and timing in Yiddish theater where only 40% of the show was in English. He had hits with "Just My Luck," "What a Guy" and "The Scotsman from Orchard Street," all accentuating the fumbling ways of the somewhat sad, shy little Skulnik.

Skulnik recorded 78 rpm novelty tunes—using a high nasal voice and a lot of Yiddish—a style later employed by Mickey Katz. The humor, as with Katz, was in the funny voice, the accent and the idea of a Jew as anything but himself. "Cordova the Bronx Casanova" was first a joke at the idea of little Menasha as a lover; any double entendres were strictly secondary: "I'm Cordova the Bronx Casanova. I am famous from Paris to Dover. When I make love I'm in demand. Each old maid wants to put her future in my hand. . . . The girls all say I'm just their type, for every new romance I get a service stripe!"

Jackie Mason recalled, "Skulnik had a big Second Avenue following, but then times changed. The kids didn't want to know from him because he was too Jewish, so he played to half-empty houses. Just to the old people. Then he took a chance, and he came to Broadway. . . . Suddenly, after all those years, it became chic for audiences to watch Menasha Skulnik and he was a big hit."

The doleful little man with the sad face and shrugging shoulders won Broadway audiences with *The Flowering Peach* by Clifford Odets ("A masterpiece of acting," said Brooks Atkinson in the *New York Times*) and then *The Fifth Season*. Wolcott Gibbs in *The New Yorker* raved over the "unique actor, with a sad, withdrawn, wistful quality that is apparently a special invention of his own."

Skulnik was a special talent, and though he chose to perform for 35 years in Yiddish theater in New York and did most of his other fine work on Broadway, he remains unforgettable to those who saw him and a legend for those who missed him.

BROADWAY: *In a Tenement House* (1932), *God Man and Devil* (1935), *The Perfect Fishel* (1935), *Laugh Night* (1936), *Schlemihl* (1936), *Yossel and His Wives* (1937), *The Little Tailor* (1938), *The Wise Fool* (1938), *Mazel Tov, Rabbi* (1938), *Three Men and a Girl* (1939), *The Flowering Peach* (1954), *The Fifth Season* (1953), *The Zulu and the Zayda* (1965)
TV: "Menasha the Magnificent" (1950)

## YAKOV SMIRNOFF

### (Yakov Pokhis, January 24, 1951–   )

Yakov Smirnoff's life in Russia was tough: "I lived with my parents in a single apartment room with five families. There was one bathroom but we had to go down the street and pay money to shower with 200 other men. I shared the same bed with my parents. And there was one stove for everyone to use."

Yakov Smirnoff was grateful to get out of Russia—and that became his comedy act, which was especially popular until the 1990's, when the weakened nation was no longer considered an enemy. With mild manners, a hopeful gaze and a smile of delight (and slight bewilderment), he spoke thankfully of his new life in America: "When I got to America, I saw an ad in the paper: 'We guarantee our furniture and stand behind it for six months.' That's why I left the Soviet Union! I don't want any people standing behind my furniture!" His catch phrase showed his unabashed delight in his newly adopted nation: "What a country!"

Smirnoff's father was an inventor, his mother taught Russian literature in school. Yakov studied to be a refrigeration mechanic but, once in the army, began to perform in the Russian equivalent of the USO. Later he hosted beauty contests and shows, and worked cruise ships on the Black Sea. He had to submit his jokes to the Ministry of Culture. He recalled, "They have no sense of humor about kidding politics—or almost anything else." In 1977 he moved to Queens, New York, where his parents worked for a company that made holiday wreaths. He said, "I knew I wanted to be American and speak English so I moved to Manhattan, took a course in bartending and got a job at Grossingers." Part Christian, part Jewish, he claimed Smirnoff was his grandmother's maiden name.

Within a few years he was a rising comic in comedy clubs. He wanted the big venues—the music fairs and the casinos. Thanks to his likable personality and clean, well-constructed jokes, he got them. He starred on radio and television commercials, turned up doing one-minute jokes on Saturday morning kid shows, got his own joke phone line and even had his own syndicated television show for a while, about a mixed group of ethnics learning the customs of the country.

For the man who believed in the American dream—who said "What a country"—the dream came true. He became a U.S. citizen in 1986, rebuilt and moved into the house Lenny Bruce once owned, and installed a doorbell that played "The Star Spangled Banner." His Ferrari sported the license plate EX RED. On Memorial Day in 1988 he brought his girlfriend, Linda Dreeszen, on stage and asked her to marry him. "You know, the Soviets do a lot of things in public, because they don't have much privacy."

In 1990 he went back to Russia and, thanks to the reforms there, he was allowed to perform in Russian and tell jokes about the government that would have gotten him into severe trouble years earlier. Impressed that Soviet citizens were now buying VCRs, he told them, "Now you can watch the video that the KGB took of you earlier!" Back home he told Americans how the Russian version of McDonald's had brought new happiness to the citizenry. One man took the wrapper from his hamburger and told Yakov, "This is wonderful! Not only do they give you food, but free toilet paper with it!"

BOOK: *America on Six Rubles a Day* (1987)
FILMS incl.: *Moscow on the Hudson* (1984), *Adventures of Buckaroo Bonzai* (1984), *Brewster's Millions* (1985), *Heartburn* (1986)
TV: "What a Country" (1986)

## SMITH and DALE

**Joe Smith: Joe Sultzer, February 16, 1884–February 11, 1981**
**Charlie Dale: Charles Marks, September 6, 1881–November 16, 1971**

Now probably best known as the team that inspired Neil Simon's play *The Sunshine Boys,* Smith and Dale were one of the classic comedy duos of vaudeville, their routines so beautifully polished and engagingly played that they remained as welcome as grandfathers with birthday gifts, bringing out their "Dr. Kronkheit and His Only Living Patient" for new generations to enjoy in the 1940s, '50s and '60s.

Comfortably corny, loaded with character comedy and dialect, the "Dr. Kronkheit" sketch always brought a smile similar to Abbott and Costello's "Who's on First," or the 50th rerun of a piece of well-timed Laurel and Hardy slapstick. With its odd catch phrases ("Take off the coat, my boy!" "The coat is o-o-o-offf!") and clockwork gag lines ("I'm dubious" "I'm glad to know you, Mr. Dubious"), the routine's appeal was a bit like watching an old jukebox or gumball machine; in its polished but mundane way the machinery was somehow fascinating to watch over and over again.

Smith (the tall and dubious one) and Dale (the short and preposterously dignified one) in action, patient battling doctor: "Before you I saw another doctor. He said I had snoo in my blood." "Snoo? What's snoo?" "Nothing, what's snoo with you! But Doctor, I'm sick, every time I eat a heavy meal I don't feel so hungry after." "Maybe you don't eat the right type of vitaminees! What type of dishes are you eating?" "I should eat dishes? What am I, a crocodile?" "No, no . . . please, my time is liniment." "Don't rub it in." "I have no patience!" "I shouldn't be here either."

The duo met by accident—literally. In 1898 they bashed into each other on bicycles down on Delancey Street in Manhattan. A storekeeper watched them bicker and told them they sounded like a comedy team. Joe and Charlie cooled off, found they did have a lot in common and became friends. They eventually worked together, singing, telling jokes and around 1901 joined Avon Cafe waiters Will Lester and Jack Coleman to become The Avon Comedy Four. Lester and Coleman were replaced later by Harry Goodwin and Irving Kaufman. The foursome made singles such as "The Professor's Birthday" and "Ginsberg's Stump Speech" and even played before the King and Queen of England in 1914. The group moved to Broadway in 1916 with *Why Worry.*

Joe and Charlie had begun building their doctor-and-patient sketch as early as 1906 and performed it in 1915's "Hungarian Rhapsody." By then the duo worked under the name Smith and Dale. As with their meeting, they got their names by accident. A team by that name had broken up, leaving the printer with 100 "Smith and Dale" business cards to get rid of.

Smith and Dale became stars in *The Passing Show of 1919,* and regularly played vaudeville, London's Palladium and Broadway. They remained together in films, revues and radio shows through the 1940s and met President Truman in 1946. "Are you a doctor?" The president said to Joe Smith, "I'm dubious!" Naturally, Joe shot back: "How do you do, Mr. Dubious!"

Smith and Dale's tried-and-true material won them a spot with Judy Garland when she headlined The Palace in 1951. They guested on television many times over the years and in 1968 marked their 70th year together. They performed for the last time together that very year at The Lambs Club in New York City.

They always claimed they never argued off stage because they did so much bickering in the act. Both widowers, they eventually moved to the Actors Fund of America Home in Englewood, New Jersey. Charlie Dale died there in 1971. Joe Smith lived to see *The Sunshine Boys* open on Broadway in 1972 and enjoyed it, though he always insisted, "I never did poke Charlie hard. I'd point my finger at him and, if necessary, give him a little jab when I said, 'You're making a mountain out of a mothball,' but I never hurt him. . . . And as for all that about my spitting in his face during the act when I pronounced my 't's, why, it was *he* who spit in *my* face when he pronounced his 'p's!"

Joe appeared at a Friar's Roast honoring the stars of the film, George Burns and Walter Matthau. On the dais, he said, "I just want to add a little ode to Charlie Dale. We've been together since 1898—over 70 years together. It's a great age we've lived in from the horsecar to the jet planes . . . but it seems like yesterday . . . we shared each other's sorrows, we shared each other's joys. In all phases of show business since we were a couple of boys. Over 70 years together. As close as two peas in a pod—and the only one that could separate us was God."

For nearly a decade after that the lively old star continued to give interviews, attend Friar's Roasts, speak at local schools and even perform on a "Dial-a-Joke" phone line. And over the years he autographed copies of the Smith and Dale record with the famous routine about Dr. Kronkheit (the German word for "sick"). By the end of the routine the doctor finally did discover what was wrong with his patient:

"The whole trouble with you is you need eyeglasses." "My eyes are all right!" "You owe me $10." "For what?" "For my advice." "Well, Doctor, here's $2. Take it, that's my advice!" "You cheapskate, you chiseler, you come in here you cockamamie—" "One more word and you only get a dollar." "Why—" "That's a word! Here's the dollar!"

AUDIO: *Two Black Crows/Smith and Dale* (Timestu), *The Great Radio Comedians* (Murray Hill), *Golden Age of Comedy* (Evolution), *At the Palace with Smith and Dale* (Jubilee)
BROADWAY: *Why Worry* (1916), *Mendel Inc.* (1929), *Crazy Quilt* (1931), *The Sky's the Limit* (1934), *Frank Fay's Vaudeville* (1939), *Laugh Town Laugh* (1942), *Old Bucks and New Wings* (1962)
FILMS incl.: *Anything But Ham* (1929), *The False Alarm Fire Co.* (1929), *When East Meets West* (1929), *Knights in Venice* (1929), *S.S. Malaria* (1930), *La Schnapps Inc.* (1930), *The Heart of New York* (1932), *Manhattan Parade* (1932), *A Nag in the Bag* (1939), *Mutiny on the Body* (1939), *Two Tickets to Broadway* (1951)

## THE SMOTHERS BROTHERS

**Tom Smothers, February 2, 1937–**
**Dick Smothers, November 20, 1939–**

The Smothers Brothers mirrored their generation. They were young and naive folkies in the early 1960s, social and political protestors in the late '60s, aimless and unsure in the '70s, and mellowed and family oriented into the '80s and '90s.

Born in New York, the brothers grew up in California along with the younger sisters, Sherry and Michelle. Their father, Major Thomas Smothers, died in a prisoner-of-war camp. The boys attended Southwestern Military Academy, Redondo Beach High School and then San Jose State College, where they performed folk music together. Their between-song patter evolved into comedy. As Tom recalled, "We were a little surprised at first—people liked to listen to two brothers argue!"

Tom and Dick, better known as The Smothers Brothers, have made several generations laugh at their brand of sibling rivalry. Photo from the author's collection.

Though actually the older brother, on stage Tommy evolved a "younger brother" character, one audiences identified with. Tommy refused responsibility, even if it was simply singing a solo chorus of a song: "Take it, Tom!" "No . . ." He used his baby-faced blamelessness to deliberately antagonize his brother. Tom, singing: "Jimmy crack corn, and I don't care. I don't care, I don't care." Dick: "That's not the way the song goes!" Tom: "I don't care. . . ."

As Tommy told the author in 1990, "We were the most unquoted comics. We had only one line: 'Mom always liked you best.' The rest of it was the relationship. . . . We did 'puberty comedy' on the awkwardness of going into adulthood from childhood, from 12 to 13 years old. And I stayed on the other side of it. I studied children and used it. . . . there were very few real jokes on our old albums. It was our attitude. It was all in the timing." He admitted, "Once you have a style, people can't steal it." If anyone was an influence on Tommy's comedy style, it was sly but unassuming George Gobel, a favorite of Tom's during his teen years.

After the tumult of the "sicknik" '50s comedians Lenny Bruce, Shelley Berman and Mort Sahl, the Kennedy era marked a rebirth of youth-oriented comedy. The president had young children in the White House, and childlike comics including Bill Cosby, Marty Allen and Tommy Smothers provided a welcome relief from adult problems and woes. But after Kennedy's death and the escalation of the Vietnam War, childhood was over. Tommy found that out in 1965 when he was clubbed by a cop in Elkhart, Indiana, during an argument about receipts at a local concert.

After a mild comedy-fantasy television sitcom (Tom as an angel coming back to earth to guide and misguide brother Dick), the boys starred in their notorious comedy variety show. It had begun innocuously enough, but over the years, as the brothers and their writers became more and more aware of social issues, they booked Mort Sahl, Joan Baez and Pete Seeger. Censorship battles erupted over anti-Vietnam songs, drug humor and political comedy that attacked the president. The more the brothers were frustrated, the harder they fought back. At this point, their brand of political comedy seems surprisingly tame. Consider Tommy's theory that "you can tell who's running the country by how much clothes people wear." Dick: "You mean some people can afford more clothes on, and others less on?" "The ordinary people are the less-ons." "Then who's running the country?" "The more-ons!"

After several skirmishes CBS canceled the program, even though it had been the only series to beat NBC's powerhouse western of the era, "Bonanza." The Smothers Brothers sued the network and won, but by the time they did, in 1973, it was too late. The brothers had lost their momentum. Times had changed, political comedy was out, folk music was dead and they were a bit too old to go back to "Mom always liked you best." It was a restless, unhappy time for the brothers. Tommy made unwanted headlines for himself as he joined John Lennon for some drinking and partying in West Coast nightclubs. He didn't have much luck with a 1971 television show ("Tom Smothers' Organic Space Ride") or the 1973 film *Get to Know Your Rabbit.*

The brothers called it quits in 1976, then re-teamed in 1978 to star together on Broadway in *I Love My Wife*. In 1981 they played Fitz and Bones, a pair of reporters in a television comedy/drama series. Dick took time off to race cars and ride horses. Tom starred in a few films, including the role of a ridiculously upright Mountie in *Pandemonium*. The boys found a lucrative second profession when they began producing wine from their own California vineyard. Their on-again off-again touring continued, until a tour with Joan Rivers in 1983 and a political comedy special for HBO in 1984 brought them back into the spotlight. The Baby Boomers who grew up with them wanted them back again. The Smothers Brothers were booked for concerts, television commercials and once again had their own television variety show, this time featuring mostly the light songs and gentle humor that had marked them as "family entertainment" years earlier.

The boys had come full circle. When they started, they were offering mild songs and comedy everyone could enjoy. Now, for their fans and the children in the audience, the brothers were back with songs, comedy, and Tom's new "Yo-Yo Man" segment of Yo-Yo tricks that harkened back to the nostalgic Duncan Yo-Yo craze of the 1950s. Like their fans, the boys had been through a lot, had gone through some changes but had emerged with their personalities intact. In November of 1989 they received their own star on the Hollywood Walk of Fame.

On stage Tommy was still clowning around, Dick: "I thought maybe you'd changed a little bit. You have not done one *responsible* thing tonight! You have not acted like a *responsible* adult yet!" Tom, shaking his head, his eyes wide with disbelief: "Right now, I'm wearing a condom!"

Off stage Tommy, "the dumb one," is well known for his intensity and intelligence. Dick, the exasperated "mean" one, enjoys a reputation for being friendly, courteous and quick with funny adlibs. But after all these years, is the bickering really a put-on? Dick says no: "We honestly have differences of opinions on everything. What we bring on stage is just exaggerated, that's all."

And how does it feel to be performing together for so long? Says Tom: "I like what Dick said about

it." Says Dick, "It's kind of like an old marriage—all fighting and no sex."

AUDIO: *At the Purple Onion* (Mercury), *Two Sides of the Smothers Brothers* (Mercury), *Think Ethnic* (Mercury), *Curb Your Tongue, Knave* (Mercury), *It Must Have Been Something I Said* (Mercury), *Tour De Farce American History* (Mercury), *Aesop's Fables* (Mercury), *Mom Always Liked You Best* (Mercury), *Smothers Comedy Brothers Hour* (Mercury), *It's Smothers Brothers Month* (Mercury Promotional), *Sibling Revelry* (Rhino)

TV: "The Steve Allen Show" (1961), "The Smothers Brothers Show" (1965–66), "The Smothers Brothers Comedy Hour" (1967–69), "The Smothers Brothers Summer Show" (1970), "The Smothers Brothers Show" (1975), "Fitz and Bones" (1981), "The Smothers Brothers Show" (1988–89)

VIDEO: *And If I'm Elected; Yo-Yo Man*

# JACK SOO

## (Goro Suzuki, October 28, 1916–January 11, 1979)

One of the most gifted stars of subtle comedy, Jack Soo did his best work when he did little or nothing at all. A deadpan reaction, a stoic disregard for the proceedings or a mumbled comeback line generated big laughs when he was in a sitcom scene. Though he was often subjected to the strains of stereotypical Oriental comedy parts, he made the most of the good ones he landed.

After his father—a tailor—died in 1929, his dressmaker mother supported the family. Jack pitched in working on farms and selling melons from a truck. While a student at University of California in San Francisco, he began using "Carl" as a more easily understandable first name. The first time he tried stand-up comedy, in the early 1940s, "the laughter was polite." In the mid '40s, Soo and many other Japanese Americans sat out World War II at Camp Topaz in Utah.

After the war he worked in burlesque and nightclubs. "I did your standard [master-of-ceremonies] one-liners, not all of them clean, all stolen, but not one of them demeaning to any race." He teamed with Joey Bishop in the '40s, but neither could avoid cornball jokes. "You better learn those lyrics, Soo," said Bishop, "there's a lot of slow boats leaving." Soo evidently learned his lyrics well, for in 1950 he was performing as a straight singer. *Variety* reviewed him at The Palace in New York: "As the only vocalist on the show, Jack Soo registers okay with a brace of romantic ballads. Chinese [sic] crooner closes strongly with a powerful baritone rendition of 'Lucky Old Sun.' "

Soo's big break came in 1958 when he played Frankie Wing in *Flower Drum Song* on Broadway. He was in the show and various touring companies for six years and appeared in the film version. A few years later television viewers got to know him as Anthony Franciosa's hip sidekick on the short-lived "Valentine's Day." Soo was taking pains to avoid ethnic comedy. As he told *TV Guide* magazine in 1965, "We're not a bunch of ricky-ticky stereotypes who do nothing but wash shirts and cook Sukiayki." Unfortunately, his career included some embarrassing stereotypical roles such as a goofy bald Oriental in *Thoroughly Modern Millie*. Among the better ones was a wrestler on an episode of "The Odd Couple." Soo's home life was quite assimilated, with a Yugoslavian wife, Jan Zdelar, and three children.

Danny Arnold, the executive producer of "Barney Miller," had been a stand-up comic and worked with Soo 30 years earlier. "I always loved his style, his timing, that superb comic understatement he does. I wanted him . . . not because I wanted a Japanese cop. I wanted Jack's humor." Soo was at the height of his comic powers as Sergeant Nick Yemana, the perfect counterpoint to the action on the show. Some of the funniest moments on the show were from the deadpan Soo. He got laughs where there seemed to be none: "Japanese got a lot of willpower. We eat raw fish." "You like it?" "No. We don't." One of his funniest scenes was the time he got high on pot-laced brownies. While other high officers made faces or jokes, mournful Jack merely gripped Barney Miller's face, muttering "Mooshy mooshy!" Then he tearfully burst into song.

Soo was still starring in the show when he was diagnosed as having cancer of the esophagus. "It must have been my coffee," he joked. He underwent an operation in January 1978. When the story broke, he got over 12,000 well-wishing letters from fans. He rallied but a year later his last appearance on "Barney Miller" came in the form of a tribute show that highlighted the late actor in some of his finest moments.

BROADWAY: *Flower Drum Song* (1958)
FILMS incl.: *Flower Drum Song* (1961), *Who's Been Sleeping in My Bed?* (1963), *Thoroughly Modern Millie* (1967)
TV: "Valentine's Day (1964–65), "Barney Miller" (1975–78)

## ANN SOTHERN

### (Harriette Lake, January 22, 1909–   )

A sitcom star before the term existed, Ann Sothern played "Maisie" in a series of low-budget 1940s films. While most of the films don't hold up in reruns, Sothern does, synthesizing qualities in earlier performers from Joan Blondell to Jean Arthur—and adding her own unique personality. As Maisie she was attractive, independent, able to wisecrack and yet never lose an audience's sympathy. She was equally cool, calm and yet lovably human on her own television sitcom, "The Ann Sothern Show." And on voice alone, she was the only bright spot on the legendary disaster, "My Mother the Car."

Born in Valley City, North Dakota, the five-foot-one, blue-eyed beauty studied music at the University of Washington, both composing and singing. She was on Broadway in *Smiles* in 1930 and appeared in several more productions before moving to Hollywood. She made her first films under her real name. By the time she starred in hit movie musicals such as *Kid Millions* with Eddie Cantor, she was working under her new name. She married Roger Pryor, a band leader, and together they toured with a nightclub act.

She made her first "Maisie" film in 1939, and it soon yielded not only a film series but a radio show on CBS (1945–47, 1949–52; an attack of hepatitis had forced a brief sabbatical). In the "Maisie" films she always had a quip ready. At the depot she put off a man's advances with "My bag doesn't want to be picked up and neither do I." Audiences responded to her working-class values. She was tough but a "good girl" who didn't drink or fool around. There was a distinct lack of romance in the plots. She wasn't exactly bowled over by Robert Sterling in *Ringside Maisie,* even though he was actually her second husband in real life. She had similar disdain for Red Skelton in *Maisie Gets Her Man.* Skelton: "I pay for my mistakes—" Ann: "That must keep you broke all the time." She rarely flaunted her beauty or used it to charm her way to the top. In the sitcoms she got into trouble through her heart of gold—not a head of fluff—and got out of it with plucky comic invention.

Into the 1950s Sothern moved on to sitcoms, both her own starring series and the recurring role of "The Countess" on "The Lucy Show." She was alone among comic heroines in her smoothness and cool, characteristics that would influence the modern stylings of Jane Curtin and others. Sothern's wry and knowing attitude suggested she could take or leave whatever man or whatever sitcom problem was bothering her. Her style of not "going over the top" in comedy, as Lucille Ball did, cost her some mass appeal, but earned her respect from the rest. At the height of her fame the cool, composed star admitted, "I can live happily behind cameras. I've never had that gnawing, burning desire to act." In later years she turned to painting and through the 1980s held many art exhibitions. Her last major acting role was in *The Whales of August,* for which she was nominated for an Academy Award. In an early scene an actress played Ann as a young woman. The part was played by Ann's real-life daughter, Tisha Sterling.

AUDIO: *Ann Sothern* (Tiara), *Sothern Exposure* (Tops)
BROADWAY: *Smiles* (1930), *America's Sweetheart* (1931), *Everybody's Welcome* (1931), *Faithfully Yours* (1951)
FILMS incl.: *The Shows of Shows* (1929), *Doughboys* (1930), *Let's Fall in Love* (1933), *Kid Millions* (1934), *The Girl Friend* (1935), *Walking on Air* (1936), *There Goes the Groom* (1937), *She's Got Everything* (1937), *Maisie* (1939), *Brother Orchid* (1940), *Congo Maisie* (1940), *Lady Be Good* (1941), *Ringside Maisie* (1941), *Maisie Gets Her Man* (1942), *Panama Hattie* (1942), *Swing Shift Maisie* (1943), *Maisie Goes to Reno* (1944), *The Judge Steps Out* (1947), *A Letter to Three Wives* (1949), *Chubasco* (1967), *Golden Needles* (1974), *The Little Dragons* (1980), *A Letter to Three Wives* (1985), *The Whales of August* (1987)
TV: "Private Secretary" (1953–57), "The Ann Sothern Show" (1958–61), "My Mother the Car" (1965–66)

## JEAN STAPLETON

### (Jeanne Murray, January 19, 1923–   )

As a character actress, for years Jean Stapleton tended to play cheerful, ditsy housewives, such as the doting, goofy baseball fan who goes nuts over baseball player Joe Hardy (Tab Hunter) in *Damn Yankees,* and the frowsy, perpetually sneezing frump married to Vincent Gardenia in *Cold Turkey*—a woman whose main passion seemed to be eating gherkins wrapped in salami. One of her earliest roles was Myrtle Mae in a 1948 touring production of *Harvey.*

Stapleton became the ultimate "dingbat" when she played opposite Carroll O'Connor on "All in the Family," winning Emmy awards in 1971, 1972 and 1978. Ironically, in the first year of the show her role as Edith Bunker included a lot of deadpan putdowns of her blustery husband. As the show progressed, Edith blossomed into a dithery but good-natured soul, the only member of the household that viewers might actually want to know. Even if she sometimes blabbered on too much or got a bit giddy after a few glasses of wine, fans knew she was honest, caring and thoughtful. While the rest of the family seemed to do the taking, the shouting, the pushing and the shoving, Edith did the giving. And for this she was usually ordered by her husband, "Stifle yourself!"

Jean Stapleton has tried to distance herself from the Queens-accented ninny she played. When she left the show, she successfully pursued dramatic television movies and played Eleanor Roosevelt in *Eleanor, First Lady of the World.* She also performed often at the Totem Pole Playhouse in Pennsylvania, which was run by her husband, Bill Putch. Stapleton, born in New York City and educated at Hunter College, had married him in 1957. Through the

1980s, a time marred by Putch's death in 1983, Stapleton picked and chose her roles carefully.

If there is any similarity between her and Edith Bunker, it is her kindness and consideration once a decision is made. She had agreed to sing opera in a small theater in Baltimore, a low-paying venue obviously, but one that called attention to the young woman who wrote the piece. Nothing could deter her once she'd made that commitment, even an offer to go to Hollywood to test for the lead in a new mystery television show called "Murder She Wrote."

In 1986 she went to Broadway for *Arsenic and Old Lace* and in 1989 appeared in Harold Pinter's *The Birthday Party*. She played a housewife, which caused some to wonder if she'd play it like Edith. Stapleton quickly set the rumors to rest: "If I did see a connection, I would not dwell on it or even discuss it because my objective is always to separate Edith from my other work. I keep the distance. I must. It helps the audience if I do, also."

It was a full ten years before Stapleton returned to the television sitcom world. It was for "Bagdad Cafe," co-starring Whoopi Goldberg. Jean played a thoughtful, only mildly giddy ex-teacher now living away from her husband. In the very first episode it was clear that Stapleton's character Jasmine was not going to be another Edith Bunker. After the car stalls in the desert, her husband shouts, "You idiot, you moron!" She answers, "Don't talk to me like that. Remember your blood pressure. . . ." "You're gonna kill me one way or another," the man cries. She walks out on him, saying, "Ralph, you've been promising me for 25 years that you were going to die. Well, I'm sick of waiting."

The show didn't last, something she attributes to "a lack of vision by the people in charge." She vows, "Unless the standard rises in the sitcom area, I can say now definitely that I'm not interested in doing another half-hour series." She busied herself with challenging stage work, from her version of Ruth Draper's monologue "The Italian Lesson" to the part of Julia Child in a 1989 musical about the "French Chef" called *Bon Appetit!* She starred in a West Coast production of *Oklahoma* with Larry Storch in 1990 and has frequently appeared in off-Broadway theatrical productions, including Moliere's *The Learned Ladies* in 1991.

She acknowledges that audiences will always remember her as Edith Bunker in one of the most famous sitcoms of all time, but adds, "The role of Edith would have buried me if I continued it." She had fond memories of every member of the cast: "We had our ups and downs. We all learned from them, but I'd never repeat them. They're our own private business."

AUDIO: *Bells Are Ringing* (Columbia), *All in the Family 1 and 2* (Atlantic), *Archie and Edith Side by Side* (RCA)

BROADWAY incl.: *In the Summer House* (1953), *Damn Yankees* (1955), *Bells Are Ringing* (1956), *Rhinoceros* (1961), *Funny Girl* (1964), *Arsenic and Old Lace* (1986)

FILMS incl.: *Damn Yankees* (1958), *Bells Are Ringing* (1960), *Something Wild* (1961), *Up the Down Staircase* (1967), *Cold Turkey* (1970), *Klute* (1971), *Aunt Mary, Angel Dusted* (1981), *Eleanor, First Lady of the World* (1982), *A Matter of Sex* (1984), *The Buddy System* (1984), *Grownups* (1985), *Dead Man's Folly* (1986)

TV: "All in the Family" (1971–80), "Bagdad Cafe" (1990)

## DAVID STEINBERG

**(August 9, 1942–   )**

Basically a quiet, cerebral performer with a slow, methodical cadence, David Steinberg's conversational style was always brightened by a Groucho Marx-inspired penchant for iconoclasm and whimsy. He combined both traits in his famous mock sermons, the carefully enunciated lectures on biblical figures that always contained Marxian asides.

After telling the stories of Jezebel and Lot, he paused to add, "I can't do Onan tonight—I suggest you go home tonight and do it yourself." In his retelling of Moses and the burning bush, God urges Moses to take off his shoes and approach. Moses burns his feet and God gleefully shouts, "Aha! Third one today!"

At a time when religious comedy was strictly taboo, The Smothers Brothers invited Steinberg to appear on their show. The second time was enough for CBS. They shut the show down. Steinberg's monologue was the last straw in the network's on-going battle with the brothers. David had offered the story of Jonah on April 6, 1969. It ended like this:

". . . And the Gentiles, as is their wont from time to time, threw the Jew overboard. The Old Testament scholars say that Jonah was in fact swallowed by a whale. The Gentiles (the New Testament scholars) said 'Hold it, Jews. No.' They literally grabbed the Jews by the Old Testament. They said, 'Jonah could not have been swallowed by a whale . . . because whales have tiny gullets and cannot swallow whole prophets.' Therefore they offered their own theory. That Jonah was in fact swallowed by a gigantic guppy. . . .'"

Though harmless and silly by today's standards, as performed with grand seriousness by David Steinberg, it was deemed subversive and dangerous. So was Steinberg, a mild-mannered fellow from Winnipeg whose father, a rabbi, now made his living as a grocer.

Steinberg studied theology in Israel then enrolled at the University of Chicago, earning a master's in English literature. His show business career took off after joining the Second City improvisational group in 1964. He was part of *The Mad Show* off-Broadway and then, branching out into straight acting, appeared in several Broadway productions. When his friends suggested he try stand-up, he was surprised. "I felt this was very insulting! I'm an *actor,* I had a pompous image of myself."

In the summer of 1968 at The Bitter End he developed his sermons and resurrected from his Second City days a Groucho Marx routine in which he played a madcap psychiatrist stalking members of the audience and shouting "Booga booga!" (a cry not far removed from Groucho's "boogie" jeer at a singer in *A Night at the Opera*). As Steinberg recalled, "It did not work. The audience didn't like me . . . they didn't get me." At least the waitresses did, which helped the young comic's spirits. "If a waitress will sleep with you when you're dying on stage . . . that's some acceptance." A reviewer from the *New York Times* dropped by, gave him a glowing review and then, suddenly, there were lines around the block and audiences were now laughing uproariously at material that hadn't gotten a chuckle before.

In the 1960s, a time that saw a mild resurgence of interest in intellectual comedians, including Woody Allen and Dick Cavett, David Steinberg became a regular on talk shows and in clubs. Like Allen and Cavett, Steinberg was a quiet monologist, short but intense, able to keep a crowd quiet and listening. His most distinctive trademark aside from his slight build and mop of black hair was the discernible scar on the left side of his chin. He got it when he was four years old, after stumbling onto a ginger ale bottle. He turned the incident into an anecdote; typically it involved his Jewish upbringing, and the notion that if his father hadn't kept driving and looking for a particular hospital, the cut would have been tended to earlier and more efficiently.

Like Woody Allen, Steinberg sometimes obsessed on being Jewish. The result was occasionally a pointless if not anti-Semitic generalization: "Jews could go to the Nautilus from today till a year from now. When they take off their shirts—the breasts sag." Other times he was bristling with satire, as in his description of the Orthodox rabbi concerned that his bride was "a Jewess." Said Steinberg, "Yes—and I am the Jewee!"

Most of his act was secular. Some lines echoed Woody Allen, such as his ultimate goal "to sexually satisfy the entire King Family right before their big Thanksgiving special." He offered observations more than jokes: "The reason I feel guilty about masturbation is I'm so bad at it." Like Fred Allen, he enjoyed creating images: "President Nixon has a face that looks like a foot." He savored words and drew his audience into each word thanks to his measured cadence and the confidence to speak slowly and calmly without worrying about the amount of laughter.

One of his classic routines described, in grandly slow phrasing and multisyllables, a sexual encounter with an airheaded girl named Judy Disney: "Imagine. You have attained undreamed of horizons of virtuosity. You have devised and executed maneuvers that would mystify even Masters and Johnson. You have become to sex what Julia Child is to a chicken. And as you're lying there in the afterglow of a moment that poets devote their whole lifetimes to describe, she turns to you and says, 'Hey. That was cute.' "

Steinberg remains a popular talk show raconteur and has occasionally starred in a cable television concert special, but over the years has been far busier behind the scenes directing television sitcoms (notably "Designing Women") and several films, including *Paternity* and *Going Berserk*.

AUDIO: *The Incredible Shrinking God* (Uni), *Disguised as a Normal Person* (Elektra), *Booga Booga* (Columbia), *Goodby to the 70s* (Columbia)

BROADWAY: *Return of Second City* (1966), *Little Murders* (1967), *Carry Me Back to Morningside Heights* (1968)

FILMS incl.: *Night Train to Terror* (1973)

TV: "The Music Scene" (1969–70), "The David Steinberg Show" (1972)

VIDEOS: *Evening at the Improv; David Steinberg in Concert; Comedy Tonight; Showbiz Ballyhoo*

## FORD STERLING (See also THE KEYSTONE KOPS.)

### (George Ford Stitch, November 3, 1889–October 13, 1939)

Best remembered as the squinting, sputtering, grimacing little leader of the Keystone Kops, Ford Sterling began his comedy career as a child. When the circus came to his hometown, LaCrosse, Wisconsin, he joined as "Keno, The Boy Clown."

After working as an acrobat with Forepaugh's Circus and appearing in vaudeville, Sterling joined Keystone in 1911. At first, he took on all sorts of film parts. His snarling lips and glaring, intense eyes under heavy eyebrow makeup typed him for comic villain roles. He also played in Sennett's rather anti-Semitic "Meyer and Cohen" comedies, taking the part of Cohen, complete with stereotypical beard and mustache.

Replacing the now-forgotten Fred Mace, a chubby, mild-mannered comic who had played the police chief in 1913's *The Bangville Police* and other formative Keystone Kop films, the lively Sterling used wire-rimmed glasses and a round blob of chin whiskers for his role as Chief Teheezal. Sterling seemed to spend most of his time growling into the phone or gasping at the ineffectiveness of his troops. His caricatured expressions of chagrin, confusion and

irritation helped him become the biggest star on the Sennett lot. When he demanded a raise in salary from $250 a week to $500, Sennett balked.

Joining Universal Studios for his own "Sterling Comedies," he remained a star but saw competition from Sennett's new performers, including Charlie Chaplin. Sterling bickered with Universal and returned to Sennett in 1915. Chaplin had just moved on to Essanay, but even so Sterling couldn't quite regain his old success, especially in films without his trademark Teheezal glasses and beard. Sterling worked for many companies through the decade, but sporadic supporting roles were all he seemed able to find. Without the eccentric makeup (now too much of a cliché to use) he was rather bland.

Sterling's flagging career was finished in 1939, the year his left leg was amputated due to thrombosis. A few months later, he was dead.

FILMS incl.: *Cohen Collects a Debt* (1912), *On his Wedding Day* (1913), *Toplitsky and Company* (1913), *Cohen Saves the Flag* (1913), *Love and Dynamite* (1914), *Court House Crooks* (1915), *His Wild Oats* (1916), *His Torpedoed Love* (1917), *Stars and Bars* (1917), *Her Screen Idol* (1918), *Yankee Doodle in Berlin* (1919), *Love, Honor and Behave* (1920), *An Unhappy Finish* (1921), *Oh Mabel Behave* (1922), *The Spoilers* (1923), *So Big* (1923), *Stage Struck* (1925), *The Show Off* (1926), *The American Venus* (1926), *Casey at the Bat* (1927), *Gentlemen Prefer Blondes* (1928), *The Fall of Eve* (1929), *Showgirl in Hollywood* (1930), *Kismet* (1930), *Her Majesty Love* (1931), *Alice in Wonderland* (1933)

## McLEAN STEVENSON

### (November 14, 1929–   )

Mclean Stevenson seemed to make a career portraying comically average, muddled mid-Americans. In *The Cat from Outer Space* he's the guy who spends most of his time betting on television sports, smoking cigars and drinking a lot of beer. "Did you forget my beer," he asks a visiting friend, "or did I drink it already?"

On television, he was Colonel Henry Blake on "M*A*S*H," playing with sympathy as well as satire an average man thrust into a position of power he can barely cope with. "This place is a shambles!" he cries. Then he pauses in confusion. "So we've got to—as soon as possible—deshambilize!"

Born in Normal, Illinois, Mclean grew up to become the head of "Young Democrats for Stevenson," an organization supporting one of his relatives—Adlai Stevenson. After attending Northwestern University, he served in the navy medical corps during World War II.

Following work in summer stock and cabaret revues such as Manhattan's "Upstairs at the Downstairs," Stevenson appeared on television sitcoms ("Car 54, Where Are You?" among others) and wrote for "That Was the Week That Was" and "The Smothers Brothers Comedy Hour." His first major television break was playing Doris Day's boss on her sitcom. On "M*A*S*H" he was able to display a full range of emotions, including the serio-comic moment when Colonel Blake learns that his stateside wife has had an affair: "Al Franklin? Do I know him . . . the Pumpkin Dance at the Country Club? Lorraine . . . Oh, Lorraine . . . an orthodontist! Yes, I know the movie—*Brief Encounter*—Lorraine, that's only a movie!"

Finding that 20th Century-Fox was as snafu-filled as the army, the rising star began complaining about the lack of air conditioning, the inconvenient bathrooms and other problems on the "M*A*S*H" set. Eventually Stevenson left the show and was written out with a vengeance—his character's death. The emotional episode had many "M*A*S*H" staffers in tears, including Stevenson, who cried in his dressing room and left early rather than become part of a difficult farewell scene.

McLean Stevenson's name became somewhat of an industry joke after that. Stand-up comics got a lot of mileage out of his stop-start sitcom career. One sitcom after another failed. He and the networks seemed determined to keep trying. Only three months after he played a priest in "In the Beginning," he was back on the air as a disc jockey with "Hello, Larry." Critics loathed these admittedly minor sitcoms, but it seemed that he took more than his share of abuse. The Hollywood community seemed to enjoy the "comeuppance" of a man who had the nerve to leave a hit show, and were especially gleeful that every time he got a second chance

it failed. It was an embarrassing time for Stevenson, but he emerged with his own Las Vegas act, became involved in the Equal Rights movement and other causes, and in the late 1980s and early '90s has returned to television for plentiful guest-starring roles and game show appearances.

FILMS incl.: *Win, Place or Steal* (1972), *The Cat from Outer Space* (1978)

TV: "The Doris Day Show" (1969–71), "The Tim Conway Comedy Hour" (1970), "M*A*S*H" (1972–75), "The McLean Stevenson Show" (1976–77), "Celebrity Challenge of the Sexes" (1978), "In the Beginning" (1978), "Hello, Larry" (1979–80), "Condo" (1983), "America" (1985)

VIDEO: *Big City Comedy*

## STILLER and MEARA

**Jerry Stiller, June 8, 1928–**
**Anne Meara, September 20, 1929–**

A thousand-dollar answer on the quiz show "Jeopardy" in July of 1989: "Married couple who've done commercials for Blue Nun wine and Jack-in-the-Box." Answer: Jerry Stiller and Anne Meara.

They've done a lot more than that. The most realistic husband-and-wife team in stand-up, through the 1950s and '60s Jerry and Anne gained fame for their domestic comedy sketches as Hershey Horowitz and Elizabeth Doyle. Since then they have performed more often in separate film, television and Broadway productions.

Short, chunky and curly-haired Jerry married tall, red-headed Anne in 1954. They were both struggling actors at the time. Jerry recalled, "She was the first person who ever really liked me for myself . . . and I liked how she would throw spaghetti on the wall to test whether it was al dente." They appeared in productions of Shakespeare in New York's Central Park together. Audiences were not used to seeing culture al fresco. Stiller: "I remember hearing them yell at Romeo in perfect Spanish, 'Give it to that Juliet!'"

Stiller became a member of The Compass Players in 1959, a St. Louis-based improvisational group. Anne Meara joined a short time later. After touring in a revue called *The Happy Medium* in Chicago and the birth of their daughter, Stiller and Meara became a stand-up duo. In 1962 they took over for Vaughn Meader at Phase II, a Greenwich Village club, and soon after appeared on television's "Ed Sullivan Show." They were a favorite of Sullivan's and appeared dozens of times.

At first their humor was sharp, somewhat influenced by their comedy duo friends, Will Holt and Dolly Jonah, and the team of Nichols and May: "I hate you!" "You hate me? I hate you!" "You don't know what hate is, the kind of hate I have for you." "Listen, my hate for you is such a hot hate, I hate you with hot heaping hunks of hate!" "The heat of your hot hate could not begin to approximate the hateful hatredness with which I'm hatefully hating you right now." "If it was possible to write the word 'Hate' on each grain of sand in the Sahara desert all that hate on each of those hateful grains wouldn't equal one one-millionth of the hate that I'm hating you with right now!" "You know how much you hate me?" "Yeah?" "Double it! That's my hate for you!"

Jerry and Anne evolved character-oriented comedy based in part on their personalities. Jerry was the deadpan, befuddled Jewish guy, Anne the lively, heart-of-gold Irish woman who loved him. The "Horowitz and Doyle" routines had a mix of gags and poignancy as the couple struggled through their differences: "I couldn't come over. It's Friday. I can't eat meat on Friday . . . ." "Didn't they change the rule on that?" "Sure, they changed the rule, but my family don't go along with it. . . . Why don't you come to my house for Sunday dinner . . . my mother always has a big spread, roast stuffed pork, baked Virginia ham—oh! I'm sorry! You don't have to eat any of that stuff. I'll fix you bacon and eggs. . . ."

The smooth, slice-of-life style that Stiller and Meara created led them to advertising deals, most prominently a set of commercials for Blue Nun wine between 1969 and 1979. The company went from selling 43,000 cases in the United States to over a million a year. Eventually Stiller and Meara set up their own company to handle all of their ad assignments. Nationally (though more prominently in New York) their comical conversational commercials were a radio perennial.

Into the late 1970s and '80s nightclub performing held less interest for the veteran actors. Their fame

had won them inroads into stage and film roles and they eagerly took them. Jerry went to Broadway for *The Ritz* and *Hurlyburly*, while Anne scored a stage triumph in *The House of Blue Leaves* and *Eastern Standard*. Jerry parlayed his put-upon feistiness and woeful demeanor into television comedy, including the series "Joe and Sons." Anne's ability to imitate earthy lower-middle-class women helped her land a continuing role as a cook on "Archie Bunker's Place." Her most satisfying video role was as "Kate McShane," a tough but tender lawyer.

Together Stiller and Meara appeared in the films *Nasty Habits* and *The Other Woman*. Their daughter, Amy, has become a performer as has their son, Ben, who entered the business in the late 1980s, writing for "Saturday Night Live" and later starring in his own MTV show. As Ben explained it: "I grew up with people saying hello to my parents on the street every day. Deep down, I've always wanted people to say hello to me too."

AUDIO: *Sex Life of the Primate* (Verve), *Presenting Stiller and Meara* (Verve), *Last Two People on Earth* (Columbia), *Laugh When You Like* (Atlantic)

FILMS incl.: *Nasty Habits* (1977), *The Other Woman* (1983)

TV: "The Paul Lynde Show" (1972)

## COLONEL LEMUEL Q. STOOPNAGLE

### (Frederick Chase Taylor, October 4, 1897–May 29, 1950)

Fred Allen admiringly called Colonel Stoopnagle the "pinup boy in many of the country's leading psychopathic wards." A heavyset fellow with a slight resemblance to Jonathan Winters, Stoopnagle appeared in some films but was mainly a star on radio, with announcer Budd Hulick serving as his straight man.

Born in Buffalo, New York, the Colonel went to the University of Rochester and later worked as a stockbroker. The dullness got to him. In 1925 he began taking local radio work on WMAK in Buffalo as part of the team of Nip and Tuck. He worked mostly as a writer until he met announcer Budd Hulick in October 1930. When a hurricane knocked out the feed from the CBS network, Hulick called him in to help fill the time. They ad-libbed comedy and, before long, they were "Stoopnagle and Budd," the "gloomchasers."

They were pioneers in utilizing subtle comedy and also sound effects. Stoopnagle might casually ask, "Budd, will you please scratch my back?" Then there'd be the frenzied sound of scratching. Rather than having a snazzy theme song, an announcer remarked with bitter disappointment, "It's Stoopnagle, and, er, Budd . . ." And a dreary, barely on-key tune sawed its way slowly through a ponderous accordion or organ. The offbeat team went national in 1931, though their unorthodox style took so much getting used to they didn't even have a sponsor at first.

Occasionally viewers got a chance to see the duo. In the film *International House,* Stoopnagle unveiled his fish bowl for tired fish: "The bowl revolves, so the fish doesn't have to swim." On radio, bewildered audiences listened to bits like this:

"Ladies and gentlemen, if the lady who sat in the plate of syrup here in Town Hall last Wednesday will kindly return the plate nothing further will be said about the syrup. Thank you. Well, now what, Budd?" "How about an invention or two?" "Well, I have a sort of double invention, Budd. It is salt that looks like pepper and pepper that looks like salt, so if anyone takes the wrong one by mistake, it's all right . . . (and) luminous butter. This luminous butter gives off a bright, shining glow. It is especially useful for people who never know which side their bread is buttered on."

Stoopnagle split with Budd late in 1937. He starred in his own radio show in 1939, appeared on Vaughn Monroe's show in the late '40s and returned to writing, producing a variety of comedy and novelty books.

BOOKS: *You Wouldn't Know Me from Adam; My Tale Is Twisted; My Back to the Soil; Father Goosenagle*

## LARRY STORCH

### (January 8, 1923–  )

Though he's best known as the alternately querulous and agonizing Corporal Agarn of the hit television show "F-Troop," Larry Storch has also won praise for his stand-up act, a balance of story telling and mimicry.

Born in New York City, Larry imitated the foreign accents of people he knew in his neighborhood. He joined the navy at 17, amusing shipmates (including Tony Curtis) with his mimicry. Storch returned to New York to play clubs and even open his own night spot for a while. At 23 he was using his vocal talents on radio. He appeared on Frank Morgan's series and, when Morgan misplaced his glasses during a rehearsal, Larry stepped in and read the part—in Morgan's voice. The impressive stunt won him a 13-week contract.

Storch appeared in the Chicago revue *Red, White and Blue* in 1951 and that year replaced Jackie Gleason for the summer run of television's "Cavalcade of the Stars." In 1953 he had his own series. Storch appeared in several Broadway productions after that and played a Russian spy in *Who Was That Lady?* He went to Hollywood for the film version that reunited him with Tony Curtis.

Back in the 1950s, Storch had developed a penchant for character comedy, in both stand-up and revues. Dick Shawn recalled, "Most of the comics were doing standard jokes. Larry was one of the first ones to do characters." According to Cary Grant himself, it was Larry who created the "Judy, Judy, Judy" catch phrase that Grant imitators used for decades after. In Storch's routine, Grant was talking to Judy Garland. He cut an album for Jubilee in 1960, married his wife, Norma, in 1961 and continued to make films and take stand-up assignments.

He was a seasoned pro by the time he co-starred on "F-Troop" as Randolph Agarn, a character with quite a bit of depth for a sitcom buffoon. He was crafty but gullible, suspicious but open-minded, a tough soldier who bullied his underlings and fawned over his superiors. Storch went on to appear as a feisty sidekick to "F-Troop" star Forrest Tucker on the Saturday morning series "Ghost Busters" and would play similar roles in many sitcoms and movies.

His private life sometimes seems like a sitcom. In 1972 he underwent surgery for the insertion of a plastic hip. "I'd just had four hours surgery. They were going to move me from the operating table to my room. And they dropped me on the floor." When they scraped him up, they realized they had to operate—again. Eventually Storch was back on his feet, performing in theatrical productions, including a West Coast production of *Oklahoma* in 1990 and the 1991 off-Broadway comedy *Breaking Legs.* He is also busy with his stand-up concerts. His act, still a mix of conversation, old-fashioned stories and mimicry, amused a *Variety* critic who said he was still as hilarious as ever, "mixing new material with tales he's been telling for decades."

A dialect Storch classic concerns a delicate girl named Esther, a shy and frail and very sweet young thing. As Esther's Jewish granny, Storch says, "That goil must have come down from heaven on a moonbeam. . . . She fell in love mit a truck driver . . . a bull in a China Shoip! That big ape fell in love mit that girl. He proposed marriage. . . . At de wedding ceremony, well, date big bull backed into the canopy . . . when de rabbi gave him dat sacred glass of wine to drink, drank whole glass of wine, stomped on the glass, made by him such a racket that the poor delicate child had a miscarriage right there!"

AUDIO: *At the Bon Soir* (Jubilee), *Epstein* (Lively Arts)
BROADWAY: *Red, White and Blue* (1950), *Curtain Going Up* (1952), *The Littlest Revue* (1956), *Who Was That Lady I Saw You With?* (1958)
FILMS incl.: *The Prince Who Was a Thief* (1951), *Who Was That Lady?* (1960), *40 Pounds of Trouble* (1963), *Captain Newman, MD* (1963), *Sex and the Single Girl* (1964), *Wild and Wonderful* (1964), *That Funny Feeling* (1965), *The Monitors* (1969), *The Couple Takes a Wife* (1972), *The Happy Hooker Goes to Washington* (1977), *Without Warning* (1980), *Sweet Sixteen* (1981)
TV: "Cavalcade of Stars" (1951–52), "The Larry Storch Show" (1953), "F Troop" (1965–67), "The Queen and I" (1969), "Ghost Busters" (1975–78)
VIDEO: *Miss Casino Comedy Show*

## STRINGBEAN

### (David Akeman, June 17, 1915–November 11, 1973)

A beloved "Hee-Haw" performer for years, the lanky, six-foot-two banjo-playing "Stringbean" was born in Anneville, Kentucky and got his first big break on WLAP in Lexington in the 1930s.

After joining the Grand Ole Opry in 1942, he began to record tunes such as "I Wonder Where Wanda Went," along with albums that mostly featured his straight banjo picking. He developed into a memorable comedian. He looked the part—tall and thin with a sad-sack expression—but accentuated it by wearing a pair of pants that couldn't go down past his thighs.

He developed a nationwide audience on television's "Hee-Haw." Then one night of brutality cut short Stringbean's career. Following a performance at the Grand Ole Opry, he and his 59-year-old wife, Estelle, came home to discover two burglars in the house. They had been waiting for them, had even listened to WSM and heard Stringbean perform that evening on the radio. What they were after was the thousands in cash they had heard he kept at home instead of in the bank. In the struggle that followed, the comedian was shot dead. Estelle ran but was caught before she could even get past the lawn of her own home. On her hand and knees, pleading for her life, Estelle was shot three times and left facedown in the grass.

The killers, a pair of young cousins named Brown, fled with whatever they could carry. They didn't find the money in the house. They also missed the $3,000 Stringbean had in a pocket of his pants and a packet containing $2,000 Estelle had tucked away in her brassiere.

Archie Campbell, a co-star from "Hee-Haw," recalled the incident: "Such a horrible, senseless thing! If you ever knew String, you just couldn't see how anyone could ever harm a hair on his head; he was such a gentle person. He did have a lot of money. He had made a lot and hadn't spent much of it because he didn't really want much out of life except to go fishing every day. So I guess the people who did that awful thing thought that he would be carrying it around on him."

The killers were sentenced to life in prison, but the shocking ending to the fun-loving Stringbean was a jolt that still lingers. Fans can smile at the memory of his humor; but it's a sad smile, tainted by the tragic circumstances of his death.

AUDIO: *Me and My Old Crow* (Nugget)
TV: "Hee Haw" (1969–74)

## SALLY STRUTHERS

### (July 28, 1947–    )

Twice an Emmy winner for television's "All in the Family," Sally Struthers appeared in comedies before and after the hit show, but remained firmly identified with her role as Gloria Bunker. The show was a radical departure from standard sitcoms and, in her own way, Struthers bridged standard sitcom behavior (comical bawling) with more modern comic reactions (slow burns of feminist anger and frustration).

Born in Portland, Oregon, her father Scots-English, her mother Norwegian, she was a chubby child whose appearance was not enhanced by the silver front tooth that replaced the one knocked out in a fall. She remained short (five foot one) but during her years at U.S. Grant High School and the Pasedena Playhouse lost some of her pudgy baby fat. Over the years she amassed a very mixed bag of credits; she danced on a Herb Alpert television special, understudied Margaret O'Brien in a Los Angeles production of *Barefoot in the Park* and toured with the Spike Jones Jr. Band.

She endured some typical moments of starlet angst. There was an interview in which a male agent insisted on getting a better view of her by demanding she raise her skirt. And there was the female agent who complained that she'd never make it with her "fat face." Sally tried to compensate for her round face by adopting a curly hair style, one that so appalled her roommates they finally took matters into their own hands and cut it.

After the haircut, her luck changed. She played a bowling alley pickup in Jack Nicholson's film *Five Easy Pieces*. The only problem was a nude scene. She recalled, "I locked myself in the bathroom for an hour debating it. I couldn't drop that towel in front of six or seven men. When I got to Jack, I stayed glued to him. . . . I finally went home and bit my nails for six months hoping they'd cut the scene out but they didn't" Her mother went to the film alone saying 'If I don't like it, I don't want anybody to see me with you.' "

The perky, busty blonde played cheerleaders, dancers and had some minor comedy parts on "The Summer Brothers Smothers Show" and "The Tim Conway Comedy Hour." When she auditioned for

"All in the Family"—a midseason replacement series based on a British sitcom—she turned out to be one of the few young comic actresses whose round features resembled Carroll O'Connor's. She *looked* like the daughter of Archie Bunker.

The show was a tremendous hit, but Struthers knew that to avoid typecasting she had to branch out. She starred in a summer stage production of *A Girl Could Get Lucky*, put a nightclub act together, and starred in the television movie *Aloha Means Goodbye*. Gloria Bunker grew into womanhood and outgrew the show. Struthers' own series "Gloria" was not a major hit, but she had some success in 1985 taking the all-female version of *The Odd Couple* on tour and to Broadway opposite Rita Moreno. She made more films and even turned up doing voices on Saturday morning cartoon shows, including the teenage "Pebbles Flintstone." She also starred in the syndicated sitcom "9 to 5."

In the late '80s Struthers began working with the Christian Children's Fund. In 1991 she received a Presidential End Hunger Award from President Bush for her charity work, and has been seen in many public service television commercials.

She's tried very hard to stay slim, and help others stay slim, through her own *Sally Struthers Walking Video*. She said: "Walking is the one exercise almost anyone can do . . . and it's easier to learn because you've been doing the basic form ever since you took you first step." Fans still ask her about "All in the Family," wondering how closely the Gloria Bunker character matched the real Sally Struthers. She notes one main difference: "My mother wasn't a dingbat."

BROADWAY: *Wally's Cafe, The Odd Couple* (1985)

FILMS incl.: *The Phynx* (1970), *Five Easy Pieces* (1970), *The Getaway* (1972), *Aloha Means Goodbye* (1974), *Hey I'm Alive* (1975), *Intimate Strangers* (1977), *And Your Name Is Jonah* (1979), *A Gun in the House* (1981)

TV: "The Summer Smothers Show" (1970), "The Tim Conway Comedy Hour" (1970), "All in the Family" (1971–78), "Gloria" (1982–83), "9 to 5" (1986–88)

VIDEO: *Sally Struthers' Walking Video*

## MACK SWAIN

### (February 16, 1876–August 25, 1935)

A big, good-natured bear of a man, Mack Swain was beloved by audiences not as a screen heavy but as a jolly-built, harmlessly oafish clown. He was instantly identifiable: the garrulous, toothy smile, the wide eyes, the dark limp noodle of hair that curved directly down his forehead and sloppy thick black rectangle of a mustache that extended far up the sides of his nose.

The ex-vaudevillian began making films for Mack Sennett in 1913. The following year he starred in his own "Ambrose" comedies. As Ambrose he was the big but bullied husband—often henpecked, but sometimes childlike with a gleaming look in his roving eye as he chased after a girl far prettier than his wife. Tiny Chester Conklin was often a contrasting foil for Swain, but subsequently the big man ended up as the foil for other comics. He was the blustery cuckold opposite Mabel Normand (in *Mabel Lost and Won*) and lost many a battle to little Charlie Chaplin.

It was Chaplin who washed away the stereotyped "Ambrose" makeup and used Swain in a variety of guises, in *The Pilgrim, The Idle Class, Pay Day* and the classic *Gold Rush.* In the latter, Swain played Big Jim McKay, balancing just the right amount of menace and forgivable gluttony, playing a starving prospector who deliriously believes poor Charlie is a delectable chicken just waiting to be caught and cooked.

*The Gold Rush* was the high point for the aging funny man, coming ten years after he seemed to peak with his "Ambrose" film series. He appeared in several early talkies before his death in 1935.

FILMS incl.: *Laughing Gas* (1914), *Ambrose's First Falsehood* (1914), *The Battle of Ambrose and Walrus* (1915), *The Idle Class* (1921), *Pay Day* (1922), *The Pilgrim* (1923), *The Gold Rush* (1925), *Finnegan's Ball* (1927), *The Beloved Rogue* (1927), *Gentlemen Prefer Blondes* (1928), *The Cohens and Kellys in Atlantic City* (1929), *Finn and Hattie* (1931), *Lighthouse Love* (1932)

## ALFALFA SWITZER (See also OUR GANG.)

### (Carl Switzer, August 7, 1926–January 21, 1959)

The most comic-looking member of "Our Gang," Alfalfa was the freckle-face kid with the slicked-down hair, flying cowlick and look of nauseous fear. That fear, which included grimaces and a lot of dry-throated gulping, usually came when he tried to impress his girlfriend, Darla Hood. The results were laughable, as he sang love songs in a memorably strained, cracking, off-key voice.

Alfalfa's antics, pretty much the same in every short film, amused audiences but not his co-workers. To them he was a spoiled brat, practical joker and pest. His "girlfriend" Darla recalled, "The worst kid in the gang was Alfalfa. His dad told him he was God's gift to the world and he thoroughly believed it. . . . Maybe it wasn't Alfalfa's fault, Basically I think he was a nice boy, but his father was German and had drilled into his son that he was a member of the master race."

The child star was in the "Our Gang" series from 1935 to 1942. He was less in demand as he aged, taking minor roles in the '40s and early '50s. He had a cameo as a brat in Bob Hope's *My Favorite Blonde.* One of his better assignments was Ensign Kein in *The High and the Mighty.* In 1954 he got married, but it lasted barely five weeks. That same year he was arrested for drunkenness. In the '50s Switzer worked mainly as a hunting guide. Hunting pal Roy Rogers put him on his television show a few times in 1956, but the one-time brat had become increasingly hostile and sullen over the years, brawling in bars and turning on his friends.

The last brawl involved a lost dog. Alfalfa had lost friend Bud Stiltz's hunting dog. Stiltz offered a $35 reward for it. Eventually Alfalfa found the dog, but there was a dispute about the reward money. Alfalfa had evidently paid $35 to get the dog back and now was demanding that Stiltz repay him—plus an extra $15 for all of the times he'd treated Stiltz to drinks at the local bar. He pushed his way into Stiltz' home demanding $50 and smashed Stiltz in the face with a clock. The two struggled until Stiltz managed to push Switzer into an open closet.

Stiltz and the frightened witnesses in the house figured that was the end of it, but the furious Switzer broke out of the closet brandishing a hunting knife.

Stiltz grabbed a gun. "I'm gonna kill you," Switzer shouted as he charged forward. Stiltz fired one shot into Switzer's stomach. It stopped him.

Stiltz was tried for Switzer's death and acquitted. The case was not considered very important at the time and was not widely reported. Few who saw the movie *The Defiant Ones,* released after the incident, recognized Switzer in the bit part of Angus.

FILMS incl.: *General Spanky* (1936), *Wild and Woolly* (1937), *The War Against Mrs. Hadley* (1942), *My Favorite Blonde* (1942), *Johnny Doughboy* (1943), *The Human Comedy* (1943), *The Gas House Kids* (1946), *State of the Union* (1948), *Pat and Mike* (1952), *The Defiant Ones* (1958)

# T

## EVA TANGUAY

### (August 1, 1878–January 11, 1947)

W. C. Fields' appraisal of Eva Tanguay's talents: "Her singing and dancing was assault and battery." It didn't seem to matter.

One of vaudeville's most charismatic stars, an outrageous personality who flaunted her buxom, slightly chubby figure in bizarre costumes, Eva Tanguay was energetic and extroverted to mythic proportions. She was "The I Don't Care Girl" and in her own odd, comedic way had the same kind of appeal as modern "I Don't Care" pop stars. Long before Cher or Madonna, there was Eva Tanguay drawing crowds obsessed less with her singing than what she was wearing and how she was behaving. Eva didn't disappoint. One dress was just memo pads and pencils glued together, another an avalanche of dollar bills. She was often billed as "The Genius of Mirth and Song" and "The Evangelist of Joy."

Her songs included: "I May Be a Nut, But I'm Not a Crossword Fan," "I Want Somebody to Go Wild with Me" and "It's All Been Done Before, But Not the Way I Do It." Sometimes billed as the "Cyclonic Comedienne," Tanguay would take each city by storm, spending a fortune on publicity and advertising. Each new outfit was the talk of the town. As *Variety* wrote, her "dynamic salesmanship . . . made her unique, albeit a freak."

Born in Canada, Eva grew up in Massachusetts. Her father, Octave, died when she was just six. By the age of eight, she was already touring alone, appearing in *Little Lord Fauntleroy.* In her teens she learned how to stand out in a chorus and steal scenes in bit parts. She didn't let anyone get in her way. The fiery Tanguay sometimes choked and beat other chorus girls, once bashing a chorine's head against a wall. When her antics turned up in the papers, she realized the value of tangy publicity. It was probably temper—and an eye on the newspapers—that caused her to slash theater curtains and push a stagehand down a flight of stairs after one performance. What did anyone expect from a girl who sang "That's Why They Call Me Tabasco" and "I've Got to Be Crazy"?

After forming her own "Eva Tanguay Comedy Company" in 1903, the singer/comedienne appeared in "The Office Boy," "The Sambo Girl" (1904) and "A Good Fellow" (1906). She had a hit with the tune "I Don't Care" around that time and her earnings zoomed from $500 to $3,500 a week. Her production of *Salome* featured such a provocative costume that decency groups had her photos banned from theater lobbies. Before Mae West started to sell sex, Eva Tanguay was quipping "When I put on tights, my name went up in lights!"

The aging Tanguay had the same thing as aging liquor—the ability to still pack a wallop. *Variety* wrote late in her career, "What Ruth is to baseball, Dempsey to pugilism and Chaplin to pictures, Tanguay is to vaudeville. She embodies the spirit of youth in her work, her personality is elusive and baffling as ever, and she has the color that penetrates beyond the four walls of a theatre and cashes in at the box office."

Finally, Eva faded away with vaudeville itself. She lost $2 million in the stock market crash. She went blind in 1933 but her sight was restored after admirer Sophie Tucker paid for an eye operation. Arthritis slowed her in 1937, and the thrice-married star became more and more reclusive. When she died, her fortune was reduced to $500.

In 1952 Mitzi Gaynor made a film about her, *The I Don't Care Girl*, which at least proved that some people remembered—and still cared.

# JACQUES TATI

### (Jacques Tatischeff, October 9, 1908–November 5, 1982)

A student of human nature, Jacques Tati had a huge international hit with what was practically a silent movie, 1953's *Mr. Hulot's Holiday*. The film, a whimsical, mild-mannered study of a vacation by the sea, has been called a classic of observational humor. Tati's gentle, quaint and curious brand of humor has a cult of devotees. Those outside it find him numbing and bland.

Tati was clearly influenced by Keaton. The difference was that Keaton was active and Tati passive. Tati adapted Keaton's habit of walking with tentative, awkward stiffness, trying to be unassuming and inobtrusive. He would study the world around him with the mute stare of confusion, as if he was from another planet and had never seen a piece of machinery or a barking dog before. If Tati was a cartoon character, he would have had a "?" balloon over his head in every frame. Keaton balanced this passivity with action chases and lively acrobatics. Tati seemed to be content with chuckles over belly laughs.

Tati as a comic character is an enigma. One of the least known of the "classic" comedians, Tati's anonymity is in part due to his own philosophies in humor. Rather than facial expressions, the six-foot-four-inch comedian stressed a funny walk. He was known not by his features but by his props; the pipe

and umbrella he usually carried. The average comedy fan could not recognize Tati's face, unlike Chaplin's or Keaton's. Despite his blank personality and passive nature, Tati had many supporters. Jerry Lewis called him "a great technician, a craftsman, He knew every nuance of comedy and he made no bones about the fact that he was influenced greatly by Keaton."

Tati's Russian parents emigrated to France. There he played professional rugby; later he explored music hall comedy. Touring England in the late 1930s, he began to move from clownish humor to a more realistic style. After a show in which he had gotten few laughs, he recalled his inspiration:

"I took off my makeup and went out into the streets. And there suddenly, I understood. How could I be so ambitious as to want to make people laugh, when they were all of them wonderful mimes already, when the most ordinary passerby knew more about it than I did? That day I saw, really saw, the workman slinging bricks over to his mate who stacked them up, the cyclist distributing newspapers to the shops, the grocer displaying his fruit, weighing, wrapping and ringing up the change: the precision of their gestures, their wonderful exactness, the flexibility, the ease, the confidence and everything that movement and bearing can reveal about a man." He discovered that "basically everybody is amusing."

Tati had some success with a few short films in France, but hit his stride after World War II, starring in *L'Ecole des Facteurs* as an absent-minded mailman who somehow wins the day by inventing a new, efficient delivery system. *Mr. Hulot's Holiday* was his biggest success, a Cannes Film Festival winner and Oscar nominee (for Best Story and Screenplay), but the slow-working comedian took years before making another film.

He made only four films in 20 years. *Mon Oncle*, a study of modern times and gadgets, was fairly well received. Typical of the gentle running gags was the series on a woman who owned a fancy water fountain that she turned on only when guests arrived. As soon as they left, it was shut off. If an unimportant person arrived, the fancy fountain wasn't even put on at all.

Tati took six years plotting *Playtime*, a movie about tourism. Production took another three years. *Traffic*, a mild car chase, showed only flashes of his old form. The 1974 documentary *Parade* was his last film. Part of the reason was a lack of financial support, understandable considering his last hit was in 1958.

Tati was self-effacing about his genius and about his great comic character, Hulot: "He promenades, that's all. He takes a walk. Innocent and tranquil. He simply looks at things . . . he is not funny himself, not at all. He conducts himself according to strict rules of courtesy that do not ever allow him to express surprise. . . . He is not the cause of funny situations. He is in the middle of them."

BIOGRAPHIES: *Jacques Tati* (Harding, 1984), *Jacques Tati* (Gilliatt, 1976), *The Films of Jacques Tati* (Maddock, 1977), *Jacques Tati, a Guide to References and Resources* (Fischer, 1983)

FILMS: *Oscar—Champion de Tennis* (1932), *On Demande Une Brute* (1934), *Gai Dimanche* (1935), *Soigne Ton Gauche* (1936), *Retour à la Terre* (1938), *Sylvie et le Fantome* (1945), *Le Diable au Corps* (1946), *L'Ecole des Facteurs* (1947), *Jour de Fête* (1949), *Mr. Hulot's Holiday* (1953), *Mon Oncle* (1958), *Playtime* (1967), *Traffic* (1970), *Parade* (1974)

## RIP TAYLOR

### (Charles Elmer Taylor, January 13, 1934–   )

A campy, anything-for-a-laugh personality, outrageous Rip Taylor showered his audience with gags—and confetti as well. It was his trademark. He declared, "Confetti is my favorite thing. It's New Year's Eve, an ocean liner to the Caribbean and my last divorce all rolled up into one."

The confetti throwing began as an ad lib on Merv Griffin's talk show. He got laughs ripping up Griffin's question sheet and tossing the pieces all over the bewildered host. Before long he was punctuating zany gags with outbursts of confetti and assaulting ringsiders with it in mock bursts of temperament.

Taylor's other trademarks included a thick white mustache flying out toward his rounded cheeks, a huge meringue of a blond toupee, and a table full of props to whip out for one-liner gags.

While at George Washington University Taylor first experimented with comedy, appearing on stage miming and making faces to records by straight

singers. Figuring that "a tailor keeps you in stitches," he became "Rip" Taylor. In his early years he was billed as "The Crying Comedian," offering comic tales of woe with exaggerated tears and bawling.

Ultimately he made his mark as one of the first popular prop comics in modern stand-up. His delivery was overpowering, campy and flamboyant. After years in burlesque and the Catskills, he guested on television's "Ed Sullivan Show" in 1963. He became a hit through the '60s, but over 25 years later, he never forgot the sting of his early years in show business. Whenever he'd go to New York, he'd make a point of walking past his old apartment house at 146 West 46th Street—just so he could spit on it.

Unabashedly tacky, Taylor was the perfect host for the "$1.98 Beauty Show," in which unappetizing women paraded themselves for laughs and prizes. Taylor has remained a top draw at the casinos, winning "Comic of the Year" honors in Las Vegas (his hometown) three years in a row. Through the years Taylor has toured in companies of *Damn Yankees*, *Oliver!* and *Sugar Babies*, but no show could be as fast and furious as Rip's own stand-up act, with its props, confetti and constantly popping, corny gags: "Two Jewish lawyers are opening a Japanese restaurant. They're calling it 'So Sue Me!'" "Raymond Burr had an out-of-body experience—and a family of six moved in."

FILMS incl.: *I'd Rather Be Right* (1964), *The Gong Show Movie* (1980), *Things Are Tough All Over* (1982), *Amazon Women on the Moon* (1986)

TV: "The Beautiful Phyllis Diller Show" (1968), "Dean Martin Presents Bobby Darin" (1972), "The Gong Show" (1976–80), "The $1.98 Beauty Show" (1978–80)

## JUDY TENUTA

### (November 7, 1951–   )

Controversial, original and outrageous, Judy Tenuta—self-proclaimed "Goddess of Comedy"—has developed a cult of chuckling acolytes. Following her almost religiously, delighting in the slightly campy rituals of her religion "Judyism," they cheer her entrance on stage with cries of "Jooodee, Jooodee," as she parades regally in either silk and satin thrift-

Judy Tenuta, self-proclaimed "Goddess of Comedy."
Photo from the author's collection.

shop gowns or sparkling jump suits that look like Elvis Presley's pajamas.

After false smiles of "fairy princess" modesty, and perhaps a chortling trill of Billie Burke-ish laughter, the Goddess thuds to earth with a growling "Hi, pigs" and a stream of disgusted one-liners and sarcastic rages, disdaining mortal men ("stud puppets!"), mortal women ("pseudovirgins") and subhumans merely dubbed "sponges." Her ability to load up on audience participation insult routines has made her especially hot on the comedy club circuit. In a classic bit that appalled several television critics of her 1989 HBO special, Judy spit out her gum and shouted at a ringsider, "Crawl for it!" In her early years she would often grab a "love slave" from the audience and stuff her used gum into his willing mouth.

Weighed down by a clanky accordion—a symbol of human invention at its worst—the Goddess punc-

tuates lines with a few discordant notes. She even sings (one effort was a growly love ballad to the pope, whom she always insisted she "was just *using* to get to God"). Discovering the shock value of bad-taste humor, Judy occasionally skewers gays, foreigners and stars. Her most notorious single line was on the John Lennon assassination. After slanting her eyes with her fingers and putting on an outrageous Japanese accent to mock Yoko Ono, she grunted that if Lennon's killer "aimed a little to the right—he would've been a hero!" As the crowd giggled and gasped she cried, "You thought it but I *said* it! Oh, come and get me!"

After using that line while guesting on Joan Rivers' daytime talk show, Joan rasped between fits of her own laughter, "You're the funniest woman in the world!"

While some were as appalled by Judy as they were by the male shock comics, most could clearly see the sense of fun. Off stage the five-foot-three star enjoys remaining in character, like a little girl play-acting in costumes, all smiles and mischief. To those who can't quite figure out the bizarre vision they were seeing, she once explained, "I'm a cross betweeen Groucho Marx, Lady Macbeth and Tinkerbell."

Raised in Oak Park, Illinois, her mother Polish, her father Italian, Judy attended the University of Illinois at Chicago majoring in theater. Around 1976 she took a course in improvisation at Second City and began her comedy career. Judy's cult expanded after opening for George Carlin in 1987 and created controversy in 1988 co-hosting a "Friday Night Videos" program. She had dressed up as Cher, which caused co-host Sonny Bono to walk out in shocked dismay. She starred in cable specials and made a record album, capping the 1980s as the star of diet Dr. Pepper television commercials and gaining prime national exposure. In one commercial in a health club she chortled, "You can't get a body like mine in a bottle . . . unless you push real hard."

In the fall of 1991 Harper-Perennial released her book *The Power of Judyism*, filled with advice, pet peeves and even recipes for "Mass Murderer Mousse" and "Sexist Pigs in a Blanket." *Vogue* magazine declared, "Tenuta is to female stand-up comics what Carrie was to high school girls."

Tenuta, whose style influenced "Domestic Goddess" Roseanne Arnold toward gum-chewing, salty sass, had an edge over the hefty comic in her ability to write and create evocative comic imagery. She described her horrible family life: "Mom boiled the hot dogs—and we got to drink the juice." While contemporaries Sandra Bernhard and Elayne Boosler were often cited as strong, independent women, it was Judy who said she didn't join her college sorority because "I already had a personality of my own."

Judy's feminism is frank and sarcastic. She says on stage, "Yeah, you can probably tell just by lookin' at me—that I want to be a *wife and mother!*" She said she refused a date with one man: "I told him I was looking for something a little closer to the *top* of the food chain." Even her "standard" jokes cause shudders. Her line on Dr. Ruth, the diminutive sex therapist: "A sex therapist? I would be too if I came up to everyone's belt buckle!" A desultory report on growing up: "My mom told me, 'You won't amount to anything because you procrastinate.' I said, 'Just wait!'"

Tenuta waited many years before her unique style caught on, but it doesn't seem to bother her. Her catch phrase ending for every show remains the same: "Thank you—you people mean nothing to me!"

AUDIO: *Buy This, Pigs!* (Elektra)
BOOK: *The Power of Judyism* (1991)

## TERRY-THOMAS

### (Thomas Terry Hoar-Stevens, July 14, 1911–January 8, 1990)

Jolly good fun was what Terry-Thomas was about, whether playing stereotyped silly Englishmen or a wide array of dastardly amusing villains. His gleaming, malicious smile was comically marked by a gap between his front teeth.

Thomas grew up in London, enjoyed the comforts of a wealthy family and graduated from Ardsley College. "I was a film extra in the thirties," he recalled. He appeared in mostly B pictures: "When I came out of the army, I became a star in C, D, and E pictures! I gave that up and started off again."

He achieved early success as a mimic, taking off on the leading music hall stars of the day. Originally "Thomas Terry," he reversed it and then added a hyphen to symbolize the trademark of his spaced front teeth. The London revue "Piccadilly Hayride" in 1946 marked his first major triumph.

Thomas's stand-up career included mystifying shaggy dog stories told in a variety of British accents and parody madrigals—material (preserved on the album *Strictly T-T*) difficult for Americans to comprehend. He referred to it as "the English sense of humor. One must be able to see large laughs in very poor jokes." His film career took off in the late '50s, capped by an autobiography published in England in 1959.

By that time many of his films were being imported to America. He was the lovable, scheming but inept rogue in a series of hits, including *School for Scoundrels* and *Make Mine Mink.* In the latter, he solved a comic dilemma with typical British ridiculousness. Ditching his fake policeman's uniform when the real police are after him, he ducks into a men's

Americans never thought of the British in quite the same way after watching Terry-Thomas and his hilarious gap-toothed stereotypes. Photo from the author's collection.

room and emerges with "7" written on a sheet of toilet paper and fastened to his back. He jauntily race-walks down the street in T-shirt and undershorts as a marathoner.

In 1963 Thomas recorded a comedy album for American audiences, which included a British version of Allan Sherman's "Hello Muddah, Hello Faddah," titled "Hello Mater, Hello Pater." He went on to co-star in two blockbuster comedies of the era, *It's a Mad Mad Mad Mad World* and *Those Magnificent Men in Their Flying Machines*. As always, his roles called for cheerful larceny, the proper Englishman reduced to nefarious deeds—and relishing it.

Thomas' magnificent career began to slow due to Parkinson's disease. Through the 1980s, his physical state worsened. Some days he was fine, he told interviewers, but on others, "I cannot say the simplest possible word." The frustrating illness sapped his strength and his money. A benefit for him in the spring of 1989 helped pay off debts, but he was barely aware of it. The tall, smiling gent with the thick mustache and bright grin was now almost unrecognizable. Video cameras showed him slumped in his chair, eyes unfocused and half shut, hair thinned, a beard obscuring most of his face. He died less than one year later.

For his many fans, the tragedy of Terry-Thomas's last years cast a pall that could be erased only by the highest comedy—watching him in his golden years of the 1950s and '60s in sparkling film comedies that, like fine champagne, never seem to lose their bubbling brightness.

AUDIO: *Strictly T-T* (London), *Terry-Thomas Discovers America* (WB), *Three Billion Millionaires* (UA), *Jeeves* (Caedmon)

AUTOBIOGRAPHY: *Filling the Gap* (1959), *Terry-Thomas Tells Tales* (1990)

BOOKS: *How Many Times a Week Is Bi-Annually?*, *A Bidet-Full of Fruit*, *The Freckled Ferret of Effingham*

FILMS: incl. *Private's Progress* (1956), *Blue Murder at St. Trinian's* (1957), *The Naked Truth* (1958), *Tom Thumb* (1958), *Carleton Browne of the F.O.* (1958), *I'm All Right, Jack* (1959), *School for Scoundrels* (1960), *Make Mine Mink* (1960), *His and Hers* (1961), *A Matter of Who* (1962), *Bachelor Flat* (1962), *Wonderful World of the Brothers Grimm* (1963), *Kill or Cure* (1963), *It's a Mad Mad Mad Mad World*

(1963), *Those Magnificent Men in Their Flying Machines* (1963), *The Mouse on the Moon* (1963), *How to Murder Your Wife* (1965), *You Must Be Joking* (1965), *Munster Go Home* (1966), *Kiss the Girls and Make Them Die* (1966), *The Perils of Pauline* (1967), *Those Fantastic Flying Fools* (1967), *Where Were You When the Light Went Out?* (1968), *2000 Years Later* (1969), *Those Daring Young Men in their Jaunty Jalopies (Monte Carlo or Bust)* (1969), *The Abominable Dr. Phibes* (1971), *The Vault of Horror* (1973), *Spanish Fly* (1976), *The Last Remake of Beau Geste* (1977)

## THEODORE (See BROTHER THEODORE.)

## BUCKWHEAT THOMAS (See also OUR GANG.)

### (William Thomas, March 12, 1931–October 10, 1980)

Some may appreciate his precociousness, but it seems likely that the fondness viewers feel for "Buckwheat" lately is tainted with campy disdain at best, racism at worst.

During the years of "Our Gang," and through the 1950s and '60s when the old shorts were rerun on television, the cheerful little boy Buckwheat was considered an amusing, somewhat minor member of those little rascals. Like the rest of the gang, he spoke with a piping, declarative little voice, rolled his eyes when amazed and had a silly blameless grin when happy. But the grin and the rolling eyes were, for a black child, uncomfortably close to stereotype.

In the 1980s Eddie Murphy parodied Buckwheat on television's "Saturday Night Live." It was hard to tell if the audience was laughing at the stereotype of a grinning, inarticulate black child or the lampoon of that stereotype. Either way, the routine was a hit. On one show Murphy imitated "Buh-wheat" singing. Lines from Lionel Richie's hit song "Three Times a Lady" came out: "Unce, tice, fee tines a mady!" Murphy made a happy catch phrase out of "Otay!" which was the closest the child could get to "okay." It led to a slew of "Otay!" Buckwheat T-shirts, watches and other paraphernalia, and a complaint from Eugene Lee (who played *Porky*,

Buckwheat's little white pal) that it was he who originally said "otay" in the old shorts.

Darla Hood, the sweet little girl of the "gang," remembered no racism on the Hal Roach lot and said making the films was a happy time for Buckwheat. Unfortunately, outside the film studio there was less enthusiasm for integration. Hood said, "When we went on the road to make personal appearances . . . Buckwheat and his mother couldn't sit in the same car on the train with the rest of us. . . . he could never stay in the same hotels we did, and mind you, this wasn't in the South; this happened in Minneapolis, Chicago and Detroit." It was especially sad and striking for Darla, since she considered him her "favorite" of the gang.

After Murphy made Thomas notorious, several aging black men tried to win fame and fortune claiming to be Buckwheat. In the fall of 1990, ABC's news show "20/20" aired a segment featuring a man they said was Buckwheat, now working in a supermarket. As Leonard Maltin reported on "Entertainment Tonight" in exposing this and other imposters, "They're all phonies . . . [ABC] didn't seem to investigate this story at all. It's so simple to check." He ran a few clips showing the real Buckwheat in 1960s interviews and an interview with Buckwheat's son.

The real Buckwheat, William Thomas, died of a heart attack in 1980; he was spared the knowledge of how much of a "favorite" he'd become to a new gang of mocking fans.

# DANNY THOMAS

## (Muzyad Yakhoob, later Amos Jacobs, January 6, 1912–February 6, 1991)

Older fans of Danny Thomas remember him as a monologist and singer who excelled at dialect stories and changed the pace with songs. But most recall him primarily as a television sitcom star. On "Make Room for Daddy" he played a nightclub star perplexed by his wife and two kids. He got a lot of mileage out of comic shock: staring eyes, tight lips and exasperated frustration. Years later he played a crusty doctor on "The Practice," a polished example of the gruff old-timer with a heart of gold.

One of nine kids, Thomas was born in Michigan. His Lebanese parents assimilated a short time later and changed the family name to Jacobs, with "Muzyad" becoming "Amos." He attended Woodward High in Toledo and worked in a burlesque theater selling candy. An early influence was an obscure burlesque dialect comic, Abe Reynolds. Danny began entertaining as early as 1932 on a local Detroit radio show, "The Happy Hour Club." It was in 1940 at Chicago's 5100 Club that he established his reputation as a comedian and singer. By then he adopted the names of his youngest and eldest brothers, Danny and Thomas. He appeared on radio with Fanny Brice and was a regular on "The Bickersons" as the irritating Cousin Amos. From 1944 to 1949 he had his own radio series.

In the 1950s Thomas's pleasant way with a song and his dialect stories—especially those done with a Yiddish accent—made him a nightclub favorite around the country. His natural speaking voice and cadence suggested he was Jewish, but whenever asked, he proudly described his true heritage. Even so, he was embraced as a performer in the Jewish tradition. As Leo Rosten rhapsodized, "He has a face like a foot wiper and a nose of such size and splendor that it merits comparison only to Cyrano's. . . . He is the perfect fall guy, the mournful image of innocence kicked around by indignities. Collar buttons tighten around his throat . . . nails follow him, trying to get into his shoes . . . but he is blessed with a wonderful eye for characterization, a faultless ear for dialects and an outlandish gift for comic invention."

In clubs the somewhat sad-looking comic with the soulful eyes liked to tell stories he could act out. Along the way, a few one-liners would slip in, along with philosophy: "If you're worried about your job or making a payment on your car, if you're worried whether she loves you or not, just try wearing a pair of tight shoes! You'll forget the other things."

Moving from stand-up star to fall-guy parent, Thomas won an Emmy for "Make Room for Daddy" during the show's long run. The story of a nightclub star at home mirrored aspects of Danny's life and warm sense of humor. Even the show's character "Uncle Tonoose" was based on a real relative by that name. Danny was surprised it was a hit: "I was sure that this face was not going to be considered white, Protestant American fare." The show proved durable in rerun right into the 1990s, even with its share of sitcom clichés. Thomas was aware of them. On a January 8, 1991 appearance on David Letterman's show, Danny delighted the crowd by demonstrating a "spit take," drinking water and suddenly spurting it out on hearing something startling. Marlo Thomas came by a few weeks later to try one, just like her famous Dad.

Thomas became an important figure off stage, producing "The Andy Griffith Show," "The Dick Van Dyke Show" and many others. He attempted "Make Room for Granddaddy" in 1970, but by that time the big star in the family was his daughter Marlo (in "That Girl).

Thomas continued performing at his own pace, in sitcoms and in nightclubs, meeting with only one major disappointment, the short run of his sitcom "The Practice," about a lovable cantankerous doctor. In one episode he tried to examine a skittish patient (Lucille Ball) convinced he was going to hurt her. "I won't hurt you! I won't hurt you!" he exclaimed with exasperation. "I had less trouble on my honeymoon!" At 76 Thomas co-starred in *Side by Side,* a television movie with Milton Berle and Sid Caesar; he also joined them for a "Legends of Comedy" tour in 1988. Thomas always kept up his charity work. "Every other weekend I'm somewhere in America for St. Jude Children's Research Hospital." He was a founder of the Tennessee facility and was one of its major supporters.

Danny wrote his autobiography in 1990 and had just finished a long tour promoting it when he suffered a fatal heart attack. He had also completed a guest spot on the sitcom "Empty Nest" (a show produced by his son Tony) playing an 80-year-old pediatrician. In one scene the wise old doctor pointed to a health poster showing four basic food groups: "This is what they told the kids to eat so they'd stay healthy and live to be a hundred! Milk, eggs, meat and white bread. Today, this is a death chart!"

The good-hearted Thomas was often gently kidded by other comics for his well-known "holier than thou" image and tendency toward pious sentimentality on stage. Walter Winchell once called him "The Preacher." Thomas replied, "To me the entertainment of people is a calling just like the ministry. You have to want to entertain people."

AUTOBIOGRAPHY: *Make Room for Danny* (1991)
FILMS incl.: *The Unfinished Dance* (1947), *Big City* (1948), *Call Me Mister* (1951), *The Jazz Singer* (1953), *Looking for Love* (1964)
TV: "All Star Revue" (1950–52), "Make Room for Daddy", "aka The Danny Thomas Show" (1953–64), "The Danny Thomas Hour" (1967–68), "Make Room for Granddaddy" (1970–71), "The Practice" (1976–77), "I'm a Big Girl Now" (1980–81), "One Big Family" (1986)

## THE THREE STOOGES (See also SHEMP HOWARD, TED HEALY and JOE BESSER.)

**Moe Howard: Moses Horwitz, June 19, 1897– May 4, 1975**
**Curly Howard: Jerome Horwitz, October 22, 1903–January 18, 1952**
**Larry Fine: Louis Feinberg, October 5, 1902–January 24, 1975**
**Shemp Howard: Samuel Horwitz, March 17 1895–November 23, 1955**
**Joe Besser, August 12, 1907–March 1, 1988**
**Joe DeRita: Joseph Wardell, July 12, 1909–**

The Marx Brothers were the intellectuals' idea of anarchists. The Three Stooges were everybody else's. The ultimate moment in Stooge comedy: a pie fight in which members of society are dismayed by the unseemly violence—then gleefully lose all inhibitions and start slinging pies too.

Moe, Larry and Curly were never called "the stooges" by fans. They were always "the boys." That was part of their appeal. The trio were adults who behaved like children.

Moe, in his little-boy bangs, play-acted the parent, slapping the other two, uttering comically outrageous threats ("I'll tear your esophagus out and shove it right in your eye!"). He frowned, glowered and bullied: every kid's fantasy of what being an adult boss was like. Underrated as a comedian, no one made meanness and malice funnier than Moe Howard.

Curly, a true child with his dumpling body, high voice and baby-bald skull, only wanted to play. He wanted to laugh and "nyuk" his way through life. Like a little boy, he was reduced to squeals, guttural

They called themselves "phenomenal, sensational—and even mediocre." They were right the first time. The cult for The Three Stooges is a phenomenon that has grown stronger than that of any other comedians in recent years. Photo from the author's collection.

grunts and frenzied yowls when, for no reason he could see, he was disciplined by Moe. If not a comic genius, Curly was humor's greatest savant. Curly Howard had more recognizable mannerisms and catch phrases than any film comedian, ranging from pinwheel spins on the floor, inane finger snapping and sudden cries of "wub-wub-woo!" to snarls of "Oh, a backbiter!" or bleats of "I'm a victim of soicumstance!"

Larry, with messy uncombed curls spilling over his ears, was every kid who ever said "I wasn't doin' nothin'." He was the passive one whose eyes often

glazed over in a stupor. He minded his own business—and got clobbered anyway. After fans reran the shorts to cheer Moe or Curly, they soon began to appreciate the subtle (often unintentional) hilarity of "the stooge in the middle."

For years their eye-poking, nostril-gouging, pie-throwing antics were ignored by critics and abhorred by parents and teachers. Even other comics, even *Jerry Lewis,* insisted the boys were journeymen using sure-fire slapstick "basics." It was only in the 1980s that these "human cartoons" were finally appreciated. Kids who grew up loving Stooge television reruns in the 1950s refused to give them up. Critics began to realize that the boys had original and identifiable comic characters and performed their slapstick with a great deal of skill and style. Anybody might throw a pie or poke an eye; but not everybody could get a real belly laugh doing it.

Moe and Curly were brothers from Bensonhurst, Brooklyn, Larry was born in Philadelphia. Their parents were all Jewish immigrants, the Horwitzes from Lithuania, the Feinbergs from Russia. Moe was a child actor in New York films before joining friend Ted Healy for a vaudeville act. His brother Shemp joined, and Larry made it three. The act became known as Ted Healy and His Stooges. Shemp was the first to rebel against the unpleasant Healy and quit to become a solo comedian.

Another Howard brother, eager young Jerome, wanted to take Shemp's place. Healy was doubtful. What kind of distinctive look could he create to match Moe's bangs and Larry's friz? Jerome had his head shaved and joined as "Curly." The team took off, making several films, but Healy the on-screen wise guy/disciplinarian was even tougher off stage, paying his "stooges" as if they really were just stooges. The trio left Healy, with Moe assuming the dominant role; in 1934 they began making two-reelers for Columbia. They didn't stop until 1958 when Columbia abandoned its short subject department. Nobody in comedy had a continuous contract that long and none matched the Stooges' record for appearing in some 200 films.

Over the years there were a few changes. After Curly had a stroke in 1946, brother Shemp came back to replace him. "Curly was a genius," Larry said years later, "he worked so fast. When we lost him we lost something, I'll admit it." What they lost was a lot of their childlike innocence, but Shemp's combination of gruff exterior and mindless interior earned him his own dedicated core of fans. The aging new stooges used more adult plots involving wives and gangsters. After Shemp's sudden death from a heart attack in 1955, Joe Besser joined the act. Besser acted like a child, with his blameless smile, balding dome and effeminate whining and pinching. Moe felt he was fairly close to Curly as a chubby innocent, but Besser's effeminacy didn't fit in well with Moe and Larry's personalities; viewers

also missed the wild slapstick that had been a trademark even in the later Shemp shorts.

Movie theaters in the 1950s didn't want filler interfering with the quick turnover of customers. For economic reasons, the single feature became the rule. Columbia disbanded its short subjects department and after Besser balked at touring, the Stooges disbanded. Fortunately, when the old shorts were sold to television, the boys became famous all over again. They staged a comeback for feature films. Since the shorts with Curly earned the best ratings, Moe and Larry found crew-cutted Joe DeRita, an ex-burlesque comic who once had his own series of shorts for Columbia in the 1940s. Moe was still the leader and fans still loved their stooges. Despite the storybook level of the sitcom plots, DeRita's amusing but undynamic personality and the mildness of the slapstick, the films did very well, especially among children.

In the late 1960s, poor health kept sidelining one member of the trio or another. After Larry Fine's stroke in the early 1970s, Joe and Moe planned to continue with Emil Sitka, an actor who had co-starred in many shorts. Then Moe became ill, De-Rita briefly enlisted two men for a tour as The Three Stooges, but there wasn't much interest; after his eyesight became worse, that group disbanded. Moe was often invited to appear at colleges and to demonstrate pie throwing on a variety of television shows in the late 1960s and 70s. Larry recovered from his stroke enough to make some "nostalgia" appearances for his fans. They both lived to see the beginnings of "Stoogemania," which reached a peak on January 4, 1982 when the *Wall Street Journal* ran a front-page story on the burgeoning sales of videos, books and other memorabilia.

Though in their day the boys seldom received praise from critics, they always had devoted fans. And late in life, they did get the last laugh, and nyuk, before going to that big pie in the sky.

AUDIO: *The Nonsense Songbook* (Coral, reissued by MCA), *Six Funny Bone Stories* (Peter Pan), *Madcap Musical Nonsense* (Golden, reissued by Rhino), *Christmas Time* (Rhino)
AUTOBIOGRAPHIES: *Moe Howard and the Three Stooges*

(Howard), *A Stroke of Luck* (Fine), *Not Just a Stooge* (Besser)

BOOKS incl.: *The Three Stooges Scrapbook* (Lenburg, Maurer, Lenburg, 1982), *The Stooge Chronicles* (Forrester, 1981), *The Stooges' Lost Episodes* (Forrester, 1988), *The Films of the Three Stooges* (Volk, 1988), *Curly: The Superstooge* (Howard, 1985), *My Brother Larry, the Stooge in the Middle* (Feinberg, 1984), *The Stooge Fans' I.Q. Test* (R. Smith)

FILMS incl.: shorts: *Beer and Pretzels* (1933), *Woman Haters* (1934), *Punch Drunks* (1934), *Men in Black* (1934), *Three Little Pigskins* (1934), *Pop Goes the Easel* (1935), *Hoi Polloi* (1936), *Tassels in the Air* (1938), *Violent Is the Word for Curly* (1938), *Yes We Have No Bonanza* (1939), *You Nazty Spy* (1940), *Dutiful But Dumb* (1941), *An Ache in Every Stake* (1941), *In the Sweet Pie and Pie* (1941), *Spook Louder* (1943), *A Gem of a Jam* (1943), *Micro Phonies* (1945), *Hold That Lion* (1947), *Brideless Groom* (1947), *Don't Throw That Knife* (1951), *Spooks* (1953), *Rip Sew and Stitch* (1953), *A Merry Mix-Up* (1957); features: *Soup to Nuts* (1930), *Meet the Baron* (1933), *Have Rocket Will Travel* (1959), *Snow White and the Three Stooges* (1961), *The Three Stooges Go Around the World in a Daze* (1963), *The Outlaws Is Coming* (1965)

VIDEOS: *The Three Stooges Columbia Shorts* (various volumes); *The Making of the Three Stooges; Joy of Stooging; Stoogephile Trivia Movie; Stooges Lost and Found; Goofs of the Trade; T.V. Jitters*

# THELMA TODD

## (July 29, 1905–December 16, 1935)

Along with Carole Lombard, Thelma Todd was considered one of the most promising blond comediennes of the sound era. Vivacious in romantic comedies, a toughie in slapstick shorts, she was versatile enough to co-star with everyone from Harry Langdon, Ed Wynn and Buster Keaton to Wheeler and Woolsey, Laurel and Hardy, and the Marx Brothers. Like Lombard, her life and career were cut short suddenly and tragically.

Born in Lawrence, Massachusetts, a student at the State Normal School, Thelma won a "Miss Mas-

sachusetts" beauty pageant, which earned her a Paramount film contract. Initially she had little to do. In 1929's *Unaccustomed as We Are* she played Edgar Kennedy's wife who loses her dress amid Laurel and Hardy slapstick and has to hide in a trunk to avoid her angry husband.

Most viewers remember Todd best in her two films with The Marx Brothers. In *Monkey Business* she's married to a gangster but enjoys flirting and dancing with Groucho Marx, crying, "You know what I want, I want life, I want laughter, I want gaiety. I want to ha-cha-cha!" She hates her husband: "From the time he got the marriage license, I've led a dog's life." Groucho: "Are you sure he didn't get a dog's license?"

As the flirty "college widow" in *Horse Feathers*, she was the object of all The Marx Brothers' attention, which made for a rousingly raucous marriage ceremony. The highlight was Thelma's coy baby-talk routine aboard a canoe with Groucho, which got her kicked overboard.

Hal Roach decided to team her with ZaSu Pitts and create a female Laurel and Hardy, the first female comedy team since the duo of Dressler and Moran. They became the most popular female comedy team in film history, but the strain on Thelma was great. She took diet pills to keep her weight down and had a failed marriage to a thug with connections to Lucky Luciano. Her private life had been strewn with tragedies and violence, from the questionable business dealings of her political boss father to the accidental death of her ten-year-old brother in a farmhouse accident.

Looking for a good business outside the acting world, Thelma opened Thelma Todd's Sidewalk Cafe in 1934. Most theorists believe it was not her Hollywood fame but her restaurant that led to her death. Through her ex-husband she met Lucky Luciano and began an affair with him. He was more interested in getting a piece of her restaurant and turning it into a gambling den.

Mystery surrounded the party she attended on Saturday night, December 14, and her whereabouts on Sunday. She was found dead in her garage on Monday morning, behind the wheel of her car, wearing her evening gown and mink coat. Evidence in the case was botched and the exact time of death was also in doubt. Rumors abounded concerning her ex-husband (a guest at the party), her relationship with business partner and ex-lover Roland West (he had directed her 1931 attempt at straight drama, *Corsair*) and her connection to Lucky Luciano.

The official cause of death was carbon monoxide poisoning. Dismissing fractured bones to her body and face as having been caused by her fall against the steering wheel, the verdict was suicide. Todd's mother immediately announced it was murder. Later she changed her story. Others, including key witnesses, also seemed hazy on the facts. They acted as if they had been threatened to keep quiet. There were reports that Thelma Todd had made an appointment with the police just a week before her death and that she had been receiving threatening notes. One recovered note read: "Our San Francisco boys will lay you out. We'll wreck that Santa Monica cafe of yours."

Few dared to point a finger at the powerful mobster Lucky Luciano. Among the insiders in Hollywood, though, there was little doubt that Luciano had been involved. In the late 1960s David Niven admitted in print that Clark Gable had told him about the thug violence that had taken Thelma Todd's life and the price of stardom and fan adulation. Gable said that fans "expect us to pay the price for it all . . . we have to 'get it' in the end. So, when we get knocked off by gangsters, like Thelma did, or get hooked on booze or dope or get ourselves thrown out of the business because of scandals or because we just grow old . . . that's the pay-off and the public feels satisfied."

In the late 1980s Andy Edmonds wrote a book about Todd in which she firmly documented the case against Luciano.

BIOGRAPHY: *Hot Toddy* (Edmonds, 1990)
FILMS incl.: *Rubber Heels* (1927), *The Haunted House* (1928), *Her Private Life* (1929), *Aloha* (1930), *The Hot Heiress* (1931), *Monkey Business* (1931), *Broad Minded* (1931), *Maltese Falcon* (1931), *Horse Feathers* (1932), *Klondike* (1932), *This Is the Night* (1932), *Speak Easily* (1932), *Air Hostess* (1933), *Sitting Pretty* (1933), *Fra Diavolo* (1933), *Hips Hips Hooray* (1934), *Bottoms Up* (1934), *Cockeyed Cavaliers* (1934), *Lightning Strikes Twice* (1935), *Two for Tonight* (1935), *Bohemian Girl* (1936)

## LILY TOMLIN

### (Mary Jean Tomlin, September 1, 1939–   )

She was Ernestine, the snorting, grimacing, nasal-voiced phone operator. She was sticky-mouthed brat Edith Ann. Then she was a bag lady, the quadraplegic Crystal and a dozen more vivid characters. And along the way, Lily Tomlin's reputation grew from a funny lady on television to a successful tragicomic stage artist and film star.

Born in Detroit, where her Kentucky-bred father went to find factory work, Lily was a joker early on. At seven she was buying "sleazy stuff advertised in the back of a comic book, like itching powder and hand buzzers. It came C.O.D. and cost $11. My poor mother was intimidated enough to pay for it, but when I got home from school, she said, 'You can't have it until you can pay me back.' " Tomlin began running errands and at 14 went to work as a shop clerk, skipping school for weeks at a time.

In high school Lily liked to hang out with a girl gang called "The Scarlet Angels." That didn't get in the way of her studies, though; she entered Wayne State University as a pre-med student. In a college variety show she adopted the character of Mrs. Earbore, the Tasteful Lady, and her comic acting career had begun.

In 1965 she went to New York hoping for acting jobs, but she ended up as a waitress at Howard Johnson's on Broadway and 49th Street. She lived above the B&H Dairy Luncheonette on 2nd Avenue in the East Village, making the rounds and eventually appearing in a revue, *Below the Belt,* and performing a routine on an early "Merv Griffin Show." She appeared on "The Garry Moore Show" but most video viewers recognized her for a television commercial for Vapo-Rub. "The Music Scene" television show proved to be her big break, a springboard to "Laugh-In," in December 1969.

Her phone operator, Ernestine, was the first exciting new character "Laugh-In" had seen in years, even though it was really just a snorty burlesque of the phone character Elaine May had used years earlier. The next success, Edith Ann, obviously had Baby Snooks as an ancestor, but was modern and uncompromising: "I didn't ask to be born. If I did, Mama would have said no!" Both characters had a little more reality to them than the average "Laugh-

Lily Tomlin, one of the few performers who has won a Grammy, a Tony and an Emmy award. Photo from the author's collection.

In" character. Tomlin admitted, "Ernestine is probably the only vindictive character I have." And Edith Ann was the first character Tomlin created that did more than crack jokes. Edith Ann's childhood angst included a description of anger: "Your face gets just like a fist, and then your heart gets like a bunch of bees and flies up and stings your brain."

Lily wrote the Edith Ann material with Jane Wagner, a writer she sought out in 1972 after noting her name among the credits for a television special. They became friends and have shared a house together for two decades. Wagner also helped Lily with the thoughtful one-liners that became a trademark of her monology: "There will be sex after death—we just won't be able to feel it. . . . Things are going to get a lot worse before they get worse. . . . Maybe if we listened to it, history would stop repeating itself. . . . If truth is beauty, how come no one has her hair done at the library. . . . Why is it when we talk to God, we're said to be praying, but when God talks to us, we're schizo-

phrenic? . . . If love is the answer, could you re-phrase the question?"

Lily won Emmy awards and Grammy awards for her early comedy and then a Tony when she went to Broadway with *Appearing Nitely*. Her pioneering 1977 one-woman show ignited the dormant "performance artist" genre that seemed to have died years ago with Ruth Draper. New comic characters included a colorfully crazed, battered bag lady and Sister Boogie, the elderly evangelist: "I say think of yourself as a chicken leg and life as Shake 'n Bake!" Audiences and critics were enthralled by Tomlin's ability to magically transform herself into characters, and they were empathic to her as a personality, knowing of her fight to put morality, feminism and humanity into stand-up comedy.

Of her tendency toward psychodrama above one-liners, she said, "Most sketch comedy . . . has no intelligence behind it. I want a glimmer of hope, a little spirit. It's not that I don't want a laugh; I want both—but I'd rather have the spirit."

Bright and hilarious on television, dramatic on stage, Tomlin seemed destined for film stardom as well, but her movie success has been spotty. There was a career-staggering bomb (*Moment by Moment* with look-alike John Travolta) and the disappointing *Incredible Shrinking Woman* balanced against a variety of solid co-starring roles from *The Late Show* to *All of Me*. Lily wasn't interested in *All of Me* at first, but after discussing some script changes with director Carl Reiner, the film became something she could be proud of: "I liked the idea of the male and female in the [same] body and I thought it had a lot of potential for that kind of expression, and then coming together, and the intimacy of it. And the kind of unconditional acceptance of another . . . because you're sharing a physical body. It was the ultimate in intimacy. Unconditional love."

She returned to the stage for her brightest success, *The Search for Signs of Intelligent Life In the Universe*, in collaboration with Jane Wagner. She toured with it all over the country for many years before bringing it to the screen. One reason for its acclaim was, in Wagner's words, its balance of "black humor and sentimentality. . . . It's so easy to be shrewd and mean. I thought we needed something else. We needed something loving. . . . We wanted a reflection, a balance of the absurdity and the realism, and we decided that after all, what is more absurd than real life?"

It affirmed Tomlin as one of the most independent and original women in comedy. As far as Lily is concerned, the audience is taking more of a chance than she: "For people to laugh . . . it's submissive. When people laugh they're vulnerable."

AUDIO: *This Is a Recording* (Polydor), *And That's the Truth* (Polydor), *Modern Scream* (Polydor), *Lily Tomlin on Stage* (Arista)
BIOGRAPHY: *Lily Tomlin* (Sorensen, 1989)
BROADWAY: *Appearing Nitely* (1977), *The Search for Signs of Intelligent Life in the Universe* (1985)
FILMS incl.: *Nashville* (1975), *The Late Show* (1977), *Moment by Moment* (1978), *9 to 5* (1980), *The Incredible Shrinking Woman* (1981), *All of Me* (1984), *Lily Tomlin* (documentary, 1987), *Big Business* (1988), *The Search for Signs of Intelligent Life in the Universe* (1991), *The Player* (1992), *Shadows and Fog* (1992)
TV: "The Garry Moore Show" (1966), "The Music Scene" (1969), "Rowan and Martin's Laugh-In" (1969–73)

## SOPHIE TUCKER

### (Sophia Abuza, January 13, 1884–February 9, 1966)

Along with Mae West, Sophie Tucker was a purveyor of racy songs delivered with a mockingly sophisticated, heavily cadenced delivery. One 1928 tune "He Hadn't Up Till Yesterday But I Guess He Will Tonight," featured Sophie as the comic sexual aggressor. She sang in the chorus: "He may be the slowest man under the sun, but wait till I get him under the moon!"

One big difference between West and Tucker was Sophie's love of schmaltz. She endeared herself to audiences with sentimental ballads such as "My Yiddische Mama." The other big difference was that Sophie was literally big and got stockier over the years, eventually billed as "The Last of the Red Hot Mamas." Despite her girth she sang "I May Be Getting Older Every Day, but Getting Younger Every Night."

Tucker's parents were named Kalish, but when the family left Russia for the United States and detoured through Italy, the name was changed to Abuza to help insure a trouble-free trip. After her birth, the family settled in Hartford, Connecticut. As a teen Sophie married Louis Tuck, giving her a logical stage name. Once she became famous and he merely Mr. Sophie Tucker, the marriage broke up.

Originally a blackface "coon shouter" singing raucous Dixieland tunes, she reached The Palace in 1914 with a collection of boisterous comic numbers. Her tune "Who Paid the Rent for Mrs. Rip Van Winkle When Rip Van Winkle Went Away?" was actually banned in some theaters. She offered a parody of "Bye Bye Blackbird" ("Bye Bye Greenburg") and, into the 1930s when she went from 145 to 200 pounds, "Nobody Loves a Fat Girl."

Sophie's strong personality kept fans coming back year after year. Along with contemporaries Jimmy Durante and Eddie Cantor, she could put over almost any lame tune or lame joke on sheer nerve and verve. Sometimes called the "female Jolson" (she belted out straight hits "Some of These Days" and "After You've Gone" with gusto), by the '50s she was offering mildly racy tunes such as "I'm Living Alone and I Like It." The song suggested that, unlike Mae West, tubby Tucker had to pay for her pleasures: "If I wanna have some fun, if I get bothered and hot, I phone one of those young tall dark handsomes that I've got. So it costs me a twenty or a fifty, so what . . ."

Somewhat of a self-parody in the 1960s, Sophie's act, along with her chubbiness and sweating, were satirized by young comics such as Lenny Bruce. Even the usually tactful Steve Allen, author of the music and lyrics for the 1963 Broadway musical *Sophie*, wrote: "True enough she isn't funny . . . 'Look at me,' she says in effect. 'I'm seven million years old but, by God, I'm still doin' business at the same old stand. I'm the last of the red-hot mammas, so you'd better take a look at me now because I won't be around forever.' " Folks kept looking, right up until the year she died.

AUDIO incl.: *Miff Mole's Molers* (Swaggie), *Cabaret Days* (Mercury), *Spice of Life* (Mercury), *Bigger and Better Than Ever* (Mercury), *Sophie Tucker* (Mercury), *Golden Jubilee* (Mercury), *Last of the Red Hot Mommas* (Columbia), *Sophie Tucker* (Decca), *The Great Sophie Tucker* (Decca), *Her Latest and Greatest Spicy Songs* (Mercury)

AUTOBIOGRAPHY: *Some of These Days*

BROADWAY: *Ziegfeld Follies* (1909), *Shubert Gaities* (1919), *Earl Carroll's Vanities* (1924), *Leave It to Me* (1938), *High Kickers* (1941)

BROADWAY BIOGRAPHY: *Sophie* (1963, Libi Staiger in title role)

FILMS incl.: *Honky Tonk* (1929), *Gay Love* (1934), *Broadway Melody of 1937* (1937), *Thoroughbreds Don't Cry* (1937), *Atlantic City* (1944), *Follow the Boys* (1944), *Sensations of 1945* (1945)

## BEN TURPIN

**(Bernard Turpin, September 17, 1873–July 1, 1940)**

Make a funny face and you might get a laugh once. Or twice. But to have a successful career in comedy, you need a little more than that. Ben Turpin had it. Though his crossed eyes were an instantly identifiable trademark, Turpin was an underrated comedian whose gestures had hilarious comic nuance. He was extremely athletic, able to flip and pratfall with great dexterity. Turpin was particularly proud of his ability to perform a "108," a trade term for a backward somersault from a standing position. Without much coaxing at all, Ben would startle onlookers with his sudden complete turn-around.

Born in New Orleans (and bearing a slight French-Louisiana accent), Ben encountered misfortune early. According to a 1919 *Toledo Times*, "Turpin met with an accident when a boy that affected his eyes. He failed to have them cared for and they grew steadily worse until now Turpin is exactly what his pictures show him to be—cross-eyed."

Ben left home as a teenager and for a time lived a hobo lifestyle. In the 1890s he joined Sam T. Jack's burlesque company in Chicago but had to retire due to problems with his eyesight. He went to Europe to have his condition treated and was well enough to continue in show business. After taking voice lessons but failing to make a dent in the opera world, Ben returned to comedy, as a circus

Ben Turpin, the ultimate silent film funny face. Photo from the author's collection.

clown and vaudevillian. He worked solo and later developed "Happy Hooligan," a sketch with a partner. He played in it for years, ultimately moving to Los Angeles in 1908 to work in films as a prop man, assistant and finally comic actor at Essanay and Sennett studios. Thus began a career in films—as well as an object lesson for parents who pointed to Ben and said, "Don't cross your eyes—they'll freeze like that!" Various stories in newspapers claimed that Ben had indeed suffered that fate. One report insisted Ben's eyes "go that way through his being hit on the head while in vaudeville, and a doctor told him that if he ever got another crack like that it might jar them back into shape."

Turpin co-starred in early Charlie Chaplin comedies such as *The Champion* and *A Night Out*. Before long he was starring in his own short films. He was reportedly not an original thinker and didn't contribute many gags to his comedies, but he knew how to get the most out of a performance.

Ben played a variety of hilarious, cock-eyed optimists, often cast as an unlikely hero or improbable lover. His Valentino send-up, *Shriek of Araby,* remains one of his most memorable efforts. Turpin's interest in comedy may have faded in 1925. His wife, Carrie le Mieux, died that year, after suffering three strokes, the last of paralyzing intensity. They had been married since 1908.

Well invested in real estate, Ben Turpin had his eye on retirement. He made few appearances in the 1930s and '40s, getting laughs in the short subject *Keystone Hotel,* appearing in W. C. Fields' *Million Dollar Legs* as an unlikely cross-eyed spy, singing a few lines in *Show of Shows* and making a farewell cameo in Laurel and Hardy's *Saps at Sea.*

FILMS incl.: *The Champion* (1914), *A Night Out* (1914), *His New Job* (1915), *Caught in the End* (1917), *Two Tough Tenderfeet* (1918), *Uncle Tom Without the Cabin* (1919), *A Small Town Idol* (1921), *The Shriek of Araby* (1923), *Romeo and Juliet* (1924), *Raspberry Romance* (1925), *Hogan's Alley* (1925), *The Eyes Have It* (1928), *Show of Shows* (1929), *Make Me a Star* (1932), *Million Dollar Legs* (1932), *Saps at Sea* (1940), *When Comedy Was King* (1960, compilation), *Days of Thrills and Laughter* (1961, compilation)

VIDEOS incl.: *Ben Turpin Rides Again; Charlie Chase and Ben Turpin; The Eyes of Turpin Are Upon You; Ben Turpin's an Eye for an Eye*

## THE TWO BLACK CROWS (See MORAN and MACK.)

## TRACEY ULLMAN

### (December 30, 1959– )

Though her syndicated television show tended to dwell at the bottom of the ratings, Tracey Ullman had the demographically potent audience—young, hip and trendy—that advertisers wanted to reach. Critics were also kind to Tracey, praising her ability to use a variety of wigs, costumes and accents to satirize a wide range of American womanhood in her "skitcoms," experimental playlets and minimusicals.

The charismatic young British star was initially likened to Carol Burnett for her ability to create realistic characters, but in live performance and on talk shows she was closer to Robin Williams, chattering nonstop, switching voices and dialects at almost unintelligible speeds. "I'm definitely a parrot," she admitted. "It must be irritating for people. If I describe something, I start acting out the whole thing and doing these stupid voices."

Calling her style in comedy "British sarcasm mixed with American optimism," the plucky, precocious Ullman first made waves in the United States as a slightly campy singer of 1960s-style tunes. Her 1984 album *You Broke My Heart in 17 Places* parodied the Connie Francis style of love songs and featured a top-10 hit "They Don't Know," with a video co-starring Paul McCartney. Her ability to embrace the mundane grinningly—only to gnash it with sarcastic overkill—led to her own American television show, even though she was far from a household word at the time. High-profile supporters such as Billy Crystal and Steven Spielberg turned up in guest spots. Tracey had come a long way.

Tracey's Polish-born father died when she was six. Her mother worked at a food testing lab and brought samples home for dinner. At ten, the gift of a Liza Minnelli album inspired Tracey to sing all over the house. At 12 she won a scholarship to the Italia Conti Stage School, but by 16 the cheeky lass was expelled and out making a living. "I wanted to have a good time and make some money. Great pressure is put on kids who don't have dads to get out and make money, and make life easier for everybody. It was always 'Hurry up, grow up, make money, there's no man to do it for us.' " She worked as a chorus girl in Berlin. One night she got unexpected cheers from the audience: "I'd forgotten to put on my knickers."

Back in England, she appeared in *The Rocky Horror Show,* a BBC soap called "MacKenzie" and won a London Theater Critics Award in 1981 for *Four in a Million.* She said, "I knew I wasn't a real pretty girl, but I hoped I made up for it in personality." She did. Two television shows followed, "Kick Up the Eighties" and the successful "Three of a Kind," a British variant on "Saturday Night Live" co-starring England's version of Eddie Murphy, Lenny Henry. Married to a millionaire producer in Britain,

Allen McKeown, Tracey took time off in 1986 to have her first child, Mabel.

"The Tracey Ullman Show" premiered in the United States in 1987, and she won a Golden Globe in 1988. In 1989 her show beat out David Letterman and "Saturday Night Live" at the Emmy awards, the first Fox network show to be honored. The logical move to films didn't pan out immediately. Her 1990 black comedy *I Love You to Death* suffered from miscasting and a creaky plot. The *New York Post* called Ullman "astoundingly miscast . . . drably straight . . . drudgily unattractive."

In 1991 she starred in a one-woman show portraying the mother of Beverly Aadland (the teen who had a scandalous affair with Erroll Flynn). While Broadway critics generally felt Ullman's work demonstrated flashy mimicry and caricature without depth, her peers disagreed. On opening night actress Glenn Close proclaimed, "I think she's one of the most gifted people around."

Though the perky, sardonic star hadn't made the big film splash expected after her television show, she planned to stay in Hollywood for more films and television: "I love California. Who wouldn't? And there's so many Brits here anyway!" Though her realistic sitcom roles seemed to win her an enthusiastic female following, she admitted, "I don't have much respect for other women and much prefer men. Men don't gossip or get catty, and most of my friends are men."

BROADWAY: *The Big Love* (1991)

FILMS incl.: *Give My Regards to Broad Street* (1984), *Plenty* (1985), *Jumpin' Jack Flash* (1986), *I Love You to Death* (1990)

TV: "The Tracey Ullman Show" (1987–90)

# V

## VIVIAN VANCE

### (Vivian Roberta Jones, July 26, 1912–August 17, 1979)

Forever "Ethel Mertz," the slightly frumpy and always cautious sidekick to Lucille Ball on television's "I Love Lucy," Vivian Vance initially didn't want the role. In fact, her career nearly ended in shambles years before the two ladies even met.

Born in Cherryvale, Kansas (some sources say 1903 or 1907), Vivian grew up in Independence, Kansas and blossomed in Albuquerque, New Mexico where she became the star at the local Albuquerque Little Theater. She went to New York thanks to money raised by local supporters and managed to get a job in the Broadway musical *Music in the Air*. She understudied for Ethel Merman in *Anything Goes* in 1934, and when star Kay Thompson left *Hooray for What!* just before opening night, understudy Vivian Vance saved the day.

Her triumph in the 1937 production seemed the start of good fortune, but in 1945, while touring in *The Voice of the Turtle*, her world collapsed. The show was in Chicago at the time. "One day," she recalled, "I was up and around, the next I was lying in bed in my hotel room, my hands shaking helplessly, in a state of violent nausea, weeping hysterically from causes I didn't know."

A few more of these attacks, and she was forced to quit the show. Diagnosis: a nervous breakdown.

She retired from the stage. For two years she didn't do much of anything. Then she began therapy. In 1949 she and her husband, actor Philip Ober, moved to Albuquerque where she started to work again. She even dared to appear in another production of the ill-fated *Voice of the Turtle*.

Meanwhile, in Hollywood, director Marc Daniels was trying to help Lucille Ball and Desi Arnaz find a television wife for William Frawley on "I Love Lucy." He suggested Vivian Vance, a complete unknown. When *The Voice of the Turtle* came to San Diego, Daniels persuaded Arnaz to see the show. Before the play was over, Arnaz knew he'd found Ethel Mertz. When offered the part, Vance turned it down. She had her eye on movies—why should she bother with television?

Once Vivian changed her mind and joined the show, Lucy insisted that her co-star keep at least ten extra pounds of flab on her frame. Though miffed at having to remain chubbier and dowdier than her glamorous co-star, Vance became a true friend of Lucy's off screen and on. An underrated comic talent, Viv worked best as a reaction comedienne, getting giggles from her timerous or horrified reactions to Lucy's ridiculous schemes. Usually coerced into participation, her frowning, uncertain "welllll . . ." was a well-known catch phrase among fans.

"I Love Lucy" lasted for six years. The show ended not only Lucy and Desi's marriage but Vivian's as well. She and Ober divorced in 1959 and she married a literary agent, John Dodds. She lived with him in Connecticut but became bicoastal when she was asked to co-star in Lucy's new show. At least this time she got to use her real first name, as Lucy did. She was "Vivian Bagley" to "Lucy Carmichael." Gradually tiring of her dual life, Vance retired. She lectured at colleges, wrote her autobiography (but then decided against publishing it, valuing her privacy) and rarely went back to sitcoms. A special appearance on the sitcom "Rhoda" was one of her few exceptions.

BROADWAY: *Anything Goes* (1934), *Red Hot and Blue* (1936), *Hooray for What!* (1937), *Skylark* (1939), *Out from Under* (1940), *Let's Face It* (1941), *It Takes Two* (1947), *The Cradle Will Rock* (1947), *My Daughter, Your Son* (1969)

FILMS incl.: *Secret Fury* (1950), *The Blue Veil* (1951), *The Great Race* (1965), *Getting Away from It All* (1972), *The Great Houdini* (1976)

TV: "I Love Lucy" (1951–57), "The Lucy-Desi Comedy Hour" (1957–60), "The Lucy Show" (1962–65)

Dick Van Dyke has it all: wit, charm and grace in taking a fall. Here he is seen in a promotional still from *Mary Poppins.* Photo courtesy of Walt Disney Productions.

# DICK VAN DYKE

### (December 13, 1925–   )

"He's one of the very, very few comedians around who knows how to use his body for real comedy," said Stan Laurel. Tall, lean, rubber-bodied Dick Van Dyke differed greatly from other 1960s masters of the pratfall, Jerry Lewis and Red Skelton. Van Dyke had the average man's sensibilities and reactions. When he tripped over the ottoman (as he did for several seasons in the opening credits of "The Dick Van Dyke Show"), he was every man who was ever embarrassed by his own bumbling. He was believable as a pleasant, nice-looking, average suburbanite; his particular brand of comedy, which included a slight nervous stutter and physical awkwardness in moments of stress, made him the quintessential sitcom star.

Van Dyke got into situations that were comical. Lewis and Skelton made comedy out of situations, even if they had to mug, mime and throw themselves around the room to do it. Realism was a key to "The Dick Van Dyke Show." As creator, pro-

ducer, and frequent writer, Carl Reiner noted, the part of Rob Petrie "required a performer who doesn't want to get up in front of an audience, but who can perform in a room at a party."

"The Dick Van Dyke Show" was a landmark television program, often called the first "adult sitcom." It did away with a lot of the artficiality of sitcom slapstick (the "I Love Lucy" variety) and the "homey" pretense and cutesy antics of the "Ozzie and Harriet" school. The stories involving Van Dyke as comedy writer Rob Petrie, both at the office and in suburbia, were intelligent and believable, from domestic scenes of recognition humor (Rob convinced he's losing his hair) to the comedy of embarrassment (his paranoia over believing the hospital switched babies on him), to shows about comedy as an art form itself (an office demonstration of why slapstick comedy is no longer funny).

Van Dyke's genius was in his ability to update slapstick and make it believable. His visual comedy was subtle, whether in capturing the nuances of everyday misery (trying to watch television in bed without a pillow to support his head) or in creating wild visual humor using the smallest gestures (as in an episode where he is bandaged from a ski accident and can barely walk).

Born in West Plains, Missouri, Van Dyke got his start in a mime act, The Merry Mutes, a group that lip-synched to records. In 1953 he began working for a local television station in Atlanta, ultimately moving to New York as host of a 1956 cartoon show. He appeared on "The Andy Williams Summer Show" in 1958, turned up on quiz programs and "The Ed Sullivan Show," and won a Tony Award for his role as the comic, romantic lead in the hit Broadway musical *Bye Bye Birdie*.

Carl Reiner had starred in a pilot episode of a series about a comedy writer, but when it came time to actually produce the show the choice came down to two men—Van Dyke and a quiz show host named Johnny Carson. Van Dyke won out and earned Emmy awards for his show in 1964, 1965 and 1966. He decided to quit the show while it was still on top (in itself, a precedent-setting event), but his first films, such as *Mary Poppins,* were mild and family oriented and considered disappointingly "safe." After all, here was a man who facially resembled Stan Laurel and moved with a bit of Chaplin's grace. Ironically, when he made a film that tried to make use of his talents in slapstick and depth as an actor, *The Comic,* it failed at the box office. Another role, as a suspiciously motivated preacher in the cynical, satiric *Cold Turkey,* was too unsympathetic to help his career. Though now considered a minor classic, at the time the film was not well received and critics were again frank in their impatience for Van Dyke to become either a new Stan Laurel or at least another handsome comic hero like Jack Lemmon.

Van Dyke tried a comeback on television but his new show was not the big success his early sitcom was. Fans seemed to love him only as Rob Petrie and were unhappy seeing him with a new name, new profession and new sitcom family. The show managed to stay on the air for a respectable amount of time but did nothing to enhance Van Dyke's standing as a major comic talent. Dick's struggles professionally were nothing compared to the battle he waged with alcoholism. He went into therapy and came out with *The Morning After,* a powerful television drama about drinking.

Dick tried a song-and-dance variety show, but as Bill Cosby, Mary Tyler Moore, Julie Andrews and many others discovered, that particular form of entertainment had died out with Ed Sullivan. The show won him an Emmy, but not much respect in an industry that seemed to think his best years were behind him. One project, a sitcom called "Harry's Battles," didn't even get past the pilot. Van Dyke turned up as a semiregular on "The Carol Burnett Show," proving that he was indeed a durable, reliable veteran.

Into the 1980s Dick once again starred in a sitcom blend of sight gags and one-liners, but there weren't many laughs when the aging star bent his body into pretzel positions or flopped from his grandson's bunk bed. His white hair made audiences worry for him. Unlike Jerry Lewis and Red Skelton, still pratfalling after so many years, Van Dyke's character was too realistic (and now too middle-aged) to take such comic abuse. He was also expected to act his age; he couldn't be the comically embarrassed, flustery Rob Petrie. Audiences expected him to be a little more sensible. Without his main comic tools— the mobile body and sympathetic moments of indecision—Van Dyke had to come up with something different, and that took more time than impatient networks were now alloting to new shows. Ironically, the original "Dick Van Dyke Show" almost was canceled in its first season, but was allowed to continue and find its own rhythm and style.

Fortunately, Dick Van Dyke has always managed to find a part to rekindle interest in him (such as the Emmy Award–winning *The Wrong Way Kid* and a very amusing television movie, *Found Money,* with Sid Caesar). He was chosen, "against type," to play a straight role in *Dick Tracy,* which was very helpful exposure and has led to more dramatic roles, including a crime-solving doctor in a series of TV films. Like his co-star Mary Tyler Moore, who had a sitcom hit and then suffered through "great expectations" in subsequent tries, Van Dyke spent many long years looking for good roles that would if not do justice to his talents, at least keep up with them.

BOOKS: *Alter Egos* (1967), *Those Funny Kids* (1976)
BROADWAY incl.: *The Girls Against the Boys* (1959), *Bye Bye Birdie* (1960)

FILMS incl.: *Bye Bye Birdie* (1963), *What a Way to Go* (1964), *Mary Poppins* (1964), *The Art of Love* (1965), *Lt. Robinson Crusoe* (1965), *Never a Dull Moment* (1967), *Divorce American Style* (1967), *Fitzwilly* (1967), *Chitty Chitty Bang Bang* (1968), *Some Kind of a Nut* (1969), *The Comic* (1969), *Cold Turkey* *(1971)*, *The Morning After* (1974), *The Runner Stumbles* (1979), *The Country Girl* (1982), *Found Money* (1983), *The Wrong Way Kid* (1984), *Ghost of a Chance* (1987), *Dick Tracy* (1990), *Diagnosis of Murder* (1992)

TV: "CBS Cartoon Theatre" (1956), "The Chevy Showroom" (1958), "Pantomime Quiz" (1958–59), "Laugh Line" (1956), "The Dick Van Dyke Show" (1961–66), "The New Dick Van Dyke Show" (1971–74), "Van Dyke and Company" (1976), "The Carol Burnett Show" (1977), "The Dick Van Dyke Show" (1988)

# JERRY VAN DYKE

## (July 27, 1931–   )

Jerry Van Dyke has always been known as a pleasant, cheerful performer; remarkable considering how many years he had to put up with comparisons to his older brother Dick and kidding over his legendary sitcom bomb, "My Mother the Car."

Born in Danville, Illinois, Jerry had his own talk show in Terre Haute, Indiana before putting together a nightclub act of light patter and banjo playing. Back in the late 1950s, with vaudeville still fondly remembered and folk music the rage, audiences actually stayed in their seats when someone walked on stage carrying a banjo. At least they did for Jerry, a clean-cut, crew-cutted young fellow with a shy grin and an easygoing personality.

The sunny, gentle Jerry might have made a fine Gilligan on television's "Gilligan's Island." He was up for the part along with Carroll O'Connor as the Skipper, but instead he ended up in "Picture This," a mediocre summer replacement game show. His next assignment was to play second banana to Judy Garland on her variety series. The show was a notorious debacle for the star, and for Jerry, who was written insult jokes completely out of character. "What's an old lady like you doing on television?"

Jerry jested. Before long both he and the old lady were off television.

Jerry's best early exposure was on his brother's series. In a memorable two-part episode he played Rob's eccentric brother, a mild-mannered nerd until he falls asleep. Then he "sleepwalks" and turns into a wild, banjo-playing life of the party who calls everyone "Berford." Jerry's nightclub act at the time was similar to the joking and playing on the show. He came across as an affable younger version of Dick, one with sitcom star potential.

Jerry's first starring sitcom was "My Mother the Car." Even though previous years had seen talking horses, babies and basset hounds in sitcoms—as well as shows about lovable ghosts—critics seemed to think it was time to take a stand. The concept of a man's mother reincarnated into a talking auto was just too much!

"My Mother the Car" was no worse than the lovable silly "Gilligan's Island" in its plot and jokes (a typical episode had Mom the car "drunk" on antifreeze and careening along the highway). It had a good supporting cast (Avery Schreiber as a comically villainous car collector and the voice of Ann Sothern as Jerry's mother, now a 1928 Porter auto). Still, despite lasting a full year, the show folded and became a convenient target for any critic lamenting the state of modern television.

Initially Jerry had no trouble landing a new show, but "Accidental Family" was a harmless, sappy little family comedy that went the way of most other harmless, sappy little family comedies. Unfortunately, it tagged Van Dyke as a two-time loser.

In the 1970s he was a two-time loser again, having the bad luck of starting and ending the decade with short-lived television shows. Jerry spent more time working clubs and summer theaters. Like his brother, he seemed to have an increasingly hard time reaching his potential. There was never any doubt that Jerry had a marketable personality, similar to his brother, but perhaps with more of the mild, slightly goofy likability of Tommy Smothers.

Eventually—a very long eventually—Jerry found a successful comedy character for himself. He became Luther, an assistant to Craig Nelson on "Coach," a top-10 sitcom about antics at Minnesota State College. It brought him his best notices in years, his first Emmy nomination and his first brush with controversy. Since he played a football coach, he was asked to make a prediction on a Cleveland Browns football game on ABC's "Monday Night Football." He announced that the Browns had to lose no matter what happened; even if they won, they'd have to return to Cleveland! Citizens of Cleveland protested and Van Dyke apologized during a subsequent football broadcast. He insisted, "I love the town." Then he was asked about an upcoming Browns game. Would they win? Van Dyke answered, "Not Cleveland. They haven't got a shot!"

In his spare time a "gentleman rancher" on a 500-acre farm in Arkansas, he appraises his success late in life with an ironic smile. "It couldn't be much later—this is as late as it gets!" Van Dyke continues to appear in dinner theater, and in 1990 brought his "Red Hot and Rowdy Revue" to the casinos of Atlantic City. It features his banjo playing and clowning. "I have never been one of those guys you laugh with," the affable star admitted. "I don't tell these great stories with wonderful endings or hot one-liners that bring down the house. I'm a guy you can laugh at. I act silly and talk silly and I think the key to it all is that I kind of stir up a good feeling in people in the club. I put them at ease, give them a night of easy laughs. I like doing that. This is, I think, what a comic's job is."

FILMS incl.: *The Courtship of Eddie's Father* (1963), *Palm Springs Weekend* (1963), *Love and Kisses* (1965), *Angel in My Pocket* (1969), *Run If You Can* (1987)
TV: "Picture This" (1963), "The Judy Garland Show" (1963), "My Mother the Car" (1965–66), "Accidental Family" (1967–68), "The Headmaster" (1970–71), "13 Queens Boulevard" (1979), "Coach" (1989–   )

## JACKIE VERNON

### (Ralph Verrone, 1928–November 10, 1987)

He didn't look sad—he looked dilapidated, like a broken-down car left at the dump. The ultimate sad sack of stand-up comedy, Jackie Vernon deadpanned his jokes in a mournful, hollow tenor voice, his eyes glazed, his body immobile. He was so far gone that he could see only the negative in any

situation: "The meek shall inherit the Earth—they won't have the nerve to refuse it."

Vernon grew up in East Harlem and the Bronx, New York and attended Theodore Roosevelt High School. After serving in the air force, he played trumpet in a band called The Looney Lunatics. In 1955 he went out on his own as a comic. "Well, in the beginning I was doing a different kind of comedy. I was doing what I thought was funny—running around, making a lot of noise. I sang a Jolson song, played the trumpet, did all these real quick impressions. It didn't suit me. And I found out later just standing there, staying in a character, maybe a little more of an extension of the way I really was, worked for me."

He charted his success: "After groping for years, not knowing what I was doing, just memorizing a bunch of jokes, I found I was getting nowhere." He stayed nowhere for a long time. Watching him make the rounds of cheap nightclubs, his wife dubbed him "the Willy Loman of comedy."

At the turn of the 1960s Vernon experimented with offbeat material in keeping with sick comedy trends of the day. "I got a strange gift—a bowling ball with a thumb in it." Asked by the author to recall one of his first gags, he noted this one: "I used to be an atheist, but I gave it up. No holidays." He paused and said softly, "That was mine. Milton Berle started using it, everyone . . . since then everybody's used it." What Berle didn't have that Jackie developed to perfection was a deadpan style, one often too subtle for the harsh booze 'n' broads atmosphere of the local nightclubs. "My grandfather had to leave the West because he broke the code of the West. He said a discouraging word."

With the help of comedy writer Danny Davis, Vernon honed his loser comedy character. He played on his pathetic look on stage. "If you don't like me, how about a nice hand for the suit?" Dubbed "Mr. Excitement" by Johnny Carson, Vernon ultimately created entire routines based on his sorry lifestyle: "A dull guy is a fellow who usually runs away from home when he's 38 . . . if he has a job it's as a piano player in a marching band. A dull guy is a man who buys a painting of Lady Godiva because he likes horses."

He described his "dull man" persona as incorporating "a look of innocence" and "controlled bewilderment. I get bewildered at things that happen in life. So the attitude is what sells me more than anything, the voice and the attitude."

Lenny Bruce was a friend of Jackie's, and Jackie still remembers Lenny's advice to him. "He said, 'Never lose your attitude.' Don't deceive the audience. Once they don't believe you any more, you're finished. They want to see you a certain way, so that's the way you should stay." Vernon never veered out of character in his act, never hinted that he was anything but the sad and sorry dull man. The only variation in his act was his penchant for offbeat material. A trademark was his imaginary vacation "slide show," using a hand-held clicker to imitate the sound of the machine as he pointed to an imaginary screen in back of him. "Here I am in Alaska. It's cold up there. All you see are dogs stuck to trees." Usually he brought along his inept guide, "Guido," forever a victim of bizarre accidents. Another classic surreal routine had him so lonely he made a watermelon his pet. He also favored odd routines on losers in history, such as Ponce de Leon. It ended this way: "Ponce de Leon left Spain in 1541, to search for the Fountain of Youth. And last week he died in Miami, still searching. You might say he ended his life by dying . . . I miss you, Ponce."

In real life, Vernon was pretty similar to his character, a mild mannered type. Asked if he had any hobbies, anything that was different from how the public perceived him, he said softly, "No. I don't have any real hobbies. Once in a while I like to take a camera out and shoot pictures. I don't really have any hobbies, come to think of it. I work, and when I'm not working, I just stay home."

Vernon got a lot of mileage out of his dull loser character and the depressed irony of his catch phrase, "Hello again, fun seekers." Unfortunately, Vernon was so utterly passive and his humor so subtle that he was easily upstaged by another loser comic, Rodney Dangerfield. While Jackie Vernon was swallowing his pride and biting his lip in shyness, Rodney spat out his frustration and railed against his lack of respect.

Vernon influenced several comedians, including Steven Wright, but by the late 1970s he faded out of the limelight. He had nothing to fight back with.

The dull man persona, he admitted, was accurate. He quietly went on his way, touring clubs and playing the resorts, actually modifying his passive show by inserting some risqué material and familiar, "sure-fire" comic material. He said in 1986, "I maintain the same attitude but I'm working a bit more commercial. Because you can't do that way off-the-wall stuff for the common denominator audience. So it's working okay, it works fine in Vegas."

On stage he was "just being myself—or an extension of myself—"the kind of guy you feel sorry for." In the 1980s his best national success was behind the scenes, doing commercials for Bud Lite and the voice for "Frosty the Snowman." The Christmas cartoon special has now become a perennial. Each year audiences are touched again by the sweet sorrow that was Jackie Vernon.

AUDIO: *A Wet Bird Never Flies at Night* (Jubilee), *A Night in New York* (Ethicon), *A Man and His Watermelon* (United Artists), *The Day the Rocking Horse Died* (United Artists), *Sex Is Not Hazardous to Your Health* (Beverly Hills), *Frosty's Winter Wonderland* (Disneyland)
BROADWAY: *At Home at the Palace* (1967)
FILMS incl.: *The Gang That Couldn't Shoot Straight* (1971), *Microwave Massacre* (1979)
VIDEOS: *Hungry i Reunion, Young at Heart Comedians Special, A Toast to Lenny Bruce*

## VIC and SADE

**Victor Gook: Art Van Harvey (Arthur H. van Berschoot), August 23, 1883–July 7, 1957
Sade Gook: Bernardine Flynn, January 2, 1904–March 10, 1977**

"The best American humor of its day," according to poet Edgar Lee Masters, came from Vic and Sade. They were "Radio's Home Folks," living in that "little house halfway up the next block." Each episode was a humdrum, homey slice of Americana. Those who listen to an episode or two today often walk away unsmiling and bored, but regular listeners during the show's heyday got to know each character and enjoyed the show's subtle nuances.

Vic Gook, who worked for the Consolidated Kitchenware Company, was played by Indiana-born ex-advertising executive Art Van Harvey. Sade was Bernardine Flynn, a drama student from the University of Wisconsin. Bill Idelson, who played Skeezix on "Gasoline Alley," played their son Rush. He would later go to television as Herman, Rose Marie's timorous boyfriend on "The Dick Van Dyke Show." Chicago radio announcer Clarence Hartzell, who had played Pappy Yokum on radio's "Li'l Abner," was Uncle Fletcher. Vic and Sade's evocatively named friends included Gumpos the garbageman, Blue-Tooth Johnson, Gus Plink, Robert and Slobbert Hink, Reverend Kidneyslide and Ruthie Stembottom.

No doubt Bob and Ray were influenced by Vic and Sade's style and characters such as Y. Y. Flirtch who worked for the "Ohio State Home for the Bald." Garrison Keillor could easily have found a spot in Lake Wobegon for "The Little Tiny Petite Feathered Pheasant Tea Shoppe." A typical example of the gentle smiles and small talk in Paul Rhymer's scripts, with Uncle Fletcher talking:

"Arnie Gupples give Gwendolyn Yowtch this fancy shoe scraper for her birthday . . . well, sir . . . Gwendolyn went to scrape some mud off her shoes with that shoe scraper, twisted her ankle, had to have the doctor, got mad, an' give Arnie the mitten. Two months afterwards she married Art Hungle and moved to North Dakota. Arnie felt so bad he quit his job at the shoe store. . . . Stuff happens, don't it?"

Vic on vacation: "I go sit in the yard and read the Chicago paper. I play a couple records on the phonograph. I turn on the radio. I don't know what to do with myself. . . . I go chew the rag with Whitey a little while. I come back and sit in the yard. . . . I try to take a nap. I sit in the yard some more. . . . I know that Wednesday's going to be the same as Tuesday, and Thursday's gonna be the same as Wednesday. . . ."

Vic and Sade ran 15 minutes a day, five days a week. Viewers got into the mundane habit of visiting their home folk from 1932 to 1944, and many continue to enjoy the show on disc and tape. A book of scripts, *The Small House Halfway Up the Next Block*,

can help turn any four fans into a quadrangle of Gooks.

AUDIO: *Vic and Sade* (Radiola), *Vic and Sade* (Golden Age), *Vic and Sade* (Mark 56)
BOOK: *The Small House Halfway Up the Next Block* (Rhymer, 1972)

## ABE VIGODA

### (February 24, 1921– )

A grim, Karloffian looking actor, Abe Vigoda spent years on television ("Dark Shadows," "Kojak," etc.) and in crime films (Tessio in *The Godfather*) before turning up on the side of the law as the stoic Phil Fish, an old-time detective on "Barney Miller."

Vigoda had few lines at first but delivered them with a winning blend of deadpan and mocking sarcasm. Before long, the subtle actor stole many scenes. A classic in simplicity was his reaction to office conflict—his weary trudge to the bathroom. A weak bladder, flat feet and consistent tiredness made him a downtrodden character viewers identified with; he accepted each new burden with gentle cynicism and sighing resignation.

"People respond to what's human," said co-star Max Gail. "The [Fish] character is so complete, so human. Things like going to the bathroom or being tired—simple, human things—Abe finds a kind of poetry in them and people connect with it. He's a wonderful actor."

Showing just the right amount of cranky, feisty spirit amid his depressed, pessimistic complaints, weary, weatherbeaten Fish became a comic working-class hero. "Dry humor is something I had as a young boy," said Vigoda. "Because I'm basically a serious person, I try not to take myself too seriously."

In his teens, the serious-looking boy was often cast as an old man in school plays. After attending New York City's Thomas Jefferson High and serving in World War II, he studied acting and appeared in everything from a 1961 Shakespeare in the Park production of *King Richard II* (as John of Gaunt) to *The Last Analysis* in 1965, a show that earned him praise from the *San Francisco Examiner:* "Watching Abe Vigoda work in the lead role is a joy. There's been nobody like it since Groucho Marx, comic acting of that great tradition."

After becoming the surprise hit of "Barney Miller," Vigoda wanted the show retitled "Fish and Barney." Soon after he left to star in his own sitcom. The split from "Barney Miller" was acrimonious and led to a 1977 tangle of mutual lawsuits. The new show "Fish" flopped and was fried. "Barney Miller" was still on the air, but Vigoda was not invited back. Of the "Fish" show, Vigoda complained, "The character shouldn't have been a retired policeman. He should have been more active." Vigoda remained active since, but hasn't yet hooked a comic character quite like Phil Fish.

FILMS incl.: *The Godfather* (1972), *The Godfather Part II* (1974), *The Cheap Detective* (1978), *The Great American Traffic Jam* (1980), *Vasectomy* (1986), *Plain Clothes* (1988), *Look Who's Talking* (1989), *Joe Versus the Volcano* (1990), *Keaton's Cop* (1990)

TV: "Barney Miller" (1975–77), "Fish" (1977–78)

# W

## JIMMIE WALKER

### (June 25, 1949–   )

A six-foot-tall, scrawny string bean with a smile that seemed wider than his head, Jimmie Walker meteorically shot from a chuckling, streetwise stand-up comic to a fad sitcom superstar.

A high school dropout from the South Bronx's Melrose project, Walker realized he wasn't going anywhere without an education. He worked days, studied for his high school diploma at night, then used the government-funded SEEK (Search of Education, Evaluation and Knowledge) program to train as a disc jockey at the RCA Technical Institute. In 1967 he began working at New York radio station WMCA.

He had a tougher time breaking into comedy. Local community center talent shows mostly featured singers, and the struggling comic was often booed. Once he managed to get on as an opener for the pioneer rap/poetry group The Last Poets. Fortunately, he armed himself with tried-and-true material (swiped from old comedy records). In 1967 and 1968 he honed his skills performing with the group.

Walker needed his arrogant, jiving personality to survive the early days. The comic bravado became his trademark. After working the local club scene in the early 1970s, Walker won a guest spot on Jack Paar's short-lived comeback talk show. Shortly after he was chosen for the role of "J. J. Evans" on television's "Good Times." Young viewers immediately identified with his silliness and sass, but many critics felt he was a little *too* ethnic in his comedy.

As J. Fred MacDonald wrote in *Blacks and White TV,* Walker was "the coon character, that rascalish, loud, pushing and conniving stereotype." His shouting catch phrase, on the lips of thousands of adolescents in the country, was an irritating "Dyn-o-miiiite!" His bright-eyed, wide-mouthed face appeared on T-shirts and school notebooks as well as on a quickly made comedy album.

In 1991 Walker looked back and insisted that the troubles on his television show were mostly "jealousy." He wasn't billed as the star but he'd become the undeniable favorite. Others in the cast simply felt that the more scripts catered to the broad humor of "J. J. Evans," the more offensive it became. Co-star Esther Rolle huffed, "He's 18 and he doesn't work. He can't read or write. He doesn't think."

The fever pitch of his fad success didn't last. Viewers no longer were laughing at the mere sight of the funny-looking street kid. The comical swaggerer who once got laughs from nonjoke references to himself ("I'm the Black Prince!") now had to earn every giggle. Amid walkouts and bickering by cast members, "Good Times" hit bad times and was canceled.

In an early film appearance (the Bill Cosby hit *Let's Do It Again*), Walker was excellent as a ridiculously scrawny boxer who somehow possesses a knockout punch. Unfortunately, the one-joke of Walker's gruesomely funny physical appearance couldn't sustain interest. He made a few more movies and sitcoms, none particularly successful. He maintained his career in comedy clubs, but rarely had jokes as strong as his personality.

In the late 1980s Walker staged a minicomeback co-starring with Dom DeLuise in the harmless kiddie safari film *Going Bananas*. He landed the lead in the syndicated "Bustin' Loose" television show, based on the Richard Pryor movie. He still swaggered into nightclubs from time to time but was working in the shadow of newer models of youthful black bravado including Chris Rock of "Saturday Night Live." For fans who still enjoyed his personality, Jimmie Walker never grew up. In 1990 he was still offering the same kind of corny racial humor he used nearly two decades earlier. On "Hollywood Squares" he was asked, "How many calories in a chocolate kiss?" Walker's answer: "It depends on the chocolate person you're kissing!"

AUDIO: *Dynomite!* (Buddah)

FILMS incl.: *Let's Do It Again* (1975), *The Greatest Thing That Almost Happened* (1977), *Rabbit Test* (1978), *Concorde: Airport 79* (1979), *Murder Can Hurt You* (1980), *The Jerk, Too* (1984), *Going Bananas* (1987)

TV: "Good Times" (1974–79), "B.A.D. Cats" (1980), "At Ease" (1983), "Bustin' Loose" (1987–89)

VIDEOS incl.: *NBA/Comic Relief: The Great Blooper Caper*

# NANCY WALKER

## (Anna Myrtle Swoyer, May 10, 1921–March 25, 1992)

Nancy Walker wanted to be a serious singer; but when she sang for Broadway impresario George Abbott, he laughed instead. Then he signed her up for *Best Foot Forward* and she became a comedy star. At first compared to Bea Lillie and Fanny Brice, the little (four-foot-eleven) lady later earned praise for her own stylish approach to playing no-nonsense

Jewish mothers, man-hungry wallflowers and a variety of eccentric maids.

Born in Philadelphia, Nancy traveled with her vaudevillian parents all across the country. Her acrobat father changed his name to Dewey Barto when he joined The Three Bartos and later was half of a comedy team, Barto and Mann. Nancy didn't envision a comedy career, but after her "funny girl" role in *Best Foot Forward*, she played the cab driver in *On the Town*, starred in Max Schulman's *Barefoot Boy with Cheek* and had a musical written for her, *Look Ma, I'm Dancing*. Brooks Atkinson in the New York Times called her "the best slapstick comedienne of her generation."

Despite the praise, she admitted, "It took me about seven years to adjust to my stage personality. I was uncomfortable being funny. People expected me to be 'on' and I wasn't. I never am. But I kept at it, and learned to do comedy well." One of her most popular (and deceptively easy-looking) roles in films, was as the mute maid in *Murder by Death*. The comedy was all in Nancy's long-suffering shrugs and subtle expressions of anguish.

On television, Walker's first major exposure came in 1955 on "The Buick-Berle Show." She became familiar to viewers as Mildred, the wisecracking maid on "McMillan and Wife" (earning three Emmy nominations), and then made memorable appearances as Ida Morgenstern, the good-hearted, concerned but slightly pushy mother on "Rhoda." Her light touch in playing working-class people earned her a different kind of fame in television commercials. As "Rosie," the coffeeshop waitress, she spent over a decade dutifully cleaning up spills with Bounty paper towels, the "quicker picker upper!"

A key supporting comedienne, Walker wasn't quite able to make the jump to solo star on television. Her "Nancy Walker Show" and "Blansky's Beauties" shows were failures. A television movie, *Human Feelings*, nearly became a series, but was turned down. A switch on the movie *Oh God*, Nancy Walker played God, with Billy Crystal as her favorite angel. Walker also slipped behind the camera to direct the movie musical *Can't Stop the Music*, which featured a briefly popular, campy disco group, The Village People. It was yet another disaster for the plucky comedienne.

A quick "picker upper" herself, Walker picked up her career in the 1980s co-starring with Eve

Arden in a dinner theater production of *The Odd Couple*. She resumed her identity as a salty, disapproving mother with "True Colors," a sitcom about an interracial marriage. Though suffering from lung cancer, she completed a full season of shows before her death. Valerie Harper said at the time, "She was as good as it gets. She was unique, absolutely unique."

BROADWAY: *Best Foot Forward* (1941), *On the Town* (1944), *Barefoot Boy with Cheek* (1947), *Look Ma, I'm Dancin'* (1948), *Along Fifth Avenue* (1949), *Phoenix '55* (1955), *Fallen Angels* (1956), *Wonderful Town* (1958), *The Girls Against the Boys* (1959), *Do Re Mi* (1960), *The Cherry Orchard* (1968), *The Cocktail Party* (1968)
FILMS incl.: *Stand Up and Be Counted* (1972), *The World's Greatest Athlete* (1973), *Forty Carats* (1973), *Murder by Death* (1976), *Human Feelings* (1978)
TV: "Family Affair" (1970–76), "McMillan and Wife" (1971–76), "Rhoda" (1974–78), "The Nancy Walker Show" (1976), "Blansky's Beauties" (1977), "True Colors" (1990–92)

## MARCIA WARFIELD

### (March 5, 1955–  )

In stand-up, stocky five-foot-eleven Marcia Warfield is a toughie with a hard edge. "How can you sleep with Prince?" she asked. "He's so little. I guess you sort of grab him by his feet and use his whole body as a vibrator." She brought the same no-nonsense attitude to her role as the bailiff on the television sitcom "Night Court."

She had to be tough to climb out of The Pickle Barrel, the Chicago nightclub where she got her start. Marcia was born in Chicago, where her mother was a phone operator. Her stepfather worked for the Chicago Public Library. After graduating from Calumet High, she went to work for the phone company, got married and settled down. Then she was divorced at 20.

Her fortunes changed the night she opened at The Pickle Barrel with the shock laugh line, "I'm a virgin." Before long she was signed to Laff Records for an album by that title and won a comedy competition in San Francisco in 1979. She was one of the few black women in comedy, but looking back, she was too busy trying to make it to really care.

She recalled, "I had no idea I was one of the few black women doing comedy. That never entered my mind. Being black was not a reason, or being female was not a reason to do comedy. I don't think it is today. You have the funny bone, you have the desire to do that or you don't. I think if you tried to say, 'There are no crippled Puerto Rican comics' and you tried to make a crippled Puerto Rican comic it wouldn't work. There has to be a person who wants to do that. And then you find out later you're filling some sort of void."

Warfield has had to tone down her risqué act for national television but still has plenty of material. "I hate skinny women, especially when they say things like 'Sometimes I forget to eat.' Now, I've forgotten my mother's maiden name, and my keys, but you've got to be a special kind of stupid to forget to eat."

She was doing stand-up when she caught the attention of the "Night Court" staff. Reinhold Weege, who had previously worked on "Barney Miller," liked one of her lines: "There's absolutely no ladylike way to eat a hot dog." She got the job, replacing the late Florence Halop, who in turn had replaced Selma Diamond. Both were older women. Because of her youth and size, as well as black streetwise presence, Warfield offered a different type of tough bailiff. She was a standout on the show and parlayed it into her own series.

On March 26, 1990 she premiered her morning talk show on NBC. She intended to keep things amusing. "I want to celebrate the positive; if you want pain, go to the afternoon shows." Though she put on a tough-lady act, fans knew there was another side to Marcia. She admitted, "Performing is asking people you don't know to give you a hug—and it's devastating if they don't like you."

FILMS incl.: *Mask* (1985), *D.C. Cab* (1983), *Whoopee Boys* (1986), *Caddy-Shack II* (1988)
TV: "The Richard Pryor Show" (1977), "Night Court" (1986–  ), "The Marcia Warfield Show" (1990–  )
VIDEOS: *Laughing Room Only; Tommy Chong Roast*

## RUSTY WARREN

### (Ilene F. Goldman, March 20, 1930–  )

Billed as "The Knockers Up Gal," risqué comedienne Rusty Warren is best known for her "knockers-up" shock comedy routine, in which to a marching song she railed at the giggling women in her audience to stand up and dance:

"Knockers up! Knockers up! Ladies get your knockers up! Come on girls, throw those shoulders back! Get those shoulders back, get those knockers up! Now doesn't that make your navel tingle? Throw your knockers up and out! Up two three four, up two three four, up, up, up, up! There we go! Ladies, get up and march through the room, knockers high! Are you ready to commence the march of the knockers? Ladies! March! Ladies? You're not marching . . ."

Warren made most of her albums in the repressed late 1950s and early '60s, each disc loaded with corny party tunes and energetic ranting: "What's the favorite word of the men? Sex! All the girls in the audience who really like sex, holler *I like sex!*" What made her different from Belle Barth and Pearl Williams was her audience participation style, observational humor and a tendency to talk more to and for the women in the audience than the men. "Am I right, girls? After 15 years of marriage you're lucky to get it! And when you do it's a present. He brought it all the way home from the office for you! On the bus! Under his hat!"

In 1959 *Variety* was unamused: "Her approach," a reviewer wrote, "is as direct as a sidewalk-hawker's bark, her repartee a monument to the lack of innuendo." Even so, she issued a string of albums, beginning with that year's *Songs for Sinners* and followed by 1960's *Knockers Up.*

Born in New York, raised in Milton, Massachusetts (a suburb of Boston), Rusty got her last name "from the corner of the street where I lived in." She characterized herself back then as "open, brash and loud." These traits would become a part of her comic persona, but she wasn't complaining. She also knew she was a "forceful, aggressive and efficient business woman," and pointed out that she owned the rights to all her recordings and successfully formed a corporation to handle everything from the manufacture of novelty gifts to real estate and industrial investments.

Rusty studied piano at the New England Conservatory of Music, graduating with a Bachelor of Arts degree. She once played in a concert with Arthur Fiedler. Around 1954 she switched from

singing and playing piano in clubs to performing risqué stand-up and songs. She claimed to have sold over 8 million party albums and earned seven gold records, but these figures come from NARM (The National Association of Record Merchandisers). It is the RIAA (The Record Industry Auditors of America) that certifies sales and issues world-recognized gold and platinum albums.

Rusty, the most attractive of the risqué comediennes, continued to issue albums, many with eye-catching covers, right through the 1970s. In 1978 she received a Woman of the Year Humanitarian Award from the Massachusetts House of Representatives and into the 1980s was on the board of directors of Project Prevention, a group that used live plays produced for schools to educate children on drug and alcohol abuse.

Warren performed on the Playboy cable channel and produced a video in 1988, *Rusty Warren . . . Does It Again* live at the Celebrity Theater in Phoenix. She sometimes appeared on the same bill with the new generation of shock comics but was appalled at what she heard. She always said, "I hold up a mirror for people to see themselves as they are. I don't do warped stuff. I don't do vulgarity."

Based in Arizona, she continues to tour and to offer comic "lectures" for civic groups, turning down or turning up the heat, depending on the crowd. She always had the women in the audience applauding when she delivered this observation: "Women enjoy sex more than men. And if you don't believe it, put your little finger in your ear. Wiggle it around. Now which feels better, your finger or your ear?"

AUDIO: *Songs for Sinners* (Jubilee), *Knockers Up* (Jubilee), *Banned in Boston* (Jubilee), *Rusty Bounces Back* (Jubilee), *In Orbit* (Jubilee), *Portrait on Life* (Jubilee), *Sex X Ponent* (Jubilee), *Sinsational* (Jubilee), *More Knockers Up* (Jubilee), *Bottoms Up* (Jubilee), *Look What I've Got for You* (compilation, Jubilee), *Knockers Up '76* (GNP Crescendo), *Sexplosion* (GNP Crescendo), *Lays It on the Line* (GNP Crescendo), *Knockers Up/Songs for Sinners* (reissue, GNP Crescendo), *Bounces Back/Sinsational* (reissue, GNP Crescendo)

VIDEO: *Rusty Warren Does It Again!*

## WAYNE and SCHUSTER

**Johnny Wayne, May 28, 1918–July 18, 1990**
**Frank Shuster, September 5, 1916–**

In the late 1950's and through the '60s, "The Ed Sullivan Show" was America's favorite television variety series and Wayne and Shuster were Ed's favorite comedy team. He had them on his show 67 times—a record no act ever came close to topping.

Another amazing record was the team's longevity. They starred on radio in Canada and, when television arrived there, the duo starred in at least one new comedy special each year. While a few teams were technically "together" longer, however inactive they might be, Wayne and Shuster were consistently in front of an audience for nearly 50 years.

The Toronto-born comedians made their radio debut in 1941. In the late 1940s and early '50s they began to make appearances on American television, from "The Dinah Shore Show" to "The Ed Sullivan Show." Their style was vaudevillian, presenting old-fashioned comedy sketches and parodies. Their best-known routines were "Rinse the Blood Off My Toga" (a parody of *Julius Caesar*) and "Shakespearian Baseball." It was silly and harmless stuff.

"One more time at bat do we have to win the game. Who's next . . . see how the valiant Yogi stands at the plate." "But soft, here is the windup. Here is the pitch!" "Oooh!" "The ball did strike his head. The pitcher bean-ed him! He staggers from the plate and rolls his eyes. . . . Oh, his noggin hath taken a floggin' . . . concussion thou hath made its masterpiece . . . with this bucket shall I pour water on his pate." "Oh! Good fortune smiles upon our club again! The game has been called off on account of rain!"

The pattern rarely changed. Thirty years later they did a parody of *Macbeth* taking place at a McDonald's restaurant: "Bubble, bubble, toil and trouble, give me a burger and make it a double!"

Wayne and Shuster remained a big attraction during the golden years of "The Ed Sullivan Show" and had their own summer series for CBS in 1966. While critics considered the duo as pleasantly bland as a hamburger and fries, and most audience members could never distinguish between the two, the team flourished in Canada after Ed Sullivan left the air and television variety shows in general sank in America. The duo were not overly concerned with their dip in popularity South of the border. The Canadians were family men who preferred to live in Toronto; Johnny was raising three daughters, Frank a son and daughter.

Wayne and Shuster packaged 80 half-hour shows for worldwide syndication in the late 1980s, though America's continued lack of appreciation for family-oriented vaudeville limited their exposure in the States. "We pride ourselves in always being a family show," said Frank in 1989. "It is sort of a legacy because a lot of people who have their own kids now say, 'Hey, I used to watch them when I was a kid.'"

Ironically, Frank's daughter Rose married next-door neighbor Lorne Michaels, producer of "Saturday Night Live." Though Lorne helped make that series notoriously irreverent, his technique of sketch comedy was basically similar to Wayne and Shuster's work and showed the influence of that early, harmless team. Rose Shuster became a writer for the show. She and Lorne divorced eventually, and each remarried, but they remained friends.

Wayne and Shuster remained a working team and prided themselves on never offending, never doing political material, topical jokes, or even hospital or dentist sketches—since some of their listeners may be in hospitals or worried about the pain of a dental visit. Johnny said, "I don't want anybody sitting at home with his daughter or grandson and saying 'Why did they say that?' We keep away from anything that would offend anybody. When you offend somebody, it's a form of violence."

Wayne and Shuster acknowledged that their light style wasn't going to win them much critical acclaim, especially in the volatile 1970s and '80s, but there was always a family audience waiting to watch. In the late 1980s the trend toward family comedy, spurred by Bill Cosby's sitcom comeback, helped make Wayne and Shuster's last years together as successful as ever. Said Johnny Wayne at the time, "Today's challenge is for a comic to be outrageous or different, but with so much 'outrageous' and 'sick' comedy around, being clean is outrageous . . . so what we're doing is fresh."

AUDIO: *In Person* (Columbia), *Selected Shorts* (Columbia)

TV: "Holiday Lodge" (1961), "Wayne and Shuster Take an Affectionate Look At . . . " (1966)

## CHARLEY WEAVER

### (Cliff Arquette, December 28, 1905–September 23, 1974)

Spry, whimsical Charley Weaver was a humble fellow from the mythical small town of "Mt. Idy." The creation of Cliff Arquette, who had played similar types of cheerful fogeys and cracker-barrel wits on radio, he became a favorite on Jack Paar's "Tonight Show" and later "The Hollywood Squares" television quiz program. Charley was a cuddly rascal who enjoyed injecting sly double entendres and sharp wit into his down-home corn. He dressed like a bumpkin, sporting a fuzzy mustache, wire-rimmed glasses that skidded down his nose, a beaten-up hat, suspenders and an askew necktie.

Originally Arquette was part of a band called Cliff Arquette and His Purple Derbies, but he soon formed a comedy team, The Three Public Enemies. It was on radio that he began specializing in elderly characters, including "Grandpaw Sneed" on Fred Astaire's show and "The Oldtimer" with Fibber McGee and Molly. He even played old women: Mrs. Wilson on "The Dick Haymes Show" and later Mrs. Butterworth in some television commercials.

As "Charley Weaver," Cliff had starred on several television shows before retiring in 1957 to run a Civil War museum in Gettysburg, Pennsylvania. He had been married and divorced twice and had a son. It was only after Jack Paar mused "What ever became of Cliff Arquette?" one night that Charley Weaver returned. Once he did, he never retired. He recorded a Grammy-nominated album of odd country tunes about Mt. Idy, as well as a record of his "Letters to Mamma."

The chubby, aging star found that by reading letters aloud on Paar's show he solved the problem of memorizing his routines. Pieced together from various letters: "Dear Castor Oil: (Mamma always said I was hard to take.) Things are fine in Mounty Idy (she goes on). . . . Leonard Box was arrested yesterday. Somebody told him his wife was as pretty as a picture, so he hung her on the wall. . . . Elsie Krack dropped by yesterday. My, she looked lovely. She just had her hair done. She waited at our house until they sent it over. . . . Well son, I must close now and go help your father. He just kissed a bride and got himself a black eye. I know everyone does it, but not seven years after the wedding. Love, Mamma."

Lovable Charley won over even more fans when he aged into the sprightly old fox on "The Hollywood Squares." Chubby, blameless and cheerful, he hardly seemed the type to give zingers. But he did. Question: "On the average Miss America, would her bust be larger than her hips?" "Out at the home we have one of the first Miss Americas. Her bust meets her hips."

The man who had planned to retire in 1957 stayed with the quiz show through the 1960s. After suffering a stroke in 1972, he returned to the show and stayed with it until his death.

AUDIO: *Charley Weaver Sings for His People* (Columbia), *Letters from Mamma* (Coral)

BOOKS: *Charley Weaver's Letters from Mamma* (1959), Charley Weaver's Family Album (1960), *Things Are Fine in Mt. Idy: More Letters from Mamma* (1960)

TV: "Dave and Charley" (1952), "The RCA Victor Show" (1952–54), "Do It Yourself" (1955), "The Jack Paar Show" (1958–62), "Hobby Lobby" (1959–60), "The Roy Rogers and Dale Evans Show" (1962), "The Jonathan Winters Show" (1968–69), "Hollywood Squares" (1968–74)

## DOODLES WEAVER

### (Winstead Sheffield Weaver, May 11, 1911–January 13, 1983)

Two of the saddest words in comedy are "Doodles Weaver." His silly name suggests an anything-for-a-laugh personality; but it was just that kind of personality that doomed him. Weaver was "anything for a laugh" to the extreme, which included ancient jokes, corny slapstick and desperate mugging and miming. He was the funmaker at the party who tells bad jokes and tries to punctuate them with an elbow in the ribs. Eventually everyone walks away.

As a child, Weaver's mother looked at his goofy freckled face, long nose, button eyes and huge looping ears and nicknamed him "Doodlebug," which became "Doodles." Weaver didn't seem to mind. He was the class clown; there was the time his affluent parents went away for the weekend and he used up all their credit at local stores to hire a band and cater a nonstop party for his high school pals.

After minor film roles (as Hannibal Hobbs he had some of the very few laughs in the original *Li'l Abner*), Doodles hooked up with Spike Jones' band in the 1940s. This was the perfect outlet for Weaver's ridiculous brand of cornball genius. And genius it was; Doodles was the master of lightning-fast spoonerisms. His classic was "Man on the Flying Trapeze," in which every word seemed to perplex him: "He floats through the air with the aidest of grease! With the latest of fleas! With plates full of cheese. No no. With the birds and the bees . . . the manning young dare—the daring young mare—he's not a horse." After a while he'd abandon the lyrics entirely in favor of laughably terrible jokes: "A man came up to me and said, 'Doodles, did you put the cat out?' 'I didn't know he was on fire!' Haaaa! Isn't that a killer?"

Another fast-paced classic was his routine as a manic commentator, accompanying "The William Tell Overture" with the frenzied call of a horse race ("Banana coming up to the bunch! Girdle in the stretch! It's Mother-in-Law nagging in the rear!"). The ending always saw the inept horse "Feetlebaum" somehow emerging with a victory.

As amusing as these hits were, they were intended as "novelties." No one wanted an entire evening of it. Two or three songs by Weaver were plenty. Into the 1950s, Doodles went to television for low-budget comedy shorts and variety show appearances. He always had young fans and for a time succeeded with a local "Day with Doodles" and "Doodles' Club House" shows in Los Angeles. But, like Spike Jones, he found himself out of favor as times changed and audiences grew more "sophisticated."

Doodles' career was sagging, and so was his private life. He went through four marriages. In a sad appearance on Groucho Marx's "You Bet Your Life" show, Doodles turned up strictly as a contestant. Groucho asked what he did for a living. Doodles:

"I'm lookin' for a job." Groucho: "Not mine I hope. How long have you been out of work?" Doodles: "I haven't had a steady job in three years."

After admitting that his profession was "comedian," Doodles delivered as many desperate joke-book jests as he could: "My wife's a good cook. Ever taste fried water? Her cooking is so bad that our garbage disposal has ulcers. . . . I live in Burbank. Luther Burbank crossed hybrids. He crossed a potato with a sponge. He got something that tastes awful but it holds a lot of gravy. . . . I crossed a bee with a doorbell. Know what I got? A humdinger."

Groucho kindly remarked, "You're a much better comedian than many I see making big salaries . . . I don't understand why you're not working." Neither could fans, who knew that Doodles' brother was the powerful Sylvester "Pat" Weaver, president of NBC. About the best Doodles could do late in life was to play "Crier Tuck" on an episode of "Batman" and "Eddie Hoyle" in a few episodes of "Starsky and Hutch." He made an embarrassingly corny album for a small West Coast label in the 1970s and lived in obscurity. He wasn't even the funniest-named person in the family anymore. That honor went to his niece, Susan, now calling herself Sigourney Weaver.

Perhaps in the right setting and with the right discipline he might have purveyed silly jokes as Soupy Sales did, or become a variation on Spike Milligan's persona of the desperate but sympathetic tragi-comic vaudevillian. But Doodles never seemed to know good gags from bad, and young sitcom producers who'd never even heard of him considered his name the biggest joke of all, the comedy equivalent of failed actor Sonny Tufts.

Weaver was bitter. He told one fan/interviewer, Jordan Young, "The guys you see on TV—David Letterman, Jonathan Winters, Dom DeLuise, Richard Pryor—they're not a bit funny, not to me. If I did stuff like Pryor does they'd take me and put me in jail. My competition were guys who worked to be funny . . . Phil Foster would walk out and say, 'How do you like me so far?' That's funny. I'd come out and say, 'You know how to milk a mouse? First you get a small stool. . . .'"

Ultimately Weaver had nothing to go on but his heart. When his heart began to fail him and his health began to deteriorate, Doodles Weaver shot and killed himself.

AUDIO: *The Best of Spike Jones* (RCA Victor), *Feetlebaum Returns* (Fremont)
BROADWAY: *Meet the People* (1940)
FILMS incl.: *Behind the Headlines* (1937), *Topper* (1939), *Lil' Abner* (1940), *A Girl, A Guy and a Gob* (1941), *Winchester 73* (1950), *The 30-Foot Bride of Candy Rock* (1959), *The Ladies' Man* (1961), *The Birds* (1963), *It's a Mad Mad Mad Mad World* (1964), *The Spirit Is Willing* (1967)
VIDEO: *The Best of Spike Jones*

## WEBER and FIELDS

**Joe Weber: Moisha Weber, August 11, 1867–May 10, 1942**
**Lew Fields: Moisha Schanfield, January 1, 1867–July 20, 1941**

FIELDS: Who vas dat lady I saw you vit?
WEBER: Dat vas no lady, dat vas my wife!

And that was Weber and Fields, the originators of several classic two-man comedy routines and pioneers in slapstick as well. They originated comic eye-poking, choking and some violence too shocking for even The Three Stooges: Fields slamming a hatchet into his chubby little pal's head (and with such force Weber had to use not only cork padding but a steel-plated wig). They were the first successful "anti team." Rather than working smoothly together, much of their comedy came from antagonism. On stage one of their hit routines mostly involved Fields hitting Weber. While trying to explain the game of pool to Weber, Fields is driven to pelting and smacking his fat partner, first for messing up the game and later for becoming too good at it. Abbott and Costello based many routines on the same premise.

Of their verbal routines, Weber and Fields had great success with their "Drinking Sketch." In it, Fields discovers he has "only five cents" and cautions Weber that "when we go into the saloon, I'll have a beer and you say you don't want any . . . say in a sort of careless way, 'Oooh, I don't care for anything.'" They rehearse their lines before they enter the bar. But once there, Fields puts on too much of a show. "Take something small," he says. Weber,

thinking Fields has had a change of heart, pipes up, "I'll take a small bottle!" And so it goes, with endless coaxing from Fields and predictable forgetfulness from Weber.

Most comedy fans remember this routine done by Laurel and Hardy (in the short *Men 'o War*) and Abbott and Costello (in the feature *In the Navy*). Sadly, the memory of Weber and Fields has been tarnished by the years. Not only are there few films or recordings of the team, but what survives—slow-paced and damaged by stereotypical Dutch dialect—can't compete with the newer versions by subsequent teams.

Weber and Fields were both sons of Polish immigrants. Both originally named Moisha, Weber changed his first name to Morris, and Fields became Moses. They grew up in poverty, living in rat-infested New York apartments. The friends danced for money on the street, then performed in vaudeville, ultimately owning their own Weber and Fields Music Hall where they staged many hit productions. Excellent at various dialects, they seemed to combine elements of Dutch, German and Jewish accents for their identities as "Mike and Myer."

Audiences could easily tell the two apart. Fields was the tall one. Weber, in fake goatee and sporting a huge pillow under his shirt, was the short chubby one. His part was simple. He recalled, "All the public wanted to see was Fields knock the hell out of me."

As showmen, the duo pioneered techniques used by others. Before Flo Ziegfeld, they were using a chorus line of pretty girls. Way before Ed Sullivan, they brought in a family audience by staging clean shows and spending money for the biggest guest stars of the day, including Lillian Russell. In 1904 they split up. Weber staged hits in his own theater, including *The Climax*, a drama that earned over a million dollars. Fields appeared in productions such as *Old Dutch* and *The Henpecks*.

They reteamed in 1912 and made some films, records and even appeared at The Palace in 1915, but theirs was an off-again, on-again partnership. They played The Palace again in 1925 and in 1932, but were not together consistently through the years. The arguments between Weber and Fields were mostly over business situations—what to charge, whom to book. Later in their careers Weber seemed more content to produce shows. Lew Fields remained in the spotlight, appearing in *The Jazz King*

(1924), *Henky* (1924), *The Melody Man* (1924), *Money Business* (1926), *The High Cost of Loving* (1928) and *Hello Daddy!* (1928).

Weber and Fields played themselves in Alice Faye's *Lillian Russell* film biography and had hopes of starring in a film about themselves. But as the fast-paced Abbott and Costello shot to stardom in 1940, the slower Weber and Fields faded away. Lew Fields, troubled with heart problems and pneumonia, died with his partner Weber by his bedside. His daughter Dorothy Fields became a famous lyricist, his son Herbert wrote "Du Barry Was a Lady" and his other son Joseph co-wrote "My Sister Eileen."

Weber, who had holdings of over a half-million dollars at one time, saw his investments erode. His West End theater on 125th Street had been a good location, but it wasn't anymore. When he died, not long after his partner, the money for his burial came from The Actors Fund.

Some saccharine writers of the day eulogized the team, hoping that at least Weber and Fields were reunited in heaven. But if they were, chances are they opened with some lines from one of their old sketches:

WEBER: I am delightfulness to meet you!

FIELDS: Der disgust is all mine.

AUDIO: *They Stopped the Show* (Audio Rarities), *Golden Age of Comedy* (RCA Victor)

BIOGRAPHY: *Weber and Fields* (Isman, 1924)

BROADWAY incl.: *Hurly Burly* (1898), *Helter Skelter* (1899), *Fiddle-Dee-Dee* (1900), *Hoity Toity* (1901), *Twirly Whirly* (1902), *Whoop-Dee-Doo* (1903), *Friar's Club Frolic* (1922)

FILMS incl.: *The Best of Enemies* (1915), *Fatty and the Broadway Stars* (1915), *The Worst of Friends* (1916), *The Corner Grocer* (1918), *Friendly Enemies* (1925), *Mike and Meyer* (1927), *Two Flaming Youths* (1927), *Blossoms on Broadway* (1937), *Lillian Russell* (1940)

VIDEO: *Tape #760: The Oyster Routine* (Video Yesteryear)

## SENOR WENCES

### (Wenceslao Moreno, April 20, 1912– )

One of the most unique and memorable ventriloquists in comedy, Señor Wences got laughs from three bizarre creations: "Johnny," which was just a face painted on the side of his fist (complete with a wig over the knuckles); a chicken puppet named "Cecilia"; and "Pedro," a disembodied head kept in a box. Much of the humor of Wences' act came from his fast talk and idiosyncratic voices. There was the back-and-forth singsong between himself and high-voiced Johnny ("Be nice." "Nice." "Are you nice?" "Yes." "Nice.") and the macabre comedy between himself and the deep-voiced, stoic Pedro. Whenever Wences opened the lid to look in on him, the catch-phrase dialogue was always the same: "S'all right?" "S'all right. Shut the door."

Wences was born in Penaranda, Spain, where his father, a Sephardic Jew, restored paintings and gave guitar lessons. Wences recalled, "I was a mischievous boy. Spirited. In school I began to use the voice. When some pupil is sick I answer for him. During a measles epidemic I answer for six kids. . . . My mother had 17 children, and she say she hopes never another like me."

From 12 to 17, the boy trained to be a bullfighter, but after his left arm was severely gored and his ribs damaged, he became a juggler. When a retired circus performer gave him a bunch of monkeys, Wences created an animal act, complete with a monkey dressed as a policeman. The act ended permanently when the monkey escaped and ran into a convent. A nun cried, "You are the devil! You are the devil!" when the strangely dressed monkey was captured.

In 1935 Wences went to New York for the first time. His "hand" puppet, Johnny, was charming. Pedro added the bizarre touch to the act. Pedro was originally a full-size dummy, but a train wreck that hit the baggage car splintered him to pieces. The sentimental Señor Wences managed to find a way of using Pedro's head in the act.

Wences usually inserted some shaky plate spinning and juggling into his show, but the highlight was the ventriloquism—his ability to sing and create amusing byplay for his puppet while he smoked or drank, and the ping-pong effect of his quick shifts from high voice to low: "Throat specialists always want to look down my throat," he recalled, "but I do not know if it is different from anybody's. The most important thing in my work is the breath . . . a cold in the head is the worst that can happen."

The 1947 film *Mother Wore Tights* contained a portion of his routine with "Johnny." He had his hand in another film, *History's Made at Night*. It was his expressive digits, not those of star Charles Boyer, seen in the closeups. Constantly in demand around the world, Señor Wences went to Broadway for *The Danny Kaye Show* (an evening of variety performers hosted by Kaye), guested on "The Ed Sullivan Show" on television regularly and starred in his own half hour of the syndicated "One Man Show" series in 1970. After a long absence he returned to America in 1980 to star at New York's Chateau Madrid. "It's all fresh and charming," *Variety* reported of the venerable ventriloquist.

Able to speak Portuguese, Spanish, Italian, French and English, and managed by his British wife, Señor Wences maintained homes in Los Angeles, New York and Paris and was consistently in demand. His uniquely appealing act, with its catch phrases ("Is difficult." "Is easy!" "Is easy for you—is difficult for me.") delighted fans of all ages. With his main comic character, little Johnny, he won his fame single-handed.

BROADWAY: *The Danny Kaye Show* (1963)
FILM: *Mother Wore Tights* (1947)

## BILLY WEST

### (Roy Weissberg, September 22, 1892–July 21, 1975)

Some comics have been compared to Charlie Chaplin—but Billy West *was* Charlie Chaplin. As the silent film era's foremost Chaplin imitator, he not only dressed the part and donned a Chaplin mustache, he even had his hair permed into the familiar Little Tramp mop. When his films were screened some theater owners announced them as new Chaplin films and many fans never knew the difference.

West was born in Russia but raised in Chicago. While in vaudeville, he made himself up as Charlie Chaplin for a parade. When the crowds cheered him as if he was the real Chaplin, Billy was persuaded to create a new vaudeville sketch, "Is He Charlie Chaplin?" Backed by some local filmmakers, West began to ask that question in movies.

The year was 1917. Chaplin was at his peak. The demand for his films was at an all-time high, so West helped fill that demand with his highly popular imitations. While West didn't copy actual Chaplin film plots, he aped Chaplin's mannerisms and had other cast members duplicate members of the Chaplin stock company. A young Oliver Hardy was made up to resemble Chaplin villain Eric Campbell. The real Chaplin, though seething on the inside, refused to add to Billy's fame by filing a lawsuit. The true silent film star remained silent.

West's popularity began to wane in the 1920s. He tried a more original character, playing a snappy young man in a straw hat, but audiences were not amused. He drifted behind the scenes, working as an assistant director at Columbia Pictures. With his wife, Marian, he owned the Columbia Grill, which he ran for 19 years. Ironically, in his old age West once again found fan appreciation. Some critics were actually rescreening his old comedies and admiring the skill of his Chaplin impersonations! He died of a heart attack while leaving the Hollywood Park racetrack in 1975.

FILMS incl.: *His Waiting Career* (1916), *His Day Out* (1917), *The Slave* (1918), *He's in Again* (1918), *A Wild Woman* (1919), *Sweethearts* (1921), *Don't Be Foolish* (1923), *Lucky Fool* (1927), *Motive for Revenge* (1935)
VIDEO: *Slapstick*

## MAE WEST

### (Mary Jane West, August 17, 1893–November 22, 1980)

Comedy's classic vamp was born in Brooklyn, where as a child she imitated Eva Tanguay, the reigning star of teasing sex and outrageous costuming. Billed as "Baby Mae" and later "The Baby Vamp," Mae West graduated from talent shows to a Brooklyn stock company. At 18 she was in Broadway revues and a married woman. Her Broadway career soared, but her marriage quickly dissolved. She left husband Frank Wallace and never remarried. They were officially divorced in the 1940s, after he had the temerity to tour as "Mr. Mae West."

In 1915 Mae raised eyebrows by donning a leopard skin and singing a novelty number called "The Cave Girl." In 1918 she was in *Sometime* on Broadway doing a sexy shimmy dance. Her unique, tough-

Mae West, the most recognizable film comedienne of all time. Her leering sexuality made her a top-grossing star in the 1930s. She was a legend in her own time when she made this appearance in *Myra Breckinridge*. Photo from the author's collection.

but-tender style may have come from her parents; her father was a pro boxer who owned a stable of horses. Her mother was a model for corsets.

Mae hit her stride in the roaring '20s, writing and starring as a prostitute in a show called *Sex*. The show ran for nearly a year until she was jailed for "corrupting the morals of youth." She took advantage of the publicity, demanding the right to wear her own silky underwear rather than itchy prison garb. Sentenced to 10 days in jail, she was out in eight due to "good behavior." She subsequently wrote but did not appear in *The Drag*, a play on the then-daring topic of homosexuality. She wrote a novel, *Babe Gordon*, about a prostitute who enters society. After it was cut and censored, she brought out a new edition called *The Constant Sinner* and then adapted it into a play. She scored her biggest hit with *Diamond Lil*, the show that offered her taunting, sexy catch phrase, "Come up and see me sometime." (It was in *She Done Him Wrong* that Mae uttered the

film variation to Cary Grant: "Why don't you come up sometime and see me?") She remarked, "I used humor so I could do and say what I wanted and get over the sex. And then they started classifying me as a great comedienne."

By this time Mae had just about perfected her persona, which she wrapped herself in like one of her form-fitting gowns. She realized, "It isn't what I do, but how I do it. It isn't what I say, but how I say it, and how I look when I do it and say it." When she went to Hollywood in 1932, the tough New Yorker announced, "I'm not a little girl from a little town making good in a big town. I'm a big girl from a big town making good in a little town."

She was not the star of her first film, George Raft's *Night After Night,* but she stole every scene she was in. Everyone was quoting her wisecracks. After an admiring woman whispered, "Goodness, what lovely diamonds," West cracked, "Goodness had nothing to do with it!"

Through the 1930s the Mae West "formula" remained the same. All she really seemed to do was mince and swing about in her gowns (she never wore anything remotely revealing) and utter well-timed risqué one-liners. Many were predictable plays on words: "I'm no angel but I've spread my wings a bit." "A figure with curves always offers a lot of interesting angles." "It's not the men in my life that count, it's the life in my men."

While modern viewers find that her stagy films creak badly, the charismatic Mae West personality still shimmers and fascinates. Many essays have been written exploring Mae West as everything from a liberated feminist who controlled her men to a stereotypical man-pleaser who couldn't do without them.

West was outrageous and controversial throughout her career. After her first (and best) films had earned millions at the box office, William Randolph Hearst in 1936 wrote that she was a "monster of lubricity . . . Is it not time Congress did something about Mae West?" In 1937 she was "banned" from radio for one too many double entendres on Edgar Bergen's radio show.

In the early 1930s West as both actress and screenwriter commanded $400,000 per film, a top salary. In 1941 the busty star had an inflatable life jacket named after her by GIs, and the term turned up in the dictionary. She remarked, "I've been in

*Who's Who* and I know what's what, but it'll be the first time I ever made the dictionary." However, the 1940s were a slow time for the aging star. *My Little Chickadee* was actually a comeback film for her, following the faltering *Every Day's a Holiday*. But while co-star W. C. Fields went on to make more classic comedies, West's *The Heat's On* was received coldly. She later toured in revivals of her old Broadway shows and in the 1950s had a then-racy nightclub act that featured the novelty of scantily clad muscle men.

She put out an album in 1955 featuring some of her best risqué songs and published her autobiography in 1959. Still as witty and risqué as ever, her 1960 "Person to Person" interview with Ed Murrow was considered too suggestive to air. Into the 1960s, with nostalgia and camp riding high, Mae West issued rock albums offering sexy, sultry, laughable renditions of hits such as "Light My Fire" and "Great Balls of Fire." She undulated her way into the 1970s, with a little pushing and shoving, and edged co-star Raquel Welch out of the spotlight for her comeback film *Myra Breckenridge*. She followed it with *Sextette*, a film that many found a self-parody. There was an unbecoming crudity to her modern brand of risqué comedy. Of a six-foot-seven Adonis she cracked: "Let's forget about the six feet and talk about the seven inches."

In interviews, West was still good copy. Modern fashion was a favorite topic for her comedy. "God gave women their curves," she lectured. "Effeminate dressmakers took them away by designing garments which could be worn only by women shaped like scarecrows. . . . Most men like women when they look like women. You can get a handful of toothpicks in a restaurant—free of charge."

Through the years, West managed to remain a comic sex symbol of some kind. Careful about her health, never smoking, never drinking, a great believer in daily enemas, Mae was in good physical shape. With careful makeup and a few tricks of the trade, she managed to look presentable, if not actually sexy, in her 70s. As West admitted, "I concentrate on myself most of the time. Everything I do pertains to myself."

She had an amazing sense of self, and for 60 years, Mae West worked to keep up her image. She created her own legend and became a legend in her own time.

AUDIO: *Voicetracks from Her Films* (Decca), *Mae West on the Chase and Sanborn Hour* (Radiola), *Mae West on Radio* (Mark 56), *Mae West on the Air* (Sandy Hook), *Mae West and Her Guys* (Caliban), *Fabulous Mae West* (Decca), *Wild Christmas* (Dagonet, reissued as *Mae in December)*, *Fields and West* (Proscenium), *Great Balls of Fire* (MGM), *Way Out West* (Capitol)

AUTOBIOGRAPHY: *Goodness Had Nothing to Do With It* (1981)

BIOGRAPHIES: *Come Up and See Me Sometime* (Hanna), *The Films of Mae West* (Tuska, 1973), *Wit and Wisdom of Mae West* (Weintraub, 1977), *Mae West: A Bio-Bibliography* (Ward, 1989), *Mae West* (Eells and Musgrove, 1982)

BOOKS: *Diamond Lil* (1932); *Babe Gordon; Sex, Health and ESP* (1975); *Pleasure Man* (1975)

BROADWAY: *A la Broadway* (1911), *Vera Violetta* (1917), *A Winsome Widow* (1917), *Sometime* (1918), *The Mimic World of 1921* (1921), *Sex* (1926), *The Wicked Age* (1927), *Diamond Lil* (1928), *The Constant Sinner* (1931), *Catherine Was Great* (1944), *Diamond Lil* (1948)

FILMS: *Night After Night* (1932), *She Done Him Wrong* (1933), *I'm No Angel* (1933), *Goin' to Town* (1934), *Belle of the Nineties* (1934), *Klondike Annie* (1936), *Go West Young Man* (1937), *Every Day's a Holiday* (1938), *My Little Chickadee* (1939), *The Heat's On* (1943), *Myra Breckenridge* (1969), *Sextet* (1977)

## WHEELER and WOOLSEY

**Bert (Albert) Wheeler, April 17, 1895–January 18, 1968**
**Robert Woolsey, August 14, 1889–October 31, 1938**

Unlike Mae West, The Marx Brothers or W. C. Fields, who all made some early 1930s films that creak, Wheeler and Woolsey's personalities are as dated as their material. Bert Wheeler, the "pixie" leading man with the wavy hair and toothy smile, had a whining nasal voice and an irritating brand of childlike pluck. Bespectacled, cigar-wagging Robert Woolsey, the blunt-nosed, big-eared one who looked and acted amazingly like George Burns, is equally trying with his affected wise-guy delivery style and inane cry of "Wayyyy oh!" in moments of panic.

At the time, the team no doubt had fans who preferred realistic-looking men to more "cartoonish" specimens such as Laurel and Hardy, The Three Stooges and The Marx Brothers. Wheeler was probably considered a sympathetic boy-next-door type and Woolsey a sharp wise guy, crossing as he did the styles of Groucho Marx and George Burns. In 1935's *The Nitwits*, he even serves up a Groucho one-liner from 1932's *Horsefeathers*. To his partner Wheeler: "Johnny, you've got the brain of a six-year-old boy, and I'll bet even money he was glad to get rid of it."

Even then critics were complaining that the duo's material had whiskers. Some familiar waiter-to-customer patter in *Half Shot at Sunrise:*

Customer: "Do you have a wild duck?" Woolsey: "No, but we could take a tame one out and aggravate it for ya!" Wheeler: ". . . and listen! Don't ask him if he has frog's legs." Customer: "I can't eat this duck. Send for the manager." Wheeler: "It's no use, he can't eat it either."

Even with fresh material (S. J. Perelman co-wrote *Hold 'Em Jail*), the team wasn't very memorable. In that one, Perelman gave Woolsey lines that might have been classic if Groucho Marx had said them. Dowager Edna May Oliver wants advice on her singing. Before she begins, she notes, "I spent four years in Paris. Of course, I'm not a virtuoso." Woolsey: "Not after four years in Paris. . . ." "Are you trying to play fast and loose with me?" "I'll play fast but you play loose—out in the outfield."

Wheeler and Woolsey did try to vary their subject matter, picking different occupations and settings for their films. In fact, when Universal Studios needed ideas for new Abbott and Costello films, they often copied the settings of old Wheeler and Woolsey comedies.

Both Wheeler and Woolsey had independent careers before teaming. Wheeler was the better known of the two, both for his stage work with first partner and first wife Betty and for his solo efforts. He'd brashly bring out a joke book, sit on the edge of the stage, eat a sandwich and read from it. He'd interrupt this to let the audience in on confidential gags about his wife and then do a cry routine, wiping his eyes with his sandwich.

Woolsey was a jockey until a horse threw him in 1907. He excelled at Gilbert and Sullivan and eventually starred on Broadway in *The Rich Girl* (1921), *Poppy* with W. C. Fields (1923) and *Mayflowers* (1925). The duo teamed in 1927 for *Rio Rita* on Broadway and moved to films soon after. They knew they were never the critics' favorites. In *Caught Plastered*, Wheeler opened: "The manager said he didn't allow any profanity in his theater." "We didn't use any profanity." "No, but the audience did."

After Woolsey died of a kidney disease, Wheeler appeared in a few films (*Cowboy Quarterback* in 1939 and *Las Vegas Nights* in 1941) and took over for Frank Fay in *Harvey* on Broadway. He was also on Broadway in *New Priorities of 1943* (1943), *Laugh Time* (1943), *Three Wishes for Jamie* (1952), *The Gang's All Here* (1959) and *Seven Scenes for Yeni* (1963). On television Wheeler was best remembered as "Smokey Joe" on the "Brave Eagle" series in 1955. Wheeler kept active, well respected and remembered by his many friends in show business. He even found new partners for comedy work on stage, teaming with Sid Slate and later Jack Pepper in the 1950s, and Tommy Dillon in the 1960s.

BROADWAY: *Rio Rita* (1927)
FILMS incl.: *Rio Rita* (1929), *The Cuckoos* (1930), *Dixiana* (1930), *Half Shot at Sunrise* (1930), Hook Line and Sinker (1930), *Cracked Nuts* (1931), *Caught Plastered* (1931), *Peach O'Reno* (1931), *Girl Crazy* (1932), *Hold 'em Jail* (1932), *So This Is Africa* (1933), *Diplomaniacs* (1933), *Hips Hips Hooray* (1934), *Cockeyed Cavaliers* (1934), *Kentucky Kernels* (1934), *The Nitwits* (1935), *The Rainmakers* (1935), *Silly Billies* (1936), *Mummy's Boys* (1936), *On Again Off Again* (1937), *High Flyers* (1937)

# BETTY WHITE

## (January 17, 1922–  )

In a career that has seen her comic persona change from sweet, to sweetly poisonous to sweetly dumb,

Betty White has displayed such gentle charm and pleasant humor that it's easy to take her effortless grace for granted. But staying around so long in show business has proven both her talent and tenacity.

Born in Oak Park, Illinois, a Chicago suburb, Betty grew up in Los Angeles and attended Beverly Hills High. She appeared on the "Blondie" and "Great Gildersleeve" radio shows among others and was one of the first stars to work regularly on television, co-hosting "Hollywood on Television" with Al Jarvis and having her own Emmy-winning sitcom in 1953, "Life with Elizabeth." She recalled of that early effort, "We were more two-dimensional cartoon characters than three-dimensional real people." More sitcoms followed, plus talk and variety shows on daytime television. Her 1954 "Betty White Show" was nominated for an Emmy. She was a quiz show panelist, a frequent guest on Jack Paar's show and had her own "Ask Betty White" radio advice program.

In 1962 Betty appeared in a summer theater production of *Critic's Choice* with actor/quiz show host Allen Ludden. Divorced from her first husband in 1949, she resisted marriage for a while, but Ludden won her over. Theirs was a long, happy union that lasted until his death in 1981.

White's wholesome image was well known over the years and continued with "The Pet Set," a talk show about celebrities and their pets in 1971. Two years later, working deliciously against type, White scored her best success in years playing the artificially sweet, cheerfully nasty and unexpectedly promiscuous local television personality "Happy Homemaker," Sue Ann Nivens, on "The Mary Tyler Moore Show." She won two Emmys for her role and in 1977 had her own series again, playing a modification of Sue Ann. "There's bitchiness," she said of her character Joyce Whitman, "but she doesn't strike first. She waits until somebody else strikes and then she lets 'em have it."

Through the 1970s and early '80s Betty often guested on "The Tonight Show" in good-natured, sometimes sexy sketches with Johnny Carson. She won another Emmy for the game show "Just Men" in 1983. While some comediennes seemed to fade away, Betty proved durable and was proud of it. She wasn't about to go in for plastic surgery to compete with younger stars. "I've worked hard to get these sags and lines. Besides, my friends with facelifts all look alike."

Originally set to play the flirty and vain Blanche on "The Golden Girls," she got the part of Rose instead. It was another departure from typecasting, playing the slightly dumb, but (of course) nicest and most sympathetic member of the cast. She won an Emmy for the role, which included a variety of peculiar comic episodes (dating a midget, purchasing condoms, finding her lover dying in her bedroom). Middle-age sexual desire is a big snickering point on the show. Rose was often inclined toward action, but if there was no opportunity, she made other plans. One of the girls complained that on a cruise "We never even had to use those [condoms they bought]." Rose: "You didn't? I used every one of mine! Late at night I filled 'em with water and threw 'em at the people in the limbo line!"

An animal rights activist, Betty wrote a book on pets and today lends her support to "People for the Ethical Treatment of Animals." Pets helped her through the tragedy of her husband's illness and death. Of her dogs and cat she says, "I don't know how I would exist without my 'kids.' When I come home at night, no matter how bad my day, I'm the most important thing in the world to them."

AUTOBIOGRAPHY: *Betty White in Person* (1988)
BOOKS: *Betty White's Pet Love: How Pets Take Care of Us* (1983)
FILMS incl.: *With This Ring* (1978), *The Gossip Columnist* (1980)
TV: "Life With Elizabeth" (1953–55), "Make the Connection" (1955), "Date with the Angels" (1957–58), "The Betty White Show" (1958), "The Jack Paar Show" (1959–62), "The Mary Tyler Moore Show" (1973–77), "Match Game PM" (1975–82), "Liar's Club" (1976–78), "The Betty White Show" (1977–78), "Mama's Family" (1983–84), "Golden Girls" (1985–   )

# GENE WILDER

## (Gerald Silberman, June 11, 1935–   )

A likable actor with woolly straw-colored hair and bright, friendly blue eyes, Gene Wilder usually plays on-the-edge types, mild-mannered fellows reduced by anxiety and frustration to comically childish rages.

After attending the University of Iowa, Milwaukee-born Wilder appeared in a variety of off-Broadway and Broadway productions, earning a New York Drama Critics nomination for *One Flew over the Cuckoo's Nest*. He also earned praise in *Mother Courage* with Anne Bancroft.

Wilder played an undertaker in an early film appearance, *Bonnie and Clyde*. When he appeared in Mel Brooks' *The Producers*, he turned in one of his best performances as a shy, nervous accountant duped by con man Zero Mostel and getting into the kind of trouble that could make even a mild man scream.

Though Wilder had some luck with roles that accentuated his mild, lovable side (Woody Allen cast him as a gentle sheep-loving pervert in *Everything You Always Wanted to Know About Sex But Were Afraid to Ask*), he returned to major stardom with Mel Brooks, first as a washed-up lawman in *Blazing Saddles*, and then in a major starring role in the tense and intense *Young Frankenstein*. He co-wrote that film with Brooks.

Having mastered the Brooks formula of parody, Wilder then wrote and directed himself in films that might have passed for Brooks' efforts. *Sherlock Holmes' Smarter Brother* was an effective farce, and in *The World's Greatest Lover* he continued to indulge in frantic slapstick, including a scene in which the Harpo-haired, excitable "lover" hoarsely shouts out numbered instructions to his bride during sex.

His best effort was as The Frisco Kid in the film of that title, as an alternately friendly and fiery Polish rabbi determined to cross the country and become the spiritual leader for a needy synagogue in San Francisco. Though his naiveté led to swindles and beatings, and he suffered through predictable comic highlights trying to catch fish and ride a horse, he came through with a winning combination of resolve and vulnerability, stubbornness and warmth. The film was rich in ironic Jewish humor. In one scene, dubious sidekick Harrison Ford has helped guide the rabbi along part of his journey but can't understand why he'll risk capture by Indians to protect his Torah. "I don't ride on Saturday," the rabbi insists. When Ford decides to leave, the rabbi announces, "Thanks for everything you did for me—up until the time I needed you most."

In later years, Wilder made a suitably jumpy foil for Richard Pryor. In the hit *Stir Crazy*, his inept attempts at matching Pryor's cool (including imitating a black strut and even doing a scene in blackface shouting "We bad, we bad") helped make the film a lot funnier than the script. Fans wanted more from the "team" of Wilder and Pryor, but more important to him was the emerging team of "Wilder and Radner."

Wilder and Gilda Radner were paired in *Hanky Panky* and eventually they married. It was the second marriage for both, and it was a happy one. Sadly, the promising beginning to their career in films and their life off-camera ended in tragedy with Gilda's death after a long struggle with cancer.

Wilder has continued on, playing a cartoonist in the critically panned *Funny About Love* and reteaming with Richard Pryor in two more films, *See No Evil, Hear No Evil* and *Another You*. In September 1991 Wilder married a hearing specialist, Karen Webb.

BROADWAY: *Roots* (1961), *One Flew over the Cuckoo's Nest* (1963), *Dynamite Tonight* (1964)

FILMS incl.: *Bonnie and Clyde* (1967), *The Producers* (1968), *Start the Revolution Without Me* (1969), *Quackser Fortune Has a Cousin in the Bronx* (1970), *Willy Wonka and the Chocolate Factory* (1971), *Everything You Always Wanted to Know About Sex But Were Afraid to Ask* (1972), *Rhinoceros* (1973), *The Little Prince* (1973), *Blazing Saddles* (1974), *Young Frankenstein* (1974), *Thursday's Game* (1974), *Adventures of Sherlock Holmes' Smarter Brother* (1975), *Silver Streak* (1976), *The Frisco Kid* (1979), *Stir Crazy* (1980), *Hanky Panky* (1982), *The Woman in Red* (1984), *See No Evil, Hear No Evil* (1989), *Funny About Love* (1990), *Another You* (1991)

# BERT WILLIAMS

## (Egbert Austin Williams, November 12, 1876– March 4, 1922)

W. C. Fields called Bert Williams "the funniest man I ever saw—the saddest man I ever knew."

Unfortunately, it is the second half of the statement that is easiest to verify. The Jackie Robinson of vaudeville, Williams was the first black on many all-white bills; the miseries and indignities he suffered ruined the enjoyment of his triumphs.

In fact, his on-stage success made things worse. On stage he received cheers. Off stage he was treated as so many blacks were: ostracized in restaurants; forced to use a black entrance to his hotel; treated with suspicion or contempt. He solemnly told Eddie Cantor, "It wouldn't be so bad, Eddie, if I didn't still hear the applause ringing in my ears."

Cantor was one of many who idolized Williams. He admitted, "Whatever sense of timing I have, I learned from him."

Since Williams worked mainly in vaudeville and *The Ziegfeld Follies*, very limited archival material is available on him. Some old and scratchy recordings hardly do him justice, though his lilting sense of irony and his wry delivery shine through on even the weakest novelty tunes. Most anyone will appreciate "Nobody," the brilliant tune of comic melancholy he co-wrote and sang with such eloquence:

"When life seems full of clouds and rain, and I am filled with naught but pain, who soothes my thumping, bumping brain? Nobody. When winter comes with snow and sleet, and me with hunger and cold feet, who says, 'Here's two bits, go and eat?' Nobody . . ."

His song "Nobody," with its plea for friendship, was mirrored in real life. He told an interviewer of having to wait to enter a restaurant or saloon, needing a white friend to go in with him, "waiting for anybody . . . anybody who'd breeze in and say, 'Hello, Bert! what you doing here?' and give me a chance to chum and make myself at home. Funny what a man'll do for human companionship."

On stage, Williams wore the minstrel's burnt cork, white gloves and a shabby coat. Even so, not all his monologues and songs were performed in such downcast, hapless attire. He scored success with outlandishly hilarious costumes and performed in *Ziegfeld Follies* sketches in a variety of roles. He won laughs with his extravagantly humorous gestures (he could make removing his gloves or lighting a cigarette an elaborate art form) and his debonaire facial expressions (from a raised eyebrow of surprise to a mild frown of disapproval).

Born in the West Indies, Bert's light complexion came from a Danish grandfather and a grandmother who was, using the term of the day, "a quadroon." Williams originally worked with a black partner, George Walker. In the 1890s they offered the standard smart-guy versus patsy routines, with Williams the gullible fool.

In one sketch, Walker tries to talk Bert into stealing money from a bank, insisting by the time the theft is discovered, "we'll be far, far away, where the birds are singing sweetly and the flowers are in bloom." Williams: "And if they catch us, they'll put us so far, far away we never will hear no birds singin'. And everybody knows you can't smell no flowers through a stone wall!"

Williams and Walker were inserted into Broadway shows so they could perform a specialty song or routine, and at the turn of the century were making $40,000 a year. The money came in handy. Down South, Bert went into a bar, ordered a drink and was told "It will cost you $50." The star comedian was unruffled. Peeling off some hundred-dollar bills, he said, "I'll take six."

They appeared on Broadway in *The Gold Bug* (1896) and *In Dahomey* (1903), which was such a success they went to England and played a command performance for King Edward VII. *Abyssinia* (1906) and *Bandanna Land* (1908) followed, with *Theatre* magazine raving that Williams was "vastly funnier . . . than any white comedian now on the American stage."

After Walker became ill, Bert went solo for *Mr. Lode of Koal* (1909) and, after Walker's death in 1911, began appearing in *The Ziegfeld Follies*. Williams was recording as early as 1901, the first black man on record: "I'm in the Right Church but the Wrong Pew" and "Come After Breakfast, Bring Along Your Lunch, and Leave Before Suppertime." Most of his best recordings were made between 1913 and 1919.

In addition to songs he performed monologues: "Where I'm living now is a nice place, but you have to go along a road between two graveyards to get to it. One night last week I was coming home kind of late, and I got about halfway home when I happened to look over my shoulder and saw a ghost following me. I started to run. I run till I was 'most ready to drop. And then I looked around. But I didn't see no ghost, so I sat down on the curbstone to rest. Then out of the corner of my eye I could see something white, and when I turned square around, there was that ghost sitting alongside of me. The ghost says, 'That was a fine run we had. It was the best running I ever saw.' I says, 'Yes, and soon as I get my breath you're going to see some more.' "

Williams appeared in all editions of *The Ziegfeld Follies* of the decade except 1913 and 1918. He made a film, *A Natural Born Gambler* in 1916. He was touring in *Under the Bamboo Tree* when he collapsed on stage in Detroit. He went back home to his wife Lottie, and their home at 2309 Seventh Avenue in New York, where he died of pneumonia. Having joined the Masons while in Scotland in a play, Williams, even in death, was a pioneer, the first black man to be buried by a white Masonic lodge. He was buried in the Bronx's Woodlawn Cemetery.

Said Eddie Cantor: "As a man, he was everything the rest of us would like to have been. As a friend, he was without envy or jealousy."

AUDIO: *Nobody* (Folkways)

BIOGRAPHIES: *Son of Laughter* (Rowlands, 1969), *Nobody: The Story of Bert Williams* (Charters, 1970)

BROADWAY: *Mr. Lode of Koal* (1909), *The Ziegfeld Follies* (1910–12, 1914–17, 1919–20), *Broadway Brevities* (1920)

FILM: *A Natural Born Gambler* (1916)

## PEARL WILLIAMS

### (Pearl Wolfe, September 10, 1914–September 18, 1991)

One of the best risqué comedians of the 1950s and '60s, Pearl Williams' gags were not very different from those told by Belle Barth, B. S. Pully or a dozen other party record favorites. What made the difference was her delivery: stories told in the manic Jewish dialect of a Lenny Bruce; one-liners spat out with the comic aggressiveness of a Leo Gorcey; rhymes told with the same self-confidence of admirer/imitator Andrew "Dice" Clay. As a female comedian, there was a touch of Mae West to her style, but it was a tougher version: "Shut yer hole, girlie," Pearl would yell to a gabby ringsider, "mine's makin' money!"

"Makin' money" in comedy was not Pearl's first career choice. She was a legal stenographer by profession and a part-time piano player/singer. When she helped a friend by playing piano accompaniment for an audition, Pearl was hired instead. In 1938 she landed a job on the same bill with Louis Prima, and through the 1940s she learned to mix straight songs with snappy Joe E. Lewis patter and risqué tunes. Sophie Tucker told the young performer, "You're me at your age, only better." Jack Benny said, "I've never heard a woman comedian with your pace and timing and delivery."

Williams issued the first of her best-selling party albums in 1962 and might have been able to move into the "straight" world of comedy as Redd Foxx eventually did, but her manager Joe Glazer died. "I didn't bother getting a new manager," Williams recalled, "I just settled down in Florida and bought a house . . . had I gotten another manager, I probably would've gone on to bigger and better things."

Williams, who retired in 1984, spent 18 years performing at the Place Pigalle in Miami. She made periodic trips to venues around the country during that time, especially Las Vegas where she recorded many more albums, all loaded with frisky quickies: "Definition! Indecent: If it's long enough, hard enough and in far enough, it's in decent!" "Hear about the guy who bought his wife a gold diaphragm? He wanted to see how it feels to come into money!"

Pearl Williams was unabashed about her comedy. Though off stage she had a strong distaste for X-rated films and resented fans who thought she was bawdy in real life, on stage she refused to be censored, or censured. As she said on stage: "I get broads come in here, they sit in front of me and they stare at me. Everything I do, they stare at me. Then they walk out saying 'She's *so dirrrr-ty!*' If they're so refined how come they understand what I'm saying?"

AUDIO: *A Trip Around the World Is Not a Cruise* (After Hours), *2nd Trip Around the World* (Surprise), *Pearl Williams at Las Vegas* (Riot), *All the Way* (Riot), *Battle of the Mothers* (Riot), *You'll Never Remember It, Write It Down* (Laff), *Bagels and Lox* (Laff)

Robin Williams' fast-paced ad libs made him a phenomenon in stand-up. After starring in "Mork and Mindy," he's become one of the biggest stars in modern film comedy. Photo from the author's collection.

## ROBIN WILLIAMS

### (July 21, 1952–   )

With his trademark of exuberance and energy, Robin Williams became a blazing star in stand-up, television and ultimately films. Though he rose in show business like a meteor, his early years were more like life on a cold, distant planet.

As a youth, Robin lived a lonely life fulfilled only in fantasy. His father was a wealthy executive with Ford Motors and Robin lived in a 30-room mansion. He had an entire floor to himself, as well as the use of the large basement that housed his 2000 toy soldiers. The chubby kid played down there, bringing his soldiers to life with sound effects and voices. When the family moved to California, the teenager went out for sports and turned into a slim, rather

attractive young man well suited for his chosen career: acting. He attended Juilliard on a scholarship and trained with one of the severe-but-fun masters of the acting profession, John Houseman.

Williams enjoyed improvisations and found an outlet in comedy clubs. Influenced strongly by Jonathan Winters, Williams discovered he too could blitz audiences with the virtuosity of his voices and the hectic pace of his quick-change characterizations. In hip clubs where the clientele was often on booze, drugs or both, Williams seemed like a human cartoon; every now and then there was a scripted joke but the thrill was in the funny faces, funny voices and the energetic, improbable contortions.

If Morey Amsterdam had been a "human joke machine," Williams was the modern computer, programmed with old jokes and new twists, the best influences of both great comedians and great actors, fueled by inexhaustible energy. What came out was like a computer gone berzerk: All of the ad libs, improvisations, jokes and vocal impressions spewed out at once like confetti.

Other comics grumbled when Robin borrowed their jokes or catch phrases, but he wasn't intentionally stealing. He was a computer on overload, spitting out everything in his memory. The material was sometimes an extension of acting class (his bit "inside the mind" of a bombing comic), sometimes silly (Jack Nicholson doing *Hamlet,* Elmer Fudd singing rock songs) and often typical of the nightclub (a quick grab for the crotch to make sure "Mr. Happy" was home). But it was a fresh and innovative mix circa 1981. Like a brilliant rock guitarist or jazz musician, the virtuosity was enough at first. After several years he became smoother, structured the improv with a steady beat and serious, identifiable themes. He reached a peak in 1986 with his concert at the Metropolitan Opera House. The once-merry prankster wasn't sweating over his impression of "The Fly" in a '50s horror movie or making fun of ringsiders' drinks. He was straining and gasping over world problems, drugs, women's rights and children facing the future. While there was still plenty of schtick and George Jessel impressions, the underlying theme was innocence crying out for change in the world and *to* change the world.

By this time, there were many other avenues for his creativity, many ways to experiment with roles that often used his strengths as a youthful idealist or innocent. On television, Williams had begun his career as one of the "zanies" on the new version of "Laugh-In." Then he landed the role that made him a national star (something his stand-up hadn't quite accomplished). He was Mork, the naive alien from the planet Ork on "Mork and Mindy." The premise allowed Williams to do what every child does—point out the strange and foolish world of the adults. Most of the comedy was light and cute, the emphasis more on silly space-alien catch phrases ("Na-nu na-nu") and his ability to mimic everything in sight. But the show was still a great success in its first few seasons.

Finally, in films, Williams progressed beyond easy laughs. It was a difficult transition. Director Robert Altman's film version of *Popeye* was strangely dark and moody, and though Williams could mimic the familiar voices and mannerisms of the heroic sailor, this was not his strength. A few more films like this, and film studios began doubting Williams' box office potential.

*Moscow on the Hudson* was a mild hit, the sentimental story of a naive, eccentric Russian searching for a new life in America and facing a whole baffling new world. But his first bona fide hit was *Good Morning Vietnam*, in which he played a sarcastic disc jockey. In his Academy Award–nominated *Dead Poet's Society*, Williams' optimism and energy influenced naive schoolkids as they began facing the realities of the world.

Off stage, fans saw how the realities of stardom affected Robin. As he went from $25,000 for a 1978 HBO special to $750,000 for a 1983 concert, Williams lived in a fast lane that included drug abuse. On a Barbara Walters television special, Williams admitted his cocaine use was "a great way of escaping." The overdose death of his friend John Belushi was a sad, sobering event.

Williams' first marriage was another casualty of his change in lifestyle. He married a second time, and with his children Zachary and Zelda found a stable home environment matched by healthful regimes of yoga, exercise and a vegetarian diet.

Williams continues to amaze both critics and fans with his depth as an actor and versatility as a comedian. In three hit films in a row, Williams was dazzling, clearly on equal footing with his legendary co-stars and directors. He played a compassionate doctor trying to reach out to the dormant Robert De Niro in *Awakenings*, danced naked in Central Park as the manic homeless man in Terry Gilliam's *The Fisher King*, and was Peter Pan in the splashy Steven Spielberg fantasy *Hook* co-starring Dustin Hoffman.

Williams' professional life has become a balance of the two things that bring him the most satisfaction—acting and stand-up. When he is out promoting a new film, he'll still jump into a local club and surprise the cheering crowd with a half hour of ad libs and comic frenzy. "For me it's therapy. Stand-up is the freest form of comedy, and also the scariest. . . . I went to a therapist for a while, but I think that I can deal with my fears better up on stage . . . it's healthier for me." Just how he creates his comedy remains a mystery: "Analyzing comedy is like peeling an onion. You peel a layer, peel a layer, peel a layer, and then you go: 'There's nothing there.' "

AUDIO: *Reality, What a Concept* (Casablanca), *Throbbing Python of Love* (Casablanca), *A Night at the Met* (Columbia), *Good Morning Vietnam Soundtrack* (Columbia), *Comedy Relief I–IV* (Rhino)

FILMS incl.: *Can I Do It Till I Need Glasses?* (1980), *Popeye* (1980), *The World According to Garp* (1982), *The Survivors* (1983), *Moscow on the Hudson* (1984), *Seize the Day* (1986), *The Best of Times* (1986), *Club Paradise* (1986), *Good Morning Vietnam* (1987), *The Adventures of Baron Munchausen* (1989), *Dead Poets Society* (1989), *Cadillac Man* (1990), *Awakenings* (1990), *The Fisher King* (1991), *Shakes the Clown* (1992)

TV: "Laugh-In" (1979), "Mork and Mindy" (1978–82)

VIDEOS: *Comedy Tonight; Catch a Rising Star's 10th Anniversary Reunion; All Star Toast to the Improv; An Evening with Robin Williams; Comic Relief I, II, III; Robin Williams Live*

# FLIP WILSON

## (Clerow Wilson, December 8, 1933–   )

In the late 1960s and early '70s Flip Wilson repopularized black ethnic comedy with all of its funk and flamboyance. The decade had begun with the banning of "Amos and Andy" and saw the rise of Bill Cosby, whose routines were nonracial. Wilson found a way of making elements of "stereotype" comedy respectable again. He did it performing a good portion of his monology without dialect, which allowed the audience to accept him as an equal, as they had Cosby. Then, when performing dialect material, he gave the characters more dimension. He underlined the dignity behind his comic preacher "The Reverend Leroy" and the independent spirit underneath the strutting "Geraldine."

An orphan at eight, Wilson got into reform school trouble, but fortunately found the care and support he needed to straighten out. He joined the air force at 16, and it was there that he amused the troops with routines, including a favorite bit in which he turned everyday situations into high drama using mock-Shakespearean phrases. One guy pointed and shot back, "He flippeth his lid," leading to his nickname.

Around 1954 while working as a bellhop, Wilson began to double as hotel comedian, then nightclub comic, evolving a style similar to that of Redd Foxx, the most successful of the black nightclub comics of the day. In the dour, smoky confines of the clubs,

Flip Wilson was a fine stand-up performer, but it was his drag characterizations of "Geraldine" that most fans delight in remembering. Photo from the author's collection.

Wilson put on a hostile deadpan, lit a cigarette and gave audiences the adult tales they wanted to hear. This one about his wife: "I'm rollin' up a few reefers to bring to work with me tonight. About 11:30 my old lady came in, and her wig was amuss . . . her blouse was torn to shreds, you could see the imprint of fingers . . . this really threw me off. So I asked her, 'Where the hell have you been?' And she said she spent the night with her sister. You dig it? I knew she was lyin' because I had spent the night with her sister."

Wilson developed more family-oriented humor for television, gradually dropping the risqué and drug humor and becoming known for puns, shaggy dog stories and character comedy. "If you are a comedian, your first obligation is to be funny," he said early in his career. "I'll confess that I tuck in a little message here and there in my routines, but it's carefully placed so that it doesn't interfere with the audience's fun. The message has to be secondary to the humor. Like Max Eastman said 30 years ago: 'The first law of humor is that things can be funny only if they are in fun.'"

Wilson found his best success with his drag routines as the hilariously cocksure and cocky "Geraldine," who confidently pointed to her body and crowed, "What you see is what you get!" Geraldine had an answer for everything. When her husband complained that she bought a dress, she cried, "The Devil made me do it! I said Devil, stop it! Please! Then he made me try it on! Devil pulled a gun! Made me sign your name to a check!"

Wilson's show had a respectable run. The Geraldine catch phrases became something of a fad. When the fad cooled, audiences moved on to something else. Both Wilson and Bill Cosby were eclipsed in the late 1970s by the next rage—Richard Pryor.

Flip continued to tour and worked on a number of projects over the years, but never returned to the splashy national prominence that was his in the early 1970s. In the fall of 1985, after Bill Cosby's sitcom comeback, Wilson was brought back for "Charlie and Company." As *TV Guide* magazine noted, "Here's an idea for a sitcom: middle-class black parents cope with exasperating but lovable kids. What's that you say? It sounds like 'The Cosby Show'? What a coincidence." One thing the two shows didn't have in common was ratings.

Once again Wilson flipped back to stand-up comedy. Audiences still love his one-liners, his character Geraldine and a little of both: "Love is a feeling you feel when you're about to feel a feeling you never felt before! Whooooo!"

AUDIO: *Flip Wilson's Pot Luck* (aka *Funny and Live at the Village Gate*, Sceptor), *Flippin'* (Minit), *Cowboys and Colored People* (Atlantic), *You Devil You* (Atlantic), *The Devil Made Me Buy This Dress* (Little David), *The Flip Wilson Show* (Little David), *Geraldine* (Little David)

BROADWAY: *Old Bucks and New Wings* (1962)

FILMS incl.: *Uptown Saturday Night* (1974), *Skatetown USA* (1979), *The Fish That Saved Pittsburgh* (1979)

TV: "The Flip Wilson Show" (1970–74), "People Are Funny" (1984), "Charlie and Company" (1985–86)

## JONATHAN WINTERS

### (November 11, 1925– )

One of the most original and influential comedians in stand-up comedy, Jonathan Winters can dazzle and delight audiences as both a zany clown and a caustic satirist. Incredibly, he can be both at the same time. The same routines that might amuse a country fair crowd accustomed to Red Skelton would also draw knowing chuckles and approval from nightclub sophisticates accustomed to Mort Sahl.

As a clown, the moon-faced comic twists his features and changes his voice to become an entire country of funny characters—rural types, city slickers, old women, young kids, pressured businessmen, laconic gas station attendants and sharp politicians. As a satirist, the laughs are brutally on target. His characterizations, warts, clichés and all, are mirrors that gently distorted each person's weaknesses and folly so that they are made not only crystal clear but hilarious as well.

One of the keys to Winters' comedy is a line he used in his early monologues. He believed "most men are little boys." As for the rich businessmen and powerful politicians, "they just have bigger toys."

Winters was born in Dayton, Ohio. When he was only seven his parents split up. The boy was frustrated in school; he was never a very good student.

Lightning-fast characterizations and satiric impressions have made Jonathan Winters a legend in comedy since the 1950s. Here he is shown as the paranoid assistant chief in the film *The Russians Are Coming, The Russians Are Coming.* Photo from the author's collection.

He enlisted in the marines when he was 17, and after World War II held a succession of odd jobs, ultimately turning up as a disc jockey and television personality on WBNS in Columbus. In 1953 he went to New York but lost as a stand-up comic on "Arthur Godfrey's Talent Scouts." He did win some walk-on parts on a Saturday morning kids' show called "Rod Brown of the Rocket Rangers." The show's star, Cliff Robertson: "During our rehearsals, or even when he wasn't on the air, he'd go behind a flat and the most amazing and weird sounds would come our way—all kinds of things like machine guns, bomb blasts, and everything imaginable." He was simply referred to around the set as "the nut."

"The nut" was an amazing chameleon, able to change identities and stay in the new character as if it were real. Like a chameleon, his actions were really reactions. He was "on" all of the time, all the world becoming his stage. It wasn't enough to mimic people's pathetic foolishness, pomposity or pretensions for audience approval. It was as important to confront them one-to-one off stage, playing the game for his own amusement. Sometimes it would take the form of a benign put-on, but sometimes it was more sinister. Once he silenced a gabby cab driver by intimating he was The Mad Bomber, complete with furtive glances and veiled threats.

Winters didn't merely have talented vocal cords or a sensitive ear. He had a sensitive heart and skin, and every person who crossed his path made an impression. Some were reflected back to an audience with love, such as the rube "Elwood P. Suggins" or feisty old lady "Maude Frickert." But many characters were etched in acid: caricatures of the giggling jeering schoolmates he knew as a kid; the blustery officers who ruled over him in the marines; or those he called "the Babbitts, the pseudointellectuals, the little politicians" he encountered in his everyday life.

When Winters arrived, he was considered breathtakingly unique. While some comics had dabbled in routines involving sound effects and even visual and verbal mimicry of characters, no one had done it as well, or with such a sharp satiric eye or with such a bewildering arsenal of ad libs and stream-of-conscious allusions.

Many have wondered who inspired Winters. He said in 1989, "I'd have to go back to James Thurber. Writers, more than performers. I think that Laurel and Hardy are still two of the funniest guys in the world. The Marx Brothers were funny guys. W. C. Fields was a funny man. Chaplin, a very unique talent who also made statements about the times. . . . I think that these guys were unique in their own right. . . . you try to be just a little bit different. I learned a lot from Peter Sellers. I was one of his biggest admirers."

Called the "John O'Hara of Sound," Winters appeared on television in 1954 doing sound effects while Mickey Spillane read from his detective book, *I, the Jury.* The odd sound effects and lightning-fast ad-lib impressions made him a novelty on talk shows hosted by Jack Paar and Steve Allen, and in 1957 Winters had his own 15-minute television series. The time was too short and the format too pressured

really to show him at his best; it was the first of many disappointments with executives who recognized but did not fully understand his talent.

In nightclubs in the late 1950s Winters developed dozens of six-minute routines, little minimovies in a style that was coming into vogue at the time with Will Jordan and Lenny Bruce. Many were actual parodies of films, as Winters acted out all the characters of *The Prison Scene,* or a western "Scratchy" or an adventure epic "The Lost Island" or a variety of horror films. Often Winters peopled the stage with one-man sketches that were bizarrely original: an inventor who vows to fly ("he Scotch-taped a hundred twenty-six pigeons to his arms"); a nagging old lady at a funeral; a jaundiced look at the average amateur "talent show"; a scene in a pet shop selling used, defective or damaged animals; or a monologue about a turtle trying to cross a road of constantly speeding cars so he could see his girlfriend.

The lifestyle of a touring nightclub comic involved endless travel, gruelling gigs of two and three shows a night, and a reliance on alcohol and coffee to deaden the strain or pump life into a late-show performance. The crash came in May 1959 when, half in fun and half in desperation, Winters climbed into the rigging of a ship moored at Fisherman's Wharf. "I'm John Q. from Outer Space," he shouted at an arriving police officer. Winters was forcibly taken away in handcuffs as photographers snapped pictures of the angry, grimacing comedian.

Winters had now earned his reputation as "the nut," the wild man of comedy. Talk show hosts, friends, fellow comedians and audiences all urged him to even wilder escapades. And now he had gone over the edge. Fortunately, though the publicity around the incident would dog him for decades, Winters recuperated within a few weeks and, remarkably, was able to resume his on-the-edge comedy style.

In 1961 Winters made an impressive appearance on "The Twilight Zone" as a stark and serious pool hustler. Comedy was still his domain though, and in the 1960s Winters hosted a television variety show for a few seasons, began to make films and found audiences willing to indulge him when he decided to "wing it" on stage, forsaking unfulfilling set routines for suggestions from the crowd. It was on his own terms now: He told the audience that some of their suggestions would pay off and others wouldn't, but that the show would at least be something unique and different.

Winters continued to influence performers all around him. Admirer Johnny Carson clearly patterned his "Aunt Blabby" after "Maude Frickert." On talk shows, actor Burt Reynolds copied Winters' hip conversational style (including meaningful comic glares and indulgent mock chuckling) to great success. Reynolds' ex-wife Judy Carne remembered his fondness for performing entire Winters routines for friends. And Robin Williams applied Winters' stream-of-conscious techniques to the needs of comedy club audiences in the 1980s.

Though Winters often complained that he was "on the bench" more often than out on the field, his fans could always count on seeing him from time to time in concert or on a talk show, in a somewhat muted film role or in a sitcom (as "Mearth," son of Mork on Robin Williams' "Mork and Mindy" and later as Randy Quaid's eccentric and feisty father on "Davis Rules").

When not busy with comedy, Winters, married and father of two, pursues his other interests. A capable announcer, he is often in demand for commercial voiceovers and narrates stories for children's albums. In 1991 his resemblance to war hero General Norman Schwarzkopf led to a series of print ads with Winters dressed up in army outfits. A well-trained painter, Winters has won praise from many critics and his works are highly prized among collectors. A book of his short fables and observations, *Winters Tales,* turned out to be a best seller.

The book, along with the comedian's stand-up albums, films and videotaped television appearances, belong to posterity. Not so the physical body. Winters doesn't want any fuss or monument after he is gone:

"I'm going to be cremated and have my ashes put in a Campbell's soup can and taken out to the dump and mashed or something. I don't even want an urn. I don't want people around the house thinking it's pipe tobacco, or hitting it and saying, 'What's in that?' 'Oh, that's Dad.' I would level cemeteries. The ground is for the living. The ground is for food, for animals, for people. We don't need to put

a lot of stones up. The dead don't get up . . . I don't see people coming back. If they are, God love 'em, then they're coming back as squirrels or beavers."

FILMS incl.: *It's a Mad Mad Mad Mad World* (1963), *The Loved One* (1965), *The Russians Are Coming, The Russians Are Coming* (1966), *Penelope* (1966), *Oh Dad Poor Dad* (1967), *Eight on the Lam* (1969), *Viva Max* (1968), *The Fish That Saved Pittsburgh* (1976), *More Wild Wild West* (1980), *The Longshot* (1985), *Say Yes* (1986), *Moon Over Parador* (1988)

TV: "And Here's the Show" (1955), "NBC Comedy Hour" (1956), "The Jonathan Winters Show" (1956–57), "Masquerade Party" (1958), "The Andy Williams Show" (1965–67), "The Jonathan Winters Show" (1967–69), "The Andy Williams Show" (1970–71), "The Wacky World of Jonathan Winters" (1972–74), "Mork and Mindy" (1981–82), "Hee Haw" (1983–84), "Davis Rules" (1991)

VIDEOS: *Hungry i Reunion Concert, The NFL TV Follies*

## STEVEN WRIGHT

### (December 6, 1955–   )

Steven Wright—morose, frizzy-haired and balding—looks and sounds as if he's just awakened from a daydream. His one-liners take a moment to reach and destroy the audience. First comes the shock and surprise, then the explosion of laughter.

"It's a good thing there's gravity. If birds died they'd just stay up there. . . . Sponges grow in the ocean. I wonder how much deeper the ocean would be if that didn't happen. . . . What's the youngest you can die of old age? . . . I got food poisoning today—I don't know when I'm gonna use it."

Wright's slightly dazed persona is somewhat the same on stage and off. On stage he might say, "I'm living on a one-way dead-end street—I don't know how I got there." In an interview with the author he said he wasn't even sure how he makes up the jokes: "Something hits me. Just walking down the street. Something comes into my head. I might be talking to you now and all of a sudden write a joke about underwater photography. Like my subconscious is working on these jokes all the time, and the guy runs up to the conscious and says, 'Here's another one.'" After a pause he asks, "What was I saying?" Intentionally, but often unintentionally, it's hard to know for sure where the stage persona ends and the real Wright begins.

Factually, it all began in Cambridge, Massachusetts. That's where, late at night, young Steven listened to comedy albums on a local radio station. He memorized some of the Cosby and Carlin routines and performed them for his classmates. One strong influence on his style was sad-sack Jackie Vernon. Wright recalled a Vernon gag he always liked: "My father died. We buried him because he would've wanted it that way."

After graduating from Emerson College, Wright began performing stand-up around 1979 in local clubs. "I watched a show in Boston with five guys, and I thought—this is going to be harder than I thought. They were very funny. It kind of scared me. I auditioned the next week. I didn't have a plan, I didn't have a style, I was just trying to be funny. I got some stuff together and tried to make them laugh. Not 'I'll be different, I'll be weird.' That never entered my mind." His first gag: "I was in a bookstore, and I started talking to a French-looking girl. She was a bilingual illiterate. She couldn't read in two different languages."

Peter LaSally of "The Tonight Show" caught his act in Cambridge and booked him for his first major television appearance on August 6, 1982. He was such a smash that, in a very unusual break from tradition, he was invited back a week later. Wright became a favorite on the comedy club circuit, recorded a Grammy-winning comedy album in 1986 and after some cable specials wrote and starred in *The Appointments of Dennis Jennings* for HBO. The film was shown in theaters and earned him a 1988 Academy Award for Best Live Action Short Subject. That a made-for-television piece of comedy ended up winning an Oscar was strange, but not in the strange world of Steven Wright.

All of Wright's jokes have one thread in common, a deliberately skewed view of the world around him. He describes his act as "seeing the world through the eyes of a child and getting to use the words of an adult." On the street, Wright admits, "People still stop me and say 'You're the guy who doesn't smile.' But it's just what happens when I'm working. Like

Clever, bizarre one-liners mark the inimitable style of Steven Wright. Photo from the author's collection.

a carpenter doing a house. If he was laughing hysterically while he was building a house—it's insane."

Wright's particular brand of madness has a definite method: weaving some 300 jokes into an hour-long show with nearly 600 jokes discarded along the way. Even personal favorites of his are dropped if the audience didn't laugh, a line such as: "Babies don't need a vacation but I still see 'em at the beach." He admitted, "You have to fail so much to go ahead."

At a time when audiences are unaccustomed to "thinking man's humor," a one-liner style out of favor since the prime days of Woody Allen, Dick Cavett and Jackie Vernon, Wright has flourished. Though his future seems secure, Wright still has his doubts. He says, "I'm a peripheral visionary. I can see into the future, but only way off to the side." Asked in 1990 where he planned to be in ten years he said, "In ten years I'll be dead eight years." The world may or may not have joined him: "I think God's going to come down and pull civilization over for speeding."

AUDIO: *I Have a Pony* (Warner Bros.)

FILMS incl.: *Desperately Seeking Susan* (1986), *Stars and Bars* (1988), *The Appointment of Dennis Jennings* (1988)

VIDEOS: *Evening at the Improv, Young Comedians All-Star Reunion, Steven Wright Live, NBA/Comic Relief: The Great Blooper Caper*

## ED WYNN

### (Isaiah Edwin Leopold, November 9, 1886–June 19, 1966)

Ed Wynn loved corny gags and puns. He wrote most of them himself and giggled along with the audience. It didn't seem to matter how silly his humor was. Audiences loved him. He looked funny and he sounded funny. There was always an expression of wide-eyed surprise on his large, bulb-nosed face, which was crowned with a too-small hat that forced his hair to spring out from the sides. He spoke with a little boy's cracked voice that skidded into a yodel when he was excited. He lisped with thick-tongued confusion and amazement. He had a high-pitched "heh-hoo!" giggle that punctuated some of his most ridiculous lines.

For over 50 years, Wynn lived up to his billing. He was "The Perfect Fool."

His began to play the fool in 1902 when, not long after attending Central High School in Philadelphia, he starred as a college kid in a vaudeville sketch called "The Freshman and the Sophomore" with Jack Lewis. Wynn claimed, "We revolutionized the two-man comedy act. Up to then the straight man used to swat his partner with a bladder or rolled-up newspaper after every joke and chase him around the stage. We stood still and cut out the swatting."

His most quotable line was the breezy cheer, "Rah Rah Rah! Who pays my bills? Ma and Pa!" On stage he was the devil-may-care college clown, but in real life he and his father had a warring relationship. Ed's father was a Czech immigrant who had struggled to build his own very successful hat manufacturing company. When Ed defied his prominent father and chose show business, it made newspaper headlines. One read: "Millionaire's Son Quits College for Stage."

Ed didn't have an easy time. In his first show business attempt the 16-year-old runaway was stranded by a touring company in Maine. The team of Wynn and Lewis (often billed as "Win and Lose") was not an instant success, but they had a powerful ally, Lewis' pal Gentleman Jim Corbett, the boxing champ. When Corbett made a personal appearance at a Harlem theater, he brought the duo along. After some modest success, Wynn went solo, billed as "The Boy with the Funny Hat," an irony considering his father's profession. Throughout his career, funny hats were an important part of his act. He even had a hat-buying routine in his first big film, *The Chief,* in which a German woman comes in with her little boy and asks, "Do you have a hat that would fit my little Heine?"

Wynn's first big routine was "The King's Jester," a vaudeville sketch about a jester trying to make his monarch laugh. Nothing works until he whispers something to the king. The king laughs out loud and Wynn shouts, "Why didn't you tell me you wanted to hear that kind of a story!" The act played The Palace in 1913 and was used in the *Ziegfeld Follies* the following year. Wynn was an incorrigible clown. In that *Follies* show he hid under W. C. Fields' pool table and mugged to the audience until Fields cracked him over the head with a cue stick.

Ed was a big Broadway star over the next decade in a variety of revues that featured breezy whiz-bang gags. Stooge: "Did you give me a dirty look?" Ed: "I didn't give you a dirty look. You've got one, but I didn't give it to you!" After supporting the Actors' Equity strike in 1919, Wynn was briefly blacklisted by irate Broadway producers. Ed staged his own show and remained one of the great comedians of his era. Elaborate sight gags were part of his act, wild and crazy stunts unheard of at the time. In 1927's *Manhattan Mary* he played a waiter. When a customer declared, "I'm so hungry I could eat a horse," in came Wynn with a real horse, shouting "Will you have mustard or ketchup?"

Wynn brought his infectious silliness to movies, but despite his cartoonish looks he flourished on radio instead. In 1932 he began his 17-year radio career. Disliking the eerie quiet of a broadcast booth, Wynn became one of the first comedians to invite a live studio audience. He thrived on the hysterical atmosphere, his own giggling and mugging for the audience fueling the euphoria. His ad libs, mangling of sponsor commercials and on-air kidding about reading from a script were imitated by many radio and television comedians to come, including his major disciple, Red Skelton. His trademark high-pitched voice was an accident of live radio performance. For one early show he recalled being "pretty well keyed up. When I rushed out and started to speak, it was in that high register, and unconsciously I stayed with it through the broadcast."

In 1932 a Herbert Hoover speech cut into Wynn's show. *The Nation* magazine called this an "outrage," declaring "Whose hour was it anyhow? Ten million husbands and wives retired to bed in a mood of bitter rebellion. . . ." The magazine insisted that Hoover had lost a lot of potential voters that night, voters who would elect Franklin D. Roosevelt! The following year Wynn formed the Amalgamated Broadcasting Company, with the "EW" in flagship WNEW named for him. WNEW, eventually independent, lasted longer than Amalgamated, which lost Wynn $250,000.

The 1930s turned sour for him. He and his wife, Hilda Keenan, married in 1914, divorced in 1937. They had a son, Keenan, who was later a popular character actor and wrote an autobiography describing Ed's serious and difficult off-stage personality. Wynn married twice more, both ending in divorce. After W. C. Fields turned down $150,000 to play the title role in *The Wizard of Oz,* Ed passed on the film as well, feeling the role was too small.

Wynn's radio career declined in the 1940s but he retained his stage stardom in *Boys and Girls Together* which the *New York Times* called "funny to the point of tears . . . the peak of Ed's career." He arrived on television in good form, the bulb-nosed, potato-headed clown still getting laughs for his zany costumes and silly gags. He won two Emmy awards in 1949 despite the mechanics of early television. His live audiences couldn't see past the camera crew. He complained to one writer, "You just can't get laughs out of cameramen's asses." The aging clown fretted over losing his appeal as the demands of television ate up his sure-fire material.

Wynn took a bold step into serious drama. He said at the time, "Suddenly after 54 years to come out and be a human being—that gives me a good deal of apprehension." He won raves for the 1956 television production of *Requiem for a Heavyweight* but asked, "What kind of a medium is it that has Dinah Shore getting laughs and Ed Wynn making people cry?" He received an Academy Award nomination for *The Diary of Anne Frank* and was able late in life to achieve some kind of balance between dramatic work and comedy. In later years he often played eccentric grandfather types, often livening up family and children-oriented movies. The new generation loved the man whose funny clothes, funny face and funny voice had tickled Broadway and radio audiences 50 years earlier.

It was Ed Wynn who first said "A comic says funny things. A comedian says things funny." By his own definition, Ed Wynn was a great comedian.

AUDIO: *The Fire Chief* (Mark 56)

BROADWAY: *The Deacon and the Lady* (1910), *Ziegfeld Follies* (1914), *Ziegfeld Follies* (1915), *The Passing Show* (1916), *Doing Our Bit* (1917), *Over the Top* (1917), *Sometime* (1918), *The Shubert Gaieties* (1919), *Ed Wynn Carnival* (1920), *The Perfect Fool* (1921), *The Grab Bag* (1924), *Manhattan Mary* (1927), *Simple Simon* (1930), *The Laugh Parade* (1931), *Hooray for What* (1937), *Boys and Girls Together* (1940), *Laugh, Town, Laugh* (1942)

FILMS incl.: *Rubber Heels* (1927), *Follow the Leader* (1930), *The Chief* (1933), *Stage Door Canteen* (1943), *The Great Man* (1956), *The Diary of Anne Frank* (1959), *The Absent Minded Professor* (1960), *Cinderfella* (1960), *Babes in Toyland* (1961), *Son of Flubber* (1963), *Mary Poppins* (1964), *That Darn Cat* (1965), *Dear Brigitte* (1965), *The Greatest Story Ever Told* (1965), *The Gnome Mobile* (1967)

TV: "The Ed Wynn Show" (1949–50), "All Star Revue" (1950–52), "The Ed Wynn Show" (1958–59)

# Y

## WEIRD AL YANKOVIC

### (October 23, 1959–  )

Kids loved him. He looked like one of them, with his wild curly hair, loud Hawaiian shirts and pubescently sketchy mustache ("the worst mustache in show business" said *TV Guide* magazine). "Weird" Al Yankovic's schtick—kid-subtle and childishly goofy—was parodying rock songs with silly new lyrics. Sometimes he even fractured the music, intentionally adding a lame accordion and polka beat (in homage to '50s musician Frankie Yankovic—no relation—but the man who inspired his parents to give Al an accordion).

Most of Weird Al's parodies were aural food fights: Michael Jackson's "Beat It" became "Eat It," The Knack's "My Sharona" became "My Bologna," Joan Jett's "I Love Rock and Roll" became "I Love Rocky Road" and Cyndi Lauper's "Girls Just Want to Have Fun" became "Girls Just Want to Have Lunch."

Though Yankovic demonstrated little singing talent, often screaming out the lyrics—and critics quickly tired of his albums after hearing one or two cuts—Yankovic did hit his target now and then. His best efforts were "Eat It" (both the song and the video), "Hey Ricky," a send-up of both "I Love Lucy" and the Toni Basil tune "Hey Micky," and the song about quiz show failure, "I Lost on Jeopardy," based on Greg Kihn's "Our Love's in Jeopardy."

Yankovic's original comic songs failed to elicit much interest and his attempt to move from comic rock videos to feature films failed. His debut movie *UHF,* which included fake commercials for a funeral home ("Plots R Us"), distressed both film critics Siskel ("injurious to your sense of humor . . . you don't laugh once") and Ebert ("this parody of television . . . is defeated by the requirements of feature-length comedy"). Though his film career hasn't materialized, Yankovic remains a hero to his cult of young fans who flock to his concerts. He remains a dangerous parodist when the right song comes along.

AUDIO: *Weird Al Yankovic* (Rock n Roll), *In 3-D* (Rock n Roll), *Dare to Be Stupid* (Rock n Roll), *Polka Party* (Rock n Roll), *Weird Al's Greatest Hits* (Epic), *UHF Soundtrack* (Epic), *Worse* (Epic), *Peter and the Wolf with Wendy Carlos* (Epic)
FILMS: *UHF* (1989), *The Naked Gun* (1989)
VIDEO: *The Compleat Al*

## HENNY YOUNGMAN

### (Henry Youngman, January 12, 1906–  )

"Take my wife—please!"

The ultimate dumb "wife joke" of the standard stand-up comedian, this line ended up the "so corny it's hip" catch phrase for a journeyman comic named Henny Youngman, a man who endured over 50 years to become a legend, the "King of the One-Liners." Like Bob Hope, another impersonal performer who dispensed gags like a candy machine drops gumballs, Youngman became an institution to the bafflement of his contemporaries.

Born in England (his parents were en route to Brooklyn), Youngman learned enough at the Manual Training High School and the Brooklyn Vocational School to earn a living printing business cards. He formed a musical group The Syncopaters and did fairly well playing the Coney Island and Catskill resorts of the late 1920s. It was at the Swan Lake Inn in 1932 that he worked as a master of ceremonies and ultimately switched to comedy. Soon all that remained of his musical career were the few snatches of "Smoke Gets in Your Eyes" he'd play between jokes on his violin.

Youngman struggled for several years as a comedian during the depression: "All those nights I'd wake up, gasping for breath, strangling because I had no money . . . I couldn't breathe! So many disappointments! So many!" Millions first heard Henny in 1936 when he guested on "The Kate Smith Show."

For subsequent radio and television guest spots, Youngman spent the next 50 years telling practically the same 50 jokes. While he drew criticism for this through the 1940s and '50s, his hard-headed determination to rotate only a portion of his jokes seemed to pay off. He made his one-liners "classics." While his contemporaries fretted to come up with new material, Youngman was booked by anyone wanting a "surefire" comedian, especially if the audience was so young or so forgetfully old that the jokes seemed new.

While a few others used old gags and wheezes from joke books, they didn't have the appeal of Youngman, who not only told "classic" one-liners but made many "classic" through his delivery. Tall, granite-faced and somewhat bleary-eyed, he looked like everybody's salesman uncle. His delivery was the verbal equivalent to sticking a foot in the door; he wore down resistance with constant patter. With an amiably light voice, a hopeful half smile and the humility that comes from peddling secondhand merchandise, Henny would keep offering joke after joke until his audience gave up and gave in. Henny simply told another joke until one broke the ice.

Into the 1960s and '70s when a door-to-door salesman giving a spiel would have been considered an amusing novelty by the average housewife, Youngman was considered a camp novelty by audiences. It was hilarious to see Henny stand up and tell the same jokes, making the same deliberate mistakes, using the same deliberate cadence. Sometimes the audience would join in on a punchline. On Rowan and Martin's "Laugh-In" a catch phrase for any old joke was "Oh, *that* Henny Youngman!"

An amused and grateful Youngman simply kept going, putting out joke books and record albums duplicating earlier joke books and record albums, and appearing at any banquet, bar mitzvah, comedy club or convention that would book him. He was in the phone book, ready to arrange a show.

Though not a legend like George Burns, or a beloved piece of Americana like Bob Hope, Youngman moved into his sixth decade of comedy with many admirers respecting both his longevity and his unique personality. As Steve Allen put it, "I don't see why a man should be criticized for memorizing thousands of jokes . . . to me it seems a tremendous feat. I wish I could do it." Among the classics Youngman used for most every show:

"I just had a physical. I said, 'Doc, how do I stand?' He said, 'That's what puzzles me.' " "I told my mother-in-law my house is your house. So she sold it." "I miss my wife's cooking. As often as I can." "What good is happiness? It can't buy you money."

In 1990 Youngman sold a mail order album *Henny Youngman in Person,* played a cameo role in *GoodFellas* and completed a new autobiography. He even celebrated the 50th anniversary of his "take my wife, please" joke:

"I used that line for the first time 50 years ago on 'The Kate Smith Show.' It was a half-hour until the show started, my wife was backstage. I asked one of the ushers, 'Take my wife, please.' I meant to get a seat, but that was the beginning."

Youngman's "take my wife, please" gag even outlived his wife, who died in 1987 after 58 years of marriage.

Youngman never stopped telling the oldies and people never stopped laughing. As he always insisted, "An old joke is new if you've never heard it before." In comedy, Youngman proved something else. An old joke can get a laugh even if it has been heard a thousand times.

AUDIO: *Primitive Sounds* (NRC), *The Best of the Worst* (Certron), *And a Little Barbecue on the Side* (Youngman), *Take My Album, Please* (Waterhouse), *128 Greatest Jokes* (Rhino), *Take My Project, Please* (Ryerson and Haynes), *Horse and Auto Race Game* (Urania), *Henny Youngman in Person* (Ballymote Tape Library)

AUTOBIOGRAPHIES: *Take My Wife . . . Please!* (1973), *My Life and Laughs* (1973), *Take My Life, Please!* (1991)

BOOKS: *Don't Put My Name on This Book, Insults for Everyone, Henny Youngman's Five Hundred All-Time Greatest One-Liners* (1988), *Henny Youngman's Giant Book of Jokes* (1983), *Encyclopedia of One-Liners* (1989), *Take My Jokes, Please* (1988)

FILMS incl.: *A Wave, a Wac and a Marine* (1944), *Nashville Rebel* (1966), *Won Ton Ton, The Dog Who Saved Hollywood* (1976), *Silent Movie* (1976), *History of the World, Part I* (1981), *National Lampoon Goes to the Movies* (1981), *GoodFellas* (1990)

TV: "The Henny and Rocky Show" (1955), "Joey and Dad" (1975)

VIDEO: *The Young (At Heart) Comedians Special*

**Z**

## ZEB and ZARROW

**Zeb Ferguson, 1875–September 29, 1908**
**Walter Hightower Zarrow, 1874–August, 1906**

Probably no comedy team suffered such a quick demise as Zeb and Zarrow. The ill-fated comic bicycling team had their partnership shattered by a bullet and the lone survivor didn't survive long after.

In 1906 the duo played at an amusement park in Houston. It's unclear whether Zarrow was horsing around in an outdoor restaurant, or whether he was doing stunts to call attention to the duo's appearance in town. Whichever it was, a policeman objected to Zarrow bicycling atop a table and got into an argument with him. There was a scuffle. Angry at Zarrow for "resisting arrest," the policeman drew his gun. Zarrow started running and was shot in the back. The policeman was arrested for murder.

The wheels of Zeb and Zarrow screeched to a halt. The remaining spokesman, Zeb, worked the burlesque circuit as a monologist. He joined "The Ducklings" burlesque show and toured the country. On September 21 he collapsed after a matinee performance in Brooklyn. Typhoid and pneumonia were diagnosed and a week later Zeb rejoined Zarrow—bicycling through parts unknown.

# APPENDIXES

# APPENDIX A:
## NICKNAME AND CHARACTER NAME INDEX

| | |
|---|---|
| Maude ("Granny") Frickert | JONATHAN WINTERS |
| Geraldine | FLIP WILSON |
| Gilligan | BOB DENVER |
| Reginald Van Gleason | JACKIE GLEASON |
| The Goddess | JUDY TENUTA |
| Molly Goldberg | GERTRUDE BERG |
| The Great One | JACKIE GLEASON |
| The Great Stone Face | BUSTER KEATON |
| Ed Grimley | MARTIN SHORT |
| Horace Debussy Jones | HUNTZ HALL |
| Monsieur Hulot | JACQUES TATI |
| The Human Joke Machine | MOREY AMSTERDAM |
| The I Don't Care Girl | EVA TANGUAY |
| The Italian Golf Pro | PAT HARRINGTON JR. |
| George Jefferson | SHERMAN HEMSLEY |
| Joe the Bartender | JACKIE GLEASON |
| José Jimenez | BILL DANA |
| Karnak the Magnificent | JOHNNY CARSON |
| Kingfish | TIM MOORE |
| Corporal Klinger | JAMIE FARR |
| The Knockers Up Gal | RUSTY WARREN |
| Alice Kramden | AUDREY MEADOWS |
| Ralph Kramden | JACKIE GLEASON |
| Dr. Kronkheit and his only living patient | SMITH AND DALE |
| The Last of the Red Hot Mamas | SOPHIE TUCKER |
| The Little Tramp | CHARLES CHAPLIN |
| Lonesome George | GEORGE GOBEL |
| Terence Aloysius Mahoney | LEO GORCEY |
| Maude | BEATRICE ARTHUR |
| Mr. Magoo | JIM BACKUS |
| Muggs McGinnis | LEO GORCEY |
| Meathead | ROB REINER |
| Ethel Mertz | VIVIAN VANCE |
| Fred Mertz | WILLIAM FRAWLEY |
| Moms | MOMS MABLEY |
| Herman Munster | FRED GWYNNE |
| Ed Norton | ART CARNEY |
| Mrs. Nussbaum | MINERVA PIOUS |
| Officer Judy | BOB EINSTEIN |
| The Old Philosopher | EDDIE LAWRENCE |
| One Long Pan | FRED ALLEN |
| Our Miss Brooks | EVE ARDEN |
| Guido Panzini | PAT HARRINGTON JR. |
| Mr. Peepers | WALLY COX |
| The Petite Flower | JUDY TENUTA |
| Hawkeye Pierce | ALAN ALDA |
| Pigmeat | PIGMEAT MARKHAM |
| Poor Soul | JACKIE GLEASON |
| Professor | IRWIN COREY |
| Queen of Candy Pants | JUDY TENUTA |
| The Question Man | STEVE ALLEN |
| The Question Man | ERNIE KOVACS |
| Radio's Home Folks | VIC AND SADE |
| Redhead | IRENE FRANKLIN |
| Redhead | LUCILLE BALL |
| Rhoda | VALERIE HARPER |
| Lucy Ricardo | LUCILLE BALL |
| Ricky Ricardo | DESI ARNAZ |
| Chester Riley | WILLIAM BENDIX |
| Rochester | EDDIE ANDERSON |
| Roseanne Roseannadanna | GILDA RADNER |
| Fred Sanford | REDD FOXX |
| Satch | HUNTZ HALL |
| Schnozzola | JIMMY DURANTE |
| Shemp | SHEMP HOWARD/THE THREE STOOGES |
| Josh Shmenge | JOHN CANDY |
| Slip | LEO GORCEY |
| Maxwell Smart | DON ADAMS |
| The Sneezer | BILLY GILBERT |
| Spanky | SPANKY MCFARLAND |
| The Stuttering Comic | JOE FRISCO |
| Super Dave Osborne | BOB EINSTEIN |

| | | | |
|---|---|---|---|
| Elwood P. Suggins | JONATHAN WINTERS | The Two Black Crows | MORAN AND MACK |
| The Thinking Man's Hillbillies | HOMER AND JETHRO | The 2000 Year Old Man | MEL BROOKS |
| Topsy and Eva | THE DUNCAN SISTERS | Uncle Fester | JACKIE COOGAN |
| Mr. Tudball | TIM CONWAY | Mr. Warmth | DON RICKLES |

# APPENDIX B:
## CATCH PHRASE INDEX

"Ain't that weird?"    BROTHER DAVE GARDNER

"All I know is what I read in the papers."    WILL ROGERS

"Am I bothering you?"    PETER FALK

"And away we go!"    JACKIE GLEASON

"And don't call me Shirley."    LESLIE NIELSEN

"And now for something completely different."    JOHN CLEESE/MONTY PYTHON'S FLYING CIRCUS

"Anyway, onward."    MORT SAHL

"Booga booga!"    DAVID STEINBERG

"But I wanna tell ya . . ."    BOB HOPE

"Can we talk?"    JOAN RIVERS

"Check and double check."    AMOS AND ANDY

"Come up and see me sometime . . ."    MAE WEST

"Confidentially . . ."    JERRY COLONNA

"Dave's not here."    CHEECH AND CHONG

"The Devil made me do it!"    FLIP WILSON

"Don't ever dooooo that!"    JOE PENNER/THE GREAT GILDERSLEEVE

"Don't get me started."    BILLY CRYSTAL

"Dyn-o-mite!"    JIMMIE WALKER

"Ever notice . . ."    ANDY ROONEY

"Everybody wants ta get inna the act!"    JIMMY DURANTE

"Feetlebaum!"    DOODLES WEAVER

"Funny you should ask."    MOREY AMSTERDAM

"Gladda see ya."    PHIL SILVERS

"Godfrey Daniels!"    W. C. FIELDS

"God'll get you for that."    BEATRICE ARTHUR

"Golly!"    JIM NABORS

"Good evening, anybody."    HENRY MORGAN

"Good night, Mrs. Calabash, wherever you are!"    JIMMY DURANTE

"Greetings, Gate!"    JERRY COLONNA

"Hang by your thumbs."    BOB AND RAY

"Hardy Har Har"    JACKIE GLEASON

"Hello again, fun seekers."    JACKIE VERNON

"Hello dere!"    ALLEN AND ROSSI

"Hello dummy"    DON RICKLES

"Hello, good evening and welcome!"    DAVID FROST

"Hello, Mama?"　GEORGE JESSEL

"Here come de Judge."　PIGMEAT MARKHAM

"Here's another fine mess you've gotten me into!"　OLIVER HARDY/LAUREL AND HARDY

"He's fallen in the water!"　THE GOONS

"Hey there, Ralphie boy!"　ART CARNEY

"Hi, guys!"　TED KNIGHT

"Hi Ho, Steverino!"　LOUIS NYE

"The Ho-Ho Song"　RED BUTTONS

"How-deeee!"　MINNIE PEARL

"How sweet it is."　JACKIE GLEASON

"Huh?" "Yeah." "Huh?" "Yeah."　BURNS AND SCHREIBER

"I don't get no respect."　RODNEY DANGERFIELD

"I dood it!"　RED SKELTON

"I gotta million of 'em."　JIMMY DURANTE

"I kid you not."　JACK PAAR

"I'll clip ya so help me I'll mow ya down."　CHARLIE MCCARTHY (EDGAR BERGEN)

"I'll kill you a million times!"　MILTON BERLE

"I'm a ba-a-a-a-ad boy!"　ABBOTT AND COSTELLO

"I'm a victim of soicumstance!"　CURLY HOWARD

"I'm Chevy Chase—and you're not!"　CHEVY CHASE

"I'm outta here."　DENNIS MILLER

"I'm so glad we've had this time together."　CAROL BURNETT

"I must say!"　MARTIN SHORT

"I never met a man I didn't like."　WILL ROGERS

"Inka Dinka Do!"　JIMMY DURANTE

"Is easy for you, is deefeecult for me!"　SENOR WENCES

"Is it bigger than a breadbox?"　STEVE ALLEN

"Is not my job."　FREDDIE PRINZE

"Isn't that speical?"　DANA CARVEY

"Is there any group I haven't offended?"　MORT SAHL

"It is now post time!"　JOE E. LEWIS

"It's *good* to be the king!"　MEL BROOKS

"It's always something!"　GILDA RADNER

"Ize regusted."　AMOS AND ANDY

"Lookin' good!"　FREDDIE PRINZE

"Look that up in your Funk & Wagnall's."　ROWAN AND MARTIN

"Missed me by that much!"　DON ADAMS

"Mom always liked you best."　TOMMY SMOTHERS

"My name . . . José Jimenez."　BILL DANA

"My next story is a little risqué."　BELLE BARTH

"Never give a sucker an even break."　W. C. FIELDS

". . . never got a dinner!"　RED BUTTONS

"Nevermind."　GILDA RADNER

". . . nobody."　BERT WILLIAMS

"Nobody expects the Spanish Inquisition!"　MICHAEL PALIN/MONTY PYTHON'S FLYING CIRCUS

"Not so *rough*!"　JOE BESSER

"Now cut that out!"　JACK BENNY

"Nyuk nyuk nyuk!"　CURLY HOWARD

"Ooh! Ooh!"　JOE E. ROSS

"Oooh, I'll haaaarm you!"　JOE BESSER

"Pick two."　MOE HOWARD

"Picky, picky, picky."　PAT PAULSEN

" 'S'all right?' " " 'S'all right."　SENOR WENCES

"Shazam!"　JIM NABORS

"Sí."　MEL BLANC

"Smock, smock!"　STEVE ALLEN

"Some fun, ay kid?"　BERT LAHR

"Sorry about that, Chief."　DON ADAMS

"So who's to know?"　GERTRUDE BERG

"Tain't a fit night out for man nor beast."
W. C. FIELDS

"Tain't funny, McGee."    MOLLY MCGEE

"Take my wife—please!"    HENNY
YOUNGMAN

"Take off the coat, my boy!"    CHARLIE DALE

"Thanks for the memory . . ."    BOB HOPE

"Vas you dere, Sharlie?"    JACK PEARL

"Verrrry interresting!"    ARTE JOHNSON

"Wanna buy a duck?"    JOE PENNER

"Well!"    JACK BENNY

"Well execuuuuuuse me!"    STEVE MARTIN

"Well, I'll be a dirty bird"    GEORGE GOBEL

"What a country!"    YAKOV SMIRNOFF

"What a revoltin'
development . . ."    WILLIAM BENDIX

"What can I tell you. . . ."    DENNIS MILLER

"What you see is what you get!"    FLIP
WILSON

"What's a matter wit you?"    MOE HOWARD/
THE THREE STOOGES

"What's the matter, Bunky?"    EDDIE
LAWRENCE

"Who's Yehoodi?"    JERRY COLONNA

"Why bring that up?"    MORAN AND MACK

"Why not!"    DAYTON ALLEN

"(I'm a) Wild and crazy guy!"    STEVE
MARTIN

"Would you believe . . ."    DON ADAMS

"Write if you get work."    BOB AND RAY

"Yadeeyada."    LENNY BRUCE

"Yoo hoo, Mrs. Bloom!"    GERTRUDE BERG

"You bet your bippy!"    ROWAN AND
MARTIN

"You look Mahvelous!"    BILLY CRYSTAL

"You must come over!"    BERT SAVOY/SAVOY
AND BRENNAN

"You nasty man!"    JOE PENNER

"You're a haaaaard man."    THE GREAT
GILDERSLEEVE

"You're a good group!"    JACKIE GLEASON

"You really know how to hurt a guy."    DON
ADAMS

"You said a mouthful!"    JOE E. BROWN

# APPENDIX C:
# CATEGORICAL INDEX

## British Comedians

Cleese, John

Cook and Moore

Guinness, Sir Alec

Hill, Benny

Idle, Eric

Lauder, Harry

Milligan, Spike

Monty Python's Flying Circus

Moore, Dudley

Palin, Michael

Ullman, Tracey

## Country/Rural Comedians

Canova, Judy

Gardner, Brother Dave

Griffith, Andy

Homer and Jethro

Knotts, Don

Lum and Abner

Nabors, Jim

Pearl, Minnie

Stringbean

## Dialect Comedians

Buckley, Lord

Cheech and Chong

Cohen, Myron

Cooper, Pat

Dana, Bill

Fetchit, Stepin

Lauder, Harry

Mabley, Moms

Markham, Pigmeat

Moore, Tim

Parkyakarkus

Pearl, Jack

Pinchot, Bronson

Pious, Minerva

Prinze, Freddie

Sarducci, Father Guido

Skulnik, Menasha

Smirnoff, Yakov

Weber and Fields
Wences, Señor
Wilson, Flip

## Film Comedians

Abbott and Costello
Albertson, Jack
Alda, Alan
Allen, Woody
Arden, Eve
Arkin, Alan
Arthur and Dane
Arthur, Beatrice
Arthur, Jean
Aykroyd, Dan
Backus, Jim
Ball, Lucille
Belushi, John
Benchley, Robert
Bendix, William
Benny, Jack
Berle, Milton
Bracken, Eddie
Brooks, Mel
Brown and Carney
Brown, Joe E.
Burnett, Carol
Burns, George
Caesar, Sid
Cantor, Eddie
Carney, Art
Carson, Jack
Chaplin, Charles
Chase, Chevy
Cleese, John
Colbert, Claudette
Coleman, Dabney
Colonna, Jerry

Conway, Tim
Cosby, Bill
Crosby, Bing
Crystal, Billy
Dangerfield, Rodney
Day, Doris
DeLuise, Dom
Demarest, William
De Vito, Danny
Dumont, Margaret
Dunne, Irene
Durante, Jimmy
East Side Kids, The
Errol, Leon
Falk, Peter
Feldman, Marty
Fernandel
Fields, W. C.
Finlayson, James
Garr, Teri
Gilbert, Billy
Gilford, Jack
Gleason, Jackie
Goldberg, Whoopi
Goldthwait, Bob
Gorcey, Leo
Grant, Cary
Griffith, Andy
Griffith, Raymond
Guinness, Sir Alec
Hackett, Buddy
Hall, Huntz
Hanks, Tom
Hawn, Goldie
Henry, Buck
Herman, Pee-Wee
Holliday, Judy
Hope, Bob
Howard, Shemp

Idle, Eric

Kahn, Madeline

Kaye, Danny

Keaton, Buster

Keaton, Diane

Kennedy, Edgar

Klugman, Jack

Knotts, Don

Korman, Harvey

Lahr, Bert

Langdon, Harry

Lasser, Louise

Laurel and Hardy

Leachman, Cloris

Lembeck, Harvey

Lemmon, Jack

Levenson, Sam

Lewis, Jerry

Lloyd, Christopher

Lloyd, Harold

Lombard, Carole

Loy, Myrna

Lynde, Paul

Martin and Lewis

Martin, Steve

Marx Brothers, The

Matthau, Walter

McCormick, Pat

Midler, Bette

Milligan, Spike

Monty Python's Flying Circus

Moore, Dudley

Moran, Polly

Moranis, Rick

Morgan, Harry

Mostel, Zero

Mulligan, Richard

Murphy, Eddie

Murray, Bill

Nielsen, Leslie

Oakie, Jack

Olsen and Johnson

Our Gang

Palin, Michael

Pangborn, Franklin

Penner, Joe

Pinchot, Bronson

Poston, Tom

Powell, William

Pryor, Richard

Radner, Gilda

Randall, Tony

Raye, Martha

Ritz Brothers, The

Rogers, Will

Rooney, Mickey

Russell, Rosalind

Rutherford, Margaret

Segal, George

Sellers, Peter

Shawn, Dick

Short, Martin

Silvers, Phil

Sothern, Ann

Switzer, Alfalfa

Tati, Jacques

Terry-Thomas

Thomas, Buckwheat

Three Stooges, The

Todd, Thelma

Tomlin, Lily

Van Dyke, Dick

Wheeler and Woolsey

Wilder, Gene

Williams, Robin

Wynn, Ed

## Impressionists

Allen, Dayton

Blanc, Mel

Crystal, Billy

Frees, Paul

Frye, David

Gorshin, Frank

Hill, Benny

Jordan, Will

Little, Rich

Meader, Vaughn

Piscopo, Joe

## International Comedians

Cantinflas

Fernandel

Frick and Frack

Grock

Linder, Max

Marceau, Marcel

Marceline

Tati, Jacques

Wences, Señor

## Musical Comedians

Borge, Victor

Brice, Fanny

Burns, George

Buttons, Red

Cantor, Eddie

Colonna, Jerry

Durante, Jimmy

Harris, Phil

Homer and Jethro

Jones, Spike

Kabibble, Ish

Katz, Mickey

Kaye, Danny

Lauder, Harry

Lehrer, Tom

Lewis, Joe E.

Lillie, Beatrice

Midler, Bette

Moore, Dudley

Mostel, Zero

Mull, Martin

Piscopo, Joe

Sherman, Allan

Yankovic, Weird Al

## Radio Comedians

Abbott and Costello

Ace, Goodman, and Jane Ace

Amos and Andy

Anderson, Eddie "Rochester"

Benny, Jack

Bergen, Edgar

Bickersons, The

Blanc, Mel

Bob and Ray

Brice, Fanny

Burns, George

Cantor, Eddie

Colonna, Jerry

Davis, Joan

Firesign Theatre

Freberg, Stan

Goons, The

Great Gildersleeve, The

Hope, Bob

Kabibble, Ish

Lum and Abner

McGee, Fibber, and Molly

Moore, Garry

Morgan, Henry

Pearl, Jack

Penner, Joe
Pious, Minerva
Rogers, Will
Vic and Sade

## Silent-Film Comedians

Arbuckle, Fatty
Chaplin, Charles
Chase, Charley
Conklin, Chester
Keaton, Buster
Kennedy, Edgar
Keystone Kops, The
Langdon, Harry
Laurel and Hardy
Linder, Max
Lloyd, Harold
Moran, Polly
Normand, Mabel
Our Gang
Pollard, Snub
Purviance, Edna
Ritchie, Billy
Semon, Larry
Sterling, Ford
Swain, Mack
Turpin, Ben
West, Billy

## Stand-Up Comedians

Adams, Don
Adams, Joey
Allen and Rossi
Allen, Steve
Allen, Woody
Altman, Jeff
Amsterdam, Morey
Arnold, Roseanne

Barth, Belle
Bean, Orson
Benny, Jack
Berle, Milton
Berman, Shelley
Bernhard, Sandra
Bishop, Joey
Bob and Ray
Borge, Victor
Brenner, David
Brooks, Albert
Brother Theodore
Bruce, Lenny
Buckley, Lord
Burns and Schreiber
Burns, George
Buttons, Red
Byner, John
Cambridge, Godfrey
Carlin, George
Carson, Johnny
Carter, Jack
Cavett, Dick
Cheech and Chong
Clay, Andrew Dice
Close, Del
Cohen, Myron
Cooper, Pat
Corey, Irwin
Cosby, Bill
Crosby, Norm
Crystal, Billy
Dana, Bill
Dangerfield, Rodney
Diller, Phyllis
Douglas, Jack
Fay, Frank
Fields, Totie
Foxx, Redd

Frisco, Joe

Frost, David

Frye, David

Gardner, Brother Dave

Gayle, Jackie

Gobel, George

Goldberg, Whoopi

Goldthwait, Bob

Gorshin, Frank

Gottfried, Gilbert

Graham, Ronny

Greene, Shecky

Gregory, Dick

Griffith, Andy

Hackett, Buddy

Hall, Arsenio

Hope, Bob

Jessel, George

Jordan, Will

Kaplan, Gabe

Kaufman, Andy

Kelly, Lew

King, Alan

King, Alexander

Kinison, Sam

Klein, Robert

Landesberg, Steve

Lawrence, Eddie

Leno, Jay

Leonard, Jack E.

Letterman, David

Levenson, Sam

Lewis, Joe E.

Lewis, Richard

Little, Rich

Mabley, Moms

Mandel, Howie

Markham, Pigmeat

Martin, Steve

Marx, Groucho

Mason, Jackie

Meader, Vaughn

Miller, Dennis

Milligan, Spike

Mull, Martin

Murphy, Eddie

Murray, Jan

Newhart, Bob

Nichols and May

Paar, Jack

Paulsen, Pat

Pearl, Minnie

Philips, Emo

Piscopo, Joe

Prinze, Freddie

Professor Backwards

Pryor, Richard

Radner, Gilda

Rickles, Don

Rivers, Joan

Rogers, Will

Rudner, Rita

Russell, Mark

Russell, Nipsey

Sahl, Mort

Sales, Soupy

Seinfeld, Jerry

Shandling, Garry

Shawn, Dick

Shepherd, Jean

Skelton, Red

Smirnoff, Yakov

Smothers Brothers, The

Steinberg, David

Stiller and Meara

Storch, Larry

Taylor, Rip

Tenuta, Judy

Thomas, Danny

Tomlin, Lily

Vernon, Jackie

Walker, Jimmie

Warfield, Marcia

Warren, Rusty

Wences, Señor

Williams, Pearl

Williams, Robin

Wilson, Flip

Winters, Jonathan

Wright, Steven

Youngman, Henny

## Stage/Broadway Comedians

Arthur, Beatrice

Berg, Gertrude

Borge, Victor

Brice, Fanny

Burnett, Carol

Caesar, Sid

Cantor, Eddie

Clark and McCullough

Colbert, Claudette

Cook, Joe

Draper, Ruth

Dressler, Marie

Dunne, Irene

Durante, Jimmy

Gilford, Jack

Gleason, Jackie

Holliday, Judy

Hope, Bob

Howard, Willie

Kaye, Danny

Klugman, Jack

Lahr, Bert

Lavin, Linda

Lawrence, Eddie

Lemmon, Jack

Lillie, Beatrice

Marceau, Marcel

Marceline

Marx Brothers, The

Mason, Jackie

Matthau, Walter

Midler, Bette

Mostel, Zero

Nichols and May

Olsen and Johnson

Penn and Teller

Questel, Mae

Randall, Tony

Rooney, Mickey

Russell, Rosalind

Savo, Jimmy

Silvers, Phil

Skulnik, Menasha

Stapleton, Jean

Williams, Bert

Wynn, Ed

## Television Comedians

Adams, Don

Albertson, Jack

Alda, Alan

Allen, Steve

Anderson, Eddie "Rochester"

Arden, Eve

Arnaz, Desi

Arnold, Roseanne

Arthur, Beatrice

Astin, John

Aykroyd, Dan

Backus, Jim

Ball, Lucille

Belushi, John

Bendix, William

Benny, Jack

Berg, Gertrude

Berle, Milton

Bishop, Joey

Burnett, Carol

Burns and Allen

Buzzi, Ruth

Caesar, Sid

Candy, John

Carney, Art

Carson, Johnny

Carvey, Dana

Cavett, Dick

Chase, Chevy

Coca, Imogene

Colonna, Jerry

Conway, Tim

Coogan, Jackie

Cosby, Bill

Cox, Wally

Crystal, Billy

Curtin, Jane

Davis, Joan

Day, Doris

DeLuise, Dom

Denver, Bob

De Vito, Danny

Douglas, Jack

Einstein, Bob

Falk, Peter

Farr, Jamie

Feldman, Marty

Foxx, Redd

Frawley, William

Frost, David

Gleason, Jackie

Gobel, George

Goldberg, Whoopi

Griffith, Andy

Guillaume, Robert

Gwynne, Fred

Hall, Arsenio

Harper, Valerie

Harrington, Pat, Jr.

Hawn, Goldie

Hemsley, Sherman

Herman, Pee-Wee

Hill, Benny

Hope, Bob

Idle, Eric

Johnson, Arte

Kaplan, Gabe

Kaufman, Andy

Kaye, Danny

Klugman, Jack

Knight, Ted

Knotts, Don

Korman, Harvey

Kovacs, Ernie

Landesberg, Steve

Lavin, Linda

Leachman, Cloris

Lee, Pinky

Lembeck, Harvey

Leno, Jay

Lester, Jerry

Letterman, David

Lewis, Al

Lewis, Richard

Lynde, Paul

Mandel, Howie

Marshall, Penny

Martin, Steve

Marx, Groucho

McCormick, Pat

Meadows, Audrey

Meadows, Jayne
Miller Dennis
Monty Python's Flying Circus
Moore, Garry
Moore, Mary Tyler
Moore, Tim
Moranis, Rick
Morgan, Harry
Morgan, Henry
Morris, Howard
Mull, Martin
Mulligan, Richard
Murphy, Eddie
Murray, Bill
Nabors, Jim
Newhart, Bob
Nielsen, Leslie
Nye, Louis
O'Connor, Carroll
Paar, Jack
Palin, Michael
Paulsen, Pat
Pinchot, Bronson
Poston, Tom
Prinze, Freddie
Radner, Gilda
Randall, Tony
Raye, Martha
Reiner, Carl
Reiner, Rob
Rickles, Don
Rivers, Joan
Rooney, Andy
Rooney, Mickey
Rose Marie
Ross, Joe E.
Rowan and Martin
Russell, Mark
Sales, Soupy

Seinfeld, Jerry
Short, Martin
Silvers, Phil
Skelton, Red
Smothers Brothers, The
Soo, Jack
Sothern, Ann
Stapleton, Jean
Stevenson, McLean
Storch, Larry
Struthers, Sally
Thomas, Danny
Tomlin, Lily
Ullman, Tracey
Vance, Vivian
Van Dyke, Dick
Van Dyke, Jerry
Vigoda, Abe
Walker, Nancy
Warfield, Marsha
Wayne and Shuster
Weaver, Charley
Weaver, Doodles
White, Betty
Williams, Robin
Wilson, Flip
Winters, Jonathan

## Teams

Abbott and Costello
Allen and Rossi
Bickersons, The
Bob and Ray
Brown and Carney
Bunny and Finch
Burns and Allen
Burns and Schrieber
Cheech and Chong

Clark and McCullough

Cook and Moore

Duffy and Sweeney

Duncan Sisters, The

East Side Kids, The

Frick and Frack

Gallagher and Shean

Goons, The

Homer and Jethro

Keystone Kops, The

Laurel and Hardy

Lum and Abner

Martin and Lewis

Marx Brothers, The

McGee, Fibber, and Molly

Miller and Lyles

Montgomery and Stone

Monty Python's Flying Circus

Moran and Mack

Nichols and May

Olsen and Johnson

Our Gang

Penn and Teller

Ritz Brothers, The

Rowan and Martin

Savoy and Brennan

Smith and Dale

Smothers Brothers, The

Stiller and Meara

Three Stooges, The

Vic and Sade

Wayne and Shuster

Weber and Fields

Wheeler and Woolsey

## Vaudeville/Burlesque Comedians

Abbott and Costello

Allen, Fred

Benny, Jack

Besser, Joe

Burns and Allen

Cook, Joe

Demarest, William

Duffy and Sweeney

Faye, Joey

Fields, W. C.

Foy, Eddie

Franklin, Irene

Frisco, Joe

Healy, Ted

Howard, Willie

Jessel, George

Kelly, Lew

Lahr, Bert

Lauder, Harry

Lee, Pinky

Marx Brothers, The

Miller and Lyles

Moran and Mack

Pearl, Jack

Rogers, Will

Savo, Jimmy

Savoy and Brennan

Smith and Dale

Tanguay, Eva

Three Stooges, The

Tucker, Sophie

Weaver, Doodles

Weber and Fields

Wences, Señor

Williams, Bert

Zeb and Zarrow